THIRD EDITION

# INTERNATIONAL COOKING
## A Culinary Journey

### Patricia A. Heyman

Boston   Columbus   Indianapolis   New York   San Francisco   Upper Saddle River
Amsterdam   Cape Town   Dubai   London   Madrid   Milan   Munich   Paris   Montreal   Toronto
Delhi   Mexico City   São Paulo   Sydney   Hong Kong   Seoul   Singapore   Taipei   Tokyo

Executive Editor: Daryl Fox
Editorial Director: Andrew Gilfillan
Editorial Assistant: Lara Dimmick
Program Manager: Susan Watkins
SVP Field Marketing: David Gesell
Senior Marketing Manager: Darcy Betts
Field Marketing Manager: Thomas Hayward
Vendor Project Manager: Melissa Sacco, Lumina Datamatics, Inc.
Operations Specialist: Deidra Skahill
Senior Art Director: Diane Ernsberger

Cover Designer: Carie Keller, Cenveo
Image Lead Manager/P&C: Lori Whitley
Cover Art: Pearson
Full-Service Project Management: Saraswathi Muralidhar,
    Lumina Datamatics, Inc.
Composition: Lumina Datamatics, Inc.
Printer/Binder: LSC Communications, Kendallville
Cover Printer: LSC Communications, Kendallville
Text Font: 10.25/12.25 ITC Garamond STD

Credits and acknowledgments borrowed from other sources and reproduced, with permission, in this textbook appear on appropriate page within text.

**Library of Congress Cataloging-in-Publication Data**
Names: Heyman, Patricia A., author.
Title: International cooking : a culinary journey / Patricia A. Heyman.
Description: Third edition. | Boston : Prentice Hall, [2017] | Includes
    bibliographical references and index.
Identifiers: LCCN 2015050384| ISBN 9780133815238 | ISBN 0133815234
Subjects: LCSH: International cooking. | LCGFT: Cookbooks.
Classification: LCC TX725.A1 H48 2017 | DDC 641.59--dc23 LC record available at http://lccn.loc.gov/2015050384

ISBN 10:    0-13-381523-4
ISBN 13: 978-0-13-381523-8

35 2022

*Dedicated to four who are in my heart forever—*
*for limitless love and support:*
*Lisa Heyman, my mom*
*and*
*Alan Roer, my husband*
*I wish you could see this book;*
*Julius Heyman, my dad*
*and*
*Emma Frank, my Oma*

# Contents

## PART 4  Asia

>>**CHAPTER 11**

### China *348*

>>**CHAPTER 12**

### Japan and Korea *382*

>>**CHAPTER 13**

### Vietnam, Thailand, Indonesia, and the Philippines *414*

## >>CHAPTER 18

### Caribbean Islands  575

# Preface

People say the world is becoming smaller. Of course, the world is not shrinking, but more accessible travel, familiarity with people from foreign lands, and efficient communication make faraway destinations seem less remote.

No longer reserved for the wealthy, travel to foreign lands is attainable for many people. The price of an airline ticket to Europe often costs less than flying from New York to California, and myriad flights travel overseas every day. While college spring break used to mean a trip to Florida for the lucky, now a week in Paris or scuba diving in Belize fits into the realm of spring break possibilities.

With the help of telephones, computers, wireless technology, satellites, airplane travel, and continually developing technologies, business and pleasure truly span the globe. As a result, more and more people are familiar with foods from foreign lands, and dishes from all corners of the world penetrate the menus of other cuisines.

Culinary schools used to teach continental cookery, which primarily covered the cuisines of Europe; however, that no longer suffices. Offering a much broader range of cuisines, international cookery is the necessary course now. As travel to Asia, Latin America, and destinations throughout the world has increased, so has the interest and knowledge of cuisines spanning the globe.

Today many businesses operate globally. Companies from around the world relocate employees to other countries for varied periods of time. This adds to the ethnic diversity of neighborhoods all over the globe. In addition, when people move to foreign lands, they learn about other cultures and cuisines, and they adopt the aspects they like.

Demographic changes also have altered our perspective of the world. Great increases in the number of immigrants play a significant part in the cultural composition of cities, schools, and neighborhoods. Of course, ethnic restaurants thrive in areas with substantial ethnic populations, and then these cuisines become more mainstream. According to the last census, the fastest growing ethnic groups in the United States are Hispanics and Asians. Mexican and Asian restaurants proliferate. No wonder salsa has replaced ketchup as the leading condiment in the United States.

Immigration and increased birth rates continue to change the demographics of the world. Predictions released from the United Nations estimate that people from Asia, Africa, and Latin America will represent about 87 percent of the world's population by 2050. The remaining 13 percent will reside in other regions, including North America and Europe. People from densely populated developing countries continue to seek opportunities in more prosperous nations. As a result, many immigrate to the more affluent countries. So, although the world is not shrinking, it certainly is changing, and that change results in people's being exposed to more countries, more cultures, and more cuisines.

## >> GOAL OF THE BOOK

The goal of this book is to provide a comprehensive picture of cuisines found though-out the world and an explanation of their development and evolution. This is accomplished by information about the food and culture, as well as recipes from each area. Discussion in each chapter focuses on the development of the cuisine and the many issues that molded and influenced it. With this knowledge, each cuisine's evolution can seem both logical and natural.

Additionally, understanding the cuisine and familiarity with its traditional recipes allow the cook or chef to adapt and create recipes. With this information, he or she can incorporate current trends, characteristics of any geographical area, or personal preferences into the traditional recipes.

## >> PREMISE OF THE BOOK

What makes each cuisine unique? This book shows that neither random selection nor chance caused a cuisine to develop as it did. First, many of a cuisine's culinary traits result from conditions that naturally exist in the region or country—factors such as the geography, topography, climate; what can be grown or raised there; and historical influences from settlers, invaders, and bordering countries.

Second, and often determined by the factors listed earlier, many food preferences and cultural traits create the differences that distinguish one cuisine from another. The preferred carbohydrate, whether rice, pasta, bread, or corn, makes a significant impact on the cuisine. How can one think of Asian cuisines without thinking of rice? The herbs, spices, and other flavorings utilized create the taste associated with each country. For example, chili peppers and salsa are identified with Mexican cookery. The variety of protein consumed in the region further defines the cuisine. The Jewish and Muslim strictures against eating pork in the Middle East (as well as other places), the abstinence from beef in India, and the abundance of seafood and fish in areas near water characterize the cuisines of these places. All these issues clearly affected the cookery in each region and country, causing it to evolve into the cuisine it is today.

## >> ORGANIZATION OF THE BOOK

Each chapter is divided into six sections: history, topography, common food ingredients and flavorings, cooking methods, regions, and general characteristics of the cuisine. The development and the evolution of each cuisine become apparent through an understanding of the issues discussed in these sections. Following this dialogue, each chapter contains a glossary (a master glossary is located in the back of the book), a chart summarizing the material covered in the chapter, and a selection of recipes characteristic of the cuisine and its heritage, with dishes representing all segments of the menu. In addition to the entrées, the collection of recipes contains at least two first courses, soups, salads, vegetables, starches, breads, and desserts. When appropriate, the choice of entrées includes a selection of meats, poultry, fish and/or seafood, and vegetarian dishes to offer sufficient variety. The group of recipes is well rounded enough to prepare a successful buffet representing the country(ies) in the chapter.

Throughout history and today, wine has been valued for enhancing food as well as the whole dining experience. Food and wine pairing is an important aspect of dining today and, therefore, must be included in a book of this type.

Jerry Comfort, senior manager of wine education at Foster's Wine Estates (Beringer Vineyards, Château St. Jean, Château Souverain, Stags' Leap Winery, St. Clement, Greg Norman, Meridian, Lindeman, and many other wineries) has provided wine recommendations for each first course, soup, and entrée in the first two editions.

Wine pairings for the new recipes in this third edition are created by Leo Schnee-mann. Currently, his jobs include Wine Director for KG-NY Restaurant Group (Wallsé, Café Sabarsky, Blaue Gans, and Upholstery Store: Food and Wine), Managing Co-Owner of the Upholstery Store: Food and Wine, and General Manager of the New York City restaurant, Wallsé. Born in Austria, Schneemann received his education and extensive training in restaurants and wineries of Austria, France, and Switzerland. With especially broad knowledge of Austrian and German wines, he is a member of the American Sommelier Association.

The cooking method(s) employed appear at the top of each recipe. My colleague Bob Chapman always told his students that there are only six ways to cook—no matter what you're cooking. Whether the cuisine is American, French, or Chinese, the six cooking methods remain bake/roast, grill/broil, braise, boil/simmer/poach/steam, sauté, and deep-fry. Braising is braising, regardless of what spices and flavorings surround the foods. Please let that thought demystify the recipes you encounter in your cookery from around the world.

Some chapters cover one country, others include two or more countries, and still others contain a whole continent. Choosing to group some countries together and exclude others from this book altogether is the result of both the time limitations of a course and the magnitude of covering every country in the world. As a result, I have tried to include countries that are culinary representatives of the world cuisines.

Many of the European countries covered in a continental cookery course need their own chapter. Theirs remain the most familiar cuisines to many dining customers, and they still guide many of the cookery principles and standards in the Western world. This does not lessen the profound, significant, and growing influence of a myriad of other "lesser known" cuisines that are included in this book. Realize that the popularity and influence of any particular cuisine continually changes. Triggered by a limitless number of factors, trends come and go, leaving today's hottest cuisines passé tomorrow.

Although this book may contain too many chapters for a one-semester course, I am including more countries knowing that the instructor might need to omit some. Rather than write a textbook that fits neatly into a semester, I want to offer a valuable book for one's personal library covering cuisines from every continent.

## >> WHY I WROTE THIS BOOK

The idea for this book began when I was the program coordinator for the culinary arts program at Jefferson Community College in Louisville, Kentucky. Searching in vain for a book on international cuisine for our students, I called colleagues across the country only to find that they did just what we did—lectured on the cuisine and distributed lots of handouts. So, finally, here is the book I wanted to find!

## >> MY HOPE

Writing this book has been a joy on many levels. For more than two years, I submerged myself into researching and learning about the cultures and cuisines of other lands and testing more than 250 recipes. For this edition, I modified the text, tested and added more than 65 recipes, and included at least one bread recipe in each chapter. Although I have barely scratched the surface of knowledge about the world's cuisines, it's been a fascinating culinary journey!

As I always tell my students before espousing strong personal opinions, "This is from the world according to Patsy." So here are some thoughts from my world: I strongly believe that knowledge of a cuisine is an important part in understanding the culture and the people who live there. Armed with this knowledge, we can understand and appreciate others for both their similarities to and differences from us. It is my sincere hope that this book will open some doors to knowledge of other cuisines and cultures, which will lead to greater tolerance for others.

# Notes on Using This Book

Always read the entire recipe before beginning. Reading through the recipe makes it easy to understand the preparation and assembly, giving you an overview of what the recipe involves. Gather all the needed ingredients, and then begin cooking.

In the recipes, I make some assumptions regarding ingredients. Unless otherwise specified:

1. Garlic cloves and onions have been peeled.
2. Bell peppers have been cored and seeded.
3. All fresh fruits and vegetables have been washed.
4. All meat, poultry, fish, and seafood have been washed.
5. Stems have been removed from fresh herbs.
6. "Pepper" is ground black pepper.

A topic that must be addressed is homemade stock versus stock prepared from bases. For better or worse, because of labor and money issues, the majority of cooks and chefs use prepared bases for stocks. Of course, the recipes in this book do not designate homemade or stock prepared from bases; however, most prepared bases are quite salty. As a result, recipes containing stock include little or no salt in the ingredients. Toward the end of every recipe, instructions call for correcting the seasonings. At that point, you should taste the recipe and add salt or any other needed seasonings. Remember that it is easier to add more salt at the end of the recipe than to remove salt from the dish!

Every recipe in this book includes both weight and volume measurements. Although all the culinary schools I have visited use scales, that might not be the case in every restaurant or catering kitchen. Certainly, I have worked in restaurants without scales or with only one digital scale. With both measurements available, anyone can prepare the recipes in this book.

Finally, this international cookery book obviously contains many ingredients not commonly used in North American cookery. Throughout this book, my goal was to keep the unusual ingredients to a minimum so people living in areas that do not have large ethnic communities can prepare the recipes. Don't let the foreign-sounding ingredients intimidate you! A large supermarket stocks most of the ingredients listed in this book. An Asian market will carry many of the ingredients needed for Indian as well as the Asian and Middle Eastern cuisines. I even bought a few of the dried peppers needed for the Mexican recipes from a Mexican restaurant in town. A natural foods store or co-op will probably sell all or most of the herbs or spices needed for the recipes.

If an ingredient cannot be found, substitute. Look on the Internet for a suitable substitute for the ingredient. Many foreign cheeses are similar to ones easily obtained in the United States. Although the taste or melting quality might not be exactly as it is in the native country, it should be close enough to prepare the dish and enjoy it.

Substitute freely, if necessary, but do try to use the listed ingredients, if at all possible, to create the most authentic dish.

## >> DOWNLOAD INSTRUCTOR RESOURCES FROM THE INSTRUCTOR RESOURCE CENTER

To access supplementary materials online, instructors need to request an instructor access code. Go to www.pearsonhighered.com/irc to register for an instructor access code. Within 48 hours of registering, you will receive a confirmation e-mail including an instructor access code. Once you have received your code, locate your text in the online catalog and click on the Instructor Resources button on the left side of the catalog product page. Select a supplement, and a login page will appear. Once you have logged in, you can access instructor material for all Pearson textbooks. If you have any difficulties accessing the site or downloading a supplement, please contact Pearson 24/7 Technical Support at http://247pearsoned.custhelp.com.

## >> NEW TO THIS EDITION

The third edition of International Cooking: A Culinary Journey contains more material in both the dialogue of the chapter and the recipes. It has updated information from the second edition of the textbook and additional recipes in each of the 18 chapters. In addition, the book is formatted into smaller sections to enable the student to absorb the information more easily.

- More than 65 new recipes added, with three to five new recipes per chapter.
- All chapters now contain at least one bread recipe. In this edition, the collection of recipes in every chapter includes two or more first courses, two or more soups, two or more salads, two or more vegetables, two or more starches, one or more bread, and two or more desserts, as well as an assortment of entrées with at least one beef dish, one pork dish, one lamb dish, one poultry, and one seafood or fish (when appropriate to the country/region). This allows the students to prepare a comprehensive buffet of the cuisines covered in each chapter.
- The revised and updated text contains new information and additional sidebars giving the student more knowledge. With our changing world, some new countries were noted, while nonexistent countries were deleted.
- Over 700 photographs, with many of the older photos replaced. It also contains more how-to photographs, which provides more clarity for the students.
- Maps have been enlarged and new regions/areas noted in the chapter openers.
- Updated PowerPoint slides for use with the lectures on each chapter.

# Websites

A world of information exists on the Web, but obtaining that information often presents a formidable challenge. After much searching, I have compiled a list of websites that contain more recipes, as well as information about some of the food products and countries discussed in this book. There are literally thousands of websites with information and/or recipes on international cuisines. This list represents just a small portion of the sites available in "cyberland."

Websites for embassies, consulates, and national tourism agencies often contain worthwhile information about the history, customs, foods, and food traditions of a given country. Food companies and organizations feature particular products and recipes that utilize their products. Of course, try searching using each country or cuisine followed by the words "cooking," "culinary," "cookery," or "recipes."

A disclaimer: Websites come and go, so realize that this list is constantly changing and some of these sites may disappear. View this merely as a start for further research....

| Website | Countries |
|---|---|
| www.allrecipes.com | Search for individual countries |
| www.food-links.com | Many countries |
| www.recipesource.com | Many countries |
| www.kitchenlink.com | Many countries |
| www.globalgourmet.com | Many countries |
| www.about.com | Many countries |
| www.sallybernstein.com | Many countries |
| www.foodtimeline.org | Many countries |
| www.internationalrecipes.net | Many countries |
| www.worldtravelguide.net | Many countries (go to individual country for information on food and drink) |
| www.goya.com | Latin America, Caribbean |
| www.justmexico.org | Mexico |
| www.caribbeantraveler.com | Caribbean Islands (go to Caribbean Culture, then click on Food at bottom of the page) |
| www.visitjamaica.com | Jamaica |
| www.sbs.com.au/food/cuisine/brazilian | Brazil |
| www.ziyad.com | Middle East |

| Website | Countries |
| --- | --- |
| www.egypt.cl/typical-food.htm | Egypt |
| www.allaboutturkey.com | Turkey |
| www.syriancooking.com | Syria |
| www.denmark.dk | Denmark |
| www.norway.org | Norway |
| www.visitnorway.com | Norway |
| www.italianmade.com | Italy |
| www.italiantourism.com | Italy |
| www.sbs.com.au/food/cuisine | Portugal |
| www.spain.info | Spain |
| www.russianfoods.com | Russia and Eastern Europe |
| www.poland.travel/en-us | Poland |
| www.gotohungary.com | Hungary |
| www.orientalfood.com | Asian countries |
| www.tourismthailand.org | Thailand |
| www.visitkorea.or.kr | Korea (click on Food) |
| www.bento.com | Japan |
| www.jnto.go.jp | Japan |
| www.koreanrecipes.org | Korea |
| www.discoverhongkong.com | Hong Kong |
| www.tourismchina.org | China |
| www.filipinofoodrecipes.net | Philippines |
| www.tourismofindia.com | India |
| www.australia.com | Australia |

**Meat**

| Website | Countries |
| --- | --- |
| www.beefandlamb.com.au/Home | Beef and lamb |
| www.nzbeeflamb.co.nz | New Zealand—beef and lamb |
| www.vealfoodservice.com | Veal |
| www.beeftips.com | Beef (Wisconsin Beef Council) |
| www.beef.org | Beef |
| www.certifiedangusbeef.com | Beef |
| www.beeffoodservice.com | Beef |
| www.porkbeinspired.com | Pork |

**Poultry**

| Website | Countries |
| --- | --- |
| www.mapleleaffarms.com | Duck |
| www.eatchicken.com | Chicken |
| www.tyson.com | Chicken |

**Seafood**

| Website | Countries |
| --- | --- |
| www.seafood.no | Norwegian Seafood Export Council |
| www.nfi.org | National Fisheries Institute |
| www.alaskaseafood.org | Alaska seafood |

| Website | Countries |
|---|---|
| **Cheese** | |
| www.cheesefromspain.com | Spanish cheeses |
| www.cheese.com | Cheeses from many countries |
| **Beans** | |
| www.pea-lentil.com | USA Dry Pea & Lentil Council |
| **Fruits and Vegetables** | |
| www.idahopotato.com | Potatoes |
| www.mainepotatoes.com | Potatoes |
| www.pma.com | Produce |
| **Olive Oil** | |
| www.villabertolli.com | |
| www.colavita.com | |
| www.asoliva.com | Spanish olive oil |
| **Seasonings** | |
| www.astaspice.org | American Spice Trade Association |
| www.kikkoman.com | Soy sauce and other products |
| **Miscellaneous** | |
| www.almonds.com | Almonds |
| www.dececco.it | Pasta |
| www.pasta.com | Pasta |
| www.ilovepasta.org | Pasta |
| www.professionalpasta.it | Pasta |
| www.landolakes.com | Butter |
| www.aeb.org | American Egg Board |
| www.recipes.wuzzle.org | International recipes |

# Acknowledgments

So many people have helped and supported me in this endeavor. First and foremost are my husband, Alan Roer, and my mom, Lisa Heyman. They have listened; offered advice; encouraged me; and given as much help, support, and love as possible. Many friends cared about this project and me. I thank all the people who tasted the 400 plus recipes that I tested for this book—years of dinner parties and get-togethers that Alan and I will never forget. More thanks to my entire family, including my stepchildren, and to my father-in-law, Irving Roer, who really wanted to see this book in print—I wish he could have. In the life of this book, Samantha and David have grown from "Why do you always have to make new recipes?" to "Sure, I'd love to try a new recipe. What country is it from?" The difference of a few years is remarkable, and perhaps the exposure to diverse foods creates adventurous diners.

Wine has become an intrinsic part of the dining experience, and I think all culinary textbooks should include wine pairings with the recipes. I am thrilled for the collaboration with Foster's Wine Estates and Jerry Comfort, wine educator at Foster's Wine Estates. When I first spoke with Jerry about the idea of including a wine pairing suggestion with each recipe, his initial response was "What a great idea!" His enthusiasm for this project never wavered. Jerry, I appreciate your hard work and know that your input increases the value of this book as a reference tool for the student/cook/chef/manager in the future. I hope we have started a trend so that future textbooks will include this valuable asset, too. Thank you, Jerry, for writing the pairings for the first two editions of this book. Leo Schneemann, the wine director for KG-NY Group prepared the wine pairings for this edition.

I also want to thank the many individuals representing organizations around the world that provided photographs for use in this book or who helped me track down someone who had the "right" photograph. Through countless e-mails sent, I encountered many, many helpful individuals who went out of their way to help me (a stranger) find some of the beautiful photographs in this book. Often, it made me pause and think about how many kind people are out there.

The following reviewers should also be acknowledged for their input on the third edition Vickie Brown-Racy, Northeastern State University; Kristin Goss, Erie Community College; David Jones, Laney College; and Sherry Sipho, Tarrant County College - Southeast Campus.

Unfortunately, I cannot name everyone, but many more are in my heart. Thank you all—I realize what a lucky woman I am.

# British Isles

## >> LEARNING OBJECTIVES

By the end of this chapter, you will be able to:

- Name foods that are available in the British Isles and explain why those particular foods are prevalent
- Identify similarities and differences between the cuisines of the various countries of the British Isles
- Identify cooking methods commonly used in the British Isles
- Name some foods typically served at tea and in a pub
- Prepare a variety of dishes from the British Isles

## >> HISTORY

The British Isles consists of the islands of Great Britain, Ireland, several larger islands, and about 5,500 small islands. The countries of England, Scotland, and Wales make up the island of Great Britain while Ireland contains two countries, Northern Ireland and Ireland. Protected by the surrounding water, the British Isles endured relatively few invasions throughout history.

Evidence found in caves confirms the existence of Old Stone Age people in Britain more than 10,000 years ago. By 3000 B.C., inhabitants of this land were raising cattle, pigs, sheep, and crops.

### ROMANS AND OTHER CONQUERORS

Julius Caesar discovered Britain in 55 B.C. Soon after, the Romans gained control of most of the land. Leaving numerous contributions throughout these countries, the Romans built many cities, as well as roads that were used for transportation and trading. In addition, they introduced and spread Christianity throughout the British Isles. In terms of their culinary legacy, the Romans are credited with bringing artichokes, asparagus, carrots, cucumbers, endive, parsnips, and turnips, as well as pheasants, peacocks, and guinea fowl. They also imported almonds, dates, olives and olive oil, and wine and introduced cheese-making techniques to the British Isles. The Romans ruled until the early 400s, when the Saxons gained control.

Following the rule of the Romans, Germanic tribes and Danes invaded at various times before the Norman Invasion took place in 1066. At that time, a group of Vikings, the Normans, sailed across the English Channel and conquered England. The Vikings introduced the techniques of smoking and drying fish to preserve it. Simplicity and heartiness characterizes the food of the British Isles, with the most profound culinary influences coming from the Celtics, Germans, and Normans. Among their many contributions, the Franco-Normans brought nutmeg, mace, saffron, ginger, pepper, and sugar to the British Isles.

### KINGDOMS AND RELIGION

Around the time the Romans left, the British Isles consisted of many small kingdoms. Through fighting, marriages, and other mergers, eventually many of the kingdoms united. Finally, in 1603, one monarch ruled England and Scotland.

At different times in Britain's history, the Catholic and Protestant religions became the national religion. For example, King Henry VIII changed the official religion from Catholicism to the Church of England (Episcopalian) when he wanted to divorce his wife. Since Catholics did not eat meat on Fridays and many holy days, the cuisine of Britain includes many fish entrées and dishes that contain no meat. Many areas had access to plenty of fish and seafood through lakes, rivers, or the seas surrounding this island.

In 1536, Wales and England united. Scotland remained independent until the 1700s, when it joined England and Wales.

### AN EMPIRE

From the 1700s to the 1900s, Britain built a huge empire that covered one-quarter of the world. Its colonies stretched around the globe, including islands in the Caribbean, parts of North and South America, Africa, the Middle East, India, the Far East, Australia, and islands in the Pacific. This far-reaching colonization resulted in a strong British influence around the world and significant influences from faraway lands on Britain. Exposure to cooking techniques and food ingredients, as well as dishes from these worldwide colonies, greatly impacted the culinary scene of the British Isles.

The British adopted many foods and dishes from their colonies. Still today, tea from China remains the popular drink throughout the British Isles. Although they contrast

*According to reports, the British consume 163 million cups of tea each day.*

sharply with the typically bland foods of Britain, curries, chutneys, condiments, and highly spiced foods from India have become a permanent part of Britain's cuisine.

## IRELAND

Introduced to Ireland from the New World in the 1600s, potatoes quickly became a staple and major part of the diet in this poor country. In the 1840s, Ireland was hit with a potato blight. A fungus destroyed the potato crop, and starvation raged throughout the country. A million people died, and more than a million fled Ireland during that time. The population of Ireland today remains just a bit over half of what it was before the potato blight.

Today, Ireland remains torn by religious strife, as it has been for many, many years. The Protestants of Northern Ireland wished to align with predominately Protestant Great Britain; however, the people living in the south of Ireland, who are mostly Catholic, did not wish to become the religious minority of the United Kingdom. In 1920, the British Parliament passed the Government of Ireland Act, which allowed the people of Ireland to choose many aspects of self-government. As a result, the northeastern corner of Ireland became Northern Ireland and united with Britain. The remaining section of Ireland chose not to join the United Kingdom and, in 1921, became the independent country of Ireland. Still experiencing ongoing political troubles with the United Kingdom, in 1949, Ireland declared independence from anything to do with the British.

## >> TOPOGRAPHY

Situated to the northwest of Europe, the British Isles are bordered by the English Channel, Strait of Dover, North Sea, and Atlantic Ocean. The English Channel lies to the south and separates Britain from France. The North Sea is to the east, and the Atlantic lies to the west.

Although the British Isles lie at quite a northern latitude, they experience temperate weather. This mild climate results from warm ocean currents that moderate the temperature, causing mild summers and cool, damp winters with almost no snow.

Scotland composes approximately one-third of Great Britain and lies in the northern part of the island. Wales is situated in the southwest corner, and England covers the southern two-thirds of Great Britain.

The topography of Great Britain is quite varied, ranging from the windswept land of Northern Scotland to the rugged mountains and deep valleys of Wales, to the gently rolling plains and meadows of England. The coastline also differs greatly, with some parts rocky, some consisting of steep cliffs, and others sandy beaches.

### ENGLAND

England consists of three regions. The Pennines lies in the northern half and contains coast, mountains, hills, and lakes. The Southwest Peninsula comprises low plateaus, highlands, and coast. The rest of England is known as the English Lowlands and consists of fertile farmland, plains, hills, valleys, coast, and the Thames River.

Numerous lakes and rivers are found throughout England. More than 2,000 miles of waterways flow through this land. The River Tweed and the Cheviot Hills form the border between England and Scotland.

### SCOTLAND

Rugged Scotland contains many mountains, valleys, and lakes (called "lochs" in Scotland). The northern two-thirds consists of barren and mountainous highlands, conducive to raising sheep and cattle. The only fertile land in Scotland is found in the lowlands of the "central" section, the top part of the last third. Rivers, valleys, rolling hills, and fertile

> **Ingredients and Foods Commonly Used throughout the Cuisines of the British Isles Include**
>
> - lamb and mutton
> - beef
> - seafood including cod, haddock, salmon, herring, mackerel, shrimp, and oysters
> - ham and bacon
> - potatoes
> - winter vegetables including kale, cabbage, cauliflower, Brussels sprouts, rutabagas, carrots, and peas
> - cucumber and celery
> - oats
> - scones and crumpets

farmland make up this central area. In addition to the potato, grains for feeding both livestock and people grow well in this region. These include oats, barley, and wheat. The south contains rugged highlands, rolling treeless moors, and pastureland for grazing sheep and cattle. Known for milk production, many dairy products come from this area.

## WALES

Wales is situated on the western coast of Great Britain. With England to its east, the rest of the land is surrounded by the Atlantic Ocean. Wales consists of low, broad mountains and deep valleys.

The northern section contains rugged mountains, which provide a good place for raising sheep and cattle for beef. In the central section, the mountains become more rounded, and lots of sheep and cattle graze there also. The southern area consists of plateaus and valleys. Although much cattle is raised in the north for dairy production, most of the crops produced in Wales grow in the south.

## IRELAND

A separate island about the size of Maine, Ireland lies to the west of Great Britain. The Irish Sea separates Ireland from Great Britain, and the Atlantic Ocean borders the north and west of Ireland. Northern Ireland occupies the northeast corner, while the country of Ireland comprises the remaining five-sixths of the island. Composed of low mountains and rolling hills, Ireland is dotted with lakes and rivers. The central portion contains lowlands and rolling green pastures, and mountains lie near the coasts.

## >> COOKING METHODS

Roasting, braising, and frying remain the most common cooking methods used in meat preparation. The ample amounts of mutton (old sheep) and tough cuts of meat often appear braised in stews. Pies, puddings, and larger cuts of meat usually are baked or roasted. Whether deep-frying or sautéing, the British often fry foods. Fish and chips is a popular deep-fried dish served throughout the British Isles.

Surrounded by seas, very fresh, high-quality seafood abounds, so poaching is often the preferred cooking method. With the bounty of fish, fish and seafood frequently are smoked, providing a method of preserving seafood for times when less of it is available.

Many identify boiling and blandness with British cookery. Indeed, boiled foods appear frequently, including all sorts of vegetables and meats.

## >> REGIONS

With lots of sheep and cattle grazing in the hills and mountains throughout the British Isles, lamb, mutton, and beef remain the most popular meats. Mint sauce often accompanies lamb. Ample dairy products are produced, and cheese consumption is high all through the British Isles.

### ENGLAND

Several dishes are associated with the cuisine of England. Fish and chips—deep-fried fish and thickly cut French fries—is served accompanied by malt vinegar. Steak and kidney pie consists of a stewlike combination of kidneys and steak topped with a pastry crust. "Bangers and mash" translates into sausages and mashed potatoes. Another dish made with those ubiquitous mashed potatoes, shepherd's pie, combines ground or minced beef with them as a topping.

England's abundant coastline, lakes, and rivers yield plenty of fish and seafood. Favorite fish include cod, haddock, Dover sole, and plaice. Prawns (large shrimp), oysters, and other shellfish are consumed often.

Condiments rank high in English cuisine. Horseradish sauce accompanies roast beef; strong mustards, chutneys, vinegars, and Worcestershire sauce appear frequently.

### SCOTLAND

Scottish cooking includes plentiful seafood, especially cod, haddock, salmon, and mackerel. Salmon from the waters of Scotland is considered some of the finest in the world. Most commonly, the salmon is served grilled, smoked, or poached. Another popular fish is herring, including *kippers*, smoked herring, which are eaten throughout the British Isles.

Scotland's rugged terrain supports game including boar, venison, and many types of wild fowl as well as wild berries and mushrooms. Because abundant sheep thrive in this mountainous land, lamb remains the most often consumed meat. All parts of the animal are used, as demonstrated by the famous dish, *haggis*. A Scotch delicacy, *haggis* consists of sheep's offal mixed with oatmeal, stuffed in a sheep's stomach, and boiled. Oatmeal appears often, both as a filler combined with other ingredients and eaten alone as porridge or cooked cereal.

*Steak and Kidney Pie*
Elzbieta Sekowska © Shutterstock

In 1762, the sandwich was invented. An avid gambler, the 4th Earl of Sandwich, John Montagu, ordered roast beef with two slices of bread while sitting at the gambling table. By placing the meat between the slices of bread, Montagu could eat at the table while still playing cards and manage to keep his hands clean. Named after its creator, this culinary delight gained great popularity and became known as the "sandwich."

### WALES

With many herds of sheep in Wales, lamb reigns as the most popular meat here too. Providing dairy products and meat, cattle also thrives. People in areas near waterways consume fish and seafood.

The cuisine of Wales reflects the workingman—farmers, fishermen, laborers, and coal miners. Easily grown leeks, cabbage, turnips, and potatoes are popular vegetables. Welsh *rarebit*, a melted cheese dish served on toast, originated in Wales. Breweries have existed here since the 1800s.

### IRELAND

Known as the Emerald Isle, Ireland contains rolling farmland and lush, green lands because of its high annual rainfall. Potatoes rank as *the* dietary staple, and seafood, mutton, lamb, and beef are consumed regularly. Irish stew, a stew containing mutton or lamb cooked with potatoes and onions, remains a favorite. Cabbage also appears often. With plentiful pastureland in the interior portions of this country, sheep, cattle for meat and dairy, and hogs thrive. The staggering range of available seafood includes cod, herring, mackerel, whiting, shrimp, lobster, salmon, and trout. With so much access to the ocean, seaweed functions as an important ingredient in the diet on this small island, as it does on the island of Japan.

## >> CUISINE

Simple cooking prevails throughout the British Isles. On Sunday, the typical main meal consists of roast beef (or perhaps mutton, lamb, or pork) with potatoes and one or two vegetables. Yorkshire pudding, a savory battercake cooked in the fat drippings from the roast, usually accompanies the meat. The remainders from Sunday's roast often form the basis for several meals later in the week. Two popular dishes, shepherd's pie and bubble and squeak, begin with leftover meats.

Much of British cookery includes few spices, resulting in a reputation for bland dishes. With lots of cool, damp weather, soups play a substantial role in the diet in these countries. *Cawl*, clear broth with vegetables, is a creation from Wales. *Cockaleekie* hails from Scotland and is their version of very thick chicken soup containing leeks and barley.

*Individual Meat Pudding*
© Joe Gough

With miles and miles of shoreline surrounding this large island, seafood remains a staple. Cod and haddock appear everywhere; fish and chips is widely consumed. They smoke all sorts of seafood to preserve it. In addition, game remains an important part of the cuisine.

As a result of the short growing season, winter vegetables, including cabbage, turnips, rutabagas, cauliflower, Brussels sprouts, carrots, and peas, are most available and frequently served. The British prepare most vegetables simply by boiling and seasoning with salt, pepper, and butter.

Puddings and pies are popular fare throughout the British Isles. The main difference between a pie and a pudding depends on the dish in which it is baked. A pie comes in a dish about 2 or 3 inches high, whereas a pudding is prepared in a bowl or basin-type dish. Unlike the typical American version of pie, the British prepare both sweet and savory puddings and pies. From steak and kidney to vegetarian, a wide assortment of meats and/or vegetables fills the pies and puddings. Often, the sweet varieties are prepared with dried fruits and/or treacle (sweet syrup like maple syrup or molasses). Whether sweet or savory, they appear frequently in the cuisines found in all of these countries. A variation of the pie, the *pasty*, resembles a turnover. Cornish pasties, filled with meat, potatoes, and sometimes vegetables, remain a popular snack, first course, or light entrée. Schoolchildren frequently eat a Cornish pasty after school.

### PUBS AND BEVERAGES

The pub, short for public house, is the British name for a bar. Truly a British/Irish institution, people gather together to meet friends, watch sports on television, listen to music, eat, and, of course, drink. Typically, one can order food to accompany the drink. Pub food includes such favorites as fish and chips, bangers and mash, sandwiches, cheese plates, and many other dishes.

The most popular alcoholic beverages include all sorts of beers, ale, lager, and stout. However, the British Isles have certainly made a mark on the world of hard liquor. Commonly known as Scotch, Scottish whiskey was first produced in Scotland in the 1400s. Irish whiskey is also quite well known. Gin originated in England. The most popular nonalcoholic beverage, tea, is brewed until quite strong and served with cream and sugar, as we serve coffee in the United States.

*Bangers and Mash*
© Joe Gough

## THE ORIGINS OF WHISKY

References to whisky date from as early as 1494 in Scotland. By 1500, it reigned as the favorite drink of Scottish royalty. The popularity of whisky soared by the 1600s, and distilleries opened throughout Scotland. Over the centuries, Scotch whisky has evolved and improved; the Scotch available today is described with adjectives like complex, aromatic, smoky, and smooth.

The name derived from the Gaelic *uisge beatha* or *usquebaugh*, meaning "water of life." Eventually, *uisge* became pronounced as "usky," which evolved into "whisky."

Scotch whisky is distilled from barley. Some say they made the first whisky to use "ruined" rain-soaked barley.

Now, the first step in making Scotch whisky is to malt (germinate) the barley. To do this, the barley soaks in tanks with spring water for several days. When the grain germinates, it changes the composition of the grain from starch to starch and sugars. Since sugars ferment, this is crucial to the development of the whisky. At the end of this stage of production, they dry the grain in a kiln. The type of wood or peat (coal) used for the drying greatly affects the final flavor of the whisky. After the malting, the liquid undergoes four more processes: mashing, fermenting, distilling, and finally blending and maturing the liquor. Like wine and other liquors, the techniques, length of time, and countless other variables determine the quality and flavor of the final product.

Scotch whisky matures in casks (barrels). Often, those casks were used earlier for the storage of other wines or spirits like sherry, bourbon, rum, or port. Of course, the history of the cask affects the flavor and the color of the finished Scotch whisky.

Single malt Scotch is made from a single distillery. The rest are a blend of whiskies from different distilleries. In theory, blending whiskies combines the best characteristics of all the components to produce a particular flavor palate for the final product.

In order to be called "Scotch," the whisky must be made in Scotland. Today, Scotch whisky ranks as one of Scotland's most important industries.

## MEALS

Hearty breakfasts are customary throughout the British Isles. Eggs, breakfast meat (bacon, sausage, and/or ham), toast, marmalade, oatmeal or porridge, fruit, and kippers frequent breakfast plates.

As in the United States, lunch consists of a sandwich, cold meats, or cheese. Around four or five o'clock in the afternoon, many still consume what is known as "tea," a meal of assorted sweet and savory foods served with tea. Many types of sandwiches, fish, cold meats, cheeses, pickled vegetables, scones, crumpets, breads, cookies (known as "biscuits" throughout the British Isles), and/or cakes may accompany the tea. The selection of foods served can be quite simple or very elaborate. Therefore, the size of the evening meal depends on whether the diner had tea and how much food was consumed at tea.

| REGION | AREA | WEATHER | TOPOGRAPHY | FOODS |
|---|---|---|---|---|
| England | Pennines (northern half) | Mild, damp winters, mild summers | Coast, mountains, hills, lakes | Seafood, cattle, sheep, chicken, eggs, milk |
| | Southwest Peninsula (southwest) | Mild, damp winters, mild summers | Coast, low plateaus, highlands | Seafood, barley, beets, wheat, potatoes, fruit |
| | English Lowlands (remaining southern half) | Mild, damp winters, mild summers | Coast, valleys, fertile farmland, plains, hills, Thames River | Seafood, vegetables, fruits |
| Scotland | Northern two-thirds | Mild, damp winters, mild summers | Coast, mountains, treeless moors, valleys, lakes | Seafood, sheep, cattle |
| | Central | Mild, damp winters, mild summers | Rivers, valleys, fertile farmland, rolling hills | Seafood, wheat, oats, barley, potatoes |
| | South | Mild, damp winters, mild summers | Rolling treeless moors, pastures, highlands | Seafood, sheep, cattle, milk, dairy products |
| Wales | North | Mild, damp winters, mild summers | Mountains, coast, valleys | Seafood, sheep, cattle |
| | Central | Mild, damp winters, mild summers | Rounded mountains, coast, valleys, lakes, plateaus | Seafood, sheep, cattle, dairy |
| | South | Mild, damp winters, mild summers | Plateaus, valleys, coast, forests, lakes, pasture, plains | Seafood, cattle, dairy, oats, barley, potatoes, cauliflower, cabbage |
| Northern Ireland | North | Mild, damp winters, mild summers | Low mountains, coast, lakes, rolling hills | Seafood, sheep, cattle, potatoes |
| | Central | Mild, damp winters, mild summers | Plains, fertile farmland | Seafood, sheep, cattle, chicken, eggs, dairy, potatoes, cabbage, turnips, pears, plums, apples, mushrooms |
| Ireland | Coasts | Mild, damp winters, mild summers | Mountains, coast | Seafood, sheep, cattle, potatoes, seaweed |
| | Central | Mild, damp winters, mild summers | Pastureland, rolling hills | Sheep, cattle, fruits, winter vegetables, potatoes |

## CHEESES FROM THE BRITISH ISLES

### England

**Cheddar** Made from cow's milk; sharp deep flavor, firm texture

**Cheshire** Made from cow's milk; the oldest variety of English cheese from the twelfth century, tangy yet mild flavor, firm crumbly texture; a tall cheese

**Derby** From Derbyshire, made from cow's milk; mild flavor, firm yet flaky texture, often mixed with sage

**Gloucester** Made from cow's milk; mild with a little sharpness in flavor, firm texture

**Lancashire** Made from cow's milk; tangy yet mild flavor, firm crumbly texture

**Leicester** Made from cow's milk; sweet yet sharp flavor, creamy texture

**Stilton** Made from cow's milk; a blue cheese, creamy texture

**Wensleydale** From Yorkshire, made from sheep's milk in the early days but now made from cow's milk; mild with buttermilklike taste, crumbly firm texture

### Scotland

**Bonnet** Made from goat's milk; hard, at least 6 months to mature; named for town of Stewarton, which had a mill where they made bonnets

**Crowdie** Made from cow's milk; fresh cheese; hails from the time of the Vikings; slightly tart flavor, creamy yet crumbly texture

**Orkney Extra Mature Cheddar** Made from cow's milk; aged at least one year; firm texture

**Seriously Strong Cheddar** Made from cow's milk; aged one and a half to two years; strong flavor, firm texture

### Wales

**Caerphilly** Made from cow's milk; mild flavor, creamy, semifirm texture; first made in 1830

**Llanboidy** Made from cow's milk; Cheddar-like flavor, creamy, crumbly texture

### Ireland

**Cashel Blue** Made from cow's milk; a blue cheese, soft texture

## >> Review Questions

1. Discuss the geographic factors of the British Isles as they relate to the cuisines of the various countries.
2. How does the weather influence the cuisines of these countries?
3. Name four food ingredients that are prevalent in the British Isles.
4. Name beverages (alcoholic and nonalcoholic) that are favored in the countries of the British Isles.
5. What is tea, and what foods are served for tea?
6. What is a pub, and what foods are typically served there?
7. Name and describe four dishes served in the British Isles. Tell whether they are regional dishes or are served throughout the British Isles.

## >> Glossary

**bangers and mash** Sausages and mashed potatoes

**biscuits** British word for cookies

*cawl* Clear broth containing vegetables, served in Wales

**chips** Thickly cut french fries served throughout the British Isles

*cockaleekie* A thick chicken soup containing leeks and barley from Scotland

*colcannon* An Irish dish of potatoes mixed with kale or cabbage

**fish and chips** Deep-fried fish and thickly cut french fries, served with malt vinegar

*haggis* Scottish dish consisting of sheep's heart, liver, and lung mixed with oatmeal, stuffed in a sheep's stomach, and boiled

*kippers* Smoked herring, frequently served at breakfast or tea

**mutton** Old lamb, which contains a stronger flavor and tougher texture than younger lamb

*pasty* A turnover usually filled with meat, potatoes, and vegetables

**porridge** Cooked cereal, usually oatmeal

**potato crisps** British term for the American version of potato chips

**prawns** Large shrimp

**scone** A slightly sweetened bread product (like an American biscuit) containing dried currants

**shepherd's pie** A dish containing cooked beef topped with a crust of mashed potatoes

**steak and kidney pie** A stewlike combination of kidneys and steak in a pastry crust

**treacle** A sweet syrup like maple syrup or molasses

**Yorkshire pudding** A savory battercake cooked in meat fat, usually served with roast beef

## SCOTCH EGGS (SCOTLAND)
### HARD BOILED EGGS SURROUNDED BY SAUSAGE

Pearson Education, Inc.

**Number of Servings:** 8
**Serving Size:** 1 egg, about 4 oz. (114 g)
**Total Yield:** 2 lb., 1 1/2 oz. (950 g)
**Wine Style:** Medium- to full-bodied dry white wine, from an old world cool climate region. Possible grape varietals are Pinot Blanc, Pinot Gris, Riesling, Gruner Veltliner, and Silvaner.
**Example:** Pinot Blanc GG "im Sonnenschein" 2011, Rebholz (Pfalz/Germany)

**Cooking Method:** Boil, deep-fry

| | WEIGHT | | VOLUME | |
|---|---|---|---|---|
| INGREDIENTS | U.S. | METRIC | U.S. | METRIC |
| pork sausage | 1 lb. | 454 g | | |
| Worcestershire sauce | 1 oz. | 28 g | 2 tablespoons | 30 mL |
| mace | sprinkling | | | |
| flour | 2 1/2 oz. | 71 g | 1/2 cup | 120 mL |
| eggs, hard boiled, peeled | 14 1/2 oz. | 411 g | 8 each | |
| egg | 3 1/2 oz. | 104 g | 2 each | |
| water | 1 oz. | 28 g | 2 tablespoons | 30 mL |
| breadcrumbs, dried | 5 oz. | 142 g | 1 cup | 240 mL |
| oil, for deep-frying | | | | |

**Accompaniment:**
mustard, English or brown

### TWIST ON THE CLASSIC

For an entrée salad, prepare a lettuce salad with mustard vinaigrette. Top salad with a Scotch egg cut in half. Nest each half in the greens so the hard boiled egg faces the diner.

Scotch eggs developed as food for farmers or shepherds to take to the fields for later consumption. The fried egg sausage combination was easy to carry, tasty, and full of protein. Today, Scotch eggs are a popular pub food served throughout the British Isles.

1. Mix sausage with Worcestershire sauce and mace.
2. Pat 2 to 2 1/4 oz. (57 to 64 g) of sausage mixture into patty about 1/4-inch (0.5-cm) thick on piece of plastic wrap.
3. Place flour on plate. Roll egg in flour; shake egg to remove excess. Place hard boiled egg in center of sausage. Using plastic wrap, fold sausage around egg. Seal tightly so it covers egg completely. Chill.
4. Set up standard breading station: Flour is already on plate. Mix egg with water in bowl. Place breadcrumbs on plate.
5. Roll sausage-covered egg in flour. Dip in egg wash. Roll in breadcrumbs. Refrigerate until needed.
6. At time of service, heat oil to 375 degrees (190°C) for deep-frying. Add sausage eggs, a few at a time to maintain oil temperature. Fry until golden, about 3 to 4 minutes on each side. Turn to fry all sides until golden. Remove to drain on absorbent paper.
7. Serve accompanied by mustard either hot, room temperature, or cold.

**Note:** When preparing hard boiled eggs for Scotch eggs, do not overcook the eggs. Place eggs in saucepan of water, bring to a gentle boil, reduce heat, and simmer about 6 minutes. Cool with cold water and refrigerate until needed.

# PICKLED ONIONS (ENGLAND)

**Note:** Pickled onions make a good accompaniment to a sandwich. Use any place a traditional pickle might appear.

**Total Yield:** 1 pint (480 mL)
**Cooking Method:** Boil
**Food Balance:** Sweet/sour
**Wine Style:** Light and fruity Riesling, Pinot Blanc, soft-style reds—Shiraz
**Example:** Beringer Vineyards Pinot Grigio

**TWIST ON THE CLASSIC**

Replace the raw onions with pickled onions on any meat, poultry, seafood, or vegetable kabob before grilling.

| | WEIGHT | | VOLUME | |
| --- | --- | --- | --- | --- |
| **INGREDIENTS** | **U.S.** | **METRIC** | **U.S.** | **METRIC** |
| small white boiling onions | 1 lb. | 454 g | | |
| kosher salt | 2 1/4 oz. | 64 g | 1/4 cup | 60 mL |
| malt vinegar | | | 2 cups | 480 mL |
| sugar | 3 3/4 oz. | 107 g | 1/4 cup | 60 mL |
| pickling spices | 1/4 oz. | 8 g | 1 tablespoon | 15 mL |
| whole cloves | | | 3 each | |
| black peppercorns, whole | | | 5 each | |

1. Place onions in pot of boiling water, boil 1 minute, drain, rinse with cold water.
2. Peel onions, place in bowl, sprinkle with salt, stir to coat evenly.
3. Cover bowl, set in cool place for 12 hours.
4. Drain onions, rinse well with cold water, let drain.
5. Combine vinegar, sugar, pickling spices, cloves, and peppercorns in nonreactive pan.
6. Bring to boil, stir to dissolve sugar, boil for 5 minutes.
7. Add onions, adding water if liquid does not cover onions.
8. Return to boil for 10 minutes, uncovered, until onions show slight resistance when pierced with sharp knife.
9. Remove pan from heat, let mixture cool.
10. For quicker use place in jar or other nonreactive covered container and store in refrigerator at least 2 weeks before serving. For longer storage, process pickled onions in canning jars.

© Monkey Business

# CORNISH PASTY (ENGLAND)
## BEEF, ONION, AND POTATO TURNOVER

© Joe Gough

### TWIST ON THE CLASSIC

Pasties can hold an endless variety of fillings. In addition to beef, prepare them with lamb, pork, chicken, or vegetarian fillings. How about a wild mushroom pasty flavored with truffle oil or duck with hoisin as the filling?

**Note:** Serve Cornish pasties as a snack, first course, luncheon entrée, or at tea.

**Number of Servings:** 12 or 24      **Cooking Method:** Bake
**Serving Size:** 1 or 2 turnovers
**Total Yield:** 24 turnovers
**Food Balance:** Balanced protein
**Wine Style:** Wide variety of wines: Sauvignon Blanc, Chardonnay, Pinot Noir, Merlot, Shiraz
**Example:** Beringer Founders' Estate Pinot Noir

| | WEIGHT | | VOLUME | |
|---|---|---|---|---|
| INGREDIENTS | U.S. | METRIC | U.S. | METRIC |
| **Pastry:** | | | | |
| flour, all-purpose | 1 lb., 4 oz. | 567 g | 4 1/2 cups | 1.8 L |
| salt | | | 1/4 teaspoon | 2 mL |
| butter, shortening, or combination, chilled, cut into 3/4-inch (2-cm) pieces | 12 oz. | 341 g | 1 1/2 cups or 3 sticks | 360 mL |
| cold water | 6 to 8 oz. | 171 to 227 g | 3/4 to 1 cup | 180 to 240 mL |
| **Filling:** | | | | |
| beef, top round, trimmed and minced | 1 lb. | 454 g | | |
| potatoes, white, waxy, or all-purpose, peeled and cut into small dice | 10 1/2 oz. | 298 g | 3 medium | |
| onions, medium dice | 8 oz. | 227 g | 2 medium | |
| salt | 3/4 oz. | 22 g | 1 tablespoon | 15 mL |
| pepper | 1/4 oz. | 8 g | 2 teaspoons | 10 mL |
| fresh parsley, minced | 1/2 oz. | 15 g | 1/4 cup | 60 mL |
| **Assembly:** | | | | |
| egg, lightly beaten | 1 3/4 oz. | 50 g | 1 each | |

### PASTRY:

1. Place flour and salt in bowl of food processor fitted with knife blade. Pulse to mix.
2. Add butter, shortening, or combination, pulse to mix until clumps the size of peas form.
3. With machine running, add water through feed tube; dough should form a ball quickly. If it does not, pulse until dough comes together.
4. Wrap ball in film, refrigerate until well chilled, several hours or overnight. For quicker chilling, pat into disk and place in freezer.

### FILLING:

1. Combine all filling ingredients in bowl, mix well.
2. Cover and refrigerate until ready to use.

### ASSEMBLY:

1. Preheat oven to 400 degrees (205°C). Position oven rack in center of oven.
2. On lightly floured surface, roll pastry thin, 1/8 to 3/16 inch (30 mm to 45 mm) thick.
3. Cut 5- to 5 1/2-inch (13 to 14 cm) circles, place 1 1/2 oz (43 g) or 3 tablespoons (45 mL) of filling just under center of each circle of dough.

4. Brush edges of dough with cold water, fold dough over filling until edges meet to form half-circle, and crimp edges to seal well.
5. Place on baking sheet, brush with egg.
6. Bake for 12 minutes, reduce heat to 325 degrees (160°C), bake another 45 minutes. Serve immediately or slightly cooled.

---

## CREAM OF PEA SOUP

**Note:** This soup presents a strong green color of spring, and it delivers a very fresh flavor. With a base similar to vichyssoise, cream of pea soup can be served hot or cold.

**Number of Servings:** 12
**Serving Size:** 8 oz. (227 g)
**Total Yield:** 6 lb., 3 3/4 oz. (2.8 kg)
**Food Balance:** Sweet/protein
**Wine Style:** Low-oaked to unoaked whites and soft, fruity reds
**Example:** Souverain Sauvignon Blanc or Château St. Jean Merlot

**Cooking Method:** Sauté, boil

© Viktorija

| | WEIGHT | | VOLUME | |
|---|---|---|---|---|
| INGREDIENTS | U.S. | METRIC | U.S. | METRIC |
| butter | 1 oz. | 28 g | 2 tablespoons | 30 mL |
| leeks, washed thoroughly and sliced | 10 3/4 oz. | 305 g | 2 each | |
| potato, white, waxy, or all-purpose, peeled and cut into large dice | 9 oz. | 256 g | 2 medium | |
| all-purpose flour | 1 oz. | 28 g | 3 tablespoons | 45 mL |
| stock, ham, chicken, or vegetarian, hot | 3 lb., 8 oz. | 1.6 kg | 1 quart + 3 cups (7 cups) | 1.68 L |
| frozen peas | 2 lb. | 908 g | | |
| fresh parsley, minced | 1/4 oz. | 8 g | 1 tablespoon | 15 mL |
| fresh mint, minced | 1/4 oz. | 8 g | 2 tablespoons | 30 mL |
| salt | to taste | | | |
| pepper | | | 1/2 teaspoon | 3 mL |
| heavy cream | 4 oz. | 114 g | 1/2 cup | 120 mL |

**Garnish:**
fresh mint, minced

### TWIST ON THE CLASSIC

For a lighter version, substitute milk for the cream in this recipe. Also, this refreshing soup could be thinned and used as a sauce for vegetables or chicken.

1. Melt butter in large pan over medium heat. Add leeks and potato, sauté about 5 minutes.
2. Lower heat to medium-low, add flour. Stir until blonde *roux*.
3. Slowly whisk in hot stock. Cook about 30 minutes.
4. Add peas, parsley, and mint. Remove from heat, purée in batches in food processor fitted with knife blade.
5. Return to pan, heat over medium-low heat until simmering. Add salt, pepper, and cream. Be careful not to boil once cream is added.
6. Correct seasonings. Serve, garnished with mint.

# COCKALEEKIE (SCOTLAND)
## CHICKEN AND LEEK SOUP

**Number of Servings:** 23　　　　　　**Cooking Method:** Braise
**Serving Size:** 8 oz. (227 g)
**Total Yield:** 11 lb., 10 oz. (5.3 kg)
**Food Balance:** Protein
**Wine Style:** Light- to medium-bodied Viognier or Chardonnay, and soft reds, such as Merlot or Shiraz
**Example:** Souverain Chardonnay or Stone Cellars Merlot

| INGREDIENTS | WEIGHT | | VOLUME | |
| --- | --- | --- | --- | --- |
| | U.S. | METRIC | U.S. | METRIC |
| stewing chicken, washed | about 6 lb. | 2.8 kg | | |
| cold water | | | 5 quarts (20 cups) | 4.8 L |
| leeks, washed thoroughly and sliced 1/2-inch (1 1/3-cm) thick, including 2 inches (5 cm) of the green stems | 1 lb., 7 oz. | 652 g | 6 each | |
| barley | 4 oz. | 114 g | 1/2 cup | 120 mL |
| salt | 3/4 oz. | 22 g | 1 tablespoon | 15 mL |
| pepper | to taste | | | |
| grated nutmeg | to taste | | | |
| **Garnish:** | | | | |
| fresh parsley, minced | 1/4 oz. | 8 g | 2 tablespoons | 30 mL |

1. Remove excess fat from cavity of chicken.
2. Place water and chicken in large pot.
3. Bring to boil over high heat, skimming when necessary.
4. Add leeks, barley, and salt, reduce heat to low, simmer about 3 hours, until chicken is well done.
5. Remove chicken, set aside to cool slightly. Remove and discard skin and bones, cut meat into pieces no larger than 2 inches (5 cm). Cover and refrigerate until needed.
6. Cool soup in cold water bath, refrigerate overnight to solidify fat. Remove fat and discard.
7. Return meat to soup, heat thoroughly.
8. Add pepper and nutmeg. Correct seasonings. Serve, garnished with parsley.

# CULLEN SKINK (SCOTLAND)
## SMOKED HADDOCK CHOWDER

**Number of Servings:** 13
**Serving Size:** 8 oz. (227 g)
**Total Yield:** 6 lb., 12 oz. (3.1 kg)
**Wine Style:** Medium-bodied red wine with well-integrated oak and a balanced acidity.
Possible grape varietals are St. Laurent, Zweigelt, Blaufrankisch, and Pinot Noir.
**Example:** St Laurent "Schafleiten," Judith Beck (Neusiedlersee/Austria)

**Cooking Method:** Boil

© Fanfo/Fotolia

| INGREDIENTS | WEIGHT | | VOLUME | |
|---|---|---|---|---|
| | U.S. | METRIC | U.S. | METRIC |
| Finnan haddock or smoke haddock, undyed | 1 lb. to 1 lb., 4 oz. | 454 g to 567 g | 2 each | |
| bay leaves | | | 2 each | |
| onion, chopped | 12 oz. | 340 g | 2 large | |
| water | 2 lb. or to barely cover | 908 g | 1 quart | 946 mL |
| potatoes, red, peeled, cut into chunks | 2 lb. | 908 g | about 6 each | |
| milk, whole | 3 lb. | 1.4 kg | 1 quart, 2 cups | 1.4 L |
| salt | 1/2 oz. | 15 g | 2 teaspoons | 10 mL |
| pepper | | | 1/2 teaspoon | 3 mL |
| butter | 2 oz. | 57 g | 4 tablespoons or 1/2 stick | 60 mL |

**Garnish:**
chives, minced
parsley, minced

### TWIST ON THE CLASSIC

Use this thick soup as a sauce for fish. For another idea: parboil florets of broccoli and cauliflower, place in ovenproof dish and pour some of the Cullen skink over it. Top with grated cheddar and heat in a 425-degree (220°C) oven until vegetables are done and dish is hot and cheese browns (broil if needed to brown cheese).

1. Wash haddock; place in pot large enough to hold it without folding the fish. Add bay leaves and onion. Barely cover with water.

2. Bring to boil over medium heat; lower heat and simmer until fish flakes, about 10 minutes.

3. Gently remove fish from stock; allow to cool. After it cools, remove skin and all bones. Flake fish and refrigerate until needed.

4. Add potatoes to stock; partially cover pot and cook until done. If liquid becomes too little, add some of the milk. Remove bay leaves and discard.

5. Purée potato mixture until smooth in food processor fitted with knife blade. Return to saucepan. Add milk, salt, pepper, butter, and reserved fish. Heat gently until hot over medium-low heat.

6. Correct seasonings. Garnish with minced chives and/or parsley. Serve.

**Note:** If smoked haddock is unavailable, substitute another smoked fish. Use any firm fish, if available.

# PICKLED RED ONION SALAD

© Azurita

**Note:** Allow at least 1 hour for onions to marinate. Chill salad plates in advance.

**Number of Servings:** 8          **Cooking Method:** Boil
**Serving Size:** 4 oz. (114 g)
   1 1/4 oz. (36 g) lettuce
   1/2 oz. (15 g) cheddar cheese
   1 3/4 oz. (50 g) onions
   1/2 oz. (15 g) vinaigrette
**Total Yield:**
   1 lb., 1 1/2 oz. (497 g) onions in marinade
   4 1/4 oz. (120 g) vinaigrette
**Food Balance:** Balanced
**Wine Style:** Wine friendly—Try your favorite
**Example:** Chardonnay, Zinfandel

| | WEIGHT | | VOLUME | |
|---|---|---|---|---|
| INGREDIENTS | U.S. | METRIC | U.S. | METRIC |
| red wine vinegar | | 43 g | 3 tablespoons | 45 mL |
| port | | 29 g | 2 tablespoons | 30 mL |
| Dijon mustard | 1/4 oz. | 8 g | 1 teaspoon | 5 mL |
| salt | | | 1/4 teaspoon | 2 mL |
| pepper | | | 1/8 teaspoon | 1 mL |
| olive oil | | 86 g | 1/4 cup + 2 tablespoons | 90 mL |
| red onion, cut in half and sliced 1/4-inch (1/2-cm) thick | 12 1/4 oz. | 348 g | 1 large | |
| *VINAIGRETTE:* | | | | |
| red wine vinegar | | 29 g | 2 tablespoons | 30 mL |
| port | | 15 g | 1 tablespoon | 15 mL |
| curry powder | | | 1/4 teaspoon | 2 mL |
| salt | | | 1/4 teaspoon | 2 mL |
| pepper | | | 1/8 teaspoon | 1 mL |
| olive oil | | 86 g | 1/4 cup + 2 tablespoons | 90 mL |
| salad greens, variety of choice | 10 oz. | 284 g | | |
| cheddar cheese, grated | 5 oz. | 142 g | 1/2 cup | 120 mL |

1. Place vinegar, port, mustard, salt, pepper, and olive oil in nonreactive saucepan. Bring to boil.
2. Add onion, reduce heat, and simmer about 4 minutes.
3. Remove from heat, let cool in marinade until room temperature. Correct seasonings. Marinate at least 1 hour. Refrigerate until needed.

## VINAIGRETTE:

1. Place red wine vinegar, port, curry powder, salt, and pepper in bowl of food processor fitted with knife blade.
2. With processor running, slowly add olive oil through feed tube. Process until mixture emulsifies (thickens). Correct seasonings.

## ASSEMBLY:

1. Place 1 1/4 oz. (36 g) salad greens on each chilled plate. Sprinkle 1/2 oz. (15 g) cheddar cheese over greens.
2. Top with 1 3/4 oz. (50 g) marinated onions. Drizzle about 1/2 oz. (15 g) or 1 tablespoon (15 mL) vinaigrette over salad. Serve.

## WATERCRESS AND ORANGE SALAD (IRELAND)

**Note:** If watercress is unavailable, substitute spring mix or another variety of lettuce. Chill salad plates in advance.

**Number of Servings:** 15
**Serving Size:** 3 oz. (86 g)
**Total Yield:** 2 lb., 13 oz. (1.28 kg)

| | WEIGHT | | VOLUME | |
| --- | --- | --- | --- | --- |
| INGREDIENTS | U.S. | METRIC | U.S. | METRIC |
| **Dressing:** | | | | |
| fresh lemon juice | | 57 g | 1/4 cup | 60 ml |
| salt | | | 1/2 teaspoon | 3 mL |
| white pepper | | | 1/8 teaspoon | 1 mL |
| olive oil | | 57 g | 1/4 cup | 60 mL |
| watercress, washed, tough stems removed, and dried | 8 1/2 oz. | 241 g | 2 bunches | |
| celery, thinly sliced | 12 1/2 oz. | 355 g | 6 stalks | |
| onion, minced | 4 oz. | 114 g | 1 small | |
| oranges, peeled, pith removed, and sliced thinly | 1 lb., 2 oz. | 511 g | 4 each | |

1. Place all dressing ingredients in a jar or bowl of food processor fitted with knife blade. Beat or process until mixture thickens (emulsifies).

2. Place watercress, celery, and onion in bowl, top with oranges.

3. Pour dressing over salad, mix gently to distribute dressing. Correct seasonings.

4. Serve immediately, making sure at least one orange slice tops each serving.

© FoodPhotogr Eising/StockFood/AGE Fotostock

# BEEF STEW BRAISED IN GUINNESS (IRELAND)

**Note:** Serve this hearty stew with bread to sop up the remaining sauce.

**Number of Servings:** 11                    **Cooking Method:** Braise
**Serving Size:** 8 oz. (227 g)
**Total Yield:** 5 lb., 14 oz. (2.7 kg)
**Food Balance:** Protein
**Wine Style:** Light- to medium-bodied, fruity Sauvignon Blanc, Merlot, Shiraz, or Cabernet
Sauvignon
**Example:** Souverain Cabernet Sauvignon

| | WEIGHT | | VOLUME | |
| --- | --- | --- | --- | --- |
| **INGREDIENTS** | **U.S.** | **METRIC** | **U.S.** | **METRIC** |
| prunes | 12 oz. | 341 g | 2 cups | 480 mL |
| oil | | 57 g | 1/4 cup | 60 mL |
| bay leaves | | | 6 each | |
| beef, chuck or round, trimmed and cut into 2-inch (5-cm) chunks | 4 lb. to 4 lb., 8 oz. | 1.8 kg to 2.1 kg | | |
| onion, sliced 1/4-inch (1/2-cm) thick | 1 lb., 2 oz. | 511 g | 2 large | |
| flour | 1 oz. | 28 g | 1/4 cup | 60 mL |
| Guinness | | 341 g | 1 1/2 cups | 360 mL |
| water | | 454 g | 2 cups | 480 mL |
| fresh parsley, minced | 1/4 oz. | 8 g | 2 tablespoons | 30 mL |
| carrots, peeled and cut into 1-inch slices | 1 lb. | 454 g | 5 each | |
| salt | 1/4 oz. | 8 g | 1 teaspoon | 5 mL |
| pepper | | | 1/2 teaspoon | 3 mL |

**Garnish:**
fresh parsley, minced, *optional*

© Annamavriita

1. Preheat oven to 300 degrees (150°C). Cover prunes with hot water, set aside.
2. Heat oil in large ovenproof pan or braiser on medium-high heat, add bay leaves and sauté.
3. Add beef, sauté until seared on all sides.
4. Add onion, sauté until lightly browned.
5. Reduce heat to medium, sprinkle flour over mixture in pan, mix until browned.
6. Reduce heat to low, slowly whisk in Guinness and water, a little at a time. If necessary, add more water to cover meat.
7. Add parsley, carrots, salt, and pepper; stir to distribute seasonings.
8. Place in oven and braise for 2 to 2 1/2 hours, until meat is tender. Stir occasionally. Add soaked prunes 30 minutes before serving.
9. Correct seasonings and serve, garnished with minced parsley, if desired.

## SHEPHERD'S PIE (ENGLAND)

### BEEF TOPPED WITH MASHED POTATOES

**Note:** This common British dish was prepared from leftovers of the beef roast traditionally served on Sundays. For easier restaurant service, make shepherd's pie in individual casseroles.

**Number of Servings:** 12

**Serving Size:** 5 oz. (142 g) or 1/6 pie

**Total Yield:** Two 9-inch pies (23 cm)

**Food Balance:** Protein

**Wine Style:** Light- to medium-bodied Chardonnay, Merlot, Shiraz, Zinfandel, or Cabernet Sauvignon

**Example:** Beringer Founders' Estate Merlot

**Cooking Method:** Boil, bake

© Fudio

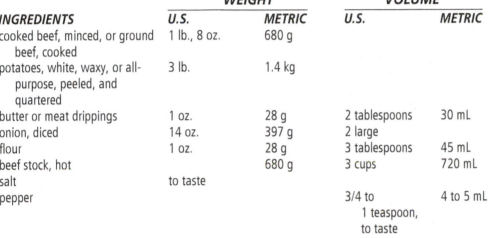

| INGREDIENTS | WEIGHT | | VOLUME | |
|---|---|---|---|---|
| | U.S. | METRIC | U.S. | METRIC |
| cooked beef, minced, or ground beef, cooked | 1 lb., 8 oz. | 680 g | | |
| potatoes, white, waxy, or all-purpose, peeled, and quartered | 3 lb. | 1.4 kg | | |
| butter or meat drippings | 1 oz. | 28 g | 2 tablespoons | 30 mL |
| onion, diced | 14 oz. | 397 g | 2 large | |
| flour | 1 oz. | 28 g | 3 tablespoons | 45 mL |
| beef stock, hot | | 680 g | 3 cups | 720 mL |
| salt | to taste | | | |
| pepper | | | 3/4 to 1 teaspoon, to taste | 4 to 5 mL |

**Topping:**

butter, melted

> **TWIST ON THE CLASSIC**
>
> Prepare shepherd's pie with any filling substituted for the traditional beef filling, covered with mashed potatoes. Try curried chicken or slices of a sausage such as English bangers, Italian sweet or hot sausage, or Spanish chorizo.

 While preparing beef, boil potatoes in water until tender. Process into mashed potatoes. Season potatoes with salt and pepper, to taste.

2. Preheat oven to 425 degrees (220°C).

3. Melt butter or meat drippings in skillet, add onion, sauté over medium-low heat until soft, about 4 minutes.

4. Add flour and cook until light brown in color.

5. Slowly whisk in stock. Add meat, salt, and pepper, and simmer at least 10 minutes. Add more stock if too thick. Correct seasonings.

6. Place meat mixture into pie pans, steam table pan, or individual ovenproof dishes. Top with mashed potatoes, which can be spread or decoratively piped over meat. Dot or brush with melted butter.

7. Bake for 25 to 30 minutes. If needed, brown under broiler until golden. Serve immediately, accompanied by your choice of vegetable.

# IRISH STEW (IRELAND)

**Note:** Originally, long-cooking Irish stews made use of tough, strongly flavored mutton.

**Number of Servings:** 9

**Cooking Method:** Braise

**Serving Size:** 8 oz. (227 g)
**Total Yield:** 4 lb., 10 oz. (2.1 kg)
**Food Balance:** Balanced protein
**Wine Style:** Wide variety: Sauvignon Blanc, Pinot Blanc, Pinot Noir, Merlot
**Example:** Château St. Jean Pinot Noir

| INGREDIENTS | WEIGHT | | VOLUME | |
| --- | --- | --- | --- | --- |
| | U.S. | METRIC | U.S. | METRIC |
| potatoes, white, waxy, or all-purpose, peeled, and cut into 1/4-inch slices | 1 lb., 8 oz. | 680 g | | |
| onions, 1/4-inch slices | 1 lb. | 454 g | 4 each | |
| lean boneless lamb, neck or shoulder, 1 1/2-inch cubes | 2 lb. | 908 g | | |
| salt | 1/2 oz. | 15 g | 2 teaspoons | 10 mL |
| pepper | | | 1/2 teaspoon | 3 mL |
| thyme | | | 1 teaspoon | 5 mL |
| fresh parsley, minced | 1/4 oz. | 8 g | 2 tablespoons | 30 mL |
| stock or water | | 227 g | 1 cup | 240 mL |

1. Preheat oven to 300 degrees (150°C). Place oven rack in lower half of oven.
2. Place half of potatoes (12 oz./341 g) in ovenproof pan.
3. Top with half of onions (8 oz./227 g), then lamb.
4. Sprinkle half of seasonings (salt, pepper, thyme, and parsley) over lamb.
5. Place remaining onions over lamb.
6. Arrange remaining potatoes on top.
7. Sprinkle with remaining seasonings.
8. Pour in stock or water.
9. Cover pan, place in oven. Bake for 2 to 2 1/2 hours, until lamb is tender. Add more water if becoming too dry; remove lid if too soupy. Correct seasonings. Serve.

Courtesy of the Idaho Potato Commission

# DUCK WITH PEAS AND ONIONS

**Number of Servings:** 8  **Cooking Method:** Bake, sauté

**Serving Size:** 1/4 duck, 6 oz. (171 g) peas and onions

**Total Yield:** 10 lb., 6 1/2 oz. (4.72 kg)

**Wine Style:** You can pair this dish with a more full-bodied white wine with some age on it or a lighter red wine.

Possible grape varietals are Riesling, Gruner Veltliner, Sauvignon Blanc, Pinot Noir or St. Laurent.

**Example:** 2013 Domaine Reverdy-Ducroux Sancerre 'Les Vignes Silex' (France/Upper Loire)

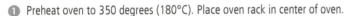

© Nicol/Photocuisine/AGE Fotostock

| | WEIGHT | | VOLUME | |
| --- | --- | --- | --- | --- |
| **INGREDIENTS** | **U.S.** | **METRIC** | **U.S.** | **METRIC** |
| duck, neck and giblets removed | 10 lb., 13 1/2 oz. | 4.8 kg | 2 each | |
| salt, coarse | as needed | | | |
| bacon, cut into 3/4-inch (2-cm) pieces | 5 oz. | 142 g | 6 slices | |
| boiling onions, peeled | 14 oz. | 397 g | 24 each | |
| pepper | as needed | | | |
| chicken stock | | 114 g | 1/2 cup | 120 mL |
| honey | 2 1/2 oz. | 71 g | 1/4 cup | 60 mL |
| peas, frozen | 2 lb. | 908 g | | |

1. Preheat oven to 350 degrees (180°C). Place oven rack in center of oven.

2. Place duck on rack in roasting pan with breast side up. Using fork, stick the duck all over. Sprinkle salt over duck. Place in oven and bake for 1 hour. Remove from oven, discard fat from bottom of pan.

3. Turn duck over so the breast side is down. Stick with fork, sprinkle with salt, and return to oven for 1 hour. Remove from oven, discard fat from bottom of pan.

4. Turn duck over so the breast side is up. Return to oven and bake another 45 minutes or until duck is almost done. From this point, the duck cooks another 30 minutes. (Thermometer inserted into fully cooked duck thigh should read 175 degrees [80°C].)

5. While duck is cooking this final time, place bacon pieces and whole onions into skillet over medium heat. Sauté until bacon is crisp (onions will brown), about 10 minutes. Season with pepper.

6. After 45 minutes, remove duck from oven, pour off excess fat. Remove duck and rack from pan. Deglaze pan with stock, stirring to release baked-on bits from bottom of pan. Add honey and cook to combine.

7. Stir onion and bacon mixture into liquid in duck pan. Return rack and duck to pan. Return to oven for 15 minutes.

8. Remove from oven. Add frozen peas to pan. Bake another 15 minutes.

9. Correct seasonings. Serve duck with vegetables, making sure each portion receives three onions.

## TWIST ON THE CLASSIC

If duck with crisp skin is desired, broil duck until golden on all sides before deglazing the pan and adding the vegetables. Then continue with the recipe as written.

# COD CAKES (SCOTLAND)

**Note:** Like many recipes from the British Isles, this recipe is a bit bland. If you want to spice it up, add some nutmeg and cayenne pepper. Be careful not to overdo it.

**Number of Servings:** 9
**Serving Size:** Two 3-oz. patties (86 g)
**Total Yield:** 3 lb., 7 oz. (1.6 kg)
**Food Balance:** Protein
**Wine Style:** Soft and fruity Viognier, Marsanne, Chardonnay, Dolcetto, or Beaujolais
**Example:** Greg Norman Chardonnay

**Cooking Method:** Sauté

Courtesy of the Idaho Potato Commission

## TWIST ON THE CLASSIC

Try substituting cheddar cheese for the béchamel sauce for a different flavor. Serve the cod cake over a salad for a luncheon dish or warm weather entrée.

| | WEIGHT | | VOLUME | |
|---|---|---|---|---|
| **INGREDIENTS** | **U.S.** | **METRIC** | **U.S.** | **METRIC** |
| **Béchamel Sauce:** | | | | |
| butter | 1 oz. | 28 g | 2 tablespoons | 30 mL |
| flour | 1 oz. | 28 g | 2 tablespoons | 30 mL |
| milk, hot | | 227 g | 1 cup | 240 mL |
| salt | to taste | | | |
| pepper | to taste | | | |
| cod or haddock, poached, then flaked | 1 lb., 1 oz. | 482 g | 3 cups | 720 mL |
| onion, finely minced | 2 oz. | 57 g | 1/4 cup | 60 mL |
| potatoes, white, waxy, or all-purpose, cooked and mashed | 1 lb., 8 oz. | 680 g | 3 cups | 720 mL |
| salt | | | 3/4 teaspoon | 4 mL |
| pepper | | | 1/2 teaspoon | 2 mL |
| dried thyme, crushed | | | 1/2 teaspoon | 2 mL |
| fresh parsley, minced | 1/2 oz. | 15 g | 3 tablespoons | 45 mL |
| prepared mustard | | | 1 1/2 teaspoons | 8 mL |
| egg | 5 oz. | 142 g | 3 each | |
| frying oil | as needed | | | |

**Garnish:**
lemon, minced parsley, and/
or tartar sauce

## BÉCHAMEL SAUCE:

1. Melt butter in pan over medium heat, add flour, and whisk until a blond *roux* (very lightly colored).
2. Reduce heat to low, add milk slowly, whisking constantly until thickened to medium consistency.
3. Season with salt and pepper.
4. Correct seasonings. Strain through China cap or *chinois* to remove any lumps. Cover and refrigerate if not using immediately.

## ASSEMBLY:

1. Add béchamel sauce and all other ingredients, except oil, to bowl. Stir gently until blended.
2. Form 3-oz. (86-g) patties with floured hands. Refrigerate until ready to sauté.
3. Heat 1/4- to 1/2-inch (1/2-cm to 1.3-cm) oil in skillet over medium heat.
4. Sauté cakes until golden brown on both sides.
5. Drain on absorbent paper.
6. Serve, garnished with lemon, parsley, and/or tartar sauce.

# DOVER SOLE MEUNIÈRE (ENGLAND)

## DOVER SOLE WITH BUTTER SAUCE

**Number of Servings:** 9      **Cooking Method:** Sauté

**Serving Size:** 6 oz. (171 g) fish + 1 oz. (28 g) sauce

**Total Yield:** 3 lb., 7 oz. (1.6 kg) fish

**Wine Style:** For this dish, a full-bodied white wine with creaminess and oak flavors is required. Possible grape varietals are Chardonnay, Gruner Veltliner, Sauvignon Blanc.

**Example:** 1994 Domaine aux Moines Savennières Roche aux Moines (France/Loire Valley)

© Marco Mayer

| INGREDIENTS | WEIGHT | | VOLUME | |
| --- | --- | --- | --- | --- |
| | U.S. | METRIC | U.S. | METRIC |
| flour, all purpose | 5 oz. | 142 g | 1 cup | 240 mL |
| salt | 1/4 oz. | 8 g | 1 teaspoon | 5 mL |
| white pepper | | | 1/4 teaspoon | 2 mL |
| butter, unsalted | as needed for frying | | | |
| oil, vegetable or canola | as needed for frying | | | |
| sole fillets | 3 lb., 6 oz. | 1.5 kg | | |
| **Meunière Sauce:** | | | | |
| butter, unsalted | 5 oz. | 142 g | 10 tablespoons or 1 stick + 2 tablespoons | 148 mL or 1 stick + 30 mL |
| salt | | | 1/2 teaspoon | 3 mL |
| white pepper | to taste | | | |
| lemon juice | | 28 g | 2 tablespoons | 30 mL |
| parsley, minced | 1 oz. | 28 g | 1/4 cup | 60 mL |

**Garnish:**

lemon wedges

> ### TWIST ON THE CLASSIC
>
> For a different taste and presentation, top the Dover sole with a seafood stuffing or place the stuffing under the sole.

1. Mix flour, salt, and pepper on plate. Preheat oven to 300 degrees (150°C).
2. Mix equal parts of butter and oil in skillet. Use enough butter/oil mixture to coat skillet. Heat over medium-high heat until hot.
3. Dredge fish in flour; shake off excess. Fry fish until golden, a few minutes. Turn, sauté other side until golden. Remove to pan and keep warm in preheated oven.
4. Wipe out pan if needed. Again add more butter and oil. Repeat until all fish is sautéed.

## FOR MEUNIÈRE SAUCE:

1. Melt butter in saucepan over medium-high heat. Cook until butter turns lightly browned, 1 or 2 minutes. Remove from heat.
2. Add salt, pepper, and lemon juice. Be careful: It might splatter. Add parsley. Stir to combine.
3. Serve fish drizzled with 1/2 oz. (1 tablespoon) butter mixture. Garnish with lemon wedges.

**Note:** In the past, cooks sautéed the Dover sole in only butter. Because oil has a higher smoke point, the cook can sauté the fish at a higher temperature by using a mixture of butter and oil.

# WELSH RAREBIT (WALES)

## CHEDDAR CHEESE SAUCE OVER TOAST

**Note:** Every collection of classic British cooking includes a version of Welsh Rarebit. There are countless variations on this recipe.

**Number of Servings:** 8
**Cooking Method:** Simmer, broil
**Serving Size:** 2 1/2 oz. (71 g) cheese sauce on toast
**Total Yield:** 1 lb., 5 oz. (596 g)
**Food Balance:** Protein
**Wine Style:** Soft and fruity blush, Pinot Blanc, Chenin Blanc, Merlot, Shiraz, or Zinfandel
**Example:** Souverain or Greg Norman Zinfandel

| | WEIGHT | | VOLUME | |
| --- | --- | --- | --- | --- |
| INGREDIENTS | U.S. | METRIC | U.S. | METRIC |
| toast, crusts removed | | | 8 each | |
| sharp Cheddar cheese, grated | 1 lb. | 454 g | 6 cups | 1.44 L |
| flour | 1/2 oz. | 15 g | 2 tablespoons | 30 mL |
| beer or ale | | 114 g | 1/2 cup | 120 mL |
| butter | 1 oz. | 28 g | 2 tablespoons | 30 mL |
| Worcestershire sauce | | | 2 teaspoons | 10 mL |
| dry mustard | | | 1/2 teaspoon | 3 mL |
| cayenne | | | pinch | |
| egg yolk | 1 1/2 oz. | 43 g | 2 each | |

1. Place toast in individual shallow ovenproof dishes, set aside. Preheat broiler.
2. In top of double boiler or saucepan, mix cheese with flour, then add beer, butter, Worcestershire sauce, mustard, and cayenne.
3. Stirring constantly, melt in top of double boiler over simmering water or in saucepan over medium-low heat. Do not let mixture boil.
4. Place yolk in small bowl, whisk briefly.
5. Stirring constantly, slowly add some melted cheese to yolk to temper it.
6. Take cheese mixture off heat. Stir yolk mixture into cheese. Correct seasonings.
7. Pour cheese evenly over toast.
8. Place cheese dishes under broiler until lightly brown, about 1 or 2 minutes. Serve immediately.

© Fanfo

## TURNIPS AND LEEKS (SCOTLAND)

**Note:** If desired, bake in ramekins or individual dishes. Serve in the individual dishes or unmold the Turnips and Leeks onto plates.

**Number of Servings:** 9
**Serving Size:** 4 oz. (114 g)
**Total Yield:** 2 lb., 4 oz. (1.1 kg)

**Cooking Method:** Bake

| | WEIGHT | | VOLUME | |
|---|---|---|---|---|
| *INGREDIENTS* | *U.S.* | *METRIC* | *U.S.* | *METRIC* |
| turnips, peeled and thinly sliced | 1 lb., 6 oz. | 624 g | 5 medium | |
| leeks, core removed, washed thoroughly, and sliced thinly, leaving about 3 inches of green | 10 1/4 oz. | 292 g | 2 each | |
| salt | as needed | | | |
| pepper | as needed | | | |
| grated nutmeg | as needed | | | |
| cream | | 57 g | 1/4 cup | 60 mL |
| chicken stock | | 177 g | 3/4 cup | 180 mL |
| butter | 1 oz. | 28 g | 2 tablespoons | 30 mL |

**Garnish:**
paprika, *optional*

1. Pan-spray or grease 3-quart ovenproof pan. Preheat oven to 350 degrees (180°C).
2. Place layer of turnips on bottom of pan. Place layer of leeks over turnips. Sprinkle with salt and pepper.
3. Repeat layering turnips, leeks, salt, and pepper. Sprinkle every few layers with nutmeg.
4. Sprinkle top layer (either leeks or turnips) with salt, pepper, and nutmeg. Pour cream over top, then chicken stock.
5. Dot with butter. Cover dish and bake 1 hour. Uncover and bake another 15 minutes. Serve, garnished with sprinkling of paprika, if desired.

Richard Embery © Pearson Education, Inc.

# CAULIFLOWER CHEESE

© Lilyana Vynogradova

**Number of Servings:** 11

**Serving Size:** 4 oz. (114 g)

**Total Yield:** 2 lb., 12 1/4 oz. (1.3 kg)

**Cooking Method:** Boil, bake

**Wine Style:** Cauliflower with cheese would pair very well with a fuller bodied white wine from a cool climate region.

Possible grape varietals are Pinot Gris, Pinot Blanc, Gruner Veltliner, Riesling, Chardonnay.

**Example:** Grauburgunder "Pluris" 2011, Hirtzberger (Wachau/Austria)

| | WEIGHT | | VOLUME | |
|---|---|---|---|---|
| INGREDIENTS | U.S. | METRIC | U.S. | METRIC |
| **Béchamel Sauce:** | | | | |
| butter, unsalted | 1 oz. | 28 g | 2 tablespoons | 30 mL |
| flour, all purpose | 1 oz. | 28 g | 1/4 cup | 60 mL |
| milk, hot | | 227 g | 1 cup | 240 mL |
| clove, whole | | | 2 each | |
| onion, cut in half | 3 oz. | 86 g | 1 small | |
| salt | | | 1/4 teaspoon | 2 mL |
| white pepper | | | 1/8 teaspoon | 1 mL |
| mustard, dry | | | 1/8 teaspoon | 1 mL |
| nutmeg | | | sprinkling | |
| cheddar cheese, grated | 4 oz. | 114 g | 1 1/2 cups | 360 mL |
| cauliflower, core and leaves removed | 1 lb., 12 oz. | 794 g | 1 head | |
| breadcrumbs, dried | 2 3/4 oz. | 78 g | 1/2 cup | 120 mL |
| cheddar cheese, grated | 2 oz. | 57 g | 3/4 cup | 180 mL |

Cauliflower cheese is served throughout the British Isles as a side dish or a vegetarian entrée. Sometimes, some chopped ham is added to the dish, and it is served as an entrée.

1. Preheat oven to 425 degrees (220°C). Pan spray ovenproof dish.
2. Melt butter in small saucepan over medium heat. Whisk in flour and cook until blonde *roux*.
3. Reduce heat to medium-low; slowly whisk in hot milk until all milk is incorporated. Stick one clove in each onion half. Add onions, salt, pepper, mustard, and nutmeg to milk mixture.
4. Whisk occasionally and simmer for 15 to 20 minutes until thick.
5. Remove from heat. Remove onions and discard. Add 4 oz. (1 1/2 cups, 114 g or 360 mL) cheese to sauce. Stir to incorporate. Set aside until needed.
6. Break cauliflower into florets. Place water in saucepan about 1-inch (2 1/2-cm) deep.
7. Add cauliflower to water, bring to boil over medium-high heat. Boil 3 to 4 minutes to cook until half done. Remove florets from saucepan, place in prepared dish.
8. Mix breadcrumbs and 2 oz. (3/4 cup [57 g or 180 mL]) cheese together in small bowl. Set aside until needed.
9. Pour sauce over cauliflower. Top with breadcrumb cheese mixture. Bake for 20 to 25 minutes until bubbly and golden brown. Serve.

## COLCANNON (IRELAND)

### MASHED POTATOES WITH KALE OR CABBAGE

**Note:** An intrinsic ingredient in Irish cookery, the ever available and inexpensive potato is added to countless dishes to extend the food.

**Number of Servings:** 13
**Serving Size:** 4 oz. (114 g)
**Total Yield:** 3 lb., 6 oz. (1.5 kg)

**Cooking Method:** Boil, sauté

| | WEIGHT | | VOLUME | |
|---|---|---|---|---|
| **INGREDIENTS** | **U.S.** | **METRIC** | **U.S.** | **METRIC** |
| milk | | 227 g | 1 cup | 240 mL |
| scallions, with 3 inches green, sliced | 2 1/2 oz. | 71 g | 1 bunch | |
| potatoes, white, waxy, or all-purpose, peeled and quartered | 2 lb. | 908 g | | |
| kale or green cabbage, washed and cut finely or shredded | 1 lb. | 454 g | | |
| butter | 1 oz. | 28 g | 2 tablespoons | 30 mL |
| salt | 1/4 oz. | 8 g | 1 teaspoon | 5 mL |
| pepper | | | 1/4 teaspoon | 2 mL |
| ground mace | | | 1/4 teaspoon | 2 mL |

**Garnish:**

fresh parsley, minced

1. Place milk and scallions in small pan, heat.
2. Boil potatoes in water until tender, drain well.
3. While potatoes boil, in a pan over medium heat, sauté kale in butter until tender. If using cabbage, boil until tender and then sauté in butter.
4. Mash potatoes using milk and scallions for liquid.
5. Stir cooked kale or cabbage and seasonings into potatoes.
6. Correct seasonings. Serve, garnished with minced parsley if desired.

> **TWIST ON THE CLASSIC**
>
> Try replacing the mashed potatoes with mashed rutabaga or sweet potatoes for color.

Courtesy of the Idaho Potato Commission

Monkey Business Images © Shutterstock

# BOXTY (IRELAND)

## POTATO PANCAKES

Courtesy of the Idaho Potato Commission

**Note:** There are endless variations on this traditional Irish dish. To utilize leftover mashed potatoes, many cooks combine mashed potatoes with grated potatoes to make this pancake. Often, this dish is served on Halloween and Shrove Tuesday (the day before Ash Wednesday, the beginning of Lent).

**Number of Servings:** 11 pancakes

**Serving Size:** 3-oz. pancake (86 g)

**Total Yield:** 2 lb., 1 oz. (936 kg)

**Cooking Method:** Sauté

| | WEIGHT | | VOLUME | |
|---|---|---|---|---|
| INGREDIENTS | U.S. | METRIC | U.S. | METRIC |
| flour | 4 oz. | 114 g | 1 cup | 240 mL |
| salt | 1/4 oz. | 8 g | 1 teaspoon | 5 mL |
| pepper | | | 1/2 teaspoon | 3 mL |
| caraway seeds | | | 1 teaspoon | 5 mL |
| milk | | 114 g | 1/2 cup | 120 mL |
| potatoes, white, waxy, or all-purpose, peeled and grated | 2 lb. | 908 g | 6 each | |
| butter, for frying | 2 to 4 oz. | 57 to 114 g | 4 to 8 tablespoons or 1/2 to 1 stick | 60 to 120 mL |

1. Mix flour, salt, pepper, caraway seeds, and milk in bowl. Refrigerate until needed.
2. In colander, squeeze excess moisture from potatoes.
3. Add potatoes to milk-flour mixture, correct seasonings. Form into 3-oz (86-g) patties (flour hands if necessary).
4. Heat 3 tablespoons (45 mL) butter, or enough for sautéing, in skillet over medium-high heat. Sauté pancakes until golden and crisp on edges, about 3 minutes on each side. Serve immediately.

# YORKSHIRE PUDDING (ENGLAND)

Monkey Business Images © Shutterstock

**Note:** Yorkshire pudding typically accompanies roast beef or other large pieces (joints) of meat.

**Note:** To prepare Yorkshire pudding in individual servings, pour the batter into small dishes or muffin tins instead of a baking pan.

**Number of Servings:** 9

**Serving Size:** 3-inch × 4 1/4-inch (8-cm × 11 1/2-cm) piece

**Total Yield:** 9-inch × 13-inch (23-cm × 33-cm) pan

**Cooking Method:** Bake

| | WEIGHT | | VOLUME | |
|---|---|---|---|---|
| INGREDIENTS | U.S. | METRIC | U.S. | METRIC |
| all-purpose flour | 4 1/2 oz. | 128 g | 1 cup | 240 mL |
| salt | | | 1/2 teaspoon | 3 mL |
| eggs | 3 1/2 oz. | 104 g | 2 each | |
| milk | | 227 g | 1 cup | 240 mL |
| pan drippings or butter | 1 oz. | 28 g | 2 tablespoons | 30 mL |

1. Place flour and salt in bowl of food processor fitted with knife blade, pulse to mix.
2. With processor running, add eggs and milk through tube, pulse to mix well.
3. Remove batter to bowl, refrigerate at least 1 hour. Meanwhile, preheat oven to 400 degrees (205°C).
4. Place pan drippings or butter in 9- by 13-inch (23-cm by 33-cm) pan or 1/2-steam table pan; heat in oven until hot.
5. Stir batter, pour batter into pan, bake for 15 minutes. Reduce heat to 350 degrees (180°C), bake another 10 to 15 minutes, until puffy, crisp, and golden.
6. Remove from oven, cut into squares. Serve immediately.

© Joe Gough

# SCONES (ENGLAND)

## RICH BISCUITS WITH CURRANTS

**Note:** Served warm with butter and jam, honey, or lemon curd, scones appear regularly accompanied by tea.

**Total Yield:** 12 biscuits  **Cooking Method:** Bake

| | WEIGHT | | VOLUME | |
| --- | --- | --- | --- | --- |
| INGREDIENTS | U.S. | METRIC | U.S. | METRIC |
| all-purpose flour | 9 1/2 oz. | 270 g | 2 cups | 480 mL |
| baking powder | 1/4 oz. | 8 g | 2 teaspoons | 10 mL |
| sugar | 1 oz. | 28 g | 2 tablespoons | 30 mL |
| salt | | | 1/2 teaspoon | 3 mL |
| unsalted butter, cold, cut into 12 equal pieces | 3 oz. | 86 g | 6 tablespoons | 90 mL |
| egg | 1 3/4 oz. | 50 g | 1 each | |
| milk | | 114 g | 1/2 cup | 120 mL |
| dried currants | 1 3/4 oz. | 50 g | 1/3 cup | 80 mL |

1. Preheat oven to 400 degrees (205°C). Place oven rack in center of oven. Grease baking sheet or cover with parchment paper.
2. Place flour, baking powder, sugar, and salt in bowl of food processor fitted with knife blade, pulse to mix.
3. Place butter pieces on top of flour mixture, pulse to mix until clumps the size of peas form.
4. In a separate bowl, mix egg and milk. With processor running, pour egg and milk through feed tube, pulse until dough forms ball. Add currants, and pulse once or twice.
5. Remove dough from processor bowl to lightly floured counter; knead gently, if necessary, to mix in currants.
6. Divide dough into three even parts, pat each part into 4- to 5-inch (10-cm to 13-cm) circle.
7. Cut each circle into quarters, place pieces on prepared baking sheet.
8. Bake for about 15 minutes, until lightly brown. Serve immediately with butter and jam, honey, or lemon curd.

### TWIST ON THE CLASSIC

Bakers prepare myriad variations of this classic recipe. Some replace the currants with dried blueberries, cherries, cranberries, chopped apricots, or any other variety of fruits. Still others add nuts or replace part of the flour with cornmeal to add crunch.

David Murray and Jules Selmes © Dorling Kindersley

Courtesy King Arthur Flour

# LEMON TART

**Note:** Traditionally, lemon curd is spread on toast like jam. The applications for this versatile, pungent cream are endless. It is a great addition to any dessert repertoire.

**Number of Servings:** 8
**Serving Size:** 1/8 of 9-inch (23-cm) tart
**Total Yield:** one 9-inch (23-cm) tart

**Cooking Method:** Simmer, bake

Finished lemon curd

| INGREDIENTS | WEIGHT U.S. | WEIGHT METRIC | VOLUME U.S. | VOLUME METRIC |
|---|---|---|---|---|
| **Lemon Curd:** | | | | |
| egg yolks | 6 3/4 oz. | 191 g | 10 each | |
| sugar | 7 1/4 oz. | 206 g | 1 cup | 240 mL |
| lemon juice | | 256 g | 1 cup + 2 tablespoons | 270 mL |
| lemon zest, grated | 1 oz. | 28 g | 3 tablespoons | 45 mL |
| butter, cut into pieces | 4 oz. | 114 g | 1/2 cup (1 stick) | 120 mL |
| pie dough | 13 oz. | 369 g | | |
| egg white | 1 oz. | 28 g | 1 each | |
| semisweet chocolate, in chips, shaved, or in small pieces | 1 1/2 oz. | 43 g | | |
| Chantilly cream | 12 oz. | 341 g | | |

© JJAVA

## LEMON CURD:

1. With wooden spoon, mix egg yolks and sugar in nonreactive pan. Cook over low heat, stirring constantly for a couple minutes.
2. Stirring constantly, add lemon juice and zest. Slowly add butter, a piece or two at a time. Continue stirring, cook until mixture thickens, about 20 to 30 minutes.
3. Remove from pan, cool completely. Stir frequently or cover with parchment paper to prevent skin from forming on top. Store in refrigerator, tightly covered.

## ROLLING OUT DOUGH:

1. Place chilled ball of pie dough on table. If dough is made with butter, it will be stiff. With rolling pin, hit ball to flatten into disk about one-inch (2.5-cm) thick. Lightly flour table and rolling pin if needed.
2. Roll dough from middle to sides. Release dough from table with icing spatula after every few rolls. After each roll or two, turn dough one-quarter turn to keep dough round. Roll into circle of desired thickness, between 1/8 and 1/4 inch (30 and 60 mm).
3. Release dough from table with spatula. Fold gently in half. Lift and position over tart pan so dough covers pan when unfolded.
4. Press dough into all corners of pan. Flute edges of dough. Prick bottom of pie shell with fork in several places to prevent buckling of dough during baking.
5. If possible, chill thoroughly before baking.

Constantinos Loumakis © Shutterstock

## BAKING:

1. Place rack in bottom half of oven, preheat oven to 375 degrees (190°C). Line inside of pie shell with aluminum foil with shiny side down (to prevent dough from buckling). Make sure foil reaches into all "corner" seams (where sides and bottom of pan join).
2. Bake for about 10 minutes, until just set. Remove from oven, remove foil.
3. Brush bottom of crust with egg white, return to oven for another 15 to 20 minutes until golden. Remove from oven, cool about 10 minutes.

## ASSEMBLY:

1. Layer chocolate over bottom crust. Allow to sit a few minutes to melt. Using icing spatula, spread evenly over bottom of crust. Cool crust completely.
2. Spread lemon curd about 1/2-inch (1.3-cm) thick in prepared pie shell. Remove rim and bottom of pan. Place tart on serving plate or cardboard round.
3. Decoratively pipe top with Chantilly cream. Refrigerate until serving.

Tightly covered, lemon curd stores well in the refrigerator.

When removing zest from lemon, be careful to avoid the white pith that is just under the yellow zest. While the zest contains the oils and the lemon flavor, the pith is bitter.

## TWIST ON THE CLASSIC

This pungent, tart lemon cream (curd) makes a wonderful filling for a tart or between layers of white, yellow, or chocolate cake. Lemon curd easily replaces jams or preserves in almost any application. To create a variation on the classic British trifle, make a lemon blueberry trifle: moisten the cake pieces with simple syrup or rum, top with some lemon curd (substituted for the traditional raspberry preserves), add blueberries over the lemon curd, and top with whipped cream. Repeat layers to fill an attractive clear glass bowl or individual martini glasses.

Chantilly cream is lightly sweetened whipped cream. To make 12 ounces (341 g) of Chantilly cream, begin with about 1 1/2 cups (360 mL) of heavy whipping cream. Whip the cream on low speed until it starts to thicken, about 1 minute. Increase speed to high, and whip until about half thickened. Add a little sifted confectioner's sugar (about 1 tablespoon or 15 mL) and vanilla extract. Continue whipping until soft peaks form.

Use the pie dough recipe of choice or use the one for Pâte Brisée in Chapter 3, France.

If available, prepare this dessert in a 9-inch (23-cm) tart pan with a removable bottom.

# PASTRY CREAM

## CUSTARD

**Note:** Use a stainless steel saucepan because whisking against aluminum can cause the custard to become gray in color. Pastry cream should be used within 24 hours.

**Total Yield:** 1 lb., 8 oz. (680 g), or 3 cups (720 mL)    **Cooking Method:** Boil

| | WEIGHT | | VOLUME | |
| --- | --- | --- | --- | --- |
| INGREDIENTS | U.S. | METRIC | U.S. | METRIC |
| sugar | 5 1/2 oz. | 156 g | 2/3 cup | 160 mL |
| milk | | 511 g | 2 1/4 cups | 540 mL |
| cornstarch | 1 1/4 oz. | 36 g | 1/4 cup | 60 mL |
| egg yolks | 4 oz. | 114 g | 6 each | |
| butter, unsalted | 1 oz. | 28 g | 2 tablespoons | 30 mL |
| vanilla | | | 2 teaspoons | 10 mL |

*Whisking pastry cream while cooking*

1. Combine sugar and 1 1/2 cups (360 mL) of the milk in nonreactive pan, stir, bring to boil over medium heat.
2. Whisk cornstarch and remaining 3/4 cup (180 mL) milk together in bowl, add yolks, whisk well.
3. While whisking, very slowly pour hot milk into yolk mixture to temper eggs.
4. Return mixture to pan, whisk constantly over medium-low heat until mixture boils. Make sure to whisk into corners of pan to prevent sticking and burning.
5. Cook for 1 minute, scrape into nonreactive bowl using the whisk. (Using a spatula adds overcooked pastry cream from the corners of the pan.)
6. Add butter and vanilla, stir well.
7. Stirring frequently, chill in ice water bath until cool, then cover with plastic wrap and refrigerate until needed.

*Adding butter to pastry cream*

*Sprinkling sherry on cake pieces*

*Assembling the trifle — placing preserves over cake pieces*

## TWIST ON THE CLASSIC

Change the flavor combinations of a trifle to use available fresh fruits or to match the season.

- Tropical Trifle: Substitute pineapple preserves for the raspberry preserves (or omit the preserves for this variation), add chopped tropical fruits over the pastry cream, and sprinkle the cake pieces with rum instead of sherry
- Chocolate Trifle: Use apricot or raspberry preserves and replace the vanilla pastry cream with chocolate pastry cream or chocolate pudding
- Christmas Trifle: Place a layer of raspberries and chopped kiwi over the raspberry preserves

# TRIFLE (ENGLAND)

## SHERRY-FLAVORED CAKE LAYERED WITH VANILLA CUSTARD, RASPBERRY PRESERVES, AND WHIPPED CREAM

**Note:** Trifle looks beautiful layered in a glass bowl or oversized brandy snifter; however, it may be prepared in individual bowls or glasses for easy service. Martini or marguerita glasses work well because the top is wide enough to easily accommodate a spoon. Many prefer pound cake instead of sponge cake for their trifle.

**Number of Servings:** 10
**Serving Size:** 5 oz. (142 g)
**Total Yield:** 3 lb., 4 oz. (1.5 kg)

| INGREDIENTS | WEIGHT | | VOLUME | |
|---|---|---|---|---|
| | U.S. | METRIC | U.S. | METRIC |
| sponge cake, homemade or purchased, cut into 1-inch (2.5 cm) cubes | 15 oz. | 426 g | 6 1/2 cups | 1.56 L |
| sherry, dry | | 170 g | 3/4 cup | 180 mL |
| heavy cream | | 341 g | 1 1/2 cups | 360 mL |
| confectioner's sugar | 3/4 oz. | 22 g | 2 tablespoons | 30 mL |
| vanilla | 1/4 oz. | 8 g | 1 1/2 teaspoons | 8 mL |
| raspberry preserves | 4 to 8 oz. | 114 to 227 g to taste | 1/4 to 1/2 cup | 60 to 120 mL to taste |
| vanilla pastry cream or custard, *recipe on p. 31* | 1 lb. | 454 g | 2 cups | 480 mL |

**Garnish:**
raspberry preserves

① Place cake pieces in bowl, sprinkle with sherry to taste. Do not add more sherry than the cake can absorb without collapsing.

② Whip heavy cream until half thickened and barely holding peaks. Scrape down sides of bowl with spatula.

③ Add confectioner's sugar and vanilla, whip until thickened and holding peaks.

④ Place whipped cream in pastry bag filled with large star tip.

⑤ Place 1/3 or 1/2 of cake pieces in bowl, depending on width of bowl, to cover bottom.

⑥ Top with 1/3 or 1/2 of raspberry preserves (drop bits of preserves from a spoon on top of cake pieces).

⑦ Using pastry bag or spoon, cover with layer of pastry cream, about 1/4 inch thick (use 1/3 or 1/2).

⑧ Pipe layer of whipped cream over pastry cream (use about 1/3 or 1/2).

⑨ Repeat layers (if using thirds, repeat all layers twice; if 1/2, repeat layers once), decoratively piping the final layer of whipped cream.

⑩ Garnish with dollop of raspberry preserves. Cover and refrigerate until serving time.

⑪ Spoon onto plates to serve.

*Trifle for a crowd and an individual serving*

# Spain and Portugal

## >> LEARNING OBJECTIVES

By the end of this chapter, you will be able to:

- Identify differences and similarities in the regional cuisines of Spain and Portugal
- Explain how the topography and climate influence the cuisines found on the Iberian peninsula
- Know which food products are prevalent in various regions of Spain and Portugal
- Prepare several Iberian dishes

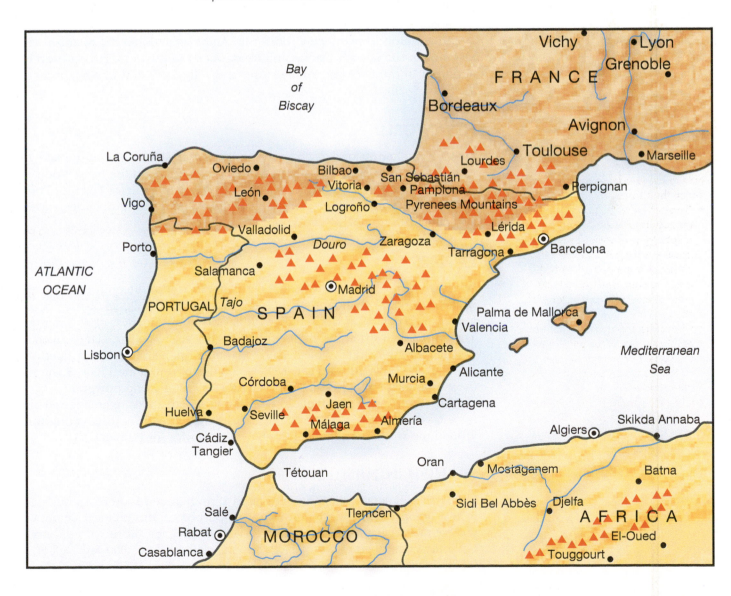

## >> HISTORY

Lying in southeastern Europe, the Iberian Peninsula contains the countries of Spain and Portugal. Archeologists believe people first inhabited this peninsula about 100,000 years ago. The Iberians settled there 5,000 years ago and built the first cities in Spain. Throughout history, many invading countries left a great impact on the cuisines of Iberia. Around 200 B.C., the Romans entered Spain from the south, bringing grapes for wine, garlic, wheat, and olives.

### MOORS

The Moors, who were Arabs from North Africa, entered the south of Spain in 711 A.D. Eventually they conquered most of Spain and ruled the country for hundreds of years, until the late fifteenth century.

Reflecting the culinary world of northern Africa and various countries of the Middle East, the Moors introduced the Spaniards to oranges, lemons, watermelon, pomegranates, grapes, artichokes, spinach, eggplants, rice, dates, almonds, marzipan, herbs, fruits, vegetables, and a variety of spices, including nutmeg, saffron, and pepper. The Spanish adopted combining sweet with savory, as well as the use of honey, from the Moors.

Another major contribution from the Moors, *tapas* resemble Middle Eastern *meze*, appetizers or small plates. Of course, this type of food became very popular throughout Spain and reigns as a very well known and popular food.

In addition to many new foods, the Arabs acquainted the Spanish with cooking techniques such as marinating and frying foods in olive oil. Strong Arab influence is apparent in the cooking, architecture, and religion found in Andalusia, a region in southern Spain.

### NEW WORLD

Finally, another major influence on the Iberian cuisines came in the late 1400s when Christopher Columbus and other explorers returned from the New World. Along with their triumphs of discovering new lands and claiming them for Spain or Portugal, these explorers returned to their homeland with tomatoes, corn, potatoes, sweet peppers, and chocolate from the New World.

### EMPIRES

When all of the invaders were gone at the end of the fifteenth century, Spain finally became a unified country. At that time, Spain began to build its own empire. The Spaniards gained control of lands in South America, North America, Asia, Africa, and Europe. They ruled their extensive empire for about 100 years, until the late sixteenth century.

In 1588, the British defeated the invading Spanish Armada, a fleet of ships that sailed to the British Isles to attack. Between this time and the 1700s, Spain lost many of the countries it had ruled and lost its rank as a major world power.

The Portuguese also built an empire in the late 1400s, which lasted about a century. Like the Spanish, their empire began with explorers discovering foreign lands around the world and claiming these new territories for Portugal.

### SPANISH INQUISITION

Under the leadership of King Ferdinand II and Queen Isabella I, the Spanish established the Spanish Inquisition in 1478. The purpose of this political action was to purge the country of Jewish, Muslim, and Protestant people. Those who did not convert to Catholicism escaped or were killed. Reports claim that 160,000 Jews left Spain or were killed there in 1492. In 1502, the Spanish expelled most Muslims.

# >> TOPOGRAPHY

Containing mountains, coastlines, plateaus, hills, rivers, and streams, Spain and Portugal's topography is characterized by great diversity. Spain makes up five-sixths of the Iberian Peninsula; Portugal occupies the remaining one-sixth.

## SPAIN

Spain ranks as both the third largest country in Europe and the third most mountainous European country. Only Switzerland and Austria contain more mountains.

The Atlantic Ocean borders Spain on the northwest, the Bay of Biscay on the north, and the Mediterranean Sea lies to the east and south. Only 8 miles of water separate Africa from the south of Spain. France neighbors Spain on the northeast; Portugal joins on the west.

The majority of Spain has a dry climate and consists of poor soil and *meseta*—high, dry plateaus. Because the land is not very fertile, it is used primarily for the grazing of sheep and goats.

The coastal areas receive more rainfall than the interior, where dry conditions prevail. Also, the north of Spain receives more precipitation than the south. Hot, sunny summers and cold winters dominate Spain's climate. The southern areas near the Mediterranean Sea enjoy a warmer climate, and the mountainous regions are colder.

Situated in the northwest of Spain, the dramatic landscape in Galicia contains beaches, mountains, and valleys. The Pyrenees Mountains lie in the northeast, forming the border with France. They actually stretch for almost 270 miles across the entire country from the Mediterranean Sea to the Bay of Biscayne (in the Atlantic Ocean). In essence, the Pyrenees form a barrier separating Spain and Portugal from the rest of Europe. Because, historically, travel over these mountains was so difficult, this rugged mountain range created significant isolation.

The central portion of Spain is a large, open expanse of land. With poor soil and a fairly dry climate, this area produces thin cattle that yield tough meat.

The southwest of Spain consists of dry basin; however, any land in this area that is supplied with water—whether by rivers, streams, or irrigation—transforms into fertile farmland. The area along the Mediterranean in the south contains fertile plains.

## PORTUGAL

Because of moderation from ocean breezes, Portugal experiences a more temperate climate than Spain. Cooler summers and warmer winters reign in Portugal.

The entire west and south side of Portugal borders the Atlantic Ocean, yielding lots of coastline and plentiful seafood. Plains line the coasts.

Spain joins Portugal on its east. Generally, this country consists of two regions—the mountainous, cooler, and humid north and the drier, more temperate south. Actually, the mountains lie in the northeastern, central, and southwestern areas, whereas most of the remainder of the country consists of flat land.

---

### Ingredients Commonly Used throughout the Cuisines of Spain and Portugal Include

- *seafood*
- pork and lamb
- *serrano* ham and chorizo sausage
- blood sausage
- dried beans
- olive oil and olives
- garlic
- saffron and Spanish paprika
- parsley
- citrus fruits
- honey
- almonds

## >> COOKING METHODS

During the Middle Ages, when shepherds and nomads roamed the countryside, the Spanish began using one-pot cookery. They cooked any available ingredients in one pot over a fire. Because most of the flocks were sheep, lamb was the most prevalent meat. As a result, braising remains a common cooking method there.

Actually Arabs from North Africa, the Moors used cooking methods that came from the Arabians who cooked over an open fire while traveling through the desert. They introduced grilling and frying to the southern region of Andalusia, where they entered Spain. As the Moors extended their rule throughout Spain, their cooking techniques permeated the cuisine of the country.

With the introduction of the olive by the Romans hundreds of years before the Moors entered Spain, olive oil became a popular cooking fat. When the Moors popularized frying, olive oil became the preferred cooking fat. Today Spain produces an enormous quantity of olive oil, and the export of olive oil is a major industry for Spain.

## >> REGIONS

The various regions of Spain and Portugal exhibit huge diversity in topography, climate, and influences from their many invaders throughout history. Differences in the foods that grow, the selection of herbs and spices, and the cultural aspects of each area cause vast variations in the regional cuisines found in these two countries. Although many of the same dishes are prepared in the regions of Spain and Portugal, the recipes have pronounced regional adaptations.

### GALICIA

Lying in the northwest corner of Spain, Galicia is known for simple, fresh food and its bounty of fish and seafood from the cold waters of the Atlantic Ocean bordering on the north and the many rivers. This region supports many fishermen and farmers. Plenty of dairy for milk and cheese and cold weather vegetables like cabbage, potatoes, and apples come from this region.

Galicia is the home of the *empanada*, traditionally a meat pie or turnover with a soft, flaky crust that appears as a first course or entrée throughout Spain and Latin America. Fillings range from pork to seafood to vegetable mixtures.

### BASQUE

Situated in the north of Spain, the Basque region contains a rugged terrain that led to significant isolation. Many think the finest and most simple food in Spain comes from this region. The Basque cuisine exhibits strong influence from its neighbor, France. The Basque region and bordering Catalonia are known for their use of many sauces. Because of the terrain, game and many types of mushrooms abound.

### LA MANCHA

Lying in the central part of the country, this landlocked region experiences more extreme climates than other regions. Pigs thrive with the sparse grazing available, so pork and sausages appear often. While common throughout Spain, the well-known air-dried hams and chorizo hail from this region.

With a sparse population and large, open expanse of land, much of the central portion of Spain is known as the land of "the hunt." To the south of Madrid lies La Mancha, an area with many windmills and sheep. In addition to lots of sheep, wheat thrives in La Mancha. This provides flour for many of the breads consumed throughout Spain.

*Olla podrida*, a casserole containing almost anything that can be stewed, originated in this region. Literally translated *rotten pot*, every region has its own version of this national dish. Meat is the protein of choice in the central part of Spain, but the inhabitants of the coastal areas consume ample amounts of seafood.

## VALENCIA

Bordering the Mediterranean Sea, Valencia is situated on the eastern coast. Typical Mediterranean foods including oranges and other citrus fruits, olives, peppers, tomatoes, and grapes grow here as well as in much of southern Spain. In addition, warm water fish and shellfish thrive. Of course, the northeast is cooler than the southeast, and the food products reflect this.

A profusion of rice-based dishes come from this eastern part of Spain. The most well-known Spanish dish, *paella*, probably originated in this region. Named for the pot in which it is cooked, *paella* is a casserole of saffron-flavored rice with a variety of meats, chicken, seafood, and vegetables. Countless variations of *paella* flourish throughout Spain, but the constant ingredients include saffron, rice, a variety of seafood, sausage, chicken, and peas.

| AREAS OF SPAIN |
| --- |
| *North - Galicia, Basque* |
| *East - Valencia* |
| *Central - La Mancha* |
| *South - Andalusia* |
| *West - Extremadura* |

## ANDALUSIA

Situated in southern Spain, the Moors came to Andalusia more than 800 years ago. They developed irrigation systems that allowed a wide variety of produce to thrive. Eggplant, tomatoes, peaches, and dates are just a few of the many fruits and vegetables that grow in this region. Exhibiting the Moorish influence, many Andalusian recipes contain cloves, cumin, cinnamon, and other aromatic spices.

With borders on the Mediterranean and the Atlantic, this region has access to lots of fish and seafood. It is known for fried foods and as the home of *gazpacho*, the famous cold tomato vegetable soup.

## EXTREMADURA

Situated in the west, Extremadura consists primarily of farmland. Pigs thrive in this region, and a myriad of pork dishes originated here. The profusion of sausages and cured meats found throughout Iberia hails from the western part of Spain, from the times when the rich people kept all the "good parts" of the hogs and gave the peasants the "insides" and less desirable parts. To make these parts palatable, the peasants ground them into sausages or created sauces from the blood and other undesirable scraps.

## PORTUGAL

This small country measures 150 by 350 miles. The ocean breezes create a milder climate in Portugal than in Spain, and that affects the foods that grow there. Many crops, including potatoes, tomatoes, and corn, flourish. Grapes for wine and port thrive in the river valleys. The ocean lying on Portugal's west and south yields abundant seafood, the primary protein consumed here.

## >> CUISINE

Culinary similarities among the regions of Spain and Portugal include the simplicity of the food and a strong emphasis on fresh ingredients. Although Spain was a trade center for spices in the fifteenth century, Spanish cooking has remained very simple. Fresh parsley and garlic flavor many recipes, but Iberian dishes do not contain an overabundance of spices. Contrary to what many believe, the dishes served in Spain and

Portugal are *not* hot and spicy. Many people confuse the Iberian cuisines with those found in Mexico and other Spanish-speaking countries.

## SAFFRON

Spain currently produces and exports lots of saffron. Known as the world's most expensive spice by weight, labor-intensive saffron is actually the three red stigmas present in a specific variety of crocus flowers, and it must be hand-harvested. After the stigmas are roasted and dried, the saffron is ready for use. Saffron serves as an important component in the famous Spanish dish *paella*. In this dish, the flavor of saffron permeates the rice, and it tints the rice with saffron's characteristic golden color.

## PROTEIN

As is true in many countries, the people who live near the oceans, seas, rivers, and lakes consume lots of seafood. Both Spain and Portugal have miles and miles of coastline where fishing provides plenty of fine-quality fish and shellfish. The many varieties of seafood form the basis of the cuisine in all of the coastal areas. Cod, sardines, and tuna are particularly popular in Portugal. Both fresh and dried (salted) cod are widely consumed in the north. In fact, according to Portuguese folklore, a bride must know at least 10 different recipes for cod before she can marry. Anchovies, cod, squid, and many types of shellfish are among the fish that abound in Spain. In the central interior regions, lamb, mutton, goat, and pork prevail as the main source of protein.

## CHEESE

Many high-quality cheeses are made in Spain from cow, sheep, and goat milk or a combination of all three. As in most countries that produce cheese, different regions specialize in making certain types of cheeses. The governments of many European countries, including Spain, regulate production of some of the cheeses. There are currently more than 20 Designation of Origin (DO) cheeses in Spain.

*It takes 50,000 to 75,000 crocus flowers to yield one pound of dried saffron.*

### PDO STATUS

*The governments in most European countries have instituted PDO (Protected Designation of Origin) for some agricultural and food products. Simply stated, this is a government-controlled quality program. This designation (often called DO) means that the government guarantees the origin of the product, preparation methods, where in the country it was produced, and its quality.*

*Currently, twelve countries regulate cheese. They are France, Italy, Spain, Portugal, Greece, Switzerland, the United Kingdom, Ireland, Austria, Germany, Holland, and Belgium. The number of DO cheeses changes as new cheeses obtain this status. Government control is not limited to cheeses. Many countries control wine and all sorts of other products. For example, Spain controls Serrano ham, Italy controls balsamic vinegar and prosciutto di parma ham, and the list goes on and on.*

*Harvesting Saffron*
Gts © Shutterstock

## SOME SPANISH DO CHEESES

**Cabrales** Made from cow's milk mixed with goat's or sheep's milk; a type of blue cheese; semifirm texture; from northern Spain

**Cantabria** Made from cow's milk; mild flavor, soft creamy texture; from Cantabrian

**Idiazábal** Made from sheep's milk; smoked cheese with sharp flavor, dry crumbly firm texture; from Basque region

**La Serena** Made from sheep's milk; nutty pungent flavor, soft texture; from Extremadura

**Mahon** Made from cow's milk; slightly acidic and salty taste, smooth firm texture; used for grating; from the island of Minorca in the Mediterranean

**Majorero** Made from goat's milk; aged cheese, buttery texture; from Canary Islands

**Manchego** Made from sheep's milk; aged, tangy taste, crumbly texture; from La Mancha in central Spain

**Picón** Made from cow's, goat's, and sheep's milk; aged, robust full flavor; a type of blue cheese from northern Spain

**Quesucos de Liebana** A group of several cheeses from northern Spain, made from cow's milk or mixed with sheep's and goat's milk; fresh or aged, smoked or unsmoked

**Roncal** Made from sheep's milk; nutty flavor, firm smooth texture; from northern Spain

**Tetilla** Made from cow's milk; aged, mild flavor, soft creamy texture; from Galicia

**Zamorano** Made from sheep's milk; aged, intense sharp flavor, firm yet crumbly texture; from northwest Spain

## PORTUGAL

The Portuguese use more herbs and spices than the Spanish. Fresh cilantro appears in many recipes. The addition of cream and butter makes Portuguese cooking richer than the cuisines found in Spain. Besides providing fruits and nuts, the numerous orange, lemon, and almond trees lead to significant honey production in Portugal.

## TAPAS

In Madrid and throughout Spain, people typically go to bars in the early evening for sherry and *tapas,* small snacks or appetizers. Often, *tapas* are eaten in the late morning or early afternoon as a snack before the main meal. Similar to Chinese *dim sum, tapas* have gained much popularity outside of Spain in recent years.

There is an endless variety of *tapas*—seafood in various sauces, olives in all sorts of herbs and brines, meats, sausages, vegetables, fillings wrapped in pastry dough, and on and on. Many *tapas* are just small portions of popular Iberian dishes; for example, small turnovers become the *tapas* version of *empanadas.* A slice of *tortilla,* the popular egg dish that resembles an unfolded omelet, is served as *tapas.* Usually eaten at room temperature, *tortillas* can be filled with almost anything. Potatoes and onion make the classic *tortilla* filling.

## BEVERAGES AND MEALS

Although Portugal produces excellent port, Spain is known for sherry, most of which comes from a small, hot, flat area in Andalusia. Both sherry and port are fortified wines. In addition, much wine production exists throughout Iberia, with each region producing its own varieties. Wine usually accompanies both the afternoon and evening meals. Another popular drink, *sangria,* consists of red wine with brandy, soda water, and fresh fruits. Favorite nonalcoholic beverages include strong coffee and hot chocolate.

Throughout Spain and Portugal, breakfast usually is eaten at a coffee shop rather than at home. People often buy *churros, choux* pastry dough deep-fried in olive oil, from a street vendor. Typically, coffee or hot chocolate accompanies the *churros.* In the late morning, *tapas,* or a snack, may be consumed to hold the diner until *comida,* the main meal of the day. Served after two in the afternoon, *comida* begins with a course of soup or salad, followed by a fish or *tortilla* course, then meat, and finally dessert, which is usually fruit. A *siesta,* or rest, follows this large meal, which occurs during the hottest part of the day. After the *siesta*, people return to work. In the early evening, around six or seven, people go to a *tapas* bar for sherry and *tapas*. *Cena*, a light supper, is consumed after nine in the evening.

| REGION | AREA | WEATHER | TOPOGRAPHY | FOODS |
|---|---|---|---|---|
| **Spain** | | | | |
| Galicia | Northwest | Lush and green, temperate climate | Borders Atlantic, coast, mountains, valleys | Seafood, *empanadas* |
| Basque | North | Cool | Mountains, coast | Seafood, trout, game, sheep's cheese, mushrooms, sauces |
| Castile | Central | Flat and arid | Plateau, *meseta* | Livestock, sheep, goats, *tapas* |
| La Mancha | South of Madrid | Arid, cold winters and hot summers | Mountainous plateau, *meseta* | Lamb, mutton, goats, sheep's cheese, *olla podrida* |
| Valencia | East | Warm summers, mild winters | Borders Mediterranean Sea, coast | Seafood, *paella*, rice, olives, citrus fruit, oranges, grapes, wine |
| Andalusia | South | Hot summers, mild winters | Coast, flat land | Seafood, *gazpacho*, olives, citrus fruit, oranges, grapes, wine, sherry |
| Extremadura | West | Warm summers, mild winters | Farmland | Pigs, sausages, cured hams |
| **Portugal** | | | | |
| Northern Portugal | | Temperate: Warm and dry spring and summer, cool and rainy winter and fall | Coast, forests, mountains, plains, *meseta* | Seafood, cod, grapes, wine, port |
| Southern Portugal | | Temperate: Warm and dry spring and summer, cool and rainy winter and fall | Coast, forests, rolling, mountains, *meseta*, plains | Seafood, sardines, lemons, oranges, melons, almonds, grapes, wine, port |

## >> Review Questions

1. What ingredients were brought to Spain and Portugal from the explorers who returned from the New World?
2. What is *paella,* and in which region did this dish originate?
3. Give examples of the Moorish influence on the cuisine of Spain.
4. What are *tapas*? Give at least three examples.

5. How do the weather and topography influence the cuisines of Spain and Portugal?
6. Name at least four regions in Spain and tell what types of foods are most common in each region.
7. Discuss differences and similarities between the cuisines of Spain and Portugal.

## >> Glossary

**aioli** Mayonnaise flavored with garlic

**chorizo** A sausage flavored with garlic and paprika

**churros** *Choux* pastry dough deep-fried in olive oil and eaten at breakfast; sold by street vendors

**empanada** A meat pie or turnover with a soft, flaky crust that is served throughout Spain; originated in Galicia

**gazpacho** Cold tomato vegetable soup; originated in Andalusia

**jambon serrano** Cured ham with a sweet-salty taste similar to the *prosciutto* of Italy

**meseta** High, dry plateaus

**olla podrida** A casserole containing almost anything that can be stewed; literally translated, "rotten pot"; originated in central Spain

**paella** A casserole of saffron rice with a variety of meats, chicken, seafood, and vegetables named for the pot in which it is cooked; originated in Valencia; every region has its own variation on this national dish

**tapas** Small snacks or appetizers

## EMPANADA DE CERDO Y PIMIENTOS (SPAIN)

### PORK AND PEPPER PIE

**Note:** Start preparation of dough and meat several hours in advance or the day before.
This dish may be served as *tapas* or an entrée.

**Number of Servings:** 12 to 16 *tapas*  **Cooking Method:** Bake
**Total Yield:** Two 10-inch (25-cm) pies
**Food Balance:** Protein
**Wine Style:** Light- to medium-bodied Chenin Blanc, Pinot Grigio, soft Chardonnay, Pinot Noir, or Chianti
**Example:** Castello di Gabbiano Pinot Grigio or Chianti

*Folding empanada dough into thirds*

| INGREDIENTS | WEIGHT | | VOLUME | |
| --- | --- | --- | --- | --- |
| | U.S. | METRIC | U.S. | METRIC |
| **Dough:** | | | | |
| flour | 12 1/2 oz. | 355 g | 3 cups | 720 mL |
| salt | | | 1 1/2 teaspoons | 8 mL |
| cold water | | 171 g | 3/4 cup | 180 mL |
| vinegar | | | 1 1/2 tablespoons | 23 mL |
| egg, lightly beaten | 1 3/4 oz. | 50 g | 1 each | |
| lard, shortening, or butter | 8 oz. | 227 g | 1 cup (2 sticks) | 240 mL |
| **Filling:** | | | | |
| paprika | 1/4 oz. | 8 g | 1 tablespoon | 15 mL |
| olive oil | | 71 g | 1/4 cup + 1 tablespoon | 75 mL |
| fresh parsley, minced | | | 1 tablespoon | 15 mL |
| garlic, minced | | | 1 large clove | |
| thyme | | | 1/2 teaspoon | 3 mL |
| oregano | | | 1/2 teaspoon | 3 mL |
| salt | | | 1/2 teaspoon | 3 mL |
| pork shoulder or loin, cut into 1/8- by 2 1/2-inch strips | 12 oz. | 341 g | | |
| bell peppers, green or mix of green and red, cut into thin strips | 12 oz. | 341 g | 2 each | |
| water | | 14 g | 1 tablespoon | 15 mL |
| onions, thinly sliced | 10 oz. | 284 g | 2 medium | |
| dry white wine | | 29 g | 2 tablespoons | 30 mL |
| **Glaze:** | | | | |
| egg | 1 3/4 oz. | 50 g | 1 each | |
| water | | | 1 teaspoon | 5 mL |

*Empanada dough folded into thirds*

*Placing filling ingredients on rolled dough*

*Crimping edge of dough*

## DOUGH:

1. Mix flour and salt in large bowl, form a well in center. Place water, vinegar, and egg in well.
2. Stir until stiff, then work by hand until dough forms smooth ball.
3. Cover, let sit for 30 minutes.
4. Roll dough into 10- by 15-inch (25-cm by 37 1/2-cm) rectangle.
5. Spread two-thirds of dough with 1/3 cup (80 mL) of the lard, shortening, or butter. Fold into thirds business-letter style, folding uncovered dough over half of buttered dough. Fold last third over folded dough. (This folding pattern alternates layers of fatted dough with plain dough.)
6. Wrap in plastic wrap and refrigerate at least 15 minutes.
7. Repeat from step 4, using another 1/3 cup (80 mL) lard, shortening, or butter. Refrigerate again.
8. Repeat with remaining fat. Refrigerate at least 1 hour, preferably overnight.

## FILLING:

1. Combine paprika, 3 tablespoons (45 mL) of the oil, parsley, garlic, thyme, oregano, and salt in small nonreactive bowl.
2. Add meat and stir to coat well. Cover and refrigerate to marinate for several hours or overnight.
3. Heat 1 tablespoon (15 mL) of the oil in skillet over medium-high heat. Add peppers and sauté for 1 minute.
4. Add 1 tablespoon (15 mL) water, reduce heat to low, cover, and cook about 15 minutes, until peppers are tender. Remove peppers from skillet.
5. Heat remaining tablespoon of oil in same skillet and sauté onions over low heat until tender but not brown. Remove onions from skillet.
6. Turn heat to high, add marinated meat mixture, fry until it loses its color. Add wine and cook another minute.
7. Add peppers and onions to meat, mix well. Correct seasonings, making sure it is well seasoned, because it will be surrounded by dough.

## ASSEMBLY:

1. Preheat oven to 350 degrees (180°C).
2. Roll dough into 10-inch × 15-inch (25-cm × 37 1/2-cm) rectangle, fold into thirds as before.
3. Cut dough in half, roll each half of dough into 10-inch × 20-inch (25-cm × 50-cm) rectangle and cut each into two 10-inch (25-cm) squares.
4. Trim each square into 10-inch (25-cm) circle. Place one circle on parchment-lined half-size sheet pan.
5. Cover the dough with half of filling, not quite reaching to edges. Dip finger into water, moisten edges of dough with wet finger. Cover with another circle of dough. Roll edges and press firmly to seal. Repeat with remaining half of filling and two circles of dough.
6. Lightly beat egg with 1 teaspoon (5 mL) water for glaze, brush over dough. Using a sharp knife, make several slits in top of dough. Bake about 35 minutes, until golden.
7. Cool slightly or wait until room temperature. Cut into wedges and serve.

*Cutting slits in empanada so steam can escape*

# PATATAS BRAVAS (SPAIN)

## SPICY POTATOES

**Number of Servings:** 9
**Serving Size:** 4 oz. (114 g)
**Total Yield:** 2 lb., 7 1/2 oz. (1.12 kg)
**Wine Style:** White wine with a little sweetness and a medium body, high acidity, and minerality. Possible grape varietals are Riesling, Gruner Veltliner, Sauvignon Blanc.
**Example:** Jorge Ordonez Number 1 Seleccion Especial 2011 (Spain)

**Cooking Method:** Boil, sauté

© MediablitzImages

| INGREDIENTS | WEIGHT | | VOLUME | |
| --- | --- | --- | --- | --- |
| | U.S. | METRIC | U.S. | METRIC |
| potatoes, Russet, peeled, cut into 1-inch chunks | 4 lb. | 1.8 kg | about 10 medium | |
| olive oil | | 57 g | 1/4 cup | 60 mL |
| garlic, peeled, smashed | 1/4 oz. | 8 g | 2 cloves | |
| tomato sauce | 2 1/2 oz. | 71 g | 1/4 cup | 60 mL |
| red wine vinegar | | 28 g | 2 tablespoons | 30 mL |
| Tabasco or other hot sauce | 1/4 oz. | 8 g | 2 teaspoons | 10 mL |
| paprika | | | 2 teaspoons | 10 mL |
| cayenne pepper | sprinkling, to taste | | | |
| olive oil, for frying | as needed | | | |
| salt | 1/4 oz. | 8 g | 1 teaspoon | 5 mL |

**Garnish:**

*aioli* [garlic-flavored mayonnaise]

① Place potatoes in saucepan, cover with water. Bring to boil over high heat. Reduce to medium-high and continue boiling for 5 minutes. Drain well, spread on towel or absorbent paper to cool and dry. (If there is no time to thoroughly dry on towel, place in low oven [225 to 250 degrees (110°C to 120°C)] to dry.)

② Preheat oven to 300 degrees (150°C). Place absorbent paper on sheet pan; set aside until needed.

③ Heat olive oil (57 g, 1/4 cup [60 mL]) in skillet over medium-low heat until hot. Add garlic and cook about 1 minute, until just beginning to brown. Remove from heat.

④ Add tomato sauce, red wine vinegar, Tabasco, paprika, and cayenne. Stir constantly, return to medium heat and cook a few minutes until well blended and simmering. Remove from heat, set aside until needed.

⑤ Heat about 1/2 inch (1.3 cm) olive oil in large skillet over medium-high heat until hot and beginning to shimmer. Test by placing one piece of potato in hot oil—oil is ready when it quickly bubbles and sizzles around potato. Using large spoon or metal spatula, gently add one layer of potatoes to hot oil. Cook potatoes in batches so there is a single layer of potatoes in skillet.

⑥ Cook a few minutes, until golden. Turn potatoes, cook other side until golden. Remove from oil with slotted spoon, drain and place on prepared pan lined with absorbent paper. Keep warm in oven until remaining potatoes are sautéed. Add more oil to skillet, if needed for remaining potatoes.

⑦ Heat oil-paprika mixture until hot. Transfer cooked potatoes to bowl; sprinkle with salt. Pour oil-paprika mixture over potatoes. Mix gently to thoroughly coat with oil mixture and distribute salt. Correct seasonings. Serve immediately, accompanied by a dollop of *aioli* (garlic-flavored mayonnaise), if desired.

### TWIST ON THE CLASSIC

For a breakfast or brunch dish, serve *Patatas Bravas* topped with a poached or fried egg. For another idea: create "Spanish Eggs Benedict" replacing the English muffin base of the Eggs Benedict with *Patatas Bravas*.

If available, use hot paprika instead of mild. In that case, eliminate the cayenne and add half of the Tabasco. Taste and add remaining Tabasco, as needed, depending on the amount of spice in the paprika. This dish should have a little "kick" of heat from pepper.

Served throughout Spain, this popular *tapas* originated in Madrid.

# MEJILLONES CON LINGUIÇA Y TOMATE (PORTUGAL)

## MUSSELS WITH LINGUIÇA AND TOMATO

**Note:** Discard any mussels that are open before cooking. Live mussels are closed; they open when cooked. Discard any mussels that are closed after cooking.

**Number of Servings:** 11                          **Cooking Method:** Sauté, boil
**Serving Size:** 11 oz. (308 g)
**Total Yield:** 7 lb., 13 oz. (3.51 kg)
**Food Balance:** Spicy and acid-based
**Wine Style:** Crisp, low-oaked whites, such as Pinot Grigio and Australian Riesling, and fruity, rich reds, such as Shiraz, Merlot, and Zinfandel
**Example:** Penfolds Thomas Hyland Riesling and Thomas Hyland Shiraz

© martiapunts

|  | WEIGHT | | VOLUME | |
|---|---|---|---|---|
| **INGREDIENTS** | **U.S.** | **METRIC** | **U.S.** | **METRIC** |
| linguiça, chorizo, or sausage of choice | 1 lb. | 454 g | | |
| olive oil | | 29 g | 2 tablespoons | 30 mL |
| onion, thinly sliced | 12 1/2 oz. | 355 g | 2 large | |
| garlic, minced | 1 1/2 oz. | 43 g | 12 cloves | |
| tomatoes, fresh or canned, peeled and diced | 1 lb., 12 oz. | 794 kg | 3 cups | 720 mL |
| shrimp stock | | 454 g | 2 cups | 480 mL |
| dry white wine | | 227 g | 1 cup | 240 mL |
| red pepper flakes, optional | | | 1/2 teaspoon | 3 mL |
| fresh parsley, minced | 1 1/2 oz. | 43 g | 1/2 cup | 120 mL |
| mussels, scrubbed, debearded | 4 lb. | 1.8 kg | | |
| salt | as needed | | | |

1. Remove casing from sausage; crumble sausage into braiser over medium-high heat.
2. Sauté until sausage is done and texture is firm. Remove from pan and set aside until needed.
3. Put olive oil in braiser, then add onions. Cook over medium heat until softened, about 4 minutes.
4. Add garlic, sauté another minute. Add tomatoes, stock, wine, and pepper flakes, if desired. Bring to boil and cook about 2 minutes so flavors meld and liquid reduces a little.
5. Add parsley and mussels, shake pan to distribute evenly over tomato mixture. Cover pan and cook about 4 to 6 minutes, until mussels open. Discard any mussels that do not open.
6. Add reserved sausage, stir, add salt to taste. Correct seasonings. Serve mussels and sauce accompanied by bread to soak up sauce.

## TORTILLA A LA ESPAÑOLA (SPAIN)

### POTATO AND ONION OMELET

**Note:** Instead of making one large pie and serving wedges, consider baking individual tortillas.

**Number of Servings:** 8 to 10  **Cooking Method:** Sauté
**Serving Size:** Small wedge
**Total Yield:** 1 lb., 14 oz. (850 g), 9- or 10-inch (23-cm or 25-cm) round
**Food Balance:** Protein
**Wine Style:** Light- to medium-bodied Riesling, Pinot Blanc, Sauvignon Blanc, mild Chardonnay, or Pinot Noir
**Example:** Beringer Founders' Estate Chardonnay or Pinot Noir

Courtesy of the Idaho Potato Commission

|  | WEIGHT | | VOLUME | |
|---|---|---|---|---|
| **INGREDIENTS** | **U.S.** | **METRIC** | **U.S.** | **METRIC** |
| olive oil |  | 171 g | 3/4 cup | 180 mL |
| Russet potatoes, peeled and cut into 1/8-inch slices | 1 lb., 5 oz. | 596 g | 4 large | |
| onion, thinly sliced | 6 oz. | 171 g | 1 large | |
| salt | to taste | | | |
| eggs | 8 1/2 oz. | 241 g | 5 each | |

1. Heat oil in 9- or 10-inch (23- to 25-cm) skillet over medium heat.
2. One at a time, add enough potato slices to form single layer. Top with layer of onion slices. Sprinkle lightly with salt.
3. Continue layering, using all potatoes and onions. Turn occasionally with spatula so all potatoes and onions cook evenly. Layers will mix. Cook until potatoes are tender but remain separate and are not browned, about 10 minutes.
4. Drain potatoes and onions in colander, reserve oil.
5. In large bowl, beat eggs with fork until slightly foamy. Add pinch salt.
6. Add potatoes and onions to eggs, stirring to cover potatoes and onions with egg. Let mixture rest 15 minutes.
7. Heat 1 to 2 tablespoons (15 to 30 mL) reserved oil in skillet over high heat until smoking point. Add potato and egg mixture to skillet, tilting and shaking pan to spread evenly. Lower heat to medium-high, shake pan often to prevent sticking.
8. When brown on bottom, invert plate over skillet and flip omelet onto plate. Slide omelet back into skillet to cook other side. Lower heat to medium, cook until browned yet juicy inside.
9. Place on serving platter, cut into small wedges. Serve warm or at room temperature.

### TWIST ON THE CLASSIC

Add some color with the addition of minced red and green bell peppers and some tomato *concassé*. For a luncheon item, serve the tortilla over or next to a salad.

## SALSA ROMESCO (TARRAGONA)

### ROMESCO SAUCE

**Total Yield:** 2 lb., 1/2 oz. (921 g) or 2 cups (480 mL)  **Cooking Method:** Bake, fry
**Wine Style:** Medium-to full-bodied white wine with higher acidity.
Possible grape varietals are Gruner Veltliner, Riesling, Pinot Blanc.
**Example:** Gruner Veltliner Smaragd "Bergdistel" 2011, Tegernseerhof (Wachau/Austria)

Pearson Education, Inc.

|  | WEIGHT | | VOLUME | |
|---|---|---|---|---|
| **INGREDIENTS** | **U.S.** | **METRIC** | **U.S.** | **METRIC** |
| almonds, blanched | 1/2 oz. | 15 g | 12 each | |
| hazelnuts, skinned | 1/4 oz. | 8 g | 6 each | |
| tomato | 7 1/2 oz. | 213 g | 1 medium to large | |

### TWIST ON THE CLASSIC

Use Romesco sauce as an accompaniment to skirt steak or use it as a spicy topping on a hamburger. For a Spanish flair to French fries, replace the usual catsup with Romesco.

| | WEIGHT | | VOLUME | |
|---|---|---|---|---|
| garlic, peeled | 1/4 oz. | 8 g | 3 cloves | |
| olive oil | | 114 g | 1/2 cup | 118 mL |
| French bread, sliced | 3 slices or as needed | 43 g | | |
| red pepper, roasted, peeled, seeds and membranes removed | 4 oz. | 114 g | 1 each | |
| crushed red pepper flakes | | | 1/2 teaspoon | 3 mL |
| salt | | | 1/2 teaspoon | 3 mL |
| red wine vinegar | | 43 g | 3 tablespoons | 45 mL |
| cayenne pepper, ground, *optional* | as desired | | | |

**Garnish:**

parsley, minced

A common *tapas*, Romesco sauce usually accompanies shrimp. Make the sauce as mild or spicy as desired by adding ground cayenne pepper.

1. Bake almonds and hazelnuts in oven at 300 degrees (150°C) until starting to brown and fragrant. Set aside until needed.
2. Place tomato and garlic on baking tray. Place in 350-degree (180°C) oven for 15 minutes. Turn and bake another 15 minutes. Remove from oven. Peel tomato when cool enough to handle.
3. Cover bottom of skillet with some of the olive oil. Heat over medium heat until hot. Add bread, sauté until golden.
4. With motor running, drop nuts and garlic through feed tube of running food processor fitted with knife blade. Stop processor, scrape sides. Add tomato, roasted red pepper, crushed red pepper flakes, salt, vinegar, and bread to food processor. Run processor until mixture is smooth. Scrape sides as needed. Mixture should be thick enough to coat dipped shrimp. If too runny, add more sautéed bread.
5. Add cayenne to desired spiciness. The sauce should have a "kick." Correct seasonings.
6. Serve with shrimp or other seafood, garnished with minced parsley.

## ESPINACAS A LA CATALANA (SPAIN)

### CATALAN SPINACH

© mariontxa

**Note:** This may be served as *tapas*, first course, or vegetable.

**Number of Servings:** 11  
**Serving Size:** 4 oz. (114 g)  
**Total Yield:** 2 lb., 15 oz. (1.4 kg)  
**Food Balance:** Protein/sweet  
**Wine Style:** Soft and fruity Riesling, Pinot Blanc, blush, or soft Syrah  
**Example:** Rosemount Shiraz

**Cooking Method:** Sauté

### TWIST ON THE CLASSIC

To serve as *tapas*, present the spinach on top of a bread crouton.

| | WEIGHT | | VOLUME | |
|---|---|---|---|---|
| INGREDIENTS | U.S. | METRIC | U.S. | METRIC |
| raisins | 3 3/4 oz. | 107 g | 1/2 cup + 1 tablespoon | 135 mL |
| fresh spinach, washed, tough stalks removed | 4 lb., 8 oz. | 2.1 kg | | |
| olive oil | | 71 g | 1/4 cup + 1 tablespoon | 75 mL |
| garlic, smashed and minced | | | 3 cloves | |
| pine nuts | 3 3/4 oz. | 107 g | 1/2 cup + 1 tablespoon | 135 mL |
| salt | | | 1 1/2 teaspoons | 8 mL |
| pepper | | | 3/4 teaspoon | 4 mL |

1. Soak raisins in warm water. Set aside.
2. Steam spinach in a few drops of water in covered saucepan over medium-high heat for a few minutes, until wilted. Remove from pan.
3. Drain and press spinach to remove excess water. Chop roughly.
4. Drain raisins and roughly chop them.
5. Heat oil in skillet over medium heat, add garlic and sauté about one minute. Be careful not to burn garlic.
6. Add spinach, pine nuts, and raisins, sauté another minute.
7. Season with salt and pepper, sauté about 5 minutes. Correct seasonings.
8. Serve immediately.

## CHAMPIÑONES AL AJILLO

### MUSHROOMS IN GARLIC SAUCE

**Number of Servings:** 7                  **Cooking Method:** Sauté
**Serving Size:** 3 oz. (86 g) *tapas*
**Total Yield:** 1 lb., 6 oz. (624 g)
**Food Balance:** Protein/acid-balanced
**Wine Style:** Light- to medium-bodied Pinot Gris, dry sherry, Gewürztraminer, or Beaujolais
**Example:** Beringer Gewürztraminer or Castello Di Gabbiano Chianti

Paul Brighton/Fotolia

| INGREDIENTS | WEIGHT | | VOLUME | |
| --- | --- | --- | --- | --- |
| | U.S. | METRIC | U.S. | METRIC |
| olive oil | | | 3 tablespoons | 45 mL |
| wild or cultivated mushrooms, cleaned and left whole if small or cut if larger | 1 lb. | 454 g | | |
| garlic, smashed and minced | 1 oz. | 28 g | 8 cloves | |
| stock, mushroom, veal, or beef | | 114 g | 1/2 cup | 120 mL |
| dry sherry | | 57 g | 1/4 cup | 60 mL |
| fresh lemon juice | | | 1 tablespoon + 1 teaspoon | 20 mL |
| red pepper flakes | | | 1/2 teaspoon | 3 mL |
| salt | | | 1/2 teaspoon | 3 mL |
| pepper | | | 1/4 teaspoon | 2 mL |
| fresh parsley, minced | 1/2 oz. | 15 g | 1/4 cup | 60 mL |

> ### TWIST ON THE CLASSIC
>
> Serve this dish cold, like a salad. Either present it on a bed of lettuce greens or serve it alone.

1. Heat oil in skillet over high heat until hot.
2. Add mushrooms and garlic, sauté for about 3 or 4 minutes.
3. Add stock, sherry, lemon juice, red pepper flakes, salt, and pepper; cook 3 minutes.
4. Add parsley, cook another 2 minutes. Correct seasonings. Serve.

# GAZPACHO (SPAIN)
## COLD TOMATO VEGETABLE SOUP

© olynia

**TWIST ON THE CLASSIC**

Give gazpacho a spicy twist by substituting Bloody Mary mix for the tomato juice in the recipe. Add a healthy dash of Worcestershire sauce.

© mizina

**Note:** Allow time to chill the soup and soup bowls.

**Number of Servings:** 9
**Serving Size:** 6 oz. (171 g)
**Total Yield:** 3 lb., 6 oz. (1.5 kg)
**Food Balance:** Protein/sweet/acid
**Wine Style:** Light-bodied Pinot Gris, Pinot Grigio, Sauvignon Blanc, Chablis-style Chardonnay, blush, or rosé
**Example:** Etude Rose of Pinot Noir

| | WEIGHT | | VOLUME | |
|---|---|---|---|---|
| INGREDIENTS | U.S. | METRIC | U.S. | METRIC |
| **Soup:** | | | | |
| fresh or canned tomatoes, peeled and coarsely chopped | 1 lb., 12 oz. | 794 g | 5 medium or 1 can | |
| cucumbers, peeled and diced | 9 1/2 oz. | 270 g | 1 large | |
| onion, diced | 7 oz. | 199 g | 1 large | |
| green bell pepper, diced | 6 oz. | 171 g | 1 each | |
| garlic, minced | 1/4 oz. | 8 g | 2 cloves | |
| red wine vinegar | | 57 g | 1/4 cup | 60 mL |
| olive oil | | 15 g | 1 tablespoon | 15 mL |
| stale white bread, crumbled | 3/4 oz. | 22 g | 1 slice | |
| salt | 1/4 oz. | 8 g | 1 teaspoon | 5 mL |
| tomato juice | | | 1 1/2 cups | 360 mL |

**Garnish:**
bread, 1/4-inch (1/2-cm) cubes
onions, finely chopped
cucumbers, peeled and finely chopped
green bell peppers, finely chopped

1. Combine all soup ingredients in bowl, stir.
2. Put some of mixture in bowl of food processor fitted with knife blade. Purée in batches.
3. Strain mixture through sieve or China cap.
4. Chill thoroughly for several hours or overnight. Correct seasonings.
5. Serve in chilled soup bowls. Pass bowls of garnishes for guests to add to soup.

## CALDO VERDE (PORTUGAL)

### POTATO AND KALE SOUP

**Number of Servings:** 8
**Serving Size:** 7 oz. (199 g)
**Total Yield:** 3 lb., 13 oz. (1.7 kg)
**Food Balance:** Protein
**Wine Style:** Light- to medium-bodied Riesling, Pinot Blanc, Sauvignon Blanc, Pinot Grigio, or Pinot Noir
**Example:** Souverain Sauvignon Blanc

**Cooking Method:** Boil

© uckyo

| INGREDIENTS | WEIGHT | | VOLUME | |
|---|---|---|---|---|
| | U.S. | METRIC | U.S. | METRIC |
| potatoes, white, waxy, or all-purpose, peeled and cubed | 1 lb. | 454 g | 3 large | |
| water | | | 1 quart + 2 cups (6 cups) | 1.44 L |
| salt | 1/2 oz. | 15 g | 2 teaspoons | 10 mL |
| garlic, smashed and minced | 1/4 oz. | 8 g | 2 cloves | |
| pepper | | | 1/4 teaspoon | 2 mL |
| olive oil | | 28 g | 2 tablespoons | 30 mL |
| kale, washed, deribbed, cut into thin ribbons | 8 oz. | 227 g | | |

**TWIST ON THE CLASSIC**

In the style of vichyssoise, try serving this soup cold.

1. Combine potatoes, water, and salt in saucepan. Bring to boil. Cover and simmer for 25 minutes. Add garlic, remove from heat.
2. Put in bowl of food processor fitted with knife blade and purée until almost smooth. Some potato chunks are fine.
3. Return to saucepan. Add pepper and oil, bring to boil over high heat.
4. Add kale, boil uncovered about 5 minutes. Correct seasonings. Serve.

## ENSALADA DE ARROZ (SPAIN)

### RICE SALAD

**Note:** Prepare this dish several hours in advance so the flavors will marry.

**Number of Servings:** 8
**Serving Size:** 4 oz. (114 g)
**Total Yield:** 2 lb. (908 g)

**Cooking Method:** Sauté, boil

Monkey Business Images © Shutterstock

| INGREDIENTS | WEIGHT | | VOLUME | |
|---|---|---|---|---|
| | U.S. | METRIC | U.S. | METRIC |
| **Rice:** | | | | |
| olive oil | | 15 g | 1 tablespoon | 15 mL |
| onion, small dice | 1/2 oz. | 15 g | 1 tablespoon | 15 mL |
| short- or medium-grain rice | 8 oz. | 227 g | 1 cup | 240 mL |
| chicken stock | | 227 g | 1 cup | 240 mL |
| boiling water | | 227 g | 1 cup | 240 mL |
| fresh parsley | | | 1 sprig | |
| dried thyme | | | 1/4 teaspoon | 2 mL |
| dried tarragon | | | 1/8 teaspoon | 1 mL |

### TWIST ON THE CLASSIC

For a different presentation, serve this salad in a tomato. Hollow out a tomato or cut it almost into eighths, leaving wedges attached at the bottom, and spread to create a nest for the rice salad.

**Salad:**

| | | | | |
|---|---|---|---|---|
| mushrooms, chopped | 4 oz. | 114 g | 1 1/3 cups | 320 mL |
| fresh lemon juice | | 15 g | 1 tablespoon | 15 mL |
| olive oil | | 43 g | 3 tablespoons | 45 mL |
| red wine vinegar | | 15 g | 1 tablespoon | 15 mL |
| sugar | | | 1/4 teaspoon | 2 mL |
| garlic, smashed and minced | | | 1 clove | |
| Dijon mustard | | | 1/4 teaspoon | 2 mL |
| dried thyme | | | 1/4 teaspoon | 2 mL |
| fresh parsley, minced | | | 1 tablespoon | 15 mL |
| salt | | | 1/4 teaspoon | 2 mL |
| pepper | | | 1/8 teaspoon | 1 mL |
| anchovy, finely chopped | | | 1 each | |
| anchovy oil (from anchovy can) | | | 1/2 teaspoon | 3 mL |
| roasted red pepper or pimento, diced | 1 1/2 oz. | 43 g | 1 each | |

### RICE:

1. Preheat oven to 400 degrees (205°C). Heat oil on stovetop in ovenproof pan.
2. Add onion and sauté until wilted. Add rice, stir to coat.
3. Add chicken stock, water, parsley, thyme, and tarragon to rice, cover. Transfer to oven, bake for 15 minutes.
4. Remove from oven, discard parsley, recover. Let sit for 10 minutes.
5. Uncover and cool completely.

### SALAD:

1. Combine mushrooms with lemon juice in bowl, set aside.
2. Mix oil, vinegar, sugar, garlic, mustard, thyme, parsley, salt, pepper, anchovy, and anchovy oil in small bowl.
3. Place cooled rice in large bowl, pour oil and vinegar mixture over rice.
4. Fold in roasted red pepper and reserved mushrooms/lemon juice mixture.
5. Let salad sit several hours. Correct seasonings. Serve at room temperature or chill and serve cold.

## ENSALADA DE PIMENTO Y TOMATE (SPAIN)

### PEPPER AND TOMATO SALAD

### TWIST ON THE CLASSIC

Heat this colorful pepper and tomato mixture, and serve it with grilled chicken or meat.

**Note:** Allow at least 1 hour for the mixture to marinate. You may prefer to marinate overnight.

**Note:** This popular salad is served all over Spain. It also appears as *tapas*.

**Number of Servings:** 13      **Cooking Method:** Grill
**Serving Size:** 6 oz. (171 g)
**Total Yield:** 5 lb., 1 1/2 oz. (2.4 kg)

| | WEIGHT | | VOLUME | |
|---|---|---|---|---|
| INGREDIENTS | U.S. | METRIC | U.S. | METRIC |
| red bell peppers, whole | 1 lb., 7 oz. | 652 g | 6 each | |
| green bell peppers, whole | 1 lb., 7 oz. | 652 g | 6 each | |
| onion, sliced into thin rings | 5 oz. | 142 g | 1 medium | |
| tomatoes, peeled and cut into 8 wedges | 1 lb., 11 oz. | 762 g | 4 medium | |
| sherry vinegar | | 86 g | 1/4 cup + 2 tablespoons | 90 mL |

| garlic, smashed and minced | 1/4 oz. | 8 g | 2 cloves | |
|---|---|---|---|---|
| anchovies, minced | 1 oz. | 28 g | 1 tablespoon | 15 mL |
| salt | 1/2 oz. | 15 g or to taste | 2 teaspoons | 10 mL or to taste |
| pepper | | | 1 teaspoon | 5 mL or to taste |
| olive oil | | | 1/2 cup | 120 mL |

**Garnish:**
fresh parsley, minced
cured black olives

1. Char peppers on grill, over flame of burner, or in 500-degree (260°C) oven, turning until blackened and blistered all over.
2. Place peppers in bag, seal, let rest 15 minutes.
3. Remove peppers from bag, peel off skin and discard. Cut pepper in half, remove seeds and ribs, rinse with cold water, and cut into 1/2-inch (1.3-cm) strips.
4. Place pepper strips, onions, and tomatoes in bowl. Set aside until needed.
5. Whisk vinegar, garlic, anchovies, salt, pepper, and olive oil together. Pour over reserved peppers, onions, and tomatoes.
6. Let salad sit at least 1 hour. Serve, garnished with parsley and olives.

## CHULETA DE TERNERA HORTELANA (SPAIN)

### VEAL CHOPS WITH HAM, MUSHROOMS, AND PIMIENTO

**Number of Servings:** 8
**Serving Size:** 1 chop; 1 1/4 oz. (36 g) sauce
**Total Yield:** 10 1/2 oz. (298 g) sauce
**Food Balance:** Protein/acid-balanced
**Wine Style:** Wide variety—very balanced dish: Enjoy wine of your choice, such as Pinot Blanc, Chardonnay, Pinot Noir, Merlot, Cabernet Sauvignon, or Rioja
**Example:** Souverain Chardonnay or Cabernet Sauvignon

**Cooking Method:** Sauté

| | WEIGHT | | VOLUME | |
|---|---|---|---|---|
| **INGREDIENTS** | **U.S.** | **METRIC** | **U.S.** | **METRIC** |
| olive oil | | 57 g | 1/4 cup | 60 mL |
| onion, minced | 4 1/2 oz. | 128 g | 1 cup | 240 mL |
| garlic, minced | 1/4 oz. | 8 g | 2 cloves | |
| cured *serrano* ham, minced | 2 oz. | 57 g | 1/4 cup | 60 mL |
| mushrooms, finely chopped | 7 oz. | 199 g | 2 cups | 480 mL |
| pimientos or roasted red pepper, finely chopped | 5 oz. | 142 g | 4 each | |
| salt | | | 1/2 teaspoon | 3 mL |
| pepper | | | 1/4 teaspoon | 2 mL |
| dried thyme | | | 1/2 teaspoon | 3 mL |
| veal rib chops, about 1-inch thick (2.5-cm) | about 4 lb., 8 oz. | (2.1 kg) | 8 each | |
| dry white wine | | 114 g | 1/2 cup | 120 mL |
| bay leaf | | | 1 each | |
| **Garnish:** | | | | |
| fresh parsley, minced | | | 2 tablespoons | 30 mL |

### TWIST ON THE CLASSIC

This could be prepared with veal scaloppini or boneless chicken breasts instead of veal chops.

1. Heat 2 tablespoons (30 mL) oil in skillet over medium heat, sauté onion for 2 minutes, add garlic. Sauté until onion is wilted.
2. Add ham, mushrooms, pimientos, salt, pepper, and thyme. Cook 5 minutes more. Remove from skillet and refrigerate until needed.
3. Sprinkle chops with salt and pepper.
4. Place ovenproof platter in oven to warm. Set oven to 200 degrees (95°C).
5. Heat remaining 2 tablespoons (30 mL) oil in skillet. Add chops to skillet and sauté chops over medium-low heat until cooked, about 10 to 15 minutes. Remove them to warm platter.
6. Deglaze skillet juices with wine over medium heat, add salt and pepper and bay leaf. Stir constantly, scraping pan drippings from bottom of skillet.
7. Reduce heat to medium-low and cook slowly 2 or 3 minutes, adding water or veal or chicken broth if necessary. Add refrigerated ham and vegetable mixture and heat thoroughly. Correct seasonings.
8. To serve, top each chop with ham and vegetable mixture, then coat center two-thirds of chop with sauce. Sprinkle with parsley.

# LOMBODE PORCO ASSADO EN SALSA DE NARANJAS (SPAIN)

## PORK TENDERLOIN WITH ORANGE GLAZE

© Mike Richter

**TWIST ON THE CLASSIC**

Serve slices of this meat topped with the onion sauce as the filling for a hoagie (sub sandwich).

**Number of Servings:** 9  
**Cooking Method:** Braise  
**Serving Size:** 5 oz. (142 g) meat, 2 1/2 oz. (71 g) sauce  
**Total Yield:** 2 lb., 15 1/4 oz. (1.3 kg) meat, 1 lb., 8 oz. (680 g) sauce  
**Wine Style:** Full-bodied white wine with well-integrated oak and higher acidity. Possible grape varietals are Sauvignon Blanc, Chardonnay, Gruner Veltliner.  
**Example:** Sauvignon Blanc "500" 2011, Von Winning (Pfalz/Germany)

| | WEIGHT | | VOLUME | |
| --- | --- | --- | --- | --- |
| INGREDIENTS | U.S. | METRIC | U.S. | METRIC |
| olive oil | | 43 g | 3 tablespoons | 45 mL |
| pork tenderloin, trimmed of fat and silver | 3 lb., 10 1/2 oz. | 1.7 kg | 3 each | |
| onion, small dice | 15 oz. | 426 g | 2 large | |
| garlic, peeled, smashed | 3/4 oz. | 22 g | 5 cloves | |
| orange juice | | 340 g | 1 1/2 cups | 360 mL |
| sherry, medium dry | | 340 g | 1 1/2 cups | 360 mL |
| bay leaf | | | 3 each | |
| thyme | 1/4 oz. | 8 g | 2 teaspoons | 10 mL |
| salt | 1/4 oz. | 8 g | 1 teaspoon | 5 mL |
| pepper | | | 1/2 teaspoon | 3 mL |

**Garnish:**  
orange slices

1. Heat olive oil in large skillet over medium-high heat. Add tenderloins, brown on all sides. Move meat to one side of pan.
2. Add onions, cook until softened, stirring often, about 2 to 3 minutes. Add garlic, cook another minute.
3. Add orange juice, sherry, bay leaves, thyme, salt, and pepper. Bring to boil, reduce heat, cover and simmer for 10 minutes.
4. Turn pork, cover and continue cooking another 5 to 10 minutes, until desired internal temperature. Remove pork from pan, cover to keep warm and rest a few minutes before slicing.
5. Turn heat to medium-high, stir constantly while reducing sauce until thick and syrup-like in consistency. Correct seasonings.
6. Slice tenderloins. Serve the meat napped with sauce and garnish with orange slices.

## JARRETE DE CORDERO CON AJO (SPAIN)

### LAMB SHANKS WITH GARLIC

**Note:** If fresh rosemary is unavailable, substitute dried. Remember that dried is more concentrated, so use about half the weight of fresh. Both minced garlic and whole unpeeled heads of garlic flavor this dish. Serve each portion (one lamb shank) with a roasted head of whole, unpeeled garlic. With scissors or sharp knife, cut the top off the head so the diner can extract the roasted garlic. Serve with crusty bread for spreading with the roasted garlic.

**Number of Servings:** 8

**Serving Size:** 1 lamb shank with sauce, 10 1/2 oz. (298 g)

**Total Yield:** 8 lb., 13 oz. (4 kg)

**Food Balance:** Balanced

**Wine Style:** Try your favorite!

**Example:** Chateau St. Jean Chardonnay or Beringer Knights Valley Cabernet Sauvignon

**Cooking Method:** Braise

© jb325

| INGREDIENTS | WEIGHT U.S. | WEIGHT METRIC | VOLUME U.S. | VOLUME METRIC |
|---|---|---|---|---|
| olive oil | | 57 g | 1/4 cup | 60 mL or as needed |
| flour for dredging | as needed | | | |
| lamb shanks | 6 lb., 6 oz. | 2.9 kg | 8 each | |
| onion, diced | 12 oz. | 341 g | 2 large | |
| garlic, minced and smashed | 1 oz. | 28 g | 8 cloves | |
| red wine | | 680 g | 3 cups | 720 mL |
| tomato paste | 1 oz. | 28 g | 2 tablespoons | 30 mL |
| fresh rosemary sprigs | 1/2 oz. | 15 g | 12 each | |
| pepper | | | 1/2 teaspoon | 3 mL |
| garlic, unpeeled whole heads | 13 1/2 oz. | 383 g | 8 heads | |
| stock, lamb or chicken | | 908 g or as needed | 1 quart (4 cups) | 960 mL or as needed |
| salt | to taste | | | |

**Garnish:**

| | | | | |
|---|---|---|---|---|
| fresh rosemary sprigs | | | 8 small | |

1. Place half the oil in braiser (if using larger pan, use all oil or as needed to cover bottom of pan). Heat over medium-high heat.

2. Place flour on plate. Dredge lamb shanks in flour on all sides. Preheat oven to 350 degrees (180°C).

3. Sauté lamb shanks on all sides until browned. Remove from pan when browned.

4. Reduce heat to medium, add more oil if needed. Add onion, sauté a few minutes. Add minced garlic, sauté another 1 or 2 minutes.

5. Stir in red wine, then stir in tomato paste, rosemary, and pepper. Add lamb shanks and whole garlic heads.

6. Add stock as needed to cover lamb shanks halfway. Cover and place in oven. After 45 minutes, turn lamb shanks in sauce and add more stock if needed. Bake another 45 minutes or until very tender and meat pulls away from bone. Turn lamb shanks as needed and add more stock if necessary.

7. Remove pan from oven, remove lamb shanks from pan and keep warm. Place pan with sauce over high heat to reduce. Boil over high heat for about 10 minutes or as needed to reduce liquid and thicken sauce. Correct seasonings.

8. Remove top of unpeeled garlic heads with scissors or sharp knife so diner easily can remove the roasted garlic cloves. Serve one lamb shank, one head of unpeeled garlic, and extra sauce for each serving. Garnish with fresh rosemary sprig and accompany with rice or other starch of choice.

# PAELLA A LA VALENCIANA (SPAIN)

## CHICKEN AND SEAFOOD RICE

© Douglas Freer

**Note:** This dish originated in Valencia.

**Number of Servings:** 13          **Cooking Method:** Sauté, boil, bake
**Serving Size:** 13 oz. (369 g)
**Total Yield:** 10 lb., 13 oz. (4.9 g)
**Food Balance:** Protein/spicy
**Wine Style:** Light- to medium-bodied Riesling, Pinot Blanc, light Chardonnay, or Pinot Grigio, and soft reds
**Example:** Beringer Founders' Estate Chardonnay or Merlot

© kuvona

| | WEIGHT | | VOLUME | |
|---|---|---|---|---|
| **INGREDIENTS** | **U.S.** | **METRIC** | **U.S.** | **METRIC** |
| shrimp | 1 lb. | 454 g | | |
| live lobsters | 3 to 4 lb. | 1.4 to 1.8 kg | 2 each | |
| chicken stock, strong | | 1.4 kg | 1 quart + 2 cups (6 cups) | 1.44 L |
| dry white wine | | 114 g | 1/2 cup | 120 mL |
| saffron threads, crumbled | | | 1/2 teaspoon | 3 mL |
| olive oil | | 86 g | 1/4 cup + 2 tablespoons | 90 mL |
| chicken, cut into small pieces (breast into 4, thigh into 2 pieces) | 2 lb., 8 oz. to 3 lb. | 1.1 to 1.4 kg | 1 each | |
| chorizo sausage, 1/4-inch slices | 4 oz. | 114 g | | |
| cured *serrano* ham, diced | 4 oz. | 114 g | | |
| lean pork, 1/2-inch cubes | 4 oz. | 114 g | | |
| red bell pepper, small dice | 7 oz. | 199 g | 1 each | |
| onion, small dice | 5 oz. | 142 g | 1 medium | |
| garlic, minced | 1/2 oz. | 15 g | 4 cloves | |
| rice, short- or medium-grain | 1 lb., 6 1/2 oz. | 640 g | 3 cups | 720 mL |
| fresh parsley, minced | 3/4 oz. | 22 g | 1/4 cup + 1 tablespoon | 75 mL |
| salt | to taste | | | |
| peas, fresh or frozen | 4 oz. | 114 g | 1 cup | 240 mL |
| mussels, cleaned | 12 oz. to 1 lb. | 341 g to 454 g | 12 each | |
| clams, cleaned | about 1 lb. | 454 g | 12 each | |
| roasted red pepper or pimiento, sliced | 1 1/2 oz. | 43 g | 1 each | |

**Garnish:**

lemon wedges
fresh parsley, minced

1. Peel and devein shrimp, reserve shells for stock.
2. Bring stockpot of water to full boil. Place lobsters in pot. Bring back to boil, lower heat, and simmer until shells turn bright red, about 10 to 15 minutes. Remove lobsters from pot and cool enough to handle.
3. Separate tail section and claws from lobster. Cut each tail in half. Crack lobster claws and remove meat. Reserve shells, small feelers, and head for stock.

4. Cook chicken stock with shrimp and lobster shells in a large pot for 1 hour. Strain, reserving 5 1/2 cups (1.32 L) of stock. Add wine and saffron to stock. Refrigerate until needed.

5. Heat oil in *paella* pan, braising pan, or ovenproof dish over high heat. Add chicken pieces, fry until golden. Remove and refrigerate until needed.

6. Sauté chorizo, ham, pork, shrimp, and lobster about 3 minutes. Remove shrimp and lobster. Refrigerate until needed.

7. Add red peppers, onions, and garlic to meat in pan, sauté over medium heat about 5 minutes.

8. Add rice and parsley, coating well. *Can be prepared in advance to this point.*

9. Preheat oven to 325 degrees (160°C). Bring reserved broth to boil on stovetop. Add broth to meat and rice mixture in pan. Stir.

10. Bring to boil, cook uncovered, stirring occasionally, over medium-high heat about 10 minutes. Add salt if needed.

11. Mix peas into rice, bury cooked shrimp and chicken in rice. Place mussels and clams in rice so the side that will open faces up. Arrange pepper strips and cooked lobster pieces over rice.

12. Transfer pan to oven, bake uncovered for 20 minutes. Remove from oven, tent with foil, let rest about 10 minutes.

13. Serve from *paella* pan, garnished with lemon wedges and parsley.

# POLLO AL AJILLO (SPAIN)

## GARLIC CHICKEN

**Number of Servings:** 8
**Serving Size:** 1/4 chicken
**Total Yield:** 3 lb., 14 oz. (1.8 kg)
**Food Balance:** Protein/salt
**Wine Style:** Light and fruity Riesling, White Merlot, low-oak Chardonnay, rosé, Shiraz, Zinfandel
**Example:** Greg Norman Chardonnay or Zinfandel

**Cooking Method:** Sauté

Neil Mersh © Dorling Kindersley

| INGREDIENTS | WEIGHT U.S. | WEIGHT METRIC | VOLUME U.S. | VOLUME METRIC |
|---|---|---|---|---|
| chicken | 5 to 6 lb. | 2.3 to 2.8 kg | 2 each | |
| garlic, minced | 5 oz. | 142 g | 2 heads | |
| olive oil | | 57 g | 1/4 cup | 60 mL |
| pepper | | | 1/4 teaspoon | 2 mL |
| brandy or cognac | | 114 g | 1/2 cup | 120 mL |
| Kosher salt | to taste | | | |

1. Cut chicken into small serving pieces: cut each thigh, split breast, and wing into 2 parts. Dry well.

2. In food processor fitted with knife blade, mince garlic by dropping it through tube with machine running. Reserve 2 tablespoons (30 mL) for later use.

3. Heat oil in pan or skillet over medium heat. Sauté chicken until pieces are browned.

4. Add garlic (except reserved portion), pepper, and brandy. Be careful: it may flame.

5. Cover and cook over low heat about 12 to 15 minutes, or until done.

6. Sprinkle with the remaining garlic and salt to taste. Serve chicken pieces topped with sauce and garlic from pan.

# SCALLOPS IN GREEN SAUCE (SPAIN)

**Note:** This versatile dish may be prepared with any variety of seafood or a combination. Try shrimp, clams, mussels, lobster, or a combination of fish and shellfish.

**Number of Servings:** 8
**Serving Size:** 7 oz. (199 g)
**Total Yield:** 3 lb., 12 oz. (1.7 kg)
**Food Balance:** Protein
**Wine Style:** Light- to medium-bodied Riesling, Sauvignon Blanc, Pinot Grigio, blush, or rosé
**Example:** Souverain Sauvignon Blanc

**Cooking Method:** Braise

**TWIST ON THE CLASSIC**

A puff pastry shell makes a great base for holding the scallops in green sauce.

| INGREDIENTS | WEIGHT | | VOLUME | |
| --- | --- | --- | --- | --- |
| | U.S. | METRIC | U.S. | METRIC |
| olive oil | | 43 g | 3 tablespoons | 45 mL |
| onion, finely chopped | 7 oz. | 199 g | 1 1/2 cups | 360 mL |
| garlic, minced | 1 1/2 oz. | 43 g | 2 tablespoons + 2 teaspoons | 40 mL or 10 to 12 cloves |
| fresh parsley, finely chopped | 4 1/2 oz. | 128 g | 2 1/2 cups | 600 mL |
| scallops | 3 lb. | 1.4 kg | | |
| all-purpose flour | 2 1/2 oz. | 71 g | 1/2 cup | 120 mL |
| strong chicken stock, hot | | 567 g | 2 1/2 cups | 600 mL |
| dry sherry | | 151 g | 2/3 cup | 160 mL |
| salt | to taste | | | |

1. Heat oil in large skillet or braising pan over medium heat.
2. Sauté onion for 1 or 2 minutes.
3. Add garlic, parsley, and scallops, sauté for another 4 or 5 minutes.
4. Add flour and stir for 1 minute. Reduce heat to low.
5. Slowly whisk in stock, whisking constantly (but gently so scallops do not break) for 5 minutes.
6. Add sherry and cook for another 3 minutes. Add salt, if needed.
7. Correct seasonings. Serve over rice.

# BATATAS À PORTUGUÊSA (PORTUGAL)

## FRIED POTATOES

**Number of Servings:** 9
**Serving Size:** 4 oz. (114 g)
**Total Yield:** 2 lb., 4 oz. (1.1 kg)

**Cooking Method:** Sauté

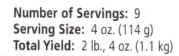

| INGREDIENTS | WEIGHT | | VOLUME | |
| --- | --- | --- | --- | --- |
| | U.S. | METRIC | U.S. | METRIC |
| butter | 2 1/2 oz. | 71 g | 5 tablespoons | 74 mL |
| olive oil | | 71 g | 1/4 cup + 1 tablespoon | 75 mL |
| red potatoes, peeled, sliced 1/4-inch thick | 4 lb., 8 oz. | 2 kg | 15 to 18 each | |
| salt | | | 1 1/4 teaspoons | 6 mL |
| pepper | | | 1/2 teaspoon | 3 mL |
| **Garnish:** | | | | |
| fresh parsley, minced | 1/4 oz. | 8 g | 2 to 3 tablespoons | 30 to 45 mL |

1. Melt butter and heat with olive oil in heavy skillet over medium-high heat until hot.
2. Add potatoes. Turning often with spatula, cook until tender and golden brown, about 20 minutes. Lower heat if getting dark too quickly.
3. Season with salt and pepper. Correct seasonings, and sprinkle with parsley just before serving.

### TWIST ON THE CLASSIC

To change the visuals of this dish, try preparing it with a variety of potatoes in different colors. Add sweet potatoes and purple potatoes.

## COLIFLOR AL AJO ARRIERO (SPAIN)
### CAULIFLOWER, MULE DRIVER'S STYLE

**Number of Servings:** 9
**Serving Size:** 4 oz. (114 g)
**Total Yield:** 2 lb., 6 oz. (1.1 kg)
**Cooking Method:** Boil, sauté
**Wine Style:** White wine with a medium body and residual sugar. Possible grape varietals are Riesling, Chenin Blanc.
**Example:** Riesling "Ürziger Würzgarten" Alte Reben, Dr. Loosen (Mosel/Germany)

Fanfo/Fotolia

| INGREDIENTS | WEIGHT | | VOLUME | |
| --- | --- | --- | --- | --- |
| | U.S. | METRIC | U.S. | METRIC |
| cauliflower, separated into florets | 2 lb., 3 oz. | 994 g | 1 large | |
| olive oil | | 43 g | 3 tablespoons | 45 mL |
| salt | | | 1 1/2 teaspoons | 8 mL |
| garlic, peeled, smashed | 3/4 oz. | 22 g | 5 cloves | |
| reserved cooking liquid | | 15 g | 1 tablespoon | 15 mL |
| red wine vinegar | | 15 g | 1 tablespoon | 15 mL |
| paprika | 1/2 oz. | 15 g | 1 tablespoon | 15 mL |
| pepper | | | 1/2 teaspoon | 3 mL |
| cayenne pepper | sprinkling, to taste | | | |
| parsley, minced | 1/2 oz. | 15 g | 3 tablespoons | 45 mL |

### TWIST ON THE CLASSIC

To create an entrée, add strips of grilled chicken to the cauliflower and serve over pasta.

Serve this as a side dish or *tapas*.

1. Steam or boil cauliflower florets in a little water until al dente, about three-quarters done. Remove cauliflower from water, drain well, reserve cooking water. Cover cauliflower to keep warm.
2. While cauliflower cooks, prepare sauce. Heat olive oil in small skillet over medium heat. Add salt and garlic, cook stirring constantly until just beginning to brown, about 45 seconds. Remove skillet from heat.
3. Stir in reserved cooking liquid, vinegar, paprika, pepper, cayenne, and parsley. Mix well. Correct seasonings.
4. Pour over cauliflower and gently stir cauliflower to coat evenly. Correct seasonings. Serve.

## GUISANTES A LA ESPAÑOLA (SPAIN)

### PEAS WITH CURED HAM

© DueDiDenari

**Number of Servings:** 11      **Cooking Method:** Sauté
**Serving Size:** 4 oz. (114 g)
**Total Yield:** 2 lb., 15 oz. (1.3 kg)

|  | WEIGHT | | VOLUME | |
|---|---|---|---|---|
| **INGREDIENTS** | **U.S.** | **METRIC** | **U.S.** | **METRIC** |
| olive oil |  | 57 g | 1/4 cup | 60 mL |
| onion, minced | 5 1/2 oz. | 156 g | 1 cup | 240 mL |
| carrot, minced | 5 oz. | 142 g | 1 cup | 240 mL |
| cured *serrano* ham, minced | 6 oz. | 171 g | 1 cup | 240 mL |
| peas, fresh or frozen | 2 lb. | 908 g |  |  |
| salt | to taste |  |  |  |
| pepper |  |  | 1/2 teaspoon | 3 mL |

1. Heat oil in pan on medium heat, sauté onion and carrot until onion is wilted, about 3 minutes.
2. Add ham and cook one minute.
3. Add peas, salt, and pepper. Be careful not to oversalt if ham is salty.
4. Cover tightly, cook on low heat about 15 minutes, or until peas are tender. Serve.

### TWIST ON THE CLASSIC

Add cream when peas are halfway cooked to make creamed peas. If desired, add corn to the peas and carrots in this recipe (with or without the cream).

## BROA (PORTUGAL)

### CORNBREAD

© David Smith

**Number of Servings:** 14      **Cooking Method:** Bake
**Serving Size:** 2-inch (5-centimeter) wedge
**Total Yield:** 9-inch (23-centimeter) round
**Dough:** 2 lb., 11 3/4 oz. (1.24 kg)

|  | WEIGHT | | VOLUME | |
|---|---|---|---|---|
| **INGREDIENTS** | **U.S.** | **METRIC** | **U.S.** | **METRIC** |
| cornmeal | 12 1/2 oz. | 355 g | 2 cups | 480 mL |
| salt | 1/4 oz. | 8 g | 1 teaspoon | 5 mL |
| milk, warm |  | 171 g | 3/4 cup | 180 mL |
| water, warm |  | 227 g | 1 cup | 240 mL |
| olive oil |  | 15 g + as needed | 1 tablespoon + as needed | 15 mL + as needed |
| water, warm |  | 57 g | 1/4 cup | 60 mL |
| sugar | 1/4 oz. | 8 g | 1 teaspoon | 5 mL |
| yeast, dry, granulated | 1/2 oz. | 15 g | 1 tablespoon | 15 mL |
| bread flour | 14 1/2 oz. or as needed | 411 g or as needed | 2 3/4 cups | 660 mL |

1. Mix cornmeal and salt in large nonreactive bowl, make well in center of mixture. Add milk, water (227 g [1 cup or 240 mL]), and olive oil. Stir with wooden spoon until thoroughly mixed.
2. Mix water (57 g [1/4 cup or 60 mL]) and sugar in small nonreactive bowl. Sprinkle yeast on top, mix with wooden spoon. Set aside until foamy, several minutes.
3. Add yeast mixture to cornmeal, stir well. Add flour until stiff enough to knead.
4. Knead 8 to 10 minutes, until elastic, adding more flour as needed. Be careful to add only enough flour to prevent dough from sticking to counter while kneading. Too much flour will result in a dry finished product.
5. Return dough to bowl, cover and let rise until doubled, about 1 hour. Meanwhile, lightly coat 9-inch (23-centimeter) pie pan with olive oil; set aside until needed.
6. Punch down dough, knead briefly, and form into round loaf. Place into prepared pan. Cover and allow to rise until doubled, about 45 to 55 minutes. Place oven rack in center of oven. Preheat oven to 350 degrees (180°C).
7. Bake for 40 minutes, until bread is done and sounds hollow when tapped. Remove from oven and pan. Cool on rack.

### TWIST ON THE CLASSIC

Bake in muffin tins for individual portions. If desired, add minced jalapeno peppers and/or minced bell peppers in several colors (green, red, yellow, orange, etc.).

While this bread originated in northern Portugal, now it is served throughout the country. Traditionally, *Broa* accompanied the popular soup, *Caldo Verde* (potato and kale soup).

## TARTA DE ALMENDRAS DE SANTIAGO (SPAIN)

### ALMOND CAKE

**Note:** In many variations, this cake is served in regions throughout Spain.

**Note:** This light cake has a coarse texture and a pleasant, lemony flavor. Because of the lack of fat in the recipe, it can become dry, so be careful not to overbake it. A sauce complements this cake well.

**Number of Servings:** 12 or 16  **Cooking Method:** Bake
**Serving Size:** 1 wedge
**Total Yield:** 10-inch (25-cm) cake

ampFotoStudio © Shutterstock

| | WEIGHT | | VOLUME | |
|---|---|---|---|---|
| **INGREDIENTS** | **U.S.** | **METRIC** | **U.S.** | **METRIC** |
| eggs | 10 oz. | 284 g | 6 each | |
| sugar | 5 1/2 oz. | 156 g | 3/4 cup | 180 mL |
| lemon zest | 1/4 oz. | 8 g | 2 teaspoons | 10 mL |
| lemon juice | | 15 g | 1 tablespoon | 15 mL |
| cinnamon | | | 1/2 teaspoon | 3 mL |
| almonds, blanched, lightly toasted, and ground | 1 lb. | 454 g | 3 cups | 720 |
| flour | 2 1/2 oz. | 71 g | 1/2 cup | 120 mL |
| confectioner's sugar | for dusting top of cake | | | |

### TWIST ON THE CLASSIC

Serve a piece of this cake topped with lemon sorbet and hot fudge sauce.

1. Pan-spray or grease 10-inch (25-cm) springform pan. Place a piece of parchment paper about 3 inches × 5 inches (8 cm × 13 cm) in bottom of pan. Pan-spray or grease parchment. Place oven rack in upper third of oven. Preheat oven to 350 degrees (180°C).
2. In large bowl, mix eggs, sugar, lemon zest, lemon juice, and cinnamon with electric mixer fitted with wire beater at high speed until light colored and very fluffy.
3. Meanwhile, place almonds in small bowl, sift flour over almonds, mix gently to combine.
4. Using rubber spatula, gently fold one-third of almond mixture into egg mixture. Repeat twice with remaining almond mixture.
5. Pour into prepared pan. Rap pan on counter once to remove large air pockets. Bake for 30 to 35 minutes, until knife inserted in cake comes out clean.
6. Remove sides of pan. Cool completely on rack.
7. Dust top of cake with sifted confectioner's sugar. If desired, serve accompanied by apricot purée or another fruit purée, orange- or frangelica-flavored custard sauce, ice cream, or topping of choice.

# PORTO PUDIM FLAN (PORTUGAL)
## PORTUGUESE BAKED CARAMEL CUSTARD

*Brushing sugar crystals from side of pan*

**Note:** Consider wrapping a kitchen towel around the hand you use to stir the heated cream mixture into the caramelized sugar because it will bubble and splatter.

**Note:** Allow time for the flan to chill 3 hours or overnight. Chill plates for service.

**Number of Servings:** 8 to 12         **Cooking Method:** Bake
**Total Yield:** One 8-inch (20-cm) or 10 to 12 individual

| INGREDIENTS | WEIGHT | | VOLUME | |
| --- | --- | --- | --- | --- |
| | U.S. | METRIC | U.S. | METRIC |
| **Caramel:** | | | | |
| sugar | 7 1/4 oz. | 206 g | 1 cup | 240 mL |
| water | | 57 g | 1/4 cup | 60 mL |
| **Custard:** | | | | |
| milk | | 340 g | 1 1/2 cups | 360 mL |
| heavy cream | | 340 g | 1 1/2 cups | 360 mL |
| sugar | 4 3/4 oz. | 135 g | 3/4 cup | 180 mL |
| egg yolks | | 114 g | 6 each | |
| port | | 15 g | 1 tablespoon | 15 mL |

## CARAMEL:

1. Combine sugar and water in small pan, mixing until all sugar is wet.
2. Bring to boil over high heat. Do not stir. Use pastry brush dipped in cold water to wash any sugar crystals from sides of pan.
3. Reduce heat to medium-high, cook without stirring until golden brown color.
4. Immediately pour into flan dish(es), tip to coat bottom and up part of sides. Set dish(es) aside.

## CUSTARD:

1. Place oven rack in middle of oven. Preheat oven to 350 degrees (180°C). Put a pot of water on the stovetop to boil.
2. Heat milk and heavy cream in pan over medium heat until small bubbles appear around the edge of the pan. Set aside.

**TWIST ON THE CLASSIC**

Prepare individual baked tart shells, and make the custard in individual molds the same size or a little smaller than the size of the tart shell. Just before service, unmold the custard into the tart shell. The flan will stand in the tart shell and the caramelized sugar will pool around the flan.

*Coating dish with caramelized sugar*
Jerry Young © Dorling Kindersley

*Pouring custard into prepared dish*

③ Place sugar in medium-sized heavy pan over medium heat to caramelize: stir with wooded spoon until it melts and turns golden brown. Remove from heat.

④ Pour hot cream mixture very slowly into caramelized sugar, stirring with wooden spoon. Be careful; it will bubble and splatter. Stir until caramel has dissolved. Return to heat if needed to dissolve caramel.

⑤ Beat egg yolks in large bowl with mixer or whisk until well blended.

⑥ Slowly pour cream mixture into eggs, stirring constantly.

⑦ Stir in port, then strain mixture through fine sieve. Pour into prepared dish(es).

⑧ Put roasting pan on middle shelf of oven, place dish(es) in pan. Pour boiling water into pan until it comes halfway up sides of dish(es) *(baine-marie)*.

⑨ Bake until knife inserted in center of custard comes out clean, about 1 hour and 10 minutes for large dish or 40 minutes for individual molds.

⑩ Cool, then refrigerate until chilled, at least 3 hours, or overnight.

⑪ To unmold, run sharp knife around inside edge of mold, invert on chilled serving plate.

© Grafvision

# France

## >> LEARNING OBJECTIVES

By the end of this chapter, you will be able to:

• Explain the origins of classical French cookery
• Understand and explain differences in classical and regional French cookery
• Name dishes from various regions of France and explain why they originated there
• Name countries and cultures that influenced French cuisine and describe how their impact affected the cuisine of France
• Name food items that flourish in various areas of France
• Prepare a variety of regional and classical French dishes

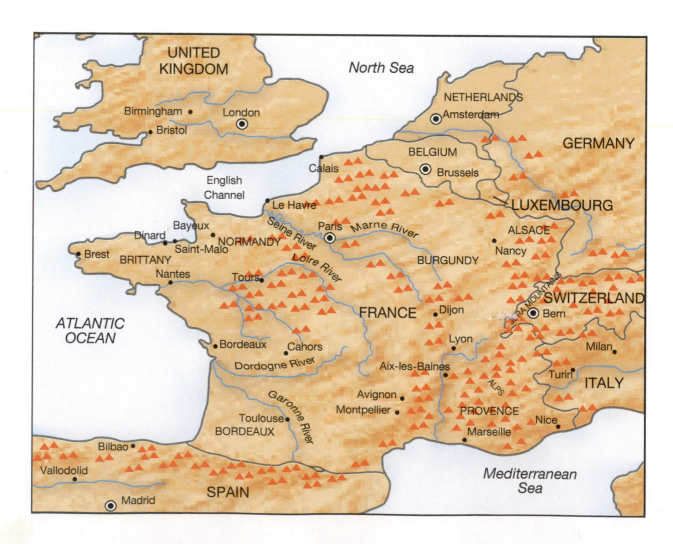

## >> HISTORY

Drawings discovered on the walls of caves in southwest France confirm the presence of prehistoric man. Researchers believe Cro-Magnon people lived in this area as early as 25,000 B.C.

### INVADERS

Because of its geographic location, France was subjected to invasions on all sides by many different groups of people throughout history. In about 125 B.C., the Romans conquered Provence in the south of France from the Gauls. Roman rule existed until the late fifth century A.D., when the Roman Empire declined. At that time, France came under the power of the Franks and Germans.

Sharing a border with Germany, the northeastern areas of Alsace and Lorraine exhibit strong German culinary influence. A rich, fertile land, this area exchanged nationalities numerous times throughout history, sometimes won by the Germans, other times under the rule of France.

Fifteen hundred years ago, the Celtics came to Brittany from England, and the Vikings from Scandinavia landed in Normandy around 1000 A.D. The Arabs entered the south of France around 720 A.D. Besides bringing goats to France, their influence is apparent in dishes from that area such as *cassoulet*, a one-pot braised dish containing meats and beans.

### CATHERINE DE' MEDICI

In 1533, Catherine de' Medici of Italy moved to France to marry the future king, Henry II. She brought fine Italian chefs with her, and she introduced the French aristocracy to the Italian splendor of table setting, as well as new foods including broccoli, peas, artichokes, sauces, and fine pastries. The course of dining in France changed forever.

From the time of Catherine de' Medici until the French Revolution was an era of great opulence and wealth for the aristocracy and extreme poverty for the lower class. While the rich feasted on abundant food including roasts, poultry, and rich pastries, the poor ate stale bread, grains, and anything they could find. Of course, this eventually led to the poor people's overthrowing the monarchy.

### FRENCH REVOLUTION

The French Revolution began in 1789. It resulted in the end of the ruling aristocracy, and France becoming an independent nation. The concept of the restaurant developed during the Revolution. Supposedly, anyone who could afford it went into restaurants and ordered soup.

In 1804, Napoleon Bonaparte became the ruler of France and conquered much of Europe. The French Revolution brought an important culinary change to France and to the world: the proliferation of the restaurant. After the Revolution, the cooks who had worked for the aristocracy found themselves without jobs, so they found work in the restaurants of France. These chefs and cooks transformed many French restaurants into world-renowned eating establishments, a reputation that still exists today.

### NOUVELLE CUISINE

In the 1900s, Fernand Point initiated a change in the French culinary world called *nouvelle cuisine*. This transformed classic French dishes into healthier ones. Instead of heavy sauces of butter, *roux*, and cream, the chefs seasoned and thickened with items like butter, puréed vegetables and/or fruits, herbs, vinegars, and lemon juice. Vegetables and many types of meat were cooked for a shorter time to maintain their fresh flavor and crispness. Steaming became an often-used cooking technique. In general, this lighter cooking used less butter, fat, and cream.

Haute cuisine, *literally "high cooking," began with Catherine de' Medici and reached its pinnacle of perfection with the famous chef Georges Auguste Escoffier (1846–1935). Characteristics of haute cuisine include large, elaborate meals consisting of numerous courses of rich foods with grand presentation. Fine wines, beautiful serving pieces, and excellent service added to the ambience and pleasure of* haute cuisine. *Historically, this is the cuisine served in the finest restaurants. Over the years, the foods and dishes have changed as the trends in cooking and cuisine evolve.*

The word restaurant *comes from the French word* restaurer. *Literally translated "to restore," the idea was that restaurants were restorative (for health).*

In addition to simpler preparations and presentations, all of these modifications brought real change to classical French cuisine. In the 1970s, French chefs including Paul Bocuse, Roger Vergé, Jean and Pierre Troisgros, Michel Guérard, and pastry chef, Gaston Lenôtre spearheaded this cookery and spread it to the United States.

## >> TOPOGRAPHY

France lies in western Europe. Belgium and Luxembourg border on the north; Germany, Switzerland, and Italy are situated to the east; Spain and the Mediterranean Sea are to the south; and the Bay of Biscayne and English Channel lie to the west.

Two major mountain chains stand in France. Situated on the eastern and southeastern side of France, the Alps forms the border between France and Italy and Switzerland. The highest peak in the Alps, Mont Blanc, actually lies in France. Joining Spain on the southwest, the Pyrenees Mountains create a difficult, rugged terrain that also historically contributed to significant isolation.

Two bodies of water form miles and miles of coastline in France. On the southern side lies the Mediterranean Sea; the Atlantic Ocean borders the west and northwest.

Several rivers transect France, resulting in fertile farmlands and valleys where vineyards flourish and world-famous wines are produced. The longest river, the Loire, runs through central and western France; the Seine and the Marne lie in the central area; the Dordogne transects the southwest; and the Rhine and Rhone flow in the east.

In the northwest, Normandy contains coastline, rolling hills, and forests. Just south in Brittany, the landscape changes to rugged coast, rocky terrain, and forests. With the exception of the central highlands, most of the land in France consists of fertile farmland. The French grow grains, fruits, and vegetables on this productive land and raise cattle and sheep for both meat and dairy.

### Ingredients and Foods Commonly Used throughout the Cuisine of France Include

- lamb
- pork
- duck, chicken, and goose
- beef
- fish and seafood
- *foie gras*
- butter
- cream
- cheese
- apples, pears, and cherries
- truffles and all types of mushrooms
- numerous vegetables, including peas and *haricots*
- shallots, leeks, onions, and garlic
- wine and brandy

## >> COOKING METHODS

The cooks and chefs of France use virtually all preparation methods. The famous French fries are among the deep-fried food items; the list of dishes prepared by sautéing goes on and on. Poaching is commonly used for fish. Baking, roasting, and broiling appear frequently.

From *bouillabaisse* to *cassoulet* to *confit*, braising and one-pot cookery appear often in traditional regional cookery. One-pot dishes characterized the cooking of the Arabs who traveled the desert and cooked any available ingredients in one pot over an open fire. After entering the southwest of France around 720 A.D., Arabs left their influence on the cuisine with many braised dishes and spices like pepper, cumin, anise, cinnamon, and ginger.

## >> REGIONS

### NORTH

The north and northwest receive ample rainfall, resulting in fertile soil that produces abundant crops. Many orchards thrive in this area, which is particularly known for apples. Although temperatures on the coasts remain more moderate, inland areas experience cold winters and hot summers.

Located in the northwest, Normandy borders the English Channel, which provides plentiful fish and seafood. In addition, this region is known for its farmland and dairy products. They produce very high-quality butter, cream, cheese, and eggs. Apple orchards thrive in Normandy, where *calvados*, apple brandy, originated. Cream sauces, Camembert cheese, fresh seafood (especially sole), sheep for meat and cheese, and apple desserts are trademarks of this region. Butter is the cooking fat of choice here.

© Taratorki

Just to the south of Normandy, the people of Brittany prefer heavy, simple food—quite a contrast to the cuisine of Normandy. Buckwheat, whole grains, pork, and seafood remain staples. Excellent shellfish, particularly oysters, are bred here. *Crêpes*, thin, delicate pancakes that are rolled around a filling, originated in Brittany. Situated just across the channel from Great Britain, the Welsh influence appears prominently here. *Beurre blanc*, butter sauce, accompanies many dishes in Brittany.

Known as Ile de France, the north-central region includes Paris and the surrounding countryside. Surprisingly, most of this region remains quite rural. All types of soups are appreciated here, from consommés to cream soups and from thick purées to the classic French onion soup with its topping of cheese and bread. Pâtés are widely consumed; Brie cheese hails from this region. Finally, Ile de France is the home of the very popular *pomme frittes*, better known as French fries.

*Ham and Cheese Crêpe*
© Fanfo

In the northeast, the valleys around the Rhine River create fertile farmland suitable for lots of crops. Bordering Germany and Belgium, the culinary influence of those countries is strongly felt. Alsace contains very fertile farmland and produces a bounty of fruits and vegetables. Known for onion tart and *choucroute*, a dish containing sauerkraut cooked with sausages and meats and accompanied by boiled potatoes, this region serves some of the hearty foods of its neighbor, Germany. Noodles, dumplings, and *spaetzel* (a German specialty that is a cross between a noodle and dumpling) are regular menu items here. Pork ranks as the favorite meat, and *charcuterie* is prevalent. In addition to sharing the fondness for wine so prevalent throughout France, the people of this region serve beer often.

### CENTRAL

The Jura Mountains and French Alps lie in the southeast. Potatoes, milk, cream, cheese, freshwater fish, and beef dominate the cuisine here. Gruyère cheese, a type of Swiss cheese, comes from the French Juras, while several creamy cheeses including Reblochon are produced in the French Alps.

The region of Burgundy in central France boasts excellent wines and is the birthplace of the famous culinarian Jean Brillat-Savarin. This area contains rivers supplying fish, forests abounding with mushrooms and game, and the city of Dijon, which is famous for its mustards. The cooking in Burgundy often incorporates wine and cream. Pork fat is the fat of choice here; many dishes contain bacon. Two dishes braised in wine, *boeuf bourguignon* and *coq au vin* originated in this area. *Escargot*, snails prepared with garlic butter, is another famous specialty from this region. Chalky caves found in Burgundy and in the Champagne district to its north provide excellent storage for the aging of fine wines.

*"Escargot in Garlic Butter"*
© Maksim Shebeko

To the south of Burgundy lies the city of Lyon, reputed to be the gastronomical capital of France, and perhaps the world. Pork, all sorts of sausages, onions, and potatoes are popular in this area. *Quenelles*, a dumpling of puréed fish, originated here. Much of the gastronomical splendor of this area comes from its proximity to other areas in France that produce the finest food products. For example, beef from Charlois, poultry from Bresse, lamb from Auvergne, forests providing a variety of mushrooms, abundant rivers and streams yielding freshwater fish and seafood, and some of the best wines in the world come from areas lying close to Lyon.

Much of the central region contains poor soil and highlands. This land is good for grazing livestock and sheep but not great for crops. As a result, this area yields a lot of meat and dairy products. In addition, wild mushrooms and much game thrive in the central to west-central area. This region claims the invention of *tarte Tatin*, apple pie that is baked with a top crust only and then inverted on a plate immediately after baking.

The Loire Valley in the west produces an abundance of fruits and vegetables from its rich soil, grapes for wine, and numerous types of goat cheeses. Shallots flavor many of the dishes here. Throughout French history, kings chose this beautiful area to the west of Paris to build *châteaux*, country homes.

## SOUTH

The Mediterranean Sea borders the south of France in the area called the Riviera. The mild winters and hot, dry summers result in a proliferation of crops, including olives and grapes. Olive oil replaces butter or pork fat as the fat of choice here.

Provence, a southern province, displays food products typical of the Mediterranean cuisines. Tomatoes, olives, olive oil, garlic, bell peppers, anchovies, and a variety of herbs are widely used and are characteristic of dishes called *provençal*. Goat cheeses, which often appear seasoned with herbs, come from this southern region.

The southwestern border with Spain contains the high, rugged Pyrenees Mountains, creating incredibly difficult terrain. These mountains are so rugged that the French used to travel by sea to reach Spain rather than by crossing this mountainous barrier. Known as the Basque region, seafood, pork, tomatoes, and both mild and spicy red peppers frequent many dishes in this region. Besides the obvious Spanish influence on the food, people in this rugged, mountainous area consumed a variety of dried beans in soups and stews.

South-central France contains the region called Languedoc. From this region comes oysters and other shellfish; *confit*, a method of slow cooking goose or duck in its own fat; *foie gras*, the highly prized goose liver; and *cassoulet*, a one-pot dish containing various meats, white beans, and herbs. Famous for the sheep's cheese of the same name, the town of Roquefort lies in Languedoc. Lots of caves dot this area, providing an excellent place for aging cheeses.

In the southwest of France lies Perigord, an area known for black truffles, cheeses, mushrooms, walnuts, red wine, cognac, game, pork, goose, duck, *foie gras*, *pâté*, and *confit*. As in Languedoc, the many caves here are used for aging cheeses.

"Cassoulet"
© Sollub

## >> CUISINE

Throughout history, the people of France displayed extraordinary interest in food and dining. As a result, the French embraced all types of culinary influences from other groups, adapting ones that improved their dining experience. In addition, France has had many talented chefs whose goal was to improve and refine French foods and the culinary experience.

Two distinctly different cuisines are associated with the cooking of France. The first—classical cookery—initially existed only for the upper class and aristocracy. Definite rules governed classical cooking in its early days, as they still do today. In classical preparations, the marriage of sauces with dishes held the utmost importance, with the goal of achieving gastronomical perfection.

The second type of cuisine—regional cookery—involves much simpler preparations than classical cooking and utilizes the foods available in each region. Although quite different from each other, both classical and regional cuisines remain very important components of the cookery of France. First, French classical cookery is addressed.

## CLASSICAL COOKING

The Greeks achieved a level of dining sophistication. They felt dining should be a relaxing and enjoyable time, and music, dancing, and dinner conversation accompanied the food. The Greeks taught two momentous lessons about eating and drinking:

1. Moderation and balance in both eating and drinking
2. An association of these two tasks (eating and drinking) with great joy and pleasure

From the Romans, the French learned overindulgence in eating. The rich partook in huge banquets featuring hundreds of varieties of fish, meat, and other dishes. In the meantime, the poor subsisted on a diet of porridge and gruel.

Throughout the Middle Ages until the fourteenth century, the food was heavily spiced and without a lot of variety. In those days before refrigeration, the heavy spices hid the taste and smell of sometimes rancid food.

Culinary issues changed during the Renaissance in the fifteenth century. An emphasis on fine cuisine, tableware, and service began in Italy. This trend toward culinary opulence spread to France, helped along when Italian Catherine de' Medici married the future king of France in 1533. The Italian chefs who accompanied her to France introduced sweetbreads, truffles, the Italian tradition for splendid foods and table settings, and the Italian pastries that became the basis for French pastries. The French nobility embraced the lavish banquets with many courses, extravagant centerpieces, and carvings made from foods.

Since the 1700s, the *haute cuisine* of France has set the standard for excellence. The French have made remarkable contributions to the culinary world, especially with their repertoire of sauces. From growing it to selling it to cooking it, the French treat food with great respect. In the past and still today, food and wine rank as some of life's greatest pleasures throughout France. By the 1700s, under the rule of Louis XIV, the heavy spices had disappeared, and the emphasis became the flavors found in natural foods. During this time, chefs began serving magnificent meals in separate courses. Opulence defined the culinary world during the reign of Louis XIV.

The nobility continued their grandiose banquets, until the execution in 1793 of King Louis XVI and his wife Queen Marie Antoinette, which marked the French Revolution. Not realizing that the poor people were starving while the aristocracy consumed lavish banquets, Marie Antoinette made the famous "let them eat cake" statement when told that the people had no bread to eat.

During the rule of Napoleon following the French Revolution, food became even more elegant. Considered the father of French classical cuisine, Marie-Antoine Carême (1784–1833) trained as a cook and then as a pastry chef around 1800. He made several significant contributions to the culinary world, one being the introduction of symmetry and order to French cooking. Also, Carême initiated the concept of balancing the flavors and textures of the foods both within individual courses and throughout the meal. This led to the belief that the entire meal must unite to form a pleasing, whole experience.

During his lifetime, Carême wrote several cookbooks. These were the first books to contain actual recipes and menus in addition to defining cooking methods. Carême's recipes included precise amounts of ingredients, exacting directions, and the feeling of artistic execution for each dish.

Always interested in architecture, from pastry materials Carême created centerpieces that were replicas of architectural masterpieces found throughout the world. These pastry feats adorned opulent tables of food, some of these tables holding dozens of different cold or hot dishes. Among the well-known dishes invented by

According to accounts, Louis XIV had an enormous appetite. His meal might consist of several bowls of different types of soup, a whole partridge or other poultry, a large piece of mutton or other meat, salads and vegetables, and several desserts. He loved vegetables, and many were planted in the gardens at Versailles. In 1644, he first drank coffee, and soon many of the aristocracy adopted this habit.

Stocks form the foundation of classical cooking; sauces are prepared from stocks. The five mother sauces are béchamel, velouté, tomato, espagnole, and hollandaise. All the other sauces are derived from these five sauces.

**RULES FOR CLASSICAL COOKERY**

- Offer a variety of textures in the different foods—soft, puréed, firm, crunchy, and so on.
- Food items should not be repeated within a meal—for example, if potato soup is served, potatoes should not accompany the entrée.
- Offer an interesting array of colors on the plate to stimulate the appetite.

### FAMOUS CHEFS AND GASTRONOMES

- *Pierre François de la Varenne (1618–1678)*—*Began the trend toward modern French cooking by emphasizing the natural flavor of foods; credited with inventing béchamel sauce and mushroom duxelles; wrote cookbook* Le Cuisiner Francóis *in 1651*
- *Jean Anthelme Brillat-Savarin (1755–1826)*—*Great gastronome*
- *Marie-Antoine Carême (1784–1833)*—*Father of classical cuisine; created ornate and elaborate table decorations as well as beautifully presented foods*
- *Urbain Dubois (1818–1901)*—*Promoted Russian table service, which resulted in meals being served by courses*
- *Georges Auguste Escoffier (1846–1935)*—*Father of modern cooking; reorganized setup of kitchen personnel by initiating cooking stations in the kitchen to expedite food preparation*
- *Prosper Montagné (1865–1948)*—*Wrote* Larousse Gastronomique; *simplified classical cuisine by eliminating many garnishes*
- *Maurice Edmond Sailland (1872–1956)*—*Gastronome, professional food critic, wrote forerunner for Guide Michelin (which rates restaurants and hotels)*
- *Fernand Point (1897–1955)*—*Excellent restaurateur who owned the restaurant La Pyramide in Vienne, France; developed many recipes and trained many chefs; instrumental in the* nouvelle cuisine *movement, which emphasizes creating lighter versions of traditional French Dishes*

Carême is *charlotte russe*, a confection featuring a core of vanilla Bavarian cream folded with whipped cream surrounded by ladyfinger biscuits. Considered "the queen of all entrées" by Carême, *chartreuse* consists of a molded dish with a decorative outside of colorful vegetables around a center containing vegetables, game, and/or poultry.

Another prominent French chef who left a significant culinary legacy was Georges Auguste Escoffier (1846–1935). Known as "the king of chefs and the chef of kings," he is credited with adapting classical cooking for the modern world.

Among his many contributions, Escoffier reorganized the kitchen, developing stations for the kitchen personnel that are still used in many kitchens today. Instead of having one cook responsible for each dish, cooks were assigned to *brigades,* or teams, that prepared items according to the type of cooking technique. For example, the *saucier* was responsible for the sauces; the *garde manger* prepared cold foods and garnishes; the *rôtisseur* handled the foods requiring roasting.

Prior to Escoffier's time, all the foods in a meal were presented at the same time in an elaborate display on one or more tables. Escoffier and another French chef, Urbain Dubois, initiated serving the meal in courses. This resulted in hot food's being served hot, and cold foods served cold. The *brigade* system in the kitchen helped achieve this, because it expedited the delivery of food to the diner after an order was placed.

Escoffier established several changes that affected the presentation of food; many of these changes are still followed today. He said all garnishes and centerpieces should be edible and that food and its presentation should reflect simplicity. He greatly reduced the size of menus, making them more manageable for the kitchen staff. Leaving a lasting legacy, Escoffier wrote several cookbooks containing a total of more than 5,000 recipes for future generations of cooks.

Escoffier became associated with Cesar Ritz and ran the kitchens in Ritz's elite hotels in many cities in Europe, Canada, and the United States. In this position, he cooked for many prominent patrons, including nobility, actors and actresses, and many of the most wealthy people of the time. Escoffier invented numerous dishes that were named for the event or the patron for whom they were created. Peche Melba and Melba toast were named after Nellie Melba, a famous soprano. The actress Sarah Bernhardt had several dishes named in her honor, too.

Although Carême's legacy depicts him as the father of classical cuisine, Escoffier is remembered as the father of modern classical cooking. He made numerous profound contributions to the culinary world, and many of these form the foundation of today's culinary ideas.

## REGIONAL COOKING

The second type of cooking, regional cookery, developed from the strong variations existing between the cuisines of the different regions. As in most countries, the creation of dishes depended on what grew best and what animals were raised in each area. A number of factors, including the topography, climate, neighboring countries, and the groups who invaded, influenced the cuisine found in each region.

Availability and selection of wines, cheeses, produce, cooking fat, meats, fish, and poultry as well as preparation methods vary with the different regions. Sauces found in regional cookery often derive from liquids added to the ingredients in the pot, rather than being prepared as a separate sauce, as is customary in classical cookery. Frequently, regional specialties are prepared in other areas also; however, they often appear with great differences. Originating in the Mediterranean area, variations on *bouillabaisse*, the traditional fish stew, show up in many coastal areas. The same is true for *cassoulet*, which is served throughout France.

Bouillabaisse has a long history in the areas bordering the Mediterranean Sea where they prepared this fish soup from a variety of available fish and shellfish. Often, it was made with whatever fish the fishermen had left over at the end of the day. In Marseilles, they say the soup should contain at least seven types of fish, while in most of Provence, they require five different varieties.

## BOUNTY OF FOODS

As a country, France has a rich bounty of crops. Abundant apples, cherries, peaches, pears, and grapes grow. Many vegetables, including sugar beets, beans, peas, carrots, potatoes, cauliflower, and tomatoes, thrive in various regions of France. Besides plentiful produce, all sorts of seafood, fish, and animals for meat flourish here. Sheep, cattle, poultry, and game, as well as freshwater fish and saltwater seafood from the Atlantic, Mediterranean, and the many rivers, provide a wide variety of animal protein products.

With an abundance of dairy products available, France produces more than 500 varieties of cheese. Most agree that French cheeses rank as some of the world's best. Most regions make cheeses that are known as specialties of that particular area. Cow, goat, and sheep milk are used for cheese making. Many cooks think the exceptionally high quality of French cream and butter accounts for recipes' not tasting the same when prepared outside of France.

*Charcuterie* shops selling all sorts of sausages and cured meats are found throughout the various regions of France. As with their cheeses, regions have their own meat specialties, which often are available only in that particular region.

Known throughout the world, the fine breads and pastries of France actually evolved from Italian pastries. With bread served at every meal, the French consume a tremendous amount of bread daily. A person walking down the street carrying a baguette or two is a common sight in both large cities and small towns throughout France. To ensure high quality, the government regulates bread standards. Most French bakers in shops prepare bread twice each day so that only very fresh bread is sold.

Second only to Italy in wine production, France is renowned for creating some of the finest wines and other spirits in the world. Excellent quality grapes flourish in a number of regions throughout France. Each area specializes in grapes that grow best in that region, and based on the type of grape and the growing conditions, one or more specific types of wine are produced there. By government regulation, a sparkling wine can be called Champagne only if it is produced in the Champagne district of France. Brandy and cognac come from the southwest, while Burgundy, Bordeaux, Alsace, Champagne, and the Loire Valley are known for fine wines.

## MEALS

Typically, breakfast in France consists of bread and coffee. The bread may be *croissant, brioche,* or a crusty hard roll. *Café au lait,* strong coffee mixed with warmed milk, remains the morning beverage of choice.

The main meal includes several courses and is eaten midday. People used to return home and take two hours for this meal, but with modern jobs often situated in cities, many take a standard one-hour midday meal break. For the main meal, a first course of soup or appetizer precedes the entrée. A salad and then a fruit or cheese course follows the entrée. For a special occasion, a fish course is added before the entrée and a dessert follows the cheese.

The evening meal, which is much lighter than the midday meal, is not eaten until eight or nine o'clock at night. Often, two hot meals are consumed daily. Depending on the area of France, wine or beer accompanies meals. Another popular alcoholic beverage, *pastis,* is anise-flavored liquor that is served mixed with water.

---

**MAJOR COOKBOOKS IN FRENCH HISTORY**

*1300s— by Taillevent— Demonstrates the heavily spiced foods of that time, using lots of cinnamon, ginger, clove, and nutmeg; sauces are thickened with bread rather than roux; emphasizes soups, meats, and poultry; exhibits little variety in the foods*

*1600s— by La Varenne—Le Cuisiner Francóis—First cookbook that moved toward classical cuisine and away from heavily spiced foods; first cookbook with alphabetized recipes; includes directions for cooking vegetables; uses roux instead of bread to thicken sauces; emphasizes the natural flavors of foods*

*1800s— by Brillat-Savarin—The Physiology of Taste—Took twenty-five years to write; chronicles the food of the time*

*1800s— by Carême—Describes classical cookery in great detail; contains precise recipes*

*1800 to 1900s— by Montagné— Larousse Gastronomique, the basic French cooking encyclopedia*

*1900s— by Escoffier—Many books, containing a total of more than 5,000 recipes documenting classical cuisine*

---

*The Greeks and Romans introduced cheese making to France.*

| REGION | AREA | WEATHER | TOPOGRAPHY | FOODS |
|--------|------|---------|------------|-------|
| North and northwest | Normandy, Brittany | Coast: Cool winters, mild summers<br>Inland: cold winters, hot summers | Coast, rolling hills, plains, Seine River | Seafood, pork, beef, butter, cream, cheeses, wheat, buckwheat, apples, sugar beets, *calvados* |
| Northeast | Rhine Valley | Cold winters, hot summers | Mountains, valleys, flat bottomlands, plateaus, forests, Rhine River | Cattle, sheep, pork, *choucroute, charcuterie*, noodles, *spaetzel*, grapes, various crops, fruit orchards |
| Central | Burgundy, Champagne | Cool winters, hot summers | Hills, rivers, valleys | Fish, game, beef, pork, snails, cheeses, mushrooms, mustards, vegetables, fruits, wine |
| Central | Central highlands | Cold winters, hot summers | Hills, mountains, grasslands, forest, Loire River | Cattle, sheep, game, cream, milk, cheeses, rye, mushrooms |
| Southwest | Bordeaux, Perigord | Coast: Cool winters, mild summers<br>Inland: Cold winters, hot summers | Coast, forests, rolling plains, Garonne River | Seafood, pork, goose, duck, game, *confit, foie gras, pâté*, cheeses, truffles, mushrooms, walnuts, grapes |
| Southwest | Pyrenees | Cold winters, mild summers | Mountains | Seafood, pork, red peppers, tomatoes |
| Southeast | Riviera | Mild winters, hot, dry summers | Mountains, hills, valleys, lowlands, Rhone River | Seafood, anchovies, goats, goat cheese, vegetables, olives, olive oil, herbs, peppers, tomatoes, fruits, grapes |
| East | French Alps, Jura Mountains | Cold winters, mild summers | Mountains, valleys | Beef, fish, cheeses, cream, butter, potatoes |
| Corsica (island) | 100 miles southeast of France | Mild | Hills, mountains | Seafood, sheep, goats, cheeses, grains, vegetables, olives, fruits, grapes |

## SOME FRENCH CHEESES

**Brie** Made from cow's milk; full flavored yet mild; buttery soft texture that oozes; rind-ripened cheese from Ile de France

**Brillat-Savarin** Made from cow's milk; mild rich, savory flavor, buttery soft texture; a triple-cream cheese from Normandy

**Camembert** Made from cow's milk; full flavored yet mild, buttery soft texture that oozes; rind-ripened cheese from Normandy

**Crottin de Chavignol** Made from goat's milk; becomes stronger flavored and more firm as it ages; natural rind cheese from Loire

**Epoisses de Bourgogne** Made from cow's milk; mild to pungent flavor depending on age; heady, yeasty aroma, smooth semisoft texture; from Burgundy

**Munster** Made from sheep's milk; full flavored and aromatic, heady aroma, creamy semisoft texture; from Alsace

**Neufchâtel** Made from sheep's milk; bitter, salty flavor, creamy and soft yet grainy texture; similar to cream cheese; from Normandy

**Port-Salut** Made from cow's milk; mild, smoky flavor, buttery, semisoft texture; from Loire

**Reblochen** Made from sheep's milk; fresh flower taste, creamy oozing texture like Brie; from mountainous area in the east

**Roquefort** Made from sheep's milk; blue cheese, crumbly yet soft texture with holes and cracks; from Rouergue

**Tomme de Savoie** Made from cow's milk, complex flavor with several levels, semisoft texture; from mountainous area in the east

**Vacherin du Haut-Doubs** Made from cow's milk; woody flavor, heady aroma, creamy, runny semisoft texture; like the Swiss Vacherin Mont d'Or; from mountainous area in the east

## >> Review Questions

1. Who were Carême and Escoffier? What contributions did each make to the culinary profession?
2. What is the difference between classical and regional French cookery? Give examples of each.
3. How did the Greeks and Romans influence classical cookery? What were some later influences on the development of classical cuisine?
4. Name four regions, explain the type of dishes prepared in each region, and discuss why those dishes traditionally have been prepared there.
5. What is the cooking fat of choice in the south of France and the rest of France? Why are they different?
6. How did the Italian influence come to the French culinary scene? Give examples of some of the culinary traits the French learned from the Italians.

## >> Glossary

**beurre blanc** Butter sauce

**brigades** Teams of people working in the kitchen who prepare food items according to the type of cooking techniques involved in their preparation

**café au lait** Strong coffee mixed with warmed milk

**calvados** Apple brandy made in Normandy in the northwest of France

**cassoulet** A one-pot dish containing various meats, white beans, and herbs; originated in Languedoc

**charcuterie** Refers to all sorts of sausages and cured meats

**charlotte russe** A molded dessert consisting of a core of Bavarian cream folded with whipped cream and surrounded by ladyfinger biscuits

**chartreuse** A molded dish with a decorative outside of colorful vegetables and an inside containing vegetables, game, and/or poultry

**choucroute** A dish served in Alsace containing sauerkraut cooked with sausages, meats, and served accompanied by boiled potatoes

**confit** A method of slow cooking goose or duck in fat

**crêpes** Thin, delicate pancakes, served rolled around a savory or sweet filling; originated in Brittany

**foie gras** The highly prized goose liver, produced for this delicacy by force-feeding geese so they develop large livers

**garde manger** Preparation of cold foods and garnishes

**haricots** Thin, tender green beans

**rôtisseur** Person in kitchen responsible for foods that require roasting

**saucier** Person in kitchen responsible for preparation of sauces

**spaetzel** A homemade noodle/dumpling that is popular in Germany and areas in France near the German border

**tarte Tatin** An upside-down apple pie: apples, butter, and sugar are caramelized, then topped with pie dough and baked; the cooked tart is inverted on a plate after baking

## COQUILLES ST. JACQUES À LA PARISIENNE (CLASSIC)

### SCALLOPS AND MUSHROOMS IN WHITE WINE SAUCE

**Number of Servings:** 12                          **Cooking Method:** Poach
**Serving Size:** 5 oz. (142 g)
**Total Yield:** 4 lb. (1.8 kg)
**Food Balance:** Protein/acid balanced
**Wine Style:** Light- to medium-bodied Pinot Blanc, Pinot Grigio, Chardonnay, Viognier, or Pinot Noir, and light reds
**Example:** Beringer Napa Valley Chardonnay or Pinot Noir

<table>
<tr><th rowspan="2">INGREDIENTS</th><th colspan="2">WEIGHT</th><th colspan="2">VOLUME</th></tr>
<tr><th>U.S.</th><th>METRIC</th><th>U.S.</th><th>METRIC</th></tr>
<tr><td>dry white wine</td><td></td><td>454 g</td><td>2 cups</td><td>480 mL</td></tr>
<tr><td>salt</td><td>1/4 oz.</td><td>8 g</td><td>1 teaspoon</td><td>5 mL</td></tr>
<tr><td>white pepper</td><td></td><td></td><td>1/4 teaspoon</td><td>2 mL</td></tr>
<tr><td>bay leaf</td><td></td><td></td><td>2 each</td><td></td></tr>
<tr><td>shallots, minced</td><td>1 1/2 oz.</td><td>43 g</td><td>1/4 cup</td><td>60 mL</td></tr>
<tr><td>water</td><td></td><td>114 to 227 g</td><td>1/2 to 1 cup</td><td>120 to 240 mL</td></tr>
<tr><td>scallops, bay or sea, washed</td><td>2 lb.</td><td>908 g</td><td></td><td></td></tr>
<tr><td>fresh mushrooms, sliced</td><td>1 lb.</td><td>454 g</td><td></td><td></td></tr>
<tr><td colspan="5">Sauce:</td></tr>
<tr><td>butter</td><td>3 oz.</td><td>86 g</td><td>1/4 cup + 2 tablespoons</td><td>90 mL</td></tr>
<tr><td>flour</td><td>2 1/2 oz.</td><td>71 g</td><td>1/2 cup</td><td>120 mL</td></tr>
<tr><td>milk, heated</td><td></td><td>340 g</td><td>1 1/2 cups</td><td>360 mL</td></tr>
<tr><td>egg yolks</td><td>2 3/4 oz.</td><td>78 g</td><td>4 each</td><td></td></tr>
<tr><td>heavy cream</td><td></td><td>227 g</td><td>1 cup</td><td>240 mL</td></tr>
<tr><td>salt</td><td>to taste</td><td></td><td></td><td></td></tr>
<tr><td>white pepper</td><td>to taste</td><td></td><td></td><td></td></tr>
<tr><td>lemon juice</td><td></td><td></td><td>1/4 teaspoon</td><td>2 mL or to taste</td></tr>
<tr><td colspan="5">Assembly:</td></tr>
<tr><td>Swiss cheese, grated</td><td>4 oz.</td><td>114 g</td><td>3/4 cup</td><td>180 mL</td></tr>
<tr><td>fresh parsley, minced</td><td></td><td></td><td></td><td></td></tr>
</table>

### TWIST ON THE CLASSIC

Substitute shrimp or chunks of boneless chicken breast for the scallops.

© fotogal

1. Place wine, salt, white pepper, bay leaf, shallots, and water in pan over medium heat. Bring to boil, reduce heat, simmer for 5 minutes.
2. Add scallops and mushrooms to pan, cover, simmer gently for another 5 minutes. Remove scallops and mushrooms with slotted spoon, refrigerate until ready to use.
3. Increase heat, bring to boil, and reduce cooking liquid to 2 cups (480 mL).

### SAUCE:

1. Over medium heat, melt butter, add flour, whisk until white to blonde roux, about 2 minutes.
2. Remove from heat, slowly whisk in hot reduced cooking liquid *(from above)*, then milk.
3. Return to medium heat, boil 1 minute.
4. Blend egg yolks and heavy cream together in medium bowl, add hot liquid very slowly while whisking to temper eggs.
5. Return mixture to pan, bring to simmer over low to medium-low heat, stirring constantly. Simmer for 1 minute.
6. Season to taste with salt, white pepper, and lemon juice. Strain.

### ASSEMBLY:

1. Heat broiler. Butter scallop shells or ovenproof serving dishes.
2. Blend two-thirds of sauce with reserved scallops and mushrooms. Correct seasonings.
3. Place scallop mixture into prepared dishes, cover with remaining sauce.
4. Sprinkle with Swiss cheese, broil about 8 or 10 inches (20 or 25 cm) from broiler until golden brown.
5. Place hot dish on serving plate. Serve immediately, sprinkled with minced parsley, if desired.

Photographer: Stuart West

© fotogal

# PÂTÉ (CLASSIC AND REGIONAL)

**Note:** From classic recipes to regional variations, there are countless pâté recipes. Traditionally, French bread and cornichons (small, tart, crisp pickles) accompany pâté.

**Note:** Allow time to chill the pâté overnight or 24 hours.

**Number of Servings:** 10        **Cooking Method:** Bake
**Serving Size:** 3 oz. (86 g), or 1 slice about 1/2-inch (1.3-cm) thick
**Total Yield:** 2 lb., 10 1/4 oz. (1.2 kg) raw mixture before cooking
           2 lb., 6 1/2 oz. (1.1 kg) cooked mixture before trimming
           2 lb., 3/4 oz. (930 g) trimmed, cooked mixture
**Food Balance:** Protein
**Wine Style:** Low-oaked whites and fruity, soft reds
**Example:** Etude Pinot Gris or Pinot Noir

*Ground meat in food processor*
Pearson Education/PH College

*Lining terrine pan with fatback*
Pearson Education/PH College

*Filling terrine pan*
Pearson Education/PH College

| | WEIGHT | | VOLUME | |
|---|---|---|---|---|
| **INGREDIENTS** | **U.S.** | **METRIC** | **U.S.** | **METRIC** |
| bay leaf | | | 2 each | |
| ground allspice | | | 3/4 teaspoon | 4 mL |
| dried thyme | | | 3/4 teaspoon | 4 mL |
| dried basil | | | 3/4 teaspoon | 4 mL |
| ground ginger | | | 3/4 teaspoon | 4 mL |
| pepper | | | 1/2 teaspoon | 3 mL |
| salt | | | 1 1/2 teaspoons | 8 mL |
| pork fat, not cured or smoked | 1 lb. | 454 g | | |
| butter | 1/2 oz. | 15 g | 1 tablespoon | 15 mL |
| onion or shallot, minced | 1 1/4 oz. | 36 g | 3 tablespoons | 45 mL |
| ground veal | 1 lb. | 454 g | | |
| ground pork | 12 oz. | 341 g | | |
| cognac | | 57 g | 1/4 cup | 60 mL |
| liver-calf, beef, pork, or chicken, cleaned of membrane and rinsed | 8 oz. | 227 g | | |
| egg | 1 3/4 oz. | 50 g | 1 each | |

**Accompaniments:**

cornichons
French bread
mustard, *optional*

① Grind bay leaf, allspice, thyme, basil, ginger, pepper, and salt in spice grinder or clean coffee grinder until fine powder. Set aside until needed.

② Using a slicer, if available, cut half of pork fat into very thin sheets. Note: It is easier to cut pork fat that is half frozen.

③ Line sides and bottom of 1 1/2 quart (1.4 L) terrine pan with the cut sheets of pork fat, leaving enough fat hanging over the long sides of pan to fold over top of filled pan. Set aside until needed.

④ Place oven rack in middle of oven. Preheat oven to 350 degrees (180°C). Choose pan to hold water that comes halfway up sides of terrine pan, for a *bain-marie*. Set aside until needed. Heat pot of water until boiling while preparing the pâté mixture.

⑤ Heat butter in skillet over medium heat. Add onions, sauté until softened. Remove from heat.

⑥ In food processor fitted with knife blade, pulse veal, pork, and 8 oz. (227 g) pork fat until smooth. Add onions and butter from skillet, process until smooth.

⑦ Add cognac to skillet and boil until reduced by half. Remove from heat.

⑧ Meanwhile, add liver to food processor, pulse until smooth. Transfer meat mixture to bowl of mixer fitted with flat paddle beater.

⑨ Add cognac and egg to mixture in mixer bowl, mix until light and fluffy, several minutes.

⑩ Pour mixture into prepared terrine pan. Smooth top of meat mixture, rap pan on counter to eliminate air pockets and settle mixture. Fold fat over top of meat. Cover pan with heavy-duty aluminum foil or several layers of regular aluminum foil.

⑪ Place terrine pan in large reserved pan, add boiling water until halfway up sides of pan. Bake for 1 1/2 to 2 hours, until juices are clear and pâté reaches proper internal temperature. Remove from oven.

⑫ Set terrine on cooling rack that is placed on sheet pan to catch dripping fat. Place board and weight on top of pâté, allow to cool. Refrigerate 24 hours or at least overnight.

⑬ Remove from refrigerator, unmold, and remove excess fat that solidified in pan. If desired, remove some fat surrounding the pâté. Slice and serve with cornichons, French bread, and mustard, if desired.

*Slicing pâté*
Pearson Education/PH College

### TWIST ON THE CLASSIC

Many prepare terrines with poultry, fish and seafood, or vegetables instead of meat.

If desired, add other items to the pâté for visual and taste interest. Strips of ham, pieces of liver, pistachios, hazelnuts, diced truffles, and a limitless list of other items can be layered in the mixture or added randomly.

© Monkey Business

© pass

# CRÊPE AUX CHAMPIGIONS, ÉPINARDS, ET GRUYÈRE (SOUTHEAST, AREAS NEAR JURA MOUNTAINS AND ALPS)

## PANCAKES FILLED WITH MUSHROOMS, SPINACH, AND GRUYÈRE

**Number of Servings:** 10  
**Cooking Method:** Sauté  
**Serving Size:** 2 crêpes, 6 oz. (171 g)  
**Total Yield:** 20 filled crêpes, 4 lb., 1 1/4 oz. (1.9 kg)  
           22 crêpes, 1 lb., 10 3/4 oz. (759 g), 3 cups (720 mL) batter  
           1 lb., 15 oz. (880 g) filling  
**Wine Style:** Full-bodied red wine with a medium-plus alcohol content. Possible grape varietals are Gamay, Chardonnay.  
**Example:** 2011 Domaine Bernard Baudry Chinon Le Clos Guillot (France/Loire Valley)

| INGREDIENTS | WEIGHT U.S. | WEIGHT METRIC | VOLUME U.S. | VOLUME METRIC |
|---|---|---|---|---|
| **Crêpes:** | | | | |
| flour, all purpose | 7 3/4 oz. | 220 g | 1 1/2 cups | 360 mL |
| salt | 1/4 teaspoon | | | 1 mL |
| eggs | 5 oz. | 142 g | 3 each | |
| milk, whole | | 284 g | 1 1/4 cups | 300 mL |
| water | | 57 g + as needed | 1/4 cup + as needed | 60 mL + as needed |
| butter, unsalted, melted, cooled | 1 1/2 oz. | 43 g | 3 tablespoons | 45 mL |
| butter or oil | for frying | | | |
| **Filling:** | | | | |
| spinach, stems removed | 1 lb., 8 oz. | 680 g | | |
| butter | 1 oz. | 28 g | 2 tablespoons | 30 mL |
| mushrooms, small button or variety of choice, sliced 1/8 inch thick | 1 lb., 8 oz. | 680 g | | |
| salt | | | 1 1/2 teaspoons | 8 mL |
| pepper | | | 3/4 teaspoon | 4 mL |
| Gruyère cheese or Swiss, grated | 4 1/2 oz. | 128 g | 1 1/2 cups | 360 mL |
| **Topping:** | | | | |
| heavy cream, hot | | 425 g | scant 2 cups | 480 mL |
| nutmeg | sprinkling | | | |
| salt | sprinkling | | | |
| white pepper | sprinkling | | | |
| Gruyère cheese or Swiss, grated | 4 1/2 oz. | 128 g | 1 1/2 cups | 360 mL |
| **Garnish:** | | | | |
| parsley, minced | | | | |

*Coating pan with batter.*

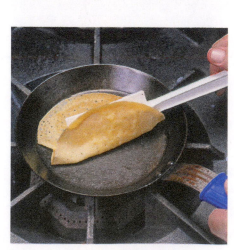

*Turning the lightly browned crepe.*

## CRÊPES:

1. Place flour, salt, eggs, milk, and water in food processor fitted with knife blade. Pulse to mix until incorporated.
2. With processor running, add butter through feed tube. Process just until incorporated.
3. Chill batter for at least 1 hour.

## FILLING:

1. Wash spinach. Place in colander to drain.

2. Melt butter in skillet over high heat. Add mushrooms and sauté until softened and liquid is evaporated, a few minutes. Transfer to bowl, set aside until needed.

3. Heat same skillet over high heat. Add spinach (with some water clinging to leaves) and cook until done, stirring frequently, about 2 or 3 minutes. Transfer to colander. When cool enough to handle, squeeze to remove excess liquid. Add to mushrooms in bowl.

4. Add salt and pepper. Mix thoroughly. Add cheese when completely cool. Correct seasonings.

## TOPPING AND FINISH:

1. Melt very thin coating of butter in a 7- or 8-inch (18- or 20-cm) crêpe pan or a skillet over medium heat. When hot enough to sizzle a drop of water, add 1 oz. (28 g) (2 tablespoons [30 mL]) crêpe batter. If batter is too thick, thin with a teaspoon or so of water until correct consistency. While pouring in batter, quickly rotate pan to spread batter very thinly. Note: This amount of batter yields a 6- to 7-inch (15- to 18-cm) crêpe. It might not totally cover pan, but swirling batter as pouring results in a round pancake.

2. Sauté about a minute, until just starting to get some brown dots. Flip crêpe, cook other side another minute. Remove to plate. Repeat with remaining batter, stacking crêpes on top of each other. If not using immediately, cover and refrigerate.

3. Pan spray half sheet pan. Place oven rack in middle of oven. Preheat oven to 400 degrees (205°C).

4. To fill crêpes, lay pancake on counter. Place 1 1/2 oz. (43 g) filling across crêpe about 1 inch (2.5 cm) from bottom. Roll pancake around filling. Transfer filled crêpe to prepared pan. Repeat with remaining pancakes, placing filled crêpes closely next to each other.

5. Mix cream, nutmeg, salt, and white pepper together. Pour over crêpes. Sprinkle cheese over crêpes and topping.

6. Bake about 20 minutes, until hot, bubbly, and cheese is golden. Serve immediately, garnished with minced parsley.

Two of these crêpes is a hearty appetizer. One crêpe is perfect for a "small plate." Serve three for a luncheon entrée. Alternately, make the crêpes in a 12-inch (30-cm) pan to serve one larger crêpe for an appetizer.

## GRATINÉE LYONNAISE (LYONNAIS)

### ONION SOUP

**Note:** To alter the flavor of the soup, try using chicken or vegetable stock instead of beef stock. Warm the bowls for this soup before serving.

**Number of Servings:** 13
**Serving Size:** 12 oz. (341 g)
**Total Yield:** 10 lb., 2 oz. (4.6 kg)
**Food Balance:** Sweet/protein
**Wine Style:** Soft and fruity Johannisberg Riesling; fruity, mild Chardonnay or Viognier; blush; and rich mild reds, such as Syrah
**Example:** Meridian Santa Barbara Chardonnay or Syrah

**Cooking Method:** Braise

Adding onions to pan for sweating
David Murray and Jules Selmes © Dorling Kindersley

| | WEIGHT | | VOLUME | |
|---|---|---|---|---|
| INGREDIENTS | U.S. | METRIC | U.S. | METRIC |
| **Croûtons:** | | | | |
| olive oil | | 57 g | 1/4 cup | 60 mL |
| garlic, peeled and cut in half | 1/2 oz. | 15 g | 4 cloves | |
| French bread, 1-inch (2.5-cm) thick slices | | | 13 each | |

*Brushing bread with butter to make* croûtons

David Murray and Jules Selmes © Dorling Kindersley

**Soup:**

| | | | | |
|---|---|---|---|---|
| butter | 4 oz. | 114 g | 8 tablespoons (1 stick) | 120 mL |
| oil | | 28 g | 2 tablespoons | 30 mL |
| onions, thinly sliced | 4 lb. | 1.8 kg | | |
| flour | 1 1/2 oz. | 43 g | 1/4 cup + 2 tablespoons | 90 mL |
| rich beef stock, hot | | | 1 gallon (4 quarts) | 3.8 L |
| pepper | | | 1/2 teaspoon | 3 mL |
| port | | 156 g | 2/3 cup | 160 mL |
| salt | to taste | | | |

**Topping:**

| | | |
|---|---|---|
| Gruyère cheese, grated or sliced | 1 lb., 10 oz. | 738 g |

### CROÛTONS:

1. Place oil and garlic in small bowl, set aside. Preheat oven to 325 degrees (160°C).
2. Place bread slices on sheet pan, bake for 15 minutes, turn over, bake another 5 or 10 minutes, until dry. Remove from oven.
3. Brush both sides of bread with oil, rub with garlic.

### SOUP:

1. Heat butter and oil in large saucepan, add onions and cook slowly over medium-low heat about 30 minutes, until carmelized to rich golden color. Stir occasionally.
2. Sprinkle with flour, stir well.
3. Slowly add beef stock, whisking constantly. Add pepper, simmer for 40 minutes.
4. Add port and salt, if needed. Correct seasonings.

### ASSEMBLY:

1. Pour soup into heated bowls, float *croûton* on top of each, sprinkle generously with cheese (about 1 1/2 to 2 oz. [43 to 57 g] per bowl).
2. Place bowl under broiler until cheese is melted and golden brown. Serve immediately.

*Assembling the soup — sprinkling cheese over* croûtons

David Murray and Jules Selmes © Dorling Kindersley

David Murray and Jules Selmes © Dorling Kindersley

# POTAGE CRÉCY

## CARROT CREAM SOUP

**Note:** This soup was named Potage (soup) Crécy after the region Crécy, which is known for growing the best, most flavorful carrots. Warm the bowls for this soup before serving.

**Number of Servings:** 14
**Serving Size:** 7 oz. (199 g)
**Total Yield:** 6 lb., 2 oz. (2.8 kg)
**Food Balance:** Sweet/protein
**Wine Style:** Soft and fruity Riesling, Gewürztraminer, Pinot Blanc, or blush
**Example:** Rosemount Traminer Riesling or Chardonnay

**Cooking Method:** Sauté, boil

| INGREDIENTS | WEIGHT | | VOLUME | |
| --- | --- | --- | --- | --- |
| | U.S. | METRIC | U.S. | METRIC |
| butter | 2 1/2 oz. | 71 g | 5 tablespoons | 74 mL |
| onion, diced | 12 oz. | 340 g | 2 large | |
| carrots, peeled and diced | 2 lb. | 908 g | | |
| flour | 1 1/2 oz. | 43 g | 1/4 cup | 60 mL |
| chicken or vegetable stock, hot | | | 2 quarts (8 cups) | 1.9 L |
| sugar | | | 2 teaspoons | 10 mL |
| pepper | | | 1/2 teaspoon | 3 mL |
| nutmeg | | | few grindings, to taste | |
| heavy cream | | 454 g | 2 cups | 480 mL |

**Garnish:**

fresh parsley, minced

1. Heat butter in pan over medium-low heat, add onions, sauté a couple of minutes.
2. Add carrots, sauté to sweat them, about 10 minutes.
3. Sprinkle flour over carrots, stirring constantly, continue to cook a few minutes.
4. Slowly whisk stock into carrots. Add sugar, pepper, and nutmeg, simmer for 30 minutes, or until vegetables are soft.
5. Purée mixture in food processor or strain through food mill or China cap. Refrigerate for later use or return to pan.
6. Before serving, reheat soup, add heavy cream, simmer gently to heat thoroughly. Do not boil. Correct seasonings.
7. Serve in warmed bowls, garnished with parsley.

© Natalia Mylova

# HARICOT BLANC ET SOUPE OLIVE (SOUTHWEST)
## WHITE BEAN AND OLIVE SOUP

© Flayols

**Note:** If possible, begin this soup the day before service.

**Number of Servings:** 12  
**Serving Size:** 8 oz. (227 g)  
**Total Yield:** 6 lb., 2 1/4 oz. (2.8 kg)  
**Cooking Method:** Boil

**Wine Style:** Fuller-bodied white wine with a medium-plus alcohol content. Possible grape varietals are Gruner Veltliner, Riesling, Chardonnay.  
**Example:** Gruner Veltliner "Wachtberg" 2012, Stadt Krems (Kremstal/Austria)

| INGREDIENTS | WEIGHT U.S. | WEIGHT METRIC | VOLUME U.S. | VOLUME METRIC |
|---|---|---|---|---|
| white beans, dried, Tarbais, cannellini, baby limas, Great Northern, or variety of choice | 1 lb. | 454 g | | |
| water | to cover | | | |
| leeks, cleaned, white and 1 inch of green, thinly sliced | 7 oz. | 199 g | 2 each | |
| garlic, peeled, smashed | 1/2 oz. | 15 g | 4 cloves | |
| potatoes, red, peeled, medium dice | 10 oz. | 284 g | 2 medium | |
| rosemary sprig | 1/4 oz. | 8 g | 1 each | |
| pepper | | | 1 teaspoon | 5 mL |
| olives, pitted, Picholine or variety of choice, cut into quarters | 5 oz. | 142 g | 1 cup | 240 mL |
| chicken base or chicken stock | as needed | | | |
| salt | as needed | | | |

**Garnish:**

rosemary sprig  
croûton from French bread rubbed with cut garlic clove

1 Place beans in pot and cover with water. Soak in refrigerator overnight. If time is short, add beans to pot of rapidly boiling water. Turn off flame and allow beans to sit at least 1 hour before cooking.

2 Add leeks, potatoes, garlic, rosemary, and pepper. Make sure beans are covered with water (and flavor with chicken base later) or chicken stock.

3 Bring to boil, reduce heat and boil gently for 1 to 1 1/2 hours or until beans are almost soft. Remove rosemary sprig.

4 Add olives, continue cooking until beans are soft. Add chicken base and/or salt as needed. Correct seasonings.

5 Serve, garnished with a sprig of rosemary and a garlic-infused croûton.

## SALADE DE BETTERAVES AUX NOIX (NORTH)
### BEET SALAD WITH WALNUTS

**Note:** Chill plates before serving the salad.

**Number of Servings:** 8
**Serving Size:** 3 oz. (86 g)
**Total Yield:** 1 lb., 8 oz. (680 g)

| | WEIGHT | | VOLUME | |
|---|---|---|---|---|
| INGREDIENTS | U.S. | METRIC | U.S. | METRIC |
| **Vinaigrette:** | | | | |
| red wine vinegar | | 15 g | 1 tablespoon | 15 mL |
| Dijon mustard | 1/4 oz. | 8 g | 1 teaspoon | 5 mL |
| salt | to taste | | | |
| pepper | to taste | | | |
| oil | | 43 g | 3 tablespoons | 45 mL |
| **Salad:** | | | | |
| Belgian endive, washed and cut into 3/4-inch slices | 8 oz. | 227 g | 2 each | |
| mesclun mix, lettuce, or other greens | 4 oz. | 114 g | | |
| beets, cooked or canned, diced | 15 oz. | 426 g | 2 fresh or 1 can | |
| salt | to taste | | | |
| pepper | to taste | | | |
| walnuts, toasted and coarsely chopped | 2 1/4 oz. | 64 g | 1/2 cup | 120 mL |

1. Mix vinaigrette ingredients together in bowl, set aside until needed. Refrigerate for longer storage.
2. Place endive and lettuce in bowl.
3. Add beets to lettuce, toss, adding enough vinaigrette to coat each salad ingredient.
4. Correct seasonings; sprinkle with walnuts. Serve.

### TWIST ON THE CLASSIC

For a visual variation, prepare this salad with golden beets or a mixture of red and golden beets.

*Beet and walnut mixture ready for salad greens*
© Comugnero Silvana

# SALADE DE CONCOMBRES ET TOMATES (SOUTH)
## CUCUMBER AND TOMATO SALAD

**Note:** This amount of cucumber and tomato requires about 4 oz. (114 g) of vinaigrette. If increasing this recipe, realize it makes an extra 2 oz. (57 g) of vinaigrette.

**Number of Servings:** 9
**Serving Size:** 5 oz. (142 g)
**Total Yield:** 2 lb., 15 3/4 oz. (1.4 kg)
6 1/4 oz. (177 g) or 7/8 cup (210 mL) vinaigrette

© Photographee.eu

| INGREDIENTS | WEIGHT U.S. | WEIGHT METRIC | VOLUME U.S. | VOLUME METRIC |
|---|---|---|---|---|
| **Vinaigrette:** | | | | |
| red wine vinegar | | 71 g | 1/4 cup + 1 tablespoon | 75 mL |
| Dijon mustard | 1/4 oz. | 8 g | 1 teaspoon | 5 mL |
| salt | | | 1/2 teaspoon | 3 mL |
| pepper | | | 1/8 teaspoon | 1 mL |
| dried tarragon | | | 1 teaspoon | 5 mL |
| olive oil | | 114 g | 1/2 cup | 120 mL |
| cucumber, peeled and thinly sliced | 2 lb., 5 1/4 oz. | 1.1 kg | 2 large | |
| tomatoes, sliced 1/4-inch (1/2-cm) thick | 1 lb., 3 1/4 oz. | 546 g | 2 medium to large | |
| Roquefort cheese, crumbled | 5 oz. | 142 g | | |
| fresh parsley, minced | 1/2 oz. | 15 g | 3 tablespoons | 45 mL |

## TWIST ON THE CLASSIC

If desired, try this salad with all cucumber or tomato. Also, the type of cheese can be changed to goat cheese, brie, or a variety of your choice.

### VINAIGRETTE:

1. Place vinegar, mustard, salt, pepper, and tarragon into food processor fitted with knife blade.
2. With processor running, slowly add olive oil through feed tube. Process until dressing emulsifies (thickens).
3. Refrigerate until needed.

### SALAD:

1. Place cucumbers, tomatoes, and Roquefort cheese in bowl.
2. Add vinaigrette (about 4 to 5 oz. [114 to 142 mL]) as needed to coat ingredients. Toss gently. Correct seasonings.
3. Add most of parsley, mix gently, sprinkle remaining parsley on top. Serve.

# BOEUF BOURGUIGNON (BURGUNDY AND LYON)

## BEEF BURGUNDY STEW

**Note:** Allow 1 or 2 days to marinate meat.

**Number of Servings:** 13    **Cooking Method:** Braise
**Serving Size:** 10 oz. (284 g)
**Total Yield:** 8 lb., 2 oz. (3.7 kg)
**Food Balance:** Acid/protein balanced
**Wine Style:** Wide variety—very balanced dish: Enjoy with the wine of your choice
**Example:** Beringer Chenin Blanc, Chardonnay, Pinot Noir, or Private Reserve Cabernet Sauvignon

© Joe Gough

| INGREDIENTS | WEIGHT | | VOLUME | |
| | U.S | METRIC | U.S | METRIC |
| --- | --- | --- | --- | --- |
| **Marinade:** | | | | |
| black peppercorns | | | 12 each | |
| whole cloves | | | 4 each | |
| bay leaves | | | 2 each | |
| dried thyme | | | 1 teaspoon | 5 mL |
| red wine | | | 1 quart + 2 cups (6 cups) | 1.44 L |
| onion, sliced | 10 oz. | 284 g | 2 medium to large | |
| carrot, sliced | 5 oz. | 142 g | 2 each | |
| garlic, minced | 1/4 oz. | 8 g | 2 cloves | |
| beef rump, trimmed and cut into 2-inch cubes | 4 to 5 lb. | 1.8 to 2.3 kg | | |
| bacon, chopped | 12 oz. | 340 g | | |
| pearl or small boiling onions, peeled | 1 lb., 6 oz. | 624 g | 32 each | |
| mushrooms, sliced | 1 lb. | 454 g | 28 medium | |
| red wine | | 227 g | 1 cup | 240 mL |
| oil | | 43 g | 3 tablespoons | 45 mL |
| flour | 2 oz. | 57 g | 1/4 cup + 2 tablespoons | 90 mL |
| beef stock, hot | | 680 g | 3 cups | 720 mL |
| salt | | | 1/4 teaspoon | 2 mL |
| pepper | | | 1/2 teaspoon | 3 mL |
| **Garnish:** | | | | |
| fresh parsley, minced | | | | |

© Joe Gough

1. Place peppercorns, cloves, bay leaves, and thyme in cheesecloth bag. Mix 1 quart + 2 cups (1.44 L) red wine, onion, carrot, and garlic in nonreactive bowl. Add cheesecloth bag containing spices.
2. Add meat to marinade, cover, and marinate in refrigerator for 1 to 2 days.
3. Drain meat and vegetables well, reserving marinade liquid. Put meat and vegetables in two separate bowls. Discard cheesecloth bag.
4. Preheat oven to 300 degrees (150°C).
5. Sauté bacon in skillet over medium to medium-high heat until well done, remove from skillet.
6. Sauté pearl onions in same skillet until browned, remove.
7. Sauté mushrooms in same skillet until tender, remove. Refrigerate bacon, onions, and mushrooms until needed.
8. Add well-drained meat pieces to skillet in one layer, sauté until seared on all sides, remove from skillet and place in ovenproof pan.

⑨ Pour 1 cup (240 mL) red wine into skillet, deglaze by stirring and scraping any bits from bottom of pan into wine, pour over meat.

⑩ Add oil to heavy-bottomed pot, heat over medium heat.

⑪ Sauté marinated vegetables slowly until soft, add flour, cook, stirring constantly, until mixture is rich brown color.

⑫ Whisk in hot stock, then marinade liquid and salt and pepper to taste.

⑬ Add stock mixture to meat pieces, cover pan, place in oven, and braise, stirring occasionally, for about 3 to 4 hours, until tender.

⑭ Add reserved bacon, onions, and mushrooms for last 15 to 20 minutes of cooking. Correct seasonings.

⑮ Serve with wide noodles or boiled potatoes. Garnish with minced parsley, if desired.

---

## GIGOT À LA BRETONNE (BRITTANY)

### LEG OF LAMB WITH HARICOT (WHITE) BEANS

**Note:** Allow time to soak beans overnight. To expedite the process, bring a pot of water to boil, add beans, and remove beans from heat. Allow to soak for 1 or 2 hours.

**Number of Servings:** 12          **Cooking Method:** Bake

**Serving Size:** 4 oz. (114 g) meat; 4 oz. (114 g) beans; 1 oz. (28 g) sauce

**Total Yield:** 3 lb., 3 oz. (1.5 kg) meat
           3 lb., 5 oz. (1.5 kg) beans
           12 oz. (340 g) sauce

**Food Balance:** Protein/acid balanced

**Wine Style:** Wide variety—very balanced dish: Enjoy with the wine of your choice

**Example:** Château Souverain Sauvignon Blanc, Chardonnay, Zinfandel, or Cabernet Sauvignon

Jules Selmes/David Murray/Dorling Kindersley, Ltd.

| INGREDIENTS | WEIGHT U.S. | WEIGHT METRIC | VOLUME U.S. | VOLUME METRIC |
|---|---|---|---|---|
| **Beans:** | | | | |
| dried white beans | 1 lb. | 454 g | | |
| whole onion, peeled and stuck with 4 cloves | 4 oz. | 114 g | 1 small | |
| carrot, diced | 2 oz. | 57 g | 1 each | |
| onions, diced | 7 oz. | 199 g | 2 small | |
| garlic, minced | | | 1 clove | |
| bay leaf | | | 1/2 each | |
| dried thyme | | | 1/2 teaspoon | 3 mL |
| pepper | | | 1/4 teaspoon | 2 mL |
| salt | 1/4 oz. | 8 g | 1 teaspoon | 5 mL |
| **Lamb:** | | | | |
| leg of lamb, boned and trimmed of all but thin layer of fat | 4 lb., 6 oz. | 2 kg | | |
| garlic, slivered | 1/2 oz. | 15 g | 4 cloves | |
| carrots, peeled and cut into thick chunks | 8 oz. | 227 g | 4 each | |
| onions, 3/8-inch slices | 14 oz. | 397 g | 4 each | |
| dried rosemary | 1/2 oz. | 15 g | 1 tablespoon + 1 teaspoon | 20 mL |
| pepper | to taste | | | |
| dried thyme | to taste | | | |

**Sauce:**

| | | | | |
|---|---|---|---|---|
| white wine | | 227 g | 1 cup | 240 L |
| stock, lamb or beef | | 454 g | 2 cups | 480 L |

**Garnish:**

| | | | | |
|---|---|---|---|---|
| fresh parsley, minced | 1/4 oz. | 8 g | 2 tablespoons | 30 mL |
| fresh rosemary sprigs | | | | |

## BEANS:

1. Wash beans well, cover with water, refrigerate and soak overnight.
2. Drain beans. Add onion stuck with cloves, carrot, diced onions, garlic, bay leaf, thyme, and pepper. Cover with fresh water, cook until beans are tender, about 1 hour.
3. Add salt, discard onion stuck with cloves. Correct seasonings. Keep beans warm until service, or cool and refrigerate until needed.

## LAMB:

1. Position oven rack in center of oven. Preheat oven to 450 degrees (230°C). Rinse meat under cold water.
2. With point of knife, make small incisions in meat and push garlic slivers into them.
3. Place onions and carrots in roasting pan, place lamb on top of vegetables. Sprinkle with rosemary, pepper, and thyme.
4. Place pan in oven, cook for 10 minutes. Reduce heat to 400 degrees (205°C), cook for about 1 hour more, basting occasionally, until meat thermometer reads proper internal temperature.
5. Remove from oven, move lamb to plate or board, let rest for 10 minutes before carving.
6. Meanwhile, remove excess fat from roasting pan. Pour white wine and stock in pan, heat on stovetop, scraping bits from bottom of pan to deglaze. Simmer 5 to 10 minutes, correct seasonings.
7. Strain sauce. Keep hot until service or refrigerate until needed.

## ASSEMBLY:

1. Portion beans on warm plate either in the center or on the side. Place sliced lamb on beans or beside. Nap with sauce.
2. Sprinkle beans with parsley, garnish lamb with rosemary sprig, if desired.

---

## CÔTES DE PORC NORMANDE (NORMANDY)

### PORK CHOPS WITH APPLES AND CREAM

**Note:** Instead of placing the deglazed pan with pork chops in the oven, you can simmer them on top of the stove until done.

**Number of Servings:** 8      **Cooking Method:** Sauté, bake
**Serving Size:** 9 oz. (256 g), or 2 pork chops, apple, and sauce
**Total Yield:** 4 lb., 9 oz. (2.1 kg)
**Food Balance:** Protein/sweet
**Wine Style:** Soft and fruity Riesling, Viognier, mild Chardonnay, blush, Amarone, mild reds, Shiraz, or Merlot
**Example:** Beringer Founders' Estate Chardonnay, Shiraz, or Merlot

© Joe Gough

| INGREDIENTS | WEIGHT | | VOLUME | |
|---|---|---|---|---|
| | U.S. | METRIC | U.S. | METRIC |
| butter | 2 oz. | 57 g | 1/4 cup | 60 mL |
| pork chops | about 4 lb. (4 oz. each) | about 1.8 kg (114 g each) | 16 each | |
| salt | to taste | | | |
| pepper | to taste | | | |
| bread crumbs | 2 oz. | 57 g | 1/2 cup | 120 mL |
| firm, tart apples, such as Granny Smith, peeled, cored, and sliced into 1/2-inch (1.3 cm) rings | 1 lb., 12 oz. | 794 g | 4 each | |
| heavy cream | | 454 g | 2 cups | 480 mL |

1. Melt butter in skillet, butter ovenproof pan. Preheat oven to 450 degrees (230°C).
2. Season pork chops with salt and pepper, sauté quickly over medium-high to high heat until lightly brown.
3. Remove chops, place in prepared pan, top with bread crumbs.
4. Add apple rings to skillet, sauté until beginning to soften and lightly brown. Remove apples from skillet, place apples on top of pork chops.
5. Add heavy cream to skillet, scrape bits at bottom of pan to deglaze while it comes to a boil.
6. Pour immediately over pork, place in oven, cook for 10 to 15 minutes. Be careful not to overcook.
7. Add a bit more cream to thin sauce if necessary, correct seasonings. Serve immediately.

## COQ AU VIN (BURGUNDY)

### CHICKEN IN RED WINE

**Note:** The total weight and serving size numbers look odd, but the number of servings is limited by the amount of chicken, not the amount of sauce.

**Number of Servings:** 8 each 1/4-chicken or 10 each 1/2-chicken breast
**Cooking Method:** Boil, braise
**Serving Size:** about 11 oz. (308 g) chicken and sauce
**Total Yield:** about 12 lb. (5.4 kg)
**Food Balance:** Acid/protein balanced
**Wine Style:** Wide variety—very balanced dish, enjoy this with the wine of your choice (try the unexpected)
**Example:** Château St. Jean Gewürztraminer, Chardonnay, Pinot Noir, or Merlot

| INGREDIENTS | WEIGHT | | VOLUME | |
|---|---|---|---|---|
| | U.S. | METRIC | U.S. | METRIC |
| lean slab bacon or salt pork, diced | 5 oz. | 142 g | | |
| butter | 2 oz. | 57 g or as needed | 4 tablespoons | 60 mL or as needed |
| chicken, whole, cut into quarters, or bone-in breasts, cut in half (10 each) | 6 to 8 lb. | 2.8 to 3.6 kg | 2 whole or 5 breasts | |
| button mushrooms, cut into halves or quarters if large | 1 lb. | 454 g | | |

| | | | | | |
|---|---|---|---|---|---|
| small white onions, peeled | 2 lb. | 908 g | | | |
| celery, minced | 7 oz. | 199 g | 4 stalks | | |
| garlic, smashed and minced | 1/2 oz. | 15 g | 4 cloves | | |
| flour | 2 1/2 oz. | 71 g | 1/4 cup | 60 mL | |
| chicken stock, hot | | 454 g | 2 cups | 480 mL | |
| cognac | | 57 g | 1/4 cup | 60 mL | |
| red Burgundy wine | | | 1 quart + 2 cups (6 cups) | 1.44 L | |
| bay leaves | | | 2 each | | |
| dried thyme | 1/4 oz. | 8 g | 1 1/2 teaspoons | 8 mL | |
| salt | 1/4 oz. | 8 g | 1 teaspoon | 5 mL | |
| pepper | | | 1/2 teaspoon | 3 mL | |

**Garnish:**

fresh parsley, minced

1. Simmer bacon or salt pork in water for 10 minutes, drain thoroughly, dry.

2. Melt 2 tablespoons (30 mL) of butter in large, heavy-bottomed pan over medium-high heat, sauté bacon or salt pork several minutes until golden (lower heat if butter is burning). Remove from pan.

3. Sauté chicken in same pan until brown on all sides, adding remaining butter when needed. Remove from pan.

4. Add mushrooms to pan, sauté several minutes, stirring often. Remove from pan and refrigerate until last 30 minutes of cooking.

5. Add onions and celery to pan, sauté, stirring often, for 3 minutes or until softened. Add garlic, sauté another couple of minutes.

6. Sprinkle flour over vegetables, stir constantly a couple of minutes, until flour begins to color. Slowly whisk in hot stock, then add cognac, wine, bay leaves, thyme, salt, and pepper.

7. Stirring constantly, bring to boil. Add chicken and bacon, reduce heat, cover, simmer 30 minutes.

8. Add mushrooms, cover, continue simmering another 30 minutes. Correct seasonings.

9. Skim excess fat from sauce, remove bay leaves, serve immediately accompanied by boiled, mashed, or preferred style of potatoes. Garnish with parsley.

© PhotoEd

# CANARD MONTMORENCY (CLASSIC)
## ROAST DUCK WITH CHERRY SAUCE

**Note:** For crisp duck, place duck in broiler while deglazing the pan. Broil until crisp and golden on all sides.

**Note:** Unlike a roux, arrowroot sauce reaches its maximum thickness when it comes to a boil. Continuing to boil a sauce with arrowroot will cause it to become thin.

**Number of Servings:** 4 or 8
**Serving Size:** 1/2 or 1/4 duck
**Food Balance:** Sweet/sour
**Wine Style:** Light- to medium-bodied Riesling, Gewürztraminer, blush, Grenache, Pinot Noir, mild Shiraz, or Zinfandel
**Example:** Meridian Gewürztraminer, Pinot Noir, Syrah, or Zinfandel

**Cooking Method:** Bake

© gryfot

© chamillew

|  | WEIGHT | | VOLUME | |
|---|---|---|---|---|
| INGREDIENTS | U.S. | METRIC | U.S. | METRIC |
| ducks, washed, giblets removed from neck cavity | 11 to 12 lb. | 5 kg to 5.4 kg | 2 each | |
| salt | to taste | | | |
| pepper | to taste | | | |
| small onion, sliced | 6 oz. | 171 g | 2 each | |
| carrot, peeled and sliced | 4 oz. | 114 g | 2 small to medium | |
| medium onion, sliced | 10 oz. | 284 g | 2 each | |
| **Cherries:** | | | | |
| canned cherries, red or black, pitted | 1 lb., 2 1/2 oz. | 526 g | two #2 cans, drained | |
| fresh lemon juice | | 28 g | 2 tablespoons | 30 mL |
| sugar | 2 oz. | 57 g | 1/4 cup | 60 mL |
| port | | 86 g | 1/4 cup + 2 tablespoons | 90 mL |
| **Sauce:** | | | | |
| arrowroot | 1 oz. | 28 g | 1/4 cup | 60 mL |
| port | | | 1/4 cup + 2 tablespoons | 90 mL |
| sugar | 3 oz. | 86 g | 1/4 cup + 2 tablespoons | 90 mL |
| red wine vinegar | | 114 g | 1/2 cup | 120 mL |
| strong duck stock | | | 1 quart (4 cups) | 960 mL |
| **Deglazing:** | | | | |
| port | | 86 g | 1 cup | 240 mL |
| butter, *optional* | 1 to 2 oz. | 28 to 57 g | 2 to 4 tablespoons | 30 to 60 mL |

---

**TWIST ON THE CLASSIC**

If desired, prepare this with a grilled, roasted, or sautéed boneless duck breast instead of whole duck. For service, slice the duck breast on a bias and fan on the plate. Place the cherry sauce over or under the duck.

1. Position oven rack in center of oven. Preheat oven to 425 degrees (220°C).
2. Season inside cavity of ducks with salt and pepper, place sliced small onion inside cavity of each duck.
3. Place ducks on rack in a roasting pan, breast side up. Place carrot and sliced medium onion in pan, bake for 20 minutes.
4. Reduce oven temperature to 350 degrees (180°C), drain fat from pan, turn duck over on breast.
5. Cook another 30 minutes, drain fat, and turn duck breast side up.
6. Continue baking, draining fat occasionally, until duck reaches proper internal temperature, about 2 to 2 1/2 hours total.

## CHERRIES:

1 Mix all ingredients in bowl.
1 Soak for at least 30 minutes.

## SAUCE:

1 While duck cooks, prepare sauce. Mix arrowroot with port in a small bowl, set aside until needed.
2 In saucepan, boil sugar and vinegar over moderately high heat for several minutes until mixture turns into brown syrup.
3 Remove from heat, add 1 cup (240 mL) of the stock. Be careful pouring, it might splatter. Return to heat, simmer 1 minute, stirring to dissolve caramel.
4 Add remaining stock to saucepan, mix in arrowroot mixture. Continue stirring, simmer about 3 to 4 minutes, just bringing to boil, until sauce is clear and lightly thickened.
5 Correct seasonings. Set aside until needed.

© vaspakulov

## DEGLAZING:

1 Remove cooked duck from roasting pan, cover to keep warm. Remove as much fat as possible from roasting pan.
2 Put roasting pan on stovetop over high heat, add port, stirring to scrape bits from bottom of pan. Boil rapidly, until reduced to couple of tablespoons.
3 Strain deglazing liquids and add to sauce. Do not boil.
4 Add cherries and its marinade to sauce, simmer for 3 to 4 minutes. Correct seasonings.
5 Remove from heat. If desired, add butter to sauce, swirl to melt.

## SERVE:

Cut duck into serving pieces and place on plates. Nap sauce over duck or place it on plates then top with duck.

---

## FILETS DE ROUGET AUX CREVETTES, ARTICHAUTS, ET TOMATES (CÔTE D'AZUR)

### RED SNAPPER FILLETS WITH SHRIMP, ARTICHOKES, AND TOMATOES

**Note:** The weight of the shrimp depends on the size of the shrimp. If possible, use very large shrimp.

**Note:** While this recipe calls for two shrimp on top of the fish, one jumbo or colossal shrimp could be used instead, if desired.

**Number of Servings:** 9  **Cooking Method:** Sauté
**Serving Size:** 7 oz. (199 g); about 4 oz. (114 g) snapper
        1 oz. (28 g) shrimp
        2 oz. (57 g) sauce)
**Total Yield:** 4 lb., 4 oz. (1.9 kg)
**Food Balance:** Acid/protein/salt balanced
**Wine Style:** Very wine friendly—Pick a winner!
**Example:** Beringer Napa Valley Sauvignon Blanc, Pinot Noir, or Merlot

© Alexandre Kuhl de Oliveira

| | WEIGHT | | VOLUME | |
| --- | --- | --- | --- | --- |
| **INGREDIENTS** | **U.S.** | **METRIC** | **U.S.** | **METRIC** |
| flour | 3 oz. | 86 g | 2/3 cup | 160 mL |
| salt | | | 1/2 teaspoon | 3 mL |
| pepper | | | 1/4 teaspoon | 2 mL |
| olive oil | | 114 g | 1/2 cup | 120 mL or as needed |
| red snapper fillets, washed | 2 lb., 5 oz. | 1.1 kg | | |

| large shrimp, peeled and deveined | 7 to 8 oz. | 199 g to 227 g | 18 each | |
| onion, minced | 1 1/2 oz. | 43 g | 1/4 cup | 60 mL |
| tomato, canned, or fresh, peeled, seeded, and diced | 1 lb., 1 oz. | 482 g | 2 cups | 480 mL |
| red wine vinegar | | 28 g | 2 tablespoons | 30 mL |
| canned artichoke hearts, quartered, drained | 1 lb., 1 1/2 oz. | 497 g | 2 each 14 oz. (397 g) cans or 3 1/2 cups | 840 L |
| olives, variety of choice, pitted and chopped | 2 oz. | 57 g | 1/4 cup | 60 mL |
| fresh parsley, minced | 1/2 oz. | 15 g | 2 tablespoons | 30 mL |
| salt | to taste | | | |
| pepper | to taste | | | |

**Garnish:**

| fresh parsley, minced | | | 2 teaspoons | 10 mL |

1. Mix flour with salt and pepper on plate. Set aside until needed.
2. Heat 2 tablespoons (30 mL) of oil in large skillet over high heat; it should just coat bottom of skillet with about 1/4 inch (1/2 cm) of oil. Preheat oven to low temperature to keep sautéed fish warm.
3. Dredge fish and shrimp in seasoned flour.
4. Add fish to skillet with skin side down, using only enough fish to cover skillet in one layer. Sauté until golden and cooked through, about 3 or 4 minutes depending on thickness of fish. Turn fish and sauté other side until golden and done. Remove to warm oven.
5. Add more oil to pan, as needed. Continue sautéing fish until all is cooked. Keep warm in oven. Heat additional oil in skillet. Add shrimp and sauté until cooked, about 1 minute depending on size of shrimp. Remove shrimp and add to fish in warm oven.
6. Add another tablespoon (15 mL) oil to skillet. Reduce heat to medium-high. Add onion, stir, and sauté until softened. Add tomato, stir, and cook another minute.
7. Add vinegar, artichokes, olives, and parsley. Cook about 1 minute to heat thoroughly. Add salt and pepper, if needed. Correct seasonings.
8. Place tomato–artichoke mixture on plates, top with fish, then shrimp. Garnish with parsley. Serve immediately.

# BOUILLABAISSE A LA MARSEILLAISE (SOUTH)

## MEDITERRANEAN FISH SOUP

© kab-vision

**Note:** Of course, fish caught in the Mediterranean is used to make the bouillabaisse; however, any non oily variety of fish works well. Large fish hold together better, while the thin ones tend to fall apart. A mixture of the two types is fine, but be careful to choose mostly thicker fish. Some examples of firm-fleshed, gelatinous fish are halibut, eel, and cod. Tender and flaky fish (that will fall apart sooner) include sole, whiting, and more.

Traditionally, they present the fish on a platter and the broth in a tureen. The diner places some of the fish in a large soup plate and pours some of the broth over it. French bread and the spicy *rouille* accompany the soup, but there are endless variations on the presentation. Some toast the bread; others leave it fresh. While some cooks place a piece at the bottom of the bowl and ladle the broth over it, others top the bowl with the bread or omit it from the bowl and pass bread separately. Most pass the *rouille* after the soup is served which allows the diner to add as much of the spicy sauce as desired.

**Number of Servings:** 14
**Serving Size:** 14 oz. (397 g)
**Total Yield:** 13 lb., 11 oz. (6.2 kg) bouillabaisse
        8 oz. (227 g) rouille
**Wine Style:** Full-bodied white wine with a touch of oxidation.
**Example:** Riesling Smaragd "Loibenberg" 1999, Alzinger (Wachau/Austria)

**Cooking Method:** Boil

| INGREDIENTS | WEIGHT | | VOLUME | |
|---|---|---|---|---|
| | U.S. | METRIC | U.S. | METRIC |
| *Rouille* (Spicy Garlic Pepper Sauce): | | | | |
| bread, soft, cut into cubes | 1 1/2 oz. | 43 g | 1 cup | 240 mL |
| water | as needed | | | |
| garlic, peeled | 1/4 oz. | 8 g | 3 cloves | |
| hot pepper, Serrano or pepper of choice, roasted, peeled, seeds and membrane removed if desired | 1/4 oz. or to taste | 8 g or to taste | 1 each | |
| red pepper, roasted, seeds and membranes removed | 1 1/2 oz. | 43 g | 1/2 each | |
| olive oil | | 78 g | 1/3 cup | 80 mL |
| **Stock:** | | | | |
| shrimp with shells fish bones, from fish filets below | 2 lb. | 908 g | | |
| water, cold | | 2.8 kg | 3 quarts | 2.8 L |
| parsley stems | 2 to 3 oz. | 57 to 86 g | 1 to 2 bunches | |
| leeks, chopped, separate green and white parts | 15 1/2 oz. | 439 g | 2 each | |
| fish or shrimp base, optional (if needed for flavorful stock) | | | | |
| **Soup:** | | | | |
| Pernod or other anise liquor | | 308 g | 2/3 cup | 160 mL |
| saffron | large pinch | | | |
| olive oil | | 57 g | 1/4 cup | 60 mL |
| onion, chopped | 12 oz. | 340 g | 2 large | |
| fennel, chopped | 1 lb., 4 oz. | 567 g | 2 each | |
| garlic, peeled, smashed | 1/2 oz. | 15 g | 4 cloves | |
| orange peel | 1/2 oz. | 15 g | 2 each 3-inch (8-cm) strips | |
| tomatoes, chopped, canned or fresh | 1 lb., 13 oz. | 822 g | 3 cups | 720 mL |
| salt | to taste | | | |
| pepper | to taste | | | |
| fish filets, varieties of choice, cut into 1 1/2-inch (4-cm) pieces, *see note above regarding choice of fish* | 4 lb. | 1.8 kg | | |
| mussels, shells tightly closed | 2 lb. | 908 g | | |
| **Garnish:** | | | | |
| French bread slices, toasted or plain (as desired) | | | | |
| parsley, minced | | | | |

### TWIST ON THE CLASSIC

Mix some of the *rouille* into the bouillabaisse broth and serve this spicy seafood mixture over linguine.

## FOR *ROUILLE:*

1. Place bread in bowl, cover with water. Allow to soak thoroughly. Squeeze to remove as much water as possible.
2. Drop garlic through feed tube of running food processor fitted with knife blade. Process to pulverize. Scrape sides of processor, add hot and red peppers. Process until smooth. Add bread, process until smooth.
3. Slowly add oil through feed tube while processor is running. Allow to process until emulsified. Refrigerate and store until needed. This will keep at least several days in refrigerator.

If fish bones are not available, use fish or seafood base or clam juice to make stock.

## FOR STOCK:

1. Remove shells from shrimp. Cover and refrigerate shrimp until needed. Place fish bones and shrimp shells in stock pot with water.
2. Add parsley stems and green portion of leeks to stock pot. Reserve white leeks for later use.
3. Bring to boil over medium heat, lower heat, cover and simmer for 30 minutes.
4. Strain through a *chinois* or cheesecloth-lined strainer. Push on all solids to extract as much liquid as possible. Discard solids, refrigerate stock when cool if not using right away.

## FOR SOUP:

1. Place Pernod in bowl, add saffron. Set aside until needed.
2. Heat olive oil in stock pot over medium heat. Add onions, sauté a few minutes. Add white portion of leeks, fennel, garlic, orange peel, and tomatoes. Cook 15 minutes.
3. Add Pernod/saffron mixture and reserved fish stock. Season with salt and pepper, as needed. Bring to boil, reduce heat, cover and simmer for 40 minutes.
4. Strain using a *chinois* or cheesecloth-lined strainer. Push on all solids to extract as much liquid as possible. Discard solids. *May be made ahead to this point. If not using immediately, cool, cover, and refrigerate.*

## TO FINISH SOUP:

1. Bring stock to a boil. Add thick fish, cook 5 minutes. Add thin fish, reserved shrimp, and mussels, cook another 5 minutes. (Fish will look opaque, shrimp looks pink, and mussels or clams open.) Correct seasonings.
2. Serve as desired (*see note*). Place slice of bread at bottom of bowl and ladle soup on top or garnish top with slice of bread. Sprinkle parsley over soup. Pass rouille separately.

## RATATOUILLE (PROVENCE)

### VEGETABLE STEW

Pearson Education/PH College

**TWIST ON THE CLASSIC**

For a vegetarian entrée, add sautéed tofu to the *ratatouille* about 25 minutes before it is finished cooking. This allows time for the tofu to absorb flavoring from the *ratatouille*.

**Note:** This vegetable can be prepared ahead and partially cooked, then reheated gently at service. The flavors marry well for the second day.

**Number of Servings:** 11  
**Serving Size:** 5 oz. (142 g)  
**Total Yield:** 3 lb., 8 oz. (1.6 kg)  
**Food Balance:** Protein/sweet  
**Wine Style:** Light- to medium-bodied Riesling, Pinot Blanc, Sauvignon Blanc, White Zinfandel, and mild reds, such as Grenache, Beaujolais, Shiraz  
**Example:** Wolf Blass Riesling or Shiraz

**Cooking Method:** Braise

| INGREDIENTS | WEIGHT | | VOLUME | |
| --- | --- | --- | --- | --- |
| | U.S. | METRIC | U.S. | METRIC |
| eggplant | 1 lb., 9 oz. | 708 g | 1 medium | |
| salt | as needed | | | |
| olive oil | | 28 g | 2 tablespoons | 30 mL |
| onions, sliced thin | 15 oz. | 426 g | 3 medium | |
| garlic, smashed and minced | 1/2 oz. | 15 g | 4 cloves | |
| zucchini, cut in 3/4-inch (2-cm) pieces | 1 lb., 7 oz. | 652 g | 3 medium | |
| bell peppers, red, yellow, or green, cored and sliced into 2- to 3-inch (5- to 8-cm) strips | 1 lb. | 454 g | 2 large | |
| plum tomatoes, fresh or canned, peeled and chopped | 1 lb. | 454 g | 4 medium | |

| | | | | |
|---|---|---|---|---|
| ground anise seed | | | 1/8 teaspoon | 1 mL |
| dried basil | | | 1 teaspoon | 5 mL |
| dried thyme | | | 1 teaspoon | 5 mL |
| pepper | | | 1/2 teaspoon | 3 mL |
| salt | | | 1/2 teaspoon | 3 mL |
| bay leaf | | | 1 each | |
| ground coriander | | | 1/2 teaspoon | 3 mL |
| **Garnish:** | | | | |
| fresh parsley, minced | 1/2 oz. | 15 g | 2 tablespoons | 30 mL |

Alain Wacquier/Fotolia

1. Cut eggplant into 1/2- to 3/4-inch (1.3- to 2-cm) cubes. Place in colander either in sink or on a plate, sprinkle with salt. Let stand for 30 minutes, then rinse well and dry with paper towels.
2. Heat oil in large skillet or braising pan. Add onions, cook about 3 minutes.
3. Add eggplant, cook another 3 minutes.
4. Add garlic, zucchini, peppers, tomatoes, and seasonings.
5. Simmer, uncovered, for about 40 minutes, until vegetables are tender but not mushy.
6. Remove bay leaf, correct seasonings.
7. Serve hot or at room temperature, garnished with fresh parsley.

## PETITS POIS FRAIS À LA FRANCAISE (CLASSICAL)
### PEAS BRAISED WITH LETTUCE AND ONIONS

**Number of Servings:** 12
**Serving Size:** 4 oz. (114 g)
**Total Yield:** 3 lb. (1.4 kg)

**Cooking Method:** Braise

Mathieu Viennet/Getty Images

| INGREDIENTS | WEIGHT | | VOLUME | |
|---|---|---|---|---|
| | U.S. | METRIC | U.S. | METRIC |
| Boston bibb lettuce | 15 oz. | 426 g | 2 heads | |
| dried thyme or chervil | | | 1 teaspoon | 5 mL |
| fresh parsley sprigs | | | 5 each | |
| butter | 3 oz. | 86 g | 6 tablespoons | 90 mL |
| scallions, bottom 2 inches with bulb, cut into 1-inch sections | 5 oz. | 142 g | 24 each | |
| shelled peas, fresh or frozen | 2 lb. | 908 g | | |
| boiling water | | 78 g | 1/3 cup | 80 mL |
| sugar | 1 1/2 oz. | 43 g | 3 tablespoons | 45 mL |
| salt | 1/4 oz. | 8 g | 1 teaspoon | 5 mL |
| pepper | | | 1/4 teaspoon | 2 mL |
| more butter, *optional* | 1/2 oz. | 15 g | 1 tablespoon | 15 mL |

**TWIST ON THE CLASSIC**

For an interesting presentation, serve this in a hollowed out and baked tomato.

1. Wash lettuce, cut into strips, discarding core. Place thyme or chervil and parsley in cheesecloth bag.
2. Melt 6 tablespoons (90 mL) butter in pan, add scallions, lettuce, and peas; stir to coat with butter. Add water, sugar, salt, pepper, and spice bag to pan.
3. Cover, cook over low heat until peas are tender, about 10 minutes (for frozen). Add more water if necessary.
4. Discard cheesecloth bag, correct seasonings. Mix 1 tablespoon (15 mL) butter into peas, if desired. Serve.

# EPINARDS À LA BASQUAISE (BASQUE)

## GRATIN OF SPINACH AND POTATOES WITH ANCHOVIES

**Number of Servings:** 9
**Serving Size:** 4 oz. (114 g)
**Total Yield:** 2 lb., 5 oz. (1.1 kg)

**Cooking Method:** Bake

| | WEIGHT | | VOLUME | |
|---|---|---|---|---|
| **INGREDIENTS** | **U.S.** | **METRIC** | **U.S.** | **METRIC** |
| spinach | 1 lb., 4 oz. | 567 g | two 10-oz. bags | two 284-g bags |
| Swiss cheese, grated | 3 1/2 oz. | 104 g | 1/2 cup + 1/3 cup | 200 mL |
| potatoes, white, waxy, or all-purpose, peeled and sliced 1/8-inch thick | 1 lb., 2 oz. | 511 g | 3 each | |
| anchovies | 1 1/4 oz. | 36 g | 2 tablespoons | 30 mL |
| butter, softened | 1 oz. | 28 g | 2 tablespoons | 30 mL |
| pepper | | | 1/8 teaspoon | 1 mL |
| dry bread crumbs | 3/4 oz. | 22 g | 3 tablespoons | 45 mL |
| butter, melted | 1 oz. | 28 g | 2 tablespoons | 30 mL |

1. Remove stems from spinach and coarsely chop leaves. Wash well.
2. Braise spinach in sauté pan until cooked, about 5 minutes. Water clinging to leaves should provide enough moisture.
3. Stir 1/2 cup (120 mL) of the cheese into the braised spinach. Set aside until needed.
4. Cook potatoes in boiling water until just tender, about 5 minutes. Drain.
5. Mash anchovies with 2 tablespoons (30 mL) softened butter and pepper in small bowl. Set aside.
6. Mix remaining 1/3 cup (80 mL) cheese with bread crumbs in a small bowl.
7. Butter baking dish. Preheat oven to 375 degrees (190°C).
8. Place half of potatoes in bottom of baking dish. Dot with half of anchovy mixture. Place half of spinach mixture over potatoes.
9. Repeat layering with remaining potato, anchovy, and spinach mixtures. Spread mixed cheese and bread crumbs over spinach, pour melted butter over top.
10. Bake 30 minutes, until golden brown. Serve immediately.

### TWIST ON THE CLASSIC

As in the following recipe for potato Savoyard, to create a round serving, cut with individual metal rings and unmold on the serving plate. Otherwise, bake potatoes in rings and unmold on serving plate.

Courtesy of the Idaho Potato Commission

## GRATIN SAVOYARD (PROVENCE)

### SCALLOPED POTATOES

**Note:** Countless variations of scalloped potatoes appear all over France. Many replace the stock and olive oil used in this recipe from the south of France with cream and butter. This potato dish makes a fine accompaniment for a chop or roast chicken.

**Note:** These can be baked in individual dishes.

**Number of Servings:** 14
**Serving Size:** 4 oz. (114 g)
**Total Yield:** 3 lb., 10 oz. (1.7 kg)

**Cooking Method:** Bake

*Pouring stock over Gratin Savoyard*
Pearson Education, Inc.

| INGREDIENTS | WEIGHT U.S. | WEIGHT METRIC | VOLUME U.S. | VOLUME METRIC |
|---|---|---|---|---|
| olive oil | | 15 g | 1 tablespoon | 15 mL |
| potatoes, white, waxy, or all-purpose, peeled and sliced very thin, about 1/16-inch (15-mm) thick | 2 lb., 8 oz. | 1.1 kg | about 6 medium | |
| onion, cut in half through root end then sliced thinly | 6 oz. | 171 g | 1 large | |
| pepper | | | 1/4 to 1/2 teaspoon | 2 to 3 mL |
| cheese, Swiss or other strong variety, grated | 5 oz. | 142 g | 1 1/2 cups | 360 mL |
| salt | as needed | | | |
| strong stock, beef or chicken, hot | | 397 g | 1 3/4 cups | 420 mL |

1. Spread oil in shallow ovenproof dish. Preheat oven to 350 degrees (180°C).
2. Mix potatoes, onion, and pepper in bowl, layer half in prepared dish.
3. Top with half of cheese, layer remaining potatoes over cheese.
4. Sprinkle with salt if stock is not salty, then pour stock over potatoes.
5. Cover tightly, bake for 30 minutes. Remove cover, top with remaining cheese. Bake another 30 to 40 minutes, uncovered, until potatoes are done and top is golden brown. Serve immediately.

> **TWIST ON THE CLASSIC**
>
> To create a round serving, cut with individual metal rings and unmold on the serving plate. Alternatively, bake the potatoes in rings and unmold on serving plate.

Courtesy of the Idaho Potato Commission

# BRIOCHE

## TWIST ON THE CLASSIC

For a luncheon entree, remove "top knot" of brioche, fill hole with the filling of choice like tuna salad, pulled pork, or Indian curried chicken. Let filling overflow hole, so there is plenty to eat at the base of the brioche. Replace top knot and serve two per order.

This very buttery bread product is delicious when served with jam. The French use this dough to make a variety of breads by baking it in different shapes or adding ingredients like dried or candied fruits to the dough.

There are many recipes for brioche containing less butter. Many require shorter rising times and/or do not need overnight refrigeration to firm the butter. I decided to use the higher amount of butter because it produces a wonderful, rich brioche that is more like what I have had in France.

**Number of Servings:** 31 rolls
**Scaling:** 1 1/2 oz. (43 g) for individual (muffin tin size)
**Total Yield:** 3 lb. (1.4 kg)

**Cooking Method:** Bake

| | WEIGHT | | VOLUME | |
|---|---|---|---|---|
| INGREDIENTS | U.S. | METRIC | U.S. | METRIC |
| yeast, dried | 1/2 oz. | 15 g | 1 tablespoon | 15 mL |
| water, warm | | 43 g | 3 tablespoons | 44 mL |
| sugar | 1 oz. | 28 g | 2 tablespoons | 30 mL |
| salt | 1/2 oz. | 15 g | 2 teaspoons | 10 mL |
| flour, all purpose | 1 lb., 3 oz. | 540 g | 3 3/4 cups | 900 mL |
| eggs | 10 oz. | 284 g | 6 each | |
| butter, slightly softened, cut into 1 to 2 tablespoon-sized (15 g-sized) pieces | 1 lb. | 454 g | | |
| flour | as needed | | | |

**Glaze:**

| | WEIGHT | | VOLUME | |
|---|---|---|---|---|
| egg yolk | 3/4 oz. | 22 g | 1 each | |
| water | | | about 1/4 teaspoon or as needed | about 2 mL or as needed |

1. Place yeast and 1 oz. (28 g, 2 tablespoons [30 mL]) water in small nonreactive bowl. Stir to mix. Place sugar, salt, and remaining 1/2 oz. (15 g, 1 tablespoon [15 mL]) water in another small nonreactive bowl. Stir to mix. Let both bowls rest a couple of minutes to hydrate contents.

2. Place sugar/salt mixture into bottom of mixing bowl of electric mixer. Top with flour, then place yeast mixture over flour. Using dough hook, beat on low speed for 2 minutes.

3. Stop mixer, add 6 3/4 oz. (191 g, 4 each) eggs, continue beating on low until well incorporated, for about 5 minutes. Scrape sides with rubber spatula, as needed.

4. Add remaining 3 1/2 oz. (104 g, 2 each) eggs, one at a time, beating well after each addition. Beat at medium speed for 10 to 15 minutes, until smooth, light, and no longer sticky.

Adding butter to brioche dough.

Shaping brioche

5. Turn mixer to low speed. Smash a piece of butter between fingers, add to mixer. Quickly repeat with all of butter.

6. Cover bowl loosely with plastic wrap, allow to rise at room temperature until doubled, 1 1/2 to 2 1/2 hours. Punch down dough, pull the dough twice to stretch it, cover as before and refrigerate until doubled, 2 or 3 hours. Punch down, cover again, and refrigerate overnight.

7. Butter or pan spray brioche molds. Use a dusting of flour, only if needed to prevent sticking on hands and counter. Remove dough from refrigerator. Quickly form into log. Cut off correct amount of dough for scaling. Remove one-quarter of scaled piece of dough, form into ball, and set aside. Form remainder into ball, place in individual mold, and flatten slightly to fill pan. Make indentation in center of dough, place reserved ball of dough securely into indentation. Repeat with remaining dough.

8. Cover loosely with plastic wrap, allow to rise until doubled, about 1 hour and 30 minutes. Meanwhile, place oven rack in middle of oven and preheat to 425 degrees (220°C).

9. Brush risen brioche with egg yolk mixed with a few drops of water. Bake for 13 to 15 minutes, until golden brown. Remove from pans immediately. Cool.

© superfood

## TARTE DES DEMOISELLES TATIN (CENTRAL)

### UPSIDE-DOWN CARAMELIZED APPLE TART

**Note:** Use any variety of firm apple suitable for baking.

**Number of Servings:** 8
**Serving Size:** 1/8 tart
**Total Yield:** One 10-inch tart (25 cm)

**Cooking Method:** Bake

| INGREDIENTS | WEIGHT U.S. | WEIGHT METRIC | VOLUME U.S. | VOLUME METRIC |
|---|---|---|---|---|
| unsalted butter | 2 oz. | 57 g | 4 tablespoons | 60 mL |
| sugar | 5 1/2 oz. | 156 g | 3/4 cup | 180 mL |
| apples, peeled, cut into quarters cored, and sliced 1/4 to 3/8 inch (1/2 to 1 1/2 cm) thick | 2 lb., 3 oz. | 994 g | about 5 large | |
| cinnamon | | | 1 teaspoon | 5 mL |
| **Dough:** | | | | |
| Pâte Brisée, well chilled, *recipe follows* | 7 to 7 1/2 oz. | 199 to 213 g | | |
| **Garnish:** | | | | |
| *crème frâiche* or whipped cream, *optional* | | | | |

Arranging apple slices on top of caramelized sugar

Reversing direction of apples forming second ring of apples

*Cutting slits in top of tart*

*Baked tarte Tatin in skillet*

1. Position oven rack in middle of oven. Preheat oven to 350 degrees (180°C).
2. Melt butter in heavy, ovenproof 10-inch (25-cm) skillet over medium heat, add sugar.
3. Cook, stirring, until sugar caramelizes to light golden brown, remove from heat. (It will continue to cook a bit from the heat held in the pan, so do not caramelize to dark brown.)
4. Place apple slices in overlapping concentric circles over sugar.
5. Sprinkle cinnamon over first layer of apples, repeat layering apples and cinnamon.
6. Roll out *pâte brisée* 3/16 (45 mm) or 1/8 inch (30 mm) thick, at least 10 inches (25 cm) in diameter, big enough to cover pan.
7. Cover apples with dough, trimming edges if necessary. With sharp knife, make two or three 2-inch (5-cm) slits in crust so steam can escape.
8. Bake until golden, about 40 to 45 minutes.
9. Remove from oven, let cool a couple of minutes, invert pan on serving dish. (Be careful when inverting pan so that tart flips over entirely. The key is to invert the pan quickly.)
10. Serve immediately, accompanied by *crème frâiche* or whipped cream, if desired.

*Unmolded Tarte des Demoiselles Tatin (Upside-down Caramelized Apple Tart)*

*Slice of Tarte des Demoiselles Tatin (Upside-down Caramelized Apple Tart)*

# PÂTE BRISÉE (CLASSIC)

## ALL-BUTTER PASTRY (PIE) DOUGH

**Note:** This pastry dough is a recipe from French pastry chef Gaston Lenôtre.

**Note:** The recipe works well for both sweet and savory purposes.

**Note:** Be careful not to overwork dough. Working the dough develops the gluten, and too much gluten leads to dough that is tough. To avoid excess gluten formation, manipulate the dough only as much as needed to mix it and form it into a ball.

**Scaling**: 11 oz. (308 g) ball of dough for 9-inch (23-cm) tart pan, 2 1/2 balls for 1/2-sheet pan, 5 balls for full sheet pan
**Total Yield**: 2 lb., 3 oz. (994 g), or 3 balls of dough

*Butter cut into flour mixture*
Pearson Education, Inc.

| | *WEIGHT* | | *VOLUME* | |
|---|---|---|---|---|
| *INGREDIENTS* | *U.S.* | *METRIC* | *U.S.* | *METRIC* |
| all-purpose flour | 1 lb., 1/2 oz. | 467 g | 3 3/4 cups | 900 mL |
| salt | 1/2 oz. | 15 g | 2 teaspoons | 10 mL |
| sugar | 3/4 oz. | 22 g | 1 1/2 tablespoons | 23 mL |
| unsalted butter, cold | 13 1/2 oz. | 383 g | 1 2/3 cups (about 3 sticks + 3 tablespoons) | 400 mL |
| eggs | 3 1/2 oz. | 104 g | 2 each | |
| milk | | 28 g | 2 tablespoons | 30 mL |

### PREPARATION IN FOOD PROCESSOR:

1. Place flour, salt, and sugar in bowl of food processor fitted with knife blade, pulse a couple of times to mix.
2. Cut cold butter into small pieces, about half-tablespoon size. Place on top of dry ingredients, pulse several times, until clumps the size of peas form.
3. Whisk together eggs and milk in a small bowl. With processor running, pour mixture through feed tube. Pulse until dough comes together into ball.
4. Remove dough from processor, divide into three equal balls. Wrap in plastic wrap, refrigerate until well chilled, several hours or overnight.

### PREPARATION IN MIXER:

1. With flat paddle beater, mix salt and sugar in mixing bowl. Add butter cut into small pieces, about half-tablespoon size, continuing to beat, then add eggs and milk.
2. Beat for a few seconds, stop mixer, then add flour all at once.

### TWIST ON THE CLASSIC

Besides working for any type or size of tart shells, this dough can be used for a turnover. Chill turnover before baking to firm the butter; this way the turnover won't spread too quickly while baking.

*Pâte brisée* freezes very well, baked or unbaked. Excess balls of dough or rolled out, unbaked dough fitted into the pie tin or sheet pan store well in the freezer if properly wrapped. If freezing baked dough, be careful to wrap securely so it does not break when jostled in the freezer. Wrap dough tightly; eliminating contact with air prevents freezer burn.

*Rolling Pastry Dough*
Gerard Brown/Dorling Kindersley, Ltd.

*Finished Pie Shell*
© sugar0607

③ Beat ingredients just long enough to blend. Small pieces of butter visible in dough are fine. Do not overwork dough.

④ Remove dough from mixer, divide into three equal balls. Wrap in plastic wrap, refrigerate until well chilled, several hours or overnight.

## PREPARATION BY HAND:

① Place flour on table in mound, make well in center. Sprinkle salt and sugar around edges, place butter cut into small pieces, milk, and eggs in well.

② Mix together until crumbly, working very quickly with tips of your fingers. Knead dough gently by pushing it away from you against table with your palm (called *fraiser*).

③ Gather dough into ball and *fraiser* once more, working quickly and gently.

④ Form dough into three equal balls. Wrap in plastic wrap, refrigerate until well chilled, several hours or overnight.

## TO ROLL DOUGH:

① Place chilled ball on table. With rolling pan, hit ball to flatten into disk about one inch thick. Lightly flour table and rolling pin, if needed (only if dough is sticking to table or pin).

② Roll out dough, from middle to sides, releasing dough from table with icing spatula every few rolls. Turn dough one-quarter turn to keep dough even and roll into circle of desired thickness.

③ Release from table with spatula. Fold gently in half. Lift and move dough to pan. Position dough over pan, unfold to cover pan.

④ Press dough into all corners of pan. Either flute edges or cut flush with top of pan.

⑤ If possible, chill for at least 1 hour in the refrigerator or 10 minutes in the freezer before baking.

Recipe © *Gaston Lenôtre*

## GASTON LENÔTRE

### PASTRY CHEF & RESTAURATEUR (1920–2009)

*In the 1930s, Gaston Lenôtre began baking in his native Normandy, where he passed his professional exams and began working by the age of 15. He purchased his first boulangerie/pâtisserie in 1947. Ten years later, Lenôtre opened a pastry shop in Paris.*

*In order to train workers, in 1971 he began a training program that became the famous school L'école Lenôtre. Because of a shortage of qualified people to work with breads and pastry, Lenôtre expanded the school from a training facility for his employees to a school open to the public. Today, L'école Lenôtre remains a highly esteemed pastry school.*

*Considered the father of modern French pastry by many, Lenôtre was instrumental in bringing to pastry making the nouvelle cuisine trend of lightening up French cooking. Having created variations on numerous traditional pastries and baking techniques, he received many honors and accolades throughout his career.*

*Besides writing several books on the topic of French pastry, candies, and ice cream, Lenôtre inspired countless bakers and pastry chefs with both his creativity and his professionalism. Pastry shops bearing his name are found around the world, in places including England, Switzerland, Germany, Brazil, Las Vegas, and Orlando.*

# SOUFFLÉ AU CITRON (CLASSIC)
## LEMON SOUFFLÉ

**Note:** Soufflés make excellent desserts or savory first courses. Whether sweet or savory, the preparation and techniques involved remain the same.

**Number of Servings:** 6  **Cooking Method:** Bake
**Serving Size:** 1/6 of soufflé, about 1 cup (about 240 mL)
**Total Yield:** One 1 1/2-quart (1.4 L) soufflé dish

*Placing collar on soufflé dish*
Clive Streeter © Dorling Kindersley

| INGREDIENTS | WEIGHT | | VOLUME | |
| --- | --- | --- | --- | --- |
| | U.S. | METRIC | U.S. | METRIC |
| unsalted butter | 1/4 oz. | 8 g | 1/2 tablespoon | 7 mL |
| sugar | 4 1/4 oz. | 120 g | 1/2 cup + 1 tablespoon | 135 mL |
| egg yolks | 3 1/2 oz. | 104 g | 5 each | |
| lemon zest, grated | 1/2 oz. | 15 g | 2 tablespoons | 30 mL |
| lemon juice | | 57 g | 1/4 cup | 60 mL |
| egg whites | 7 oz. | 199 g | 7 each | |
| cream of tartar | | | 1/2 teaspoon | 2 mL |
| confectioner's sugar for dusting | | | | |

1. Butter bottom and sides of soufflé dish, dust with 1 tablespoon (15 mL) of sugar.
2. Place collar on soufflé dish by folding parchment paper to make double-thick sheet 6 or 8 inches (15 or 20 cm) wide, then wrap around dish and tie with string. (You may need to overlap two pieces of parchment paper so it is long enough to wrap dish.) Butter or pan-spray parchment paper on inside (where soufflé will touch it).
3. Place oven rack in upper half of oven. Preheat oven to 425 degrees (220°C). Prepare pan of hot water for bottom of double boiler.
4. With wire beater on mixer, beat yolks and remaining 1/2 cup (120 mL) sugar until thick and pale yellow, several minutes. Prepare pan of ice water.
5. Place mixing bowl over pan of barely simmering water, vigorously whisk until mixture is almost too hot to touch and it ribbons. (Test for ribbon: Write an "M" with mixture as it drops from the whisk. The beginning line of "M" still remains on top of mixture when the last line is formed.)
6. Whisk in lemon zest and lemon juice, cool pan in ice water bath, refrigerate until ready to use. *Can be prepared ahead to this point.*
7. With wire beater on mixer, beat egg whites and cream of tartar in a clean bowl. Beat on medium speed until frothy, then turn to high speed and beat until stiff peaks form.
8. With rubber spatula, stir large spoonful of whites into yolk mixture to lighten, fold remaining whites into mixture in two parts.
9. Transfer mixture to prepared soufflé dish, gently smooth top.
10. Bake for 2 minutes, reduce heat to 400 degrees (205°C), bake another 20 or 30 minutes, until lightly browned.
11. Remove from oven, sift confectioner's sugar over top. Soufflés do not hold well; they deflate. Serve immediately.

Martin Brigdale © Dorling Kindersley

### TWIST ON THE CLASSIC

Instead of baking in a soufflé dish, bake this in hollowed lemon shells.

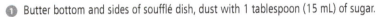

# MOUSSE AU CHOCOLAT
## CHOCOLATE MOUSSE

**Number of Servings:** 9

**Serving Size:** 4 oz. (113 g)

**Total Yield:** 2 lb., 4 1/4 oz. (about 1 kg)

**Cooking Method:** Boil

|  | WEIGHT | | VOLUME | |
|---|---|---|---|---|
| **INGREDIENTS** | **U.S.** | **METRIC** | **U.S.** | **METRIC** |
| chocolate, semisweet or bittersweet chips or cut into small pieces | 12 oz. | 340 g | | |
| coffee, strong | | 57 g | 1/4 cup | 60 mL |
| butter, unsalted, room temperature, cut into pieces | 3 oz. | 86 g | 6 tablespoons | 90 mL |
| sugar | 5 oz. | 142 g | 2/3 cup | 160 mL |
| egg yolks | 4 oz. | 114 g | 6 each | |
| orange liqueur | | 57 g | 1/4 cup | 60 mL |
| whipping cream | | 227 g | 1 cup | 240 mL |

**Garnish:**

whipped cream

chocolate, rolled or grated, if desired

1. Place chocolate and coffee in medium bowl that fits tightly over pot of gently simmering water (bain-marie). Stir once or twice until chocolate is almost melted. (Be careful the water is *not* too hot; that can cause the chocolate to burn or become grainy.)

2. Remove from heat, stir with whisk. Whisk in butter, a piece at a time. Mixture will be smooth. Set aside until needed.

3. Whisk sugar and egg yolks together in bowl of mixer or stainless steel bowl that fits tightly over pot of gently simmering water (bain-marie).

*Whisking the egg yolks and sugar over pan of simmering water*

*Texture of mixture after whipping with mixer*

④ Whisk in orange liqueur, whisk constantly until mixture is fluffy and registers 160 degrees (70°C). Remove from heat, beat at high speed with mixer until room temperature.

⑤ Fold egg mixture into chocolate mixture with rubber spatula. Whip whipping cream until it forms soft peaks. Fold into chocolate mixture.

⑥ Store, covered in refrigerator until time of service. When served, garnish with dollop of whipped cream topped with a chocolate roll, grating of chocolate, and/or a fresh raspberry.

Traditionally, many chocolate mousse recipes incorporate raw eggs. If using pasteurized eggs, this is acceptable.

*Folding whipped cream into chocolate mixture*

*Final folding of ingredients in chocolate mousse*

## >> LEARNING OBJECTIVES

By the end of this chapter, you will be able to:

- Identify differences and similarities in the regional cuisines of Italy
- Explain how the topography of the various regions in Italy affect their cuisine
- Know what food products are prevalent in various regions of Italy
- Identify and explain the courses served at a typical Italian meal
- Prepare a northern and a southern Italian meal

## >> HISTORY

Throughout history, Italy's geographic location made it an ideal stopping place for traders and sailors traveling between Europe and the Middle or Far East. The travelers stopped in Italy, replenished their supplies, and traded goods. Venice, in northeastern Italy, and Naples in the south became bustling port cities and trading centers for spices and other goods on this well-traveled route between the east and west.

One country after another invaded and occupied Sicily, an Italian island in the Mediterranean. Many of these countries left their culinary mark, but the Arabs, who ruled for about 400 years during the time of the Middle Ages, left a huge impact. They introduced pastries, ice cream, many spices, pasta, rice, raisins, honey, almonds, and pine nuts, as well as many types of stuffed vegetable dishes that still remain popular today. Every nationality of traders, sailors, invaders, and conquerors that entered Italy left some of their cuisine behind.

*When the Greeks occupied the southern part of Italy, they introduced the Italians to their sumptuous eating and drinking.*

### INVADERS

Coming from the eastern Mediterranean or Asia Minor, Etruscans occupied central Italy from as early as 1200 B.C. to about 100 B.C. Their extensive culinary influence included growing rye and barley as well as seasoning with garlic, onions, rosemary, and bay leaves. They planted a wide variety of fruits and vegetables like legumes, figs, pomegranates, and grapes. In addition, the Etruscans raised cows, pigs, goats, sheep, chickens, ducks, and geese for food and dairy. They are credited with introducing wine, huge banquets, and irrigation of land to Italy.

As early as 500 B.C., the Roman Empire began in southern Italy, where it slowly flourished and grew. With the city of Rome as the center of the Empire, the Romans conquered and ruled many nations until their fall in 400 A.D. Much of the foundation for the Italian cuisine came from the Roman Empire, with significant influence from the foods of Greece and Asia Minor, the area from the Black Sea to the Mediterranean.

*In the time of the Roman Empire, salt had great importance both in flavoring foods and preserving. It was so valuable that soldiers' salaries were paid in salt.*

Leaving a legacy that still lives today, the Greeks introduced all sorts of fish and seafood and planted olive trees, grapevines, and wheat in Italy. Pungent, full-flavored sauces reflect the Middle Eastern influence. The Italians added their own rich bounty of local ingredients such as cheeses, seafood, nuts, and native fruits and vegetables to the foreign recipes. Those adapted recipes became a permanent part of the Italian cuisine.

In the mid-500s, Germanic groups came into northern Italy. They introduced Germanic culinary traits into the cuisine found in those regions. When the Saracens from northern Africa invaded Sicily around 800, they brought many culinary changes. Besides peaches, dates, melons, citrus fruits, cloves, and cinnamon, they introduced rice and sugarcane. Most important, the Saracens taught the Italians to irrigate more efficiently, which changed their agriculture forever.

*Although no one knows for sure, many believe the origins for ice cream and sherbet came from the Roman emperor Nero. He had snow brought from the mountains to chill his drinks, and he combined the snow with fruits and honey, creating what may have been the forerunner of sherbet.*

### CATHERINE DE' MEDICI

Many consider the cuisine of Italy to be the most imaginative of the European cuisines. According to *Larousse Gastronomique*, Italy is the mother of all European cuisines. Beginning with Catherine de' Medici, Italian cooking played a major role in the development of the French cuisine.

In 1533, Catherine de' Medici married future king Henri II of France. When she took Italian cooks with her to France, the French learned and adopted much from the Italian cuisine. The Italians introduced broccoli, peas, artichokes, sauces, fine pastries, and much more to the French during this time. For the first time, they served meals in courses. This marked the start of *haute cuisine*.

### LATER INFLUENCES

Another major culinary impact on the cuisine of Italy occurred in the sixteenth century when explorers returned from the New World bearing vegetables previously unknown in Italy. Vegetables like corn, bell peppers, hot peppers, tomatoes, and beans quickly became an intrinsic part of the Italian cuisine.

In the 1800s, Napoleon conquered Italy and made it part of the French Empire. That rule lasted until the latter part of the nineteenth century. In 1870, the regions of Italy finally unified into a nation.

## >> TOPOGRAPHY

Situated in the southern part of Europe, Italy is a boot-shaped peninsula jutting out into the Mediterranean Sea. In fact, Italy contains almost 1,000 miles of coastline. Two large islands lying to the south and west, Sicily and Sardinia, as well as some smaller islands, compose the nation of Italy.

Because of this peninsula's long, narrow shape, most regions contain both seashore and mountains. Obviously, plentiful seafood exists near the coasts, and meats from herding and hunting are prevalent in the mountainous areas. In particular, game, pork, and lamb grace menus in homes and restaurants. Generally, beef is consumed less often because cattle graze in pastures and flatter land, which many consider more valuable for growing crops. Sheep thrive on mountains, so they are raised in many areas of Italy.

Italy contains two mountain ranges. The highest mountains in Europe, the Alps, lie across the northern part bordering France, Switzerland, and Austria. The Apennine Mountains run from the north to the south through the middle of the country. The resulting topography provides hilly terrain for herding, fertile valleys for agriculture, and caves for aging cheese.

As in Scandinavia, the mountains in Italy exerted a profound effect on the cookery, causing considerable differences among the regional cuisines because of two factors. First, difficult travel through the mountainous areas led to significant isolation; that isolation resulted in limited sharing between regions of both food products and recipes. Second, growing conditions change with the varied terrain, and those conditions determined the products produced in each area. As a result, the available food items differed from region to region.

In addition, Italy contains diverse climates. Of course, cooler conditions exist in the mountainous areas, whereas the coastal regions have warmer weather. The north experiences cool winters, warm summers, and average rainfall; the south has mild winters and hot, dry summers with very limited rainfall in parts of the south.

---

### Ingredients and Foods Commonly Used throughout the Cuisine of Italy Include

- seafood
- cured hams, sausages, and other pork products
- veal
- game
- pasta
- olives and olive oil
- garlic and onions
- anchovies
- dried beans
- fresh herbs—including parsley, basil, oregano, rosemary, fennel, marjoram, mint, and thyme
- cheeses—used in a number of ways: grated over finished dishes from salad to pasta to entrées, used as an ingredient in dishes before cooking, and for eating
- tomatoes, eggplant, and peppers
- all sorts of mushrooms and truffles
- wine

---

## >> COOKING METHODS

The Italian cuisine uses virtually all of the cooking methods. Sautéing, deep-frying, braising, roasting, grilling, or spit roasting are commonly used meat preparations. A well-known dish, *ossobuco*, is braised veal shanks. Preparation of veal scaloppini involves pounding the meat until thin, then sautéing it. Pizza, *calzone*, and *focaccia*, as well as a number of pasta dishes, are just a few of the baked dishes. *Fritto misto di pesce* is deep-fried mixed seafood.

The most usual cooking methods for vegetables include boiling, sautéing, and baking. Generally, vegetables and pastas are cooked until *al dente*, meaning "to the tooth." This term refers to foods cooked until done but still crisp or maintaining a little "bite."

## >> REGIONS

Often the cuisines of Italy are classified into two large regions with distinct culinary differences: the more affluent, industrial north and the poorer, hotter, more sparsely populated south. Generally, butter is the fat used in the north whereas olive oil prevails in the south. The north is known for vegetables, creamy sauces, red meats, fresh pastas, rice, polenta, and potato *gnocchi* (potato and flour dumpling served with a sauce like pasta). Dried pastas, pizza, white meats, garden spices, red sauces, and more highly seasoned foods typify dishes from the south. People from the north tend to cook with wine, but the southern cooks incorporate tomatoes into many dishes. All Italian cooks use pepper, but those in the north prefer black pepper while southerners use spicy hot peppers. Although these generalizations apply to the cookery of the north and south, it is an oversimplification, as distinct regional cuisines flourish throughout Italy.

*Making gnocchi*
© Lsantilli

### OVERVIEW

Many independent regions form the country of Italy, and each of these regions claims its own history, culture, and culinary traditions. Depending on the source, Italy is divided into anywhere from 14 to 20 regions. Great diversity exists among the cuisines of these regions based on what is grown and raised in the area, the methods of food preparation, topography, affluence of the region, cultural differences, and historical influences by other countries. Prior to World War II, the regions maintained separate and distinct identities. In the aftermath of World War II, however, a weakening of culinary boundaries between the various regions occurred.

Each region in Italy produces its own preferred cured meats, cheeses, and wine. The type of wine is based on the variety of grapes that grow best in that region. With varying climates and topography as well as diverse soil conditions, including volcanic ash in the central section, a wide range of wines come from Italy. Furthermore, the wines produced in each region influence the cooking of that area.

*Gnocchi with pesto*
© silberkorn73

### NORTHERN ITALY

Strong influence from neighboring countries affected the cuisines of several regions in the north. The Piedmont region shares a border with France; Austria and Switzerland lie next to Trentino-Alto Adige, Veneto, and Lombardy; and Austria and Slovenia border Venezia Giulia. Each of these regions exhibits strong culinary influences from its bordering countries. Adopting culinary traits from neighboring countries explains the Germanic style and French influence found in northern Italy, where sauerkraut, potato *gnocchi*, and *au gratin* dishes appear on menus.

In addition to their favored polenta, people of the Piedmont consume plenty of butter, milk, cheese, beef, game, and rice. Pronounced French influence shows in the cuisine here, too. *Barolo* wine hails from this region.

Situated in the northwest, Liguria borders the Mediterranean Sea. Honey and a wide range of produce including citrus fruits come from Liguria. A very large port on the Mediterranean, Genoa is known for seafood dishes; *focaccia*, a flatbread; and *pesto Genovese*, the famous sauce/paste made from puréed basil, garlic, pine nuts, olive oil, and Parmesan cheese.

*Attracting lots of tourists, the Italian Riviera lies in Liguria.*

Very fresh seafood is available throughout the northeastern region of Veneto. The city of Venice, the famous port city with canals and boats instead of paved streets and cars, lies in this region.

Refined cookery reigns in Veneto. The seafood served here is delicately cooked, with an absence of strong or overpowering sauces. Veneto produces a bounty of high-quality fruits and vegetables comparable to that of any other region in Italy. Peas, asparagus, many varieties of mushrooms, pumpkin, zucchini, and radicchio are a sampling of the vegetables grown here. Although many think of pasta as Italy's only starch, the Arabs introduced rice to Veneto, and it thrives in this region. Many rice dishes, including a local variation of risotto, prevail in the north of Italy. Serving as a major trade center linking Europe and the Middle East, Venice and the other ports of Italy experienced culinary influences from countries around the world.

The city of Milan is in Lombardy, Italy's richest region. Nestled between the Po Valley and the Alpine area, it is an area where cattle for meat thrives. Called the industrial capital of Italy, Milan is known for several dishes, including *ossobuco*, braised veal shanks, and *risotto*, a creamy dish made from arborio rice prepared by constantly stirring the rice while it cooks. Flavored with any variety of ingredients, many types of risotto are served. One of the best known, *risotto alla milanese*, takes its golden color from saffron.

Corn also grows well here, providing cornmeal for polenta, which is a thick cornmeal mixture similar to the cornmeal mush consumed in the United States. Italians either serve polenta by the spoonful after cooking, or they chill it, then slice and sauté.

From the Emilia region comes Parma ham, Parmesan cheese, high-quality pork, and balsamic vinegar. In addition to abundant dairy cattle providing milk for cheese and butter, many claim this region has the best agriculture in Italy. Emilia is known for its love of food and fine cuisine. Called the culinary capital of Italy since the 1100s, Bologna lies in this region. Famous for bologna, sausages, tomato sauce containing meat (*Bolognese*), and many other dishes, the town of Bologna produces the robust, rich, Italian food that characterizes the cooking of Emilia. With the Adriatic Sea bordering on the west and the Po River flowing through this region, people in Emilia have access to a variety of fish and seafood.

## CENTRAL ITALY

Lying in the region of Tuscany, Florence reached its peak during the Renaissance in the fifteenth century, when some of the greatest artists and architects of the period resided there. Tuscany lies in the heartland of Italy, and many claim Italian cooking began here. Some say the cooking of Tuscany represents the simplest of all the regional cooking, with an emphasis on the flavors found in fresh, high-quality ingredients.

Located in the center of Italy, Umbria remains a poor area with simple, straightforward food. Black truffles, many varieties of mushrooms, and olives proliferate in this region and appear in all sorts of dishes. Excellent olive oil comes from Umbria. Pork and cured pork products, including salami, sausage, and cured ham dominate menus. Meat is often grilled or spit roasted, giving it the characteristic flavor of wood.

People in Marche, a region located in the east, eat pasta every day. More truffles come from this region than any other area in Italy. Bordering the Adriatic Sea, they have access to lots of seafood like squid, shrimp, lobster, sole, and more. Each town in Marche prepares their unique version of *brodetto*, a fish soup.

## SOUTHERN ITALY

Moving toward the south, Naples, in Campania, claims to be the home of pizza. From Naples, pizza spread throughout the regions of Italy and eventually to countries around the world. Incredible vegetables grow in this region. Lots of seafood and cheese are consumed, but little meat.

---

*Rice production in Italy is higher than in any other country in Europe, and the 530-bushel-per-acre yield of rice found in Italy is greater than any in the world.*

*Traditional balsamic vinegar is aged for at least 12 years in a wooden barrel!*

*Tuscany is known for Chianti wine.*

*From Campania, pungent pasta puttanesca features tomato sauce containing garlic, dried hot peppers, olives, capers, and anchovies. Believed to originate in the 1950s, this modern sauce is named for prostitutes. Several colorful stories surround the name of this sauce.*

- *Puttanesca is hot, spicy, and pungent, like a prostitute.*
- *Its quick preparation allowed prostitutes to make the sauce between customers.*
- *Because it contains no meat, this sauce is inexpensive.*
- *Prostitutes used the fragrant aroma of the pot of puttanesca to help them lure customers into the brothel.*

Situated in the "toe of the boot" of the Italian peninsula, Calabria displays prominent Greek influence from Greece's control in the 900s B.C. Many other powers, including Normans and Byzantines, dominated Calabria in the past. A poor region, the cuisine here can be described as simple peasant food. Eggplant dishes, pasta, and olive oil abound. In addition to eggplant, Calabrians grow onions, peppers, tomatoes, and citrus fruits.

Sicily, an island just off the toe of the boot, shows culinary influences from the series of invaders who occupied the island throughout history. Some of those include the Greeks, Romans, Arabs, Spanish, Turks, French, Germans, English, and Austrians. Seafood and fresh vegetables remain cherished foods in the Sicilian diet. Besides supplying high-quality tuna and swordfish from the seas around the island, Sicily made several contributions to the cuisine of Italy, including a sweet-and-sour sauce called *agrodolce*, ice cream, and *zabaglione*, a dessert sauce containing eggs, sugar, and Marsala wine. Further west, the island of Sardinia obtains very large lobsters from the sea, while sheep graze in the mountainous interior.

*Zabaglione is the Italian version of French sabayon. While white wine flavors sabayon, Italians flavor zabaglione with marsala. Other desserts of Sicilian origin include cassata, a frozen layer cake, and cannoli, a deep-fried pastry tube filled with a mixture of ricotta cheese, dried fruits, and chocolate.*

## >> CUISINE

Many attribute the excellence of Italian cooking to the fact that high-quality, fresh ingredients are combined simply. Historically, Italy was a country of hardworking farmers who toiled long hours on their land. As a result, much of the cuisine consisted of the freshest ingredients growing on the farm, which were prepared simply and quickly. Even now, the sauce that will accompany the meat course is often served on pasta as the first course. Allowing the natural flavors of the foods to dominate the dish, Italians do not serve the heavy sauces so prominent in the cooking of France.

Very high-quality fruits and vegetables thrive throughout Italy, and fresh produce plays an important part in each region's cuisine. Some attribute the exceptional quality of the fruits and vegetables, including the grapes for wine, to the high volume of volcanic ash found in the soil. Many of the most popular varieties of fresh vegetables, such as tomatoes, eggplant, zucchini, and artichokes, appear in dishes from antipasto and salads to pasta and pizza. As stated earlier, Italians cook vegetables, pasta, and rice *al dente*, meaning cooked yet still a bit crunchy or firm, never overcooked and mushy.

### PROTEIN

With many miles of coastline, all sorts of fish and seafood play an important role in the Italian cuisine. A variety of fish soups and chowders are served along the coasts. Many types of fish are available, including tuna, red mullet, sardines, sole, sea bass, anchovies, and eel. Shellfish, octopus, and squid are widely consumed. Anchovies function as a flavoring in sauces, as well as appearing on pizza and in a myriad of other dishes.

In terms of meat, veal and pork remain the most popular. The many Italian veal dishes include *ossobuco* (braised veal shanks), *saltimbocca* (veal with a slice of *prosciutto* braised in white wine), veal *piccata* (veal in a lemon and white wine sauce), and veal *marsala* (veal in a sherry sauce). Used alone or as a flavoring for other dishes, pork products, cured hams, and a variety of sausages made from pork, wild game, and/or veal are widely available. *Prosciutto*, a well-known, cured, air-dried ham, flavors many dishes and also is served in *antipasti* (appetizers). A typical meal that a farmer or shepherd might take to the fields or mountains consists of sausage, cheese, bread, and wine.

### PASTA

Pasta spread through Italy after the Arabs introduced it in Sicily. Of course, it still remains a staple throughout the country. The size and shape of pasta varies from *acini di pepe*, tiny bead-shaped pasta used in soups, to *lasagna*, three-inch-wide sheets of

Veal saltimbocca
© Oran Tantapakul

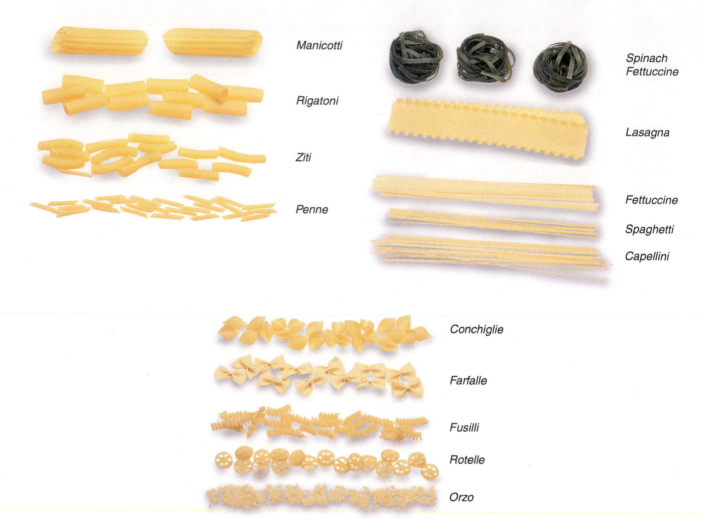

Manicotti

Rigatoni

Ziti

Penne

Spinach Fettuccine

Lasagna

Fettuccine

Spaghetti

Capellini

Conchiglie

Farfalle

Fusilli

Rotelle

Orzo

Pasta shapes

pasta layered with meats and/or vegetables, cheeses, and sauce in a casserole. The plethora of other pasta shapes include large tubes such as manicotti for stuffing with cheese and/or meat and many sizes of small tubes that allow the sauce to coat the pasta on the inside and outside. Sometimes pasta dough is shaped to enclose a filling (e.g., ravioli and tortellini). Many shapes of pasta are named for things they look like: *farfalle*, butterflies (sometimes called bow ties); *fusilli*, spindles (sometimes called corkscrews); *ditalini*, little thimbles; and *conchiglie*, conch shells. Obviously, pasta comes in a huge assortment of sizes and shapes to fit any need.

In the north, pasta recipes contain egg, but pasta made in the south omits the egg. Pasta can be dried and stored, or it can be cooked fresh after the dough is rolled out and cut into the desired shape. Fresh pasta cooks in just a few minutes. Although people in northern Italy often replace pasta with other starches such as polenta or rice, people in the south consume pasta at least once each day.

## CHEESES

Over 450 types of cheeses are produced throughout Italy, and they play an important part in each region's cuisine. While lots of cheeses appear in many regions, numerous cheeses are available only in the specific region or regions where they are made. Grated cheese is frequently served as a condiment and functions as an important flavoring. Parmesan, Gorgonzola, and Bel Paese are just a few of the many cheeses found in the north, and mozzarella and sharp sheep cheeses like Pecorini are prevalent in the south.

Ricotta is made from the whey left when producing other cheeses like provolone or mozzarella. Used often in both sweet and savory dishes, this creamy, soft cheese (similar to cottage cheese) is found throughout Italy.

## SOME CHEESES OF ITALY

**Asiago** Made from cow's milk; sharp flavor; hard granular texture

**Bel Paese** Made from cow's milk; yellow tender cheese with mild, slightly salty flavor; soft creamy texture

**Caciocavallo** A delicate, creamy cheese for the first two or three months; after that it becomes sharp and spicy; provolone is a variety of Caciocavallo

**Fontina** Made from cow's milk; sweet, creamy with mild, delicate flavor; semihard texture with a few holes; melts well

**Gorgonzola** Made from cow's milk although some use goat's milk; type of blue cheese

**Mascarpone** Made from cow's milk; fresh cheese, white cream cheese made from fresh cream; buttery, delicate flavor

**Mozzarella** Made from the milk of cows or buffaloes; mild flavor; rubbery texture

**Parmesan** Made from cow's milk; sharp, full flavor, hard granular texture; found throughout Italy; eaten as is or grated and used as a condiment

**Pecorini** Made from sheep's milk; sharp flavor; hard texture; found throughout much of Italy

**Provolone** Made from cow's milk; aromatic; aging sharpens the flavor and firms the texture

**Ricotta** Made from sheep's and buffalo's milk; fresh cheese, mild flavor; moist, unsalted cooking cheese similar to cottage cheese in texture

**Robiola** Made from goat's, sheep's, or cow's milk, or a mixture of milks; can be mild or strong in flavor; smooth, soft, and delicate texture

**Stracchino** Made from cow's milk; strong and tart, full flavor; soft creamy texture that oozes from rind

**Taleggio** Made from cow's milk; full flavor; smooth, soft, creamy, melt-in-your-mouth texture

| REGION | CHEESE |
|---|---|
| Piedmont | Fontina, Robiola, Parmesan, Gorgonzola |
| Lombardy | Gorgonzola, Taleggio, Stracchino, Bel Paese, Mascarpone, Parmesan, Reggiano |
| Veneto | Asiago, Grana Padano |
| Liguria | Fiore Sardo |
| Emilia-Romagna | Parmesan Reggiano, Grana Padano |
| Tuscany | Fiore Sardo |
| Rome-Lazio | Pecorino Romano, Fiore Molle |
| Naples-Campagna | Fiore Sardo |
| Apulia | Provole di Bufala, Mozzarella, Ricotta |
| Sicily | Pecorino Siciliano |
| Sardinia | Pecorino Romano, Fiore Sardo |

## OTHER FOOD ITEMS

An inexpensive item, beans appear in every section of the Italian menu, including *antipasti*, soups, pasta dishes, and entrées. Some of the many varieties consumed are white kidney beans (*cannellini*), red kidney beans, garbanzo beans (chickpeas), and navy beans.

Italian cooking features an abundance of herbs, creating variety in the flavors. Italian kitchens often contain herbs like basil, parsley, oregano, rosemary, fennel, juniper, marjoram, mint, bay leaves, and thyme. Pesto, a basil-garlic sauce that originated in Genoa, is used as a sauce for pasta, as well as a flavoring in other dishes. In addition to herbs, liberal amounts of garlic and onion flavor most dishes.

While France claims the black truffle, the prized white truffle comes from Italy. Found primarily in the Piedmont area, the exorbitant white truffle can sell for thousands of dollars.

## SOUPS

Soup remains an important part of the diet in Italy. Of course, soups utilize any available ingredients and function as an inexpensive, filling menu item. Italian menus feature many soups.

- *Minestrone*—Italian vegetable soup.
- *Pasta e fagioli*—A tomato-based soup containing pasta and beans, this appears on menus throughout the country.
- *Zuppa alla Pavese*—Translated as "Pavia soup," it comes from the region of Lombardy. According to the story, in the mid-sixteenth century, Francis I, the king of France, was losing the battle of Pavia. Retreating before the surrender, he stopped at a peasant's cottage and asked for a meal. A pot of *minestrone* was on the stove, but the peasant thought that was not good enough for a king. Since the peasant had limited ingredients, he put slices of toasted and buttered stale bread in a bowl, placed some eggs over the bread, and topped it with Parmesan cheese. When the boiling soup was poured over this concoction, *zuppa alla Pavese* was created.
- Each town on the coast has its own version of a fish chowder or soup. *Brodetto*, an assortment of seafood in broth similar to the French *bouillabaisse,* is well known in the Marches region.
- Another popular soup, *brodo* appears frequently. Pasta, bread, vegetables, or meats are sometimes added to this clear broth.

*Pizza margherita*
© Jillian Alexander

## PIZZA

A popular snack or meal throughout Italy, a whole pizza or a slice can be purchased from open-air shops or in restaurants. There are countless flavor combinations. Some of the well-known ones are as follows:

- *Pizza margherita*—Named for the first queen of Italy; topped with basil, tomato, and mozzarella, representing the green, red, and white of the Italian flag
- *Napoletana*—Contains tomatoes, mozzarella, anchovies, oregano, and oil
- *Capricciosa*—With mozzarella, tomato, mushrooms, artichokes, olives, and sometimes cooked ham and/or anchovies
- *Quattro formaggi*—With tomatoes and four cheeses (mozzarella and three others, which vary)

## DESSERTS

Numerous street vendors and shops selling *gelato* (ice cream) and *granita* (ices) are prevalent all over Italy. In fact, some think Italian ice creams and ices rank as the best in the world. For sure, Italians consume a lot of frozen confections! Sicily is known for a variety of fine desserts. *Cannoli*, a fried pastry tube filled with a mixture of creamed cheeses, candied fruits, nuts, and chocolate, originated on this island. Each region has their favorite desserts, and many versions of the same dessert flourish within each region. Below is a list of some of the Italian confections.

**amaretti**  The Italian version of macaroons, an almond cookie
**biscotti**  A twice-baked cookie; many like to dip them in sweet wine or coffee
**cannoli**  Fried pastry tube filled with a mixture of creamed cheeses, candied fruits, nuts, and chocolate; from Sicily
**panforte**  Christmas cake, which comes from the city of Siena; contains almonds, hazelnuts, cocoa, spices, and fruits

*Cannoli*
© Lsantilli

***pannettone*** Spiced Christmas cake which they say the Milanese invented; contains citron and raisins

***tiramisu*** Layered confection consisting of espresso- and/or liquor-soaked ladyfinger biscuits and a mascarpone cheese mixture

***torta di ricotta*** Pie with a filling of sweetened ricotta cheese containing citron and nuts; often served around Easter

***zabaglione*** Custard sauce flavored with marsala; usually served over fresh fruits; the same sauce in France is flavored with white wine instead of marsala and called *sabayon*

## GOVERNMENT REGULATION

As in other countries in the European Union, the government in Italy guarantees the authenticity and quality of some of Italy's food products. In addition to DOC, which means *denominazione di origine controllata*, DOCG adds "guarantee" to the "controlled place of origin." Still other designations regulate different aspects of the foods. Some of the wines, cheeses, balsamic vinegars, and olive oils carry these government-sanctioned acronyms on their labels, ensuring the area of origin, quality, and/or standards of the products. The list of government-controlled foods is growing as the goverment decides to place more items under regulation.

Olive trees grow well in poor soil and on hillsides, so they thrive in Italy. An important crop, olives are valued for both the fruit and the oil that is pressed from them. Black and green olives as well as capers (a bud from a shrub, preserved by pickling or salting) appear on antipasto plates and as a flavoring for many Italian dishes and sauces.

Like wines, olive oils all taste different. Numerous grades of olive oil are available, and the type selected depends on its intended use. The most common olive oil and the least expensive is marketed as "olive oil." If heating the oil, this olive oil is usually the best choice. However, if the oil is intended for use in a cold dish, an extra virgin or virgin olive oil is preferred. Considered the finest, extra virgin olive oil has an excellent, delicate flavor. Virgin olive oil is the next-best type.

As explained in the chapter on Spain, various growing conditions, weather, and soil conditions yield olive oils with different characteristics. Because olive trees grow in many regions of Italy, a wide range of olive oils with varying flavors is available throughout the country.

## MEALS

A typical Italian breakfast consists of *cappuccino* (a coffee drink combining espresso and steamed milk) and bread. Served at the end of a meal or in the late afternoon with a pastry or ice cream, many Italians drink espresso, very strong coffee served in a small cup called *demitasse*.

The largest meal of the day is served midday. Shops close for part of the afternoon, and people usually dine at home. Several small courses make up this main meal, yet the incorrect generalization (outside of Italy) is that the main meal consists of a huge plate of pasta. In fact, if pasta is served, it is the course served before the entrée.

When the meal begins with *antipasto*, it precedes the pasta course. Most likely, *antipasto* appears with a Sunday or holiday meal, or it may be served alone as the light evening meal. Examples of the *antipasto* include cheese, salami, sausage, marinated vegetables, fresh fruit wrapped with *prosciutto* (cured ham), or other simple foods. The typical first course, *primo piatto*, consists of soup, pasta, rice, or polenta. Comprised of carbohydrates, this course filled the diner before the *secondi piatto*, the second course. This second or main course consists of meat, seafood, or an egg dish accompanied by vegetables and perhaps salad. Fruit and/or cheese for dessert follow the main course. The beverage of choice, wine, accompanies the midday and evening meals. The local wine produced in each region goes with meals in that area.

---

### CULINARY CAPITALS

- Many believe the city of Bologna has the richest and best cooking in all of Italy, and certainly in the north.
- Tuscany and the city of Florence are reputed to have the purist cooking in the country.
- Naples is known as the culinary capital of the south.

---

### GRADES OF OLIVE OIL

*extra virgin* Contains less than 1 percent of free acidity

*virgin* Contains less than 2 percent of free acidity

*refined olive oil* Refined virgin olive oil made with oils containing higher acidity and/or inferior taste

*olive oil* Blend of refined olive oil and virgin olive oil

| REGION | AREA | WEATHER | TOPOGRAPHY | FOODS |
|---|---|---|---|---|
| Piedmont | Northwest | Cool winters, warm summers | Mountains, hills, plains | Trout, *fontina* cheese, butter, corn, barley, rye, wheat, rice, polenta, vegetables, garlic, white truffles, mushrooms, nuts, fruits, grapes, *zabaglione* |
| Lombardy | North-central | Cool winters, warm summers | Rivers, lakes, plateaus, mountains, hills, fertile farmland | Livestock, dairy, *ossobuco*, pork products, game, salami, butter, *gorgonzola*, polenta, corn, rice, risotto, saffron, *zuppa alla pavese*, *panettone* |
| Veneto | Northeast | Cool winters, warm summers | Coast | Fish, seafood, cows, pigs, *bacala*, cheese, rice, polenta, vegetables, radicchio, peas, asparagus, mushrooms, fruits, grapes, *grappa*, wine, tiramisu |
| Liguria | Northwest | Cool winters, warm summers | Coast, mountains | Shellfish, olives, olive oil, pesto, herbs, vegetables, fruits, grapes |
| Emilia-Romagna | North-central | Cool winters, warm summers | Mountains, valleys, plains | Pork products, sausages, cured hams, *ragu*, pasta, Parmesan cheese, white truffles, mushrooms, balsamic vinegar |
| Tuscany | East-central | Mild winters, dry, hot summers | Mountains, coast, hills, plains | Grilled meats, seafood, polenta, olive oil, spinach, vegetables, pine nuts, chestnuts, fruits, grapes |
| Umbria | Midcentral | Mild winters, hot, dry summers | Mountains, hills | Pork, lamb, spit roasted meats, game, seafood, fish soups, wheat, black truffles, mushrooms, beets, olive oil |
| Marches | Mideast | Mild winters, hot, dry summers | Coast, mountains | Seafood, cattle, sheep, pigs, wheat, corn, vegetables, truffles, mushrooms, *brodetto* |
| Rome-Lazio | Midwest | Mild winters, hot, dry summers | Mountains, coast, forests, lakes | Sheep, lamb, pork, seafood, *saltimbocca*, Pecorino cheese, spicy red sauces, pasta, artichokes |
| Abruzzo-Molise | Mideast | Mild winters, hot, dry summers | Mountains, coast, lakes, forests, hills, valleys | Lamb, pork, ham, salami, game, Pecorino cheese, pasta, wheat, mushrooms, hot peppers |
| Naples-Campagna | Mid-southwest | Mild winters, hot, dry summers | Volcanoes, mountains | Seafood, mozzarella, cheeses, pizza, wheat, pasta, olives, vegetables, tomatoes, fruits, grapes, wine |
| Calabria-Lucania | South | Mild winters, hot, dry summers | Coast, mountains, forests, plateaus, plains | Seafood, swordfish, pork, lamb, sausage, sheep, cheese, bread, chili peppers, eggplant, black pepper |
| Apulia | Southeast | Mild winters, hot, dry summers | Coast, plains, mountains, fertile farmland | Fish, seafood, mozzarella, cheeses, pasta, olives, olive oil, vegetables, tomatoes, almonds, grapes, wine |
| Sicily | South island | Mild winters, hot, dry summers | Mountains, coast, hills, volcanoes | Seafood, swordfish, tuna, sardines, sheep, goats, pigs, cheese, wheat, pasta, olives, olive oil, tomatoes, eggplant, artichokes, citrus fruits, nuts, almonds, ice cream, grapes, wine |
| Sardinia | Midwest island | Mild winters, hot, dry summers | Barren, rocky mountains, hills, plains, coast | Sheep, game, fish, seafood, lobster, sheep's cheese, bread, artichokes, grapes |

## >> Review Questions

1. Name four foods associated with the north of Italy and four foods associated with the south of Italy.
2. Name four food products and flavorings that are prevalent throughout Italy.
3. What two topographical features are found in most regions of Italy?
4. According to Larousse, how does the cuisine of Italy compare with that of other European countries?
5. Describe polenta, risotto, and pasta, including from which grain each is made and in which areas of Italy each of these is commonly served.
6. Explain the courses served at a typical Italian midday meal, and give examples of dishes for each course.

## >> Glossary

**al dente** Literally, "to the tooth," meaning cooked until done but still crisp

**antipasto** An assorted appetizer platter usually containing salami, cheese, olives, and grilled vegetables

**bacala** Salted codfish

**brodetto** Fish soup resembling the French *bouillabaise*

**Campari** Bitter red liqueur served as an aperitif from the region of Lombardy

**cannellini** White kidney beans

**capers** Bud from a shrub that grows in Mediterranean areas; usually preserved by pickling or salting

**frito misto di mare** Assorted deep-fried fish and seafood

**gnocchi** Potato and flour dumpling served in northern Italy; served with a sauce, like pasta

**grappa** Clear-colored, sharp-tasting brandy

**gremolada** Aromatic ingredients, including lemon zest, parsley, rosemary, sage, and garlic, which are added to braised veal shanks (*ossobuco*) a few minutes before serving

**marinara** A tomato-based sauce containing no meat

**minestrone** Italian vegetable soup

**ossobuco** Braised veal shanks

**pancetta** Unsmoked pork used for flavoring

**pasta e fagioli** Tomato-based soup containing pasta and beans

**pesto** Basil-garlic sauce served with pasta and in other dishes; originated in the city of Genoa

**polenta** Starch made of cornmeal that sometimes replaces pasta in the north of Italy

**primo piatto** Literally "first course," this usually consists of soup, pasta, rice, or polenta and is followed by the meat course

**prosciutto** Salted, air-cured ham

**ragu** A tomato-based sauce containing meat

**risotto** Creamy rice dish popular in the north of Italy

**saltimbocca** Dish consisting of pounded veal with a thin slice of *prosciutto*, seasoned and braised in white wine

**Sambuca** Clear, anise-flavored liqueur served as an after-dinner cordial

**zabaglione** Dessert sauce containing eggs, sugar, and Marsala wine

## SCAROLA CON FABIOLI (SOUTHERN ITALY)

### ESCAROLE GREENS AND BEANS

**TWIST ON THE CLASSIC**

To change this first course into an entrée with zip, add cooked rotini (or shape of choice) and some red pepper flakes to the beans and greens. If desired, also add sautéed hot or sweet Italian sausage, salami cut in julienne, or pieces of prosciutto. Top with plenty of grated Parmesan cheese.

**Note:** Wash the leaves carefully to remove all the sand and grit.

This dish originated in southern Italy as peasant food. They combined any type of bitter greens with beans and sometimes some scraps of prosciutto for flavoring.

**Number of Servings:** 10
**Serving Size:** 7 oz. (199 g)
**Total Yield:** 4 lb., 9 oz. (2.2 kg)
**Food Balance:** Protein
**Wine Style:** Light- to medium-bodied Pinot Grigio, Sauvignon Blanc, Grenache, Pinot Noir, or mild Chianti
**Example:** Castello di Gabbiano Pinot Grigio or Chianti, Meridian Vineyards Sauvignon Blanc or Pinot Noir

**Cooking Method:** Boil, sauté

| | WEIGHT | | VOLUME | |
|---|---|---|---|---|
| INGREDIENTS | U.S. | METRIC | U.S. | METRIC |
| escarole | 2 lb., 10 oz. | 1.2 kg | 2 large heads | |
| olive oil | | 28 g | 2 tablespoons | 30 mL |
| garlic, pulverized | 2 1/2 oz. | 71 g | 12 cloves | |
| salt | 1/4 oz. | 8 g | 1 teaspoon | 5 mL |
| pepper | | | 1/2 teaspoon | 3 mL |
| white beans (*cannellini*), cooked or canned | 1 lb., 14 oz. | 851 g | 4 cups | 960 mL |
| Parmesan cheese, grated | | | to taste | |

1. Cut off bottom of escarole and discard, separate leaves. Wash well, removing dirt from ribs.
2. Slice in pieces across ribs, add to pot containing a few inches of boiling water.
3. Parboil stirring often, until tender, a few minutes.
4. Meanwhile, heat oil in large skillet or braising pan over medium heat. Sauté garlic, do not let it brown.
5. Remove greens from pot using spoon so some cooking liquid comes with them, add greens to skillet.
6. Sauté a few minutes, add salt and pepper. Sauté a few minutes more.
7. Add beans and cook until hot.
8. Correct seasonings. Serve sprinkled generously with grated Parmesan cheese.

# CALAMARI FRITTI (VENETO)

## FRIED SQUID

**Note:** The key to tender calamari is not to cook them too long. Fry only 2 to 4 minutes, until they are light golden. If overcooked, they become tough and rubbery.

**Note:** While marinara sauce usually accompanies fried calamari served in the United States, Italians sprinkle the calamari with salt and squeeze lemon juice over it.

**Note:** Recipes for calamari fritti differ in various areas of Italy.

**Number of Servings:** 12
**Serving Size:** 4 oz. (114 g)
**Total Yield:** 3 lb., 3/4 oz. (1.5 kg)
**Food Balance:** Protein/salt balance
**Wine Style:** Wine friendly—What are you in the mood for?
**Example:** Castello di Gabbiano Pinot Grigio or Chianti

**Cooking Method:** Deep-fry

| INGREDIENTS | WEIGHT | | VOLUME | |
| --- | --- | --- | --- | --- |
| | U.S. | METRIC | U.S. | METRIC |
| squid, body and tentacles, cleaned | 3 lb., 14 1/2 oz. | 1.9 kg | | |
| flour | 1 lb., 1 oz. | 482 g | 4 cups | 960 mL |
| salt | 1 oz. | 28 g | 1 tablespoon + 1 teaspoon | 20 mL |
| pepper | 1/4 oz. | 8 g | 2 teaspoons | 10 mL |
| paprika | 1/2 oz. | 15 g | 1 tablespoon + 1 teaspoon | 20 mL |
| vegetable oil | | | as needed | |
| salt | | | for sprinkling | |

**Garnish:**
lemon wedges

1. Cut squid body into 1/2-inch (1.3-cm) rings. (The body is round, so slicing it produces rings.) If tentacles are too large, cut in half. Refrigerate until needed. Mix flour, salt, pepper, and paprika in bowl.
2. Place absorbent paper on sheet pan, and preheat oven to 250 degrees (120°C) for warming if needed (for holding fried squid before service).
3. Place squid pieces in flour, mix to coat thoroughly. Remove from flour and place on another sheet pan until ready to fry.
4. Place about 2 inches (5 cm) of oil in pan or use deep-fryer. Heat oil to 375 degrees (190°C).
5. Add squid to hot oil in batches. (Be careful not to fry too many at once so the temperature of oil stays constant.) Fry for 2 to 4 minutes, until light golden. Be careful: Overcooking yields tough calamari.
6. Remove from oil. Drain well on absorbent paper or in hanging fryer basket.
7. Serve immediately, sprinkled with salt and accompanied by lemon wedges.

In Italy, ordinary olive oil, not extra virgin olive oil, probably would be used for frying the *calamari*. Because olive oil has a lower smoking point than many other vegetable oils, canola or vegetable oil is recommended for deep-frying.

### TO CLEAN SQUID

Grasp the body while pulling the head and tentacles. When the head pulls away, the insides will come with it. Discard head and insides. Slice the tentacles above the eyes. Remove the ink bladder. (Cleaning the squid well removes the ink bladder, bone, eyes, and yellow liquid from the head.) Cut pointed end of sac and thoroughly rinse the body with water to remove all sand and dirt.

*Cutting calamari into strips*
Clive Streeter and Patrick McLeavy
© Dorling Kindersley

Ramon Grosso Dolarea © Shutterstock

# PASTA E FAGIOLI (THROUGHOUT ITALY)

## PASTA AND BEAN SOUP

David Munns © Dorling Kindersley

**Note:** Begin preparation for this dish the night before to allow time for the beans to soak.

**Note:** This soup appears in countless variations all over Italy. Some recipes use no tomato; others add cut up tomatoes or tomato paste. Traditionally a very thick soup, some people mash a few of the beans to thicken it while others cook the pasta in the soup so the starch from the pasta acts as a thickener.

**Number of Servings:** 15

**Serving Size:** 8 oz. (227 g)

**Total Yield:** 7 lb., 15 oz. (3.6 kg)

**Food Balance:** Protein

**Wine Style:** Light- to medium-bodied Pinot Blanc, mild Chardonnay, Pinot Noir, or mild Shiraz

**Example:** Stone Cellars Chardonnay or Shiraz

**Cooking Method:** Boil

| INGREDIENTS | WEIGHT U.S. | METRIC | VOLUME U.S. | METRIC |
|---|---|---|---|---|
| white kidney beans (*cannellini*), dried | 15 oz. | 426 g | 2 cups | 480 mL |
| *prosciutto*, minced | 6 oz. | 171 g | | |
| onion, small dice | 8 oz. | 227 g | 2 medium | |
| celery, small dice | 4 1/2 oz. | 128 g | 2 stalks | |
| carrot, small dice | 6 oz. | 171 g | 2 large | |
| garlic, minced | 1/2 oz. | 15 g | 4 cloves | |
| potato, white, waxy, or all-purpose, peeled and cut into small dice | 8 oz. | 227 g | 2 small | |
| tomato paste | 1 1/2 oz. | 43 g | 2 tablespoons | 30 mL |
| bay leaf | | | 1 each | |
| salt (omit if using salty stock) | to taste | | 1 1/2 teaspoons or to taste | 8 mL or to taste |
| pepper | | | 1 teaspoon | 5 mL |
| chicken or beef stock or water | as needed | | | |
| dry pasta, small shape like ditalini | 10 oz. | 284 g | 2 cups | 480 mL |
| Parmesan cheese, grated | | | | |

1. Wash beans well, cover with water, soak overnight in refrigerator. If time is limited, add beans to pot of boiling water, turn off heat and let beans soak 1 or 2 hours before proceeding.

2. Drain beans, cover with fresh water, add *prosciutto*, onion, celery, carrot, garlic, potato, tomato paste, and bay leaf. Simmer until tender, about 2 hours.

3. Add salt, pepper, and stock or water, adding enough liquid to cook pasta.

4. Bring to boil, add pasta, cook until pasta is *al dente*. Correct seasonings and add more liquid if too thick.

5. Serve accompanied by Parmesan cheese.

# MINESTRA DI ORZO (TRENTINO)

## BARLEY SOUP

**Note:** If enlarging the recipe, realize that this recipe makes almost 9 servings.

**Number of Servings:** 8
**Serving Size:** 8 oz. (227 g)
**Total Yield:** 4 lb., 6 1/2 oz. (2 kg)
**Food Balance:** Protein/salt balanced
**Wine Style:** Wine friendly—Full-bodied wines, too
**Example:** Château St. Jean Robert Young Chardonnay, St.Clement Merlot

**Cooking Method:** Boil

Monkey Business/Fotolia, LLC–Royalty Free

| INGREDIENTS | WEIGHT U.S. | METRIC | VOLUME U.S. | METRIC |
|---|---|---|---|---|
| smoked ham hock, ham bone, or shank bone from *prosciutto* | 10 oz. | 284 g | 1 each | |
| bay leaves | | | 2 each | |
| beef stock or water | as needed | | | |
| onion, small dice | 7 1/2 oz. | 213 g | 1 large | |
| celery, small dice | 5 1/2 oz. | 156 g | 2 stalks | |
| carrots, small dice | 3 1/2 oz. | 104 g | 2 each | |
| garlic, minced | 1/4 oz. | 8 g | 2 cloves | |
| potatoes, white, waxy, or all-purpose, peeled and cut into medium dice | 12 1/2 oz. | 355 g | 3 small | |
| pepper | | | 1/2 teaspoon | 3 mL |
| barley | 4 oz. | 114 g | 1/2 cup | 120 mL |

**Garnish:**
fresh parsley, minced
Parmesan cheese, grated

1. Place ham hock and bay leaves in large pot. Cover with beef stock or water to several inches above bone.
2. Bring to boil, reduce heat, cover, and simmer for 1 or 2 hours to extract flavor from bone. Add more liquid as needed.
3. Remove ham hock from liquid. When cool enough to handle, remove meat and cut into small pieces. Return meat to pot of liquid. Discard bone.
4. Add onion, celery, carrots, garlic, potatoes, pepper, and barley to pot. Simmer another hour or so, until barley is puffed and tender. Again, add liquid as needed to keep soup proper thickness.
5. Correct seasonings. Depending on the saltiness of the ham hock or bone, salt is probably not needed. Serve, garnished with parsley and grated Parmesan cheese.

**TWIST ON THE CLASSIC**

Spice it up by adding minced hot peppers when cooking the soup or red pepper flakes to the finished soup.

This soup appears in northern Italy in the mountainous areas, particularly in the region of Trentino. Lots of barley grows in this region, and they cure meats there. Many refer to soups like this as peasant food because the ingredients are plentiful and cheap in the area. Although this recipe includes just a small amount of meat, the meat functions as an important flavoring.

# PANZANELLA (TUSCANY)

## BREAD SALAD

**Note:** Use stale Italian or French bread for this salad.

**Number of Servings:** 11
**Serving Size:** 5 oz. (142 g)
**Total Yield:** 3 lb., 10 oz. (1.6 kg)

| | WEIGHT | | VOLUME | |
|---|---|---|---|---|
| **INGREDIENTS** | **U.S.** | **METRIC** | **U.S.** | **METRIC** |
| crusty white bread, medium dice | 8 oz. | 227 g | | |
| red wine vinegar | | 71 g | 1/4 cup + 1 tablespoon | 75 mL |
| cold water | | 28 g | 2 tablespoons | 30 mL |
| ripe tomatoes, large dice | 1 lb. | 454 g | 6 small | |
| red onion, minced | 4 oz. | 114 g | 1 small | |
| cucumber, peeled and diced | 6 oz. | 171 g | 1/2 each | |
| celery, diced | 4 1/2 oz. | 128 g | 2 stalks | |
| fresh basil, shredded | 1/4 oz. | 8 g | 10 leaves | |
| salt | 1/4 oz. | 8 g | 1 teaspoon | 5 mL |
| pepper | | | 1/2 teaspoon | 3 mL |
| olive oil | | 86 g | 1/4 cup + 2 tablespoons | 90 mL |

1. Place bread in bowl, mix vinegar and water, sprinkle over bread.
2. Depending on how stale the bread is, sprinkle more water, if needed, to moisten lightly. Set aside for 30 minutes.
3. Add tomatoes, onion, cucumber, celery, basil, salt, and pepper to bread, mix gently.
4. Sprinkle oil over, mixing well, correct seasonings. Refrigerate for at least 30 minutes before serving.

Pearson Education/PH College

# INSALATA di ARANCE, FINOCCHIO, e CIPOLLE (SOUTHERN ITALY)

## SALAD WITH ORANGES, FENNEL, AND ONION

**Number of Servings:** 13
**Serving Size:** 1/2 oz. (14 g) or 1 1/2 cups (360 mL) spring mix
 2 1/4 oz. (64 g) fennel/orange mixture
 1 oz. (28 g) vinaigrette
**Total Yield:** 6 1/2 oz. (184 g) spring mix
 1 lb., 13 1/2 oz. (837 g) fennel/orange mixture
 16 oz. (454 g) or 2 cups (480 mL) vinaigrette

© sarsmis

| INGREDIENTS | WEIGHT | | VOLUME | |
| --- | --- | --- | --- | --- |
| | U.S. | METRIC | U.S. | METRIC |
| oranges, navel, blood oranges, or variety of choice | 2 lb., 10 1/2 oz. | 1.2 kg | 6 medium | |
| fennel, thinly sliced or julienne | 14 oz. | 397 g | 2 small to medium | |
| red onion, thinly sliced | 4 oz. | 114 g | 1 small | |
| **Vinaigrette:** | | | | |
| orange juice | | 114 g | 1/2 cup | 120 mL |
| balsamic vinegar | | 57 g | 1/4 cup | 60 mL |
| salt | 1/4 oz. | 8 g | 1 teaspoon | 5 mL |
| pepper | | | 1/4 teaspoon | 2 mL |
| olive oil | | 284 g | 1 1/4 cups | 300 mL |
| lettuce, spring mix, arugula, or variety of choice | 6 1/2 oz. weight depends on variety used | 184 g | 19 1/2 cups | 4.7 L |
| **Garnish:** | | | | |
| Parmesan cheese, shaved strips or grated | 2 1/2 oz. | 71 g | 1/2 cup | 120 mL |

1. Place bowl on counter to catch juices from oranges while cutting. With sharp paring knife, peel oranges, removing rind and pith. To remove membrane, cut on each side of membrane, staying as close to the membrane as possible. Discard peel and membrane, reserve orange sections.
2. Place fennel, onion, and orange sections in a bowl. Refrigerate until needed.
3. Place orange juice, vinegar, salt, and pepper in a bowl of food processor fitted with knife blade. Process to mix. With processor running, slowly pour olive oil through feed tube. Process until emulsified, thickened. Correct seasonings.
4. Pour a little vinaigrette (about 3 oz. [86 g] or 1/4 cup + 2 tablespoons [90 mL]) over fennel/orange mixture. Place lettuce in mixing bowl, pour enough vinaigrette over greens to lightly coat (about 13 oz. [369 g] or 1 + 2/3 cups [400 mL] vinaigrette).
5. Place lettuce portion on chilled plate. Top with fennel/orange mixture. Garnish with Parmesan cheese. Serve.

# INSALATA DI PATATE CON CAPPERI E OLIVE

## POTATO SALAD WITH CAPERS AND OLIVES

**Number of Servings:** 14
**Serving Size:** 5 oz. (142 g)
**Total Yield:** 4 lb., 8 1/2 oz. (2.1 kg)

**Cooking Method:** Boil

| | WEIGHT | | VOLUME | |
|---|---|---|---|---|
| *INGREDIENTS* | *U.S.* | *METRIC* | *U.S.* | *METRIC* |
| red potatoes | 4 lb. | 1.8 kg | | |
| garlic, smashed and minced | 1/2 oz. | 15 g | 6 cloves | |
| fresh parsley, minced | 1 oz. | 28 g | 1/2 cup | 120 mL |
| capers, drained | 2 oz. | 57 g | 1/4 cup | 60 mL |
| Italian olives, pitted and chopped | 6 oz. | 171 g | 1 cup | 240 mL |
| anchovies, minced | 1 oz. | 28 g | 1 tablespoon + 1 teaspoon | 20 mL |
| red or white wine vinegar | | 114 g | 1/2 cup | 120 mL |
| olive oil | | 114 g | 1/2 cup | 120 mL |
| salt | as needed | | | |
| pepper | as needed | | | |

**Garnish:**

fresh parsley, minced

1. Put potatoes in large pot, cover with water. Cook until done yet still firm; time will depend on size of potatoes.
2. Meanwhile, place garlic, parsley, capers, olives, anchovies, vinegar, and olive oil in bowl. Whisk to combine, set aside until needed.
3. As soon as potatoes are done, drain them and cool until can be handled. Peel hot potatoes, cut into 3/4-inch (2-cm) dice. Place in large bowl.
4. Add olive mixture, salt, and pepper, stir gently with rubber spatula to combine well. Cover, allow to marinate at least 30 minutes before serving.
5. Correct seasonings. Sprinkle with parsley and serve at room temperature.

Ekaterina Nikitina © Shutterstock

Courtesy of the Idaho Potato Commission

# RAVIOLI DI MELANZANE E POMODORI
## RAVIOLI FILLED WITH EGGPLANT AND TOMATO

**Note:** Serve as an appetizer or an entrée.

**Number of Servings:** 9  **Cooking Method:** Boil
**Serving Size:** Four 2-inch (5-cm) raviolis
**Total Yield:** 1 lb., 9 oz. (710 g) pasta dough
  1 lb., 11 oz. (762 g) filling
**Food Balance:** Protein
**Wine Style:** Light- to medium-bodied Pinot Gris, Viognier, Gewürztraminer, or blush, and fruity reds, such as Grenache, Dolcetto, Pinot Noir, Zinfandel
**Example:** Beringer Gewürztraminer or Viognier, Beringer Founders' Estate Zinfandel

| INGREDIENTS | WEIGHT | | VOLUME | |
|---|---|---|---|---|
| | U.S. | METRIC | U.S. | METRIC |
| **Pasta:** | | | | |
| all-purpose flour | 13 oz. | 369 g | 2 3/4 cups | 660 mL |
| semolina flour | 3 oz. | 86 g | 1/2 cup | 120 mL |
| eggs | 8 1/2 to 10 oz. | 241 to 284 g | 5 or 6 each | |
| **Filling:** | | | | |
| eggplant, peeled and diced | 1 lb., 1 oz. | 482 g | 1 each | |
| salt | 1/2 oz. | 15 g | 2 teaspoons | 10 mL |
| sun-dried tomatoes, diced | 1 1/4 oz. | 36 g | 1/2 cup | 120 mL |
| olive oil | | 43 g | 3 tablespoons | 45 mL |
| onions, finely diced | 6 oz. | 171 g | 1 large | |
| garlic, minced | 1/2 oz. | 15 g | 4 cloves | |
| tomatoes, ripe or canned, peeled and diced | 8 oz. | 227 g | 4 plum | |
| pepper | | | 1/8 teaspoon | 1 mL |
| fresh parsley, minced | 1/2 oz. | 15 g | 1/4 cup | 60 mL |
| fresh basil, minced | 1/2 oz. | 15 g | 1/4 cup | 60 mL |
| Parmesan cheese, grated | 2 1/4 oz. | 64 g | 1/2 cup | 120 mL |

**Garnish:**

sauce of choice—light tomato sauce, garlic-herb olive oil, or as desired
Parmesan cheese, grated

*Stirring egg into dry ingredients*
Pearson Education/PH College

*Kneading pasta dough*
Pearson Education/PH College

## PREPARATION:

1. Place eggplant in colander, sprinkle with salt, let sit 30 to 60 minutes. Set colander in sink or on plate to catch liquid.
2. Place sun-dried tomatoes in bowl, cover with warm water, let sit at least 30 minutes.

## PASTA:

1. Place both flours in bowl, form a well in center. Add eggs. Mix with fork until well combined.
2. Knead dough on table until smooth, add more flour if too wet or a little water if too dry.
3. Cover with plastic wrap, let rest 30 minutes.

*Rolling pasta dough through pasta machine*
Pearson Education/PH College

*Pressing dough around filling to seal*
Pearson Education/PH College

## FILLING:

1. Rinse eggplant with water, dry. Drain sun-dried tomatoes, chop.
2. Heat olive oil in skillet over medium-high heat, add onions, sauté until lightly browned.
3. Add garlic and eggplant, sauté over high heat for about 5 minutes.
4. Add canned or ripe tomatoes and sun-dried tomatos, cook over low heat until mixture breaks down, about 5 minutes.
5. Remove from skillet, add pepper, parsley, basil, and Parmesan. Stir to combine, correct seasonings.

## ASSEMBLY:

1. Divide pasta dough into 6 pieces.
2. Roll one piece at a time through pasta machine to form thin sheet, place on lightly floured table.
3. Place 1 teaspoon (5 mL) filling on dough, spaced at regular intervals (1 1/2 to 2 inches [4 to 5 cm] apart) to form raviolis.
4. Wet finger and make line of water around edges of dough and between mounds (wherever top sheet of dough will meet bottom dough). Cover with second sheet of dough, press between mounds of filling with handle of dough cutter or hand to seal well and mark squares.
5. Cut out squares, seal edges with tines of fork or crimper.
6. Place prepared ravioli on lightly floured pan.
7. Refrigerate or freeze until ready to cook and serve.

## COOKING RAVIOLI:

1. Add ravioli to pot of boiling water.
2. Cook until *al dente*, about 10 minutes. Serve immediately or shock (rinse with cold water to stop cooking) for later use. If cooking for later service, undercook pasta because it will cook more when reheated later.
3. Serve accompanied by sauce of choice and grated Parmesan cheese.

*Ravioli ready to boil.*
© Joe Gough

*Ravioli with tomato sauce—finished plate*
© Monkey Business

*Ravioli with herbs and oil—finished plate*
© FomaA

# PIZZA DOUGH

**Note:** From appetizer to dessert, pizza dough offers unlimited possibilities.

**Note:** Can be prepared one day ahead and refrigerated. Also, this dough freezes well. Freeze in balls of an appropriate size.

**Total Yield:** 6 lb., 6 oz. (2.9 kg)
**Scaling:** about 1 lb., 7 oz. (653 g) for half sheet pan

*Kneading pizza dough*
© vladi59

| INGREDIENTS | WEIGHT | | VOLUME | |
|---|---|---|---|---|
| | U.S. | METRIC | U.S. | METRIC |
| warm water | | 850 g | 3 cups + 3/4 cup | 900 mL |
| sugar | 1 1/4 oz. | 36 g | 3 tablespoons | 45 mL |
| granulated yeast | 1 oz. | 28 g | 2 tablespoons + 1 teaspoon | 35 mL |
| all-purpose flour | 3 lb., 3 1/2 oz. | 1.5 kg | 12 cups | 2.9 L |
| semolina flour | 8 3/4 oz. | 248 g | 1 1/2 cups | 360 mL |
| salt | 2 oz. | 57 g | 3 tablespoons | 45 mL |
| olive oil | | 86 g | 1/4 cup + 2 tablespoons | 90 mL |

1. Place 3/4 cup (180 mL) of warm water in nonreactive bowl. Add sugar and yeast, stir to dissolve with wooden spoon or plastic spatula. Let stand until foamy, about 5 minutes.
2. In large bowl, mix 7 1/2 cups (1.8 L) of flour, semolina, and salt.
3. Using a wooden spoon, gradually mix remaining 3 cups (720 mL) water in with flour mixture. Add oil, stir until well blended, about 2 minutes.
4. Fold in yeast mixture with rubber spatula. Stir in remaining 4 1/2 cups (1.1 L) flour, adding as much as needed.
5. Knead on lightly floured surface until smooth and elastic, about 10 minutes. Add more flour if sticking.
6. Place dough in bowl, smooth side up. Cover with plastic wrap, allowing room to double. Let rise in warm area until doubled, about 1 hour.
7. Punch dough down. Refrigerate, well covered with plastic wrap, until ready to use. Allow to rest 20 minutes at room temperature, punch down dough.
8. Roll into pizza crust of desired thickness.

*Punching down risen dough*
Pearson Education/PH College

*Rolling pizza dough*
© schankz

**TWIST ON THE CLASSIC**

Substitute part or all of the white flour with whole wheat.

# PESTO (LIGURIA)
## BASIL AND GARLIC SAUCE

**Note:** Traditionally, pesto is served as a coating for pasta. After draining the cooked hot pasta, stir the pesto into it. Reheat if needed.

**Note:** Many cooks now incorporate pesto into many dishes, using it as a flavoring for chicken, a spread on canapés, or whatever the imagination creates.

**Serving Size:** 8 oz. (227 g) or 1 cup (240 mL) pesto for 1 lb. (454 g) dry pasta
**Total Yield:** 10 oz. (284 g) or 1 1/4 cups (300 mL)
**Food Balance:** Protein
**Wine Style:** Light- to medium-bodied Orvieto or Verdicchio, Sauvignon Blanc, Chenin Blanc, or blush, and mild reds, such as Beaujolais, Grenache, Shiraz, or Merlot
**Example:** Meridian Sauvignon Blanc or Syrah

| INGREDIENTS | WEIGHT U.S. | WEIGHT METRIC | VOLUME U.S. | VOLUME METRIC |
|---|---|---|---|---|
| fresh basil leaves | 3 1/4 oz. | 92 g | 2 cups, firmly packed | 480 mL |
| salt | 1/4 oz. | 8 g | 1 teaspoon | 5 mL |
| garlic, smashed and minced | 1/4 oz. | 8 g | 2 cloves | |
| pine nuts | 3/4 oz. | 22 g | 2 tablespoons | 30 mL |
| olive oil | | 114 g | 1/2 cup | 120 mL |
| Parmesan cheese | 2 1/2 oz. | 71 g | 1/2 cup | 120 mL |

1. Wash basil leaves and dry.
2. Place basil, salt, garlic, pine nuts, and olive oil in bowl of food processor fitted with knife blade, process until smooth paste, stopping to scrape sides if necessary.
3. Add Parmesan cheese and pulse just to mix.

*Pesto ingredients in food processor*
Pearson Education/PH College

*Finished pesto in food processor*
Pearson Education/PH College

*Pesto (basil and garlic sauce) on pasta*
Piotr Rzeszutek © Shutterstock

*Bowl of pesto*
© Dani Vincek

## PASTA ALLE OLIVE (UMBRIA)

### PASTA WITH OLIVE AND MUSHROOM SAUCE

**Serving Size:** Use 11 oz. (308 g) of the sauce for 1 lb. (454 g) pasta

**Cooking Method:** Sauté

**Total Yield:** 11 oz. (308 g) sauce
**Food Balance:** Protein/salt balanced
**Wine Style:** Light- to medium-bodied Johannesburg Riesling, Sauvignon Blanc, Pinot Grigio, mild Chardonnay, Pinot Noir, or Merlot
**Example:** Beringer Sauvignon Blanc or Red Alluvium (rich Merlot)

© Morenovel

| INGREDIENTS | WEIGHT | | VOLUME | |
|---|---|---|---|---|
| | U.S. | METRIC | U.S. | METRIC |
| olive oil | | 15 g | 1 tablespoon | 15 mL |
| mushrooms, any variety, thinly sliced | 8 oz. | 227 g | | |
| garlic, smashed and minced | | | 1 clove | |
| black olives, Greek or Italian variety, pitted and chopped | 6 oz. | 171 g | 1 1/4 cups | 300 mL |
| fresh parsley, minced | 1/2 oz. | 15 g | 3 tablespoons | 45 mL |
| cayenne | | | 1/4 teaspoon | 2 mL |
| dry pasta | 1 lb. | 454 g | | |
| water or mushroom stock, to thin | as needed | | | |

**Garnish:**

Parmesan cheese, grated
heavy cream, whipped

> **TWIST ON THE CLASSIC**
>
> Add artichoke hearts and *prosciutto* to the puréed olive and mushroom sauce just before tossing with the pasta.

1. Heat oil in skillet over medium-high heat, add mushrooms, sauté until tender, remove from heat.
2. Place mushrooms, garlic, olives, parsley, and cayenne in bowl of food processor fitted with knife blade, process into paste.
3. Cook pasta until *al dente.*
4. Transfer sauce from food processor to saucepan, heat. If needed, add water or stock to thin sauce until coating consistency.
5. Mix sauce with pasta, toss well, correct seasonings.
6. Serve accompanied by Parmesan cheese and a dollop of whipped cream.

## BRACIOLE AL RAGÙ (SOUTHERN ITALY)

### STUFFED MEAT ROLLS IN SAUCE

**Number of Servings:** 14
**Serving Size:** 7 oz. (199 g)
**Total Yield:** 11 lb., 4 1/2 oz. (5.1 kg) (meat rolls and sauce)
**Cooked meat rolls:** 6 lb., 2 oz. (2.8 kg)
**Filling:** 1 lb., 7 1/2 oz. (667 g)
**Wine Style:** Chardonnay with a few years bottle aging would pair very well with this dish.
**Example:** Chardonnay "Gloria" 2010, Kollwentz (Neusiedlersee/Austria)

**Cooking Method:** Sauté, braise

© Mi.Ti.

| INGREDIENTS | WEIGHT | | VOLUME | |
|---|---|---|---|---|
| | U.S. | METRIC | U.S. | METRIC |
| breadcrumbs, dried | 5 oz. | 142 g | 1 cup | 240 mL |
| pecorino cheese, grated | 8 oz. | 227 g | 1 1/2 cups | 360 mL |
| garlic, peeled, minced, smashed | 1/2 oz. | 15 g | 4 cloves | |
| parsley, minced | 2 oz. | 57 g | 1 cup | 240 mL |
| pine nuts | 3 oz. | 86 g | 1/2 cup | 120 mL |
| raisins | 4 oz. | 114 g | 2/3 cup | 160 mL |
| salt | 1/4 oz. | 8 g | 1 teaspoon | 5 mL |
| pepper | | | 1/4 teaspoon | 2 mL |
| beef round roast, trimmed of all fat | 5 lb. | 2.3 kg | | |
| salt | as needed | | | |
| pepper | as needed | | | |
| olive oil | as needed for frying | | | |
| onion, medium dice | 11 oz. | 308 g | 2 medium | |
| garlic, peeled, minced, smashed | 1/4 oz. | 8 g | 2 cloves | |
| red wine | | 454 g | 2 cups | 480 mL |
| tomatoes, canned | 4 lb. | 1.8 kg | 1 quart + 3 cups or 7 cups | 1.7 L |
| tomato paste | 4 oz. | 114 g | 1/4 cup + 2 tablespoons or 6 tablespoons | 90 mL |

**Garnish:**

rosemary sprig or minced
parsley

- In the typical course sequence of Italian meals, the first course is pasta with the red sauce in which the meat rolls cooked. The second course consists of the meat rolls.
- Some place a slice of prosciutto on the pounded beef before spreading the filling.
- Cooks in southern Italy often prepare this dish for the Sunday meal; however, the pot of red sauce might contain a variety of meats including *braciole* (meat rolls), meatballs, and/or sausages.

1. Mix breadcrumbs, pecorino, garlic (1/2 oz. [15 g], 4 cloves), parsley, pine nuts, raisins, salt (1 teaspoon [5 mL]), and pepper (1/4 teaspoon [2 mL]) together in a bowl. Set aside until needed.
2. Slice beef into 1/2-inch (1.3-cm) slices. Place slice between two pieces of film wrap and pound with meat mallet until thin, about 1/4-inch (0.5-cm) thick. Repeat with remaining meat slices. Season each slice with a sprinkling of salt and pepper.
3. Divide reserved breadcrumb mixture evenly among beef slices (about 1 oz. [28 g] filling). Spread filling over meat leaving a 1-inch (2.5-cm) border at the side that will roll last. Fold in sides and roll tightly in jellyroll fashion. Tie each roll with butcher twine or secure with toothpicks.
4. Cover bottom of skillet with olive oil. Heat over medium heat until hot, add meat rolls, and brown all sides. Add more oil as needed. Remove meat rolls from skillet.
5. Add oil so bottom of skillet is coated, heat over medium heat until hot. Add onion, cook 2 minutes. Add garlic, cook another minute. Add wine, bring to boil.
6. Add tomatoes and tomato paste, stir to combine. Add meat rolls, reduce heat to simmer, cover and cook 2 hours on cooktop (or in oven at 325 degrees [160°C]) until tender. Occasionally, gently move meat rolls so they do not stick to pan. If needed, add more wine or water so the sauce covers the meat rolls. Correct seasonings.
7. Remove meat rolls from sauce. Remove twine or toothpicks. Slice on the diagonal into 1/2-inch (1.3-cm) pieces. Serve with some sauce, garnished with rosemary or parsley.

# OSSOBUCO ALLA MILANESE (LOMBARDY)

## BRAISED VEAL SHANKS

**Note:** Traditional recipes for ossobuco call for the addition of gremolada at the end of cooking the veal shanks. The aromatic ingredients that make up gremolada are the same as those used in this recipe as "Gremolada Seasoning." The gremolada is added at the end, and the dish continues to cook until just heated. Some people serve ossobuco with a garnish of gremolada on top. If desired, prepare extra gremolada for this purpose.

**Number of Servings:** 8

**Serving Size:** 1 shank piece

**Total Yield:** 8 lb., 4 oz. (3.7 kg)

**Food Balance:** Protein/acid balanced

**Wine Style:** Wide variety, very balanced, enjoy the wine of your choice

**Example:** Château Souverain Sauvignon Blanc or Zinfandel

**Cooking Method:** Braise

### TWIST ON THE CLASSIC

Remove meat from the bones, mix with the sauce and use the *ossobuco ragu* (sauce) to top pasta or *gnocchi.*

*Browning veal shanks*

David Murray and Jules Selmes © Dorling Kindersley

| INGREDIENTS | WEIGHT | | VOLUME | |
| --- | --- | --- | --- | --- |
| | U.S. | METRIC | U.S. | METRIC |
| **Gremolada Seasonings:** | | | | |
| fresh parsley, minced | 1 oz. | 28 g | 1/4 cup + 2 tablespoons | 90 mL |
| rosemary | 1/4 oz. | 8 g | 2 teaspoons | 10 mL |
| sage | | | 2 teaspoons | 10 mL |
| garlic, smashed and minced | 1/4 oz. | 8 g | 2 cloves | |
| lemon zest, grated | 1/2 oz. | 15 g | 2 tablespoons | 30 mL |
| veal shanks, about 2-inches (5-cm) thick, washed | about 8 lb. | 3.6 kg | 8 each | |
| flour, for dredging | as needed | | | |
| butter | 3 oz. | 86 g | 6 tablespoons | 90 mL |
| white wine | | 340 g | 1 1/2 cups | 360 mL |
| Italian plum tomatoes, fresh or canned, peeled and diced | 1 lb. | 454 g | 2 cups | 480 mL |
| pepper | | | 1/2 teaspoon | 3 mL |
| stock, veal or mixture of beef and chicken, to cover meat | | | about 2 1/2 quarts (10 cups) | 2.4 L |

*Adding stock to browned veal shanks*

David Murray and Jules Selmes © Dorling Kindersley

Pearson Education/PH College

1. Mix *gremolada* seasoning ingredients (parsley, rosemary, sage, garlic, and lemon zest) together in a small bowl, set aside.
2. Coat veal shanks with flour in another bowl.
3. Over medium heat, heat butter in pan large enough to hold all shanks in single layer (or divide into 2 pans), then brown meat in butter on both sides.
4. Add wine, simmer until almost evaporated, about 10 minutes.
5. Add tomatoes, pepper, reserved *gremolada* seasoning, and just enough stock to almost cover meat.
6. Cover and simmer for about 2 hours, stirring occasionally, until very tender (meat comes away from bone).
7. If sauce is not thick, remove meat and cook sauce over medium-high heat to reduce. Skim impurities and scum from surface, if necessary. Return meat to pan, correct seasonings.
8. Serve hot, accompanied by risotto or plain rice.

William Shaw © Dorling Kindersley

## BRACIOLA DI AGNELLO CON BALSAMICO E ROSMARINO (EMILIA-ROMAGNA)

### LAMB CHOPS WITH BALSAMIC VINEGAR AND ROSEMARY

msheldrake © Shutterstock

**Note:** It is very difficult to estimate the number of lamb chops in one portion or the exact weight. The size of the lamb chops will determine the portion size.

**Note:** Allow several hours or overnight to marinate the meat.

**Number of Servings:** 9
**Serving Size:** 8 oz. (227 g), about 3 lamb chops
**Total Yield:** 4 lb., 15 oz. (2.2 kg) meat, 8 oz. (227 g) or 1 cup (240 mL) sauce
**Food Balance:** Sweet and sour
**Wine Style:** Stronger wines, barrel fermented, and full bodied
**Example:** Sbragia Family Vineyards Chardonnay, Stags' Leap Petite Syrah

**Cooking Method:** Grill, boil

| | WEIGHT | | VOLUME | |
|---|---|---|---|---|
| **INGREDIENTS** | **U.S.** | **METRIC** | **U.S.** | **METRIC** |
| garlic, smashed and minced | 2 oz. | 57 g | 1/4 cup | 60 mL |
| fresh rosemary, minced | 1 oz. | 28 g | 1/4 cup + 2 tablespoons | 90 mL |
| salt | 1/2 oz. | 15 g | 2 teaspoons | 10 mL |
| pepper | 1/4 oz. | 8 g | 2 teaspoons | 10 mL |
| balsamic vinegar | | 305 g | 1 1/3 cups | 320 mL |
| red wine | | 227 g | 1 cup | 240 mL |
| olive oil | | 86 g | 1/4 cup + 2 tablespoons | 90 mL |
| lamb chops, loin, washed | 6 lb., 4 oz. | 2.8 kg | | |
| sugar | 1/2 oz. | 15 g | 1 tablespoon + 1 teaspoon | 20 mL |

**Garnish:**
fresh rosemary sprigs

1. In bowl, mix garlic, rosemary, salt, pepper, vinegar, and wine. Whisk in olive oil.
2. Place lamb chops in nonreactive dish. Pour vinegar and oil mixture over lamb. Cover and refrigerate several hours or overnight.
3. Preheat grill. Remove lamb from marinade. Transfer marinade to pan. Add sugar to marinade.
4. Bring marinade to boil, reduce marinade by half, until thickened to correct consistency to serve as sauce over lamb chops. (The more reduced the marinade, the stronger the flavor.) Correct seasonings.
5. While marinade reduces, grill lamb chops until desired internal temperature.
6. Serve with about 1 teaspoon (5 mL) sauce over each lamb chop. Garnish with rosemary sprig.

# ARISTA DI MAIALE (CENTRAL ITALY)

## ROASTED PORK LOIN

**Note:** Allow a few extra hours for marinating so the flavors permeate the meat.

**Note:** Since this recipe is a common one for preparing suckling pig, some call this recipe porcette, which means "suckling pig." Today, pork loin usually replaces the suckling pig, but the flavorful filling remains the same.

**Number of Servings:** 15

**Serving Size:** 5 oz. (142 g)

**Total Yield:** 4 lb., 12 oz. (2.2 kg) meat, 1 lb. 1/2 oz. sauce (2 cups [480 mL])

**Food Balance:** Balanced

**Wine Style:** Wine friendly

**Example:** Souverain Sauvignon blanc, Chardonnay, Merlot, Cabernet Sauvignon

**Cooking Method:** Bake

| INGREDIENTS | WEIGHT | | VOLUME | |
| --- | --- | --- | --- | --- |
| | U.S. | METRIC | U.S. | METRIC |
| **Filling:** | | | | |
| whole garlic cloves, peeled | 1 oz. | 28 g | 6 each | |
| fresh fennel, diced | 6 1/2 oz. | 184 g | 1 1/2 cups | 360 mL |
| fennel seeds | 1/4 oz. | 8 g | 1 teaspoon | 5 mL |
| fresh rosemary leaves | 1 oz. | 28 g | 1/4 cup + 2 tablespoons | 90 mL |
| dried thyme | 1/4 oz. | 8 g | 2 teaspoons | 10 mL |
| salt | 1/4 oz. | 8 g | 1 teaspoon | 5 mL |
| pepper | | | 1 teaspoon | 5 mL |
| olive oil | | 28 g | 2 tablespoons | 30 mL |
| boneless pork loin, center cut, trimmed and washed | 5 lb., 4 1/2 oz. | 2.4 kg | 1 or 2 pieces | |
| carrots, medium dice | 5 oz. | 142 g | 2 small or 1 cup | 240 mL |
| celery, medium dice | 4 oz. | 114 g | 2 stalks or 1 cup | 240 mL |
| onion, medium dice | 5 oz. | 142 g | 1 medium or 1 cup | 240 mL |
| chicken stock | | 454 g | 2 cups | 480 mL |
| white wine | | 227 g | 1 cup | 240 mL |

**Garnish:**

fresh rosemary sprigs

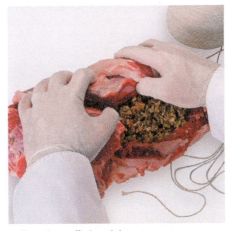

*Rolling the stuffed pork loin*

Pearson Education/PH College

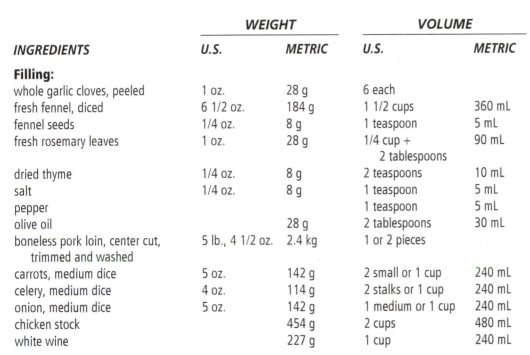

© Joe Gough

## ASSEMBLY:

1. With food processor fitted with knife blade running, drop garlic through feed tube. Pulse a few times, scrape sides of processor as needed.
2. Add fresh fennel, fennel seeds, rosemary, thyme, salt, and pepper. Pulse until finely chopped.
3. Add olive oil, pulse until chunky paste. Set filling aside until needed.
4. Butterfly pork loin by cutting through middle (on long side) and stopping about 1 inch (2.5 cm) from other side. Do not cut through the whole loin. Open meat by laying top half of meat away from bottom half.
5. Reserve 2 tablespoons (30 mL) of filling mixture. Spread remaining filling evenly over inside of meat. Fold top of meat over bottom to enclose filling. Tie meat with butcher twine to hold closed. Spread reserved filling over out-side of meat. Cover and refrigerate for several hours to marinate.

## COOK:

1. Preheat oven to 450 degrees (230°C). Place carrots, celery, and onion in bottom of roasting pan. Place pork loin on top of vegetables. Bake 15 minutes.

2. Reduce heat to 350 degrees (180°C). Add chicken stock and wine to pan. Bake about 40 to 45 minutes until proper internal temperature (about 155 degrees (70°C)—temperature will rise as the meat rests and the internal heat keeps cooking the meat). Remove meat from pan, cover, and keep warm.

3. Place vegetables and pan juices in bowl of food processor fitted with knife blade. Process until paste. Remove from processor and push through sieve placed over bowl, extracting as much liquid as possible. Discard remaining "vegetables" in sieve.

4. Correct sauce seasonings. Reheat if necessary.

5. Slice meat and serve with sauce. Garnish with a sprig of fresh rosemary.

---

# POLLO ALLA CACCIATORA (SOUTHERN ITALY)

## HUNTER STYLE CHICKEN

© Fanfo

**Number of Servings:** 8

**Serving Size:** 1/4 chicken

**Total Yield:** 9 lb., 12 oz. (4.4 kg)

**Food Balance:** Protein/acid

**Wine Style:** Light- to medium-bodied Johannesburg Riesling, blush, or Sauvignon Blanc, and mild reds, such as Grenache, Shiraz, or Zinfandel

**Example:** Beringer Founders' Estate Sauvignon Blanc or Zinfandel

**Cooking Method:** Braise

| | WEIGHT | | VOLUME | |
|---|---|---|---|---|
| **INGREDIENTS** | **U.S.** | **METRIC** | **U.S.** | **METRIC** |
| chicken, cut in quarters | about 6 lb. | 2.8 kg | 2 each | |
| flour, for dredging | 3 oz. | 86 g | 2/3 cup | 160 mL |
| olive oil | | 57 g | 1/4 cup | 60 mL |
| pancetta, diced | 6 oz. | 171 g | | |
| onion, diced | 14 oz. | 397 g | 2 large | |
| garlic, minced | 1 oz. | 28 g | 8 cloves | |
| mushrooms, button or any variety, sliced | 1 lb. | 454 g | | |
| dried rosemary | 1/4 oz. | 8 g | 2 teaspoons | 10 mL |
| dried marjoram | 1/4 oz. | 8 g | 2 teaspoons | 10 mL |
| dried sage | | | 1 teaspoon | 5 mL |
| bay leaves | | | 4 each | |
| salt | 1/2 oz. | 15 g | 2 teaspoons | 10 mL |
| pepper | | | 1 teaspoon | 5 mL |
| tomatoes, peeled and chopped | 2 lb. | 908 g | | |
| dry white wine | | 284 g | 1 1/4 cups | 300 mL |

1. Wash chicken, dredge with flour.

2. Heat oil in large pot over medium-high heat, sauté pancetta a couple of minutes. Add chicken pieces, sauté until starting to brown.

3. Add onion and garlic, sauté another couple minutes, until softened.

4. Add mushrooms, rosemary, marjoram, sage, bay leaves, salt, pepper, tomatoes, and wine.

5. Bring to gentle boil, turn down heat, cover, and simmer 25 minutes. Turn chicken over. Simmer until done, about 25 to 35 additional minutes.

6. If desired, remove cover for last 10 or 15 minutes for thicker sauce. Correct seasonings.

7. Serve immediately over rice or pasta.

# TONNO IN AGRODOLCE (SICILY)

## SWEET AND SOUR TUNA

**Note:** This dish originated in Sicily, where sweet-and-sour recipes are common.

**Number of Servings:** 9

**Serving Size:** 5 oz. (142 g)

**Total Yield:** 3 lb. (1.4 kg)

**Food Balance:** Acid/spicy

**Wine Style:** Wide variety—Gewürztraminer, Pinot Gris, Pinot Grigio, Grenache, or Chianti

**Example:** Castello Di Gabbiano Pinot Grigio or Chianti

**Cooking Method:** Sauté

| INGREDIENTS | WEIGHT U.S. | WEIGHT METRIC | VOLUME U.S. | VOLUME METRIC |
|---|---|---|---|---|
| fresh tuna steaks, cut 1 inch thick | 3 lb. | 1.4 kg | | |
| salt | to taste | | | |
| pepper | to taste | | | |
| olive oil | | 28 g | 2 tablespoons | 30 mL |
| onion, sliced thinly | 12 oz. | 340 g | 3 medium | |
| red pepper flakes | | | 1/8 teaspoon | 1 mL |
| sugar | 1/2 oz. | 15 g | 1 tablespoon | 15 mL |
| red wine vinegar | | 86 g | 1/4 cup + 2 tablespoons | 90 mL |
| white wine | | 114 g | 1/2 cup | 120 mL |
| fresh mint leaves, coarsely chopped | 1 1/2 oz. | 43 g | 1/4 cup + 2 tablespoons | 90 mL |

1. Wash tuna, dry it, and sprinkle with salt and black pepper. Heat oil in large skillet over medium-high heat.
2. Place tuna, onion, and crushed red pepper in skillet, sear (sauté until light brown to seal in juices) on both sides.
3. Reduce heat to medium-low, cover, cook until desired doneness, turning fish after 3 minutes (8 minutes total cooking time for no pink flesh, which is typical where this dish originates).
4. Remove tuna from skillet, keep warm.
5. Turn heat to high, add half the sugar and vinegar and all the wine to skillet, deglaze the pan, stirring constantly, until liquid is syrupy.
6. Add remaining sugar and vinegar, simmer a few seconds.
7. Correct seasonings, stir mint leaves into sauce, pour sauce over tuna. Serve immediately.

© Comugnero Silvana

# PARMIGIANA DI MELANZANE (SICILY)
## EGGPLANT PARMIGIANA

David Murray and Jules Selmes © Dorling Kindersley

**Note:** For a lower calorie version, grill the eggplant slices instead of frying them.

**Note:** Although many recipes for eggplant Parmigiana prepare the eggplant slices with a standard breading procedure before frying, this recipe calls for sautéing the eggplant in olive oil without breading.

**Number of Servings:** 27 side dishes, 11 entrées    **Cooking Method:** Sauté, bake
**Serving Size:** 4 oz. (114 g) side dish, 10 oz. (284 g) entrée
**Total Yield:** 6 lb., 14 oz. (3.1 kg)
**Food Balance:** Protein/sweet
**Wine Style:** Soft and fruity Gewürztraminer, Pinot Blanc or Pinot Grigio, blush, and mild Reds, such as Grenache, Dolcetto, Merlot, or Shiraz
**Example:** Château St. Jean Gewürztraminer, Pinot Blanc, or Merlot

| INGREDIENTS | WEIGHT | | VOLUME | |
| --- | --- | --- | --- | --- |
| | U.S. | METRIC | U.S. | METRIC |
| eggplant, sliced about 1/2 inch thick | 4 lb., 4 oz. | 1.9 kg | 4 each | |
| salt | as needed | | | |
| **Tomato Sauce:** | | | | |
| olive oil | | 28 g | 2 tablespoons | 30 mL |
| onion, small dice | 9 oz. | 256 g | 2 medium | |
| garlic, smashed and minced | 1/4 oz. | 8 g | 2 cloves | |
| Italian plum tomatoes, fresh or canned, peeled and diced | 2 lb., 10 oz. | 1.2 kg | 5 cups | 1.2 L |
| sugar | | | 2 teaspoons | 10 mL |
| salt | | | 1/4 teaspoon | 2 mL or to taste |
| pepper | | | 1/4 teaspoon | 2 mL or to taste |
| fresh basil or mint leaves, minced | 1 oz. | 28 g | 1/2 cup | 120 mL |
| olive oil, for frying | as needed | | | |
| mozzarella cheese, grated | 1 lb. | 454 kg | 5 cups | 1.2 L |
| Parmesan cheese, grated | 5 oz. | 142 g | 1 cup | 240 mL |

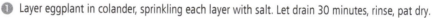

1. Layer eggplant in colander, sprinkling each layer with salt. Let drain 30 minutes, rinse, pat dry.
2. Meanwhile, heat 2 tablespoons (28 g or 30 mL) oil in pan over medium heat. Add onion, sauté until soft. Add garlic, sauté another minute.
3. Add tomatoes, sugar, salt, pepper, and basil (or mint), cook until thick.
4. Correct seasonings. If sauce is too chunky, purée, if desired.
5. Cover bottom of another skillet with olive oil, heat over high heat until hot.
6. Add eggplant slices, fry until golden on both sides, remove to paper toweling to drain.
7. Adding more oil if needed, fry remaining eggplant slices.

## ASSEMBLY:

1. Mix both cheeses together in bowl, preheat oven to 350 degrees (180°C).
2. Spread small amount of tomato sauce on bottom of ovenproof casserole or pan.
3. Place layer of eggplant over sauce.
4. Top with layer of tomato sauce, then sprinkle with cheese.
5. Repeat layering eggplant, sauce, and cheese until all ingredients are used. (Cheese should be the last layer.)
6. Bake for 30 minutes, serve hot.

© Marco Mayer

# ASPARAGI IN SALSA VERDE (LOMBARDY)
## ASPARAGUS IN GREEN SAUCE

**Note:** Serve this pungent sauce with any steamed or boiled vegetables and with boiled or grilled meats. The vinegar can be replaced with lemon juice or eliminated, if desired. The weight of asparagus in this recipe is a little over the weight needed so that 3 oz. (86 g) per person is available without breaking the asparagus. Depending on the thickness of the asparagus, estimate weight and how many spears are needed for each serving.

**Number of Servings:** 14
**Serving Size:** 1/2 oz. (15 g) sauce on 3 oz. (86 g) asparagus
**Total Yield:** 7 oz. (199 g), or 1 cup (240 mL) sauce

**Cooking Method:** Boil

> ### TWIST ON THE CLASSIC
>
> To create a first course or entrée, coat pasta or gnocchi with *salsa verde*. If it is too pungent, thin with extra olive oil.

| | WEIGHT | | VOLUME | |
| --- | --- | --- | --- | --- |
| **INGREDIENTS** | **U.S.** | **METRIC** | **U.S.** | **METRIC** |
| fresh parsley, washed and stems removed | 2 1/4 oz. | 64 g | 2 cups | 480 mL |
| capers, drained | 1 oz. | 28 g | 2 tablespoons | 30 mL |
| garlic, peeled | | | 1 clove | |
| anchovies | | | 2 each | |
| pepper | | | 1/8 teaspoon | 1 mL |
| wine vinegar | | 57 g | 1/4 cup | 60 mL |
| olive oil | | 114 g | 1/2 cup | 120 mL |
| asparagus, trimmed | 3 lb. | 1.4 kg | | |

1. Chop parsley, capers, garlic, and anchovies by hand or in processor fitted with knife blade until finely chopped but not puréed.
2. Transfer to bowl, stir in pepper and wine vinegar.
3. Whisk in oil, adding it in slow trickle.
4. Refrigerate until ready to serve, warm for service.
5. Meanwhile, steam or boil asparagus until *al dente*. (Check after 4 minutes depending on thickness of asparagus.)
6. Place asparagus on plate or platter, drizzle with green sauce using about 1/2 tablespoon (7 g or 7 mL) per 3 oz. (86 g) cooked asparagus.

Clive Streeter © Dorling Kindersley

# RADICCHIO E FINOCCHIO (NORTHERN ITALY)
## SAUTÉED RADICCHIO AND FENNEL

**Note:** The anise flavor of the fennel juxtaposes the bitter radicchio.

**Number of Servings:** 8
**Serving Size:** 4 oz. (114 g)
**Total Yield:** 2 lb. (908 g)

**Cooking Method:** Braise

|  | WEIGHT | | VOLUME | |
|---|---|---|---|---|
| INGREDIENTS | U.S. | METRIC | U.S. | METRIC |
| olive oil |  | 28 g | 2 tablespoons | 30 mL |
| onion, sliced thinly | 2 oz. | 57 g | 1/2 cup or 1/2 medium | 120 ml |
| fennel (sometimes called anise), stalks and 1/4-inch of bottom of bulb removed, sliced thinly across bulb | 1 lb., 12 oz. | 794 g | 2 each | |
| radicchio, sliced thinly | 5 oz. | 142 g | 1 head | |
| salt | | | 3/4 teaspoon | 4 mL |
| pepper | | | 1/4 teaspoon | 2 mL |

1. Heat olive oil in skillet on medium heat, add onions, sauté until soft.
2. Add fennel, radicchio, salt, and pepper, turn heat to low.
3. Cover and sauté until fennel is tender, about 30 minutes. Serve.

© audaxl

# SPINACI IN TEGAME

## SAUTÉED SPINACH

**Note:** Use this preparation for any type of greens. If using escarole or a bitter green, first parboil it to remove some of the bitterness.

**Number of Servings:** 8
**Serving Size:** 4 oz. (114 g)
**Total Yield:** 2 lb., 2 oz. (965 g)
**Food Balance:** Protein
**Wine Style:** Light- to medium-bodied Pinot Gris, Pinot Grigio, Sauvignon Blanc, Grenache, or Beaujolais
**Example:** Campanile Pinot Grigio

**Cooking Method:** Sauté

© Comugnero Silvana

| INGREDIENTS | WEIGHT | | VOLUME | |
|---|---|---|---|---|
| | U.S. | METRIC | U.S. | METRIC |
| olive oil | | 86 g | 1/4 cup + 2 tablespoons | 90 mL |
| garlic, minced | 1 1/4 oz. | 36 g | 8 cloves | |
| spinach, washed, stems removed, and coarsely cut | 2 lb., 5 oz. | 1.1 kg | four 10-oz. bags | four 300-mL bags |
| salt | 1/4 oz. | 8 g | 1 teaspoon | 5 mL |
| pepper | | | 1/2 teaspoon | 3 mL |

1. Heat olive oil in large sauté pan over medium-high heat until hot. Add garlic, sauté until golden but not burned, about 1 minute or less.
2. Add spinach, stirring constantly, sauté until wilted and tender, about 4 or 5 minutes. (Enough water should cling to leaves from washing, but, if necessary, add a teaspoon of water to prevent burning.)
3. Add salt and pepper, correct seasonings.
4. Serve immediately.

> **TWIST ON THE CLASSIC**
>
> For a brunch item, top the spinach with a fried or poached egg.

# RISOTTO AI FUNGI (LOMBARDY)

## SAFFRON MUSHROOM RISOTTO

**Note:** This dish usually appears as a first course on Italian menus; however, saffron risotto is the traditional accompaniment for ossobuco.

**Number of Servings:** 21 side dishes or 9 entrées
**Serving Size:** 4 oz. (114 g) side dish; 9 oz. (256 g) entrée
**Total Yield:** 5 lb., 4 oz. (2.4 kg)
**Food Balance:** Protein
**Wine Style:** Light- to medium-bodied Riesling, Pinot Blanc, Viognier, Chardonnay, light Pinot Noir, or Chianti
**Example:** Meridian Santa Barbara Chardonnay or Pinot Noir

**Cooking Method:** Braise

> **TWIST ON THE CLASSIC**
>
> There are countless creative, unusual variations of risotto. Try adding any of the following to risotto:
>
> - Roasted corn and crisply fried pancetta
> - Sautéed bay scallops
> - Shrimp scampi
> - Any vegetables

*Sautéing rice for risotto*
Richard Embery, Pearson Education/PH College

| INGREDIENTS | WEIGHT | | VOLUME | |
|---|---|---|---|---|
| | U.S. | METRIC | U.S. | METRIC |
| butter | 4 oz. | 114 g | 8 tablespoons (1 stick) | 120 mL |
| onion, small dice | 10 oz. | 284 g | 2 medium | |
| Arborio rice | 1 lb., 4 oz. | 568 g | 2 2/3 cups | 641 mL |
| white wine | | 227 g | 1 cup | 240 mL |
| stock, chicken, mushroom, or combination, hot | | 1.8 kg | 2 quarts (8 cups) | 1.9 L |
| saffron threads soaked in 2 tablespoons (28 g or 30 mL) stock | | | 3/4 to 1 teaspoon | 4 to 5 mL |
| assorted wild mushrooms, sliced | 14 oz. | 397 g | | |
| Parmesan cheese, grated | 2 1/2 oz. | 71 g | 2/3 cup | 160 mL |

1. Melt 4 tablespoons (57 g or 60 mL) of the butter in large pan or skillet over medium heat, add onion, sauté until soft. Add rice, stir to coat grains well.
2. Stirring constantly over medium heat, add wine and 1/2 cup (114 g or 120 mL) of the boiling stock gradually.
3. When almost absorbed, add another 1/2 cup (114 g or 120 mL) stock, still stirring. Continue this process of stirring and adding stock as it is absorbed.
4. After about 15 minutes, add saffron to risotto.
5. Meanwhile, in separate pan, sauté mushrooms in remaining 4 tablespoons (57 g or 60 mL) butter until mushrooms release liquid, then add to risotto and continue cooking risotto.
6. Continue stirring risotto and adding stock until all stock is almost absorbed. Cook until rice is *al dente* but sauce is creamy. Add extra stock if needed.
7. Correct seasonings, stir Parmesan into risotto. Serve immediately, accompanied by extra Parmesan cheese if desired.

*Adding stock to risotto*
Richard Embery, Pearson Education/PH College

© PhotoEd

© matteocozzi

# POLENTA (NORTHERN ITALY)

## CORNMEAL MUSH OR PUDDING

**Number of Servings:** 12
**Serving Size:** 6 oz. (171 g)
**Total Yield:** 4 lb., 10 1/4 oz. (2.1 kg)

**Cooking Method:** Boil

| INGREDIENTS | WEIGHT | | VOLUME | |
| --- | --- | --- | --- | --- |
| | U.S. | METRIC | U.S. | METRIC |
| water | | 1.8 kg | 2 quarts | 1.9 L |
| salt | 1/2 oz. | 15 g | 2 teaspoons | 10 mL |
| cornmeal, coarse | 13 oz. | 369 g | 2 cups | 480 mL |

*Spreading cooked polenta in pan for chilling*

*Cutting chilled polenta*

*Plating grilled polenta*

*Creamy cooked polenta*

1. Prepare double boiler for cooking polenta.
2. Place water and salt in a large saucepan. Bring to rapid boil over medium-high heat.
3. Stir water briskly with wooden spoon and slowly pour cornmeal into vortex [hole] in center of the swirling water. Pour cornmeal from measuring cup or release slowly from fist, so cornmeal "falls like rain" into the boiling water. Continue stirring mixture constantly for 5 minutes.
4. Move cornmeal mixture to the top of double boiler. Cook for 1 hour and 25 minutes, stirring every 20 to 30 minutes.
5. If desired, flavor polenta with ingredients of choice. Traditionally, polenta is served in one of two ways: soft, which is right after cooking, or in a firm form. To make the firm polenta, place polenta in pan lined with parchment paper or film wrap, then cover and chill the pan for several hours or overnight. (The amount in this recipe fits in a 9-by-13-inch [23-by-33-cm] pan making a slice 1 1/4 inch (3.2 cm) thick. Cut chilled polenta into desired serving pieces (12 pieces from the 9-by-13-inch [23-by-33-cm] pan) and fry in skillet with olive oil, grill, or bake the polenta to heat thoroughly. Serve plain or with topping of choice.

Coarse cornmeal for polenta is available in Italian markets as well as many health food stores and supermarkets.

Like pasta, polenta often functions as the base for many toppings. Also, it is served frequently as the starch side dish (like a potato).

To prepare polenta in the traditional method, the cornmeal is added to the boiling water and then the mixture is stirred constantly for 40 minutes.

# FOCACCIA (LIGURIA)

## LEAVENED FLAT BREAD

**Serving Size:** 1 wedge, 1/12 of 8-inch (20-cm) round
**Cooking Method:** Bake
**Total Dough:** 3 lb., 3 1/4 oz. (1.5 kg)
**Scaling:** 12 oz. (340 g) dough for 8-inch (20-cm) round
1 lb., 14 oz. (850 g) dough for half sheet pan

### TWIST ON THE CLASSIC

Focaccia makes a great warm sandwich. Split the bread and fill it with ham, sliced tomato, Swiss cheese, sliced Italian sausages, mozzarella, and marina sauce, or any combination imaginable. Heat the sandwich by grilling, baking, or in a Panini press.

| | WEIGHT | | VOLUME | |
| --- | --- | --- | --- | --- |
| **INGREDIENTS** | **U.S.** | **METRIC** | **U.S.** | **METRIC** |
| water, warm | | 511 g | 2 1/4 cups | 540 mL |
| sugar | 1/4 oz. | 8 g | 1 teaspoon | 5 mL |
| yeast, dried, granulated | 1/4 oz. | 8 g | 1 tablespoon | 15 mL |
| bread flour | 1 lb., 11 3/4 oz. | 787 g | 6 cups | 1.4 L |
| salt | 1/4 oz. | 8 g | 1 teaspoon | 5 mL |
| olive oil | | 43 g | 3 tablespoons | 45 mL |

**Toppings:**
olive oil
coarse salt
coarse pepper
rosemary, minced
garlic, minced

*Dimpling focaccia dough*

*Focaccia*
© giotti52

1. In small nonreactive bowl, place 1/2 cup (114 g or 120 mL) warm water, sugar, and yeast. Mix to hydrate yeast and set aside until yeast foams, several minutes.
2. Meanwhile, put flour and salt in a bowl of mixer fitted with dough hook, if available. (If not available, place in a large nonreactive bowl.) Mix flour and salt to blend.
3. Add remaining water (397 g, 1 3/4 cups, or 420 mL), olive oil, and yeast mixture. Mix at low speed until incorporated, then continue mixing at medium speed for 7 minutes or knead by hand for 10 to 15 minutes, until dough is smooth and elastic. If dough seems too dry, add a little more water. If dough seems too wet, add a little more flour.
4. Cover and allow to double in size, about 1 hour. Meanwhile, cover baking pans (half sheet pans or cookie sheets) with parchment paper or grease them. Place oven rack in top of oven and preheat to 450 degrees (230°C).
5. Punch down dough; knead briefly. Scale dough and press or roll into either rounds or into half sheet pan; dough should be about 3/8-inch (1-cm) thick. Brush coating of olive oil over top of bread, then press top of dough all over with fingertips to "dimple the dough." Sprinkle with salt, pepper, rosemary, and garlic, or any combination of toppings. Cover and allow to rise until double, about 30 minutes.
6. Bake for 12 to 15 minutes, until golden. Remove from oven, brush with olive oil, if desired. Cool on racks. Serve warm or room temperature. Wrap tightly to store.

Some of the endless topping variations for focaccia include:

- thinly sliced onions marinated in balsamic vinegar
- thinly sliced onions
- caramelized onions
- sun-dried tomato pieces
- crushed red pepper
- olives
- minced garlic
- minced sage

Some use focaccia as the base for a pizza.

## ZABAGLIONE (PIEDMONT)

### MARSALA-FLAVORED DESSERT SAUCE

**Note:** Traditionally, zabaglione is served over fresh fruit. After cooking, serve this sauce immediately; it does not hold well. If it becomes too thick, thin with a little Marsala.

**Note:** This same sauce appears in France with white wine replacing the Marsala. In France, the sauce is called sabayon.

**Number of Servings:** 12
**Serving Size:** 1 oz. (28 g)
**Total Yield:** 14 oz. (397 g)

**Cooking Method:** Boil (bain-marie)

**TWIST ON THE CLASSIC**

Use any liquor to change the flavor. Try replacing the Marsala with bourbon or whiskey and serving it over bread pudding. Substitute *limoncello* for a delicious topping over rice pudding.

| INGREDIENTS | WEIGHT | | VOLUME | |
| --- | --- | --- | --- | --- |
| | U.S. | METRIC | U.S. | METRIC |
| egg yolks, room temperature | 8 oz. | 227 g | 12 each | |
| sugar | 3 1/2 oz. | 104 g | 1/2 cup | 120 mL |
| dry Marsala wine | | 78 g | 2/3 cup | 160 mL |

Whisking ingredients for zabaglione
David Murray © Dorling Kindersley

Whisked ingredients forming a ribbon
David Murray © Dorling Kindersley

Anneka © Shutterstock

1. Place all ingredients in heatproof nonreactive bowl (stainless steel, for example). Place bowl over pan of barely simmering water *(bain-marie)*, whisk constantly.
2. Continue whisking until mixture is pale yellow, thick, and 185 degrees (85°C), about 8 minutes. If water becomes too hot, the eggs will cook, so immediately remove pan from heat if water starts to boil and let it cool a bit.
3. Serve immediately over fresh fruit.

## TORTA DI RICOTTA (SOUTHERN ITALY)
### RICOTTA CHEESE PIE

**Note:** Sometimes called torta di Pasquale (Easter pie), ricotta pie is a favorite dessert served at Easter.

**Number of Servings:** 8 or 10  
**Serving Size:** 1 slice, or 1/8 or 1/10 of pie  
**Total Yield:** One 10-inch (25-cm) pie

**Cooking Method:** Bake

Neil Mersh © Dorling Kindersley

| | WEIGHT | | VOLUME | |
|---|---|---|---|---|
| **INGREDIENTS** | **U.S.** | **METRIC** | **U.S.** | **METRIC** |
| **Dough:** | | | | |
| all-purpose flour | 9 3/4 oz. | 276 g | 2 cups | 480 mL |
| salt | | | 1/4 teaspoon | 2 mL |
| sugar | 1 1/2 oz. | 43 g | 3 tablespoons | 45 mL |
| unsalted butter, cold | 4 oz. | 114 g | 8 tablespoons (1 stick) | 120 mL |
| egg | 1 3/4 oz. | 50 g | 1 each | |
| water | | 15 to 28g | 1 to 2 tablespoons | 15 to 30 mL |
| **Filling:** | | | | |
| pine nuts | 1 1/2 oz. | 43 g | 1/4 cup | 60 mL |
| citron, minced | 1 1/2 oz. | 43 g | 3 tablespoons | (45 mL) |
| eggs | 6 3/4 oz. | 191 g | 4 each | |
| sugar | 5 1/2 oz. | 156 g | 3/4 cup | 180 mL |
| orange liqueur | | 15 g | 1 tablespoon | 15 mL |
| vanilla | | | 1/2 teaspoon | 3 mL |
| ricotta cheese | 1 lb. | 454 g | | |
| **Garnish:** | | | | |
| confectioner's sugar | | for dusting | | |
| almonds or pine nuts, *optional* | | | | |

There are countless variations of *torta di ricotta*. Some omit nuts from the filling; others use chopped almonds or a combination of pine nuts and almonds. Some cooks include orange rind, chocolate bits, or raisins in the filling instead of (or in addition to) citron.

### DOUGH PREPARATION IN FOOD PROCESSOR:

1. Place flour, salt, and sugar in bowl of food processor fitted with knife blade, pulse a couple of times to mix.
2. Cut cold butter into small pieces, about half-tablespoon size. Place on top of dry ingredients; pulse several times, until clumps the size of peas form.
3. Whisk egg and 1 tablespoon (15 g or 15 mL) water in small bowl. With processor running, pour egg mixture through feed tube. Pulse until dough comes together into a ball. Add remaining 1 tablespoon (15 g or 15 mL) water, if needed.
4. Remove dough from processor. Wrap in plastic wrap and refrigerate until well chilled, several hours or overnight. For quick chilling, pat into disk and place in freezer.

## DOUGH PREPARATION BY HAND:

1. Place flour, salt, and sugar in bowl.
2. Cut cold butter into small pieces, about half-tablespoon size. Place on top of dry ingredients; mix with fingertips, pastry cutter, or two knives until clumps the size of peas form.
3. With fork, mix in egg and 1 tablespoon (15 g or 15 mL) water. Add remaining water if too dry.
4. Knead dough gently a few times, form into ball. Wrap in plastic wrap and refrigerate until well chilled, several hours or overnight. For quick chilling, pat into disk and place in freezer.

## ROLLING OUT DOUGH:

1. Pan-spray 10-inch (25-cm) pie pan. Place chilled ball of dough on table. With rolling pin, hit ball to flatten into disk about 1 inch (2.5 cm) thick. Lightly flour table and rolling pin, if needed. Cut off three-quarters of dough, refrigerate remainder until needed.
2. Roll dough, from middle to sides, releasing dough from table with icing spatula every few rolls. Turn dough one-quarter turn to keep dough even, roll into circle of desired thickness.
3. Release dough circle from table with spatula. Fold gently in half. Lift and move dough to pan. Position dough over pan, so it covers pan when unfolded.
4. Press dough into corners of pan. Leave about 1/2 to 3/4 inch (1.3 to 2 cm) of dough hanging over edge of pan. Refrigerate until needed.

## FILLING:

1. Position rack in lower half of oven. Preheat oven to 375 degrees (190°C). Combine pine nuts and citron in small bowl, set aside until needed.
2. Beat eggs, sugar, orange liqueur, and vanilla together in medium bowl. Add ricotta cheese, mix well to combine.
3. Add reserved pine nuts and citron. Refrigerate until needed.

## ASSEMBLY:

1. Roll out remaining dough. Cut into strips about 1/2 inch (1.3 cm) wide. Pour ricotta mixture into prepared pie shell. Place strips of dough in lattice pattern on top of filling. Press edges to seal lattice dough to shell. Flute edges.
2. Bake for 40 to 45 minutes, until crust is golden and filling is almost set.
3. Remove from oven, place on rack, cool completely. Sift light coating of confectioner's sugar over top of pie. If desired, decorate with nuts.

© eZeePics Studio

# Germany

>> **LEARNING OBJECTIVES**

By the end of this chapter, you will be able to:

- Identify food products prevalent in Germany and discuss why those particular foods thrive there
- Understand the effects of climate on the cuisine of Germany
- Describe how its geographic location and bordering countries have affected Germany's cuisine
- Identify differences and similarities between the cuisines of the various regions in Germany
- Prepare a variety of German dishes

## >> HISTORY

As early as 1000 B.C., tribes from northern Europe inhabited the area of central Europe that is now Germany. First settling near the Baltic Sea, they lived in Scandinavia and northern Germany. Eventually, they migrated toward the south.

### ROMAN EMPIRE

By 100 B.C., these people had moved into the middle and southern sections of present-day Germany, where the Romans ruled. At that time, most Germans lived as hunters, farmers, or nomads with a simple diet consisting of grains, wild fruits and berries, milk and cheeses, and game that they hunted. These early Germans learned lots from the Romans about both food and civilization. Among other contributions, the Romans introduced gardens, orchards, and gold and silver dining implements. In fact, Romans planted the first grapes for wine along the steep banks of the Rhine and Mosel rivers about 2,000 years ago. The Roman rule lasted until 9 A.D., when the Roman army was defeated in battle. The Germanic tribes continued moving southward, taking lands the Romans ruled. Through many invasions, Germany conquered Rome and ruled much of the former Roman Empire by the tenth century. That rule lasted until the early 1800s.

### MIDDLE AGES

Charlemagne, king of the Franks, conquered Germany in 800 A.D. He restored the vineyards, which had fallen into disrepair. In addition, Charlemagne imparted knowledge about many foods, planting herbs, and meal planning. Around the early tenth century, Germany was divided into five regions.

By the Middle Ages, the German diet included lots of fish, goose, and game. As was true in many other countries during this time period, heavily spiced foods prevailed, partially to cover the spoiled or rancid taste so common in these times before refrigeration. During the Middle Ages, banquets contained many courses, and for the first time here, the visual aspects of food became an important consideration.

### RENAISSANCE

The Renaissance brought awareness of luxury and opulence in all sorts of things, including food and dining. Table settings and food decoration acquired new importance. Silver and porcelain became prized serving pieces. French influence on the food and customs dominated during the seventeenth and eighteenth centuries. While the upper class enjoyed the lavish food of this period, the peasants still subsisted on grains, gruel, sauerkraut, dumplings, and bacon.

In the sixteenth century, the Protestant Reformation began in northern Germany. This started as an attempt to reform the Catholic Church and some of its doctrine. In 1517, Martin Luther published *95 Theses*, which questioned some practices of Catholicism. In addition to Luther, many other religious leaders were involved in this movement. In the end, Protestant religions including Lutheranism, Mennonitism, Calvinism, Presbyterianism, Huguenotism, and Puritanism developed in countries throughout Europe.

### LATER HISTORY

From 1806 until 1813, Napoleon of France ruled western Germany. Following Napoleon's fall, Germany became 39 states in 1814; however, the nation of Germany did not become united under one sovereign until 1871. As a result, great differences exist between the various regions, and culinary specialties and traits characterize each of the regions.

In 1884, Germany began to expand to territories outside of Europe. Like many other European powers, it established colonies in Africa. Germany lost all colonies in 1919 as part of the Treaty of Versailles.

Prior to World War I, many Germans enjoyed an affluent lifestyle. People entertained frequently and indulged in lavish food. The aftermath of World Wars I and II left the country and people of Germany shattered, both physically and emotionally.

At the end of World War I in 1918, Germany was a devastated country. Between the effects of losing the war and the Treaty of Versailles, Germany lost its colonies and much of its territory. For example, Alsace-Lorraine again became part of France, and Denmark gained territory. Much of eastern Europe controlled by Germany was returned to Poland, Czechoslovakia, Lithuania, and other countries.

By 1923, the German economy collapsed. The worldwide economic depression of 1929 further eroded the Germans' economy and morale, making the climate ripe for political extremism. The Nazis became a strong political force by 1933. The leader of the Nazi Party, Adolf Hitler, planned to conquer Europe, beginning with the east. Of course, Hitler's actions led to the Holocaust and World War II.

After World War II, Germany was destroyed again. This time, the country was divided into East and West Germany. Isolated from the democratic west, East Germany was under the Communist rule of Russia until 1990, when they tore down the Berlin Wall and Germany was united as a democracy.

Throughout Germany's history, many battles and different rulers ensued. Borders changed, and the various European countries fought and gained control over each other. This explains a lot of the overlap in foods and cuisine with Belgium, France (especially Alsace-Lorraine), Austria, the Czech Republic, and Poland.

## >> TOPOGRAPHY

Germany lies in the middle of western Europe and consists of mostly fertile land with plenty of rivers that supply water. The land supports ample agriculture for crops and animals that provide both dairy products and meat.

Surrounded by nine countries, the only coastline in Germany lies to the north, at the North and Baltic seas. Denmark also borders on the north; Poland and the Czech Republic are situated to the east; Switzerland and Austria are on the south; and the Netherlands, Belgium, Luxembourg, and France lie to the west.

The northern part of Germany consists of flat terrain, the central section is hilly, and the south contains hills and mountains. The Alps lies in the southern section and forms the border with Austria and Switzerland.

Germany has two large forests—the Black Forest in the southwest and the Bohemian Forest in the east. In addition, many smaller forests are scattered throughout the country. The forests yield a bounty of game as well as numerous varieties of mushrooms and berries.

Transecting the countryside, several rivers provide fertile floodplains for crops, and grapes for wine thrive in the hills and valleys. The Rhine and Mosel rivers lie in the west, the Danube in the south, the Oder in the east, and the Elbe and Weser rivers in the north.

## >> COOKING METHODS

Boiling ranks high in popularity as a cookery method used throughout Germany, where they boil all sorts of foods, including vegetables, potatoes, dumplings, meats, and even fresh fish. *Forelle blau*, literally blue trout, is prepared by dropping a live trout that has been gutted (or dressed) in boiling water that contains a little vinegar. The vinegar causes the skin of the fish to take on a blue cast, therefore the name.

*Forelle blau*
© Jörg Lantelme

| Ingredients and Foods Commonly Used Throughout the Cuisine of Germany Include |
| --- |

- sausages
- pork and veal
- goose
- lentils and split peas
- rye bread
- potatoes
- red and white cabbage, sauerkraut
- turnips, kohlrabi, cauliflower, Brussels sprouts, beets, carrots, and spinach
- white asparagus
- vinegar
- juniper berries and caraway seeds
- onions
- hops
- fruits including apples, cherries, apricots, and plums
- many berries
- grapes and wine
- nuts
- honey

While Germans broil, sauté, or braise smaller pieces of meat, large pieces of meat are either braised or roasted. Often, they marinate tough cuts of meat in buttermilk, wine, beer, or vinegar, and then braise them in the acidic marinade. Made with a tough cut of beef, *sauerbraten* exemplifies this cooking technique. Roasting is the usual cooking method for game as well as other meats.

Sautéing is another favored cooking method. From veal, sausages, and fish to potatoes and *spaetzle,* Germans fry all sorts of foods in butter and/or oil.

Germans frequently smoke and pickle meats, fish, and vegetables. In earlier days, this preserved the foods, prevented spoilage, and provided sustenance during the long winters. Pickling, marinating, smoking, and sausage making extended the freshness of many food products in this country with a short growing season. Some examples of these preparations include sauerkraut, pickled cabbage, and *sauerbraten*. Sausages use many leftover or unused parts of the animal. Even in early days, Germans had access to plenty of meat, poultry, and fish through agriculture, hunting, and fishing. Of course, they preserved their excess bounty of protein products for lean times.

The Tartars, who learned of fermented cabbage when they invaded China, brought sauerkraut in the 1200s. Introducing it in Hungary and then in Austria, sauerkraut finally made its way to Germany, where it became a staple of the diet.

*In mountainous areas containing the freshwater streams where the trout or salmon thrive, often a tank of live fish stands in the lobby of restaurants so customers can choose the desired fish for their meal. While lobsters receive this same treatment in many areas of the United States, trout or salmon are the usual fish swimming in the fish tanks in Germany.*

## >> REGIONS

Distinct differences exist between the foods of the northern, central, and southern areas of Germany. Each of the regions exhibits significant culinary influences from the countries that share its border.

In the regions of the north, typical cold-climate cooking prevails, and the cookery in the north reflects the cuisines of Scandinavia. The eastern section demonstrates influence from eastern Europe, including the countries of Poland, Russia, and Lithuania; the west shows the effect of Holland and France; and the cookery in the south resembles that of Austria.

People throughout Germany consume countless varieties of sausages (*würst* in German) and cold cuts; in fact, many consider this a staple of the German diet. *Braunschweiger,* a liverwurst or liver sausage, hails from the town of Braunschweig in the north.

*It is estimated that Germans prepare more than 1,500 types of sausages!*

### NORTH

Major cities of northern Germany include Berlin and Hamburg. Pork, beef, goose, game, and lamb come from this area, with the game served primarily in the fall. Frequently, meats are cooked with fruits and vegetables. Sweet-and-sour dishes enjoy much popularity in the north. Bacon and bacon grease flavor myriad dishes, including appetizers, soups, salads, and entrées.

In this region, the North Sea and the Baltic Sea provide abundant seafood, with eel and herring being favorites. Both pickled and smoked fish and meats appear often. Typical cold-weather crops such as potatoes, beets, cabbage, barley, hops, and rye grow well in the north and remain an important part of the diet there.

From the eastern European influence, the Germans adopted the use of both sweet and soured cream in the cuisine found in the north. As a result, they prepare many cream sauces and soups. From hearty stews to fruit soups, a wide variety of soups are served in this northern region. Popular beverages include beer and *schnapps*, a strong-tasting, clear, colorless liquor made from fruit.

## CENTRAL GERMANY

*Stollen*
© Lilyana Vynogradova

Famous for Westphalian ham and pumpernickel bread, central Germany thrives on hearty foods like pork, dumplings, sauerkraut, beer, rye bread, cheese, and butter. Sausages and stews such as *pfefferpotthast*, a stew of beef short ribs containing lots of pepper, remain favorites.

This region of Germany includes the cities of Dresden, Westphalia, Cologne, and Frankfurt, for which the frankfurter, or hot dog, is named. Founded in 38 B.C., Cologne became a trade center because of its location on the Rhine River, which positioned the city between trade coming from the east and west. As a result, a lot of spices were available in Cologne. The traditional Christmas bread, *stollen*, originated in the town of Dresden, located in this region.

Onions receive special prominence in the western part of the central region, whether sautéed as an accompaniment to meat or in *zwiebelkuchen*—literally onion pie—a quiche-like pie consisting of a pastry shell with a filling of bacon, eggs, cream, and onions. Another much-loved food, the ubiquitous dumpling is made from potatoes, bread, flour, or oats. Dumplings appear often and in a number of varieties, as a side dish as well as in soup.

Fruits grow in orchards throughout this region, and the forests provide abundant berries that often become part of pastries. Vineyards thrive on the banks rising from the Rhine and Mosel rivers, and lots of wine is produced in this area. After the harvest in the fall, many towns throughout the grape-growing region celebrate with wine festivals.

## SOUTH

The southern regions claim many specialties. Here, as in the rest of Germany, residents consume potatoes, dumplings, sausage, and beer in great quantities, but some of the preparations are a bit lighter than those from regions to the north. The cookery in southern Germany places more emphasis on salads and desserts.

Four states lie in the south—Bavaria, Swabia, Baden, and Alsace-Lorraine. Bavaria, lying in the southeast, borders Austria. Swabia lies to its west, and Baden is west of Swabia. Alsace-Lorraine is tucked in the southwest corner, sharing a border with France. This region shows strong French culinary influence mixed into the German cuisine. Likewise, the cuisine of the area bordering Austria exhibits lots of Austrian characteristics. These borders have changed through the years as one country gained control over the other. Alsace-Lorraine is a perfect example, having belonged to France or Germany at many different times throughout its history. As a result, the cuisine found in Alsace-Lorraine blends the cooking traits of Germany and France.

Lush fields and meadows make up the southern part of Bavaria. This is beer country, and breweries observe stringent government-controlled standards to ensure the high quality of the beer they produce. Besides generating fine wines from the vineyards along the Rhine and Mosel rivers, the northern part of Bavaria's fertile countryside yields a bounty of vegetables.

Radishes, white asparagus, and cabbage rank supreme as vegetables here. Most meals include at least one type of salad, which might consist of lettuces or any variety

In 1516, Duke Wilhelm IV of Bavaria instituted the "Beer Purity Law" that stated beer can contain only hops, yeast, barley, and water. This ranks as the world's oldest regulation of food.

of vegetables tossed with vinegar and oil dressing. Many varieties of plums, cherries, apples, and berries grow well in this area and appear in many desserts.

Every region boasts its own sauerkraut recipes. Although pig's feet and snout in sauerkraut continues as a northern treat, sauerkraut in Swabia is cooked with apples, onions, and white wine. Hunting and fishing remain popular throughout the south. As a result, game and freshwater fish from the mountain streams are served often. *Spaetzle*, a cross between a dumpling and a noodle, accompanies many plates. Served as a light meal, *käsespaetzle* is *spaetzle* combined with *emmentaler* (a type of Swiss cheese) and sometimes onions. Several fine cheeses come from Bavaria, including *emmentaler* and beer cheese.

The Black Forest area in the southwest is known for several specialties. Besides yielding numerous varieties of mushrooms, the forest produces ample berries and game. It is perhaps most famous for *Schwartzwälder kirschtorte*, Black Forest cherry cake, a torte that features cake layers flavored with *kirschwasser*, a cherry liqueur, layered with whipped cream and a cherry filling. Although this specialty comes from the Black Forest region, countless variations of Black Forest cake are served throughout Germany.

## >> CUISINE

Basically, the German diet consists of many soups, salads, vegetables, meat, and potatoes. Their hearty cooking includes plenty of starches: dumplings, *spaetzle*, and of course, potatoes.

### POTATOES

Potatoes were brought to Germany from South America in the seventeenth century. Considering their importance in the German cuisine, it is hard to believe they were not widely grown until about the nineteenth century. However, once they started growing potatoes, the Germans embraced them heartily, and potatoes became the starch of choice. Today, they are consumed daily and prepared in a plethora of recipes—fried, boiled, mashed, and puréed, in pancakes, soup, salad, dumplings, stews, and on and on. Potatoes appear in every part of the menu from appetizers, salads, entrées, and side dishes to desserts.

### PROTEIN

Meat plays a large role in the German diet, with pork ranking as the most popular meat, followed by veal. Dating from the times of the Romans, the Germanic tribes consumed pork (wild boar), deer, and rabbit. Today as in the past, Germans use all parts of the pig. Bacon and other cured pork products flavor many German dishes, including soups and salads. Westphalian ham, a delicate, smoked ham similar to Italian *prosciutto,* is sliced very thinly and served with buttered rye or pumpernickel bread.

Of course, both pork and veal are frequent ingredients in the endless varieties of *würst*, German sausages. Every region has its own specialty, but *würst* certainly ranks as a German national food. Prepared in any imaginable way, *würst* appears in a range of dishes from *würstsalat* (sliced würst and other ingredients in vinegar and oil) to *choucroute*, the popular casserole served in Alsace-Lorraine containing sauerkraut, various meats, and sausage. German street vendors sell *würst* like American hot dogs, on a roll accompanied by mustard.

*Schnitzle*, veal cutlets that are pounded thin and sautéed, appear on menus with a variety of toppings. These cutlets are sometimes breaded, as in *wiener schnitzle,* or sautéed plain as with *schnitzle natur.*

Goose, the traditional Christmas meal, is prepared in several ways. Some stuff the goose with fruit, while others prefer smoked goose. Duck also graces tables in homes and restaurants.

*Piece of black forest cake*
© Bernd Jürgens

### SOME WELL KNOWN SAUSAGES

*Bratwürst* – made of beef and pork
*Blutwürst* – sausage containing blood, meats, grains, and/or bread that is congealed
*Frankfurter* – originated in Frankfurt, like a hot dog
*Knockwürst* – usually all beef, thicker than a Frankfurter
*Landjäger* – dried sausage containing beef and pork; similar to salami; "Jäger" means hunter and this sausage was taken on hunting trips since it requires no refrigeration
*Leberwürst* – made with liver, comes in many varieties, is soft enough to spread on bread
*Leberkäse* – contains no liver or cheese although that's the literal translation; like a meatloaf of corned beef and pork
*Teewürst* – also called Mettwürst; spreadable smoked meat mixture in casing, available in coarse or fine texture
*Weisswürst* – veal sausage

## TYPES OF *SCHNITZLE* (FRIED VEAL CUTLET)

**jaeger schnitzle** Served with a sauce containing mushrooms, onions, white wine, and cooked tomatoes

**paprika schnitzle** Served with a paprika and sour cream sauce

**rahmschnitzle** Served with a cream sauce that often contains mushrooms

**schnitzle a la Holstein** Topped with a fried egg, garnished with anchovy and capers

**schnitzle a la Oscar** Topped with asparagus tips and crabmeat, then napped with Béarnaise sauce

**schnitzle natur** Plain, fried cutlet, served with juices from the pan deglazed with water or stock and lemon juice

**wiener schnitzle** Breaded with standard breading procedure using flour, egg, and bread crumbs, then pan fried; garnished with lemon, caper, and anchovy

*Würst*
© Nataliia Pyzhova

*Schnitzle a la Holstein*
© Mike Richter

*Schnitzle a la Oscar*
© Quade

Germany's most famous beef dish, *sauerbraten*, starts with a beef roast that is marinated for at least three days in an acidic liquid (usually vinegar) and spices. The acid from the vinegar tenderizes the tough meat. Like many dishes, the preparation of *sauerbraten* varies with the region. In the north, the beef is marinated in buttermilk instead of vinegar, while vinegar and red wine are used in the south. Some even marinate with beer. After marinating, the beef is braised until tender. Variations on the recipes involve more than the choice of marinating liquid. *Sauerbraten* from the Rhineland contains raisins; in other areas the gravy is thickened with broken gingersnap cookies in addition to flour. *Rouladen*, another popular beef dish, consists of beef pounded thin, spread with mustard, rolled around a dill pickle spear or sauerkraut, and then braised.

Often German meat recipes incorporate fruit with the meats, either in the cooking process or as an accompaniment. Dried fruits appear frequently in stuffing.

Since the Middle Ages, hunting has remained a strong tradition in Germany. In the fall of the year, menus found both in restaurants and homes prominently feature all sorts of game. Offal, including liver, tongue, heart, kidneys, brains, and sweetbreads, are frequently eaten. Germans waste none of the animal.

Much fish is consumed. In the southern regions, freshwater fish such as trout and salmon from the mountain streams reigns supreme, while ocean fish from the Baltic and North Sea remains popular in the north. Prevalent in all regions, the ever-popular herring is prepared in a number of manners, including *rollmops*, where the pickled herring is rolled around a dill pickle. Many Germans choose herring marinated in vinegar instead of the milder wine marinade preferred in most countries. Still others like herring cloaked in a sour cream sauce or mixed with diced apple to create a sweet/salty dish.

## VEGETABLES AND FRUITS

Because of the cold, northern climate, winter vegetables thrive. This includes many varieties of cabbage, turnips, carrots, cauliflower, Brussels sprouts, kohlrabi, spinach, and more. Major crops grown in Germany include sugar beets, hops, potatoes, wheat, barley, oats, and rye.

One exception to the winter vegetables is a German passion—white asparagus. Available in the spring, restaurants often display banners announcing their arrival. Unlike the American preference for thin asparagus, Germans prize thick ones. Wasting none of the vegetable, they use the tough bottom part of the stalks to make cream of asparagus soup.

Vegetables occupy an important place in the German cuisine. Cooks carefully choose vegetables to accompany the other foods. They cook vegetables so they are thoroughly cooked but maintain their integrity, that is, done but not mushy. Also, they transform almost any vegetable or combination of vegetables—both cooked and raw—into a salad by dressing it with vinegar and oil.

Heartier fruits such as apples grow extremely well here, but all sorts of fruits, including cherries, apricots, plums, grapes, and many berries, thrive in different areas of Germany. While some of these are paired with meats, many become part of the extensive dessert repertoire.

## FLAVORINGS

With a preference for sour tastes, Germans flavor numerous foods with vinegar, including lentil soup and countless varieties of salads. Vinegar and/or lemon juice is added to many entrées, often forming the basis for the sauce.

The most popular condiments are mustard and horseradish. The many varieties of mustard range from sweet mustard to medium-sharp to sharp.

Dating from early days, parsley, celery, and dill flavor many dishes. Juniper berries often season meats, game, and marinades. Caraway seeds appear in all sorts of recipes including meats, vegetables, and breads.

Butter, lard, and bacon grease remain the cooking fats of choice. Bacon or other cured or smoked pork imparts flavor to many dishes. Germany is also known for fine cheeses with specialties produced in the various regions.

## SOUPS

From clear soups to thick bean or pea soups to cream soups, the Germans usually include some variety of soup in any major meal. In past times, soup was actually served three times a day. Clear soups frequently contain dumplings, *spaetzle*, noodles, or thin slices of crêpelike pancakes. Thick soups use flour, cream, or egg to achieve the desired thickness.

## FOOD STORES

All but the smallest towns have open markets where they sell fruits and vegetables. Supermarkets now exist, but many people still prefer to shop at individual markets for their food items. These include *konditorei*, bakeries for pastries; *backerei*, bakeries for breads; butcher shops carrying raw meats; *metzgerei*, selling cold cuts and sausages; *molkerien* for milk, cheeses, and other dairy products; stores for fresh produce; and other stores for grocery items. Clustered close together, the shoppers go from one store to the next for their shopping.

## BREADS AND PASTRIES

Famous for their breads, shops called *backerei* are devoted to preparing and selling the many types and varieties of breads. Ranging from light to dense, rye breads abound. Excellent fine white breads, many varieties of rolls, and large, soft pretzels sprinkled with coarse salt are also quite popular. It is said that more than 300 types of breads are sold in German bakeries!

Well known throughout the world, German pastries include *torten* (cakes), *kuchen* (pie or single-layer cake), cookies, and a number of pastries from puff pastry, *choux* pastry, and yeast dough. *Lebkuchen*, honey cookies, become the foundation of the gingerbread houses made around Christmastime.

Many pastries contain nuts. Quite popular in Germany, *marzipan*, almond paste, is dyed with food coloring and formed into miniature fruits, vegetables, animals, and other whimsical shapes. Most *konditorei* have a counter filled with homemade truffles, candies, and marzipan pieces for sale.

Austrian and German pastries are very similar to one another, but remain quite different from French pastries. Many of the same pastries are served in *konditorei* in both countries, particularly in southern Germany, which borders Austria.

In earlier times, the Germans valued asparagus fields so much that they became part of a woman's dowry.

*Marzipan fruits*
© emf-images

Germany boasts the production of at least 5,000 types of beer made in more than 1,200 breweries throughout the country.

Hops are used for making beer, and Germany ranks as one of the largest producers of hops in the world.

## MEALS

A simple breakfast of coffee and bread with butter and jam is standard fare, sometimes accompanied by a soft-boiled egg or cheese and cold cuts. Another snack, or "second breakfast," used to be eaten in the late morning. For school children or farmers, this consisted of a sandwich. Most no longer have this meal, since *mittagessen*, the main meal of the day, is served around twelve or one o'clock. Soup followed by meat with vegetables and a starch makes up this hearty main meal. In the late afternoon, people meet at a *konditorei* or at home for *kaffeestunde*, literally translated "coffee hour." Similar to the English tea, at this meal people consume a pastry with a cup of coffee. This remains a popular time for entertaining friends, particularly on the weekends. Like our lunch, the light evening meal consists of sausage, cold cuts, cheese, bread, and often salad.

## BEVERAGES

Consumption of both beer and wine remains high. Beer often is brewed using natural fermentation, a brewing method dating from the Middle Ages. The Germans invented the lagering process for making beer. Beer pairs well with the hearty German foods, and they produce many types of beer in breweries throughout the countryside. The northern Germans generally prefer a lighter beer served well chilled, whereas the southerners like darker beer at room temperature.

Most of the wine production occurs around the Rhine and Mosel rivers and primarily consists of varieties of white wine. *Kirschwasser* is a cherry liqueur produced in the Black Forest, where many cherry trees thrive. Brandies also come from Germany.

## GERMAN CHEESES

**Butterkäse** Made from cow's milk; buttery flavor, semisoft texture

**Cambozola** Made from cow's milk; cross between Brie and Gorgonzola; flavor of blue cheese, smooth soft texture

**Emmentaler** Made from cow's milk; type of Swiss cheese; flavor of Swiss cheese, contains holes; from Bavaria in southern Germany

**Limburger** Made from cow's milk; very sharp pungent flavor, soft creamy texture

**Muenster** Made from cow's milk; mild flavor, semisoft texture

**Tilsiter** Made from cow's milk; full-bodied strong flavor, tiny holes

**Quark** Made from cow's milk; fresh cheese with mild fresh flavor, smooth soft texture; resembles a soft cream cheese with a yogurt flavor

| REGION | AREA | WEATHER | TOPOGRAPHY | FOODS |
|---|---|---|---|---|
| North | Baltic Sea and North Sea | Cold winters, mild summers | Coast, sand dunes | Seafood, eel, herring, turbot, plaice |
| | Inland | Cold winters, mild summers | Lowlands, plains, sandy soil, rich farmland, lakes, forest in northeast | Cattle, sheep, geese, pigs, *würst*, game, fish, rye, barley, wheat, hops, potatoes, winter vegetables, cabbage, sugar beets, mushrooms, fruits, apples, berries |
| Central | Rhine and Mosel rivers | Cold winters, mild summers | Hills, forests, valleys, plateaus, rivers, vineyards | Sheep, pigs, *würst*, Westphalian ham, rye, wheat, dumplings, potatoes, turnips, sugar beets, cabbage, onions, fruits, berries, grapes, wine |
| South | Bavaria, Swabia, Baden, Alsace-Lorraine | Cold winters, mild summers | Hills, mountains, streams, forests, fertile farmland, orchards, vineyards | Cattle, *würst*, fish, trout, salmon, game, *Emmentaler* cheese, dairy, barley, wheat, *spaetzle*, vegetables, white asparagus, cabbage, radishes, mushrooms, fruits, cherries, plums, grapes, wine, beer |

## >> Review Questions

1. Name countries that border Germany and give examples of their influence on Germany's cuisine.
2. How has the climate and topography in Germany affected the cuisine?
3. Name at least five food products and/or flavorings that appear commonly in Germany.
4. Discuss the prevalence and types of starches in the German diet.
5. Discuss the meals eaten in the normal German's day, including the types of foods that would be served at each meal.

## >> Glossary

**backerei** Bakeries that sell all sorts of breads and rolls

**braunschweiger** Liverwurst or liver sausage that originated from the town of Braunschweig in the north

**choucroute** Popular casserole containing sauerkraut, various meats, and sausage served in Alsace-Lorraine

**Emmentaler** Type of Swiss cheese from Bavaria

**forelle blau** Literally meaning blue trout, this fish is prepared by dropping a live trout in boiling water containing a little vinegar; the vinegar causes the skin of the fish to take on a blue cast, therefore the name

**kaffeestunde** Literally translated "coffee hour," a late-afternoon snack consisting of pastry and coffee or other beverage

**kirschwasser** A strong cherry liqueur produced in the Black Forest

**konditorei** Bakeries that sell pastries; they usually contain tables and chairs where customers can sit and order a slice of pastry or ice cream and coffee or other beverages

**lebkuchen** A spiced honey cookie eaten alone or baked in large pieces and used as the base for gingerbread houses

**metzgerei** Shops where cold cuts and sausages are sold

**mittagessen** The main meal of the day, served in the afternoon around twelve or one o'clock

**molkerien** Shops selling milk, cheeses, and other dairy products

**pfefferpotthast** A stew of beef short ribs containing lots of pepper

**sauerbraten** Beef marinated in an acidic liquid (often vinegar, but it depends on the region), then braised

**schnitzle** Veal cutlets that are pounded thin, sometimes breaded, and then pan-fried

**Schwartzwälder kirschtorte** Black Forest cherry cake, a torte featuring cake layers flavored with *Kirschwasser,* a cherry liqueur, filled with whipped cream and a cherry filling; originated in the Black Forest region

**spaetzle** A starch that is a cross between a dumpling and a noodle

**stollen** Traditional Christmas bread that originated in Dresden

**Westphalian ham** A delicate, smoked ham similar to Italian *prosciutto,* served sliced very thinly on buttered rye or pumpernickel bread

**würst** Any of the countless varieties of sausages

**zwiebelkuchen** Quichelike pie consisting of a pastry shell with a filling of bacon, eggs, cream, and onions

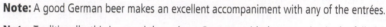

## ZWIEBELKUCHEN

### ONION TART

*Maille*

**Note:** A good German beer makes an excellent accompaniment with any of the entrées.

**Note:** Traditionally, this is served throughout Germany with the new wine in the fall. This tart may be prepared as one large pie (which is traditional) that is cut into wedges or as individual tarts.

**Note:** To serve this as a first course/salad, place mixed-lettuce salad in a vinegar and oil dressing either next to the Zwiebelkuchen or with the Zwiebelkuchen partially on top of the salad.

**Number of Servings:** 8 to 10
**Total Yield:** 9-inch (23-cm) tart
**Food Balance:** Sweet/protein
**Wine Style:** Soft and fruity Alsatian Riesling or Liebfraumilch, Viognier, rosé, Pinot Noir
**Example:** Beringer Viognier or Rosé de Saignee

**Cooking Method:** Bake

---

<table>
<thead>
<tr><th rowspan="2">INGREDIENTS</th><th colspan="2">WEIGHT</th><th colspan="2">VOLUME</th></tr>
<tr><th>U.S.</th><th>METRIC</th><th>U.S.</th><th>METRIC</th></tr>
</thead>
<tbody>
<tr><td>pie shell</td><td></td><td></td><td></td><td></td></tr>
<tr><td>bacon, diced</td><td>4 oz.</td><td>114 g</td><td>5 slices</td><td></td></tr>
<tr><td>onion, finely chopped</td><td>1 lb., 2 oz.</td><td>511 g</td><td>3 1/2 cups, about 4 medium</td><td>840 mL</td></tr>
<tr><td>pepper</td><td></td><td></td><td>1 teaspoon</td><td>5 mL</td></tr>
<tr><td>caraway seeds</td><td></td><td></td><td>1/8 teaspoon</td><td>1 mL</td></tr>
<tr><td>eggs</td><td>3 1/2 oz.</td><td>104 g</td><td>2 each</td><td></td></tr>
<tr><td>egg yolk</td><td>3/4 oz.</td><td>22 g</td><td>1 each</td><td></td></tr>
<tr><td>sour cream</td><td>6 oz.</td><td>171 g</td><td>3/4 cup</td><td>180 mL</td></tr>
</tbody>
</table>

1. Prepare pie shell. Do not dock (make small holes in bottom crust), but weight shell, by placing a piece of aluminum foil (shiny side down) in shell, making sure to push it into corners of pie pan. Bake until halfway done. Remove from oven and remove aluminum foil. Set aside until needed.
2. Fry bacon in skillet over medium heat until translucent, then add onions. Sauté, stirring frequently, until onions are clear yellow in color.
3. Add pepper and caraway seeds. Remove from heat and cool.
4. Place oven rack in lower portion of oven. Preheat oven to 400 degrees (205°C).
5. Beat eggs and yolk into sour cream in bowl. Spread onion mixture in bottom of pie crust, pour sour cream mixture over slowly so that it penetrates through onion mixture.
6. Bake for 15 minutes, then reduce temperature to 350 degrees (180°C) and bake another 20 minutes, until golden brown.
7. Cut into wedges, serve warm.

---

## KÖNIGSBERGER KLOPSE

### MEATBALLS IN CAPER SAUCE

**Note:** The portion size versus the weight is skewed because of the weight of the sauce.

**Note:** Königsberger Klopse is normally served as an entrée. To serve this as an entrée, double the size of the meatballs, to 2 oz. (57 g), and double the portion size of this appetizer, to about 6 oz. (171 g). As an appetizer, try serving the meatballs on a bed of mashed potatoes or spaetzle. Alternately, serve the meatballs (like Swedish meatballs) as a passed hors d' oeuvre with toothpicks, or place them in a chafer for a buffet.

**Number of Servings:** 11

**Cooking Method:** Boil

**Serving Size:** about 3 oz. (86 g), or 4 meatballs with sauce (1 oz. [28 g] raw meat per meatball)

**Total Yield:** 2 lb., 12 1/2 oz. (1.3 kg) meatballs in sauce

2 lb., 6 1/2 oz. (1.1 kg) raw meat mixture

1 lb., 10 1/4 oz. (746 g) cooked meatballs

44 meatballs

**Food Balance:** Balanced

**Wine Style:** Wine friendly—Choose your favorite

**Example:** Château St. Jean Chardonnay, Pinot Noir, or Cabernet Sauvignon

© Viktorija

| INGREDIENTS | WEIGHT | | VOLUME | |
| --- | --- | --- | --- | --- |
| | U.S. | METRIC | U.S. | METRIC |
| **Meatballs:** | | | | |
| white bread or roll | 2 oz. | 57 g | | |
| lukewarm water | | 227 g | 1 cup | 240 mL |
| onion, cut into quarters | 5 oz. | 142 g | 1 medium | |
| ground beef, veal, and pork in equal weights or any combination desired | 1 lb., 8 oz. | 680 g | | |
| anchovies | 3/4 oz. | 22 g | 5 fillets | |
| grated lemon zest | | | 1 teaspoon | 5 mL |
| fresh parsley, minced | 1/2 oz. | 15 g | 3 tablespoons | 45 mL |
| salt | | | 1/2 teaspoon | 3 mL |
| pepper | | | 1/4 teaspoon | 2 mL |
| eggs | 3 1/2 oz. | 104 g | 2 each | |
| beef stock, hot | | 1.4 kg | 1 quart + 2 cups (6 cups) | 1.44 L |
| **Sauce:** | | | | |
| butter | 1 oz. | 28 g | 2 tablespoons | 30 mL |
| onion, minced | 1/2 oz. | 15 g | 1 tablespoon | 15 mL |
| all-purpose flour | 1 oz. | 28 g | 3 1/2 tablespoons | 52 mL |
| beef stock, hot *from above* | | 454 g | 2 cups | 480 mL |
| lemon juice | | 43 g | 3 tablespoons | 45 mL |
| capers | 1 1/2 oz. | 43 g | 3 tablespoons | 45 mL |

## TWIST ON THE CLASSIC

Serve the *Königsberger Klopse* on French bread or a hoagie roll as a submarine sandwich.

This Prussian dish originated in an area of northern Germany that is now part of Russia and Eastern Europe. Today, they serve variations of *Königsberger Klopse* throughout Germany. In Bavaria, they add sour cream to the sauce.

## MEATBALLS:

1. Cut or tear rolls into pieces and soak in lukewarm water for 15 minutes. Squeeze to remove all excess water from bread. Set aside until needed.
2. Fit food processor with knife blade. With processor running, drop onion through feed tube. Pulse until minced, scraping sides as needed.
3. Add meat, bread, anchovies, and lemon zest to processor. Pulse until well blended, scraping sides as needed.
4. Add parsley, salt, pepper, and eggs. Process until smooth paste and well blended. Meanwhile, heat beef stock until gently boiling.
5. With wet hands, form a round meatball with 1 oz. (28 g) meat mixture (about 1 1/4- to 1 1/2-inches, 3- to 4-cm, in diameter). Place on plate, continue forming meatballs with remaining meat mixture. Place meatballs in stock. Cook for 10 to 12 minutes. Remove from stock. Reserve stock for sauce. Refrigerate meatballs until needed.

## SAUCE:

1. Melt butter in saucepan or skillet over medium heat. Add onion and cook a few minutes until softened and beginning to brown.
2. Whisk in flour, reduce heat to low. Cook, whisking, until dark blonde *roux*, a light brown color. Slowly whisk in hot stock.
3. Add lemon juice. Bring to boil, reduce heat, simmer until thickened, about 15 minutes.
4. Add meatballs and capers, continue cooking over low heat for 15 minutes. Correct seasonings. Serve as a passed hors d' oeuvre or plated and accompanied by boiled potatoes, mashed potatoes, or *spaetzle*.

# LEBERKNÖDEL SUPPE
## LIVER DUMPLING SOUP

© silencefoto

**Note:**
- Allow several hours to chill mixture before forming into balls.
- Warm bowls for serving soup.
- The portion for this recipe is two liver dumplings in a bowl of soup. A cup of soup needs only one dumpling.

**Note:** Leberknödel sometimes are served as an entrée with sauerkraut and potatoes.

**Number of Servings:** 15      **Cooking Method:** Boil
**Serving Size:** 11 oz. (308 g), or 2 dumplings and soup
**Scaling:** 2 1/2 oz. (71 g) raw meat per dumpling
**Total Yield:** 5 lb., 2 1/2 oz. (2.3 kg) cooked liver dumplings
                4 lb., 12 oz. (2.2 kg) raw liver mixture
                30 liver dumplings
**Food Balance:** Protein
**Wine Style:** Off-dry or low-oaked whites and soft-tannin reds
**Example:** Beringer Sauvignon Blanc or Napa Valley Pinot Noir

## TWIST ON THE CLASSIC

Prepare a submarine sandwich with a filling of sauerkraut, liver dumplings, and melted Swiss cheese.

© silencefoto

| | WEIGHT | | VOLUME | |
|---|---|---|---|---|
| **INGREDIENTS** | **U.S.** | **METRIC** | **U.S.** | **METRIC** |
| French bread, cut or torn into pieces | 6 oz. | 171 g | | about 6-inch (15-cm) piece |
| lukewarm water | | 454 g | 2 cups | 480 mL |
| onion, cut into quarters | 6 oz. | 171 g | 1 medium to large | |
| liver, trimmed of all membrane and gristle, washed | 1 lb., 12 oz. | 794 g | | |
| dried marjoram | | | 2 teaspoons | 10 mL |
| fresh parsley, minced | 1/2 oz. | 15 g | 1/4 cup | 60 mL |
| lemon zest | 1/4 oz. | 8 g | 2 teaspoons | 10 mL |
| nutmeg | | | 1/2 teaspoon | 3 mL |
| salt | 1/4 oz. | 8 g | 1 teaspoon | 5 mL |
| pepper | | | 1 teaspoon | 5 mL |
| eggs | 6 3/4 oz. | 191 g | 4 each | |
| breadcrumbs | 1 lb. or as needed | 454 g | 3 cups or as needed | 720 mL |
| beef stock, hot | | 3.6 kg | 1 gallon (4 quarts) | 3.84 L |

**Garnish:**
fresh chives, minced

1. Place bread in bowl, pour warm water over it. Let soak for 15 minutes. Squeeze dry, discard water, set aside.
2. Fit food processor with knife blade. With processor running, drop onion through feed tube. Pulse until finely chopped. Scrape down sides of processor as needed.
3. Add liver, pulse until fine. Add soaked bread, pulse to incorporate. Add marjoram, parsley, lemon zest, nutmeg, salt, pepper, and eggs. Process until paste. Scrape down sides of processor as needed.
4. Add two-thirds of breadcrumbs, pulse to combine. Add more breadcrumbs as needed to form soft mixture.
5. Cover and chill for a few hours to firm mixture.
6. Form into 2 1/2 oz. (71 g) balls (about 2 inches [5 cm] in diameter). Drop into boiling stock, simmer for 20 to 25 minutes, until done.
7. Serve liver dumplings in bowl of beef stock, garnished with chives, if desired.

# BLUMENKOHLSUPPE

## CREAM OF CAULIFLOWER SOUP

**Note:** Warm bowls for serving this soup.

**Number of Servings:** 9
**Serving Size:** 6 oz. (171 g)
**Total Yield:** 3 lb., 7 oz. (1.6 kg)
**Food Balance:** Sweet/protein
**Wine Style:** Light and fruity Sauvignon Blanc, fruity Chardonnay, or Beaujolais
**Example:** Souverain Sauvignon Blanc

**Cooking Method:** Boil

| INGREDIENTS | WEIGHT | | VOLUME | |
|---|---|---|---|---|
| | U.S. | METRIC | U.S. | METRIC |
| cauliflower | approx 2 lb., 3 oz. | 994 g | 1 large | |
| chicken stock | | 908 g | 1 quart (4 cups) | 960 mL |
| water | | 227 g to 454 g | 1 to 2 cups | 240 to 480 mL |
| butter | 2 oz. | 57 g | 4 tablespoons (1/2 stick) | 60 mL |
| flour | 1 1/2 oz. | 43 g | 1/4 cup + 1 tablespoon | 75 mL |
| milk | | 227 g | 1 cup | 240 mL |
| white pepper | | | 1/2 teaspoon | 3 mL |
| ground nutmeg | | | 1/4 teaspoon | 2 mL |
| egg yolk | 3/4 oz. | 22 g | 1 each | |

**Garnish:**

paprika

### TWIST ON THE CLASSIC

Use this thick soup as a sauce for other vegetables. Another idea is to top a piece of grilled chicken with provolone cheese and a slice of tomato, broil it until the cheese melts, then place it on a bed of this cauliflower purée.

1. Remove and discard core and outer green leaves of cauliflower. Separate flowerets, wash well. Reserve some small florets to add to puréed soup at end. Chop remaining cauliflower.

2. Bring stock to boil, add chopped cauliflower, cook until almost soft. Add 1 cup (227 g or 240 mL) water. Remove cauliflower from stock. Set aside until needed.

3. Melt butter in saucepan over moderate heat, add flour, whisk briefly over low heat until it becomes a white roux.

4. Slowly whisk hot stock into roux, a ladle-full at a time, cook until smooth and thick. If needed, add remaining 1 cup (227 g or 240 mL) water.

5. Add reserved cauliflower to roux. Whisk in milk, white pepper, and nutmeg, cook about 10 to 15 minutes, until cauliflower is soft. Add remaining 1 cup (227 g or 240 mL) water if too thick.

6. Purée mixture, using food processor or ricer.

7. Return to saucepan, add reserved uncooked cauliflower florets, cook until almost soft.

8. Place yolk in separate bowl. Whisking continually, add hot soup by tablespoons to temper yolk. Add yolk to soup, cook another few minutes, stirring occasionally. Be careful not to boil, or soup could curdle.

9. Correct seasonings. Serve immediately in warmed bowls. If desired, garnish with sprinkling of paprika.

## KALTER KARTOFFELSALAT

### COLD POTATO SALAD

**Note:** Allow several hours for this potato salad to sit before serving. The potatoes absorb the flavorings, so it is important to taste the salad and correct the seasonings.

**Number of Servings:** 8
**Serving Size:** 4 oz. (114 g)
**Total Yield:** 2 lb., 3 oz. (994 g)

**Cooking Method:** Boil

**TWIST ON THE CLASSIC**

To serve this warm, sauté minced onions until they soften, and then add potato salad to the skillet. Sauté until hot.

| INGREDIENTS | WEIGHT U.S. | WEIGHT METRIC | VOLUME U.S. | VOLUME METRIC |
|---|---|---|---|---|
| red potatoes, scrubbed | 2 lb. | 908 g | 6 medium to large | |
| onion, finely minced | 3 oz. | 86 g | 1 small | |
| oil | | 43 g | 3 tablespoons | 45 mL |
| vinegar | | 57 g | 1/4 cup | 60 mL |
| salt | 1/4 oz. | 8 g | 1 teaspoon | 5 mL |
| pepper | | | 3/4 teaspoon | 4 mL |
| fresh parsley or dill, minced, *optional* | 1/2 to 1 oz. | 15 g to 28 g | 2 to 4 tablespoons | 30 mL to 60 mL |

1. Place potatoes in pan, cover with cold water. Bring to gentle boil, cook until tender.
2. Drain, saving 1/3 cup (78 g or 80 mL) cooking liquid. Let potatoes cool slightly until able to handle, then peel potatoes, slice thinly into nonreactive bowl.
3. Add onion, oil, and reserved cooking liquid to potatoes, mix gently.
4. Add vinegar, salt, and pepper, mix gently.
5. Let sit at room temperature for several hours.
6. Add parsley or dill, if desired. Correct seasonings. Serve.

© Quade

# WARMER KARTOFFELSALAT MIT SPECK
## WARM POTATO SALAD WITH BACON

**Number of Servings:** 13
**Serving Size:** 4 oz. (114 g)
**Total Yield:** 3 lb., 5 oz. (1.5 kg)

**Cooking Method:** Boil, sauté

| | WEIGHT | | VOLUME | |
|---|---|---|---|---|
| **INGREDIENTS** | **U.S.** | **METRIC** | **U.S.** | **METRIC** |
| red potatoes, scrubbed | 3 lb. | 1.4 kg | 9 medium | |
| bacon, finely diced | 8 oz. | 227 g | | |
| onion, minced | 3 oz. | 86 g | 1 small | |
| cider vinegar | | 156 g | 2/3 cup | 160 mL |
| water | | 57 g | 1/4 cup | 60 mL |
| salt | 1/4 oz. | 8 g | 1 teaspoon | 5 mL |
| pepper | | | 3/4 teaspoon | 4 mL |
| fresh parsley, minced | 1/2 oz. | 15 g | 2 tablespoons | 30 mL |

1. Place potatoes in pot and cover with water. Bring to boil and cook until three-quarters done. Do not overcook.
2. Drain potatoes, peel while still quite warm. Cut into 1/8- to 1/4-inch (30-mm to 60-mm) slices, place in bowl. Cover to keep warm.
3. Cook bacon in skillet over moderate heat until brown and crisp, remove bacon from skillet, drain well on paper towels.
4. Add onions to bacon fat and cook, stirring frequently, 5 minutes, until onions are soft and transparent.
5. Stir in vinegar, water, salt, and pepper, and cook, stirring constantly, for a minute or so.
6. Pour hot sauce over potatoes, turning gently with spatula to coat evenly. Be careful not to break potatoes.
7. Gently stir reserved bacon pieces into salad. Correct seasonings.
8. Serve at once or cover and store at room temperature until service. For longer storage, refrigerate, then serve at room temperature.
9. At service, stir salad gently and sprinkle with parsley.

### TWIST ON THE CLASSIC

Use this potato salad as the filling for an omelet or frittata: Sauté the potato salad, add beaten eggs. Lift the eggs with a spatula so the raw eggs run under the cooked ones. When set, flip the entire "egg pancake" to briefly cook the other side or place a lid on the skillet to steam the top of the eggs.

*Courtesy of the Idaho Potato Commission*

# SAUERBRATEN

## MARINATED BEEF ROAST

**Note:** Begin marinating the meat two to three days before cooking.

| | |
|---|---|
| **Number of Servings:** 8 | **Cooking Method:** Braise |

**Serving Size:** 4 oz. (114 g) meat with 2 oz. (57 g) sauce
**Total Yield:** 2 lb., 1 oz. (936 g) meat
1 lb., 1 oz. (482 g) sauce
**Food Balance:** Acid/balanced
**Wine Style:** Wide variety of wines: Sauvignon Blanc, Pinot Grigio, Pinot Noir, Shiraz, Chianti, or Barbera
**Example:** Castello di Gabbiano Chianti

*Marinating meat*
© M. Schuppich

© ExQuisine

| | WEIGHT | | VOLUME | |
|---|---|---|---|---|
| **INGREDIENTS** | **U.S.** | **METRIC** | **U.S.** | **METRIC** |
| **Marinade:** | | | | |
| red wine | | 114 g | 1/2 cup | 120 mL |
| red wine vinegar | | 114 g | 1/2 cup | 120 ml |
| water | | 114 g | 1/2 cup | 120 mL |
| onion, sliced thin | 5 oz. | 142 g | 1 medium | |
| whole peppercorns | | | 6 each | |
| whole cloves | | | 6 each | |
| bay leaves | | | 2 each | |
| kosher salt | 1/4 oz. | 8 g | 1 teaspoon | 5 mL |
| beef roast, bottom round, chuck, rump, or shoulder | 4 lb. | 1.8 kg | | |
| oil | | 28 g | 2 tablespoons | 30 mL |
| onion, finely diced | 3 oz. | 86 g | 1 small onion or 1/2 cup | 120 mL |
| celery, finely diced | 2 3/4 oz. | 78 g | 1/2 cup | 120 mL |
| carrot, finely diced | 2 1/2 oz. | 71 g | 1/2 cup | 120 mL |
| flour | 1/2 oz | 15 g | 2 tablespoons | 30 mL |
| gingersnap crumbs | 2 1/4 oz. | 64 g | 1/2 cup | 120 mL |

### MARINATE:

1. Place wine, vinegar, water, onion, peppercorns, cloves, bay leaves, and salt in nonreactive saucepan. Bring to boil, remove from heat. Cool.
2. Trim meat of excess fat, wash well. Place in nonreactive bowl. Pour cooled marinade over meat. Add more red wine, if needed, to cover meat halfway.
3. Cover and refrigerate for 2 to 3 days, turning two or three times daily.

### COOK:

1. Remove meat from marinade, pat dry. Strain marinade and reserve liquid. Measure 2 cups (480 mL) marinade (adding water if necessary), place in saucepan and heat. Set aside any extra marinade.
2. Place oil in braising or roasting pan over medium to medium-high heat and heat until hot. Sear meat on all sides, browning lightly. Remove meat from pan.
3. Over medium heat, add onion, celery, and carrot, sauté until soft and lightly browned, about 5 to 7 minutes. Sprinkle flour on vegetables and cook, stirring about 2 to 3 minutes.
4. Slowly whisk in 2 cups (480 mL) hot reserved marinade. Return meat to pan and cover tightly.
5. Braise on top of stove, simmering until meat is tender, about 2 to 2 1/2 hours, or cook in 300-degree (150°C) oven for 2 to 3 hours.

⑥ Remove meat and keep warm.

⑦ Strain liquid, discard vegetables. Put 2 1/2 cups (600 mL) liquid in saucepan, adding more reserved marinade or water if necessary. Skim excess fat. Add gingersnap crumbs.

⑧ Cook sauce 10 minutes over medium heat. Strain, if lumpy. If too thick, add more marinade or water. Bring to boil.

⑨ Correct seasonings. To serve, slice meat in thin slices against grain. Nap with sauce. Serve with *spaetzle*, mashed potatoes, boiled potatoes, or potato pancakes.

## WIENER SCHNITZLE

### VEAL CUTLET VIENNESE STYLE

**Number of Servings:** 2      **Cooking Method:** Sauté
**Serving Size:** 4 oz. (114 g)
**Total Yield:** 8 1/4 oz. (234 g)
**Food Balance:** Balanced
**Wine Style:** Wide variety of wines: Riesling, Chardonnay, Pinot Noir, Merlot
**Example:** Souverain Merlot

> **TWIST ON THE CLASSIC**
>
> Instead of veal, prepare the *schnitzle* with chicken or pork. For an interesting presentation, serve *wiener schnitzle* topped with a salad dressed with vinaigrette.

| | WEIGHT | | VOLUME | |
|---|---|---|---|---|
| **INGREDIENTS** | **U.S.** | **METRIC** | **U.S.** | **METRIC** |
| boneless veal cutlets, (scaloppine) | 6 to 7 oz. | 171 g to 199 g | 2 each | |
| salt | to taste | | | |
| pepper | to taste | | | |
| **Breading:** | | | | |
| egg | 1 oz. | 28 g | 1/2 each | |
| milk | | 28 g | 2 tablespoons | 30 mL |
| flour | 1 1/4 oz. | 36 g | 1/4 cup | 60 mL |
| bread crumbs | 1 1/4 oz. | 36 g | 1/4 cup + 1 tablespoon | 75 mL |

oil and/or clarified butter for frying

**Garnish:**
lemon wedge
rolled anchovy

*Dripping veal in egg*
David Murray and Jules Selmes © Dorling Kindersley

*Dredging veal in flour*
David Murray and Jules Selmes © Dorling Kindersley

*Dredging veal in bread crumbs*
David Murray and Jules Selmes © Dorling Kindersley

*Frying veal cutlets*

David Murray and Jules Selmes © Dorling Kindersley

© Quade

1. Lightly flatten each piece of veal with meat mallet until 1/16- to 1/8-inch (15-mm to 30-mm) thick. Be careful not to tear meat.
2. Season with salt and pepper.
3. Set up breading ingredients, as for standard breading. Mix egg and milk in shallow dish. Place flour in flat dish. Place bread crumbs in flat dish.
4. Coat each piece of veal with flour, dunk into egg mixture, then coat with bread crumbs. Make sure meat is thoroughly coated with each ingredient.
5. Heat about 1/4-inch (1/2-cm) oil or butter in skillet over medium to medium-high heat until hot. Sauté cutlets until golden brown on both sides.
6. Garnish with lemon and anchovy, serve immediately.

## SCHWEINE-FILET

### PORK TENDERLOIN (IN A LEMON SAUCE)

**Number of Servings:** 6 to 8      **Cooking Method:** Braise
**Serving Size:** 4 to 5 oz. (114 to 142 g)
**Total Yield:** 1 lb., 10 oz. to 2 lb., 2 oz. (738 to 965 g) meat (depending on size of tenderloins)
**Food Balance:** Acid balanced
**Wine Style:** Wide variety of wines: Pinot Grigio, Chardonnay, Merlot, Cabernet Sauvignon
**Example:** Beringer Knights Valley Cabernet Sauvignon

|  | WEIGHT | | VOLUME | |
|---|---|---|---|---|
| **INGREDIENTS** | **U.S.** | **METRIC** | **U.S.** | **METRIC** |
| pork tenderloin, trimmed of fat | 12 oz. to 1 lb. | (340 to 454 g) each | 3 each | |
| flour, all-purpose or bread | 2 oz. | 57 g | 1/4 cup + 3 tablespoons | 105 mL |
| oil | | 43 g | 3 tablespoons | 45 mL |
| onions, sliced in 1/8-inch (30-mm) rings | 9 oz. | 256 g | 1 to 1 1/2 large | |
| hot water, as needed | | | | |
| lemon juice | | | 1 to 1 1/2 lemons | |
| salt | to taste | | | |
| pepper | to taste | | | |

**TWIST ON THE CLASSIC**

Give this dish flair by adding capers and artichoke hearts to the sauce.

1. Dredge pork in flour. Heat oil in skillet or braising pan over medium heat until hot. Sear pork on all sides, then add onions. Sauté until brown.
2. Add remaining flour to pan, whisk until lightly brown.
3. Whisk in hot water very slowly to make medium-thin sauce. Add more water as necessary, if sauce becomes too thick.
4. Add lemon juice, salt, and pepper. Cover and braise over medium-low heat about 45 minutes, until pork is done. Stir occasionally to keep meat from sticking. Add water as necessary to make medium-thin sauce. Correct seasonings.
5. Slice and serve with *spaetzle*, fried potatoes, or pasta.

## SCHWEINE FLEISCH MIT SAUERKRAUT

### PORK WITH SAUERKRAUT

**Number of Servings:** 12
**Cooking Method:** Braise
**Serving Size:** 1 chop and 1/2 sausage with kraut
**Total Yield:** 9 lb., 10 oz. (4.4 kg)
**Food Balance:** Acid/protein
**Wine Style:** Acid-balanced-to-strong dry Riesling, Pinot Grigio, Chianti, or strong Cabernet
**Example:** Castello Di Gabbiano Chianti Classico or Riserva

| INGREDIENTS | WEIGHT | | VOLUME | |
| --- | --- | --- | --- | --- |
| | U.S. | METRIC | U.S. | METRIC |
| sauerkraut, drained and rinsed | 3 lb., 6 oz. | 1.5 kg | two 27-oz. cans | 1.531 kg |
| red potato, peeled and grated | 11 1/2 oz. | 326 g | 2 medium | |
| tart apple, peeled, cored, and grated | 11 oz. | 312 g | 2 medium | |
| onion, peeled and grated | 8 oz. | 227 g | 2 medium | |
| caraway seeds | 1/2 oz. | 15 g | 1 tablespoon + 1 teaspoon | 20 mL |
| country style ribs, pork chops, sausage, or any combination | 6 lb. | 2.8 kg | | |

1. Preheat oven to 325 degrees (160°C).
2. Combine sauerkraut, potato, apple, onion, and caraway seeds in ovenproof pan or roaster.
3. Top with ribs and/or chops, bury sausages in sauerkraut.
4. Bake, uncovered, for about 1 1/2 hours, until done.

### TWIST ON THE CLASSIC

Transform this into a duck dish by substituting duck for the pork. Remove any excess fat and skin from the duck so the dish will not be greasy.

## ENTE MIT APFELFÜLLUNG

### DUCK WITH APPLE DRESSING

**Note:** If serving 1/2 duck for a portion, double the amount of duck and prepare 6 ducks.

**Number of Servings:** 12
**Cooking Method:** Bake
**Serving Size:** 1/4 duck, about 10 oz. (284 g)
4 oz. (114 g) dressing
1 oz. (28 g) sauce
**Total Yield:** about 7 lb., 10 1/4 oz. duck (3.5 kg), or 3 ducks
3 lb., 2 1/4 oz. (1.4 kg) dressing
12 3/4 oz. (377 mL) sauce
**Food Balance:** Sweet/protein
**Wine Style:** Off-dry or low-oaked whites and soft-tannin reds
**Example:** Rosemount Traminer Riesling or Semillon or Pinot Noir

©Viktor1

**TWIST ON THE CLASSIC**

Try adding apple juice and some brandy to the sauce and replacing the bone-in duck with a boneless duck breast fanned around the stuffing.

To toast the bread crumbs, bake in 250-degree (120°C) oven until dried. They can be lightly browned, but it is not necessary.

| INGREDIENTS | WEIGHT | | VOLUME | |
|---|---|---|---|---|
| | U.S. | METRIC | U.S. | METRIC |
| duck, giblets and excess fat removed, washed | about 14 lb., 5 1/2 oz. | 6.5 kg | 3 each | |
| **Dressing:** | | | | |
| raisins | 3 oz. | 86 g | 1/2 cup | 120 mL |
| German white wine | | 227 g | 1 cup | 240 mL |
| bread, stale or lightly toasted, cubed | 8 oz. | 227 g | about 7 cups | 1.7 L |
| butter | 1 oz. | 28 g | 2 tablespoons | 30 mL |
| apples, peeled, cored, and cut into large dice | 2 lb. | 908 g | about 4 large | |
| ham, small dice | 4 oz. | 114 g | | |
| fresh parsley, minced | 1/4 oz. | 8 g | 1 tablespoon | 15 mL |
| nutmeg | | | 1/4 teaspoon | 2 mL |
| pepper | | | 1/2 teaspoon | 3 mL |
| chicken stock | | 114 to 170 g | 1/2 to 3/4 cup | 120 to 180 mL |
| salt, *optional* | as needed | | | |
| **Sauce:** | | | | |
| all-purpose flour | 1 oz. | 28 g | 3 tablespoons | 45 mL |
| chicken stock, hot | | 114 to 170 g | 2 cups | 480 mL |
| German white wine | | 114 g | 1/2 cup | 120 mL |
| salt | as needed | | | |
| pepper | as needed | | | |
| **Garnish:** | | | | |
| apple rings, sautéed | | | | |
| fresh parsley, minced | | | | |

## DUCK:

1. Position oven rack in center of oven. Preheat oven to 450 degrees (230°C). Place a rack in the bottom of a roasting pan and add about 1/2 inch (1.3 cm) water (so duck will not touch water). Stick duck with a fork all over, to dock skin so fat will be rendered. Prepare dressing while duck roasts.

2. Place duck on rack in pan with the breast side down, put in oven, and reduce oven temperature to 350 degrees (180°C). Remove after 45 minutes, drain fat if necessary. Turn duck over so breast side is up. Stick all over with fork again. Return to oven, bake for another 45 minutes. Remove from oven, drain grease, if needed.

3. Return to oven, bake another 30 minutes to 1 hour (total baking time 2 to 2 1/2 hours) until proper internal temperature is reached and juices run clear. If broiling duck to crisp the skin, undercook the duck slightly.

4. To obtain a crisp skin, pour all fat from pan. Broil duck on all sides until crisp. Keep warm in oven while preparing sauce.

## DRESSING:

1. While duck cooks, prepare dressing. Place raisins in nonreactive bowl, pour wine over them. Allow to sit at least 30 minutes. Pan-spray ovenproof pan and set aside.

2. Place bread cubes in large bowl. Melt butter in skillet over medium heat. Add apples, sauté until beginning to soften, about 5 to 10 minutes, depending on the hardness of the apple variety.

3. Add apples and liquid from skillet, ham, parsley, nutmeg, pepper, and 1/2 cup (114 g or 120 mL) chicken stock to bread cubes. Add more stock if mixture seems too dry, but just moisten mixture, do not soak it with liquid. Add salt if needed.

4. Correct seasonings. Transfer mixture to prepared pan. Cover and bake with duck for 30 minutes. Remove cover and bake for 30 to 45 minutes, depending on wetness of mixture.

## SAUCE:

1. Place roasting pan (with fat drained off) over medium heat. Sprinkle flour over pan. Whisk until light brown in color.
2. Slowly whisk in hot stock. Whisk in wine.
3. Season with salt and pepper, as needed. Correct seasonings.

## ASSEMBLY:

1. Place 4 oz. (114 g) dressing on plate. Top with duck (either 1/4 duck or 1/2 duck, as desired) sitting at an angle over dressing.
2. Nap with 1 oz. (28 g) sauce.
3. Garnish with sautéed apple rings or slices and a sprinkling of parsley.

## FORELLE IN RAHM

### TROUT IN CREAM

svry © Shutterstock

**Note:** If desired, remove head of trout before serving.

**Number of Servings:** 8

**Cooking Method:** Sauté

**Serving Size:** 1 trout, or about 7 oz. (199 g) with 2 1/4 oz. (64 g), or about 1/4 cup (60 mL) sauce

**Total Yield:** 8 trout, or about 3 lb., 8 oz. (1.6 kg)
1 lb., 2 3/4 oz. (532 g), or about 2 cups (480 mL) sauce

**Food Balance:** Protein/sour

**Wine Style:** Off-dry or low-oaked whites and soft-tannin reds

**Example:** Beringer Chenin Blanc, Stone Cellars Chardonnay or Merlot

| INGREDIENTS | WEIGHT U.S. | METRIC | VOLUME U.S. | METRIC |
|---|---|---|---|---|
| all-purpose flour | as needed for dredging | | | |
| salt | to taste | | | |
| pepper | to taste | | | |
| trout, sliced open on one side, bones removed, head and tail intact (if desired), washed | about 3 lb., 8 oz. | 1.6 kg | 8 each | |
| butter | about 4 oz. | 114 g | 8 tablespoons (1 stick) | 120 mL |
| **Sauce:** | | | | |
| butter or oil | | 28 g | 2 tablespoons | 30 mL |
| onion, minced | 6 oz. | 171 g | 1 large | |
| flour, all-purpose | 1 oz. | 28 g | 3 tablespoons | 45 mL |
| sour cream | 13 1/2 oz. | 383 g | 1 1/2 cups | 360 mL |
| salt | | | 1/2 teaspoon | 3 mL |
| white pepper | | | 1/2 teaspoon | 3 mL |
| lemon juice | | 43 g | 3 tablespoons | 45 mL |
| water | | 15 g | 1 tablespoon | 15 mL or as needed |

**Garnish:**
fresh parsley, minced
lemon wedges

### TWIST ON THE CLASSIC

For an elegant presentation, serve fish in a puff pastry shell (made to fit the whole fish). Alternatively, remove bones and skin from cooked trout, mix fish with the sauce, and serve in a puff pastry shell.

1. Season flour for dredging fish with salt and pepper. Place on plate or flat surface like sheet pan. Dredge both sides of fish (inside and outside) with flour.

2. Melt enough butter to cover bottom of large skillet over medium heat. When hot, add trout. Sauté until golden on each side.

3. Remove trout from pan, keep warm in oven. Repeat with remaining fish, adding butter as needed. Do not wash skillet—use it to prepare sauce.

## SAUCE:

1. Place butter or oil in skillet (if butter remains in skillet from sautéing trout, add enough additional butter or oil so there is 2 tablespoons (28 g or 30 mL) in skillet. Heat until hot over medium heat.

2. Add onion to pan, sauté until golden. Lower heat to medium-low, sprinkle flour over onions, whisk until dark blonde *roux*, just beginning to brown.

3. Whisk in sour cream. Add salt, pepper, and lemon juice. Whisking constantly, cook until mixture thickens and begins to boil. If too thick, add 1 tablespoon (15 g or 15 mL) water to thin. Add additional water if needed to obtain desired thickness.

4. Correct seasonings. If desired, remove head from fish. Place fish on plate, and nap with about 1/4 cup (60 mL) sauce. Garnish with parsley and lemon, serve at once.

---

## SPAETZLE

### SMALL NOODLELIKE DUMPLINGS

**Note:** To expedite cutting the dough into the boiling water, place dough in large pastry bag fitted with 3/8-inch (1-cm) diameter round tip. Push dough through the bag by pulsing the bag so the dough extrudes in pieces that break off and fall into the boiling water.

**Number of Servings:** 14
**Serving Size:** 3 oz. (86 g)
**Total Yield:** 2 lb., 10 oz. (1.2 kg)

**Cooking Method:** Boil, sauté

| | TWIST ON THE CLASSIC |
|---|---|

Use *spaetzle* instead of gnocchi or pasta in countless dishes. Try cutting slices of *sauerbraten* into strips, mix with *spaetzle,* top with your cheese of choice, and bake in a 400-degree (205°C) oven until it's hot and the cheese bubbles.

*Pushing spaetzle dough into boiling water*
Jerry Young © Dorling Kindersley

| | WEIGHT | | VOLUME | |
|---|---|---|---|---|
| **INGREDIENTS** | **U.S.** | **METRIC** | **U.S.** | **METRIC** |
| all-purpose flour | 13 oz. | 369 g | 3 cups | 720 mL |
| salt | | | 1/2 teaspoon | 3 mL |
| nutmeg | | | 1/8 teaspoon | 1 mL |
| eggs | 6 3/4 oz. | 191 g | 4 each | |
| water | | about 227 g | about 1 cup | 240 mL |
| butter | as needed | | | |
| salt | to taste | | | |
| pepper | to taste | | | |
| dill, finely chopped, *optional* | to taste | | | |

1. Place flour, salt, and nutmeg in bowl, form a well (indentation in center).

2. Beat eggs in small bowl to blend, pour into well in dry ingredients. Add about half the water, beat well.

3. Add more water, a little at a time, and beat mixture until bubbles start to appear and smooth batter no longer adheres to the spoon. Batter will be thick but wet.

4. Fill large pot with water, bring to boil.

5. Moisten a small board with a little boiling water, take a little bit of dough, and press it flat on board with an icing spatula or dull side of a chef's knife.

6. Cut off fine strips of dough, push them off edge of board into boiling water with spatula. Dip spatula into boiling water if sticking to dough. *Note: This is difficult and takes practice. For a simpler way to form the* spaetzle, *extrude dough through a pastry bag (as described above) or push dough through a perforated hotel pan.*

7. Remove *spaetzle* with skimmer when they float to surface. Place in bowl of cold water to remove excess starch and hold until service.

8. To serve, drain well, sauté in butter to reheat. Season with salt, pepper, and finely chopped dill, if desired.

*Removing cooked spaetzle from boiling water*

Jerry Young/Dorling Kindersley, Ltd

© Magrit Hirsch

## KAESESPAETZLE

### NOODLELIKE DUMPLINGS WITH CHEESE

**Note:** Serve this as a side dish or a luncheon entrée. Traditionally, this is served in Germany as a light entrée accompanied by a salad.

**Number of Servings:** 15 side dishes or 8 entrées    **Cooking Method:** Sauté, broil
**Serving Size:** 4 oz. (114 g) side dish or 7 oz. (199 g) entrée
**Total Yield:** 3 lb., 12 oz. (1.7 kg)
**Food Balance:** Protein
**Wine Style:** Light- to medium-bodied Pinot Blanc, Chardonnay, Merlot, or Zinfandel
**Example:** Château St. Jean Pinot Blanc

| INGREDIENTS | WEIGHT | | VOLUME | |
| --- | --- | --- | --- | --- |
| | **U.S.** | **METRIC** | **U.S.** | **METRIC** |
| butter | 2 oz. | 57 g | 4 tablespoons (1/2 stick) | 60 mL |
| *Spaetzle* (recipe above) | 2 lb., 10 oz. | 1.2 kg | 10 cups | 2.4 L |
| salt | 1/2 oz. | 15 g | 2 teaspoons | 10 mL |
| pepper | | | 1 teaspoon | 5 mL |
| *Emmentaler* or other Swiss cheese, grated | 1 lb., 4 oz. | 567 g | 4 cups | 960 mL |

© kab-vision

1. Preheat broiler. Melt butter in ovenproof skillet over medium heat.

2. Spread single, thin layer of *spaetzle* in skillet. Sprinkle with salt and pepper.

3. Sauté lightly, sprinkle cheese on top.

4. Place pan in broiler, broil until lightly brown. Serve immediately.

**TWIST ON THE CLASSIC**

For a different breakfast dish, make individual *kaesespaetzle* and top with a poached egg and Hollandaise (Benedict-style) or top with a fried egg.

# HIMMEL UND ERD

## POTATO AND APPLE MASH

"Himmel und Erd" means "heaven and earth." While the apples are heaven, potatoes represent the earth. This dish has many variations and supposedly originated in the Rhineland area.

Blutwürst often accompanies this dish.

**Number of Servings:** 11
**Serving Size:** 4 oz. (114 g)
**Total Yield:** 2 lb., 14 3/4 oz. (1.3 kg)
**Potato Apple Mixture:** 2 lb., 10 oz. (1.2 kg)
**Topping:** 4 3/4 oz. (135 g)

**Cooking Method:** Boil, sauté

| | WEIGHT | | VOLUME | |
|---|---|---|---|---|
| **INGREDIENTS** | **U.S.** | **METRIC** | **U.S.** | **METRIC** |
| bacon | 5 oz. | 142 g | | |
| potatoes, Russet or starchy variety, peeled, cut into pieces | 1 lb., 8 oz. | 681 g | | |
| apples, tart variety, peeled, cored, cut into 1-inch (2 1/2-cm) pieces | 1 lb. | 454 g | | |
| sugar | 1/2 oz. | 15 g | 1 tablespoon | 15 mL |
| lemon juice | | 15 g | 1 tablespoon | 15 mL |
| water | | 57 g | 1/4 cup | 60 mL |
| onion, thinly sliced | 12 3/4 oz. | 361 g | 2 medium | |
| salt | 1/4 oz. | 8 g | 1 teaspoon | 5 mL |
| pepper | | | 1/2 teaspoon | 3 mL |
| nutmeg | | | 1/4 teaspoon | 2 mL |
| butter | 1 1/2 oz. | 43 g | 3 tablespoons | 45 mL |

1. Cut bacon into pieces 1/2- to 3/4-inches (1- to 2-cm) wide. Sauté in skillet until crisp. Drain on absorbent paper and reserve until needed. Do not discard bacon grease.
2. Boil potatoes in water until soft but not falling apart.
3. Combine apples, sugar, lemon juice, and water in saucepan. Cook apples until soft like chunky applesauce.
4. Cook onions in skillet with bacon grease over medium-high heat until browned, about 20 minutes. If heat becomes too hot, reduce to medium.
5. Drain water from potatoes, mash them. Add apples, salt, pepper, nutmeg, and butter. Mash together. Correct seasonings.
6. Serve, topped with fried onions and bacon.

© creative studio

# BLAUKRAUT

## SWEET AND SOUR RED CABBAGE

**Note:** This cabbage may be cooked a day ahead. Some say the flavors actually marry better when reheated.

**Number of Servings:** 8
**Serving Size:** 4 oz. (114 g)
**Total Yield:** 2 lb., 2 oz. (965 g)

**Cooking Method:** Boil

| | WEIGHT | | VOLUME | |
| --- | --- | --- | --- | --- |
| **INGREDIENTS** | **U.S.** | **METRIC** | **U.S.** | **METRIC** |
| red cabbage, cored and thinly sliced across the grain | 2 lb. | 908 g | 1 medium head, about 10 cups | 2.4 L |
| apple, cored and cut into 12 pieces | about 6 oz. | 171 g | 1 medium or large | |
| water | | 340 g | 1 1/2 cups | 360 mL as needed |
| sugar | 2 3/4 oz. | 78 g | 1/3 cup | 80 mL |
| red wine vinegar | | 284 to 340 g | 1 1/4 to 1 1/2 cups | 300 to 360 mL |
| ground cloves | | | 1/8 teaspoon | 1 mL |
| salt | 1/4 to 1/2 oz. | 8 to 15 g | 1 1/2 teaspoons | 8 mL |
| pepper | | | 1/4 teaspoon | 2 mL |

1. Place cabbage, apple, and 1 cup (227 g or 240 mL) of the water in large pan over medium heat until starting to cook.
2. Add about three-quarters of the sugar and vinegar. Add cloves.
3. Reduce heat to low, cover, cook about 1 hour, adding more water, if needed, to prevent scorching.
4. Add salt and pepper. Taste, add more vinegar and sugar to balance sweet and sour. Continue cooking until cabbage is soft.
5. Correct seasonings and serve.

Pearson Education/PH College

© Tanja/Fotolia

## SÜSS UND SAURE GRUENE BOHNEN

### SWEET AND SOUR GREEN BEANS

© Wiktory

**Number of Servings:** 10
**Serving Size:** 4 oz. (114 g)
**Total Yield:** 2 lb., 10 oz. (1.2 g)

**Cooking Method:** Boil

| | WEIGHT | | VOLUME | |
|---|---|---|---|---|
| **INGREDIENTS** | **U.S.** | **METRIC** | **U.S.** | **METRIC** |
| butter | 1 oz. | 28 g | 2 tablespoons | 30 mL |
| all-purpose flour | 1 oz. | 28 g | 1/4 cup | 60 mL |
| water, hot | | 340 g | 1 1/2 cups | 360 mL |
| sugar | 2 oz. | 57 g | 1/4 cup | 60 mL |
| cider vinegar | | 142 g | 1/2 cup + 2 tablespoons | 150 mL |
| salt | 1/4 oz. | 8 g | 1 teaspoon | 5 mL |
| pepper | | | 1/2 teaspoon | 3 mL |
| green beans, stems and strings removed, broken, if desired | 2 lb. | 908 g | | |

① Make white roux: Melt butter over medium heat, add flour and mix with whisk. Cook briefly so it does not color. Whisking constantly, slowly add water.
② Add sugar, vinegar, salt, and pepper to sauce. Add green beans.
③ Cook until beans reach desired doneness, about 15 minutes. Add more water if necessary.
④ Correct seasonings and serve.

---

**TWIST ON THE CLASSIC**

Give these green beans a brighter look by adding diced or sliced red pepper in the last 5 or 10 minutes of cooking (depending on the size of the cut).

---

## LAUGENBREZELN

### PRETZELS

**TWIST ON THE CLASSIC**

Roll scaled dough into rectangle. Place pepperoni, salami, ham, or combination of choice on top of dough. Roll to seal meat within dough and press edges well to seal. Proceed with directions to simmer and then bake roll.

**Number of Servings:** 17 pretzels
**Scaling:** 2 1/2 oz. (71 g)
**Total Yield:** 2 lb., 12 1/4 oz. (1.3 kg) dough

**Cooking Method:** Boil, bake

| | WEIGHT | | VOLUME | |
|---|---|---|---|---|
| **INGREDIENTS** | **U.S.** | **METRIC** | **U.S.** | **METRIC** |
| water, lukewarm | | 57 g | 1/4 cup | 60 mL |
| sugar | 1/2 oz. | 15 g | 2 teaspoons | 10 mL |
| yeast, dry, granulated | 1/2 oz. | 15 g | 1 tablespoon + 1 teaspoon | 15 mL + 5 mL |
| butter, unsalted | 1 1/2 oz. | 43 g | 3 tablespoons | 45 mL |
| milk | | 227 g | 1 cup | 240 mL |
| water | | 227 g | 1 cup | 240 mL |
| bread flour | 1 lb., 7 1/4 oz. or as needed | 660 g | 5 cups or as needed | 1.2 L or as needed |
| salt | 1/2 oz. | 15 g | 2 teaspoons | 10 mL |

**Boiling Mixture:**

| | | | | |
|---|---|---|---|---|
| water | | | 3 quarts | 2.8 L |
| baking soda | 1 3/4 oz. | 50 g | 3 tablespoons | 45 mL |
| salt | 1/4 oz. | 8 g | 1 teaspoon | 5 mL |

**Toppings:**
coarse salt
poppy seeds, optional
caraway seeds, optional
sesame seeds, optional

*Forming laugenbrezeln*

1. Mix water (1/4 cup, 57 g, or 60 mL) and sugar in a small nonreactive bowl. Sprinkle yeast on top, mix with wooden spoon. Set aside until foamy, about 5 minutes.

2. Meanwhile, melt butter with milk. Add water and heat until lukewarm.

3. Mix 1 lb., 3 oz. (540 g, 4 cups, or 960 mL) flour and salt in a large nonreactive bowl. Make well in center of mixture, add butter mixture and stir with wooden spoon to combine.

4. Add yeast mixture. Stir with wooden spoon until thoroughly mixed. Add more flour as needed until dough is just stiff enough to knead. Knead for 10 minutes, until smooth and elastic, adding a little flour when needed. Be careful to add only enough flour to prevent dough from sticking to counter while kneading. Too much flour will result in a dry finished product.

5. Return dough to bowl, cover and let rise until doubled, about 1 hour.

> To create a glossy finish, brush pretzels with beaten egg before baking.

6. Meanwhile, cover sheet pan with parchment paper or pan spray it. Prepare boiling mixture by combining water, baking soda, and salt in a large pan. Stir mixture to dissolve baking soda. Place oven rack in center of oven. Preheat to 425 degrees (220°C).

7. Punch down dough, knead briefly to remove any air bubbles, then scale into 2 1/2 oz. (71 g) pieces. Form into pretzel shape.

> If desired, form into a plain round roll or a crescent roll (*Salzstangen*) instead of a pretzel.

8. To form pretzel, roll dough into logs about 14- or 16-inches (36- or 41-cm) long. Make log a little thinner toward ends and thicker in the middle. Twist the ends to form a loop, then twist ends again. Flip dough over and press two loose ends into bottom part of loop to form pretzel shape. Press ends well to seal.

9. Place pretzels on prepared pan. Cover until all are formed and allow them to rest 15 minutes. Ready paper toweling or towels for draining boiled pretzels. Bring boiling mixture to full boil.

10. Place 1 or 2 pretzels in water, reduce heat to simmer. Simmer for 15 seconds, turn and simmer for 15 seconds on other side. Remove with skimmer or slotted spoon and drain well on toweling. Place pretzels back on sheet pan.

11. Brush pretzels with boiling water. Sprinkle with coarse salt and/or poppy seeds, caraway seeds, or sesame seeds. Place pans in oven, reduce temperature to 400 degrees (205°C). Bake for 20 to 25 minutes, until golden.

12. Cool on baking rack, serve lukewarm or at room temperature.

*Laugenbrezeln*

*Laugenbrezeln with butter*
© Bernd Jürgens

## LINZERTORTE

### SPICED DOUGH FILLED WITH RASPBERRY PRESERVES

Pearson Education/PH College

**Note:** This confection actually is named after Linz, Austria; however, southern Germany and neighboring Austria serve many of the same food items.

**Note:** Allow time to chill dough several hours in the refrigerator or at least 30 to 45 minutes in the freezer (depending on the temperature of the freezer). Chilling this fragile dough makes it much easier to handle.

**Number of Servings:** 10 to 12      **Cooking Method:** Bake
**Total Yield:** 9- or 10-inch (23-cm to 25-cm) tart, 1 lb., 11 3/4 oz. (787 g) dough, in French tart pan with removable bottom or springform pan
**Scaling:** 1 lb., 5 oz. (596 g) dough for 9-inch (23-cm) French tart pan

<table>
<tr><td rowspan="2">INGREDIENTS</td><td colspan="2">WEIGHT</td><td colspan="2">VOLUME</td></tr>
<tr><td>U.S.</td><td>METRIC</td><td>U.S.</td><td>METRIC</td></tr>
<tr><td>all-purpose flour, sifted</td><td>6 1/2 oz.</td><td>184 g plus more for rolling out dough</td><td>1 1/2 cups</td><td>360 mL plus more for rolling out dough</td></tr>
<tr><td>baking powder</td><td></td><td></td><td>1 teaspoon</td><td>5 mL</td></tr>
<tr><td>salt</td><td></td><td></td><td>1/4 teaspoon</td><td>2 mL</td></tr>
<tr><td>ground cinnamon</td><td>1/4 oz.</td><td>8 g</td><td>2 teaspoons</td><td>10 mL</td></tr>
<tr><td>ground cloves</td><td></td><td></td><td>1/4 teaspoon</td><td>2 mL</td></tr>
<tr><td>ground nutmeg</td><td></td><td></td><td>1/2 teaspoon</td><td>3 mL</td></tr>
<tr><td>unsalted butter</td><td>8 oz.</td><td>227 g</td><td>1 cup (2 sticks)</td><td>240 mL</td></tr>
<tr><td>sugar</td><td>7 1/2 oz.</td><td>213 g</td><td>1 cup</td><td>240 mL</td></tr>
<tr><td>grated lemon peel</td><td></td><td></td><td>1 1/2 teaspoons</td><td>8 mL</td></tr>
<tr><td>grated orange peel</td><td></td><td></td><td>1 tablespoon</td><td>15 mL</td></tr>
<tr><td>egg yolks</td><td>1 1/2 oz.</td><td>43 g</td><td>2 each</td><td></td></tr>
<tr><td>almonds, blanched and ground</td><td>4 oz.</td><td>114 g</td><td>1 cup</td><td>240 mL</td></tr>
<tr><td>raspberry preserves</td><td>13 1/2 oz.</td><td>383 g</td><td>1 cup + 2 tablespoons</td><td>270 mL</td></tr>
</table>

**Garnish:**
confectioner's sugar, sifted
whipped cream, slightly
  sweetened

1. Sift together flour, baking powder, salt, cinnamon, cloves, and nutmeg into bowl. Set aside until needed.
2. Cream butter, sugar, and lemon and orange peel in mixer fitted with flat paddle beater. Add egg yolks, one at a time, mixing well after each one.
3. Add sifted dry ingredients to creamed mixture. Mix just to combine.
4. Add nuts. Mix well, by hand if necessary, until smooth.
5. Wrap dough and chill thoroughly for several hours or overnight.
6. Place over rack in middle of oven. Preheat oven to 350 degrees (180°C).
7. Press dough into pan, making a crust about 1/4- to 3/8-inch (60- to 90-mm) thick. If using springform, press dough about 1 inch (2.5 cm) up sides; if using French tart pan or pie pan, press dough to top edge of pan. (This will use about two-thirds to three-quarters of the dough.)
8. Spread preserves over dough to depth of about 3/8 to 1/2 inch (90 to 120 mm).
9. Flour rolling surface, roll out remaining dough, cut into long strips, about 3/8 to 1/2 inch across, and place over tart in lattice pattern.
10. Bake for 40 to 50 minutes, until golden brown. Remove from oven, cool thoroughly on rack.
11. Sift lightly with confectioner's sugar. Serve, garnished with slightly sweetened whipped cream.

# ZWETSCHGEN KUCHEN

## PLUM PIE

**Note:** *Zwetschgen* are known as prune plums or Italian plums in different areas of the United States. This confection is served only in the fall when these plums ripen.

**Note:** *Muerbe Teig* is sweet butter dough similar to the French *pâte sucrée* or a sugar cookie.

**Number of Servings:** 8
**Total Yield:** 9-inch (23-cm) pie

**Cooking Method:** Bake

| | WEIGHT | | VOLUME | |
|---|---|---|---|---|
| **INGREDIENTS** | U.S. | METRIC | U.S. | METRIC |
| **Muerbe Teig (Butter Dough):** | | | | |
| unsalted butter, cut into pieces | 2 oz. | 57 g | 4 tablespoons (1/2 stick) | 60 mL |
| sugar | 3 3/4 oz. | 107 g | 1/2 cup | 120 mL |
| all-purpose flour | 4 1/2 oz. | 128 g | 1 cup | 240 mL |
| egg | 1 3/4 oz. | 50 g | 1 each | |
| **Filling:** | | | | |
| plums, prune or Italian type | 2 lb. to 2 lb, 4 oz. | 908 g to 1 kg | | |
| cinnamon | | | 1/2 teaspoon | 3 mL |
| sugar | | | 1 to 3 tablespoons, to taste | 15 to 45 mL |
| **Garnish:** | | | | |
| whipped cream, slightly sweetened | | | | |

**TWIST ON THE CLASSIC**

For a different look and flavor, alternate the rows of plums with rows of apples.

*First cut in plum along crease*
Courtesy of Patricia Heyman

*Removing pit from plum*
Courtesy of Patricia Heyman

*Cutting slit in top of plum half*
Courtesy of Patricia Heyman

*Cut plum ready for placing in pie*
Courtesy of Patricia Heyman

*Placing plums in Zwetschgen Kuchen (Plum Pie)*
Photo by Jean-Louis Vosgien © Shutterstock

Photo by Jean-Louis Vosgien © Shutterstock

## MUERBE TEIG:

1. Lightly pan-spray 9-inch (23-cm) pie pan (with sloped sides, not French tart pan).
2. Soften butter slightly, until a little colder than room temperature. Cut in sugar with fingertips.
3. Add flour, mix with fingertips, then add egg.
4. Mix until well blended and dough forms ball. Do not overmix.
5. Pat evenly into prepared pie pan. If dough sticks, lightly dampen fingers. Refrigerate while preparing filling.

## FILLING:

1. Wash plums. Position rack in center of oven. Preheat oven to 350 degrees (180°C).
2. Hold plum in hand, cut through half of plum along crease line on one side only, do not cut plum in half.
3. Open plum and remove pit. Parallel to first cut, slice halfway down each half. Plum can be opened like a book with two cuts splaying top.
4. Repeat with remaining plums.
5. Starting at outer edge of pie shell, place plums, standing upright, in tight concentric circle around pie until center is filled.
6. Sprinkle with cinnamon and sugar.
7. Bake for 25 minutes. If desired, sprinkle another tablespoon sugar over tart, return to oven.
8. Bake another 5 to 15 minutes, until crust is golden. Cool to room temperature.
9. Serve, garnished with slightly sweetened whipped cream.

# SCHWARZWÄLDER KIRSCHTORTE

## BLACK FOREST CHERRY CAKE

**TWIST ON THE CLASSIC**

Change the fruit used in this cake to raspberries, blackberries, or peeled orange sections.

**Number of Servings:** 12 to 16
**Serving Size:** 1 wedge
**Total Yield:** 1 each 9-inch (23-cm) cake

**Cooking Method:** Bake, boil

| INGREDIENTS | WEIGHT | | VOLUME | |
|---|---|---|---|---|
| | U.S. | METRIC | U.S. | METRIC |
| **Cake:** | | | | |
| flour, all-purpose | 4 oz. | 114 g | 1 cup | 240 mL |
| cocoa | 1/2 oz. | 15 g | 3 tablespoons | 45 mL |
| baking powder | 1/4 oz. | 8 g | 2 teaspoons | 10 mL |

| | | | | |
|---|---|---|---|---|
| butter, unsalted | 4 oz. | 114 g | 1/2 cup | 120 mL |
| sugar | 3 3/4 oz. | 107 g | 1/2 cup | 120 mL |
| eggs, separated | 10 oz. | 284 g | 6 each | |
| vanilla | | | 1 teaspoon | 5 mL |
| almond extract | | | 1/4 teaspoon | 2 mL |
| chocolate, semisweet, grated | 4 oz. | 114 g | | |
| salt | | | pinch | |
| sugar | 1 oz. | 28 g | 2 tablespoons | 30 mL |
| almonds, blanched, ground | 2 oz. | 57 g | 1/2 cup | 120 mL |

© Marina Lohrbach

**Filling:**

| | | | | |
|---|---|---|---|---|
| sour cherries, drained, reserve syrup | 1 each 15-oz. | (426-g) can | | |
| cornstarch | 1/4 oz. | 8 g | 1 tablespoon | 15 mL |
| sugar | 1 oz. | 28 g | 2 tablespoons | 30 mL |
| Kirsch | | 28 g | 2 tablespoons | 30 mL |

**Dessert Syrup:**

| | | | | |
|---|---|---|---|---|
| sugar | 1 1/2 oz. | 43 g | 3 tablespoons | 45 mL |
| Kirsch | | 43 g | 3 tablespoons | 45 mL |

**Frosting:**

| | | | | |
|---|---|---|---|---|
| heavy whipping cream | | 794 g | 3 1/2 cups | 840 mL |
| vanilla | | | 1/2 teaspoon | 3 mL |
| confectioners' sugar | 1 oz. | 28 g | 1/4 cup | 60 mL |

© viperagp

**Garnish:**
chocolate shavings
cherries

## FOR CAKE:

1. Pan spray 9-inch (23-cm) springform pan. Place rectangle of parchment paper about 3 by 4-inches (8 by 10-cm) on bottom of pan. Pan spray parchment. Place oven rack in middle of oven. Preheat to 350 degrees (180°C).
2. Sift flour, cocoa, and baking powder together. Set aside until needed.
3. Beat butter and sugar with mixer until light and fluffy. Add egg yolks, one at a time. Beat well after each addition. Add vanilla and almond extract. Add chocolate and beat well.
4. Whip egg whites with salt until starting to stiffen. Sprinkle in half of remaining sugar (1 oz or 28 g), beat and sprinkle in remainder. Continue whipping until stiff peaks form. Fold into butter mixture.
5. Sift 1/3 of flour mixture over batter, fold in gently. Repeat with remaining two parts. Fold in almonds.
6. Transfer batter to prepared pan. Tap once on counter to remove any air bubbles. Bake for 35 to 40 minutes, until tester comes out clean, cake pulls away from sides of pan, and it is springy to the touch. Cool on rack for 10 minutes, remove side of springform pan and cool completely.

## FOR FILLING:

1. In small saucepan, whisk 4 oz. (114 g, 1/2 cup, or 120 mL) reserved cherry juice, cornstarch, sugar, and Kirsch until smooth. Whisking, bring to boil over medium heat, cook until thickened.
2. Add cherries, stir occasionally and bring back to boil. Remove from heat, cool.

## FOR DESSERT SYRUP

1. Add enough water to remaining cherry juice to make 2 3/4 oz. (78 g, 1/3 cup, or 80 mL). Place in a small saucepan with sugar. Bring to boil.
2. Remove from heat, add Kirsch.

Instead of preparing the cherry filling using canned cherries, many use prepared cherry preserves for the filling.

For easier slicing, bake in a loaf pan or make individual cakes.

## TO ASSEMBLE:

1. Whip cream in a mixer using wire whip, if available, until it thickens and begins to form soft peaks. Turn off mixer, add vanilla and sifted confectioners' sugar. Continue beating until peaks form and it holds its shape.

2. Using long serrated knife (like a bread knife), slice cake horizontally into three even layers. Place one layer with cut side up on cardboard round or flat plate.

3. With pastry brush, moisten cake layer with dessert syrup. Be careful not to use too much liquid or cake will collapse.

4. Spread half of cherry filling over cake, top with whipped cream (about 3/4-inch [about 2-cm] thick). Top with another cake layer and repeat (brushing with dessert syrup, cherries, whipped cream). Top with final layer. Brush top and sides with dessert syrup.

5. Using an icing spatula, frost sides and top of cake with whipped cream. Decorate as desired with piped whipped cream, cherries, and chocolate curls or shavings.

6. Refrigerate until service.

# Scandinavia

## >> LEARNING OBJECTIVES

By the end of this chapter, you will be able to:

- Know which foods are prevalent in Scandinavia, why those foods are available, and how they are used in various dishes
- Identify similarities in the cooking methods and cuisines of the countries of Scandinavia
- Understand the concept of a *smörgåsbord*
- Prepare a variety of Scandinavian dishes

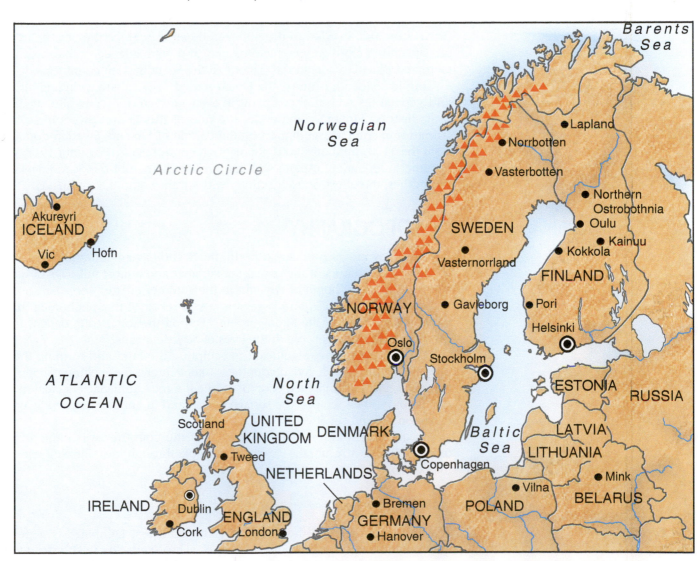

Leaving a great culinary heritage, the Vikings occupied Norway for two centuries, ending in 994. From the Viking legacy, Norwegians adopted the serving of elk in the north and lamb in the south. They also learned to feast on salmon from the mountain streams; herring, cod, and mackerel from the ocean; and game, mushrooms, and berries from the forests.

## >> HISTORY

Situated at the far northern end of Europe, the area known as Scandinavia consists of four countries: Denmark, Norway, Sweden, and Finland. (Some sources include Iceland as the fifth Scandinavian country.) Throughout history, these four countries politically united with each other in various combinations in attempts to rule the others. Today, each of the countries is an independent nation, yet people often group them together because of their many similarities and geographic proximity.

### VIKING INFLUENCE

From about 800 A.D.. to 1050 A.D.., the Vikings departed from Scandinavia and sailed the seas fortified with all sorts of smoked meats and dried, salted fish. Using techniques that they learned from the Vikings, the Scandinavians became very proficient at preserving meats, fish, fruits, and vegetables. In addition, the Vikings introduced many customs and traditions including a fondness for wine that still remains throughout Scandinavia.

### IMPACT OF OTHER EUROPEAN COUNTRIES

Sharing a border with Denmark, Germany became a significant influence there. Around the 1600s and 1700s, the nobility of Denmark started imitating the royalty of France, resulting in strong French impact on the foods throughout Denmark. French influence became even more pronounced when one of Napoleon's generals joined the nobility of Norway and Sweden in the nineteenth century. Since the Scandinavian countries are situated in close geographic proximity and were aligned politically, the French and German influences spread throughout all the Scandinavian countries.

In the sixteenth century, the Dutch settled in Denmark, bringing all sorts of fruits and vegetables with them to plant in their new land. Meanwhile, at different times in its history, Finland came under the rule of Russia and Sweden, so both of these countries exerted a large impact on the cuisine of Finland. Sweden dominated Finland from the 1100s until the 1800s. Russia took control from 1809 until 1917, when Finland became independent. Again, with the great influence of the Scandinavian nations on each other, the effect of each country was felt throughout Scandinavia.

## >> TOPOGRAPHY

Because they are situated so far north, the Scandinavian countries experience daylight for most of the hours of the day in the summer and almost full days of darkness in the winter. The many hours of daylight in the summer creates very high-quality produce including berries, fruits, and vegetables. As a result of this phenomenon, Scandinavia is called the "Land of the Midnight Sun." During the long, cold, dark winter, food and drink play a prominent role in the lives of Scandinavians.

Glaciers were very significant in sculpting the land and forming the topography throughout the Scandinavian countries. Interestingly, the melting glaciers left different features on the land in each country. While the retreating glaciers created mountains in one country, they scraped the surface of the land in another country, leaving it with an elevation around sea level.

In the early days, travel within each of the countries was limited by the rugged topography. As a result, the products available through local farming and fishing determined the cuisine in that area.

### DENMARK

Denmark is almost twice the size of Massachusetts.

The most southern of the Scandinavian countries, Denmark is a peninsula with Germany situated on its southern border. The North Sea lies to the west, and bays and the Baltic Sea are to the east. Although separated by water, Norway lies to the north, and Sweden to the east. Denmark also claims over 480 islands. The country consists of coasts, rolling hills, many lakes, and fertile farmland that formed when the glaciers melted; however, the retreating glaciers left most of the land at about sea level.

## NORWAY

The most barren of the Scandinavian countries, Norway contains mostly high, mountainous plateaus, mountains, fjords (inlets), forests, and rocky shores. In fact, mountains cover about two-thirds of Norway's land. Counting the fjords and peninsulas along the coast, this country contains over 13,000 miles of coastline!

The melting glaciers formed deep valleys and many lakes. When the glaciers left, they scraped the soil away, and bare rock covered the mountainous plateaus, creating a terrain of mountains in northern Norway.

Sweden joins the eastern side of Norway. Finland and Russia border on the northeast. The North Sea lies to the west and south. Denmark is beyond the waters situated on the south. Southern Norway lies at about the same latitude as southern Alaska.

*Norway contains just over four and a half million people. Primarily because of the small population, most of the land remains unspoiled and well preserved.*

*Norway is a bit larger than New Mexico.*

## SWEDEN

As remnants of the glaciers, thousands of lakes dot Sweden and Finland. Large areas of forest grow in both countries. With the Baltic Sea on the east, Sweden has lots of coastline, as well as mountains, rivers, rocky islands, forests, and of course, lakes. Glaciers still remain in the mountains in the north of Sweden, a cold, barren land where it is too cold even for trees to grow. Sweden claims the most land and the largest population of any of the Scandinavian countries.

*Sweden is slightly larger than California.*

## FINLAND

Finland shares a border with Russia on the east. Forest covers two-thirds of Finland, and over 100,000 lakes dot the countryside. Most of the land is plateaus with gentle hills and valleys. There are some mountains, but the majority of land is fairly low. Finland claims many thousands of islands.

Only about 10 percent of Finland's land is cultivated. With about one-third of Finland lying in the Arctic Circle, much of the land is too cold for growing crops. Luckily, the warmth from the Gulf Stream leads to temperate summers and the ability to grow a variety of fruits, vegetables, and grains. Finns grow lots of potatoes, rye, and oats. Pork is the most available meat, and they frequently smoke it or make it into sausages. In addition to pork, many Finns in the north consume reindeer.

*Finland is about the size of Great Britain.*

## >> COOKING METHODS

To survive the long, hard, cold winters, the Scandinavians preserved all sorts of foods to provide sustenance through the winter. They salted, smoked, and pickled a wide variety of meats, fish, and seafood. On the other hand, the high quality and incredible freshness of fish and seafood have led to simple preparations such as grilling, sautéing, boiling, poaching, or cooking on a spear or plank over an open fire.

Because meat was not abundant in the early days, Scandinavians used all parts of the animal. Braising (in the popular stews) functioned as a method of using the tougher cuts of meat as well as extending the meager meat supplies. Baking and slow one-pot cookery remain common, as plentiful wood for fuel comes from the many forests, and the heat from a long-burning oven also helps combat the cold weather.

> **Ingredients and Foods Commonly Used throughout the Cuisine of Scandinavia Include**

- all sorts of seafood including herring, cod, and salmon
- game including elk, hare, and reindeer
- cheese, cream, sour cream, and butter
- dill, fennel, anise, and horseradish
- cardamom, allspice, caraway, nutmeg, and cinnamon

- winter vegetables, including cabbage, beets, winter squash, rutabagas, and carrots
- apples and berries
- potatoes
- cucumbers
- rye bread

## >> REGIONS

The lines between the culinary traditions in Denmark, Norway, and Sweden blur. In the past, these three countries have ruled each other, and they have been united under one monarch. As a result, although they maintain individual traits, their culinary heritage is intertwined.

The inland portions of Sweden, Norway, and Finland experience extremely cold temperatures. As a result, most people live in the southern coastal areas. Since the northern portions of these three countries lie in the Arctic Circle, they endure extremely cold weather. People residing in the north, the Lapps, mostly herd reindeer.

### DENMARK

Denmark contains the most fertile land of the four Scandinavian countries. The countryside consists of green and rolling land, conducive to raising animals that produce both top-quality meat and milk for butter and cheese. Dairy cows and pigs are raised most often; pork reigns as the most commonly consumed meat. It is said that more pigs than people live in Denmark. Goose is also very popular.

With miles of coastline and many lakes, fishing remains an important industry here; in fact, the Danes export the majority of their catch. Favorite fish are herring, salmon, eels, and crabs.

The Danish people are known for their love of food and raising livestock. Sweet cream appears in many dishes including soups, salads, sauces, and desserts. Meat and potatoes remain staples. Although the Danes produce ample amounts of meat, they export significant quantities of both pork and beef, so meat is rather expensive. As a result, the Danes prepare and serve meat conservatively. Every household possesses their favorite recipe for *frikadeller*, a ground meat mixture formed into meatballs, patties, or used as forcemeat.

*Smørrebrød*
© Bernd Jürgens

### Danish Meals

Breakfast in Denmark consists of coffee with either "Danish" (a sweet roll) or rye bread and cheese. Typically, the afternoon meal is *smørrebrød,* literally meaning "buttered bread." Actually a canapé, a base of thin bread or cracker is spread with butter and then topped with meat, seafood, or cheese. Eye-catching garnishes top these beautiful, opened-faced sandwiches. Accompanied by cold beer, *smørrebrød* is truly a Danish institution. Shops serving these beautiful canapés are found all over the larger cities such as Copenhagen. As early as the eighteenth century, *smørrebrød* became unique in Denmark because it was eaten with a knife and fork rather than by being picked up and eaten like a sandwich. Endless varieties of *smørrebrød* exist; the only constant is that the base consists of thinly sliced bread or cracker spread evenly with butter. There is no limit to the topping possibilities.

The hearty evening meal served in Denmark usually consists of roasted meat or fish accompanied by potatoes and vegetables. For most Danes, dinner is the only hot

*Smørrebrød*
© Petersen

meal they eat during the day. Later in the evening, people often partake of dessert and coffee.

Quite popular, dessert might simply consist of fresh fruits and cheeses or a more involved confection such as cake, tart, mousse, pudding, or crêpelike pancakes filled with lingonberries, a native berry often used in desserts and on the famous pancakes served throughout Scandinavia.

## NORWAY

Although comprised of very beautiful countryside, only about 4 percent of the land in Norway is suitable for cultivation. As a result, Norwegians rely on the sea for much of their food, with fish and potatoes forming the foundation of their cuisine. Many call Norway the land of cod and potatoes.

With miles and miles of fjords, long coastal channels, mountain streams, and coastline, many varieties of fresh fish and seafood abound. While the seas yield herring, cod, turbot, plaice, and sole, the streams are abundant with trout and salmon. Because the fish is so fresh, Norwegians choose simple preparations such as poaching or boiling. They smoke and salt lots of fish to eat through the long winter. Salted cod, *klippfisk*, remains a popular food item.

Goats and sheep survive in this mountainous land, which accounts for the popularity of goat cheeses. Available meat is usually mutton, lamb, or game. Since many Norwegians hunt, a wide variety of game is served in homes and restaurants. In the northern region, reindeer are hunted. Sour cream appears in all sorts of dishes from appetizers to desserts. As in the other Scandinavian countries, cabbage is omnipresent.

Because of the rugged, mountainous terrain, severe isolation within the country made it difficult to share recipes. Therefore, each family has its own recipes for many common dishes, and those recipes vary widely from one family to the next.

Norway claims several national dishes. *Rømmegrøt,* a porridge made with sour cream, is served at all important functions including weddings and harvest celebrations. Also gracing many Norwegian celebrations, *lefsa,* a thin pancake made with mashed or riced potatoes, is served with butter and sugar. Another favorite dish, *får i kål,* is a stew made of mutton or lamb, cabbage, and peppercorns. Salt-cured meats, called *spekemat,* are dried, cured, and/or salted mutton or pork. These resemble dried ham or salami.

### Norwegian Meals

Breakfast in Norway is a large, hearty meal of cold meat and fish, cheese, eggs, and a variety of breads and jams. Herring remains a breakfast staple. The light lunch typically consists of a sandwich. Consumed early, when the children arrive home from school and the adults return from work, the evening meal often includes fish accompanied by boiled potatoes, vegetables, and dessert. Served in the late evening, supper is ordinarily a sandwich.

## SWEDEN

Only about 10 percent of Sweden's land can be farmed, and most of that farmland lies in the southern portion. They raise pigs as well as cows for both meat and dairy. Main crops include oats, potatoes, sugar beets, and wheat. Of course, seafood continues as a staple both for consumption and for export.

Forests of fir trees and thousands of lakes dot the landscape of Sweden and Finland. In addition to ample access to the sea and seafood, Sweden has myriad lakes that provide fish and forests that yield many varieties of berries, mushrooms, and game.

Although the Swedes are the most affluent of the Scandinavians, simplicity describes the everyday cooking of Sweden. A tradition continuing from the Middle Ages, many homes have very thick, hearty yellow-pea soup every Thursday night for dinner, followed by Swedish pancakes.

*Norwegian king Harold Hårfagre first unified Norway in 900. Beginning in the late fourteenth century, Denmark and Norway united for more than 400 years. In 1815, Norway joined forces with Sweden until 1905, when Norway became independent.*

*Norway reigns as the largest producer of salmon.*

*The traditional Easter dinner features roasted leg of lamb. For Sunday dinner, the most popular meat is roast pork.*

*In 1901, the first Nobel Prize award ceremony was held in Stockholm, Sweden. This annual tradition still continues, with an elaborate dinner to commemorate the awards.*

*Buffet table of hot foods*
Adisa/Fotolia

More than 200 species of wild mushrooms thrive in Finland.

## Swedish Smörgåsbord

The most lavish *smörgåsbord* of any of the Scandinavian countries is found in Sweden. The *smörgåsbord* consists of a buffet table laden with all sorts of meats, seafood, vegetables, salads, cheeses, and breads. No one actually knows when the tradition of the *smörgåsbord* began. Many believe it hails from the time of the Vikings a thousand years ago; others think it first appeared in the sixteenth century. Regardless of its origin, the *smörgåsbord* had become a tradition in Swedish homes by the eighteenth century.

Served in both homes and restaurants, the *smörgåsbord* contains as many as 60 food items. Guests serve themselves, usually beginning with a herring course that offers a choice of several preparations of herring. Another fish course follows, then a cold meat course consisting of pâté, smoked meat, or pork accompanied by salads. After that, the hot dishes are served, followed by cheeses with dessert or fruit.

## Swedish Meals

A light breakfast of cereal or pastry with coffee starts the day. Lunch consists of an open-faced sandwich. Dinner comprises meat or fish accompanied by boiled potatoes. A Swedish staple, the potato, frequently is eaten at both lunch and dinner.

## FINLAND

Like the rest of Scandinavia, Finland experiences relatively mild winters along the coasts and very cold temperatures inland. Although the average winter temperature is around 30 degrees near the coast, very long winters and quite short summers are normal. Most of the population resides in the southern coastal regions.

The cuisine of Finland remains simple, straightforward, and plentiful. Finland's cookery reflects culinary influences from both Sweden and neighboring Russia, both of whom ruled them in the past. *Kalakukko*, a specialty served in central Finland, reflects Russian and eastern European influence. Resembling a baked loaf of bread, *kalakukko* is a combination of fish and pork wrapped in pastry dough.

The most often-consumed fish, salmon is smoked on a plank over a fire, poached, preserved, or prepared in any number of ways. Finns consume lots of fish and seafood in addition to salmon, particularly herring, pike, and perch. Finns also enjoy abundant caviar from the waterways and a bounty of game, mushrooms, and berries from the forests. Popular game includes moose, deer, reindeer, hare, and duck. They prepare a wide variety of soups; porridge and gruel remain favorites. Boiled potatoes topped with butter accompany most dinners.

In August, the crayfish season arrives, and the crayfish and vodka parties begin. The people of Finland are known for high consumption of beer and cognac. In addition, more milk is used per capita here than in any other nation.

*Buffet table of cold meats*
Nikitos77/Fotolia

*Buffet table of fish*
Nikitos77/Fotolia

### Finnish Meals

In Finland, an early morning light breakfast of coffee and bread with butter and cheese is followed by a hearty breakfast in the late morning or even at noon. The hearty breakfast consists of two courses: meat or fish and porridge. The other substantial meal of the day is dinner at seven or eight o'clock.

## >> CUISINE

### ISOLATION

Water, rough terrain, and long, harsh winters of snow and ice created the isolation that historically has cut off these four countries from the rest of the world. This isolation affected Scandinavia's cuisine in two significant ways. First, culinary traditions in each of these four countries were preserved and stayed within Scandinavia instead of spreading throughout the world. Second, influence from much of the rest of the world's culinary traits stayed out of Scandinavia.

### SEASONS AND DIET

The common threads in the cuisines of Scandinavia are the simplicity of the dishes and the connection to the seasons. With long, harsh winters and short, mild, lush summers, the preservation of meats, seafood, fruits, and vegetables remains integral to the Scandinavian diet. In early days, people's survival depended on the preservation of foods.

Short summers mean a short growing season, so the profusion of hardy "winter" vegetables, including potatoes, carrots, turnips, parsnips, winter squashes, rutabagas, cabbage, cauliflower, and spinach dominates the Scandinavian diet. They store great amounts of these root and cold-weather vegetables for use during the winter.

The Scandinavians heartily feast on the bounty of fruits and vegetables that grow in the summer, and then they preserve all that is left. Dried, smoked, pickled, and salted meats and seafood help extend the food supplies throughout the winter. The Scandinavians even ferment fish and milk. Soured milk and cream are used extensively in Norway, Sweden, and Finland. Yet the cuisine of Scandinavia can be described as pure, natural, simple, plain, and fresh. Heavy spices do not appear in Scandinavian cookery.

### FISH, SEAFOOD, AND MEAT

Throughout history, protein claimed a prime spot in the Scandinavian diet. Because of the short growing season, vegetables and fruits often were unavailable. While the miles of coastline, fjords, and rivers yielded a bounty of fish and seafood, wild games including elk, wild boar, deer, and duck flourish in the acres and acres of forests, mountains, and waterways throughout Scandinavia. Sheep and goats thrived in the mountains, and there was plenty of land suitable for grazing cattle.

Surrounded by ocean and filled with rivers and inlets, both freshwater and saltwater fish and seafood play a major role in the Scandinavian diet. *Gravlax,* salmon cured in salt, sugar, and dill, remains a famous Scandinavian dish. Needed for the preserving of meats and seafood, salt was a very important commodity. Even though sea surrounds Scandinavia, only the rich people in these countries had access to adequate salt in the past.

The Scandinavian fondness for herring dates back to the time when the Europeans were still nomads. Greatly prized in all of the countries of Scandinavia, herring appears in several different preparations on every smörgåsbord. This fatty fish commands much respect throughout these countries. Surely, if there were a national fish, the ubiquitous herring would win the title.

*Until the late 1600s, people in northern Sweden paid their taxes with salmon instead of money.*

## SCANDINAVIAN CHEESES

### Denmark

**Blue Castello** Made from cow's milk; a cross between blue cheese and brie, similar to Saga cheese; soft, creamy texture

**Danbo** Made from cow's milk; mild flavor; semisoft texture

**Esrom** Made from cow's milk; mild but full flavor; semifirm texture; called Danish Port-Salut

**Havarti** Made from cow's milk; mild flavor; creamy, semisoft texture containing tiny holes; sometimes with added ingredients such as dill or caraway seeds

**Saga** Cross between blue and brie cheeses; flavor of mild blue cheese; soft creamy texture

### Sweden

**Graddost** Made from cow's milk; mild, similar to Gruyere in flavor; creamy, semihard texture

**Hushållsost** Made from cow's milk; mild with fresh flavor; smooth texture with some holes

### Norway

**Gammelost** made from skimmed cow's milk; semisoft blue cheese; dense, moist, grainy texture

**Gjetost** Made from mixture of cow's and goat's milk; fresh cheese; sweet caramel-like flavor; semihard texture

**Jarlsberg** Made from cow's milk; similar to "baby Swiss"; firm texture

### Finland

**Juustoleipä** Made from cow and reindeer's milk; mild flavor; creamy, smooth, semifirm texture

**Turunmaa** Made from cow's milk; aromatic tangy flavor; smooth, creamy, semifirm texture

When meat is available, every bit of the animal is used, from the blood to the organs. Cooks use blood in both soups and sausages throughout Scandinavia. Over 1,000 years ago, the Vikings originated *svartsoppa,* known as black soup, which contains the blood of pig and goose. Blood sausage remains popular in Scandinavia as well as in Germany.

## DAIRY

Because of the high production of dairy cattle, butter and cheese are consumed in substantial quantity throughout Scandinavia. In addition, goats and sheep that graze in the mountainous areas yield milk to make cheeses. Scandinavian cookery incorporates plenty of dairy products, and they are well known for their wide variety of high-quality cheeses.

## PRODUCE

Hearty winter vegetables including beets, cabbage, rutabagas (often called "swedes" in England), carrots, peas, cauliflower, and potatoes thrive in this rich soil and short growing season. All sorts of mushrooms and berries, including the famous Scandinavian lingonberries, come from the many forests. They prepare lingonberry preserves as well as use these berries in sauces to accompany all sorts of dishes from meat and game entrées to desserts.

## FLAVORINGS

Scandinavians incorporate lots of dill, parsley, fennel, and horseradish in their recipes. They add cardamom to many baked goods. Like Germans, Scandinavians display a fondness for sweet-and-sour dishes. Vinegar provides the sour in meats, marinades, vegetables, and sauces, which they juxtapose with a sweet fruit, molasses, honey, or sugar. Often, currant, lingonberry, raspberry, and other fruits and berries flavor sauces that accompany meats or fowl.

## SOUP

Soup continues as a staple in the diet of the Scandinavians and is served daily in many homes. While hot soups appear often in the winter, cold fruit or vegetable soups are popular in the summer. Sometimes the cold soups function as a dessert instead of a soup course. The hot soups consumed during the winter often incorporate dried and preserved vegetables, fish, and meats.

## BEVERAGES

Beer and aquavit remain the most popular alcoholic beverages in Scandinavia. Many varieties of these two beverages appear within each country. Excellent with the hearty Scandinavian foods, both beer and aquavit accompany meals.

First made in the 1400s, aquavit literally means "water of life." A strong liquor made from potatoes or grains, its flavoring comes from caraway, anise, fennel, coriander, star anise, or any combination of these herbs. Traditionally, a shot of aquavit is drunk in one gulp. Although imported, wine is greatly appreciated and widely consumed.

Scandinavians generally love coffee, drinking it at all three meals as well as between meals. Strong coffee accompanies pastries, particularly cookies, pound cakes, and yeast breads.

*Eighty percent of Norwegians drink coffee.*

## DESSERTS

Well known for desserts, Scandinavians enjoy their sweets. Served daily in many homes, dessert and coffee follows the meal, is served as a separate course in the afternoon, or is eaten a few hours after the evening meal.

Countless varieties of cookies come from the Scandinavian kitchen. In fact, many people always keep cookies on hand to serve unexpected guests along with a cup of coffee. A traditional Swedish party in the past, coffee "klatch" consisted of coffee served with seven different types of cookies.

A rich, sweet roll or coffeecake dough with folded-in butter like puff pastry, Danish pastry was actually invented by the Viennese. Danish bakers improved it so much that it became known as Danish pastry. Today, it ranks as a Scandinavian specialty and appears with endless variations of shape and flavor.

Desserts can be as complex as Danish pastry or as simple as the apple cake that appears frequently in many homes throughout Scandinavia. This very simple dessert consists of sautéed breadcrumbs or *zweiback* layered with applesauce and then baked. Almonds, almond paste, fresh fruits, and berries appear in many desserts. No scrimping of butter or cream occurs in Scandinavian pastries.

Scandinavians produce a bounty of yeast breads, flatbreads, and crackers for which they are well known. Light and dark rye breads as well as limpa rye, pumpernickel, and wheat serve both as the base for sandwiches and an accompaniment to meals. Many breads are aromatic due to the addition of fennel, anise, caraway, cardamom, and/or orange peel. Crackers and hard breads remain popular because they store well in the cooler temperatures of Scandinavia.

*Assorted Danish pastries*
© Elenathewise

*Assorted breads*
© stevem

| REGION | AREA | WEATHER | TOPOGRAPHY | FOODS |
|---|---|---|---|---|
| Denmark | North of Germany | Mild and damp, moderated by surrounding seas | Coast on three sides, lakes, flatland, rolling hills (central), granite in the north | Seafood, fish, beef, game, pork, bacon, ham, cream, butter, cheese, potatoes, apples, cherries |
| Norway | | Moderate on coasts, extremely cold winters and short summers inland | Coast on three sides, high, mountainous plateaus, fjords, lakes, mountains, streams | Seafood, fish, sheep, goats, livestock, goat cheese, smoked meats, salted cod, game, rye bread, potatoes, sour cream |
| Sweden | North | Cold winters; short, cool summers | Coast, lakes, mountains, hills | Seafood, fish, herring |
| | Central and south | Somewhat milder winters; short, cool summers | Coast, forests, lakes, plains, highlands, fertile farmland | Seafood, fish, herring, game, beef, dairy, pork, cream, oats, wheat, dill, potatoes, sweet-and-sour dishes, sugar beets, lingonberries |
| Finland | North | Very cold winters; short, cool summers | Many lakes and forests | Seafood, fish, reindeer |
| | Central and south | Moderately cold winters; short, cool summers | Many lakes, forests, plateaus, small hills, and valleys | Seafood, fish, caviar, trout, salmon, crayfish, game, livestock, dairy, oats, rye, barley, wheat, beets, potatoes, mushrooms, berries |

## >> Review Questions

1. Discuss geographic and topographical factors that created the isolation in Scandinavia.
2. How has the weather in Scandinavia affected the cuisines?
3. What did the Vikings contribute to the cuisines of Scandinavia?
4. Name at least five food products and flavorings that are prevalent throughout Scandinavia.
5. Discuss which animal proteins are consumed in various areas of Scandinavia and why.

## >> Glossary

**aquavit** Literally, "water of life," a strong liquor made from potatoes or grains, its flavoring comes from caraway, anise, fennel, coriander, star anise, or any combination of these herbs; first made in the 1400s

**fjords** Inlets

**frikadeller** Ground meat mixture that is made into meatballs, patties, or used as forcemeat

**gravlax** Salmon cured with salt, sugar, and dill

**klippfisk** Salted fish, usually cod, served in Norway

**rømmegrøt** Porridge made with sour cream that is popular in Norway

**smörgåsbord** A buffet laden with all sorts of meats, seafood, vegetables, salads, cheeses, and breads; contains as many as 60 food items

**smørrebrød** Literally, "buttered bread," an open-faced sandwich with a base of thin bread or cracker that is spread with butter, then topped with meat, seafood, or cheese and crowned with an eye-catching garnish; the Danes are known for these sandwiches, which resemble canapés

## GRAVLAX (SCANDINAVIA)

### SUGAR AND SALT CURED, MARINATED SALMON

**Note:** Allow 2 to 3 days to marinate the salmon.

**Total Yield:** 2 1/2 to 3 lb. (1.1 to 1.4 kg)
**Food Balance:** Protein
**Wine Style:** Light- to medium-bodied Champagne or Sparkling Wine, Gewürztraminer, Pinot Blanc, Viognier, White Zinfandel, or rosé
**Example:** Greg Norman Sparkling Chardonnay

| | WEIGHT | | VOLUME | |
| --- | --- | --- | --- | --- |
| INGREDIENTS | U.S. | METRIC | U.S. | METRIC |
| fresh salmon, center-cut, skin left on | 2 1/2 to 3 lb. | 1.1 to 1.4 kg | | |
| fresh dill | | | 1 large bunch | |
| kosher salt | 1 3/4 oz. | 50 g | 1/4 cup | 60 mL |
| sugar | 1 3/4 oz. | 50 g | 1/4 cup | 60 mL |
| crushed peppercorns | 3/4 oz. | 22 g | 2 tablespoons | 30 mL |

**Garnish:**
fresh dill
lemon wedges

1. Wash salmon thoroughly. Cut in half lengthways through center (like fillet) and remove all bones.
2. Place one piece of fish, skin side down, in deep glass dish. Spread dill over fish. Sprinkle salt, sugar, and crushed peppercorns over dill. Top with other fish fillet, skin side up.
3. Cover with foil and weight with 5-lb. (2.3-kg) weight placed on a board. Refrigerate for 48 to 72 hours, turning the salmon and basting every 12 hours with juices from pan.
4. Color and texture of fish change when cured. Texture becomes more firm and color is darker orange.
5. To serve, remove fish from marinade, scrape away dill and spices, pat dry. Slice salmon very thinly on the diagonal. Arrange on platter or plate, garnish with lemon wedges and fresh dill. Serve with thin rye bread or crackers. May be accompanied by *Laxås* (mustard sauce) and *Agurkesalat* (pickled cucumbers) (*recipes follow*).

*Sprinkling salt mixture over salmon*
Pearson Education/PH College

> **TWIST ON THE CLASSIC**
>
> Prepare a pizza by spreading a thin layer of dilled mustard sauce on partially baked pizza dough. Top the mustard with pieces of *gravlax* and grated havarti cheese.
>
> For a salad, serve *gravlax* on a bed of greens and top with dill and mustard vinaigrette.

*Placing weights over salmon*
Pearson Education/PH College

Alexnika © Shutterstock

© Martin Turzak

# LAXÅS (SCANDINAVIA)

## MUSTARD DILL MAYONNAISE

© Dar1930

**Total Yield:** 7 1/2 oz. (213 g)

| | WEIGHT | | VOLUME | |
|---|---|---|---|---|
| **INGREDIENTS** | **U.S.** | **METRIC** | **U.S.** | **METRIC** |
| Dijon-style mustard | 2 1/4 oz. | 64 g | 1/4 cup | 60 mL |
| dry mustard | | | 1 teaspoon | 5 mL |
| white vinegar | | 28 g | 2 tablespoons | 30 mL |
| sugar | 1 1/4 oz. | 36 g | 3 tablespoons | 45 mL |
| cardamom | | | 1/8 teaspoon | 1 mL |
| vegetable oil | | 114 g | 1/2 cup | 120 mL |
| fresh dill, minced | 3/4 oz. | 22 g | 3 tablespoons | 45 mL |

1. Combine both mustards in a small bowl, blend in vinegar, sugar, and cardamom to make a paste. Transfer to bowl of food processor fitted with knife blade, if using.
2. Slowly whisk in oil by hand or, if using food processor, drop oil very slowly through feed tube into running processor. Mixture should emulsify to become thick mayonnaise. Stir in dill.
3. Cover and refrigerate to store. Let sauce stand at room temperature 25 minutes before serving.

# KÖTTBULLAR (SWEDEN)

## SWEDISH MEATBALLS

**Number of Servings:** 9

**Cooking Method:** Sauté, braise

**Serving Size:** 4 3/4 oz. (135 g), 3 meatballs with sauce

**Total Yield:** 2 lb., 14 3/4 oz. (1.3 kg) total

**Sauce:** 1 lb., 5 1/2 oz. (611 g)

**Raw meat mixture:** 1 lb., 14 oz. (851 g)

**Wine Style:** Wide variety – Pinot Blanc; Chardonnay; soft, fruity red wines; Beaujolais; or soft Merlot

**Example:** Ruby Nouveau – Wollersheim Winery, Prairie du Sal, WI – This wine is young and fruity made using traditional Beaujolais methods.

© Brent Hofacker

| | WEIGHT | | VOLUME | |
|---|---|---|---|---|
| **INGREDIENTS** | **U.S.** | **METRIC** | **U.S.** | **METRIC** |
| **Meatballs:** | | | | |
| ground beef, lean | 1 lb. | 454 g | | |
| ground pork | 8 oz. | 227 g | | |
| breadcrumbs | 2 oz. | 57 g | 1/2 cup | 120 mL |
| milk | | 57 g | 1/4 cup | 60 mL |
| egg | 1 3/4 oz. | 50 g | 1 each | |
| cardamom | | | 1/4 teaspoon | 2 mL |
| nutmeg | | | 1/4 teaspoon | 2 mL |
| allspice | | | 1/8 teaspoon | 1 mL |
| ginger | | | 1/8 teaspoon | 1 mL |
| salt | | | 1/2 teaspoon | 3 mL |
| pepper | | | 1/4 teaspoon | 2 mL |

© Brent Hofacker

| INGREDIENTS | WEIGHT | | VOLUME | |
| --- | --- | --- | --- | --- |
| | U.S. | METRIC | U.S. | METRIC |
| butter or oil | 2 oz. | 57 g | 1/4 cup or 4 tablespoons | 60 mL |
| **Sauce:** | | | | |
| butter or drippings | 1 1/2 oz. | 43 g | 3 tablespoons | 45 mL |
| onion, minced | 2 3/4 oz. | 78 g | 1/2 cup or 1 small | 120 mL |
| flour, all purpose | 1 1/2 oz. | 43 g | 1/4 cup | 60 mL |
| beef stock, hot | | 454 g | 2 cups | 480 mL |
| salt | | | 1/2 teaspoon | 3 mL |
| pepper | | | 1/4 teaspoon | 2 mL |
| sour cream | 4 1/4 oz. | 120 g | 1/2 cup | 120 mL |

### FOR MEATBALLS:

1. Combine beef, pork, breadcrumbs, milk, egg, cardamom, nutmeg, allspice, ginger, salt, and pepper in bowl. Mix gently to combine well.
2. With moistened hands, shape into balls of desired size (about 1 1/2-oz. [43-g] meat mixture for 1 1/2-inch [4-cm] meatball). Cover and refrigerate until needed.
3. Heat butter or oil (2 oz., 57 g, 1/4 cup, or 60 mL) in skillet over medium heat.
4. Add meatballs, sauté until browned on all sides. If necessary, sauté meatballs in batches to avoid crowding.
5. Remove to platter lined with absorbent paper, keep warm in low oven for immediate service or cool, cover, and refrigerate until needed.

### FOR SAUCE AND FINISH:

1. Heat butter or drippings (1 1/2 oz., 43 g, 3 tablespoons, or 45 mL) in pan, add onion and sauté until softened, about 5 minutes.
2. Sprinkle flour over mixture, whisk about 2 minutes; whisking constantly, gradually add beef stock, a little at a time into flour.
3. Bring to boil, reduce heat and simmer about 10 minutes, until thickened.
4. Add salt, pepper, and sour cream. Correct seasonings.
5. Strain sauce to remove onion and any lumps.
6. Pour sauce over meatballs or add meatballs to sauce, cook over low heat until meatballs are hot. Serve immediately.

This versatile dish functions as hors d' oeuvre at a cocktail party, a first course, or an entrée served over wide egg noodles.

---

## SILLSALLAD (NORWAY)

### HERRING AND APPLE SALAD

**Note:** Variations on this recipe are served all over Scandinavia.

**Note:** Allow several hours to chill salad. Chill plates for serving salad.

**Number of Servings:** 6 or 9
**Serving Size:** 4 oz. or 3 oz. (114 g or 86 g)
**Total Yield:** 1 lb., 11 oz. (766 g)

| INGREDIENTS | WEIGHT | | VOLUME | |
| --- | --- | --- | --- | --- |
| | U.S. | METRIC | U.S. | METRIC |
| pickled herring, cut into 1/2-inch (1.3-cm) pieces | 7 1/2 oz. | 213 g | 1 cup | 240 mL |
| onion, minced | 6 oz. | 171 g | 1 large | |
| apple, peeled, cored, and cut into large dice | 10 oz. | 284 g | 1 large | |

Clive Streeter © Dorling Kindersley

| INGREDIENTS | WEIGHT | | VOLUME | |
| --- | --- | --- | --- | --- |
| | **U.S.** | **METRIC** | **U.S.** | **METRIC** |
| celery, small dice | 3 oz. | 86 g | 1/2 cup | 120 mL |
| lemon juice | | 28 g | 1/2 lemon or 2 tablespoons | 30 mL |
| sugar | | | 1 teaspoon | 5 mL |
| apple cider vinegar | | 28 g | 2 tablespoons | 30 mL |
| heavy cream | | 114 g | 1/2 cup | 120 mL |
| white pepper | to taste | | | |

**TWIST ON THE CLASSIC**

Present this in a puff pastry shell.

1. Combine herring, onions, apples, and celery in a nonreactive bowl. Sprinkle with lemon juice.
2. Dissolve sugar in vinegar. In separate bowl, whip cream until stiff peaks. Fold in vinegar, season with white pepper. Fold cream dressing into herring salad.
3. Cover and chill for several hours before serving. Correct seasonings. Serve on bed of lettuce or as part of *smörgåsbord*.

## CABBAGE SOUP (SWEDEN, DENMARK)

**TWIST ON THE CLASSIC**

For a hearty entrée, add small meatballs to the soup.

**Number of Servings:** 8
**Serving Size:** 8 oz. (227 g)
**Total Yield:** 4 lb., 7 oz. (2 kg)
**Food Balance:** Protein/sweet
**Wine Style:** Soft and fruity Johannisberg Riesling, Gewürztraminer, blush, or Shiraz
**Example:** Château St. Jean Gewürztraminer or Penfolds Bin 28 Shiraz

**Cooking Method:** Sauté, boil

| INGREDIENTS | WEIGHT | | VOLUME | |
| --- | --- | --- | --- | --- |
| | **U.S.** | **METRIC** | **U.S.** | **METRIC** |
| butter | 2 oz. | 57 g | 4 tablespoons (1/2 stick) | 60 mL |
| cabbage, cored and cut thin or shredded | 2 lb., 9 oz. | 1.2 kg | 1 large head | |
| brown sugar | 1 oz. | 28 g | 2 tablespoons | 30 mL |
| beef stock | | | 1 1/2 quarts (6 cups) | 1.4 L |
| pepper | | | 1/2 teaspoon | 3 mL |
| ground allspice | | | 1/2 teaspoon | 3 mL |

1. Melt butter in pan over medium heat. Add cabbage, sauté until lightly brown.
2. Add sugar, cook a few minutes, stirring often.
3. Add stock, pepper, and allspice and simmer, covered, for 1 hour. Correct seasonings.
4. Serve with dumplings, if desired.

© cook_inspire

# ÄRTSOPPA (SWEDEN)

## YELLOW PEA SOUP

**Note:** The traditional Thursday night dinner in Sweden consists of this thick soup followed by crêpelike pancakes for dessert.

**Note:** Allow time to soak the peas overnight. If not enough time is available, bring water to boil, add peas, turn off flame, and allow to soak for at least an hour or two. Cooking time may need lengthening.

**Number of Servings:** 9
**Serving Size:** 8 oz. (227 g)
**Total Yield:** 4 lb., 8 1/4 oz. (2.1 kg)
**Food Balance:** Protein
**Wine Style:** Low-oaked whites and soft reds
**Example:** Matua Sauvignon Blanc, Greg Norman Pinot Noir

**Cooking Method:** Boil

Courtesy of Canola Oil @ canolainfo.org

| INGREDIENTS | WEIGHT | | VOLUME | |
| --- | --- | --- | --- | --- |
| | U.S. | METRIC | U.S. | METRIC |
| dried yellow peas, washed | 1 lb. | 454 g | | |
| water | | | 2 quarts (8 cups), as needed | 1.9 L |
| salt pork, lean | 12 oz. | 340 g | | |
| whole onion, studded with 2 cloves | 3 1/4 oz. | 92 g | 1 small | |
| onions, minced | 9 oz. | 256 g | 2 medium | |
| carrot, minced | 3 1/2 oz. | 104 g | 1 each | |
| dried thyme | | | 1 teaspoon | 5 mL |
| dried marjoram | | | 1 teaspoon | 5 mL |
| ground ginger | | | 1/2 teaspoon | 3 mL |
| pepper | | | 1/4 teaspoon | 2 mL |
| grainy brown mustard | 1/4 oz. | 8 g | 1 teaspoon | 5 mL |
| salt | as needed | | | |

**Garnish:**
grainy brown mustard

1. Soak peas and water overnight or at least for several hours.
2. Place peas, soaking water, salt pork, onions, carrot, thyme, marjoram, ginger, and pepper in large pan. Bring to boil over high heat. Reduce heat to medium-low, partially cover pot, and simmer until peas are tender and starting to fall apart, about 2 hours and 30 minutes. Add water as needed, if peas are sticking or soup is too thick.
3. Remove whole onion studded with cloves and salt pork. Discard onion.
4. Trim fat from salt pork, cut pork into small dice and return to pan. Stir in mustard.
5. Correct seasonings, serve. If desired, garnish with extra mustard.

### TWIST ON THE CLASSIC

Prepare two pots of this soup—one with yellow peas and the other with green peas. For service, place a ladle of each in the bowl. Leave straight or curve into yin/yang design. This thick soup will remain separated.

For a thinner soup, add a little more water. Also, swirled mustard makes an attractive garnish.

If yellow peas are unavailable, substitute green split peas. The cooking time is less for green split peas.

# AGURKESALAT (DENMARK)

## PICKLED CUCUMBER SALAD

**Note:** Serve as a salad, a garnish on smørrebrød, or to accompany seafood, meat, and poultry.

**Note:** Allow a couple of hours to drain the cucumbers.

**Number of Servings:** 10
**Serving Size:** 2 1/2 oz. (71 g)
**Total Yield:** 1 lb., 10 oz. (738 g)

| INGREDIENTS | WEIGHT | | VOLUME | |
| --- | --- | --- | --- | --- |
| | U.S. | METRIC | U.S. | METRIC |
| cucumbers | 3 lb., 3 oz. | 1.4 kg | 4 large | |
| salt | 1 oz. | 28 g | 2 tablespoons | 30 mL |
| white vinegar | | 227 g | 1 cup | 240 mL |
| sugar | 2 oz. | 57 g | 1/4 cup | 60 mL |
| white pepper | | | 1/2 teaspoon | 3 mL |
| fresh dill, finely chopped | 1 oz. | 28 g | 1/4 cup | 60 mL |

**TWIST ON THE CLASSIC**

Try preparing this salad with any variety of vegetables such as blanched carrots, cauliflower, or asparagus.

1. Peel cucumbers, slice very thin. Layer with salt in colander, drain for a couple of hours to eliminate water and bitterness (place colander in bowl or sink to catch liquid).
2. Press cucumbers lightly to expel liquid, thoroughly blot with towel. Place them in a bowl.
3. Combine vinegar, sugar, and white pepper in a small bowl. Pour over cucumbers and mix well. Mix in dill. Chill for 2 or 3 hours. Correct seasonings. Drain before serving.

---

# INLAGDA RÖDBETOR (SWEDEN)

## PICKLED BEETS

**Note:** Pickled beets appear often throughout Sweden. Use them as part of a recipe (like the following potato and beet salad), as a garnish, an accompaniment, or in any imaginable way.

**Note:** Allow at least 24 hours for the beets to pickle.

**Total Yield:** 12 oz. (340 g) without brine          **Cooking Method:** Boil

**TWIST ON THE CLASSIC**

Add an assortment of vegetables with the beets or omit the beets and pickle other vegetables. For example, replace the beets with cauliflower and carrots.

| INGREDIENTS | WEIGHT | | VOLUME | |
| --- | --- | --- | --- | --- |
| | U.S. | METRIC | U.S. | METRIC |
| beets, cooked or canned, whole | 15 oz. | 426 g | one 15-oz. can | one 426-g can |
| onion, sliced thinly | 4 oz. | 114 g | 1 small | |
| vinegar, white | | 227 g | 1 cup | 240 mL |
| water | | 227 g | 1 cup | 240 mL |
| sugar | 2 oz. | 57 g | 1/2 cup | 120 mL |
| bay leaf | | | 1 each | |
| caraway seeds, enclosed in sachet | 1/4 oz. | 8 g | 1 1/2 teaspoons | 8 mL |

© natalikaevsti

© Viktor

1. In a nonreactive bowl or jar, layer beets and onions.
2. Place vinegar, water, sugar, bay leaf, and caraway seeds in a nonreactive saucepan. Bring to boil and pour hot liquid over beets and onions.
3. Cover and refrigerate at least 24 hours. Discard bay leaf and sachet of caraway seeds before serving (unless some caraway seeds are desired).

## POTATIS OCH RÖDBETSALLAD (SWEDEN)

### POTATO AND BEET SALAD

**Note:** If desired, alter the amount of potatoes and beets in this salad. Consider using the same amount of pickled beets as potatoes for a more pungent flavor. Also, add some of the caraway seeds from the pickled beets, if desired.

**Number of Servings:** 13
**Serving Size:** 4 oz. (114 g)
**Total Yield:** 3 lb., 6 3/4 oz. (1.6 kg)

**Cooking Method:** Boil

| | WEIGHT | | VOLUME | |
|---|---|---|---|---|
| **INGREDIENTS** | **U.S.** | **METRIC** | **U.S.** | **METRIC** |
| **Dressing:** | | | | |
| sour cream | 8 oz. | 227 g | 3/4 cup | 180 mL |
| dill pickle, minced | 1 1/2 oz. | 43 g | 1/4 cup | 60 mL |
| mustard, Swedish, brown, or variety of choice | 1/4 oz. | 8 g | 1 teaspoon | 5 mL |
| beet juice, *from pickled beets* | | 15 g | 1 tablespoon | 15 mL |
| salt | 1/4 oz. | 8 g | 1 teaspoon | 5 mL |
| white pepper | | | 1/2 teaspoon | 3 mL |
| **Salad:** | | | | |
| pickled beets and onions, *from previous recipe* (Inlagda Rödbetor), drained and cut into large dice | 12 oz. | 340 g | | |
| apple, peeled, cored, and cut into large dice | 10 1/4 oz. | 292 g | 2 small | |
| red potatoes, cooked, peeled, and cut into large dice | 1 lb., 8 1/4 oz. | 688 g | 4 medium | |
| **Garnish:** | | | | |
| fresh parsley or dill, minced | | | | |

© Gayvoronskaya_Yana

### DRESSING:

1. Mix sour cream, pickle, mustard, beet juice, salt, and pepper in a nonreactive bowl.
2. Correct seasonings. Cover and refrigerate until needed.

### SALAD:

1. Gently mix drained pickled beets and onions, apple, and potatoes in a nonreactive bowl. Be careful not to break potatoes.
2. Gently fold dressing into mixture, folding to coat all ingredients but not mashing or breaking the potatoes.
3. Cover and refrigerate until service. Correct seasonings. Serve cold, garnished with minced parsley or dill. If desired, serve on a bed of lettuce.

# FRIKADELLER (DENMARK)

## MEAT PATTIES OR MEATBALLS

© Aynia

**Note:** Serve as an hors d'oeuvres or entrée. An equal amount of ground veal may be substituted for either one of the ground meats.

**Number of Servings:** 11                   **Cooking Method:** Sauté
**Serving Size:** 5-oz. (142-g) patty or five 1-oz. (28-g) meatballs
**Total Yield:** 3 lb., 8 oz. (1.6 kg)
**Food Balance:** Protein/salt balanced
**Wine Style:** Wide variety of wines: Pinot Blanc, Chardonnay, blush, Beaujolais, Merlot, or Cabernet Sauvignon
**Example:** Beringer Knights Valley Cabernet Sauvignon

| INGREDIENTS | WEIGHT | | VOLUME | |
| --- | --- | --- | --- | --- |
| | *U.S.* | *METRIC* | *U.S.* | *METRIC* |
| ground beef | 1 lb. | 454 g | | |
| ground pork | 1 lb. | 454 g | | |
| salt | 1/4 oz. | 8 g | 1 teaspoon | 5 mL |
| pepper | | | 1 teaspoon | 5 mL |
| all-purpose flour | 3 oz. | 86 g | 2/3 cup | 160 mL |
| onion, minced | 8 oz. | 227 g | 2 medium | |
| egg | 3 1/2 oz. | 104 g | 2 each | |
| water | | 340 g | 1 1/2 cups | 360 mL |
| butter, for frying | | | | |

① Combine all ingredients except butter, blend thoroughly. Let stand for 15 minutes so flour absorbs water. Shape into patties or meatballs.

② Heat 1/8 to 1/4 inch (30 mm to 60 mm) butter in skillet until very hot. Reduce heat to medium and fry meat until golden brown, about 5 minutes per side.

③ Serve hot.

# FÅR I KÅL (NORWAY)

## LAMB AND CABBAGE

Frits Solvang © Dorling Kindersley

**Note:** Many consider this the national dish of Norway. They serve a very similar version in Finland.

**Note:** In Norway, they commonly cut lamb breast or lamb shoulder (which includes bone) into pieces for this dish. This recipe uses boneless lamb.

**Number of Servings:** 8                   **Cooking Method:** Braise
**Serving Size:** 9 oz. (256 g)
**Total Yield:** 4 lb., 13 3/4 oz. (2.2 kg)
**Food Balance:** Protein/salt
**Wine Style:** Wine friendly—Try your favorite
**Example:** Beringer Pinot Grigio, Greg Norman Zinfandel

| INGREDIENTS | WEIGHT | | VOLUME | |
| --- | --- | --- | --- | --- |
| | U.S. | METRIC | U.S. | METRIC |
| oil | | 15 g | 1 tablespoon | 15 mL |
| boneless lamb, trimmed and cut into 2-inch (5-cm) cubes | 2 lb., 5 1/2 oz. | 1.1 kg | | |
| stock or water | | 454 g | 2 cups | 480 mL |
| all-purpose flour | 1 1/4 oz. | 36 g | 1/4 cup | 60 mL |
| cabbage, cored and cut into 1-inch (2.5-cm) slices | 2 lb., 2 3/4 oz. | 986 g | 1 medium head | |
| whole peppercorns | 1/4 oz. | 8 g | 1 tablespoon | 15 mL |
| salt | as needed | | | |

**Accompaniment:**

potatoes, boiled

1. Heat oil in large pan over medium-high heat. Brown lamb in batches, remove sautéed lamb to bowl until all lamb is cooked.
2. Remove pan from heat, add about 1/2 cup (114 g or 120 mL) of the stock, deglaze pan by scraping bottom to remove browned bits. Set pan aside until needed.
3. Sprinkle flour over meat, toss to coat.
4. Place a layer of meat over bottom of pan, top with layer of cabbage. Repeat layers using all meat and cabbage, ending with cabbage on top. Sprinkle peppercorns over cabbage and pour remaining stock over it.
5. Cover and simmer over medium-low heat until meat is tender, about 1 1/2 to 2 hours.
6. Add salt as needed. Correct seasonings. Serve, accompanied by boiled potatoes.

### TWIST ON THE CLASSIC

For an interesting presentation, serve this in a partially hollowed out loaf of rye bread.

Typically, *får i kål* is served with the peppercorns throughout the dish, and diners either eat or discard the peppercorns. If desired, place peppercorns in cheesecloth so they can be removed before service.

# DILL SÅS (SWEDEN)

## DILL SAUCE

**Note:** This sauce often accompanies lamb or veal in Sweden. Boiled lamb with dill sauce is a popular entrée.

**Note:** If desired, substitute fresh dill for the dried. Add cream or an egg yolk at the end of preparation to make the sauce creamier.

**Total Yield:** 12 3/4 oz. (362 g), or 1 2/3 cups (400 mL)  
**Food Balance:** Protein  
**Wine Style:** Low-oaked whites and soft reds  
**Examples:** Campanile Pinot Grigio, Rosemount Shiraz

**Cooking Method:** Boil

Paul Cowan © Shutterstock

| INGREDIENTS | WEIGHT | | VOLUME | |
| --- | --- | --- | --- | --- |
| | U.S. | METRIC | U.S. | METRIC |
| butter | 1 oz. | 28 g | 2 tablespoons | 30 mL |
| all-purpose flour | 1 oz. | 28 g | 3 tablespoons | 45 mL |
| stock, chicken, lamb, beef, or variety of choice, hot | | 454 g | 2 cups | 480 mL |
| dried dill | | | 2 teaspoons | 10 mL |
| white vinegar | | 22 g | 1 1/2 tablespoons | 23 mL |
| sugar | 1/4 oz. | 8 g | 2 teaspoons | 10 mL |
| salt | as needed | | | |

### TWIST ON THE CLASSIC

Use this dill sauce instead of hollandaise over eggs Benedict.

① Melt the butter in saucepan over medium-low heat. Whisk the flour into the butter, continue whisking until blonde *roux*.

② Slowly whisk hot stock into *roux*. Add dill. Barely simmer over low heat, whisking occasionally, for at least 15 minutes.

③ Add vinegar and sugar, simmer another 5 minutes. Add salt if needed. Correct seasonings.

# MØRBRAD MED SVEDSKER OG AEBLER (DENMARK)

## PORK LOIN STUFFED WITH PRUNES AND APPLES

**Number of Servings:** 10
**Serving Size:** 6 oz. (171 g)
**Total Yield:** 3 lb., 12 oz. (1.7 kg)
**Food Balance:** Sweet and sour
**Wine Style:** Light- to medium-bodied, rich Chenin Blanc, blush, Chardonnay, Zinfandel, or rich Merlot
**Example:** Beringer Alluvium Merlot

**Cooking Method:** Bake

| | WEIGHT | | VOLUME | |
|---|---|---|---|---|
| **INGREDIENTS** | **U.S.** | **METRIC** | **U.S.** | **METRIC** |
| prunes, pitted | 5 oz. | 142 g | 18 each | |
| tart apple, peeled, cored, and cut into 1-inch (2.5-cm) dice | 7 oz. | 199 g | 1 large | |
| lemon juice | as needed | | | |
| center-cut pork loin, boned, fat trimmed | 4 lb., 8 oz. to 5 lb. | 2 to 2.3 kg | | |
| butter | 3/4 oz. | 22 g | 1 1/2 tablespoons | 23 mL |
| oil | | 22 g | 1 1/2 tablespoons | 23 mL |
| dry white wine | | 156 g | 2/3 cup | 160 mL |
| heavy cream | | 156 g | 2/3 cup | 160 mL |
| red currant jelly | 1 1/2 oz. | 43 g | 1 1/2 tablespoons | 23 mL |
| salt | to taste | | | |
| pepper | to taste | | | |

① Place prunes in saucepan, cover with cold water, bring to a boil. Remove from heat, let prunes soak in water for 30 minutes. Drain well, cut prunes in half.

② Sprinkle apple with a little lemon juice to prevent discoloring, mix apples with prunes.

③ With knife, make opening about 1/2 to 1 inch (1.3 to 2.5 cm) in diameter through center of pork. Either make opening with knife or start with knife and then use sharpening steel to push through center of meat to form cavity. Be careful not to break through back end of meat.

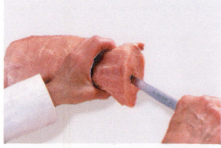

*Inserting point of knife in pork to start hole for filling*

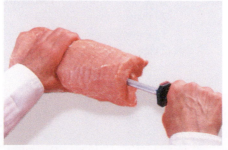

*Pushing sharpening steel through pork to create cavity*

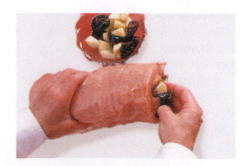

*Filling cavity of pork with fruit*

*Searing meat*

*Removing meat from oven*

④ Stuff fruits tightly into cavity. If meat must be held together, tie pork with string at 1-inch (2.5-cm) intervals to keep shape while cooking.

⑤ Preheat oven to 350 degrees (180°C).

⑥ Melt butter and oil over moderate heat in ovenproof pan just large enough to hold pork. Sauté pork until brown on all sides. Remove pork from pan.

⑦ Remove excess fat from pan. Deglaze with wine, then whisk in heavy cream, bring to simmer, then add pork.

⑧ Cover pan, cook in center of the oven for 1 to 1 1/4 hours, until meat reaches correct internal temperature with meat thermometer.

⑨ Remove pork from pan, rest on warm plate. Skim fat from liquid in pan, place pan over heat, boil to reduce liquid by half.

⑩ Stir in red currant jelly, simmer until sauce is smooth. Add salt and pepper to taste. Correct seasonings.

⑪ Remove strings from pork, slice. Arrange pork slices on plate. Nap with sauce or place sauce under slices.

## HØNS I ASPERGES (DENMARK)

### CHICKEN WITH ASPARAGUS

**Number of Servings:** 9    **Cooking Method:** Boil
**Serving Size:** 9 oz. (256 g)
**Total Yield:** 5 lb., 7 3/4 oz. (2.5 kg)
           2 lb., 1 3/4 oz. (958 g) chicken meat
**Wine Style:** Sauvignon Blanc with a medium body and moderate acidity pairs well.
**Example:** Sauvignon Blanc "Moarfeitl" 2007, Neumeister (Syria/Austria)

> **TWIST ON THE CLASSIC**
>
> To create a more visually appealing dish, use half white asparagus and half green asparagus. Also, add some red pepper strips with the asparagus for more color.

| | WEIGHT | | VOLUME | |
|---|---|---|---|---|
| **INGREDIENTS** | **U.S.** | **METRIC** | **U.S.** | **METRIC** |
| chicken | 5 lb., 1/4 oz. | 2.3 kg | 1 each | |
| onion, chopped | 8 oz. | 227 g | 1 large | |
| carrots, peeled, sliced | 2 1/4 oz. | 64 g | 2 small | |
| celery, chopped | 3 1/2 oz. | 99 g | 2 stalks | |
| asparagus, white | 1 lb., 7 1/2 oz. | 667 g | | |
| bay leaf | | | 1 each | |
| peppercorns | 1/4 oz. | 7 g | 2 teaspoons | 10 mL |
| salt | 3/4 oz. | 21 g | 1 tablespoon | 15 mL |
| water | as needed | | | |
| butter | 1 1/2 oz. | 43 g | 3 tablespoons | 44 mL |
| flour | 1 1/2 oz. | 43 g | 1/3 cup | 79 mL |
| reserved chicken stock, hot | | 1 kg | 1 quart + 1/2 cup or 4 to 4 1/2 cups, as needed | 960 mL to 1.1 L |

© lidi

For an hors d'oeurve or first course, this chicken and asparagus dish sometimes is used as filling in a pre-baked tart shell.

| INGREDIENTS | WEIGHT | | VOLUME | |
|---|---|---|---|---|
| | U.S. | METRIC | U.S. | METRIC |
| heavy cream | | 114 g | 1/2 cup | 120 mL |
| pepper | to taste | | | |

**Garnish:**

parsley, minced

1. Place chicken, onion, carrots, celery, bottom woody part of asparagus stalks, bay leaf, peppercorns, and salt in a large pot. Cover with cold water and heat until it comes to gentle boil. Reduce heat, cover partially, and simmer for 1 hour or until chicken is tender and done. Skim surface to remove any foam and scum as needed throughout cooking.

2. Remove chicken from stock, set aside until cool enough to handle. Meanwhile, boil stock to reduce liquid.

3. When chicken is cool enough, remove skin, bones, and any cartilage. Cut chicken meat into bite-sized pieces. Refrigerate until needed. Return bones to stock for boiling to make richer stock.

4. Peel asparagus stalks. Cut into pieces about 1 1/2-inches (about 4-cm) long, place heads separate from stalk portions. Set aside until needed.

5. Melt butter over medium heat in medium-sized saucepan. Whisk flour into butter, cook until blonde roux. Slowly whisk hot chicken stock into roux. Add about 1 to 1 1/2 lb. (454 to 681 g, 3 to 4 cups, or 720 to 960 mL) of stock. Allow to come to boil, reduce heat and simmer about 20 minutes to eliminate raw flour taste. Whisk in additional stock as needed to make enough sauce to hold chicken and cook asparagus.

6. Add chicken to sauce, heat just until simmering. Add asparagus stalk portions, cook 3 minutes. Add asparagus tips, cook another 3 minutes. Add cream and pepper, gently stir until hot. Correct seasonings.

7. Serve immediately, garnished with parsley. For accompaniments, serve over rice or with boiled new potatoes.

# ÆNDER MED ÆBLER OG SVEDSKER (DENMARK)

## ROAST DUCK WITH APPLES AND PRUNES

© Thinkstock/Getty Images

**Note:** This recipe is popular for cooking goose or duck in Denmark and Sweden. In fact, many Scandinavians serve it for Christmas dinner.

**Number of Servings:** 6 or 12

**Serving Size:** 1/2 duck or 1/4 duck

**Food Balance:** Protein/sweet

**Wine Style:** Low-oaked whites and soft reds

**Example:** Stags' Leap Viognier, Cellar #8 Zinfandel

**Cooking Method:** Bake

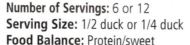

| INGREDIENTS | WEIGHT | | VOLUME | |
|---|---|---|---|---|
| | U.S. | METRIC | U.S. | METRIC |
| prunes, pitted and cut into pieces | 12 oz. | 340 g | 2 cups | 480 mL |
| apples, peeled, cored, and cut into pieces | 1 lb., 12 oz. | 794 g | 5 each | |
| onions, cut into eighths | 8 oz. | 227 g | 2 each | |
| duck, giblets and excess fat removed, washed | about 14 lb., 5 1/2 oz. | 6.5 kg | 3 each | |
| lemon juice | as needed | | | |
| pepper | as needed | | | |

**Garnish:**

lingonberry preserves or
   poached apples with prunes

**Accompaniments:**
red cabbage, cored, sliced, and
    cooked
*brunede kartofler* (caramelized
    potatoes), *recipe on page 203*

1. Place prunes in dish. Cover with boiling water. Set aside for at least 30 minutes to hydrate. If needed immediately, boil prunes with water for a few minutes, until plumped.

2. Gently mix prunes, apples, and onions in bowl. Set aside until needed.

3. Position oven rack in center of oven. Preheat oven to 450 degrees (230°C). Place a rack in the pan (so duck will not touch water) and add about 1/2 inch (1.3 cm) water to bottom of roasting pan. Stick duck with a fork all over to dock skin so fat is released.

4. Lightly sprinkle inside cavity of ducks with lemon juice and pepper. Fill the cavity of each duck with one-third of the prune mixture.

5. Place duck on rack in pan with the breast side down, put in oven, and reduce oven temperature to 350 degrees (180°C). Remove after 45 minutes, drain fat if necessary. Turn duck over so breast side is up. Stick all over with fork again. Return to oven, bake for another 45 minutes. Remove from oven, drain fat, if needed.

6. Return to oven, bake another 30 minutes to 1 hour (total baking time 2 to 2 1/2 hours) until proper internal temperature and juices run clear. If broiling duck to crisp the skin, undercook duck slightly.

7. To obtain a crisp skin, pour all fat from pan. Broil duck on all sides until crisp.

8. Cut duck into desired serving size (quarter or half). Discard stuffing (because it contains too much fat from the duck).

9. Serve duck with a garnish of lingonberry preserves or poached apples and prunes. Accompany with red cabbage and *Brunede Kartofler* (see recipe).

---

This classic preparation for roasted goose or duck is typically served without a sauce. If desired, serve with a lingonberry sauce or the sauce of choice.

To prepare poached apples and prunes, soak prunes in port for several hours to plump. Poach apple slices in a small amount of lightly sugared water until half soft. Add prunes and port, continue poaching until tender.

---

## FISKEPUDDING (NORWAY)

### FISH MOUSSE

**Note:** This common Norwegian dish is made with very fresh fish. It may be served as an entrée or first course. Leftovers are served either cold or hot.

**Number of Servings:** 8
**Serving Size:** 6 oz. (171 g)
**Total Yield:** 3 lb., 2 oz. (1.4 kg)
**Food Balance:** Protein
**Wine Style:** Light- to medium-bodied Chenin Blanc, Sauvignon Blanc, soft Chardonnay, blush, or rosé
**Example:** Meridian Vineyards Santa Barbara Chardonnay

**Cooking Method:** Bake

Arturo Limon © Shutterstock

| INGREDIENTS | WEIGHT | | VOLUME | |
|---|---|---|---|---|
| | U.S. | METRIC | U.S. | METRIC |
| butter, for greasing pan | | | | |
| breadcrumbs, for dusting pan | 3/4 to 1 oz. | 22 to 28 g | 3 to 4 tablespoons | 45 to 60 mL |
| cod, skinned and boned | 3 lb. | 1.4 kg | | |
| salt | | | 1 1/2 teaspoons | 8 mL |
| pepper | | | 1/2 teaspoon | 3 mL |
| ground cardamom | | | 1/2 teaspoon | 3 mL |
| ground mace | | | 1/2 teaspoon | 3 mL |

**TWIST ON THE CLASSIC**

Use cold slices as a sandwich filling, or coat the cold slices with breadcrumbs or flour and sauté to serve warm.

| INGREDIENTS | WEIGHT | | VOLUME | |
| --- | --- | --- | --- | --- |
| | U.S. | METRIC | U.S. | METRIC |
| cornstarch | 1 oz. | 28 g | 3 tablespoons | 45 mL |
| milk | | 114 g | 1/2 cup | 120 mL |
| heavy cream | | 567 g | 2 1/2 cups | 600 mL |

**Accompaniments:**
butter flavored with lemon fresh
  dill, finely chopped shrimp
  sauce

1. Butter 2- to 3-quart (1.9 to 2.8 L) pan, ring mold, or terrine pan; dust with breadcrumbs. Turn pan upside down and tap to remove excess crumbs.
2. Position rack in middle of oven. Preheat oven to 350 degrees (180°C). Boil a couple quarts of water for *bain-marie*.
3. Cut fish into pieces and place in food processor fitted with knife blade. Add salt, pepper, cardamom, mace, and cornstarch.
4. Mix milk and cream together in small bowl. Turn on processor, add cream mixture slowly through feed tube while processing until mixture is smooth and fluffy.
5. Pour purée into prepared mold. Tap it once or twice on counter to remove air bubbles. Smooth surface with spatula. Cover pan tightly with aluminum foil, seal well.
6. Place pan inside larger pan (for *bain-marie*) and place in oven. Pour boiling water into larger pan to depth of about 3/4 inch (2 cm).
7. Bake for 50 to 60 minutes, until knife comes out clean. The water should not boil while baking or mousse will have holes in it.
8. Remove pan from *bain-marie*. Let stand about 5 minutes.
9. Drain any liquid from pan containing mousse. Unmold mousse: invert on warm serving platter. Remove any excess liquid from platter.
10. Serve with melted butter flavored with lemon and finely chopped fresh dill or a shrimp sauce.

# TORSK PÅ FAD (DENMARK)

## BAKED COD

### TWIST ON THE CLASSIC

To add zip to this dish, mix a little cayenne pepper into the breadcrumb/salt mixture that tops the cod. Also, add lemon juice to the caper sauce.

© Stephanie Frey

**Number of Servings:** 9
**Serving Size:** 6 oz. (171 g)
**Total Yield:** 3 lb., 8 oz. (1.6 kg) total
**sauce:** 10 oz. (284 g)
**fish:** 2 lb., 14 1/2 oz. (1.3 kg)
**Wine Style:** Lighter white wine without oak. Possible grape varietals are Sauvignon Blanc, Riesling, Zierfandler.
**Example:** Sauvignon Blanc STK 2013, Tement (Sudsteiermark/Austria)

**Cooking Method:** Bake, boil

| INGREDIENTS | WEIGHT | | VOLUME | |
| --- | --- | --- | --- | --- |
| | U.S. | METRIC | U.S. | METRIC |
| white wine | | 227 g | 1 cup | 240 mL |
| cod fillets | 3 lb., 1 1/2 oz. | 1.4 kg | | |
| breadcrumbs, dried | 5 oz. | 142 g | 1 cup | 240 mL |
| salt | 1/4 oz. | 8 g | 1 teaspoon | 5 mL |
| butter, melted | 2 oz. | 57 g | 4 tablespoons (1/4 cup) | 60 mL |

| INGREDIENTS | WEIGHT | | VOLUME | |
| --- | --- | --- | --- | --- |
| | U.S. | METRIC | U.S. | METRIC |
| **Caper Sauce:** | | | | |
| white wine | | 114 g | 1/2 cup | 120 mL |
| onion, minced | 1 oz. | 28 g | 2 tablespoons | 30 mL |
| thyme | | | 1 teaspoon | 5 mL |
| pepper | | | 1/2 teaspoon | 3 mL |
| salt | | | 1/2 teaspoon | 3 mL |
| butter | 5 oz. | 142 g | 10 tablespoons | 148 mL |
| capers | 2 oz. | 57 g | 1/4 cup | 60 mL |
| parsley, minced | 1/2 oz. | 15 g | 1/4 cup | 60 mL |

**Garnish:**

red pepper, minced

1. Position oven rack in upper half of oven. Preheat oven to 400 degrees (205°C). Place rack in ovenproof dish large enough to hold fish in single layer. Pour white wine (227 g, 1 cup, or 240 mL) in pan.
2. Place cod on rack in single layer. Mix breadcrumbs and salt together. Spread evenly over fish. Drizzle with melted butter. Place in oven. Begin preparing sauce while fish bakes.
3. Bake until fish is flaky and opaque. Check after 18 minutes; actual time will depend on thickness of cod.
4. Remove from oven, cover with aluminum foil while finishing sauce.

## FOR CAPER SAUCE AND ASSEMBLY:

1. Put white wine (114 g, 1/2 cup, or 120 mL), onion, thyme, pepper, and salt in saucepan. Bring to boil, reduce heat and simmer until wine reduces by half.
2. Over low heat, add butter and capers. Heat thoroughly, remove from heat, add parsley. Correct seasonings.
3. If serving from platter or steam table pan, remove fish to platter or pan and pour caper sauce over fish. For individual portion, place about a 5-oz. (142-g) portion of cod on plate and top with about 1 oz. (28 g) of caper sauce. If desired, garnish plate or platter with minced red pepper.

> Baked cod is served throughout Scandinavia.
>
> If a rack to hold the fish above wine in pan is unavailable, use stalks of fennel or celery laid in the pan to elevate the fish.

## PAISTETUT SIENET (FINLAND)

### MUSHROOMS WITH SOUR CREAM

**Number of Servings:** 6
**Serving Size:** 3 oz. (86 g)
**Total Yield:** 1 lb., 2 oz. (511 g)

**Cooking Method:** Sauté

| INGREDIENTS | WEIGHT | | VOLUME | |
| --- | --- | --- | --- | --- |
| | U.S. | METRIC | U.S. | METRIC |
| butter | 1 oz. | 28 g | 2 tablespoons | 30 mL |
| onions, minced | 1 1/4 oz. | 36 g | 1/4 cup | 60 mL |
| fresh mushrooms, button or any variety, thinly sliced | 1 lb. | 454 kg | | |
| fine, dry breadcrumbs | 1 oz. | 28 g | 1/4 cup | 60 mL |
| sour cream | 4 1/2 oz. | 128 g | 1/2 cup | 120 mL |

**Garnish:**

fresh herbs, minced

paprika

Kiselev Andrey Valerevich © Shutterstock

**TWIST ON THE CLASSIC**

Serve these mushrooms as an appetizer by placing them in a puff pastry shell or a tart shell.

1. Melt butter over moderate heat. Sauté onions until soft and transparent but not brown.
2. Add mushrooms and cook another 3 to 5 minutes, until light brown.
3. Sprinkle in breadcrumbs, mix. Turn heat to low.
4. Add sour cream and mix until evenly coated. Correct seasonings.
5. Serve as a vegetable accompaniment to meat or fish dishes. If desired, garnish with minced fresh herbs or paprika.

# LANTTULAATIKKO (FINLAND)

## RUTABAGA PUDDING

**Number of Servings:** 9　　　　　　　**Cooking Method:** Boil, bake
**Serving Size:** 4 oz. (114 g)
**Total Yield:** 2 lb., 4 oz. (1.1 kg)

© Dorling Kindersley

| INGREDIENTS | WEIGHT U.S. | WEIGHT METRIC | VOLUME U.S. | VOLUME METRIC |
|---|---|---|---|---|
| rutabagas, peeled and cut into 1/4-inch (1/2-cm) dice | 2 lb., 7 oz. | 1.1 kg | 2 medium | |
| breadcrumbs | 1 oz. | 28 g | 1/4 cup | 60 mL |
| heavy cream | | 57 g | 1/4 cup | 60 mL |
| salt | 1/4 oz. | 8 g or to taste | 1 teaspoon | 5 mL or to taste |
| pepper | | | 1/4 teaspoon | 2 mL |
| ground nutmeg | | | 1/2 teaspoon | 3 mL |
| sugar, *optional* | | | 2 teaspoons | 10 mL |
| eggs, lightly beaten | 3 1/2 oz. | 104 g | 2 each | |
| butter | 1 3/4 oz. | 50 g | 3 1/2 tablespoons | 52 mL |

1. Place rutabagas in pan, cover with cold water, partially cover and cook until tender.
2. Combine breadcrumbs and cream in bowl, let sit a few minutes. Add salt, pepper, nutmeg, sugar, and eggs.
3. Preheat oven to 350 degrees (180°C), grease baking dish.
4. Drain liquid from rutabagas and mash as for mashed potatoes using some reserved liquid, if needed. Add breadcrumb mixture and 2 tablespoons (30 mL) of butter to rutabagas. Correct seasonings.
5. Place rutabaga mix in prepared dish. Dot with remaining 1 1/2 tablespoons (23 mL) butter.
6. Bake uncovered for 1 hour, until lightly browned. Serve.

**TWIST ON THE CLASSIC**

Prepare this in individual serving dishes instead of one large dish.

# GRONKAAL MED FLØDE (DENMARK)

## CREAMED KALE

**Number of Servings:** 9　　　　　　　**Cooking Method:** Boil, sauté
**Serving Size:** 4 oz. (114 g)
**Total Yield:** 2 lb., 6 oz. (1.1 kg)

**TWIST ON THE CLASSIC**

For a breakfast dish, use the creamed kale as the base and top it with a poached egg.

| INGREDIENTS | WEIGHT U.S. | WEIGHT METRIC | VOLUME U.S. | VOLUME METRIC |
|---|---|---|---|---|
| water | as needed | | | |
| kale, tough stems removed | 1 lb., 8 oz. | 680 g | | |
| butter | 1 oz. | 28 g | 2 tablespoons | 30 mL |

| INGREDIENTS | WEIGHT | | VOLUME | |
| --- | --- | --- | --- | --- |
| | U.S. | METRIC | U.S. | METRIC |
| flour | 1 oz. | 28 g | 2 tablespoons + 2 teaspoons | 30 mL + 10 mL |
| milk, warm | | 511 g | 2 1/4 cups | 540 mL |
| salt | | | 1 1/2 teaspoons | 8 mL |
| pepper | | | 1/4 teaspoon | 2 mL |
| sugar | 3/4 oz. | 22 g | 1 tablespoon | 15 mL |
| nutmeg | | | 1/8 teaspoon, or to taste | 1 mL |

© fkruger

1. Bring pot of water to boil over medium-high heat. Add kale and simmer for 3 to 4 minutes, until wilted. Remove to colander, drain well.
2. When well drained, chop. Set aside until needed.
3. Melt butter in a saucepan over medium heat. Sprinkle flour over butter, whisk until incorporated and smooth. Whisking constantly, gradually add warm milk, a little at a time into flour.
4. Add salt, pepper, sugar, and nutmeg. Whisking occasionally, bring to gentle boil, reduce heat and simmer about 10 minutes, until thickened.
5. Add kale to sauce, stir gently to combine thoroughly. Correct seasonings. Serve.

> Instead of making the cream sauce with a *roux* made with milk, some use cream and a little cornstarch for the sauce.

## BRUNEDE KARTOFLER (DENMARK)

### CARAMELIZED POTATOES

**Note:** Good served with pork roasts, ham, braised or sautéed pork chops, roast beef, and poultry.

**Number of Servings:** 8  
**Serving Size:** 4 oz. (114 g)

**Cooking Method:** Boil, sauté

### TWIST ON THE CLASSIC

Substitute turnips and parsnips for the potatoes, or use a combination of all three.

| INGREDIENTS | WEIGHT | | VOLUME | |
| --- | --- | --- | --- | --- |
| | U.S. | METRIC | U.S. | METRIC |
| red potatoes, small | 2 lb. | 908 g | 10 to 12 each | |
| sugar | 2 1/4 oz. | 64 g | 1/4 cup + 1 tablespoon | 75 mL |
| unsalted butter | 1 1/2 oz. | 43 g | 3 tablespoons | 45 mL |
| fresh dill, minced | 1/4 oz. | 8 g | 1 tablespoon | 15 mL |

1. Place unpeeled potatoes in pot, cover with cold water. Bring to boil, simmer until potatoes are tender.
2. Drain potatoes. Peel as soon as cool enough to handle.
3. In heavy skillet over medium heat, stir sugar until melted and light brown.
4. Add butter and stir until thoroughly blended into sugar.
5. Add some potatoes (do not crowd in pan). Coat them with caramelized mixture by shaking pan or rolling potatoes with wooden spoon.
6. Remove glazed potatoes and keep them warm while glazing next batch(es).
7. Just before service, sprinkle potatoes with dill.

© Olaf Speier/Fotolia

# JANSSON'S FRESTELSE (SWEDEN)

## JANSSON'S TEMPTATION (POTATO CASSEROLE)

**Number of Servings:** 9
**Serving Size:** 4 oz. (114 g)
**Total Yield:** 2 lb., 6 oz. (1.1 kg)

**Cooking Method:** Bake

|  | WEIGHT | | VOLUME | |
|---|---|---|---|---|
| INGREDIENTS | U.S. | METRIC | U.S. | METRIC |
| potatoes, white, waxy, or all-purpose, peeled and cut into 1/4-inch (1/2-cm) strips | 2 lb., 15 oz. | 1.3 kg | 7 medium | |
| butter | 1 to 2 oz. | 28 to 57 g | 2 to 4 tablespoons | 30 to 60 mL |
| onions, thin rings | 13 oz. | 369 g | 3 medium | |
| anchovy fillets | 2 oz. | 57 g | 1 small can | |
| white pepper | to taste | | | |
| heavy cream | | 227 g | 1 cup | 240 mL |
| milk | | 114 g | 1/2 cup | 120 mL |
| breadcrumbs | 1 1/2 oz. | 43 g | 1/2 cup | 120 mL |

1. Place potatoes in cold water to prevent discoloring.
2. Preheat oven to 350 degrees (180°C), butter 2-quart (1.9-L) pan.
3. Melt 2 tablespoons (30 mL) of butter in skillet over medium heat, add onion and sauté until soft but not browned, about 5 to 10 minutes. Remove from heat.
4. Place alternate layers of potatoes, onion rings, and anchovies in prepared pan, ending with layer of potatoes. Sprinkle a little white pepper on potato layers.
5. Mix cream and milk in bowl. Pour over potatoes. Top with breadcrumbs. If desired, dot with remaining butter.
6. Bake for 45 to 60 minutes, or until potatoes are tender and most liquid is absorbed.

© vera-g

© Dorling Kindersley

# HILVALEIPÄ (FINLAND)

## RYE BREAD

**Note:** This is a very basic rye bread.

**Scaling:** 15 1/2 oz. (439 g) per loaf  **Cooking Method:** Bake
**Total Yield:** 1 lb., 15 1/4 oz. (888 g) dough, or 2 small loaves

| | WEIGHT | | VOLUME | |
|---|---|---|---|---|
| **INGREDIENTS** | **U.S.** | **METRIC** | **U.S.** | **METRIC** |
| water, lukewarm | | 57 g | 1/4 cup | 60 mL |
| honey | | | 2 tablespoons | 30 mL |
| granulated yeast | 3/4 oz. | 22 g | 2 tablespoons | 30 mL |
| water, hot | | 227 g | 1 cup | 240 mL |
| salt | 1/2 oz. | 15 g | 2 teaspoons | 10 mL |
| butter, cut into pieces | 2 oz. | 57 g | 4 tablespoons (1/2 stick) | 60 mL |
| rye flour | 10 1/4 oz. | 292 g | 2 cups | 480 mL |
| whole wheat flour | 6 oz. | 171 g, as needed | 1 1/4 cups | 300 mL, as needed |
| oil | as needed | | | |
| butter, melted | for brushing loaves | | | |

**TWIST ON THE CLASSIC**

If desired, add caraway, fennel, or other seeds of choice to this bread.

1. Mix lukewarm water, 1 tablespoon (15 mL) of honey, and yeast in a nonreactive bowl. Set aside for about 5 minutes, until foamy.

2. Mix hot water, remaining 1 tablespoon (15 mL) honey, salt, and butter together in a bowl. Stir until butter melts and mixture is lukewarm.

3. Place rye flour in large bowl. Add yeast mixture, mix well with wooden spoon. Add whole wheat flour and reserved salt/butter water. Stir well to form dough. Add flour if needed to prevent sticking, but add a little at a time. Too much flour will make the bread dry.

4. Knead until smooth, about 10 minutes. Place in oiled bowl, turn to oil top of dough. Cover (leaving room for dough to expand) and place in warm area to rise until doubled, about 1 hour and 15 minutes. Meanwhile, pan-spray two 8 1/2- by 4 1/2-inch (22-by-11-cm) loaf pans.

5. Punch down dough, let rest for 10 minutes. Form into two loaves (about 15 1/2 oz., 439 g each) and place in prepared pans. Cover and let rise until doubled, about 45 minutes. While dough rises, preheat oven to 400 degrees (205°C).

6. Bake for 30 minutes, until done. Bread should sound hollow when tapped. Remove from oven, remove loaves from pans, brush tops with melted butter, and cool completely on racks. Wrap tightly to store.

Kamenecskly Konstantin © Shutterstock

# KNÄKEBRÖD (SWEDEN)

## CRISPBREAD

stocksnapp © Shutterstock

**Note:** Scandinavians consume lots of hard breads or crackers. These breads hark from the early days—they have the advantage of storing well because they are dry.

**Scaling:** about 3 1/2 oz. (104 g) per disk
**Total Yield:** 1 lb., 11 1/4 oz. (770 g) dough, or 8 disks about 8 inches (20 cm) in diameter

| | WEIGHT | | VOLUME | |
|---|---|---|---|---|
| **INGREDIENTS** | **U.S.** | **METRIC** | **U.S.** | **METRIC** |
| milk, lukewarm | | 284 g | 1 1/4 cups | 300 mL |
| sugar | 1/2 oz. | 15 g | 1 tablespoon | 15 mL |
| granulated yeast | 3/4 oz. | 22 g | 2 tablespoons | 30 mL |
| whole wheat flour | 8 oz. | 227 g | 1 3/4 cups | 420 mL |
| rye flour | 8 oz. | 227 g, as needed | 1 1/2 cups | 360 mL, as needed |
| fennel seeds, crushed with mortar and pestle | | | 1 teaspoon | 5 mL |
| salt | 1/4 oz. | 8 g | 1 teaspoon | 5 mL |

1. Mix milk, sugar, and yeast in a nonreactive bowl. Set aside for about 5 minutes, until frothy.
2. Mix whole wheat flour, half of rye flour, fennel seeds, and salt together in a bowl. Add to yeast mixture and mix to combine. Stir and add remaining rye flour as needed to form fairly firm dough.
3. Knead for several minutes, until smooth dough. Cover and let rest for 20 minutes. Preheat oven to 400 degrees (205°C).
4. Divide dough into eight pieces (about 3 1/2 oz., 104 g each). Roll each piece into disk about 8 inches (20 cm) in diameter and 1/16-inch (2-mm) thick. Dock with fork or docker.
5. Bake for 10 to 15 minutes, until crisp. Cool completely on racks. Store in an airtight container.

### TWIST ON THE CLASSIC

Form the dough into 1- by 5- by 1/16-inch (2.5-cm by 13-cm by 2-mm) crackers and use them as a garnish for soup or a salad.

---

# MAZARINTÅRTA (SWEDEN)

## SWEDISH ALMOND RASPBERRY TORTE

**Note:** Best prepared a day ahead.

**Number of Servings:** 12 to 16     **Cooking Method:** Bake
**Total Yield:** 9-inch (23-cm) fluted tart pan or 9-inch (23-cm) springform pan

| | WEIGHT | | VOLUME | |
|---|---|---|---|---|
| **INGREDIENTS** | **U.S.** | **METRIC** | **U.S.** | **METRIC** |
| **Dough:** | | | | |
| all purpose flour, sifted | 5 1/4 oz. | 149 g | 1 1/3 cups | 320 mL |
| baking powder | | | 1 teaspoon | 5 mL |
| sugar | 2 3/4 oz. | 78 g | 1/3 cup | 80 mL |
| unsalted butter, cold | 4 oz. | 114 g | 1/2 cup (1 stick) | 120 mL |
| egg | 1 3/4 oz. | 50 g | 1 each | |
| **Filling:** | | | | |
| unsalted butter | 4 oz. | 114 g | 1/2 cup (1 stick) | 120 mL |
| sugar | 5 1/2 oz. | 156 g | 2/3 cup | 160 mL |
| blanched almonds, ground | 3 1/2 oz. | 104 g | 1 cup | 240 mL |

| INGREDIENTS | WEIGHT | | VOLUME | |
| --- | --- | --- | --- | --- |
| | *U.S.* | *METRIC* | *U.S.* | *METRIC* |
| vanilla | | | 1/2 teaspoon | 3 mL |
| eggs | 3 1/2 oz. | 104 g | 2 each | |
| raspberry preserves | 7 1/2 oz. | 213 g | 2/3 cup | 160 mL |
| **Topping:** | | | | |
| confectioner's sugar, sifted | 4 oz. | 114 g | 1 cup | 240 mL |
| fresh lemon juice | | 15 g | 1 tablespoon | 15 mL |
| water | | | about 1 teaspoon | 5 mL |

**TWIST ON THE CLASSIC**

Use any flavor of preserves in this recipe. Apricot preserves work well. Prepare this in individual tart pans.

## DOUGH:

1. Sift flour, baking powder, and sugar together. Place in bowl of food processor fitted with knife blade and pulse to mix.
2. Cut butter into 8 or 10 pieces. Place on top of dry ingredients. Pulse to cut in butter until clumps the size of peas form. Add egg and mix until dough comes together.
3. Remove from bowl, knead once or twice, if necessary, to form ball. Wrap in plastic wrap and refrigerate until needed.

## FILLING:

1. Cream butter and sugar in mixer fitted with flat paddle beater, beat until fluffy.
2. Add almonds and vanilla. Mix.
3. Add eggs, one at a time, beating well after each addition.

## ASSEMBLY:

1. Position oven rack in lower half of oven. Preheat oven to 350 degrees (180°C).
2. Roll chilled dough between sheets of parchment or waxed paper. Remove top paper, invert into springform pan or tart pan. Release dough from paper, press evenly on bottom and about an inch or so up sides of pan. Make sure any holes are covered so filling won't leak out while baking.
3. Spread half of raspberry preserves over bottom of dough. Top with filling; smooth top with spatula.
4. Bake about 40 minutes or until a knife inserted into filling comes out clean. Cool torte 10 minutes. Remove sides of pan, cool completely.

## TOPPING:

1. Mix confectioner's sugar and lemon juice. Add water, a few drops at a time, until it reaches spreading consistency.
2. Let topping rest 5 to 10 minutes.
3. Spread remaining raspberry preserves over cooled torte. Drizzle topping over torte or pipe decoratively over preserves. (Pipe a traditional spider-web design or a design of your choice.)

# TOSKAKAKE (NORWAY)
## ALMOND CARAMEL CAKE

**Number of Servings:** 12 to 16  **Cooking Method:** Bake
**Total Yield:** 11-inch (28-cm) tart pan or 10-inch (25-cm) springform pan

© Comugnero Silvana

| INGREDIENTS | WEIGHT | | VOLUME | |
| --- | --- | --- | --- | --- |
| | U.S. | METRIC | U.S. | METRIC |
| **Cake:** | | | | |
| all-purpose flour | 7 1/2 oz. | 213 g | 1 1/2 cups | 360 mL |
| sugar | 7 1/2 oz. | 213 g | 1 cup | 240 mL |
| baking powder | 1/4 oz. | 8 g | 2 teaspoons | 10 mL |
| salt | | | 1/2 teaspoon | 3 mL |
| heavy cream | | 227 g | 1 cup | 240 mL |
| eggs | 3 1/2 oz. | 104 g | 2 each | |
| vanilla | | | 1 teaspoon | 5 mL |
| **Topping:** | | | | |
| unsalted butter | 2 1/2 oz. | 71 g | 1/3 cup | 80 mL |
| sugar | 2 3/4 oz. | 78 g | 1/3 cup | 80 mL |
| almonds, chopped | 4 1/4 oz. | 120 g | 3/4 cup | 180 mL |
| all-purpose flour | 1/4 oz. | 8 g | 1 tablespoon | 15 mL |
| heavy cream | | 15 g | 1 tablespoon | 15 mL |

## CAKE:

1. Position oven rack in center of oven. Preheat oven to 350 degrees (180°C). Butter tart or springform pan.
2. Sift together flour, sugar, baking powder, and salt in bowl.
3. In separate bowl, whip cream until stiff peaks form, add eggs and vanilla and mix. Add flour mixture, mix just to combine.
4. Pour into prepared pan.
5. Bake 30 to 35 minutes or until cake slightly pulls away from side of pan and knife comes out almost clean. Do not overbake.

## TOPPING:

1. Meanwhile, melt butter in small saucepan over medium heat. Add remaining ingredients and bring to boil, stirring constantly.
2. Cook about 2 to 3 minutes, until slightly thickened.
3. Pour hot topping over hot cake. Spread with icing spatula to cover top. Return to oven and bake about 10 minutes, until golden brown.
4. Serve warm or cold.

# SPRITSAR (SWEDEN)

## ALMOND SUGAR COOKIES (SPRITZ)

**Number of Cookies:** 30
**Scaling:** 3/4 oz. (22 g) per cookie
**Total Yield:** 1 lb., 7 1/4 oz. (660 g)

**Cooking Method:** Bake

| INGREDIENTS | WEIGHT | | VOLUME | |
|---|---|---|---|---|
| | U.S. | METRIC | U.S. | METRIC |
| vanilla bean | 1/4 oz. | 8 g | 1 each | |
| sugar | 5 1/2 oz. | 156 g | 3/4 cup | 180 mL |
| butter, unsalted | 5 oz. | 142 g | 10 tablespoons (1 stick + 2 tablespoons) | 148 mL (1 stick + 30 mL) |
| egg | 1 3/4 oz. | 50 g | 1 each | |
| almond extract | | | 1/4 teaspoon | 2 mL |
| flour, sifted | 7 1/4 oz. | 206 g | 1 3/4 cups | 420 mL |
| almonds, blanched, ground | 4 oz. | 114 g | 1 cup | 240 mL |

1. Place parchment paper on baking sheet. Position oven rack in center of oven. Preheat oven to 400 degrees (205°C). Cut vanilla bean vertically to expose seeds, then cut bean horizontally into 1-inch (2.5-cm) pieces.
2. Place vanilla bean and sugar in food processor fitted with knife blade, process until bean is incorporated with sugar and looks like tiny flecks of dark, several minutes.
3. Transfer sugar to mixer fitted with whisk attachment. Add butter, cream on medium speed until light and fluffy, several minutes. Add egg and almond extract, beat until well blended, light, and fluffy. Add flour and almonds, mix on low speed just to incorporate.
4. Using pastry bag fitted with large star tip, form dough into circle about 1 1/2 to 2 inches (4 to 5 cm) in diameter (3/4 oz., 22 g dough) on prepared pan. Repeat with remaining dough. Alternately, form cookies into "S" shape. If pastry bag is unavailable, form dough into ropes and shape into circles.
5. Bake for 9 to 12 minutes, until beginning to lightly brown. Remove and cool on racks.

### TWIST ON THE CLASSIC

To create a sandwich cookie, place preserves or melted chocolate on the bottom (flat side) of a cookie and top it with another cookie placed with the bottom against the filling.

© Brad Pict

These popular butter almond cookies appear throughout Scandinavia with each country having many recipes and variations.

# Russia and Eastern Europe

## >> LEARNING OBJECTIVES

By the end of this chapter, you will be able to:

- Identify similarities and differences among the cuisines of the Eastern European countries and Russia
- Understand the historical, geographic, and climatic influences on the cuisines of these countries
- Identify food products prevalent in the cuisines of Russia and Eastern Europe and explain why they appear so frequently
- Prepare a variety of dishes from Russia and Eastern Europe

*Although this chapter covers a lot of area spanning portions of both Europe and Asia, the similarities among the cuisines of Russia and Eastern Europe facilitate discussing these countries together.*

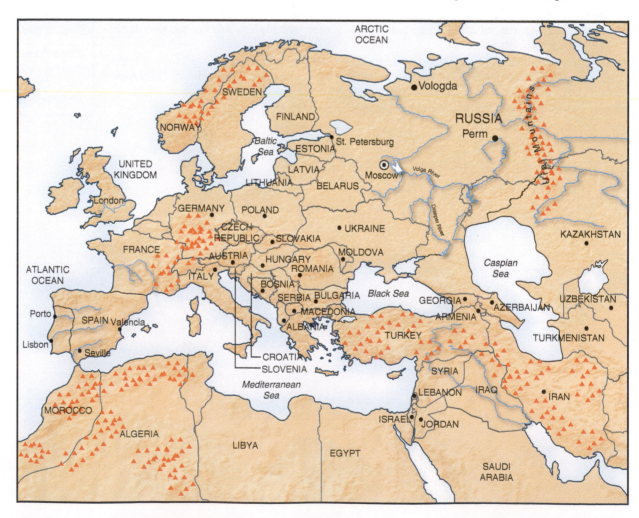

## >> HISTORY

### CHANGING BORDERS

The Eastern European countries lie east of Germany, Austria, and Italy. Some of these countries include Poland, Hungary, the Czech Republic, Slovenia, Macedonia, Croatia, Serbia, Montenegro, Kosovo, Bosnia, Romania, Albania, Lithuania, Bulgaria, Ukraine, and the part of Russia that is in Europe.

Throughout history, Russia and the countries of Eastern Europe have intertwined, conquering one another and then losing control. Boundaries in Eastern Europe continue to change. Some countries previously found in Eastern Europe no longer exist, having been annexed by more powerful nations. On the other hand, new nations form: for example, Czechoslovakia became the Czech Republic and Slovakia in 1989. The history of the area formerly called Yugoslavia is another recent change of countries. At the end of World War I, Yugoslavia was created in an area occupied by more than 20 ethnic groups. Tensions among some of these ethnic groups increased dramatically in the 1980s. Ultimately, Russia lost control over Yugoslavia in 1991, and the countries of Slovenia, Macedonia, Croatia, Serbia, Montenegro, Kosovo, and Bosnia came into existence in the years after the Communist rule ended. Unfortunately, intense fighting and genocide continued in Bosnia in the 1990s, and more than 100,000 people died.

### EARLY SETTLERS

One common thread among these countries is their Slavic ancestry. Evidence exists of Slavic tribes in Poland as early as 2000 B.C. These tribes migrated to the south from Poland and Russia during the sixth century. By the 800s A.D., tribes of Slavic origin inhabited most of the lands covered in this chapter. Around that time, Polane tribes settled in Poland, Magyars came to Hungary, and East Slavs inhabited Ukraine.

### RUSSIA

Being such a large country, Russia has felt the effects of diverse groups of invaders from both Asia and Europe; however, the long, bitter winters have stopped many aggressors throughout Russia's history. Iranians conquered Russia around 700 B.C., and Germanic tribes entered about 500 years later. In the 800s A.D., the Vikings came to Russia. They introduced herring. The Mongols invaded around the 1200s and brought spices as well as the techniques of grilling, souring milk, and pickling cabbage. During medieval times, trade with the Byzantine Empire brought buckwheat, rice, and spices to Russia. Because of their location on the trade route between China and Europe, Russians had access to many new foods and spices.

Czars ruled Russia from the middle 1500s until the Bolshevik Revolution in 1917. Under the leadership of the czars, Russia had frequent battles and exchanges of power with Eastern European countries, particularly with Ukraine and Poland.

During the rule of Peter the Great from 1682 to 1725, Russia developed into a modernized country. From 1697 to 1698, Peter the Great traveled throughout Europe using a pseudonym, so no one knew he was the czar of Russia. He learned about shipbuilding, weapons, military issues, and much more. When he returned to Russia, he brought experts in many of these fields with him. Besides establishing important ties with Europe, he transformed Russia into a powerful country. Those liaisons led to strong influences between the various European countries and Russia. The infatuation with Europe continued, and, during the time of Napoleon's conquests in the early nineteenth century, the Russians almost idolized France and all things French. While the peasants subsisted on grains, cereals, and some vegetables, the wealthy enjoyed dining on the classical cuisine of the French aristocracy.

In 1922, the Communists in Russia created the United Soviet Socialist Republic (USSR). The USSR extended its control to include many Eastern European countries

*As a result of the transformation he caused in Russia, many consider Peter the Great as the most important czar in Russia's history. Because of his relationship with European leaders, Russians learned a lot about food, cooking, and dining during this time. This led to more refined foods and cookery. For example, Russians learned about frying pans, spoons for straining, and other cooking utensils during the reign of Peter the Great.*

during the 1940s, after World War II ended. This control lasted until the late 1980s, when these countries began to regain their freedom and the Communist Empire dissolved.

## ROMANIA

Because of its desirable location, numerous tribes and countries including the Romans, Turks, Greeks, Hungarians, Germans, and Russians conquered and ruled Romania until the middle of the nineteenth century. At that time, Romania finally became an independent country.

Romania was named after the Romans, who ruled the land in the first two centuries A.D. Besides building roads and bridges, the Romans influenced the language and culture of this country. Unfortunately, none of the many countries that ruled Romania throughout its history developed the country into an independent or economic power. As a result, Romania has a lower standard of living than most of Eastern Europe.

## POLAND

With many invaders throughout its history, Poland's borders have changed many times. Hungarians, Turks, Germans, French, Spanish, and Dutch all occupied Poland at some time, and each group left its imprint on the cookery of Poland.

In the 1500s, Poland's borders reached from the Black Sea to the Baltic Sea. With the marriage of King Sigismund to Italian Bona Sforza in 1518, Italian vegetables were planted in the gardens, and Italian foods, such as pasta, cakes, and ice cream were introduced.

## HUNGARY

Magyars settled in Hungary in the late ninth century. They discovered a land with a bounty of game and fish that was very suitable for planting crops and raising livestock.

King Matthius Corvinus ruled Hungary in the 1400s. Historians say his Italian wife, Beatrice, introduced the cookery of Italy and the Renaissance to Hungary. Garlic, onions, cheese, and pasta became common ingredients during this time. Also, the Hungarians learned to prepare gravies from the natural juices of meat and poultry.

More than 150 years of Turkish rule began in 1526. The Turks brought paprika, tomatoes, corn, cherries, phyllo dough, stuffed vegetables, and coffee into the Hungarian cuisine. Even today paprika flavors many Hungarian dishes.

## >> TOPOGRAPHY

### RUSSIA

The largest country in the world, Russia, encompasses part of the continents of Europe and Asia. Almost twice the size of the United States, this mammoth country contains eight time zones. The country experiences cold weather with long, hard winters and short summers. Situated in the north, vast and desolate Siberia endures subarctic conditions. Moving toward the south, the climate becomes more moderate; however, a cold climate dominates Russia.

Running through Russia, the Ural Mountains form the boundary that divides Europe and Asia. Mountain ranges tower in the eastern and southern part of Russia. Large areas of plains also cover much land. Besides mountains and plains, the varied topography includes forests, tundra, and swamps. While the forests yield plentiful game, mushrooms, berries, and nuts, the rivers and seas provide a bounty of fish and seafood. Grains like rye, wheat, millet, and oats flourish on the plains.

Bordered by four bodies of water, Russia spans from the Arctic Ocean on the north to the Black Sea on the south. The Baltic Sea lies to the east and the Pacific Ocean to the west. In addition to having access to oceans or seas in each direction, Russia contains many major rivers.

## UKRAINE

The second largest country in Europe, Ukraine is about the size of the combined states of Arizona and New Mexico. Russia and Belarus lie to the north of Ukraine; Russia is to the east; the Black Sea, Moldova, and Romania border on the south; Poland, Slovakia, and Romania are to the west.

Favorable for agriculture, gently rolling hills dominate much of Ukraine. There are some highlands, forests, and some mountains in the far western and southern portion of the country. Almost 3,000 rivers flow through Ukraine.

## POLAND

Although mountains fill the landscape in the southern part of Poland, the rest of the country consists of flat plains, rolling hills, and lakes. The Baltic Sea, Russia, and Lithuania lie on its northern side; Belarus and Ukraine to the east; Slovakia and Czech Republic to the south; and Germany on the western border. In size, Poland is slightly smaller than Germany.

## SLOVENIA, MACEDONIA, CROATIA, SERBIA, MONTENEGRO, KOSOVO, AND BOSNIA

Miles of coastline along the Adriatic Sea form the western side of this area. The interior section contains a more rugged terrain of mountains, hills, and plains. Dominating the northern section, the plains support a bounty of crops, particularly grains. Mountains tower in the east, and cold winters reign there. The south and coastal areas have a typical Mediterranean climate, where orchards, vineyards, olives, and figs thrive. There are miles of coastline along the Adriatic Sea on the western side of this area.

## CZECH REPUBLIC

About the size of South Carolina or Scotland, the Czech Republic borders no ocean or sea. The countryside consists of forests, mountains, plains, plateaus, and rivers. Poland and Germany lie north of the Czech Republic; Poland and Slovakia are to the east; Austria, Slovakia, and Germany are to the south; and Germany is situated on the west.

## HUNGARY

Nestled among the Czech Republic, Romania, Slovenia, Macedonia, Croatia, Serbia, Montenegro, Kosovo, Bosnia, and Austria, Hungary consists of fertile low-lying plains. Most of the land in the eastern part of this small country is flat, and rolling hills and low mountains define the terrain found in the west. Hungary is about two-thirds the size of England, or the size of Indiana.

*Hungary is situated in the center of Europe.*

## ROMANIA

Ukraine lies north of Romania; Moldova and the Black Sea are to the east; Bulgaria borders on the south; and Serbia and Hungary are to the west. The Romanian cuisine exhibits strong influence from bordering countries. While the western portion shows Hungarian traits, with the use of paprika and spicier dishes, Turkish culinary influence shows up in the south.

A range of mountains runs through the north and central portions of the country, with fertile land found at the base of the mountains. Forests abound in Romania, yielding mushrooms, berries, and game. Many rivers and lakes transect the land, providing fish.

## >> COOKING METHODS

### COOKING TECHNIQUES

The nomadic tribes who inhabited these lands in the early days frequently braised stews in a pot over an open flame. Braising allowed the tough cuts of meat to become tender and extended the small amount of available meat into larger meals. As a result, the popularity of stews continues throughout Russia and all of Eastern Europe. Grilling is another carryover from the nomadic tribes, who also cooked directly over an open fire.

In the early days, Russian homes used stoves for both heating and cooking. These early stoves contained a large oven but no burners. As a result, braising and baking were the most prevalent cooking methods; even preparation of the ever-popular soups took place in the oven. In the 1700s, the rich acquired stoves with burners. Peasants did not obtain burners until about 150 years ago; however, with plenty of lard and oils available, frying became common.

### PRESERVATION

To survive the long winters, the people in Russia and Eastern Europe preserve their summer bounty. They pickle all sorts of fruits and vegetables and preserve fruits into jellies, jams, and preserves for use during the many cold months. Cabbage becomes sauerkraut; cucumbers and mushrooms become some of the many forms of pickled vegetables; apples, watermelons, and other fruits enter brines for winter consumption.

Pickled fish and sausages, which originated from the necessity of preserving seafood and meat for use during the long winter, remain popular. Another method of preservation—drying—still prevails for both fruits and vegetables.

---

**Ingredients and Foods Commonly Used throughout the Cuisines of Russia and Eastern Europe Include**

- beef
- pork
- potatoes
- dumplings
- winter vegetables, including cabbage, beets, carrots, cauliflower, kohlrabi, and turnips
- grains, including rye, buckwheat, barley, and millet
- dairy products, including frequent use of sour cream
- mushrooms
- dill and caraway seeds
- pickled and brined vegetables and fruits
- smoked and pickled fish

## >> REGIONS

### INFLUENCE BASED ON GEOGRAPHY

Influences on the cuisines in this area depended heavily on geographic area. The countries lying in the southern part of this block, Bulgaria and Albania, show strong Turkish and Middle Eastern overtones. The countries situated near the Baltic Sea in the north exhibit pronounced Scandinavian impact, and those located near Austria resemble the Germanic cuisines. Eastern Poland and Romania trace strong Russian influence.

Many lump the cuisines of Russia, Ukraine, and Poland together, since there are so many similarities in what grows in these three cold-climate countries and, therefore, in their recipes. Although similar recipes appear in these countries, each adds special touches and variations, creating recipes unique to the region.

### RUSSIA

Because of the very short growing season and the lack of rainfall, only a small percentage of the land in Russia is suitable for agriculture. Russia experiences a harsh, cold climate with long, bitter winters and short, cool summers. Most of the population resides in the western portion of Russia, which lies within Europe. Because of its extremely rugged terrain, the Asian section remains quite remote.

Straddling Europe and Asia, Russia exhibits influences from both continents. Scandinavians taught the Russians about drying, smoking, and pickling all sorts of foods, including fish, meat, vegetables, and fruits. Russians adopted pilafs and many other dishes from their Middle Eastern neighbors as well as from both China and India. Now staples in the Russian diet, noodles, dumplings, and tea came from the Turks and the Chinese. When contact with Europe intensified during the 1700s, German, Dutch, and French effects on Russia's cuisine arrived.

The still flourishing Russian Orthodox Church had a great impact on the cuisine of Russia. With more than 200 fast days that exclude meat throughout the year, fish entrées and hearty vegetable dishes play an important role.

Of course, Russia's history of territorial expansion heavily affected the cuisine. As borders changed, so did the cuisines of both Russia and the country it invaded. The foods of Eastern Europe penetrated into the cuisine of Russia, and the foods of Russia entered the cuisines of the other Eastern European countries.

*Buckwheat groats*
© Fanfo

### Russian Dishes

Some well-known Russian dishes include beef *stroganoff*, a stewlike dish consisting of pieces of beef cooked with mushrooms, onions, and sour cream; *blinis*, pancakes; *borscht*, a soup made from beets; *shchi*, cabbage soup; and *piroshki*, baked or fried dumplings filled with meat and cabbage. An often-consumed grain, *kasha* (buckwheat groats) shows up as a side dish, an entrée, or as stuffing for meat (e.g., roast chicken or veal breast) or vegetables (e.g., cabbage leaves). Many varieties of mushrooms appear regularly in soups, meat dishes, vegetable dishes, and sauces. They are also served pickled and as a condiment. Salads often contain mayonnaise or sour cream. A popular dessert, *vareniki*, is a sweet dumpling filled with cheese or fruits. Favorite beverages include tea, vodka, beer, and wine.

*Zakuska*, assorted hors d'oeuvres or bite-size morsels of food, were traditionally served with vodka before dinner. This custom developed into the *zakuska* table, reminiscent of the Scandinavian *smörgåsbord*, an elaborate table laden with salads, cold and hot smoked fish, caviar, pâtés, aspics, galantines, and pastries. The *zakuska* table was popular in the nineteenth century.

> *Zakuska* resemble Spanish tapas. They might be salads, pickled vegetables, or a variety of small savory dishes.

*Varenyky*
© Dmytro Sukharevskyy

*In the early days, people in Poland hunted lots of wild boar and venison. They caught a multitude of freshwater fish including carp, sturgeon, pike, and perch from the rivers and lakes. Those settlers planted wheat, rye, and barley on the plains. In summary, plentiful food sources insured survival for the early inhabitants.*

## UKRAINE

Much of the land in Ukraine consists of fertile, flat plains that are some of the best farmland in Eastern Europe. Abundant grains grow in this region, including rye, wheat, buckwheat, millet, and oats. As a result of the bounty of grain, the people of Ukraine are known for making many wonderful varieties of breads.

### Ukrainian Dishes

The diet in Ukraine includes pork products, fish, chicken, potatoes, kasha, and rye or oat breads. Again, hearty soups, stews, and breads are favored; mushroom and potato dishes remain very popular. Some of the traditional dishes include *varenyky*, boiled dumplings filled with potatoes, sauerkraut, cheese, or fruits and garnished with sour cream, fried onions, or bacon bits; *borscht*; and *holubtsi*, stuffed cabbage rolls filled with meat, kasha, and rice.

## POLAND

Poland's climate ranges from mild, temperate weather in the coastal areas to very cold in the mountains. Basically, Poland experiences cold winters and mild summers. The diverse climate creates favorable conditions for growing a variety of crops and for raising livestock.

Plains make up most of Poland, but there are some mountains and lots of forests. While the forests yield mushrooms, berries, nuts, and game, the plains prove excellent for growing many types of grains. Another rich source of food, the Baltic Sea in the north and numerous lakes and rivers provided an assortment of freshwater and saltwater fish.

### Polish Dishes

The same hearty foods reign in Poland as in Russia. Meat stews, beet or cabbage soups, potatoes, mushrooms, and rich desserts appear regularly. Favorite meats include pork and sausages. As with Russia, frequent use of sour cream and flavoring with dill and horseradish prevail. Both the Russians and the Poles have a fondness for sweet-and-sour dishes.

## SLOVENIA, MACEDONIA, CROATIA, SERBIA, MONTENEGRO, KOSOVO, AND BOSNIA

Like Poland, mild weather exists along the coast while a harsh climate with very cold winters prevails in the interior areas. About half of the land in this area is farmland; one-quarter of the country remains as forest.

Because each ethnic group adds its own contributions to the cookery, great diversity within the cuisines can be found in this area. For example, Serbian cooks use many spices and commonly grill meats. On the other hand, the northern part of the country follows the typical Slavic cooking pattern, which includes stews, soups, and the hearty cooking commonly seen throughout most of Eastern Europe.

Having ruled this area for five centuries, the Turks left a strong mark on the cuisine. As a result, many dishes incorporate ingredients commonly used in the Middle East such as rice, eggplant, tomatoes, and lamb. *Moussaka, pilaf, mezze* (Middle Eastern appetizers), stuffed grape leaves, and strong coffee appear here, particularly in the southern portions of the country.

### Dishes of Slovenia, Macedonia, Croatia, Serbia, Montenegro, Kosovo, and Bosnia

The cuisine in the north contains great similarity to that of Germany and Austria, but the southern areas exhibit pronounced Middle Eastern, Mediterranean, and

Italian influences. Pork reigns as the most popular meat, with seafood prevalent near the coasts. Dumplings, sauerkraut, potatoes, pickled herring, and desserts such as apple strudel appear often, but unlike most Eastern European food, hot peppers and some highly seasoned dishes appear here. In addition, they flavor with ample amounts of onions and garlic. Excellent beers are produced here; wine also is consumed.

## CZECH REPUBLIC

The climate in the Czech Republic consists of warm summers and cold winters. Good agricultural conditions exist for the production of barley, rye, corn, hops, wheat, potatoes, beets, vegetables, and fruits. Hogs, cattle, poultry, and sheep thrive here.

### Czech Dishes

The rich, heavy Czech cuisine uses lots of bacon and caraway for flavoring. The typical Czech diet includes ample amounts of starches and meats, particularly pork and beef. Also, game, chicken, and duck are frequent menu items.

*Knedliky*, dumplings, appear everywhere. This ubiquitous food is either sweet or savory and appears in any segment of the menu from soup or side dish to meat or dessert. Bread (wheat) dumplings are most popular, followed by potato dumplings. Two favorite recipes for roast pork both include dumplings. They are roast pork with sauerkraut and dumplings and *svickova*, roast pork with dumplings and gravy. Sauce (or gravy) usually accompanies the entrée, and the dumplings soak up much of the excess sauce. Cooks often serve cream sauces.

Soups of all types abound, and they are consumed for any meal, including breakfast. This cuisine also includes a variety of fine pastries. They fill the *crêpe*like pancakes, *palacinky*, with sweetened cheese or fruits.

The beverage of choice remains beer in much of the Czech Republic, which is the home of pilsner beer. They make excellent quality beer and serve it with snacks like cheeses or sausages that are grilled, boiled, or pickled.

## HUNGARY

Landlocked, Hungary experiences cold winters and hot summers. Fertile soil and a good climate for agriculture create a favorable situation for growing crops. Lots of hogs and chickens are raised, followed by cattle and sheep. Hungarians grow grapes, which are made into excellent Hungarian wines. As in much of Eastern Europe and Russia, beets and potatoes thrive here.

### Hungarian Dishes

Like some of the other countries in the southern parts of Eastern Europe, the Hungarians also prefer highly seasoned foods, which is characterized by their liberal use of paprika. Hungarian paprika ranges from sweet to smoky to hot in flavor, and the spiciness and flavoring of the food vary according to the type of paprika chosen. Tomatoes and garlic appear in many dishes.

As in the rest of Eastern Europe, the Hungarian diet includes daily soup and abundant starches like noodles, dumplings, and potatoes. Pork remains the most popular meat, but Hungarians also eat poultry and beef. Well-known Hungarian dishes include *goulash*, a beef stew containing onions, tomatoes, and potatoes, and *paprikash*, another stew-type dish containing plenty of paprika. Hungarian pastries are famous, and Hungarian strudel remains a trademark dessert.

*Roast pork and dumplings*
© manulito

*Plum dumplings*
© Grafvision

*Czech beer consumption ranks as the highest in the world per capita.*

*Romania ranks as the tenth largest producer of wine in the world.*

*People in Russia and other Eastern European countries relied on a diet with lots of complex carbohydrates to sustain them through the long winters. Breads, porridge, beans and peas, and winter vegetables formed the foundation of the diet. Meals often centered on one-pot dishes.*

*The very large beluga sturgeon from the Caspian Sea yields the most expensive caviar known as beluga.*

Pancakes with caviar
© olgavolodina

## ROMANIA

Fertile land suitable for crops composes the plains and plateaus in Romania. Corn, wheat, beets, potatoes, grapes, and other fruits flourish there. Romanians raise sheep, cattle, pigs, and poultry.

Romanians adopted foods from both their neighbors and their conquerors. From the former country of Yugoslavia that was situated south of Hungary, they learned of stuffed cabbage. While Germans introduced potatoes to the Romanian cuisine, Austrians brought pastries like torte and strudels. Hungarian influence shows in the *goulash* and *paprikash* dishes. The Russians contributed hearty dark breads as well as *blini* and sour soups known as *ciorba*.

In the 1500s and 1600s, the Turks introduced corn to the Venetians. Subsequently, the northern Italians and Romanians planted corn for polenta (Italy) and mămăligă (Romania).

### Romanian Dishes

Grilled meats remain popular in Romania, where pork ranks as the favorite meat. Grilled *mititei*, garlic-infused meatballs, are a national favorite. *Mămăligă*, cornmeal mush, is a Romanian staple that resembles Italian polenta. Favorite beverages include wine and plum brandy called *tuica*.

## >> CUISINE

### HEARTY AND HEAVY FOODS

The foods prepared and consumed in Russia and Eastern Europe can best be described as hearty cuisine. Much of the cuisine derives from the harsh winters and short growing season. Root vegetables, winter vegetables, pickled fruits and vegetables, dried fruits and vegetables, and grains remain mainstays in the diet of people from these countries. Some of the winter and root vegetables include cabbage, beets, cauliflower, potatoes, carrots, turnips, kohlrabi, rutabagas, onions, and horseradish.

A wide variety of grains play a prominent role in the diets of Eastern Europeans because many grains grow quickly and tolerate a cold climate. Rye grows particularly well in cold-weather countries like Russia, Poland, and Ukraine. Forests provide ample mushrooms, game, and berries for cooking in Ukraine, Russia, and much of the Eastern Europe. Apples also thrive in the cold climate found in many of these countries.

Heavy foods dominate the meals, frequently featuring meats, stews, and vegetables in sour cream sauces. The cuisines in these countries include lots of soup, as well as abundant use of dairy products and sugar.

### FISH

Sturgeon flourishes in cool waters, particularly in the Caspian Sea. Besides being prized for eating, this fish yields very high-quality black caviar. Carp, freshwater salmon (the source of red caviar), pike, and perch also thrive here. Probably the most widely consumed fish throughout Eastern Europe, lots of herring comes from the Baltic Sea. Sardines, halibut, and haddock are another source of food swimming in the Baltic.

### STARCHES

Dumplings, potatoes, and noodles appear regularly; in fact, multiple starches often accompany the entrée. With a strong liking for foods wrapped in dough, both large and small savory pies are widely consumed for appetizers, to accompany soup, or as an entrée.

Noodles and pancakes of all sorts abound. Many of these countries serve thin, *crêpe*like pancakes rolled around a savory filling for an entrée or around sweetened cheese or fruit purée for dessert. When filled with slightly sweetened cheese and sautéed, this becomes the popular *blintz* from Israeli cookery. A well-known hors d'oeuvre or appetizer, *blinis* from Russia are thicker, small pancakes served with a garnish of sour cream and salmon, caviar, or other topping.

Dumplings come in a myriad of sizes, shapes, and varieties. Whether served unfilled as a solid dumpling or filled with meat, grain, or cheese, this ubiquitous starch shows up everywhere on the menu. Made from potatoes, flour, bread, cottage cheese, or a combination of these ingredients, dumplings appear floating in soup, as a side dish, entrée, or dessert.

Usually made with rye, oat, buckwheat, or barley, heavy bread accompanies every meal. Bread products differ based on the type of flour and the cooking method used. Baking produces bread, frying results in fritters, and boiling yields the ever-popular dumplings.

*Dessert crêpe*
© annamavritta

## CABBAGE

In many recipes and guises, sauerkraut and cabbage appear regularly in all of these countries. Sauerkraut soup, cabbage soup, sauerkraut salad, stuffed cabbage rolls, as well as all sorts of sauerkraut and meat dishes emerge as just a few of the diverse cabbage creations. The national dish of Poland, *bigos*, consists of sauerkraut cooked with a variety of meats and sausages. Often referred to as "hunter's stew," this sweet-and-sour dish is flavored with apples, mushrooms, prunes, tomatoes, or other ingredients. *Bigos* resembles the French dish *cassoulet*.

Even though each of the countries creates its own version of stuffed cabbage rolls, a cabbage roll by any other name is still a cabbage roll. Usually filled with rice and pork or a mixture of beef and pork, a sweet-and-sour tomato-based sauce surrounds the Polish *golabki*. The Russian *golubtsi* is served in a sour cream sauce. Hungarians call them *töltött kaposzta*, the Romania version is *sarmale*, and *holubtsi* are served in Ukraine. Grains sometimes fill these popular items, particularly on fast days or in times of meager meat supplies. While some prefer wrapping the filling with pickled cabbage leaves, others use boiled fresh leaves of cabbage. When using fresh leaves, some cook the cabbage rolls on a bed of sauerkraut. Obviously, endless variations of cabbage rolls exist, depending on the country and the region within the country.

*Quite important in all the Slavic cuisines, bread and salt are long considered symbols of hospitality. According to folklore, Ukrainian guests are offered bread and salt as a greeting. The bread symbolizes hospitality and health (as the staff of life), and the salt represents friendship because, it is said, salt maintains its same quality, does not become stale, and retains its same taste in spite of its age.*

## FLAVORINGS

People of Eastern Europe and Russia share a liking for sour foods. Vinegar, sour cream, and horseradish appear often both in their sauces and in their many pickled foods. The combination of sour cream and dill flavors many dishes. Dill reigns as the most popular herb. Cooks use dill seeds as well as the leaves of the plant. As stated earlier, paprika is used widely in Hungary and some of the other Eastern European countries.

Used as a filling and as a decoration for the outside of pastries and breads, poppy seeds show up often. Cooks sometimes add poppy seeds to savory dishes. Poppy-seed fillings appear in cakes, strudels, cookies, sweet rolls, and more.

## MEALS

Russians and most Eastern Europeans typically begin the day with a hearty breakfast that might consist of eggs, porridge, cheese and/or sausage accompanied by bread, butter, and jam. The main meal occurs around midday and starts with salad or appetizer followed by soup, then meat or fish with potatoes and/or another grain, and dessert. The evening meal is light.

## CHEESES OF RUSSIA AND EASTERN EUROPE

**Abertam** Made from sheep's milk; robust flavor, firm texture

**Daralagjazsky** Made from sheep's or cow's milk; salty with added garlic and thyme, soft texture

**Feta** Made from sheep's milk but sometimes made from goat's milk; fresh cheese stored in brine; salty flavor, crumbly soft texture; used in cooking, as well as eaten as an appetizer

**Kashkaval** Made from sheep's milk; a "stretched" curd cheese, which refers to the process of handling the curds when making the cheese; springy texture that resembles cooked chicken

**Liptauer** Made from sheep's milk or a combination of sheep's and cow's milk; spicy flavor, often with added caraway, onion, capers, and paprika; soft texture

**Oszczypek** Made from sheep's milk; salty flavor, semifirm texture; traditional cheese made by shepherds in the mountains of Poland

**Sirene** Made from sheep's and cow's milk; fresh clean flavor, soft slightly grainy texture

**Urdu** A fresh cheese produced from the whey remaining after making feta cheese; nutty flavor and texture similar to ricotta cheese; used in cooking sweet and savory foods as well as eaten plain

| REGION | AREA | WEATHER | TOPOGRAPHY | FOODS |
|---|---|---|---|---|
| Russia | Northwestern Europe, northern Asia | Long, bitter winters, short summers | Tundra, forests, plains, mountains, semidesert, four seas on borders, numerous rivers | Cattle, sheep, hogs, game, cod, haddock, herring, salmon, sturgeon, caviar, flax, barley, oats, wheat, rye, buckwheat, potatoes, vegetables, beets, mushrooms, fruits, vodka |
| Poland | West of Russia | Warmer at coast, very cold in mountains | Plains, hills, lakes, Baltic Sea in north, mountains in south | Hogs, cattle, sheep, potatoes, rye, barley, beets |
| Ukraine | Southeast of Poland, southwest of Russia | Cold winters, warm summers | Fertile, flat plains, forests, Black Sea to south | Beef, dairy cattle, hogs, mackerel, tuna, carp, trout, perch, pike, game, wheat, barley, beets, corn, potatoes, mushrooms, rye, berries |
| Slovenia, Macedonia, Croatia, Serbia, Montenegro, Kosovo, and Bosnia | West of Hungary, Romania, and Bulgaria; south of Austria | Temperate coast, harsh interior | Hills and plains on coast, mountains in interior | Cattle, hogs, sheep, wheat, potatoes, corn, grapes, olives, fruits, beer |
| Czech Republic | South of Poland, north of Hungary, east of Germany and Austria | Cold winters, warm summers | Forests, mountains, plains, plateaus, rivers | Hogs, cattle, poultry, sheep, game, wheat, rye, corn, barley, oats, potatoes, hops, beets, mushrooms, berries, vegetables, fruits, beer |
| Hungary | Bosnia to southwest, Serbia to south, Czech Republic to north, Romania to east | Cold winters, warm summers | Flat in east, hills and low mountains in west, fertile soil | Hogs, poultry, cattle, sheep, wheat, corn, potatoes, beets, fruits, apricots, grapes, wine |
| Romania | Baltic Sea and Ukraine to east, Bulgaria to south, Serbia and Hungary to west, Moldova to north | Hot summers, cold winters | Mountains in north and central, plateaus, plains, forests, lakes, rivers | Sheep, pigs, cattle, poultry, game, wheat, corn, potatoes, beets, mushrooms, fruits, grapes, berries, wine, *tuica* |

## >> Review Questions

1. Name five foods or ingredients that frequently appear in the cuisines of Russia and Eastern Europe.
2. Name three methods of food preservation. Explain why these methods are so important in these countries.
3. How has the weather affected the cuisines of Russia and Eastern Europe?
4. Discuss countries that have influenced these cuisines from a historical or geographic standpoint and why they became an influence.

## >> Glossary

***bigos*** The national dish of Poland, consists of sauerkraut cooked with a variety of meats and sausages

**beef *stroganoff*** A stewlike dish consisting of pieces of beef cooked with mushrooms, onions, and sour cream

***blinis*** Small, buckwheat pancakes traditionally topped with sour cream, smoked salmon, caviar, or other toppings

***borscht*** Soup made from beets and other ingredients

***golabki*** Polish stuffed cabbage roll in a tomato-based sweet-and-sour sauce

***golubtsi*** Russian stuffed cabbage roll surrounded by a sour cream sauce

***goulash*** Hungarian beef stew containing onions, tomatoes, and potatoes

***holubtsi*** Ukrainian stuffed cabbage rolls filled with meat, kasha, and rice

***kasha*** Buckwheat groats, which is a grain

***knedliky*** Dumplings served frequently in the Czech Republic

***mămăligă*** Cornmeal mush served in Romania, resembles Italian polenta

***mititei*** Garlic-infused meatballs from Romania

***paprikash*** Hungarian stew-type dish containing plenty of paprika

***piroshki*** Baked or fried dumplings filled with meat and cabbage popular in Russia

***sarmale*** Romanian stuffed cabbage roll

***töltött kaposzta*** Hungarian stuffed cabbage roll

***vareniki*** A sweet dumpling filled with cheese or fruit

***varenyky*** Boiled dumplings with potatoes, sauerkraut, cheese, or fruits, garnished with sour cream, fried onions, or bacon bits, served in the Ukraine

***zakuska*** Assorted hors d'oeuvres or bite-size morsels of food

Stormur © Shutterstock

## PIEROGI (POLAND)
### FILLED DUMPLINGS

**Total Yield:** 1 lb., 4 oz. (567 g) filling
1 lb., 15 oz. (880 g) dough
or 50 dumplings made with 3 1/2-inch (9-cm) cutter

**Cooking Method:** Boil, sauté

**Food Balance:** Protein
**Wine Style:** Light- to medium-bodied Chenin Blanc, Sauvignon Blanc, blush, Pinot Noir, or mild Merlot
**Example:** Souverain Sauvignon Blanc or Merlot

| | WEIGHT | | VOLUME | |
| --- | --- | --- | --- | --- |
| INGREDIENTS | U.S. | METRIC | U.S. | METRIC |
| **Dough:** | | | | |
| flour | 1 lb., 1 oz. | 482 g | 4 cups | 960 mL |
| eggs | 6 3/4 oz. | 191 g | 4 each | |
| water, cold | | 156 g | 2/3 cup | 160 mL |
| salt | | | 1/2 teaspoon | 3 mL |
| **Filling:** | | | | |
| onions, minced | 8 oz. | 227 g | 1 cup or 2 small | 240 mL |
| butter | 1 oz. | 28 g | 2 tablespoons | 30 mL |
| mushrooms, button or any variety, washed and minced | 1 lb. | 454 g | | |
| salt | | | 1/2 teaspoon | 3 mL |
| pepper | | | 1/4 teaspoon | 2 mL |
| ground nutmeg | | | 1/8 teaspoon | 1 mL |
| fresh dill, minced | 1 1/2 oz. | 43 g | 1/4 cup + 2 tablespoons | 90 mL |
| sour cream | 4 1/2 oz. | 128 g | 1/2 cup | 120 mL |
| **Cooking:** | | | | |
| butter | as needed for sautéing | | | |
| **Garnish:** | | | | |
| fresh dill | | | | |
| sour cream | | | | |

© B. and E. Dudzinscy

© B. and E. Dudzinscy

## DOUGH:

1. Place flour in mixing bowl, form a well in center.
2. Place eggs, water, and salt in well, mix thoroughly with wooden spoon.
3. Knead for several minutes on lightly floured table. Cover until ready to use.

## FILLING:

1. Sauté onions in butter until tender.
2. Add mushrooms, sauté about 4 minutes, until soft and almost dry.
3. Season with salt, pepper, and nutmeg.
4. Remove from heat and stir in dill and sour cream. Correct seasonings. Let cool.

## ASSEMBLY:

1. Roll out one quarter of dough on lightly floured table until thin, about 1/8-inch (30-mm) thick.
2. Cut out circles with 3- or 3 1/2-inch (8- or 9-cm) cutter. Moisten edge of each disk with water.
3. Place rounded teaspoonful of filling (between 1/4 and 1/2 oz., 8 to 15 g) just off center on each disk. Fold disk in half to cover filling. Seal well, crimping edges with fork.
4. Repeat with remaining dough. Reroll scraps.
5. Place on floured, parchment-lined sheet pan until ready to cook. If not using immediately, seal sheet pan well and refrigerate.

## COOKING:

1. Boil large pot of water. Place *pierogi* in boiling water. Do not crowd in pot.
2. When *pierogi* rise to the surface, they are cooked. Remove to plate with slotted spoon.
3. Melt butter in skillet over moderate heat. Sauté *pierogi* until lightly brown, a couple of minutes.
4. Serve immediately, garnished with a sprig of dill and a dollop of sour cream.

*Forming pierogis*
© robert6666

*Boiling pierogis*
© Liaurinko

*Eggs in well of flour*
© nestonik

# BLINI (RUSSIA)

## BUCKWHEAT PANCAKES

**Note:** This is a classic Russian appetizer. The buckwheat gives the pancake a unique flavor.

**Number of Servings:** 8

**Cooking Method:** Sauté

**Serving Size:** 4 blini (1/2 oz., 15 g batter per blini)
**Total Yield:** 1 lb., 1/2 oz. (469 g) batter, or 33 blini
**Food Balance:** Protein
**Wine Style:** Low-oaked whites and crisp wines
**Example:** Greg Norman Sparkling, Etude Pinot Gris, Beringer Napa Valley Sauvignon Blanc

*Cooking blini (buckwheat pancakes)*

Pearson Education/PH College

*Blini (buckwheat pancakes) topped with smoked salmon and caviar*

Monkey Business Images © Shutterstock

| INGREDIENTS | WEIGHT | | VOLUME | |
|---|---|---|---|---|
| | U.S. | METRIC | U.S. | METRIC |
| all-purpose flour | 3 oz. | 86 g | 2/3 cup | 160 mL |
| buckwheat flour | 3 oz. | 86 g | 2/3 cup | 160 mL |
| salt | | | 1/2 teaspoon | 3 mL |
| granulated yeast | | | 1 teaspoon | 5 mL |
| milk, lukewarm | | 227 g | 1 cup | 240 mL |
| butter, melted | 1 oz. | 28 g | 2 tablespoons | 30 mL |
| egg, separated | 1 3/4 oz. | 50 g | 1 each | |
| oil, as needed for frying | | | | |

**Garnish:**

sour cream or crème fraîche
caviar, smoked salmon, or
   smoked fish of choice
fresh dill

1. Into a large nonreactive bowl, sift together both flours and salt. Add yeast, mix to combine. Make well in center of flour mixture.

2. Add milk, stir until smooth. Cover with plastic wrap; set aside to rise until doubled, about 1 hour.

3. Stir batter. Add butter and egg yolk. Stir to combine.

4. Beat egg white in mixer fitted with wire beater until stiff but not dry. Fold egg white into batter. Cover with plastic wrap and let rise for 20 minutes.

5. Pour enough oil into griddle or skillet to just coat bottom. Heat over medium heat until hot. Place 1/2 oz. (15 g) batter on pan. Repeat with remaining batter until pan is filled.

6. Sauté pancake about 1 minute on first side. Bubbles will form in batter and edges will look set. Turn pancake and cook other side about 30 to 45 seconds, until golden. Serve immediately or keep warm in low-temperature oven. Garnish with a dollop of sour cream or crème fraîche and top that with caviar or a small piece of smoked fish and a sprig of fresh dill.

### TWIST ON THE CLASSIC

Use these pancakes like any other variety of pancakes. Prepare them in a larger size, add fruit (like blueberries or raspberries), and serve with maple syrup and a dollop of yogurt. Also, try them as an appetizer topped with oxtail ragu, smoked duck, crabmeat, or a topping of choice.

# BORSHCH UKRAÏNSKY (UKRAINE)

## UKRAINIAN BEET SOUP

**Note:** Unlike most borscht served in the United States, Ukrainian borscht resembles thick vegetable soup. Apparently, the sign of a good pot of borscht is one thick enough so that a spoon will stand up in the pot.

**Number of Servings:** 13

**Cooking Method:** Boil

**Serving Size:** 10 oz. (284 g)
**Total Yield:** 8 lb., 2 oz. (3.7 kg)
**Food Balance:** Protein/acid balanced

**Wine Style:** Light- to medium-bodied Riesling, Pinot Gris, blush, rosé, soft reds, Shiraz, or Zinfandel
**Example:** Meridian Vineyards Syrah or Zinfandel

Ekaterina Pokrovskaya © Shutterstock

| INGREDIENTS | WEIGHT | | VOLUME | |
| --- | --- | --- | --- | --- |
| | U.S. | METRIC | U.S. | METRIC |
| beef short ribs, chuck, or brisket | 1 lb. | 454 g | | |
| ham bone | 8 oz. | 227 g | 1 each | |
| water or light beef stock | | | 3 quarts + 2 or 3 cups | 2.8 L + 480 to 720 mL |
| butter | 1/2 oz. | 15 g | 1 tablespoon | 15 mL |
| onions, small dice | 6 oz. | 171 g | 1 large | |
| garlic, smashed and minced | 1/2 oz. | 15 g | 4 cloves | |
| plum tomatoes, fresh or canned, peeled and chopped | 1 lb. | 454 g | 2 cups | 480 mL |
| beets, peeled and coarsely grated | 1 lb., 3 oz. | 540 g | 5 each | |
| celery bunch, bottom 3 inches (8 cm), coarsely grated | 3 oz. | 86 g | 1 each | |
| parsnip, peeled and coarsely grated | 4 oz. | 114 g | 1 each | |
| carrot, peeled and coarsely grated | 4 oz. | 114 g | 1 each | |
| sugar | | | 1/2 teaspoon | 3 mL |
| red wine vinegar | | 57 g | 1/4 cup | 60 mL |
| potatoes, white, waxy, or all-purpose, peeled and cut into 1 1/2-inch (4-cm) chunks | 1 lb. | 454 g | 3 to 4 large | |
| cabbage, cored and coarsely shredded | 1 lb. | 454 g | 1/2 small head | |
| ham, 1-inch (2.5-cm) cubes | 8 oz. | 227 g | | |
| salt | to taste | | | |

**Garnish:**

sour cream
fresh dill or parsley, minced

**TWIST ON THE CLASSIC**

Instead of preparing this as a soup, make it into a short ribs entrée. Start by reducing the amount of liquid for cooking the meat. Do not remove the meat from bones of the short ribs, but reserve meat as the recipe states. In step 4, cook onions and garlic in butter, then add flour to make a roux. Proceed with the recipe, adding the other vegetables and only enough liquid to cook the vegetables without scorching. In the end, add short ribs to thickened sauce with vegetables to create a short rib entrée with Eastern European flair.

1. Wash beef and ham bone, place in pot with about 2 quarts (1.9 L) of water or light beef stock, to cover.
2. Simmer about 1 1/2 hours, until meat is tender; skim stock occasionally to remove scum.
3. Strain, reserve stock and meat. Remove meat from bones and cut into 1-inch (2.5-cm) cubes. Discard bones.
4. Melt butter in a pan. Add onions, sauté a few minutes. Add garlic, sauté, stirring frequently, until soft and lightly colored, a few minutes.
5. Stir in tomatoes, grated beets, celery, parsnip, and carrot, sugar, vinegar, and 1 quart (960 mL) of stock. Bring to boil over medium-high heat, reduce heat, partially cover, and simmer 40 minutes.
6. Meanwhile, place remaining 2 to 3 cups (480 to 720 mL) stock into another pot with potatoes and cabbage. Bring to boil, lower heat, simmer partially covered about 20 minutes, until potatoes are tender but not falling apart.
7. Combine vegetables and potatoes in one large pot. Add reserved meat and ham, and simmer about 10 or 15 minutes. Salt to taste.
8. Correct seasonings, serve with sour cream and a sprinkling of parsley or dill.

# CIORBĂ DE PERISOARE (ROMANIA)

## SOUR SOUP WITH MEATBALLS

© JJAVA

**Number of Servings:** 15

**Serving Size:** 8 oz. (227 g)

**Total Yield:** 7 lb., 10 1/4 oz. (3.5 kg)

**Meatball Mixture:** 1 lb., 8 1/2 oz. (695 g)

**Meatball Scaling:** 1/2 oz. (15 g)

**Wine Style:** Medium-bodied red wine fermented in used oak. Possible grape varietals are Pinot Noir, St. Laurent, Zweigelt.

**Example:** Pinot Noir "Premium" 2010, Fischer (Thermenregion/Austria)

**Cooking Method:** Boil

| | WEIGHT | | VOLUME | |
|---|---|---|---|---|
| **INGREDIENTS** | **U.S.** | **METRIC** | **U.S.** | **METRIC** |
| beef shank, bones, or cut of choice | 1 lb., 6 oz. | 624 g | | |
| water | | | 2 quarts | 1.9 L |
| onion, medium dice | 10 oz. | 284 g | 1 large | |
| carrot, medium dice | 4 oz. | 114 g | 2 medium | |
| celery, medium dice | 5 3/4 oz. | 163 g | 3 stalks | |
| tomatoes, diced, canned or fresh | 15 oz. | 426 g | | |
| tomato paste | 3/4 oz. | 22 g | 1 tablespoon | 15 mL |
| salt | 1/2 oz. | 15 g | 2 teaspoons | 10 mL |
| pepper | | | 1 teaspoon | 5 mL |
| fennel, ground | | | 1/2 teaspoon | 3 mL |
| green or red pepper, medium dice | 3 1/2 oz. | 104 g | 1/2 each | |
| sauerkraut juice | | 340 to 454 g | 1 1/2 to 2 cups | 360 to 480 mL |
| **Meatballs:** | | | | |
| rice | 2 oz. | 57 g | 1/4 cup | 60 mL |
| beef, ground | 1 lb. | 454 g | | |
| onion, minced | 1 3/4 oz. | 50 g | 1/4 cup | 60 mL |
| parsley, minced | 1/2 oz. | 15 g | 2 tablespoons | 30 mL |
| salt | 1/4 oz. | 8 g | 1 teaspoon | 5 mL |
| pepper | | | 1/4 teaspoon | 2 mL |
| egg | 1 3/4 oz. | 50 g | 1 each | |
| flour, for dredging | | | | |

**Garnish:**

sour cream

crushed red pepper, *optional*

1. Place beef shank and water in stockpot. Bring to boil, reduce heat and simmer for 1 hour. Skim any scum as needed.
2. Add onion, carrot, celery, tomatoes, tomato paste, salt, and pepper. Boil gently for another 30 minutes.
3. Add fennel, green pepper, and sauerkraut juice. Boil gently for another 20 minutes.
4. Remove beef shank, remove bone and cut or shred meat into small pieces. Return meat to soup.
5. While soup cooks, prepare meatballs. Place rice in a small saucepan. Cover with water and boil for 10 minutes. Drain.
6. Mix rice with ground beef, onion, parsley, salt, pepper, and egg. Mix to combine well.

## TWIST ON THE CLASSIC

- To serve this as an entrée, use a double portion (1 lb., 454 g) and accompany it with cornbread or Romanian mămăligă and a salad.

- For a healthier version, use chicken stock for the soup and make the meatballs with ground turkey.

- Often, this soup is made with lamb instead of beef. Substitute lamb shanks or bones for the beef bones and ground lamb for the ground beef.

- Some use a combination of beef and veal or beef, veal, and pork for the meatballs in the beef-based version.

Instead of sauerkraut juice, use lemon juice or vinegar to give the soup a mildly sour flavor. Start with about 1/3 to 1/2 cup (80 to 120 mL) lemon juice and taste for correctness.

7. Scale into 1/2 oz. (15 g) meatballs or desired size. Dredge meatballs with light coating of flour. Refrigerate until needed while soup continues cooking.

8. Add meatballs to soup, boil gently for 25 to 30 minutes, checking meatballs for doneness. Correct seasonings.

9. Remove fat from top of soup. Either refrigerate overnight until fat congeals or spoon liquid fat from top. Serve hot, garnished with sour cream. If desired, provide crushed red pepper.

# ZELLER KRÉMLEVES (HUNGARY)
## CREAM OF CELERY SOUP

**Note:** This recipe calls for celeriac, or celery root, which contains a more pronounced and stronger flavor than stalks of celery. If celeriac is not available, substitute celery stalks. If the soup is stringy after puréeing, strain it.

**Number of Servings:** 11
**Serving Size:** 8 oz. (227 g)
**Total Yield:** 5 lb., 12 oz. (2.6 kg)
**Food Balance:** Protein/sweet
**Wine Style:** Low-oaked whites
**Example:** Castello di Gabbiano Pinot Grigio, Beringer Chenin Blanc

**Cooking Method:** Boil

© Pawel Strykowski

**TWIST ON THE CLASSIC**

With the strong celery flavor from the celeriac, adding diced potatoes creates a delicious cream of potato-celery soup. Just add the potatoes to the puréed soup and cook slowly until they soften. If needed, add more stock to thin the soup.

| INGREDIENTS | WEIGHT | | VOLUME | |
|---|---|---|---|---|
| | U.S. | METRIC | U.S. | METRIC |
| butter | 2 oz. | 57 g | 4 tablespoons (1/2 stick) | 60 mL |
| onion, medium dice | 12 oz. | 340 g | 2 medium to large | |
| celeriac (celery root), peeled and cut into large dice | 1 lb., 8 oz. | 680 g | 2 bulbs | |
| russet potato, peeled and cut into large dice | 10 oz. | 284 g | 2 medium | |
| garlic, minced | 1/4 oz. | 8 g | 2 cloves | |
| bay leaf | | | 2 each | |
| white pepper | | | 1 teaspoon | 5 mL |
| chicken stock | | | 1 quart + 2 cups (6 cups) | 1.4 L |
| heavy cream | | 227 g | 1 cup | 240 mL |
| salt | to taste | | | |

**Garnish:**
celery leaves, minced
sour cream

1. Melt butter in a large pan over medium heat. Add onion, sauté a couple of minutes.

2. Add celeriac, potato, and garlic. Stir and sauté another 3 or 4 minutes. Add bay leaves, pepper, and stock. Cook about 20 minutes, until celeriac is soft.

3. In food processor fitted with knife blade, purée in batches. If desired, strain soup to remove pulp. Return to pan.

4. Add cream, bring to simmer. Correct seasonings, adding salt to taste or additional stock if too thick.

5. Serve, garnished with celery leaves and a dollop of sour cream.

# SALAT IZ KRASNOI KAPUSTY (RUSSIA)

## RED CABBAGE SALAD

**TWIST ON THE CLASSIC**

Try this as a hot vegetable instead of a salad.

**Note:** May be used as an hors d'oeuvre or a side dish.

**Number of Servings:** 13 or 9  
**Serving Size:** 3 or 4 oz. (86 or 114 g)  
**Total Yield:** 2 lb., 7 oz. (1.1 kg)

**Cooking Method:** Boil

| INGREDIENTS | WEIGHT | | VOLUME | |
| --- | --- | --- | --- | --- |
| | U.S. | METRIC | U.S. | METRIC |
| bay leaf | | | 2 each | |
| whole allspice | | | 1/4 teaspoon | 2 mL |
| peppercorns | | | 8 each | |
| whole cloves | | | 4 each | |
| cider vinegar | | 340 g | 1 1/2 cups | 360 mL |
| water | | 454 g | 2 cups | 480 mL |
| sugar | 2 3/4 oz. | 78 g | 1/4 cup + 2 tablespoons | 90 mL |
| salt | | | 1 1/2 teaspoons | 8 mL |
| red cabbage, cored and julienned | 2 lb., 8 oz. | 1.1 kg | 2 small heads | |
| olive oil | | 28 g | 2 tablespoons | 30 mL |

1. Place whole spices (bay leaf, allspice, peppercorns, and cloves) in cheesecloth bag for marinade.
2. Combine vinegar, water, sugar, salt, and spice bag in a nonreactive pan. Bring to boil.
3. Add cabbage, return to boil, lower heat, and simmer until cabbage is tender but not mushy, about 15 minutes.
4. Chill well. Correct seasonings.
5. Before serving, drain, discarding spice bag and marinade. If desired, sprinkle with olive oil immediately before serving.

© Stuart Monk

© PHB.cz

## SALATKA z KISZONEJ KAPUSTY (POLAND)

### SAUERKRAUT SALAD

**Number of Servings:** 11
**Serving Size:** 4 oz. (114 g)
**Total Yield:** 2 lb., 12 1/2 oz. (1.3 kg)

© Nitr

| INGREDIENTS | WEIGHT U.S. | WEIGHT METRIC | VOLUME U.S. | VOLUME METRIC |
|---|---|---|---|---|
| sauerkraut, drained | 2 lb. | 908 g | | |
| carrot, shredded | 8 oz. | 227 g | 4 each | |
| onion, minced | 2 1/2 oz. | 71 g | 1/4 cup + 2 tablespoons | 90 mL |
| sugar | | | 2 teaspoons | 10 mL |
| salt | | | 1/2 teaspoon | 3 mL |
| pepper | | | 1/2 teaspoon | 3 mL |
| olive oil | | 57 g | 1/4 cup | 60 mL |

**Garnish:**

parsley or dill, minced

1. Combine all ingredients together in a nonreactive bowl. Correct seasonings.
2. Chill at least 30 minutes. Serve. Garnish with minced parsley or dill, if desired.

## SALATA MIZERJA (POLAND)

### CUCUMBER SALAD

**Note:** This may be served as a salad or an item for a *zakuska* table.

**Number of Servings:** 12
**Serving Size:** 4 oz. (114 g)
**Total Yield:** 3 lb. (1.4 kg)

© graletta

| INGREDIENTS | WEIGHT U.S. | WEIGHT METRIC | VOLUME U.S. | VOLUME METRIC |
|---|---|---|---|---|
| cucumbers | 3 lb., 3 oz. | 1.4 kg | 4 large | |
| salt | as needed | | | |
| cider vinegar | | 57 g | 1/4 cup | 60 mL |
| white pepper | | | 1/2 teaspoon | 3 mL |
| fresh dill, finely chopped | 1 1/2 oz. | 43 g | 1/4 cup + 2 tablespoons | 90 mL |
| sour cream | 8 1/2 oz. | 241 g | 1 cup | 240 mL |

1. Peel cucumbers, slice very thin. Layer with salt in colander, place colander in sink or bowl to catch liquid, drain at least 1 hour to eliminate water and bitterness.
2. Press cucumbers lightly to expel liquid, blot with towel.
3. Combine remaining ingredients with cucumbers in a small nonreactive bowl, mix gently.
4. Chill. Correct seasonings. Serve.

# GOLABKI (POLAND)

## STUFFED CABBAGE ROLLS

Brett Mulcahy © Shutterstock

**Number of Servings:** 14
**Serving Size:** 9 oz. (256 g), or 2 rolls
**Total Yield:** 8 lb., 5 oz. (3.8 kg), or about 30 rolls
**Food Balance:** Protein/sweet
**Wine Style:** Soft and fruity Riesling, Pinot Blanc, soft Chardonnay, blush, soft Merlot, Shiraz, or Zinfandel
**Example:** Beringer Founders' Estate Chardonnay or Shiraz

**Cooking Method:** Boil, sauté, bake

| INGREDIENTS | WEIGHT | | VOLUME | |
| --- | --- | --- | --- | --- |
| | **U.S.** | **METRIC** | **U.S.** | **METRIC** |
| cabbage | 2 to 3 lb. | 908 g to 1.4 kg | 1 or 2 heads | |
| **Filling:** | | | | |
| oil or butter | 1 oz. | 28 g | 2 tablespoons | 30 mL |
| onion, small dice | 1 lb., 4 oz. | 567 g | 4 medium | |
| ground beef | 1 lb. | 454 g | | |
| ground pork | 1 lb. | 454 g | | |
| white rice, uncooked | 7 oz. | 199 g | 1 cup | 240 mL |
| water | | 227 g | 1 cup | 240 mL |
| salt | 1/4 oz. | 8 g | 1 teaspoon | 5 mL |
| pepper | | | 1/4 to 1/2 teaspoon | 2 to 3 mL |
| fresh dill, minced | 1 oz. | 28 g | 1/4 cup | 60 mL |
| **Sauce:** | | | | |
| plum tomatoes, fresh or canned, peeled and chopped | 4 lb. | 1.8 kg | | |
| apples, peeled, cored, and chopped | 12 oz. | 340 g | 2 each | |
| cider vinegar | | 57 g | 1/4 cup | 60 mL |
| sugar | 3 1/2 oz. | 104 g | 1/2 cup | 120 mL |
| honey | 1 1/2 oz. | 43 g | 2 tablespoons | 30 mL |
| raisins | 3 1/2 oz. | 104 g | 1/2 cup | 120 mL |
| salt | | | 1/2 teaspoon | 3 mL |
| pepper | | | 1/4 teaspoon | 2 mL |

**Garnish:**
fresh dill, minced
sour cream

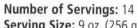

> **TWIST ON THE CLASSIC**
>
> For a lower-fat option, prepare this dish using ground chicken or turkey instead of ground beef and ground pork.

## CABBAGE LEAVES:

1. Core cabbage, separate leaves. If leaves tear when detaching, place cabbage head in boiling water for couple of minutes, until leaves can be removed. Place leaves in boiling water for about 5 minutes, until pliable. Do not use small inner leaves.

2. Drain and set aside to cool.

## FILLING:

1. Heat oil or butter in skillet, add onions, sauté several minutes until soft. Transfer to bowl.

2. Add beef, pork, rice, water, salt, pepper, and dill to bowl with onions, mix well.

3. Refrigerate until ready to use.

## SAUCE:

1. Combine tomatoes, apple, vinegar, sugar, honey, raisins, salt, and pepper together in a saucepan.
2. Heat briefly.

## ASSEMBLY:

1. Preheat oven to 325 degrees (160°C).
2. Trim center rib of leaf by cutting thick part even with leaf. (This is necessary to roll leaf around filling.) *Note: If uniform-size rolls are desired, use cabbage leaves of the same size. Trim large ones and use two overlapping leaves for small ones. Also, overlap two leaves to cover a torn leaf.*
3. Place about 2 oz. (57 g) filling (depending on size of leaf—more for large leaves, less for small) on lower third of cabbage leaf.
4. Fold bottom of leaf over filling, fold in sides, then roll leaf to top. Place, seam side down, in baking pan.
5. Continue, until all filling is used. Pour sauce over cabbage rolls.
6. Bake, covered, for 1 to 1 1/2 hours, until meat filling almost reaches appropriate internal temperature when tested with meat thermometer.
7. Uncover, bake for another 30 minutes. Baste if rolls seem too dry. Remove from oven. Correct seasonings.
8. Serve two or three rolls, depending on size, napped with sauce. If desired, serve with sprinkling of minced fresh dill and/or dollop of sour cream.

## GULYÁS (HUNGARY)

### HUNGARIAN GOULASH

**Number of Servings:** 8
**Serving Size:** 8 oz. (227 g)
**Total Yield:** 4 lb., 3 oz. (1.9 kg)
**Food Balance:** Protein
**Wine Style:** Light- to medium-bodied Riesling, Gewürztraminer, White Zinfandel, rich Merlot, or Zinfandel
**Example:** Beringer White Zinfandel or Alluvium Merlot

**Cooking Method:** Braise

| | WEIGHT | | VOLUME | |
|---|---|---|---|---|
| **INGREDIENTS** | **U.S.** | **METRIC** | **U.S.** | **METRIC** |
| lean beef, boneless chuck or stew meat, cubed | 2 lb. | 908 g | | |
| oil | | 28 g | 2 tablespoons | 30 mL |
| onions, medium dice | 12 oz. | 340 g | 2 large | |
| Hungarian paprika | 1/2 oz. | 15g | 2 tablespoons | 30 mL |
| garlic, smashed and minced | 1/4 oz. | 8g | 2 cloves | |
| caraway seeds | | | 1 teaspoon | 5 mL |
| water | | 340 g | 1 1/2 cups | 360 mL |
| tomatoes, peeled and diced | 10 oz. | 284 g | 2 medium | |
| salt | 1/4 oz. | 8g | 1 teaspoon | 5 mL |
| pepper | | | 1/2 teaspoon | 3 mL |
| potatoes, white, waxy, or all-purpose, peeled and cut into large dice | 2 lb. | 908 g | 8 medium | |

**TWIST ON THE CLASSIC**

For a different taste, try replacing a half-cup of the water with red wine.

© blende40

1. Wash meat and pat dry.
2. Heat oil in pan over medium heat, brown meat on all sides. Add onions and sauté until tender.
3. Add paprika, garlic, and caraway seeds, cook for 1 minute. Add just enough water to cover meat. Tightly cover pan and simmer for 1 hour.
4. Add tomatoes, salt, and pepper. Continue cooking until almost tender.
5. Add potatoes, cook another 30 minutes, until tender. If necessary, add more water, but not too much—final gravy should be thick without additional thickeners.
6. Correct seasonings. Serve over *galuska* (dumplings) or wide noodles.

# BEF STROGANOV (RUSSIA)

## BEEF STROGANOFF

Pearson Education/PH College

**Number of Servings:** 9
**Serving Size:** 7 oz. (199 g)
**Total Yield:** 4 lb., 3 oz. (1.9 kg)
**Food Balance:** Protein/acid balanced
**Wine Style:** Light- to medium-bodied Chenin Blanc, Pinot Blanc, Chardonnay, or Pinot Noir
**Example:** Château St. Jean Pinot Blanc, Chardonnay, or Pinot Noir

**Cooking Method:** Braise

| | WEIGHT | | VOLUME | |
|---|---|---|---|---|
| **INGREDIENTS** | **U.S.** | **METRIC** | **U.S.** | **METRIC** |
| beef, sirloin or tenderloin | 3 lb. | 1.4 kg | | |
| butter | 2 oz. | 57 g | 4 tablespoons (1/2 stick) | 60 mL |
| onion, small dice | 12 oz. | 340 g | 2 large | |
| mushrooms, button or any variety, cleaned and sliced | 1 lb., 8 oz. | 680 g | | |
| flour | | | 1 1/2 tablespoons | 23 mL |
| beef stock, hot | | 340 g | 1 1/2 cups | 360 mL |
| Dijon mustard | 3/4 oz. | 22 g | 1 1/2 tablespoons | 23 mL |
| sugar | | | 1 1/2 teaspoons | 8 mL |
| pepper | | | 1/4 teaspoon | 2 mL |
| sour cream | 13 1/2 oz. | 383 g | 1 1/2 cups | 360 mL |
| salt | to taste | | | |

1. Trim meat of all fat, cut into strips 1/4- to 1/2-inch (0.5- to 1.3-cm) thick.
2. Heat 2 tablespoons (30 mL) of butter in skillet over high heat. Sauté meat to sear, remove to plate. (If meat gives off too much liquid, drain and reserve for sauce.)
3. Reduce heat to medium, add remaining 2 tablespoons (30 mL) of butter and sauté onions until soft, about 4 minutes. Add mushrooms, sauté until almost dry, about 5 to 10 minutes.
4. Lower heat to medium-low, add flour, stir, and sauté a couple of minutes until light brown. Whisk in stock and any reserved juice from meat.
5. Add mustard, sugar, and pepper and bring to boil. Lower heat, cover, and simmer for 10 minutes, adding more liquid, if needed.
6. Stir in sour cream and meat, simmer another 3 to 5 minutes, until thoroughly hot. Correct seasonings, adding salt if needed. Serve over wide noodles.

© Joe Gough

# TOCANĂ DE MIEL (ROMANIA)

## SHEPHERD'S LAMB STEW

**Note:** This stew has a fairly large amount of sauce. As the dish sits, the sauce seems to thicken from the starch in the potatoes. Traditionally, tocană de miel is served with bread to soak up excess sauce.

**Number of Servings:** 10
**Serving Size:** 9 oz. (256 g)
**Total Yield:** 6 lb., 1 oz. (2.8 kg)
**Food Balance:** Sour/protein
**Wine Style:** Any white wine and most reds, except those with the strongest tannins
**Example:** Château St. Jean Chardonnay, Penfolds Shiraz, Souverain Merlot and Cabernets

**Cooking Method:** Braise

© JAY

| INGREDIENTS | WEIGHT | | VOLUME | |
|---|---|---|---|---|
| | U.S. | METRIC | U.S. | METRIC |
| oil | | 15 g | 1 tablespoon | 15 mL |
| boneless lamb, trimmed of fat and cut into 2-inch (5-cm) pieces | 2 lb., 3 3/4 oz. | 1 kg | | |
| flour | 1/4 oz. | 8 g | 1 tablespoon | 15 mL |
| onions, medium dice | 1 lb. | 454 g | 3 medium to large | |
| pepper | | | 1/2 teaspoon | 3 mL |
| bay leaves | | | 2 each | |
| stock, lamb or light beef, or water, hot | | 908 g | 1 quart (4 cups) | 960 mL |
| red potatoes, peeled and cut into 2-inch (5-cm) cubes | 2 lb. | 908 g | | |
| sour cream | 6 oz. | 171 g | 2/3 cup | 160 mL |
| cider vinegar | | 15 g | 1 tablespoon | 15 mL |

**Garnish:**

sour cream, optional

> **TWIST ON THE CLASSIC**
>
> Serve this stew in a hollowed round of bread. The bread will soak up some of the sauce for a tasty addition.

1. Heat oil in large pot over medium heat. Dredge lamb with flour. Add lamb to pan, cook, stirring, until it begins to brown about 1 minute.
2. Add onions, stir and sauté until onions are softened and meat is browned, about 10 minutes.
3. Whisk in pepper, bay leaves, and stock. Bring to boil, reduce heat, cover and simmer 1 hour, until meat is almost tender.
4. Add potatoes, cover, and simmer about 15 minutes. Uncover and continue cooking 15 to 20 minutes, until meat is tender and potatoes are done.
5. Stir in sour cream and vinegar. Correct seasonings. Serve, garnished with a dollop of sour cream, if desired. Serve accompanied by bread.

# PYSHNA PECHENIA (UKRAINE)

## STUFFED PORK LOIN

**Note:** To butterfly the pork loin, cut through the center of the meat and cut about three-quarters through the loin. Open the two sides of the meat, laying the pork flat as one rectangle. If needed, pound the meat slightly to flatten so it is even.

**Number of Servings:** 14
**Serving Size:** 7 oz. (199 g), or 2 to 3 slices
**Total Yield:** 6 lb., 5 1/2 oz. (2.9 kg)

**Cooking Method:** Bake

B.G. Smith © Shutterstock

© Joe Gough

**Food Balance:** Protein/sweet
**Wine Style:** Low-oaked whites and soft reds
**Example:** St. Clement Sauvignon Blanc, Beringer Founders' Estate Merlot

| INGREDIENTS | WEIGHT | | VOLUME | |
| --- | --- | --- | --- | --- |
| | U.S. | METRIC | U.S. | METRIC |
| **Filling:** | | | | |
| bacon | 11 1/2 oz. | 326 g | 10 slices | |
| ground pork | 2 lb. | 908 g | | |
| eggs | 6 3/4 oz. | 191 g | 4 each | |
| fresh parsley, minced | 1/2 oz. | 15 g | 1/4 cup | 60 mL |
| dried dill | | | 2 teaspoons | 10 mL |
| dried basil | | | 2 teaspoons | 10 mL |
| salt | 1 oz. | 28 g | 1 tablespoon + 1 teaspoon | 20 mL |
| pepper | | | 1 teaspoon | 5 mL |
| garlic, minced | 1/4 oz. | 8 g | 2 cloves | |
| breadcrumbs, fresh | 4 oz. | 114 g | 2 cups | 480 mL |
| **Basting Liquid:** | | | | |
| honey | 5 oz. | 142 g | 1/2 cup | 120 mL |
| dry sherry | | 57 g | 1/4 cup | 60 mL |
| boneless pork loin, trimmed, butterflied | 5 lb., 4 oz. | 2.4 kg | | |
| bacon | 11 1/2 oz | 326 g | 10 slices | |

**Garnish:**
fresh dill or parsley, minced

## FILLING:

1. Cook bacon until crisp. Drain well on absorbent paper. Crumble into pieces and set aside until needed.
2. Mix pork, eggs, parsley, dill, basil, salt, pepper, garlic, breadcrumbs, and cooked bacon. Mix to combine well.
3. If not needed immediately, cover and refrigerate until needed.

## ASSEMBLY:

1. Position oven rack in center of oven. Preheat oven to 350 degrees (180°C). Mix honey and sherry together. Set aside until needed.
2. Place butterflied pork on work surface. Arrange filling evenly over meat leaving a 1-inch (2.5-cm) border along one side. (Filling will move as it is rolled, so it will cover that area.) Roll meat tightly, beginning at side opposite the side with no filling.
3. Place bacon strips over outside of meat. Wrap and tie meat securely with butcher's twine. Transfer meat to baking pan.
4. Bake about 1 hour. Baste with prepared mixture and continue basting every 10 minutes. Cook meat until almost done and internal temperature reaches about 155 degrees (70°C) (temperature will continue to rise as it sits). Total cooking time should be about 1 1/2 to 1 3/4 hours.
5. Remove from oven, cover with aluminum foil, and allow to rest about 20 minutes before cutting. Cut into slices, serve garnished with dill or parsley.

## SERBIAN DUCK WITH SAUERKRAUT (SERBIA)

**Number of Servings:** 8
**Cooking Method:** Bake
**Serving Size:** 1/4 duck (with about 5 oz., 142 g sauerkraut)
**Total Yield:** 8 lb., 5 oz. (3.8 kg), 2 ducks
**Food Balance:** Protein/acid balanced
**Wine Style:** Wide variety of wines: Very balanced—Enjoy the wine of your choice
**Example:** Beringer Riesling, Chardonnay, Pinot Noir, or Cabernet Sauvignon

| INGREDIENTS | WEIGHT | | VOLUME | |
| --- | --- | --- | --- | --- |
| | U.S. | METRIC | U.S. | METRIC |
| duck, cleaned, excess fat removed | 8 to 10 lb. | 3.6 to 4.5 kg | 2 each | |
| oil | | 8 g | 1/2 tablespoon | 7 mL |
| onions, small dice | 1 lb., 2 oz. | 511 g | 3 large | |
| paprika | 3/4 oz. | 22 g | 3 tablespoons | 45 mL |
| sauerkraut, drained and rinsed | 3 lb. | 1.4 kg | | |
| water | | 680 g | 3 cups | 720 mL |
| fresh dill, minced | 3/4 oz. | 22 g | 3 tablespoons | 45 mL |

① Preheat oven to 425 degrees (220°C). Place ducks on rack in roasting pan. Prick with fork all over. Place about 1/4-inch (1/2-cm) water in bottom of pan.

② Bake for 30 minutes. Remove from oven. Drain fat and water. Prick ducks again with fork. Put 1/4 inch (1/2 cm) water in pan. Return to oven for another 30 minutes.

③ Drain again. Lower temperature to 325 degrees (160°C), return to oven.

④ Meanwhile, heat oil in saucepan, add onions, and sauté a couple of minutes. Add paprika, cook 1 minute. Stir in sauerkraut, add 3 cups (680 g or 720 mL) water.

⑤ Cook sauerkraut slowly, covered, for 30 minutes.

⑥ When duck is done, about 1 1/2 hours, remove from oven. Remove ducks from pan and cut into quarters. Pour off all fat from roasting pan, transfer sauerkraut to pan. Top with duck pieces. Return to oven. Bake about 30 to 45 minutes.

⑦ Serve each piece of duck on bed of sauerkraut and sprinkle with dill. Accompany with boiled potatoes or dumplings.

© papa1266

© fox17

# CSIRKE PAPRIKÁS (HUNGARY)

## CHICKEN PAPRIKA

**TWIST ON THE CLASSIC**

Replace the bone-in chicken with strips of boneless chicken breast. Sauté the chicken strips until golden, remove from pan. After returning them to pan, cook only a few minutes and then proceed with the recipe.

Ian O'Leary © Dorling Kindersley

**Number of Servings:** 8 or 10
**Serving Size:** 1/4 chicken or 1 bone-in split breast
**Total Yield:** 7 lb., 14 oz. (3.6 kg)
**Food Balance:** Protein
**Wine Style:** Light- to medium-bodied Chenin Blanc, Pinot Gris, Sauvignon Blanc, blush, Dolcetto, or Shiraz
**Example:** Stone Cellars Shiraz

**Cooking Method:** Braise

| | WEIGHT | | VOLUME | |
|---|---|---|---|---|
| **INGREDIENTS** | **U.S.** | **METRIC** | **U.S.** | **METRIC** |
| fryer chickens, cut into quarters | 5 to 6 lb. | 2.3 to 2.8 kg | 2 each | |
| *or* | | | | |
| bone-in split chicken breasts | 5 to 6 lb. | 2.3 to 2.8 kg | 10 each | |
| oil | | 28 g | 2 tablespoons | 30 mL |
| onions, medium dice | 12 oz. | 340 g | 2 large | |
| bell pepper, green or red, medium dice | 12 oz. | 340 g | 2 small | |
| garlic, smashed and minced | 1/2 oz. | 15 g | 4 cloves | |
| tomatoes, peeled and chopped | 10 oz. | 284 g | 2 medium | |
| Hungarian paprika | 3/4 oz. | 22 g | 3 tablespoons | 45 mL |
| pepper | | | 1/2 teaspoon | 3 mL |
| chicken stock | | 284 g | 1 1/4 cups | 300 mL |
| flour | 1/2 oz. | 15 g | 2 tablespoons | 30 mL |
| sour cream | 1 lb., 2 oz. | 511 g | 2 cups | 480 mL |

**Garnish:**

fresh parsley, minced
paprika

1. Wash chicken pieces, wipe dry. Heat oil in a pan over medium heat, sauté chicken pieces on both sides until golden. Set aside.
2. Add onions and bell peppers to pan, cook until soft. Add garlic, tomatoes, paprika, and pepper, sauté another minute or so.
3. Mix in chicken stock, bring to a boil. Return chicken to pan. Lower heat, cover, and simmer until chicken is done, about 45 minutes. Remove chicken from pan and keep warm.
4. Combine flour and sour cream, add to pan. Cook slowly, stirring, until thickened and smooth. Correct seasonings.
5. Return chicken to sauce for a few minutes. Serve chicken on a bed of dumplings, wide noodles, or rice, napped with sauce. Sprinkle with parsley and paprika, if desired.

# KULEBYAKA (RUSSIA)

## SALMON IN PUFF PASTRY

**Note:** This classic Russian dish was created in the late 1800s. They served this popular fish pie on fast days when the people abstained from eating meat. Some of the many variations of *kulebyaka* include the addition of mushrooms.

**Number of Servings:** 11 to 12

**Cooking Method:** Bake

**Serving Size:** about 8 oz. (227 g), or about 1/6 of rectangle

**Total Yield:** 5 lb., 14 1/2 oz. (2.7 kg), or two 9- by 11-inch (23- by 28-cm) pastry rectangles

**Food Balance:** Protein

**Wine Style:** Low-oaked whites, rosé, or sparkling

**Example:** Greg Norman Chardonnay, Etude Rose

Clive Streeter © Dorling Kindersley

| INGREDIENTS | WEIGHT | | VOLUME | |
|---|---|---|---|---|
| | U.S. | METRIC | U.S. | METRIC |
| butter | 2 oz. | 57 g | 4 tablespoons (1/2 stick) | 60 mL |
| onions, minced | 8 oz. | 227 g | 2 small to medium | |
| dill, fresh or dried | 1/2 oz. | 15 g (fresh) | 3 1/2 tablespoons | 52 mL (fresh) |
| | | | 1 tablespoon | 15 mL (dried) |
| lemon juice | | 28 g | 2 tablespoons | 30 mL |
| salt | 1/2 oz. | 15 g | 2 teaspoons | 10 mL |
| pepper | | | 1/2 teaspoon, plus a sprinkling | 3 mL, plus a sprinkling |
| long-grain rice, cooked | 1 lb. | 454 g | 3 cups | 720 mL |
| puff pastry, homemade or purchased | 2 lb., 1 1/2 oz. | 951 g | | |
| egg, beaten | 1 3/4 oz. | 50 g | 1 each | |
| fresh salmon, sliced thinly, in 2-inch (5-cm) pieces | 2 lb. | 908 g | | |
| eggs, hard boiled and diced | 11 oz. | 312 g | 6 each | |

**Garnish:**

sour cream, mustard, or mixture of sour cream and mustard

fresh dill

**TWIST ON THE CLASSIC**

If desired, bake in individual portions. Also, a small serving of *kulebyaka* makes a great first course.

1. Place oven rack in center of oven. Preheat oven to 425 degrees (220°C). Cover sheet pan(s) with parchment paper, set aside.

2. Melt butter in a pan over medium heat. Add onion and sauté until softened, about 8 to 10 minutes. Remove from heat.

3. Add 2 tablespoons (30 mL) fresh or 2 teaspoons (10 mL) dried dill, lemon juice, 1 teaspoon (5 mL) of the salt, pepper, and rice. Stir gently to combine. Set aside until needed.

4. Divide puff pastry into four parts. Roll each into a 12- by 10-inch (30- by 25-cm) rectangle about 1/8 inch (30 mm) thick. Brush outer 1/2-inch (1.3-cm) edge of two rectangles with beaten egg. (Those two will be the bottom pieces.) Place the bottom pieces on prepared sheet pan(s).

5. Spread rice mixture over bottom two rectangles up to 1/2 inch (1.3 cm) from outer edge.

6. Top rice with salmon pieces. Sprinkle salmon with remaining 1 teaspoon (5 mL) salt, sprinkling of pepper, and remaining 1 1/2 tablespoons (23 mL) fresh or 1 teaspoon (5 mL) dried dill. Place hard-boiled eggs over salmon.

7 Place remaining pieces of puff pastry over bottom puff pastry. Seal edges tightly and decoratively crimp. Brush pastry with beaten egg. If desired, decorate with pieces of puff pastry. Brush decorations with egg. Cut a few slits in top pastry to allow steam to escape.

8 Bake for 20 minutes. Lower heat to 350 degrees (180°C). Continue baking another 20 minutes. If dough becomes too brown, tent with aluminum foil.

9 Remove from oven. Cool slightly, if desired. Cut into pieces of the desired size. Serve, accompanied by sour cream, mustard, or a mixture of sour cream and mustard. Garnish with springs of fresh dill.

## MORAVSKÉ ZELÍ (CZECH REPUBLIC)

### MORAVIAN CABBAGE

© fox17

**Number of Servings:** 10
**Serving Size:** 4 oz. (114 g)
**Total Yield:** 2 lb., 10 oz. (1.2 kg)

**Cooking Method:** Boil, sauté

| INGREDIENTS | WEIGHT | | VOLUME | |
|---|---|---|---|---|
| | U.S. | METRIC | U.S. | METRIC |
| cabbage, shredded | 3 lb. | 1.4 kg | 2 small heads | |
| water | | 454 g | 2 cups | 480 mL |
| onions, small dice | 10 oz. | 284 g | 2 medium | |
| oil | | 43 g | 3 tablespoons | 45 mL |
| flour | 2 oz. | 57 g | 1/4 cup | 60 mL |
| caraway seeds | | | 1 teaspoon | 5 mL |
| sugar | 1 1/2 oz. | 43 g | 3 tablespoons | 45 mL |
| salt | 1/4 oz. | 8 g | 1 teaspoon | 5 mL |
| vinegar | | 156 g | 2/3 cup | 160 mL |

> **TWIST ON THE CLASSIC**
>
> Bring color to this dish by adding carrot to the cabbage.

1 Simmer cabbage in water for 5 minutes. Drain, reserving cooking liquid.

2 Over medium heat, sauté onion in oil until soft, about 3 minutes. Add flour and stir for a minute or so. Slowly whisk in hot liquid from cabbage, whisk until smooth. Add more water if necessary.

3 Add cabbage, caraway, sugar, salt, and vinegar. Simmer for 20 minutes, adding more water if needed. Correct seasonings. Serve.

## FAZOLOVÉ LUSKY NA PAPRICE (CZECH REPUBLIC)

### GREEN BEANS PAPRIKA

> **TWIST ON THE CLASSIC**
>
> Substitute other vegetables or a mixture of vegetables for the green beans. Try this with a combination of mushrooms and cauliflower.

**Number of Servings:** 12
**Serving Size:** 4 oz. (114 g)
**Total Yield:** 3 lb., 2 oz. (1.4 kg)

**Cooking Method:** Sauté, boil

| INGREDIENTS | WEIGHT | | VOLUME | |
|---|---|---|---|---|
| | U.S. | METRIC | U.S. | METRIC |
| butter | 2 oz. | 57 g | 4 tablespoons (1/2 stick) | 60 mL |
| onions, small dice | 11 oz. | 312 g | 2 medium | |
| salt | 1/4 oz. | 8 g | 1 teaspoon | 5 mL |

| INGREDIENTS | WEIGHT | | VOLUME | |
| --- | --- | --- | --- | --- |
| | U.S. | METRIC | U.S. | METRIC |
| sweet paprika | 1/2 oz. | 15 g | 2 tablespoons | 30 mL |
| water | | 227 g | 1 cup | 240 mL |
| green beans, stems removed, cut into 1-inch (2.5-cm) pieces | 2 lb. | 908 g | | |
| flour | 1/2 oz. | 15 g | 2 tablespoons | 30 mL |
| sour cream | 14 1/2 oz. | 411 g | 1 1/2 cups | 360 mL |

① Melt butter in a saucepan over medium heat. Add onions, sauté until softened, about 8 to 10 minutes.

② Add salt, paprika, water, and green beans. Mix to combine. Bring to boil, reduce heat to medium or medium-low, cover and simmer until beans are done, about 15 minutes.

③ Meanwhile, whisk flour into sour cream in bowl. When beans are done, gently stir sour cream mixture into beans.

④ Simmer over low heat for about 5 minutes. Correct seasonings, serve.

## GALUSKA (HUNGARY)

### SMALL DUMPLINGS

**Number of Servings:** 11
**Serving Size:** 5 1/2 oz. (156 g)
**Total Yield:** 3 lb., 15 oz. (1.8 kg)

**Cooking Method:** Boil

| INGREDIENTS | WEIGHT | | VOLUME | |
| --- | --- | --- | --- | --- |
| | U.S. | METRIC | U.S. | METRIC |
| flour, unsifted | 1 lb., 8 oz. | 680 g | 5 2/3 cups | 1.3 L |
| salt | | | 1 1/2 teaspoons | 8 mL |
| butter, melted | 1 1/2 oz. | 43 g | 3 tablespoons | 45 mL |
| eggs | 5 oz. | 142 g | 3 each | |
| water | | 340 g | 1 1/2 cups | 360 mL |

① Sift flour and salt together. Set aside until needed. In another bowl, mix butter and egg. Add water.

② Stir flour mixture into egg mixture, mix just until combined. Let rest in cool place for 1 hour.

③ With floured hands, drop small pieces of dough (size of a dime to a quarter) into pot of boiling salted water.

④ Cook until done, about 10 to 15 minutes. Dumplings will rise to surface and no longer look floury when done. Serve with sauce to accompany stew or any dish.

> ### TWIST ON THE CLASSIC
>
> Serve these in the manner of *Käsespaetzel* from Chapter 5, Germany. Sauté the *galuska* in butter, transfer them to an ovenproof dish, top with salt, pepper, dill, and the grated cheese of choice. Broil until the cheese browns lightly.

Tobik © Shutterstock

# BRAMBOROVÉ KNEDLÍKY (CZECH REPUBLIC)
## BOHEMIAN POTATO DUMPLINGS

**Note:** This fluffy dumpling may be prepared with half semolina and half all-purpose flour or only all-purpose flour.

**Number of Servings:** 14 or 7      **Cooking Method:** Boil
**Serving Size:** one or two 1 3/4-oz. (50 g) dumplings
**Total Yield:** 14 dumplings, or 1 lb., 9 oz. dough (710 g)

| | WEIGHT | | VOLUME | |
|---|---|---|---|---|
| **INGREDIENTS** | **U.S.** | **METRIC** | **U.S.** | **METRIC** |
| potatoes, white, waxy, or all-purpose, cooked, cooled, and riced | 1 lb., 1 1/2 oz. | 497 g | 2 cups, about 4 or 5 each | 480 mL |
| eggs | 3 1/2 oz. | 104 g | 2 each | |
| salt | 1/4 oz. | 8 g | 1 teaspoon | 5 mL |
| flour | 2 oz. | 57 g | 1/2 cup | 120 mL |
| semolina | 3 oz. | 86 g | 1/2 cup | 120 mL |

**Garnish:**
butter, melted
fine dry bread crumbs

1. Place a large pan of water over high heat to bring to boil. Meanwhile, combine riced potatoes, eggs, and salt in bowl, beat thoroughly with wooden spoon.
2. Add flour and semolina, mix well. Dough should be stiff.
3. With floured hands, shape dough into 1 1/2-inch (4-cm) balls.
4. Drop dumplings into pan of boiling water, bring water to slow boil again.
5. Cook about 12 to 15 minutes, until dumplings rise to top. Test by tearing a dumpling apart with two forks. Remove all with slotted spoon to colander and drain.
6. Serve with melted butter and sprinkling of bread crumbs, if desired.

*Boiling dumplings*
© unpict

© mrr

# KASHA (RUSSIA)

## BUCKWHEAT GROATS WITH MUSHROOMS AND ONIONS

**Number of Servings:** 11 or 8          **Cooking Method:** Braise
**Serving Size:** 3 or 4 oz. (86 to 114 g)
**Total Yield:** 2 lb., 2 oz. (965 g)
**Food Balance:** Protein
**Wine Style:** Light- to medium-bodied Pinot Blanc, Sauvignon Blanc, blush, or rich Cabernet Sauvignon
**Example:** Souverain Sauvignon Blanc or Cabernet Sauvignon

**TWIST ON THE CLASSIC**

Use the *kasha* as a stuffing for pork chops. Use one of these two methods of stuffing: either cut a pocket into the side of the pork chop and stuff with *kasha* or place a chop over a mound of *kasha* and bake until done and proper internal temperature.

| INGREDIENTS | WEIGHT | | VOLUME | |
|---|---|---|---|---|
| | U.S. | METRIC | U.S. | METRIC |
| *kasha*, coarse | 6 oz. | 171 g | 1 cup | 240 mL |
| egg | 1 3/4 oz. | 50 g | 1 each | |
| salt | | | 1 1/4 teaspoons | 6 mL |
| pepper | | | 1/4 teaspoon | 2 mL |
| water, boiling | | 454 to 680 g | 2 to 3 cups | 480 to 720 mL |
| butter | 1 1/2 oz. | 43 g | 3 tablespoons | 45 mL |
| onions, small dice | 9 1/2 oz. | 270 g | 2 cups or 2 medium | 480 mL |
| mushrooms, button or any variety, diced | 8 oz. | 227 g | 2 1/2 cups | 600 mL |

1. Place *kasha* and egg in bowl, mix until grains are thoroughly coated.
2. Place *kasha* mixture in ungreased skillet and cook, stirring constantly, over medium heat, until *kasha* is lightly toasted and dry.
3. Add salt, pepper, and 2 cups (454 g or 480 mL) of the boiling water. Stir well. Cover pan, reduce the heat to low, and simmer for 20 minutes. If *kasha* is not yet tender and seems dry, stir in remaining cup of boiling water and cook, covered, for 10 minutes, or until water is absorbed and grains are separate and fluffy.
4. Remove pan from heat, let sit undisturbed for 10 minutes.
5. Meanwhile, melt butter in skillet. Add onions and sauté over medium heat until soft, about 3 minutes. Add mushrooms and sauté over high heat until liquid evaporates, about 3 minutes.
6. Add onions and mushrooms to cooked kasha. Correct seasonings, serve.

© Maksim Shebeko

# POTATOES AND MUSHROOMS IN SOUR CREAM (POLAND)

**Number of Servings:** 17
**Serving Size:** 4 oz. (114 g)
**Total Yield:** 4 lb., 5 oz. (2 kg)

**Cooking Method:** Braise

| | WEIGHT | | VOLUME | |
|---|---|---|---|---|
| **INGREDIENTS** | **U.S.** | **METRIC** | **U.S.** | **METRIC** |
| potatoes, white, waxy, or all-purpose, peeled | 3 lb. | 1.4 kg | 6 to 8 large | |
| onions, small dice | 15 oz. | 426 g | 3 medium to large | |
| butter | 1 1/2 oz. | 43 g | 3 tablespoons | 45 mL |
| mushrooms, button or any variety, diced | 1 lb., 8 oz. | 680 g | | |
| salt | | | 1 to 1 1/2 teaspoons | 5 to 8 mL |
| pepper | | | 1/2 to 3/4 teaspoon | 3 to 4 mL |
| sour cream | 13 1/2 oz. | 383 g | 1 1/2 cups | 360 mL |
| fresh dill, minced | 1 1/2 oz. | 43 g | 1/4 cup + 2 tablespoons | 90 mL |

1. Place potatoes in a saucepan, cover with cold water. Bring to boil, continue boiling for 5 minutes. Drain well, slice into 1/4-inch (1/2-cm) rounds. Set aside until needed.
2. Sauté onions in butter over medium heat until tender, about 4 minutes. Add mushrooms, sauté until liquid has evaporated.
3. Add potatoes, salt, pepper, sour cream, and dill. Mix gently.
4. Cover, cook slowly until tender, about 20 minutes. Stir frequently, adding more sour cream or water, if necessary, to prevent sticking.
5. Correct seasonings. Serve.

# KRUMPLIS KENYER (HUNGARY)

## POTATO BREAD

**Serving Size:** 1 large or 2 small loaves
**Total Yield:** 3 lb., 10 oz. (1.6 kg) dough

**Cooking Method:** Boil, bake

| | WEIGHT | | VOLUME | |
|---|---|---|---|---|
| **INGREDIENTS** | **U.S.** | **METRIC** | **U.S.** | **METRIC** |
| potato, Russet, unpeeled | 11 1/2 oz. | 326 g | 2 medium | |
| sugar | 1/2 oz. | 15 g | 1 tablespoon | 15 mL |
| yeast | 1/2 oz. | 15 g | 1 tablespoon | 15 mL |
| bread flour | 1 lb., 11 3/4 oz. or as needed | 788 g or as needed | 6 cups or as needed | 1.4 L |
| salt | 1/2 oz. | 15 g | 2 teaspoons | 10 mL |
| caraway seeds | 1/4 oz. | 8 g | 1 teaspoon | 5 mL |

1. Scrub potatoes well. Place in a saucepan, cover with water, bring to boil, and cook until tender but not falling apart.
2. Drain water, reserving 1 lb., 2 oz. (511 g, 2 1/4 cups, or 540 mL). Cool potatoes until able to handle. Peel, discard peels, put potatoes through ricer, set aside until needed.

③ In a small nonreactive bowl, mix 2 oz. (57 g, 1/4 cup, or 60 mL) lukewarm potato water with sugar. Add yeast and stir to mix. Allow to sit until foamy, about 5 to 10 minutes.

④ Place 1 lb., 2 3/4 oz. (532 g, 4 cups, or 960 mL) flour in a large mixing bowl, make well in center. Pour yeast mixture into center. Incorporating just enough flour to make paste, mix a little flour into yeast with a wooden spoon. Cover and allow to sit for 20 minutes.

⑤ Meanwhile, prepare baking sheet. Pan spray and lightly sprinkle with flour.

⑥ With wooden spoon, add potatoes and remaining potato water to flour, mix well. Add salt and caraway seeds, mix well. Add flour until soft dough. Knead using dough hook or by hand until smooth dough, 10 to 15 minutes. Add just enough flour, as needed, to keep dough from sticking. Return to bowl, cover, rise until doubled, about 1 hour.

⑦ Punch down dough, knead briefly to remove all air bubbles and form dough into one large round loaf or two small ones. Lightly sprinkle top of loaf with flour. Cover, allow to rise until doubled, about 30 minutes.

⑧ Meanwhile, place oven rack in center of oven. Preheat to 400 degrees (205°C).

⑨ Using sharp knife, make three slashes into top of loaf. Bake for about 35 minutes (for large loaf) or until done. Loaf will be lightly brown on top and bottom and sound hollow when tapped.

⑩ Cool on rack. Store tightly wrapped.

> Some Hungarian breads use fennel seeds. If desired, replace caraway with fennel seeds.

## JABLKOV 'Y ZÁVIN (CZECH REPUBLIC)

### APPLE STRUDEL

**Note:** Although typical of strudel dough found in many countries of Eastern Europe, this dough is quite tough. It lacks the large amount of butter or fat used in many doughs. Personally, I prefer strudel wrapped with phyllo dough. For instructions on working with phyllo dough, see the recipe for *spanikopita* in Chapter 9 on the Middle East.

**Number of Servings:** 10          **Cooking Method:** Bake
**Serving Size:** 3-inch (8-cm) slice
**Total Yield:** Two 17-inch (43-cm) strudels

Kneading strudel dough

| | WEIGHT | | VOLUME | |
| --- | --- | --- | --- | --- |
| **INGREDIENTS** | **U.S.** | **METRIC** | **U.S.** | **METRIC** |
| **Dough:** | | | | |
| flour | 13 1/4 oz. | 377 g | 2 2/3 cups | 641 mL |
| salt | | | 1/8 teaspoon | 1 mL |
| egg | 1 3/4 oz. | 50 g | 1 each | |
| water, lukewarm | | 114 g | 1/2 cup | 120 mL |
| vinegar | | | 1/2 teaspoon | 3 mL |
| lard or butter, melted | 1/2 oz. | 15 g | 1 tablespoon | 15 mL |
| **Filling:** | | | | |
| breadcrumbs | 2 1/4 oz. | 64 g | 3/4 cup | 180 mL |
| unsalted butter, melted | 5 1/2 oz. | 156 g | 1/2 cup + 3 tablespoons | 120 mL + 45 mL |
| apples, peeled and sliced | 2 lb. | 908 g | about 6 | |
| walnuts, chopped | 1 3/4 oz. | 50 g | 1/3 cup | 80 mL |
| raisins | 1 3/4 oz. | 50 g | 1/3 cup | 80 mL |
| sugar | 3 3/4 oz. | 107 g | 1/2 cup | 120 mL |
| cinnamon | 1/4 oz. | 8 g | 2 teaspoons | 10 mL |
| flour, for rolling out dough | | | | |
| **Garnish:** | | | | |
| confectioner's sugar | to dust | | | |

Rolling strudel dough on table

Stretching strudel dough until thin

### TWIST ON THE CLASSIC

Use any filling in the strudel dough. Substitute pears for the apples, or make a savory strudel with an assortment of vegetables and herbs bound with sour cream.

## DOUGH:

1. Sift flour and salt into bowl, form a well.
2. Place egg, water, vinegar, and lard or butter into well, stir with fork until moistened. Knead dough until smooth and elastic.
3. Shape into ball, cover, let rest about 30 minutes. Meanwhile, make filling.

## FILLING:

1. Make filling while dough rests. Preheat oven to 375 degrees (190°C). Pan-spray sheet pan or cover with parchment paper. In skillet, brown breadcrumbs in 3 tablespoons (45 mL) of butter. Set aside.
2. Combine apples, walnuts, raisins, sugar, and cinnamon in bowl, mix gently.

## ASSEMBLY

1. Cover table with clean cloth, sprinkle with flour. Place dough in center, roll out to 1/8-inch (30-mm) thick.
2. Slide hands under dough, stretch dough with backs of clenched fists, working from center in all directions until dough is paper-thin.
3. Lightly brush stretched dough with some of remaining 1/2 cup (120 mL) of melted butter. Sprinkle with bread crumbs.
4. Arrange filling in a horizontal log about 5 inches (13 cm) from bottom edge of dough.
5. Bring bottom of dough over apples to begin roll, then grasp cloth and use it as guide to roll dough like a jellyroll. Roll dough, brushing underside with butter as you roll. Pinch ends to seal when finished.
6. Transfer strudel to prepared pan. Brush top with melted butter. Slit top of dough in several places, so steam can escape. Bake for 35 to 45 minutes, until golden.
7. Cool slightly, dust with sifted confectioner's sugar. Slice and serve while warm or at room temperature.

*Filling placed at bottom of dough; lifting dough to roll over filling*

*Lifting cloth to help roll dough over filling*

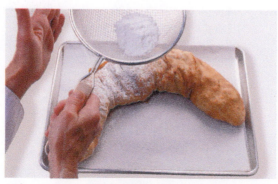

*Sifting confectioner's sugar over baked strudel*

*Slice of Jablkovy' Závin (Apple Strudel) on plate decorated with caramelized sugar*

# RIGÓ JANCSI (HUNGARY)
## CHOCOLATE CREAM CAKE

**Note:** This confection is named after a Gypsy violinist, Rigó Jancsi, who lived in the late nineteenth century. Born into poverty, he rose to fame as a violinist and performed throughout Europe. According to the story, he met Belgium's Prince Chimay and his beautiful wife when they dined in the Parisian restaurant where he played. Rigó and the princess fell in love; in fact, she left her husband and children to live with Rigó. Although their love affair did not last, the pastry created in their honor still thrives!

**Note:** If possible, begin preparation of this dessert the day before service, so the filling chills overnight.

**Number of Servings:** 14  
**Serving Size:** One 2 3/4- by 2 1/8-inch (7- by 5-cm) piece  
**Total Yield:** One 5 1/2- by 15 1/2-inch (14- by 39-cm) cake cut into 14 pieces

**Cooking Method:** Bake, boil

| INGREDIENTS | WEIGHT | | VOLUME | |
| --- | --- | --- | --- | --- |
| | U.S. | METRIC | U.S. | METRIC |
| **Filling:** | | | | |
| heavy cream | | 340 g | 1 1/2 cups | 360 mL |
| semisweet chocolate, chopped | 10 oz. | 284 g | 1 1/2 cups | 360 mL |
| vanilla | | | 1 teaspoon | 5 mL |
| dark rum | | 28 g | 2 tablespoons | 30 mL |
| **Cake:** | | | | |
| all-purpose flour | 3 oz. | 86 g | 2/3 cup | 160 mL |
| cocoa | 3/4 oz. | 22 g | 3 tablespoons | 45 mL |
| unsalted butter | 3 oz. | 86 g | 6 tablespoons | 90 mL |
| eggs, separated | 10 oz. | 284 g | 6 each | |
| sugar | 5 1/2 oz. | 156 g | 3/4 cup | 180 mL |
| salt | | | pinch | |
| **Glaze:** | | | | |
| cocoa | 1/2 oz. | 15 g | 2 tablespoons | 30 mL |
| sugar | 1 3/4 oz. | 50 g | 1/4 cup | 60 mL |
| water, cold | | 28 g | 2 tablespoons | 30 mL |
| heavy cream | | 28 g | 2 tablespoons | 30 mL |
| semisweet chocolate, chopped | 3 oz. | 86 g | 1/2 cup | 120 mL |
| **Assembly:** | | | | |
| apricot preserves | 2 1/2 oz. | 71 g | 3 tablespoons | 45 mL |

© pelena

## FILLING:

1. Heat cream in a pan over medium heat until small bubbles form around edge of the pan.
2. Remove from heat, add chocolate. Whisk occasionally until chocolate dissolves.
3. Whisk in vanilla and rum. Transfer to a nonreactive bowl. Cover with plastic wrap, placing plastic wrap directly on top of chocolate mixture, so it does not form a skin. Refrigerate until cold, several hours or overnight.

## CAKE:

1. Sift together flour and cocoa into a bowl. Set aside until needed. Melt butter, then carefully pour melted butter from pan into a small bowl, leaving the white solids behind to discard. Set this clarified butter aside until needed.
2. Pan-spray or grease half sheet pan or jelly roll pan. Cover with parchment paper, pan-spray again. Place oven rack in center of oven. Preheat oven to 350 degrees (180°C).

3. In mixer fitted with wire beater, mix egg yolks and sugar for several minutes at high speed until light, fluffy, and pale yellow.

4. Into egg mixture carefully fold flour mixture alternately with clarified butter (half of the flour, half of the butter, remaining half of the flour, remaining half of butter).

5. With whisk or mixer fitted with wire beater, beat egg whites with a pinch of salt in a clean bowl until frothy. Increase speed to high and continue beating until stiff peaks form. Stir one-quarter of egg whites into batter. Gently fold in remaining egg whites.

6. Transfer batter to prepared pan. Tap once on counter to remove air pockets. Place in oven and bake for about 12 minutes, until top is springy and cake starts to pull away from the sides of the pan. Do *not* overbake.

7. Flip from pan to a piece of parchment paper. Cool completely. Cover tightly and store until needed or use immediately to prepare dessert.

## GLAZE:

1. Thoroughly mix cocoa, sugar, water, and cream in top of double boiler. Add chocolate.

2. Place over pan of barely simmering water. Stirring frequently, cook until chocolate melts and mixture is smooth. Remove from heat.

## ASSEMBLY:

1. Cut cake in half lengthwise (two pieces about 5 1/2 by almost 16 inches [14 by 41 cm]). Reserve best (most smooth) piece for top and set aside. Place other piece on cake board or serving platter.

2. Spread apricot preserves over cake on board or platter.

3. Place cold filling mixture in a bowl of mixer fitted with wire beater. Beat mixture until fluffy, like dense whipped cream. *Do not overmix.* Spread filling evenly over cake with preserves.

4. Place reserved cake on top of filling. If glaze is too cool (thick) to spread, warm briefly over double boiler. Using icing spatula, frost top of cake with glaze.

**Note:** If preferred, frost top layer before placing on top of filling. Place cake on rack and pour glaze over cake. Then spread until smooth with icing spatula. When set, move frosted cake to top filling.

5. Score cake into serving sizes. For dessert-size portions, cut cake in half lengthwise, and then cut each side into 7 pieces. This yields 14 pieces.

# The Countries of Africa

## >> LEARNING OBJECTIVES

By the end of this chapter, you will be able to:

- Identify various areas of Africa and the types of foods consumed in those areas
- Understand why the cuisine of northern Africa differs so greatly from that of the area lying south of the Sahara
- Explain why soups and stews dominate the diet in Africa
- Understand the role of starches and fat in the African diet
- Explain how the weather conditions impact the cuisine of Africa
- Prepare a variety of dishes from different African countries

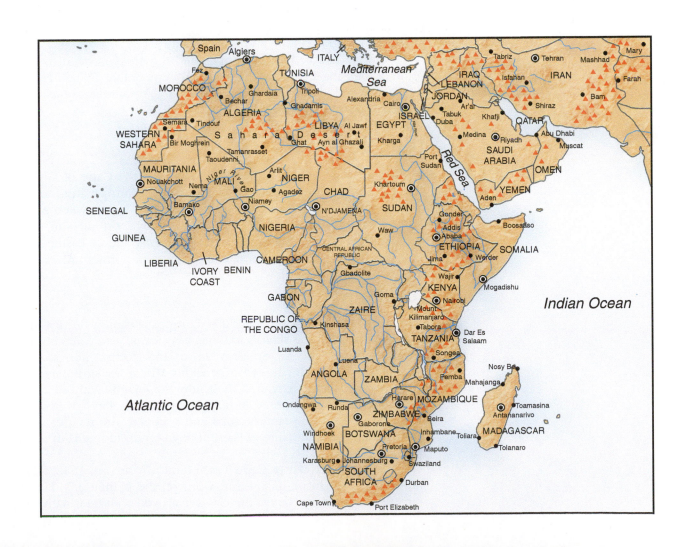

>> **HISTORY**

Archaeologists believe people inhabited eastern Africa two million years ago. Those early Africans were the first humans to roam the earth, and this was the beginning of civilization. Evidence shows that, later, Stone Age people lived in Africa and that cereals, grains, and tubers played a major role in their diet.

## NORTHERN AFRICA

Further archaeological evidence indicates that as early as 6000 B.C. people lived in communities near the Nile River (in Egypt), raised animals, and built large structures. The first written history tells of Egypt's civilization, settlements along the Nile River, and Egypt as a unified state in about 3000 B.C. We know that the early Egyptians built canals, irrigated their crops, and consumed bread and grains as staples. Of course, the Nile provided fish for the Egyptian diet. At that time, an estimated 1.8 million people lived along the Nile River.

The yearly flooding of the Nile River deposited rich, fertile soil on the land, which yielded bountiful crops. Using the excess from their harvest, these Egyptians traded for other foods and needed goods.

Alexander the Great entered Egypt around 330 B.C. Under Greek rule, the port city of Alexandria was established on the Mediterranean Sea, and it became the capital of Egypt as well as a thriving port and center for trade. The Greeks also improved roads, canals, irrigation, and travel in general, which allowed better movement of goods from area to area.

Around the year 100 A.D., the Romans came to northern Africa, and they spread Christianity throughout the area. In the 700s, the Arabs came into northern Africa and introduced Islamic culture and religion.

Although Arabic heritage dominated the areas north of the Sahara, inhabitants south of the Sahara consisted of blacks from more than 800 different ethnic tribes. Each tribe possessed its own culture, religion, language, and cuisine, and this great diversity still exists throughout Africa.

## TRADE ROUTE

In the quest for spices, Phoenicians rounded the Cape of Good Hope as early as 600 B.C. Situated in the Pacific Ocean between Europe and the Spice Islands, Africa became an important part of the trade route that ran between Asia and Europe about 1,000 years ago. Like several port cities in Italy, port cities in Africa developed into major trading centers during this time. The heavy Middle Eastern influence that arrived then is still apparent in the cuisine and culture of northern Africa.

## EUROPEANS

During the late 1400s and the 1500s, Europeans came to Africa in search of gold and slaves. Because of the slave trade, many Africans were forced to live in distant lands, including the Caribbean, South America, and North America. While Europeans left their mark on the cuisines of Africa, the African cuisine permeated other cultures when African slaves arrived at their new homelands with their recipes and culinary heritage. The climates found in many of these new lands were similar to their native Africa, so the slaves planted crops and prepared the recipes from their homeland. Soon, other cooks in many of these foreign lands adopted African culinary traits into their cuisines.

The Dutch arrived in Cape Town, South Africa, in 1652. Before too long, they imported slaves from Malaysia to work on the plantations. Like the African slaves transported to foreign lands, these slaves arrived with their native recipes, spices, and

---

*During the period from about 2500 B.C. to 2100 B.C., Egyptians built pyramids to entomb their pharaohs (kings). The bodies were preserved and wrapped into mummies, and then sealed in the pyramids with all sorts of items thought to be needed in the next world. Some of those items included pottery, art, gold, furniture, and various foods. Evidence shows that bread was included among the necessities and treasures sealed in pyramids.*

cooking techniques. As a result, significant culinary influence in South Africa comes from the Dutch and the Malaysians. When the French came to South Africa, they brought vine cuttings to grow grapes for wine. A legacy of those French settlers, today the wine industry in South Africa flourishes.

Initially, explorers to Africa stayed along the coasts in search of gold, slaves, spices, and/or ivory. Beginning in the late 1700s, exploration of the interior sections began.

Colonization in Africa occurred rapidly in the late 1800s and early 1900s, with the governments of France, United Kingdom, Germany, Italy, Spain, Belgium, and Portugal each controlling some areas of Africa. The French and British dominated most of the western coast, while the British governed much of the eastern and southern sections of the continent. The country in power exerted heavy influence over the customs and cuisine of each nation it controlled. By the second half of the 1900s, much strife and resistance toward the ruling Europeans erupted as the people of Africa sought independence from European control. In 1951, Libya became the first of the colonized countries to claim independence. The rest of the countries followed over the next decades. Unfortunately, several countries have experienced many coups, civil wars, and fighting between different ethnic or religious groups within the country. Some of these have resulted in massive genocide, such as in Rwanda in the 1990s when over one million people died in the fighting between the Hutus and Tutsis. Often, borders have changed or countries divided to separate dissenting factions.

## AFRICAN COUNTRIES, RULING COUNTRIES, DATES OF INDEPENDENCE

### Countries of North Africa
Algeria, France, 1962
Egypt, United Kingdom, 1922
Libya, Italy, 1951
Morocco, France, 1956
Tunisia, France, 1956
Western Sahara, Spain, 1976, but currently occupied by
  Morocco

### Countries of West Africa
Benin, United Kingdom and France, 1960
Berkina Faso, France, 1960
Côte d' Ivoire, France, 1960
Gambia, United Kingdom, 1965
Ghana, United Kingdom, 1957
Guinea, France, 1959
Guinea-Bassau, Portugal, 1974
Liberia—never a territory
Mali, France, 1960
Mauritania, France, 1960
Niger, France, 1960
Nigeria, Britain, 1960
Senegal, France, 1960
Sierra Leone, United Kingdom, 1961
Togo, France, 1960

### Countries of Central Africa
Cameroon, France, 1960, and United Kingdom, 1961
Central African Republic, France, 1960
Chad, France, 1960
Democratic Republic of the Congo, Belgium, 1960
Equatorial Guinea, Spain, 1968
Gabon, France, 1960

### Countries of East Africa
Burundi—split from Rwanda in 1962
Djibouti, France, 1977
Eritrea, Ethiopia, 1991
Ethiopia, Italy, 1941
Kenya, United Kingdom, 1963
Rwanda, Germany and Belgium, 1962
Somalia, Italy and United Kingdom, 1960
Sudan, United Kingdom and Egypt, 1956
Tanzania—formed in 1964 from Tanganyika, Germany, 1961,
  and Zanzibar, United Kingdom, 1963
Uganda, United Kingdom, 1962

### Countries of South Africa
Angola, Portugal, 1975
Botswana, United Kingdom, 1966
Lesotho, United Kingdom, 1966
Malawi, United Kingdom, 1964
Mozambique, Portugal, 1976
Namibia, South Africa, 1990
South Africa, United Kingdom, 1934, and White ruling
  minority, 1994
Swaziland, United Kingdom, 1968
Zambia, United Kingdom, 1964
Zimbabwe, United Kingdom, 1965

### Islands
Cape Verde, Portugal, 1975
Comoros, France, 1975
Madagascar, France, 1960
Mauritius, United Kingdom, 1968
Sao Tome and Principe, Portugal, 1975
Seychelles, United Kingdom, 1976

## CURRENT SITUATION

Today, there are more than 50 countries containing over 900 million people on the continent of Africa. With a huge number of tribes and cultural backgrounds, more than 1,000 languages are spoken in Africa.

Throughout history and into the present, two factors are responsible for widespread hunger and starvation in many areas of Africa. First, a number of the countries experience poverty and poor living conditions as a result of poor soil and unfavorable growing conditions. Second, numerous natural disasters routinely plague the continent, including droughts, floods, and insect infestations. These create huge crop losses and the ensuing devastation of land and life.

## >> TOPOGRAPHY

Africa reigns as the second largest continent. Desert covers two-fifths of Africa; another two-fifths consists of grasslands; forests and other land types occupy the remaining one-fifth. The equator runs through central Africa, so a tropical, hot, and humid climate predominates. In fact, 90 percent of the country lies in the tropics. Although some of the areas are situated near the equator, high elevations cause a temperate rather than a tropical climate. This is apparent in parts of Ethiopia and Tanzania.

### WATERWAYS

Africa contains about 20,000 miles of coastline, with borders on the Mediterranean Sea in the north, the Atlantic Ocean in the west, the Indian Ocean in the east, and the Red Sea on the northeastern side. This yields ample seafood for the areas with coastline. Two large rivers, the Nile and the Congo, provide freshwater fish. The longest river in the world, the Nile flows for more than 4,000 miles! In addition, several large lakes in eastern Africa, Lake Victoria, Lake Tanganyika, and Lake Malawi, provide abundant fish. In areas with access to the waters, fish and seafood provide the main source of protein for the inhabitants.

### NORTH AFRICA

Lying in the northwest corner of Africa, Morocco is bordered by the Atlantic Ocean on the west and the Mediterranean Sea on the north. Only eight miles and the Strait of Gibraltar separate Spain (and the continent of Europe) from Morocco. The Atlas Mountains run through the center of the country in the north, and the Sahara Desert forms the southern section of Morocco. The land of Morocco has a diverse topography, including five mountain ranges, coastline, fertile agricultural land, and desert.

Egypt is situated in the northeastern corner of Africa. Like Morocco, the Mediterranean Sea lies to its north. Connecting Africa to the Middle East, Israel lies to the northeast of Egypt. The Red Sea is to the east, Sudan to the south, and Libya to the west. The Nile River runs from north to south through Egypt, and its delta is situated in the north. The capital of Egypt, Cairo, grew around the fertile lands of the delta. Although the majority of Egypt was too arid to farm, the Nile River Valley, particularly at the delta, contains rich, productive soil used for farmland. As a result, much of the early population settled in areas near the Nile. Later, irrigation from the Nile transformed much of this once barren land into fertile farmland.

### SAHARA DESERT

The largest desert in the world, the Sahara lies across northern Africa, forming a barrier separating the northern and southern portions of the continent. The resulting isolation has led to very limited mixing of the cultures and cuisines on either side of this arid divider.

> **Ingredients and Foods Commonly Used throughout the Cuisine of Africa Include**
>
> - beans
> - fish and seafood
> - rice, millet, and corn
> - cassava
> - bananas and plantains
> - okra
> - peanuts
>
> - tomatoes
> - yams
> - greens
> - peppers and chilies
> - cilantro and cumin
> - palm oil
> - coconuts and tropical fruits

## SOUTH OF THE SAHARA

The western part of Africa contains rain forests, lots of palm trees, and generally tropical conditions. The Niger River runs from east to west across Nigeria. The southern side of Nigeria borders the Atlantic Ocean. With so many water sources, seafood remains the mainstay here.

High plateau and some lush, fertile areas make up the central portion of Africa lying south of the Sahara. Some rain forests exist in this section, too. Hot, dry summers and rainy winters characterize the climate. Depending on location within the region, very windy conditions or cold winters prevail.

Eastern Africa has the most spectacular scenery in Africa, containing huge plains with spots of grass and trees, dramatic mountains such as Mount Kilimanjaro, incredible rock formations, vast vistas, and varied wildlife. The large lakes in this area provide the people who live there with fish.

On the south side of South Africa, Cape Town is situated on the Atlantic Ocean. With an elevation of 3,500 feet, Table Mountain lies at the Cape of Good Hope. The interior of South Africa consists of vast, semiarid plains surrounded by mountains that lead to green, fertile land along the coast.

## >> COOKING METHODS

The most frequently used cooking methods are braising, frying, and grilling. One-pot cookery is prevalent throughout Africa, a remnant of cooking over an open fire. Benefits of braising (one-pot cookery) are twofold: it extends the small amount of available meat and tenderizes tough meat through the slow cooking process. As a result, the African mainstay remains stews and soups.

With plenty of oil available, frying continues as an often-used cooking technique. Besides providing a frying medium, the oil also functions as a significant source of calories in a land that often yields too little food for its inhabitants. In some areas, cooks add oil to a dish at the end of cooking. This creates a dish with a layer of oil floating on top, but it adds needed calories and helps to fill the diner.

Like one-pot cookery, grilling is another carryover from cooking over an open fire. Baking and roasting occur infrequently.

With unpredictable growing conditions due to either too much or not enough rainfall, salting and pickling continue as two methods of preserving foods in many African countries. These preservation techniques are important because the condition of the next crop is always an unknown.

## >> REGIONS

Nomads still herd livestock in the dry and desert areas of Africa. Dates grow in the oases found in the Sahara Desert, but not much else thrives there. The northern area contains the most fertile regions on the continent of Africa. Wheat, barley, fruits, and vegetables grow in this region. The eastern and southern areas produce peanuts, corn, millet, and sorghum. The wetter western and central areas yield bananas, plantains, rice, cassava, and yams. People living in the east consume lots of yams and cassava. In the southeast, choice foods include seafood and yam stews. Cassava, okra, and spinach appear regularly in soups and stews throughout the southwest. In fact, most of the world's cassava, yams, cashews, cocoa beans, and vanilla beans come from Africa.

## NORTH AFRICA

The countries north of the Sahara Desert bear more resemblance to the countries of the Middle East and Mediterranean than to the rest of Africa. Most inhabitants claim Middle Eastern ancestry; in fact, Arabic is spoken in much of this area, and the Islamic religion dominates. Many dishes served in northern Africa are the same or a variation of those served in the Middle East. With more crops available, the cuisine in the north is richer and contains more gastronomic possibilities than the cuisines found in the regions south of the Sahara.

Although North Africans use many spices and herbs, they lean toward the aromatic rather than the spicy, hot flavorings preferred in much of the south. Favored spices in the north include cumin, caraway, garlic, coriander, pepper, cinnamon, saffron, ginger, and hot red peppers. Because abundant fresh fruits thrive in northern Africa, dishes from those areas often include fresh and dried fruits cooked in the savory dishes. Commonly seen in the areas north of the Sahara, sweet components combined with sour ones like vinegar or lemon often flavor savory dishes. Preserved lemons and many types of olives appear in numerous dishes both in Morocco and throughout northern Africa. *Tagine*, a meat stew often containing fruit, is associated with Moroccan cookery. This dish is named after a cooking pot that has a cone-shaped lid with a hole in the top that allows some steam to escape during cooking.

The cuisine of Morocco shows a long history combining the influences of different people and their civilizations, and it reflects the cultures of Africa, Europe, and the Middle East. In 683, the Arabs invaded and left their indelible mark on the Moroccan culture and cuisine. The famous, ancient walled city of Fez was founded in 808 A.D. and remains the capital of Morocco. Influences from the Middle East and France are particularly strong throughout Morocco.

*Couscous*
© joanna wnuk

Although bordering the Atlantic and the Mediterranean, Moroccans consume surprisingly little seafood. They do consume ample amounts of wheat products, including flatbreads and *couscous*. A well-known Moroccan dish, *couscous* is actually tiny pasta made from durum wheat semolina. Regional variations of *couscous* abound. Some prefer *couscous* plain, some like it sweet, and others combine it with meat or vegetables.

With high regard for fragrances in both the food and dining experience, Moroccans often incorporate orange flower water or rose water into desserts and coffee, and even sprinkle it on the table. Like those of the Middle East, the people of northern Africa favor very sweet desserts. Tea remains the beverage of choice.

Quite different from the cuisines found in the rest of Africa, where a pot of soup or stew functions as the entire meal, a North African meal includes multiple courses. Unlike most African countries, Moroccans serve their guests generous amounts of food, as well as a variety of different dishes. Guests encounter tables laden with more food than could possibly be consumed. As in many Asian cuisines, great care is taken to juxtapose sweet, salty, bitter, and spicy tastes within dishes, courses, and/or the entire meal. North African cooks devote considerable effort to creating culinary interest and excitement with a meal.

Moroccans prefer to eat with their hands rather than with silverware. To facilitate eating without forks, knives, and spoons,

*A tagine*
Laurent Renault © Shutterstock

meats are cut into cubes before cooking and thick sauces prevail. Bread is used to pick up the remaining sauces and bits of food left in the bowl.

Archaeologists trace the earliest leavened bread to ancient Egypt. Like residents in much of northern Africa and the Middle East, Egyptians consume ample amounts of bread (*aysh* in Egyptian). Pita bread stuffed with all sorts of fillings replaces the sandwich and remains very popular. It is said that an adult in Egypt eats three pounds of bread daily!

As in the Middle East, legumes (beans) and grains play a large part in the Egyptian diet. Rice accompanies many dishes. A typical Egyptian breakfast includes fava beans.

Directly connected to the Middle East, Egypt displays prominent Middle Eastern traits in both food and customs. Although Rome and Greece ruled Egypt prior to the Arabs taking control in 640 A.D., the strongest influence is obviously from the Middle East. Arabic is the official language, and the Muslim religion is prevalent. Many dishes served in Egypt are the same or very similar to those of the Middle East.

## WEST AFRICA

Although the hot, humid climate prevailing in western Africa is conducive to the production of abundant agriculture, most of the land consists of poor soil, resulting in meager crops. A profusion of tropical fruits thrive here, in spite of the poor soil. Stews appear most often. They have the advantage of using any available foods, as well as extending the volume of limited food supplies. Generous use of chili peppers produces the hot, spicy food served in much of this area. Besides their use as a seasoning, peppers are highly valued for medicinal purposes.

The most common foods found in Nigeria include beans, plantains, bananas, yams, okra, and cassava. Primarily Muslim, the diet in northern Nigeria centers on beans.

Countries on the western coast take advantage of their proximity to the ocean, and the inhabitants consume much seafood. These people often use salted and dried fish. An astounding amount of hot chilies are eaten here, often too much for the American palate. Okra stew appears frequently in this part of Africa.

Located in the Sahara Desert yet with the Niger River running through it, Mali became the most important center of trading for the Islamic people in medieval times. Situated on the trade route across the Sahara, Mali served as the seat for the ancient empires that traveled the trade route. Founded in the eleventh century, the city of Timbuktu lies on the Niger River in central Mali. Although Mali is a landlocked country, the people eat lots of freshwater fish from the river. A rapid-growing fish that thrives in warm waters, tilapia remains a popular variety.

## CENTRAL AFRICA

The central part of Africa lying south of the Sahara consists of poor soil, high plateaus, some rain forests, and occasional fertile growth regions. Poor growing conditions and poor soil result in sparse food supplies and a narrow range of available ingredients. The people of this region subsist on any available food, and as a result, they eat a repetitive diet, consuming the same foods over and over. The primary staple, corn appears everywhere in this area. Combined with any obtainable vegetables or meat, corn functions as the major portion of the diet in the poorer areas of the central region. Much like cornmeal mush, *samp* is prepared alone or combined with other ingredients such as peanuts or beans. With the exception of Congo and Gabon, the dishes in central Africa are not spicy hot. In those countries, abundant chilies regularly appear, and the heat level even surpasses that of western Africa.

## EAST AFRICA

The famous safaris and Mount Kilimanjaro hail from the eastern section of Africa. Parts of this area experience temperate rather than tropical climate due to the high

**THE ART OF EATING WITH ONE'S HANDS**

In several African countries, including Ethiopia and Morocco, it is customary to eat with one's hands. The right hand replaces the silverware. Do not think this way of eating lacks manners. Quite the contrary, there exists a different set of "rules" and etiquette for eating with hands.

Before the meal begins, everyone washes his or her hands. Often, bowls of water are brought to the table and everyone partakes in the washing ritual.

The food for the entire table is served on one platter. Each guest eats the portion directly in front of him or her. Only the right hand is used to pick up food—never the left hand. In Morocco, diners use only the first three fingers of the right hand for handling food. Licking fingers is considered very poor manners. Moroccans use bread to scoop the food and clean the plate at the end of the meal. In Ethiopia, injera, a spongy flatbread much like a pancake, is used to scoop the food and soak up the last bits of sauce remaining on the platter.

According to archaeologists, yeast was used in Egypt around 4000 B.C. Many believe this allowed the Egyptians to prepare leavened bread and brew alcoholic beverages. Evidence indicates wheat and barley were grown in ancient times. They used wheat to make bread and barley to make beer.

*Basket of injera*
© paul _brighton

*Injera with Ethiopian meal*
© paul _brighton

elevations. Like other areas of Africa, the lack of rainfall in some years creates severe droughts that severely limit food supplies in this region.

The influence of the United Kingdom and India remains apparent in most of eastern Africa. Having been under British rule, bland, not spicy cooking prevails in Kenya, Uganda, and Tanzania; however, hot chili peppers often are passed separately as a condiment to accompany the food. Curry powder appears frequently, a remnant of the Indian influence. Ethiopia, which was never colonized or under the control of a foreign country, uses generous amounts of spicy, hot flavoring. The basis of the diet consists of stews and soups accompanied by starch, usually rice, corn, and/or bananas.

The cuisine of Ethiopia developed without the addition of sugar. When the Italian Fascists came to Ethiopia in 1935, they introduced sugar. Before that time, Ethiopians added salt or spices to coffee in the way we use sugar. Ethiopians developed a spicy seasoning called *berbere*. With countless recipes around for this spice blend, it may contain all or a combination of spices including cumin, coriander, ginger, cardamom, nutmeg, cinnamon, allspice, paprika, fenugreek, salt, pepper, and cayenne. *Berbere* flavors many Ethiopian dishes. A similar seasoning mixture, *piripiri*, is commonplace in Mozambique. Hot, spicy food remains the norm in both of these countries. *Wot*, the Ethiopian term for stew, is served regularly, eaten with hands, and scooped with the flatbread, *injera*. Traditionally, *injera* is made with teff flour and water that ferments for 2 or 3 days. The resulting batter makes a spongy pancake with a slightly sour taste. All meats except pork are eaten here; pork consumption violates Islamic religious laws. As a result, *wot* contains any meat or variety of meats or it can be vegetarian with beans, vegetables, or a combination.

The land in Tanzania yields a wide variety of fruits, and many of their recipes incorporate fruit into them. The exotic cuisine of Tanzania includes curries and other foods exhibiting the influence of people from India, Portugal, and Iraq who came there to trade.

Situated in southeastern Africa, Zimbabwe also has experienced a number of droughts. In an attempt to ensure food through the winter, the people dry any excess foods remaining after the wet summer season. Having no ocean borders and no major rivers running through it, the cuisine of Zimbabwe features much more meat.

## SOUTHERN AFRICA

Southern Africa includes many countries: Botswana, Angola, Lesotho, Malawi, Namibia, Mozambique, Swaziland, South Africa, Zambia, and Zimbabwe. Of course this large area has a variety of terrains and climates. Within southern Africa, there is coastline, mountains, valleys, desert, and lots of plateaus. The range of climates spans from tropical to temperate.

The southern African cuisine shows influence from the United Kingdom, Malaysia, Holland, and northern Europe. As a result of the British, Indian, and Malaysian influences, curries are widely consumed in southern Africa. A stew containing lamb or mutton, onion, and other vegetables, *bredie* appears often in South Africa. With coasts on the Indian and Atlantic Oceans, seafood is plentiful.

Like much of Africa, great diversity in the diet is often based on a person's wealth. For example, in South Africa, poor people consume lots of *mealies*, a porridge made from corn and *bourewors*, a popular Afrikaner sausage dish. The wealthy have access to a large quantity and a wide variety of foods.

## >> CUISINE

### OVERVIEW

Africa's economy remains poor for a number of reasons. Much of the soil is poor and yields meager crops. Unpredictable weather conditions lead to droughts and floods. Insect infestations often destroy crops. Many farmers produce only enough food to feed their families. Starvation remains a reality in Africa and accounts for numerous deaths.

An incredibly diverse continent, Africa hosts climates that range from tropical to arid to temperate. The terrain includes coasts, rain forests, snow-capped mountains, grasslands, and desert. With so many topographical and climatic variations, it is no wonder that the cuisines differ greatly. The countries with borders on the oceans and seas consume much seafood; however, inland countries rely on hunting and herding for meat. Most Africans' diets consist primarily of fruits, vegetables, legumes, and grains.

## AVAILABLE INGREDIENTS

Corn, beans, okra, cassava, plantains, yams, greens, and *dendê* (palm oil) remain staple ingredients in many of the African countries. Whether mixed with coconut milk, combined with meats, mixed into cornmeal mush, or added to one of the many other preparations, large quantities of greens are consumed by Africans. Similarities exist between the cuisines of Africa and those of Central America, South America, and the Caribbean because of the similarity of the available ingredients and the influences from the people of these countries on each other. Depending on the area, hot chilies appear in many recipes.

As in many countries in Latin America, the Middle East, and Asia, meat is not plentiful enough to be served alone as an entrée. As a result, particularly in the countries south of the Sahara, any available food ingredients—meats, seafood, and/or vegetables—are combined in a pot and cooked into soup or stew. Meat becomes one of several ingredients making up the entrée or is even served alone as a condiment. The difference between soup and stew is the amount of liquid incorporated; both preparations contain the same ingredients and flavorings.

*Groundnut soup*
© Eva Gruendemann

Starches and grains play a crucial role in the African diet. Perhaps consumed three times a day, generous portions of starch accompany the soup or stew and function as a filling staple. Whether served alone or combined with other foods, bland grains and starches complement the spicy entrées consumed in many areas.

Which of the variety of starches is available depends on the geographic location on the continent. Choices include rice, corn, millet, teff (a grain grown at high elevations), plantains (green varieties of bananas), yams, cassava, wheat, and others. Semolina, the primary ingredient in *couscous*, grows in the north of Africa. Yams and cassava root grow in the west, corn in the south and central areas, and bananas and plantains in the very wet areas. From each of these products comes the starch for that region, usually prepared as a stiff porridge resembling cornmeal mush.

An abundance of tropical fruits and palm trees grow in Africa's hot, humid climate. All sorts of foods and objects are made from parts of the palm tree. Heavy and strongly flavored palm oil remains the major cooking fat. Valued for both its meat and milk, the coconut appears in all areas of the menu. Among the myriad uses of the precious palm tree, palm sap becomes wine while materials from the palm tree are used in clothing and for building. The major cash crop for this area, peanuts, appears in many dishes, in paste form (peanut butter) or coarsely ground, adding texture as well as flavor to the dish.

## ONE-POT DISHES

Some of the one-pot dishes commonly served throughout Africa include *tagines* from the north, groundnut stews (containing ground nuts, often peanuts) from the west, and curries from the east and south. Accompanied by appropriate grains or bread from the region, these one-pot dishes function as the complete meal. The cuisines of the countries in the western portion of Africa use more seafood, while meat consumption is higher in eastern Africa. Legumes, however, are widely consumed in all of Africa.

*Groundnut stew*
© teleginatania

## FAT

Many of the African cuisines include a lot of fat by American standards. At the beginning of cooking, meats and vegetables are sautéed in fat before adding liquid. In addition, Africans often incorporate fat into the dish near the end of cooking to create a sauce based on fat. Although food supplies remain sparse in many of these countries, oil from palms, peanuts, and other vegetables are abundant throughout tropical Africa. By weight, fats contain a higher amount of calories than other foods, and those extra calories are needed to augment the meager calories obtained from the normal diet.

## MEALS

Because of limited food, inhabitants in many areas south of the Sahara consume only one meal a day with snacks at other times. Meals usually consist of one-pot dishes except in the extreme north and south of Africa.

Breakfast is a robust meal consisting of beans and rice or other foods that we normally think of as entrées. Africans believe that people need to consume a hearty breakfast containing ample calories before departing for work. If available, both the afternoon and the evening meals typically consist of soup or stew served with a starch. In northern Africa, guests receive feastlike meals; however, families still consume the one-pot dish and a starch.

| REGION | AREA | WEATHER | TOPOGRAPHY | FOODS |
|---|---|---|---|---|
| Morocco | Northwest | Rainy from September or October until April or May; dry rest of year | Coast, desert, mountains, fertile plains | Seafood, sugar, beans, barley, corn, wheat, tomatoes, onions, citrus fruits, potatoes, vegetables, olives, figs, almonds, dates |
| Egypt | Northeast | North and east: hot | Coastal, Nile Valley | Fruits, wheat, rice, legumes, vegetables, sugar |
|  |  | West and central: hot | Desert | Sheep, goats, camels |
| Mali | West | Tropical, hot | Sahara Desert, semiarid, grasslands | Seafood, fish, peanuts, corn, millet, rice, vegetables, cassava, yams, fruits |
| Ivory Coast | West | Tropical, temperate on coast with ocean currents | Coast, savanna, tropical rain forest | Cocoa, coffee, corn, rice, cassava, yams, plantains, bananas, pineapple, sweet potatoes |
| Ghana | West | Tropical, temperate on coast with ocean currents | Forests, plateaus, savanna, grasslands | Seafood, poultry, millet, rice, plantains, corn, cassava, yams, tropical fruits, cocoa, coffee |
| Nigeria | West | Tropical | Niger River, swamps, plains, plateaus, forests, mountains | Livestock, corn, peanuts, rice, millet, wheat, cassava, yams, bananas, plantains, tropical fruits, coffee, cocoa |
| Central Africa | Central | Hot, dry summers; wet, cool winters | High plateaus, isolated lush areas, rain forests, mountains | Freshwater fish, poultry, corn, rice, cassava, yams, bananas, plantains, honey |
| Ethiopia | East | Temperate in high elevations; very hot in lowlands; rainy summers but subject to droughts | Highlands, mountains, deserts | Cattle, sheep, goats, grains, corn, teff, vegetables, onions, sugar, coffee |
| Kenya | East | Tropical, hot and dry | Rift Valley, some arid land, grasslands | Cattle, sheep, goats, seafood, beans, fruits, vegetables, corn, sugar, coffee, tea |
| Tanzania | East | Varies from hot and rainy coasts to temperate mountains | Plateaus, mountains (Mount Kilimanjaro), Great Rift Valley | Seafood, cattle, poultry, peanuts, rice, corn, grains, vegetables, plantains, yams, coconuts, bananas, sugar, coffee, spices, cashews, tea |
| South Africa | South | Mostly temperate, mild and sunny | Coasts, plateaus, mountains, desert | Beef, game, seafood, sheep, corn, peanuts, soy, wheat, apples, grapes, coffee, wine |

## >> Review Questions

1. Explain the differences in cuisine between the north, south, east, west, and central portions of Africa.
2. What factors created the differences between these regions?
3. What historical and geographic influences contributed to the contrasting cuisines of northern Africa and the rest of the continent?
4. Discuss the spices used in the foods in various parts of Africa.
5. How does the weather influence the foods and cuisine of Africa?
6. Explain the role and importance of starches and fats in the African diet.
7. What is one-pot cookery, and why is it so prevalent in Africa?

## >> Glossary

**berbere** Spicy seasoning mixture used in Ethiopia containing cumin, coriander, ginger, cardamom, nutmeg, cinnamon, allspice, paprika, fenugreek, salt, pepper, and cayenne

**bourewors** A popular Afrikaner sausage dish

**bredie** A stew served in South Africa containing lamb or mutton, onions, and other vegetables

**couscous** A tiny pasta shaped like a grain and made from semolina

**dendê** Palm oil

**injera** A spongy flatbread served in Ethiopia, used to scoop food

**mealies** A porridge made from corn

**millet** A grain

**piripiri** Spicy seasoning mixture used in Mozambique

**samp** A cornmeal mush

**tagine** A type of stew containing meat and often fruit served in Morocco; the pot used for cooking a *tagine*, with a cone-shaped lid containing a hole on the top that allows some steam to escape

**teff** A grain grown at high elevations

**tilapia** A rapid-growing freshwater fish that thrives in warm waters

**wot** Ethiopian term for stew

**Author's Note:** Preparation of many African dishes includes a lot of oil or fat by American standards. The reason for this is that several varieties of fat are available, whereas other food supplies are often quite limited. As a result, fat functions as a significant source of calories for many Africans. To maintain authenticity, originally I was not going to reduce the fat in the recipes. After much pondering, I decided to cut much of the fat from the recipes because I think the average American customer would want less fat. If that is not what your clientele wants, add extra fat to the recipes.

## AKARA (ETHIOPIA)

### BLACK-EYED PEA FRITTERS

© Viktor

**Number of Servings:** 14
**Serving Size:** 4 fritters
**Total Yield:** 3 lb., 8 1/2 oz. (1.6 kg)
**Scaling:** 1 oz., 28 g (1 tablespoon, 15 mL)
**Wine Style:** Fruit forward, dry white wine with medium body. Possible grape varietals are Pinot Blanc, Riesling.
**Example:** Pinot Blanc trocken "Schiefer" 2012, Wagner Stempel (Rheinhessen/Germany)

**Cooking Method:** Boil, deep-fry

| INGREDIENTS | WEIGHT | | VOLUME | |
| --- | --- | --- | --- | --- |
| | U.S. | METRIC | U.S. | METRIC |
| black-eyed peas | 1 lb., 4 oz. | 567 g | 3 cups | 720 mL |
| onion, roughly chopped | 11 oz. | 312 g | 2 medium | |
| cayenne, ground | 1/4 oz. or to taste | 8 g or to taste | 2 teaspoons or to taste | 10 mL |
| salt | 1/2 oz. | 15 g | 2 teaspoons | 10 mL |
| water | | 227 g | 1 cup | 240 mL |
| oil for deep-frying | | | | |

**Accompaniment:**
hot sauce

1. Bring pot of water to boil. Turn off heat, add peas, allow to sit in water until cool enough to handle.
2. Meanwhile, purée onion, cayenne, and salt until paste in food processor fitted with knife blade. Set aside until needed.
3. Rub peas between hands to remove outer skins. Discard skins. Place peas in food processor fitted with knife blade. Pulse to grind the peas. Add water (4 oz., 114 g, or 1/2 cup, 120 mL) as needed, using only as much water as necessary to grind finely.
4. Transfer ground peas to bowl, add onion paste. Mix vigorously with wooden spoon.
5. Heat oil in frying pan, pot, or deep-fryer to 365 to 375 degrees (185 to 190°C). Scale pea batter into 1 oz. (28 g) (1 tablespoon, 15 mL) portions. Carefully place in hot oil, fry for a few minutes on each side, until golden.
6. Remove and drain on absorbent paper. Serve, accompanied by hot sauce.

### TWIST ON THE CLASSIC

Try serving the *akara* on a bed of greens accompanied by a *sambal* aioli.

To create a spicier fritter, some use minced habanero pepper instead of cayenne.

Popular throughout much of western Africa, *akara* often is sold as "street food." In addition, Nigerians frequently eat *akara* for breakfast.

*Sambal* makes a nice accompaniment for these fritters.

## MOROCCAN OLIVES (MOROCCO)

**Note:** These store well in the refrigerator.

**Note:** Begin preparation for these olives at least 2 or 3 days in advance.

**Total Yield:** 1 lb. (454 g)
**Food Balance:** Spicy and salt/acid
**Wine Style:** Medium-bodied fruity—White Zinfandel, Riesling, fruity Chardonnay, or Shiraz
**Example:** Beringer Founders' Estate Chardonnay or Shiraz

| INGREDIENTS | WEIGHT U.S. | METRIC | VOLUME U.S. | METRIC |
|---|---|---|---|---|
| olives, black or green | 1 lb. | 454 g | | |
| fresh parsley, minced | 1 oz. | 28 g | 1/4 cup + 2 tablespoons | 90 mL |
| fresh cilantro, minced | 1 1/4 oz. | 36 g | 1/4 cup + 2 tablespoons | 90 mL |
| garlic, minced | | | 3 cloves or 1 1/2 teaspoons | 8 mL |
| red pepper flakes | | | 1 teaspoon | 5 mL |
| ground cumin | | | 1/2 teaspoon | 3 mL |
| fresh lemon juice | | 28 g | 2 tablespoons | 30 mL |
| lemon zest, grated | | | 1/2 teaspoon | 3 mL |

1. Rinse olives, crack them with a mallet or flat side of knife, cover with cold water and refrigerate overnight.
2. Drain well.
3. Combine parsley, cilantro, garlic, pepper flakes, cumin, lemon juice, and zest. Mix with olives.
4. Refrigerate at least 2 or 3 days before serving.

© Mariusz Prusaczyk

### TWIST ON THE CLASSIC

Purée this and create a tapanade. Use the tapanade for a dip with vegetables, a spread for crackers or pieces of French bread, or as a sandwich spread.

© Floydine

© Monkey Business

# CAMARÃO GRELHADO PIRI PIRI (MOZAMBIQUE)
## GRILLED SHRIMP PIRI PIRI

Courtesy of Canola Oil @ canolainfo.org

**Note:** Allow 3 to 4 hours to marinate the shrimp.

**Note:** *Piri piri* shrimp makes a great entrée. Use a 5- or 6-ounce (142- to 171-g) portion.

**Note:** This is a spicy dish, so adjust the quantity of hot peppers according to taste.

**Number of Servings:** 8　　**Cooking Method:** Grill
**Serving Size:** 2 1/2 oz. (71 g)
**Total Yield:** 1 lb., 5 1/2 oz. (610 g)
**Food Balance:** Spicy/protein
**Wine Style:** Low-oaked whites and soft reds
**Example:** Campanile Pinot Grigio and Rosemount Shiraz

*Piri piri* is a sauce made from oil and hot chili peppers. In the Portuguese colonies of Mozambique and Angola, *piri piri* means "bird's-eye pepper." While the bird's-eye pepper is commonly used in Mozambique, any very hot pepper can be substituted. Also spelled "peri peri" and "pilli pilli," this sauce appears throughout much of western Africa. Normally, plain rice accompanies this dish.

| INGREDIENTS | WEIGHT U.S. | METRIC | VOLUME U.S. | METRIC |
|---|---|---|---|---|
| garlic, peeled | 1/2 oz. | 15 g | 4 small cloves | |
| fresh hot peppers, bird's-eye or variety of choice, seeds and membranes removed if desired | 1/4 oz. | 8 g or to taste | 2 teaspoons | 10 mL or to taste |
| salt | 1/4 oz. | 8 g | 1 teaspoon | 5 mL |
| lemon juice | | 28 g | 2 tablespoons | 30 mL |
| oil | | 114 g | 1/2 cup | 120 mL |
| extra-large shrimp 16/20, peeled with tails left attached, deveined | 1 lb., 10 oz. | 738 g | | |

**Accompaniment:**
cooked rice, hot

**Garnish:**
fresh parsley, minced
lemon, sliced or quartered

1. Turn on food processor fitted with knife blade, drop garlic and pepper through feed tube. Scrape sides of processor with rubber spatula as needed, process until finely chopped.
2. Add salt and lemon juice, pulse. Scrape sides.
3. Slowly add oil. Scraping sides as needed, process until oil thickens and emulsifies.
4. Wash shrimp and drain thoroughly. Place shrimp in a nonreactive bowl, add oil mixture. Stir to coat all shrimp well. Cover and refrigerate for at least 3 or 4 hours. Turn once or twice while marinating.
5. Preheat grill. Remove shrimp from marinade and place on grilling rack. Grill for 2 or 3 minutes per side, until done. If desired, bring remaining marinade to boil. Add more oil, if needed.
6. Place shrimp on plates. If desired, drizzle some additional spiced oil over shrimp. Add serving of rice next to shrimp. Garnish with parsley and lemon wedge, serve.

# CREAM OF BLACK-EYED PEA SOUP (WESTERN AFRICA)

**Note:** Begin soaking the black-eyed peas the night before cooking. If the peas were not soaked the night before, they can be added to boiling water and then allowed to soak for a couple of hours.

**Note:** This soup is spicy! To judge the amount of spice, start by adding half the amount of cayenne pepper to the soup. Depending on the amount of spiciness the diners would enjoy, add the remaining cayenne or more after tasting.

**Number of Servings:** 10

**Serving Size:** 7 oz. (199 g)

**Total Yield:** 4 lb., 6 1/4 oz. (2 kg)

**Food Balance:** Spicy/protein

**Wine Style:** Low-oaked whites and soft reds

**Example:** Beringer Sauvignon Blanc, Lindeman's Merlot

**Cooking Method:** Boil

**TWIST ON THE CLASSIC**

Add shrimp pieces to this soup at the end of cooking.

| INGREDIENTS | WEIGHT | | VOLUME | |
|---|---|---|---|---|
| | U.S. | METRIC | U.S. | METRIC |
| dried black-eyed peas | 8 oz. | 227 g | 1 cup | 240 mL |
| onion, diced | 7 1/4 oz. | 206 g | 1 medium to large | |
| tomatoes, canned or fresh, diced | 14 1/2 oz. | 411 g | 1 1/2 cups | 360 mL |
| stock, chicken, beef, vegetarian, or variety of choice | | 908 g | 1 quart (4 cups) | 960 mL |
| curry powder | 1/4 oz. | 8 g | 1 teaspoon | 5 mL |
| cayenne | | | 1/4 teaspoon | 2 mL |
| half and half | | 114 g | 1/2 cup | 120 mL |
| salt | as needed | | | |

1. Wash peas, place in pan or bowl. Add enough water to cover peas with a couple of inches of water above the top of the peas. Cover and refrigerate 5 hours or overnight.

2. Drain peas and place in pot. Add onion, tomatoes, stock, curry powder, and cayenne. Bring to boil, reduce heat, cover, and simmer until beans are done. Add more stock or water if needed.

3. Add half and half. Be careful not to boil soup because it might curdle. Add salt to taste, correct seasonings. Serve.

© ZEF

# HARIRA (MOROCCO)
## VEGETABLE AND MEAT SOUP

**Note:** Ramadan, a holy month in the Muslim religion, includes fasting every day from dawn to sunset. *Harira* is the traditional food served at the end of the day to break the fast.

**Number of Servings:** 8
**Serving Size:** 8 oz. (227 g)
**Total Yield:** 4 lb., 6 oz. (2 kg)
**Food Balance:** Sweet/protein
**Wine Style:** Soft- to medium-bodied Gewürztraminer or Pinot Noir to lighter Merlots or Cabernet Sauvignon
**Example:** Souverain Merlot

**Cooking Method:** Sauté, boil

Elzbieta Sekowska © Shutterstock

| INGREDIENTS | WEIGHT | | VOLUME | |
| --- | --- | --- | --- | --- |
| | U.S. | METRIC | U.S. | METRIC |
| butter | 1/2 oz. | 15 g | 1 tablespoon | 15 mL |
| onion, diced | 5 oz. | 142 g | 1 cup or 1 medium | 240 mL |
| fresh parsley, minced | 1 1/2 oz. | 43 g | 1 cup | 240 mL |
| pepper | | | 1 teaspoon | 5 mL |
| ground turmeric | | | 1 teaspoon | 5 mL |
| ground cinnamon | | | 1/2 teaspoon | 3 mL |
| lamb shoulder, trimmed and cut into 1/2-inch (1.3-cm) cubes | 8 oz. | 227 g | | |
| wings and back of 1 chicken | | | | |
| dried lentils | 3 3/4 oz. | 107 g | 1/2 cup | 120 mL |
| plum tomatoes, fresh or canned, peeled and seeded | 2 lb. | 908 g | | |
| fresh cilantro, minced | 1/2 oz. | 15 g | 2 tablespoons | 30 mL |
| water | | | 1 quart + 2 1/2 cups (6 1/2 cups) | 1.6 L |
| fine soup noodles | 1 oz. | 28 g (dry) | 1/2 cup | 120 mL |
| semolina or substitute all-purpose flour | 1 1/4 oz. | 36 g | 3 tablespoons | 45 mL |
| salt | 1/4 oz. | 8 g | 1 teaspoon | 5 mL |

**Garnish:**
lemon wedges

1. Melt butter in large pot over medium heat. Sauté onion, parsley, pepper, and turmeric for 3 to 4 minutes, then add cinnamon, lamb, and chicken.
2. Cook slowly until golden brown, about 15 minutes.
3. Wash lentils. Purée tomatoes. Add lentils, tomatoes, and cilantro to meat mixture. Cook 15 minutes over low heat.
4. Add 6 cups (1.4 L) of water to pot. Cook until lentils are soft, about 45 minutes to 1 hour. Heat pot of water for cooking roodles.
5. Cook noodles in pot of boiling water. Mix semolina and remaining 1/2 cup (120 mL) of water thoroughly in bowl.
6. Just before service, add noodles and salt to soup. Boil for two minutes.
7. Stir semolina into soup. If substituting all-purpose flour, mix the flour with a little water to make a thin paste before adding. Cook 3 minutes, stirring constantly. Correct seasonings.
8. Serve with lemon wedges.

## COOKED CARROT SALAD (MOROCCO)

**Note:** Allow at least 30 minutes for salad to rest so flavors marry.

**Number of Servings:** 9
**Serving Size:** 4 oz. (114 g)
**Total Yield:** 2 lb., 6 oz. (1.1 kg)

**Cooking Method:** Boil

### TWIST ON THE CLASSIC

Substitute any vegetable for the carrots. To make a salad plate, place some green bean salad, this Cooked Carrot Salad, a grilled chicken breast, and some Moroccan Olives *(see recipe in this chapter)* over a bed of lettuce.

| INGREDIENTS | WEIGHT | | VOLUME | |
| --- | --- | --- | --- | --- |
| | U.S. | METRIC | U.S. | METRIC |
| water | | 454 g | 2 cups | 480 mL |
| carrots, peeled and cut into 1/4-inch (1/2-cm) rounds | 2 lb., 13 oz. | 1.3 kg | 16 medium | |
| garlic, smashed and minced | 1/4 oz. | 8 g | 2 cloves | |
| paprika | | | 1/2 teaspoon | 3 mL |
| ground cumin | | | 1/2 teaspoon | 3 mL |
| olive oil | | 15 g | 1 tablespoon | 15 mL |
| red wine vinegar | | 28 g | 2 tablespoons | 30 mL |
| pepper | | | 1/4 teaspoon | 2 mL |
| salt | | | 1/2 teaspoon | 3 mL |
| fresh parsley, minced | | | 1 tablespoon | 15 mL |

1. Bring water to boil. Add carrots and garlic, cook until just tender, about 10 minutes.
2. Drain carrots, rinse with cold water to stop cooking. Place them in bowl, set aside.
3. Mix paprika, cumin, oil, vinegar, pepper, salt, and parsley in small bowl. Pour over salad, mix well.
4. Cover with plastic wrap, leave at room temperature for at least 30 minutes to allow flavors to blend. Correct seasonings.
5. Serve at room temperature.

© mariontxa

# M'RAAD (EGYPT)

## EGGPLANT SALAD

Milarka/Getty Images

**Note:** Allow time for the eggplant to rest with the salt and then for this salad to marinate for several hours or overnight so flavors will permeate the eggplant.

**Number of Servings:** 9

**Serving Size:** 4 oz. (114 g)

**Total Yield:** 2 lb., 4 1/2 oz. (1 kg)

**Cooking Method:** Sauté

| INGREDIENTS | WEIGHT | | VOLUME | |
|---|---|---|---|---|
| | U.S. | METRIC | U.S. | METRIC |
| eggplant | 2 lb., 11 oz. | 1.2 kg | 2 large | |
| salt | 1 1/2 oz. | 43 g, as needed | 2 tablespoons | 30 mL, as needed |
| cumin seeds | | | 1 teaspoon | 5 mL |
| caraway seeds | | | 1/2 teaspoon | 3 mL |
| paprika | | | 1 teaspoon | 5 mL |
| ground turmeric | | | 1/8 teaspoon | 1 mL |
| olive oil, as needed for frying | | | | |
| onions, cut in half, then thinly sliced | 12 1/2 oz. | 355 g | 2 medium to large | |
| garlic, smashed and minced | 1 oz. | 28 g | 6 cloves | |
| tomato paste | 1 oz. | 28 g | 2 tablespoons | 30 mL |
| salt | | | 1/2 teaspoon | 3 mL |
| pepper | | | 1/4 teaspoon | 2 mL |
| water | | 340 g | 1 1/2 cups | 360 mL |
| red wine vinegar | | 57 g | 1/4 cup | 60 mL |

**Accompaniment:**

lettuce, variety of choice, chiffonade
   or torn into bite-sized pieces,
   lightly coated with vinaigrette or
   dressing of choice at time of service

**Garnish:**

fresh parsley, minced
dates, pitted and cut in half

① Peel eggplant and cut into large dice. Place eggplant in colander, sprinkle salt all over eggplant. Place colander in sink or in large bowl (to catch liquid). Allow to sit for 30 to 45 minutes to draw water and bitterness from eggplant. After allotted time, rinse eggplant with water and let drain well.

② In spice grinder or with mortar and pestle, grind cumin, caraway seeds, paprika, and turmeric together until powdered. Set aside until needed.

③ Cover bottom of large skillet with oil, heat over medium-high heat until hot. Add eggplant, stir often, and sauté until softened. Remove from skillet and place in bowl.

④ Add oil to cover bottom of skillet, heat over medium-high heat until hot. Add onion, stir often, and sauté until softened. Remove from skillet and add to eggplant.

⑤ Add a little oil to skillet, heat over medium heat until hot. Add garlic, sauté a few seconds, stirring constantly. Add reserved ground spices, tomato paste, salt, pepper, and water. Stir, simmer for 5 minutes.

⑥ Stir in vinegar. Remove from heat, pour over eggplant and onions. Mix to coat. Cover and refrigerate until needed, at least several hours or overnight.

⑦ Serve over a bed of lettuce. Garnish with minced parsley and dates, if desired.

# PEIXE A LUMBO (MOZAMBIQUE)

## FISH AND SHRIMP STEW

**Number of Servings:** 9
**Serving Size:** 7 oz. (199 g)
**Total Yield:** 4 lb. (1.8 kg)
**Food Balance:** Protein/sweet/spicy
**Wine Style:** Soft and fruity Chenin Blanc or Pinot Gris, Beaujolais
**Example:** Beringer Chenin Blanc

**Cooking Method:** Sauté, braise

Geff Reis/AGE Fotostock

| INGREDIENTS | WEIGHT U.S. | WEIGHT METRIC | VOLUME U.S. | VOLUME METRIC |
|---|---|---|---|---|
| **Coconut Milk:** | | | | |
| water, boiling | | 227 g | 1 cup | 240 mL |
| unsweetened coconut | 1 1/2 oz. | 43 g | 1/2 cup | 120 mL |
| medium-size shrimp, uncooked | 1 lb. | 454 g | | |
| sea bass, red snapper, or other white fish, about 1 inch (2.5 cm) thick | 2 lb. | 908 g | | |
| olive oil | | 15 g | 1 tablespoon | 15 mL |
| onions, finely diced | 12 oz. | 340 g | 2 large | |
| red bell peppers, finely diced | 14 oz. | 397 g | 2 large | |
| plum tomatoes, fresh or canned, peeled and chopped or drained and chopped | 7 oz. | 199 g | 2 medium or 2/3 cup | 160 mL |
| fresh cilantro, minced | 1/2 oz. | 15 g | 2 tablespoons | 30 mL |
| salt | 1/4 oz. | 8 g | 1 teaspoon | 5 mL |
| hot chili peppers, birds-eye or variety of choice, minced, seeds and ribs removed, if desired | | | 1 teaspoon | 5 mL, or to taste |

**Accompaniment:**

hot cooked rice

### TWIST ON THE CLASSIC

Serve this in the style of paella. Place the rice in an ovenproof pan, top with fish, shellfish, and precooked sausages, pour the coconut milk over the dish, and bake.

1. Pour boiling water over coconut, let sit for at least 15 minutes.
2. Strain through fine mesh strainer or cheesecloth, pressing coconut to extract all liquid. Discard solid coconut, reserve coconut milk.
3. Peel and devein shrimp. Wash in cold, running water. Wash fish. Drain seafood well. Refrigerate until ready to use.
4. Heat oil in skillet over medium-high heat, sauté onions and bell peppers until soft, stirring frequently, about 5 minutes.
5. Add tomatoes, stirring frequently, cook until most of liquid evaporates.
6. Remove pan from heat, add cilantro, salt, and chili peppers. Correct seasonings.
7. Place half of fish in bottom of separate pan, top with half of shrimp, then half of sautéed vegetables. Repeat layers with remaining ingredients.
8. Pour in coconut milk, partially cover pan, and bring to simmer over moderate heat, then reduce heat to low and cook until done, about 10 to 15 minutes. Alternately, bake in 325-degree (160°C) oven until done. Correct seasonings.
9. Serve over bed of rice.

# TANZANIAN CHICKEN STEW (TANZANIA—EAST AFRICA)

Joe Gough © Shutterstock

**Note:** Because this recipe does not contain a lot of vegetables, I recommend that each diner receive a piece of chicken.

**Note:** This dish can be very spicy, so adjust the hot peppers to your guests' palates. Since the seeds and ribs of peppers contain the most heat, consider removing them from the peppers and/or use only one pepper to reduce the spiciness of this stew.

**Number of Servings:** 12
**Serving Size:** 14 oz. (397 g)
**Total Yield:** 10 lb., 8 oz. (4.8 kg)
**Food Balance:** Sweet/spicy
**Wine Style:** Soft and fruity Gewürztraminer or Fume Blanc
**Example:** Château St. Jean Gewürztraminer

**Cooking Method:** Braise

## TWIST ON THE CLASSIC

Cook this dish with one chicken breast per serving. Instead of serving on a bed of rice, serve over mashed potatoes.

| | WEIGHT | | VOLUME | |
|---|---|---|---|---|
| **INGREDIENTS** | **U.S.** | **METRIC** | **U.S.** | **METRIC** |
| onions, sliced | 14 oz. | 397 g | 2 large | |
| oil | | 57 g | 1/4 cup | 60 mL |
| canned tomatoes, chopped | 1 lb., 1 oz. | 482 g | 2 cups | 480 mL |
| garlic, smashed and minced | 1/2 oz. | 15 g | 4 cloves | |
| chili peppers, ribs and seeds removed if desired | | | 2 or 3 each | |
| curry powder | 1/2 oz. | 15 g | 1 tablespoon + 1 teaspoon | 20 mL |
| whole cloves | | | 6 each | |
| green bell peppers, cut into strips | 1 lb., 14 oz. | 851 g | 4 each | |
| whole chicken, cut into pieces | 6 to 7 lb. | 2.7 to 3.2 kg | 2 each | |
| chicken stock | | 454 g | 2 cups | 480 mL |
| coconut milk | | 454 g | 2 cups | 480 mL |
| potatoes, white, waxy, or all-purpose, peeled and sliced very thinly | 1 lb., 12 oz. | 794 g | 4 each | |
| salt | to taste | | | |

**Accompaniment:**
hot cooked rice

1. Sauté onion in hot oil in pan over medium-high heat until softened. Add tomatoes, garlic, chili peppers, curry powder, cloves, and bell peppers. Sauté about 5 minutes.
2. Add chicken, sauté about 5 minutes. Add chicken stock, 1 cup (227 g or 240 mL) of coconut milk, and potatoes. Reduce heat and simmer for 30 minutes, uncovered, stirring occasionally.
3. Add remaining coconut milk, simmer until all is tender, about 20 minutes. Add salt to taste.
4. Remove chicken pieces to serving platter. Stir stew to break up and slightly mash potatoes. Correct seasonings.
5. Serve chicken on a bed of rice topped with sauce.

## MAFE (SENEGAL)

### CHICKEN PEANUT STEW

**Note:** Any variety of vegetables may be used in this dish. Most Africans do not eat as much meat as Americans, so the portion size is less than the usual quarter chicken served in America. Each portion contains some meat and a lot of vegetables.

**Number of Servings:** 8
**Serving Size:** 13 oz. (369 g)
**Total Yield:** 6 lb., 12 oz. (3.1 kg)
**Food Balance:** Sweet/spicy
**Wine Style:** Soft and fruity blush wines, Gewürztraminer, or Pinot Noir
**Example:** Meridian Vineyards Pinot Noir

**Cooking Method:** Braise

| INGREDIENTS | WEIGHT | | VOLUME | |
| --- | --- | --- | --- | --- |
| | U.S. | METRIC | U.S. | METRIC |
| chicken, whole | 3 lb., 8 oz. | 1.6 kg | 1 each | |
| or | | | | |
| bone-in chicken breasts | 2 lb., 8 oz. | 1.1 kg | 2 whole | |
| oil | | 28 g | 2 tablespoons | 30 mL |
| onions, diced | 7 oz. | 199 g | 1 large | |
| canned plum tomatoes | 4 oz. | 114 g | 1/2 cup | 120 mL |
| tomato paste | 1 1/2 oz. | 43 g | 2 tablespoons | 30 mL |
| water, boiling | | 794 g | 3 1/2 cups | 840 mL |
| salt | | | 1/2 teaspoon | 3 mL |
| peanut butter | 4 3/4 oz. | 135 g | 1/2 cup | 120 mL |
| sweet potatoes, peeled and cut into 1-inch (2.5-cm) cubes | 14 oz. | 397 g | 1 large | |
| turnips, cut into 1-inch (2.5-cm) cubes | 8 oz. | 227 g | 2 each | |
| carrots, peeled and cut into 1-inch (2.5-cm) pieces | 5 oz. | 142 g | 2 each | |
| cabbage, cored and chopped into 1 1/2- to 2-inch (4- to 5-cm) pieces | 14 oz. | 397 g | 1/2 small head | |
| green bell pepper, diced | 8 1/2 oz. | 241 g | 1 large | |
| chili pepper, serano or cayenne, minced | 1/4 oz. | 8 g or to taste | 1 each or to taste | |
| okra, sliced | 4 oz. | 114 g | 1 cup | 240 mL |

**TWIST ON THE CLASSIC**

Prepare *Mafe* with strips of boneless chicken breasts and serve it in a puff pastry shell. Substitute chicken stock for the water and remove the chicken from the pan before adding tomatoes. Add the chicken strips back to dish with the okra.

1. Cut chicken into small pieces. If using only breasts, cut each half breast in half. Wash chicken well, pat dry.
2. Heat oil in pot over medium-high heat, add chicken, sauté until browned. Add half the onion, stir, cook until golden brown. Drain fat.
3. Chop tomatoes into chunks, add to chicken. In bowl, thin tomato paste in boiling water, add to pot. Add salt.
4. Thin peanut butter with some of liquid from pot, then stir it in gradually, reduce heat, simmer for half an hour.
5. Add sweet potatoes, cook 5 minutes.
6. Add turnips, cook another 5 minutes.
7. Add carrots, cook another 5 minutes.
8. Add cabbage, cook another 5 minutes.
9. Add green pepper, cook another 5 minutes.
10. Grind remaining onion and chili pepper in food processor fitted with knife blade. Add to pot.
11. Add okra, let cook 5 to 10 minutes, until chicken and all vegetables are tender.
12. Correct seasonings. Serve over rice or other grain.

# CHICKEN AND APRICOT TAGINE (MOROCCO)

Travellinglight/iStockphoto/Getty Images

**Note:** The smaller amount of cayenne in this recipe makes the dish fairly hot, so add more after tasting it. This recipe may be prepared with lamb, chicken, or a combination. Lamb requires a longer cooking time by about 45 minutes to 1 hour.

**Number of Servings:** 8  
**Serving Size:** 1/4 chicken  
**Total Yield:** 6 lb., 14 oz. (3.1 kg)  
**Food Balance:** Spicy/sweet  
**Wine Style:** Soft and fruity white or red low-tannin/low-oaked reds  
**Example:** Beringer Founders' Estate Merlot

**Cooking Method:** Braise

| INGREDIENTS | WEIGHT | | VOLUME | |
|---|---|---|---|---|
| | U.S. | METRIC | U.S. | METRIC |
| dried apricots | 12 oz. | 340 g | 2 cups | 480 mL |
| olive oil | | 15 g | 1 tablespoon | 15 mL |
| chicken, cut into quarters or bone-in breasts or leg quarters | 4 to 5 lb. | 1.8 to 2.3 kg | 2 each whole or 8 pieces | |
| garlic, smashed and minced | 1/2 oz. | 15 g | 4 cloves | |
| ground turmeric or saffron threads | | | 1 teaspoon | 5 mL |
| ground coriander | | | 1 teaspoon | 5 mL |
| ground cumin | | | 1 teaspoon | 5 mL |
| ground ginger | | | 1/2 teaspoon | 3 mL |
| salt | 1/4 oz. | 8 g | 1 teaspoon | 5 mL |
| pepper | | | 1 teaspoon | 5 mL |
| ground cayenne | | | 1/2 to 2 teaspoons | 3 to 10 mL |
| *or* | | | | |
| hot chili peppers of choice | | | 2 to 4 each | |
| onions, finely sliced | 1 lb., 4 oz. | 567 g | 4 medium to large | |
| fresh lemon juice | | 86 g | 2 lemons or 1/4 cup + 2 tablespoons | 90 mL |

1. Soak apricots in enough water to cover apricots for several hours or overnight.
2. Heat oil in large heavy pan or braiser over medium-high heat. Add chicken, sauté until brown.
3. Stir in garlic, tumeric or saffron, coriander, cumin, ginger, salt, pepper, and cayenne or chili peppers. Cook for 2 to 3 minutes.
4. Add onions, soaking water from apricots (not apricots), and more water to just cover meat, if necessary.
5. Bring to boil, reduce heat to low, cover, simmer for 30 minutes.
6. Add apricots and lemon juice, cook 30 minutes, or until done.
7. Correct seasonings. Serve chicken and sauce on top of rice or *couscous*.

---

## TWIST ON THE CLASSIC

Besides changing the type of meat used in the *tagine*, substitute the type of dried fruit. For example, prepare the dish with dates and lamb.

By chopping the meat, the *tagine* mixture could serve as the filling for a Shepherd's Pie (*see recipe in Chapter 1, British Isles*).

# BOEREWORS (SOUTH AFRICA)

## BEEF AND PORK SAUSAGE

**Note:** This recipe is an adaptation of *boerewors*. It contains less fat, and the meat is formed into a patty and grilled. Because the recipe contains sausage, weight is lost when cooking. As a result, I am recommending a larger raw weight portion size.

**Note:** The number of servings indicated for this recipe leaves about 6 3/4 oz. (191 g) of meat. If increasing this recipe, take that into account.

**Note:** *Boerewors* hail from the Afrikaners of South Africa. *Boer* means "farmer" and *wors* means "sausage."

**Number of Servings:** 9

**Serving Size:** 1 patty: 8 oz. (227 g) raw; 5 1/2 oz. (156 g) cooked

**Total Yield:** 4 lb., 14 3/4 oz. (2.2 kg)

**Food Balance:** Balanced

**Wine Style:** Wine friendly—Try your favorite

**Example:** Château St. Jean Cabernet Sauvignon

**Cooking Method:** Grill

*Boerewors (Beef and Pork Sausage) in its traditional form*

Elzbieta Sekowska © Shutterstock

| INGREDIENTS | WEIGHT | | VOLUME | |
|---|---|---|---|---|
| | U.S. | METRIC | U.S. | METRIC |
| ground beef, preferably chuck | 3 lb. | 1.4 kg | | |
| ground pork | 1 lb., 8 oz. | 680 g | | |
| Worcestershire sauce | | 28 g | 2 tablespoons | 30 mL |
| red wine vinegar | | 86 g | 1/4 cup + 2 tablespoons | 90 mL |
| ground coriander | 1/2 oz. | 15 g | 3 tablespoons | 45 mL |
| nutmeg | | | 3/4 teaspoon | 4 mL |
| ground allspice | 1/4 oz. | 8 g | 2 1/2 teaspoons | 12 mL |
| ground cloves | | | 3/4 teaspoon | 4 mL |
| dried thyme | 1/4 oz. | 8 g | 1 1/2 teaspoons | 8 mL |
| salt | 1/2 oz. | 15 g | 1 tablespoon | 15 mL |
| pepper | 1/4 oz. | 8 g | 2 teaspoons | 10 mL |

1. Combine all ingredients together in bowl. Mix thoroughly until fluffy with spoon or by kneading.
2. Cover and refrigerate for at least 1 hour to marinate. Check seasonings: cook a small portion of meat (sauté in skillet or grill), taste, then correct sausage seasonings. Preheat grill.
3. Form into 8 oz. (227 g) patties or oblongs that are 1/2 to 3/4 inches (1.3 to 2 cm) thick. The oblong should measure 6 by 3 1/2 inches (15 by 9 cm).
4. Grill until cooked to proper internal temperature, about 3 to 5 minutes per side. Serve.

## TWIST ON THE CLASSIC

Form this meat mixture into meatballs, bake until done, and pass as hors d'oeuvres or use in a meatball sandwich.

Typical of sausages, *boerewors* were made from any spare meat or parts. The meat mixture for these sausages normally contains more fat than in this recipe. When cooks fill the casing for this sausage, they make it into one long link that is curled into concentric circles when cooked. To cook, these sausages are first boiled to thoroughly cook them and remove some of the fat, and then they are grilled or fried.

# COUSCOUS IN THE FEZ MANNER (MOROCCO)

## *COUSCOUS* WITH LAMB AND VEGETABLES

### TWIST ON THE CLASSIC

Prepare this couscous as a side dish by omitting the lamb. Sauté the onions with spices and herbs, then add the vegetables in the order given in the recipe. Add stock for the liquid. Serve the couscous with the vegetables as a side dish or vegetarian entrée.

Appearing frequently as an accompaniment to Moroccan and Tunisian dishes, *harissa* is a hot sauce made from hot chilies, garlic, caraway, cumin, olive oil, and sometimes other ingredients. Purchase it in a store selling Middle Eastern foods or prepare it from scratch.

**Note:** This couscous recipe may be changed to include any available vegetables, meat, or poultry. Just be sure to alter the cooking times and to add each ingredient at the appropriate time, so none of the ingredients is overcooked and mushy.

**Note:** If using dried chickpeas instead of canned, use half the amount of beans and soak them overnight before cooking. If there is no time to soak overnight, add washed chickpeas to boiling water, turn off heat, and allow them to sit at least an hour before cooking.

**Number of Servings:** 9
**Serving Size:** 10 oz. (284 g)
**Total Yield:** 6 lb., 3 oz. (2.8 kg)
**Food Balance:** Spicy/sweet
**Wine Style:** Light- to medium-bodied Viognier, fruity Chardonnay, Cote-du-Rhône, or Zinfandel
**Example:** Greg Norman Zinfandel

**Cooking Method:** Braise

| | WEIGHT | | VOLUME | |
|---|---|---|---|---|
| **INGREDIENTS** | **U.S.** | **METRIC** | **U.S.** | **METRIC** |
| raisins | 3 oz. | 86 g | 3/4 cup | 180 mL |
| water, boiling | as needed | | | |
| lamb shoulder, trimmed and cut into 1 1/2-inch (4-cm) cubes | 1 lb. | 454 g | | |
| onions, diced | 10 oz. | 284 g | 2 medium | |
| olive oil | | 28 g | 2 tablespoons | 30 mL |
| fresh cilantro, minced | 1/2 oz. | 15 g | 2 tablespoons | 30 mL |
| saffron or ground turmeric | | | 1/2 teaspoon | 3 mL |
| ground ginger | 1/4 oz. | 8 g | 1 teaspoon | 5 mL |
| pepper | 1/4 oz. | 8 g | 1 1/2 teaspoons | 8 mL |
| salt (omit if using salty stock) | 1/4 oz. | 8 g plus more for sprinkling eggplant | 1 teaspoon | 5 mL plus more for sprinkling eggplant |
| water or stock | as needed | | | |
| eggplant, peeled and cut into 1-inch (2.5-cm) cubes | 11 oz. | 312 g | 1 small to medium | |
| *couscous* | 1 lb. | 454 g | 2 1/2 cups | 600 mL |
| water, cold | | 454 g | 2 cups | 480 mL |
| carrots, peeled and cut into 1 1/2-inch (4-cm) strips | 12 oz. | 340 g | 4 medium | |
| turnips, peeled and cut into quarters | 12 oz. | 340 g | 3 medium | |
| zucchini, cut into quarters | 13 oz. | 369 g | 2 medium | |
| jalapeño, minced | 1/4 oz. | 8 g or to taste | 1/2 each or to taste | |
| chickpeas, cooked | 1 lb. | 454 g | one 1-lb. can | one 454-g can |
| pine nuts | 1 1/2 oz. | 43 g | 1/4 cup | 60 mL |
| *harissa* sauce, *optional* | | | | |

1. Place raisins in bowl. Cover with boiling water and let sit.

2. Place lamb, onions, 1 tablespoon (15 g or 15 mL) of oil, cilantro, saffron or turmeric, ginger, pepper, and salt in pan (in which colander can fit snugly hanging from top of pan). Gently cook over medium heat, while stirring, for 10 minutes.

3. Add enough water or stock to cover meat. If using uncooked chickpeas, add the presoaked beans to pan now. If using canned, they will be added later.

4. Bring to boil, reduce heat, cover, and simmer for 1 hour. Meanwhile, place eggplant cubes in colander and sprinkle with salt to remove excess moisture and bitterness. Let sit for at least 30 minutes in sink or place colander in larger bowl to catch liquid. Rinse well to remove excess salt. Drain well.

5. While meat is cooking, place *couscous* in large bowl, gently stir in 2 cups (454 g or 480 mL) cold water. Immediately drain and allow grains to stand for 10 to 15 minutes. Fluff with fingers to remove any lumps.

6. Add carrots and turnips. Cook for 5 minutes. Place *couscous* in colander or *couscousier*. Set colander over pot of stew to steam *couscous*. Continue cooking for 5 more minutes.

7. Lift colander briefly, add eggplant, cook and steam another 15 minutes.

8. Lift colander, add zucchini, jalapeño, and canned chickpeas (if using), cook and steam another 10 minutes. Meat and vegetables should be tender. Correct seasonings in stew.

9. Meanwhile, sauté pine nuts in remaining 1 tablespoon (15 g or 15 mL) of oil. When lightly browned, add drained raisins to pan and heat through.

10. To serve, place *couscous* in mound on platter. Remove meat and vegetables with slotted spoon and put over *couscous*. Pour half of liquid over *couscous*. Garnish with pine nuts and raisins.

11. Serve with bowl of remaining broth and *harissa* sauce.

*Sautéing meat and spices*

*Fluffing soaked couscous*

*Adding carrots and turnips*

*Colander of couscous fitted into pot, ready to cover and steam*

*Sautéing pine nuts and raisins*

*Couscous in the Fez Manner (Couscous with Lamb and Vegetables)*

# KERRIEBOONTJIES BREDIE (SOUTH AFRICA)

## CURRIED LAMB AND BEANS

**Note:** Curries reflect the Malaysian and Indian influence in South Africa.

**Number of Servings:** 13

**Serving Size:** 6 oz. (171 g)

**Total Yield:** 4 lb., 15 oz. (2.2 kg)

**Food Balance:** Protein/spicy

**Wine Style:** Fruity, low oak/tannins, Zinfandel, Châteauneuf-du-Pape, Viognier, Gewürztraminer, rosé, or soft Merlot

**Example:** Souverain Zinfandel

**Cooking Method:** Braise

| INGREDIENTS | WEIGHT U.S. | WEIGHT METRIC | VOLUME U.S. | VOLUME METRIC |
|---|---|---|---|---|
| onions, thinly sliced | 1 lb., 12 oz. | 794 g | 6 medium | |
| oil | | 43 g | 3 tablespoons | 45 mL |
| lamb, ribs or shoulder, trimmed of fat and cut into pieces | 4 lb. | 1.8 kg | | |
| salt | 1/4 oz. | 8 g | 1 teaspoon | 5 mL |
| pepper | | | 1/2 teaspoon | 3 mL |
| curry powder | 1/4 oz. | 8 g | 2 teaspoons | 10 mL |
| jalapeño pepper, minced | 1/4 oz. | 8 g or to taste | 1/2 pepper or to taste | |
| garlic, smashed and minced | 1/2 oz. | 15 g | 4 cloves | |
| black-eyed peas, cooked and drained | 4 lb. | 1.8 kg | four 1-lb. cans | four 454-g cans |
| fresh lemon juice | as needed | | | |

**Accompaniment:**

hot rice cooked

1. Brown onion in oil until golden over medium-high heat.
2. Add lamb, salt, and pepper. Sauté until meat begins to lose red color.
3. Cover and simmer until meat is about half-cooked, about 45 minutes to 1 hour. (Add a little water if necessary.)
4. Add curry powder, jalapeño, and garlic. Cook until meat is almost tender, about 30 to 45 minutes.
5. Add beans, continue to simmer until meat is tender and flavors are blended. Correct seasonings.
6. Drizzle with lemon juice before serving. Accompany with rice.

# MISIR WAT (ETHIOPIA)

## LENTIL STEW

**Number of Servings:** 14
**Cooking Method:** Sauté, boil
**Serving Size:** 8 oz. (227 g) or depends on other entrées served with it
**Total Yield:** 7 lb., 1 oz. (3.2 kg)
**Wine Style:** Cool climate dry white wine with high minerality. Possible grape varietals are Riesling, Gruner Veltliner and Sauvignon Blanc.
**Example:** Riesling "Hollerin" 2009, Alzinger (Wachau/Austria)

Typically, Ethiopians serve their entrées on top of *injera* (a pancake-like flatbread). The different foods are placed in mounds on top of the *injera*, and all of the diners share the meal.

| INGREDIENTS | WEIGHT U.S. | WEIGHT METRIC | VOLUME U.S. | VOLUME METRIC |
|---|---|---|---|---|
| ginger, peeled, small dice | 1 oz. | 28 g | 2-inch (5-cm) piece | |
| garlic, peeled | 1 oz. | 28 g | 6 cloves | |
| onion, roughly chopped | 2 lb. | 908 g | 4 large | |
| oil | | 114 g | 1/2 cup | 120 mL |
| *berberé* recipe follows | 1 oz. or to taste | 28 g or to taste | 1/4 cup + 2 tablespoons or to taste | 90 mL or to taste |
| red lentils | 1 lb., 5 oz. | 596 g | 3 cups | 720 mL |
| water | | | 2 quarts | 1.9 L |
| salt | 1/2 oz. | 15 g | 2 teaspoons | 10 mL |

1. With food processor fitted with knife blade running, drop ginger and garlic through feed tube. Pulse and scrape down sides. Turn processor on and add onion. Process until thick paste.

2. Heat oil in large pan over medium heat. Add *berberé*, sauté until fragrant, about 1 minute. Add onion paste, sauté another 5 to 10 minutes with frequent stirring. Do not let it burn.

3. Add lentils and 1 quart, 2 cups (1.4 L) water, bring to boil. Reduce heat, stir occasionally, and simmer for 30 to 40 minutes until lentils are soft and mixture is thick. Add more water, if needed. Add salt after cooking for about 25 minutes.

4. Correct seasonings. Serve with *injera* or other flat bread.

© paul-brighton

# BERBERÉ (ETHIOPIA)

## SPICE BLEND

**Cooking Method:** Dry sauté
**Total Yield:** 2 1/4 oz. (64 g) or 1/3 cup + 2 tablespoons (79 mL + 30 mL)

| | WEIGHT | | VOLUME | |
|---|---|---|---|---|
| *INGREDIENTS* | *U.S.* | *METRIC* | *U.S.* | *METRIC* |
| coriander seeds | 1/4 oz. | 8 g | 2 teaspoons | 10 mL |
| cardamom seeds | 1/4 oz. | 8 g | 2 teaspoons | 10 mL |
| fenugreek seeds | 1/4 oz. | 8 g | 1 teaspoon | 5 mL |
| allspice seeds | | | 1/4 teaspoon | 2 mL |
| peppercorns, whole | | | 1/2 teaspoon | 3 mL |
| chili powder, mild | 1/2 oz. | 15 g | 2 tablespoons | 30 mL |
| paprika | 3/4 oz. | 22 g | 3 tablespoons | 45 mL |
| cayenne, ground | | | 1 teaspoon | 5 mL |
| ginger, ground | | | 1 teaspoon | 5 mL |
| nutmeg | | | 1/4 teaspoon | 2 mL |
| cloves, ground | | | 1/8 teaspoon | 1 mL |
| salt | 1/4 oz. | 8 g | 1 teaspoon | 5 mL |

1. Place coriander, cardamom, fenugreek, allspice, and peppercorns in skillet over medium heat. Stirring frequently, sauté for a few minutes until very fragrant and beginning to brown.

2. Allow mixture to cool, transfer to spice grinder or mortar and pestle. Process until ground.

3. Mix all other ingredients with coriander mixture in jar. Cover tightly and store until needed. For long storage, refrigerate or freeze spice mixture to preserve freshness.

© Serghei Velusceac

## SPINACH STEW (CENTRAL AFRICA)

**Note:** In many parts of Africa, cooks must create an entrée from any available food ingredients.

**Number of Servings:** 11

**Serving Size:** 7 oz. (199 g)

**Total Yield:** 5 lb., 3 oz. (2.4 kg)

**Food Balance:** Sweet/spicy

**Wine Style:** Low-oaked whites and soft reds

**Example:** Black Opal Shiraz

**Cooking Method:** Braise

**TWIST ON THE CLASSIC**

Use this spinach stew as the base for a grilled steak.

| | WEIGHT | | VOLUME | |
|---|---|---|---|---|
| INGREDIENTS | U.S. | METRIC | U.S. | METRIC |
| oil | | 28 g | 2 tablespoons | 30 mL |
| onions, diced | 1 lb., 2 oz. | 511 g | 4 medium | |
| fresh tomatoes, peeled and chopped | 1 lb., 8 oz. | 680 g | 4 each | |
| green bell pepper, diced | 12 oz. | 340 g | 2 each | |
| fresh spinach, washed and chopped | 4 lb. | 1.8 kg | | |
| salt | 1/2 oz. | 15 g | 2 teaspoons | 10 mL |
| hot chili peppers, minced | | | 1 to 4 fresh | |
| or | | | | |
| red pepper flakes | | | 1 to 2 tablespoons | 15 to 30 mL |
| peanut butter | 9 1/2 oz. | 270 g | 1 cup | 240 mL |
| water | | 15 to 28 g | 1 to 2 tablespoons | 15 to 30 mL |

1. Heat oil in pan over medium heat, add onions, and sauté until tender but not brown.
2. Add tomatoes and bell peppers, sauté 1 or 2 minutes.
3. Add spinach, salt, and chili peppers or red pepper flakes. Cover and simmer about 5 minutes.
4. Mix peanut butter with 1 or 2 tablespoons (15 to 28 g or 15 to 30 mL) of water to make smooth paste. Add to spinach, stir well.
5. Stirring frequently, continue cooking on low heat for about 10 minutes.
6. Correct seasonings. Serve with rice or another starch.

# CURRIED CORN (KENYA)

**Number of Servings:** 9
**Serving Size:** 4 oz. (114 g)
**Total Yield:** 2 lb., 7 oz. (1.1 kg)

**Cooking Method:** Boil

© Eva Gruendemann

| | WEIGHT | | VOLUME | |
|---|---|---|---|---|
| INGREDIENTS | U.S. | METRIC | U.S. | METRIC |
| oil | | 15 g | 1 tablespoon | 15 mL |
| onion, medium dice | 5 oz. | 142 g | 1 medium | |
| garlic, smashed and minced | | | 1 clove | |
| hot Madras curry powder | | | 1/2 to 1 teaspoon | 3 to 5 mL, to taste |
| corn, frozen kernels or fresh and cut from cob | 1 lb., 7 1/2 oz. | 667 g | 5 cups | 1.2 L |
| coconut milk | | 227 g | 1 cup | 240 mL |
| cornstarch | | | 1/2 teaspoon | 3 mL |
| fresh tomatoes, peeled, seeded, and diced | 7 oz. | 199 g | 2 medium | |
| salt | | | 1/2 teaspoon | 3 mL |
| pepper | | | 1/4 teaspoon | 2 mL |

1. Heat oil in pan over medium-high heat until hot, add onion and garlic, cook, stirring occasionally, until lightly browned.
2. Add curry powder, stirring to coat well.
3. Add corn, continue cooking a few minutes. Meanwhile, combine coconut milk and cornstarch in bowl.
4. Add coconut milk–cornstarch mixture and tomatoes, salt, and pepper to corn, stir well.
5. Lower heat and cook, stirring occasionally, for 7 minutes, or until most of coconut milk is absorbed and corn is tender.
6. Correct seasonings. Serve.

# GREEN PEAS AND YAMS (WEST AFRICA)

**Note:** Like many recipes from this part of Africa, the original recipe contains a large amount of oil.

**Number of Servings:** 12
**Serving Size:** 4 oz. (114 g)
**Total Yield:** 3 lb., 2 1/4 oz. (1.4 kg)

**Cooking Method:** Boil, sauté

| | WEIGHT | | VOLUME | |
|---|---|---|---|---|
| INGREDIENTS | U.S. | METRIC | U.S. | METRIC |
| yams, peeled, large dice | 1 lb., 5 1/4 oz. | 603 g | 4 small | |
| water | as needed | | | |
| oil | | 15 g | 1 tablespoon | 15 mL |
| onion, medium diced | 5 oz. | 142 g | 1 medium | |
| hot pepper, variety of choice, ribs and seeds removed, if desired, and minced | 3/4 oz. | 22 g or to taste | 1 each or to taste | |
| salt | 1/4 oz. | 8 g | 1 teaspoon | 5 mL |
| tomato paste | 1 1/4 oz. | 36 g | 2 tablespoons | 30 mL |
| green peas, fresh or frozen | 1 lb. | 454 g | | |

1. Place yams in saucepan, cover with water. Bring to boil, lower heat to medium, and cook until yams are almost tender. Drain and set aside until needed.

2. Heat oil in large skillet or saucepan over medium-high heat. Add onion, sauté about 3 or 4 minutes. Add hot pepper, sauté another 2 minutes.

3. Add salt and tomato paste and continue cooking about 5 minutes, stiring constantly. If necessary to prevent sticking, add a little water, only as needed. *At this point, this mixture can be set aside until time of service.*

4. Add cooked yams and peas (if frozen). If using fresh peas, add a few minutes before yams to allow them a longer cooking time. Add water, as needed, to prevent sticking.

5. Cook until peas and yams are hot. Correct seasonings. Serve.

## TATALE (GHANA)

### CORNCAKES WITH PLANTAIN

**Note:** Add cayenne to make these as hot as desired. The ripe plantain adds a sweetness that balances the spice.

**Number of Servings:** 15  
**Serving Size:** 1 corncake with 1 1/2 oz. (43 g) raw batter  
**Total Yield:** 1 lb., 7 oz. (653 g)

**Cooking Method:** Fry

| INGREDIENTS | WEIGHT | | VOLUME | |
|---|---|---|---|---|
| | U.S. | METRIC | U.S. | METRIC |
| onion, cut into quarters | 5 oz. | 142 g | 1 medium | |
| very ripe plantain, (yellow with black spots), peeled and cut into chunks | 11 1/2 oz. | 326 g | 2 each | |
| cornmeal | 7 oz. | 199 g | 1 cup | 240 mL |
| ground cayenne | | | 1/4 to 1/2 teaspoon | 2 to 3 mL |
| ground ginger | 1/4 oz. | 8 g | 1 teaspoon | 5 mL |
| salt | | | 1/2 teaspoon | 3 mL |
| oil, as needed for frying | | | | |

1. Fit food processor with knife blade. With machine running, drop onion through feed tube. Pulse until finely chopped, stopping to scrape down sides of bowl.

2. With machine running, drop plantain through feed tube. Pulse and scrape down sides of bowl until puréed.

3. Mix cornmeal, cayenne, ginger, and salt together in bowl. Add to plantain mixture. Pulse to combine.

4. Heat oil in skillet over medium-high heat. Form 1 1/2 oz. (43 g) of batter into 2-inch (5-cm) ball. Flatten ball into flat corncake, about 3/8 inch (1 cm) thick.

5. Fry until golden on both sides. Drain on absorbent paper. Serve warm.

Olinchuk © Shutterstock

# YEMARINA YEWOTET DABO (ETHIOPIA)
## HONEY SPICE BREAD

**Serving Size:** 2 loaves

**Total Yield:** 4 lb., 3 1/2 oz. (1.9 kg) dough

**Cooking Method:** Bake

Typically, this bread is served at breakfast with honey and butter or a chickpea spread.

| INGREDIENTS | WEIGHT U.S. | WEIGHT METRIC | VOLUME U.S. | VOLUME METRIC |
|---|---|---|---|---|
| water, lukewarm | | 57 g | 1/4 cup | 60 mL |
| yeast | 1/2 oz. | 15 g | 1 1/2 tablespoons | 23 mL |
| honey | 9 oz. | 256 g | 3/4 cup | 180 mL |
| water | | 454 g | 2 cups | 480 mL |
| oil or melted butter | 2 oz. | 57 g | 1/4 cup | 60 mL |
| egg | 1 3/4 oz. | 50 g | 1 each | |
| coriander, ground | 1/4 oz. | 8 g | 1 tablespoon | 15 mL |
| cinnamon | 1/4 oz. | 8 g | 1 teaspoon | 5 mL |
| cloves, ground | | | 1/4 teaspoon | 2 mL |
| flour, all purpose | 3 lb., 3 oz., + as needed | 1.4 kg + as needed | 7 cups + as needed | 1.7 L + as needed |
| salt | 1/2 oz. | 15 g | 2 teaspoons | 10 mL |

1. Place lukewarm water (57 g, 1/4 cup, or 60 mL) in a small nonreactive bowl. Add yeast and stir to mix. Allow to sit until foamy, about 5 minutes.

2. Meanwhile, whisk honey, water (454 g, 2 cups, or 480 mL), oil, egg, coriander, cinnamon, and cloves in a large nonreactive bowl.

3. Add half the flour, mix well. Stir in salt and more flour until it forms soft dough that is firm enough to knead. Add just enough flour, as needed, to keep dough from sticking. Knead for 5 to 7 minutes, until smooth and elastic. Return to bowl, cover, rise until doubled, about 1 to 1 1/2 hours.

4. Meanwhile, pan spray 2 loaf pans or sheet pan (if making braid or round loaves). Position oven rack in center of oven. Preheat oven to 350 degrees (180°C).

5. When doubled, punch down dough and knead briefly. Form into two loaves, make one large braid, or one or two round loaves. For round loaves, either bake in pan-sprayed round pans or form rounds and place on prepared sheet pan.

6. Cover, allow to rise until doubled, about 20 to 30 minutes.

7. Bake for about 50 to 60 minutes or until done. Loaf will be lightly brown on top and bottom and sound hollow when tapped.

8. Cool on rack. Serve warm or at room temperature with butter and honey. Store tightly wrapped.

© pawel70

# BASBOUSA (EGYPT)

## SEMOLINA CAKE

**Note:** Allow time to refrigerate the cake overnight. In fact, this cake improves with age and seems more moist even a couple of days after baking.

**Number of Servings:** 13  
**Serving Size:** 3 squares  
**Total Yield:** One 9- by 13-inch (23- by 33-cm) cake, cut into 40 pieces

**Cooking Method:** Bake

Hohenhaus/iStockphoto/Getty Images

| INGREDIENTS | WEIGHT | | VOLUME | |
|---|---|---|---|---|
| | **U.S.** | **METRIC** | **U.S.** | **METRIC** |
| **Syrup:** | | | | |
| whole lemon (for zest and juice) | 4 3/4 oz. | 135 g | 1 each | |
| sugar | 11 3/4 oz. | 334 g | 1 1/2 cups | 360 mL |
| water | | 340 g | 1 1/2 cups | 360 mL |
| honey | 3/4 oz. | 22 g | 1 tablespoon | 15 mL |
| **Cake:** | | | | |
| semolina | 13 oz. | 369 g | 2 cups | 480 mL |
| baking powder | 1/4 oz. | 8 g | 1 teaspoon | 5 mL |
| baking soda | | | 1/2 teaspoon | 3 mL |
| salt | | | 1/2 teaspoon | 3 mL |
| almonds, ground | 1 oz. | 28 g | 1/3 cup | 80 mL |
| butter, softened | 4 oz. | 114 g | 8 tablespoons (1 stick) | 120 mL |
| sugar | 5 1/2 oz. | 156 g | 3/4 cup | 180 mL |
| eggs | 3 1/2 oz. | 104 g | 2 each | |
| plain yogurt | 6 1/4 oz. | 179 g | 3/4 cup | 180 mL |

**Garnish:**  
almond slices, toasted  
candied lemon peel, reserved  
   from syrup

## TWIST ON THE CLASSIC

Place several small pieces of *basbousa* on a bed of crème anglaise and garnish with raspberry purée and fresh raspberries.

## SYRUP:

1. Using potato peeler, remove zest from lemon, being careful not to remove white pith (which is bitter). Set zest aside. Juice lemon, set juice aside until needed.
2. Place sugar, water, and lemon zest in nonreactive saucepan. Bring to full boil, reduce heat, and simmer a minute or two.
3. Add lemon juice and honey. Simmer 5 minutes. Remove from heat, cool completely.

## CAKE:

1. Sift semolina, baking powder, baking soda, and salt into bowl. Add ground almonds. Set aside until needed.
2. Pan-spray 9- by 13-inch (23- by 33-cm) pan. Position oven rack in center of oven. Preheat oven to 350 degrees (180°C).
3. In mixer fitted with wire beater, if available, beat butter and sugar until light and fluffy. Add eggs, one at a time, beating well after each one. Scrape sides of bowl as needed.
4. Add semolina mixture alternately with yogurt. Add one-third of semolina mixture, mix just to combine. Add one-half of yogurt, mix just to combine. Add half of remaining semolina mixture, mix just to combine. Add remaining yogurt, mix just to combine. Add remaining semolina, mix just to combine.
5. Transfer the thick batter into prepared pan. Smooth top. Bake about 20 minutes, until point of knife inserted in cake comes out clean. Remove from oven.

## ASSEMBLY:

1. Immediately, pour cooled syrup evenly over hot cake. If desired, reserve lemon peel from syrup for garnish. Cut lemon peel into very thin (1/16-inch, 1.5-mm) strips, set aside to dry.

2. Let cake sit a few minutes, then cut into small squares or diamonds. Five cuts on the short side and 8 cuts on the long side yields 40 small pieces. Cutting diamonds yields fewer pieces. Cool cake completely.

3. Cover and refrigerate overnight. If desired, decorate each piece with sliced almonds and candied lemon zest. Serve three small pieces accompanied by fresh fruit.

---

# BEIGNETS DE BANANES (WEST AFRICA)

## BANANA FRITTERS

**Note:** Start the batter the day before using.

**Note:** Other fruits also work well in this recipe.

**Number of Servings:** 8

**Cooking Method:** Deep-fry

**Total Yield:** 9 1/2 oz. batter (270 g)

| INGREDIENTS | WEIGHT | | VOLUME | |
|---|---|---|---|---|
| | U.S. | METRIC | U.S. | METRIC |
| **Batter:** | | | | |
| flour, sifted | 3 oz. | 86 g | 3/4 cup | 180 mL |
| sugar | 1 oz. | 28 g | 2 tablespoons | 30 mL |
| salt | | | dash | |
| eggs | 3 1/2 oz. | 104 g | 2 each | |
| water | | 28 g | 2 tablespoons | 30 mL |
| milk | | 28 g | 2 tablespoons | 30 mL |
| lemon zest, grated | | | 1/4 teaspoon | 2 mL |
| nutmeg | | | few gratings | |
| peanut oil for deep frying | | | | |
| firm, ripe bananas | 1 lb., 8 oz. | 680 g | 4 large | |

**Garnish:**

confectioner's sugar for dusting

## BATTER:

1. Sift flour, sugar, and salt into bowl. Set aside.
2. Mix eggs, water, milk, lemon zest, and nutmeg in another bowl. Mix thoroughly.
3. Add flour mixture to egg mixture. Whisk well.
4. Cover bowl and refrigerate for one day.

## COOKING:

1. Heat 1 1/2 inches (4 cm) of oil to 375 degrees (190°C) in pan or deep fryer.
2. Peel bananas and cut crosswise into 1-inch (2.5-cm) pieces.
3. Dip pieces into batter, fry until golden brown on each side.
4. Drain on absorbent paper.
5. Serve warm, sprinkled with sifted confectioner's sugar.

---

### TWIST ON THE CLASSIC

For a modern version, try one of these variations using any combination of peanut, coconut, and pineapple in the sauce and ice cream.

- Place the banana fritters on top of chocolate peanut sauce and accompany them with coconut ice cream.
- Place the banana fritters on top of chocolate sauce and accompany them with coconut ice cream. Decorate plate with shelled peanuts.
- Place the banana fritters on top of a coconut, pineapple, or coconut-pineapple sauce and accompany them with chocolate peanut butter ice cream.

# Lebanon, Jordan, Iraq, Saudi Arabia, Syria, Iran, Greece, and Turkey

## >> LEARNING OBJECTIVES

By the end of this chapter, you will be able to:

- Identify food ingredients and dishes frequently served in the Middle Eastern countries
- Explain how the spice route in the 1400s impacted the cuisine of the Middle East
- Explain how religions influenced the cuisine of the Middle East
- Describe the significance of the desert for the Middle Eastern cuisine
- Prepare a variety of Middle Eastern dishes

This section on the Middle East includes the countries of Iran, Iraq, Syria, Lebanon, Saudi Arabia, and Jordan, which are traditionally thought of as the Middle East, as well as Greece and Turkey. Although Greece lies in Europe and Turkey straddles southwestern Asia and southeastern Europe, their cuisines contain so many similarities to those of the Middle East that they are discussed in this chapter. Even though Israel is located within the Middle East, it is covered in a separate chapter because the culinary history and culinary traits of that country differ in many ways from those of the rest of the Middle East.

## >> HISTORY

Evidence indicates that around 100,000 B.C. Stone Age man lived near the Jordan River. About 9,000 years ago, man first learned to farm and raise livestock in Mesopotamia, which is located in the area known as the Middle East. Olive trees were cultivated in this area by 4000 B.C. Obviously, a very long culinary history exists in this part of the world. Because of the extensive travel that has occurred between and throughout the Middle Eastern countries, the nations influenced each other's cuisines greatly. As a result, the culinary differences between these countries often seem more like the regional variations found within other countries.

### EARLY INFLUENCES

> In Greek, Mesopotamia means "between the rivers."

Creating one of the world's earliest civilizations (from about 5000 B.C. to 1000 B.C), Sumerians flourished in Mesopotamia on the fertile land between the Euphrates and Tigris rivers, in what is now Iraq. These people were the first to farm throughout the year, which enabled them to create settlements instead of living a nomadic life. As a result, they are credited with building the first cities, known as city-states because they were walled cities, each with its own ruler. Around 3500 B.C., the Sumerians invented the first writing system.

In the 1400s, the Middle East was situated on the "spice route" through Europe, the Far East, and central Africa. This location affected their culinary history in two ways: the introduction of many foods from other areas and the opportunity to regularly obtain a variety of foods from Asia, including citrus fruits, almonds, rice, new fruits and vegetables, sugar, and many spices. From India, they adopted rice, eggplant, and numerous spices, including saffron. While the New World provided Middle Easterners with tomatoes and sweet peppers, they learned about *couscous* from Morocco in northern Africa.

Because the land is so arid throughout much of the Middle East, nomads roamed the area moving their herds of sheep and goats in search of the sparse grasses. This greatly influenced the types of foods eaten as well as the cooking techniques used. Basically, any available food ingredients were cooked over an open fire in the desert.

### OTTOMAN EMPIRE

> Unlike most conquering powers, the Ottomans did not try to culturally subjugate the people they ruled. Rather, they took parts of the culture and cuisine of those they conquered and assimilated those into their own. They adopted spices from Asia, olives from the Greeks, dates from Egyptians, and more. In summary, they created a melting pot of the many cuisines. The Ottoman Empire did not have one common language; each region kept its own. Groups of people coexisted peacefully. For example Jews, Christians, and Muslims kept their own faith and lived as neighbors.

Lasting from 1299 to 1923, the Ottoman Empire ranks as one of the most widespread and longest-lived empires in history. Beginning in Turkey, the Ottomans gained control of southeastern Europe, the Middle East, and northern Africa at the peak of their rule. Their vast empire stretched from Baghdad to Tripoli and from Cairo to Budapest.

Culinary issues were very important during the Ottoman Empire. Undoubtedly, the Ottomans changed many cuisines in the lands they ruled by introducing people to dishes and foods from other regions and countries. According to reports, 1,300 people worked in the palace kitchen preparing food for the sultan during the 1600s! Some claim they prepared banquets with as many as 130 courses.

### RELIGIOUS INFLUENCES

Three major religions, Islam, Christianity, and Judaism, began in the Middle East. Although 90 percent of the inhabitants in this area are Muslim (Islamic), much religious strife continues here. Religion heavily influenced the cuisines in this part of the world. Forbidden in both the religions of Islam and Judaism, pork is rarely served in most of the Middle Eastern countries and Turkey. Lamb remains the most often consumed meat in this part of the world, both because sheep adapt well to nomadic herding and because they survive better than cattle in the barren, arid areas that exist here. In addition, Muslims are forbidden the consumption of alcohol, so drinking and cooking with alcohol are uncommon.

## GREECE

Historians say western civilization began in Greece 2,500 years ago. Even though Greece lies in Europe, their foods and methods of preparation were so influenced by the cuisines to the east that many consider the cuisine of Greece to be Middle Eastern. About 7000 B.C., inhabitants from the east entered Greece, bringing with them sheep and new foods such as lamb, peas, and beans. Later, people from the north moved into Greece. Unlike in most countries in the Middle East, Christianity is the most prevalent religion in Greece, where Catholicism and the Greek Orthodox religion reign. As a result, pork and alcoholic beverages are consumed here, which, again, is not true of most of the Middle East.

The tradition of chefs wearing a tall white hat comes from the Greeks during the Middle Ages. Many of the fine cooks of that time were scholars who decided to cook in the Orthodox monasteries. To distinguish themselves from the other scholars, who wore tall black hats, the cooks donned a tall white hat, and this tradition still exists today.

## INFLUENCES FROM THE NEW WORLD

In the 1700s and 1800s, foods like peppers, tomatoes, string beans, pumpkins, sweet potatoes, and white potatoes from the New World were introduced to the Middle East by Europeans. These foods penetrated the Middle Eastern cuisine and still play a dominant role.

## >> TOPOGRAPHY

Since the Middle East lies between three continents, Asia, Africa, and Europe, this area was important for travel between the continents. As a result, a wide range of food products were transported through the Middle East, and residents obtained many foods, herbs, and spices not indigenous there.

## WATER AND WATERWAYS

The arid Middle East is composed of huge areas of sand, rocky mountains, sparsely vegetated hills, and high plateaus. Water was and is the key to existence throughout these countries. Although the majority of the land remains expansive desert, the areas that have sufficient rainfall, border rivers or the sea, or have installed irrigation systems produce large, flavorful fruits and vegetables.

The Mediterranean Sea lies to the west of Lebanon, and the Lebanese Mountains dominate much of the interior of the country. In Syria, the area around Damascus and the Barada River in the southwest contains very fertile land. The rest of the country consists of desert.

Two major rivers, the Tigris and the Euphrates, run from Turkey through Syria and Iraq to the Persian Gulf. Land around these rivers as well as other small rivers in Syria, Iran, and Lebanon is very lush and contains rich soil, and is known as the "Fertile Crescent." The Persian Gulf borders Iran, Iraq, and Saudi Arabia. The Caspian Sea lies on

*Muslim dietary laws come from the Koran. Those laws forbid the following:*

- *consumption of pig*
- *eating animals killed for any reason other than being slaughtered for food*
- *consuming alcoholic or fermented liquids*

> **Ingredients and Foods Commonly Used throughout the Cuisines of the Middle East Include**
>
> - lamb and mutton
> - yogurt
> - chickpeas and lentils
> - bread, wheat, and wheat products
> - rice
> - eggplant, spinach, and okra
> - olives and olive oil
> - garlic
> - lemon
>
> - many herbs and spices, including mint, dill, flat-leaf parsley, cilantro, hot red peppers, cinnamon, paprika, cumin, coriander, ginger, allspice, and saffron
> - figs and dates
> - honey
> - pine nuts

the northern border of Iran. Greece, Turkey, Syria, Lebanon, Israel, and Egypt border the Mediterranean Sea. Other than the regions where the rivers flow, desert, mountains, salt lakes, and high plateaus compose most of Iran.

## TURKEY

Lying between two continents, Turkey straddles southeastern Europe and southwestern Asia. It is a mountainous peninsula situated between Greece and Syria. The Mediterranean Sea lies to the south and west, and the Black Sea is to the north.

Turkey's diverse climate and topography helped mold its culinary profile. Long, cold winters dominate the eastern section of Turkey. Far from the sea and close to the Middle East, residents eat plenty of meat, grains, and dairy, and have a fondness for honey. Its deserts and hot climate define southeastern Turkey. The people in this region often consume spicy foods and *kebobs*. Lying near the Mediterranean Sea and Greece, western Turkey experiences a temperate climate. In addition to olive oil, plenty of fish and seafood is available here. A fertile plain runs along the northwestern coast. For those Turks living near the more than 5,000 miles of coast, fish and seafood play a significant role in their diet.

*Many believe Mount Ararat in eastern Turkey was the landing place of Noah's Ark.*

## GREECE

Thick forests make up the northern part of Greece, while the south is arid and quite dry. Hundreds of Greek islands dot the Mediterranean Sea. In fact, no land in Greece lies more than 85 miles from a sea.

## >> COOKING METHODS

Basically, the most common cooking methods come from the time when the nomads roamed the deserts and cooked over an open fire. Grilling tops the list of cooking methods. Meats are often roasted or cooked on a spit over a fire as they were in ancient times. Larger, tender meats such as a whole young lamb appear grilled or cooked over a fire in this manner. Smaller cubes of meat are often placed on a skewer, *shish kebob,* and grilled over fire. Credit for inventing *shish kebob* goes to Turkish warriors who skewered chunks of mutton on their swords and held it over the campfire. Frequently, ovals of ground meat are placed on a skewer and grilled.

Stewing or braising the smaller cuts of meat is prevalent throughout the Middle East. Placing any available ingredients in a pot and cooking that over the fire also hails from the days of the nomads traveling the desert with their herds of sheep and/or goats.

As in other hot climates, people in the Middle East needed to preserve their harvest in the days before refrigeration. In addition to pickling all sorts of vegetables, they pickled cheeses and fruits, as well as preparing jams and preserves.

*Kebobs*
©VP

*Ground meat kebobs*
©Joe Gough

## >> REGIONS

Because borders of the countries lying within the Fertile Crescent (including Syria, Jordan, Kuwait, Iraq, Israel, and the southwestern section of Iran) often changed, there is great similarity in dishes throughout much of the Middle East. On the other hand, distinct and subtle differences exist in the various countries and regions.

### LEBANON, JORDAN, SYRIA, AND TURKEY

Lebanon, Jordan, Syria, and Turkey share a fondness for olive oil, salads, and flavoring with garlic, cilantro, mint, dill, and parsley. Residents in these countries often season meat with pungent spices like allspice, cinnamon, and cloves.

There are many differences, too. Using lots of red pepper, they prepare spicy foods in Syria. Cooks in Jordan often use cumin. Besides liking sauces containing walnuts, hazelnuts, or almonds, the Turks enjoy pilafs and desserts. Both pilafs and desserts (other than the compote or fresh fruit commonly served for dessert) hail from the time of the Ottomans.

### IRAN AND AFGHANISTAN

The cuisine of Iran does not include spicy peppers or garlic. Iranians favor saffron, mint, cilantro, parsley, tarragon, fenugreek, and turmeric. Besides adding pomegranate juice or lime to make sour dishes, Iranians often transform recipes into popular sweet-and-sour dishes by including dried fruits for the sweet component. People in Afghanistan like spicy dishes.

### NUTS

Throughout the Middle East, nuts appear frequently in both sweet and savory recipes. Walnuts and hazelnuts are the choice in Turkey, walnuts in Iran, and pine nuts in Syria and the Mediterranean regions. Pistachios and almonds remain popular throughout all of these countries.

### GREECE

Lemon and egg often show up in Greek cookery, exemplified by the famous egg and lemon soup, *avgolemono*. *Ouzo*, an anise-flavored alcoholic beverage that turns cloudy when mixed with water, is a popular Greek beverage. *Retsina*, a sharp-tasting Greek wine, is another drink frequently consumed with *mazza*, appetizers much like Spanish *tapas*.

## >> CUISINE

Throughout the Middle East, countless varieties of *mazza* (appetizers) are served. People enjoy these small portions in the evening with alcoholic drinks in Greece and throughout the rest of the Middle East accompanied by either nonalcoholic or alcoholic beverages. Some examples of *mazza* include small portions of any of the many salads, meat, chicken, fish, seafood, or vegetable dishes; marinated meats or cheeses; olives; pickles; nuts; or raw vegetables.

### GRAINS

Grains, legumes, and vegetables form the foundation of the Middle Eastern diet. Bread is truly the staff of life in the Middle East. From *pita* bread (pocket bread) to flat breads to crackers and yeast breads, every Middle Eastern meal includes some type of bread.

Early settlements developed in the lands around the Tigris and Euphrates Rivers and the Nile River. Of course, these rivers provided necessary and otherwise scarce water as well as fertile soil for agriculture.

Served throughout the Middle East, kibbe is the national dish of Lebanon.

Like ouzo, pernod and pastis are other anise-flavored alcoholic beverages that turn cloudy when mixed with water. Appearing frequently in Mediterranean countries, star anise flavors these liqueurs. Popular as aperitifs, many recipes include these anise liquors for flavoring.

Courtesy of Canola Oil @ canolainfo.org

## THE BEGINNINGS OF WHEAT

*Archaeologists discovered evidence of wheat farming in the Middle East 8,000 to 10,000 years ago. Eventually, wheat became the foundation for bread and pasta. The Etruscans made pasta, and from there it spread east to the Chinese around 3000 B.C. and then west again, to the Romans and Greeks. Although Italy is the country known for pasta, the Arabs actually introduced pasta to Sicily when they ruled there. Evidence proves that the Arabs actually dried pasta to make it easier to carry while traveling. In addition, Marco Polo returned to Italy from China in the 1200s and brought pasta with him.*

Gyros
©Faraways

*The Ottomans receive credit for introducing dishes like moussaka, stuffed vegetables, Turkish shish kebab, and a number of pastries including baklava.*

Besides being ground into flour for bread, wheat appears in other forms in the Middle Eastern diet. Cracked wheat is boiled and dried to become *bulgur*, a grain that rehydrates quickly and is used in salads, in stuffings, and as a side dish.

Rice runs a close second to wheat in popularity. In some areas of the Middle East, almost all entrées incorporate rice, and it often functions as a side dish, too. *Chelo kebah*, a dish consisting of rice, marinated lamb, spices, and yogurt, is the national dish of Iran. *Chelo kebah* comes in countless variations, depending on where it is prepared. These variations involve the type of meat used and whether vegetables are included. *Chelo*, steamed rice, and *polo*, a steamed rice casserole containing combinations of fruits, vegetables, nuts, and meats, remain two Iranian favorites. In one form or another, rice is included with meals throughout much of the Middle East and Turkey. Middle Eastern cooks prepare dry, fluffy, well-separated grains of rice, none of the sticky rice that is preferred in the Orient.

## LEGUMES

Combined with grains, legumes (beans) function as a significant source of protein throughout the Middle East. Two favorite legumes, lentils and chickpeas, appear often in a variety of dishes. Chickpeas form the base of *hummus*, a spread combining chickpeas with garlic, lemon juice, and *tahini* (sesame seed paste). Another chickpea product, *falafel*, is a spicy fritter sold by street vendors. In the Middle East, the popularity of *falafel* tucked into pita bread rivals that of the hot dog in the United States. Lentils hail from Biblical times and are cooked in many ways. A well-liked dish, *mujaddarah* is a mixture of lentils and rice.

## PROTEIN

Whether prepared as a whole piece of meat, cubed and marinated, or ground, lamb remains the most often-served meat throughout the Middle East. It is cooked in many ways. Pork is rarely served in the Middle East because Muslims are not allowed to consume it.

Ground meat in a variety of forms appears on the Middle Eastern table. Extremely popular in Syria and Lebanon, *kibbe neyya* consists of a mixture of raw ground lamb or sometimes beef mixed with onions, bulgur, and seasonings. Formed into a patty, *kibbe* is served both raw and cooked.

Greece is known for *gyros*, lamb cooked on a rotisserie then shaved into thin slices and eaten plain or in pita bread. Because no part of the animal is wasted here, organ meats, including tripe, heart, lungs, liver, brains, and sweetbreads, are widely consumed.

Cooks in the Middle East frequently prepare poultry in soups, stews, or alone as the entrée. While chicken remains the favorite, they also consume turkey and pigeon. Commonly, they stuff poultry with rice or bulgur instead of a bread stuffing.

Although most of the land is desert, the areas by the many seas and rivers have access to ample seafood. Caviar, roe, shellfish, and fish are prevalent in these areas. The Caspian Sea, which borders Iran on the north, produces sturgeon and the prized beluga caviar.

## DAIRY

Dairy products, especially cheeses and yogurt, appear commonly. Sheep, goats, and cows all provide milk in this region, but sheep and goats thrive more easily on the terrain and are used most often. *Feta*, a goat's milk cheese, is served as an appetizer with drinks, as a salad, or combined with other ingredients in a main course such as *spanakopita*, a spinach and feta mixture layered with phyllo dough. Several other strongly flavored cheeses made from goat's or sheep's milk flavor many dishes.

A significant food in Middle Eastern cuisine, yogurt is a fermented, cultured milk product. Used in countless ways, yogurt appears in soups, beverages, marinades, side dishes, snacks, and desserts. It is extremely important in the cuisine of Iran, and many

## CHEESES OF THE MIDDLE EAST

**Feta** Usually made from sheep's milk but sometimes made from goat's milk; fresh cheese stored in brine; salty flavor, crumbly soft texture; used in cooking as well as eaten as an appetizer

**Halloumi** Made from sheep's milk; mild flavor; often contains fresh mint, which lends a mint flavor to this mild cheese; a stretched curd cheese, which refers to the process of handling the curds when making the cheese, resulting in a springy texture resembling that of cooked chicken

**Kasseri** Made from sheep's milk or a combination of goat's and sheep's milk; pungent salty flavor, firm yet rubbery and stringy texture; a stretched curd cheese

**Labneh** Made from sheep's or goat's milk; fresh cheese made by draining soured milk or yogurt; tangy flavor, soft texture; also called Lebbene, Lebney, and Gibne

**Manouri** Made from sheep's milk; mild nutty flavor, soft and buttery, slightly crumbly texture

**Myzithra** Made from sheep's milk; a fresh cheese produced from the whey remaining after making feta cheese; also called Anthotiro; nutty flavor and texture similar to ricotta cheese; used in cooking sweet and savory foods and eaten plain

---

say no meal is complete without some form of yogurt. Some people attribute health benefits including long life to this food.

## VEGETABLES AND FRUITS

Throughout the Middle East, many recipes combine small amounts of meat extended with vegetables and/or grains. Stuffed vegetables remain popular, including such classics as stuffed eggplant, zucchini, peppers, tomatoes, or onions. Stuffings contain ground meats with grain or may be vegetarian consisting of grains and vegetables. Rice or bulgur instead of bread stuffing reigns in this part of the world.

People consume all sorts of *dolma*, a filling enclosed in an edible wrapper. Fillings include a ground lamb and pine nut filling, rice and mint, or anything imaginable. The wrappers are often grape leaves or cabbage leaves. Aromatic spices and herbs are an important ingredient in *dolma* fillings, as well as in most other dishes served in the Middle East.

Where the rivers transect the land, the ground is transformed into fertile farmland. Through irrigation, areas that once were barren desert now produce abundant crops and high-quality fruits and vegetables.

Main dishes often combine meats with fruits. Figs, dates, pomegranates, quince, and citrus fruits are consumed widely. Except on special occasions, fresh fruit or fruit compote normally ends the meal.

Brought to the Middle East from India about 1,500 years ago, the eggplant appears often and in many guises. It functions as an appetizer, vegetable, and entrée. Served sautéed, stewed, or mashed, many know it best as part of the Middle Eastern and Greek dish, *moussaka*, which consists of alternating layers of ground lamb, fried eggplant, and sauce.

Preparation of eggplant usually begins with one of two methods. The first method of preparation involves slicing or dicing the eggplant, then sprinkling it with salt and allowing it to sit at least a half-hour to remove excess water and bitterness from the eggplant. The salt is then rinsed from the eggplant before it is used in the recipe. The second method is to char the eggplant over an open flame (or gas burner or electric burner, or under a broiler) until the skin is blistered and black. At that point, the peel of the eggplant is easily removed, and the eggplant flesh is cooked with other ingredients or used in a myriad of other preparations.

Another frequently used vegetable in the Middle East, bell peppers usually are peeled with a similar but different procedure. Peeling peppers requires charring in the same manner as eggplant, but then immediately placing them in an enclosed container (such as a paper bag) to steam. After steaming, the peels are removed.

Stuffed eggplant
© mallivan

Olive oil is held in high esteem in the Middle East. Many claim it cures all sorts of illnesses, and some believe it is an aphrodisiac.

Known as Turkish coffee, small cups of very strong and very sweet coffee are served throughout the Middle East. To prepare this coffee, the cook boils sugar water, then adds coffee and brings it to boil several more times. Like bars in other countries, popular coffeehouses in the Middle East function as gathering places for men. Since Muslims do not drink alcoholic beverages, they go to coffeehouses to drink coffee, tea, and other nonalcoholic drinks.

In addition to eggplant, okra, peppers, and beans remain popular throughout the Middle East. Usually, vegetables are cooked thoroughly, not in the *al dente* style common in much of the West. Cooks often add a lot of olive oil and/or tomatoes to vegetables. In some areas, hot peppers flavor the vegetables.

## SALADS

People in the Middle East enjoy a plethora of salads. In fact, a salad accompanies most meals. All sorts of vegetables, legumes, and grains become salads. *Tabouli* is a well-known salad composed of bulgur, mint, parsley, lemon juice, olive oil, chopped tomato, and sometimes chickpeas.

Salad dressings usually consist of lemon juice and sometimes vinegar mixed with oil or a yogurt-based dressing. If affordable for the cook, olive oil is the oil of choice. Ample mint and parsley in salads create the flavoring palate associated with the Middle East. Onion and garlic season many salads.

## FLAVORINGS

Abundant spices and herbs flavor the foods throughout the Middle East. Some of these include mint, dill, flat-leaf parsley, cilantro, ground red pepper, cinnamon, paprika, cumin, coriander, ginger, allspice, and saffron. Garlic and onions also play a significant part in the cuisine. Sesame seeds are widely used, both in their natural state as the whole seed and ground into paste to form *tahini*. When ground and mixed with sugar, sesame seeds transform into *halvah*.

## BEVERAGES

Water or a yogurt drink such as *aryan*, a frothy, salty yogurt beverage, accompanies meals in the Middle East. Tea is the national drink of Iran, and strong, sweet Turkish coffee also remains an important part of Middle Eastern life. A demitasse (small cup) of Turkish coffee begins all business transactions and is offered at all visits.

Whether the meal ends with fresh fruit, fruit compote, or a confection, a demitasse of very strong, sweetened coffee is served. Middle Easterners frequently flavor desserts or beverages with fragrant orange flower water or rosewater.

## DESSERTS

Used throughout the Middle East, phyllo dough is paper-thin dough made from flour and water. It appears in a wide range of preparations for both sweet and savory dishes, from *spanakopita* to *baklava*. Phyllo and *kadayif*, a shredded variety of phyllo dough that resembles shredded wheat, often form the base of the cloyingly sweet desserts preferred in these countries. Honey and dried fruits in the fillings enhance the sweetness.

## MEALS

Because of the hot climate, the main meal is served in the afternoon, followed by a *siesta*. The evening meal occurs late in the evening. This light meal often consists of *mazza* followed by a salad.

In the Middle East and much of Africa, food is scooped up and eaten with the fingers or pieces of flat bread instead of forks and knives. Traditionally, the hands are washed at the beginning and end of the meal at the dining table. Only the thumb and the first two fingers on the right hand pick up the food. Dining while sitting on the floor is customary.

| REGION | AREA | WEATHER | TOPOGRAPHY | FOODS |
|--------|------|---------|------------|-------|
| Syria | Western Middle East | Southwest: hot | Coast, plains, Barada River, fertile farmland | Livestock, wheat, legumes, vegetables, fruits |
| | | Northeast: hot | Euphrates River | Sheep, fruits |
| | | Remaining: hot | Plateaus, desert | Sheep, goats |
| Lebanon | Western Middle East | Hot | Coastal plains, mountains, Mediterranean Sea | Sheep, vegetables, fruits |
| Jordan | Western Middle East | West: mild | Mountains, valleys, plains | Wheat, barley, olives, cabbage, eggplant, cucumbers, tomatoes, nuts, citrus fruits, melons |
| | | Remaining: hot | Desert | Sheep, goats |
| Iraq | Central Middle East | Northwest: cool, moderate | Hilly; Tigris and Euphrates rivers | Sheep, goats, fish, legumes, wheat, figs |
| | | Remaining: hot | Desert, plains, mountains | Dates, olives |
| Iran | Eastern Middle East | Hot desert and plateaus, cold in mountains | Caspian Sea, rivers, desert, mountains, salt lakes, plateaus | Sheep, goats, cattle, seafood, fish, sturgeon, caviar, yogurt, wheat, rice, barley, lentils, dates |
| Saudi Arabia | Southwest and Central Middle East | East: hot | Desert, plateaus, plains, mountains | Sheep, goats, cattle, dates, wheat, melons, tomatoes |
| | | West: hot | | |
| Turkey | Northwestern Middle East | Southeast and interior: hot summers and cold winters | Fertile plains, hills, valleys, mountains, desert | Sheep, goats, livestock, fish, seafood, kebobs, dairy, grains, wheat, barley, corn, beets, olives, nuts, fruits, vegetables, honey |
| | | Northeast: cold winters and mild summers | | |
| | | South and west: mild winters and hot summers | | |
| Greece | Eastern Europe | Mild, wet winters, hot, dry summers | Mountains, rocky terrain, coasts, pastures | Sheep, cattle, poultry, fish, seafood, wheat, corn, olives, beets, grapes, raisins, fruits |

## >> Review Questions

1. Discuss influences that molded the cuisine of the Middle East, including the weather, the topography, and religion.
2. What cooking methods are most prevalent in the Middle East and why?
3. What role do grains and legumes play in this cuisine? Give examples of dishes using these foods.
4. What is phyllo dough? How is it used?
5. What is *mazza*? Give examples.
6. Which meat is most widely consumed and why?
7. Name and describe five dishes associated with the Middle East.

## >> Glossary

**bulgur** Cracked wheat that is boiled and then dried (dehydrated)

**chelo** Steamed rice

**chelo kebab** A dish consisting of rice, marinated lamb, spices, and yogurt; the national dish of Iran

**couscous** A tiny, grainlike semolina pasta

**dolma** A filling usually of meat and/or rice enclosed in an edible wrapper such as grape leaves or cabbage leaves

**falafel** A spicy chickpea fritter

**feta** A goat or sheep's milk cheese with a salty flavor and crumbly texture; quite popular throughout the Middle East

**gyros** Lamb cooked on a rotisserie, which is sliced in thin shavings and served in pita bread or plain

**hummus** A spread combining chickpeas with garlic, lemon juice, *tahini,* and other ingredients

**kadayif** A shredded variety of phyllo dough that looks like shredded wheat

**kibbe** A ground lamb and grain patty that is served either raw or cooked

**mazza** Appetizers

**moussaka** A dish consisting of alternating layers of ground lamb, fried eggplant, and sauce

**ouzo** An anise-flavored alcoholic beverage that turns opaque when mixed with water; a popular drink in Greece

**pita bread** Also called pocket bread; a yeast bread dough formed into a disk then baked in a very hot oven, a pocket forms in the bread during baking

**polo** An Iranian favorite dish consisting of steamed rice with combinations of fruits, vegetables, nuts, and meats

**retsina** A Greek sharp wine

**shish kebob** Smaller cubes of meat and sometimes vegetables placed on a skewer, then grilled over fire

**spanakopita** A dish consisting of phyllo dough layered with a spinach and feta mixture

**tahini** Sesame seed paste, like peanut butter made from sesame seeds

## DOLMADES (GREECE)

### MEAT STUFFED GRAPE LEAVES

**Note:** With variations on seasonings and fillings, dolmades are served throughout the Middle East.

**Serving Size:** 2 1/2- to 3-inch (6- to 8-cm) roll
**Total Yield:** 40 to 50
**Food Balance:** Protein/acid balanced
**Wine Style:** Wide variety of wines: Pinot Grigio, Pinot Blanc, Sauvignon Blanc, Grenache, or Zinfandel
**Example:** Souverain Merlot

**Cooking Method:** Boil, sauté

**TWIST ON THE CLASSIC**

Use any filling the imagination creates. For a vegetarian alternative, many omit the meat and serve the grape leaves stuffed with a rice or bulgur filling.

| INGREDIENTS | WEIGHT | | VOLUME | |
| --- | --- | --- | --- | --- |
| | U.S. | METRIC | U.S. | METRIC |
| **Filling:** | | | | |
| olive oil | | 15 g | 1 tablespoon | 15 mL |
| onion, minced | 6 oz. | 170 g | 1 medium | |
| lean ground lamb or beef | 1 lb., 8 oz. | 680 g | | |
| white rice, uncooked | 3 1/2 oz. | 104 g | 1/2 cup | 120 mL |
| fresh mint, minced* | 1/2 oz. | 15 g | 2 tablespoons | 30 mL |
| fresh dill, minced* | 1/2 oz. | 15 g | 2 tablespoons | 30 mL |
| salt | to taste | | | |
| pepper | to taste | | | |
| water | | 170 g | 3/4 cup | 180 mL |
| lemon juice | | 28 g | 1/2 lemon or 2 tablespoons | 30 mL |
| **Assembly:** | | | | |
| preserved grape leaves | | | 1 jar, or 50–60 leaves | |
| boiling water | | | | |
| lemons, thinly sliced | | | 2 each | |
| lemon juice | | | to taste | |
| **Garnish:** | | | | |
| lemon | | | | |
| mint | | | | |

*If fresh mint and dill are unavailable, substitute 1/4 oz. (8 g) or 2 teaspoons (10 mL) of the dried herb.

*Rolling leaf*
David Murray and Jules Selmes © Dorling Kindersley

*Placing dolmades in pan*
David Murray and Jules Selmes © Dorling Kindersley

## FILLING:

1. Heat olive oil in large skillet over medium heat, add onion and sauté until tender but not brown.
2. Add meat, sauté over medium heat until crumbly and browned. Drain excess oil.
3. Add rice, mint, dill, salt, and pepper, stir until rice is glazed. Add 3/4 cup (170 g or 180 mL) water, simmer and cook, uncovered, for 5 minutes, until liquid is absorbed.
4. Stir in lemon juice, set aside to cool. Correct seasonings.

## ASSEMBLY:

1. Cut stems from grape leaves. Place leaves in bowl, pour boiling water over leaves to cover. Drain and rinse. Set aside to cool.
2. Line bottom of large saucepan with two or three large leaves.
3. Place each leaf shiny side down on work surface. Place one tablespoon of filling in center of leaf. Fold sides in just to cover the edge of the filling (burrito style), then roll from stem end to tip.
4. Stack rolls, seam side down, in an even layer in prepared saucepan. Place three lemon slices over rolls, repeat layering rolls and lemon slices. Place inverted plate on top of rolls to prevent their moving while cooking. Pour boiling water to within 1 inch of saucepan rim. Cover and simmer over low heat until rice is tender, about 40 minutes. Leaves should be tender yet slightly chewy.
5. Cool slightly. Arrange on platter. Sprinkle with lemon juice to taste. If desired, garnish with lemon and mint.

David Murray and Jules Selmes © Dorling Kindersley

© uckyo

## BABA GHANNOUJ (ARABIC)

### EGGPLANT SESAME DIP

**Total Yield:** 1 lb., 4 1/2 oz. (582 g)          **Cooking Method:** Bake

© keko64

| INGREDIENTS | WEIGHT | | VOLUME | |
| --- | --- | --- | --- | --- |
| | U.S. | METRIC | U.S. | METRIC |
| eggplant | 1 lb., 5 oz. | 596 g | 1 large | |
| garlic, smashed and minced | 1/4 oz. | 8 g | 2 cloves or 1 teaspoon | 5 mL |
| *tahini* | 4 1/2 oz. | 128 g | 1/2 cup | 120 mL |
| fresh lemon juice | | 57 g | 1/4 cup | 60 mL |
| salt | | | 1/2 teaspoon | 3 mL |
| pepper | | | 1/4 teaspoon | 2 mL |
| fresh parsley, finely chopped | 1/4 oz. | 8 g | 1 tablespoon | 15 mL |

**Garnish:**

fresh parsley, minced

1. Preheat oven to 400 degrees (205°C). With fork, pierce whole eggplant in several places.
2. Place eggplant on rack in oven and bake until soft, about 45 minutes. Cool enough to handle.
3. Peel. Cut eggplant into pieces and place in bowl of food processor fitted with knife blade.
4. Add garlic, *tahini*, lemon juice, salt, and pepper. Pulse to mix thoroughly. Eggplant does not need to be completely smooth.
5. Add parsley and pulse a few more times. Correct seasonings.
6. Place in serving bowl or mound on platter. Garnish with minced parsley, if desired. Serve with raw vegetables or pieces of pita bread to scoop the dip.

---

**TWIST ON THE CLASSIC**

For a combination appetizer plate, prepare three 5-inch (13-cm) crêpes, and wrap one around *baba ghannouj*, one around *hummus*, and the third around *tabouli*.

---

## HUMMUS (ARABIC)

### CHICKPEA SESAME DIP

**Total Yield:** 1 lb., 3 1/2 oz. (558 g)

Pearson Education/PH College

| INGREDIENTS | WEIGHT | | VOLUME | |
| --- | --- | --- | --- | --- |
| | U.S. | METRIC | U.S. | METRIC |
| chickpeas (garbanzo beans), cooked or canned | 11 1/2 oz. | 326 g | 2 cups | 480 mL |
| garlic, smashed and minced | | | 3 cloves | |
| *tahini* | 6 3/4 oz. | 191 g | 3/4 cup | 180 mL |
| fresh lemon juice | | 57 g | 1/4 cup | 60 mL |
| salt | 1/4 oz. | 8 g | 1 teaspoon | 5 mL |
| pepper | | | 1/4 teaspoon | 2 mL |
| ground cayenne | | | dash | |
| fresh parsley, finely minced | 1/4 oz. | 8 g | 1 tablespoon | 15 mL |

**Garnish:**

fresh parsley, minced

1. Place chickpeas in bowl of food processor fitted with knife blade. Process until smooth.
2. Add garlic, *tahini*, lemon juice, salt, pepper, and cayenne. Process until well blended.
3. Add parsley and pulse a few times. Correct seasonings.
4. Place in serving bowl or mound on platter. Garnish with more minced parsley, if desired. Serve with raw vegetables or pieces of pita bread to scoop the dip.

# DUGH KHIAR (IRAN)
## CHILLED CUCUMBER YOGURT SOUP

**Note:** Allow at least 2 hours to chill this soup before serving. Chill bowls for serving soup.

**Note:** This soup presents a wonderful juxtaposition of flavors. The yogurt and buttermilk provide tartness and acidity while the raisins and mint add sweetness. Cucumbers offer a smooth, cooling component that contrasts nicely with the onions, which give it a sharp, pungent character.

**Number of Servings:** 9
**Serving Size:** 6 oz. (170 g)
**Total Yield:** 3 lb., 8 oz. (1.6 kg)
**Food Balance:** Protein/acid balance
**Wine Style:** Light- to medium-bodied Chenin Blanc, Pinot Blanc, White Merlot, soft Chardonnay, or Grenache
**Example:** Stone Cellars Chardonnay

| | WEIGHT | | VOLUME | |
|---|---|---|---|---|
| **INGREDIENTS** | **U.S.** | **METRIC** | **U.S.** | **METRIC** |
| cucumbers, peeled and coarsely shredded | 1 lb., 6 1/2 oz. | 639 g | 2 large | |
| garlic, smashed and minced | 1/4 oz. | 8 g | 2 cloves | |
| fresh mint, minced | 1/2 oz. | 15 g | 2 tablespoons | 30 mL |
| plain yogurt | 1 lb., 1 oz. | 482 g | 2 cups | 480 mL |
| buttermilk | | 454 g | 2 cups | 480 mL |
| salt | 1/4 oz. | 8 g | 1 teaspoon | 5 mL |
| raisins | 1 1/4 oz. | 36 g | 1/4 cup | 60 mL |
| green onions, chopped | 1/4 oz. | 8 g | 1 tablespoon | 15 mL |

1. Combine cucumbers, garlic, mint, and yogurt in large bowl. Stir gently to mix well.
2. Stir in buttermilk, salt, raisins, and green onions.
3. Chill at least 2 hours. Correct seasonings. Serve in chilled bowls.

David Murray and Jules Selmes © Dorling Kindersley

# SOUPA AVGOLEMONO (GREECE)

## EGG AND LEMON SOUP

**Number of Servings:** 13
**Serving Size:** 6 oz. (170 g)
**Total Yield:** 5 lb., 3 oz. (2.4 kg)
**Food Balance:** Protein/acid
**Wine Style:** Low-oaked whites and soft reds
**Example:** Château St. Jean Pinot Blanc

**Cooking Method:** Boil, sauté

| INGREDIENTS | WEIGHT | | VOLUME | |
|---|---|---|---|---|
| | **U.S.** | **METRIC** | **U.S.** | **METRIC** |
| chicken stock | | | 1 1/2 quarts (6 cups) | 1.4 L |
| onion, finely diced | 5 oz. | 142 g | 1 medium | |
| olive oil | | 28 g | 2 tablespoons | 30 mL |
| white rice, uncooked | 2 3/4 oz. | 78 g | 1/3 cup | 80 mL |
| pepper | | | 1/4 teaspoon | 2 mL |
| eggs | 6 3/4 oz. | 191 g | 4 each | |
| lemon juice | | 57 g | 2 large or 1/4 cup | 60 mL |

**Garnish:**
fresh mint, finely chopped

1. Bring chicken stock to a boil in large saucepan.
2. Sauté onion in olive oil in skillet over medium-high heat until soft. Add rice and sauté until starting to brown.
3. Add rice, onions, and pepper to stock, bring to boil, reduce heat to low and simmer, partially uncovered, about 15 minutes, until rice is *al dente*.
4. In bowl, beat eggs with whisk, add lemon juice.
5. Whisking constantly, slowly add about one cup hot chicken stock to eggs to temper them.
6. Over low heat, slowly pour egg mixture into stock, whisking constantly.
7. Cook over low heat for a few minutes, until soup thickens enough to coat back of spoon lightly. Do not boil, or eggs might curdle. Correct seasonings.
8. Garnish with mint, if desired.

© Elzbieta Sekowska

# FATTOUSH (LEBANON AND THROUGHOUT MIDDLE EAST)

## BREAD SALAD

**TWIST ON THE CLASSIC**

To add a wider range of color, use an orange pepper instead of a green one.

**Note:** Add pita pieces to each portion at time of service. The vegetable portion of this salad keeps well in the refrigerator, but the pita pieces absorb lots of dressing and become soggy.

**Number of Servings:** 10
**Serving Size:** 5 oz. (142 g)
**Total Yield:** 3 lb., 3/4 oz. (1.4 kg)

| | WEIGHT | | VOLUME | |
|---|---|---|---|---|
| *INGREDIENTS* | *U.S.* | *METRIC* | *U.S.* | *METRIC* |
| **Dressing:** | | | | |
| lemon juice | | 43 g | 3 tablespoons | 45 mL |
| olive oil | | 43 g | 3 tablespoons | 45 mL |
| salt | 1/2 oz. | 15 g | 2 teaspoons | 10 mL |
| pepper | | | 1 teaspoon | 5 mL |
| garlic, peeled, minced, smashed | | | 1 clove | |
| **Salad:** | | | | |
| cucumber, peeled | 13 oz. | 369 g | 1 large | |
| pita, cut into 1 1/2-inch (4-cm) pieces | 5 oz. | 142 g | 2 to 3 each | |
| tomato, large dice | 1 lb., 1 3/4 oz. | 504 g | 3 medium | |
| green pepper, seeds and membranes removed, medium dice | 7 1/2 oz. | 213 g | 1 large | |
| green onions, trimmed leaving about 3-inches (8 cm) green, thinly sliced | 3 oz. | 86 g | 5 each | |
| parsley, flat leaf, chopped | 1/2 oz. | 15 g | 1/3 cup | 80 mL |
| mint, chopped | 1/4 oz. | 8 g | 3 tablespoons | 45 mL |
| lettuce, romaine, sliced into strips | 3 1/2 oz. | 104 g | 2 cups | 480 mL |

1. Whisk all dressing ingredients together in a small nonreactive bowl. Set aside until needed.
2. Cut cucumber in half lengthwise, then cut into 1/4-inch (0.5-cm) slices. Pull pita pieces apart (divide where pocket lies). If pita is fresh or if more of a crouton is desired, toast lightly. Otherwise, use pita as is.
3. Mix cucumber, tomato, green pepper, onions, parsley, mint, and romaine together in a large bowl. Add pita pieces before mixing dressing or after, depending on service timing.
4. Pour dressing over salad, mix thoroughly so dressing covers all ingredients. Correct seasonings. Serve.

© ramzi hachicho

## TABOULI

### BULGUR SALAD

**Note:** Allow at least 2 hours to marinate.

**Note:** Bulgur wheat is available in health food stores, many supermarkets, and Middle Eastern food stores.

**Number of Servings:** 8
**Serving Size:** 4 oz. (114 g)
**Total Yield:** 2 lb., 3 oz. (994 g)

<table>
<tr><th rowspan="2">INGREDIENTS</th><th colspan="2">WEIGHT</th><th colspan="2">VOLUME</th></tr>
<tr><th>U.S.</th><th>METRIC</th><th>U.S.</th><th>METRIC</th></tr>
<tr><td>bulgur wheat</td><td>7 1/2 oz.</td><td>213 g</td><td>1 cup</td><td>240 mL</td></tr>
<tr><td>water, boiling</td><td></td><td>340 g</td><td>1 1/2 cups</td><td>360 mL</td></tr>
<tr><td>fresh mint, finely minced</td><td>1 oz.</td><td>28 g</td><td>1/4 cup</td><td>60 mL</td></tr>
<tr><td>fresh parsley, finely minced</td><td>2 oz.</td><td>57 g</td><td>1 cup</td><td>240 mL</td></tr>
<tr><td>fresh lemon juice</td><td></td><td>114 g</td><td>1/2 cup</td><td>120 mL</td></tr>
<tr><td>onion, finely minced</td><td>3 oz.</td><td>86 g</td><td>1 small</td><td></td></tr>
<tr><td>garlic, smashed and minced</td><td>1/4 oz.</td><td>8 g</td><td>2 cloves</td><td></td></tr>
<tr><td>salt</td><td></td><td></td><td>1 1/4 teaspoons</td><td>6 mL</td></tr>
<tr><td>pepper</td><td></td><td></td><td>1/8 teaspoon</td><td>1 mL</td></tr>
<tr><td>olive oil</td><td></td><td>57 g</td><td>1/4 cup</td><td>60 mL</td></tr>
<tr><td>chickpeas (garbanzo beans), cooked or canned, optional</td><td>3 to 6 oz.</td><td>86 to 170 g</td><td>1/2 to 1 cup</td><td>120 to 240 mL</td></tr>
<tr><td>tomatoes, diced</td><td>9 oz.</td><td>256 g</td><td>2 medium</td><td></td></tr>
</table>

① Place bulgur in bowl, cover with boiling water. Let sit until cool, at least 15 to 20 minutes.

② Add mint, parsley, lemon juice, onion, garlic, salt, pepper, oil, and chickpeas. Refrigerate at least 2 hours.

③ Correct seasonings. Add tomatoes and serve.

### TWIST ON THE CLASSIC

For a vegetarian luncheon entrée, serve *tabouli* in a tomato (cut into eighths, but not all the way through, so the sides of the tomato open like a flower).

© lenushkab

# SALATA KHODRA (MIDDLE EAST AND TURKEY)
## DICED SALAD

Kheng Guan Toh © Shutterstock

**Note:** Some refer to this as shepherd's salad, because shepherds would take a tomato, cucumber, onion, and radishes with them to the mountains to cut up and prepare into a salad.

**Note:** Allow at least 20 minutes to marinate so the flavors marry.

**Number of Servings:** 13
**Serving Size:** 5 oz. (142 g)
**Total Yield:** 4 lb., 4 oz. (1.9 kg)

|  | WEIGHT | | VOLUME | |
|---|---|---|---|---|
| INGREDIENTS | U.S. | METRIC | U.S. | METRIC |
| tomato, medium dice | 1 lb., 12 1/2 oz. | 809 g | 4 medium | |
| cucumber, peeled and cut into medium dice | 1 lb., 9 1/2 oz. | 724 g | 2 large | |
| onion, red or sweet (like Vidalia), small dice | 8 oz. | 227 g | 1 large | |
| radishes, cut into eighths | 9 oz. | 256 g | 12 each | |
| fresh parsley, minced | 1 1/2 oz. | 43 g | 2/3 cup | 160 mL |
| **Dressing:** | | | | |
| lemon juice | | 114 g | 1/2 cup | 120 mL |
| olive oil | | 114 g | 1/2 cup | 120 mL |
| salt | 1/2 oz. | 15 g | 2 teaspoons | 10 mL |
| pepper | | to taste | | |

1. Place tomato, cucumbers, onion, radishes, and parsley in bowl.
2. Whisk lemon juice, olive oil, salt, and pepper together in small bowl. Taste and correct seasonings.
3. Pour dressing over vegetables. Mix gently.
4. Refrigerate to marinate for 20 minutes. Correct seasonings and serve immediately.

# KIBBEYET (SYRIA AND LEBANON)
## STUFFED GROUND LAMB AND BULGUR MIXTURE

**Note:** Bulgur wheat is available in health food stores, many supermarkets, and Middle Eastern food stores.

**Number of Servings:** 11
**Serving Size:** 6 oz. (170 g)
**Total Yield:** 4 lb., 6 oz. (2 kg)
**Food Balance:** Balanced
**Wine Style:** Wine friendly—Try your favorite
**Example:** Beringer Chardonnay or Cabernet Sauvignon

**Cooking Method:** Bake, sauté

|  | WEIGHT | | VOLUME | |
|---|---|---|---|---|
| INGREDIENTS | U.S. | METRIC | U.S. | METRIC |
| **Raw Lamb Mixture:** | | | | |
| bulgur wheat, fine | 9 oz. | 256 g | 1 1/2 cups | 360 mL |
| water, cold | as needed | | | |
| onions, minced | 1 lb., 3 oz. | 540 g | 4 medium or 4 cups | 960 mL |

© paul_brighton

| INGREDIENTS | WEIGHT | | VOLUME | |
| --- | --- | --- | --- | --- |
| | U.S. | METRIC | U.S. | METRIC |
| salt | 1/2 oz. | 15 g | 2 teaspoons | 10 mL |
| ground cinnamon | | | 1/2 teaspoon | 3 mL |
| ground allspice | | | 1/2 teaspoon | 3 mL |
| pepper | | | 1/2 teaspoon | 3 mL |
| ground lamb | 1 lb., 8 oz. | 680 g | | |
| **Filling:** | | | | |
| butter | 1 oz. | 28 g | 2 tablespoons | 30 mL |
| pine nuts | 3 oz. | 86 g | 2/3 cup | 160 mL |
| onion, finely diced | 9 oz. | 256 g | 2 medium or 2 cups | 480 mL |
| ground lamb | 1 lb. | 454 g | | |
| ground cinnamon | | | 1/2 teaspoon | 3 mL |
| ground allspice | | | 1/2 teaspoon | 3 mL |
| salt | to taste | | | |
| pepper | to taste | | | |
| fresh mint, minced | 1 oz. | 28 g | 1/4 cup | 60 mL |
| **Assembly:** | | | | |
| butter, melted | 1 oz. | 28 g | 2 tablespoons | 30 mL |

© paul_brighton

## RAW LAMB MIXTURE:

1. Place bulgur wheat in bowl, cover with cold water, let soak 10 minutes. Drain well, squeezing gently to eliminate water.
2. Place onions, salt, cinnamon, allspice, pepper, and a little iced water (about 1 to 2 tablespoons, 28 to 57 g, or 15 to 30 mL) in food processor fitted with knife blade. Blend until thick paste.
3. Add 1 lb., 8 oz. (680 g) lamb, process until very smooth. Scrape bowl of food processor several times.
4. Add bulgur, process until smooth.

## FILLING:

1. Melt butter in pan over medium heat. Add pine nuts and sauté until beginning to brown. Add onions and sauté until softened.
2. Add 1 lb. (454 g) lamb, cinnamon, allspice, salt, pepper, and mint. Stirring so meat does not clump, sauté until lightly browned. Remove from heat.

## ASSEMBLY:

1. Pan-spray half hotel pan (steam table insert). Preheat oven to 375 degrees (190°C).
2. Spread half of raw lamb mixture in pan, top with filling mixture.
3. Spread remaining raw lamb mixture on top.
4. Brush with melted butter, cut diamond pattern into top of *kibbe*, using diagonal knife strokes.
5. Bake for about 30 to 35 minutes, until browned and crisp.

## ALTERNATIVE SHAPING AND COOKING:

Form 2 1/2 to 3 oz. (71 to 86 g) of raw lamb mixture into oval shape. Make hollow ridge along the length of top of meat with index finger. Place about 3/4 oz. (22 g) filling into ridge. Seal top to enclose filling. If necessary, dip finger into cold water to smooth meat. Place *kibbe* ovals on greased baking sheet. Brush with melted butter and bake for about 20 to 25 minutes, until browned. *Kibbe* ovals are often deep-fried instead of baked.

# MOUSSAKA (GREECE)

## BAKED EGGPLANT, LAMB, AND BÉCHAMEL SAUCE

Bratwustle © Shutterstock

**TWIST ON THE CLASSIC**

Omit the lamb and otherwise prepare the *moussaka* as directed for a vegetarian entrée.

**Number of Servings:** 9
**Serving Size:** 8 oz. (227 g)
**Total Yield:** 4 lb., 11 oz. (2.1 kg)
**Food Balance:** Protein
**Wine Style:** Low-oaked whites and soft reds
**Example:** Beringer Chenin Blanc or Stone Cellars Merlot

**Cooking Method:** Boil, sauté, broil, bake

| INGREDIENTS | WEIGHT U.S. | WEIGHT METRIC | VOLUME U.S. | VOLUME METRIC |
|---|---|---|---|---|
| **Béchamel Sauce:** | | | | |
| milk | | 794 g | 3 1/2 cups | 840 mL |
| onion, finely diced | 4 to 5 oz. | 114 to 142 g | 1 medium | |
| whole cloves | | | 2 each | |
| bay leaf | | | 1 large | |
| salt | 1/4 oz. | 8 g | 1 teaspoon | 5 mL |
| butter | 1 1/2 oz. | 43 g | 3 tablespoons | 45 mL |
| flour | 1 3/4 oz. | 50 g | 3 1/2 tablespoons | 52 mL |
| nutmeg | | | few gratings, to taste | |
| **Filling:** | | | | |
| eggplant, peeled and cut into 1/2-inch (1.3-cm) slices | 3 to 3 lb., 12 oz. | 1.4 to 1.7 kg | 3 medium | |
| salt | as needed | | | |
| onions, diced | 7 1/2 oz. | 213 g | 1 1/2 cups | 360 mL |
| lean ground lamb | 1 lb., 8 oz. | 680 g | | |
| canned plum tomatoes, chopped | 13 oz. | 369 g | 1 1/2 cups | 360 mL |
| tomato purée | 6 oz. | 170 g | 3/4 cup | 180 mL |
| garlic, smashed and minced | | | 3 cloves or 1 1/2 teaspoons | 8 mL |
| dried oregano | | | 1 1/2 teaspoons | 8 mL |
| ground cinnamon | 1/4 oz. | 8 g | 1 teaspoon | 5 mL |
| salt | | | 1 1/2 teaspoons | 8 mL |
| pepper | to taste | | | |
| olive oil | | 43 g | 3 tablespoons | 45 mL |
| kefalotiri or Parmesan cheese, grated | 2 1/4 oz. | 64 g | 1/2 cup + 1 tablespoon | 135 mL |

## BÉCHAMEL SAUCE:

1. Over low heat, simmer milk, onion, cloves, bay leaf, and salt in pan for 20 minutes.
2. Melt butter in separate pan over medium-low heat, whisk in flour, and cook, whisking, until a white roux, just a couple of minutes.
3. Slowly whisk milk mixture into roux. Add few gratings of nutmeg. Let cook slowly for 20 to 25 minutes. Correct seasonings. Strain.

## PREPARATION:

1. Sprinkle eggplant slices lightly with salt, place in colander in sink or in another bowl to catch liquid. Place weight on top and let sit at least 30 minutes.
2. Place onions and lamb in skillet over medium heat, stir frequently to break up any lumps, cook until no traces of pink remain and onions are soft, about 8 minutes. Drain excess fat from pan.
3. Add tomatoes, tomato purée, garlic, oregano, cinnamon, salt, and pepper. Bring to boil over high heat, stirring frequently, and cook until most of liquid evaporates. Correct seasonings. Cool, then refrigerate until needed or use right away.
4. Preheat broiler. Rinse eggplant slices thoroughly to remove salt. Pat dry. Lay slices on sheet pan, brush lightly with oil.
5. Broil until lightly brown. Turn slices over, brush with oil, broil other side.

## ASSEMBLY:

1. Place oven rack in middle of oven. Preheat oven to 325 degrees (160°C).
2. Spread half of eggplant slices in overlapping rows in bottom of 1/2-pan steam table insert. Sprinkle one-third of grated cheese over eggplant, pour lamb mixture on top, spreading evenly in pan. Arrange remaining eggplant on top, sprinkle with half of remaining cheese. Pour Béchamel sauce over eggplant, sprinkle with remaining cheese.
3. Bake for 30 minutes, increase heat to 400 degrees (205°C) and bake for 15 minutes longer, or until top is golden brown.
4. Remove the dish from the oven, let it rest at room temperature for 5 or 10 minutes before serving.

*Individual moussaka*
© Jérôme Rommé

# ARPACIK SOĞAN YAHNISI (TURKEY)

## PEARL ONION STEW

**Number of Servings:** 13
**Serving Size:** 8 oz. (227 g)
**Total Yield:** 6 lb., 11 1/2 oz. (3.1 kg)
**Meatball Mixture:** 2 lb., 9 1/2 oz. (1.2 kg)
**Meatball Scaling:** 3/4 oz. (22 g)

**Cooking Method:** Sauté, braise

**Wine Style:** White wine with higher acidity and high minerality content. Possible grape varietals are Neuburger, Riesling.
**Example:** Neuburger "Wallse Edition" 2011, Donabaum (Wachau/Austria)

FoodPhotogr. Eising/ AGE Fotostock

| INGREDIENTS | WEIGHT U.S. | WEIGHT METRIC | VOLUME U.S. | VOLUME METRIC |
|---|---|---|---|---|
| onion, roughly chopped | 10 oz. | 284 g | 2 medium | |
| salt | 1/2 oz. | 15 g | 2 teaspoons | 10 mL |
| pepper | | | 1 teaspoon | 5 mL |
| ground beef | 2 lb. | 908 g | | |
| olive oil, as needed for frying | | | | |
| pearl onions, peeled, frozen or fresh | 2 lb. | 908 g | | |
| green pepper, seeds and membranes, removed, medium dice | 15 oz. | 426 g | 2 large | |
| tomatoes, diced | 2 each 15-oz. cans | | 2 each 426-g cans | |
| tomato paste | 1 1/2 oz. | 43 g | 2 tablespoons | 30 mL |
| garlic, peeled, minced, smashed | 1/2 oz. | 15 g | 4 cloves | |
| white vinegar | | 57 g | 1/4 cup | 60 mL |
| paprika | 1/4 oz. | 8 g | 2 teaspoons | 10 mL |
| cayenne, ground | | | 1/2 teaspoon | 3 mL |
| water | | 454 g | 2 cups, as needed | 480 mL |
| salt | | | to taste | |

1. With food processor fitted with knife blade running, drop onion through feed tube. Scraping sides of processor often, pulse until almost paste. Add salt, pepper, and ground beef. Pulse to make the beef finely ground.
2. Scale meat mixture into 3/4 oz. (22 g) portions and form into meatballs. Refrigerate until needed.
3. Over medium heat, heat enough oil in skillet to just coat bottom of pan. Add meatballs, fry until browned, remove from skillet. Repeat with remaining meatballs.
4. Add onions and green peppers to skillet, cook about 10 minutes.
5. Add tomatoes, tomato paste, garlic, vinegar, paprika, cayenne, and 1 3/4 cups (397 g or 420 mL) water. Add more water, if needed, to almost cover ingredients. Bring to boil, reduce heat to medium-low and cook 25 to 30 minutes.
6. Correct seasonings. Serve over rice or rice pilaf.

## TWIST ON THE CLASSIC

To transform this stew as a leftover, turn it into a filling for a burrito. Cut the meatballs in half, drain most of the liquid, and heat it in a skillet (for a wide surface area and plenty of evaporation). Generously add cumin, chili powder, and cayenne as needed, then heat until liquid reduces and the mixture is spicy hot. Use this as the filling for a burrito by itself or mixed with refried beans.

## ORDAK FESANJAN (IRAN)

### DUCK IN POMEGRANATE WALNUT SAUCE

**Note:** This recipe yields an ample amount of sauce, but extra sauce is good to serve with the rice that usually accompanies this dish.

**Note:** Traditionally, this dish is prepared by braising the duck in the sauce. In that case, start the recipe by sautéing the duck, then sauté the onions. Pour off any excess fat before adding the walnuts, and continue with the recipe as written. The duck simmers in the pomegranate sauce for about 2 hours, until done.

**Number of Servings:** 8  
**Serving Size:** 1/4 duck with sauce  
**Total Yield:** 3 lb., 11 1/2 oz. (1.7 kg)  
**Food Balance:** Protein/bitter  
**Wine Style:** Low-oaked whites and soft reds  
**Example:** Château St. Jean Fume Blanc or Rosemount Shiraz

**Cooking Method:** Bake, braise

**TWIST ON THE CLASSIC**

Substitute beef or chicken for the duck in this recipe. If using chicken, place lightly grilled boneless chicken breasts in the sauce to finish cooking them. If using beef, prepare the recipe with a tougher cut of meat like brisket and braise the meat in a combination of stock and pomegranate juice.

| INGREDIENTS | WEIGHT | | VOLUME | |
| --- | --- | --- | --- | --- |
| | U.S. | METRIC | U.S. | METRIC |
| duck, washed and trimmed, if needed | about 10 to 12 lb. (5 to 6 lb. each) | 4.5 to 5.4 kg | 2 each | |
| oil | | 28 g | 2 tablespoons | 30 mL |
| onion, thin slices | 1 lb., 2 oz. | 511 g | 2 large | |
| walnuts, toasted and finely ground | 12 oz. | 340 g | 3 cups | 720 mL |
| chicken stock | | 227 g | 1 cup | 240 mL |
| pomegranate juice | | | 1 1/2 quarts (6 cups) | 1.4 L |
| pepper | | | 1 teaspoon | 5 mL |
| cardamom | 1/4 oz. | 8 g | 2 teaspoons | 10 mL |
| salt, *optional* | to taste | | | |
| sugar, *optional* | to taste | | | |
| lemon juice, *optional* | to taste | | | |

**Garnish:**  
pomegranate seeds  
walnuts, toasted and chopped  
fresh parsley, minced

**Accompaniment:**  
hot cooked rice

Obtain pure pomegranate juice in the supermarket, health food store, or Middle Eastern grocery. Be careful not to buy a blend because blends usually contain a large percentage of other, very sweet juices. Pure pomegranate juice is quite tart with a sweet component, which gives this dish a sweet-and-sour flavor. If necessary to intensify and balance the sweet-and-sour flavor, add a little sugar and/or lemon juice.

© evgenyb

To grind walnuts, pulse in food processor or in coffee grinder just until finely ground. Be careful not to grind too long, because the nuts will become oily and form a paste. Toasting nuts accentuates their flavor.

## DUCK:

1. Place oven rack in middle of oven. Preheat oven to 425 degrees (220°C).

2. Place duck on rack in roasting pan, breast side up, and prick all over with fork (to allow fat to drain from duck). Place about 1/2 inch (1.3 cm) hot water in bottom of roasting pan. Bake for 20 minutes.

3. Reduce oven temperature to 350 degrees (180°C), bake another 30 minutes, and then turn duck over onto breast. Again, prick all over with fork, bake another 30 to 40 minutes.

4. Drain fat and water from pan, turn duck breast side up, and continue baking, draining fat occasionally, until duck reaches proper internal temperature, about 2 hours total.

## SAUCE:

1. Heat oil in large pan over medium heat. Add onion, sauté until golden, about 10 minutes.

2. Add walnuts, sauté for a minute, then add chicken stock, pomegranate juice, pepper, and cardamom. Cover and simmer for about 30 minutes, then uncover and simmer another 30 minutes. The sauce should have the consistency of heavy cream. If too thick, thin with stock or pomegranate juice. If too thin, uncover and cook a little longer.

3. If needed, add salt and add sugar and/or lemon juice to balance flavor of sweet/sour sauce.

## ASSEMBLY:

1. Cut ducks into quarters. Either add duck quarters to sauce and braise a short time to thoroughly coat with sauce or serve roasted duck accompanied by sauce.

2. Garnish with pomegranate seeds (if in season), walnuts, and parsley. Serve with rice.

# SAMAK TARATOR (SYRIA AND LEBANON)

## FISH WITH NUT SAUCE

**Note:** Grilled fish with *tarator* sauce appears all over the Middle East. The type of nut in the sauce varies with the region. In Turkey, walnuts or hazelnuts replace the pine nuts favored in Syria and Lebanon. Other variations include replacing the olive oil with *tahini*.

**Number of Servings:** 8
**Cooking Method:** Grill
**Serving Size:** 1 trout with 1 1/2 oz. (43 g), or 3 tablespoons (45 mL) sauce
**Total Yield:** 12 oz. (340 g), 1 1/2 cups (360 mL) sauce
**Food Balance:** Protein
**Wine Style:** Low-oaked whites and soft reds
**Example:** Penfolds Riesling or Shiraz

<table>
<tr><th rowspan="2">INGREDIENTS</th><th colspan="2">WEIGHT</th><th colspan="2">VOLUME</th></tr>
<tr><th>U.S.</th><th>METRIC</th><th>U.S.</th><th>METRIC</th></tr>
<tr><td colspan="5">***Tarator* Sauce:**</td></tr>
<tr><td>bread, crust removed</td><td>1 1/2 oz.</td><td>43 g</td><td>1 to 2 slices</td><td></td></tr>
<tr><td>water</td><td>as needed</td><td></td><td></td><td></td></tr>
<tr><td>whole garlic cloves, peeled</td><td>1/4 oz.</td><td>8 g</td><td>2 each</td><td></td></tr>
<tr><td>pine nuts</td><td>5 oz.</td><td>142 g</td><td>1 cup</td><td>240 mL</td></tr>
<tr><td>salt</td><td></td><td></td><td>3/4 teaspoon</td><td>4 mL</td></tr>
<tr><td>pepper</td><td>to taste</td><td></td><td></td><td></td></tr>
<tr><td>lemon juice</td><td></td><td>78 g</td><td>1/3 cup</td><td>80 mL</td></tr>
<tr><td>olive oil</td><td></td><td>78 g</td><td>1/3 cup</td><td>80 mL</td></tr>
<tr><td>trout, butterflied, with head left on, if desired</td><td>4 to 5 lb.</td><td>1.8 to 2.3 kg</td><td>8 each</td><td></td></tr>
<tr><td>olive oil</td><td>as needed</td><td></td><td></td><td></td></tr>
<tr><td>salt</td><td>as needed</td><td></td><td></td><td></td></tr>
</table>

**Garnish:**
lemon wedge
pine nuts, lightly toasted

### *TARATOR* SAUCE:

1. Place bread in bowl, cover with water, soak for a few minutes. Squeeze bread to eliminate the water.
2. Fit food processor with knife blade. With processor running, drop garlic through feed tube. Pulse a few times to pulverize garlic. Add pine nuts, bread, salt, a sprinkling of pepper, and lemon juice. Pulse to mix thoroughly.
3. Slowly add olive oil through feed tube, process until it forms smooth sauce with the consistency of mayonnaise. Correct seasonings. Cover and refrigerate until needed.

### ASSEMBLY:

1. Preheat grill or salamander. Lightly rub inside of trout with oil. Sprinkle with salt.
2. Grill trout until done, that is, until fish flakes and is opaque.
3. Serve each trout accompanied by three tablespoons (45 mL) *tarator* sauce and garnished with a lemon wedge and pine nuts.

---

**TWIST ON THE CLASSIC**

Try this sauce on sliced sirloin steak. Fan the slices on the plate and nap with the *tarator* sauce.

---

If convenient, prepare the *tarator* sauce a day ahead and refrigerate. It keeps well, and the flavors seem to intensify.

Ian O'Leary © Dorling Kindersley

# GARÍTHES ME FÉTTA (GREECE)

## SHRIMP WITH FETA CHEESE AND TOMATOES

Clive Streeter © Dorling Kindersley

**Number of Servings:** 8
**Serving Size:** 8 oz. (227 g)
**Total Yield:** 4 lb., 2 oz. (1.9 kg)
**Food Balance:** Acid/salt balanced
**Wine Style:** Wide variety—Enjoy the wine of your choice
**Example:** Beringer Sauvignon Blanc, Napa Valley Chardonnay, Knight Valley Cabernet Sauvignon

**Cooking Method:** Sauté, bake

| INGREDIENTS | WEIGHT | | VOLUME | |
|---|---|---|---|---|
| | U.S. | METRIC | U.S. | METRIC |
| **Tomato Sauce:** | | | | |
| olive oil | | 22 g | 1 1/2 tablespoons | 23 mL |
| onions, minced | 10 oz. | 284 g | 2 medium | |
| tomatoes, canned or fresh, peeled and diced | 1 lb., 10 oz. | 738 g | 3 cups | 720 mL |
| dry white wine | | 227 g | 1 cup | 240 mL |
| garlic, smashed and minced | | | 3 cloves | |
| dried oregano | 1/4 oz. | 8 g | 1 tablespoon | 15 mL |
| fresh flat-leaf parsley, minced | 2 oz. | 57 g | 2/3 cup | 160 mL |
| salt | | | 1/2 teaspoon | 3 mL |
| pepper | | | 1/4 teaspoon | 2 mL |
| **Assembly:** | | | | |
| olive oil | | 22 g | 1 1/2 tablespoons | 23 mL |
| shrimp, peeled and deveined | 2 lb., 2 oz. | 965 g | | |
| fresh lemon juice | | 57 g | 1/4 cup | 60 mL |
| tomatoes, peeled and thinly sliced | 8 oz. | 227 g | 2 each | |
| feta cheese, crumbled | 8 oz. | 227 g | 1 1/2 cups | 360 mL |

**Accompaniment:**

hot cooked rice

## TWIST ON THE CLASSIC

Prepare this recipe in individual serving dishes and accompany with feta bruschetta. To make the bruschetta, brush slices of French bread with olive oil, sprinkle with oregano, top with feta cheese, and bake until slightly crisp.

## TOMATO SAUCE:

1. Heat 1 1/2 tablespoons (22 g or 23 mL) olive oil in skillet over medium heat. Add onion and sauté until translucent.
2. Add tomatoes, then wine, garlic, oregano, parsley, salt, and pepper. Stirring occasionally, cook uncovered for about 20 minutes, until sauce thickens. Correct seasonings.
3. Remove from heat.

## ASSEMBLY:

1. Preheat oven to 450 degrees (230°C).
2. Heat olive oil in large skillet over medium-high heat until hot, add shrimp and sauté until just turning pink, about 1 minute.
3. With slotted spoon, remove shrimp from skillet, place in bowl, pour on lemon juice and toss gently.
4. Spread tomato sauce evenly in bottom of ovenproof pan, top with shrimp, then tomato slices, then sprinkle with feta cheese.
5. Bake 10 to 15 minutes, until cheese begins to melt. Serve immediately over or accompanied by rice.

# SPANAKOPITA (GREECE)

## SPINACH-FETA CHEESE PIE

**Note:** Although traditionally served as an entrée in the Middle East, a small portion makes a great appetizer.

**Number of Servings:** 8 entrée or 17 appetizer portions  **Cooking Method:** Bake, sauté
**Serving Size:** 8 oz. (227 g) entrée or 4 oz. (114 g) appetizers
**Total Yield:** 4 lb., 5 oz. (2 kg)
**Food Balance:** Salted protein
**Wine Style:** Very wine friendly—Try your favorite
**Example:** Meridian Vineyards Cabernet Sauvignon

**TWIST ON THE CLASSIC**

For a different presentation, prepare these in individual dishes or fold the filling in the phyllo dough like a turnover.

Placing buttered sheet of phyllo in baking pan so corners fan out

| INGREDIENTS | WEIGHT U.S. | WEIGHT METRIC | VOLUME U.S. | VOLUME METRIC |
|---|---|---|---|---|
| olive oil | | 57 g | 1/4 cup | 60 mL |
| onions, minced | 4 oz. | 114 g | 1 medium | |
| fresh spinach, washed, stems removed, and chopped | 2 lb. | 908 g | | |
| fresh dill, minced* | 3/4 oz. | 22 g | 1/4 cup | 60 mL |
| fresh parsley, minced | 3/4 oz. | 22 g | 1/4 cup | 60 mL |
| salt | | | 1/2 teaspoon | 3 mL |
| pepper | | | 1/4 teaspoon | 2 mL |
| milk | | 57 g | 1/4 cup | 60 mL |
| feta cheese, finely crumbled | 8 oz. | 227 g | | |
| eggs, lightly beaten | 10 oz. | 284 g | 6 each | |
| phyllo pastry dough | 1 lb. | 454 g | one 16-oz. package | one 454-g package |
| melted butter or olive oil | 2 3/4 oz. | 78 g | 1/3 cup or 5 1/2 tablespoons or as needed | 80 mL or as needed |

*If fresh dill is unavailable, you may substitute 1/4 oz. (8 g) or 2 tablespoons (30 mL) of the dried herb.

Pouring filling into phyllo-lined pan

Folding dough over filling

Cutting baked Spanakopita

1. In skillet or braiser, heat 1/4 cup (57 g or 60 mL) olive oil over moderate heat until hot. Add onions, and stirring frequently, sauté until soft and transparent but not brown.

2. Stir in spinach, cook a few minutes, until wilted. *If very wet,* drain liquid from spinach by placing in strainer and allowing liquid to drain. Press spinach to remove liquid, return spinach to skillet.

③ Add dill, parsley, salt, and pepper. Cook, stirring constantly, until most of liquid evaporates.

④ Let spinach mixture cool to room temperature, then add milk and feta. Correct seasonings. Add eggs.

⑤ Place oven rack in center of oven. Preheat oven to 375 degrees (190°C). Grease or pan-spray 9- by 13-inch (23- by 33-cm) pan.

⑥ Lay stack of phyllo sheets on counter. Keep unused phyllo dough covered with damp towel to prevent drying out. Move one sheet of dough to work surface. With pastry brush, brush with melted butter or oil. Place brushed sheet in pan (dough will hang over sides).

⑦ Move next sheet of dough to work surface, brush with fat, move into pan as above. Fit into pan with phyllo sheet slightly turned, so corners of dough start to fan out around pan.

⑧ Continue until all but three phyllo sheets are in pan. Pour in spinach mixture, smoothing to form even layer.

⑨ Fold excess dough from sides to cover filling, brush top with butter or oil.

⑩ Brush remaining sheets and place on top of pan. Fold excess dough into pan. Brush top with butter or oil.

⑪ Make three cuts in top, down to filling, so steam can escape.

⑫ Bake for about 45 to 50 minutes, until golden. Let cool a few minutes before slicing.

⑬ Cut into squares and serve hot or at room temperature.

## ZEYTINYAGH TAZE FASULYE (TURKEY)

### GREEN BEANS (IN OLIVE OIL WITH TOMATO)

**Note:** In Turkey, green beans are cooked until quite soft.

**Note:** Many Turkish green bean recipes use lots of olive oil, especially when served as meza. For example, the 1 1/2 lb. used in this recipe (before trimming) might incorporate 6 tablespoons (85 g or 90 mL) of oil.

**Number of Servings:** 9  
**Serving Size:** 4 oz. (114 g)  
**Total Yield:** 2 lb., 5 1/4 oz. (1.1 kg)

**Cooking Method:** Boil

CiprianCB/Shutterstock

| | WEIGHT | | VOLUME | |
|---|---|---|---|---|
| **INGREDIENTS** | **U.S.** | **METRIC** | **U.S.** | **METRIC** |
| olive oil | | 15 g | 1 tablespoon | 15 mL |
| onion, minced | 5 oz. | 142 g | 1 medium | |
| garlic, smashed and minced | 1/4 oz. | 8 g | 2 cloves | |
| canned diced tomato, with juice | one 14 1/2-oz. can | one 411-g can | | |
| tomato paste | 1 1/4 oz. | 36 g | 2 tablespoons | 30 mL |
| sugar | | | 1/2 teaspoon | 3 mL |
| salt | 1/4 oz. | 8 g | 1 teaspoon | 5 mL |
| green beans, trimmed | 1 lb., 5 oz. | 596 g | | |
| water | as needed | | | |

① Heat oil in pan over medium-low heat. Add onions and sauté for 5 to 8 minutes, to soften. Add garlic, sauté another minute.

② Add tomato with juice, tomato paste, sugar, and salt. Cook about 5 to 10 minutes to thicken sauce.

③ Add green beans, cook over medium heat until beans are tender and most of liquid is absorbed. Add extra water if needed during cooking. Serve.

### TWIST ON THE CLASSIC

Add shredded beef to this and make a delicious stew to serve over rice.

The flavor of the beans improves with reheating.

# MUJADDARAH (ARABIC)

## LENTIL AND RICE PILAF

**Note:** Combining legumes and grains forms complete protein.

**Note:** If possible, allow time to soak the lentils. Otherwise, increase the cooking time.

**Number of Servings:** 10 entrées or 20 side dishes     **Cooking Method:** Boil
**Serving Size:** 9 oz. (256 g) entrée or 4 1/2 oz. (128 g) side dish
**Total Yield:** 5 lb., 14 oz. (2.7 kg)
**Food Balance:** Protein
**Wine Style:** Low-oaked whites and soft reds
**Example:** St. Clement Sauvignon Blanc, Cellar #8 Zinfandel

© Belaya Katerina

| | WEIGHT | | VOLUME | |
| --- | --- | --- | --- | --- |
| INGREDIENTS | U.S. | METRIC | U.S. | METRIC |
| brown lentils, rinsed | 10 1/2 oz. | 298 g | 2 cups | 480 mL |
| water | as needed | | | |
| olive oil | | 28 g | 2 tablespoons | 30 mL |
| onion, finely diced | 10 oz. | 284 g | 2 medium | |
| long-grain rice, uncooked | 11 1/2 oz. | 326 g | 2 cups | 480 mL |
| salt | 1/4 oz. | 8 g | 1 teaspoon | 5 mL |
| pepper | | | 1/2 teaspoon | 3 mL |
| ground cumin | | | 1 teaspoon | 5 mL |
| ground allspice | | | 1/2 teaspoon | 3 mL |
| **Toppings (Optional):** | | | | |
| olive oil | | 28 g | 2 tablespoons | 30 mL |
| onions, finely sliced | 1 lb., 4 oz. | 567 g | 4 medium | |
| garlic, smashed and minced | 1/2 oz. | 15 g | 4 cloves | |

1. Cover lentils with water and soak for at least 2 hours.
2. Drain and cover with at least 5 cups (1.2 L) water, cover, and boil gently for 20 minutes.
3. Heat 2 tablespoons (28 g or 30 mL) oil in skillet over medium-high heat. Add diced onion and sauté until golden brown.
4. Add fried onion, rice, salt, pepper, cumin, and allspice to pot of lentils. Stir well, bring to boil, reduce heat to simmer, cover pot, and cook for 20 minutes, or until rice and lentils are tender and water is absorbed. Check toward end of cooking period to see that there is enough water to keep the contents moist. Add water, if needed.
5. Correct seasonings.

## TOPPING:

1. Heat 2 tablespoons (28 g or 30 mL) olive oil in pan over medium-high heat.
2. Add sliced onions, sauté about 2 or 3 minutes. Add garlic and sauté until brown in color.

## SERVE:

1. Place lentil mixture in mound on serving dish or on individual plates.
2. Garnish with fried onions and garlic.

---

**TWIST ON THE CLASSIC**

Treat the *mujaddarah* like risotto and add any food to it. For example, add sautéed scallops and peas to the cooked *mujaddarah*.

# STUFFED RED PEPPERS (ARABIC)

**Note:** This recipe calls for cooking the stuffed peppers in water or tomato sauce. If the peppers will be served with sauce, use the tomato sauce instead of water for cooking.

**Number of Servings:** 12
**Serving Size:** 1 stuffed pepper
**Total Yield:** 12 stuffed peppers
**Food Balance:** Sweet/protein
**Wine Style:** Low-oaked whites and soft reds
**Example:** Beringer Viognier or Moscato

**Cooking Method:** Bake, sauté

© Pawel Burgiel

| INGREDIENTS | WEIGHT | | VOLUME | |
| --- | --- | --- | --- | --- |
| | U.S. | METRIC | U.S. | METRIC |
| red bell peppers | about 4 lb., 8 oz. | 2 kg | 12 medium | |
| olive oil | | 28 g | 2 tablespoons | 30 mL |
| **Filling:** | | | | |
| raisins | 3 1/2 oz. | 104 g | 1/2 cup | 120 mL |
| water, boiling | as needed | | | |
| olive oil | | 28 g | 2 tablespoons | 30 mL |
| onions, finely diced | 1 lb., 2 oz. | 511 g | 4 medium | |
| long-grain rice, cooked | 3 lb., 1 oz. | 1.4 kg | 10 cups | 2.4 L |
| tomatoes, peeled and chopped | 12 1/2 oz. | 355 g | 4 medium | |
| fresh cilantro, minced | 1 oz. | 28 g | 1/4 cup | 60 mL |
| fresh mint, minced | 1 oz. | 28 g | 1/4 cup | 60 mL |
| pine nuts | 2 oz. | 57 g | 1/4 cup + 2 tablespoons | 90 mL |
| ground cinnamon | | | 1 teaspoon | 5 mL |
| ground allspice | | | 1 teaspoon | 5 mL |
| pepper | | | 1 teaspoon | 5 mL |
| salt | 3/4 oz. | 22 g | 1 tablespoon | 15 mL |
| tomato sauce or water | | 908 g | 1 quart (4 cups) | 960 mL |

① Cut tops off peppers, reserve. Remove seeds and ribs. Place oven rack in middle of oven. Preheat oven to 350 degrees (180°C).

② Heat 2 tablespoons (28 g or 30 mL) oil in skillet over medium heat, lightly sauté peppers and tops all over until they soften but still retain their shape. Set aside.

## FILLING:

① Place raisins in bowl, pour boiling water over to cover. Let sit until plump, drain.

② Heat 2 tablespoons (28 g or 30 mL) oil in skillet over medium-high heat. Add onions, sauté until softened.

③ Mix onions, raisins, rice, tomatoes, cilantro, mint, pine nuts, cinnamon, allspice, pepper, and salt together in bowl. Correct seasonings.

## ASSEMBLY:

① Stuff peppers with filling, place upright in ovenproof pan.

② Put tops on peppers. Pour tomato sauce or water in dish. (It should come about one-third to halfway up sides of peppers.)

③ Bake until peppers are tender, about 30 minutes. Serve.

© Warren Goldswain

# KHUBZ

## PITA BREAD

**Number of Servings:** 16
**Scaling:** 3 oz. (86 g)
**Dough:** 3 lb., 2 oz. (1.4 kg)

**Cooking Method:** Bake

| INGREDIENTS | WEIGHT | | VOLUME | |
| --- | --- | --- | --- | --- |
| | U.S. | METRIC | U.S. | METRIC |
| water, lukewarm | | 114 g | 1/2 cup | 120 mL |
| sugar | | | 1/4 teaspoon | 2 mL |
| yeast, dry | 1/4 oz. | 8 g | 1 tablespoon | 15 mL |
| flour, bread | 1 lb., 7 1/4 oz. to 1 lb., 11 3/4 oz. or as needed | 660 to 788 g or as needed | 5 to 6 cups or as needed | 1.2 to 1.4 L or as needed |
| salt | | | 1 1/2 teaspoons | 8 mL |
| olive oil | | 28 g | 2 tablespoons | 30 mL |
| water, lukewarm | | 454 g | 2 cups | 480 mL |

1. Place 4 oz. (114 g or 120 mL) water and sugar in a small nonreactive bowl. Add yeast, mix to combine. Set aside until frothy, about 5 minutes.
2. Mix 1 lb., 7 1/4 oz. (660 g, 5 cups, or 1.2 L) flour and salt in a large bowl. Make well in center, add yeast mixture and remaining water, stir well with wooden spoon.
3. Add olive oil, stir to combine. Knead dough until smooth, about 10 minutes. Add just enough flour, as needed, to prevent sticking, but keep dough soft.
4. Place a little oil in a bowl, return kneaded dough to bowl, turn dough so it is thinly coated with oil. Cover loosely with film wrap, allow to rise until doubled, about 1 to 1 1/2 hours.
5. Preheat oven to 500 degrees (260°C). Place oven rack in bottom half of oven. Also place sheet pans in oven to preheat.
6. Punch down dough, knead briefly. Scale into 3-oz. (86-g) pieces. (Divide dough in half, divide each half into eight even pieces (3 oz. or 86 g each).) Lightly flour work surface, as needed. Allow to rest 20 minutes.
7. Use rolling pin or pat each piece into round between 1/8- (30-mm) and 1/4-inch (0.5-cm) thick. Place on hot baking sheet. Bake for 5 to 10 minutes, until puffed and just beginning to brown.
8. Remove to cooling racks. Wrap as soon as cool to prevent drying.

*Rolling pita dough*

*Baked pita*

# BAKLAVA (GREECE)
## LAYERED NUT PASTRY

David Murray © Dorling Kindersley

**Number of Servings:** 12
**Serving Size:** 3- by 3 3/4-inch (8- to 10-cm) piece
**Total Yield:** 9- by 13-inch (23- by 33-cm) pan
**Food Balance:** Very sweet
**Wine Style:** Very sweet
**Example:** Château St. Jean Late Harvest Johannisberg Riesling

**Cooking Method:** Bake

| | WEIGHT | | VOLUME | |
|---|---|---|---|---|
| INGREDIENTS | U.S. | METRIC | U.S. | METRIC |
| **Syrup:** | | | | |
| sugar | 15 oz. | 426 g | 2 cups | 480 mL |
| water | | 227 g | 1 cup | 240 mL |
| lemon juice | | 28 g | 2 tablespoons | 30 mL |
| orange blossom water | | 28 g | 2 tablespoons | 30 mL |
| **Assembly:** | | | | |
| unsalted butter, melted | 6 oz. | 170 g, as needed | 3/4 cup (1 1/2 sticks) | 180 mL, as needed |
| phyllo dough | 1 lb. | 454 g | one 16-oz. package | one 454-g package |
| nuts (pistachios, walnuts, almonds, or combination), coarsely chopped | 10 oz. | 284 g | 2 1/2 cups | 600 mL |
| sugar | 1 oz. | 28 g | 2 tablespoons | 30 mL |

## SYRUP:

1. Combine sugar, water, and lemon juice in saucepan. Simmer until thick enough to coat back of spoon.

2. Add orange blossom water and simmer another 2 minutes.

3. Cool, chill thoroughly.

## ASSEMBLY:

Maksim Denisenko/Fotolia

1. With pastry brush, coat 9- by 13-inch (23- by 33-cm) pan with butter. Place oven rack in center of oven. Preheat oven to 350 degrees (180°C).

2. Lay stack of phyllo sheets on counter. Keep unused phyllo dough covered with damp towel to prevent drying out. Move one sheet of dough to work surface. With pastry brush, lightly coat with melted butter. Move into prepared pan, folding sides or overlapping sheets as necessary to make fit.

3. Repeat until half of phyllo sheets are used.

4. Mix nuts with sugar in bowl. Spread evenly over dough in pan.

5. Stack remaining phyllo sheets in pan buttering each one.

6. Brush top with butter. Using sharp knife, score pastry into diagonals, forming diamonds. If desired, score into squares.

7. Bake for 30 minutes at 350 degrees (180°C), raise temperature to between 400 and 425 degrees (205°C and 220°C), bake another 15 minutes, until puffy and light golden.

8. Remove from oven, pour chilled syrup evenly over *baklava*. Cool to room temperature.

9. Following cut marks, cut into diamonds. Arrange *baklava* on platter and serve.

# ASURE (TURKEY)

## NOAH'S PUDDING

**Note:** Considered Turkey's national dessert, this unusual pudding is served throughout Turkey and the Middle East. *Asure* is served at religious events as well as many celebrations.

**Note:** Begin preparation for this dessert the night before cooking to give wheat and dried beans time to soak.

**Note:** *Dövme*, wheat berries with the husk removed, cook faster and yield a lighter colored pudding. Obtain *dövme* from a Middle Eastern grocery.

**Number of Servings:** 13
**Serving Size:** 6 oz. (170 g)
**Total Yield:** 5 lb., 1 1/2 oz. (2.3 kg)

**Cooking Method:** Boil

Clive Streeter © Dorling Kindersley

| | WEIGHT | | VOLUME | |
|---|---|---|---|---|
| **INGREDIENTS** | **U.S.** | **METRIC** | **U.S.** | **METRIC** |
| wheat berries, rinsed | 11 1/2 oz. | 326 g | 1 1/2 cups | 360 mL |
| chickpeas, rinsed | 4 1/2 oz. | 128 g | 1/2 cup | 120 mL |
| white beans, such as Great Northern, rinsed | 4 1/2 oz. | 128 g | 1/2 cup | 120 mL |
| water | as needed | | | |
| raisins | 4 oz. | 114 g | 1/2 cup | 120 mL |
| dried apricots, chopped | 4 1/2 oz. | 128 g | 2/3 cup | 160 mL |
| dried figs, chopped | 4 1/2 oz. | 128 g | 2/3 cup | 160 mL |
| white rice, uncooked | 1 oz. | 28 g | 2 tablespoons | 30 mL |
| sugar | 11 to 14 1/2 oz. | 312 to 411 g | 1 1/2 to 2 cups | 360 to 480 mL |
| rosewater, *optional* | | 28 g | 2 tablespoons | 30 mL |

**Garnish:**
ground cinnamon
pomegranate seeds, if available
walnuts, toasted and chopped
hazelnuts, toasted and chopped
almonds, toasted and chopped

1. Place wheat, chickpeas, and white beans in separate bowls. Cover with water to a height at least 2 inches (5 cm) above ingredients. Cover and refrigerate overnight.
2. Boil wheat until tender, about 2 hours. Boil chickpeas and beans together until tender, about 2 hours.
3. Place raisins, apricots, and figs in bowl, cover with 2 cups (480 mL) water. Let soak for at least 1 hour.
4. Combine wheat and beans in one pot, add rice and sugar, bring to a boil, reduce heat and simmer for another hour. Add water if needed.
5. Add soaked dried fruits, cook another 15 minutes. If desired, add rosewater.
6. Cool, cover, and refrigerate until cold. Serve with a sprinkling of cinnamon and garnished with pomegranate seeds (if in season), and nuts.

### TWIST ON THE CLASSIC

Serve a portion of this confection accompanied by a bowl of vanilla custard (pudding).

The lore behind *asure* is quite interesting. According to legend, Noah made *asure* when he landed on Mount Ararat after the floodwaters receded. With little food left on the ark, he took all remaining food items and cooked them together to create a dessert to give thanks for their safety. The result was *asure*, also called Noah's pudding.

The beans and grains used in *asure* require long soaking and cooking. To expedite the process, replace the wheat berries with bulgur and the dried beans with drained canned beans. To rehydrate bulgur, cover it with boiling water and soak it a short time (15 to 30 minutes). Double the amount of canned beans to replace the dried beans, for example replace 5 oz. (142 g) of dried beans with 10 oz. (284 g) of canned.

## >> LEARNING OBJECTIVES

By the end of this chapter, you will be able to:

- Understand the diversity of cooking methods and dishes prepared in Israel
- Explain the transformation of barren land to farmland in Israel
- Describe the growing conditions that exist in Israel and why a bounty of crops is produced there
- Identify some of the kosher dietary laws
- Prepare a variety of Israeli dishes

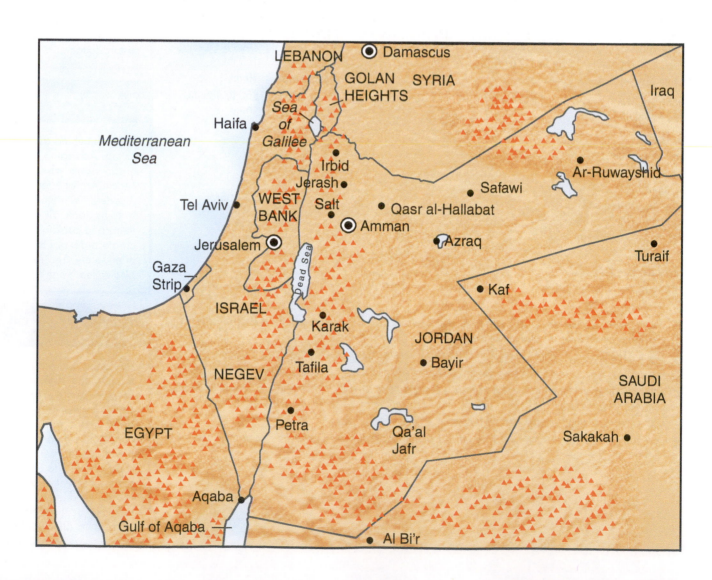

## >> HISTORY

### EARLY HISTORY

According to the Old Testament, about 4,500 years ago Israelites roamed the Sinai Desert for 40 years. As written in the Bible, they subsisted on *manna* and quails during that time.

Many years later, the Greeks took control of the land. They introduced foods and traditions from their culture, such as the preparation of large pieces of meat. Roman rule followed Greek rule. During this time, the people of Jerusalem and the Holy Land consumed the same foods as residents of the Middle East.

With an increase in the number of Muslims in this area by the 600s, Jewish people found it easier to fulfill their dietary needs. Since both groups ate no pork, they both relied on sheep and goat meat. Both sheep and goats flourished by grazing in the mountains and scruffy land here.

Taking place during the Middle Ages, the Crusades were an armed pilgrimage to the Holy Land led by the Christians in an attempt to oust the Muslim control. These wars continued for two centuries: from the end of the eleventh century to the end of the thirteenth. Because of the Crusades, thousands of people from myriad countries traveled to this sacred land. Those people brought influences from their native homelands, and they learned of foreign foods during their journey.

The Ottomans ruled in the 1500s, and of course, they introduced Turkish cookery here. They cooked meats with yogurt, made kebobs, and barbequed meats. In addition to preparing a variety of stuffed vegetables including eggplant, zucchini, peppers, and grape leaves, the Ottomans brought foods like potatoes and tomatoes.

Throughout history, Jewish people have faced persecution, imprisonment, enslavement, and/or death in various countries. To escape these conditions, many fled their homes and settled in new lands. They took their culinary history with them and adopted the cuisine of their new home. In this way, Jewish cookery evolved into its own melting pot of the world's cooking.

- *Late 1400s and early 1500s— The Spanish Inquisition forced Jewish people to flee from Spain. Since historians have no idea how many fled, estimates range from 40,000 to 800,000 people.*
- *Large-scale anti-Jewish riots known as pogroms have raged in Russia and Eastern Europe at many times throughout history. During the late 1800s and early 1900s, these pogroms were particularly violent and frequent. Hundreds of thousands (some say millions) of Jewish people fled from Russia and Eastern Europe during those years.*
- *1930s and 1940s—Adolf Hitler ruled Germany. He tried to annihilate the Jewish people and conquer the world. Six million Jewish people died under Hitler.*

### BIRTH OF A NEW NATION

On May 14, 1948, the United Nations formed the nation of Israel in spite of intense hostility from its Arab and Palestinian neighbors. That hostility still rages today, and the borders of this tiny nation frequently change as the conflict and fighting continue.

Designated as a home for people of the Jewish faith because of their persecution throughout history, Israel attracted Jewish people from around the world. As a newly established country and continuing to the present, Israel is a culinary melting pot.

The area that became Israel in 1948 primarily consisted of barren land containing mountains, canyons, swamps, and arid desert. The Israelis studied, experimented, and transformed that poor soil into fertile and productive farmland. While they drained the swampland, they irrigated the desert with massive irrigation networks. Through the use of breeding, pesticides, fertilizers, and irrigation, Israelis greatly increased the production of livestock and crops. At this point, they could raise cattle because they now had grasses for grazing. Also, now they could grow all sorts of fruits and vegetables.

In the first 20 years after becoming a nation, Israelis raised the production of dates by 38 times, increased banana production by 16, and citrus fruits by almost four. In addition to producing plenty of food for their residents, Israelis export a huge amount of very high-quality produce all over the world.

### KIBBUTZIM

Almost one-third of Israel's agricultural production comes from a *kibbutz*, a commune or agricultural collective. These collectives actually began in the late nineteenth century. Those who live and work on a particular *kibbutz* own the entire business of that *kibbutz,* including the crops, equipment, houses, and buildings. This has proved a successful venture in Israel, where about 100,000 people living in *kibbutzim* produce the agricultural needs and export for a country of over several million.

## KOSHER DIETARY LAWS

*Kashrut*, the ancient kosher dietary laws of Judaism, forbids the consumption of pork and shellfish. To be considered kosher, an animal must have cloven hooves and chew a cud. Permitted seafood needs a backbone, fins, and scales. This means that pork and shellfish, including shrimp, lobster, scallops, mussels, oysters, and clams, are among the forbidden foods under *kashrut*. In addition, special butchering procedures must be followed when processing meat. Because eating blood is not allowed, Israelis typically prepare and serve meat well done. Also, it is forbidden to mix milk and meat at the same meal, so one either eats a meat meal or a dairy meal.

## >> TOPOGRAPHY

From north to south, Israel is less than 300 miles long, and it spans only 63 miles across its widest east to west point. Despite its small size, Israel contains an incredible diversity of temperatures and terrain, ranging from desert to mountains to subtropical farmland.

In the Bible, Israel is called "the land of milk and honey." The wide variety of topography and weather conditions in Israel make it conducive to growing a wide range of crops in different areas.

Arid desert composes half of Israel's land. The western coast of Israel borders the Mediterranean Sea. The Sea of Galilee and the Dead Sea are situated on Israel's eastern border; the Red Sea lies to the south.

## TOPOGRAPHICAL AREAS

Israel has four distinct topographical areas: the coastal plain, the central hills, Jordan Rift Valley, and the Negev Desert. Lying in the west, the coastal plains contain land near the Mediterranean Sea. They experience the typical Mediterranean climate of short, rainy winters and hot, dry summers. This fertile, humid area yields abundant crops, including lots of citrus fruits and grapes for eating and wine. Galilee lies in the northern section of this region.

The central hills region consists of hills, mountains, and fertile valleys. The Jezreel Valley separates Galilee from the central mountain range. Often referred to as the West Bank, Samaria and Judea lie in central and western Israel, spanning the central hills and the Jordan Rift Valley regions.

The Jordan Rift Valley lies east of the central hills, in the eastern portion of Israel. The Jordan River flows through this region, creating the border between Israel and Jordan. With the Jordan River providing water for agriculture and climate that's conducive for agriculture throughout the year, lots of crops come from here. Known as Lake Kinneret to the Israelis, the Sea of Galilee lies in the northern part of this region, and the Dead Sea lies in the south.

In the south, the Negev Desert contains desert, cliffs, huge erosion craters unlike any in the world, and plateaus. With more than 4,600 square miles, this region encompasses more than half of Israel's land. The Red Sea borders on the south.

## >> COOKING METHODS

Truly creating a melting pot of cuisines, the Israelis have adopted and adapted cooking techniques and methods from their many diverse ancestors. Israelis use virtually all cooking methods.

---

*"Kosher" means fit or proper to eat. Developed as laws for sanitization, these dietary laws were made in the days before refrigeration, pasteurization, and other methods of safely preserving food.*

### KASHRUT (KOSHER DIETARY LAWS)

- *Dairy and meat may not be eaten together, so a meal contains either dairy or meat. A number of foods are classified parve (neutral), meaning they can accompany either meat or dairy. Eggs, fish, grains, vegetable oils and margarine, vegetables, and fruits are a few examples of parve foods.*
- *Separate dishes, silverware, cooking pans, and utensils are used for meat and dairy preparation as well as eating.*
- *Meat must come from animals with cloven hooves and who chew a cud. This eliminates pork.*
- *Fowl is allowed except birds of prey.*
- *Seafood must have a backbone as well as scales and fins, which eliminates all shellfish, eel, monkfish, catfish, and more.*
- *Special slaughtering procedures must be followed for all animals consumed.*
- *Only approved facilities may process meat and package kosher foods.*
- *No blood may be consumed, so meat must be cooked until no pink shows.*

*A profusion of kosher restaurants exist in Jerusalem and other large cities. Some serve only dairy (serving no meat products), others offer only meat (no dairy), and still others are vegetarian restaurants (serving no meat or seafood). Of course, all restaurants serve parve foods.*

> **Ingredients and Foods Commonly Used throughout the Cuisine of Israel Include**

- freshwater and saltwater fish
- lamb
- *falafel*
- hummus
- pita bread and *challah*
- citrus fruits
- all sorts of fruits and vegetables
- olives and olive oil

The grilling of meats and popularity of *shish kebobs* reflects the Middle Eastern influence, and were a natural extension of cooking over an open fire in the desert. From their European heritage, Israelis adopted the cooking techniques of baking, braising, and poaching. Because the Sabbath is a day with no work, Jewish people prepare braised dishes that can withstand a night of cooking in a very low oven. With an abundance of fresh fish flourishing here, poaching, grilling, and sautéing are frequently used cooking methods.

## >> REGIONS

### LOCATION

Israel is surrounded by Middle Eastern countries on three sides: Lebanon lies to the north of Israel, Syria to the northeast, Jordan to the east and southeast, Saudi Arabia to the south, and Egypt to the southwest. The Mediterranean Sea forms Israel's western border. The cookery of the Middle East dominates much of Israel's cuisine, and the Middle Eastern and north African influences remain the most prominent in this culinary melting pot.

### CLIMATE

In Israel, rain falls during the winter months with the possibility of snowfall only in the northern and central hills. Hot, dry summers exist throughout most of the land, particularly in the desert areas.

### NORTHERN ISRAEL

The mountainous Golan Heights and the Sea of Galilee are situated in the north. Actually a freshwater lake, the Sea of Galilee is fed by the Jordan River, which enters it from the north, exits from the south, and continues flowing to the Dead Sea. The area around the Sea of Galilee lies 700 feet below sea level, and the warm climate found here supports the growth of subtropical vegetation.

### CENTRAL AND EASTERN ISRAEL

The capital of Israel, Jerusalem, lies in the center of the country and enjoys fairly moderate temperatures. Built on a series of hills, it is located near Israel's central mountain range, which runs north to south. These mountains create a "watershed" effect that provides Jerusalem with rainfall. Lying to the east, the Dead Sea area remains hot and dry.

### SOUTHERN ISRAEL

The Negev Desert is located in the south. Eilat, the major city in this area, lies at the southern border. Although this region experiences hot days, the nights cool off drastically in the areas with high elevations.

### WESTERN ISRAEL

The coastal cities of Tel Aviv and Haifa lie on the Mediterranean Sea on the western side of the country. Tempered by the sea, this area experiences moderate temperatures. Tel Aviv, now the center of Israel's commerce, consisted of sand dunes less than a century ago.

*In size, the country of Israel is just a little larger than the state of Massachusetts.*

*Ranking as the lowest point on earth, the Dead Sea lies 1,339 feet below sea level. Measuring over 33 percent salinity, the Dead Sea is the saltiest body of water on earth. It contains six times more salt than the oceans. No fish live in this body of water.*

*Jaffa oranges flourish in Jaffa (which lies near Tel Aviv) and surrounding areas. A sweet and almost seedless orange, it tolerates cold better than most orange varieties. It is believed that the first orange trees were planted in Israel in the 1500s.*

*Shakshouka*
© signorinac

*Shwarma*
© paul _brighton

*Bourekas*
© Rafael Ben-Ari

## >> CUISINE

### MELTING POT

People from more than 80 nationalities immigrated to Israel, bringing their native cuisines with them. When the Sephardic Jews from Greece, Turkey, Spain, northern Africa, and the Middle East moved to Israel, they arrived bearing the foods from their homelands. They brought dishes like *dolmades* (stuffed grape leaves), *shakshouka* (sautéed tomatoes, onions, garlic, and herbs topped with a poached egg), and couscous (tiny pasta made from semolina) served with meats and vegetables. The Ashkenazi Jews from central and eastern Europe brought *borscht* (beet soup), *gefilte* fish (a fish dumpling served cold), *knishes* (dumplings consisting of dough surrounding one of several fillings), *challah* (braided egg bread), and *kugel* (noodle pudding). The Jews from northern Europe contributed bagels and pretzels to the foods of Israel. The cuisine of Israel formed into a culinary melting pot with representation from many ethnic cuisines added to the Middle Eastern cuisine that, of course, is native to the area.

Currently, Israeli culinary professionals are developing a cuisine of their own. Instead of centering around foods from the colder climates of Europe, this new cuisine uses the incredible bounty of available fresh ingredients in Israel and is based on the weather conditions in their country.

### MIDDLE EASTERN INFLUENCE

For several reasons, Middle Eastern cookery exerts the largest influence on the cuisine of Israel. First, the Arab countries are Israel's closest neighbors, so they influence the cookery. Second, many Muslims inhabit the countries of the Middle East, and both Judaic and Islamic dietary laws forbid eating pork. The shared dietary restrictions of these two cultures make for easy exchange of recipes.

Foods sold by street vendors are widely available in many areas in Israel, particularly in the larger cities. Some of the most popular items include Middle Eastern specialties like *hummus* (*tahini* and chickpea spread served with torn pieces or wedges of pita bread), *falafel* (referred to as Israeli hot dogs, they serve these fried chickpea patties in pita bread and top with diced salad and *tahini* sauce), *shwarma* (grilled slices of meat served in a pita with salad); *bourekas* (turnovers of phyllo dough filled with spinach or potato), and *kibbe* (fried patties of seasoned ground meat and bulgur).

*Mezze*, small appetizers, are consumed in Israel as they are throughout the Middle East. Green and red chilies frequently spice Israeli foods. Chili-based relishes often accompany meals. Borrowed from the North African cuisine, *harissa*, a hot pepper paste, is commonly used in Israel. The Yemenites and Moroccans are particularly fond of chilies and hot, spicy foods.

### STAPLES

Israeli staples include lots of food items commonly consumed in the Middle East. Foods like wheat, rice, barley, lentils, beans, yogurt, lemons, eggplant, olives, olive oil, grapes, pomegranates, dates, and figs appear often. Israeli cooks season with onions, garlic, and many herbs and spices such as mint, parsley, cumin, coriander, cardamom, rosemary, and thyme.

### FISH AND SEAFOOD

Seafood abounds, particularly along the Mediterranean, the northern coast, and in the Galilee regions. Many types of freshwater and saltwater fish including grouper, red and gray mullet, red snapper, talapia, carp, and sea bream thrive here. Fish stews or soups similar to *bouillabaisse* are common in Jaffa.

Israelis prepare fish using a variety of cooking methods; they bake, fry, braise, poach, and grill seafood. Because of the very fresh quality of the fish, it often simply is grilled or baked and served with a sauce.

## PRODUCE

Today, a staggering abundance of fruits and vegetables grow in this small country. Through irrigation, the Israelis transformed barren land into fertile farmland and because of the diverse topography, a wide range of produce thrives. Subtropical fruits and vegetables flourish in the area near the Sea of Galilee while the temperate climate of Golan and Galilee yields apples, cherries, and more. Some of the many available fruits include watermelon, figs, dates, prickly pears, all sorts of citrus fruits, apples, grapes, mangoes, kiwi, and every variety of exotic fruit. Although Israelis consume lots of fruit, they export much of this high-quality produce.

Known as Israeli salad in Israel and diced salad throughout the Middle East, a mixture containing diced cucumbers and tomatoes as well as any other desired vegetables in lemon and olive oil remains a staple throughout the Middle East. Whether used as a salad or condiment, most meals in Israel include this popular vegetable mixture. Israeli salad even tops *falafel* in a pita.

*Chapter 9 includes a recipe for diced salad.*

## BREAD

Bread accompanies meals. *Challah* is a rich egg bread traditionally formed into a braid and served every Friday night at the Sabbath meal as well as at weddings and on most holidays. For *Rosh Hashanah*, the Jewish New Year, the *challah* is formed into a circle to symbolize the never-ending circle of life. The Middle Eastern favorite pita bread appears frequently. Israelis use it as a pocket for holding sandwiches or as a scoop for hummus or other *mezze*.

## DESSERTS

Like their Middle Eastern neighbors, Israelis prefer very sweet desserts. The most common confections include fruit compotes, *baklava,* and other typical Middle Eastern pastries combining phyllo dough and nuts. *Malabi*, a popular flan-type custard, is served in a cup and topped with a sweet, syrupy fruit topping. Another well-liked confection, *halvah*, is a sesame candy that comes in several flavors—plain, chocolate, or marbled (plain marbled with chocolate). *Halvah* is sold by the slice cut from a large loaf or packaged as a candy bar.

*Halvah with nuts*
© Kybele

## MEALS

Breakfast reigns as an important meal in Israel, especially on the *kibbutz*, where manual labor produces hungry workers. Cooks serve a whole range of foods for breakfast including *labaneh*, a cheese made from curdled yogurt.

*All holidays, including the Sabbath, begin and end at sundown.*

With the exception of the Friday night Sabbath meal, the evening meal in Israel follows the late dining pattern customary in Mediterranean and Middle Eastern countries. The Friday night meal is served at sundown in celebration of the beginning of the Sabbath, the day of rest.

*Cholent*, a dish with a long culinary history, consists of a slowly cooked meat casserole containing rice or barley, beans, meat, and potatoes. This eastern European dish met north African and Middle Eastern influences in Israel. Because no work is performed on the Sabbath, preparation for the dish begins on Friday before sundown, when the Jewish Sabbath begins. Traditionally, cooks (often housewives) take the prepared *cholent* to a commercial bakery where it is baked in the oven at a very low temperature throughout the night. After services on Saturday, they pick up the *cholent* at the bakery, take it home, and dine.

Another casserole-type dish that could survive a night in a slow oven for the Saturday Sabbath meal, *kugels* consist of noodles or potatoes combined in a dish with seasonings and binding ingredients. Many refer to *kugels* as puddings.

## SOME OF THE TRADITIONAL JEWISH HOLIDAYS

**Rosh Hashanah** Jewish New Year, in the fall. Sweet foods are served to represent a sweet coming year.

**Yom Kippur** Day of Atonement, a day of fasting, occurs ten days after *Rosh Hashanah.* People abstain from all food and drink on Yom Kippur, which lasts from sunset to sunset.

**Chanukah** Festival of Lights, in December, commemorates the miracle of one day's worth of oil burning in the synagogue for eight days. All sorts of fried foods (representing the oil) and potato *latkes* are served during Chanukah.

**Purim** Festival of Esther, in the spring one month before Passover. Celebrates Jewish Queen Esther, the queen of Persia who saved the Jews from the wicked government minister, Haman, who wanted to kill all the Jews. A triangular pastry, *Hamantaschen* is served for Purim and represents Haman's triangular-shaped hat.

**Pesach** Passover, in the spring, celebrates the escape of the Jewish people from the bondage of the Egyptians. *Matzo* replaces bread, and Jews consume no bread products during the week of Passover.

| REGION | AREA | WEATHER | TOPOGRAPHY | FOODS |
|--------|------|---------|------------|-------|
| Jordan Valley | East | Hot | Fertile farmland | Winter vegetables, fruits, avocados, bananas, guava, mangos, citrus |
| Jezreel Valley | North | Hot summers, wet winters | Valley between mountains | Cereals |
| Hulah Valley | Northeast | Hot | Marsh until irrigated, fertile farmland | Corn |
| Golan | Northeast | Temperate | Mountains | Grapes, apples, fruits |
| Galilee | North | Hot summers, wet winters | Dan and Banias rivers flow from Mount Hermon into Sea of Galilee | Fish, trout, tilapia |
| Negev Desert | South | Hot | Desert until irrigated, three erosion craters, shore on south | Cereals, wheat |
| Judean Desert | Mideast | Hot | Canyons, desert, Dead Sea | Salad vegetables, tomatoes |
| West | West | Hot summers, wet winters | Mediterranean coast | Fish, seafood, citrus |
| Jerusalem Area | Central to East | Hot summers, moderate winters | Hills, mountains, forests, Dead Sea | Sheep, goats, dates, oranges, bananas, papayas |

## >> Review Questions

1. Discuss the different ethnic groups making up the population of Israel and their contributions to the cuisine.
2. What was the land in Israel like in 1948, and how has it changed?
3. Name four of the laws of *kashrut.*
4. Name and describe four Israeli dishes.

## >> Glossary

**Ashkenazi Jews** Jewish people with central or Eastern European heritage

*borscht* Beet soup

*bourekas* Turnovers of phyllo dough filled with spinach or potato

*challah* Braided egg bread traditionally served on the Sabbath and all holidays

*cholent* Known as Sabbath stew; a slowly cooked casserole containing rice or barley, beans, meat, and potatoes; traditionally cooked at a low temperature in an oven in a commercial bakery all Friday night and then eaten on Saturday, as no work may be performed on the Sabbath

*falafel* Fried chickpea patties served in pita bread topped with salad and a *tahini* sauce; known as Israeli hot dogs

*gefilte* fish A fish dumpling that is served cold and usually accompanied by horseradish

*harissa* Hot pepper paste used in Morocco

*hummus* Chickpea and *tahini* spread served with pita bread

*kashrut* The rules governing kosher diet and preparation

*kibbe* Seasoned ground meat and bulgur that is fried

*kibbutz* A farm collective where the people who live and work on the farm own the entire business

*knish* A dumpling consisting of dough surrounding one of several fillings

*kugel* Often called noodle pudding, a casserole usually consisting of noodles, cottage cheese, sour cream, raisins, and cinnamon; other vegetables can form a *kugel*

*labaneh* A cheese made from curdled yogurt

*latkes* Potato pancakes, traditionally served at Chanukah

*mezze* Appetizers

*parve* Foods that can accompany either meat or dairy products

**Sephardic Jews** Jewish people from Greece, Turkey, Spain, and northern Africa

*shakshouka* Sautéed tomatoes, onions, garlic, and herbs topped with a poached egg

*shwarma* Grilled slices of meat served in a pita with salad

*tahini* Sesame seed paste

## BOUREKAS

### FILLED TURNOVERS

© Rafael Ben-Ari

**Number of Pieces:** 24
**Cooking Method:** Bake
**Serving Size:** 1 or 2
**Scaling:** 1 oz. (28 g) filling per turnover
**Total Yield:** 1 lb., 8 oz. (680 g) filling
**Wine Style:** Full-bodied young white wine. Possible grape varietals are Gruner Veltliner, Riesling.
**Example:** Gruner Veltliner Smaragd "Urgestein Terrassen" 2014, F.X. Pichler (Wachau/Austria)

| | WEIGHT | | VOLUME | |
|---|---|---|---|---|
| INGREDIENTS | U.S. | METRIC | U.S. | METRIC |
| **Eggplant and Cheese Filling:** | | | | |
| eggplant, charred | 1 lb., 4 1/4 oz. | 576 g | 1 large | |
| feta cheese | 8 oz. | 227 g | 2 cups | 480 mL |
| parsley or cilantro, minced | 1/2 oz. | 15 g | 1/4 cup | 60 mL |
| egg | 1 3/4 oz. | 50 g | 1 each | |
| salt | | | 1/2 teaspoon | 3 mL |
| pepper | | | 1/2 teaspoon | 3 mL |
| phyllo dough | about 11 oz. | about 312 g | | |
| butter, unsalted, melted | 4 oz. or as needed | 114 g or as needed | 1/2 cup or as needed | 120 mL or as needed |
| **Glaze:** | | | | |
| egg | 1 3/4 oz. | 50 g | 1 each | |
| water | | | 2 teaspoons | 10 mL |
| sesame seeds | as needed for sprinkling | | | |

1. To char the eggplant, stick it all over with a fork, then bake it at 450 degrees (230°C) for 25 minutes, broil it, or grill it until the skin blackens and/or blisters. Allow to cool enough to handle. Remove skin and seeds. Chop pulp and allow to drain to remove excess moisture. To facilitate removing excess liquid, wipe with paper towel.

2. Place chopped eggplant in bowl. Add crumbled feta, parsley or cilantro, egg, salt, and pepper. Mix to combine. Refrigerate until needed.

3. Place parchment paper on sheet pans. Position oven rack in center of oven. Preheat oven to 350 degrees (180°C).

4. To work with phyllo dough, please review instructions in Chapter 9, the Middle East on page 288. Place one sheet of phyllo on work surface; cover remaining sheets with damp towel. Cut sheet in half lengthwise into 6-inch (15-cm) wide sheet (by 18 inches, 46 cm). Brush lightly with melted butter, fold 6-inch (15-cm) sheet in half lengthwise to form 3- by 18-inch, (8- by 46-cm) sheet. Brush top side with butter. Place 1 oz. (28 g, 1 heaping tablespoon, 15 mL) filling on strip about 1/2 inch (1.3 cm) from bottom. Fold phyllo over filling like a flag to form a triangle. Place on prepared baking pan; brush outside of triangle with butter. Sprinkle with sesame seeds.

5. Repeat with remaining phyllo and filling. Bake for 20 to 25 minutes, until golden brown. Cool on racks; serve warm or at room temperature.

---

### TWIST ON THE CLASSIC

Serve the hot *boureka* on top of or next to a salad dressed with lemon vinaigrette.

---

*Bourekas* often are eaten at breakfast, lunch, or as a snack.

*Bourekas* are filled with a variety of foods. Some of the usual fillings include:

- spinach
- cheese
- potato
- eggplant
- mushroom

When making *bourekas*, some use phyllo dough, others use puff pastry, and some cooks make a dough containing flour, water, and olive oil that is rolled like pie dough.

# CHOPPED LIVER

**Note:** Chopped liver is easily molded into shapes. Since chopped liver is brown, garnish with red peppers, radishes, or other colorful items to brighten the platter.

**Number of Servings:** 18
**Serving Size:** 1-oz. (28-g) canapé
**Total Yield:** 1 lb., 3 oz. (540 g)
**Food Balance:** Protein
**Wine Style:** Low-oaked whites and soft reds
**Example:** Château St. Jean Riesling or Viognier

**Cooking Method:** Sauté

*Sautéing chicken livers*
Pearson Education/PH College

| INGREDIENTS | WEIGHT | | VOLUME | |
|---|---|---|---|---|
| | U.S. | METRIC | U.S. | METRIC |
| chicken livers | 1 lb. | 454 g | | |
| onions, minced | 4 1/2 oz. | 128 g | 1 medium | |
| butter, melted, or chicken fat | 1 1/2 oz. | 43 g | 3 tablespoons | 45 mL |
| salt | 1/4 oz. | 8 g | 1 teaspoon | 5 mL |
| pepper | | | 1/4 teaspoon | 2 mL |
| eggs, hard cooked and diced | 6 3/4 oz. | 191 g | 4 each | |
| party rye or crackers | | | | |

1. Wash livers, let drain thoroughly.
2. Sauté liver with onions in melted butter or chicken fat until liver is done; that is, no longer pink.
3. Cool liver and onions about 5 minutes, place in bowl of food processor fitted with knife blade. Pulse a couple of times.
4. Add salt, pepper, and eggs. Pulse until fine, but not too smooth. Do not let it become a fine paste.
5. Correct seasonings. Refrigerate until serving time.
6. Place on platter and garnish, if desired. Serve with party rye bread or crackers.

## TWIST ON THE CLASSIC

Prepare a tri-level pâté by placing a layer of chopped liver in a molding pan lined with plastic wrap (to facilitate removing pâté from pan). Top the chopped liver with a layer of red pepper mousse, and place a layer of asparagus mousse over the red pepper mousse. Chill, unmold, and serve.

*Chopped liver sandwich*
© robert lerich

# PASTELICOS

## MEAT-FILLED PASTRIES

**TWIST ON THE CLASSIC**

For a passed hors d'oeuvre, prepare the meat pies in mini muffin tins.

Serve three of these meat pies for an entrée portion.

**Note:** These hail from the kitchens of Sephardic Jews. *Pastel* means "stuffed dough" in a Sephardic dialect.

**Note:** In Israel and other Middle Eastern countries, they prepare these meat pies as freestanding pies and cook them on a sheet pan or cookie sheet. For ease of preparation, make the pies in a standard muffin tin with cups 2 1/2 inches (6 cm) in diameter.

**Number of Servings:** 16
**Cooking Method:** Bake
**Serving Size:** 1 meat pie, about 2 oz. (57 g)
1 1/4 oz. (36 g) dough
1 oz. (28 g) filling
**Total Yield:** Sixteen 2 1/2-inch (6-cm) meat pies
1 lb., 6 oz. dough (624 g)
1 lb., 2 1/2 oz. filling (525 g)
**Food Balance:** Balanced
**Wine Style:** Wine friendly—Enjoy your favorite wine!
**Example:** Penfolds Chardonnay or Shiraz

| | WEIGHT | | VOLUME | |
|---|---|---|---|---|
| *INGREDIENTS* | *U.S.* | *METRIC* | *U.S.* | *METRIC* |
| **Dough:** | | | | |
| all-purpose flour | 13 oz. | 369 g | 2 3/4 cups | 660 mL |
| salt | 1/4 oz. | 8 g | 1 teaspoon | 5 mL |
| unsalted butter, cold, cut into pieces | 5 oz. | 142 g | 10 tablespoons (1 stick + 2 tablespoons) | 148 mL |
| olive oil | | 28 g | 2 tablespoons | 30 mL |
| water | | 71 g | about 1/4 cup + 1 tablespoon | 75 mL |
| **Filling:** | | | | |
| olive oil | | 15 g | 1 tablespoon | 15 mL |
| pine nuts | 1 1/4 oz. | 36 g | 3 tablespoons | 45 mL |
| onion, small dice | 9 oz. | 256 g | 1 large | |
| ground beef or lamb | 1 lb. | 454 g | | |
| ground allspice | | | 1/2 teaspoon | 3 mL |
| ground cinnamon | | | 1 teaspoon | 5 mL |
| salt | 1/4 oz. | 8 g | 1 teaspoon | 5 mL |
| pepper | | | 1/4 teaspoon | 2 mL |
| water | | 57 g | 1/4 cup | 60 mL |
| **Assembly:** | | | | |
| flour | as needed | | | |
| egg, beaten | 1 3/4 oz. | 50 g | 1 each | |
| water | | | 1 teaspoon | 5 mL |
| sesame seeds, for sprinkling | | | | |
| **Accompaniments:** | | | | |
| hard-boiled egg, quartered | | | | |
| *Salata Khodra* (Diced Salad) (*see recipe in Chapter 9*) | | | | |

## DOUGH:

1. Place flour and salt in food processor fitted with knife blade. Pulse to mix. Alternatively, mix flour and salt in bowl.

2. Place butter pieces on top, pulse until clumps the size of peas form. If mixing by hand, cut butter into flour using fingertips, two knives, or pastry cutter.

3. Add oil. Pulse or mix to combine. Add water, pulse or mix to combine. If working with food processor, dough will come together in a ball. Do not overwork dough or it will be tough. Wrap in plastic wrap and refrigerate until needed.

## FILLING:

1. Heat oil in skillet over medium heat. Add pine nuts, sauté until beginning to brown. Remove from skillet, set aside until needed.

2. Add onion to skillet. Sauté until softened, about 5 minutes.

3. Add meat, cook until it loses red color. Add allspice, cinnamon, salt, pepper, and water. Stir well.

4. Continue cooking until water evaporates. Add pine nuts and remove from heat. Set aside to cool while preparing pastry cups.

## ASSEMBLY:

1. Preheat oven to 375 degrees (190°C). Working with half the dough, roll until about 1/4-inch (1/2-cm) thick. Sprinkle flour on table and rolling pin, if needed.

2. Cut into 3- to 3 1/2-inch (8- to 9-cm) rounds to line the bottom and sides of the muffin tins. Press the rounds into the muffin cup and up the sides. Roll out second half of dough, cut 2-inch (5-cm) rounds for top lids.

3. Fill each lined muffin tin with 2 tablespoons (30 mL) of filling. Top with 2-inch (5-cm) round of dough. Press edges to seal top and bottom dough together. Continue with remaining dough and filling.

4. Whisk beaten egg and water together in bowl. Brush top of meat pies with egg mixture. Sprinkle with sesame seeds. Bake until golden, about 25 to 30 minutes.

5. Serve hot or warm, accompanied by hard-boiled eggs and *Salata Khodra* (Diced Salad).

*Placing dough in muffin tin*
Pearson Education/PH College

Pearson Education/PH College

# CHICKEN SOUP WITH CHICKEN KREPLACH
## CHICKEN SOUP WITH CHICKEN-FILLED DUMPLINGS

**Note:** Called Jewish wontons or Jewish tortellini, *kreplach* usually are filled with meat, chicken, or cheese.

**Number of Servings:** 12

**Cooking Method:** Boil

**Serving Size:** 4 *kreplach* (in 6 oz., 170 g soup)

**Total Yield:** 50 *kreplach*

**Food Balance:** Protein/neutral

**Wine Style:** Wine friendly—Enjoy a wine of your choice

**Example:** Beringer Chardonnay or Merlot

© Elzbieta Sekowska

|  | WEIGHT | | VOLUME | |
| --- | --- | --- | --- | --- |
| INGREDIENTS | U.S. | METRIC | U.S. | METRIC |
| **Dough:** | | | | |
| all-purpose flour | 8 1/2 oz. | 241 g | 1 3/4 cups + 2 tablespoons | 450 mL |
| salt | | | 3/4 teaspoon | 4 mL |
| eggs | 5 oz. | 142 g | 3 each | |
| **Filling:** | | | | |
| oil | | 15 g | 1 tablespoon | 15 mL |
| onion, finely diced | 4 oz. | 114 g | 1 medium | |
| chicken, cooked | 8 oz. | 227 g | 2 cups | 480 mL |
| egg | 1 3/4 oz. | 50 g | 1 each | |
| salt | | | 1/2 teaspoon | 3 mL |
| pepper | | | 1/4 teaspoon | 2 mL |
| nutmeg | | | few gratings, to taste | |
| chicken soup | | | 2 1/2 quarts (10 cups) | 2.4 L |

**Garnish:**

fresh parsley, minced

## DOUGH:

1. Place 1 1/2 cups (360 mL) of flour in bowl of food processor fitted with knife blade. Add salt and eggs. Pulse until dough begins to form ball.
2. Add remaining flour by the tablespoon, process a few seconds after each addition. Process until dough forms ball, about 30 seconds.
3. On lightly floured surface, knead briefly by hand until very smooth. Cover dough and let rest for 30 minutes at room temperature.

## FILLING:

1. Heat oil in skillet over medium heat, add onion, sauté until soft and just beginning to brown, about 10 minutes.
2. Chop chicken in food processor fitted with knife blade until fine. Add egg, salt, pepper, and nutmeg, process until smooth.
3. Refrigerate filling until ready to use.

## ASSEMBLY:

1. Cut dough into 2 or 3 pieces. Keep unused dough covered.
2. Flatten or roll out one piece dough. If necessary, flour lightly.
3. Put dough through pasta machine with rollers at widest setting. Continue putting dough through at this setting until smooth.
4. Reduce width setting by one notch and put dough through machine. Continue reducing setting size and feeding dough until the smallest setting is reached.
5. Lay dough on lightly floured surface. Place 3/4-teaspoon (4-mL) mounds of filling about 1 1/2 inches (4 cm) apart on dough, cut dough between mounds into about 2 1/2-inch (6-cm) squares.

6  Brush two adjacent sides of square with water, fold dough over filling to form triangle, pressing moistened sides against dry sides to make tight seal. Some people then join opposite ends of triangle together to form ring. *See photograph of preparing wontons in Chapter 11, China.*

7  Place finished triangle on floured sheet of parchment paper. Repeat rolling and shaping with remaining dough and filling. (Finished *kreplach* may be refrigerated, well wrapped, for 1 day.)

## SERVE:

1  To cook, add *kreplach* to large pot of boiling salted water. Bring to boil, reduce heat to simmer, cover, and cook over low heat 15 minutes.

2  Remove with slotted spoon, drain well. (Cooked *kreplach* can be refrigerated for 2 days or frozen.)

3  To serve, simmer *kreplach* in hot chicken soup for 10 to 15 minutes. Garnish with minced parsley.

## VEGETABLE SOUP

**Note:** Start this recipe the day before needed to allow time to soak beans. If there's not enough time, put the beans in boiling water, turn off the flame, and allow beans to soak for several hours before cooking.

**Number of Servings:** 22
**Serving Size:** 6 oz. (170 mL)
**Total Yield:** 8 lbs., 8 1/2 oz. (3.9 kg)
**Food Balance:** Balanced
**Wine Style:** Wine friendly—Try your favorite
**Example:** Château St. Jean Chardonnay or Merlot

**Cooking Method:** Boil

Chiyacat © Shutterstock

| | WEIGHT | | VOLUME | |
|---|---|---|---|---|
| **INGREDIENTS** | **U.S.** | **METRIC** | **U.S.** | **METRIC** |
| kidney beans, chickpeas, or dried beans of choice, rinsed | 4 oz. | 114 g | 1/2 cup | 120 mL |
| water or beef stock | | | 3 quarts (12 cups) | 2.9 L |
| short ribs, washed | 1 lb., 14 oz. | 851 g | | |
| onion, small dice | 8 oz. | 227 g | 1 large | |
| turnip, peeled and cut into medium dice | 4 oz. | 114 g | 1 each | |
| cabbage, shredded | 11 3/4 oz. | 334 g | 1/2 small head | |
| carrots, peeled and cut into medium dice | 9 3/4 oz. | 278 g | 3 each | |
| canned diced tomatoes | 14 1/2 oz. | 411 g | one 14 1/2-oz. can | one 411-g can |
| fresh parsley, minced | 1/2 oz. | 15 g | 2 tablespoons | 30 mL |
| bay leaf | | | 1 each | |
| ground ginger | | | 1 teaspoon | 5 mL |
| pepper | | | 1 teaspoon | 5 mL |
| green beans, trimmed and cut into about 2-inch (5-cm) pieces | 4 oz. | 114 g | | |
| salt | as needed | | | |

### TWIST ON THE CLASSIC

Serve this hearty soup in a hollowed *boule*. Also, use any desired assortment of beans and vegetables in this soup.

1  Place dried beans and water or stock in stockpot. Refrigerate and soak overnight.

2  Add short ribs, onion, turnip, cabbage, carrots, tomatoes, parsley, bay leaf, ginger, and pepper. Simmer for 2 1/2 hours until beans and short ribs are tender.

3  Add green beans and continue cooking another 30 to 45 minutes.

4  If time allows, refrigerate overnight to solidify fat on top of soup. Remove fat and discard. Otherwise, skim liquid fat from top of soup and discard.

5  Remove bones and fat from meat. Cut meat into bite-sized pieces and return to soup. Add salt, correct seasonings. Serve.

# LABANEH AND CUCUMBER SALAD

Ints Vikmanis © Shutterstock

**Note:** Begin making the *labaneh* 48 hours (2 days) in advance. If possible, use yogurt without added starch, gelatin, or pectin.

**Note:** The longer the yogurt drains, the thicker it becomes. Thin *labaneh* requires less than 48 hours. The desired thickness depends on how the cook wants to use it.

**Note:** This recipe makes more *labaneh* than needed for the cucumber salad. It tastes like a tangy sour cream and makes a delicious topping for salads or many other applications.

**Number of Servings:** 8
**Serving Size:** 4 oz. (114 g)
**Total Yield:** 2 lb., 3 1/4 oz. (1 kg) cucumber salad
Thirteen 1/2 oz. (15 g) *labaneh*, or seventeen 1/2-oz. (15-g) *labaneh* balls

| INGREDIENTS | WEIGHT U.S. | WEIGHT METRIC | VOLUME U.S. | VOLUME METRIC |
|---|---|---|---|---|
| **Labaneh:** | | | | |
| whole milk yogurt | | | 1 quart | 960 mL |
| salt | 1/4 oz. | 8 g | 1 teaspoon | 5 mL |
| olive oil | as needed | | | |
| rosemary sprig | | | 1 each | |
| chili pepper, cut in half, *optional* | | | | |
| **Salad:** | | | | |
| cucumber, peeled, medium dice | 1 lb., 10 1/2 oz. | 752 g | 2 large | |
| garlic, smashed and minced | 1/4 oz. | 8 g | 2 cloves | |
| fresh mint, minced | 1/4 oz. | 8 g | 1 tablespoon | 15 mL |
| salt | 1/4 oz. | 8 g | 1 teaspoon | 5 mL |
| olive oil | | 15 g | 1 tablespoon | 15 mL |
| *labaneh, from above* | 8 oz. | 227 g | | |
| **Garnish:** | | | | |
| fresh mint, minced or sprig | | | | |

## LABANEH:

1. Forty-eight hours (2 days) before needed, mix yogurt and salt. Place in colander lined with cheesecloth. Place colander over bowl to catch liquid.
2. Cover and refrigerate for 48 hours. Empty bowl under colander periodically so colander does not stand in liquid.
3. Place about 1/2 inch (1.3 cm) oil, sprig of rosemary, and chili pepper in dish. After 48 hours, form yogurt cheese into 1-inch (2.5-cm) balls. Place them in the olive oil. Cover and refrigerate until needed.

## CUCUMBER SALAD:

1. Place cucumber, garlic, mint, salt, and oil in bowl. Mix gently to combine.
2. Add *labaneh* to cucumber mixture. Stir gently until evenly distributed. Correct seasonings.
3. Serve cucumber salad on a bed of lettuce. Garnish with mint.

---

### TWIST ON THE CLASSIC

Use *labaneh* as a substitute for sour cream. Accompany blintzes with this Middle Eastern cheese.

Substitute *labaneh* for the buffalo mozzarella in *Caprese,* the Italian salad of sliced tomatoes, mozzarella, olive oil, and fresh basil.

---

*Labaneh* is very popular throughout Israel and the Middle East. It is sold in supermarkets all over the region. Many eat *labaneh* for breakfast or serve it as a *mezze*.

## ORANGE AND OLIVE SALAD

**Number of Servings:** 8 or 16
**Serving Size:** 1 orange if segmented without membrane, or 1/2 orange if just sliced and cut
**Yield:** 1 lb., 7 oz. (653 g) (8 oranges segmented without membrane)

| INGREDIENTS | WEIGHT | | VOLUME | |
| --- | --- | --- | --- | --- |
| | U.S. | Metric | U.S. | Metric |
| **Vinaigrette:** | | | | |
| lemon juice, fresh | | 114 g | 2 lemons or 1/2 cup | 120 mL |
| olive oil | | 114 g | 1/2 cup | 120 mL |
| garlic, smashed and minced | 1 oz. | 29 g | 5 cloves | |
| salt | | | 1/2 teaspoon | 3 mL |
| ground cumin | | | 1 teaspoon | 5 mL |
| paprika | | | 1 1/2 teaspoons | 8 mL |
| cayenne | | | up to 1/8 teaspoon | 1 mL |
| oranges | 4 lb. | 1.8 kg | 8 each | |
| **Garnish:** | | | | |
| black olives | | | as desired, 3 to 5 per serving | |

1. Combine lemon juice, oil, garlic, salt, cumin, paprika, and cayenne. Mix well, refrigerate. (May be prepared ahead.)
2. Peel oranges, removing pith with sharp paring knife. To remove membrane, cut on each side of membrane to the middle, staying as close to membrane as possible. To cut with membrane, slice oranges across grain, then cut into pieces.
3. Mix oranges with enough vinaigrette to coat well.
4. Serve alone or place on bed of lettuce drizzled with vinaigrette. Garnish with olives.

*Removing pith and skin from orange*
Pearson Education/PH College

*Cutting orange sections away from membrane over bowl to catch juices*
David Murray © Dorling Kindersley

# SHAKSHOUKA

## EGGS ON TOMATO SAUCE

© Ustinova

**Recommendation:** Leave some or all of the seeds in the jalapeño to make the dish spicy.

This makes a great brunch dish.

**Number of Servings:** 12
**Serving Size:** 1 egg + 1 3/4 oz. (50 g) sauce
**Yield:** 1 lb., 5 1/2 oz. (610 g) tomato sauce
**Wine Style:** Old world, cool climate Riesling with high minerality content.
**Example:** Riesling EG "Hölle" 2009, Kunstler (Rheingau/Germany)

**Cooking Method:** Sauté, boil

| | WEIGHT | | VOLUME | |
|---|---|---|---|---|
| INGREDIENTS | U.S. | METRIC | U.S. | METRIC |
| olive oil | | 86 g | 1/4 cup + 2 tablespoons | 90 mL |
| jalapeño, minced, remove some or all seeds and membranes, if desired | 2 oz. | 57 g | 2 each | |
| green pepper, seeds and membranes removed, small dice | 7 oz. | 199 g | 1 each | |
| garlic, peeled, minced, smashed | 2 oz. | 57 g | 12 cloves | |
| crushed tomatoes | 3 lb., 8 oz. | 1.6 kg | 6 cups | 1.4 L |
| tomato paste | 1 1/2 oz. | 43 g | 2 tablespoons | 30 mL |
| salt | 1/2 oz. | 15 g | 2 teaspoons | 10 mL |
| pepper | | | 1 teaspoon | 5 mL |
| paprika | 1/2 oz. | 15 g | 2 tablespoons | 30 mL |
| water, as needed | | | | |
| eggs | 1 lb., 4 oz. | 567 g | 12 each | |

**Garnish:**

parsley or cilantro, minced

1. Heat oil in large skillet or pan over medium heat. Add jalapeño and green pepper, sauté a few minutes to soften. Add garlic, sauté another minute.
2. Add tomatoes, tomato paste, salt, and pepper. Simmer about 20 minutes.
3. Add paprika, simmer another 10 minutes until thick sauce. Add a little water if too thick or sticking. Correct seasonings.
4. If not in large skillet, place sauce in skillet. Bring to simmer, make indents in sauce and place egg in each indent. Cover and cook until whites set but yolks are still runny or desired doneness, about 4 to 7 minutes.
5. Serve immediately, sprinkled with minced parsley or cilantro and accompanied by bread.

# CHEESE BLINTZES

## CHEESE FILLED CRÊPES

**Note:** The wrapper prepared for blintzes is very similar to a *crêpe*. To prepare smaller blintzes, use about 1/3 less filling than the larger ones and reduce size of the wrappers to 3 1/2 to 4 inches (9 to 10 cm).

**Yield:** Thirteen 5- to 5 1/2-inch (13- to 14-cm) blintzes
Thirty 3 1/2- to 4-inch (9- to 10-cm) blintzes

**Cooking Method:** Sauté

**Food Balance:** Very sweet/protein

**Wine Style:** Sweet and fruity late-harvest wines: Rieslings, Sauternes, sweet Sherry

**Example:** Château St. Jean Late Harvest Riesling

| | WEIGHT | | VOLUME | |
|---|---|---|---|---|
| INGREDIENTS | U.S. | METRIC | U.S. | METRIC |
| **Wrapper:** | | | | |
| all-purpose flour | 4 1/2 oz. | 128 g | 1 cup | 240 mL |
| salt | | | 1/4 teaspoon | 2 mL |
| eggs | 6 3/4 oz. | 191 g | 4 each | |
| milk | | 227 g | 1 cup | 240 mL |
| butter, melted | 1/4 oz. | 8 g | 1/2 tablespoon | 7 mL |
| butter, for frying | | | | |
| **Filling:** | | | | |
| cream cheese | 1 lb. | 454 g | | |
| sugar | 3 oz. | 86 g | 1/3 cup | 80 mL |
| cottage cheese | 13 oz. | 369 g | 1 1/2 cups | 360 mL |
| eggs, well-beaten | 3 1/2 oz. | 104 g | 2 each | |
| salt | | | 1/4 teaspoon | 2 mL |
| lemon peel, grated | 1/4 oz. | 8 g | 2 teaspoons | 10 mL |
| butter, melted | 1 oz. | 28 g | 2 tablespoons | 30 mL |
| vanilla | | | 1 teaspoon | 5 mL |

**Accompaniments:**

sour cream
applesauce

### TWIST ON THE CLASSIC

- Instead of rolling the filling in the *crêpe*-like wrapper, place filling in center of wrapper, gather sides and twist to close before frying. This forms a purselike container for the filling.
- Use any desired filling for the blintzes. Fill the blintzes with berries and/or fruits like a pie filling. Alternately, create a savory blintz filled with meat or mashed potatoes.
- Make small blintzes and serve as an hors d'oeuvre.

*Ladling batter into pan while tilting pan*
David Murray and Jules Selmes © Dorling Kindersley

*Releasing pancake from pan*
Dave King © Dorling Kindersley

### WRAPPER:

1. Place flour, salt, eggs, milk, and butter in bowl of food processor fitted with knife blade, pulse to mix well.
2. Chill for 10 minutes.
3. Lightly butter skillet, heat over medium heat. Pour just enough batter into skillet to cover bottom of pan with thin, even layer when pan is tilted (about 3 tablespoons [45 mL] for a 7 1/2-inch [19-cm] skillet, or about 2 tablespoons [30 mL] for a 5-inch [13-cm] skillet).
4. Cook until lightly brown on one side, then remove from pan and stack on plate with cooked side up.

### FILLING:

1. Blend cream cheese and sugar in mixer with flat paddle beater until creamy.
2. Add cottage cheese, eggs, salt, lemon peel, butter, and vanilla and mix well.

### ASSEMBLY:

1. Place crêpe on flat surface with browned side up.
2. Spoon filling across center of crêpe (larger blintzes need about 3 tablespoons [45 mL] of filling, smaller ones need about 1 tablespoon [15 mL]).
3. Fold short edges to cover some of filling, then roll crêpe.
4. Refrigerate until needed or sauté in buttered pan until lightly brown and warmed through.
5. Serve, accompanied by sour cream and applesauce.

© Jjava

## FALAFEL

### DEEP-FRIED CHICKPEA BALLS

**Note:** Sold everywhere from street corners to sporting events, the popularity of *falafel* in Israel is likened to that of the hot dog in the United States.

**Note:** Serve *falafel* in pita bread halves and top with Yogurt-*Tahini* Sauce (*recipe follows in this chapter*) and diced tomatoes and cucumbers.

**Number of Servings:** 7  **Cooking Method:** Deep-fry
**Serving Size:** Three 1-oz. (28-g) patties or balls per pita half or twenty-two 1-oz. (28-g) patties or balls for appetizers
**Total Yield:** 1 lb., 6 oz. (624 g)
**Food Balance:** Protein/balanced
**Wine Style:** Wine friendly—Try your favorite
**Example:** Château St. Jean Gewürztraminer or Pinot Noir

Clive Streeter © Dorling Kindersley

| INGREDIENTS | WEIGHT U.S. | WEIGHT METRIC | VOLUME U.S. | VOLUME METRIC |
|---|---|---|---|---|
| chickpeas (garbanzo beans), cooked or canned, drained | 11 1/2 oz. | 326 g | 2 cups | 480 mL |
| garlic, smashed and minced | | | 3 cloves | |
| celery, finely minced | 2 1/4 oz. | 64 g | 1/2 cup | 120 mL |
| scallions, finely minced | 2 oz. | 57 g | 1/2 cup | 120 mL |
| eggs | 3 1/2 oz. | 104 g | 2 each | |
| *tahini* | 2 oz. | 57 g | 3 tablespoons | 45 mL |
| ground cumin | | | 1/2 teaspoon | 3 mL |
| turmeric | | | 1/4 teaspoon | 2 mL |
| ground cayenne | | | 1/4 teaspoon | 2 mL |
| salt | | | 1 1/2 teaspoons | 8 mL |
| flour | 3/4 oz., plus more for coating | 22 g | 3 tablespoons | 45 mL, plus more for coating |
| oil, for frying | | | | |

© Brent Hofacker

1. In food processor fitted with knife blade, purée chickpeas. Transfer to bowl.
2. Add garlic, celery, scallions, eggs, *tahini*, cumin, turmeric, cayenne, salt, and 3 tablespoons (3/4 oz., 22 g, or 45 mL) flour to chickpeas, mix well to blend.
3. Chill thoroughly.
4. Heat oil in skillet for deep-frying, 375 degrees (190°C). Form mixture into 1-inch (2.5-cm) balls, flatten into patties if desired. If desired, coat lightly with flour.
5. Fry until golden brown, about 2 or 3 minutes. Drain on paper towels.

**TWIST ON THE CLASSIC**

Serve small *falafel* as a passed hors d'oeuvre with a *tahini* dip.

# YOGURT–TAHINI SAUCE

**Note:** Widely used in the Middle East, northern Africa, and many Asian countries, tahini is sesame seeds ground into paste. In the Middle East, *tahini* is made from hulled sesame seeds, which yield *tahini* that is less bitter.

**Note:** Traditionally, yogurt-*tahini* sauce is served with falafel in pita. A 3-tablespoon (45-mL) serving of sauce is enough for a half pita with *falafel*.

**Number of Servings:** 12
**Serving Size:** 2 oz. (57 g) or 3 tablespoons (45 mL)
**Total Yield:** 1 lb., 9 oz. (710 g)

| | WEIGHT | | VOLUME | |
|---|---|---|---|---|
| INGREDIENTS | U.S. | METRIC | U.S. | METRIC |
| tahini | 10 oz. | 284 g | 1 1/3 cups | 320 mL |
| unflavored yogurt | 10 oz. | 284 g | 1 1/3 cups | 320 mL |
| garlic, pulverized | 1/4 oz. | 8 g | 2 cloves | |
| fresh lemon juice | | 71 g | 1/4 cup + 1 tablespoon | 75 mL |
| fresh parsley, finely minced | 1 oz. | 28 g | 1/4 cup | 60 mL |
| scallions, finely minced | 1 oz. | 28 g | 1/4 cup | 60 mL |
| salt | | | to taste | |
| ground cayenne | | | couple of shakes | |
| paprika | | | couple of shakes | |
| ground cumin | | | 1/4 teaspoon | 2 mL |

1. Mix all ingredients together. Blend well.
2. Refrigerate until needed. Correct seasonings.
3. Serve at room temperature.

## ROAST CHICKEN

**Note:** Roast chicken is the traditional entrée for the Friday night Sabbath dinner.

**Note:** Dividing a roasting chicken into four portions is quite generous. If more portions are needed, increase the amount of vegetables placed under the chicken.

**Number of Servings:** 8 or more
**Serving Size:**   1/4 chicken
                    4 oz. (114 g) vegetables
**Total Yield:**   8 lb., 11 oz. (3.9 kg) fowl
                    2 lb., 4 1/4 oz. (1 kg) vegetables
**Food Balance:** Protein/sweet
**Wine Style:** Low-oaked whites and soft reds
**Example:** Beringer Chenin Blanc or Stonecellars Merlot

**Cooking Method:** Bake

**TWIST ON THE CLASSIC**

To use leftover roast chicken, make chicken gravy and add the diced leftover chicken and dried fruits. Serve over rice.

| | WEIGHT | | VOLUME | |
|---|---|---|---|---|
| **INGREDIENTS** | **U.S.** | **METRIC** | **U.S.** | **METRIC** |
| onions, large dice | 12 oz. | 340 g | 2 each | |
| carrots, peeled and cut into 1-inch (2.5-cm) pieces | 12 oz. | 340 g | 4 large | |
| red potatoes, peeled and cut into quarters or sixths if large | 1 lb., 6 3/4 oz. | 645 g | 5 large or 6 medium | |
| dried apricots | 3 oz. | 86 g | 1/2 cup | 120 mL |
| prunes, pitted | 3 1/2 oz. | 104 g | 1/2 cup | 120 mL |
| dried thyme | | | 1 1/2 teaspoons | 8 mL |
| salt | | | sprinkling | |
| pepper | | | sprinkling | |
| roasting chicken, washed, excess fat removed | 11 lb. | 5 kg | 2 each | |

1. Place rack in roasting pan. Preheat oven to 450 degrees (230°C).
2. Scatter onions, carrots, potatoes, apricots, and prunes on bottom of roasting pan. Sprinkle with 1/2 teaspoon (3 mL) of thyme and salt and pepper.
3. Sprinkle another 1/2 teaspoon (3 mL) of thyme inside the cavity of each chicken. Lightly sprinkle outside of each chicken with pepper. Place on roasting rack. Bake for 5 minutes, reduce heat to 350 degrees (180°C) and continue cooking until chicken reaches proper internal temperature, about 1 1/2 to 2 hours.
4. Remove from oven, let chicken rest about 10 minutes before carving. Meanwhile, if vegetables need more cooking and/or browning, increase oven temperature to 450 degrees (230°C). Return vegetables to oven while chicken rests. Cook until browned and done.
5. Serve chicken with vegetables.

© nito

# GRILLED FISH WITH CAPER VINAIGRETTE

**Number of Servings:** 12

**Cooking Method:** Grill

**Serving Size:** 4 to 5 oz. (114 to 142 g) cooked fish with 1 1/2 oz. vinaigrette (43 g)

**Total Yield:** 3 to 3 lb., 12 oz. (1.4 to 1.7 kg) fish; 1 lb., 3 oz. (540 g) vinaigrette

**Food Balance:** Acid balanced

**Wine Style:** Wide variety—Pick a winner

**Example:** Campanile Pinot Grigio or Rosemount Cabernet Sauvignon

| | WEIGHT | | VOLUME | |
|---|---|---|---|---|
| **INGREDIENTS** | **U.S.** | **METRIC** | **U.S.** | **METRIC** |
| **Vinaigrette:** | | | | |
| fresh lemon juice | | 114 g | 1/2 cup | 120 mL |
| salt | 1/4 oz. | 8 g | 1 teaspoon | 5 mL |
| pepper | | | 1/2 teaspoon | 3 mL |
| ground cayenne | | | couple of shakes, to taste | |
| olive oil | | 340 g | 1 1/2 cups | 360 mL |
| capers, drained and chopped | 3 oz. | 86 g | 1/4 cup | 60 mL |
| fresh parsley, minced | 1 oz. | 28 g | 1/4 cup | 60 mL |
| fillets of grouper, red snapper, sea bream, or other white fish, 1-inch (2.5-cm) thick | 4 lb., 8 oz. | 2 kg | | |
| vegetable or olive oil | | 15 g | 1 tablespoon | 15 mL |

1. Combine lemon juice, salt, pepper, and cayenne in small bowl.
2. Whisk in 1 1/2 cups (360 mL) oil, capers, and parsley. Refrigerate.
3. Preheat grill or broiler. Brush fish lightly with oil on both sides.
4. Cook fish until opaque and tender, about 4 or 5 minutes per side.
5. Whisk vinaigrette. Correct seasonings.
6. Serve fish hot, napped with vinaigrette. A 4- to 5-oz. (114- to 142-g) portion needs about 2 tablespoons (30 mL) vinaigrette.

Robyn Mackenzie © Shutterstock

## TWIST ON THE CLASSIC

Serve this fish over Israeli *couscous* or pasta. Prepare the vinaigrette without the parsley. Heat the vinaigrette. Place cooked fish on a bed of *couscous* or pasta, top with warm vinaigrette, and sprinkle with the parsley.

## BEEF, CARROT, AND SWEET POTATO TZIMMES
### BEEF STEW

**Note:** Many prepare *tzimmes* as a vegetable stew without meat, consisting of carrots, prunes, and perhaps other vegetables. Others cook *tzimmes* with a brisket instead of stew meat. After cooking, the brisket is removed, sliced, and served with the remaining vegetables as a side dish.

**Note:** To symbolically usher in a sweet New Year, this sweet dish graces many tables at Rosh Hashanah.

**Number of Servings:** 11

**Serving Size:** 8 oz. (227 g)

**Total Yield:** 5 lb., 11 oz. (2.6 kg)

**Food Balance:** Sweet/protein

**Wine Style:** Low-oaked whites and soft reds

**Example:** Beringer Moscato or Lindeman's Shiraz

**Cooking Method:** Braise

© Olaf Speier/Fotolia

|  | WEIGHT | | VOLUME | |
| --- | --- | --- | --- | --- |
| INGREDIENTS | U.S. | METRIC | U.S. | METRIC |
| oil |  | 15 g | 1 tablespoon | 15 mL |
| boneless chuck or stew meat, trimmed and cut into 1 1/2-inch (4-cm) cubes | 2 lb. | 908 g |  |  |
| onions, diced | 12 oz. | 340 g | 2 large |  |
| carrots, peeled and cut into 1-inch (2.5-cm) chunks | 1 lb., 4 oz. | 567 g | 6 each |  |
| salt |  |  | 1/2 teaspoon | 3 mL |
| water |  | 908 g | about 1 quart (4 cups) | 960 mL |
| potatoes, white, waxy, or all-purpose, peeled and cut into large dice | 14 oz. | 397 g | 2 large |  |
| sweet potatoes, peeled and cut into large dice | 1 lb., 6 oz. | 624 g | 2 large |  |
| honey | 3 oz. | 86 g | 1/4 cup | 60 mL |
| ground cinnamon |  |  | 1/2 teaspoon | 3 mL |
| pepper |  |  | 1/2 teaspoon | 3 mL |
| prunes, pitted | 8 oz. | 227 g | 1 1/3 cups | 320 mL |
| water, hot | as needed |  |  |  |

**Garnish:**

fresh parsley, minced

### TWIST ON THE CLASSIC

Serve the *tzimmes* in a hollowed loaf of round bread. Garnish the top with deep-fried "threads" of sweet potatoes (finely shredded sweet potatoes).

1. Heat oil in pan, add meat, brown well on all sides. Remove meat from pan.
2. Add onions to pan, sauté until lightly brown.
3. Return meat to pan, add carrots, salt, and enough of the water to just cover.
4. Bring to boil, then cover and simmer over low heat, skimming once or twice, for 1 hour.
5. Add potatoes, sweet potatoes, honey, cinnamon, and pepper to meat. Mix gently. Bring to boil, partly cover, simmer 30 minutes. Meanwhile, cover prunes with hot water, adding enough water to just cover top of prunes, soak about 30 minutes.
6. Gently stir stew once. Remove prunes from liquid, reserving liquid for later thinning if necessary. Add prunes to pan.
7. Uncover, simmer 30 minutes or until meat is very tender. To prevent sticking, shake pan occasionally, but do not stir or the vegetables may break.
8. Stew should be moist but not soupy. If there is too much liquid, let it stand for an hour to absorb excess. Use reserved prune water if more liquid is needed. Correct seasonings. Serve, garnished with minced parsley, if desired.

# CHOLENT

## SABBATH STEW

© Fanfo

**Note:** Like Boston baked beans for the Puritans, this dish cooked overnight at a low temperature and solved the problem of providing a hot meal without working on the Sabbath.

**Note:** Begin preparation for this dish the day before needed.

**Number of Servings:** 8

**Cooking Method:** Braise

**Serving Size:** 4 oz. (114 g) meat
　　　　　　　9 oz. (256 g) vegetable and sauce
**Total Yield:** 10 lb., 8 oz. (4.8 kg)
　　　　　　2 lb., 1 oz. meat (936 g)
　　　　　　8 lb., 7 oz. (3.8 kg) vegetable and sauce
**Food Balance:** Balanced
**Wine Style:** Wine friendly—Try your favorite
**Example:** Greg Norman Chardonnay or Zinfandel

### TWIST ON THE CLASSIC

Many nationalities prepare a long-simmering stew similar to *cholent*—the difference is the ingredients. To change this to a poultry dish, substitute a hen or turkey for the meat and cook about 2 to 3 hours.

| | WEIGHT | | VOLUME | |
| INGREDIENTS | U.S. | METRIC | U.S. | METRIC |
| --- | --- | --- | --- | --- |
| dried beans such as lima, great northern, or chickpeas | 8 oz. | 227 g | 1 1/3 cups | 320 mL |
| beef brisket | 3 lb., 9 oz. | 1.6 kg | | |
| flour | 1/2 oz. | 15 g | 2 tablespoons | 30 mL |
| oil | | 15 g | 1 tablespoon | 15 mL |
| salt | 1/2 oz. | 15 g | 2 teaspoons | 10 mL |
| pepper | | | 1/2 teaspoon | 3 mL |
| paprika | 1/4 oz. | 8 g | 1 tablespoon | 15 mL |
| ground cinnamon | | | 1/4 teaspoon | 2 mL |
| ground ginger | | | 1/4 teaspoon | 2 mL |
| onions, diced | 1 lb. | 454 g | 3 medium | |
| garlic, smashed and minced | 1/4 oz. | 8 g | 2 cloves | |
| barley | 7 1/2 oz. | 213 g | 1 cup | 240 mL |
| turnips | 8 oz. | 227 g | 2 small to medium | |
| carrots, peeled | 7 oz. | 199 g | 4 each | |
| potatoes, white, waxy, or all-purpose, peeled | 2 lb. | 908 g | 8 medium | |
| water, boiling | as needed | | | |

1. Cover dried beans with water in bowl, soak overnight. Drain.
2. Preheat oven to 325 degrees (160°C). Dredge meat in flour. Heat oil in heavy pan over medium heat, brown meat on all sides.
3. Place meat in roasting pan. Top with salt, pepper, paprika, cinnamon, ginger, onions, garlic, and barley. Surround with drained beans, turnips, carrots, and potatoes.
4. Cover with boiling water and bake for 3 to 4 hours, until meat is tender and beans are soft. Correct seasonings.
5. Remove meat, slice across grain, and serve with bean and vegetable sauce.

## LAMB KEBABS

**Note:** If using wooden skewers, soak them in water before using. This prevents them from burning while the meat is grilling.

**Note:** Street vendors prepare and sell these popular *kebabs*. Usually, they place them in *pita* bread and dress them with yogurt or Yogurt-*Tahini* Sauce (recipe in this chapter) and Israeli (or diced) salad (*Salata Khodra*, in Chapter 9).

**Number of Servings:** 10  
**Serving Size:** 2 kebobs:  
        each 3 oz. (86 g) raw weight  
        each 2 1/2 oz. (71 g) cooked weight  
**Total Yield:** 3 lb., 13 1/2 oz. (1.7 kg) raw weight  
**Food Balance:** Balanced  
**Wine Style:** Wine friendly—Pick your favorite  
**Example:** Souverain Sauvignon Blanc or Cabernet Sauvignon

**Cooking Method:** Grill

Lamb Kebabs © Shutterstock

| INGREDIENTS | WEIGHT | | VOLUME | |
| --- | --- | --- | --- | --- |
| | U.S. | METRIC | U.S. | METRIC |
| ground lamb | 3 lb. | 1.4 kg | | |
| onion, minced | 9 oz. | 256 g | 2 medium | |
| garlic, smashed and peeled | 1/2 oz. | 15 g | 3 cloves | |
| fresh parsley, minced | 3 oz. | 86 g | 1 1/2 cups | 360 mL |
| ground coriander | | | 1 1/2 teaspoons | 8 mL |
| ground allspice | | | 3/4 teaspoon | 4 mL |
| salt | 3/4 oz | 22 g | 1 tablespoon | 15 mL |
| pepper | | | 3/4 teaspoon | 4 mL |

**Garnish:**

fresh parsley, minced

**Accompaniments:**

Yogurt-*Tahini* Sauce  
*pita* bread  
*Salata Khodra* (diced salad  
   from Chapter 9)

1. Combine lamb, onion, garlic, parsley, coriander, allspice, salt, and pepper in bowl. Mix thoroughly.
2. Preheat grill. Divide lamb mixture into 3-oz. (86-g) portions or portions of desired size. Form each portion into long, sausage-shaped cylinder, and spear metal or soaked wooden skewer through center of meat. (It should resemble a popsicle on its stick.)
3. Grill *kebabs* until proper internal temperature is reached. Serve two per serving, accompanied by Yogurt-*Tahini* Sauce, *pita* bread and *Salata Khodra* (or diced) salad.

# CARROT TZIMMES

## HONEY-GLAZED CARROTS

**Note:** This sweet vegetable accompanies many Rosh Hashanah dinners.

**Number of Servings:** 10  
**Serving Size:** 4 oz. (114 g)  
**Total Yield:** 2 lb., 10 oz. (1.2 kg)

**Cooking Method:** Boil

| | WEIGHT | | VOLUME | |
|---|---|---|---|---|
| **INGREDIENTS** | **U.S.** | **METRIC** | **U.S.** | **METRIC** |
| butter | 2 oz. | 57 g | 4 tablespoons (1/2 stick) | 60 mL |
| carrots, peeled and sliced on the diagonal, 1/2- to 3/4-inch (1.3- to 2-cm) thick | 3 lb. | 1.4 kg | | |
| orange juice | | 78 g | 2/3 cup | 160 mL |
| salt | | | pinch | |
| ground ginger | | | 3/4 teaspoon | 4 mL |
| honey | 3 oz. | 86 g | 1/4 cup or 4 tablespoons | 60 mL |

**Garnish:**

fresh parsley, minced

1. Heat butter in pan over medium heat.
2. Add carrots, sauté a few minutes. Add orange juice, salt, ginger, and honey. Cover, simmer until three-quarters tender, about 10 to 15 minutes.
3. Uncover, cook another 10 to 15 minutes, until carrots are tender and much of liquid evaporates. Correct seasonings.
4. Serve immediately, sprinkled with parsley.

Jeff Smith/Getty Images

© Olga Lyubkin

# SPINACH WITH CHICKPEAS

**Note:** This exemplifies Sephardic cooking.

**Number of Servings:** 10
**Serving Size:** 4 oz. (114 g)
**Total Yield:** 2 lb., 8 3/4 oz. (1.2 kg)

**Cooking Method:** Braise

> ### TWIST ON THE CLASSIC
>
> Turn this into an entrée by serving it over rice.

| INGREDIENTS | WEIGHT | | VOLUME | |
| --- | --- | --- | --- | --- |
| | U.S. | METRIC | U.S. | METRIC |
| olive oil | | 15 g | 1 tablespoon | 15 mL |
| onion, medium dice | 9 oz. | 256 g | 1 large | |
| garlic, peeled, smashed, and minced | 1/4 oz. | 8 g | 2 cloves | |
| ground cumin | | | 2 teaspoons | 10 mL |
| paprika | | | 2 teaspoons | 10 mL |
| turmeric | | | 1 teaspoon | 5 mL |
| red pepper flakes | | | 1/8 teaspoon | 1 mL |
| salt | 1/4 oz. | 8 g | 1 teaspoon | 5 mL |
| sugar | | | 1 teaspoon | 5 mL |
| tomatoes, canned or fresh, diced | 14 1/2 oz. | 411 g | one 14 1/2-oz. can | one 411-g can |
| chickpeas, canned or cooked, drained | 10 oz. | 284 g | one 15 1/2-oz. can | one 439-g can |
| fresh spinach, washed, stems removed, and chopped coarsely | 1 lb., 2 oz. | 511 g | two each 9-oz. bags | two each 256-g bags |

1. Heat olive oil in large pan over medium heat. Add onion, sauté until softened, several minutes.
2. Add garlic, cumin, paprika, turmeric, red pepper flakes, salt, and sugar. Stir to combine, sauté about 2 minutes. Add tomatoes, reduce heat to medium-low, cover and cook for 30 minutes, stirring occasionally.
3. Add chickpeas, cover and continue cooking, stirring occasionally, for another 30 minutes. (Mixture should be wet but not soupy. If it is too wet, remove cover and raise heat to reduce. Spinach will need just a little liquid to wilt, and the spinach releases its own liquid.)
4. Turn heat to medium-high, add spinach, cook and stir about 5 minutes until spinach wilts. Correct seasonings. Serve.

© anayupariam

Ian O'Leary © Dorling Kindersley

# POTATO LATKES

## POTATO PANCAKES

**Note:** These reign as a Chanukah favorite.

**Yield:** Twenty-five 2-oz. (57-g) patties or seventeen 3-oz. (86-g) patties
**Total Yield:** 3 lb., 3 oz. (1.4 kg)

**Cooking Method:** Sauté

| | WEIGHT | | VOLUME | |
| --- | --- | --- | --- | --- |
| **INGREDIENTS** | **U.S.** | **METRIC** | **U.S.** | **METRIC** |
| onion, quartered | 7 oz. | 199 g | 1 large | |
| Russet baking potatoes, peeled | 2 lb., 8 oz. | 1.1 kg | 6 to 7 medium | |
| eggs, lightly beaten | 3 1/2 oz. | 104 g | 2 each | |
| matzo meal | 1 1/4 oz. | 36 g | 1/4 cup | 60 mL |
| salt | 1/4 oz. | 8 g | 1 teaspoon | 5 mL |
| pepper | | | 1/4 teaspoon | 2 mL |
| oil | | 227 g | 1 cup | 240 mL, or as needed |

**Accompaniments:**

applesauce
sour cream

1. Place onion in food processor fitted with knife blade, pulse a few times, until onion is diced. Transfer onion bits into small bowl and set aside until needed. Do not wash food processor bowl.
2. Grate potatoes into food processor using medium-coarse shredding disk.
3. Place shredded potatoes in colander placed over large bowl to catch liquid. Add onion and mix with hands, squeezing out potato liquid as much as possible. Let mixture drip for a few minutes.
4. Pour out potato liquid from bowl under colander, but leave starch that clings to bowl.
5. Combine potato mixture, eggs, matzo meal, salt, and pepper in the bowl with potato starch, stir well. Let mixture rest for about 10 minutes.
6. Form potato mixture into patties of desired size. Heat 1/4-inch (1/2-cm) oil in skillet until hot. Add latkes, reduce heat to medium. Cook about 5 minutes per side, until golden brown. Drain on paper towels.
7. Serve with applesauce and/or sour cream.

Pearson Education/PH College

Courtesy of Idaho Potato Commission

## NOODLE KUGEL
### NOODLE PUDDING

**Number of Servings:** 19       **Cooking Method:** Bake
**Serving Size:** 4 oz. (114 g)
**Total Yield:** 4 lb., 15 oz. (2.2 kg)

| INGREDIENTS | WEIGHT U.S. | WEIGHT METRIC | VOLUME U.S. | VOLUME METRIC |
|---|---|---|---|---|
| noodles, wide or medium | 12 oz. | 340 g | | |
| butter, melted | 2 oz. | 57 g | 4 tablespoons (1/2 stick) | 60 mL |
| apples, grated | 1 lb., 2 oz. | 511 g | 3 medium | |
| sour cream | 11 oz. | 312 g | 1 1/4 cups | 300 mL |
| cottage cheese | 12 oz. | 340 g | 1 1/2 cups | 360 mL |
| sugar | 2 oz. | 57 g | 1/4 cup | 60 mL |
| ground cinnamon | | | 1 teaspoon | 5 mL |
| nutmeg | | | 1/8 teaspoon | 1 mL |
| salt | | | 1/4 teaspoon | 2 mL |
| orange juice | | 227 g | 1 cup | 240 mL |
| eggs | 5 oz. | 142 g | 3 each | |

1. Cook noodles in large pot of boiling water until *al dente* (done but still firm), drain, rinse with cold water.
2. Preheat oven to 350 degrees (180°C). Pour melted butter into 9- by 12-inch (23- by 30-cm) pan, coating bottom and sides of pan.
3. Mix apples, sour cream, cottage cheese, sugar, cinnamon, nutmeg, salt, and orange juice in bowl. Correct seasonings. Beat eggs in small bowl. Gently mix eggs, noodles, and apple mixture together.
4. Pour mixture into prepared pan, turn gently to incorporate excess butter in pan. Bake, uncovered, for about 50 minutes. Serve.

**TWIST ON THE CLASSIC**

Bake the *kugel* in individual dishes or use a cutter to cut the baked *kugel* into round shapes for service.

## CHALLAH
### EGG BREAD

**Note:** Many Jewish people serve *challah* at the Friday night Sabbath meal.

**Note:** If desired, prepare this recipe into two smaller loaves instead of one large one.

**Number of Servings:** 18      **Cooking Method:** Bake
**Serving Size:** 2 slices 1/2-inch (1.3-cm) thick
**Total Yield:** 2 lb., 4 3/4 oz. (1 kg) finished loaf;
           2 lb., 7 1/4 oz. (1.1 kg) dough
           Finished loaf: 19 inches (48 cm) long

| INGREDIENTS | WEIGHT U.S. | WEIGHT METRIC | VOLUME U.S. | VOLUME METRIC |
|---|---|---|---|---|
| bread flour | 1 lb., 3 oz. to 1 lb., 8 1/2 oz. | 540 g to 695 g | 3 1/2 to 4 1/2 cups | 840 mL to 1.1 L |
| granulated yeast | 3/4 oz. | 22 g | 2 tablespoons | 30 mL |
| water | | 227 g | 1 cup | 240 mL |
| sugar | 1 1/2 oz. | 43 g | 3 tablespoons | 45 mL |
| salt | 1/2 oz. | 15 g | 2 teaspoons | 10 mL |
| oil | | 28 g | 2 tablespoons | 30 mL |
| eggs, room temperature | 6 3/4 oz. | 191 g | 4 each | |
| poppy seeds, for top, *optional* | | | | |

**TWIST ON THE CLASSIC**

Leftover *challah* makes great French toast or bread pudding.

When preparing *challah* for Rosh Hashanah, the Jewish New Year, most cooks add raisins to commemorate a sweet New Year. Also, the bread is baked in a round braid for the New Year to symbolize the circle of life, that life has no beginning and no end.

*Rolling dough into ropes for braiding*
Pearson Education/PH College

Harris Shiffman © Shutterstock

1. Pan-spray half sheet pan or cookie sheet. Place 1 3/4 cups (420 mL) of flour and the yeast in bowl of mixer fitted with flat paddle beater, mix to blend. Heat water, sugar, salt, and oil together in pan until just lukewarm.

2. Add liquid mixture and three of the eggs to flour, mix at low speed until blended, about 30 seconds. Turn off mixer, scrape sides of bowl. Turn mixer to high and mix for 3 minutes.

3. Gradually add remaining flour to mixture until just dry enough to knead. Be careful to add only the needed amount so the bread is not dry. Knead until smooth (about 5 to 8 minutes by hand). Return dough to bowl, cover, and let rest for 20 minutes.

4. Punch down dough. Divide dough into three equal pieces.

5. Remove one of the pieces and keep the other two covered. Knead the piece a few times and form it into a 20-inch (50-cm) rope. Use both hands to push and roll the dough into an even rope.

6. With a short side of the sheet pan closest to you, place the rope diagonally on the prepared sheet pan, from top left top bottom right. Repeat the kneading and rolling procedure with the other two pieces. Place the next rope so it crosses the first one in the middle – it will look like an "X". Place the last rope on top of the other two so they all cross in the middle. The last one should lie in the middle of the other two, parallel to the long sides of the pan.

7. Starting in the middle where they cross, bring rope on bottom (on right) over top rope (middle). Continue braiding loosely bringing the bottom rope over the top. (The next one is the left rope over the middle.) Seal the end tightly, tucking the loose ends of the ropes firmly under the end of the loaf.

8. Turn pan around and braid the other half in the same manner. The loaf might need to sit diagonally to fit on the pan. Cover and allow to rise until doubled, about 30 minutes. Meanwhile, place oven rack in center of oven. Preheat oven to 375 degrees (190°C).

9. In small bowl, beat remaining egg. Using pastry brush, brush loaf with beaten egg. Sprinkle with poppy seeds, if desired. Bake about 25 minutes, until golden brown and bottom of loaf sounds hollow when tapped. Remove from pan and cool on a rack.

## DRIED FRUIT COMPOTE

**Note:** A single dried fruit or any combination of fruits can form the compote. Use red or white wine according to personal preference.

**Note:** Allow several hours or overnight to soak the fruits.

**Number of Servings:** 14
**Serving Size:** 4 oz. (114 g)
**Total Yield:** 3 lb., 11 oz. (1.7 kg)

**Cooking Method:** Boil

© Dorling Kindersley

| INGREDIENTS | WEIGHT | | VOLUME | |
| --- | --- | --- | --- | --- |
| | U.S. | METRIC | U.S. | METRIC |
| dried apricots | 12 oz. | 340 g | 2 cups | 480 mL |
| dried dates | 10 oz. | 284 g | 2 cups | 480 mL |
| dried prunes, pitted | 14 oz. | 397 g | 2 cups | 480 mL |
| water | | 454 g | 2 cups | 480 mL |
| dry red or white wine | | 454 g | 2 cups | 480 mL |
| cinnamon stick | | | 2 each | |
| cloves, tied in cheesecloth | | | 4 each | |
| sugar | 1 3/4 to 3 1/2 oz. | 50 to 104 g, to taste | 1/4 to 1/2 cup | 60 to 120 mL, to taste |

**Garnish:**
almond slices, toasted
whipped cream, slightly
   sweetened

**TWIST ON THE CLASSIC**

Serve compote over ice cream, sponge cake, or sponge cake topped with ice cream.

1. Combine apricots, dates, prunes, water, wine, cinnamon stick, and cloves in nonreactive bowl or pan. Soak a couple of hours or overnight.
2. Place fruit and soaking liquid in saucepan, add sugar. Add more water, if necessary, so fruit is just covered.
3. Bring just to boil, reduce heat and simmer for 15 to 20 minutes, until tender.
4. Let cool to room temperature, then remove cinnamon stick and cloves. Refrigerate.
5. Serve cold, garnished with toasted almond slices and a dollop of whipped cream.

# RUGELACH

## FILLED CRESCENT COOKIES

© Olga_Phoenix

**Number of Pieces:** 64                    **Cooking Method:** Bake

| | WEIGHT | | VOLUME | |
|---|---|---|---|---|
| **INGREDIENTS** | **U.S.** | **METRIC** | **U.S.** | **METRIC** |
| butter, unsalted | 8 oz. | 227 g | 1 cup | 240 mL |
| cream cheese | 8 oz. | 227 g | | |
| flour, sifted | 8 oz. | 227 g | 2 cups | 480 mL |
| salt | | | 1/4 teaspoon | 2 mL |
| **Filling:** | | | | |
| sugar | 4 oz. | 114 g | 1/2 cup | 120 mL |
| cinnamon | 1/4 oz. | 8 g | 1 1/2 teaspoons | 8 mL |
| nuts, almonds, walnuts, or variety of choice, finely chopped | 2 1/2 oz. | 71 g | 1/2 cup | 120 mL |
| raisins | 3 oz. | 86 g | 1/2 cup | 120 mL |
| jam, raspberry, apricot, or flavor of choice | 12 oz. | 340 g | 1 cup | 240 mL |
| **Glaze, optional:** | | | | |
| egg | 1 3/4 oz. | 50 g | 1 each | |
| water | | | 1 teaspoon | 5 mL |

1. Place butter and cream cheese in bowl of mixer fitted with paddle beater, if available. Mix for a couple of minutes until fluffy.
2. Add flour and salt, mix at low speed until just combined. Remove from bowl, wrap in film wrap, and refrigerate for at least 2 hours or as long as overnight. (If shorter time is needed, flatten ball of dough, wrap in film wrap, and place in freezer until firm enough to roll.)
3. Mix sugar, cinnamon, nuts, and raisins together, set aside until needed.
4. Place parchment paper on sheet pans. Position oven racks in middle of oven. Preheat to 350 degrees (180°C).
5. Remove chilled dough. Divide dough into four equal parts. Refrigerate three while working on the first one.
6. Roll into circle about 9 inches (23 cm) in diameter and 1/8-inch (0.3-cm) thick. Spread thin coating of jam over dough. Top with one-fourth of filling. Press lightly to make filling adhere to dough.
7. Cut into sixteen wedges. First cut into quarters, then cut each quarter into four wedges. Beginning at widest part of wedge, roll forward to form a crescent roll. Pull widest edge a bit while rolling to elongate. Curve ends of roll slightly to form a curve. Place on prepared baking pans. Repeat with remaining dough portions.
8. If desired, brush with egg mixed with water to give a shiny surface. Bake for 25 minutes, until lightly browned. Remove from oven, cool on racks.

**TWIST ON THE CLASSIC**

Try making *rugelach* in double the size (eight from a dough portion instead of sixteen) and filling with a savory like spiced ground beef or lamb.

Sold in bakeries throughout Israel, rugelach comes from the Eastern European influence. They are prepared with a variety of fillings such as:
- jam in any flavor or no jam
- cinnamon and nuts only
- chocolate

# HAMANTASCHEN

## TRIANGULAR FILLED PASTRY

**Note:** *Hamantaschen* literally means "Haman's pockets." This pastry is served during Purim, a holiday commemorating Jewish Queen Esther's preventing the villain Haman from slaying Jews. According to lore, these triangular pastries represent the triangular hat worn by Haman. Traditionally, these "pocket" pastries hold a prune or poppy seed filling.

**Note:** This recipe encloses the filling in yeast dough, but many prepare a cookie dough or sour cream dough instead of yeast dough. Regardless of the type of dough, the pastry is formed in a circle that is folded into a triangle.

**Number of Servings:** 19                    **Cooking Method:** Boil, bake
**Serving Size:** 2 *hamantaschen*:
    1 oz. (28 g) dough each
    3/4 oz. (22 g) filling each
**Total Yield:** 38 *hamantaschen*:
    2 lb., 7 oz. (1.1 kg) dough
    1 lb., 13 oz. (823 g) filling

**TWIST ON THE CLASSIC**

Use this dough with any filling—sweet or savory.
- sweetened cheese
- apricot
- feta and ground lamb
- spicy chili
- fold dough around a sausage

| INGREDIENTS | WEIGHT | | VOLUME | |
|---|---|---|---|---|
| | U.S. | METRIC | U.S. | METRIC |
| **Filling:** | | | | |
| dried prunes | 15 oz. | 426 g | 2 cups | 480 mL |
| water | | 227 g | 1 cup | 240 mL |
| walnuts | 2 3/4 oz. | 78 g | 3/4 cup | 180 mL |
| lemon juice | | 15 g | 1 tablespoon | 15 mL |
| lemon rind | 1/4 oz. | 8 g | 1 tablespoon | 15 mL |
| honey | 2 3/4 oz. | 78 g | 1/4 cup | 60 mL |
| **Dough:** | | | | |
| water, lukewarm | | 170 g | 3/4 cup | 180 mL |
| sugar | 3 3/4 oz. | 107 g | 1/2 cup | 120 mL |
| granulated yeast | 1/2 oz. | 15 g | 1 tablespoon | 15 mL |
| all-purpose flour | 1 lb., 1 3/4 oz. to 1 lb., 7 1/4 oz. | 504 g to 660 g | 3 1/2 to 4 1/2 cups | 840 mL to 1.1 L |
| salt | | | 3/4 teaspoon | 4 mL |
| eggs | 3 1/2 oz. | 104 g | 2 each | |
| butter, melted | 4 oz. | 114 g | 8 tablespoons (1 stick) | 120 mL |
| **Finish:** | | | | |
| egg, beaten | 1 3/4 oz. | 50 g | 1 each | |

*Filling placed on dough*

Elzbieta Sekowska © Shutterstock

## FILLING:

1. Place prunes and water in nonreactive saucepan. Cover and cook over medium-low heat until prunes are soft, about 15 to 20 minutes. Remove from heat and remove cover to cool slightly.
2. Place walnuts in food processor fitted with knife blade. Process until finely chopped. Drain prunes.
3. Add prunes, lemon juice and rind, and honey. Process until smooth. Cover and refrigerate until needed.

Odelia Cohen/Getty Images

## DOUGH:

1. Place 1/2 cup (114 g or 120 mL) of lukewarm water in nonreactive bowl. Add 1 tablespoon (15 mL) of sugar and the yeast. Stir to combine. Set aside until foamy, about 5 minutes.
2. Into mixer fitted with flat paddle beater or dough hook, place 3 cups (720 mL) of flour, salt, and remaining 1/4 cup plus 3 tablespoons (105 mL) sugar. Mix to combine. Add yeast mixture and remaining 1/4 cup (57 g or 60 mL) water. Mix to combine.
3. Add eggs, one at a time, mixing thoroughly after each addition. Mix well. Add butter, mix well.
4. Slowly add flour until dough is firm enough to knead. Be careful not to add too much flour or pastry will be dry. Knead until smooth, about 5 to 7 minutes.
5. Return to bowl, cover and allow to rise until doubled, about 1 to 1 1/2 hours. Punch down dough. Cover and refrigerate until later or form into pastries.

## ASSEMBLY:

1. Cover sheet pan or cookie sheets with parchment paper. Working in batches, roll out dough on work surface until 1/4-inch (1/2-cm) thick. Cut out 4-inch (10-cm) circles.
2. Place 1 tablespoon (15 mL) filling in center of each circle.
3. Fold three sides up and pinch together to form triangle. Place finished pastry on sheet pan or cookie sheets. Cover and let rise until doubled, about 30 minutes. Meanwhile, preheat oven to 350 degrees (180°C).
4. Brush pastries with beaten egg. Bake for about 20 minutes, until golden. Cool on rack.

King Arthur Flour

>> **LEARNING OBJECTIVES**

By the end of this chapter, you will be able to:

- Understand how Chinese philosophy is reflected in the cuisine
- Identify several provinces of China and explain characteristics of the cuisines found there
- Identify which grain predominates in the north and which in the south, and explain why
- Discuss various cooking techniques used in China and the advantages of those techniques
- Prepare a variety of Chinese dishes

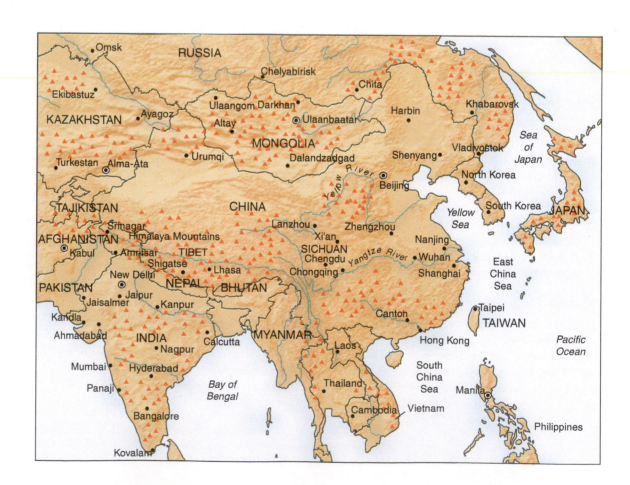

## >> HISTORY

Prehistoric people inhabited northern China more than 250,000 years ago. Written records document Chinese history from as early as the middle 1700s B.C. Having existed for more than 3,500 years, the world's oldest living civilization comes from China.

Proven by the discovery of ornate eating and drinking vessels dating from 3,500 years ago, archaeologists know that formalized culinary practices took place at that time. Throughout history and into the present, the Chinese have exhibited high culinary awareness, and the culinary traits found in this country are strongly reflected in Chinese culture, philosophy, medicine, and health. Unlike in most countries, food and cuisine impacts most aspects of life in China.

### DYNASTIES

Various dynasties ruled from 1766 B.C. until 1911. Around 221 B.C., the many small states of China united into an empire with a strong central government led by the emperor. Thousands of years of dynasties ended in 1911, when revolution erupted in China. Political unrest and turmoil ensued, and difficult times prevailed.

### HARMONY AND BALANCE

As early as 1100 B.C., tenets of Chinese philosophy affected food and cuisine. During the Chou Dynasty (1122 to 249 B.C.), foods were associated with two cosmic concepts, *yin-yang* and the Five Elements. Today, these two philosophies still influence the choice of foods both within an individual dish and in an entire meal. The Chinese believe in the importance of proper food combinations to achieve balance and harmony in the body and spirit.

*Yin-yang symbol*
© piai

## DYNASTIES

| | | |
|---|---|---|
| Shang | 1766 to 1123 B.C. | Known for excess in eating and drinking |
| Chou | 1122 to 249 B.C. | Development of philosophies including *yin* and *yang*, Five Elements, and *tsai-fan* |
| Qin | 221 to 207 B.C. | Separate regions of China united into centralized government; the Great Wall of China begun |
| Han | 206 B.C. to 220 A.D. | First written recipes; expansion of China's boundaries, which introduced different food products and cookery into the regions; prepared a stew called *keng* containing grains, vegetables, and fish and meat if available |
| T'ang | 618 to 906 A.D. | Food and medicine became intertwined; borders expanded to the south, which brought many warm-weather vegetables and fruits, like citrus fruits |
| Sung | 960 to 1279 A.D. | Great culinary advances arose from major growth of cities, and restaurants opened to meet the needs of the large city population; introduction of fast growing varieties of rice; rice became staple grain in China; major strides in agriculture and commercialism of food |
| Yuan | 1260 to 1368 A.D. | Invasion by Mongols curtailed the growth of China and the previous periods of philosophy and sophisticated culture; China's population declined by about 40 percent; the barbaric Mongols indulged in gluttony and drunkenness |
| Ming | 1368 to 1644 A.D. | The manners and sophistication lost during the Yuan Dynasty were restored; 5,000 people worked in the kitchen of the emperor; refrigerated transportation allowed the movement of perishable foods such as fish and meat from one place to another; travel between the regions increased and regional cuisines gained prominence; restaurants flourished throughout China |
| Ch'ing | 1644 to 1911 A.D. | China's population grew drastically, partially because New World crops arrived in China, increasing the food supply in areas where traditional Chinese crops did not grow; culinary sophistication spread throughout the countryside, instead of just in big cities or for the wealthy; stir-frying became a widely used cooking method |

Briefly, yin represents the feminine, dark, and cool, while yang stands for the masculine, light, and hot. Every food is labeled either yin or yang. Although yin and yang are opposites, an important issue in food, art, and numerous areas of Chinese life is the successful combining of these two opposite forces. The proper union of yin and yang elements creates harmony and balance. As a result, the Chinese possess a strong sense of balancing opposites. For example, sweet taste sensations are juxtaposed with sour tastes, and soft textures enhance crunchy ones.

In addition, careful consideration extends to the colors of the foods composing a dish, the color of the foods in relation to the plate, and many other aspects of balance within each dish and the entire meal. All this leads to the Chinese meal structure, which consists of placing all of the dishes on the table at one time. This enables the diner to choose from an assortment of flavors, textures, and taste sensations among the foods to provide his or her own balance and harmony within the meal.

A second and similar type of philosophy leading to balance and harmony is found in the Five Elements. Those elements are water, wood, fire, earth, and metal. Considered the building blocks of life, these five elements or energy forces move constantly, changing continually like life itself. The Chinese believe putting them together in the proper combination creates the natural order of things, again leading to balance and harmony. Like other Chinese philosophies, the Five Elements extend to include many issues as diverse as medicine, martial arts, and food. Each of the five elements relates to one of the five taste sensations: water represents salt, wood represents sour, fire represents bitter, earth represents sweet, and metal represents spicy or pungent. Every food is assigned an element, and the goal is the proper, balanced combination of the foods (with their corresponding flavor sensations).

This theory of balance and harmony also exhibits itself with another philosophy, *tsai-fan*. *Tsai* refers to any cooked dish of protein or vegetable, and *fan* translates to "cooked rice" or grain. In *tsai-fan* as with the Five Elements and *yin-yang*, the goal is proper balance. In order to achieve that balance, a meal must include grain with another food.

In the past as today, the Chinese strongly believe that eating should be pleasurable as well as healthful, but the end-result is harmony and balance within the foods. Creating that harmony and balance in the foods leads to harmony and balance within the body and spirit.

> *By 4 B.C., the Chinese already recognized the five taste sensations and the importance of balancing them.*

## CONFUCIUS

Confucius lived from 551 to 479 B.C., and he exerted strong influence on China's culinary heritage. Some call him the father of northern Chinese cooking. He stressed eating foods in season; fresh foods (in a time before refrigeration, when people often ate spoiled food); cutting meats and vegetables into small pieces; proper preparation, cooking methods, and condiments for recipes; and moderation in eating.

## DIET AND HEALTH

During the period from 600 to 900 A.D., Chinese physicians began attributing many culinary principles to health. The idea of balance in food and health became very important.

Doctors and pharmacists labeled herbs and spices as either hot or cool and used them to balance the foods they joined. When adding spices and herbs to a dish, considerations included the properties of the individual herbs and spices as well as their flavors. At this time, cooks used pepper, ginger, cinnamon, nutmeg, and ginseng. Doctors recommended eating whole grains and sparse amounts of meat. Throughout history and now, many Chinese believe that foods cure diseases as well as contain the key to good health and longevity.

Many consider the Chinese diet to be one of the healthiest. Ample grains and vegetables with small amounts of meats and animal products fill the consumer with plenty of nutrients, fiber, vitamins, and minerals while providing limited high cholesterol fats and "empty" calories from products like sugar. The typical Chinese diet includes lots of vegetables with the most popular ones containing lots of vitamins like greens, cabbage, and bok choy.

## EATING, DRINKING, AND SEX

From early days in China, the culture surrounding eating involved pleasure. In the time of the Sung Dynasty, cities grew and restaurants flourished. Restaurants were viewed as places of pleasure. In addition to eating and drinking to excess, men engaged sexual partners in restaurants. Some stayed in a restaurant for days at a time. The world of the *geisha* centered on the restaurant or teahouse where these women went to meet wealthy and/or powerful men. The Chinese found a profound link among dining, drinking, and sex as sensual pleasures.

## LATER CULINARY INFLUENCES

Not arriving in China until the eighteenth century, sweet potatoes, corn, red chilies, and peanuts came to China from the New World. These foods changed the culinary scene in China in a couple of ways. First, the Chinese integrated all these foods into their cuisine. Peanuts gained particular importance as a source of oil. Because it has a high smoking point, peanut oil is an excellent oil for stir-frying over high heat, a frequently used cooking technique in China. Second, the foods from the New World grew in regions where the traditional crops like rice, wheat, and millet would not grow. As a result, the food supply expanded and grew. This allowed the population to live in areas of very limited agriculture, and it yielded food for many poor people.

During the past century, China has experienced many changes. In 1911, the last dynasty was overthrown ending thousands of years of rule by various dynasties. Civil war ensued. In 1932, the Japanese invaded Manchuria and began a period in which brutality and starvation swept the land. After the Japanese defeat in World War II in 1946, civil war erupted in China.

From 1911 until 1949, China was called the Republic of China. When the Communists seized control in 1949, the leader of the nationalists, Chiang Kai-shek, fled to Taiwan. China became known as the People's Republic of China. Mao Tse-tung headed the Communist party in China until his death in 1976, and then his followers ruled.

The pro-democracy protests and uprising at Tiananmen Square in 1989 had a significant impact on the Communists' control. Although they still ruled, Chinese nationalism became stronger. Today, the Communist party continues to lead the government, but the ideology and implementation of Communist principles has changed greatly since the days of Mao.

Although numerous invaders conquered parts of China throughout history, they left relatively little influence. Explorers and invaders tended to take more contributions from China home with them than they left behind. Generally, the Chinese chose to adopt little from the culinary heritage of foreigners. In recent years that might be changing; fast food and other Western influences are appearing in China.

## >> TOPOGRAPHY

China occupies most of the eastern part of Asia. Ranking as the third largest country in the world, only Russia and Canada have more landmass.

## DIVERSE LAND AND CLIMATE

A land of many contrasts, some of the driest deserts and highest mountains as well as very fertile farmland exist in China. This country consists of a vast amount of land containing diverse topography, climates, and terrains.

While subarctic regions prevail in the north, tropical lowlands compose the south. The east contains fertile plains, but extensive desert makes up much of the west. Forests and fertile farmland cover a large portion of the northeast. Mountains lie in the east central region; the west has dry, rocky plateaus and mountains; the Himalaya Mountains loom on the southwestern border; and the northwest is desert.

Wild differences in climatic conditions follow the varying terrain. The north and west endure long, hard, cold winters, while the central and southern areas experience mild to warm winters. Hot, humid summers reign in southern Manchuria, but the arid northwest has hot, dry summers. Tibet and the Himalayas lie in the southwestern section, which experiences harsh winters and windy conditions prevailing throughout the year due to its high elevation.

*Wok*
© Dorling Kindersley

### THE UBIQUITOUS WOK

*Because of the limited amount of fuel available for cooking, the wok was developed. The design of this bowl-shaped metal pan allows food to cook quickly yet evenly. The pan's round shape eliminates corners where food can become stuck, overcook, or burn. Stirring the food in a wok causes the food to sweep the sides of the pan in a circular motion, almost a centrifugal-force-type movement. Furthermore, the wok can accommodate a stack of steamers or fit a whole fish, which gently curls to conform to the curves of the wok. Although the burners on Oriental stoves resemble deep wells that steadily hold the round-bottomed pan, the wok sits in a ring over the burner of a Western stove.*

### Ingredients and Foods Commonly Used throughout the Cuisine of China Include

- rice
- wheat and millet
- peanuts
- cabbages, greens, and bok choy
- carrots
- sweet potatoes
- water chestnuts, bamboo shoots, and bean sprouts
- mushrooms and fungi
- tofu and soybeans
- seafood and fish—both fresh and dried
- pork and poultry
- onions, garlic, and spring onions
- ginger
- soy sauce
- rice wine and rice vinegar
- tea

## WATERWAYS

Lakes dot the landscape, and many rivers, including the Yangtze and the Yellow rivers, run through China. The Pacific Ocean borders on the eastern side. As a result of this wealth of bodies of water, freshwater fish and seafood are available in many areas. Rivers in the warm southern regions yield the water needed to grow rice.

## >> COOKING METHODS

The most well-known Chinese cooking method, *chao* or stir-frying, developed as a way to save scarce cooking fuel. Cutting the food into small pieces and cooking rapidly over high heat required the least amount of cooking time and, therefore, less fuel. Besides cooking quickly, this method has two other distinct advantages: stir-frying preserves the texture of the food, and it retains valuable nutrients.

The pan used for stir-frying, a *wok*, has sloping sides and a rounded bottom. The rounded bottom eliminates corners where food might stick. To stir-fry, heat the oil in the wok over high heat until very hot, add the foods in the order of their cooking time (that is, beginning with the items requiring the most time to cook), and constantly stir the food while it cooks quickly over high heat. The Chinese cook vegetables until done but still crisp.

Another frying technique, deep-frying, appears often. Again, this method conserves fuel as foods submerged in hot fat cook quickly. Sometimes, deep-frying is combined with another method. For example, an item might be deep-fried to produce a crisp crust and then steamed.

Poaching, parboiling, and steaming are used for the cooking of soups, stews, entrées, rice, and many other items. Commonly used, steaming appears as a method for cooking whole duck, chicken, or fish, as well as individual items such as steamed buns or dumplings. Bamboo steamers, which hold the foods during the steaming process, can be stacked on top of each other in a wok. This facilitates steaming several foods at one time, another way of conserving limited heating fuel.

Sand-pot or clay-pot cooking is actually braising. The traditional pot used for this method resembles a squat, earthenware pot with a lid.

Commonly in China, a recipe uses more than one cooking method. While this is not common in most countries, it has interesting effects on the texture and taste of the dish.

Pickling, smoking, and wind drying became popular during the T'ang Dynasty (618 to 906 A.D.) as methods of preserving food for use during the long winter. To pickle foods, they used vinegar, salt, and wine. Preserved, smoked, and pickled items are still widely consumed.

*Bamboo steamer*
David Murray © Dorling Kindersley

## >> REGIONS

China is a huge country with much diversity in the climate, topography, soil conditions, and population found in its various regions. As a result, great differences exist among the regional cuisines of China. With ocean bordering China on the east, it is not surprising that most of the population resides in the eastern third of China. In addition, the majority of China's large cities are found in that area.

Because of differences in climates, terrains, and growing conditions, wheat and millet grow well in the cold, dry northern part of China, while rice thrives in the temperate, wetter south. As a result, wheat in the form of noodles, dumplings, and sometimes bread functions as the grain staple in the north. A symbol of longevity, many think noodles were actually invented in China. Millet is prepared like porridge.

People in the south eat rice instead, consuming at least one pound of rice each day. Evidence exists of rice growing in China 5,000 years ago. A symbol of life and fertility throughout China, many Western cultures have embraced this philosophy and throw rice at the bride and groom after a wedding.

*Many sources claim millet is the oldest grain grown in China. Wheat and rice came later.*

### REGIONAL DIFFERENCES

Overwhelmingly, the cuisine of each region depends on the food that grows or is raised there. Generally, favorable growing conditions result in more crops flourishing in the areas south of the Yangtze River. Lots of shrimp, crab, and fish are consumed in the eastern and southeastern coastal areas. The provinces of Sichuan and Hunan prepare spicy foods, whereas many other areas prefer mild or even bland dishes. The cooking method of choice throughout the southern regions remains stir-frying.

During the time of the Sung Dynasty from 960 A.D. to 1279 A.D., the regional cuisines began to unite into the cuisine of China. By that time, there was more transportation between regions, and foreign powers spread culinary knowledge of both other regions and their own country from one region to the next.

### NORTH

Long, cold winters and dry, arid conditions hamper the northern regions, resulting in limited crops; however, the summer yields abundant produce including tomatoes, cucumbers, eggplant, pears, grapes, and persimmons. The cuisine of the north tends to be lighter and simpler than in other areas of China. As opposed to the cooking found in the south, steaming, poaching, baking, and very fast frying are often-used cooking methods in northern China. Those techniques preserve the natural flavors of the food.

*Mongolian hot pot*
© superfood

People in the northern region of China usually marinate meat, then barbecue, boil, or roast rather than fry it. Lamb, a carryover from the nomadic Mongolian tribes of central Asia, remains popular in this region.

Mongolian hot pot consists of assorted meats, vegetables, and ginger boiled in liquid, which becomes rich stock. Nowadays, Mongolian hot pot resembles fondue because the pot of boiling stock is placed in the center of the table, and diners cook their own food by submerging it into the stock. The platter of food for cooking often includes a variety of meat, poultry, and seafood as well as all sorts of vegetables like bok choy, cabbage, and mushrooms. In addition, an assortment of condiments for dipping is offered. After cooking and eating the raw foods, diners add cellophane noodles to the stock. After the noodles absorb some of the rich stock, the diners remove them with chopsticks.

Duck and chicken also appear frequently. Peking (or Beijing) duck hails from the north and consists of crisp duck slices accompanied by thin rolled pancakes and a sweet sauce. Sweet-and-sour dishes remain a favorite here.

Due to the climate, wheat and millet not rice, grow in the north. As a result, noodles, steamed buns, and egg rolls predominate. Hot peppers do not appear here; garlic, onions, soy sauce, and ginger are the flavorings of choice. Often, a dish of thinly sliced scallions or green onions complements the other dishes. Soy sauce appears everywhere, in cooking and as a dipping sauce. A variety of dipping sauces accompanies the plainly cooked foods.

## EAST

The eastern coastal regions enjoy the best weather in China, with mild weather defining each season. The combination of fertile farmland, abundant rainfall, and a moderate climate produces a profusion of crops. Ample coastline, lakes, and rivers provide abundant seafood and freshwater fish, so eel, carp, mullet, perch, shrimp, crab, and duck dishes appear frequently here. In fact, the lower basin of the Yangtze River is a major portion of this region. Cooking in the east incorporates more sugar than any other region, and soy sauce appears less.

The provinces lying in this region generate diverse cuisines including rich stocks, gravies and sauces, soups, and stews. Red stew comes from this region. With such a bounty of foods available, the emphasis lies on very fresh tasting foods. Preferred flavorings include ginger, green onions, sugar, and some soy sauce (but not as much as other regions). Cooking in this region often includes rice wine or rice vinegar. Rice thrives in the eastern region, particularly near the Yangtze River.

## CENTRAL AND WEST

Two well-known regions, Szechwan in the west and Hunan in the central area, feature similar flavorings. The cookery in both of these provinces uses plenty of hot peppers, green onions, ginger, garlic, and fermented bean paste. Lying in lush countryside, the dishes from Hunan contain a wide variety of meats, seafood, and vegetables. In fact, Hunan is one of China's most productive agricultural areas with lots of rice growing in eastern Hunan.

Because Szechwan is in mountainous terrain, the Szechwanese have access to ample game but much less choice in the meats, fish, seafood, and vegetables available. Both the Szechwan peppercorn and hot chili peppers give dishes in Szechwan their characteristic spicy flavor. The cookery of Szechwan incorporates sugar while Hunan cooking juxtaposes the spice of the peppers with salty or sour components.

Besides red chilies, garlic, green onions, and ginger, dishes in the central region include other flavorings like rice vinegar, peanuts, and sesame oil, seeds, and paste. Hot-and-sour soup exemplifies the flavors found in the cooking here.

*Many attribute the beginnings of the Mongolian hot pot to the Mongols who invaded in the 1200s. It is reported that the soldiers put any available food items with water in their metal helmets and then heated the helmet and contents over the fire until the foods cooked. At that point, they ate the food and then drank the remaining liquid.*

Peking duck
© SS

Peking duck
© paul_brighton

Cooks marinate many foods before cooking. They use lots of foods preserved by smoking, salting, drying, and pickling. When planning meals, cooks from this region think about featuring the five elements, or taste sensations—sweet, sour, salty, pungent or spicy, and bitter. With the exclusion of pungent, the remaining four taste sensations currently are defined by scientists as those discerned by the human palate.

## SOUTH

Most agree that the south features the most fancy and sophisticated dishes of all the regional cuisines of China. Certainly, the widest range of recipes comes from this area, and most regard Canton as the heart of southern cooking. When Chinese restaurants began opening in the United States, most served Cantonese food. Some compare the Cantonese cuisine with that of France.

Located in the south-southwest, Yunnan experiences significant isolation as a result of the mountainous terrain. With ample open land, game abounds. Many say the ham of Yunnan is the finest in China. Recipes from this region incorporate all sorts of nuts, including peanuts, walnuts, pine nuts, and chestnuts.

Because the south has warm, temperate weather, rich soil, and plenty of rainfall, a huge variety of fruits and vegetables flourish here. In addition, domesticated and wild animals for meat and poultry thrive in the south. With several rivers and close proximity to the sea, fish and other seafood appear in many dishes, often mixed with meats or vegetables. Oyster sauce and shrimp paste flavor lots of dishes. In summary, the south has a plethora of food products available.

Originating in the southern region of Canton, *dim sum* is small portions of an endless variety of foods. Like hors d'oeuvres, *dim sum* resembles Spanish *tapas* or Middle Eastern *mezze*. Restaurants offer *dim sum* for lunch or any time throughout the day. Available in a whole range of forms and flavors, *dim sum* includes soups, steamed buns, stuffed dumplings, sweet and savory pastries, and much more.

Fresh foods with their natural flavor typify the cookery in the south. People here season with rice vinegar, ginger, and spring onions, which emphasize the natural flavors of the foods. To cook quickly and retain the natural flavors, stir-frying and steaming are the most frequently used cooking methods. Cooking from the southern region features many sauces.

More than in any other region, southern chefs and cooks give a lot of consideration to the visuals of a dish as well as its texture. Aesthetics including color of the foods in a dish are very important. Garnishes adorning plates and platters as well as the colors of the dish, plate, or platter command attention. In addition, cooks carefully consider the texture of foods, often pairing crisp vegetables with tender meats or fish to produce different texture sensations within each dish.

## >> CUISINE

Many claim the Chinese diet is the most nutritionally balanced diet in the world. Certainly, throughout China's history, medicine and food have been linked closely. The Chinese believe diet and food directly influence health and disease, so one's diet determines one's health.

Preparation and cooking remain two distinctly different aspects of food production here. Differing from Western cookery, it usually takes more time to prepare the food for Chinese cooking than the actual time needed to cook the food. Both meat and vegetables are meticulously chopped into small, uniform pieces to ensure quick and even cooking. The importance of evenly sized pieces cannot be overstated, because a variety of sizes results in overcooked and undercooked ingredients. In addition, all ingredients must be prepared before the cooking begins, because the actual cooking process happens very rapidly.

### RED STEW

*Although red stew originated in the eastern region, it is prepared throughout China. This slow-cooked braised dish consists of meat (or any protein) cooked in a dark broth containing dark soy sauce (which is thicker and sweeter than plain soy sauce), rice wine, sugar, green onions, and aromatic herbs and spices such as ginger, star anise, five-spice powder, and cardamom.*

Red stew
© paul_brighton

*Humid climate prevails in Hunan and Szechwan. The Chinese believe the heat from eating fiery peppers counteracts this dampness (humidity), which gives the diner balance.*

### AREAS OF CHINA

*North—Inner Mongolia*

*Northeast—Manchuria, Peking (Beijing)*

*Northwest—Xinjiang*

*Central—Hunan*

*West—Szechwan*

*East—Shanghai, Fukien*

*Southwest—Tibet*

*South—Canton, Yunnan*

## INGREDIENTS

Nothing is wasted in the Chinese kitchen. Literally all parts of the animal are consumed, from the beak to the feet. Seafood shells and heads go into the stockpot, even if the pot contains chicken stock. Leftover dishes are transformed into new creations with no semblance of their former identity.

The most important type of food remains grains followed by vegetables. The five most important grains and legumes are soybeans, rice, barley, wheat, and millet; they form the foundation of the cuisine. As stated before, the choice of grain depends on the region, with wheat preferred in the north and rice in the south. Besides grains, the most prevalent foods in the Chinese diet include soybeans, cabbages, a variety of greens, onions, and garlic.

Instead of using large amounts of meat for the center of the meal, vegetable dishes often rely on small amounts of meat, seafood, and/or fermented beans or dried or preserved foods like chili paste for flavoring. Consumed at every meal throughout the south, rice is eaten with vegetables and/or available protein, but not alone. Generally, bites of rice alternate with bites of the other food items. Although diners might put some of the sauce from a dish on the rice, the Chinese do not mix their food directly with the rice. The Chinese prefer a long-grain variety of rice to short-grain.

Widely consumed, tofu, or soybean curd, functions as a major source of protein. Pork and poultry remain the most popular meats. As a result of the huge fishing industry here, fish and shellfish play a significant role in the Chinese diet.

Vegetables are never boiled; rather, their cooking includes stir-frying and then perhaps braising. Crisp, *al dente* vegetables prevail, not the limp vegetables commonly served in many Western cuisines.

China produces more rice, wheat, and pears than any other country in the world. Many other foods grow well, including sweet potatoes, cabbage, carrots, corn, potatoes, beets, tomatoes, apples, sugar cane, peanuts, soybeans, millet, and tea. The Chinese diet is rich in fruits and vegetables.

Dairy products are almost nonexistent in this cuisine. However, a number of ingredients not used in the Western cuisines—shark's fins, tiger lily buds, snake, bear paws, and sea cucumbers—appear in Chinese dishes.

The Chinese cuisine provides ample vegetarian dishes for Buddhists, members of a religion that forbids meat consumption. The diet of Chinese Muslims resembles the kosher foods of Israel. Pork and seafood without scales or backbone are not allowed.

Cornstarch is the most often-used thickening agent in China, as opposed to the flour used in the majority of Western dishes. This eliminates the *roux* used so frequently in the West and replaces it with a mixture of cornstarch and water combined with other flavorings.

> According to historians, by 2700 B.C., the Chinese had identified 365 herbs, and they were making soy sauce by 1100 B.C.

## FLAVORINGS

Common flavorings and condiments used in Chinese cookery include soy sauce, rice wine, rice vinegar, bean paste, plum sauce, oyster sauce, sugar, salt, ginger, garlic, and sesame oil. An important ingredient used throughout China, soybeans form several products, including soy sauce, fermented beans, bean paste, and *hoisin*, in addition to tofu.

Seasonings and condiments are used to enhance the natural flavors of the foods, not to change them. Some of the frequently used spices include star anise, a licorice-flavored spice; ginger; Szechwan pepper; and a five-spice powder composed of fennel, cloves, anise seed, Szechwan pepper, and cinnamon. Ginger root comes in several forms, including fresh, crystallized, and powdered. The Chinese use marinades frequently, both to impart flavor and tenderize before the quick cooking. Because they cut food into small sizes, short marination times work well.

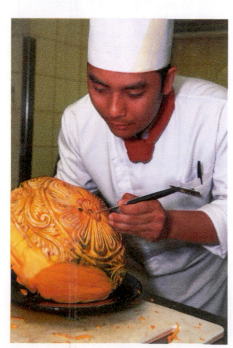

*Carving fruit*
© erwinova

## OVERVIEW

Throughout China, cooks pay a lot of attention to the balance of flavors, colors, aromas, and textures in food. The contrast between soft and smooth foods, hard and crunchy, salty and sweet, and more contrasts creates that highly prized balance and harmony. All of these issues make the food more interesting and appealing for the diner.

The aesthetics of food has always been very important to the Chinese. Both simple and intricate fruit and vegetable carvings often garnish plates and buffet tables.

## MEALS

When Chinese meals contain courses, their order differs greatly from those found in Western meals. Since soup can function as a palate cleanser between courses at a formal dinner, cooks often serve more than one variety of soup during the meal. The dessert might come in the middle of the meal, and hors d'oeuvres appear wherever their flavors fit. Again, the balance of flavors and textures throughout the meal rather than the sequence of courses remains the important concept.

Depending on the region, a typical Chinese breakfast consists of rice porridge (*congee*), chicken noodle soup, or a doughnut like fried pastry. Egg rolls or dumplings filled with meat or shrimp are served for lunch. The main meal includes vegetables with small amounts of meat or seafood, soup, and rice or noodles (depending on the region).

A typical dinner includes several dishes and often more than one type of soup. Normally, all dishes are placed in the center of the table, and diners serve themselves from each dish. Unlike Western meals, this eliminates the plating of set portions, freeing the diner to take as little or much of each dish and condiment as desired. A festive dinner will feature 10 or 12 dishes. Eating utensils are chopsticks and soup spoons.

## BEVERAGES

Gaining its popularity during the T'ang Dynasty, tea reigns as the beverage of choice throughout China. Besides being an important part of daily life and ceremonies, numerous varieties of tea have medicinal uses. Rice wine also becomes incorporated into ceremonies and rituals. In fact, brides and grooms drink rice wine during a Chinese wedding.

*Fruit and vegetable carving*
© asiancool

| REGION | AREA | WEATHER | TOPOGRAPHY | FOODS |
|--------|------|---------|------------|-------|
| North | Beijing, Shantung, Honan | Long, cold winters; dry, arid, summers; windy | Desert, mountains | Duck, lamb, chicken, seafood, wheat, corn, millet, peanuts, sorghum, soy sauce, cabbage, greens, fruits |
| East | Shanghai, Fukien | Mild to semitropical | Coast, plains, fertile farmland, Yangtze River, rolling hills, lakes | Seafood, freshwater fish, pork, poultry, red stew, ginger, onions, vegetables, fruits |
| West | Tibet | Long, cold winters; cool summers; windy, dry | Mountains, rocky plateaus, desert | Yak, barley |
| Central | Szechwan | Semitropical, hot, humid summers; mild winters | Mountains, valleys, fertile farmland, Yangtze River | Game, pork, poultry, fish, soybeans, rice, wheat, corn, hot peppers, legumes, fungus, herbs, ginger, garlic, fruits |
| | Hunan | Hot, humid summers; mild winters | Fertile farmland, lakes | Meat, fish, poultry, rice, hot peppers, ginger, garlic, vegetables |
| South | Canton | Hot, humid summers; mild winters | Mountains, valleys, fertile land, coast, rivers | Seafood, fish, poultry, game, pork, rice, *dim sum*, vegetables, ginger, sweet potatoes, fruits, tea |
| | Yunnan | Mild | Mountains, rivers, lakes | Freshwater fish, ham, game, nuts, vegetables |

Since very early days, the Chinese consumed alcoholic beverages. They learned of grapes and wine during the Han Dynasty (206 B.C. to 220 A.D.). Fermentation of grain began in the Sung Dynasty (960 to 1279 A.D.). The Chinese derived great pleasure from both food and alcoholic beverages, and both played an important part in their culture.

## >> Review Questions

1. Which grain predominates in the north and south? Why? How is it prepared (what form does it take)?
2. Name four provinces or regions and explain the differences in the flavorings and cooking of each.
3. Explain yin and yang and its affect on the cuisine of China.

4. Describe stir-frying, including the preparation of the food and the actual cooking process.
5. What are the advantages of stir-frying as a cooking method?

## >> Glossary

**chao** Cooking technique known as stir-frying

**congee** Rice (or millet or barley) porridge served for breakfast, to babies, and to ill people

**dim sum** Snack foods eaten for lunch or any time throughout the day, can include soups, steamed buns, stuffed dumplings, sweet and savory pastries, and much more; originated in the southern region of Canton

**hoisin** A sweet and spicy sauce made from soybeans and used in cooking, marinades, and dips

**tofu** Soybean curd; a cheeselike substance made from soybeans; a protein source

**tsai-fan** Protein or vegetable served with rice

**wok** A pan with sloping sides and a rounded bottom used for stir-frying and other cooking methods

**yin-yang** Complex philosophy that affects food, art, and other aspects of Chinese life; deals with combining opposites to achieve balance and harmony; *yin* represents the feminine or dark while *yang* stands for the masculine or light; the important issue remains the successful combining of these two forces to achieve the harmony and balance in the food, art, or any medium that leads to balance and harmony in the body and spirit

## CH'UN-CHÜAN (SOUTH)

### SPRING ROLLS

**Note:** Spring rolls or egg rolls probably appear on every Chinese menu in this country. In addition, most fusion restaurants offer some variety of spring rolls.

**Number of Servings:** 14
**Serving Size:** 1 spring roll with 1 1/4 oz. (36 g) filling
**Total Yield:** 1 lb., 1 1/2 oz. (497 g) filling
**Food Balance:** Protein
**Wine Suggestion:** Low-oaked whites and soft reds
**Example:** Beringer Founders' Estate Chardonnay or Merlot

**Cooking Method:** Deep-fry, stir-fry (sauté)

David Murray and Jules Selmes © Dorling Kindersley

| INGREDIENTS | WEIGHT | | VOLUME | |
|---|---|---|---|---|
| | U.S. | METRIC | U.S. | METRIC |
| **Filling:** | | | | |
| dried mushrooms, forest or any variety | 1/4 oz. | 8 g | 4 each | |
| water | as needed | 28 g | | |
| cornstarch | 1/2 oz. | 15 g | 1 tablespoon | 15 mL |
| water, cold | | | 2 tablespoons | 30 mL |
| oil | | 28 g | 2 tablespoons | 30 mL |
| ground pork | 8 oz. | 227 g | | |
| rice wine or dry sherry | | 15 g | 1 tablespoon | 15 mL |
| soy sauce | | 28 g | 2 tablespoons | 30 mL |
| sugar | | | 1/2 teaspoon | 3 mL |
| shrimp, shelled, deveined, and finely diced | 6 3/4 oz. (8 oz. in shells) | 191 g (227 g in shells) | | |
| Chinese cabbage | 7 1/2 oz. | 213 g | 2 cups | 480 mL |
| celery, finely diced | 9 1/2 oz. | 270 g | 5 stalks, about 2 cups | 480 mL |
| fresh bean sprouts | 8 oz. | 227 g | | |
| salt | 1/4 oz. | 8 g | 1 teaspoon | 5 mL |
| sesame oil | | | 1/4 teaspoon | 2 mL |
| spring roll wrappers | | | | |
| oil, peanut or other, for deep-frying | | | | |

**Accompaniments:**

dipping sauces of choice: hot mustard sauce and duck sauce, or hot chili sauce and soy sauce

> **TWIST ON THE CLASSIC**
>
> Use any filling the imagination conjures for the spring rolls. Try a combination of fresh salmon, smoked salmon, and cream cheese; or curried beef; or all vegetables for a vegetarian variety.

### FILLING:

1. Place mushrooms in bowl, cover with warm water. Let soak for 30 minutes. Drain mushrooms, dice. Mix cornstarch with 2 tablespoons (28 g or 30 mL) cold water. Set aside.
2. Heat 1 tablespoon (15 g or 15 mL) of oil in wok over medium-high to high heat until hot. Add pork, stir-fry until no longer pink, about 2 minutes.
3. Add rice wine, 1 tablespoon (15 mL) of soy sauce, sugar, shrimp, and reserved mushrooms, stir-fry until shrimp turns pink, about 1 minute. Remove to bowl and set aside.

④ Heat remaining 1 tablespoon (15 g or 15 mL) of oil in wok until hot. Add cabbage and celery, stir-fry 4 or 5 minutes, add bean sprouts and salt. Mix well.

⑤ Add pork mixture to pan, stir to mix well. Cook over medium-high heat, stirring constantly, until liquid starts to boil.

⑥ Add cornstarch mixture and sesame oil, stir constantly until slightly thickened and mixture has glaze.

⑦ Transfer to bowl, cool to room temperature. Refrigerate if not using immediately.

## ASSEMBLY:

① Place wrapper on table with point up. Place about 1 1/4 oz., or 1/4 cup (36 g) filling horizontally across center of wrapper.

② Fold lower end of wrapper over filling, tucking point under filling.

③ Using finger or pastry brush, wet exposed edges of wrapper with cold water.

④ Fold side flaps over filling, press gently to seal.

⑤ Roll wrapper into cylinder, gently pressing edges to seal.

⑥ Place filled spring rolls on sheet pan and cover well. Refrigerate until ready to fry.

⑦ Heat oil for deep-frying to 375 degrees (190°C) in wok.

⑧ Place five or six spring rolls in hot oil, fry for about 3 or 4 minutes, until crisp and golden brown.

⑨ Drain well. Repeat with remaining rolls.

⑩ Serve accompanied by hot mustard sauce and duck sauce or hot chili sauce and soy sauce.

© dreambigphotos

# CHUNG YO BING

## SCALLION PANCAKES

**Number of Servings:** 8

**Serving Size:** 1/2 pancake; 2 wedges

**Dough:** 15 1/2 oz. (439 g)

**Total Yield:** 4 pancakes

**Cooking Method:** Sauté

**Wine Style:** Medium-plus-bodied white wine from a cool climate region. Possible grape varietals are Sauvignon Blanc, Riesling, Gruner Veltliner.

**Example:** Sauvignon Blanc "Zieregg" 2009, Tement (Sudsteiermark/Austria)

© dreambigphotos

| INGREDIENTS | WEIGHT U.S. | WEIGHT METRIC | VOLUME U.S. | VOLUME METRIC |
|---|---|---|---|---|
| flour, all-purpose | 9 3/4 oz. | 278 g | 2 cups | 480 mL |
| salt | | | 3/4 teaspoon | 4 mL |
| oil | 1/2 oz. | 15 g | 1 tablespoon | 15 mL |
| boiling water | | 170 g | 3/4 cup | 180 mL |
| sesame oil | | 15 g | 1 tablespoon | 15 mL |
| oil | as needed for brushing on dough | | | |
| scallions, cut into 1/8-inch (0.3-cm) slices | 3 1/4 oz. | 92 g | 1 bunch or 1 cup | 240 mL |
| oil | as needed for frying | | | |
| coarse salt, optional | as needed for sprinkling | | | |

① Place flour and salt in bowl of food processor fitted with knife blade. Pulse to mix. Add oil (15 g, 1 tablespoon, or 15 mL) and boiling water through feed tube. Pulse until dough comes together to form a ball. Alternately, mix with wooden spoon in bowl until it forms ball.

② Remove from bowl, knead until smooth, about 1 or 2 minutes. Cover dough and allow to rest for 1 hour.

③ Form dough into log. Divide into 4 parts. Place one part on counter and roll until about 13- by 5-inch (33- by 13-cm) rectangle (about 1/16- to 1/8-inch, 0.16- to 0.3-cm thick).

## TWIST ON THE CLASSIC

For a luncheon entrée, sandwich two scallion pancakes with ham and Swiss or provolone cheese, then heat to melt the cheese.

4. Brush lightly with sesame oil, sprinkle scallions on top. Starting from the long side, fold until the dough lies past the middle. Fold the opposite long side past the middle, so the dough overlaps. Starting from the short side, tightly roll the strip like a snail or cinnamon roll. Repeat with remaining three dough portions.

5. Now repeat the rolling process on the four rounds of dough by rolling out each of the snail-like portions into a rectangle, brushing with sesame oil (use additional plain oil when the sesame oil is gone), sprinkling with scallions, folding the dough, and then rolling the dough into a snail-like shape. Allow to rest if dough becomes too tight and springy.

6. Roll each portion of dough into circle about 1/4-inch (0.5-cm) thick and about 8 inches (20 cm) in diameter. Place absorbent paper on sheet pan or plate.

7. Heat large skillet with a thin layer of oil over medium-high heat until hot. Place pancake in skillet, cook about 1 to 1 1/2 minutes on each side, until lightly browned. If browning too quickly, lower heat. Remove from skillet and place on absorbent paper. If desired, sprinkle cooked pancake with coarse salt.

8. Repeat with remaining dough. Add more oil to skillet, as needed. If desired, keep pancakes warm in low oven.

9. Cut each pancake into eight wedges. Serve four wedges or desired portion with soy sauce for dipping or the dipping sauce of choice.

> This recipe includes the process of a laminated dough as well as frying. Laminated doughs alternate layers of dough with a fat to create layers. Examples are puff pastry and phyllo dough.

## CHEN CHU JOU WAN (WEST)

### PEARL BALLS

**Note:** Allow at least 2 1/2 hours to soak and dry rice.

**Note:** Pearl balls are firm enough to use as a passed hors d'oeuvre. Include a bowl of sauce on the platter and toothpicks for spearing.

**Note:** This recipe required about 75 percent of the glutinous rice. If increasing the recipe, do not increase the rice proportionally. Use about 80 percent of the rice.

**Number of Servings:** 11  
**Serving Size:** 3 meatballs, about 3 1/2 oz. (104 g) cooked  
**Total Yield:** 33 meatballs, 2 lb., 9 oz. (1.2 kg) cooked (1 lb., 9 oz. [710 g] raw meat mixture)  
**Food Balance:** Protein  
**Wine Style:** Low-oaked whites and soft reds  
**Example:** Greg Norman Chardonnay or Zinfandel  

**Cooking Method:** Steam

Paul Williams © Dorling Kindersley

| INGREDIENTS | WEIGHT | | VOLUME | |
|---|---|---|---|---|
| | U.S. | METRIC | U.S. | METRIC |
| glutinous rice | 8 oz. | 227 g | 1 cup | 240 mL |
| water | as needed | | | |
| dried Chinese mushrooms | 3/4 oz. | 22 g | 8 each | |
| ground pork | 1 lb. | 454 g | | |
| water chestnuts, minced | 2 1/4 oz. | 64 g | 8 each | |
| fresh ginger, peeled and minced | 1/2 oz. | 15 g | 1 tablespoon | 15 mL |
| scallions, minced | 3/4 oz. | 22 g | 2 each | |
| soy sauce | | 15 g | 1 tablespoon | 15 mL |
| sugar | | | 1 teaspoon | 5 mL |
| salt | 1/4 oz. | 8 g | 1 teaspoon | 5 mL |
| egg | 1 3/4 oz. | 50 g | 1 each | |

**Accompaniment:**  
dipping sauces of choice: duck sauce, soy sauce flavored with sesame oil, sweet-and-sour sauce, or any desired

> ### TWIST ON THE CLASSIC
>
> Try preparing these meatballs with ground turkey or ground beef instead of the pork. To create a different texture, deep-fry the meatballs after steaming.

1. Rinse rice with cold water. Place in bowl, cover with cold water and soak for 2 hours. Drain rice, spread on towel to dry.

2. Soak mushrooms in warm water for 30 minutes. Remove any tough stems and then mince mushroom caps.

3. Prepare steamer by placing water at bottom of pan and bringing it to a boil.

4. Combine pork, reserved mushrooms, water chestnuts, ginger, scallions, soy sauce, sugar, salt, and egg in bowl. Mix to combine thoroughly.

5. Roll pork mixture into 3/4-oz. (22-g) meatballs about 1 inch (2.5 cm) in diameter. Roll in rice to completely coat outside with rice.

6. Place rice-coated meatballs on plate or tray or on parchment paper, place in steamer basket. Be sure that the plate does not touch the walls of the steaming pan so that steam can circulate around the plate.

7. Steam 30 minutes. Serve with dipping sauce(s) of choice.

---

## GUO TIE

### POTSTICKERS

Cooking potstickers
© uckyo

© JJAVA

**Number of Servings:** 14
**Serving Size:** 5
**Scaling:** 1/4 oz. (8 g) (1 teaspoon [5 mL]) filling per potsticker
**Total Filling:** 1 lb., 2 1/4 oz. (518 g)
**Total Potstickers:** 72
**Wine Style:** White wine with peppery aromas. Possible grape varietal is Gruner Veltliner.
**Example:** Grüner Veltliner 2013, Wess (Kremstal/Austria)

**Cooking Method:** Sauté, steam

| INGREDIENTS | WEIGHT | | VOLUME | |
| --- | --- | --- | --- | --- |
| | U.S. | METRIC | U.S. | METRIC |
| pork, ground or other ground meat | 12 oz. | 340 g | | |
| baby bok choy, fine dice | 3 1/2 oz. | 104 g | 1 cup | 240 mL |
| scallions, minced | 1 oz. | 28 g | 1/4 cup | 60 mL |
| ginger, peeled, minced | 1/4 oz. | 8 g | 2 teaspoons | 10 mL |
| white pepper | | | 1/4 teaspoon | 2 mL |
| soy sauce | | 15 g | 1 tablespoon | 15 mL |
| rice wine or dry to medium sherry | | 15 g | 1 tablespoon | 15 mL |
| sesame oil | | | 1 teaspoon | 5 mL |
| wonton wrappers | | | 72 each | |
| oil, as needed for frying | | | | |
| water needed for each skillet of potstickers | | 57 g | 1/4 cup or as needed | 60 mL |

**Accompaniment:**
dipping sauce of choice

**Garnish:**
parsley or cilantro, minced,
*optional*

1. In bowl, mix pork, bok choy, scallions, ginger, white pepper, soy sauce, rice wine, and sesame oil. Refrigerate until needed unless using right away. Cover sheet pan or cookie sheet with parchment paper; set aside until needed.

2. Remove one wonton wrapper from package; cover remaining with damp towel. Place wonton in hand or on work surface. With finger or pastry brush, lightly wet the edges of two adjacent sides with water (to moisten so the wonton seals).

③ Place 1/4 oz. (8 g, 1 teaspoon, or 5 mL) filling in center of wrapper. Fold over filling to form triangle.

④ Form pleats at top. To form pleats, pinch (or fold) one side of the wonton in the middle, then make two more pleats on each side of the middle pleat, so there are a total of five pleats on one side of the wonton. (One side has pleats; the other side is smooth.) Press top edge firmly to seal both sides together. Flatten bottom of wonton and place it with the pleats at the top on prepared pan (with the bottom flattened, the wonton will stand); cover with damp towel. Repeat with remaining filling and wonton wrappers.

⑤ Coat bottom of large skillet with oil. Heat until hot over medium-high heat. Place as many wontons (standing on flattened bottom) as skillet will hold in pan. Reduce to medium and cook about a minute until lightly brown on bottom. Cover skillet and cook for 3 minutes. Add 1/4 cup (57 g or 60 mL) water, cover and cook another 5 to 7 minutes. If necessary, add a little water to prevent burning. If needed, remove lid at end of cooking until water evaporates.

⑥ Remove from skillet, serve immediately or keep warm in low oven until service. Serve plain or with dipping sauce of choice. If desired, garnish with minced parsley or cilantro.

> Present potstickers with one or more dipping sauces. It can be as simple as plain soy sauce or soy sauce containing minced ginger, or soy sauce with minced ginger and hot oil.

## SUAN-LA-T'ANG (SZECHUAN)

### HOT AND SOUR SOUP

**Note:** Add hot chili oil to make this soup spicy.

**Number of Servings:** 11
**Serving Size:** 8 oz. (227 g)
**Total Yield:** 5 lb., 13 oz. (2.6 kg)
**Food Balance:** Acidic
**Wine Style:** Dry, crisp acidity: Pinot Grigio, Sauvignon Blanc, Chablis, Pinot Noir, cool-climate reds
**Example:** Meridian Vineyards Pinot Noir

**Cooking Method:** Boil

> **TWIST ON THE CLASSIC**
>
> For a vegetarian item, omit the pork and use vegetable stock.

| INGREDIENTS | WEIGHT U.S. | WEIGHT METRIC | VOLUME U.S. | VOLUME METRIC |
|---|---|---|---|---|
| dried Chinese mushrooms | 1/2 oz. | 15 g | 8 each | |
| water, warm | | 227 g | 1 cup | 240 mL |
| cornstarch | 2 oz. | 57 g | 1/4 cup | 60 mL |
| water, cold | | 114 g | 1/2 cup | 120 mL |
| chicken stock | | | 2 quarts (8 cups) | 1.9 L |
| soy sauce | | 57 g | 1/4 cup | 60 mL |
| canned bamboo shoots, julienne | 4 oz. | 114 g | 1 cup | 240 mL |
| boneless pork, trimmed and cut into julienne | 8 oz. | 227 g | | |
| firm tofu (bean curd), 1/2-inch (1.3-cm) dice | 1 lb., 4 oz. | 567 g | | |
| pepper | | | 1/2 teaspoon | 3 mL |
| vinegar, rice or white | | 57 g | 1/4 cup | 60 mL |
| egg, lightly beaten | 3 1/2 oz. | 104 g | 2 each | |
| sesame seed oil | | | 1 tablespoon + 1 teaspoon | 20 mL |
| hot chili oil, *optional* | to taste | | | |
| rice vinegar, *optional* | to taste | | | |
| soy sauce, *optional* | to taste | | | |
| **Garnish:** | | | | |
| scallions, including green, fine slices | 1 oz. | 28 g | 2 each | |

1. Place mushrooms in bowl, cover with 1 cup (227 g or 240 mL) warm water. Let soak for 30 minutes.
2. Mix cornstarch with 1/2 cup (114 g or 120 mL) cold water. Set aside.
3. Drain mushrooms, julienne.
4. Combine stock, soy sauce, mushrooms, bamboo shoots, and pork in large pot. Bring to boil, reduce heat, cover pan and simmer for 3 minutes.
5. Add tofu, pepper, and vinegar. Bring to boil over medium heat.
6. Stir cornstarch mixture, pour into soup. Cook, stirring, until soup thickens.
7. Slowly pour in egg, stirring gently.
8. Stir in sesame seed oil.
9. Taste to balance flavors, correct seasonings. For more spice, add hot chili oil. To make it more sour, add vinegar. For more salt, add soy sauce.
10. Serve, garnished with scallions.

# SU-MI-T'ANG (SOUTH)

## VELVET CORN SOUP

**Note:** Recipes often add pieces of chicken to corn soup.

**Number of Servings:** 9  
**Serving Size:** 8 oz. (227 g)  
**Total Yield:** 4 lb., 8 oz. (2 kg)  
**Food Balance:** Sweet/protein  
**Wine Style:** Soft and fruity Viognier, Pinot Blanc, Riesling, White Zinfandel  
**Example:** Château St. Jean Pinot Blanc

**Cooking Method:** Sauté, boil

© jreika

| INGREDIENTS | WEIGHT | | VOLUME | |
|---|---|---|---|---|
| | U.S. | METRIC | U.S. | METRIC |
| cornstarch | 1/2 to 3/4 oz. | 15 to 22 g | 1 to 1 1/2 tablespoons | 15 to 23 mL |
| water, cold | | 28 to 43 g | 2 to 3 tablespoons | 30 to 45 mL |
| oil | | 15 g | 1 tablespoon | 15 mL |
| scallions, green and white parts, chopped | 3/4 oz. | 22 g | 1 each or 3 tablespoons | 45 mL |
| fresh ginger, peeled and minced | | | 1 teaspoon | 5 mL |
| cured ham, finely chopped | 1 1/2 oz. | 43 g | 1/4 cup | 60 mL |
| Chinese rice wine or dry sherry | | 28 g | 2 tablespoons | 30 mL |
| chicken stock | | | 1 quart + 1 cup (5 cups) | 1.2 L |
| cream-style corn | 1 lb., 14 oz. | 851 g | two 15-oz. cans | two 426-g cans |
| salt | | | to taste | |
| egg whites | 2 oz. | 57 g | 2 each | |

**Garnish:**

fresh cilantro, minced

## TWIST ON THE CLASSIC

Add crab to this corn soup and create a delicious bisque.

1. Mix cornstarch with 2 to 3 tablespoons (28 to 43 g or 30 to 45 mL) cold water in small bowl. Set aside.
2. Over medium-high heat, heat oil in pot until hot.
3. Add scallions and ginger, stir for 15 seconds. Add ham, stir for 15 seconds. Add rice wine or sherry. Add stock, stir, add corn. Stirring often, heat until almost boiling.
4. Over medium heat, stir cornstarch mixture into soup, cook over low heat for several minutes to thicken slightly. Add salt, if needed, correct seasonings.

5 Beat egg whites until frothy.

6 Without stirring, pour egg whites in thin, steady stream into soup, pouring from about 6 inches (15 cm) above pot. Stir once gently, halfway through adding, then again at end.

7 Serve in bowls, garnish with cilantro.

## HÜN-T'UN-T'ANG (THROUGHOUT CHINA)

### WONTON SOUP

**Note:** There are a number of different ways to fold wontons; two are described here. Also, wonton wrappers vary in size. The amount of filling will depend on the size of the wrapper. Each wonton needs only a little filling.

**Note:** To serve wontons as an appetizer, fill them with any variety of sweet or savory filling, then deep-fry or steam them. Accompany with dipping sauces of choice.

**Number of Servings:** 10 to 13

**Cooking Method:** Boil

**Serving Size:** 5 to 6 wontons, with 1/4 oz. (8 g) filling in each

**Total Yield:** 65 wontons, with 16 1/4 oz. (462 g) filling

**Food Balance:** Protein

**Wine Style:** Low-oaked whites and soft reds

**Example:** Meridian Vineyards Chardonnay or Pinot Noir

| INGREDIENTS | WEIGHT | | VOLUME | |
|---|---|---|---|---|
| | U.S. | METRIC | U.S. | METRIC |
| **Filling:** | | | | |
| ground pork | 12 oz. | 340 g | | |
| soy sauce | | 15 g | 1 tablespoon | 15 mL |
| fresh ginger, peeled and minced | | | 3/4 teaspoon | 4 mL |
| scallions, 3/16-inch (45-mm) slices | 1/2 oz. | 15 g | 1 each | |
| fresh spinach, cooked, chopped, and squeezed dry, or use chopped frozen | 4 oz. | 114 g | 1/4 cup + 2 tablespoons | 90 mL |
| wonton wrappers | 65 each | | 65 each | |
| water, cold, for sealing wrappers | | | | |
| chicken soup | | | about 3 quarts (12 cups) | 2.8 L |

**Garnish:**

fresh spinach, chiffonade

*First fold of wrapper over filling*
David Murray and Jules Selmes © Dorling Kindersley

### FILLING:

1 Combine pork, soy sauce, ginger, and scallions in bowl. Mix well.

2 Mix in spinach.

3 Refrigerate until ready to use.

### ASSEMBLY:

1 Place wonton wrapper on table with point facing you, moisten edges with cold water.

2 Place about 1/4 oz. or 3/4 to 1 teaspoon (8 g) filling just below center of wrapper.

3 Fold bottom side of wonton wrapper over filling, tuck edge under filling.

4 Roll into cylinder, leaving 1/2-inch (1.3-cm) point of wrapper unrolled.

5 Moisten ends with cold water.

6 Using both hands, grasp two ends of the cylinder and pull them behind roll until ends overlap slightly.

7 Pinch the two ends firmly together.

8 Place formed wonton on sheet pan and cover.

*Folding the wonton*
David Murray and Jules Selmes © Dorling Kindersley

Bending the wonton
David Murray and Jules Selmes © Dorling Kindersley

Boiling the wontons
David Murray and Jules Selmes © Dorling Kindersley

David Murray and Jules Selmes © Dorling Kindersley

© Joshua Resnick

OR
1  Place wonton wrapper on table with point facing you, moisten edges with cold water.
2  Place about 1/4 oz. or 3/4 to 1 teaspoon (8 g) filling just below center of wrapper.
3  Fold one side over filling to form triangle. Press to seal seams well.
4  Moisten two corners across from each other with cold water.
5  Using both hands, grasp those two corners, twist to bring them behind wonton.
6  Pinch firmly together to seal.
7  Place formed wonton on sheet pan and cover.

## COOK:

1  Bring large pot of water to boil.
2  Add wontons, return to boil. Reduce to medium heat, cook uncovered for about 5 minutes, until tender but still *al dente*.
3  Drain wontons. Add wontons to hot chicken soup. Return to boil.
4  Garnish with chiffonade spinach and serve.

## CELERY IN GARLIC VINAIGRETTE (HUNAN)

© Rossa di sera/Shutterstock

**Note:** Almost like a pickle, this celery accompanies other dishes, becomes part of a salad, or is served with drinks.

**Note:** Allow 3 to 4 hours to marinate the celery.

**Total Yield:** 1 lb. (454 g)
**Food Balance:** Sweet-and-sour and spicy
**Wine Style:** Off-dry or unoaked whites and very soft reds
**Example:** Beringer White Zinfandel or Gewürztraminer

| | WEIGHT | | VOLUME | |
|---|---|---|---|---|
| **INGREDIENTS** | **U.S.** | **METRIC** | **U.S.** | **METRIC** |
| celery, inner stalks, cut into 2 1/2- by 1/2-inch (6- by 1.3-cm) sticks, strings removed | 1 lb. | 454 g | 5 cups | 1.2 L |
| kosher salt | 1/4 oz. | 8 g | 1 teaspoon | 5 mL |
| sugar | | | 1/2 teaspoon | 3 mL |
| **Vinaigrette:** | | | | |
| soy sauce | | | 1 tablespoon + 2 teaspoons | 25 mL |

| INGREDIENTS | WEIGHT | | VOLUME | |
| --- | --- | --- | --- | --- |
| | U.S. | METRIC | U.S. | METRIC |
| sugar | 1 oz. | 28 g | 2 tablespoons | 30 mL |
| sesame oil | | 28 g | 2 tablespoons | 30 mL |
| rice vinegar | | | 1 1/2 teaspoons | 8 mL |
| hot chili oil | | | 1/2 teaspoon | 3 mL |
| garlic, smashed and minced | 1/4 oz. | 8 g | 2 cloves, or | 8 mL |
| | | | 1 1/2 teaspoons | |

**TWIST ON THE CLASSIC**

Try this recipe with cauliflower, broccoli, carrots, or a combination of vegetables.

1. Mix celery with salt and sugar in bowl. Let stand at room temperature for 40 minutes, tossing occasionally.
2. Whisk ingredients for vinaigrette—soy sauce, sugar, sesame oil, vinegar, chili oil, and garlic—in bowl until slightly thickened. Let rest 10 minutes.
3. Drain celery, rinse with cool water, drain on paper towels to dry.
4. Place celery in bowl, pour vinaigrette over celery. Mix well.
5. Refrigerate for 3 to 4 hours, mixing often.
6. Serve slightly chilled, as an accompaniment to other dishes.

## LUN BAN DO YA (SHANGHAI - EAST)

### BEAN SPROUT SALAD

**Note:** Instead of being served as a separate course, salads add other flavors to the main part of the meal.

**Number of Servings:** 8
**Serving Size:** 4 oz. (114 g)
**Total Yield:** 2 lb., 2 oz. (965 g)
**Food Balance:** Protein/sour
**Wine Style:** Low-oaked whites and soft reds
**Example:** Castello di Gabbiano Pinot Grigio or Chianti

**Cooking Method:** Boil

© Amallia Eka

| INGREDIENTS | WEIGHT | | VOLUME | |
| --- | --- | --- | --- | --- |
| | U.S. | METRIC | U.S. | METRIC |
| bean sprouts | 1 lb., 10 oz. | 738 g | | |
| water | as needed | | | |
| rice wine vinegar | | 57 g | 1/4 cup | 60 mL |
| soy sauce | | 86 g | 1/4 cup + 2 tablespoons | 90 mL |
| sugar | 2 oz. | 57 g | 1/4 cup | 60 mL |
| sesame oil | | | 1 tablespoon + 1 teaspoon | 20 mL |
| scallions, julienne | 1 1/2 oz. | 43 g | 4 each | |

**TWIST ON THE CLASSIC**

Use the bean sprout salad as a base or accompaniment for grilled salmon or other fish.

1. Bring large pot of water to boil (for blanching bean sprouts). Add bean sprouts to boiling water for about 10 seconds.
2. Pour into colander, immediately rinse with cold water to stop cooking. Drain well.
3. Meanwhile, place vinegar, soy sauce, sugar, and sesame oil in nonreactive bowl. Whisk well to dissolve sugar.
4. Add bean sprouts and scallions to bowl, gently turn them to coat well. Correct seasonings. Serve immediately.

# POW TSAI (PEKING)

## PICKLED CABBAGE PEKING STYLE

**Note:** Serve this as a spicy condiment to accompany other dishes.

**Note:** Allow time to salt the cabbage and marinate the finished salad.

**Number of Servings:** 15
**Serving Size:** 2 oz. (57 g)
**Total Yield:** 1 lb., 14 oz. (851 g)

| INGREDIENTS | WEIGHT U.S. | WEIGHT METRIC | VOLUME U.S. | VOLUME METRIC |
|---|---|---|---|---|
| white cabbage, cored, shredded finely | 2 lb. | 908 kg | 1 small head | |
| salt | 1 1/4 oz. | 36 g | 2 tablespoons | 30 mL |
| sugar | 3 1/4 oz. | 92 g | 1/4 cup + 1 tablespoon | 75 mL |
| fresh ginger, peeled and cut into fine julienne | 1/2 oz. | 15 g | one 3/4-inch slice | one 2-cm slice |
| oil, peanut or corn | | 36 g | 2 tablespoons + 1 1/2 teaspoons | 38 mL |
| sesame oil | | 36 g | 2 tablespoons + 1 1/2 teaspoons | 38 mL |
| red chilies, dried, seeded, minced | | | 3 each | |
| Szechwan peppercorns | | | 1 teaspoon | 5 mL |
| rice vinegar | | 71 g | 1/4 cup + 1 tablespoon | 75 mL |

1. Place cabbage in large bowl, sprinkle with salt, mix well, set aside for 2 or 3 hours.
2. Squeeze excess water from cabbage, place in clean bowl.
3. Sprinkle sugar over cabbage, place ginger in a bunch on top of cabbage in center of bowl.
4. Heat both oils until very hot in small saucepan over high heat, remove from heat, add chilies and peppercorns.
5. Pour hot mixture over ginger first and then cabbage in bowl.
6. Pour on vinegar, mix well.
7. Refrigerate for 2 or 3 hours before serving. Correct seasonings.

---

**TWIST ON THE CLASSIC**

For a more interesting visual, prepare this dish with a combination of red and white cabbage.

---

# CHUN PEI NGAU YUK (WEST)

## ORANGE BEEF WITH CHILIES

**Note:** To increase the spice of this dish, add the optional hot chilies and/or cut the dried red chilies lengthwise to expose the seeds and ribs of the pepper.

**Note:** Unlike the "typical" orange beef served in American Chinese restaurants, this dish contains almost no sauce. If extra sauce is desired, increase all of the sauce ingredients and add some beef stock or water. Depending on the amount of additional sauce, thicken it with 2 teaspoons or 1 tablespoon (10 mL or 15 mL) of cornstarch dissolved in 3 tablespoons (45 mL) of cold water. After adding the cornstarch mixture to the wok, stir constantly to create a smooth sauce.

**TWIST ON THE CLASSIC**

Substitute tofu, shrimp, chicken, or pork for the beef in this recipe.

**Number of Servings:** 9
**Serving Size:** 7 oz. (199 g)
**Total Yield:** 4 lb., 2 oz. (1.9 kg)
**Food Balance:** Spicy/sour
**Wine Style:** Low-oaked whites and soft reds
**Example:** Beringer Viognier or Beringer Founders' Estate Merlot

**Cooking Method:** Deep-fry, sauté (stir-fry)

Fotolia, LLC–Royalty Free

| INGREDIENTS | WEIGHT | | VOLUME | |
|---|---|---|---|---|
| | U.S. | METRIC | U.S. | METRIC |
| **Sauce:** | | | | |
| dry sherry or Chinese wine | | 43 g | 3 tablespoons | 45 mL |
| soy sauce | | 128 g | 1/2 cup + 1 tablespoon | 135 mL |
| rice vinegar | | 43 g | 3 tablespoons | 45 mL |
| orange juice | | 86 g | 1/4 cup + 2 tablespoons | 90 mL |
| sugar | 3 oz. | 86 g | 1/4 cup + 2 tablespoons | 90 mL |
| flank steak, trimmed | 3 lb., 9 oz. | 1.6 kg | | |
| egg white | 3 oz. | 86 g | 3 each, or 3 tablespoons | 45 mL |
| cornstarch | 9 oz. | 256 g, or as needed | 2 cups | 480 mL, or as needed |
| oil, for deep frying | | | | |
| dried red chilies, cut into quarters | | | 15 each | |
| orange peel from 3 oranges, dried | 3/4 oz. | 22 g | about 24 pieces | |
| fresh ginger, peeled and minced | 1 1/2 oz. | 43 g | 3 tablespoons, or one 3-inch piece | 45 mL, or one 8-cm piece |
| garlic, smashed and minced | 3/4 oz. | 22 g | 9 cloves | |
| hot pepper, minced, *optional* | | | | |
| scallion, cut into 2-inch (5-cm) sections | 5 1/4 oz. | 149 g | 9 each | |
| sesame oil | | 43 g | 3 tablespoons | 45 mL |

If the meat is difficult to slice into thin strips, freeze it halfway and then cut it.

1. Mix all sauce ingredients—sherry, soy sauce, vinegar, orange juice, and sugar—in nonreactive bowl, set aside until needed.
2. Wash and thoroughly dry meat. Cut across grain into 2- by 1- by 1/4-inch (5- by 2 1/2- by 1/2-cm) strips.
3. Place egg white in bowl, beat with whisk until frothy. Add beef to egg white, coat well.
4. Add cornstarch, mix well to coat meat. Use more cornstarch, as needed, to lightly cover meat.
5. Heat about 2 inches (5 cm) of oil for deep-frying to 375 degrees (190°C) in wok. Add beef in batches (so the temperature of the oil does not drop too much). Fry about 1 or 2 minutes, until it loses its red color.
6. Remove meat from oil, drain. Continue until all beef is fried, then return beef to hot oil and fry another 1 or 2 minutes, until crisp. Remove from oil, drain.
7. Pour all except 1 tablespoon (15 g or 15 mL) oil from pan. Add red chilies and orange peel, fry about 30 seconds, until beginning to color.
8. Add ginger, garlic, and hot pepper. Fry until beginning to color, about 20 to 30 seconds. Add scallions, cook another 30 seconds.
9. Add beef, cook another 30 seconds. Add reserved sauce ingredients, cook until hot (sauce will be almost entirely absorbed). Sprinkle with sesame oil. Correct seasonings. Serve immediately.

# CHUNG BAO YANG RO (NORTH)

## LAMB WITH SCALLIONS

Ian O'Leary © Dorling Kindersley

**TWIST ON THE CLASSIC**

Substitute chicken or beef for the lamb.

**Note:** Technically, the yield for this recipe is nine servings, but that leaves no margin for error, and it is a modest portion. Eight servings that are a little less than 7 oz. (199 g) each is a more realistic amount.

**Number of Servings:** 8
**Serving Size:** 6 oz. (170 g)
**Total Yield:** 3 lb., 6 3/4 oz. (1.6 kg)
**Food Balance:** Balanced
**Wine Style:** Wine-friendly—Try your favorite
**Example:** Souverain Chardonnay or Cabernet Sauvignon

**Cooking Method:** Sauté (stir-fry)

| INGREDIENTS | WEIGHT | | VOLUME | |
| --- | --- | --- | --- | --- |
| | U.S. | METRIC | U.S. | METRIC |
| **Marinade:** | | | | |
| soy sauce | | 86 g | 1/4 cup + 2 tablespoons | 90 mL |
| dry sherry | | 43 g | 3 tablespoons | 45 mL |
| rice wine vinegar | | 43 g | 3 tablespoons | 45 mL |
| sugar | | | 1 1/2 teaspoons | 8 mL |
| sesame oil | | 15 g | 1 tablespoon | 15 mL |
| lean, boneless lamb, leg or shank | 2 lb., 8 1/2 oz. | 1.1 kg | | |
| **Sauce:** | | | | |
| cornstarch | 1 oz. | 28 g | 2 tablespoons | 30 mL |
| water, cold | | 86 g | 1/4 cup + 2 tablespoons | 90 mL |
| dry sherry or Chinese wine | | 43 g | 3 tablespoons | 45 mL |
| ground pepper, black or Szechwan | 1/4 oz. | 8 g | 1 1/2 teaspoons | 8 mL |
| oil, for frying | | | up to 1/2 cup | 120 mL |
| garlic, smashed and minced | 3/4 oz. | 22 g | 6 cloves | |
| scallions, 5 or 6 inches (13 to 15 cm) of green, cut in half lengthwise, then horizontally into 2-inch (5-cm) pieces | 6 oz. | 170 g | 12 each | |
| **Garnish:** | | | | |
| sesame oil | | 15 g | 1 tablespoon | 15 mL |
| scallion brushes, *optional* | | | | |

1. In nonreactive bowl, mix marinade ingredients—soy sauce, sherry, rice wine vinegar, sugar, and sesame oil.
2. Wash lamb, remove all fat and gristle. Slice lamb across the grain into strips about 2- by 1 1/2- by 1/2-inches (5- by 4- by 1.3-cm). Place into bowl of marinade, mix to coat well. Cover and refrigerate for 30 minutes.
3. Mix sauce ingredients in nonreactive bowl: First, mix cornstarch and water, then add sherry and pepper. Set aside until needed.
4. Depending on the size of the wok, the lamb may need to be cooked in batches. Using as much oil as needed, coat wok with about 1/16 inch (2 mm) of oil. Heat over medium-high to high heat until hot.
5. Add garlic and fry about 20 to 30 seconds, until starting to color.
6. Add meat with marinade; stir constantly until lamb loses its red color, about 2 minutes.

7 Add sauce, stir constantly while it begins to thicken. Add scallions, stir constantly until slightly thickened and scallions wilt.

8 Remove from heat, sprinkle with 1 tablespoon (15 g or 15 mL) sesame oil. Correct seasonings. Garnish with scallion brushes, serve with rice or Chinese bread.

---

## MA PO DO FU (SZECHWAN, WEST)

### BEAN CURD AND PORK

**Note:** High in protein, tofu is used often throughout China.

**Number of Servings:** 10          **Cooking Method:** Deep-fry, sauté (stir-fry)
**Serving Size:** 8 oz. (227 g)
**Total Yield:** 5 lb. (2.3 kg)
**Food Balance:** Protein/sweet/spicy
**Wine Style:** Low-oaked whites and soft reds
**Example:** Rosemount Semillion or Shiraz

| INGREDIENTS | WEIGHT U.S. | METRIC | VOLUME U.S. | METRIC |
|---|---|---|---|---|
| dried black mushrooms | 3/4 oz. | 22 g | 9 each | |
| water | as needed | | | |
| firm tofu (soybean curd), 1-inch (2.5-cm) cubes | 2 lb., 4 oz. | 1 kg | | |
| **Marinade:** | | | | |
| sugar | 1/2 oz. | 15 g | 1 tablespoon | 15 mL |
| light soy sauce | | 15 g | 1 tablespoon | 15 mL |
| rice wine or dry sherry | | 15 g | 1 tablespoon | 15 mL |
| cornstarch | 1 oz. | 28 g | 2 tablespoons | 30 mL |
| oil, peanut or corn | | 28 g | 2 tablespoons | 30 mL |
| fresh ginger, peeled and minced | 3/4 oz. | 22 g | 9 slices | |
| red chili peppers, minced | 3/4 oz. | 22 g, or to taste | 3 to 6 each, or to taste | |
| lean pork, julienne | 9 oz. | 256 g | | |
| **Sauce:** | | | | |
| cornstarch | 1 oz. | 28 g | 2 tablespoons | 30 mL |
| water, cold | | 57 g | 1/4 cup | 60 mL |
| chicken stock | | 680 g | 3 cups | 720 mL |
| dark soy sauce | | 43 g | 3 tablespoons | 45 mL |
| oyster sauce | | 86 g | 1/4 cup + 2 tablespoons | 90 mL |
| rice vinegar | | 15 g | 1 tablespoon | 15 mL |
| sugar | 1 oz. | 28 g | 2 tablespoons | 30 mL |
| sesame oil | | 15 g | 1 tablespoon | 15 mL |
| frying oil, peanut or corn, for deep-frying | | | | |
| green bell pepper, cut into fine dice | 14 oz. | 397 g | 3 medium | |
| carrot, peeled and cut into thin slices | 6 3/4 oz. | 191 g | 3 small | |

### TWIST ON THE CLASSIC

Add any desired vegetables to this recipe. Make it vegetarian by eliminating the pork.

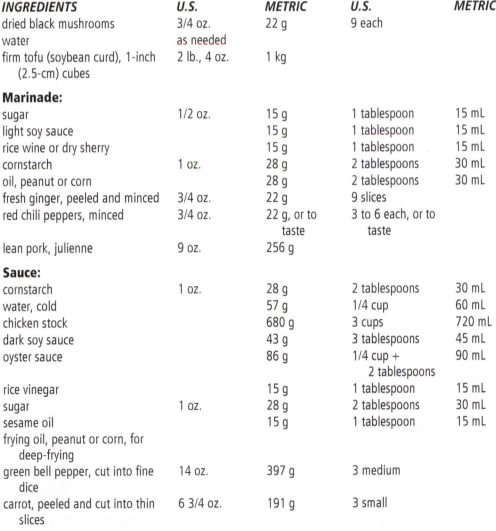

| INGREDIENTS | WEIGHT | | VOLUME | |
| --- | --- | --- | --- | --- |
| | U.S. | METRIC | U.S. | METRIC |
| bamboo shoots, cut into thin slices | 4 1/2 oz. | 128 g | 2 1/4 cups | 540 mL |
| scallions, dice | 3 oz. | 86 g | 6 each | |
| fresh ginger, peeled and minced | 3/4 oz. | 22 g | 9 slices | |
| red chili peppers, minced | 3/4 oz. | 22 g, or to taste | 3 to 6 each, or to taste | |

1. Soak mushrooms in warm water for 30 minutes. Remove from water and cut into quarters. Set aside.
2. Place tofu cubes on paper towels to remove moisture in refrigerator.
3. Mix marinade ingredients well in nonreactive bowl. Add pork, mix well, refrigerate for 15 minutes.
4. Mix 1 oz. or 2 tablespoons (30 mL) cornstarch with 1/4 cup (57 g or 60 mL) cold water in nonreactive bowl. Add stock, dark soy sauce, oyster sauce, vinegar, sugar, and sesame oil, mix well. Set sauce aside.
5. Deep-fry tofu in hot oil in wok for about 2 minutes, until lightly colored and crisp. Place on paper towels to drain.
6. Remove all but 2 tablespoons (30 mL) oil from wok. Remove pork from marinade, stir-fry until pink color is gone. Remove from wok.
7. Stir-fry bell peppers and carrots about 1 minute.
8. Add bamboo shoots, scallions, ginger, and chili peppers, stir-fry 1 to 1 1/2 minutes.
9. Add tofu, pork, and sauce. Bring to boil, stirring constantly.
10. Lower heat, simmer for 5 minutes, until tofu and meat are tender. Correct seasonings.
11. Serve with rice.

## MA YEE SONG SUE (WEST)

### HOT BEAN THREAD NOODLES WITH SHREDDED PORK

**TWIST ON THE CLASSIC**

Make this vegetarian by removing the pork and adding more vegetables. To make it more colorful add julienne carrot, and use red, orange, and green peppers instead of just green.

**Note:** These noodles are made from mung beans instead of wheat flour.

**Number of Servings:** 9
**Serving Size:** 8 oz. (227 g)
**Total Yield:** 4 lb., 13 oz. (2.2 kg)
**Food Balance:** Spicy/protein
**Wine Style:** Low-oaked whites and soft reds
**Example:** Lindemans Pinot Grigio or Moscato or Shiraz

**Cooking Method:** Sauté (stir-fry)

| INGREDIENTS | WEIGHT | | VOLUME | |
| --- | --- | --- | --- | --- |
| | U.S. | METRIC | U.S. | METRIC |
| bean thread vermicelli | 7 1/2 oz. | 213 g | | |
| water | as needed | | | |
| dried black mushrooms | 3/4 oz. | 22 g | 9 each | |
| rice wine or dry sherry | | 15 g | 1 tablespoon | 15 mL |
| cornstarch | 1/2 oz. | 15 g | 1 tablespoon | 15 mL |
| boneless pork, shredded | 7 1/2 oz. | 213 g | | |
| **Sauce:** | | | | |
| chicken stock | | 680 g | 3 cups | 720 mL |
| dark soy sauce | | 43 g | 3 tablespoons | 45 mL |
| rice vinegar | | 15 g | 1 tablespoon | 15 mL |
| sugar | | | 1 1/2 teaspoons | 8 mL |
| sesame oil | | 15 g | 1 tablespoon | 15 mL |

| INGREDIENTS | WEIGHT | | VOLUME | |
| --- | --- | --- | --- | --- |
| | U.S. | METRIC | U.S. | METRIC |
| hot chili oil | | | 2 to 3 teaspoons | 10 to 15 mL, or to taste |
| oil, peanut or corn | | 86 g | 1/4 cup + 2 tablespoons | 90 mL |
| onion, cut in half through root end, then into thin, top-to-bottom slices, separated | 15 oz. | 425 g | 3 medium | |
| green bell pepper, cut into narrow strips | 1 lb., 2 oz. | 510 g | 3 each | |
| fresh red chili peppers, seeds and ribs removed, cut into narrow strips | 1/2 to 3/4 oz. | 15 to 22 g | 3 to 5 each | |
| fresh ginger, peeled, minced | 3/4 oz. | 22 g | 6 slices | |
| garlic, minced | 3/4 oz. | 22 g | 6 cloves, or 1 tablespoon | 15 mL |
| fresh cilantro, minced | 1/2 to 3/4 oz. | 15 to 22 g | 2 to 3 tablespoons | 30 to 45 mL |

© taiftin

1. Soak vermicelli in warm water until softened. Drain and cut into 2-inch (5-cm) lengths.
2. Soak mushrooms in warm water for 30 minutes. Remove from water, dice finely.
3. Mix wine or sherry and cornstarch in nonreactive bowl. Add pork, mix well. Refrigerate for 20 minutes.
4. Combine sauce ingredients (stock, soy sauce, vinegar, sugar, sesame oil, and hot chili oil) in nonreactive bowl, set aside.
5. Heat peanut or corn oil in wok, stir-fry onion, bell peppers, and chili peppers for 2 minutes.
6. Push vegetables to side of wok, add ginger and garlic. Stir-fry about 30 seconds.
7. Drain pork, add to wok, stir-fry until white, about 45 seconds.
8. Add drained vermicelli, stir-fry briefly.
9. Pour in sauce, simmer until liquid is absorbed and noodles are tender. Correct seasonings.
10. Stir in cilantro, mix. Serve, accompanied by rice.

## BROWNED NOODLES WITH PORK (SHANGHAI—EAST)

**Note:** Noodle dishes appear often in the north and east.

**Number of Servings:** 8
**Serving Size:** 10 oz. (284 g)
**Total Yield:** 5 lb., 6 oz. (2.4 kg)
**Food Balance:** Protein
**Wine Style:** Low-oaked whites and soft reds
**Example:** Château St. Jean Fume Blanc or Pinot Noir

**Cooking Method:** Sauté (stir-fry)

### TWIST ON THE CLASSIC

Any topping works over the fried noodles. Change this to a vegetarian entrée or top with curried chicken.

| INGREDIENTS | WEIGHT | | VOLUME | |
| --- | --- | --- | --- | --- |
| | U.S. | METRIC | U.S. | METRIC |
| water | as needed | | | |
| dry Chinese egg noodles | 1 lb. | 454 g | | |
| dried mushrooms, forest or any variety | 1/2 oz. | 15 g | 12 each | |
| **Marinade:** | | | | |
| cornstarch | 1/4 oz. | 8 g | 1 1/2 teaspoons | 8 mL |

© Johnson76/Shutterstock

| INGREDIENTS | WEIGHT | | VOLUME | |
|---|---|---|---|---|
| | U.S. | METRIC | U.S. | METRIC |
| water, cold | | 28 g | 2 tablespoons | 30 mL |
| sugar | | | 1 teaspoon | 5 mL |
| thin soy sauce (regular) | | | 2 teaspoons | 10 mL |
| thick soy sauce | | | 2 teaspoons | 10 mL |
| pepper | | | 1/2 teaspoon | 3 mL |
| rice wine or dry sherry | | | 2 teaspoons | 10 mL |
| lean pork, julienne | 1 lb. | 454 g | | |
| **Sauce:** | | | | |
| cornstarch | | | 1 tablespoon + 2 teaspoons | 25 mL |
| mushroom soaking water (*from recipe*) and stock, room temperature | | 454 g | 2 cups | 480 mL |
| thin soy sauce | | | 1 tablespoon + 1 teaspoon | 20 mL |
| thick soy sauce | | | 2 tablespoons | 30 mL |
| oyster sauce | | 43 g | 3 tablespoons | 45 mL |
| frying oil, peanut or corn | | 142 g | 1/2 cup + 2 tablespoons | 150 mL |
| garlic, minced | 1 oz. | 28 g | 6 cloves | |
| scallions, cut into 1-inch (2.5-cm) sections, white and green parts separated | 5 oz. | 142 g | 12 each | |
| rice wine or dry sherry | | 28 g | 2 tablespoons | 30 mL |
| bean sprouts | 1 lb. | 454 g | | |
| Chinese red vinegar, *optional* | | | to taste | |

1. Bring large pot of water to boiling, add noodles, boil for about 4 minutes, until *al dente*.
2. Drain in colander, rinse under cold running water to stop the cooking. Let dry for 1 hour, turning occasionally to ensure even drying.
3. Meanwhile, soak mushrooms in enough warm water to cover for 30 minutes. Reserve soaking liquid (for sauce), julienne mushrooms.
4. For marinade, mix cornstarch and cold water in nonreactive bowl. Add sugar, both soy sauces, pepper, and wine or sherry. Add pork and mix well. Refrigerate for 30 minutes.
5. For sauce, mix cornstarch with the mushroom soaking water and enough stock to measure 2 cups (454 g or 480 mL) in nonreactive bowl. Add both soy sauces and oyster sauce. Set aside.
6. Heat 6 tablespoons (86 g or 90 mL) of the oil in large frying pan over high heat until hot.
7. Add noodles, arranging them in even layer in pan. Fry about 1 minute, until golden brown but not burned. Turn noodle cake over with spatula or toss. Fry other side until golden brown.
8. Remove to warm serving plate, keep warm in oven.
9. Heat wok with 2 tablespoons (28 g or 30 mL) of the oil over high heat.
10. Add garlic, then add two-thirds of white scallion pieces, stir a few times.
11. Add pork and its marinade, stir until it loses pink color. Pour in wine or sherry, stir. Add mushrooms and two-thirds of green scallion pieces, stir constantly. Remove to warm plate.
12. Wash wok. Heat with remaining 2 tablespoons (28 g or 30 mL) oil.
13. Add remaining white scallions and bean sprouts. Stir until cooked but still crunchy, about 2 minutes. Add remaining green scallions. Transfer to plate with other cooked ingredients.
14. Lower heat, stir sauce and pour into wok. Bring to boil, stirring constantly. Return cooked meat and vegetables to sauce. Heat thoroughly. Correct seasonings.
15. Pour over noodle cake. Serve by cutting noodles and serving a wedge. Accompany with red Chinese vinegar, if desired.

# KUNG PAO GAI (SZECHWAN)

## SPICY CHICKEN WITH PEANUTS

**Note:** Peanuts are both served alone before the meal and also incorporated into many dishes in China.

**Number of Servings:** 10
**Serving Size:** 8 oz. (227 g)
**Total Yield:** 5 lb., 5 oz. (2.4 kg)
**Food Balance:** Spicy/protein
**Wine Style:** Low-oaked whites and soft reds
**Example:** Beringer Founders' Estate Pinot Grigio or Merlot

**Cooking Method:** Sauté (stir-fry)

Paul Williams © Dorling Kindersley

| | WEIGHT | | VOLUME | |
|---|---|---|---|---|
| **INGREDIENTS** | **U.S.** | **METRIC** | **U.S.** | **METRIC** |
| **Marinade:** | | | | |
| soy sauce | | 86 g | 1/4 cup + 2 tablespoons | 90 mL |
| rice wine or dry sherry | | 86 g | 1/4 cup + 2 tablespoons | 90 mL |
| sugar | 1/2 oz. | 15 g | 1 tablespoon | 15 mL |
| cornstarch | 3/4 oz. | 22 g | 1 tablespoon + 1 1/2 teaspoons | 25 mL |
| scallions, finely chopped | 3/4 oz. | 22 g | 3 tablespoons | 45 mL |
| fresh ginger, peeled and minced | 3/4 oz. | 22 g | 1 tablespoon + 1 1/2 teaspoons | 23 mL |
| boneless chicken, trimmed and cut into bite-sized pieces | 2 lb., 13 oz. | 1.3 kg | | |
| **Sauce:** | | | | |
| chicken stock | | 454 g | 2 cups | 480 mL |
| soy sauce | | 86 g | 1/4 cup + 2 tablespoons | 90 mL |
| rice wine or dry sherry | | 43 g | 3 tablespoons | 45 mL |
| sugar | 3/4 oz. | 22 g | 1 tablespoon + 1 1/2 teaspoons | 23 mL |
| cornstarch | 3/4 oz. | 22 g | 1 tablespoon + 1 1/2 teaspoons | 23 mL |
| oil, peanut or other high-temperature oil | | 170 g | 3/4 cup | 180 mL |
| red chili peppers, fresh or dried, quartered and seeds removed | | | 12 small | |
| peanuts, shelled and skinned | 10 1/2 oz. | 298 g | 2 cups | 480 mL |
| scallions, 3/4-inch (2-cm) slices | 3 3/4 oz. | 107 g | 12 each | |
| garlic, sliced | 2 1/4 oz. | 64 g | 18 cloves | |
| rice vinegar | | 28 g | 2 tablespoons | 30 mL |

### TWIST ON THE CLASSIC

Substitute any protein for the chicken in this recipe. Try beef, shrimp, scallops, or deep-fried tofu.

1. Combine all ingredients for marinade in nonreactive bowl, add chicken, mix well, refrigerate for 20 minutes.

2. Combine all ingredients for sauce, mix and set aside.

3. In large wok or sauté pan, heat oil until hot over high or medium-high heat. Fry chili peppers until dark brown. Remove from oil, set aside.

4. Fry peanuts until golden. They brown quickly, so use caution not to burn them. Remove from pan, drain well.

⑤ Remove all but thick coating of oil, about 4 tablespoons (57 g or 60 mL). Drain chicken. Heat oil over high or medium-high heat, sauté chicken for 2 minutes. If necessary, sauté in batches. Return chicken to pan (if sautéed in batches).

⑥ Add scallions and garlic, sauté for 30 seconds, add chili peppers (reserving some for garnish, if desired) and sauce mixture.

⑦ Mix well, cover, lower heat and simmer until chicken is tender, about 2 minutes.

⑧ Stir in vinegar. Correct seasonings.

⑨ Stir in peanuts. Garnish with reserved fried peppers, if desired. Serve with rice.

# YOU ZHA LU YA (HUNAN)

## HUNAN CRISPY DUCK

*Cutting You Zha Lu Ya (Hunan Crispy Duck) into small pieces*

gingqing © Shutterstock

**TWIST ON THE CLASSIC**

Fuse Chinese and Mexican foods by using this duck to fill a taco or burrito.

**Note:** Chinese cookery often utilizes more than one cooking method to achieve the final texture of the dish.

**Number of Servings:** 8
**Serving Size:** 1/4 duck
**Total Yield:** 2 ducks
**Food Balance:** Sweet/protein
**Wine Style:** Low-oaked whites and soft reds
**Example:** Greg Norman Chardonnay or Zinfandel

**Cooking Method:** Steam, deep-fry

| | WEIGHT | | VOLUME | |
|---|---|---|---|---|
| INGREDIENTS | U.S. | METRIC | U.S. | METRIC |
| **Seasoning:** | | | | |
| star anise, crushed | 1/2 oz. | 15 g | 8 each | |
| fennel seeds, crushed | 1/2 oz. | 15 g | 2 tablespoons | 30 mL |
| Chinese brown peppercorns, crushed | 1/4 oz. | 8 g | 2 tablespoons | 30 mL |
| salt | 1 oz. | 28 g | 1 tablespoon + 1 teaspoon | 20 mL |
| fresh ginger, peeled and minced | 1 1/2 oz. | 43 g | 1/4 cup | 60 mL |
| scallions, finely diced | 1 oz. | 28 g | 1/4 cup | 60 mL |
| rice wine or dry sherry | | 28 g | 2 tablespoons | 30 mL |
| duck | 8 to 10 lb. | 3.6 to 4.5 kg | 2 each | |
| frying oil for deep-frying | | | | |

**Condiments:**

duck sauce

hoisin

plum sauce

① Combine seasoning ingredients in bowl.

② Wash and clean duck, rub inside and out with seasoning. Refrigerate until ready to cook.

③ Using bamboo steamer in wok or rack in pot, cover and steam duck over rapidly boiling water for 2 1/2 hours. Add more water, as necessary, while steaming.

④ Remove duck from steamer, wipe off seasonings on inside and outside.

⑤ Heat deep-frying oil in wok until hot, about 375 degrees (190°C). Carefully, lower duck into oil and fry until completely crisp.

⑥ Serve whole, to be torn into strips by the diner. Serve with rice and accompaniments of duck sauce, hoisin, and/or plum sauce.

## SHRIMP WITH PEAS AND CASHEW NUTS (SOUTH)

**Note:** Containing none of the hot peppers seen in other regions, this mild dish is typical of Canton's cookery. This region has access to plentiful seafood.

**Number of Servings:** 9
**Serving Size:** 8 oz. (227 g)
**Total Yield:** 4 lb., 9 oz. (2.1 kg)
**Food Balance:** Protein
**Wine Style:** Low-oaked whites and soft reds
**Example:** Meridian Vineyards Santa Barbara Chardonnay or Pinot Noir

**Cooking Method:** Sauté (stir-fry)

| INGREDIENTS | WEIGHT | | VOLUME | |
|---|---|---|---|---|
| | U.S. | METRIC | U.S. | METRIC |
| **Marinade:** | | | | |
| egg white, beaten | 5 oz. | 142 g | 5 each | |
| rice wine or dry sherry | | 57 g | 1/4 cup | 60 mL |
| fresh ginger, peeled and minced | 3/4 oz. | 22 g | 1 tablespoon + 1 1/2 teaspoons | 23 mL |
| cornstarch | 1 1/2 oz. | 43 g | 3 tablespoons | 45 mL |
| shrimp, peeled and deveined | 2 lb., 4 oz. | 1 kg | | |
| **Sauce:** | | | | |
| cornstarch | 1/2 oz. | 15 g | 1 tablespoon | 15 mL |
| soy sauce | | 86 g | 1/4 cup + 2 tablespoons | 90 mL |
| rice wine or dry sherry | | 43 g | 3 tablespoons | 45 mL |
| sugar | 1/2 oz. | 15 g | 1 tablespoon | 15 mL |
| pepper | | | 1 1/2 teaspoons | 8 mL |
| chicken stock | | 340 g | 1 1/2 cups | 360 mL |
| frying oil | | 142 g | 1/2 cup + 2 tablespoons | 150 mL |
| raw cashews | 9 oz. | 256 g | 2 cups | 480 mL |
| peas, fresh or frozen | 12 oz. | 340 g | 3 cups | 720 mL |

**TWIST ON THE CLASSIC**

Spice up this dish by adding some hot chili peppers.

1. Mix marinade ingredients in nonreactive bowl, add shrimp. Refrigerate for 15 minutes.
2. For sauce, mix cornstarch with soy sauce and wine in nonreactive bowl. Add sugar, pepper, and stock. Mix well, set aside until needed.
3. Heat oil to moderately hot over medium-high heat. Fry cashews about 1 to 2 minutes, until golden. Remove, drain well.
4. Add shrimp, sauté until pink, stirring frequently.
5. Add peas and sauce mixture, bring to boil, stirring constantly. Correct seasonings.
6. Simmer, stirring constantly, for 45 seconds, stir in cashews. Serve with rice.

# DUO BAN YU (SICHUAN)

## FISH WITH SPICY BEAN PASTE

© pipop kangsiri/Alamy

**TWIST ON THE CLASSIC**

Prepare this dish with shrimp, scallops, or a combination.

This is a spicy dish. Add more or less spice, as desired by increasing or decreasing the amount of chili paste.

**Number of Servings:** 2

**Serving Size:** 1 trout

**Total Yield:** 1 lb., 6 oz. (624 g)

**Cooking Method:** Sauté, braise

**Wine Style:** White wine with a balanced acidity and some residual sugar. Possible grape varietals are Riesling, Chenin Blanc, Gruner Veltliner.

**Example:** Riesling GG Kirchenstuck 2010, von Winning (Pfalz/Germany)

| INGREDIENTS | WEIGHT | | VOLUME | |
| --- | --- | --- | --- | --- |
| | U.S. | METRIC | U.S. | METRIC |
| rainbow trout, insides removed and, if desired, head | 14 1/2 oz. | 411 g | 2 each | |
| salt | as needed | | | |
| rice wine or dry sherry | | 28 g | 2 tablespoons | 30 mL |
| cornstarch | 1/2 oz. | 15 g | 1 tablespoon | 15 mL |
| water | | 15 g | 1 tablespoon | 15 mL |
| oil | | 114 g | 1/2 cup | 120 mL |
| onion, minced | 1 1/2 oz. | 43 g | 1/4 cup | 60 mL |
| garlic, peeled, minced smashed | 1/2 oz. | 15 g | 1 tablespoon | 15 mL |
| ginger, peeled, minced | 1/4 oz. | 8 g | 2 teaspoons | 10 mL |
| Sichuan chili bean paste | 1 1/2 oz. | 43 g | 2 tablespoons | 30 mL |
| sugar | | | 1/2 teaspoon | 3 mL |
| water | | 170 g | 3/4 cup or as needed | 180 mL |
| soy sauce | | | 2 teaspoons | 10 mL |
| sesame oil | | 8 g | 1 teaspoon | 5 mL |
| scallions, sliced 1/8-inch (30-mm) thick | 1 oz. | 28 g | 3 each | |
| cilantro, minced | 1/2 oz. | 15 g | 1 1/2 tablespoons | 23 mL |

1. Cut several slits into thick portion of trout on both skin sides (this facilitates marinating). Sprinkle with salt and rice wine. Refrigerate for 15 minutes, drain liquid, and pat fish dry with paper toweling. Mix cornstarch and 1 tablespoon (15 g or 15 mL) water together. Set aside until needed.

2. Heat oil in wok over high heat. Fry fish on both skin sides until brown, about 5 minutes. Remove from heat.

3. Pour off all oil except about 3 tablespoons (43 g or 45 mL). Reduce heat to medium. Add onion and stir-fry for 1 minute stirring constantly.

4. Add garlic, ginger, and chili paste. Stir constantly for a few minutes. Add sugar and water. Bring to boil.

5. Reduce heat to medium-low, add soy sauce and trout. Simmer for 5 minutes, continuously basting fish with sauce.

6. Remove fish to serving platter. Stirring constantly, add cornstarch mixture and stir until it comes to boil and thickens. If too thick, add more water, as needed. Correct seasonings. Remove from heat.

7. Stir in sesame oil and scallions. Pour over fish. Sprinkle fish with cilantro. Serve immediately, accompanied by rice.

## MAN TAU (THROUGHOUT CHINA)

### STEAMED BREAD

**Note:** Some cooks form this bread into loaves instead of buns.

**Note:** Steamed buns are served on their own or as an accompaniment to red cooked dishes, stew-type entrées, Peking duck, or ham. Originally, only people in the northern provinces consumed bread, but now it is eaten in a number of areas. Buns form the foundation of the popular *dim sum* item, filled steamed buns. They are filled with a variety of sweet and savory fillings including roast pork, bean paste, lotus seed filling, and more.

**Note:** Steamed buns reheat very well.

**Number of Servings:** 24
**Serving Size:** 1 bun
**Scaling Size:** 1 1/4 oz. (36 g) or as desired
**Total Yield:** 2 lb., 1 1/4 oz. (944 kg) dough

**Cooking Method:** Steam (boil)

© tanawatpontchour

| INGREDIENTS | WEIGHT | | VOLUME | |
|---|---|---|---|---|
| | U.S. | METRIC | U.S. | METRIC |
| water, lukewarm | | 284 g | 1 1/4 cups | 300 mL |
| granulated yeast | 1/4 oz. | 8 g | 2 teaspoons | 10 mL |
| sugar | 2 1/2 oz. | 71 g | 1/3 cup | 80 mL |
| all-purpose flour | 2 lb., 1 oz. to 2 lb., 3 1/4 oz. | 936 g to 1 kg | 3 1/2 to 4 cups | 840 to 960 mL |
| salt | 1/4 oz. | 8 g | 1 teaspoon | 5 mL |
| lard, oil, or shortening | | 43 g | 3 tablespoons | 45 mL |

1. Place water in nonreactive bowl, sprinkle yeast and 2 tablespoons (30 mL) of the sugar over water. Stir to mix. Set aside until foamy, about 5 minutes.
2. Place 3 1/2 cups (936 g or 840 mL) of flour, salt, and remaining sugar in large nonreactive bowl. Stir to combine.
3. Stir yeast mixture and lard, oil, or shortening into flour. Mix well, adding more flour as needed if dough is too soft to handle.
4. Knead until smooth and elastic, about 5 minutes. Add a little flour if dough is too sticky. Return to bowl, cover, and let rise in warm place until doubled, about 1 to 1 1/2 hours.
5. Punch down dough. Scale into 1 1/4 oz. (36 g) or desired size for buns. Form into round ball (or rectangle, if desired).
6. Place each ball of dough on a piece of parchment paper about 2 1/2 inches (6 cm) square. Cover and let rise until doubled, about 30 minutes.
7. Meanwhile, boil water in large pot for steaming. But remember, the level of water must be below food in steamer. Place buns in bamboo steamers, place steamers in pot over boiling water, and steam for 20 minutes.
8. Remove from steamers, remove paper from bottom. Serve immediately. Store leftovers well wrapped in the refrigerator and reheat when needed.

### TWIST ON THE CLASSIC

There is no limit to filling possibilities for steamed buns. Because a lot of bland bread surrounds the filling, try a highly spiced filling like lamb *vindaloo* (finely chopped), from India.

There are many methods of forming the buns around the filling. To prepare filled steam buns, follow the recipe until dough is scaled.

- Press dough into round disk. Place filling in center of disk and fold dough around filling to enclose.
- Place the filling in the center of the disk and pinch pleats of dough together around filling. This leaves the filling visible from the top.
- Make an indentation in the center of a ball of dough, place filling in the indentation, and then seal the dough around the filling. This encases the filling in the center of the ball of dough.

After filling the dough, steam buns for 15 to 20 minutes.

**Note:** Fillings are always cooked and cooled before placing in bun dough; therefore, the filling in the bun needs warming but not cooking. This eliminates the problem of getting raw meat in a filling up to the proper temperature.

© Photogrape

Tim Hall © Jupiterimages

## TSAO-NI-HÜN-TÜN

### DATE WONTONS

© oldamulet

**Note:** From appetizers to dessert, Chinese menus feature all sorts of dumplings (and wontons).

**Number of Servings:** 9    **Cooking Method:** Deep-fry
**Serving Size:** 3 wontons
**Total Yield:** 29 wontons with 1 lb., 5 oz. (596 g) filling

| | WEIGHT | | VOLUME | |
|---|---|---|---|---|
| *INGREDIENTS* | *U.S.* | *METRIC* | *U.S.* | *METRIC* |
| dates, pitted and finely chopped | 1 lb. | 454 g | 2 3/4 cups | 660 mL |
| walnuts, finely chopped | 4 1/2 oz. | 128 g | 1 cup | 240 mL |
| orange rind, finely grated | 1/4 oz. | 8 g | 2 tablespoons | 30 mL |
| five-spice powder | | | 1/4 teaspoon | 2 mL |
| water | as needed | | | |
| wonton wrappers | | | 1 package | |
| oil for deep-frying | | | | |
| confectioner's sugar | | | | |

1. Combine dates, walnuts, orange rind, and five-spice powder in bowl, knead until mixture can form ball. Add water (by drops) if necessary.
2. Place wonton wrapper on work surface with point at top, moisten edges of wonton with finger dipped in water.
3. Form about 3/4 oz. (22 g), about 1 tablespoon (15 mL), filling into cylinder about 1 1/4 inch (3 cm) long. Place across wonton just below center.
4. Roll bottom edge of wonton tightly over filling and tuck under filling, then roll wonton forward until dough forms cylinder. Press edge to seal well.
5. Stick finger into open ends of wonton, press filling gently, twist to seal ends.
6. Heat oil to 375 degrees (190°C).
7. Fry wontons, a few at a time to maintain temperature, until golden brown.
8. Remove, place on absorbent paper to drain.
9. To serve, dust wontons with confectioner's sugar.

## BA BAO FAN (THROUGHOUT CHINA)

### EIGHT-TREASURE RICE PUDDING

**Note:** This classic Chinese dessert is served at banquets, special occasions, and the New Year. The name "eight-treasure" reflects the eight ingredients used to adorn the outside of the rice pudding. Cooks choose eight different dried fruits, candied fruits, and/or nuts. Many create a pattern by arranging these ingredients on the bowl before filling with rice and red bean paste. After unmolding the pudding, the eight treasures decorate the outside. This confection requires steaming the rice twice.

**Note:** This rice pudding can be prepared ahead, refrigerated, and warmed at the time of service.

**Number of Servings:** 10    **Cooking Method:** Steam
**Serving Size:** 5 3/4 oz. (163 g) total
           4 1/4 oz. (120 g) of pudding
           about 1 1/2 oz. (43 g), or 2 to 3 tablespoons (30 to 45 mL) syrup
**Total Yield:** 2 lb., 12 3/4 oz. (1.3 kg) rice pudding
           15 1/4 oz. (434 g), or 1 3/4 cups (420 mL) syrup

| INGREDIENTS | WEIGHT | | VOLUME | |
|---|---|---|---|---|
| | **U.S.** | **METRIC** | **U.S.** | **METRIC** |
| glutinous rice, uncooked | 1 lb., 1/4 oz. | 462 g | 1 cup | 240 mL |
| water | | 397 g | 1 3/4 cups | 420 mL |
| oil | as needed | | | |
| lard, shortening, oil, or butter | 1/2 oz. | 15 g | 1 tablespoon | 15 mL |
| sugar | 2 1/2 oz. | 71 g | 1/3 cup | 80 mL |
| eight different dried fruits, candied fruits, and/or nuts of choice, cut into small pieces | approx. 8 oz. | 227 g | about 1 1/2 cups | 360 mL |
| red bean paste | 8 1/4 oz. | 234 g | 3/4 cup | 180 mL |
| **Almond Syrup (optional):** | | | | |
| cornstarch | 1/2 oz. | 15 g | 1 tablespoon + 1 1/2 teaspoons | 23 mL |
| water, cold | | 340 g | 1 1/2 cups | 360 mL |
| sugar | 4 oz. | 114 g | 1/2 cup | 120 mL |
| almond extract | | | 1 teaspoon | 5 mL |

Paul Williams © Dorling Kindersley

1. Wash rice, cover with water, and soak for 2 hours. Then set up steamer with water, bring to boil. Oil a heatproof 1 1/2-quart (1.4-L) bowl, set aside until needed.

2. Drain rice, place rice and 1 3/4 cups (397 g or 420 mL) water in heatproof bowl. Place in steamer and steam over boiling water for 30 minutes, until done. Remove from steamer, cool.

3. Mix lard and 1/3 cup (80 g) sugar with rice.

4. Arrange the eight dried fruits, candied fruits, and nuts on bottom and sides of oiled bowl. Arrange each separate item decoratively or mix them together, and place on bottom and sides of bowl.

5. Oil your hands to make handling rice easier. Using half of the rice, cover the fruits by pressing the rice over them.

6. Place bean paste in center of bowl (over rice). Fill bowl with remaining rice, covering bean paste.

7. Cover with aluminum foil and cook in steamer over boiling water for 45 minutes. Remove from steamer. Let rest 5 minutes, then run icing spatula around sides of bowl to release. Invert on serving platter. Serve hot or warm, accompanied by almond syrup, if desired.

### ALMOND SYRUP:

1. Mix cornstarch with 1/4 cup (57 g or 60 mL) of the cold water.

2. Combine sugar and remaining 1 1/4 cups (284 g or 300 mL) water in saucepan. Add cornstarch mixture.

3. Stirring constantly, bring to boil over medium-high heat. Boil until syrup thickens. Remove from heat.

4. Stir in almond extract. Store in nonreactive bowl.

Purchase canned red bean paste (made from aduki beans) and glutinous rice (or sweet rice) from an Asian market. A type of short-grain rice, glutinous rice is very sticky when cooked.

Some possible fruits for the decoration include strips of candied ginger; candied citron or mixed peels; dried dates, papaya, mango, apricots, or pineapple; lotus seeds; and any variety of nuts. Cut nuts and fruits into small pieces. Using nuts instead of dried or candied fruit cuts some of the sweetness of this cloyingly sweet dessert.

# Japan and Korea

## >> LEARNING OBJECTIVES

By the end of this chapter, you will be able to:

- Explain how the cuisines of Japan and Korea differ from each other and from the other Asian cuisines
- Describe the differences in sauces and flavorings used in Japan and Korea
- Understand how the geography and topography of these countries have influenced their cuisines
- Discuss the Japanese idea of aesthetics surrounding the food, presentation of food, the meal, and table setting
- Prepare a variety of Japanese and Korean dishes

## >> HISTORY

### JAPAN

Early descendants of Japan migrated from Asia, primarily from China and Korea. Surviving off the animals and plants native to the islands that make up Japan, these inhabitants lived as hunters and gatherers. About 400 B.C., Koreans crossed the Sea of Japan that separates Korea and Japan. They settled in southern Japan and established farming villages. Among other contributions, the Koreans brought rice to Japan. An agricultural society developed around 300 B.C., and the Japanese began growing rice and irrigating their farmland.

The strongest outside influence on Japan came from the Chinese between 400 and 800 A.D. They introduced tea, soy sauce, noodles, wheat, soybeans, and chopsticks.

#### European Influences

In the late thirteenth century, Marco Polo discovered Japan, but larger numbers of Europeans did not arrive until the middle 1500s. At that time, the Portuguese introduced sugar, corn, and the technique of battering and deep-frying foods to the Japanese. Staying true to their light, simple style of cookery and emphasis on the natural flavors of the food, the Japanese adapted this cooking technique to develop *tempura*. Well known throughout the world, *tempura* consists of an incredibly light batter that delicately coats vegetables, seafood, and/or meat for deep-frying. The batter used for *tempura* is in sharp contrast to the heavy crust of batter that coats and masks the flavor of the deep-fried food in most other countries.

#### Vegetarian Diet

Because of its large Buddhist population, vegetarian dishes abound in Japan. In fact, until a couple of centuries ago, the Japanese diet contained little or no meat. The protein basis of the diet revolved around soybeans, particularly the versatile soybean curd called *tofu,* and seafood when it was allowed.

Throughout Japan's history, taboos against eating meat and chicken have prevailed at various times. During the fifteenth century, meat and poultry consumption began increasing.

#### Present Day

Today, Japan's economy remains strong, and the Japanese people generally enjoy a high standard of living. With times changing, Western fast food and chain restaurants now flourish in the cities of Japan. The diet of the younger generation is changing from the traditional diet and style of eating that is so indicative of Japan's past culinary heritage. Some feel increased protein consumption (particularly red meat) and fewer vegetables might be responsible for the rise in heart disease and certain types of cancer that were almost nonexistent in Japan in the past.

### KOREA

The first people to settle in Korea came from areas to the north and northwest about 5,000 years ago. According to archeologists, millet grew in Korea as early as 3500 B.C., and there is evidence indicating that rice arrived from China around 2700 B.C.

In 2333 B.C., they established the first Korean state. The Chinese moved into the northern part of Korea in 108 B.C. and seized control. Exerting profound influence on this new land, the Chinese introduced Buddhism and Confucianism in the eighth century, which the Koreans adopted. Today, these remain the two major religions found in Korea. In addition, the Chinese brought cattle, pigs, poultry, cabbage, and chopsticks.

| | |
|---|---|
| 400 B.C. | Koreans introduce rice in Japan |
| 300 B.C. | Rice is prevalent in the Japanese diet; wheat and soybeans come from China |
| 500s A.D. | Buddhism becomes the official religion (and will dominate for 1,200 years); many adopt strict vegetarian diets in accordance with Buddhist principles |
| 800 A.D. | Chinese introduce tofu |

#### CH'USOK

*Food plays an intrinsic role in spiritual life in Korea. Ch'usok, the festival of the harvest moon, is held in the fall of the year. This holiday celebrates two things: the harvest and one's ancestors. To honor their ancestors, people return to their ancestral home, where they pray for the dead and leave them an assortment of foods and drink. In fact, many people cook specific dishes in advance of the holiday.*

After conquering Korea in the 1200s, Mongol tribes ruled for 150 years. Manchu armies took control in the 1600s. Both the Japanese and Chinese invaded Korea several times throughout its history. All these intruders left some effect, but the strongest influence came from the Chinese.

### Dynasties, Influences, and Rulers

From 1392 until 1910, the Yi Dynasty ruled Korea while sustaining numerous invasions from the Chinese and Japanese. During that time, a stringent class system developed. With four distinct classes of people, great differences existed between the cuisine of the royalty and that of the common people. The aristocracy enjoyed refined cookery, using a large number of ingredients, many spices, complex cooking procedures, and elaborate table settings. On the other hand, the common people ate simple foods with simple preparations.

The Portuguese introduced hot chili peppers to Korea in the 1500s, and this changed the cuisine dramatically. During the period from the seventeenth to the nineteenth centuries, no foreigners were allowed into Korea, and the country remained free from intruders for a couple hundred years.

Korea continued as an agriculture-based society until the Japanese took control in 1910, when Korea became a Japanese colony. Japan's rule lasted 35 years, until their defeat at the end of World War II in 1945. At that time, the country was divided into two countries, North Korea and South Korea. The North was set up as a Communist society under the control of the Soviet Union, while the South was established as a democracy.

## >> TOPOGRAPHY

### JAPAN

Four large islands and thousands of small ones compose the country of Japan. Although small in area, Japan ranks as one of the most densely populated countries in the world. Over 126 million people reside in this country that is slightly smaller than the state of California. Mountains run through the interior of most of Japan's islands, but flatlands containing the cities and farmland make up the coastal areas. Most of the Japanese people live in large cities along the coasts. In fact, more than 12 million people live in Tokyo and its suburbs.

Situated east of the mainland of Asia, Japan lies in the northern Pacific Ocean. The Pacific Ocean borders on the east and south; the Sea of Japan is to the west and separates it from Korea. Many rivers transect Japan and provide water for irrigating available farmland. In addition to the threat of volcanic eruption from the numerous volcanoes rising with the mountains, the country is prone to earthquakes.

Creating great diversity in the climates found in Japan, ocean currents exert a profound effect on the weather. Cold winters reign in the north, and subtropical conditions exist in the south. This leads to favorable environments for a wide variety of crops within this small country.

### KOREA

Lying in eastern Asia, the peninsula of Korea juts out from the northeastern side of China. The Soviet Union and China border on the north. Korea contains over 1,400 miles of coastline and more than 3,000 islands. The Sea of Japan (called the East Sea in Korea) lies between Korea and Japan; the Yellow Sea is situated on Korea's western side. Each of these bodies of water contains a mixture of warm and cold currents. As a result, each of the seas yields different fish and seafood, which is reflected in the regional cooking near the waters.

The entire Korean peninsula is about the size of the state of Utah, but Korea is divided into two countries, North and South Korea. The majority of the population

---

**Ingredients and Foods Commonly Used throughout the Cuisines of Japan and Korea Include**

- rice
- many varieties of seaweed
- seafood, including a wide variety of fish and shellfish, squid, crab, tuna, bonito, mackerel, trout, and sardines
- tofu
- beef (Korea)
- cabbage, Chinese cabbage, and radishes
- pickled vegetables

- *kimch'i* (Korea)
- mandarin oranges, apples, oranges, pears, and strawberries
- soy sauce
- soybean paste—*miso* (Japan) and *dhwen-jang* (Korea)
- ginger, scallions, and garlic
- rice wine (*sake* and *mirin*) and rice vinegar
- tea

---

resides in the coastal areas because, like Japan, mountains, hills, and valleys compose most of the interior portion of the country. Fertile plains make up the coasts lying to the west, northeast, and south. With mountains and hills covering two-thirds of Korea, only 20 percent of the land is suitable for agriculture.

*Monsoons,* seasonal winds, blow in the summer and winter. In the winter, the cold *monsoon* causes cold winters except on the eastern side of the mountains because they form a barrier that blocks the winds. The summer *monsoons* produce hot, humid summers. In July and August, the *monsoons* bring heavy rains.

## >> COOKING METHODS

As in other Asian countries, cooks in Japan and Korea cut ingredients into small uniform pieces before cooking. This ensures that the pieces cook evenly and are done at the same time. Because this minimizes the amount of cooking time, less fuel is needed to cook.

The Japanese use a number of cooking methods: steaming, boiling, grilling, stir-frying (sautéing), and deep-frying. Steaming emphasizes the natural flavors of the foods, which is important in Japanese cookery. An example of deep-frying, *tempura,* remains one of the most widely known Japanese dishes. While not a cooking method, Japanese consume raw foods as well as pickling or serving them in vinegar. Pickling excess seafood and vegetables preserves these food items for times when they are less plentiful.

One-pot cookery, called *nabémono,* is common, particularly in the winter. *Nabémono* resembles the Chinese hot pot. Preparation of the food occurs beforehand, and then platters containing raw, cut foods are placed before the diners. Individual diners actually cook the food at the table in a communal pot of broth placed over a heat source. They place the food ingredients in the boiling broth, adding the ingredients requiring the longest cooking time first. Diners remove and eat the ingredients as soon as they are cooked, ensuring that the food maintains its fresh quality, texture, and flavor. The cooking happens rapidly; some refer to this as "quick stew." At the end, they add noodles or rice to the flavorful broth to absorb it, and then the noodles or rice are eaten.

Like the Japanese, Koreans use a variety of cooking methods, including grilling, boiling, steaming, stir-frying, and deep-frying. Before cooking, Koreans cut, chop, and slice the foods finely. Beef preparation usually includes tenderizing the meat by pounding, slicing it thinly, and then marinating it before cooking. As in Japan, one-pot cookery is quite popular in Korea.

Preservation by pickling occurs regularly in both countries. With plenty of coastline, salt was available for pickling. Both Koreans and Japanese also preserve by drying. Many recipes include dried fish, seafood, or other products. Many Koreans eat *kimch'i,* a spicy, pickled cabbage (or other vegetable) mixture, with every meal. In

### NABÉMONO

*Sometimes called a quick-cooking stew, nabémono comes in countless varieties depending on the diners' preference and the available ingredients. Nabémono includes any assortment of ingredients such as all types of seafood, meats, tofu, and vegetables. One particularly filling type of nabémono that is popular with sumo wrestlers, chanko-nabe, contains many types of seafood, chicken, potatoes, and a variety of vegetables. Another variation of nabémono, well-known sukiyaki consists of thin slices of beef and vegetables cooked in the broth. Regardless of the type of nabémono, each diner receives a small bowl of ponzu, a citrus-based dipping sauce, to accompany it.*

addition, numerous varieties of pickled vegetables and legumes accompany meals in both countries.

## >> REGIONS

### ISLANDS OF JAPAN

The most northern of the four large islands that compose Japan, Hokkaidō has coastal plains and an interior section containing mountains, hills, and forests. Long, cold winters and cool summers exist here. Fishing and dairy farming are the main food industries on this island.

Situated south of Hokkaidō, Honshū occupies the central part of Japan. Here, too, mountains and valleys make up the interior while plains dominate the coastal areas. This island has warm, humid summers and average winters.

To the south lie two islands, Skikoku and Kyūshū. Both experience hot summers and mild winters, so rice grows very well here. Mountains and hills make up much of Skikoku, and many fruits and vegetables thrive on this island. Kyūshū contains mountains in the interior surrounded by hills, forests, and plains.

### AGRICULTURE

Only 15 percent of the land in Japan is suitable for farming. To maximize the crop production, the Japanese terrace the hills, irrigate, and fertilize. Their reverence for rice is obvious: every small tract of land that can support agriculture becomes a rice paddy.

With such limited land resources, pastures for grazing cattle are scarce. As a result, the meager cattle spend their lives confined to barns, except in northern Japan, home of the famous Kōbe beef. Producing some of the most prized and expensive beef in the world, Kōbe cattle enjoy pampered lives filled with beer and massages to create well-marbled, tender beef.

### KOREA

Although Korea is divided into two countries, the cooking in both countries remains quite similar. North and South Koreans prepare many of the same dishes; however, there are some differences. The people of North Korea eat pork while those in the south prefer beef, but basically, seafood and *tofu* form the foundation protein consumed in both countries. South Koreans prepare spicier dishes, and those in the North consume more noodles. With lots of coastline, the fishing industry continues to flourish in both North and South Korea.

North Koreans raise animals and crops on collective farms that are run by the government. Primarily grown on the plains in the northwest, major crops include rice, vegetables, fruits, corn, and potatoes.

The western and southern coasts of South Korea contain the majority of its farms. The most prevalent crops are rice, barley, wheat, fruits, and vegetables.

## >> CUISINE

In both Japan and Korea, the basis of the diet is seafood or tofu accompanied by rice and pickled vegetables. The Japanese and Koreans traditionally eat rice with every meal, both preferring the more glutinous, short-grain varieties of rice. Although noodles sometimes replace rice at a Japanese meal, bowls of hot, plain rice accompanied by pickled vegetables usually conclude the meal, whether or not noodles were served.

Because oceans surround Japan and Korea, seaweed frequently appears in the cuisines found in both countries. Recipes for lots of dishes feature many varieties of seaweed, both fresh and dried. A significant source of minerals, seaweed is used as a

The highest mountain in Japan, Mount Fuji soars over 12,000 feet and stands on the island of Honshū.

Skikoku has 88 holy temples that attract monks and many others on pilgrimages.

*Pickled vegetable*
© Xuejun li

*Seaweed salad*
© Guzel Studio

flavoring, as a frequent soup ingredient, and combined with all sorts of vegetables and seafood in salads. *Dashi*, Japanese stock made from dried bonito (a fish) and dried kelp (seaweed), forms the foundation for much Japanese cookery, including soups, braised dishes, and sauces. Depending on the type of seaweed, the flavor can seem quite foreign to many Western palates. Often, people need repeated exposure to seaweed before acquiring a taste for it.

## JAPAN

The roots of the cuisine trace back to the Buddhist religion, which reigned in Japan for 1,200 years beginning in the 500s A.D. The Buddhist influence encouraged simple, natural foods in a simple and beautiful presentation. Since Buddhism requires vegetarianism, meat played a small role in the cuisine.

Known for healthy, beautifully presented food, Japanese cooks typically prepare dishes that are low in fat and lightly cooked. The Japanese use less oil in their cookery than other Asian cuisines, which further emphasizes the light, natural flavors of the foods. The cuisine of Japan differs from other Asian cuisines in several ways. First, although portions are small, the aesthetics of each dish or plate takes on epic proportions. The Japanese attach great importance to the appearance and presentation of the food. The goal is to capture the diner's attention with the freshness and natural flavors of the food, the beauty of each dish, the atmosphere, and the whole meal. Second, although all the foods for a meal are served at once as in most of the other Asian cuisines, diners in Japan receive their own portions on individual plates and in bowls instead of serving themselves, family style, from large bowls in the middle of the table. Third, the complexity of flavors found in the sauces of other Asian countries is absent here. Japanese chefs do not want to shroud the natural flavors of the food with multi-flavored sauces.

*Japanese plate*
© Vladimir Gerasimov

### Aesthetics and Simplicity

Japanese cooks and chefs strive to create an aesthetically pleasing plate and dining experience. They take great care to place the food beautifully and artistically in every way. All aspects of appearance, including the color of both the food and the plate or bowl, the arrangement of the food on the plate, the flowers on the table, the setting of the table, and even the placement of the table in the dining room, assume paramount importance and consideration. Some describe Japanese food on the plate as minimalist, actually referring to it as a work of art.

Basically, the Japanese strive for a variety of cooking methods in each meal as well as an assortment of the five colors: white, black or purple, red or orange, green, and yellow. In addition, chefs make sure to include specific tastes in the meal representing sweet, salty, sour, spicy, and bitter. Another popular flavor sensation, *umami* is the protein or earthy taste sensation found in mushrooms and other foods. Finally, the textures of the foods served at the meal must represent a variety of textures and balance each other. For example, they might juxtapose hard with soft and creamy with crunchy.

Only absolutely fresh food products are acceptable. Menus in homes and restaurants truly change with the seasons as well as with what is available and fresh at the market that particular day. The emphasis remains on the texture, taste, smell, and appearance of the individual ingredients, the completed dish, and the entire meal. These principles are apparent in foods associated with the Japanese cuisine, such as *sushi* and *sashimi,* raw fish preparations, and the many soups consisting of a *miso* (fermented soybean paste-flavored broth containing one or just a few ingredients).

Buddhist philosophy emphasized variety in the colors and the flavor palates presented on each plate and in the entire meal. The Buddhists considered five flavors—sweet, sour, salty bitter, and spicy—and they placed importance on five colors: black, white, green, yellow, and red.

*Japanese plate*
© blue_moon_images

## Seasonings

Seasonings used in Japanese cookery reflect simplicity and allow the natural, delicate flavors of the food to dominate. Primary flavoring ingredients include *shōyu, miso,* various seaweeds, and two rice wines, *sake* and *mirin. Wasabi,* a sinus-opening, spicy-hot horseradish condiment used as a dipping sauce enhances the flavors and textures of *sushi* and *sashimi.*

## Food Items

Seafood, tofu, soup, a variety of other dishes, fresh and pickled vegetables, and steamed rice form a typical Japanese meal. The multitude of possible vegetable dishes includes pickled, raw, and cooked preparations and all sorts of salads. Like that of most Asians, the diet includes smaller amounts of protein with lots of vegetables and ample amounts of rice.

The Japanese prefer plain, boiled short- or medium-grain rice, which serves as the foundation of the meal. Short-grain rice yields sticky rice as opposed to the separated grains of the long-grain rice favored by the Chinese. Rice is so important to the meal that some refer to meals as *meshi* or *gohan,* the Japanese words for rice. Poor people extend their rice with millet.

Reflecting all the culinary goals, *sushi* is an excellent example of natural flavors and beautiful food. *Sushi* is a combination of rice, often seaweed, and a little protein or vegetable. While many think *sushi* refers to raw fish, the word means "vinegar rice." Rolled *sushi* consists of an outer wrapper of *nori* (a type of seaweed) and a thicker layer of vinegar rice with the featured ingredient in the center. Some possible fillings for the center of the rice are raw fish, cooked fish, fresh vegetables, pickled vegetables, or a combination of these. Usual accompaniments for *sushi* include *wasabi,* soy sauce, and pickled ginger. Besides preparing *sushi* by rolling the fish or other fillings in vinegar rice, they sometimes serve the filling on top of a small mound or oval of vinegar rice. *Sashimi* is raw fish.

In addition to rice, Japanese consume lots of noodles. In western Japan, they prefer *udon* noodles, made from wheat flour. People in the east like *soba* noodles, made from buckwheat flour.

Some type of soup appears at most meals. There are two popular types of Japanese soups: clear broth and a thick soup flavored with *miso.* Breakfast in Japan often consists of the thick, *miso*-based soup.

Appearing in many guises, the soybean serves as an important part of the Japanese diet. Two seasonings derived from soybeans, *miso* (fermented soybean paste) and *shōyu* (soy sauce), show up everywhere. Protein-rich *tofu* appears regularly in the cuisines of both Japan and Korea. Actually, *tofu* often is consumed at all meals of the day in Japan. Like China, cooks in these two countries use few, if any, dairy products.

## Restaurants

Many restaurants in Japan specialize so narrowly that they prepare only one type of food or use only one method of preparation in the restaurant. Noodle restaurants serve only noodle dishes; *tempura* restaurants feature only deep-fried *tempura; sushi* bars provide vinegar-flavored rice wrapped around vegetables, meat, and/or raw or cooked fish. Some restaurants specialize with such a restricted focus that they prepare only one type of fish.

## Meals

As in the rest of Asia, all dishes arrive at the Japanese table at the same time. Dishes might be served piping hot, but room-temperature foods are perfectly acceptable.

To make rice cakes, mochi, Japanese cooks pound glutinous rice until it forms a patty. Considered a high form of rice, mochi are served at feasts and special occasions.

*Sashimi*
© nickola_che

Inside-out sushi reverses the position of the vinegar rice and the nori from traditional sushi. To form inside-out sushi, place the rice on the sushi mat, cover the rice with a layer of nori, and put the filling on top of the nori. Roll and cut the sushi as normal. Rice forms the outside of this sushi, and the black nori appears as a swirl within the sushi roll.

Serving as the Japanese version of fast food, noodles remain popular throughout Japan. Noodle restaurants flourish, and they generally serve two types of noodles: soba, a buckwheat noodle, and udon, which is made from wheat.

## JAPANESE DISHES

**sashimi** Raw fish

**shabu-shabu** Features very thinly sliced beef cooked at the dining table: Similar to the Chinese hot pot, diners cook beef and vegetables in *dashi* (stock) usually flavored with soy sauce. They first cook the beef by stirring it through the stock once or twice (it is so thin it cooks very quickly), and then they cook the vegetables. Ponzu sauce (citrus-flavored soy mixture) accompanies *shabu-shabu*.

**sukiyaki** Features beef cooked at the dining table: Thinly sliced beef is grilled or sautéed in a skillet, then liquid and vegetables are added and the mixture cooks just until the vegetables are done. Diners dip *sukiyaki* in raw egg before eating.

**sushi** Combination of one or more fillings (raw or cooked fish, meat, fresh or pickled vegetables, egg, roe, or a combination) with vinegar rice

**yakitori** Grilled, skewered small pieces of chicken, often served with beer

---

Actually, the Japanese believe the natural flavors of the food come through better at room temperature.

A traditional Japanese meal consists of rice, soup, and side dishes. In fact, the name of the meal indicates the number of side dishes accompanying the rice and soup. For example, the name might be "meal plus three" which means a meal (consisting of soup and rice) with three side dishes. Generally, the side dishes represent different cooking techniques. If one dish is grilled, another might be steamed or fried. Meals end with steamed rice and pickled vegetables and perhaps fresh fruit. Dessert is served only at tea ceremonies.

## KOREA

### Flavorings

Combinations of the five flavor elements—sweet, sour, salty, bitter, and hot or pungent—create the tastes associated with Korean cookery. Common flavorings used in Korea include ginger, garlic, soy sauce, vinegar, sesame oil, sesame seeds, hot peppers, black pepper, and green onions. Whether consumed raw, pickled, or grilled, garlic appears with all foods at all meals. Koreans prefer spicy foods and use a wide variety of hot peppers in the form of chili pastes and finely sliced hot peppers. Generally, Koreans use more pungent flavorings than cooks in Japan and China.

### Foods

Koreans prefer a meal of beef, pork, seafood, or tofu, accompanied by *kimch'i,* a variety of vegetables, pickled vegetables, soup, and rice. Unlike the typical Western approach to protein foods, Koreans often mix seafood with pork, beef, and/or chicken within a dish, depending on what is available. As in other Asian countries, limited quantities of high-protein foods accompany large amounts of rice, other grains, and vegetables. Like the Japanese, Koreans eat cooked rice (called *bap*) at every meal. They also consume barley and several types of beans, often combining them with the omnipresent rice. Whether made from rice, grains, or legumes, noodles are prominent in Korean cookery.

Foods from the sea play an important role in the Korean diet. Dried cuttlefish reigns as the most popular snack in Korea. Very high in nutrients and widely consumed, seaweed is available throughout the year.

Well-seasoned foods dominate the cuisine: most foods are marinated or seasoned before cooking and then seasoned again after cooking. A popular South Korean beef dish, *bulgogi,* consists of marinated strips of beef grilled at the table.

---

### THE JAPANESE TEA CEREMONY

During the fourteenth and fifteenth centuries, the Zen Buddhists developed the tea ceremony, which remains one of the traditional arts today. This ancient ritual involves the preparation and service of powdered green tea to guests. The very simple and deliberate tea ceremony as well as its goals reflect several aspects of Zen Buddhist philosophy and bring enjoyment to the guest on all levels, including the physical and intellectual. True to Zen philosophy, the guest achieves inner peace by intently concentrating on the beauty of nature and the simplicity of the ceremony. The sound of the water (used to make the tea), the glow of the fire (on which the water is heated for tea), and the beauty of the objects used in the tea ceremony heighten the senses. All conversation focuses on these subjects and on simplicity. The guests experience a spiritual awakening through the Zen approach of appreciating and attentively living each moment.

Although not many attend or have tea ceremonies today, many Japanese spend years studying the art of the tea ceremony. Only the very rich and Buddhist monks actually have tea ceremonies.

---

### KIMCH'I

*The word kimch'i comes from the word chimchae meaning "preserved with salt." Made since the 600s, kimch'i preserves vegetables for use during the harsh winter. Kimch'i still remains a well-known staple on the Korean table. Although outside of Korea many think kimch'i is fermented cabbage, it is also prepared from radishes, cucumbers, and other vegetables. Depending on the region, different types of kimch'i are prepared. Also, the amount of spiciness and salt varies from region to region. Generally, they say people in the northern regions prepare milder kimch'i than those in the south.*

*Kimch'i recipes differ based on the main vegetable making up the kimch'i, ingredients that contribute to the flavoring, and the method of preparation and/or fermentation. Although most varieties of kimch'i are highly spiced, some Koreans prefer mild kimch'i. In addition, kimch'i preparation changes with the season, with different types favored in each season.*

*A fermented food, Koreans believe kimch'i contains all sorts of medicinal and healthful benefits. Besides aiding in digestion, its high lactic acid content helps kimch'i maintain the proper balance of flora in the intestines. Also, some believe kimch'i has anti-carcinogen effects.*

---

## Health

Like the Chinese, Koreans believe food prevents and cures disease, as well as promotes good health. Good taste and healthful eating remain priorities in the cooking of Korea.

## Meals

*The average Korean meal includes three or four dishes with rice. For special occasions, the meal might consist of 12 dishes plus rice.*

Koreans place all dishes on the table at once in large bowls. Meals include rice, soup, and at least one variety of *kimch'i.* Diners eat from bowls, not plates. Although Koreans prepare a wide variety of dishes, they consume the same foods for breakfast, lunch, or dinner.

Besides the well-known *kimch'i,* which appears with rice at every meal, including breakfast, side dishes, known as *panch'an* or *banchan* usually accompany meals. Condiments, pickles, salads, vegetables, beans, and seaweed often serve as *banchan.* Cooks choose an assortment of *banchan* that enhance the meal by balancing the flavor components and the textures of the dishes. Of course, the selection depends on the available foods.

In many Korean homes, the heartiest meal of the day is served in the morning. As in Vietnam, a typical breakfast in Korea consists of a meat-enriched soup. Koreans believe ingesting the main meal in the morning provides the most nutrients for the full day ahead. Therefore, the lunch and evening meal are both light meals.

### SOME KOREAN CUSTOMS AND MANNERS

- *Everyone at the table begins eating when the oldest person present at the table takes the first bite.*
- *No one leaves the table until the oldest person has finished eating.*
- *Leaving chopsticks standing in the rice is a ceremonial custom that occurs only at a memorial service for the dead.*

## BEVERAGES

The beverage of choice in Japan and Korea remains tea. The Japanese prefer green tea, and Koreans often drink tea made from barley or rice. Two rice wines, *sake,* served warm in the winter, and *mirin,* a sweeter wine used only for cooking, appear often in Japan. Rice wine, beer, and *soju,* a distilled grain liquor, are the most popular alcoholic beverages in Korea.

| REGION | AREA | WEATHER | TOPOGRAPHY | FOODS |
|---|---|---|---|---|
| **Japan** | | | | |
| Hokkaidō | North | Long, cold winters; cool summers | Mountains, hills, forests, coastal plains | Seafood, Kōbe beef, dairy, seaweed |
| Honshū | Central | Mild winters; warm, humid summers | Mountains, valleys, plains on coast | Seafood, seaweed, rice |
| Skikoku | South | Mild winters, hot summers | Mountains, hills, coastal plains | Seafood, tuna, bonito, mackerel, sardines, trout, crabs, shellfish, squid, seaweed, rice, vegetables, fruits |
| Kyūshū | South | Mild winters, hot summers | Mountains, hills, coastal plains, forests | Seafood, tuna, bonito, mackerel, sardines, trout, crabs, shellfish, squid, seaweed, rice, vegetables, fruits |
| **Korea** | | | | |
| North Korea | North | Cold winters; hot, humid summers; *monsoons;* moderate climate in east | North: plains, hills, coast, farmland<br>Center: mountains, forests<br>East: coast, hills, lowlands, farmland<br>South: mountains, forests, valleys, hills | Seafood, shellfish, squid, pollock, sardines, hogs, rice, barley, wheat, soybeans, corn, potatoes, vegetables, fruits |
| South Korea | South | Cold winters; hot, humid summers; *monsoons;* moderate climate in east | North: mountains, forests, valleys, hills, coasts<br>Center and east: hills, forests, mountains, valleys, coasts<br>South: hills, plains, coast | Seafood, filefish, pollock, oysters, hogs, cattle, chicken, rice, barley, soybeans, wheat, potatoes, sweet potatoes, Chinese cabbage, vegetables, melons, apples |

## >> Review Questions

1. Explain similarities and differences between the Japanese cuisine and that of other Asian cuisines.
2. Describe the Japanese philosophy on food and dining, including the goals of chefs cooking this cuisine.
3. Discuss the seasonings commonly used in the cookery of Japan and those used in the cookery of Korea.
4. Discuss food ingredients that are prevalent in both Japan and Korea because of the topography and geography of these two countries.
5. Which foods appear at all Japanese and Korean meals?
6. Describe the differences in service and presentation between a Korean and a Japanese meal.
7. What is *kimch'i* and what is its role in the Korean diet?

## >> Glossary

**banchan** Another word sometimes used for *panch'an*; side dishes like vegetables, salads, pickles, and condiments served with Korean meals

**bulgogi** Marinated strips of beef grilled at the table; a popular Korean dish

**dashi** Japanese stock made from dried bonito and dried kelp, forms the foundation for much Japanese cookery, including soups and braised dishes

**dhwen-jang** Korean bean paste

**handai** Wide wooden bowl used for cooling rice in Japan

**katsuo** Dried bonito shavings (bonito is a fish in the mackerel family)

**kimch'i** A spicy, fermented cabbage or vegetable mixture popular in Korea and served at every meal

**kombu** Dried kelp, a seaweed

**mirin** Japanese sweet rice wine used for cooking

**miso** Japanese fermented bean paste, used as a flavoring for soups or sauces

**monsoons** Seasonal winds that affect the weather

**nabémono** One-pot cookery common in Japan; similar to fondue, diners cook their own food in a pot of stock heating on the dining table

**panch'an** Side dishes like vegetables, salads, pickles, and condiments served with Korean meals; sometimes called *banchan*

**ponzu** A citrus-based dipping sauce

**sake** Japanese rice wine, served warm in the winter

**sashimi** Raw fish sliced thinly, accompanied by *wasabi*, pickled ginger, and soy sauce

**soba** A noodle made from buckwheat

**soju** Korean distilled grain liquor

**sushi** Raw or cooked fish and/or vegetables and vinegared rice, often rolled in a wrapper of *nori* seaweed and accompanied by *wasabi*, pickled ginger, and soy sauce

**tempura** Individual food items coated with a very light batter and deep-fried; a well-known Japanese dish

**tofu** Soybean curd, a protein food

**udon** A noodle made from wheat

**wasabi** Very pungent, spicy-hot, green horseradish dipping sauce served as a condiment with raw fish in Japan

## SUSHI-MESHI (JAPAN)

### SUSHI RICE

**Note:** *Sushi* rice is sticky, so it adapts well to molding.

**Number of Servings:** Depends on use
**Cooking Method:** Boil
**Serving Size:** Depends on use: 5 1/2 oz. (156 g) = 1 cup (240 mL), unpacked
**Total Yield:** 3 lb., 15 1/4 oz. (1.8 kg)

**TWIST ON THE CLASSIC**

Mold or mound this rice and use as a base for any fish, meat, or vegetable. It soaks up sauces well, but be certain the sauce goes nicely with its mild vinegar flavor.

| INGREDIENTS | WEIGHT | | VOLUME | |
|---|---|---|---|---|
| | U.S. | METRIC | U.S. | METRIC |
| **Vinegar Dressing:** | | | | |
| rice vinegar | | 86 g | 1/4 cup + 2 tablespoons | 90 mL |
| sugar | 1 1/2 oz. | 43 g | 3 tablespoons | 45 mL |
| sea salt | 1/2 oz. | 15 g | 2 1/2 teaspoons | 12 mL |
| *kombu* (kelp), 2-inch (5-cm) square, *optional* | | | | |
| short-grain or sushi rice | 1 lb., 11 3/4 oz. | 788 g | 3 1/2 cups | 840 mL |
| water | | 908 g | 1 quart (4 cups) | 960 mL |

Adding vinegar dressing to Sushi-Meshi (Sushi Rice)
Pearson Education/PH College

### VINEGAR DRESSING:

1. Place all dressing ingredients in nonreactive saucepan.
2. Bring just to boil to dissolve sugar and salt. Remove from heat. Cool until needed. Remove *kombu*.

### RICE:

1. Wash rice several times with cold water, until water is clear. Let rice dry in colander for 1 hour.
2. Place rice and 1 quart (908 g or 960 mL) water in large saucepan. Bring to boil over high heat.
3. Cover, reduce heat to medium, boil for 5 minutes. Reduce heat to low and simmer for 15 minutes. Remove from heat, let sit for 15 minutes.
4. Spread hot rice in thin layer in a *handai* (wide wooden bowl) or shallow wood, plastic, or glass vessel (a 9- by 13-inch, 23- by 33-cm glass pan works well). Do not use aluminum.
5. Gently move rice using a flat wooden spoon or rice paddle to cool it. Pour vinegar dressing over rice in a circular motion to cover all of rice. Mix gently with paddle until cool. (Traditionally, the rice is fanned to cool it faster.) Be careful to lift and mix gently, so rice does not break or mash. The process will take 5 to 10 minutes.
6. If not needed right away, cover rice to prevent it from drying. Do not refrigerate *sushi* rice; use it the day it is made.

Cooling Sushi-Meshi (Sushi Rice)
Ian O'Leary © Dorling Kindersley

# KAPPA MAKI (JAPAN)

## CUCUMBER SUSHI

A variation on rolled *sushi*: To make inside-out rolls spread the rice on the mat and top it with the sheet of *nori*. Top the *nori* with a filling like with traditional *sushi*, and then roll. This places a swirl of *nori* inside the rice instead of using it as a wrapper outside the roll.

*Inside-out sushi*
David Mager © Pearson Learning Photo Studio

**Note:** The Japanese prepare a number of varieties of *sushi* and *sashimi*. Some are mounds of vinegar rice topped with raw fish or another topping, others are shaped by a mold (like a box), and still others are called "rolls" because rice is rolled around the filling. Sometimes, *nori* (seaweed) forms the outer covering of this cucumber roll.

**Note:** If a bamboo *sushi* mat is unavailable, place the items on a piece of parchment paper and roll, using the parchment paper like a *sushi* mat.

**Number of Servings:** 10
**Serving Size:** 1 roll, cut into 8 pieces
**Total Yield:** 10 rolls
**Food Balance:** Protein/umami
**Wine Style:** Off-dry or low-oaked whites and soft reds
**Example:** Castello di Gabbiano Pinot Grigio or Chianti

| | WEIGHT | | VOLUME | |
|---|---|---|---|---|
| INGREDIENTS | U.S. | METRIC | U.S. | METRIC |
| water | | 43 g | 3 tablespoons | 45 mL |
| vinegar | | | 1 teaspoon | 5 mL |
| *nori* | | | 10 sheets | |
| vinegar rice, *recipe above* | 3 lb., 7 oz. | 1.6 kg | 10 cups, unpacked | 2.4 L |
| cucumber, peeled, seeded, and julienned in 4-inch (10-cm) lengths | 12 oz. | 340 g | 1 1/2 large | |
| carrot, peeled and cut into 1/16- by 4-inch (2-cm by 10-cm) strips, *optional* | 2 oz. | 57 g | 1 each | |

**Accompaniments:**

*wasabi*
pickled ginger
soy sauce

*Removing seeds from cucumber*
Pearson Education/PH College

*Spreading rice on nori*
Richard Embery © Pearson Education

*Placing food items on rice and nori*
shellyagami © Shutterstock

1. Mix water and vinegar. Set aside until needed.
2. Briefly toast *nori* by placing the sheet of *nori* on a high flame or burner with the shiny side toward the heat source. Heat until color of *nori* changes from brown-black to dark green.
3. Place plastic wrap over bamboo sushi mat (to make clean up easier). Place *nori* on mat with shiny side down. Place 5 1/2 oz., or 1 cup (156 g) rice on *nori*. Dip fingertips in vinegar water; using fingers, spread rice evenly about 1/4 to 1/2 inch (1/2 to 1 cm) thick over the three-fourths of the *nori* closest to you.
4. Place about 1 oz. (28 g) cucumber strips in a line across rice about one-third from bottom edge. If desired, add a few carrot strips to the cucumbers (for color). Lift *sushi* mat to begin rolling. (This procedure is the same as rolling a jellyroll.)
5. Hold plastic wrap and mat while rolling *nori* tightly over rice and cucumber. Use fingertips to hold filling in place while rolling mat forward with thumbs. Continue rolling with mat until roll is complete.
6. Place seam-side down, wrap completed roll in plastic wrap until needed.
7. To serve, slice roll in half with sharp knife. Clean knife after each cut and slice each half into four even pieces, for eight pieces.
8. Place *sushi* pieces on plate with cut side up. Serve, accompanied by *wasabi*, pickled ginger, and soy sauce or dipping sauce of choice.

> Since the cross-section of *sushi* shows in its presentation, make the filling visually attractive. Feel free to combine several items in the filling. For example, carrot shreds added to the cucumber brightens the filling in this roll.

© jreika

*Rolling nori, rice, and filling with bamboo mat*
Richard Embery © Pearson Education/PH College

*Cutting rolls into sushi*
Richard Embery © Pearson Education/PH College

## GOCHU BUCHIM (KOREA)

### PEPPERS STUFFED WITH BEEF

**Note:** Base the serving size on the size of the pepper. If Korean peppers are unavailable, substitute Anaheim peppers or poblanos. The spiciness of the pepper determines the spiciness of this dish.

**Note:** A dipping sauce of soy sauce flavored with hot pepper flakes, sesame oil, and rice wine or dry sherry compliments these stuffed peppers.

**Number of Servings:** 8

**Cooking Method:** Sauté

**Serving Size:** 3 or so stuffed peppers, depending on size, about 5 to 6 oz. (142 to 170 g) (about 1/2 oz. [15 g] raw meat per pepper half)

**Total Yield:** 2 lb., 15 1/2 oz. (1.3 kg) stuffed
1 lb., 9 oz. (710 g) raw meat

**Food Balance:** Spicy/protein

**Wine Style:** Low-oaked whites and soft reds

**Example:** Penfolds Riesling or Koonunga Hills Shiraz

*Korean chili peppers*
Dave King © Dorling Kindersley

| INGREDIENTS | WEIGHT | | VOLUME | |
| --- | --- | --- | --- | --- |
| | U.S. | METRIC | U.S. | METRIC |
| ground beef | 1 lb., 4 oz. | 568 g | | |
| soy sauce | | 28 g | 2 tablespoons | 30 mL |
| rice wine or dry sherry | | 15 g | 1 tablespoon | 15 mL |
| sugar | | | 1 teaspoon | 5 mL |
| garlic, smashed and minced | 1 1/2 oz. | 43 g | 2 tablespoons | 30 mL |
| green onion, minced | 1 oz. | 28 g | 2 each | |
| sesame oil | | 28 g | 2 tablespoons | 30 mL |
| Korean green chili peppers, medium size, or Anaheim peppers, cut in half and seeds and ribs removed | 1 lb., 9 1/2 oz. | 724 g | 24 each | |
| flour | as needed | | | |
| eggs | 6 3/4 oz. | 191 g | 4 each | |
| oil | as needed | | | |

**Accompaniment:**
dipping sauce of choice

© tab62

① Using mixer fitted with flat paddle beater, mix beef, soy sauce, wine or sherry, sugar, garlic, green onion, and sesame oil until fluffy, several minutes.

② Dust inside of each pepper half with flour. (This helps filling adhere to pepper.)

③ Portion 1/2 oz. (15 g) meat for each pepper half. Roll into log and stuff into pepper. Place flour on plate, roll pepper in flour to coat outside, being sure to coat the exposed meat with flour.

④ Beat eggs in bowl, coat entire pepper with egg. Repeat with remaining pepper halves.

⑤ Cover bottom of skillet with thin layer of oil. Heat over medium heat until hot. Add peppers in batches, cook until meat side is golden brown and reaches proper internal temperature and pepper is slightly brown and softened. Add oil by the tablespoon as needed to sauté all peppers.

⑥ Keep peppers warm in oven until all are sautéed. Depending on the size of peppers, serve three peppers (six halves) with dipping sauce of choice.

---

# DASHI (JAPAN)

## FISH AND SEAWEED STOCK

*Kombu*
Strakovskaya © Shutterstock

**Note:** *Dashi* forms the basis for many Japanese soups and sauces.

**Total Yield:** 1 quart (908 g or 960 mL)          **Cooking Method:** Boil

| INGREDIENTS | WEIGHT | | VOLUME | |
| --- | --- | --- | --- | --- |
| | U.S. | METRIC | U.S. | METRIC |
| *kombu* (kelp), dried | 1/2 oz. | 15 g | one 2- by 4-inch piece | one 5- by 10-cm piece |
| water | | 908 g | 1 quart (4 cups) | 960 mL |
| *katsuo* (dried bonito shavings) | 1/2 oz. | 15 g | 1 cup | 240 mL |

① Wipe *kombu* lightly with damp cloth, place in saucepan, cover with water.

② Bring to simmer over medium-low heat, simmer for 10 minutes.

③ Remove *kombu*, add *katsuo*, remove pan from heat, let sit few minutes until *katsuo* settles to bottom of pan.

④ Strain stock, cool, and refrigerate until needed (freeze to store more than 3 days).

## MISO SHIRU (JAPAN)

### BEAN PASTE SOUP WITH TOFU

**Number of Servings:** 9
**Serving Size:** 8 oz. (227 g)
**Total Yield:** 4 lb., 9 oz (2.1 kg)
**Food Balance:** Protein
**Wine Style:** Low-oaked whites and soft reds
**Example:** Beringer Chenin Blanc or Founders' Estate Chardonnay

**Cooking Method:** Boil

Alexey Ivanovich © Shutterstock

| INGREDIENTS | WEIGHT U.S. | WEIGHT METRIC | VOLUME U.S. | VOLUME METRIC |
|---|---|---|---|---|
| Dashi (*double recipe above*) | | | 2 quarts (8 cups) | 1.9 L |
| *aka miso* (reddish brown *miso*) | 5 1/2 oz. | 156 g | 1/2 cup | 120 mL |
| tofu (soybean curd), rinsed and cut into 1/2-inch (1.3-cm) cubes | 8 oz. | 227 g | | |
| scallions, sliced thinly, green part included | 1 1/2 oz. | 43 g | 2 each | |
| mushrooms, button or any variety, sliced | 1 1/2 oz. | 43 g | 4 each | |

1. Heat *Dashi* in saucepan until hot.
2. In small bowl, add some hot *Dashi* to *miso*, mix well.
3. Add *miso* mixture to saucepan of *Dashi*, mix well, strain if lumps remain.
4. Add tofu and scallions, heat over medium heat until just simmering.
5. Add mushroom slices, serve.

> **TWIST ON THE CLASSIC**
>
> Jazz up *miso* soup by adding minced hot pepper and rice.

## YOOK GAEJANG (KOREA)

### SPICY BEEF SOUP

**Note:** The amount of red pepper flakes depends on the heat of the pepper flakes and the desired spiciness of the soup.

**Note:** The weight of this recipe does not include the optional clear noodles.

**Number of Servings:** 11
**Serving Size:** 7 oz. (199 g)
**Total Yield:** 5 lb. (2.3 kg)
**Food Balance:** Balanced
**Wine Style:** Wine friendly—Pick your favorite
**Example:** Rosemount Chardonnay or hiraz

**Cooking Method:** Boil

> **TWIST ON THE CLASSIC**
>
> Reduce the liquid and serve as an entrée by slicing the brisket across the grain and fanning the slices over cellophane noodles.

| INGREDIENTS | WEIGHT U.S. | WEIGHT METRIC | VOLUME U.S. | VOLUME METRIC |
|---|---|---|---|---|
| beef brisket, trimmed | 1 lb. | 454 g | | |
| water or light beef stock | | | 3 quarts (12 cups) | 2.8 L |
| clear noodles, potato starch or bean thread, *optional* | 7 oz. | 199 g | | |
| red pepper flakes | | | 1 teaspoon | 5 mL, or to taste |
| garlic, smashed and minced | 3/4 oz. | 22 g | 1 tablespoon | 15 mL |

DAJ © Getty Images, Inc.–Jupiterimages

| INGREDIENTS | WEIGHT | | VOLUME | |
|---|---|---|---|---|
| | U.S. | METRIC | U.S. | METRIC |
| soy sauce | | 28 g | 2 tablespoons | 30 mL |
| sesame oil | | 28 g | 2 tablespoons | 30 mL |
| green onion, 1-inch (2.5-cm) pieces | 8 oz. | 227 g | 2 to 3 bunches | |
| eggs, beaten | 3 1/2 oz. | 104 g | 2 each | |

1. Place brisket and water or stock in large pot. Bring to boil, reduce heat and simmer for 2 hours or until tender. Remove meat from stock and cool. Shred meat into thin pieces and place in nonreactive bowl.
2. If possible, refrigerate stock overnight to allow any fat to congeal. Remove fat and discard. If there is less than 2 quarts of stock, add water or stock to bring up to 2 quarts.
3. Cover noodles with water. Soak until hydrated. Discard water.
4. Combine red pepper, garlic, soy sauce, and sesame oil, mix well. Pour over shredded meat; refrigerate and marinate for 10 minutes.
5. Place stock over medium-high heat, bring to boil. Add meat mixture and green onions. Return to boil.
6. Slowly drizzle egg into the boiling stock. Add clear noodles. Correct seasonings. Serve.

## AONA NO GOMA-AE (JAPAN)

### LEAFY GREENS WITH SESAME DRESSING

Courtesy of CanolaInfo.org

**Number of Servings:** 12
**Serving Size:** 3 oz. (86 g)
**Total Yield:** 2 lb., 5 oz. (1.1 kg)

**Cooking Method:** Boil

| INGREDIENTS | WEIGHT | | VOLUME | |
|---|---|---|---|---|
| | U.S. | METRIC | U.S. | METRIC |
| leafy greens like watercress, spinach, *komatsuna*, or combination, washed and cut into 2-inch (5-cm) pieces | 3 lb., 8 oz. | 1.6 kg | | |
| sesame seeds | 2 oz. | 57 g | 1/4 cup + 2 tablespoons | 90 mL |
| sugar | 1 1/2 oz. | 43 g | 3 tablespoons | 45 mL |
| soy sauce (*shōyu*) | | 43 to 57 g | 3 to 4 tablespoons | 45 to 60 mL |

**Garnish:**
sesame seeds, toasted

1. Place greens (with a little water clinging to leaves) in pan, making sure stems are on bottom. Cook until wilted, about 2 minutes.
2. Rinse with cold water in colander, drain well, squeeze to remove excess water.
3. Toast sesame seeds in dry skillet, being careful not to burn. Cool, grind with mortar and pestle, food processor, or coffee grinder.
4. Mix sesame seeds, sugar, and soy sauce. Set aside until ready to serve.
5. Combine sesame seed dressing with greens. Correct seasonings. Serve small portion in separate bowl to accompany other dishes and rice. Garnish with sprinkling of toasted sesame seeds, if desired.

### TWIST ON THE CLASSIC

Prepare this recipe using cold, uncooked lettuce leaves and serve as a traditional Western salad. For a different combination, place a mound of *Aona No Goma-Ae* on the plate and angle a cooked fish fillet on the salad.

## KIMCH'I (KOREA)

### PICKLED CABBAGE

**Note:** Begin preparation of *Kimch'i* at least 2 or 3 days before needed.

**Number of Servings:** 45
**Serving Size:** 2 oz. (57 g)
**Total Yield:** 5 lb., 11 oz. (2.6 kg)

| INGREDIENTS | WEIGHT | | VOLUME | |
|---|---|---|---|---|
| | U.S. | METRIC | U.S. | METRIC |
| Chinese cabbage | 2 lb., 4 oz. | 1 kg | 3/4 head | |
| water | | | 1 quart + 2 cups (6 cups) | 1.4 L |
| kosher salt | 1 3/4 oz. | 50 g | 3 tablespoons | 45 mL |
| **Stuffing:** | | | | |
| fresh ginger, peeled | 1 1/2 oz. | 43 g | two 3-inch cubes | two 8-cm cubes |
| garlic cloves, peeled | 2 oz. | 57 g | 20 each | |
| water | | 762 g | 3 1/4 cups + 2 tablespoons | 810 mL |
| daikon radish, peeled and cut into 1/8-inch (30-mm) julienne | 1 lb., 1 oz. | 482 g | 1 each | |
| scallions, finely sliced | 6 oz. | 170 g | 16 each | |
| ground cayenne | 1/4 oz. | 8 g | 1 tablespoon + 1 teaspoon | 20 mL |
| sugar | | | 2 teaspoons | 10 mL |
| anchovy fillets, drained, patted dry, and minced | 2 oz. | 57 g | one 2-oz. can | |
| kosher salt | 1 oz. | 28 g | 2 tablespoons | 30 mL |
| all-purpose flour | 1/2 oz. | 15 g | 2 tablespoons | 30 mL |

© kyogo7002

© kyogo7002

**TWIST ON THE CLASSIC**

- Replace the cabbage with any vegetable desired.
- For an interesting variation on mashed potatoes, add finely chopped *Kimch'i* to the potatoes.

① Trim bottom of the cabbage, keeping leaves attached. Quarter head lengthwise.

② Wash carefully, removing all dirt from between leaves.

③ Combine 1 1/2 quarts (1.4 L) water and 1 3/4 oz., or 3 tablespoons (50 g) salt in bowl, add cabbage, place plate and weight on top to prevent floating. Soak 4 hours.

④ Place ginger and garlic in blender or food processor fitted with knife blade, add 3 tablespoons (43 g or 45 mL) of the water, process until smooth.

⑤ Mix radish, ginger-garlic paste, scallions, cayenne, sugar, and anchovies in bowl. Add 1 oz. or 2 tablespoons (28 g) salt, mix. Set stuffing aside.

⑥ Place flour in small pan, whisk in 3 cups (720 mL) of the water, bring to simmer, cook gently until slightly thickened.

⑦ Remove cabbage from salt water, rinse several times, drain.

⑧ Place some stuffing between each cabbage leaf, place stuffed cabbage quarters in nonreactive bowl or other container, pour flour water over cabbage.

⑨ Cover, leave at room temperature for 2 days, until fermented, then refrigerate until needed. Less fermenting time is required in hot weather.

⑩ To serve, slice crossways and serve in bowl with a little fermenting liquid.

# MU SAINGCHAI (KOREA)

## RADISH SALAD

**Number of Servings:** 10
**Serving Size:** 2 oz. (57 g)
**Total Yield:** 1 lb., 4 oz. (568 g)

© tanawatpontchour/Fotolia

### TWIST ON THE CLASSIC

Serve this salad as an accompaniment to lamb chops or pork chops.

| INGREDIENTS | WEIGHT | | VOLUME | |
| --- | --- | --- | --- | --- |
| | U.S. | METRIC | U.S. | METRIC |
| **Dressing:** | | | | |
| soy sauce | | 28 g | 2 tablespoons | 30 mL |
| sesame oil | | | 2 teaspoons | 10 mL |
| rice vinegar | | 15 g | 1 tablespoon | 15 mL |
| sugar | | | 2 teaspoons | 10 mL |
| sesame seeds, toasted and ground | 1/4 oz. | 8 g | 1 tablespoon | 15 mL |
| hot red chili, seeded and minced | | | 1/2 each, or to taste | |
| daikon radish, peeled and cut into julienne | 12 oz. | 340 g | 1 each | |
| apple, peeled, cored, and cut into julienne | 4 1/2 oz. | 128 g | 1 each | |
| scallions, thin slices | 2 oz. | 57 g | 2 each | |

1. Combine all dressing ingredients (soy sauce, sesame oil, vinegar, sugar, sesame seeds, and chili) in small nonreactive bowl.
2. Combine radish, apple, and scallions in nonreactive bowl, pour in dressing, toss to mix. Correct seasonings.
3. Cover, chill before serving.

# SUKJU NAMUL (KOREA)

## BEAN SPROUT SALAD

**Number of Servings:** 15
**Serving Size:** 2 oz. (57 g)
**Total Yield:** 1 lb., 14 oz. (851 g)

**Cooking Method:** Boil

Ben Fink © Dorling Kindersley

### TWIST ON THE CLASSIC

Use this salad as a topping for a lettuce salad.

| INGREDIENTS | WEIGHT | | VOLUME | |
| --- | --- | --- | --- | --- |
| | U.S. | METRIC | U.S. | METRIC |
| bean sprouts, mung bean or other | 1 lb., 6 oz. | 624 g | 6 cups | 1.4 L |
| **Dressing:** | | | | |
| soy sauce | | 86 g | 1/4 cup + 2 tablespoons | 90 mL |
| sesame oil | | | 1 tablespoon + 1 teaspoon | 20 mL |
| rice vinegar | | 28 g | 2 tablespoons | 30 mL |
| garlic, smashed and minced | 1/4 oz. | 8 g | 2 cloves | |
| sugar | 3/4 oz. | 22 g | 1 tablespoon + 1 teaspoon | 20 mL |
| pepper | | | 1/4 teaspoon | 2 mL |
| ground cayenne | | | 1/4 to 1/2 teaspoon | 2 to 3 mL |
| scallions, finely chopped | 4 oz. | 114 g | 4 each | |

1. Bring saucepan of water to boil over high heat, add bean sprouts, cook 1 minute.
2. Drain bean sprouts in colander, rinse with cold water until cold, drain well, place in nonreactive bowl.
3. In small bowl, combine all dressing ingredients, stir well to dissolve sugar, pour over sprouts.
4. Mix well, chill. Correct seasonings. Serve.

## OI NAMUL (KOREA)

### CUCUMBER SALAD

**Number of Servings:** 8
**Serving Size:** 2 oz. (57 g)
**Total Yield:** 1 lb., 1 oz. (482 g)

| | WEIGHT | | VOLUME | |
|---|---|---|---|---|
| **INGREDIENTS** | **U.S.** | **METRIC** | **U.S.** | **METRIC** |
| cucumbers, peeled, seeded, and thinly sliced | 1 lb., 11 oz. | 766 g | 2 large | |
| kosher salt | 1/2 oz. | 15 g | 1 tablespoon | 15 mL |
| water | | 227 g | 1 cup | 240 mL |
| **Dressing:** | | | | |
| rice vinegar | | 28 g | 2 tablespoons | 30 mL |
| sugar | | | 1 teaspoon | 5 mL |
| ground cayenne | | | 1/4 teaspoon | 2 mL |
| garlic, minced | | | 1 clove | |
| scallion, minced | 1 oz. | 28 g | 1 each | |
| sesame seeds, toasted, and ground | 1/4 oz. | 8 g | 1 tablespoon | 15 mL |

1. Place cucumbers in nonreactive bowl, sprinkle with salt, add water.
2. Soak for 15 minutes, drain well.
3. Combine all dressing ingredients, pour over cucumbers, mix well.
4. Chill well, correct seasonings. Serve.

Pearson Education/PH College

> **TWIST ON THE CLASSIC**
>
> Mix tomato slices into this salad. Also, pair this with grilled, baked, or poached salmon.

## BULGOGI (KOREA)

### FIERY BEEF

**Note:** Allow time to marinate the meat overnight.

**Number of Servings:** 8
**Serving Size:** 4 oz. (114 g) meat
    1 1/4 oz. (36 g) sauce
**Total Yield:** 2 lb., 3 oz. (994 g) meat
    11 oz. (312 g) sauce
**Food Balance:** Spicy/protein
**Wine Style:** Low-oaked whites and soft reds
**Example:** Beringer Founders' Estate Sauvignon Blanc or Shiraz

**Cooking Method:** Grill

> **TWIST ON THE CLASSIC**
>
> Serve this meat without its sauce on top of a Caesar salad.

> Translated, Bulgogi means "fire meat." The name derives from the preparation of this dish—first marinated and then grilled over fire.

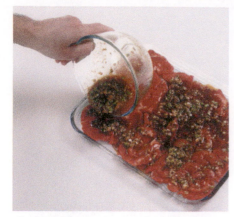

*Marinating beef*

David Murray and Jules Selmes © Dorling Kindersley

*Grilling beef*

David Murray and Jules Selmes © Dorling Kindersley

David Murray and Jules Selmes © Dorling Kindersley

| INGREDIENTS | WEIGHT U.S. | WEIGHT METRIC | VOLUME U.S. | VOLUME METRIC |
|---|---|---|---|---|
| beef, rump, top round, or fillet, sliced 1/8 inch (30 mm) thick on diagonal | 2 lb. | 908 g | | |
| **Marinade:** | | | | |
| soy sauce | | 86 g | 1/4 cup + 2 tablespoons | 90 mL |
| rice vinegar | | 57 g | 1/4 cup | 60 mL |
| sesame oil | | 57 g | 1/4 cup | 60 mL |
| sesame seeds, toasted and ground | 1/2 oz. | 15 g | 2 tablespoons | 30 mL |
| sugar | | | 1 1/2 teaspoons | 8 mL |
| scallions, minced | 1 1/2 oz. | 43 g | 4 each | |
| garlic, minced | 1 oz. | 28 g | 2 tablespoons, or 8 to 10 cloves | 30 mL |
| pepper | | | 3/4 teaspoon | 4 mL |
| sesame seeds | 1 oz. | 28 g | 3 tablespoons | 45 mL |
| **Sauce:** | | | | |
| soy sauce | | 86 g | 1/4 cup + 2 tablespoons | 90 mL |
| sesame oil | | | 1 tablespoon + 1 teaspoon | 20 mL |
| water | | 57 g | 1/4 cup | 60 mL |
| rice wine | | 57 g | 1/4 cup | 60 mL |
| sesame seeds, toasted and ground | 1/2 oz. | 15 g | 2 tablespoons | 30 mL |
| scallions, minced | 1/2 oz. | 15 g | 1 each | |
| garlic, smashed and minced | 1/4 oz. | 8 g | 2 cloves | |
| sugar | 3/4 oz. | 22 g | 1 tablespoon + 1 teaspoon | 20 mL |

**Accompaniment:**
cooked white rice

### MARINADE:

1. Place beef in stainless steel or nonreactive bowl, add marinade ingredients, mixing well into meat.
2. Cover and marinate in refrigerator overnight or 24 hours, mix occasionally.

### SAUCE:

1. Mix all sauce ingredients together in small bowl. Mix well to dissolve sugar.
2. Divide sauce into eight small bowls.

### ASSEMBLY:

1. Preheat broiler or grill.
2. Drain meat, grill meat in broiler or over coals for 25 to 40 seconds on each side, until done.
3. Serve with rice and sauce.

# CHAP CHAE (KOREA)

## CELLOPHANE NOODLES WITH BEEF AND VEGETABLES

**Note:** To roast sesame seeds: Toast seeds in a pan over medium-high heat until popping and beginning to smell. For this recipe, then grind seeds in processor or mortar and pestle.

**Number of Servings:** 11  
**Serving Size:** 7 oz. (199 g)  
**Total Yield:** 5 lb. (2.3 kg)  
**Food Balance:** Protein/sweet  
**Wine Style:** Off-dry or low-oaked whites or soft reds  
**Example:** Beringer Founders' Estate Pinot Grigio or Shiraz

**Cooking Method:** Stir-fry (sauté)

Clive Streeter and Patrick McLeavy  
© Dorling Kindersley

| INGREDIENTS | WEIGHT | | VOLUME | |
| --- | --- | --- | --- | --- |
| | U.S. | METRIC | U.S. | METRIC |
| cellophane noodles (mung bean threads) | 4 oz. | 114 g | | |
| **Marinade:** | | | | |
| sugar | 1 oz. | 28 g | 2 tablespoons | 30 mL |
| soy sauce | | 57 g | 1/4 cup | 60 mL |
| scallions | 1/2 oz. | 15 g | 2 tablespoons | 30 mL |
| garlic, minced | 1/4 oz. | 8 g | 2 cloves | |
| sesame oil | | 28 g | 2 tablespoons | 30 mL |
| pepper | | | 1/2 teaspoon | 3 mL |
| beef steak or fillet, sliced 1/8 inch (30 mm) thick across the grain | 1 lb. | 454 g | | |
| dried Chinese mushrooms | 1/2 oz. | 15 g | 12 each | |
| fresh spinach, thick stems removed | 10 oz. package | 284 g | 1 package | |
| sesame oil | | 28 g | 2 tablespoons | 30 mL |
| onions, thin slices | 8 oz. | 227 g | 2 medium | |
| carrots, julienne, in 3-inch (8-cm) lengths | 8 oz. | 227 g | 4 each | |
| garlic, minced | 1/4 oz. | 8 g | 2 cloves | |
| bamboo shoots, julienne | 8 oz. | 227 g | 1 1/2 cups | 360 mL |
| Chinese cabbage, julienne | 8 oz. | 227 g | 6 leaves | |
| **Sauce:** | | | | |
| sesame seeds, roasted, ground | 1 oz. | 28 g | 3 tablespoons | 45 mL |
| soy sauce | | 114 g | 1/2 cup | 120 mL |
| sugar | 1 oz. | 28 g | 2 tablespoons | 30 mL |
| sesame oil | | 28 to 57 g | 2 to 4 tablespoons | 30 to 60 mL |
| water | | 114 to 227 g | 1/2 to 1 cup | 120 to 240 mL |

**Accompaniment:**  
cooked rice

① Place cellophane noodles in bowl, cover with warm water, soak for 30 to 45 minutes, until soft. Drain, cut into 3-inch (8-cm) lengths.

② Mix marinade ingredients—sugar, soy sauce, scallions, garlic, sesame oil, and pepper—in nonreactive bowl, add meat, mix, refrigerate for 30 minutes.

③ Meanwhile, cover mushrooms with warm water, soak for 30 minutes, remove from water, slice thinly. Set aside until needed.

### TWIST ON THE CLASSIC

Toss the *Chap Chae* with pasta to create an Italian/Korean entrée.

© paul_brighton

4. Wash spinach, cook in skillet about 1 or 2 minutes, until soft. Remove from skillet, rinse with cold water, squeeze to remove excess water, cut into strips. Set aside until needed.

5. Heat sesame oil in wok or skillet over high heat, add onion, sauté, stirring, 1 minute, add carrot and garlic, sauté, stirring, 2 or 3 minutes, add bamboo shoots, cabbage, and spinach.

6. Remove vegetables to bowl, add beef and mushrooms to pan, cook until meat is just done, about 1 or 2 minutes.

7. Remove meat to bowl with vegetables, turn heat to medium-low.

8. Add sauce ingredients to wok, mix well. Turn heat to medium, add cellophane noodles, then meat and vegetables from bowl.

9. Correct seasonings, and serve with rice.

---

## TWIST ON THE CLASSIC

- For a low-fat version, substitute chicken, fish, or tofu for the pork belly.
- Use the ingredients from *samgyupsal gui* in a burrito shell to create a Mexican version of this Korean dish.

Koreans love barbecues and this popular dish appears frequently. When everyone at the table participates in the grilling (done on a grill in the middle of the table), it serves as perfect party food!

For service, present lettuce leaves and all ingredients to diners, so they can prepare their own wraps.

- One pound of raw pork belly yields about 6 1/4 oz. (178 g) when cooked.
- Cooks provide a wide range of ingredients for these lettuce wraps. Besides the ingredients listed above, some use sliced raw garlic or carrot.
- Some dip the cooked pork belly pieces in sesame oil flavored with salt and pepper.
- Serve one or two lettuce wraps for an appetizer.

# SAMGYUPSAL GUI (KOREA)

## GRILLED PORK BELLY

**Number of Servings:** 8
**Serving Size:** 3 lettuce wraps
**Scaling:** per lettuce wrap:

**Cooking Method:** Grill

1 oz. (28 g) cooked pork belly
1/4 oz. (8 g, 1 teaspoon, 5 mL) *Ssamjang*

**Wine Style:** Full-bodied white wine with high minerality and well integrated oak. Possible grape varietals are Riesling, Gruner Veltliner, Sauvignon Blanc.
**Example:** Riesling GG "Felsenberg", Donhoff 2010 (Nahe/Germany)

| | WEIGHT | | VOLUME | |
|---|---|---|---|---|
| **INGREDIENTS** | **U.S.** | **METRIC** | **U.S.** | **METRIC** |
| pork belly without rind, 1/8-inch (30-mm) slices | 4 lb., 4 oz. | 1.9 kg | | |
| garlic, peeled | 2 1/2 oz. or as desired | 71 g or as desired | 10 cloves or as desired | |
| lettuce leaves, Boston bib, leaf, or red leaf | | | | |
| *Ssamjang,* recipe follows | | | | |
| rice, cooked | | | | |
| *kimch'i* | | | | |
| cucumber, Korean, kirby, or European, sliced into narrow sticks about 3-inches (8-cm) long | | | | |
| green onions, sliced 1/8-inch (30-mm) thick | | | | |
| mild green chillies, sliced | | | | |

1. If using grill on table, cut pork belly into 3-inch (8-cm) pieces. If grilling on large grill, use the whole strip and cut into pieces after grilling. Grill pork belly until cooked and starting to brown a bit around edges.

2. If using table grill, place garlic or garlic slices on grill. If using large grill, bake whole garlic clove in 400 degrees (205°C) oven until starting to brown, then cut into slices.

© portokalis

3. Take lettuce leaf in hand. Spread 1/4 oz. (8 g, 1 teaspoon, 5 mL) *Ssamjang* on lettuce. Place a little rice and 1 oz. (28 g), about 3 pieces, pork belly over *Ssamjang*.

4. Put a little of all or whichever ingredients desired over the rice: cooked garlic slices, *kimch'i*, cucumber, green onions, chillies. Wrap the lettuce around the filling and eat immediately.

---

## SSAMJANG (KOREA)

### SPICY DIPPING SAUCE

**Number of Servings:** 24
**Serving Size:** 1/4 oz. (8 g, 1 teaspoon, or 5 mL)
**Total Yield:** 6 3/4 oz. (191 g)
**Wine Style:** Late harvest wine from a cool climate region. Possible grape varietals are Riesling, Chenin Blanc.
**Example:** Riesling Spatlese "Wehlener Sonnenuhr" 2012, J.J. Prum (Mosel/Germany)

| | WEIGHT | | VOLUME | |
| --- | --- | --- | --- | --- |
| **INGREDIENTS** | **U.S.** | **METRIC** | **U.S.** | **METRIC** |
| *doenjang* or *miso* | 3 oz. | 86 g | 1/4 cup | 60 mL |
| *gochujang* | 1 1/2 oz. | 43 g | 2 tablespoons | 30 mL |
| sesame oil | | 15 g | 1 tablespoon | 15 mL |
| soy sauce | | 15 g | 2 teaspoons | 10 mL |
| garlic, peeled, smashed | 1/4 oz. | 8 g | 1 clove | |
| scallion, minced | 1 oz. | 28 g | 2 each | |
| sesame seeds, toasted lightly | 1/4 oz. | 8 g | 2 teaspoons | 10 mL |
| water for thinning, if needed | | | | |

1. In nonreactive bowl, mix *doenjang*, *gochujang*, sesame oil, soy sauce, garlic, scallion, and sesame seeds. Whisk to combine thoroughly.

2. Add a little water if too thick (this will depend on the thickness of the *doenjang* and *gochujang*). Refrigerate until needed.

© paul_brighton

*Doenjang* is the Korean version of Japanese *miso*. *Gochujang* is Korean chili paste. Both of these items are available at an Oriental grocery. *Miso* also is available in health food stores.

---

## TEMPURA (JAPAN)

### DEEP-FRIED, BATTERED VEGETABLES, SEAFOOD, POULTRY, AND/OR MEAT

**Note:** Any variety of vegetables, seafood, or meat becomes *tempura*. Do not prepare *tempura* batter very far in advance, and keep it very cold.

**Number of Servings:** 8
**Total Yield:** 1 lb., 14 oz. (851 g) batter
**Food Balance:** Protein
**Wine Style:** Off-dry or low-oaked whites or soft reds
**Example:** Château St. Jean Pinot Blanc or Pinot Noir

**Cooking Method:** Boil, deep-fry

| INGREDIENTS | WEIGHT | | VOLUME | |
|---|---|---|---|---|
| | U.S. | METRIC | U.S. | METRIC |
| **Dipping Sauce:** | | | | |
| *dashi* broth | | 454 g | 2 cups | 480 mL |
| soy sauce (*sho-yu*) | | 86 g | 1/4 cup + 2 tablespoons | 90 mL |
| *sake* | | 86 g | 1/4 cup + 2 tablespoons | 90 mL |
| sugar | 1/2 to 3/4 oz. | 15 to 22 g | 1 tablespoon + 1 teaspoon | 20 mL |
| daikon radish, grated | 6 oz. | 170 g | | |
| **Batter:** | | | | |
| eggs | 3 1/2 oz. | 104 g | 2 each | |
| water, cold | | 454 g | 2 cups | 480 mL |
| all-purpose flour, sifted | 7 1/2 oz. | 213 g | 1 1/2 cups | 360 mL |
| cornstarch | 3 oz. | 86 g | 1/2 cup | 120 mL |

oil, for deep frying
flour, for dredging
assorted vegetables cut into slices, strips, or florets: peppers, broccoli, pea pods, green beans, carrots, potatoes, sweet potatoes, onion, and/or mushrooms
shrimp, peeled and deveined
boneless and skinless
  chicken, cut into strips

*Adding flour and cornstarch to egg mixture*
Richard Embery © Pearson Education/PH College

## DIPPING SAUCE:

① Combine *dashi*, soy sauce, *sake*, and sugar in pan, bring to boil, reduce heat and simmer 1 minute.
② Remove from heat, reserve.
③ Place 3/4 oz. (22 g) daikon mound in each dipping bowl. Pour reserved liquid over daikon in individual bowls.

## BATTER:

① Mix eggs and water in bowl.
② Sift together flour and cornstarch in small bowl, add to egg mixture.
③ Stir a few times with fork, mix only until combined (some lumps should remain). Refrigerate until needed.

*Dipping vegetable in batter*
Richard Embery © Pearson Education/PH College

*Frying food items*
Richard Embery © Pearson Education/PH College

Richard Embery © Pearson Education/PH College

## FRYING:

1. Heat oil in wok or deep skillet until 360 degrees (180°C). Use enough oil to cover food items.
2. Lightly dredge each vegetable, shrimp, and chicken strip with flour, then coat with batter.
3. Place a few items in hot oil—do not add too many items at once or temperature of oil will lower too much.
4. Fry until golden and food item is properly cooked (vegetables should still be crisp, and meat should reach proper internal temperature). Remove loose pieces of batter from wok.
5. Serve immediately, accompanied by dipping sauce.

# DAK JIM (KOREA)

## STEWED CHICKEN

**Note:** This dish does not contain a lot of sauce. If more is desired, increase the liquids and add some of the water from soaking the mushrooms.

**Number of Servings:** 12
**Serving Size:** 8 oz. (227 g)
**Total Yield:** 6 lb., 4 1/2 oz. (2.9 kg)
**Food Balance:** Protein/spicy
**Wine Style:** Off-dry or low-oaked whites or soft reds
**Example:** Rosemount Riesling or Shiraz

**Cooking Method:** Braise

Wizdata1 © Shutterstock

| INGREDIENTS | WEIGHT U.S. | METRIC | VOLUME U.S. | METRIC |
|---|---|---|---|---|
| soy sauce | | 114 g | 1/2 cup | 120 mL |
| sesame oil | | 57 g | 1/4 cup | 60 mL |
| garlic, smashed and minced | 1 1/2 oz. | 43 g | 2 tablespoons | 30 mL |
| red pepper flakes | | | 1 teaspoon | 5 mL, or to taste |
| scallions, minced | 4 oz. | 114 g | 8 each | |
| fresh ginger, peeled and minced | 1 oz. | 28 g | 2 tablespoons | 30 mL |
| chicken, bone in, whole, breasts, or thighs, washed and cut into 3-inch (8-cm) pieces | 5 lb., 7 oz. | 2.5 kg | 2 whole chickens | |
| dried mushrooms | 1 oz. | 28 g | 12 each | |

**Accompaniments:**

cooked rice
*kimch'i*

> ### TWIST ON THE CLASSIC
>
> For a vegetarian alternative, substitute tofu for the chicken or prepare this dish as a mushroom stew by omitting the chicken and using a number of varieties of mushrooms.

1. Combine soy sauce, sesame oil, garlic, red pepper flakes, scallions, and ginger in nonreactive bowl or pan. Add chicken, coat well with mixture. Cover and refrigerate for 2 to 3 hours.
2. Meanwhile, cover mushrooms with warm water and soak for 30 minutes. Drain mushrooms and reserve the liquid in case the dish needs more liquid. Cut mushrooms into thin strips. Set aside until needed.
3. Transfer chicken and marinade to pan. Cover and cook over medium-low heat until chicken reaches proper internal temperature, about 25 minutes. The cooking time depends on the cut of meat: dark meat requires more cooking time than white meat. Add mushrooms to chicken after 15 minutes of cooking.
4. Correct seasonings. Serve with rice and *kimch'i*.

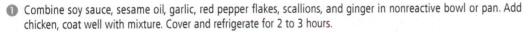

# SAENGSUN CHIGAE (KOREA)

## FISH, SHELLFISH, AND TOFU STEW

**Number of Servings:** 9  
**Serving Size:** 9 oz. (256 g)  
**Total Yield:** 5 lb., 5 oz. (2.4 kg)  
**Food Balance:** Spicy/protein  
**Wine Style:** Off-dry or low-oaked whites or soft reds  
**Example:** Cellar #8 Chardonnay or Pinot Noir

**Cooking Method:** Braise

Wizdata1 © Shutterstock

### TWIST ON THE CLASSIC

Replace any of the protein ingredients. Omit the beef and add more fish and seafood for a nonmeat dish.

| INGREDIENTS | WEIGHT U.S. | WEIGHT METRIC | VOLUME U.S. | VOLUME METRIC |
|---|---|---|---|---|
| dried Chinese mushrooms | 1/2 oz. | 15 g | 10 each | |
| tender beef, sliced very thinly | 4 oz. | 114 g | | |
| zucchini or yellow squash, 1/3-inch (3/4-cm) rounds | 5 oz. | 142 g | 1 small | |
| garlic, minced | 1/4 oz. | 8 g | 2 cloves | |
| soy sauce | | 15 g | 1 tablespoon | 15 mL |
| sesame oil | | | 1 teaspoon | 5 mL |
| hot bean paste* | 2 3/4 oz. | 78 g | 1/4 cup | 60 mL |
| fish fillets, haddock, cod, or scrod, cut across grain into 3 or 4 pieces | 1 lb. | 454 g | | |
| scallions, cut into 2-inch (5-cm) pieces | 1 1/2 oz. | 43 g | 4 each | |
| green bell pepper, 1/2-inch (1 1/3-cm) cubes | 2 oz. | 57 g | 1/4 each | |
| red bell pepper, 1/2-inch (1 1/3-cm) cubes | 2 oz. | 57 g | 1/4 each | |
| clams | | | 6 to 8 small | |
| tofu, 1-inch (2 1/2-cm) cubes | 1 lb., 2 oz. | 511 g | 1 package | |
| oil | | | 1 teaspoon | 5 mL |
| water | | 851 g | 3 3/4 cups | 900 mL |

**Accompaniment:**  
cooked rice

*If hot bean paste is unavailable, add 1 1/2 tablespoons (23 g) paprika, 1 teaspoon (5 mL) cayenne, and 1 tablespoon (15 g) sugar to 1/4 cup (59 g) bean paste.

1. Soak mushrooms in warm water for 30 minutes, drain, cut into quarters.
2. Combine mushrooms, beef, zucchini, garlic, soy sauce, sesame oil, and bean paste in nonreactive bowl. Refrigerate until needed.
3. Place fish, scallions, and peppers in bowl, refrigerate until needed.
4. Scrub clams well under cold running water, place in bowl, add tofu, refrigerate until needed.
5. In wide pot that can be brought to table, heat oil over medium-high heat until hot, add mushroom and beef mixture, stir-fry for 2 minutes.
6. Add water, bring to simmer, add fish mixture.
7. Bring to simmer, cover, simmer 5 minutes.
8. Add clams and tofu, making sure clams are submerged in liquid.
9. Cover, cook on medium-low about 5 minutes, until clams open. Correct seasonings. Serve over rice.

## SALMON TERIYAKI (JAPAN)

**Note:** *Teriyaki* sauce can be used with any desired fish (although fatty fish varieties work best), chicken, or meat. Basically, it entails marinating in the sauce, broiling, then brushing with more of the sauce while broiling.

**Number of Servings:** 8
**Serving Size:** about 4 oz. fish (114 g), or 1 salmon steak
**Total Yield:** about 2 lb. (908 g)
**Food Balance:** Sweet/protein
**Wine Style:** Off-dry or low-oaked whites or soft reds
**Example:** Castello di Gabbiano Pinot Grigio or Chianti

**Cooking Method:** Boil, broil or grill

Pearson Education/PH College

| INGREDIENTS | WEIGHT | | VOLUME | |
|---|---|---|---|---|
| | U.S. | METRIC | U.S. | METRIC |
| **Marinade:** | | | | |
| *sake* | | 170 g | 3/4 cup | 180 mL |
| soy sauce (*shōyu*) | | 170 g | 3/4 cup | 180 mL |
| sugar | 3 1/2 oz. | 104 g | 1/4 cup + 3 tablespoons | 105 mL |
| fresh ginger | | | two 1/2-inch slices | two 1 1/3-cm slices |
| garlic, minced | | | 1 clove | |
| salmon steaks | about 3 lb. | 1.4 kg | 8 small | |

**Accompaniments:**
cooked rice
sauce, if desired

1. Mix all marinade ingredients (sake, soy sauce, sugar, ginger, and garlic) in saucepan, bring to boil, lower heat, simmer for 5 minutes.
2. Remove from heat, cool to room temperature.
3. Cover fish with marinade in nonreactive bowl, cover and refrigerate for 30 minutes.
4. Preheat grill or broiler.
5. Cook fish for 5 or 10 minutes on each side, depending on thickness of fish, brushing with marinade three or four times while cooking. Fish will develop rich brown glaze.
6. Serve immediately with rice and extra sauce, if desired.

© SK

## AGDASHI DOFU, KINOKO-AN (JAPAN)

### TOFU WITH MUSHROOM SAUCE

**Number of Servings:** 8
**Serving Size:** 2 pieces tofu with 3 1/4 oz. (92 g) sauce
**Total Yield:** 1 lb., 11 oz. (766 g) tofu
        1 lb., 11 oz. (766 g) sauce
**Wine Style:** Light, crisp white wine fermented in stainless steel. Possible grape varietals are Riesling, Gruner Veltliner, Sauvignon Blanc and Neuburger.
**Example:** Riesling "Seeberg" 2002, Loimer (Kamptal/Austria)

**Cooking Method:** Deep-fry, boil

©JJAVA

## TWIST ON THE CLASSIC

Prepare this dish using a combination of proteins. For example, use an assortment of fish and/or seafood with the tofu or combine ground or thinly sliced pork with the tofu.

Use one type of mushroom or a combination. If using enoki mushrooms, add just before the *katakuriko* mixture. (They are so thin and delicate, the 1 minute is too much cooking time.)

| INGREDIENTS | WEIGHT | | VOLUME | |
| --- | --- | --- | --- | --- |
| | U.S. | METRIC | U.S. | METRIC |
| tofu, firm | 1 lb., 14 oz. | 851 g | 2 each 15-oz. blocks | 2 each 426-g blocks |
| *katakuriko* (potato starch) | 1/2 oz. | 15 g | 1 tablespoon | 15 mL |
| oil, peanut or other vegetable, for deep-frying | | | | |
| water | | 28 g | 2 tablespoons | 30 mL |
| *katakuriko* (potato starch), for dredging | | | | |
| *dashi*, recipe on page 396 | | 397 g | 1 3/4 cups | 420 mL |
| soy sauce | | 57 g | 1/4 cup | 60 mL |
| *mirin* | | 57 g | 1/4 cup | 60 mL |
| carrot, julienne | 2 oz. | 57 g | 1 small to medium | |
| onion, thinly sliced | 2 oz. | 57 g | 1 small | |
| mushrooms, wild, shitake or varieties of choice, julienne | 7 oz. | 199 g | | |

**Garnish:**

daikon radish, grated
scallions, sliced 1/8-inch (1/3-cm) thick
ginger, minced

1. Wrap tofu in clean nonterry cloth towel or paper towel, place on board slanted into sink or large bowl, and place weight on top of tofu. (Place into refrigerator if kitchen is hot.) Allow to drain for 30 to 45 minutes.

2. Meanwhile, mix *katakuriko* with water, set aside until needed.

3. Wipe tofu dry, cut into pieces about 2 by 2 3/4 inches (5 by 7 cm). Place on plate covered with paper toweling. Refrigerate until needed.

4. Preheat oven to 275 degrees (135°C) if needed to hold fried tofu before service. Dredge tofu pieces lightly in *katakuriko*. Place oil about 1/2-inch (1 1/3-cm) deep in skillet. Heat until 360 degrees (180°C). Carefully lower tofu into oil, fry for 2 to 3 minutes per side, until golden. Remove from oil, drain, keep warm in oven if not using right away.

5. Place *dashi*, soy sauce, and *mirin* in saucepan over medium heat. Add carrot and onion, cook until almost soft. Add mushrooms, cook 1 more minute. Correct seasonings. Stir in *katakuriko* mixture, stir just until it comes to boil, then remove from heat.

6. Place two pieces of tofu in bowl, top with 3 1/4 oz. (92 g) mushroom sauce. Garnish with daikon, scallions, and ginger. Serve.

## ANPAN (JAPAN)

### SWEET ROLLS FILLED WITH RED BEAN PASTE

**Number of Servings:** 14
**Serving Size:** 1 roll
**Scaling:** 2 oz. (57 g) dough, 1 1/4 oz. (36 g) *anko*
**Total Yield:** 1 lb., 11 1/2 oz. (780 g) dough
**Wine Style:** Dessert wine from botrytis-affected grapes. Possible grape varietals are Sauvignon Blanc, Semillon, Chenin Blanc and Riesling.
**Example:** Ruster Ausbruch 1999, Feiler Artinger (Neusiedlersee/Austria)

**Cooking Method:** Bake

© Arancio

| INGREDIENTS | WEIGHT | | VOLUME | |
|---|---|---|---|---|
| | **U.S.** | **METRIC** | **U.S.** | **METRIC** |
| milk, lukewarm | | 170 g | 3/4 cup | 180 mL |
| sugar | 1 1/4 oz. | 36 g | 3 tablespoons | 45 mL |
| yeast, dry | 1/4 oz. | 8 g | 1 tablespoon | 15 mL |
| bread flour | 14 3/4 oz. | 419 g | 3 cups | 720 mL |
| salt | 1/4 oz. | 8 g | 1 teaspoon | 5 mL |
| eggs (reserve 1/2 of 1 egg) | 3 1/2 oz. | 104 g | 2 each | |
| butter, room temperature | 2 oz. | 57 g | 4 tablespoons or 1/4 cup | 60 mL |
| *anko* (sweet red bean paste) | 1 lb., 2-oz. can | 511-g can | | 60 mL |

**Garnish:**

sesame seeds, black or white

① In mixing bowl of mixer fitted with dough hook, place milk, sugar, and yeast. Mix to combine and allow to sit until foamy, about 5 minutes.

② Add flour, salt, and eggs (reserving half of one egg for the glaze). Mix with dough hook for about 5 to 6 minutes, until dough forms smooth ball.

③ Add butter, knead another 5 minutes. Remove from mixer, cover mixing bowl with damp towel or plastic wrap. Allow to rise until doubled, about 1 hour. Meanwhile, cover sheet pan with parchment paper.

④ Punch down dough. Scale into 2-oz. (57-g) pieces. Roll into ball, place on prepared sheet pan, cover and allow to rise for 20 minutes.

⑤ Place oven rack in center of oven. Preheat oven to 350 degrees (180°C). Take ball of dough, flatten with hands or rolling pin into circle about 3 1/2 to 4 inches (9 to 10 cm) in diameter. Using small scoop, scale *anko* into 1 1/4-oz. (36-g) portions. Place *anko* in center of dough disk. Bring sides together and press firmly to enclose filling and seal it tightly. Place filled roll on prepared sheet pan with seam side down. Repeat with remaining dough.

⑥ Gently press center of each roll with finger to create a dent. (This will eliminate the gap between the dough and the bean paste.) Allow to rise until doubled, 40 to 50 minutes. Mix reserved egg with 1/2 teaspoon (3 mL) water.

⑦ Using a pastry brush, gently apply egg wash to rolls. Sprinkle a few sesame seeds on top. Bake for 15 minutes, until golden. Cool on rack. Eat warm or at room temperature.

## TWIST ON THE CLASSIC

Use this dough to surround any filling. Try a filling of fig paste, poppy seeds, or prune. If savory, reduce the sugar in the bread dough and use with any savory filling like pepperoni and cheese or curried chicken.

The Japanese were introduced to bread by foreigners in the nineteenth century. These rolls were created in the late 1800s.

Made from aduki beans, sweetened red bean paste comes in two varieties.

- *Tsubuan*—chunky red bean paste
- *Koshian*—smooth red bean paste

Some cooks choose smooth, while others prefer chunky for their *anpan*.

---

## KARINTO (JAPAN)

### DEEP-FRIED COOKIES

**Note:** You may want to accompany these cookies with some ice cream or sorbet.

**Number of Servings:** 9
**Serving Size:** 1 1/4 oz. (36 g)
**Total Yield:** 12 oz. (340 g)

**Cooking Method:** Deep-fry

| INGREDIENTS | WEIGHT | | VOLUME | |
|---|---|---|---|---|
| | **U.S.** | **METRIC** | **U.S.** | **METRIC** |
| all-purpose flour | 5 1/4 oz. | 149 g | 1 cup | 240 mL, plus more for rolling out dough |
| baking powder | | | 1 teaspoon | 5 mL |
| salt | | | dash | |
| white sugar | 3/4 oz | 22 g | 1 tablespoon + 1 1/2 teaspoons | 23 mL |

## TWIST ON THE CLASSIC

Using caramelized sugar, stick four or five cookies together in a mound, and serve with a scoop of caramel or toasted pecan ice cream.

© fuchi

| INGREDIENTS | WEIGHT | | VOLUME | |
|---|---|---|---|---|
| | **U.S.** | **METRIC** | **U.S.** | **METRIC** |
| egg | 1 3/4 oz. | 50 g | 1 each | |
| milk | | 43 g | 3 tablespoons | 45 mL |
| oil, for frying | | | | |
| **Icing:** | | | | |
| brown sugar | 5 oz. | 142 g | 3/4 cup | 180 mL |
| water | | 50 g | 3 tablespoons + 1 1/2 teaspoons | 53 mL |

① Line baking pan with parchment paper or oil it. Set aside until needed. Sift flour, baking powder, salt, and sugar together in bowl.

② Add egg and milk, mix just until well blended and smooth.

③ Lightly flour table, roll out dough 1/16 to 1/8 inch (1/6 to 1/3 cm) thick, cut into strips 1/2 by 2 1/2 inches (1 1/3 by 6 cm).

④ Heat oil for deep-frying (about 360 degrees, 180°C) in wok or frying pan. Add strips of cookie dough, a few at a time so oil temperature does not lower too much.

⑤ Fry until golden on both sides, remove and drain on absorbent paper.

⑥ Mix icing ingredients in saucepan. Heat, without stirring, until thickened and 242 degrees (117°C) on candy thermometer.

⑦ Add cookies (in batches) to sugar, turn over with tongs, remove to parchment-lined or oiled pan.

⑧ Repeat until all cookies are coated. Serve with ice cream or sorbet, if desired.

---

## HOTTEOK (KOREA)

### SWEET PANCAKES

Wizdata1 © Shutterstock

**Note:** Allow time for the dough to rise.

**Note:** Although usually sold by street vendors as Korean snack food, *Hotteok* are a sweet bread-like confection. These are too big to serve two as a dessert portion. If serving two, make them smaller. Try serving them accompanied by a chocolate or raspberry sauce and a scoop of ice cream.

**Number of Servings:** 14  
**Serving Size:** 1  
**Scaling:** 2 oz. (57 g) dough  
　　　　　1/2 oz. (15 g) filling  
**Total Yield:** 14 each  
　　　　　1 lb., 13 1/4 oz. (831 g) dough  
　　　　　7 oz. (199 g) filling

**Cooking Method:** Sauté

| INGREDIENTS | WEIGHT | | VOLUME | |
|---|---|---|---|---|
| | **U.S.** | **METRIC** | **U.S.** | **METRIC** |
| **Dough:** | | | | |
| water, lukewarm | | 114 g | 1/2 cup | 120 mL |
| sugar | | | 1/2 teaspoon | 3 mL |
| granulated yeast | | | 1 teaspoon | 5 mL |
| all-purpose flour | 1 lb., 3/4 oz. | 476 g | 3 cups | 720 mL |
| salt | | | 1/2 teaspoon | 3 mL |
| milk, lukewarm | | 227 g | 1 cup | 240 mL |

| INGREDIENTS | WEIGHT | | VOLUME | |
|---|---|---|---|---|
| | U.S. | METRIC | U.S. | METRIC |
| **Filling:** | | | | |
| brown sugar | 6 oz. | 170 g | 3/4 cup | 180 mL |
| cinnamon | 1/4 oz. | 8 g | 1 1/2 teaspoons | 8 mL |
| walnuts, finely chopped | 1 oz. | 28 g | 3 tablespoons | 45 mL |
| oil, as needed | | | | |

**Accompaniments:**

sauce of choice, chocolate, raspberry, or caramel

ice cream of choice

> **TWIST ON THE CLASSIC**
>
> Instead of filling these with a brown sugar filling, try a savory filling like chili or minced pulled pork.

1. In nonreactive bowl, mix lukewarm water, sugar, and yeast. Set aside for 10 minutes, until foamy.
2. Combine flour and salt in large mixing bowl, make well in center. Pour milk and yeast mixture into well, mix thoroughly with wooden spoon.
3. Cover, place in warm spot, and let rise until doubled, about 3 hours.
4. Meanwhile, mix brown sugar, cinnamon, and walnuts together. Set aside until needed.
5. Punch down dough, divide into 2-oz. (57-g, or desired size) pieces. With oiled hands, pat each piece of dough into thin disk. Place 1/2 oz., 1 tablespoon (15 g), or desired amount of filling in center of disk. Bring dough around filling to cover, and seal dough. (It should look like a smooth ball of dough.)
6. Heat oiled griddle over medium-low heat until hot. Place ball of dough on griddle and cook until set. Turn dough over, flatten with spatula, and continue frying until golden on both sides. It takes a while to cook the disk throughout. Add a little oil as needed. Continue until all disks are fried.
7. Serve warm, accompanied by sauce of choice and ice cream, if desired.

# Vietnam, Thailand, Indonesia, and the Philippines

## >> LEARNING OBJECTIVES

By the end of this chapter, you will be able to:

- Explain how the cuisines of Vietnam, Thailand, Indonesia, and the Philippines differ from other Asian cuisines
- Identify nations that have influenced the cuisines of Vietnam, Thailand, Indonesia, and the Philippines, and discuss the effects of each nation on the cuisine
- Understand how the geography and topography have influenced the cuisines of these countries
- Name prevalent food and flavoring ingredients used in the cuisines of Vietnam, Thailand, Indonesia, and the Philippines
- Prepare a variety of dishes from Vietnam, Thailand, Indonesia, and the Philippines

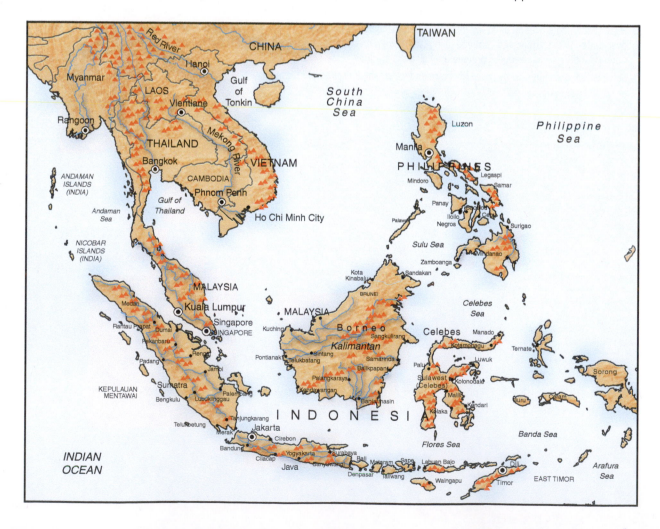

## >> HISTORY

### VIETNAM

Chinese from the north and islanders from the south first settled Vietnam. As a result, Malaysian and Chinese ancestry remains the most common heritage found among the Vietnamese. China ruled this land for about a thousand years, from 100 B.C. until 900 A.D. After that time, Vietnam became an independent country.

In the ensuing years, people from India arrived seeking spices to trade, and people from countries in the West came looking for trade as well as lands to colonize. Vietnam's independence lasted until France gained control in the late sixteenth century. Prior to the French occupation, Vietnam functioned as an agricultural society; however, the French introduced industry to this country. France's rule lasted until World War II, when Japan invaded and conquered Vietnam.

With Japan's defeat at the end of World War II, it lost control of Vietnam. France tried to regain command, but they ended up ruling the southern part while Russia ruled the northern portion of the country. What began as a civil war between the north and south of Vietnam in 1957 escalated into a war involving a number of countries that lasted until the 1970s. As a result of ongoing heavy bombing and fighting that raged throughout the country, Vietnam and the Vietnamese people changed greatly, both physically and emotionally. Many rural residents moved to the cities seeking jobs and/ or shelter. Shelling, bombing, and defoliation destroyed much land and property. Even today, many years after the fighting ended, the strong impact of the Soviet Union and the United States on Vietnam is still evident.

Although influence from the Chinese is prominent in the north, the south exhibits remnants of the Indian and French presence. The Vietnamese adopted chopsticks, stir-fries, bean curd, and a fondness for noodles from the Chinese. Curries are an Indian influence, and the French introduced pâtés, French bread, sauces, and butter into the cuisine of Vietnam.

### THAILAND

People from southeastern Asia migrated to Thailand around 4,500 years ago. Some of the tribes came from settlements on the Yangtze River in the Yunnan province of China. Most Thai claim Malaysian descent with some Chinese and Arabic ancestry. Today, Thailand remains a predominately Buddhist country with beautiful Buddhist temples called *wat* in every village. Because of the large Buddhist population, vegetarianism is common throughout Thailand. In early days, Thais consumed little meat. Even today, they cut meat into thin strips instead of adding large chunks of meat to their curries.

The Europeans entered Thailand in the 1500s; however, they never gained control of this country. In fact, Thailand is one of the few countries in Asia that was never ruled by a Western nation, and other Asian countries rarely conquered it.

Much of the culinary influences evident in Thailand today resulted from its geographic location. Situated less than 100 miles from Vietnam and China, Thailand shares borders with Cambodia, Laos, Myanmar (Burma), and Malaysia. Evidence of culinary traits from these countries appears throughout Thailand.

Middle Easterners introduced cumin and coriander, people from India brought cardamom, and the Portuguese are responsible for bringing chili peppers to Thailand. Europeans brought tomatoes, which they discovered in South America, and tapioca, which originally came from Central America.

*Until 1932, Thailand was known as Siam.*

*Although coconut milk is used extensively in Thai cooking, it was not always the case. Thai cooks added it to recipes because foreigners wanted milk or cream in dishes as was common in their native countries. Today, almost all curries contain coconut milk.*

## INDONESIA

Known as the Spice Islands, Indonesia attracted traders from India, Arabia, and Holland seeking spices. People from India arrived about 1 A.D. They introduced eggplants, cucumbers, curries, Hinduism, and Buddhism.

The Indonesians learned about *kebabs* from the Arabs. Applying their own culinary slant, the *kebabs* became *satay*, skewered marinated meats that are grilled and served with a peanut dipping sauce.

In addition to luring traders with its spices, Indonesia served as an important port on the trade route. Sailors and traders from all of the European powers used the port, and they left their religious and culinary mark on Indonesia.

Unlike Thailand, Indonesia has been controlled by many countries. At various times during its history, the Chinese, Indians, Portuguese, Dutch, and British ruled this nation. The Europeans introduced peanuts, chili peppers, avocados, pineapples, tomatoes, pumpkin, squash, and even Christianity to Indonesia. The Chinese brought the technique of stir-frying and a variety of vegetables.

The Portuguese gained control in the 1500s, the Dutch conquered in the 1670s, and the French and British ruled for a while in the 1800s until the Dutch again took over. Dutch dominance lasted until the Japanese seized control of the country during World War II, but Indonesia finally achieved independence in 1945. Each of these ruling countries also had culinary and other influences on Indonesia.

Dutch settlers developed the well-known *rijsttafel*, literally "rice table." This opulent display of rice and many different dishes required numerous servants to prepare and serve. Without the class structure that supported the keeping of so many servants, the rice table no longer exists as it once did. Today, the *rijsttafel* is more like a buffet.

## PHILIPPINES

*Spanish explorers named the Philippines after the king of Spain, King Philip.*

At least 30,000 years ago, Aborigines inhabited the islands of the Philippines. Malays came to the islands 20,000 years ago. According to evidence, people living in the Philippines interacted with residents of Indonesia and other countries in Southeast Asia during prehistoric times.

Until the arrival of the Spanish in the sixteenth century, Filipinos consumed what they caught from the sea, what they hunted, and what they gathered or planted. The forests provided abundant game, the oceans yielded a wealth of fish and seafood, and rice paddies produced plenty of rice.

In the 1000s, the Chinese moved to the Philippines and established colonies. They introduced the cooking techniques of stir-frying and deep-frying as well as foods like soybeans, tofu, soy sauce, and various Chinese vegetables. In addition to the Chinese, people from Malaysia, the Middle East, and India came to the Philippines to trade. Each group left influences on the cuisine. Malaysians brought a wide range of spices and a variety of stews.

*Islamic Malaysia, Buddhist China, and Catholic Spain all had culinary influences on the Philippines. For example, Islamic followers do not eat pork, many Buddhists are vegetarians, and Catholics observe days when meat is forbidden.*

In 1521, Spanish and Portuguese explorers landed in the Philippines. The Spanish ruled these islands from 1565 until the Spanish-American War in 1898. As a result of this hard-fought, bloody war, America gained control of the Philippines until the Japanese occupied it during World War II. In 1946, the Philippines finally became an independent country.

Besides building cities and towns, the Spanish united the Philippines as one country. Shortly after settling in the Philippines, Spaniards introduced Catholicism. Today, Catholicism is the most prevalent religion, although many Filipinos follow the Islamic, Buddhist, or Hindu faith.

For the Spanish, the Philippines served as a good place to stop on the way to China. It became a trade center, which gave these islands access to a plethora of foods, spices, and products from faraway locations. The Spanish introduced new foods from Mexico and the Americas, including hot peppers, corn, squashes, tomatoes, potatoes,

**criollo** Term for person of Spanish descent born in the Philippines

**mestizo** Term for person of Spanish and Malaysian descent born in the Philippines

tropical fruits and vegetables, peanuts, cashews, and chocolate. They planted sugar and other crops that thrived in the tropical climate of the Philippines. Because of the strong Spanish influence, Filipino food uses fewer hot spices and intense flavorings than food of the rest of Southeast Asia.

When the Suez Canal opened in the early 1800s, travel between Spain and the Philippines became much easier. This allowed easier travel to the islands for Europeans, and many came to the Philippines.

## >> TOPOGRAPHY

### VIETNAM

Vietnam lies in Southeast Asia, to the south of China. With the South China Sea bordering on its eastern side, the Gulf of Tonkin to the north, and the Gulf of Thailand in the south, Vietnam contains more than 1,400 miles of coastline as well as many rivers, which provide access to ample amounts of fish and seafood.

Although mountains, forests, and jungles make up much of the north, the land around the Red River Delta and the coastal plains in the northern region provides fertile farmland where crops flourish. The central portion contains mountains. Lowlands and fertile land for crops along the coast and the Mekong Delta compose the southern region. In fact, Vietnam ranks third in the export of rice. All of Vietnam experiences tropical weather, with hot, humid, rainy summers and drier, warm winters. The *monsoons* control the climate.

### THAILAND

Also situated in Southeast Asia, Thailand is bordered by Myanmar (Burma), Laos, and Cambodia on its west, northeast, and southeast, respectively. A narrow strip of land surrounded by the Andaman Sea to the west and the Gulf of Thailand to the east connects Thailand to Malaysia on the south.

Rivers crisscross the country and provide the main avenues for transportation. In fact, they did not build roads until the middle 1800s. Until recent times, canals functioned as roads throughout much of Thailand. Besides supplying transportation opportunities, these canals yield lots of freshwater fish. With its miles of coastline and many rivers and canals, the abundant freshwater and saltwater fish and seafood compose a major portion of the Thai diet.

Mountains, forests, dry plateaus, and some fertile river valleys compose much of the northern section of Thailand. Residents of northern Thailand use lots of coconut milk in their cooking. The central area contains plains, rivers, and very fertile farmland. This prolific growing region supplies lots of rice and all sorts of vegetables. Jungle, mountains, plains, and coastline define the humid southern region. Residents in the south use more hot peppers and prepare spicier dishes.

Rainforest covers one-quarter of the land in Thailand. Like the climates of Vietnam and Indonesia, Thailand's climate is tropical and strongly affected by the *monsoons*. Hot, dry springs; cool, dry winters; and hot, wet summers prevail throughout most of the country, with more moderate temperatures found in the mountains.

---

### SOUTHEAST ASIA

*Southeast Asia includes the countries lying south of China, east of India, and north of Australia. About the size of Europe, this area spans three time zones. All the countries within Southeast Asia share a similar climate due to the monsoons, seasonal winds. Each experiences a tropical climate with pronounced rainy and dry seasons. More than 1,000 languages are spoken throughout Southeast Asia. The major religions found in this area include Hinduism, Buddhism, Islam, and some Christianity.*

> **Ingredients and Foods Commonly Used throughout the Cuisines of Vietnam, Thailand, Indonesia, and the Philippines Include**
>
> - seafood and fish
> - rice and rice noodles
> - coconut, coconut milk, and coconut oil
> - fish sauce
> - shrimp paste
> - curry pastes
> - scallions, garlic, and ginger
> - lemongrass
> - aromatic herbs, including cilantro, basil, and mint
> - hot chili peppers and hot sauce
> - fresh fruits and vegetables
> - peanuts

## INDONESIA

Lying between Australia and southeastern Asia, more than 13,000 islands compose the country of Indonesia. About half of these islands remain uninhabited. Indonesia's land mass and population is greater than any other country in Southeast Asia. In fact, as a country Indonesia has the fifth largest population in the world. Furthermore, it is the largest archipelago.

Surrounded by the Indian and Pacific oceans, the islands of Indonesia stretch over a distance of 3,000 miles, with the equator running through them. As a result, a hot, humid, tropical climate supporting abundant plant growth prevails, except at the high altitudes of the mountains. Some of the diverse land found on these islands consists of mountains, many volcanoes, and large areas of uninhabited, dense jungle.

## PHILIPPINES

Over 7,000 islands form the Philippines. Situated in the western Pacific Ocean, this archipelago lies about 500 miles southeast of Asian land. The Philippines experience a tropical climate, with both dry and rainy seasons. Besides miles and miles of coastline, there are mountains, plains, rivers, and lakes on the islands.

This country has great diversity in topography, which, of course, impacted its cuisine. People in the inland areas consume more meat (usually pork and poultry), whereas the diet of coastal residents includes abundant fish and seafood. Freshwater fish like tilapia, carp, and catfish as well as saltwater fish and seafood, including milkfish (*bangus*), tuna, bonito, sardines, mackerel, squid, crabs, oysters, shrimp, and clams, dominate the cuisine.

## >> COOKING METHODS

Steaming, boiling or simmering, braising, grilling or broiling, stir-frying, and deep-frying are common cooking methods in these four countries. Baking is uncommon.

Grilling meats, fish, and bean curd remains popular. Meats are often cut into strips, marinated, and then placed on a skewer before grilling. People of this region steam a variety of foods, including whole fish, vegetables, custards, and rice. In the style of Japan's *nabémono,* people in both the north and south of Vietnam frequently cook foods in a pot of boiling broth at the table, adding various food items to the boiling liquid with chopsticks.

Cooks in these countries use less oil for stir-frying foods than is customary in China; however, they do cut the foods into small, uniform pieces before stir-frying, as the Chinese do. Of course, stir-frying is sautéing over high heat in a round-bottomed wok or other pan. Plenty of coconut oil is available for frying throughout these countries.

Cookery in the Philippines began with cooking over an open fire. Even today, people here boil or broil (grill) many foods. From the Spanish, Filipinos adopted sautéing in olive oil. Frequently, they boil foods in flavored stock (often with vinegar) and then sauté them.

The following three cooking styles common in Filipino cooking help to preserve foods in the tropical climate.

- *adobo* Foods cooked in vinegar, soy sauce, and garlic
- *pakisiw* Foods cooked in vinegar and garlic
- *sinigang* Foods boiled with sour fruits or vegetables

Because each of these cooking styles prepares the foods in an acidic liquid, foods are preserved longer without refrigeration. People claim these dishes taste better "the second day" because the food items have had time to absorb more of the acidic flavorings.

*Sinigang is similar to Thailand's* tomiam *and Indonesia's* sayur asam.

## >> REGIONS

### VIETNAM

The diet of the Vietnamese consists mainly of seafood, rice, and vegetables. Because North and South Vietnamese have so much access to rivers and the sea, fish and seafood remain the primary animal protein consumed in both countries. Squid, shrimp, lobster, and many varieties of fish abound. Fish sauce, *nuoc mam,* is consumed at every meal.

Because there is a lack of land for grazing, chicken and pork appear more often than beef (since cattle need the most land to graze). Poultry follows seafood in availability, and small amounts of pork appear in many dishes. Beef is reserved for special occasions except in the north, where there are some pasturelands and plains. Lamb and mutton are unknown here. Various game meats and fowl thrive in the mountainous regions as well as the jungles and forests. As in other Asian countries, meals with small amounts of meat are extended with larger quantities of vegetables and rice.

*One of the most often consumed vegetables in Vietnam, water spinach grows in every season throughout the country. Adding two textures to the dish, the stems of water spinach stay crunchy while the leaves wilt and become soft when cooked.*

#### Chinese and French Influence in Vietnam

The Chinese coveted Vietnam because of the fertile rice-growing areas in the Mekong and Red River deltas. The Chinese influence on the cuisine of Vietnam is most apparent in the northern region with its prevalence of bean curd, star anise, spring rolls, and soups. Like the Chinese, the Vietnamese prepare stir-fried dishes, and they eat rice separate from the other dishes, rather than mixing them together like people from areas to the south.

Serving as a foundation of the cuisine, rice accompanies all dishes here as in the other Southeast Asian countries. The Vietnamese prefer fluffy, separate grains of rice rather than the sticky rice favored in Japan and Korea.

Rice and noodles dominate the Vietnamese diet, but French bread adopted during the French occupation also remains quite popular. French influence on the cuisine is apparent, particularly with the use of garlic, sauces, and butter.

#### Flavorings in Vietnam

Generally, Vietnamese recipes contain a wide variety and ample amounts of fresh herbs; however, the use of spices varies from region to region. With fewer spices available in the north, the dishes tend to be less spicy here than those eaten in the south. Influence from the Indian cuisine prevails in southern Vietnam and shows up in the curries and various rice pancakes.

The Vietnamese use little oil in their cookery, even when they stir-fry. Thickening agents are rarely used; rather, food is presented in a simpler, more natural state.

*Wrapping filling in lettuce*
© Aleksander Todorovic

*Vietnamese spring rolls*
© TuTheLens

## Soups in Vietnam

Another staple of Vietnam's cuisine, soup, is consumed regularly. Breakfast in Vietnam often consists of *phở*, a North Vietnamese rice noodle soup in a beef broth strongly flavored with cilantro, garlic, and *nuoc mam* (fish sauce). Paper-thin slices of raw beef and rice noodles are placed in a bowl, then covered with boiling broth that cooks the meat. A popular soup served at any meal, many consider *phở* to be the national dish of Vietnam.

## Meals in Vietnam

As in most Asian countries, all foods composing the Vietnamese meal are served at once. Typically, various hot dishes accompany salads and lots of rice. To compose a salad, any variety of vegetables (and perhaps meat or seafood) are wrapped in a lettuce leaf, then enclosed in a rice-paper wrapper, dipped in *nuoc mam* sauce, and eaten.

The Vietnamese table setting includes a saucer at each place setting for holding *nuoc mam* dipping sauce. Condiments claim an important position in the Vietnamese meal. Basically, one or more of the four distinct types of condiments accompany a meal. They are: (1) pickles, (2) dipping sauces (which includes *nuoc mam*, fish sauce), (3) flavorings, and (4) garnishes.

To make *nuoc mam*, they layer anchovies with salt in a barrel and ferment them for months. The first pressing is returned to the barrel. At six months, they press for the second time; this is considered the best quality *nuoc mam*. Any further pressings produce a weaker fish sauce.

## THAILAND

In Thailand, the revered rice actually represents life itself. As in most countries in Southeast Asia, the foundation of the diet revolves around rice, which accompanies every meal. In fact, each Thai inhabitant consumes about one pound of rice every day! A prolific rice-growing region, this nation exports huge quantities of rice.

*Kaeng* means "liquid," and this is a very important principle in the cookery of Thailand. The amount of *kaeng* in a dish determines whether or not to mix rice directly into the dish. When planning a menu, Thai cooks strive to create a balance of dishes with and without abundant sauce, or *kaeng*.

## Curries in Thailand

While hearty curries featuring large chunks of pork are served in the north of Thailand, people in the south prefer lighter curries flavored with coconut milk and small pieces of meat, poultry, or seafood. The curries of Thailand contain a mixture of aromatics, peppers, spices, and coconut milk; they differ greatly from Indian curries.

There are three distinct types of Thai curries—yellow, red, and green. The ingredients that make up the sauce determine the color of the curry. The mildest of the curries, yellow, obtains its characteristic color from turmeric. The red ones contain red chili peppers, and the hottest variety, green, is made with green chili peppers.

## Flavorings Used in Thailand

Many characterize Thai food as "hot"; however, the food is much more complex than that single word. Aromatic herbs and coconut milk combine with a wide assortment of fiery chilies to produce complicated flavors of the dishes made in Thailand. Thai food is described as having many layers of different flavors that marry together to create an interesting and multifaceted taste sensation.

Basil, mint, cilantro, lemongrass, ginger, garlic, shallots, coriander, and fish sauce are just a few of the commonly used flavorings. Peanuts and tamarind appear in many recipes. To further heighten the appeal of the dishes, the Thai cook pays attention to the color, texture, and taste of each of the various ingredients to create a dish that attracts the diner with a variety of flavors, textures, and colors.

### Produce in Thailand

Fruits and vegetables play a major role in the cuisine of Thailand, and a typical meal includes one or more salads. All sorts of food items make their way into salads, providing healthy additions to meals. Piles of bean sprouts, lettuce, beans, and herbs accompany the spicy, hot dishes and function to cool the spiciness. Fresh fruits normally end the Thai meal, and when desserts are served they tend to be less sweet than those consumed in the other Southeast Asian countries.

## INDONESIA

Most of Indonesia's population resides in the Greater Sunda Islands to the west, which includes Borneo, Java, and Sumatra. Java ranks as the most populated island. With miles of coastline and many rivers, seafood and fish abound throughout Indonesia.

As in Vietnam and Thailand, rice forms the foundation of the Indonesian meal. In fact, Indonesians eat rice at all three meals daily. Although people from many other Southeast Asian countries eat rice separately from the other dishes, Indonesians mix rice with their foods. Combining the fiery, hot Indonesian dishes with ample amounts of rice tones down their intense spiciness.

Typically, the Indonesian cook juxtaposes sweet, sour, salty, and spicy taste sensations. Fiery *sambal,* Indonesian hot sauce, and coconut milk combine to form sweet and spicy flavorings. An important part of the Indonesian table, *sambal* accompanies the rice served at every meal.

### Religious Issues in Indonesia

Most residents of Java, the largest island, practice the Islamic faith. Although the majority of Indonesians practice the Islamic religion, the island of Bali remains a stronghold for the Hindu residents. Religion determines many culinary preferences, particularly regarding dietary restrictions on meat. Muslims do not eat pork, so other meats prevail in the Islamic areas. Although rarely served in much of Southeastern Asia, lamb appears frequently in Indonesia.

Each sect prepares ceremonial foods that continue to be an important facet of the Indonesian cuisine. *Selametan,* a ceremonial feast, marks important events in Indonesia. Many foods in Indonesia represent spiritual issues, and the foods served at *selametan* include special dishes such as *tumpeng,* which means "rice cone." Traditionally, a variety of foods decorate this ceremonial pyramid of rice. Although *tumpeng* originated in Java, it is served at important festivals throughout Indonesia, such as weddings and parties for newborn children.

### Regional Differences and Similarities in Indonesia

Significant differences exist between the cuisines of the various regions of Indonesia. The distance between islands caused great isolation, and this led to definite variations in the preparations and methods for cooking the same ingredients and dishes throughout the country. While the foods served in Sumatra are quite spicy, inhabitants of Java prefer sweeter tastes. Still, many flavor similarities are apparent throughout Indonesia. True for many countries with tropical climates, coconut milk and coconut oil appear everywhere. Also, sweet soy sauce (*kecap*), peanuts, and fermented shrimp paste (*trassi*) flavor a wide range of dishes throughout these islands.

*Gado-gado,* a salad consisting of a variety of vegetables topped with a peanut dressing, remains popular in most areas of Indonesia. Other well-known dishes include

### SOME VARIETIES OF *SAMBAL*

- *Sambal Ulek*—chili *sambal,* very hot
- *Sambal Kecap*—chilies, dark soy sauce (*kecap*), and tamarind
- *Sambal Goreng*—*sambal* with coconut milk
- *Sambal Tomaat*—tomato *sambal*

Indonesia has more Islamic residents than any other nation in the world.

*Tumpeng*
© januarandris

*Soto*
© bayu harsa

*Lumpia*
© Jose Gil

*satay,* grilled meat accompanied by a spicy peanut sauce, and *soto*, a chicken and coconut milk soup.

With tropical growing conditions, many crops thrive. Corn, rice, coffee, tea, a variety of spices, peanuts, cassava, bananas, sweet potatoes, and many other fruits and vegetables flourish here. Seventy percent of the world's nutmeg grows in Indonesia; cinnamon, cloves, and peppers also thrive on these islands. Interestingly, the Indonesians do not season food with nutmeg or cloves, but many dishes incorporate turmeric, curry, coriander, and/or ginger. They cook with all sorts of peppers, including hot chili peppers and peppercorns of various colors.

### Food Manners in Indonesia

Unlike most inhabitants of Southeast Asia, Indonesians eat with their fingers, not chopsticks. The food is rolled into a ball with the fingers on the right hand, then picked up and eaten with the same hand. The left hand is used only for passing food.

## PHILIPPINES

The cuisine of the Philippines exemplifies the fusion of cookery from the East and the West. Filipino cookery melded the cooking styles and cuisines of the many travelers and rulers who came to the Philippines.

### Influences on Filipino Cuisine

Frequent use of noodles (called *pancit* in the Philippines) and many other dishes came from the Chinese. For example, the Filipinos adapted Chinese spring rolls into *lumpia,* steamed buns with a variety of fillings called *siopao,* and dumplings called *siomai.*

Many claim that 80 percent of Filipino foods reflect Spanish heritage. The Spanish contributed rice and meat combination dishes, stews, and desserts. Often-used Spanish ingredients like tomatoes, olive oil, garlic, onions, ham, paprika, saffron, and *chorizo,* a spicy sausage, appear in Filipino cookery. The famous Spanish dish, *paella,* is popular in the Philippines. As in Spain and Portugal, flan appears on many dessert menus.

### Foods and Flavorings

Almost all meals in the Philippines include rice, coconuts, and a variety of dipping sauces and/or condiments. Like most cuisines of Southeast Asia, Filipino meals are accompanied by spicy, sour, salty, and/or sweet condiments. The difference is that Filipino spicy condiments are less spicy than the condiments served in the rest of Southeast Asia.

Filipinos prefer medium-grain rice, which is stickier than long-grain rice. Since a bounty of fish and seafood is available to the islands, it is the most common protein in the diet. Pork (in non-Islamic areas) and poultry follow seafood in popularity and availability. Cooks flavor many dishes with ginger and lemongrass.

### Regional and Religious Differences

The Philippines consist of more than 16 regions. Religion played a large role in the culinary differences between areas. While Christians dominate Luzon and Visayas, many Muslims live in the southern regions near Indonesia and Malaysia. Of course, Muslims do not eat pork or drink alcoholic beverages.

In northern Luzon, the diet consists of simple cooking, lots of native vegetables that often are boiled, and ample flavoring with *bagoong,* shrimp paste. This region contains miles of coastline and mountains. The cookery of Bicol, located on the southern tip of Luzon, features coconut and hot chilies.

---

**SOME VARIETIES OF NOODLES (*PANCIT*)**

- rice noodles
- wheat noodles
- bean or cellophane noodles
- egg noodles

---

*Hundreds of varieties of rice are available within the Philippines.*

Known as the rice-growing region, the central region contains many rice paddies. Manila, the capital of the Philippines, lies here. Known for sophisticated cookery, the central region is known for spicy sauces, higher consumption of pork and poultry, stuffed meat and poultry dishes, and vegetables sautéed with onions and garlic.

Visayas includes the central portion of the Philippines. Lots of saltwater fish as well as dried or salted fish and salty cooking dominates the menus here. Raw fish marinated in vinegar remains a popular menu item. People in this region consume ample amounts of corn.

Abundant coconuts, rice, and fruits grow in southern Tagalog. Residents consume lots of freshwater fish, and they prepare many dishes with a sour ingredient like vinegar, tamarind, or other sour fruits.

Mindanao lies in the southern part of the archipelago. People here enjoy simple cookery, no pork due to the predominantly Muslim population, and spicy, strongly flavored dishes.

## Filipino Meals

Filipinos serve all dishes at the same time instead of in courses. Planning a Filipino meal involves careful combining of tastes and textures. Meals include salty, sweet, sour, and bitter flavors.

Until introduced to forks, spoons, and knives by people from the West, Filipinos ate with their hands. They observe strict rules regarding manners for eating with hands.

Filipinos eat three meals daily and often have *merienda* in the late afternoon, which is much like British tea. Unlike those in most of Southeast Asia, Filipino meals frequently end with dessert. Their typical breakfast consists of hard rolls called *pan de sal*. Frequently, they serve sautéed leftover rice with garlic and/or dried fish, or they sauté the rice with sausage for breakfast.

# >> CUISINE

## FOOD ITEMS

The coconut holds an esteemed place in the cooking of each of these countries. While these countries do not raise many cattle for dairy and meat, the abundant coconut trees provide coconuts, coconut oil, and coconut milk that form the basis for many sauces. A common flavor combination found in curries throughout this part of the world, coconut paired with hot chilies provides a sweet taste sensation counteracting a spicy-hot. Grated or shredded, coconut meat appears in a myriad of dishes, both sweet and savory. Each of these countries feature a dish of seafood, chicken, or beef rolled in a taro or banana leaf then steamed in coconut milk. Coconuts touch every part of the menu, from appetizers to beverages and desserts.

Many varieties of bananas grow in these countries, and, like the coconut, this fruit appears in numerous forms and dishes. Sautéed, salted, underripe bananas often accompany the main meal. Ripe bananas are grilled, sautéed, cooked in custards, or coated with rice and/or coconut and eaten as a snack or dessert. As stated earlier, even the banana leaves are used. Like the cornhusks used to wrap *tamales* in Mexico and Central America, banana leaves function as a wrapper to enclose fillings for cooking (usually steaming).

Peanuts play a major role in these cuisines. Whether chopped peanuts are sprinkled over a finished dish or ground peanuts flavor the sauces, peanuts add flavor and texture to dishes throughout these countries.

## FLAVORINGS

Probably more than any other ingredient, fish flavorings contribute the characteristic tastes associated with each of these countries. Called *nám pla* in Thailand, *nuoc mam*

*Called* lechón *in the Philippines, roasted suckling pig often is served at festivals.*

### RICE

*Rice plays a major role in both diet and the culture throughout Southeast Asia and the rest of Asia. First, it functions as a staple food. As a result, rice ranks supreme in value as a food crop. Second, many festivals and celebrations revolve around the planting or harvesting of rice, which reflects the importance of rice to the society. Finally, rice assumes a prominent role in cultural events. Rice wine is often drunk as part of the wedding ceremony, and newlyweds are showered with rice as a symbol of good luck and hope for fertility and prosperity in their lives together.*

in Vietnam, and *patis* in the Philippines, fish sauce replaces the soy sauce used in other Asian countries. Fish sauce is made from fermented anchovies and salt. Paired with meat, poultry, seafood, tofu, and/or vegetables, the flavor of fish sauce permeates the dishes and functions as the major flavoring ingredient in both Vietnam and Thailand. Frequently used in Indonesia, shrimp paste (*trassi*) lends a fishlike taste to Indonesian dishes. Shrimp paste in the Philippines is called *bagoong*.

## RELIGIOUS DIETARY RESTRICTIONS

Many Muslims live in these countries, which means no pork or alcohol consumption. These dietary restrictions do not apply to Hindus or Christians, however.

### Dessert

Dessert in each of these countries usually consists of fresh fruits. Prepared desserts are reserved for special occasions. While some Filipino desserts reflect the typical cuisines of Southeast Asia, others resemble Spanish confections.

| REGION | AREA | WEATHER | TOPOGRAPHY | FOODS |
|---|---|---|---|---|
| Vietnam | North | Tropical, hot, humid, rainy summers; dry, warm winters; *monsoons* | Mountains, forests, jungles, Red River Delta, coastal plains, fertile farmland | Seafood, rice |
| | Central and south | Tropical, hot, humid, rainy summers; dry, warm winters; *monsoons* | Lowlands, mountains, Me Kong Delta, coastal plains, fertile farmland | Seafood, rice, corn, soybeans, peanuts, vegetables, fruits, sweet potatoes, coconuts, sugar |
| Thailand | North | Tropical, hot, humid, rainy summers; dry, warm winters; *monsoons* | Mountains, forests, rivers, plateaus, fertile river valleys | Fish, shellfish, tuna, herring, shrimp, rice, cassava, corn, pineapples, coconuts, sugar |
| | Central | Tropical, hot, humid, rainy summers; dry, warm winters; *monsoons* | Plains, rivers, fertile farmland | Fish, shellfish, tuna, herring, shrimp, rice, corn, cassava, pineapples, sugar |
| | South | Tropical, hot, humid, rainy summers; dry, warm winters; *monsoons* | Coasts, jungle, plains, mountains | Seafood, fish, shrimp, rice, cassava, corn, coconuts, pineapples, tropical fruits, sugar |
| Indonesia | West: Greater Sunda Islands, Borneo, Java, Sumatra | Hot, humid, wet, and dry seasons; *monsoons* | Coasts, rainforest, mountains, rivers, volcanoes, valleys, forests, plains | Fish, seafood, rice, peanuts, spices, sweet potatoes, tropical fruits, bananas, coconuts, sugar |
| | South: Bali, Timor | Hot, humid, wet, and dry seasons; *monsoons* | Coast, mountains, rivers | Seafood, fish, corn, spices |
| | East: Moluccas | Hot, humid, wet, and dry seasons; *monsoons* | Coast, mountains, equator | Seafood, fish, rice, spices |
| Philippines | Over 7,000 islands | Tropical, hot, humid, rainy summers; dry, warm winters; *monsoons* | Coast, mountains, plains, rivers, lakes | Seafood, fish, pork, poultry, *chorizo*, *paella*, rice, noodles (*pancit*), olive oil, coconut, tropical fruits and vegetables, bananas, ginger, onions, garlic, lemongrass, fish sauce, shrimp paste |
| | North | Tropical, hot, humid, rainy summers; dry, warm winters; *monsoons* | Coast, mountains, plains, rivers, lakes | Fish, seafood, pork, poultry, coconuts, rice, vegetables, fruits, shrimp paste |
| | Central | Tropical, hot, humid, rainy summers; dry, warm winters; *monsoons* | Coast, mountains, plains, rivers, lakes, rice paddies | Fish, seafood, pork, poultry, stuffed meats and poultry, coconuts, rice, corn, vegetables, fruits, chili peppers, onions, garlic |
| | South | Tropical, hot, humid, rainy summers; dry, warm winters; *monsoons* | Coast, mountains, plains, rivers, lakes | Fish, seafood, poultry, coconuts, rice, fruits, vegetables, chili peppers, vinegar, tamarind |

## >> Review Questions

1. Name flavorings and ingredients commonly used in the cuisines of Vietnam, Thailand, Indonesia, and the Philippines.
2. How do the cuisines of these four countries differ from other Asian cuisines?
3. Name at least one major difference between the cooking of North and South Vietnam.
4. Describe cooking methods often used in these four countries.
5. Discuss which animal proteins are consumed in each of these countries and why.
6. Discuss how water and the equator have affected the cuisines of these countries.
7. Which countries influenced the cuisines of Vietnam, Thailand, Indonesia, and the Philippines? Discuss those influences.

## >> Glossary

**bagoong** Shrimp paste used in the Philippines

**gado-gado** An Indonesian salad consisting of a variety of vegetables accompanied by peanut sauce dressing

**kaeng** Thai word for liquid; refers to amount of liquid in a dish

**kecap** Sweet soy sauce used in Indonesia

**lumpia** Filipino version of Chinese spring rolls

**monsoons** Seasonal winds that affect the climate

**nám pla** Fish sauce used extensively in Thailand

**nuoc mam** Fish sauce used extensively in Vietnam

**patis** Fish sauce used in the Philippines; salty, thin, and amber in color

**phó'** Rice noodle soup in a meat broth strongly flavored with cilantro, garlic, and *nuoc mam;* commonly eaten for breakfast in Vietnam but served at any meal; considered the national dish of Vietnam

**rijsttafel** Literally meaning rice table; opulent display of many different dishes accompanied by rice, requiring many servants for preparation and service; developed by the Dutch settlers

**satay** Grilled meat accompanied by a spicy peanut sauce commonly served in Indonesia

**selametan** Ceremonial feast that marks important events in Indonesia

**siomai** Filipino dumplings

**siopao** Filipino steamed buns with a variety of fillings

**soto** Indonesian chicken and coconut milk soup

**tumpeng** An Indonesian ceremonial rice dish consisting of a cone of rice decorated with a variety of foods, served at all important events

## CHA GIÒ (VIETNAM)

### SPRING ROLLS

**Note:** Accompany with *Nuoc Mam Cham (recipe follows)*.

**Number of Servings:** 9
**Serving Size:** Three 3-inch (8-cm) rolls
**Total Yield:** Twenty-eight 3-inch (8-cm) rolls
**Food Balance:** Protein
**Wine Style:** Off-dry or low-oaked whites or soft reds
**Example:** Beringer Chenin Blanc, Greg Norman Chardonnay or Pinot Noir

**Cooking Method:** Deep-fry

| | WEIGHT | | VOLUME | |
|---|---|---|---|---|
| **INGREDIENTS** | **U.S.** | **METRIC** | **U.S.** | **METRIC** |
| **Filling:** | | | | |
| dried Chinese mushrooms | 1/2 oz. | 15 g | 8 each | |
| dried tree ear mushrooms | | | 2 tablespoons | 30 mL |
| cellophane noodles | 1 oz. | 28 g | | |
| scallion, minced | 1/2 oz. | 15 g | 1 each | |
| onion, minced | 2 oz. | 57 g | 1 small | |
| ground pork | 4 oz. | 114 g | | |
| white crab meat, cooked and shredded | 4 oz. | 114 g | | |
| egg, beaten | 1 3/4 oz. | 50 g | 1 each | |
| salt | | | 1/4 teaspoon | 2 mL |
| pepper | | | 1/8 teaspoon | 1 mL |
| Vietnamese rice papers, 4-inch (10-cm) diameter | | | 28 each | |
| oil, for deep-frying | | | | |
| **Garnish:** | | | | |
| *Nuoc Mam Cham* (Fish Sauce Seasoned with Lime Juice; *recipe follows*) | | | | |
| soft lettuce like Boston, washed, and leaves separated | 10 oz. | 284 g | 1 large head | |
| fresh mint leaves, washed | | | | |

*Soaking rice paper wrappers*
Pearson Education/PH College

*Folding rice paper wrappers around filling*
Pearson Education/PH College

*Placing water on rice paper wrappers to seal*
Pearson Education/PH College

## FILLING:

1. Soak both types of dried mushrooms in hot water for 30 minutes. Remove and chop finely.
2. Soak cellophane noodles in hot water for 20 to 30 minutes. Drain, cut into 1/2-inch (1 1/3-cm) lengths.
3. Combine mushrooms, noodles, scallion, onion, pork, crab, egg, salt, and pepper in bowl. Mix well, refrigerate until needed.

## ASSEMBLY:

1. Soak rice paper in warm water just until barely softened and pliable, remove from water. If substituting 9-inch (23-cm) rice paper, cut in half or quarters (depending on desired size of spring roll) after soaking.
2. Place desired amount of filling (about 3/4 oz. or 1 tablespoon, 22 g) in log shape on lower third of rice paper.
3. Fold bottom edge (closest to you) over filling, fold in both sides. Brush top edge with water, then roll filling toward top of rice paper, encasing filling completely.
4. Place finished spring roll on parchment-lined pan, folded side down. Continue making remaining rolls. Refrigerate until ready to fry.

## FRYING:

1. Heat oil for deep-frying until 350 degrees (180°C).
2. Add spring rolls, a few at a time (so temperature is not lowered too much), fry until golden, about 5 minutes.
3. Drain on absorbent paper.

## SERVING:

1. Place bowl of *Nuoc Mam Cham* at each diner's place.
2. Place lettuce leaves and mint on platter, place spring rolls on separate platter (or for individual service, place serving of each of these three ingredients on one plate).
3. To eat, place spring roll on lettuce leaf (or part of one if leaf is too large), put a few mint leaves on top, roll lettuce around spring roll, dip in *Nuoc Mam Cham* and enjoy.

Courtesy of CanolaInfo.org

© dziewul/Fotolia

# NOUC MAM CHAM (VIETNAM)

## FISH SAUCE SEASONED WITH LIME JUICE

Pearson Education/PH College

**Note:** Purchase fish sauce from an Asian grocery.

**Number of Servings:** 8
**Serving Size:** 2 oz. (57 g) or 1/4 cup (60 mL)
**Total Yield:** 1 lb. (454 g) or 2 cups (480 mL)

| | WEIGHT | | VOLUME | |
|---|---|---|---|---|
| INGREDIENTS | U.S. | METRIC | U.S. | METRIC |
| sugar | 3 oz. | 86 g | 1/4 cup + 2 tablespoons | 90 mL |
| water, warm | | 114 g | 1/2 cup | 120 mL |
| fresh hot red or green chilies, minced and seeds and ribs removed, if desired | up to 2 oz. | 57 g | 2 to 4 each | |
| garlic, smashed and minced | 1/4 oz. | 8 g | 2 cloves | |
| lime juice | | 114 g | 1/2 cup | 120 mL |
| fish sauce | | 114 g | 1/2 cup | 120 mL |

1 Mix sugar and water in jar or bowl, shake or whisk until sugar dissolves.
2 Add chilies, garlic, lime juice, and fish sauce; mix well to combine. Refrigerate until needed.
3 Pour into individual bowls for serving.

# SATAY ATAM (INDONESIA)

## CHICKEN KEBABS WITH PEANUT SAUCE

Pearson Education/PH College

**Note:** Allow 2 to 24 hours to marinate the chicken.

**Note:** Serve with warm *Sambal Kacang* (Peanut Sauce; *recipe follows*).

**Number of Servings:** 8
**Serving Size:** 3 oz. (86 g) meat
           3/4 oz. (22 g) peanut sauce
**Total Yield:** 1 lb., 8 oz. (681 g) meat
**Food Balance:** Protein/sweet
**Wine Suggestion:** Off-dry or low-oaked whites or soft reds
**Example:** Beringer Chenin Blanc or Johannisberg Riesling, Penfolds Shiraz

**Cooking Method:** Broil

| INGREDIENTS | WEIGHT | | VOLUME | |
|---|---|---|---|---|
| | U.S. | METRIC | U.S. | METRIC |
| **Marinade:** | | | | |
| garlic, smashed and minced | 1/2 oz. | 15 g | 4 cloves | |
| ginger, peeled and minced | 1 oz. | 28 g | 2-inch cube | 5-cm cube |
| *kecap manis* (sweet soy sauce) | 1 oz. | 28 g | 2 tablespoons | 30 mL |
| soy sauce | | 28 g | 2 tablespoons | 30 mL |
| lime juice | | 28 g | 2 tablespoons | 30 mL |
| ground coriander | | | 2 teaspoons | 10 mL |
| sugar | 1/4 oz. | 8 g | 2 teaspoons | 10 mL |
| ground cayenne | | | 1/2 teaspoon | 3 mL |
| boneless, skinless, chicken, washed and cut into 1-inch (2 1/2-cm) cubes | 2 lb. | 908 g | 2 whole breasts | |
| bamboo or metal skewers | | | | |

① Combine all marinade ingredients (garlic, ginger, *kecap manis*, soy sauce, lime juice, coriander, sugar, and cayenne) in nonreactive bowl, mix well.

② Add chicken to marinade, mix well, cover and refrigerate for 2 to 24 hours.

③ Soak bamboo skewers in water for at least 30 minutes before using to prevent them from burning on the grill.

④ Thread about three chicken pieces onto each skewer.

⑤ Preheat broiler or grill, grill skewers about 4 inches (10 cm) from heat source for 5 minutes on each side, until done.

⑥ Serve with warm *Sambal Kacang* (Peanut Sauce; *recipe follows*).

### TWIST ON THE CLASSIC

To prepare this as a vegetarian dish, substitute tofu cubes or vegetables for the chicken. Alternately, replace the chicken with pork, beef, or the meat of choice.

Transform this into an entrée by mixing grilled chicken and vegetables with peanut sauce and serving it over rice.

© wong yu liang

## SAMBAL KACANG (INDONESIA)

### PEANUT SAUCE

**Note:** Prepared peanut sauce is available in Asian grocery stores and some supermarkets.

**Number of Servings:** 11
**Serving Size:** 1 oz. (28 mL)
**Total Yield:** 11 oz. (312 g) or 1 1/4 cups (300 mL)

**Cooking Method:** Boil

| INGREDIENTS | WEIGHT | | VOLUME | |
|---|---|---|---|---|
| | U.S. | METRIC | U.S. | METRIC |
| peanut butter, smooth or crunchy | 3 1/4 oz. | 92 g | 1/3 cup | 80 mL |
| garlic, smashed and minced | | | 1 clove | |
| ground cayenne | | | 1/2 teaspoon | 3 mL |
| brown sugar | 1/2 oz. | 15 g | 1 tablespoon | 15 mL |
| lime juice | | 28 g | 2 tablespoons | 30 mL |
| coconut milk | | 28 g | 2 tablespoons | 30 mL |
| *kecap manis* (sweet soy sauce) | | 15 g | 1 tablespoon | 15 mL |
| water | | 114 g | 1/2 cup | 120 mL |

Pearson Education/PH College

① Mix all ingredients in saucepan, stir often, bring to boil.
② Turn heat to medium-low, stirring occasionally, cook until thickened, about 15 to 20 minutes.
③ Correct seasonings, remove from heat, refrigerate for storage.

---

## SINIGANG NA BABOY (PHILIPPINES)
### PORK SOUR SOUP

© Lucky Dragon

A very popular soup throughout the Philippines, *sinigang* is made with seafood or beef as well as pork. Variations on the recipe are endless.

**Number of Servings:** 14 soup
8 entrée
**Serving Size:** 7 oz. (199 g) for soup
12 oz. (340 g) for entrée
**Total Yield:** 6 lb., 9 1/2 oz. (3 kg)
**Wine Style:** Full-bodied, fruit-forward red wine from a moderate climate region. Possible grape varietals are St. Laurent, Blaufrankisch, Zweigelt, and Merlot.
**Example:** St. Laurent "vom Stein" 2009, Umathum (Neusiedlersee/Austria)

**Cooking Method:** Braise

| | WEIGHT | | VOLUME | |
|---|---|---|---|---|
| **INGREDIENTS** | **U.S.** | **METRIC** | **U.S.** | **METRIC** |
| oil | | 15 g | 1 tablespoon | 15 mL |
| pork ribs, cut into 2-inch (5-cm) pieces, pork belly, pork butt, or choice, cut into 1 1/2-inch (4-cm) chunks | 2 lb. | 908 g | | |
| onion, cut in half, sliced thinly | 7 oz. | 199 g | 1 large | |
| tamarind powder or lime juice | 1 1/2 oz. (tamarind) | 43 g (tamarind) or 114 g (lime juice) | 1/2 cup | 120 mL |
| tomato, quartered, seeds removed | 14 3/4 oz. | 419 g | 2 medium | |
| fish sauce (*patis*) | 1 3/4 oz. | 50 g | 3 tablespoons | 45 mL |
| salt | 3/4 oz. | 22 g | 1 tablespoon | 15 mL |
| pepper | | | 1 teaspoon | 5 mL |
| radish, daikon or red, sliced into bite-sized pieces | 5 oz. | 142 g | 1 cup | 240 mL |
| green beans or long beans, cut into 2-inch (5-cm) pieces | 3 oz. | 86 g | about 15 each | |
| spinach, fresh | 8 oz. | 227 g | | |

**Accompaniments:**
fish sauce (*patis*)
tamarind or lime juice

① Place oil in skillet over medium heat. When hot, add pork pieces and cook until browned. Remove from skillet, place in large pot. Continue sautéing pork until all pieces are browned.
② Add onion and cover with water. Bring to boil, reduce heat, and simmer until almost tender. Remove scum from surface of soup if it forms. The amount of cooking time depends on the cut of meat—from 45 minutes to 1 1/2 hours.

③ Add sour component (tamarind or lime juice), tomatoes, fish sauce, salt, and pepper. Simmer until meat is tender.

④ Add radish and green beans; simmer another 10 to 15 minutes. Add spinach and cook another minute.

⑤ Correct seasonings. Serve over rice. Accompany with additional fish sauce and sour component, if desired.

## PHÓ' (VIETNAM)

### BEEF AND NOODLE SOUP

**Note:** The paper-thin sliced raw beef cooks in the bowl from the heat of the boiling stock poured over it. Typically, this soup is served for breakfast in many Vietnamese households, but it also appears on lunch and dinner menus.

© sugar0607

**Number of Servings:** 9

**Serving Size:** 6 oz. (170 g) soup:
    3/4 oz. (22 g) cooked meat
    2 oz. (57 g) noodles
    1/4 oz. (8 g) bean sprouts
    1 oz. (28 g) raw steak

**Total Yield:** 3 lb., 8 oz. (1.6 kg) soup

**Food Balance:** Protein/spicy

**Wine Style:** Light- to medium-bodied Gewürztraminer, Pinot Blanc, Viognier, blush, rosé

**Example:** Château St. Jean Gewürztraminer or Viognier

**Cooking Method:** Boil

| | WEIGHT | | VOLUME | |
|---|---|---|---|---|
| **INGREDIENTS** | **U.S.** | **METRIC** | **U.S.** | **METRIC** |
| beef stock | | | 2 quarts (8 cups) | 1.9 L |
| beef chuck, in one piece | 1 lb. | 454 g | | |
| onion, 1/4-inch (1/2-cm) slices | 6 1/2 oz. | 184 g | 1 large | |
| carrot, peeled and sliced | 3 oz. | 86 g | 1 each | |
| ginger, peeled and cut in half | 1 oz. | 28 g | one 2-inch piece | one 5-cm piece |
| cinnamon | | | one 2-inch stick | one 5-cm stick |
| star anise | | | 2 each | |
| whole peppercorns | | | 1 teaspoon | 5 mL |
| **Condiments:** | | | | |
| rice stick noodles | 8 oz. | 227 g | | |
| bean sprouts, blanched for 5 seconds and rinsed in cold water | 2 3/4 oz. | 78 g | 1 cup | 240 mL |
| scallions, thinly sliced, green portion included | 2 oz. | 57 g | 2 each | |
| hot chilies, thinly sliced | | | to taste | |
| fresh cilantro, minced | 3/4 oz. | 22 g | 1/4 cup | 60 mL |
| lime wedges | as needed | | | |
| fish sauce | | 57 g | 1/4 cup | 60 mL or to taste |
| tender beef steak, sliced paper thin | 10 oz. | 284 g | | |

**TWIST ON THE CLASSIC**

To change this from soup to entrée, start with less stock and add more only as needed until beef is tender. Cover the pot and simmer the meat in stock that covers meat halfway. Turn meat as needed to cook both sides. Do not add any water to recipe. Place "soup mixture" (from step 5 below) over bed of rice and top with seared beef. Deep-fry the rice stick noodles and use them as a garnish.

① Place stock, beef chuck, onion, carrot, ginger, cinnamon stick, star anise, and peppercorns in large pot. Simmer for 2 or 3 hours, until meat is tender.

② Meanwhile, soak rice noodles in water for at least 30 minutes. Prepare condiments by placing bean sprouts, scallions, chilies, cilantro, and lime wedges on a platter or in separate bowls for service.

③ Strain stock, add water to bring up to 7 cups (1.7 L), remove beef chuck, cut into thin slices.

④ Drain rice noodles, cook in pot of boiling water for 1 or 2 minutes, until tender. Drain in colander, rinse with cold water, place noodles in bowl of cold water until needed.

⑤ Heat stock, add fish sauce, taste to correct seasonings. Bring to boil. Heat noodles by dipping briefly in boiling water.

⑥ Place some noodles, sliced raw beef, and cooked beef in bowl, cover with boiling soup.

⑦ Serve immediately, let each diner add condiments as desired.

---

# TÔM YAM KÛNG (THAILAND)
## HOT AND SOUR SHRIMP SOUP

**Note:** Purchase lemongrass, fish sauce, and chili paste in an Asian food store.

**Number of Servings:** 8                **Cooking Method:** Boil
**Serving Size:** 8 oz. (227 g)
**Total Yield:** 4 lb., 5 oz. (2 kg)
**Food Balance:** Spicy/acid
**Wine Style:** Off-dry or low-oaked whites or soft reds
**Example:** Beringer White Zinfandel or Pinot Grigio, Lindemans Merlot

Kasia © Shutterstock

| INGREDIENTS | WEIGHT U.S. | WEIGHT METRIC | VOLUME U.S. | VOLUME METRIC |
|---|---|---|---|---|
| fresh lemongrass | 1/2 oz. | 15 g | 2 each | |
| chicken stock | | | 1 quart + 2 cups (6 cups) | 1.4 L |
| medium shrimp, peeled and deveined, shells reserved | 1 lb. | 454 g | | |
| lime rind, finely grated | 1/4 oz. | 8 g | 1 tablespoon | 15 mL |
| fish sauce | | 28 g | 2 tablespoons | 30 mL |
| lime juice | | 57 g | 1/4 cup | 60 mL |
| chili paste | 3/4 oz. | 22 g | 1 tablespoon | 15 mL |
| sugar | 1 oz. | 28 g | 2 tablespoons | 30 mL |
| fresh mushrooms, button or other variety, quartered and parboiled for 1 minute | 8 oz. | 227 g | 3 cups | 720 mL |
| **Garnish:** | | | | |
| fresh, hot green chilies, finely sliced into rounds | 1/2 oz. | 15 g | 2 each | |
| fresh cilantro, minced | 1/2 oz. | 15 g | 3 tablespoons | 45 mL |

① Discard dry outer leaves and dry top from lemongrass, cut remainder into 3-inch (8-cm) pieces, crush using flat part of knife.

② Place stock, shrimp shells, lemongrass, and lime rind into pan, bring to boil, lower heat and simmer for 20 minutes.

③ Strain stock, return to pan. Add fish sauce, lime juice, chili paste, and sugar, mix, correct seasonings.

④ Add mushrooms, bring to boil, add shrimp.

⑤ Cook over medium heat for 2 minutes, until shrimp become opaque.

⑥ Correct seasonings. Serve immediately, accompanied by green chilies and cilantro.

## DAU CHUA (VIETNAM)

### PICKLED CARROT AND DAIKON SALAD

**Number of Servings:** 10  
**Serving Size:** 3 oz. (86 g)  
**Total Yield:** 1 lb., 15 oz. (880 g)

**Cooking Method:** Boil

© Monkey Business

| INGREDIENTS | WEIGHT | | VOLUME | |
|---|---|---|---|---|
| | U.S. | METRIC | U.S. | METRIC |
| carrots, peeled and cut into julienne | 1 lb. | 454 g | 4 to 5 large | |
| daikon radish, peeled and cut into julienne | 1 lb. | 454 g | 4 cups | 960 mL |
| kosher salt | 1/4 oz. | 8 g | 1 teaspoon | 5 mL |
| water | | 305 g | 1 1/3 cup | 320 mL |
| rice vinegar | | 78 g | 2/3 cup | 160 mL |
| sugar | 2 oz. | 57 g | 1/4 cup | 60 mL |

1. Place carrots and daikon in strainer in sink or over bowl. Sprinkle with salt, mix well. Let stand 30 minutes.
2. Meanwhile, combine water, rice vinegar, and sugar in pan, bring to boil, remove from heat, cool to room temperature.
3. After 30 minutes, rinse carrots and daikon with cold water, squeeze dry, place in bowl.
4. Pour vinegar mixture over carrots and daikon, mix gently. Refrigerate 1 hour before serving.
5. Remove carrots and daikon from liquid. Serve as accompaniment to other dishes.

**TWIST ON THE CLASSIC**

Use this salad like a salsa as a topping for fish or chicken.

## ENSALADANG HILAW NA MANGA (PHILIPPINES)

### GREEN MANGO SALAD

**Number of Servings:** 8  
**Serving Size:** 5 oz. (142 g)  
**Total Yield:** 2 lb., 10 1/2 oz. (1.2 kg)

© MAHATHIR MOHD YASIN

| INGREDIENTS | WEIGHT | | VOLUME | |
|---|---|---|---|---|
| | U.S. | METRIC | U.S. | METRIC |
| **Dressing:** | | | | |
| *calamansi* or lime juice | | 28 g | 2 tablespoons | 30 mL |
| fish sauce (*patis*) | | 50 g | 3 tablespoons | 45 mL |
| brown sugar | 1/4 oz. | 8 g | 2 teaspoons | 10 mL |
| green mango, peeled, julienne | 1 lb., 4 1/4 oz. | 574 g | 2 each | |
| tomato, seeds removed, large dice | 15 oz. | 426 g | 2 medium | |
| red onion, sliced thinly | 3 oz. | 86 g | 1 small | |
| cilantro, minced | 1 1/2 oz. | 43 g | 1/2 cup | 120 mL |
| **Garnishes:** | | | | |
| peanuts, chopped, *optional* | | | | |
| mint leaves, minced, *optional* | | | | |
| crushed red pepper flakes, *optional* | | | | |

**TWIST ON THE CLASSIC**

Serve this green mango salad on a piece of fish topping a bed of greens.

① Whisk dressing ingredients (*calamansi* or lime juice, fish sauce [*patis*], and brown sugar) in small nonreactive bowl or jar until well combined and sugar dissolves.

② Place mango, tomato, onion, and cilantro in nonreactive bowl.

③ Pour dressing mixture over mango mixture. Mix gently to coat well. Serve immediately or refrigerate until needed. Garnish with peanuts, mint leaves, and/or crushed red pepper flakes, if desired.

Many of the countries in Southeast Asia prepare salads with green mango or green papaya.

# GADO-GADO (INDONESIA)

## MIXED VEGETABLE SALAD

Clive Streeter and Patrick McLeavy
© Dorling Kindersley

**Note:** Accompany with *Sambal Kacang* (Peanut Sauce; *see recipe earlier in this chapter*).

**Note:** Use any vegetables desired; just be sure to blanch each vegetable until still crunchy, then rinse under cold water to stop the cooking. Bean sprouts require about 15 seconds, carrots and cauliflower about 3 minutes, green beans about 2 minutes, and so on. Keep each vegetable separate for arranging attractively on the plate.

**Number of Servings:** 11
**Serving Size:** 4 oz. (114 g) vegetables
             1 oz. (30 mL) peanut dressing
**Total Yield:** 2 lb., 12 oz. (1.2 kg)

**Cooking Method:** Boil

| | WEIGHT | | VOLUME | |
| --- | --- | --- | --- | --- |
| **INGREDIENTS** | **U.S.** | **METRIC** | **U.S.** | **METRIC** |
| green beans, trimmed | 5 oz. | 142 g | | |
| carrot, peeled and cut into 3/8-inch (1-cm) matchsticks | 2 1/2 oz. | 71 g | 1 each | |
| cauliflower flowerets | 7 oz. | 199 g | 2 cups | 480 mL |
| cabbage, thin slices | 6 oz. | 170 g | 2 cups | 480 mL |
| bean sprouts | 4 oz. | 114 g | 1 cup | 240 mL |
| potatoes, white, waxy, or all-purpose, cooked, peeled and cut into 1/4-inch (1/2-cm) slices | 10 oz. | 284 g | 2 each | |
| eggs, hard-boiled, peeled, and quartered | 5 oz. | 142 g | 3 each | |
| cucumber, peeled and cut into 1/4-inch (1/2-cm) slices | 5 oz. | 142 g | 1/2 each | |
| *Sambal Kacang* (Peanut Sauce) | | | | |

① Blanch green beans, carrot, cauliflower, cabbage, and bean sprouts, each vegetable separately, in boiling water until barely tender yet still crisp, rinse with cold water, drain well.

② Set aside, keeping each vegetable separate.

③ Arrange blanched vegetables, potatoes, eggs, and cucumber on platter or individual plates, being mindful of color and texture.

④ Serve, dressed with *Sambal Kacang* (*see recipe in this chapter*) drizzled over vegetables.

### TWIST ON THE CLASSIC

To transform this into an entrée salad, top the salad with grilled salmon or shrimp.

## BO VIÊN (VIETNAM)

### BEEF BALLS

**Note:** This recipe yields almost twice the amount of broth as needed to serve with the recipe. The broth is needed to boil the beef balls. If increasing the recipe, boil meatballs in batches instead of increasing the broth mixture in proportion to the increase in meat.

**Number of Servings:** 10

**Cooking Method:** Boil

**Serving Size:** Four 1-oz. (28-g) beef balls
3 oz. (90 mL) broth

**Total Yield:** 2 lb., 8 oz. (1.1 kg) raw meat, or forty 1-oz. (28-g) beef balls
4 lb. or 2 quarts (1.9 L) broth

**Food Balance:** Protein

**Wine Style:** Off-dry or low-oaked whites or soft reds

**Example:** Campanile Pinot Grigio or Beringer Founders' Estate Pinot Noir

Annabelle Breakey © Getty Images, Inc.–Jupiterimages

| INGREDIENTS | WEIGHT | | VOLUME | |
| --- | --- | --- | --- | --- |
| | U.S. | METRIC | U.S. | METRIC |
| **Beef Balls:** | | | | |
| fish sauce | | 114 g | 1/2 cup | 120 mL |
| water | | 114 g | 1/2 cup | 120 mL |
| potato starch | 1/2 oz. | 15 g | 1 tablespoon + 1 teaspoon | 20 mL |
| sugar | | | 1 teaspoon | 5 mL |
| baking powder | 1/2 oz. | 15 g | 2 teaspoons | 10 mL |
| pepper | | | 1/4 teaspoon | 2 mL |
| boneless beef round, trimmed of fat and cut across grain into thin slices | 2 lb. | 908 g | | |
| sesame oil | | 22 g | 1 tablespoon + 1 1/2 teaspoons | 23 mL |
| **Broth:** | | | | |
| water | | | 1 quart + 2 cups (6 cups) | 1.4 L |
| fish sauce | | 8 g | 1 1/2 teaspoons | 8 mL |
| salt | | | 1/4 to 1/2 teaspoon | 2 to 3 mL |

**Garnishes:**

scallions, thin slices
pepper
chili paste

**TWIST ON THE CLASSIC**

For an Italian/Vietnamese entrée, serve the beef balls and diced fresh tomato with a little broth over linguine.

1. Mix fish sauce, water, potato starch, sugar, baking powder, and pepper in nonreactive bowl.
2. Add beef slices to bowl, mix well, cover and refrigerate for 5 hours.
3. Process meat mixture to paste in food processor fitted with knife blade. Place some sesame oil on palms of hand, form 1-oz. or 1 tablespoon (28-g) meatballs.
4. Bring 1 quart plus 2 cups (1.4 L) water to boil over high heat, add balls, boil 5 minutes until they float to surface, remove from water.
5. Add fish sauce and salt to water, boil broth, add beef balls to reheat. Correct seasonings.
6. Serve four beef balls with 1/3 cup (80 mL) broth, garnish with scallions, a sprinkling of pepper, and chili paste.

# BÁNH XÈO (VIETNAM)

## HAPPY PANCAKES

Pearson Education/PH College

**Note:** These pancakes make an excellent luncheon item, appetizer, or addition to an assortment of dishes. The *Nuoc Mam Cham* dipping sauce is a necessity with them!

**Number of Servings:** 13
**Serving Size:** 10- to 12-inch (25- to 30-cm) pancake
**Total Yield:** 3 lb., 15 oz. (1.8 kg) pancake batter
**Food Balance:** Protein
**Wine Style:** Off-dry or low-oaked whites or soft reds
**Example:** Souverain Sauvignon Blanc or Greg Norman Pinot Noir

**Cooking Method:** Sauté

| INGREDIENTS | WEIGHT | | VOLUME | |
|---|---|---|---|---|
| | U.S. | METRIC | U.S. | METRIC |
| **Batter:** | | | | |
| rice flour | 1 lb., 5 oz. | 596 g | 3 1/2 cups | 840 mL |
| water | | 908 g | 1 quart (4 cups) | 960 mL |
| turmeric | | | 1/2 teaspoon | 3 mL |
| scallion, thin slices | 1 oz. | 28 g | 2 each | |
| ground pork | 8 oz. | 227 g | | |
| pepper | as needed | | | |
| scallions, minced | 1 oz. | 28 g | 2 each | |
| garlic, smashed and minced | 1/4 oz. | 8 g | 2 cloves | |
| fish sauce | | | 2 teaspoons | 10 mL |
| shrimp, peeled and deveined | 8 oz. | 227 g | | |
| oil, for frying | | | | |
| onion, thin slices | 4 oz. | 114 g | 1 medium | |
| mushrooms, button or any variety, slices | 6 1/4 oz. | 177 g | 10 each | |
| mung bean sprouts | 10 oz. | 284 g | 3 1/4 cups | 780 mL |
| *Nuoc Mam Cham* (Fish Sauce Seasoned with Lime Juice; *recipe in this chapter*) | | | | |

1. Whisk rice flour and water together, add turmeric and sliced scallions, mix well. Refrigerate until needed.
2. In bowl, mix pork with sprinkling of pepper and half each of the minced scallions, garlic, and fish sauce, refrigerate until needed.
3. In another bowl, mix shrimp with sprinkling of pepper and other half of the scallions, garlic, and fish sauce, refrigerate until needed.
4. Heat about 1 tablespoon (15 mL) oil in large nonstick skillet over high heat.
5. Place about 3/4 oz. (22 g) pork, 3/4 oz. (22 g) shrimp, few slices of onion, and a few slices of mushrooms in skillet, cook about 1 minute over high heat.
6. Stir batter well, pour just enough batter over ingredients in pan to coat pan, about 3 oz. (90-mL) or a ladle full. Tilt pan to spread in thin even layer.
7. Cover, cook until edges of pancake turn brown, about 3 to 4 minutes.
8. Place 3/4 oz. (22 g) or 1/4 cup (60 mL) beans sprouts on half of pancake, fold other half over it (like an omelet). Keep warm in oven if not serving immediately. Continue making pancakes with remaining ingredients.
9. Serve immediately, accompanied by Nuoc Mam Cham (*see recipe in this chapter*).

---

### TWIST ON THE CLASSIC

Change the filling as desired to create a vegan or vegetarian variation by replacing the pork and shrimp with tofu and/or vegetables. Use any variety or assortment of seafood instead of pork for a seafood rendition of "Happy Pancakes."

# PAD THAI (THAILAND)

## NOODLES WITH SHRIMP AND PORK

**Number of Servings:** 8
**Serving Size:** 9 oz. (256 g)
**Total Yield:** 4 lb., 15 oz. (2.2 kg)
**Food Balance:** Acid/spicy
**Wine Style:** Off-dry or low-oaked whites or soft reds
**Example:** Meridian Vineyards Gewürztraminer, Beringer Founders' Estate Chardonnay or Shiraz

**Cooking Method:** Stir-fry (sauté)

> **TWIST ON THE CLASSIC**
>
> Use any protein desired in this recipe. Make it vegetarian with tofu, create a seafood rendition with shrimp and scallops, or prepare it with all pork or chicken.

| INGREDIENTS | WEIGHT | | VOLUME | |
| --- | --- | --- | --- | --- |
| | U.S. | METRIC | U.S. | METRIC |
| rice stick noodles, about 1/8-inch (1/3-cm) wide | 1 lb. | 454 g | one 1 lb. package | one 454-g package |
| fish sauce | | 114 g | 1/2 cup | 120 mL |
| rice vinegar | | 114 g | 1/2 cup | 120 mL |
| sugar | 2 1/2 oz. | 71 g | 1/4 cup + 2 tablespoons | 90 mL |
| catsup | 1 1/2 oz. | 43 g | 2 tablespoons | 30 mL |
| oil | | 15 g | 1 tablespoon | 15 mL |
| garlic, smashed and minced | 2 oz. | 57 g | 14 cloves | |
| medium shrimp, peeled and deveined | 8 oz. | 227 g | | |
| pork tenderloin, cut into bite-size strips | 8 oz. | 227 g | | |
| eggs, lightly beaten | 3 1/2 oz. | 104 g | 2 each | |
| Thai chili powder or ground cayenne | | | 2 teaspoons | 10 mL or to taste |
| scallions, angle-cut into 1 1/2-inch (4-cm) pieces, including greens | 4 oz. | 114 g | 8 each | |
| unsalted peanuts, shelled and finely chopped | 4 oz. | 114 g | 2/3 cup | 160 mL |
| bean sprouts | 8 1/2 oz. | 241 g | 3 cups | 720 mL |
| fresh cilantro, minced | 3/4 oz. | 22 g | 1/4 cup | 60 mL |

**Condiments:**

bean sprouts
unsalted peanuts, finely chopped
lime wedges
Thai chilies, finely sliced
fresh cilantro, minced

1. Soak rice noodles in bowl of warm water until soft, about 15 minutes. Drain noodles, set aside until needed.
2. Combine fish sauce, vinegar, sugar, and catsup in small bowl, stir to dissolve sugar.
3. Heat oil in wok over medium-high heat. Add garlic, shrimp, and pork, stir-fry until shrimp and pork lose raw color, about 1 minute.
4. Add reserved fish sauce mixture, bring to boil, add noodles, gently toss. Stir-fry until noodles absorb sauce, about 2 minutes.
5. Pour eggs into wok, mix eggs throughout noodle. Cook without stirring for 15 seconds.
6. Add chili powder or cayenne and scallions. Continue to stir-fry until the scallions are cooked, about 1 to 2 minutes.
7. Stir in peanuts and bean sprouts until well mixed. Correct seasonings.
8. Transfer to serving platter, sprinkle with cilantro, serve accompanied by condiments.

Fotolia, LIC–Royalty Free

© kazama14

## MEE KROB (THAILAND)

### CRISP RICE NOODLES WITH SHRIMP AND PORK

**TWIST ON THE CLASSIC**

For a German twist, serve the *Mee Krob* over spaetzel.

**Note:** This dish may be prepared with any combination of meats or vegetables desired.

**Note:** Purchase dried mushrooms, fish sauce, and *sambal* in an Asian food store.

**Note:** To make scallion brushes, cut root and most of green off scallion, leaving about 3 inches (8 cm) of white scallion. Make 1-inch-long (2 1/2-cm-long) vertical cuts all around both ends of scallion. Soak in ice water for 2 hours or overnight. The cuts will fan out, looking like a brush at both ends.

**Number of Servings:** 10
**Serving Size:** 5 oz. (142 g)
**Total Yield:** 3 lb., 6 oz. (1.5 kg)
**Food Balance:** Spicy/sweet-and-sour
**Wine Style:** Off-dry or low-oaked whites or soft reds
**Example:** Lindemans Moscato, Pinot Grigio, or Merlot

**Cooking Method:** Sauté (stir-fry), deep-fry

| INGREDIENTS | WEIGHT | | VOLUME | |
| | U.S. | METRIC | U.S. | METRIC |
| --- | --- | --- | --- | --- |
| dried mushrooms, forest or other type | 1/4 oz. | 8 g | 6 each | |
| oil, for deep-frying | | | | |
| eggs, lightly beaten | 3 1/2 oz. | 104 g | 2 each | |
| rice stick noodles | 8 oz. | 227 g | | |
| lean, boneless pork, 1/4-inch (1/2-cm) strips | 8 oz. | 227 g | | |
| onion, small dice | 2 1/4 oz. | 64 g | 1/2 medium | |
| garlic, minced | 3/4 oz. | 22 g | 5 large cloves | |
| shrimp, peeled and deveined | 1 lb. | 454 g | | |
| hot red chilies, seeded, minced | | | 2 each | |
| sugar | 3 3/4 oz. | 107 g | 1/2 cup | 120 mL |
| tomato paste | 3/4 oz. | 22 g | 2 tablespoons | 30 mL |
| fish sauce | | 57 g | 1/4 cup | 60 mL |
| fresh lime juice | | 57 g | 1/4 cup | 60 mL |
| lime zest | 1/4 oz. | 8 g | 1 tablespoon | 15 mL |
| green beans, julienne | 3 1/2 oz. | 104 g | 20 each | |
| *sambal* | 3/4 oz. | 22 g or to taste | 1 tablespoon | 15 mL or to taste |
| bean sprouts | 10 oz. | 284 g | 4 cups | 960 mL |
| fresh cilantro, minced | 1/2 oz. | 15 g | 1/4 cup | 60 mL |

**Garnish:**

scallion brushes

chili pepper strips

deep-fried eggs, *see recipe below*

Dripping egg from hand into hot fat

Placing rice noodles in hot oil

Removing rice noodles from hot oil

Mixing Mee Krob ingredients together in bowl

1. Soak mushrooms in 1/4 cup (57 g or 60 mL) water for 20 minutes, slice mushrooms, reserve soaking water.

2. Heat oil for deep-frying in wok or deep-fryer until 350 degrees (180°C).

3. Dribble about 1 tablespoon (15 mL) egg from gloved fingers into hot oil, moving hand in circular motion so egg falls into strands. Fry for 30 seconds, turn lacelike egg gently, fry another 30 seconds, until golden brown, drain on paper towels. Reserve until needed for garnish.

4. Dip hand in cold water, repeat process with remaining eggs. Reserve until needed.

5. Break block of rice noodles into three pieces, fry one piece at a time. Fry for 1 minute, turn gently with tongs, fry another 30 seconds, until light brown. Drain on paper towels. Reserve until needed.

6. Remove all oil except 2 tablespoons (30 mL) from wok, heat over high heat. Add pork, stir-fry 1 minute, add onions and garlic, fry another minute, add shrimp and chili peppers, fry another minute.

7. Add sugar, then add tomato paste, mushrooms, and mushroom soaking water. Bring to boil, cook for a few minutes over medium-high heat to thicken sauce.

8. Add fish sauce, and lime juice and zest, cook a few minutes. Add green beans and *sambal*, cook about 2 minutes, until beans are *al dente*. Add bean sprouts, cook 30 seconds to 1 minute. Correct seasonings.

9. Place one piece crisp noodles (one-third of noodles) in large bowl, top with one-third of stir-fry mixture. Mix gently with tongs, repeat with remaining two portions.

10. Top with cilantro, garnish with scallion brushes, chili strips, and reserved deep-fried egg. Serve immediately.

---

# ADOBONG BABOY AT MANOK (PHILIPPINES)

## CHICKEN AND PORK ADOBO

Andrea Skjold © Shutterstock

**Note:** Probably the most well-known Filipino dish, *adobo* recipes have countless variations. It is prepared with beef, pork, chicken, fish, or a combination.

**Number of Servings:** 11  
**Serving Size:** 5 1/2 oz. (156 g), or 1 piece chicken and 2 pieces pork  
**Total Yield:** 4 lb., 1/2 oz. (1.8 kg)  
**Cooking Method:** Boil, sauté  
**Food Balance:** Balanced/sour  
**Wine Style:** Wine friendly—Try your favorite  
**Example:** Château St. Jean Chardonnay or Cabernet Sauvignon

| | WEIGHT | | VOLUME | |
|---|---|---|---|---|
| **INGREDIENTS** | **U.S.** | **METRIC** | **U.S.** | **METRIC** |
| white vinegar | | 340 g | 1 1/2 cups | 360 mL |
| garlic, minced | 1 1/2 oz. | 43 g | 16 cloves | |
| salt | 1/2 oz. | 15 g | 2 teaspoons | 10 mL |
| pepper | | | 1 teaspoon | 5 mL |
| bay leaves | | | 4 each | |
| pork, shoulder or butt, trimmed and cut into 2-inch (5-cm) cubes | 2 lb. | 908 g | | |
| chicken, cut into serving pieces | 3 lb., 9 oz. | 1.6 kg | | |
| water | | 227 g | 1 cup | 240 mL |
| soy sauce | | 57 g | 1/4 cup | 60 mL |
| oil | | 28 g | 2 tablespoons | 30 mL or as needed |

**Accompaniment:**

rice, steamed

---

**TWIST ON THE CLASSIC**

For a restaurant-friendly version, replace the bone-in chicken with boneless chicken breasts, cut into pieces and cook in the dish for about 15 minutes, then add shrimp and scallops to the dish.

1. Combine vinegar, 1 oz. (12 cloves or 28 g) of garlic, salt, pepper, and bay leaves in nonreactive pan. Add pork and chicken, refrigerate and marinate for 1 hour.
2. Remove chicken from pan, refrigerate until needed. Add water to pan, cover and bring to boil over medium heat, reduce heat and simmer for 30 to 45 minutes, until pork is almost tender.
3. Add chicken, cover and simmer another 30 to 45 minutes, until tender.
4. Remove from heat. Remove meat from pan, set aside until needed. Skim excess fat from pan, discard.
5. Add soy sauce to sauce in pan, bring to boil and simmer while browning meat. Add water if necessary to bring sauce up to 2 cups (454 g or 480 mL).
6. Heat oil in skillet over medium heat until hot. Add remaining 1/2 oz. (4 cloves or 15 g) of garlic, chicken, and pork, sauté until meat lightly browns.
7. Add chicken, pork, garlic, and pan drippings from skillet to sauce. Remove bay leaves. Correct seasonings. Serve over rice.

## KAENG PET KAI NORMAI ON (THAILAND)
### CHICKEN AND BAMBOO SHOOTS IN RED CURRY

**Number of Servings:** 10
**Serving Size:** 6 oz. (170 g)
**Total Yield:** 4 lb. (1.8 kg)
**Food Balance:** Sweet/protein
**Wine Style:** Off-dry or low-oaked whites or soft reds
**Example:** Beringer Founders' Estate Chardonnay or Merlot

**Cooking Method:** Boil

| INGREDIENTS | WEIGHT | | VOLUME | |
| --- | --- | --- | --- | --- |
| | U.S. | METRIC | U.S. | METRIC |
| fresh basil | 2 1/4 oz. | 64 g | 3 cups | 720 mL |
| coconut milk, unsweetened | | | 3 cans or 5 1/4 cups | 1.3 L |
| boneless, skinless chicken, 1-inch (2 1/2-cm) cubes | 2 lb., 4 oz. | 1 kg | | |
| red curry paste, purchased or homemade (recipe follows) | 7 1/2 oz. | 213 g | 3/4 cup | 180 mL |
| lime zest, julienne | 3/4 oz. | 22 g | 2 tablespoons | 30 mL |
| bamboo shoots, julienne | 1 lb., 8 oz. | 681 g | three 8-oz. cans | three 227-g cans |
| fish sauce | | 64 g | 1/4 cup + 1 1/2 teaspoons | 68 mL |
| brown sugar | 1 1/2 oz. | 43 g | 3 tablespoons | 45 mL |

**Accompaniment:**
cooked rice

1. Break or cut basil leaves into small pieces, set aside until needed.
2. Reserve 1 cup (240 mL) thick coconut milk, place remainder in pan with chicken, bring to boil.
3. Cook on medium-high heat about 10 minutes, add curry paste, lime zest, and bamboo shoots, cook 5 minutes.
4. Lower heat, add fish sauce and brown sugar, mix well.
5. Add remaining coconut milk, bring to boil.
6. Quickly stir in basil leaves, correct seasonings, serve immediately with rice.

### TWIST ON THE CLASSIC

Instead of serving this curry over rice, try one of these presentation ideas:

- Serve in a puff pastry shell.
- Serve in a hollowed *boule* (round loaf of bread) with a very crusty outside.

## NAM PRÍK KAENG DANG (THAILAND)

### RED CURRY PASTE

© Dorling Kindersley

**Note:** Refrigerate or freeze extra curry paste.

**Total Yield:** 1 lb. (454 g) or 1 1/2 cups (360 mL)

| INGREDIENTS | WEIGHT | | VOLUME | |
| --- | --- | --- | --- | --- |
| | U.S. | METRIC | U.S. | METRIC |
| dried hot red chilies, whole, seeded | 1/2 oz. | 15 g | 16 each | |
| ginger, peeled and minced | 2 oz. | 57 g | 4-inch piece | 10-cm piece |
| lime zest | 1/2 oz. | 15 g | 2 small limes | |
| fresh lemongrass, 6 inches (15 cm) from root, outer leaves removed, sliced | 1/2 oz. | 15 g | 2 each | |
| onion, diced | 5 oz. | 142 g | 1 medium | |
| garlic, minced | 1 1/2 oz. | 43 g | 8 large cloves | |
| fresh cilantro | 1/2 oz. | 15 g | 12 to 16 sprigs | |
| shrimp paste | 1 1/2 oz. | 43 g | 2 tablespoons | 30 mL |
| paprika | 1/2 oz. | 15 g | 1 tablespoon + 1 teaspoon | 20 mL |
| ground coriander | 1/4 oz. | 8 g | 1 teaspoon | 5 mL |
| ground cumin | 1/4 oz. | 8 g | 1 teaspoon | 5 mL |
| ground cinnamon | | | 1/4 teaspoon | 2 mL |
| turmeric | | | 1/2 teaspoon | 3 mL |
| ground cardamom | | | 1/4 teaspoon | 2 mL |
| salt | 1/4 oz. | 8 g | 1 teaspoon | 5 mL |

### TWIST ON THE CLASSIC

Combine strips of grilled chicken, thinned red curry paste, and pasta for a pasta entrée with a Thai twist.

1. Chop chilies into pieces, cover with water, let soak about 45 minutes.
2. Purée all ingredients except chilies in blender or food processor fitted with knife blade, pour chilies and soaking water into blender or food processor.
3. Process into fine paste, transfer to jar, and refrigerate until needed.

## PEPES IKAN (INDONESIA)

### SPICY FISH

Dave Abram © Rough Guides

**Note:** Using 3 lb. (1.4 kg) of fish makes each serving 6 oz. (170 g) of raw fish. For an 8-oz. (227-g) raw-weight portion, start with 4 lb. (1.8 kg) of fish. Traditionally, this dish is accompanied by lots of rice.

**Number of Servings:** 8

**Serving Size:** 4 1/2 oz. (128 g)

**Total Yield:** 2 lb., 4 oz. (1 kg)

**Food Balance:** Sweet-and-sour/spicy

**Wine Style:** Off-dry or low-oaked whites or soft reds

**Example:** Beringer White Zinfandel or Gewürztraminer, Stone Cellars Shiraz

**Cooking Method:** Broil

| INGREDIENTS | WEIGHT | | VOLUME | |
| --- | --- | --- | --- | --- |
| | U.S. | METRIC | U.S. | METRIC |
| onion, diced | 4 1/2 oz. | 128 g | 1 medium | |
| garlic, minced | | | 3 cloves | |
| dried chili flakes, chopped | | | 1 1/2 teaspoons | 8 mL |
| shrimp paste | | | 3/4 teaspoon | 4 mL |
| salt | 1/2 oz. | 15 g | 2 teaspoons | 10 mL |
| sugar | 1/4 oz. | 8 g | 1 1/2 teaspoons | 8 mL |
| tamarind paste, dissolved in 3 tablespoons (45 mL) water | 3/4 oz. | 22 g | 1 tablespoon | 15 mL |
| tomato, fresh or canned, chopped | 3 3/4 oz. | 107 g | 3/4 cup | 180 mL |
| fish fillets, haddock, flounder, or sole | 3 lb. to 3 lb., 4 oz. | 1.4 to 1.5 kg | | |
| aluminum foil | 3 sheets | | | |

**Accompaniment:**
cooked rice

1. Place onion, garlic, chili flakes, shrimp paste, salt, sugar, tamarind paste, and tomato in bowl of food processor fitted with knife blade or in blender, blend until coarse paste.
2. Preheat broiler.
3. Cover both sides of fish with paste, place one-third of fish on each piece of foil, wrap tightly.
4. Place foil packet under broiler for 10 minutes, turn, cook another 10 minutes.
5. Open packet, turning back edges, and broil 5 minutes, to brown fish.
6. Serve hot, accompanied by rice.

**TWIST ON THE CLASSIC**

Accompany this fish with mango salsa.

---

## GULAI DAUN BAYEM (INDONESIA)

### SPINACH IN COCONUT MILK

**Number of Servings:** 9
**Serving Size:** 4 oz. (114 g)
**Total Yield:** 2 lb., 6 oz. (1.1 kg)

**Cooking Method:** Boil

© goytex

| INGREDIENTS | WEIGHT | | VOLUME | |
| --- | --- | --- | --- | --- |
| | U.S. | METRIC | U.S. | METRIC |
| coconut milk | | | 2 cups | 480 mL |
| fresh green chilies, minced | 3/4 oz. | 22 g | 3 each | |
| garlic, smashed and minced | 1/2 oz. | 15 g | 3 large cloves | |
| onion or shallots, thin slices | 4 oz. | 114 g | 1 medium onion or 8 shallots | |
| spinach, tough stems removed, washed and cut into 1-inch (2 1/2-cm) strips | 1 lb., 10 oz. | 738 g | | |
| salt | 1/4 oz. | 8 g | 1 teaspoon | 5 mL |

1. Place coconut milk, chilies, garlic, and onions or shallots in pan, bring to boil for 3 minutes.
2. Add spinach, cook a few minutes, until tender, add salt.
3. Correct seasonings, serve immediately.

**TWIST ON THE CLASSIC**

For a great presentation and taste combination, place a grilled steak over a bed of this spinach.

# SALA LOBAK (INDONESIA)

## CABBAGE WITH RED PEPPER SAUCE

**Number of Servings:** 9
**Serving Size:** 4 oz. (114 g)
**Total Yield:** 2 lb., 6 oz. (1.1 kg)

**Cooking Method:** Stir-fry (sauté)

Pearson Education, Inc.

| | WEIGHT | | VOLUME | |
| --- | --- | --- | --- | --- |
| **INGREDIENTS** | **U.S.** | **METRIC** | **U.S.** | **METRIC** |
| red bell pepper, diced | 8 oz. | 227 g | 1 large | |
| hot chili pepper, ribs and seeds removed if desired, minced | 1 to 1 1/2 oz. | 28 to 43 g or to taste | 2 each or to taste | |
| onion, diced | 4 oz. | 114 g | 1 medium | |
| garlic, minced | 1/2 oz. | 15 g | 4 cloves | |
| shrimp paste | 1/4 oz. | 8 g | 1 teaspoon | 5 mL |
| tamarind paste dissolved in 1/4 cup + 2 tablespoons (85 g or 90 mL) water | 1/2 oz. | 15 g | 2 teaspoons | 10 mL |
| oil | | 71 g | 1/4 cup + 1 tablespoon | 75 mL |
| cabbage leaves, outer leaves plus inner leaves to make 2 lb. (908 g), shredded | 2 lb. | 908 g | 1 small head | |
| salt | 1/4 oz. | 8 g | 1 teaspoon | 5 mL |

1. Combine bell pepper, chili peppers, onion, garlic, shrimp paste, and tamarind paste in blender or food processor fitted with knife blade, blend until coarse paste.
2. Heat oil in wok over medium heat until hot. Add paste, stirring constantly, cook for 4 or 5 minutes, until dark red.
3. Add cabbage and salt, cook, stirring for 30 seconds, lower heat to medium-low and cook for about 8 minutes, until cabbage is done. Correct seasonings.
4. Serve accompanied by rice and other dishes that contain sauce.

# NASI UDUK (INDONESIA)

## COCONUT RICE

**Number of Servings:** 9
**Serving Size:** 4 oz. (114 g)
**Total Yield:** 2 lb., 7 1/2 oz. (1.1 kg)
**Wine Style:** Medium- to full-bodied red wine with a few years of bottle aging on it. Possible grape varietals are Blaufrankisch, Zweigelt, Merlot.
**Example:** Cuvee "Gabarinza" 2008, Heinrich (Neusiedlersee/Austria)

**Cooking Method:** Boil

| INGREDIENTS | WEIGHT | | VOLUME | |
| --- | --- | --- | --- | --- |
| | U.S. | METRIC | U.S. | METRIC |
| rice, Jasmine or Thai fragrant rice | 15 oz. | 426 g | 2 cups | 480 mL |
| water | as needed | | | |
| coconut milk, unsweetened | 14-oz. can | 397-g can | | |
| salt | 1/4 oz. | 8 g | 1 teaspoon | 5 mL |
| coriander, ground | | | 1/2 teaspoon | 3 mL |
| lemongrass stem, bruised | 1/4 oz. | 8 g | 1 each | |
| cinnamon stick | 1/4 oz. | 8 g | 1/2 each | |
| bay leaf | | | 1 each | |
| ginger, 1/2-inch (1 1/3-cm) slice | | | | |

**Garnish:**

fried shallot slices

Called *nasi lemak* in Malaysia and *khao man* in Thailand, cooks in many countries throughout Southeast Asia make a version of coconut rice.

Originally from Jakarta, *nasi uduk* commonly is sold at street stands in Indonesia. Often, it accompanies an omelet, tempeh, fried chicken, salad, or is served alone.

1. Wash rice several times in cold water. Place in pan.
2. Add water to coconut milk to make 2 cups (1 pint or 480 mL). Add to pan containing rice along with salt, coriander, lemongrass, cinnamon, bay leaf, and ginger.
3. Stirring constantly, bring to boil. Reduce heat, cover, and simmer for 15 minutes. Remove from heat; allow to sit for 10 minutes.
4. Discard lemongrass, cinnamon, bay leaf, and ginger. Stir gently. Serve, garnished with fried shallot slices.

© Kicut82

© rifanny

# PAN DE SAL (PHILIPPINES)

## BREAKFAST ROLLS

**Note:** Breakfast in the Philippines includes *Pan de Sal*. Like typical dinner rolls, these hail from the Spanish influence in the Philippines. The literal translation of *Pan de Sal* is "salted bread."

**Total Yield:** 2 lb., 15 1/4 oz. (1.3 kg) dough, or about 67 small rolls

**Cooking Method:** Bake

*Kneaded dough ready to proof*
Pearson Education/PH College

| | WEIGHT | | VOLUME | |
|---|---|---|---|---|
| INGREDIENTS | U.S. | METRIC | U.S. | METRIC |
| water, lukewarm | | 57 g | 1/4 cup | 60 mL |
| sugar | 2 3/4 oz. | 78 g | 1/4 cup + 1 tablespoon | 75 mL |
| granulated yeast | 1/4 oz. | 8 g | 2 teaspoons | 10 mL |
| bread flour | 1 lb., 13 3/4 oz. | 844 g or as needed | 6 cups | 1.4 L |
| salt | | | 1 1/2 teaspoons | 8 mL |
| water | | 397 g | 1 3/4 cups | 420 mL |
| vegetable oil | | 43 g | 3 tablespoons | 45 mL |
| dry bread crumbs | 1 1/2 oz. | 43 g or as needed | 1/4 cup | 60 mL or as needed |

1. Put 1/4 cup (57 g or 60 mL) lukewarm water in nonreactive bowl. Sprinkle 1 tablespoon (15 g) of sugar and yeast over water. Mix, set aside for 5 to 10 minutes, until foamy. Line sheet pans with parchment paper, set aside until needed.
2. In large, nonreactive bowl, place 3 cups (710 g) of flour, salt, and remaining 1/4 cup (59 g) sugar. Mix to combine.
3. Make well in center, pour in remaining 1 3/4 cups (420 mL) water and oil, mix with wooden spoon to combine.
4. Add yeast mixture, mix well. Add remaining flour as needed to knead dough. Do not add too much flour or rolls will be dry.
5. Knead dough for 8 to 10 minutes until smooth and elastic. Return to bowl, cover loosely, and allow to rise until doubled, about 1 to 1 1/2 hours.
6. Punch down dough, roll out into rectangle 3/4 inches (2 cm) thick. With dough cutter or knife, slice into 1 1/2-inch (4-cm) strips. Sprinkle with 1 tablespoon (15 g) of breadcrumbs. Cover loosely and let rise for 15 minutes.
7. Cut dough strips into 1 1/2-inch (4-cm) pieces. Place on prepared sheet pans with cut side facing up. Sprinkle with remaining breadcrumbs. Cover and let rise until doubled, about 30 minutes. Meanwhile, preheat oven to 375 degrees (190°C).
8. Bake for 15 to 20 minutes until lightly brown. Serve warm.

*Punching down risen dough*
Pearson Education/PH College

*Folding punched dough*
Pearson Education/PH College

© Tony Magdaraog

## SANGKHAYA (THAILAND)

### STEAMED COCONUT CUSTARD

**Note:** Instead of steaming this custard in small cups, steam in coconut halves or small pumpkins. If steaming in a pumpkin, serve some of the meat of the pumpkin with the custard.

**Number of Servings:** 8
**Serving Size:** 8 small cups, 2 oz. (59 mL) each
**Total Yield:** 1 lb., 1 oz. (482 g)

**Cooking Method:** Steam (boil)

Alan Newham © Dorling Kindersley

|  | WEIGHT | | VOLUME | |
|---|---|---|---|---|
| **INGREDIENTS** | **U.S.** | **METRIC** | **U.S.** | **METRIC** |
| eggs | 6 3/4 oz. | 191 g | 4 each | |
| unsweetened coconut milk | | | 2 cups | 480 mL |
| brown sugar | 5 1/2 oz. | 156 g | 3/4 cup | 180 mL |
| rose water, *optional* | | | 1/8 teaspoon | 1 mL |

1. Prepare pot for steaming custard. Beat eggs lightly. Stir coconut milk well, whisk into eggs.
2. Whisk brown sugar into egg mixture.
3. Place mixture in double boiler over barely simmering water. Whisk constantly and cook until mixture thickens into custard. *Note: Be careful to keep heat low so eggs do not curdle.* Whisk in rose water, if desired.
4. Strain custard into small bowls or cups, cover with foil, steam over simmering water for 15 to 20 minutes, until custard is barely set and knife inserted into custard comes out almost clean. (If steaming in larger container, custard may require an hour to steam.)
5. Cool, and then refrigerate until serving.

### TWIST ON THE CLASSIC

At service, unmold coconut custard over a round of chocolate or vanilla cake. If using chocolate cake, decorate with chocolate sauce or ganache. Garnish with fresh pineapple pieces and/or raspberries. Serve with a small scoop of coconut ice cream.

## SANS RIVAL (PHILIPPINES)

### CASHEW MERINGUE TORTE

**Note:** The name of this confection translates from French and means "without rival." If desired, frost the long sides with filling, but leave the ends unfrosted so that no slice appears as an end piece. Using less filling (frosting) cuts down on the sweetness of this dessert.

**Number of Servings:** 10
**Serving Size:** 1 slice 1 1/2 inches (4 cm) wide
**Total Yield:** 1 torte, about 15 by 5 inches (38 by 13 cm)

**Cooking Method:** Bake, boil

### TWIST ON THE CLASSIC

For an interesting look, divide the filling in half and add melted semi-sweet or bittersweet chocolate to half of it. Fill alternate layers with chocolate and rum flavored fillings.

|  | WEIGHT | | VOLUME | |
|---|---|---|---|---|
| **INGREDIENTS** | **U.S.** | **METRIC** | **U.S.** | **METRIC** |
| **Meringue:** | | | | |
| egg whites, at room temperature | 10 oz. | 284 g | 10 each | |
| cream of tartar | | | 1/4 teaspoon | 2 mL |
| sugar | 7 1/2 oz. | 213 g | 1 cup | 240 mL |
| unsalted cashews, roasted and coarsely ground | 11 1/4 oz. | 319 g | 2 cups | 480 mL |

This dessert resembles the French almond and/or hazelnut meringue dessert *dacquoise.*

For best results, beat egg whites at room temperature or a little cooler than room temperature. Beating cold egg whites yields less volume.

*Folding ground cashews into meringue*
David Murray and Jules Selmes © Dorling Kindersley

© Ulyana Khorunzha

| INGREDIENTS | WEIGHT | | VOLUME | |
| --- | --- | --- | --- | --- |
| | U.S. | METRIC | U.S. | METRIC |
| **Filling:** | | | | |
| egg yolks | 4 oz. | 114 g | 6 each | |
| sugar | 4 oz. | 114 g | 1/2 cup | 120 mL |
| corn syrup | | | 1/2 cup | 120 mL |
| water | | 28 g | 2 tablespoons | 30 mL |
| rum | | 15 g | 1 tablespoon | 15 mL |
| unsalted butter, softened | 8 oz. | 227 g | 1 cup (2 sticks) | 240 mL |
| **Garnish:** | | | | |
| unsalted cashews, roasted and chopped | 3 1/2 oz. | 104 g | 1/2 cup | 120 mL |

## MERINGUE:

1. Preheat oven to 275 degrees (135°C). Cover three half-sheet pans (or cookie sheets) with parchment paper. Pan-spray parchment paper.
2. Place egg whites and cream of tartar in mixing bowl of mixer fitted with wire beater. Mix on low speed until frothy. Turn mixer to high speed and beat until soft peaks form. Slowly add 1 cup (213 g) sugar by the tablespoon, until all sugar is incorporated.
3. In three parts, gently fold in the ground cashews. Fold in one-third, then fold in half of the remaining cashews, and finally fold in the rest of the cashews. *Note: When folding in cashews, be careful to incorporate the pocket of nuts that often forms on the bottom of the bowl.*
4. With icing spatula, spread meringue evenly on prepared pans. Bake for 30 to 40 minutes until crisp and starting to turn lightly brown. Meringue should feel dry.\* Once crisp and dry and turning golden, remove from oven, cut meringue on each pan in half. Cut lengthwise into two strips about 15 by 5 inches (38 by 13 cm). Cool completely on the parchment paper.

\*If the meringue does not feel dry, remove from oven, cut in half (as described), and return to turned-off oven. Allow meringue to stay in oven until cool and crisp.

## FILLING:

1. In mixer fitted with wire beater, whip egg yolks on high speed until fluffy and pale yellow in color.
2. Meanwhile, place 1/2 cup (114 g) sugar, corn syrup, and water in saucepan. Mix to combine. Bring to boil over high heat. Cover and cook for 2 minutes. Remove lid and wash down sides of pan with pastry brush dipped in water to remove any sugar crystals from the sides of pan. Cook until soft ball stage, measuring about 238 degrees (114°C) on a candy thermometer.
3. Set mixer speed to low, very slowly pour sugar syrup in a thin stream into egg yolks. Set mixer to high speed and mix until room temperature.
4. Reduce mixer speed to low, add rum. Mix well. Add butter, about a tablespoon at a time. If too soft to spread at this point, refrigerate until firm. If not fluffy after refrigerating, beat at high speed until fluffy.

## ASSEMBLY:

1. Reserve best piece of meringue for the top. Place one piece of meringue on cake board or serving platter. Spread thinly with filling (about 1/8 inch, 1/3 cm thick). Repeat with remaining layers.
2. Top with reserved meringue and spread filling on that layer, too. Decorate torte with chopped cashews. Cover and refrigerate at least a couple of hours to firm filling before serving.
3. Cut into 1 1/2-inch (4-cm) or desired-size pieces and serve.

# India

>> **LEARNING OBJECTIVES**

By the end of this chapter, you will be able to:

- Discuss the major religions found in India and their role in molding India's cuisine
- Explain similarities and differences between the cuisines found in the north and south of India
- Discuss the importance and uses of spices in the cookery of India
- Define *thali* and describe the Indian method of eating a meal
- Prepare a variety of Indian dishes

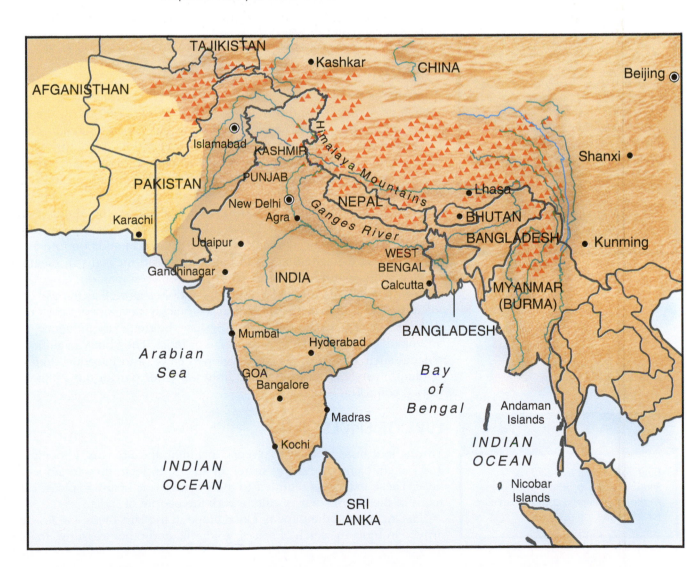

## >> HISTORY

Evidence shows people inhabited India 200,000 years ago. Around 2500 B.C., the first documented civilization in India lived in western India.

### RELIGIOUS INFLUENCE

Religion was and still remains an important part of both India's history and its culinary makeup. Throughout the history of India and into the present, Muslims and Hindus as well as people of other religions have experienced periods of violence and times of peaceful coexistence.

From about 1000 B.C., the Hindus established *Ayurveda*, which deals with health and life issues. According to this ancient tradition, life is composed of the body, mind, and soul. With that premise, matters of cuisine impact the mind and soul as well as the body, and everything that affects one of the three affects the other two. The Hindus believed that food is divided into six flavors (sour, salty, sweet, bitter, pungent, and astringent), and each of those sensations had specific outcomes. For example, they thought pungency intensified passions. Like some of the other Asian cultures, their goal was to serve dishes and meals with a variety of flavor and texture sensations to create a balanced meal.

Offshoots of the Hindu religion, Buddhism and Jainism, developed in India in the 500s and 400s B.C. Besides Hindus, Muslims, Buddhists, and Jains, India is home to Sikhs, Zoroastrians, Christians, and Jews. Many religious sects flourish in India, each with their own dietary laws.

### INVADERS AND RULERS

Residents of India have endured a seemingly endless stream of invaders throughout their history, including the Greeks in the 300s B.C., the Arabs, the Huns, and many more. When the Gupta Dynasty ruled between 320 and 500 A.D., India experienced its Golden Age. The arts, mathematics, science, and literature thrived during this time; however, after this period, a series of invasions from more aggressive Asians and Middle Eastern people ensued. This time of fighting and strife lasted until the sixteenth century when the Moghul Empire invaded and conquered.

The Muslim Moghuls entered India from Persia in the Middle East. The Moghuls left a significant mark on the Indian cuisine, which is most pronounced in the north of India. They introduced lamb and grilled *kebabs* in addition to many of their native dishes like rice pilafs, *biryani* (a baked rice and meat dish), meats marinated and cooked with yogurt, nut butters, and spices like cinnamon, cloves, cardamom, and saffron. The Indians adopted many Moghul dishes as well as the use of yogurt for marinating meats and making sauces. Indians quickly developed a preference for smooth, delicate sauces from these invaders. Besides their culinary influence, the Moghuls had an impact on many other aspects of life in India. They built magnificent mosques and palaces such as the Taj Mahal, developed cities, and introduced an extravagant and opulent lifestyle. Their rule lasted until the latter part of the 1700s when the British gained control.

### LURE OF SPICES

Throughout history, many explorers, including the Romans, Phoenicians, Portuguese, and Dutch, came to India in search of spices. Indeed, they found a bounty of spices here. These explorers returned to their homelands bearing spices, but they left remnants of their own culinary culture with the people of India.

Sailing around the Cape of Good Hope in the late 1400s, the Portuguese explorers arrived in India in search of spices, gold, silk, and other treasures. In 1498, they settled

---

The oldest modern religion, Hinduism, began between 4000 and 2200 B.C. Hinduism ranks as the third largest religion behind Christianity and Islam. Approximately 1 billion people follow the Hindu faith, and 905 million of them live in India. Thousands of different sects compose the Hindu population.

Unlike many religions, Hinduism is a way of life, incorporating religious, philosophical, and cultural aspects. Most Hindus believe in the repetition of cycles of birth and death—reincarnation—and in karma.

Like Christians' story of Jesus, who was Jewish, Buddhists say Buddha was born into a Hindu family. His followers celebrated his life and teachings, and they developed a religion around him. According to history, Buddha was born to a royal family in the 500s or 600s B.C. He lived and taught in India.

Another sect from the Hindu religion, Jainism, promotes peace and nonviolence. Jains have high regard for scholarship and education, and they claim the highest literacy of any sect in India. Followers of Jainism developed the oldest libraries in India.

---

Built from 1632 to 1653, a Moghul emperor had the Taj Mahal constructed as a mausoleum for his wife.

in Goa in western India, and then made their way to other areas. They introduced chili peppers from the New World, and hot peppers immediately became an important part of the Indian cuisine. In addition, these explorers brought cashews, potatoes, and tomatoes. The Portuguese ruled the western part of India for 400 years.

## BRITAIN

In the 1600s, the British arrived in India. By the late eighteenth century, India had become a British colony. It remained under the rule of the United Kingdom until 1947, when India became an independent nation. As a result of the long British dominance, the British strongly influenced the cuisine of India, and the Indians in turn made a lasting impact on the cuisine of the United Kingdom.

## RECENT HISTORY

In 1940, Pakistan was carved out of India and established as a primarily Muslim country. According to statistics, over 96 percent of Pakistani people are Muslims. In India today, however, about 80 percent of the inhabitants are Hindus and 15 percent are Muslims. Within densely populated India, 14 languages and at least 240 dialects are spoken.

India remains a country of extreme wealth and extreme poverty. Most Indians still follow the *caste* system, which divides people into four *castes*, or social classes. This results in four distinct levels of society, from the very poor to the privileged. Although the *castes* are not as strong today as in the past, little intermarriage or mingling takes place between people of different *castes*. As a result, people marry within their *caste*, and the children of that marriage belong to the same *caste*. In this way, the *caste* system continues, and inhabitants of India have little chance to change their social position.

## >> TOPOGRAPHY

A peninsula jutting into the Indian Ocean, India is located in southern Asia. China, Nepal, and Bhutan are found to the north; Bangladesh and the Bay of Bengal lie to the east; Sri Lanka is situated to the southeast; the Indian Ocean is on the south; and Pakistan and the Arabian Sea are to its west. Basically, the distinct regions found in India are based on topography.

## NORTH

Rising at India's northern border with China and Nepal, the towering Himalayan Mountains run through the extreme northern section of India. The climate in these snow-capped mountains consists of cold winters and cool summers, conducive to growing many crops, including fruits and walnuts. Abundant mushrooms grow wild in this terrain and sheep thrive here.

South of the mountains, the land changes to plains, valleys, and rivers. The Ganges and Indus rivers run through this area, providing rich soil for fertile farmland for a variety of crops including wheat, barley, millet, corn, and a myriad of fruits and vegetables. In addition, a bounty of fish provides food. Most of the people of India reside in this region.

## EAST

The east consists of fertile plains and coastline. Abundant seafood and fish are available here, and a bounty of crops including rice, legumes, coconuts, bananas, and many vegetables grow in this area. Eastern India receives plenty of rainfall; in fact, some of the highest recorded rainfall amounts have occurred here.

*An important man in India's history, Mohandas Gandhi became the leader of the Indian National Congress in 1920 and led the movement to gain independence from Britain. Gandhi believed in nonviolence and promoted nonviolent tactics against the British, which proved to be very effective. Under Gandhi's direction, the Indians refused to pay taxes and boycotted all things that were British, including schools, government, and goods. Ironically, this leader who stood for nonviolence was assassinated in 1948, one year after India received its independence.*

*The Himalayan Mountains reign as the world's highest mountain range.*

## WEST

Contrarily, hot, arid land with desert conditions describes the land in the west. Seafood from the coasts dominates the diet of those living in this region. Significantly fewer crops grow here.

## SOUTH

Called Deccan, the central-southern portion of the Indian peninsula contains plateaus in the center flanked by mountains on the east and west. Coastal plains lie between the mountains and the coast. Tropical conditions and jungles predominate in the south. Much of this land is fertile farmland, yielding all sorts of grains including the famous *basmati* rice, wheat, corn, millet, and barley. Legumes, many vegetables, as well as spices and peppers flourish in this region.

Lying near the equator, the extreme south experiences hot, humid, tropical weather with *monsoons*, seasonal winds. Seafood, fish, coconuts, bananas, and a myriad of tropical fruits and vegetables thrive in this area's tropical climate.

---

### Ingredients and Foods Commonly Used throughout the Cuisine of India Include

- rice and wheat
- legumes including lentils, split peas, mung beans, and chickpeas
- goat and lamb
- seafood and fish
- vegetables including spinach, cauliflower, potatoes, peas, pumpkin, and sweet potatoes
- fruits including bananas, plantains, mangoes, oranges, and coconuts

- chutneys and pickled fruits and vegetables
- garlic
- cilantro
- coriander, cumin, ginger, turmeric, cardamom, fenugreek, hot chilies, mustard, fennel, cloves, and cinnamon
- *ghee* (clarified butter)

---

## CLIMATE

The climate in India includes three distinct seasons: the cool season of the fall and winter, the hot season dominating the spring, and the rainy period found in the summer. The cool season brings cold weather in the mountainous areas but temperate, warm, or hot weather to the other regions. The southern regions experience extremely hot conditions during the hot season.

The *monsoons* have an enormous effect on the crops, making India susceptible to both flooding and droughts. Unfortunately, these unpredictable conditions often lead to crop failures and starvation.

*Fourteenth-century tandoor oven*
© aleks649

## >> COOKING METHODS

In the early days, much of the food was either grilled over an open fire or cooked in a pot placed in the embers of the fire. Of course, this one-pot cookery resulted in India's stewlike curries and was perfect for the long, slow cooking needed for legumes. To extend the available meat, they combined the tender cuts of meat with vegetables on a skewer for grilling (*kebabs*), while the tougher cuts entered the pot for braising—the slow cooking method necessary to make them tender. These techniques reflect the cookery of the Middle East, which the Moghuls brought with them.

With many rivers and lots of ocean surrounding this peninsula, fresh seafood and fish abound. Seafood preparations include frying, baking, poaching, grilling, or steaming.

## TANDOOR OVEN

People in northern India frequently bake in a *tandoor* oven. This clay oven becomes very hot from its fuel of wood or charcoal. They use the *tandoor* oven for cooking meat, poultry, seafood, fish, or vegetables on skewers, as well as for baking flatbreads. Cooks often marinate skewered foods in a yogurt and spice mixture before cooking, and then the skewers are lowered into the vat-shaped oven. Flatbreads are slapped against the inside walls of the hot oven, where they adhere and quickly cook.

## FRYING

Stir-frying remains a popular cooking technique in India, particularly with the large number of vegetable dishes served throughout this country. This is often done in a deep pan with a rounded bottom and handles on each side called a *karahi*, which is similar to the Oriental wok. Another pan found in Indian kitchens, the *tava*, is a slightly concave griddle made of cast iron. Frequently used for sautéing, an ungreased *tava* is used to fry several varieties of flatbreads. Deep-frying continues as a popular cooking method for many foods in this cuisine.

## STEAMING

In the south, steaming remains the most frequently used cooking technique. Cooks often enclose the foods in banana leaves and then steam them. They traditionally placed leaf-wrapped foods in the embers of the fire for steaming, much like the *tamale* of Mexico. Today, large and small steaming pots are standard equipment in most southern Indian kitchens.

## PRESERVATION

The preservation of fruits and vegetables is commonplace throughout India. Pickles and *chutneys* (intensely flavored, sometimes spicy relishes) function as an important part of the Indian meal. In addition, they preserve the bounty of fruits and vegetables for meager times. In the mountainous north where harsh winters limit the growing season, they dry many foods. Another preservation technique, salting, is frequently used to extend available food supplies for times when less is available. As in Africa, flooding and droughts make the condition of the next season's crops an unknown.

## >> REGIONS

India is a densely populated nation with the second largest population of any country in the world. While Hindi remains India's official language, 14 distinct languages are used widely in India as well as more than 100 others. Making communication even more difficult, many of the languages use different scripts.

The diverse topography and climate that exists here created strong regional culinary differences. In addition, dietary laws from the various religious groups in India have had pronounced effects on the cuisine. These three issues—topography, climate, and religion—molded the cuisine of each region. As a result, great differences define the cuisines found in the various regions; however, the use of aromatic herbs and spices prevails throughout all of the regions. Regional differences are particularly apparent between the north and south of India.

## DIFFERENCES BETWEEN NORTH AND SOUTH

Flatbreads made from wheat function as the predominate starch in the north, while inhabitants of the southern regions eat rice with their meals. The food prepared in the north tends toward more subtle seasoning, while hot curries and highly spiced dishes

*Tandoor oven*
© Lucky Dragon USA

*Karahi*
© paul_brighton

*India's population is second only to China. Together, these two countries claim 40 percent of the world's population. If statistics for current birth rates continue, the population of India will overtake China's by 2030, and India will become the most populous country.*

When Indian restaurants first opened in North America, almost all served the cuisine of Punjab. As a result, many still believe that is the cuisine found in all of India.

dominate southern cookery. With ample coastline on three sides, in the east, west, and south, much seafood is consumed. Although the arid regions of the west yield fewer crops, they produce peas and beans (legumes). Accompanied by bread, these legumes form a major portion of the diet in this region.

Baked flatbreads and skewers of meats, poultry, seafood, and vegetables roasted in the famous *tandoor* oven hail from the north. Usually marinated in a yogurt mixture, these meats often are seasoned with *garam masala*, a mixture of spices. The traditional orange color of the meats cooked in the *tandoor* usually comes from food coloring, not spices. Although the northerners often bake foods, the people of the south prefer to steam many of their dishes.

While high meat consumption reigns in the north, the diet of people in western, eastern, and southern India includes lots of fish and seafood and much less meat. Countless vegetarian dishes come from the south, where many Hindu vegetarians reside. Typical of inhabitants in many hot climates throughout the world, residents of the tropical south prefer hot, spicy dishes and use lots of coconut and coconut milk. In addition, tamarind and mustard seeds flavor many southern dishes.

## SPICES

Cooks in the north and south use many of the same spices, but the treatment of the spices makes them taste different. In the north, spices are cooked or roasted in a dry pan, then ground and added to the foods. People in the south prefer to mix the spices into a wet paste and then combine the spice paste with the dish.

## BEVERAGES

All Indians drink cold water with meals, but coffee or tea generally follows the meal. Northerners prefer tea, and often serve spiced tea after the meal. The people of the south choose coffee flavored with milk and sugar instead of tea.

## >> CUISINE

### DIETARY RESTRICTIONS

Hindus, Muslims, and people of numerous other religious sects live in India, each possessing their own philosophies and dietary laws. Muslims do not eat pork. Hindus consider the cow a sacred animal, so they consume no beef. Since Hindus believe in reincarnation, many abstain from eating any meat. Jains, members of another religion that developed from Hinduism, believe strongly in reincarnation. As a result, followers of that religion eat no meat, fish, poultry, or eggs, believing that the animal could have been a person in another lifetime. Many also refrain from eating root vegetables because digging them might injure a worm or other underground creature. They abstain from red foods such as tomatoes and beets because the color is reminiscent of blood. As a result of the numerous religious restrictions on meat, the Indian cuisine is rich in vegetarian dishes.

### PROTEIN

With religious dietary laws forbidding consumption of pork and beef for many people, the most popular meats remain lamb and goat. Stemming from the Moghul influence, lamb reigns as a favored meat. The Moghuls ate lots of meat in their native Persia but abstained from pork because of their Muslim faith. When they entered India, they found a country where the cow was sacred, so that left lamb, goat, and chicken for eating. Northern Indians prepare *kofta*, a ground lamb and hard-boiled egg dish reminiscent of the Middle Eastern ground lamb dish *kibbe*.

Because the state of Goa (located on the west coast) was ruled by the Portuguese for so long, they eat beef and pork unlike most Indians. Also, a large Christian

*Kofta*
© uckyo

population resides in Goa. Reflecting strong Portuguese influence with its addition of vinegar, pork vindaloo and Sorpotel (a pork curry) hail from this area.

Chicken is served often in India. To prepare it, cooks remove the skin to facilitate the absorption of spices and marinades. In addition, they make shallow cuts in the meat so more of the marinade penetrates into it. Often, chicken is cut into smaller pieces than is customary in many Western cultures for two reasons. First, as in many other Asian cuisines, less meat accompanies greater amounts of vegetables and grains in the Indian diet. Second, smaller pieces expose more surface area to absorb the spices and marinade.

Ample seafood and fish is available along the coasts and near rivers, so inhabitants in those areas consume lots of seafood and fish. Similar to Dover sole, pomfret is one of the most prevalent and popular types of fish from the coasts of India. Other frequently consumed fish include mackerel and sardines. In the coastal areas, cooks often flavor fish with *masala*, a blend of spices, and coconut or coconut oil. Shellfish also abounds, and they serve many dishes containing shrimp, clams, crabs, and other shellfish.

## GRAINS AND LEGUMES

Rice, wheat, grains, and beans form the basis of the Indian diet. In fact, an Indian meal is incomplete if not accompanied by either bread (wheat) or rice. As stated before, rice is the staple grain in the south, whereas some form of wheat accompanies meals in the north. Inhabitants of southern India eat rice three times a day. It is not unusual for a family to have 25 different recipes for rice in their repertoire.

They serve several types of unleavened flatbreads in India. Usually made from whole-grain flours such as *chapati*, a finely ground whole wheat flour, these breads are cooked by deep-frying, sautéing on a dry griddle, or baking.

Grown in the foothills of the Himalayas, *basmati* rice is a nutty-flavored, long-grain variety of rice used throughout India, but especially in the north. Since the flavor of this rice improves with aging, high-quality *basmati* rice is aged for a minimum of 6 months. Cooks prefer the aromatic *basmati* rice for *biryani*, pilafs, and other dishes; however, depending on the use, Indians also choose other types of rice. In fact, over 1,000 varieties of rice are grown in India. Like wheat, rice appears in a number of forms, including puffed rice and rice flour. Indian cooks prepare an endless variety of rice pancakes, which function as breakfast through much of southern India.

Serving as a major source of protein for the many vegetarians and people who cannot afford meat, legumes play a huge role in Indian cuisine. Lentils rank as one of the most popular legumes and appear in many recipes throughout the country. *Dal* refers to any split legume, including lentils and split mung beans. *Dal* also refers to a mild purée of lentils or beans that is commonly served in the north. Southerners prefer a spicy lentil dish called *sambar*.

*India's premier cheese, paneer, is prepared by curdling cow's milk and then pressing the curds. In a few days, the mildly flavored cheese is ready to eat. Appearing in a multitude of guises, this cheese is served deep-fried, marinated, baked in a tandoor oven, and incorporated into all sorts of dishes. Paneer is a stretched-curd cheese, which refers to the process of handling the curds when making the cheese. This handling results in cheese with a springy texture resembling that of cooked chicken.*

*Naan*
© Witty234 @ Shutterstock

## INDIAN FLATBREADS

**chapati** Cooked on an ungreased *tava*; made from *chapati* flour

**parathas** Cooked on an ungreased *tava*; the dough is laminated by rolling the dough, brushing with oil, and repeating the process

**naan** Baked in a *tandoor* (oven)

**poori** Deep-fried

## CONDIMENTS

Although pronounced regional differences in the cuisine exist, yogurt, ample amounts of fresh fruits, chutneys, and pickles accompany meals throughout India. Two condiments, chutneys and pickles, are made from a wide range of fruits and vegetables. Originating in India, the intensely flavored, often-spicy chutney joins an assortment of foods, intended to heighten the flavor sensations by adding a wide range of flavor components to the Indian meal. Chutneys and pickles can be spicy, aromatic, hot, mild, sweet, tart, and/or salty.

Another frequently served item, yogurt relishes contain any vegetable or fruit combined with yogurt. *Raita*, a yogurt salad, frequently accompanies plain roasted or grilled meats, as well as highly spiced foods. The best known variety is cucumber *raita*. Yogurt functions as a cooling component after spicy foods.

## VEGETABLES AND FRUITS

Vegetable cookery reaches new heights in India. Because of its diverse climate and topography, ranging from snow-capped mountains to tropical jungles, an incredible assortment of vegetables grows in India. With a wide selection of vegetables available year-round and many vegetarians living here, vegetables function as a major component of the diet. They appear in numerous guises, cooked alone or in combinations and flavored with an extensive range of herbs and spices. Many types of vegetable curries abound. Potatoes, spinach, cauliflower, pumpkins, peas, and sweet potatoes rank high in popularity.

With a bounty of fruits available throughout the year, Indians also consume ample amounts of fresh fruit. As in African and Latin American countries, bananas and plantains are popular. Curries frequently incorporate fruit, which counters the spiciness of the dish. Fresh fruit or fruit pastes accompany many meals, and lots of people drink fruit juices or fruit and yogurt beverages.

## SAUCES

Instead of thickening sauces with flour or cornstarch as in the Western cuisines, Indians use spices, spice pastes, yogurt, or vegetables to thicken their sauces. Unlike flour or cornstarch, these thickening items actually contribute to the flavor of the dish.

The thickness of sauces differs between the north and south. In the north, they prepare thicker sauces, which are easier to scoop with bread. The thinner sauces preferred in the south soak into the rice better.

Indian dishes are classified as "wet" or "dry," depending on how much liquid their sauce contains. Obviously, loose or liquid sauces are called "wet," and they are eaten with flatbread or rice formed into a ball. "Dry" foods contain spices and herbs but no actual sauce. Indian chefs carefully plan a meal so that it includes both wet and dry dishes to offer variety to the diner.

## HERBS AND SPICES

Many say spices distinguish the Indian cuisine from all others. Indian cookery incorporates abundant spices and herbs, both fresh and dried, into dishes. In the past, spices

## DAL AND LEGUMES COMMONLY USED IN INDIA

- red lentils—*masoor dal*
- yellow lentils—*thoor dal*
- yellow split peas—*chana dal*
- black-eyed peas—*lobbia*
- split mung beans—*moong dal*

- red kidney beans—*rajma*
- aduki beans—*ma*
- black gram beans—*ural dal*
- chickpeas—*chhole*

## FREQUENTLY USED SPICE BLENDS

**curry powder** Contains varying amounts of coriander, cumin, fennel, fenugreek, mustard, pepper, cloves, turmeric, and cayenne pepper; used throughout India

**garam masala** Contains varying amounts of black pepper, cinnamon, cloves, and nutmeg and sometimes cumin, cardamom, and coriander; frequently used in northern India

**panch phoron** Contains varying amounts of cumin, fennel, fenugreek, mustard, and nigella; frequently used in eastern India

were prized for their flavor, medicinal properties, and ability to act as a preservative for the food. Today, cooks choose spices for a particular dish primarily based on their flavor and the color they impart to the finished dish. Spices still are valued, however, for their medicinal and health properties.

Many spices are stocked in the Indian kitchen. Common spices found in this cuisine include cumin, coriander, turmeric, ginger, garlic, cardamom, mustard seeds, and cayenne pepper. Throughout India, spices are cooked to intensify their flavor before incorporating them into the dish. Typically, spices are sautéed in a dry pan or cooked in oil, which further enhances their flavor before they are added to foods. In order to obtain the maximum taste, many spices are purchased whole. Cooks toast the spices just before using, and then grind them and add them to the dish. In the end, it is the combination of spices as well as the method of handling that makes each dish unique.

Lots of spices grow in India, including peppercorns, turmeric, ginger, nutmeg, cardamom, cloves, and chili peppers. Three well-known *masalas*, spice blends, are associated with the Indian cuisine: curry powder blends, *garam masala*, and *panch phoron*. Although used throughout India, curry powder blends vary greatly from region to region, with each family preparing the combination of herbs and spices they like the best. To ensure freshness, the blends are prepared in small quantities at home and stored for short periods of time. Typically, they are not purchased already blended. *Garam masala* is found mostly in the north, and *panch phoron* appears in the east. Throughout India, curry refers to any richly spiced dish flavored with a careful blend of spices to achieve the desired taste.

## COOKING FAT

*Ghee*, clarified butter, remains the preferred cooking fat in India, but Indians also cook with vegetable oils. Several types of oils are used, each imparting its own flavor to the dish. Mustard oil appears frequently in dishes from the eastern part of India.

## DESSERT

Typical throughout most of Asia, Indian meals conclude with fresh fruit rather than dessert; however, desserts are served for special occasions. Indian desserts tend to be quite sweet and are often based on milk, grains, fruit, or nuts.

## CELEBRATIONS

Indians celebrate many festivals, and food is always part of the celebration. Sometimes they serve a particular food or dish; other times the celebration involves a feast. From harvest and religious days to weddings and births, rich and poor Indians mark important occasions with a festival.

## BEVERAGES

*Lassi*, yogurt beverages, appear either as fruit and yogurt combinations or as a salty yogurt drink. Both varieties are popular beverages, with the yogurt functioning to

### GHEE

To prepare ghee, melt butter in a saucepan. When completely melted, the clear fat of the butter floats on top and the milk solids, water, and other impurities sink. Carefully pour or ladle the clear fat into another dish—this is the ghee. Discard remaining milk solids and water at the bottom of the pan.

*Thali*
© Dorling Kindersley

counter the heat of spicy foods. Beer or nonalcoholic beer frequently accompanies the meal, but the most common beverage with meals is water. Muslims consume no alcohol.

## MEALS

Typically, Indians dine more like the Asian and Middle Eastern people than those from the Western cultures. Rather than serving the foods from bowls and platters placed in the middle of the table, every diner receives a small portion of each food served on a *thali*, a platter containing small bowls of the various foods being served at the meal. Instead of serving courses, all the foods are presented at once, including dessert.

Like Moroccans, Indians eat with their hands. To pick up their food, northerners use flatbreads while people in the south roll rice into balls to scoop the food. Only the right hand handles the food. As part of the dining ritual, diners wash their hands before the meal begins and again at its conclusion. After the meal, they serve *paan*, an assortment of aromatic spices and herbs. Indians chew these spices and herbs to clear the palate, aid digestion, and leave the diner with a pleasant flavor sensation.

Generally, breakfast is light, consisting of tea or coffee and a pastry, potato curry, rice pancake, or whatever item is customary in that region. For example, in the south, a legume and rice or a rice pancake accompanies coffee for breakfast. The main meal of the day is served midday, and the evening meal is light. A typical main meal includes a meat dish, a starch (rice or bread, depending on the region), a legume, and a vegetable dish, yogurt, fresh fruit, pickles and/or chutney, and perhaps a salad. Both the midday and evening meals are presented on a *thali*. As in many Asian countries, much care is taken to balance the textures, flavors, and colors of the foods and dishes. From the British influence, many Indians partake of tea in the afternoon. In India, tea or coffee accompanies a variety of snack-type foods, as opposed to the British custom of serving lots of sweets and some savory foods.

| REGION | AREA | WEATHER | TOPOGRAPHY | FOODS |
|--------|------|---------|------------|-------|
| Himalayas | North | Cold winters, cool summers | Mountains | Goat, lamb, milk, cheese, wheat, rice, flatbreads, walnuts, fruits, mushrooms, saffron |
| Plains | North central, Delhi | Cold winters, hot summers | Plains, valleys, Ganges River, fertile farmland | Fish, goat, chicken, lamb, milk, cheese, wheat, rice, *basmati*, millet, corn, barley, legumes, flatbreads, walnuts, mushrooms, fruits |
| Bengal | East, Calcutta | Tropical, hot and humid | Coast, rainforest, fertile plains | Seafood, fish, rice, legumes, coconuts, vegetables |
| West | West | Hot | Desert, coast | Seafood, fish, legumes, peas |
| Deccan | Central-south | Hot, tropical | Coasts, plateaus, coastal plains, mountains, hills, fertile farmland | Seafood, fish, grains, rice, *basmati*, wheat, corn, millet, barley, legumes, vegetables, coconuts, cinnamon, ginger, black pepper, turmeric |
| South | South | Tropical, hot and humid; *monsoons* | Coasts, plains | Fish, seafood, rice, tropical fruits and vegetables, coconuts, bananas, spices |

## >> Review Questions

1. Name the two most prevalent religions found in India, and discuss the impact of each on the cuisine.
2. Discuss the differences between the cuisines of the north and south, including differences in spicing, ingredients, and foods.
3. What is the role of herbs and spices in the cookery of India?
4. What is a *thali,* and how is it used?
5. Describe the Indian method of eating, including eating utensils, courses, and typical foods consumed at the main meal.
6. Name five herbs and spices commonly used in the cuisine of India.

## >> Glossary

*basmati* An aromatic type of long-grain rice preferred in India; grown in the foothills of the Himalayas

*biryani* A baked rice dish that usually contains *basmati* rice flavored with saffron and meat

*caste* One's social class; four distinct *castes,* or social levels, exist in Indian society, and relatively little intermingling occurs between these *castes*

*chapati* **flour** A finely ground whole wheat flour

**chutney** Spicy relish made from fruits or vegetables and used as a condiment to accompany many foods

*dal* Actually means "split legumes;" also refers to a dish of mildly spiced lentil purée widely consumed in the north

*ghee* Clarified butter; the cooking fat of choice throughout India

*karahi* A wok-like deep pan with a rounded bottom and handles on each side; used for frying

*lassi* A yogurt drink

*masala* A mixture of spices; also called a spice blend

*paan* An assortment of aromatic spices and herbs to clear the palate and aid digestion; served at the end of the meal

*raita* Yogurt salad

*sambar* Spicy lentil dish widely consumed in the south

*tandoori* A clay oven used to roast meats, poultry, seafood, or vegetables as well as bake flatbreads over very high heat; used in the north of India

*tava* A concave griddle made of cast iron

*thali* Actually the name for the platter or tray holding the small bowls foods are served in; the Indian method for eating meals in which each diner receives a platter containing small bowls of the various foods being served

## RAGDA PATTICE (NORTH AND WEST)
### POTATO PANCAKES WITH CHICKPEAS

**Note:** Although this is particularly popular in northern and western India, street vendors sell this *chaat* (snack) in many regions of India. Variations on this dish seem to be endless.

**Number of Servings:** 8

**Serving Size:** 2 potato pancakes:
- 1 1/2 oz. (43 g) potatoes per pancake
- 3/4 oz. (22 g) chickpeas per pancake

**Total Yield:** 1 lb., 10 3/4 oz. (759 g) potato mixture
- 13 1/4 oz. (376 g) chickpeas

**Food Balance:** Balanced

**Wine Style:** Wine friendly—Pick a winner

**Example:** Lindemans Chardonnay or Cabernet Sauvignon

**Cooking Method:** Boil, sauté

© Tobik

**TWIST ON THE CLASSIC**

Sauté the potato pancakes as directed and serve them as an accompaniment to an entrée.

*Garam masala* is a mixture of spices. It is available at Indian food stores, or you can make it yourself.

| INGREDIENTS | WEIGHT | | VOLUME | |
| --- | --- | --- | --- | --- |
| | U.S. | METRIC | U.S. | METRIC |
| **Potato Pancakes:** | | | | |
| red potatoes, peeled, cut into even pieces | 1 lb., 7 1/2 oz. | 667 g | 5 medium | |
| cumin seeds | 1/4 oz. | 8 g | 2 teaspoons | 10 mL |
| ground coriander | | | 1 teaspoon | 5 mL |
| turmeric | | | 1/2 teaspoon | 3 mL |
| *garam masala* | | | 1 teaspoon | 5 mL |
| salt | | | 1/2 teaspoon | 3 mL |
| chili powder | | | 1/2 teaspoon | 3 mL |
| onion, minced | 2 oz. | 57 g | 1/3 cup, or 1/2 medium | 80 mL |
| fresh cilantro, minced | 3/4 oz. | 22 g | 1/4 cup | 60 mL |
| oil, for frying | as needed | | | |
| **Chickpea Mixture:** | | | | |
| canned chickpeas, drained | 9 3/4 oz. | 276 g | one 15-oz. can | one 426-g can |
| garlic, smashed and minced | 1/4 oz. | 8 g | 2 cloves | |
| ground cardamom | | | 1/2 teaspoon | 3 mL |
| pepper | | | 1/4 teaspoon | 2 mL |
| ground cloves | | | pinch | |
| salt | | | 1/2 teaspoon | 3 mL |
| chili powder | | | 1/2 teaspoon | 3 mL |
| water | | 227 g | 1 cup | 240 mL |

**Optional Garnishes:**
onion, minced
fresh cilantro, minced
mint chutney
tamarind chutney
plain yogurt

## POTATO PANCAKES:

1. Cover potatoes with water. Boil until soft, and then drain and mash.
2. Add cumin, coriander, turmeric, *garam masala*, 1/2 teaspoon (3 g) salt, chili powder, onion, and cilantro to potatoes. Mix well. If not using right away, cover and refrigerate until needed.
3. Correct seasonings. Form patties about 1/2 inch (1 1/3 cm) thick using 2 tablespoons (30 g) of potato mixture each. Heat enough oil to cover bottom of skillet over medium heat until hot.
4. In batches, sauté potato cakes until golden brown and crisp on both sides. Drain on paper toweling. Keep warm in low-temperature oven while frying remaining potato cakes.

## CHICKPEA MIXTURE:

1. In food processor fitted with knife blade, chop chickpeas. Do not purée into a paste. Transfer to saucepan.
2. Add garlic, cardamom, pepper, cloves, 1/2 teaspoon (3 g) salt, chili powder, and water to chickpeas. Mix well.
3. Heat over medium to medium-high heat until boiling. Stirring constantly, continue boiling for 5 minutes. Correct seasonings.

## ASSEMBLY:

1. Place two pancakes on warm plate. Top each pancake with 1 tablespoon (15 g) chickpeas.
2. Garnish with any or all of the listed garnishes: onion, cilantro, mint chutney, tamarind chutney, and yogurt.

---

## GOBHI PAKODE (THROUGHOUT INDIA)

### CAULIFLOWER FRITTERS

**Note:** Many varieties of fritters are served in India both as snacks and with the meal. If reheating fritters, bake in a 375-degree (190°C) oven or fry them again.

**Number of Servings:** 8
**Serving Size:** 3 to 4 fritters, or 5 to 6 1/2 oz. (142 to 184 g)
**Total Yield:** About 32 fritters from 1 lb., 4 oz. (568 g) batter
**Food Balance:** Protein
**Wine Style:** Off-dry or low-oaked whites or soft reds
**Example:** Château St. Jean Pinot Blanc or Pinot Noir

**Cooking Method:** Boil, deep-fry

*Frying Gobhi Pakode (Cauliflower Fritters)*
Pearson Education/PH College

| INGREDIENTS | WEIGHT | | VOLUME | |
|---|---|---|---|---|
| | U.S. | METRIC | U.S. | METRIC |
| cauliflower flowerets | 2 lb., 6 oz. | 1.1 kg | 2 small to medium heads | |
| **Batter:** | | | | |
| chickpea flour, *besan* | 9 oz. | 256 g | 2 cups | 480 mL |
| ground coriander | 1/2 oz. | 15 g | 2 tablespoons | 30 mL |
| pepper | | | 1/2 teaspoon | 3 mL |
| ground cayenne | | | 1/4 teaspoon | 2 mL |
| salt | 1/2 oz. | 15 g | 2 teaspoons | 10 mL |
| oil | | 28 g | 2 tablespoons | 30 mL |
| cold water | | 340 g | 1 1/2 cups | 360 mL |
| oil, for deep-frying | | | | |

### TWIST ON THE CLASSIC

Serve this in the style of *tempura*. For an appetizer or entrée, use an assortment of vegetables, shrimp, and scallops. Accompany the fritters with cucumber *raita* as a dipping sauce.

1. Parboil or steam cauliflower until half cooked, rinse with cold water to stop cooking. Set aside until ready to fry.
2. Place chickpea flour, coriander, pepper, cayenne, and salt in bowl of food processor fitted with knife blade. Pulse to mix well, and then add oil and pulse to mix.
3. With processor running, add water through feed tube. Mix well, transfer to bowl, mix. Add a little water if batter is too thick.
4. Cover, let rest at least 30 minutes. Refrigerate if holding overnight.
5. Heat oil in pan to 375 degrees (190°C). Coat cauliflower with batter.
6. Fry until golden brown, a few pieces at a time so oil temperature remains fairly constant.
7. Remove fritters to absorbent toweling to drain, keep warm in low oven. Serve hot.

© Joe Gough

## RASAM (SOUTH)

### SPICY LENTIL BROTH

**Note:** Originating in the south, this spicy soup is served as a broth throughout India. The soup is either strained to remove the lentil pulp or it is allowed to settle (the broth rises and the pulp sinks) and the broth at the top is served. Some refer to this soup as the Indian version of consommé.

Barbara Pheby © Shutterstock

**Number of Servings:** 10
**Serving Size:** 7 oz. (199 g)
**Total Yield:** 4 lb., 12 oz. (2.2 kg) (not strained)
**Food Balance:** Spicy/protein
**Wine Style:** Off-dry or low-oaked whites or soft reds
**Example:** Beringer Viognier or Founders' Estate Merlot

**Cooking Method:** Sauté, boil

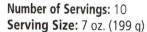

**TWIST ON THE CLASSIC**

To create a spicier version of a sauce, replace the stock in the recipe with Rasam.

| INGREDIENTS | WEIGHT | | VOLUME | |
| --- | --- | --- | --- | --- |
| | U.S. | METRIC | U.S. | METRIC |
| *thoor dal* (yellow lentils) | 7 3/4 oz. | 220 g | 1 cup | 240 mL |
| turmeric | | | 1 teaspoon | 5 mL |
| water | | | 5 cups | 1.2 L |
| *ghee* | 1/2 oz. | 15 g | 1 tablespoon | 15 mL |
| black mustard seeds | | | 3/4 teaspoon | 4 mL |
| whole cumin | 1/4 oz. | 8 g | 1 teaspoon | 5 mL |
| whole fenugreek | | | 1/4 teaspoon | 2 mL |
| whole coriander | 1/4 oz. | 8 g | 2 teaspoons | 10 mL |
| garlic, minced | 1/4 oz. | 8 g | 2 cloves | |
| jalapeño or other chili pepper, seeded, ribs removed, and minced, *optional* | 3/4 oz. | 22 g, or to taste | 1 each or to taste | |
| tomatoes, fresh or canned, chopped | 1 lb. | 454 g | 2 cups | 480 mL |
| tamarind paste | 3/4 oz. | 22 g | 1 tablespoon | 15 mL |
| salt | 1/2 oz. | 15 g | 2 teaspoons | 10 mL |
| sugar | | | 1 teaspoon | 5 mL |
| **Garnish:** | | | | |
| fresh cilantro, minced | 1/2 oz. | 15 g | 2 tablespoons | 30 mL |

1. Place *thoor dal*, turmeric, and enough water to cover, about 2 cups (454 g or 480 mL), in pan. Bring to boil, turn heat to low and simmer, partially covered, for 30 minutes, until soft.
2. Heat *ghee* in sauté pan, cook mustard seeds, cumin, fenugreek, and coriander in covered pan until beginning to pop. Add garlic and jalapeño or chili pepper, sauté to soften. Add tomatoes, tamarind, salt, and sugar, cook a few minutes.
3. Transfer tomato mixture to bowl of food processor fitted with knife blade, process until smooth.
4. Add cooked *dal* to processor, process until smooth. Return to pan.
5. Add remaining 3 cups (680 g or 720 mL) of water to pan, bring to boil. Reduce heat and simmer, partially covered, for 30 minutes.
6. Correct seasonings, serve garnished with cilantro.

## MULLIGATAWNY

### SPICY VEGETABLE SOUP

**Number of Servings:** 10
**Serving Size:** 8 oz. (227 g)
**Total Yield:** 5 lb., 6 oz. (2.4 kg)
**Wine Style:** White wine from old vines and a full body. Possible grape varietals are Riesling, Sauvignon Blanc, Gruner Veltliner.
**Example:** Gemischter Satz "Bisamberg Alte Reben" 2013, Wieninger (Vienna/Austria)

**Cooking Method:** Braise

© Szabolcs Szekeres

| INGREDIENTS | WEIGHT | | VOLUME | |
| --- | --- | --- | --- | --- |
| | U.S. | METRIC | U.S. | METRIC |
| oil | | 28 g | 2 tablespoons | 30 mL |
| onion, medium dice | 13 oz. | 369 g | 2 large | |
| carrot, medium dice | 4 1/4 oz. | 120 g | 2 large | |
| celery, medium dice | 6 oz. | 170 g | 3 stalks | |
| turnip, medium dice | 5 1/2 oz. | 156 g | 1 medium | |
| pepper, jalapeño, long green, or variety of choice, seeds and membranes removed | 1 oz. | 28 g | 1 or 2 each depending on variety | |
| garlic, peeled, minced | 1/4 oz. | 8 g | 2 cloves | |
| ginger, minced | 1/2 oz. | 15 g | 2 teaspoons | 10 mL |
| flour | 3/4 oz. | 22 g | 2 tablespoons | 30 mL |
| curry powder | 3/4 oz. | 22 g | 2 tablespoons | 30 mL |
| turmeric | 1/4 oz. | 8 g | 1 teaspoon | 5 mL |
| cumin | 1/4 oz. | 8 g | 1 teaspoon | 5 mL |
| chicken or vegetarian stock, hot | | | 1 quart + 2 1/2 cups | 1.6 kg |
| apple, peeled, cored, variety of choice, small dice | 6 oz. | 170 g | 1 each | |
| salt | 1/4 oz. | 8 g | 1 teaspoon | 5 mL |
| pepper | | | 1/2 teaspoon | 3 mL |
| rice | 3 3/4 oz. | 107 g | 1/2 cup | 120 mL |
| coconut milk, unsweetened | | 170 g | 3/4 cup | 180 mL |

**Garnish:**
cilantro, minced

### TWIST ON THE CLASSIC

Add slices of grilled hot dog, bratwurst, or the sausage of choice to a bowl of mulligatawny to turn this soup into an entrée.

Dating from the late 1700s, this Anglo-Indian soup recipe translates into "pepper water." Some say this was a sauce used in Indian cookery that the British discovered and transformed into a soup.

Countless recipes exist for mulligatawny. Among the myriad variations, some contain chicken or lamb, others purée the soup, and still others include lentils in the recipe.

① Heat oil in large saucepan over medium heat. Add onion, carrot, celery, turnip, pepper, garlic, and ginger. Stir often for about 10 minutes, until softened.

② Sprinkle flour, curry powder, turmeric, and cumin over vegetables. Stir with wooden spoon to thoroughly coat. Continue stirring and sautéing for 3 to 4 minutes.

③ Slowly, whisk or stir in hot stock, a little at a time. Bring to boil, reduce heat and simmer for 30 minutes.

④ Add apple, salt, and pepper. Continue cooking another 10 minutes.

⑤ Add rice, simmer another 20 minutes.

⑥ Add coconut milk. Correct seasonings. Serve, garnished with cilantro, if desired.

---

## LOBHIA KA SALAAD

### BLACK-EYED PEA SALAD

Courtesy of CanolaInfo.org

**Note:** Almost any bean can replace the black-eyed peas in this recipe.

**Number of Servings:** 8
**Serving Size:** 4 oz. (114 g)
**Total Yield:** 2 lb., 1 1/2 oz. (951 g)
**Food Balance:** Protein/spicy
**Wine Style:** Off-dry or low-oaked whites or soft reds
**Example:** Greg Norman Chardonnay or Pinot Noir

| INGREDIENTS | WEIGHT U.S. | WEIGHT METRIC | VOLUME U.S. | VOLUME METRIC |
|---|---|---|---|---|
| black-eyed peas, cooked or canned, drained | 1 lb., 1 1/2 oz. | 497 g | two 15 1/2-oz. cans | two 439-g cans |
| onion, minced | 3 oz. | 86 g | 1/2 cup | 120 mL |
| red bell pepper, seeds and membranes removed, minced | 3 oz. | 86 g | 1/2 cup | 120 mL |
| red potato, peeled, cut into medium dice, and boiled | 6 1/2 oz. | 184 g | 1 cup, or 2 small | 240 mL |
| salt | 1/2 oz. | 15 g | 2 teaspoons | 10 mL |
| pepper | | | 1 teaspoon | 5 mL |
| sugar | | | 1 teaspoon | 5 mL |
| ground cumin | | | 1 teaspoon | 5 mL |
| chili pepper, serrano or variety of choice, seeds and membranes removed, if desired, minced | 1/2 oz. | 15 g | 2 small | |
| fresh cilantro, minced | 1/2 oz. | 15 g | 2 tablespoons | 30 mL |
| raisins | 1 oz. | 28 g | 2 tablespoons | 30 mL |
| lemon juice | | 57 g | 1/4 cup | 60 mL |

① Mix all ingredients together in nonreactive bowl.

② Cover and refrigerate at least 2 hours to marinate. Correct seasonings. Serve on a bed of lettuce at room temperature or slightly cool.

### TWIST ON THE CLASSIC

For an interesting presentation, serve this salad in a tomato. Remove all but 1/2 inch (1 1/3 cm) of the tomato pulp, and then fill the tomato with the black-eyed pea salad.

# KHEERA RAITA (NORTH)

## CUCUMBER AND YOGURT SALAD

**Note:** *Raita* is a "cooling" salad to counter spicy foods.

**Number of Servings:** 8
**Serving Size:** 4 oz. (114 g)
**Total Yield:** 2 lb. (908 g)

**TWIST ON THE CLASSIC**

To create a cold soup with a base of *raita*, add cooked rice, plumped golden raisins, and buttermilk to the *raita*.

| | WEIGHT | | VOLUME | |
|---|---|---|---|---|
| INGREDIENTS | U.S. | METRIC | U.S. | METRIC |
| plain yogurt | 1 lb., 2 oz. | 511 g | 2 cups | 480 mL |
| salt | 1/4 oz. | 8 g | 1 teaspoon | 5 mL |
| cumin, toasted then ground | | | 1/2 teaspoon | 3 mL |
| ground cayenne | | | 1/4 teaspoon | 2 mL |
| fresh cilantro or mint leaves, minced | 1/2 oz. | 15 g | 2 tablespoons | 30 mL |
| cucumber, peeled and grated | 1 lb., 5 oz. | 596 g | 2 large | |

**Garnish:**

paprika

1. Combine yogurt, salt, cumin, cayenne, and cilantro or mint in bowl. Cover and refrigerate until needed.
2. Place cucumber in colander to drain, place colander in bowl or sink to catch liquid. Cover and refrigerate until needed.
3. At serving time, mix drained cucumber into yogurt mixture. Correct seasonings. Sprinkle with paprika. Serve.

Courtesy of Canola Oil @ canolainfo.org

# TANDOORI MURGHI (NORTH)

## CHICKEN BAKED IN TANDOOR OVEN

WITTY234 © Shutterstock

**TWIST ON THE CLASSIC**

Create a *tandoori* burrito. Wrap sliced *tandoori* chicken and cucumber *raita* in a warm tortilla. Garnish with diced tomato, diced onion, and more *raita*.

**Note:** Allow time to marinate this chicken up to 24 hours before baking. In the absence of a *tandoor* oven, bake *tandoori* foods in a very hot oven.

**Number of Servings:** 8      **Cooking Method:** Bake
**Serving Size:** 1/4 chicken
**Total Yield:** 2 chickens, or 8 pieces
**Food Balance:** Spicy/protein
**Wine Style:** Soft and fruity Gewürztraminer, Viognier, Pinot Noir, Shiraz, Merlot
**Example:** Château St. Jean Gewürztraminer or Pinot Noir

| | WEIGHT | | VOLUME | |
|---|---|---|---|---|
| INGREDIENTS | U.S. | METRIC | U.S. | METRIC |
| chickens, quartered | 5 to 7 lb. | 2.3 to 3.2 kg | 2 whole or 8 pieces | |
| **Marinade:** | | | | |
| plain yogurt | 13 1/2 oz. | 383 g | 1 1/2 cups | 360 mL |
| garlic, minced | | | 3 cloves | |
| ginger, peeled and minced | 1/4 oz. | 8 g | 1 tablespoon | 15 mL |
| paprika | 1/4 oz. | 8 g | 1 tablespoon | 15 mL |
| ground fennel | | | 3/4 teaspoon | 4 mL |
| ground coriander | 1/4 oz. | 8 g | 1 tablespoon + 1 1/2 teaspoons | 23 mL |
| ground cumin | 1/4 oz. | 8 g | 1 1/2 teaspoons | 8 mL |
| ground cardamom | 1/4 oz. | 8 g | 2 teaspoons | 10 mL |
| ground cayenne | | | 1/4 teaspoon | 2 mL |
| pepper | | | 1/4 teaspoon | 2 mL |
| ground cinnamon | | | 1/4 teaspoon | 2 mL |
| ground cloves | | | 1/8 teaspoon | 1 mL |
| fresh lemon juice | | 22 g | 1 tablespoon + 1 1/2 teaspoons | 23 mL |
| ghee, for basting, if desired | | | | |

1. Remove skin from chicken, make cuts into meat halfway to the bone about 1 inch (2 1/2 cm) apart.
2. Mix marinade ingredients in bowl of food processor fitted with knife blade, process until smooth.
3. Coat chicken pieces with marinade, making sure marinade goes into slits. Cover and refrigerate for up to 24 hours, turning at least once while marinating.
4. Preheat oven to 500 degrees (260°C).
5. Remove excess marinade from chicken. Bake until proper internal temperature is reached, about 20 to 25 minutes, turning pieces once during baking. Baste with *ghee*, if desired. Serve immediately.

# SHAH JAHANI BIRYANI (NORTH)

## LAMB AND SAFFRON RICE CASSEROLE

**Note:** Begin preparation of this dish allowing plenty of time to soak items for 3 hours and still accommodate a lengthy cooking time. Although the preparation seems quite involved, the meat for this dish can be prepared ahead of time and refrigerated until needed.

**Number of Servings:** 9
**Serving Size:** 8 oz. (227 g)
**Total Yield:** 4 lb., 13 oz. (2.2 kg)
**Food Balance:** Protein/sweet
**Wine Style:** Off-dry or low-oaked whites or soft reds
**Example:** Château St. Jean Pinot Blanc, Souverain Merlot

**Cooking Method:** Sauté, boil, braise, bake

| INGREDIENTS | WEIGHT U.S. | WEIGHT METRIC | VOLUME U.S. | VOLUME METRIC |
|---|---|---|---|---|
| *basmati* rice | 14 oz. | 397 g | 2 cups | 480 mL |
| water | | | 4 1/2 cups + 2 tablespoons | 1.1 L + 30 mL |
| saffron threads | | | 1/2 teaspoon | 3 mL |
| milk, warm | | 28 g | 2 tablespoons | 30 mL |
| whole onions, peeled | 1 lb. | 454 g | 3 medium | |
| garlic, minced | 1/2 oz. | 15 g | 4 cloves | |
| fresh ginger, peeled and minced | 1/4 oz. | 8 g | 2 teaspoons | 10 mL |
| almonds, whole or pieces | 3/4 oz. | 22 g | 2 tablespoons | 30 mL |
| *ghee* (clarified butter) | 3 oz. | 86 g | 1/4 cup + 2 tablespoons | 90 mL |
| golden raisins | 1 1/2 oz. | 43 g | 1/4 cup | 60 mL |
| blanched, slivered almonds | 1 1/2 oz. | 43 g | 1/4 cup | 60 mL |
| cashews | 1 1/2 oz. | 43 g | 1/4 cup | 60 mL |
| lean, boneless lamb 1-inch (2 1/2-cm) cubes | 1 lb., 8 oz. | 681 g | | |
| plain yogurt | 9 oz. | 256 g | 1 cup | 240 mL |
| cinnamon stick | | | one 1-inch piece | one 2 1/2-cm piece |
| whole cardamom | | | 1/2 teaspoon | 3 mL |
| whole cumin | 1/4 oz. | 8 g | 1 teaspoon | 5 mL |
| whole coriander | 1/4 oz. | 8 g | 1 teaspoon | 5 mL |
| ground cayenne | | | 1/4 teaspoon | 2 mL |
| whole cloves | | | 4 each | |
| peppercorns | 1/4 oz. | 8 g | 1 teaspoon | 5 mL |
| nutmeg | | | 1/2 teaspoon or 1/6 whole | 3 mL |
| salt | 1/4 oz. | 8 g | 1 teaspoon | 5 mL |
| **To Finish Rice:** | | | | |
| water | | | 1 quart (4 cups) | 960 mL |
| salt | 3/4 oz. | 22 g | 1 tablespoon | 15 mL |
| **Garnish:** | | | | |
| eggs, hard-boiled, peeled, quartered | | | 3 each | |

**TWIST ON THE CLASSIC**

Serve the *biryani* in individual casserole dishes or in a small tagine. If desired, replace the lamb with beef or chicken. Adjust the cooking times appropriately for the other meats.

This dish hails from the Moghul influence and appears at many festivals.

1. Rinse rice thoroughly, drain, place in bowl or pan with 4 cups (960 mL) of the water. Soak at least 3 hours.
2. Place saffron threads in small bowl with warm milk, soak at least 3 hours.
3. Cut two of the onions in half through root end, cut into thin slices (half rings). Dice remaining onion.
4. Place diced onion, garlic, ginger, whole almonds, and 2 tablespoons (30 g or 30 mL) of the water in bowl of food processor fitted with knife blade. Process into smooth paste. Set aside.
5. Heat *ghee* in pan over medium-high heat. Sauté onion slices until brown, about 5 to 10 minutes. Remove with slotted spoon, drain on absorbent paper. Place golden raisins in same pan, sauté until plump, about 45 seconds, remove to absorbent paper. Place slivered almonds and cashews in pan, sauté until golden, remove to absorbent paper.
6. Sauté lamb in same pan until browned, remove to bowl.
7. Stirring constantly, sauté onion paste in same pan until beginning to brown. If paste is sticking, add a few table-spoons of water. Return lamb and juices from bowl to pan.
8. Add yogurt, one tablespoon at a time, stirring constantly. Add remaining 1/2 cup (120 mL) water and mix well. Bring to simmer, turn heat to low, cover, and cook for 30 minutes.
9. Meanwhile, finely grind cinnamon, cardamom, cumin, coriander, cayenne, cloves, peppercorns, and nutmeg in spice grinder or coffee grinder.
10. Add ground spices and salt to lamb and sauce in pan. Cover and simmer another 30 minutes. Meat should be tender and sauce should be thick. If necessary, remove cover and reduce sauce until thick.
11. Meanwhile, preheat oven to 325 degrees (160°C). Drain and rinse rice. Boil 4 cups (960 mL) water and 1 table-spoon (15 g) salt in saucepan, sprinkle rice into boiling water, return to boil, boil rapidly for 6 minutes, drain rice.
12. Place cooked meat in bottom of ovenproof dish, top with rice, mounding rice at center to form hill. Make well into center of mound, drizzle saffron milk along sides of well. Scatter 2 tablespoons (30 g) of the fried onion rings on top of rice.
13. Cover tightly with aluminum foil, then a lid. Place in oven, bake 40 minutes.
14. Remove from oven, stir lamb and rice, if desired. Top with remaining onions, fried raisins, cashews, and slivered almonds. Cover; allow to sit a few minutes to heat toppings.
15. Garnish with hard-boiled eggs, serve immediately.

© Abeer

# SORPOTEL (GOA)

## PORK CURRY

**Number of Servings:** 14
**Serving Size:** 6 oz. (170 g)
**Total Yield:** 5 lb., 8 oz. (2.5 kg)
**Wine Style:** Off-dry white wine from a cool climate area. Possible grape varietals are Riesling and Chenin Blanc.
**Example:** Riesling Kabinett 2013, Diel (Nahe/Germany)

**Cooking Method:** Boil, Sauté

© manubahuguna

| INGREDIENTS | WEIGHT | | VOLUME | |
|---|---|---|---|---|
| | U.S. | METRIC | U.S. | METRIC |
| pork butt | 5 lb., 8 oz. | 2.5 kg | | |
| salt | 1/2 oz. | 15 g | 2 teaspoons | 10 mL |
| cloves | | | 10 each | |
| cinnamon stick | 1/2 oz. | 15 g | 4 each | |
| peppercorns | | | 16 each | |
| water, to cover | | | | |
| tamarind, seeds removed, 1 1/2-inch (4-cm) ball | 3 1/2 oz. | 104 g | 2 each | |
| cumin seeds | 1/2 oz. | 15 g | 2 teaspoons | 10 mL |
| cloves | | | 10 each | |
| chilies, dried, Kashmir or small red | 1/4 oz. | 8 g | 4 each or to taste | |
| cinnamon | 1/4 oz. | 8 g | 1 teaspoon | 5 mL |
| turmeric | 1/4 oz. | 8 g | 1 tablespoon | 15 mL |
| coriander seeds | 1/4 oz. | 8 g | 2 teaspoons | 10 mL |
| peppercorns | | | 20 each | |
| cider vinegar | | 114 g | 1/2 cup | 120 mL |
| oil | | 86 g | 1/4 cup + 2 tablespoons | 90 mL |
| onion, small dice | 1lb., 7 oz. | 653 g | 4 large | |
| garlic, peeled, minced | 2 oz. | 57 g | 16 cloves | |
| ginger, peeled, minced | 1 oz. | 28 g | 3-inch piece | 8-cm piece |
| sugar | 1/2 oz. | 15 g | 2 teaspoons | 10 mL |

① Cut pork into 5 or 6 large pieces. Place in large pan with salt, cloves, cinnamon stick, and peppercorns. Cover with water. Bring to boil, reduce heat, and simmer for 45 minutes.

② Remove meat from stock, reserve pork stock. Allow meat to cool until able to handle, cut into 1/2-inch (1 1/3-cm) cubes.

③ Heat large skillet over medium heat. Working in batches, add pork cubes to skillet to form single layer. Fry until cubes are browned on all sides and pork renders fat, about 12 to 15 minutes. Refrigerate until needed. (Alternately, place pork cubes on sheet pan and bake in hot oven or broil until brown on all sides and pork renders fat.)

④ Mix tamarind with 4 oz. (114 g, 1/2 cup, or 120 mL) hot pork stock. Stir to combine.

⑤ In dry skillet over medium heat, fry cumin, cloves, dried chilies, cinnamon, turmeric, coriander seeds, and peppercorns until fragrant. Grind all spices together. Add vinegar to form paste.

⑥ Heat oil in large pan over medium heat. Add onion, sauté until softened, about 5 minutes. Add garlic and ginger. Sauté for 2 minutes, until fragrant. Add spice mixture, sauté until fragrant and oil separates.

⑦ Add meat, tamarind, and sugar. Simmer until meat is tender, about 1 hour to 1 hour, 15 minutes. Add more reserved pork stock, as needed.

⑧ Correct seasonings, adding vinegar, sugar, and salt to balance. Serve with rice.

### TWIST ON THE CLASSIC

Make the *Sorpotel* a bit more soupy (thinning with extra pork stock) and serve in a hollowed round bread.

This dish reflects strong influence from the Portuguese who ruled Goa for centuries. Typically, Goan Catholics prepare *Sorpotel* at Christmas or for other festive occasions.

Normally, *Sorpotel* contains offal from the pig with pork liver and heart replacing part of the pork butt in the recipe. If desired, make this substitution.

The flavors of *Sorpotel* deepen as it ages. For best results, prepare the recipe at least a day in advance.

# DAHI MACHI (BENGAL)

## FISH IN YOGURT SAUCE

© Shutterstock

**Note:** Frequently served in Bengal, this fish has a thick sauce for eating with rice and fingers.

**Number of Servings:** 10
**Serving Size:** 6 oz. (170 g)
**Total Yield:** 3 lb., 14 oz. (1.8 kg)
**Food Balance:** Spicy/protein
**Wine Style:** Off-dry or low-oaked whites or soft reds
**Example:** Beringer Chenin Blanc, Rosemount Shiraz

**Cooking Method:** Sauté, poach (boil)

---

**TWIST ON THE CLASSIC**

Replace the fish with a pork chop, hamburger, or boneless chicken breast. Adjust the cooking times for the meats as needed.

| | WEIGHT | | VOLUME | |
|---|---|---|---|---|
| **INGREDIENTS** | **U.S.** | **METRIC** | **U.S.** | **METRIC** |
| dry mustard | | | 1 1/2 teaspoons | 8 mL |
| water | | 28 g | 2 tablespoons | 30 mL |
| skinless, boneless fish fillets, cod, haddock, or any firm fish, rinsed and, cut into 2-inch (5-cm) pieces | 2 lb., 8 oz. | 1.1 kg | | |
| flour | 3 oz. | 86 g | 3/4 cup | 180 mL |
| oil or *ghee* | | 170 g, as needed | 3/4 cup, as needed | 180 mL, as needed |
| onion, diced | 1 lb., 4 oz. | 568 g | 4 cups, or 4 each | 960 mL |
| fresh ginger, peeled | 1/2 oz. | 15 g | one 2-inch piece | one 5-cm piece |
| garlic, minced | 1/4 oz. | 8 g | 2 cloves | |
| turmeric | | | 1/2 teaspoon | 3 mL |
| ground cayenne | | | 1/2 teaspoon | 3 mL |
| ground cumin | | | 1/4 teaspoon | 2 mL |
| ground cinnamon | | | 1/4 teaspoon | 2 mL |
| ground cloves | | | 1/8 teaspoon | 1 mL |
| ground cardamom | | | 1/4 teaspoon | 2 mL |
| salt | | | 1 1/2 teaspoons | 8 mL |
| plain yogurt | 15 oz. | 426 g | 1 1/2 cups | 360 mL |
| **Garnish:** | | | | |
| fresh cilantro, minced | 1 1/2 oz. | 43 g | 1/4 cup + 2 tablespoons | 90 mL |
| green chilies, seeded and minced | 1 oz. | 28 g | 2 to 4 each | |

1. Mix mustard with water in bowl.

2. Lightly dredge fish with flour.

3. Heat 1/4 inch (1/2 cm) oil in pan. Sauté fish over medium-high heat until seared and lightly browned, about 1 minute per side, remove to plate when done. Add oil to pan as needed.

4. Add any remaining oil to pan, add onions, and sauté, stirring constantly, until golden, about 10 minutes. Reduce heat to medium if needed to prevent burning.

5. Add ginger and garlic, sauté another minute. Add turmeric, cayenne, cumin, cinnamon, cloves, cardamom, and salt, sauté for 15 seconds.

6. Remove from heat, add yogurt and mustard water.

7. Transfer onion mixture to bowl of food processor fitted with knife blade. Process into smooth paste, return to pan.

8. Bring sauce to simmer, add fish and any juices to sauce, cover, simmer until fish is done, 3 to 4 minutes. Be careful not to overcook fish.

9. Correct seasonings, serve garnished with cilantro and green chilies.

# CHINGRI MALAI KARI (BENGAL)

## PRAWNS IN COCONUT CURRY

**Number of Servings:** 11
**Serving Size:** 6 oz. (170 g)
**Total Yield:** 4 lb., 8 oz. (2 kg)
**Wine Style:** Full-bodied red wine with balanced acidity and well-integrated oak. Possible grape varietals are Blaufrankisch, Zweigelt, Cabernet Sauvignon, and Merlot.
**Example:** Cuvee "Comondor" 2008, Nittnaus (Neusiedlersee/Austria)

**Cooking Method:** Sauté

© FomaA

| INGREDIENTS | WEIGHT | | VOLUME | |
|---|---|---|---|---|
| | U.S. | METRIC | U.S. | METRIC |
| shrimp, jumbo, peeled with tail intact, deveined | 2 lb., 5 oz. | 1.1 kg | | |
| turmeric | 1/4 oz. | 8 g | 1 tablespoon + 1 teaspoon | 20 mL |
| salt | 1/2 oz. | 15 g | 2 teaspoons | 10 mL |
| onion, peeled | 1 lb., 8 1/2 oz. | 695 g | 4 large | |
| water, as needed | | | | |
| garlic, peeled | 1 1/2 oz. | 43 g | 12 cloves | |
| ginger, peeled | 1 oz. | 28 g | 2-inch piece | 5-cm piece |
| oil | | 57 g | 1/4 cup | 60 mL |
| bay leaf | | | 2 each | |
| cumin | 1/4 oz. | 8 g | 2 teaspoons | 10 mL |
| cardamom seeds | 1/4 oz. | 8 g | 2 teaspoons | 10 mL |
| green chilies, serrano or variety of choice, slit open | 2 oz. | 57 g | 4 each | |
| coconut milk | 1 lb., 4 oz. | 567 g | 2 1/2 cups | 600 mL |

**Garnish:**

cilantro, minced

1. Mix shrimp with half of the turmeric (2 teaspoons or 10 mL) and half the salt (1/4 oz., 8 g, 1 teaspoon, or 5 mL), coat well. Refrigerate for at least 20 minutes to marinate.
2. In food processor fitted with knife blade, chop onions until coarse paste. Add a tablespoon or so (about 15 g or 15 mL) of water if needed. Separately, purée garlic and ginger until smooth. Set both aside until needed.
3. In large skillet over medium-high flame, heat 1 oz. (28 g, 2 tablespoons, or 30 mL) oil until hot. Add shrimp in single layer just to sear on both sides. Remove from skillet, continue with remaining shrimp. Refrigerate to reserve shrimp until needed.
4. Reduce heat to medium-low, heat 1 oz. (28 g, 2 tablespoons, or 30 mL) oil until hot in same skillet. Add bay leaves, cumin, cardamom, and remaining turmeric; sauté until fragrant, about 1 to 2 minutes.
5. Add onion paste, sauté about 5 minutes at medium heat. Add garlic and ginger paste; sauté another 5 minutes.
6. Reduce heat to medium-low, add chilies and remaining salt. Cook another 3 minutes.
7. Add shrimp, cook until heated. Add coconut milk, heat thoroughly. Correct seasonings.
8. Garnish with cilantro and serve with rice.

### TWIST ON THE CLASSIC

Transform this shrimp curry into a coconut shrimp curry bisque by cutting the shrimp into small pieces and adding more coconut milk as well as milk or half-and-half.

To increase the heat from the peppers in this dish, mince peppers to expose more of the seeds and ribs (which contain the heat) or cut the peppers in separate halves instead of using whole peppers with a slit.

## MASOOR DAL (THROUGHOUT INDIA)
### SPICED LENTIL PURÉE

**Note:** *Dal* is served with most Indian meals. It functions as a sauce to moisten any dry food, including grilled meat or rice. *Dal* may be prepared with any number of legumes.

**Note:** The red lentils used in this recipe turn yellow when cooked.

**Number of Servings:** 8
**Serving Size:** 4 oz. (114 g)
**Total Yield:** 2 lb., 3 oz. (994 g)

**Cooking Method:** Boil, sauté

| | WEIGHT | | VOLUME | |
|---|---|---|---|---|
| INGREDIENTS | U.S. | METRIC | U.S. | METRIC |
| red split lentils (*masoor*), washed | 10 oz. | 284 g | 1 1/4 cups | 300 mL |
| water | | 680 g | 3 cups | 720 mL |
| fresh ginger, peeled | 1/4 oz. | 8 g | one 1/2-inch piece | one 1 1/3-cm piece |
| turmeric | | | 1/2 teaspoon | 3 mL |
| salt | 1/4 oz. | 8 g | 1 teaspoon | 5 mL |
| *ghee* | 1 1/2 oz. | 43 g | 3 tablespoons | 45 mL |
| whole cumin | 1/4 oz. | 8 g | 1 teaspoon | 5 mL |
| garlic, minced | 1/2 oz. | 15 g | 4 cloves | |
| ground coriander | | | 1 teaspoon | 5 mL |
| ground cayenne | | | 1/4 teaspoon | 2 mL |
| **Garnish:** | | | | |
| fresh cilantro, minced | 1/2 oz. | 15 g | 3 tablespoons | 45 mL |

**Accompaniments:**
cooked rice
flatbread

1. Place lentils, water, ginger, and turmeric in pan, bring to boil.
2. Reduce heat, partially cover and simmer for 20 minutes, until tender. If necessary to prevent sticking, add more water. Remove from heat, add salt.
3. Heat *ghee* in small skillet over medium heat. Add cumin, sauté until darkened, a few seconds.
4. Add garlic, coriander, and cayenne, sauté about 45 seconds, pour into lentils and mix well. Remove ginger. Correct seasonings.
5. Serve, sprinkled with cilantro. Accompany with rice and/or flatbread.

© paul_brighton

*Monkey Business Images © Shutterstock*

# SABZI MOLEE (EAST)

## MIXED VEGETABLE CURRY

**Number of Servings:** 8                 **Cooking Method:** Sauté, boil
**Serving Size:** 10 oz. (284 g)
**Total Yield:** 5 lb. (2.8 kg)
**Food Balance:** Spicy/sweet
**Wine Style:** Off-dry or low-oaked whites or soft reds
**Example:** Beringer Gewürztraminer or Viognier, Cellar #8 Zinfandel

*Clive Streeter and Patrick McLeavy*
© Dorling Kindersley

### TWIST ON THE CLASSIC

Prepare this dish with any combination of vegetables, meat, fowl, fish, and/or seafood.

| INGREDIENTS | WEIGHT U.S. | WEIGHT METRIC | VOLUME U.S. | VOLUME METRIC |
|---|---|---|---|---|
| fresh ginger, peeled and minced | 3/4 oz. | 22 g | one 1 1/2-inch piece, or 2 tablespoons | one 4-cm piece, or 30 mL |
| onion, diced | 7 oz. | 199 g | 1 large | |
| garlic, minced | 1 oz. | 28 g | 8 cloves | |
| green chilies, variety of choice, seeds removed if desired, minced | 1 1/4 oz. | 36 g, or to taste | 2 each, or to taste | |
| water | | 28 g | 2 tablespoons | 30 mL |
| *ghee* or vegetable oil | 1 1/2 oz. | 43 g | 3 tablespoons | 45 mL |
| black mustard seeds | 1/4 oz. | 8 g | 1 teaspoon | 5 mL |
| whole cumin | 1/4 oz. | 8 g | 1 1/2 teaspoons | 8 mL |
| ground coriander | 1/4 oz. | 8 g | 1 tablespoon | 15 mL |
| ground cumin | 1/4 oz. | 8 g | 1 1/2 teaspoons | 8 mL |
| turmeric | | | 1/2 teaspoon | 3 mL |
| potato, white, waxy, or all-purpose, peeled and cut into 1-inch (2 1/2-cm) dice | 7 oz. | 199 g | 1 medium | |
| sweet potato, peeled and cut into 1-inch (2 1/2-cm) dice | 7 1/2 oz. | 213 g | 1 medium | |
| carrots, peeled and cut into 1/2-inch (1 1/3-cm) slices | 7 oz. | 199 g | 2 each | |
| eggplant, 1-inch (2 1/2-cm) dice | 14 oz. | 397 g | 1 small | |
| green beans, trimmed and cut into 1 1/2-inch (4-cm) lengths | 8 oz. | 227 g | | |
| green bell peppers, large dice | 1 lb., 1 oz. | 482 g | 2 each | |
| salt | 1/2 oz. | 15 g | 2 teaspoons | 10 mL |
| sugar | | | 1/2 teaspoon | 3 mL |
| unsweetened coconut milk | 14 oz. | 397 g | | |
| fresh cilantro, minced | 1/2 oz. | 15 g | 3 tablespoons | 45 mL |
| paprika | | | 1/4 teaspoon | 2 mL |

**Accompaniment:**
cooked rice

① Place ginger, onion, garlic, green chilies, and water in bowl of food processor fitted with knife blade, purée until paste, scraping down sides of bowl as needed.

② Heat *ghee* in pan over medium heat. Add mustard seeds and whole cumin, sauté until mustard seeds begin to pop.

③ Add onion paste from processor, sauté about 3 minutes. Add coriander, ground cumin, and turmeric, sauté another 30 seconds.

4. Add potato, sweet potato, carrots, and eggplant. Stirring constantly, cook for 5 minutes.
5. Add green beans, bell peppers, salt, sugar, and coconut milk. Cover and simmer for 12 minutes.
6. Add cilantro and paprika, simmer for 5 to 10 minutes, until vegetables are tender. Correct seasonings.
7. Serve immediately with rice.

## SAAG ALOO (NORTH)

### SPINACH AND POTATOES

**Note:** This is a mild dish, so it accompanies spicy dishes quite well.

**Number of Servings:** 10
**Serving Size:** 4 oz. (114 g)
**Total Yield:** 2 lb., 11 oz. (1.2 kg)

**Cooking Method:** Sauté, braise

| | WEIGHT | | VOLUME | |
|---|---|---|---|---|
| INGREDIENTS | U.S. | METRIC | U.S. | METRIC |
| ghee | 1 1/2 oz. | 43 g | 3 tablespoons | 45 mL |
| black mustard seeds | 1/2 oz. | 15 g | 1 tablespoon | 15 mL |
| onion, cut in half through root, then into thin rings | 5 oz. | 142 g | 1 medium | |
| garlic, minced | 1/4 oz. | 8 g | 2 cloves | |
| potatoes, white, waxy, or all-purpose, peeled and cut into 1-inch (2 1/2-cm) dice | 1 lb., 3 oz. | 540 g | 5 small to medium | |
| ground cayenne | | | 1/4 teaspoon | 2 mL |
| salt | 1/4 oz. | 8 g | 1 teaspoon | 5 mL |
| fresh spinach, washed, stems removed, and sliced | 1 lb. | 454 g | two 10-oz. packages | two 284-g packages |

1. Heat *ghee* in pan over medium heat. Add mustard seeds, sauté until they begin to pop. Add onions, sauté 2 minutes.
2. Add garlic, sauté another minute or two.
3. Add potatoes, cayenne, salt, and spinach. Enough water will cling to spinach to cook, but if too dry, add 1 tablespoon (15 mL) water.
4. Cover tightly, simmer for about 35 minutes, stirring occasionally, until potatoes are done.
5. Correct seasonings. Serve.

© Joe Gough

© Joe Gough

## MASALEDAR SEM

### SPICY GREEN BEANS

**Note:** These beans get an acidic kick from the tamarind. Serve them with milder dishes.

**Number of Servings:** 12          **Cooking Method:** Sauté, boil
**Serving Size:** 4 oz. (114 g)
**Total Yield:** 3 lb., 3 oz. (1.5 kg)

© Monkey Business

| INGREDIENTS | WEIGHT U.S. | WEIGHT METRIC | VOLUME U.S. | VOLUME METRIC |
|---|---|---|---|---|
| fresh ginger, peeled and minced | 1 oz. | 28 g | 3-inch piece | (8-cm) piece |
| garlic cloves, peeled | 2 1/2 oz. | 71 g | 20 each | |
| water | | 340 g | 1 1/2 cups | 360 mL |
| vegetable oil or *ghee* | 2 1/2 oz. | 71 g | 1/4 cup + 1 tablespoon | 75 mL |
| whole cumin | 1/2 oz. | 15 g | 1 tablespoon + 1 teaspoon | 20 mL |
| dried hot chili pepper, minced | 1/4 oz. | 8 g | 2 each | |
| ground coriander | | | 1 tablespoon + 1 teaspoon | 20 mL |
| tomatoes, fresh or canned, peeled and finely chopped | 1 lb. | 454 g | 2 cups | 480 mL |
| green beans, washed, stems removed, and cut into 1/2-inch (1 1/3-cm) lengths | 2 lb., 4 oz. | 1 kg | | |
| tamarind paste | 1 1/4 oz. | 36 g | 1 tablespoon + 1 1/2 teaspoons | 23 mL |
| salt | 1/2 oz. | 15 g | 2 teaspoons | 10 mL |
| pepper | | | 1/4 teaspoon | 2 mL |
| cumin, roasted and ground | 1/4 oz. | 8 g | 2 1/2 teaspoons | 12 mL |

1. Place ginger in bowl of food processor fitted with knife blade. Turn processor on; drop garlic into bowl through feed tube. Scrape down sides of bowl, add 1/2 cup (114 g or 120 mL) of water and process until smooth paste.

2. Heat oil in pan over medium heat, add whole cumin, then chili peppers. Sauté until peppers darken.

3. Add ginger-garlic paste to pan. Sauté, stirring constantly, for about 1 minute. Add coriander, cook, stirring, for 30 seconds.

4. Add tomatoes, stir and cook for 2 minutes, crushing tomato pieces against side of pan.

5. Add beans, tamarind paste, salt, pepper, and remaining 1 cup (240 mL) water. Bring to simmer, cover and cook for about 8 minutes, until beans are tender.

6. Remove cover. If necessary, raise heat to high and reduce liquid. Correct seasonings, add ground cumin. Serve.

**TWIST ON THE CLASSIC**

To tone down the spice, add potatoes to this dish. After adding the tomatoes, add the cup of water and diced potatoes. Cover and cook until potatoes are almost tender. If necessary, add more water. Then add green beans and cook until they are done.

# MATAR PULLAO

## GREEN PEA PILAF

**Note:** To facilitate removal of the whole spices from the finished dish, enclose spices in cheesecloth after sautéing, and then add the bundle to the rice with the water.

**Number of Servings:** 13
**Serving Size:** 4 oz. (114 g)
**Total Yield:** 3 lb., 5 oz. (1.5 kg)

**Cooking Method:** Sauté, boil

| | WEIGHT | | VOLUME | |
|---|---|---|---|---|
| INGREDIENTS | U.S. | METRIC | U.S. | METRIC |
| *basmati rice*, washed (or substitute long-grain rice) | 14 oz. | 397 g | 2 cups | 480 mL |
| water, cold, for soaking | | | 1 quart (4 cups) | 960 mL |
| *ghee* | 1 oz. | 28 g | 2 tablespoons | 30 mL |
| whole cumin | 1/4 oz. | 8 g | 1 teaspoon | 5 mL |
| cinnamon stick | | | one 3-inch piece | one 8-cm piece |
| green cardamom pods | | | 6 each | |
| whole cloves | | | 6 each | |
| bay leaf | | | 2 each | |
| onion, small dice | 5 oz. | 142 g | 1 medium | |
| fresh ginger, peeled | 1/4 oz. | 8 g | one 1/2-inch piece | one 1 1/3-cm piece |
| garlic, minced | 1/4 oz. | 8 g | 2 cloves | |
| salt | 1/2 oz. | 15 g | 2 teaspoons | 10 mL |
| green peas | 10 oz. | 284 g | 2 cups | 480 mL |

1. Place rice and water in bowl, soak for 30 minutes to 2 hours. Drain, reserving soaking water.

2. Heat *ghee* in heavy pan over medium-high heat, add cumin, cinnamon, cardamom, cloves, and bay leaf. Sauté until cumin darkens.

3. Add onion and ginger. Sauté until the onion begins to brown at edges, about 4 minutes.

4. Add garlic and rice. Sauté a few minutes, until rice begins to brown.

5. Add salt and 3 cups (720 mL) of the reserved soaking water (adding more water if necessary to reach this amount). Bring to boil, reduce heat, partially cover, and simmer for 8 minutes.

6. Cover pan, reduce heat to low, simmer another 10 minutes. Remove from heat.

7. Stir in peas, cover pan, let sit 5 to 10 minutes.

8. Remove whole spices and ginger, fluff rice with fork, serve immediately.

## TWIST ON THE CLASSIC

To make this into an entrée, brown boneless chicken breasts in the *ghee*. Remove them while sautéing the remaining items. Add them to the rice and cook according to the directions.

© sugar0607

# CHAPATI (NORTH)

## WHOLE WHEAT FLATBREAD

**Note:** Chapati accompanies all Indian dishes well. *Chapati* flour is finely ground whole wheat flour containing both the bran and wheat germ.

**Serving Size:** 1 oz. (28 g), or 1 *chapati*
**Total Yield:** 14 oz. (397 g) dough

**Cooking Method:** Sauté

Linda & Colin McKie/Getty Images

|  | WEIGHT | | VOLUME | |
| --- | --- | --- | --- | --- |
| INGREDIENTS | U.S. | METRIC | U.S. | METRIC |
| *chapati* flour | 8 3/4 oz. | 248 g, plus more for rolling out dough | 2 cups | 480 mL, plus more for rolling out dough |
| water, warm | | 156 g | 2/3 cup | 160 mL |
| *ghee*, optional | | | | |

1. Place flour in bowl of food processor fitted with knife blade or in large bowl if mixing by hand.
2. With processor running, slowly pour water through feed tube, pulse until dough comes together into ball. Process another minute until smooth. If mixing by hand, add water, then knead until smooth and pliable.
3. Remove from processor. If not pliable, knead until smooth and pliable.
4. Place dough in bowl, cover and let rest 1 to 8 hours at room temperature. If holding for later use, refrigerate dough and bring to room temperature before using.
5. Divide dough into 1-oz. (28-g) pieces, form pieces into smooth balls. Pat each into a disk, roll into thin circle with rolling pin, using flour as needed to prevent sticking. Cover disks with moist towel after rolling, do not stack disks.
6. Heat griddle or heavy skillet over medium-high heat, place disk on hot griddle. Cook for about 1 1/2 minutes, until brown spots appear on underside. Turn disk with tongs, cook other side for another minute, until brown spots appear.
7. Remove from heat, stack on plate or eat immediately, brushed with *ghee*, if desired. May be kept warm, covered in low oven.

## TWIST ON THE CLASSIC

For an interesting presentation, sandwich meat or vegetable curry between three stacked 3-inch (8-cm) *chapatis*. (That is, three *chapatis* and two layers of curry.)

*Cooking Chapati*
Dave King © Dorling Kindersley

# KHEER (NORTH)

## RICE PUDDING

**Number of Servings:** 15
**Serving Size:** 5 oz. (142 g)
**Total Yield:** 4 lb., 13 oz. (2.2 kg)

**Cooking Method:** Boil

| INGREDIENTS | WEIGHT | | VOLUME | |
|---|---|---|---|---|
| | **U.S.** | **METRIC** | **U.S.** | **METRIC** |
| half-and-half | | | 2 quarts (8 cups) | 1.9 L |
| milk | | 454 g | 2 cups | 480 mL |
| *basmati* rice | 6 oz. | 170 g | 1/2 cup | 120 mL |
| sugar | 5 1/2 oz. | 156 g | 2/3 cup | 160 mL |
| ground cardamom | | | 2 teaspoons | 10 mL |
| raisins | 2 oz. | 57 g | 1/4 cup | 60 mL |
| **Garnish:** | | | | |
| sliced almonds, toasted | 3 oz. | 86 g | 1/2 cup | 120 mL |
| pistachios, chopped | 1 1/2 oz. | 43 g | 1/4 cup | 60 mL |

1. Combine half-and-half and milk in pan, bring to boil over low heat.
2. Meanwhile, wash rice, let drain. Add rice to milk, simmer for 1 to 2 hours, until rice is cooked and milk thickens.
3. Add sugar, cardamom, and raisins. Cook a few more minutes.
4. Serve warm or chilled, garnished with almonds and pistachios.

Monkey Business Images © Shutterstock

# PISTA OR BADAM KULFI

## PISTACHIO OR ALMOND ICE CREAM

**Note:** Often, this ice cream is molded in upright molds so the unmolded ice cream stands up on the plate. Small paper cups work well for molds.

**Number of Servings:** 8
**Serving Size:** 5 oz. (142 g)
**Total Yield:** 2 lb., 8 3/4 oz. (1.2 kg)

**Cooking Method:** Boil

| INGREDIENTS | WEIGHT | | VOLUME | |
| --- | --- | --- | --- | --- |
| | U.S. | METRIC | U.S. | METRIC |
| whole milk | | | 1 quart + 1 cup (5 cups) | 1.2 L |
| unsalted pistachios or blanched almonds, lightly baked | 5 1/4 oz. | 149 g | 1 cup | 240 mL |
| sugar | 5 1/2 oz. | 156 g | 3/4 cup | 180 mL |
| ground cardamom | | | 1/2 teaspoon | 3 mL |
| heavy cream | | 227 g | 1 cup | 240 mL |

**TWIST ON THE CLASSIC**

For a different presentation and combination of flavors and textures, serve the ice cream over a base of chocolate pastry cream or pudding that is topped with pieces of vanilla cake (like genoise) or pound cake. Place the ice cream over the cake pieces, so they absorb any melting.

1. Place milk in pan with thick bottom (to prevent burning). Stirring often, bring to boil over medium-high heat; allow to boil about 3 minutes. Reduce heat to medium and simmer until milk is reduced by half, about 45 minutes. Stir often while cooking.

2. Meanwhile, grind 3/4 cup (177 g) of nuts in spice grinder or food processor fitted with knife blade. Cut remaining nuts into slivers and reserve for garnish.

3. Whisk ground nuts, sugar, and cardamom into milk. Continue cooking until mixture thickens, about 10 to 15 minutes. Remove from heat. Cool completely. Refrigerate in sealed container until cold, preferably overnight.

4. Place refrigerated mixture and cream in bowl of mixer fitted with wire beater. Whip mixture for several minutes, until lightened. Pour into individual molds or a shallow pan, and place in freezer.

5. To serve, remove ice cream mold(s) from freezer a few minutes early to allow it to soften a bit. Remove from mold. Serve garnished with reserved nuts.

Stanjoman © Shutterstock

# Australia and New Zealand

>> **LEARNING OBJECTIVES**

By the end of this chapter, you will be able to:

- Discuss the influence of the Aborigines and the Māori on the cuisines of Australia and New Zealand
- Explain how the climate, geography, and topography affected Australia's and New Zealand's cuisine
- Discuss the role of the British Isles on the cuisine of Australia and New Zealand
- Prepare a variety of dishes from Australia and New Zealand

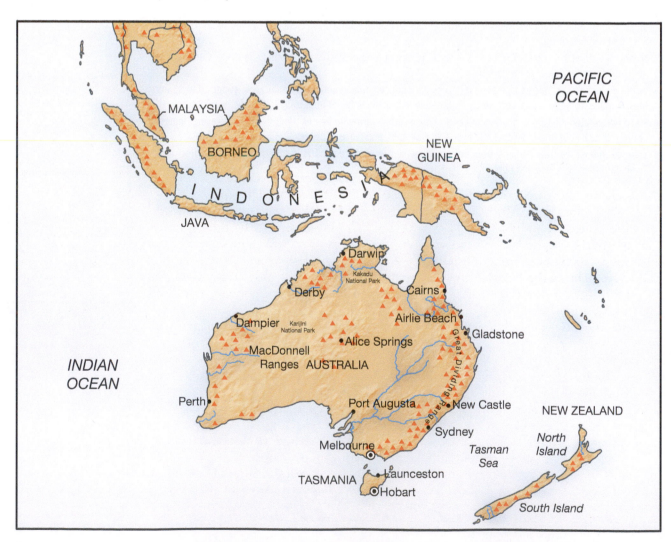

## >> HISTORY

### EARLY HISTORY OF AUSTRALIA

Historians believe the Aborigines migrated from Indonesia and inhabited Australia more than 40,000 years before white settlers arrived. Living as nomads, the Aborigines hunted and gathered food, but they planted no crops. They dried some fruits, vegetables, and meats to last them through the droughts and lean times, but they basically subsisted on the foods they found.

In the time before the arrival of the Europeans, more than 500 different tribes inhabited Australia, and all of them survived by hunting animals and foraging for plants, seeds, and berries. These people occupied both the coastal areas and the outback. "Outback" refers to the large areas of "bush country" in the interior of the country. Because of sparse population there, a person could roam the outback for days, weeks, or months without seeing another human.

### EARLY HISTORY OF NEW ZEALAND

Around 1300 A.D., eastern Polynesians called Māori crossed the Pacific Ocean in canoes and landed in New Zealand. Discovering a land with a temperate climate as opposed to the tropical one of their homeland, they found that many of their native fruits and vegetables did not grow there. *Kumara*, a type of sweet potato, thrived in this new land.

New Zealand's fertile land suited the Māori, and they settled near the coasts. Traditionally living as hunters, fishermen, and farmers, the Māori's diet in their new home included fish, birds, and produce. Since no mammals except bats lived in New Zealand at that time, they hunted all sorts of birds including the *moa*, a huge, flightless bird that stood up to 15 feet tall and was about twice the size of an ostrich.

### EUROPEAN INFLUENCE IN AUSTRALIA

Dutch explorers arrived in Australia in the early part of the seventeenth century, but they did not stay in this desolate-looking land. After World War II, many Dutch returned to Australia and settled there. Instead of introducing their native Dutch foods to Australians, they brought foods from Indonesia, their Dutch colony to the north.

In 1788, the British discovered Australia and established a penal colony there. Since the United States had recently won its freedom from Britain in the Revolutionary War, the British needed a new place to ship prisoners to relieve their overcrowded jails. Soon, Australia became the new home for many British and Irish prisoners as well as a colony of the British Commonwealth. As a result, most Australians trace their ancestry to the British and Irish, and many of their customs and culinary traditions exhibit strong influence from Great Britain and Ireland.

Since the Aborigines planted no crops, farming in Australia actually began with the British settlers in the late eighteenth century. At first, the British disregarded the tropical fruits and vegetables that flourished here and planted the "cool weather" crops that grew in their native homeland. The settlers arrived bearing seeds from their former home and introduced plants indigenous to the British Isles. Of course, those crops did not thrive in Australia's warmer and drier climate. As a result, lack of food was a serious problem for these early settlers. Eventually, they learned from the Aborigines and used the many different native plants and animals that prospered in Australia.

Several other groups of immigrants found their way to Australia. In the 1800s, Lutherans from Germany who were seeking religious freedom settled in southern Australia. They made several contributions to the Australian culinary scene, particularly in the areas of farming, growing fruits, and making wines. In the middle of the 1800s, many Irish immigrated to Australia to escape starvation during the potato famine.

### DREAMTIME

*Dreamtime, the Aborigines' story of creation, celebrates the time when powerful spirits created the land and the people who inhabit it. Although the Aborigines kept no written history, knowledge of Dreamtime comes from pictures found painted on rocks and walls.*

*The Māori named New Zealand "Aortearoa" which means "land of the long white cloud." The British explorer James Cook created the name "New Zealand."*

- *Discovered only about 1,000 years ago, New Zealand is now the youngest country.*
- *The Māori hunted the moa until it became extinct in the early 1770s.*
- *To thank the god of fishing for their catch, the Māori returned the first fish they caught back to the sea. Many New Zealanders still observe this custom.*

Also, with the discovery of gold in 1851, lots of immigrants flocked to Australia seeking their fortunes. The Chinese population rose dramatically at this time, leaving a pronounced Chinese influence on the Australian cuisine.

Since the end of World War II, more than 2 million immigrants from Greece, Italy, other European countries, and Southeast Asia have settled in Australia. Each group of people brought the culinary traditions of their homeland. As a result, the cuisine reflects great diversity, and Australia has become a melting pot.

## EUROPEAN INFLUENCE IN NEW ZEALAND

*New Zealand established itself as a progressive country regarding social welfare.*
*1893—New Zealand made history as the first country to allow women to vote.*
*1898—New Zealand established pensions for older people.*
*1907—New Zealand instituted child welfare.*

In 1642, Dutch explorer Abel Tasman became the first European to discover New Zealand. He never actually stood in New Zealand, though, because the Māori immediately sailed out to the Dutch to engage them in battle. By the end of the battle, four of Tasman's men were dead. Tasman claimed the land for Holland and continued his voyage to the Dutch East Indies.

The first British man, James Cook, landed in New Zealand in 1769; however, the first permanent settlers did not move there until the 1830s. The *Pākehā* (the Māori term for the Europeans) brought pigs, sheep, wheat, potatoes, pumpkin, and sugar to their new land. With the signing of the Treaty of Waitangi in 1840, New Zealand became a British colony. As in Australia, British recipes and traditions permeate the cuisine.

Although the immigrants wanted to prepare recipes from their homeland, they needed to substitute for many unavailable ingredients. Of course, these adaptations changed the original recipe. Another difference from the cookery in their native countries was the amount of meat consumed. Meat was scarce for all but the wealthy in the British Isles, but it was plentiful in New Zealand. For obvious reasons, these British immigrants chose to include lots of meat in their diet.

## >> TOPOGRAPHY

### AUSTRALIA

*Covering more than 1,600 miles, the Great Barrier Reef lies off the northeastern coast of Australia. Over 2,800 coral reefs and hundreds of islands in the shallow, tropical waters of the Coral Sea compose this natural wonder. It ranks as the largest coral-reef ecosystem in the world.*

Lying southeast of Asia between the Pacific and Indian oceans, the country of Australia is both a continent and a very large island. The entire country lies in the Southern Hemisphere, which means the seasons are the reverse of those found in the Northern Hemisphere. For example, January falls in the summer.

Australia consists of flat land with the exception of the Great Dividing Range and a few small mountainous areas. The Great Dividing Range lies in the east, running the entire length of the country from north to south. Plains and plateaus make up most of the Australian countryside. Flat, dry land composes the interior section. Much of that land is actually desert; in fact, one-third of the land in Australia classifies as desert. Grasslands flourish in the areas that receive enough rain, and those grasslands provide grazing for lots of livestock.

Situated close to the equator, the northern third of Australia has a tropical climate, with wet summers and dry winters as a result of the *monsoons,* tropical winds. The rest of the country experiences mild to cool winters and warm summers. Pronounced rainy seasons exist throughout Australia; droughts occur between the rainy seasons. Although many rivers and lakes contain water only during the rainy season, underground water supplies provide much of the needed water for livestock and inhabitants throughout the year.

*Forty-five percent of the land in Australia lies in the tropics.*

### NEW ZEALAND

Separated by the Cook Strait, the North Island and the South Island make up the island of New Zealand. In addition, the country of New Zealand includes at least 220 islands and many smaller ones. Located in the southwestern Pacific Ocean, New Zealand lies

> **Ingredients and Foods Commonly Used throughout the Cuisine of Australia and New Zealand Include**
>
> - beef and veal
> - lamb
> - seafood and fish
> - potatoes and sweet potatoes
> - pumpkin
> - kiwi, apples, pears, grapes, tropical fruits, and other fruits
> - sugar and sweet foods
> - beer and wine

1,250 miles southeast of Australia. The Tasman Sea is situated between New Zealand and Australia. Tonga, New Caledonia, and Fiji lie north of New Zealand. The island of New Zealand contains over 9,000 miles of coastline, giving the residents access to a bounty of fish and seafood.

Both the North and South Islands are characterized by mountains and coastal plains; however, the South Island has taller mountains and more of them. The North Island contains volcanoes as well as mountains. While the wettest area is the east coast of the South Island, the west side of the South Island claims the driest conditions. The Southern Alps run along the west coast of the South Island.

> *New Zealand is about the size of Colorado.*
> *As an island far from other lands, New Zealand experienced significant isolation.*

## >> COOKING METHODS

### OVENS

The Aborigines created an oven by digging a pit, lining it with stones, and then building a fire in the pit. When the fire burned down, the hot stones and glowing embers remained, creating a hot, smoldering oven. Using this heat source, the Aborigines employed two cooking methods that are still popular today, steaming and grilling. They steamed by wrapping vegetables, seafood, or other items in taro or banana leaves then placing them in the pit of glowing embers to cook. To grill, foods were cooked directly over the fire or embers.

The Māori also dug an oven in the ground, called *hangi,* where they baked and steamed foods. To create the *hangi,* they dug a pit, made a fire with wooden sticks, and placed stones over the fire. After placing a layer of flax over the hot stones, they arranged layers of the food (meat, poultry, fish, vegetables, or whatever) between layers of flax and poured some water over the food and stones. They covered the entire *hangi* with a mat, so the water placed on the stones steamed the foods. Today they place the foods in baskets instead of wrapping it in cloth. The baskets are placed on the hot stones, water is poured on the stones, and the *hangi* is covered to seal in the steam. Besides cooking in a *hangi,* the Māori cooked foods in the hot water of numerous natural hot springs. In particular, the North Island has many geysers and hot springs.

> *The Māori even created hot baths from the hot springs! They built tubs in the ground with channels running from the springs to the tubs to carry the hot water.*

### THE BARBEQUE

A continuation of the grilling over an open fire often used by the Aborigines, barbecuing has become a ritual in Australia and New Zealand. People here grill all sorts of foods including meats, seafood, sausages, *kebabs,* and vegetables.

Because of the limited amount of rainfall, the people of Australia and New Zealand enjoy many days of sunshine. As a result, life revolves around outdoor activities, including all sorts of sports, hiking, and picnics. This love for the outdoors leads to a national fondness for the barbecue, known as the "barbie." They cook all sorts of foods on the barbie including steaks, chops, sausages, and shrimp. For many in Australia and New Zealand, cooking on the barbie remains the cooking method of choice for many occasions, particularly when entertaining.

## OTHER TECHNIQUES

Grilling and roasting continue to be the most common methods for cooking meats. Roasted meats came from the British influence. Another carryover from the British, boiling is the usual method of vegetable cookery. Popular in New Zealand, the "boil-up" is a dish where a variety of foods are boiled together. Usually containing pork, potatoes, and dumplings, the end result is a cross between soup and stew.

## >> REGIONS

Australia and/or New Zealand are referred to as "Down Under" because they lie completely in the southern hemisphere. Australians often are called "Aussies," and New Zealanders are known as "kiwis."

## OVERVIEW

Abundant crops and animals thrive in the different areas of Australia and New Zealand, producing a bounty of fruits, vegetables, seafood, fish, and meats. Due to Australia's diverse climates and land conditions, most types of produce, fish, seafood, and animals for meat flourish somewhere on this continent.

A wide selection of fish and shellfish as well as tropical fruits and vegetables like pineapple, avocado, mango, and bananas flourish in the tropical northern sections of Australia. The southern part of the country yields produce and seafood that thrive in a temperate climate. Apples and pears grow in many areas of Australia, as do the grapes that become wine. Although the passion fruit proliferates here, and some varieties of apples and other fruits were developed in Australia, the fruit most often associated with Australia and New Zealand is the kiwi.

Although New Zealand also has diverse climates, the country is much smaller than Australia, so it does not stretch through as many climatic zones. Climates in New Zealand range from subtropical to cool-temperate.

*Two varieties of apples developed in Australia. In 1868, Maria Ann Smith first grew the tart, firm variety known as Granny Smith apples. John Cripp developed a firm apple with a pink skin in 1973. Called the Cripp Pink, most refer to the apple as "Pink Lady."*

## AUSTRALIA

### Coastal Areas

The coastal areas receive more rainfall than the interior, so most of the crops grow near the coasts. Most Australians live at or near the coasts, with the largest population found in the southeastern coastal region. In fact, 80 percent of the population resides in Australia's five largest cities, which are located near the coasts.

### Interior Lands

Cattle and sheep thrive in the vast interior lands of Australia. In areas that receive more rainfall than desert, large amounts of grasses grow that provide plenty of grasslands for grazing livestock. Huge ranches for raising cattle and sheep exist throughout Australia, supplying bountiful meat. As a result, meat consumption in this country remains very high. Australians prepare large pieces of meat like roasts, steaks, and chops as opposed to most Asians and Africans, who prepare small meat portions extended with vegetables and starches.

A wide range of wildlife lives in Australia, and several animal species thrive here that are not seen in most of the rest of the world. Kangaroos, platypuses, emus, wallabies, snakes, and lizards are just a sample of the varied forms of wildlife. Native tribes regularly consumed many of these animals, particularly in the outback regions, where rainfall is limited and food was sparse.

*Seventy-five percent of the land in Australia is "outback."*

## North

Claiming the lowest population of any region of Australia, the North contains poor soil. Much of the income in this region comes from mining. Positioned close to the equator, a tropical climate dominates most of this region.

Stretching along the coast on the northeastern side of Australia, the Great Barrier Reef is the largest coral reef in the world. Comprised of more than 3,000 individual coral reefs and hundreds of islands, the Great Barrier Reef covers more than 1,550 miles. Known as one of the Seven Wonders of the World, an incredible number and variety of birds, fish, and shellfish flourish in the Great Barrier Reef.

## East

The eastern section of Australia contains forests, fertile farmland, coasts, plains, and low mountains. This area receives more rainfall than any other region in Australia, which accounts for the fertile farmland and prolific crops. Shrimp and tuna come from the coast here; cattle, sheep, wheat, oats, rice, sugar, peanuts, vegetables, bananas, pineapple, and other fruits thrive in the east.

## Central

Grasslands, desert, and some coastline make up the central portion of Australia. Much of the land here endures very dry conditions. The coasts yield shrimp and tuna; sheep and cattle thrive in the grasslands; and wheat, barley, and grapes come from this central section of Australia.

## West

The west is composed of plateaus, grasslands, desert, and coastal plains. This region yields sheep, cattle, lobster, wheat, oats, vegetables, and a variety of fruits. Most of the crops come from the northern and southwestern parts of the western region.

## South

The southern region reigns as the premier wine area in Australia with Adelaide as the capital city of South Australia as well as the wine capital. More than 200 wineries lie within an hour's drive of Adelaide.

With long summers and mild winters, many of the great Australian wines hail from this region. Each of the areas within South Australia specializes in wines produced from the grapes that grow best there. For example, the Barossa Valley is known for Shiraz while the Clare Valley produces lots of Rieslings.

## NEW ZEALAND

A mild, temperate climate characterizes New Zealand. Situated in the southern hemisphere, the southern part of the South Island experiences the coolest weather. Because ocean currents and winds moderate the climate, the temperature rarely reaches freezing or rises above the middle 80s.

Subtropical conditions with warm weather and high humidity reign in the northern part of the North Island. The central region contains volcanoes, forests, lakes, and hills. Many vineyards and wine production define the eastern section of the North Island.

Situated in the western and central regions, the Southern Alps divide the South Island. Rolling pastures lie to the east. The rugged terrain of the west includes rainforests and fjords.

*Towering at 12,238 feet, Mount Cook in the Southern Alps is the highest mountain in New Zealand and Australia.*

*Reports state that about 4 million people and 50 million sheep live in New Zealand. That averages to over 12 sheep to each resident.*

### SOME FACTS ABOUT FARMING IN AUSTRALIA

- Statistically, each Australian farmer produces enough food to feed 600 people. Those 600 reside in Australia and in other countries.
- Farmers export 60 percent of their production.
- 93 percent of Australia's food needs is met by product from Australia.

Kangaroo steak
© Ideenkoch

Kangaroo fillet
© jay beaumont

Lamb is New Zealand's largest export. They also raise lots of deer for venison.

## >> CUISINE

Residents of both Australia and New Zealand share a love of food and wine. Some describe their cookery as that of a Pacific country with lots of European influence. The typical Australian and New Zealander diet contains lots of meat and many British and Irish dishes that reflect their strong British/Irish heritage. Some of the favorite British dishes include roasted lamb, meat pies (pasties), shepherd's pie, fish and chips, and various puddings.

Today, many chefs in these two countries focus on two things. First, they capitalize on the bounty and incredible variety of meat, seafood, fish, fruits, and vegetables available in their country. Second, they combine aspects from the many cuisines represented by immigrants from around the world. In the years since World War II, Australia and New Zealand have developed into melting pots. As a result, the cuisines reflect influences from around the globe, including that of many of the Asian and Polynesian countries lying nearby, as well as European countries. In essence, chefs are developing a new cuisine called "fusion cooking," that fuses their native food products with the cuisines from the many immigrants. Because they constantly experiment with new flavor combinations and other aspects of food and dining, the cuisine continues to grow and blossom.

### PROTEIN

Because meat is so abundant throughout these countries, inhabitants consume ample quantities of it, particularly beef, veal, and lamb. In Australia, beef ranks as the favorite meat followed by lamb, then pork, game, and poultry. Lamb is the most popular meat in New Zealand, followed by beef. Traditionally, they serve steaks, chops, meat pies, or sausages for the entrée at the main meal of the day, accompanied by potatoes and vegetables. Many consume meat three times a day—at breakfast, tea, and the main meal. A well-liked dish throughout Australia, shearer's stew, consists of lamb stew with dumplings. Colonial goose is a New Zealand favorite and features lamb stuffed with bread dressing and baked. Rabbits used to be widely consumed, and chickens were seldom eaten, but now these have reversed, and chicken appears frequently. All sorts of game, including kangaroo, crocodile, emu, venison, buffalo, and more, show up on menus.

A popular dish borrowed from their British heritage, meat pies rank as the favorite snack. They take the place of the American hot dog at a ball game. The well-liked meat pie is only one of a proliferation of sweet and savory snacks consumed by the Australians, who are known for their fondness for snacks.

Ample coastline, lakes, and rivers coupled with Australia's diverse climates yield a wide assortment of seafood and fish. With the cool waters of the south and the tropical waters in the north, countless varieties of fish and shellfish thrive here. In fact, it seems that most types of seafood flourish somewhere in Australia. Oysters, scallops, shrimp, crayfish, clams, abalone, and other shellfish abound. Australians have access to ample amounts of fresh seafood, even though they export lots of it.

Deep-frying still remains the favorite method of preparing fish. In the traditional English fish and chips, deep-fried potatoes usually accompany the deep-fried fish. Another popular Australian dish, carpetbagger steak combines two favorite food items in an unusual way. Oysters fill a pocket cut into the side of a beefsteak, and then the steak is grilled.

New Zealand also has access to abundant fish and seafood. Numerous varieties of oysters, mussels, scallops, lobster, crayfish, squid, abalone, cod, flounder, snapper, kingfish, John Dory, and freshwater fish like brown and rainbow trout thrive in the waters here.

## PRODUCE

With the bounty of fruits, vegetables, and nuts growing here, it is not surprising that they appear in many dishes in all areas of the menu. Indigenous to Australia, the macadamia nut was exported to Hawaii, where a huge trade market developed. Kiwi, melons, strawberries, raspberries, boysenberries, other berries, and grapes thrive in both countries. On the South Island of New Zealand, they also grow apricots, apples, and cherries and produce honey.

Cooks often combine fruits with meats or seafood. A variation on the traditional carpetbagger steak, they fill the pocket cut into the steak with fruit rather than oysters. Fish recipes sometimes incorporate nuts in the breading. Salads frequently mix both vegetables and fruits. Olive trees thrive in the south of Australia, and olive oil production has developed into a large market. Like the British, the Australians prefer to cook their meat and vegetables until well done. Traditional Australian cooking does not feature *al dente* vegetables or pink beef and lamb.

## CHEESE

Since the British made the first cheeses in Australia and New Zealand, British cheese varieties dominated earlier cheese production. As more and more immigrants settled Down Under, they brought their culinary heritages and prepared cheeses from their homelands. Today, hundreds of varieties of cheeses from all over the world are made in Australia and New Zealand. Depending on the type of cheese, they use milk from cows, sheep, and/or goats.

## DESSERTS

Consumption of sugar is very high, with all sorts of desserts and ice cream available. Desserts commonly follow the evening meal, and the people here consume many sweet snacks. *Pavlova*, a large meringue shell filled with whipped cream and fresh fruits, is a dessert named for the famous Russian ballerina Anna Pavlova. Residents of both Australia and New Zealand claim the *pavlova* was created in their country.

## BEVERAGES

Another tradition from their British ancestors, tea is the most popular hot drink. Beer consumption remains high, but with the proliferation of the vineyards and the wine industry in Australia and New Zealand, wine has joined beer as a popular and much consumed beverage.

The growing wine industry continues to flourish, and much wine is exported to countries around the world. Wine has developed into a huge industry. In fact, many

> The waters in and around Australia yield more than 2,500 species of fish.

> Kiwis grow on a plant similar to a grape vine. They often trellis them like grapes.

Kiwi growing on vine
© LianeM

---

## CHEESES FROM AUSTRALIA AND NEW ZEALAND

With an abundance of available milk from sheep, cows, and goats, Australians and New Zealanders produce a wide variety of cheeses including Brie, Cheddar, Gruyère, feta, mozzarella, Neufchâtel, Camembert, Gouda, and many varieties of blue cheese. They also produce cheeses that are not so widely recognized.

**Australia**

**King River Gold** Made from cow's milk; slightly sharp flavor; semi-soft texture

**Polkolbin** Made from cow's milk; sharp, spicy flavor; semi-soft texture

**Washed Rind Cheese** Sweet mild flavor; soft creamy texture

**New Zealand**

**Kikorangi** Made from cow's milk; blue cheese flavor; buttery, soft texture with some grittiness; semihard

**Hipi Iti** Māori word for "little sheep"; made from sheep's milk; caramel-like flavor; semisoft texture similar to feta

In Australia, 30 percent of the land for farming is vineyards.

rank Australia as one of the finest wine-producing regions in the world. New Zealand has ten wine regions that produce both red and white wines, depending on which type of grape grows best in the particular region.

## MEALS

Australians eat three meals per day, often partake in tea in the afternoon, and are known to snack frequently. Following the British pattern, breakfast tends to be a large meal. It might consist of porridge or cereal, eggs, bacon or a thin steak, and toast. The substantial evening meal includes a first course followed by a meat entrée and two or three side dishes. Salad either accompanies the entrée or follows it. The meal concludes with dessert.

| REGION | AREA | WEATHER | TOPOGRAPHY | FOODS |
|--------|------|---------|------------|-------|
| Australia | North | Tropical, monsoons | Poor soil, flat, low lying | Mostly fish, seafood, beef, sugarcane, nuts, tropical fruits including mango, pineapple, banana |
| | East | Warm summers, mild to cool winters | Low mountains, plains, plateaus, coast, forests, Great Dividing Range, fertile farmland | Cattle, sheep, seafood, fish, shrimp, oysters, tuna, dairy, wheat, oats, rice, corn, sugar, peanuts, potatoes, vegetables, bananas, pineapple, apples, pears, citrus, grapes, other fruits |
| | Central | Warm summers, mild to cool winters | Flat, grasslands, desert | Cattle, sheep, shrimp, tuna, wheat, barley, grapes, apples, pears |
| | West | Warm summers, mild to cool winters | Flat, grasslands, plateaus, desert, coastal plains | Cattle, sheep, lobster, wheat, oats, potatoes, rice, apples, pears, grapes, fruits, vegetables |
| | South | Temperate, long summers, mild winters | Fertile soil, valleys, hills | Fish, seafood, beef, sheep, dairy, wheat, grapes, wine, fruits, vegetables, dried fruits |
| New Zealand | North Island | Subtropical, warm weather, high humidity | Mountains, volcanoes, coastline, coastal plains, hot springs, geysers<br>North: subtropical<br>Central: volcanoes, hills, forests, lakes<br>East: vineyards | Lamb, beef, fish and shellfish like oysters, mussels, scallops, lobster, crayfish, squid, abalone, cod, flounder, snapper, kingfish, John Dory, brown and rainbow trout, dairy, kiwi, grapes, wine |
| | South Island | Temperate, cooler than North Island | Mountains, Southern Alps, coastline, coastal plains<br>East: rolling pastures<br>Central: Southern Alps, glaciers<br>West: rugged, fjords, rainforest | Lamb, beef, fish and shellfish like oysters, mussels, scallops, lobster, crayfish, squid, abalone, cod, flounder, snapper, kingfish, John Dory, brown and rainbow trout, dairy, kiwi, strawberries, raspberries, boysenberries, apricots, apples, cherries, honey, grapes, wine |

## >> Review Questions

1. Describe the ovens built by the Aborigines and the Māori. Discuss two cooking methods used with those ovens.
2. Why did the British settle in Australia?
3. Explain the British influence on the cuisine of Australia and New Zealand.
4. Explain why Australia produces such a wide range of food products.
5. Discuss how the climate, geography, and topography have affected the cuisines of Australia and New Zealand.

## >> Glossary

**barbie** The barbecue grill

**carpetbagger steak** Steak with a pocket cut into its side, filled with oysters, and then grilled

**hangi** Oven dug in the ground by Māori

**kumara** Type of sweet potato; indigenous to New Zealand

**moa** Large, flightless bird standing up to 15-feet tall, native to New Zealand, became extinct in the early 1770s

**monsoons** Tropical winds

**outback** The large areas of bush country in the interior sections of Australia

**Pākehā** Māori word for Europeans

**pavlova** An Australian/New Zealand dessert consisting of a large meringue shell filled with whipped cream and fresh fruits; named for the famous ballerina Anna Pavlova

**shearer's stew** Lamb stew with dumplings

## SCALLOPS WITH CREAM AND PERNOD

© Tsuboya

**Note:** If desired, present these scallops in a puff pastry shell or accompany with rice or Israeli couscous. To serve this as an entrée, double the portion size.

**Note:** Dry the scallops thoroughly. If they are wet, the scallops will steam rather than sauté.

**Number of Servings:** 8

**Serving Size:** 4 oz. (114 g), about 3 scallops and sauce

**Total Yield:** 2 lb., 2 oz. (965 g)

**Food Balance:** Protein

**Wine Style:** Off-dry or low-oaked whites or soft reds

**Example:** Greg Norman Chardonnay or Pinot Noir

**Cooking Method:** Sauté

### TWIST ON THE CLASSIC

- Prepare this recipe substituting oysters or shrimp for the scallops.
- For a vegetarian alternative, replace the scallops with tofu, *tempeh,* or mushrooms.
- Serve over pasta.

| INGREDIENTS | WEIGHT | | VOLUME | |
| --- | --- | --- | --- | --- |
| | U.S. | METRIC | U.S. | METRIC |
| bacon, medium dice | 10 oz. | 284 g | about 12 slices | |
| onions, small dice | 14 oz. | 397 g | 2 each | |
| garlic, smashed and minced | 1/4 oz. | 8 g | 2 cloves | |
| mushrooms, sliced | 8 oz. | 227 g | about 12 each | |
| salt | 1/4 oz. | 8 g | 1 teaspoon | 5 mL |
| pepper | | | 1/2 teaspoon | 3 mL |
| sea scallops | 2 lb. | 908 g | | |
| Pernod, Ricard, or other anise liqueur | | 170 g | 3/4 cup | 180 mL |
| cream | | 227 g | 1 cup | 240 mL |

**Garnish:**

fresh parsley, minced

© RJ Grant

1. Wash sea scallops, drain. Dry thoroughly and wrap them in paper toweling.
2. In large skillet over medium to medium-high heat, sauté bacon and onions until onions soften and bacon is thoroughly cooked, about 8 to 10 minutes.
3. Add garlic and mushrooms, sauté another 2 to 4 minutes, until mushrooms wilt. Add salt and pepper; remove vegetables from skillet and place in bowl. Set aside until needed.
4. Turn heat to medium-high, sauté scallops on one side about 2 minutes. Turn scallops over, and return reserved vegetables to skillet. Add Pernod and *carefully* flame to burn off the alcohol. Shake pan and cook until flames subside.
5. Stirring often, add cream and cook about 2 to 3 minutes, until cream thickens. Correct seasonings. Serve immediately, garnished with parsley.

# SAUSAGE ROLLS

**Number of Servings:** 14

**Cooking Method:** Bake

**Serving Size:** 1 sausage roll (1 oz. or 28 g dough)

**Total Yield:** 14 rolls (1 lb., 2 oz. or 511 g dough)

**Food Balance:** Balanced/neutral

**Wine Style:** Wine friendly—Try your favorite

**Example:** Souverain Chardonnay or Cabernet Sauvignon

### TWIST ON THE CLASSIC

Substitute any desired filling for the sausage. For example, fill with curried chicken or vegetables. Because the filling is wrapped with dough, just make sure the filling has good flavor. A bland or mild filling tastes flavorless when wrapped with dough.

| INGREDIENTS | WEIGHT | | VOLUME | |
|---|---|---|---|---|
| | U.S. | METRIC | U.S. | METRIC |
| **Pastry:** | | | | |
| all-purpose flour | 8 1/2 oz. | 241 g | 2 cups | 480 mL |
| salt | | | 1/4 teaspoon | 2 mL |
| baking powder | | | 1/2 teaspoon | 3 mL |
| unsalted butter, cold, cut into about 12 pieces | 6 oz. | 170 g | 3/4 cup (1 1/2 sticks) | 180 mL |
| water, cold | | 78 g | 1/3 cup | 80 mL |
| lean, finely ground sausage | 14 oz. | 397 g | | |
| flour | 3/4 oz. | 22 g | 2 tablespoons | 30 mL |
| egg, beaten | 1 3/4 oz. | 50 g | 1 each | |

## PASTRY

1. Place 2 cups (241 g) flour, salt, and baking powder in bowl of food processor fitted with knife blade, pulse to blend.
2. Place butter over flour, pulse to mix until clumps the size of peas form.
3. With machine running, pour water through feed tube, pulse until dough forms ball.
4. Remove dough from processor, wrap in plastic wrap, refrigerate until needed.

## ASSEMBLY:

1. Place sheet of parchment paper on sheet pan or lightly pan-spray sheet pan. Position oven rack in center of oven. Preheat oven to 375 degrees (190°C).
2. Roll about 1 oz. (28 g) pastry dough into square about 1/8 inch (30 mm) thick, brush edges with water.
3. Form 1 oz. (28 g) sausage into sausage link shape, roll in flour, place just below center of pastry.
4. Fold pastry forward over sausage to join two opposite sides, press edge to seal, crimp with fork or crimper (do not seal the two side ends). Place on prepared sheet pan.
5. Brush with egg.
6. Bake for about 30 minutes, until golden brown. Serve immediately.

© Photo Courtesy of Maille

## CREAM OF CRAB SOUP

**Number of Servings:** 10                     **Cooking Method:** Boil
**Serving Size:** 7 oz. (199 g)
**Total Yield:** 4 lb., 8 oz. (2 kg)
**Food Balance:** Sweet/protein
**Wine Style:** Off-dry or low-oaked whites or soft reds
**Example:** Beringer Viognier or Founders' Estate Merlot

SergioZ/Shutterstock

### TWIST ON THE CLASSIC

Prepare this as a thick soup (use less liquid in preparation), and use as a sauce for seafood. Serve the seafood mixture in a puff pastry shell or over pasta.

| INGREDIENTS | WEIGHT | | VOLUME | |
| --- | --- | --- | --- | --- |
| | U.S. | METRIC | U.S. | METRIC |
| butter | 1 1/2 oz. | 43 g | 3 tablespoons | 45 mL |
| onion, small dice | 12 oz. | 340 g | 2 cups, or 2 large | 480 mL |
| celery, small dice | 4 oz. | 114 g | 1 cup, or 2 stalks | 240 mL |
| flour | 2 oz. | 57 g | 1/4 cup + 2 tablespoons | 90 mL |
| milk, hot | | | 1 quart + 2 cups (6 cups) | 1.4 mL |
| salt | | | 1 3/4 teaspoons | 9 mL |
| white pepper | | | 1/4 teaspoon | 2 mL |
| ground cayenne | | | 1/8 teaspoon | 1 mL, or to taste |
| crabmeat, fresh, frozen, or canned, drained and all shell and cartilage removed | 1 lb., 8 oz. | 681 g | | |
| heavy cream | | 340 g | 1 1/2 cups | 360 mL |
| pale, dry sherry | | 57 g | 1/4 cup | 60 mL |
| lemon juice | | | 2 teaspoons | 10 mL |
| ground nutmeg | | | 1/8 teaspoon | 1 mL |

**Garnish:**
paprika

1. Melt butter in large pan over medium heat. Add onions and celery, sauté until vegetables are soft, about 5 minutes.
2. Reduce heat to medium-low. Add flour, whisk until blond *roux*, just beginning to color.
3. Slowly whisk milk into pan in thin stream, add salt, white pepper, and cayenne, stirring constantly, cook until mixture comes to boil and thickens.
4. Strain mixture through sieve, pressing on vegetables to extract all liquid, then discard vegetables.
5. Return soup to pan, add crabmeat and cream, stir over medium heat until heated, about 3 minutes. Be careful not to boil or soup might curdle.
6. Add sherry, lemon juice, and nutmeg, correct seasonings.
7. Serve, topped with sprinkling of paprika.

Frits Solvang © Dorling Kindersley

## SWEET POTATO SOUP

**Note:** The Māori introduced the *kumara,* a type of sweet potato, to New Zealand. If desired, substitute pumpkin for the sweet potatoes.

**Number of Servings:** 9
**Serving Size:** 7 oz. (199 g)
**Total Yield:** 4 lb. (1.8 kg)
**Food Balance:** Protein/sweet
**Wine Style:** Off-dry or low-oaked whites or soft reds
**Example:** Lindemans Moscato, Riesling, or Shiraz

**Cooking Method:** Sauté, boil

Courtesy of Canola Oil @ canolainfo.org

| INGREDIENTS | WEIGHT | | VOLUME | |
|---|---|---|---|---|
| | U.S. | METRIC | U.S. | METRIC |
| butter | 1 oz. | 28 g | 2 tablespoons | 30 mL |
| onion, large dice | 6 oz. | 170 g | 1 each | |
| sweet potato, peeled, large dice | 2 lb. | 908 g | about 5 medium | |
| flour | 1 oz. | 28 g | 3 tablespoons | 45 mL |
| chicken stock, hot | | | 1 quart + 1 cup (5 cups) | 1.2 L, or as needed |
| ground cayenne | to taste | | | |
| ground nutmeg | | | 1/8 teaspoon | 1 mL |
| paprika | | | 1/2 teaspoon | 3 mL |
| cream | | 114 g | 1/2 cup | 120 mL |
| salt | to taste | | | |

**Garnish:**

sour cream

paprika

1. Melt butter in large pan over medium heat. Add onions, cook several minutes until softened. Add sweet potato, sauté another few minutes.
2. Sprinkle flour over vegetables. Reduce heat to medium-low and whisk until blond *roux,* just beginning to color.
3. Very slowly whisk in hot stock. Reduce heat and simmer for 30 to 40 minutes, until potatoes are soft. Remove from heat.
4. Using food processor fitted with knife blade, purée mixture until smooth. Return to pan, add cayenne, nutmeg, and paprika. Heat thoroughly and cook at least several minutes.
5. Add cream. Heat, but do not boil. If too thick, add additional stock. Correct seasonings, adding salt if needed. Serve, garnished with a small dollop or swirl of sour cream and a sprinkling of paprika.

**TWIST ON THE CLASSIC**

For a different taste sensation, add curry powder and some plumped raisins to this soup.

## SALAD WITH AVOCADO AND MANGO

**Number of Servings:** 8
**Serving Size:** 6 oz. (170 g)
**Total Yield:** 3 lb. (1.4 kg)

**TWIST ON THE CLASSIC**

For an entrée salad, arrange grilled prawns on top of the salad with the avocado and mango slices.

| INGREDIENTS | WEIGHT | | VOLUME | |
|---|---|---|---|---|
| | U.S. | METRIC | U.S. | METRIC |
| **Dressing:** | | | | |
| olive oil | | 156 g | 2/3 cup | 160 mL |
| lemon juice | | 57 g | 1/4 cup | 60 mL |
| salt | | | 1/4 teaspoon | 2 mL |
| dry mustard | | | 1/2 teaspoon | 3 mL |

| INGREDIENTS | WEIGHT | | VOLUME | |
|---|---|---|---|---|
| | U.S. | METRIC | U.S. | METRIC |
| pepper | | | 1/8 teaspoon | 1 mL |
| prepared mustard | 1/2 oz. | 15 g | 2 teaspoons | 10 mL |
| **Salad:** | | | | |
| bacon slices, cooked, drained, and chopped | 1/2 oz. | 15 g | 2 slices | |
| mangoes, peeled and sliced | 14 oz. | 397 g | 2 each | |
| avocados, peeled and sliced | 11 1/2 oz. | 326 g | 2 each | |
| nuts, toasted and chopped, variety of choice | 4 oz. | 114 g | 2/3 cup | 160 mL |
| lettuce, Boston or any type, washed and torn into bite-size pieces | 14 oz. | 397 g | 2 heads | |

### DRESSING:

1. Mix all dressing ingredients together in jar or container with tight-fitting lid.
2. Shake well for 45 seconds, until well combined. Correct seasonings.

### SALAD:

1. Combine all salad ingredients in large bowl.
2. Just before serving, pour dressing over salad, using just enough to lightly coat ingredients.
3. Serve immediately, pulling out a few slices of avocado and mango and arranging them decoratively on top.

## SALAD WITH TOMATO, CHEDDAR, AND PINEAPPLE

**TWIST ON THE CLASSIC**

Top with grilled salmon for an entrée.

**Number of Servings:** 11
**Serving Size:** 5 oz. (142 g)
**Total Yield:** 3 lb., 8 oz. (1.6 kg)

| INGREDIENTS | WEIGHT | | VOLUME | |
|---|---|---|---|---|
| | U.S. | METRIC | U.S. | METRIC |
| **Vinaigrette:** | | | | |
| red wine vinegar | | 43 g | 3 tablespoons | 45 mL |
| orange or pineapple juice | | 86 g | 1/4 cup + 2 tablespoons | 90 mL |
| olive oil | | 86 g | 1/4 cup + 2 tablespoons | 90 mL |
| salt | | | 1/2 teaspoon | 3 mL |
| pepper | | | 1/4 teaspoon | 2 mL |
| **Salad:** | | | | |
| lettuce, torn into bite-size pieces | 14 oz. | 397 g | 9 cups | 2.2 L |
| fresh tomatoes, cut into bite-size pieces, or halved if cherry tomatoes | 1 lb., 2 oz. | 511 g | 6 small | |
| fresh pineapple, diced | 12 oz. | 340 g | 1 1/2 cups | 360 mL |
| Cheddar cheese, grated | 3 oz. | 86 g | 1 cup | 240 mL |
| nuts, toasted and chopped, variety of choice | 2 1/4 oz. | 64 g | 1/4 cup + 2 tablespoons | 90 mL |
| scallions, minced | 3/4 oz. | 22 g | 2 tablespoons | 30 mL |

1. Place all ingredients for vinaigrette in jar or food processor fitted with knife blade, shake or process until well mixed and slightly thickened. Correct seasonings.
2. Mix all salad ingredients in bowl.
3. At serving time, pour vinaigrette over salad, toss gently to coat thoroughly. Correct seasonings. Serve.

# STEAK WITH BANANA

**Note:** This is a variation on the carpetbagger steak in which the pocket is stuffed with oysters.

**Note:** Allow time to marinate the steak for 4 hours or overnight.

**Number of Servings:** 1
**Serving Size:** 1 steak
**Food Balance:** Sweet/protein
**Wine Style:** Off-dry or low-oaked whites or soft reds
**Example:** Meridian Santa Barbara Chardonnay or Pinot Noir

**Cooking Method:** Grill

© sattriani

| INGREDIENTS | WEIGHT | | VOLUME | |
|---|---|---|---|---|
| | U.S. | METRIC | U.S. | METRIC |
| steak, Delmonico or tenderloin | 8 oz. | 227 g, or desired size | | |
| dry sherry | | 57 g | 1/4 cup | 60 mL |
| banana, sliced | 3 1/2 oz. | 104 g | 1 small | |
| pepper | | | sprinkling | |
| **Garnish:** | | | | |
| fresh pineapple, slices | 3 oz. | 86 g | 1 slice | |

1. Cut deep pocket into side of steak, pour 1 or 2 teaspoons (5 or 10 mL) of sherry inside pocket.
2. Insert banana into pocket, close with wooden toothpicks, sprinkle both sides of steak with pepper.
3. Place steak in bowl, pour remaining sherry over it, cover and marinate 4 hours or overnight, in refrigerator.
4. Preheat grill or broiler.
5. Grill or broil steak to desired internal temperature, grill pineapple slice.
6. Remove toothpicks, serve immediately, topped with grilled pineapple.

### TWIST ON THE CLASSIC

Stuff the pocket of this steak with a mixture of garlic, slightly hot peppers, and an herb of choice, like rosemary or oregano for an Italian flavoring or cumin for a Hispanic slant. For another delicious alternative, try stuffing with blue cheese or a cheese of your choice.

---

# ROASTED LEG OF LAMB

**Number of Servings:** 12
**Serving Size:** 4 oz. (114 g) meat and
4 oz. (114 g) vegetables
**Total Yield:** 3 lb., 2 oz. (1.4 kg) meat
3 lb., 3 1/4 oz. (1.5 kg) vegetables
**Wine Style:** Medium-to full-bodied red wine with a few years of bottle aging on it. This lamb dish needs a heavier red wine to accompany it.
**Example:** Cabernet Franc 2011, Ryan William Vineyard, Finger Lakes N.Y.

**Cooking Method:** Bake

### TWIST ON THE CLASSIC

Turn leftover leg of lamb into lamb stew. Cut lamb into cubes, and refrigerate until needed. Sauté diced onion in butter or oil; whisk in flour and cook until the mixture turns a light brown color. Add large-diced (or chunks, if preferred) carrot and potato, and cook for another minute or so, stirring often. Slowly stir in hot lamb or beef stock to cover. Add lamb cubes, and continue cooking until carrots and potatoes are tender.

| INGREDIENTS | WEIGHT | | VOLUME | |
|---|---|---|---|---|
| | U.S. | METRIC | U.S. | METRIC |
| leg of lamb | 4 lb., 1/4 oz. | 1.8 kg | | |
| garlic, peeled, slivered | 1/2 oz. | 15 g | 4 cloves | |
| rosemary, fresh | | | several sprigs | |
| olive oil | | 15 g | 1 tablespoon | 15 mL |
| onion, peeled, cut in half | 12 3/4 oz. | 361 g | 4 small | |
| potatoes, Idaho, peeled, cut in quarters | 1 lb., 3 1/2 oz. | 558 g | 3 medium | |

From the British influence, leg of lamb is the traditional Sunday dinner.

| INGREDIENTS | WEIGHT | | VOLUME | |
| --- | --- | --- | --- | --- |
| | U.S. | METRIC | U.S. | METRIC |
| sweet potatoes, peeled, cut in quarters | 1 lb., 8 oz. | 681 g | 3 medium | |
| parsnips, peeled, cut into pieces about the size of the potatoes | 15 3/4 oz. | 447 g | 4 each | |
| salt | | | as needed | |
| pepper | | | as needed | |
| **optional au jus:** | | | | |
| stock, lamb, chicken, or beef | | 284 g | 1 1/4 cups | 300 mL |

**Garnish:**

rosemary sprig

1. Place oven rack in center of oven, preheat to 425 degrees (220°C). Place rack in bottom of roasting pan.
2. Using point of sharp knife, make 3/4-inch (2-cm) slits into lamb every couple of inches. Insert garlic sliver and a small piece of rosemary (or a few leaves) into each slit.
3. Rub lamb with olive oil. Place lamb on rack in prepared pan, place onions, both potatoes, and parsnips around meat. Bake for 30 minutes.
4. Reduce heat to 350 degrees (180°C), bake another hour to 1 hour, 20 minutes, until proper internal temperature.
5. Remove meat, cover with aluminum foil for at least 15 minutes (so juices retreat into meat) before slicing. Meanwhile, continue cooking potatoes, if necessary. Otherwise, allow them to remain in warm oven until meat is ready for slicing. Season vegetables with salt and pepper, as needed.
6. If preparing *au jus*, transfer vegetables to another pan. Pour fat from pan that contained the meat, place over medium heat and add stock. Stir with a wooden spoon to release any bits sticking to bottom of pan, and cook until slightly thickened. Season with salt and pepper, if needed.
7. Slice meat and place slices fanned on plate. Place assortment of vegetables (onion, both potatoes, and parsnips) on plate. Nap lamb with *au jus* and/or serve with mint sauce.

© jabiru

# MINT SAUCE

**Number of Servings:** 15

**Cooking Method:** Boil

**Serving Size:** 1 oz. (28 g), about 2 tablespoons (30 mL)

**Total Yield:** 15 oz. (426 g)

| INGREDIENTS | WEIGHT U.S. | WEIGHT METRIC | VOLUME U.S. | VOLUME METRIC |
|---|---|---|---|---|
| vinegar, red wine or white wine | | 511 g | 2 1/4 cups | 540 mL |
| water | | 340 g | 1 1/2 cups | 360mL |
| sugar | 7 1/2 oz. | 213 g | 1 cup | 240 mL |
| mint leaves, minced | 2 1/2 oz. | 71 g | 1 cup | 240 mL |

1. Combine vinegar, water, and sugar in nonreactive saucepan. Bring to boil, reduce heat, and simmer until reduced by half, about 12 to 15 minutes.

2. Remove from heat, cool about 5 minutes. Add mint and allow to steep at least 1 hour, 30 minutes.

3. Use immediately or refrigerate until needed.

Traditionally, they serve some type of mint accompaniment with lamb roast throughout Britain, Australia, and New Zealand. While mint jelly is often the choice, this intensely flavored mint sauce balances sweet and sour with plenty of mint.

© D. Pimborough

## SHEARER'S STEW

### LAMB STEW WITH DUMPLINGS

Paul Cowan © Shutterstock

**TWIST ON THE CLASSIC**

Replace the lamb cubes with lamb shank. Braise until tender.

© paul_brighton

**Number of Servings:** 10
**Serving Size:** 11 oz. (312 g)
**Total Yield:** 7 lb., 8 oz. (3.4 kg)
**Food Balance:** Balanced
**Wine Style:** Wine friendly—Pick a winner
**Example:** Beringer Alluvium Blanc or Red (Merlot)

**Cooking Method:** Braise

| | WEIGHT | | VOLUME | |
|---|---|---|---|---|
| **INGREDIENTS** | **U.S.** | **METRIC** | **U.S.** | **METRIC** |
| **Stew:** | | | | |
| boneless lamb shoulder, 1 1/2- to 2-inch (4- to 5-cm) cubes | 2 lb., 4 oz. | 1 kg | | |
| flour | 2 oz. | 57 g | 1/2 cup | 120 mL |
| oil | | 57 g | 1/4 cup | 60 mL |
| onion, 1/4-inch (1/2-cm) slices | 9 oz. | 256 g | 2 each | |
| carrots, 3/4-inch (2-cm) slices | 5 oz. | 142 g | 3 each | |
| parsnips, 3/4-inch (2-cm) slices | 6 1/2 oz. | 184 g | 2 each | |
| celery, dice | 5 1/2 oz. | 156 g | 2 stalks | |
| green bell pepper, cut in half, then cut into 1/4-inch (1/2-cm) slices | 4 1/2 oz. | 128 g | 1 small | |
| garlic, minced | 1/4 oz. | 8 g | 2 cloves | |
| lamb or meat stock, hot | | | 1 quart (4 cups) | 960 mL |
| Worcestershire sauce | | 15 g | 1 tablespoon | 15 mL |
| pepper | | | 1/2 teaspoon | 3 mL |
| **Dumplings:** | | | | |
| all-purpose flour, sifted | 6 oz. | 170 g | 1 1/2 cups | 360 mL |
| baking powder | 1/4 oz. | 8 g | 2 teaspoons | 10 mL |
| salt | 1/4 oz. | 8 g | 1 teaspoon | 5 mL |
| pepper | | | 1/2 teaspoon | 3 mL |
| milk | | 170 g | 3/4 cup | 180 mL |
| cucumbers, peeled, seeded, and grated | 1 lb., 3 oz. | 540 g | 2 each | |

### STEW:

1. Wash lamb, pat dry, dredge meat in flour.
2. Heat 3 tablespoons (45 g or 45 mL) of oil until hot in pot over medium to medium-high heat. Add lamb cubes and brown on all sides, then remove from pot. Sauté meat in batches so the pot is not too crowded. Set lamb aside until needed.
3. Add remaining 1 tablespoon (15 g or 15 mL) oil to pot, sauté onions, carrots, parsnips, celery, bell pepper, and garlic over medium heat until soft.
4. Sprinkle any remaining flour over vegetables, stir well. Slowly whisk stock into vegetables.
5. Add Worcestershire sauce, pepper, and lamb. Cover and simmer on low heat until lamb is tender, about 1 1/2 to 2 hours. Correct seasonings.

### DUMPLINGS:

1. Sift flour, baking powder, salt, and pepper into bowl. Add milk, stirring with fork just to blend.
2. Drop by teaspoonful into stew, cover and simmer about 10 minutes, then flip dumplings.

## FINISH:

1. Cook another 5 minutes, add cucumbers.
2. Cook about 5 minutes, correct seasonings. Serve stew immediately. Top each serving with at least one dumpling.

---

# PORK CHOPS OR CHICKEN WITH APRICOT MARINADE

**Number of Servings:** 8
**Cooking Method:** Boil, grill
**Serving Size:** 2 pork chops or 1 chicken breast, or 1 pork chop and 1/2 chicken breast
**Total Yield:** 1 lb., 4 oz. (568 g) with 2 1/4 cups (540 mL) marinade
**Food Balance:** Sweet-and-sour/balanced
**Wine Style:** Off-dry or low-oaked whites or soft reds
**Example:** Beringer Founders' Estate Pinot Grigio or Shiraz

### TWIST ON THE CLASSIC

For a different presentation, grill the marinated meats on a skewer and serve with additional marinade as per the recipe.

| INGREDIENTS | WEIGHT U.S. | WEIGHT METRIC | VOLUME U.S. | VOLUME METRIC |
|---|---|---|---|---|
| **Marinade:** | | | | |
| dried apricots | 4 1/4 oz. | 120 g | 1/2 cup | 120 mL |
| water | | 227 g | 1 cup | 240 mL |
| onion, minced | 2 1/4 oz. | 64 g | 1/2 medium | |
| white vinegar | | 114 g | 1/2 cup | 120 mL |
| catsup | 2 1/2 oz. | 71 g | 1/4 cup | 60 mL |
| honey | 3 3/4 oz. | 107 g | 1/3 cup | 80 mL |
| soy sauce | | | 1 teaspoon | 5 mL |
| oil | | 15 g | 1 tablespoon | 15 mL |
| pork chops or chicken breasts | | | 16 pork chops or 8 chicken breasts | |

## MARINADE:

1. Place apricots and water in pan. Bring to boil, lower heat and simmer for 15 minutes, until tender.
2. Purée in food processor fitted with knife blade until smooth, return to pan.
3. Add onion, vinegar, catsup, honey, soy sauce, and oil to pan, bring to boil, reduce heat, simmer for 5 minutes.
4. Cool, refrigerate until needed. This marinade will keep for several weeks refrigerated.

## ASSEMBLY:

1. Preheat grill. Place pork chops or chicken breasts on grill.
2. Brush meat with marinade whenever turned.
3. Serve meat immediately when done, accompanied by extra marinade, if desired.

Pearson Education/PH College

# SAUTÉED TROUT WITH MACADAMIA NUTS

**Number of Servings:** 8
**Serving Size:** 1 trout
**Food Balance:** Balanced/neutral
**Wine Style:** Wine friendly—Try your favorite
**Example:** Souverain Chardonnay or Merlot

**Cooking Method:** Sauté

## TWIST ON THE CLASSIC

Accompany this with a mango-kiwi salsa containing mango, kiwi, hot pepper, onion, cilantro, and macadamia nuts. If desired, prepare this dish with whole trout (with head) instead of with trout fillets.

| INGREDIENTS | WEIGHT | | VOLUME | |
|---|---|---|---|---|
| | U.S. | METRIC | U.S. | METRIC |
| flour, for coating | 6 oz. | 170 g | 1 1/2 cups | 360 mL |
| salt | 1/4 oz. | 8 g | 1 teaspoon | 5 mL |
| pepper | | | 1/4 teaspoon | 2 mL |
| eggs | 6 3/4 oz. | 191 g | 4 each | |
| macadamia nuts, ground | 8 oz. | 227 g | 1 1/2 cups | 360 mL |
| trout (without heads), bones removed | 3 lb. | 1.4 kg | 8 each | |
| butter | 2 oz. | 57 g | 4 tablespoons (1/2 stick) | 60 mL |
| oil | | 57 g | 1/4 cup | 60 mL |
| lemons | 2 oz. | 57 g | 2 each | |

**Garnish:**

| | | | | |
|---|---|---|---|---|
| lemons, quartered | | | 2 to 4 each | |
| macadamia nuts, sautéed in butter | | | | |

1. For breading, mix flour with salt and pepper and place on plate or piece of parchment paper. Beat eggs in shallow bowl. Place macadamia nuts on separate plate or piece of parchment.

2. Wash trout, pat dry. One at a time, coat trout with flour mixture, shake to remove excess flour, dip in egg, then coat with nuts. Place breaded fish on plate or rack. Refrigerate until service.

3. Heat butter and oil in skillet (enough for 1/4-inch or 1/2-cm coating in pan) over medium to medium-high heat.

4. Add fish, sauté for 3 to 5 minutes, squeeze some lemon juice over fish, turn fish over with spatula, squeeze lemon juice over fish, sauté another 3 to 5 minutes, until crisp and done.

5. Remove from pan, drain on paper towels, serve immediately, garnished with lemon wedges and sautéed macadamia nuts.

David Murray and Jules Selmes © Dorling Kindersley

## DEEP-FRIED FISH

**Number of Servings:** 8

**Serving Size:** about 6-oz. (170-g) fillet—raw weight before breading

**Total Yield:** 1 lb., 14 oz. (851 g) batter
3 lb. (1.4 kg) fish—raw weight

**Food Balance:** Protein

**Wine Style:** Off-dry or low-oaked whites or soft reds

**Example:** Campanile Pinot Grigio

**Cooking Method:** Deep-fry

David Murray and Jules Selmes © Dorling Kindersley

| INGREDIENTS | WEIGHT | | VOLUME | |
|---|---|---|---|---|
| | U.S. | METRIC | U.S. | METRIC |
| **Beer Batter:** | | | | |
| all-purpose flour | 14 oz. | 397 g | 3 cups | 720 mL |
| salt | | | 1 1/2 teaspoons | 6 mL |
| pepper | | | 1/2 teaspoon | 3 mL |
| eggs | 6 3/4 oz. | 191 g | 4 each | |
| beer | | 256 g | 1 cup + 2 tablespoons | 270 mL |
| vegetable oil, for frying | | | | |
| white, mild fish fillets, washed | 3 lb. | 1.4 kg | | |
| flour, for dredging fish | | | | |

**Accompaniments:**
French fries
malt vinegar
tartar sauce
catsup

### BATTER:

1. Sift flour, salt, and pepper into bowl, form a well in center.
2. Place eggs in well, whisk while pouring in beer, continue whisking until smooth.
3. Cover and refrigerate for at least 1 hour.

### ASSEMBLY:

1. Heat about 2 inches (5 cm) oil in pan for deep-frying; about 375 degrees (190°C).
2. Dip fish into flour for light coating, then dip into batter to coat.
3. Place fish in hot oil, two or three pieces at a time. Let oil temperature rise again before frying next batch.
4. Fry until golden, remove from oil, and drain on absorbent paper.
5. Serve immediately, accompanied by French fries (chips), malt vinegar, tartar sauce, and/or catsup.

© stocksolutions

## SPINACH WITH CURRANTS

**Number of Servings:** 9
**Serving Size:** 4 oz. (114 g)
**Total Yield:** 2 lb., 6 oz. (1.1 kg)

**Cooking Method:** Sauté

| | WEIGHT | | VOLUME | |
|---|---|---|---|---|
| INGREDIENTS | U.S. | METRIC | U.S. | METRIC |
| butter | 2 oz. | 57 g | 4 tablespoons (1/2 stick) | 60 mL |
| dried currants | 2 1/2 oz. | 71 g | 1 cup | 240 mL |
| spinach, washed, stems removed, cut into 1 1/2-inch (4-cm) slices | 2 lb., 13 oz. | 1.3 kg | | |
| salt | 1/4 oz. | 8 g | 1 teaspoon | 5 mL |
| pepper | | | 1 teaspoon | 5 mL |

1. Melt butter in large pan over low heat, add currants and cook slowly until plumped (currants soften and swell).
2. Add spinach, salt, and pepper to pan, stir well.
3. Cover pan, cook over medium heat until spinach is wilted, about 3 to 5 minutes. If necessary, add a teaspoon (5 mL) of water.
4. Stir well, correct seasonings, serve immediately.

### TWIST ON THE CLASSIC

Use this as a filling for a phyllo dough strudel, and serve a slice of the strudel as a vegetable accompaniment.

## PEAS WITH MINT

**Number of Servings:** 9
**Serving Size:** 4 oz. (114 g)
**Total Yield:** 2 lb., 5 oz. (1.1 kg)
**Wine Style:** White wine with a higher acidity and high minerality content and a floral nose.
**Example:** Gelber Muskateller Gamlitz 2011, Lackner Tinnacher, Steiermark, Austria

**Cooking Method:** Sauté

© Rachel Dewis

| | WEIGHT | | VOLUME | |
|---|---|---|---|---|
| INGREDIENTS | U.S. | METRIC | U.S. | METRIC |
| olive oil | | 28 g | 2 tablespoons | 30 mL |
| sugar snap peas, strings removed | 1 lb. | 454 g | | |
| peas | 1 lb. | 454 g | | |
| water, as needed | | | | |
| green onion, leave about 4 inches (10 cm) green, thinly sliced | 6 oz. | 170 g | 2 bunches | |
| salt | 1/2 oz. | 15 g | 2 teaspoons | 10 mL |
| pepper | | | 1 teaspoon | 5 mL |
| mint, minced | 1 oz. | 28 g | 1/2 cup | 120 mL |

1. In skillet or saucepan, heat olive oil over medium heat. Add sugar snap peas, sauté for 2 to 3 minutes until almost *al dente*, stirring often.
2. Add peas, stir gently and continue cooking until almost done. *If necessary*, add water, a tablespoon (about 15 g or 15 mL) at a time to prevent burning. Add onions, and sauté another minute or so, just until wilted.
3. Season with salt and pepper. Correct seasonings.
4. Remove from heat, stir in mint. Serve immediately.

### TWIST ON THE CLASSIC

Create a mint and pea salad. Chill the peas with mint, toss with a classic vinaigrette or the mint vinaigrette from above, and add grated sharp cheddar cheese.

## PARSNIPS WITH CHEESE

**Number of Servings:** 10
**Serving Size:** 4 oz. (114 g)
**Total Yield:** 2 lb., 8 1/2 oz. (1.1 kg)

**Cooking Method:** Boil, sauté, bake

Lulu Durand © Shutterstock

| INGREDIENTS | WEIGHT | | VOLUME | |
|---|---|---|---|---|
| | U.S. | METRIC | U.S. | METRIC |
| parsnips, large dice | 1 lb., 12 oz. | 794 g | | |
| butter | 1 oz. | 28 g | 2 tablespoons | 30 mL |
| onion, diced | 6 oz. | 170 g | 1 large | |
| flour | 1/2 oz. | 15 g | 2 tablespoons | 30 mL |
| egg | 3 1/2 oz. | 104 g | 2 each | |
| salt | 1/4 oz. | 8 g | 1 teaspoon | 5 mL |
| pepper | | | 1/2 teaspoon | 3 mL |
| ground nutmeg | | | 1/4 teaspoon | 2 mL |
| cheese, Cheddar or variety of choice | 4 oz. | 114 g | | |

1 Boil parsnips in water until tender, for about 10 to 15 minutes. Drain, set aside until needed. Pan-spray 2-quart (2-L) baking dish. Place oven rack in upper third of oven. Preheat oven to 350 degrees (180°C).

2 Melt butter in skillet over medium heat. Add onion, sauté until softened. Remove from heat.

3 Place parsnips, onion, flour, egg, salt, pepper, and nutmeg in food processor fitted with knife blade. Pulse until puréed. Scrape down sides as needed. Correct seasonings.

4 Transfer parsnip mixture to prepared pan. Top with cheese. Place in oven, bake about 20 minutes. If cheese does not brown, place under broiler. Serve.

### TWIST ON THE CLASSIC

For an interesting visual effect, substitute rutabaga for half the parsnips, prepared separately. Place the puréed rutabagas on the bottom of the pan and top with the parsnips. Proceed with this recipe by topping with cheese and baking.

For a different flavor, add pieces of cooked bacon to the parsnips before baking.

## ROASTED POTATOES AND GARLIC

**Number of Servings:** 9
**Serving Size:** 5 oz. (142 g)
**Total Yield:** 2 lb., 14 oz. (1.3 kg)

**Cooking Method:** Sauté, bake

© Shutterstock

| INGREDIENTS | WEIGHT | | VOLUME | |
|---|---|---|---|---|
| | U.S. | METRIC | U.S. | METRIC |
| potatoes, red or small white, peeled | 2 lb., 14 oz. | 1.3 kg | 18 each | |
| olive oil | | 43 g | 3 tablespoons | 45 mL |
| garlic cloves, peeled | 3 1/4 oz. | 92 g | 18 large | |
| salt | | | 1/2 teaspoon | 3 mL |
| pepper | | | 1/4 teaspoon | 2 mL |

1 Wash and dry potatoes, preheat oven to 375 degrees (190°C).

2 Heat oil in skillet, add potatoes, sauté until browned on all sides.

3 Place potatoes and garlic in ovenproof dish, sprinkle with salt and pepper, mix gently.

4 Pour oil remaining in skillet over potatoes.

5 Cover, bake until potatoes and garlic are tender, about 40 minutes.

### TWIST ON THE CLASSIC

Add parsnips, rutabaga, and an assortment of mushrooms to the potatoes before roasting.

# DAMPER

## QUICK BREAD

**Number of Servings:** About 16 slices
**Total Yield:** 1 8-inch (20-cm) round loaf

**Cooking Method:** Bake

- This bread was prepared by settlers in the Outback. Originally made with flour and water, they cooked the bread over a campfire.
- The name "Damper" refers to the flattening of the ashes before cooking this bread in the fire.

|  | WEIGHT | | VOLUME | |
|---|---|---|---|---|
| **INGREDIENTS** | **U.S.** | **METRIC** | **U.S.** | **METRIC** |
| flour, all purpose | 14 1/2 oz. + as needed | 411 g + as needed | 3 cups + as needed | 720 mL + as needed |
| baking powder | 3/4 oz. | 22 g | 1 tablespoon + 1 teaspoon | 20 mL |
| salt | 1/4 oz. | 8 g | 1 teaspoon | 5 mL |
| butter, cold, cut into pieces | 1 1/2 oz. | 43 g | 3 tablespoons | 45 mL |
| milk | | 284 g | 1 1/4 cups | 300 mL |

1. Place parchment paper on baking pan. Place oven rack in center of oven. Preheat oven to 425 degrees (220°C).
2. Sift flour, baking powder, and salt into bowl. Cut butter into flour mixture until size of peas.
3. Add milk, stir with fork to combine. Transfer dough to counter, knead about 1 minute, until smooth. Add a sprinkling of flour if needed to prevent sticking.
4. Form into round loaf about 6 to 6 1/2 inches (15 to 17 cm) in diameter. Place on prepared pan. Using sharp knife, cut "X" in top of loaf. Sprinkle top lightly with flour.
5. Bake for 15 minutes, reduce temperature to 350 degrees (180°C) and bake for 15 to 20 minutes, until golden brown and bottom sounds hollow when tapped.
6. Cool on rack, serve immediately or wrap well and store until service.

© Blue Wren

## PAVLOVA

### MERINGUE SHELL FILLED WITH WHIPPED CREAM AND FRUIT

**Note:** Top this dessert with any fruit or mixture of fruits. For best results, serve this the day it is made so the meringue stays crisp. Many prepare the meringue shell without the piped wall to hold the filling and instead top a flat disk of meringue with whipped cream and fruit.

**Number of Servings:** 8 to 10
**Total Yield:** One 9-inch (23-cm) dessert

**Cooking Method:** Bake

David Murray © Dorling Kindersley

| INGREDIENTS | WEIGHT | | VOLUME | |
| --- | --- | --- | --- | --- |
| | U.S. | METRIC | U.S. | METRIC |
| **Meringue:** | | | | |
| sugar | 7 1/2 oz. | 213 g | 1 cup | 240 mL |
| cornstarch | 1/2 oz. | 15 g | 2 tablespoons | 30 mL |
| egg whites, room temperature or a little cooler | 4 oz. | 114 g | 1/2 cup | 120 mL |
| cream of tartar | | | 1/4 teaspoon | 2 mL |
| white vinegar | | | 1/2 teaspoon | 3 mL |
| vanilla | | | 1 teaspoon | 5 mL |
| **Filling:** | | | | |
| heavy whipping cream | | 340 g | 1 1/2 cups | 360 mL |
| confectioner's sugar | | | 2 teaspoons | 10 mL |
| vanilla | | | 1 teaspoon | 5 mL |
| kiwi, peeled, cut into 1/4-inch (1/2-cm) slices | 12 oz. | 340 g | 4 each | |
| apricot glaze, *optional* | | | | |

### TWIST ON THE CLASSIC

For a chocolate variation on the *pavlova*, fill the meringue shell with chocolate mousse instead of whipped cream and top with raspberries or other fruit of choice.

For the best volume when beating egg whites, begin with egg whites that are a little cooler than room temperature. Cold egg whites do not achieve the volume of warmer ones.

### MERINGUE:

1. Set 2 tablespoons (28 g) of sugar aside. Sift remaining sugar with cornstarch in bowl, set aside.
2. Trace an 8-inch (20-cm) circle on a sheet of parchment paper; place parchment paper on sheet pan. Place oven rack in middle of oven. Preheat oven to 275 degrees (135°C).
3. Beat egg whites and cream of tartar in mixer with wire beater at low speed until frothy, then beat at high speed until half stiff, slowly add reserved 2 tablespoons (28 g) sugar. Beat until stiff peaks form, fold in sugar and cornstarch mixture, then add vinegar and vanilla.
4. Spread enough meringue on circle to cover about 3/8 inch (1 cm) thick, place remaining meringue in piping bag fitted with 3/8- or 1/2-inch (1- to 1 1/3-cm) round tip, pipe border on top of perimeter (to begin wall of shell), pipe another line on top of border.
5. Place sheet pan with meringue in middle of oven for 10 minutes to set meringue, remove, pipe another line of meringue on top of border, return to oven.
6. Bake for total of 30 minutes at 275 degrees (135°C), reduce temperature to 250 degrees (120°C) and bake another hour, until firm but not brown. If browning, lower oven temperature. Remove from oven, cool completely on rack before filling.

### FILLING:

1. Whip cream in mixer with wire beater on high speed until soft peaks form, scrape down sides of bowl, add confectioner's sugar.
2. Continue beating until medium-firm peaks form, then add vanilla.
3. Spread cream evenly over meringue shell.
4. Starting at outer edge, lay kiwi slices overlapping slightly on top, changing directions with each row (one row clockwise, the next row counterclockwise). If desired, coat kiwi with apricot glaze.
5. Refrigerate, covered tightly, until service. To serve, cut into pie-shaped wedges.

## LAMINGTONS

**Note:** These little cakes are favorites for children. There are numerous variations of lamingtons throughout Australia and New Zealand.

**Note:** Although there are several theories about the name, many think these are named for Baron Lamington, who served as the governor of Queensland from 1896 until 1901.

**Number of Servings:** 12 or 16  
**Serving Size:** 3 or 4 pieces  
**Total Yield:** 9- by 13-inch (23- by 33-cm) cake cut into 48 pieces

**Cooking Method:** Bake

Courtesy King Arthur Flour

| INGREDIENTS | WEIGHT U.S. | WEIGHT METRIC | VOLUME U.S. | VOLUME METRIC |
|---|---|---|---|---|
| all-purpose flour | 14 1/2 oz. | 411 g | 3 cups | 720 mL |
| baking powder | 1/4 oz. | 8 g | 1 tablespoon | 15 mL |
| salt | | | 1/4 teaspoon | 2 mL |
| unsalted butter, softened | 6 oz. | 170 g | 3/4 cup (1 1/2 sticks) | 180 mL |
| sugar | 7 1/4 oz. | 206 g | 1 cup | 240 mL |
| vanilla | | 8 g | 1 1/2 teaspoons | 8 mL |
| eggs | 5 oz. | 142 g | 3 each | |
| milk | | 170 g | 3/4 cup | 180 mL |
| **Icing:** | | | | |
| confectioner's sugar | 2 lb. | 908 g | 8 cups | 1.9 L |
| unsweetened cocoa powder | 2 oz. | 57 g | 2/3 cup | 160 mL |
| butter | 3 oz. | 86 g | 6 tablespoons (3/4 stick) | 90 mL |
| milk | | 227 g | 1 cup | 240 mL |
| flaked coconut | 15 oz. | 426 g | 4 cups | 960 mL |

© Fotoca

### CAKE:

1. Sift flour, baking powder, and salt together in bowl. Set aside until needed.
2. Pan-spray 9- by 13-inch (23- by 33-cm) pan. Place oven rack in middle of oven. Preheat oven to 350 degrees (180°C).
3. Cream butter and sugar in mixer until light and fluffy. Add vanilla and eggs, one at a time, beating well between each addition, until fluffy.
4. Stop mixer. Add flour mixture (in three parts) alternately with milk (in two parts), beginning and ending with flour: Add one-third of flour mixture, mix just to combine. Add half of milk, mix just to combine. Add half of remaining flour mixture, mix just to combine. Add remaining milk, mix just to combine. Add remaining flour, mix just to combine.
5. Pour batter into prepared pan. Rap once on counter to release air bubbles. Place in oven and bake for about 25 minutes, until knife inserted in middle of cake comes out clean.
6. Remove from pan and cool completely on rack.

### ICING:

1. Sift confectioner's sugar and cocoa into large bowl.
2. Heat butter and milk until butter melts. Pour into sugar-cocoa mixture, whisk until smooth.
3. Allow to sit for about 10 minutes.

### ASSEMBLY:

1. Place parchment paper on sheet pan or cookie sheet. Place wire racks on top of parchment.
2. Cut cake into 48 pieces (six even cuts on short side and eight even cuts on long side). Place cake pieces on wire rack with space between each piece. Place coconut in large bowl or on plate (for coating).
3. Pour chocolate icing over each piece so that top and sides are coated. If icing becomes too cool and thick, gently reheat icing. Reuse icing from parchment paper under wire rack, as needed.
4. Before icing sets, roll cake pieces in coconut. Set aside for icing to firm. Store in airtight container.

# Mexico

## >> LEARNING OBJECTIVES

By the end of this chapter, you will be able to:

- Describe the impact of the Mayans and Aztecs on the Mexican cuisine
- Discuss the influence of the Spanish on the cookery of Mexico
- Explain how the topography of Mexico affected the cuisine
- Name foods that the European explorers found in Mexico and then introduced to their countries
- Name foods that the Europeans introduced to Mexico
- Name foods and flavorings prevalent in the cuisine of Mexico
- Prepare a variety of Mexican dishes

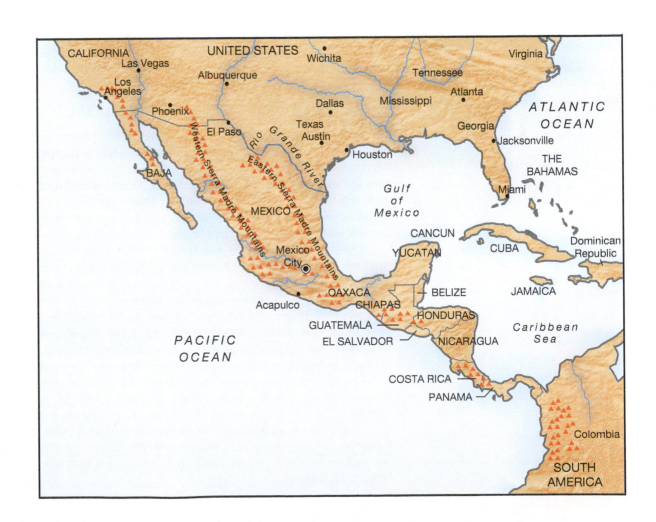

## >> HISTORY

The first known inhabitants of Mexico lived there before 8000 B.C. Although the Mayans and Aztecs remain the most recognized of the indigenous peoples who populated this land, many different native tribes dwelled in the area that now composes Mexico. During the Classic Period from 250 to 900 A.D., these civilizations constructed impressive structures such as pyramids and temples, some of which still stand today. In addition, they built cities, and the population increased dramatically during this time.

## MAYANS AND AZTECS

Thousands of years before the European explorers discovered Mexico, the native Maya and Aztec civilizations developed sophisticated cuisines. Both Mayan and Aztec leaders indulged in huge feasts. In fact, historians claim that anywhere from 60 to 500 dishes were served at these feasts!

Especially impressive considering how long ago they lived, the Mayans and Aztecs were involved in sophisticated studies and research in a number of areas. As a result, these remarkable people developed an advanced culture. They invented a calendar, a written language, an accounting system, and made significant discoveries in the fields of medicine and astronomy. The Mayans and Aztecs experimented with plants to develop better strains of their native vegetables. From the legacy of these two cultures, the Europeans learned new procedures for cultivation that they applied to their crops when they returned to their homelands.

*The Mayans settled in the Yucatan area in southeastern Mexico. In the early days, they subsisted by hunting and gathering foods. They hunted turkey, deer, and rabbit, caught lots of fish, and found tropical fruits and vegetables.*

*The Aztecs inhabited central Mexico. Cortez established Mexico City on the ruins of the Aztec capital.*

## ISOLATION

Although many different indigenous tribes inhabited this country at once, the rugged terrain prevented them from associating with each other. This isolation led to pronounced regional variations in culture and cuisine that developed throughout Mexico.

*Historians believe they cultivated corn as early as 5000 BC.*

## EXPLORERS FROM SPAIN AND PORTUGAL

In 1521, the Spanish and Portuguese discovered Mexico. They introduced almonds, citrus fruits, onions, garlic, rice, cinnamon, black pepper, sugarcane, wheat, cows, hogs, goats, chickens, and dairy products to the Mexicans. From the indigenous people, the explorers learned of many new foods, including beans, corn, tomatoes, peppers, squash, pumpkins, chocolate, bananas, avocados, cashews, exotic fruits, and new varieties of fish. They took these new foods back to their native countries, where many were readily adopted into the cuisines.

The last native tribe to rule Mexico, the Aztecs lost control of their country to the Spanish. This marked the beginning of 300 years of Spanish rule there. During that time, the foods and cooking methods of Mexico fused with those of Spain, and a great marriage occurred between these two cuisines.

In addition to all of the "new" foods, the Spanish and Portuguese brought Catholicism to Mexico. Today, almost 90 percent of the population is Catholic, and this means they celebrate Catholic holidays and festivals. In culinary terms, they observe days with no meat consumption as well as special foods for Christmas, Easter, etc.

The flavorings of the cuisine changed as Mexican cooks added onions and garlic to many of their native dishes. The introduction of hogs provided both meat and lard (pig fat). The lard was particularly important, as Mexicans had no source of cooking fat until the Spanish arrived and brought both lard and butter. This opened the world of frying to the Mexicans, who wholeheartedly embraced this cooking technique. Today, the influence of the native tribes and the Spanish remains the most prominent on the cuisine of Mexico.

| Ingredients and Foods Commonly Used throughout the Cuisine of Mexico Include | |
| --- | --- |
| • beans<br>• corn<br>• chili peppers—dried and fresh<br>• tortillas<br>• rice<br>• pork and lard<br>• onions and garlic<br>• tropical fruits and vegetables<br>• tomatoes and tomatillos<br>• squash, sweet potatoes, and pumpkins | • avocados<br>• bananas and plantains<br>• prickly pear and cactus<br>• pumpkin seeds, sesame seeds, and numerous varieties of nuts<br>• cilantro and cumin<br>• cinnamon and cloves<br>• chocolate<br>• coffee |

## LATER HISTORY

In the 1860s, the French conquered Mexico and introduced the Mexicans to pasta. The French rule lasted only a few years, and by 1867, Mexico became an independent country. A number of revolutions occurred in Mexico in the late 1800s and early 1900s. Although the economic picture improved during World War II, the country remains quite poor.

## >> TOPOGRAPHY

Located just south of the western United States, Mexico lies at the northern end of Central America. To the southeast, Guatemala and Belize link Mexico to the rest of Central America. The Pacific Ocean is situated on the west and south; the Gulf of Mexico and Caribbean Sea lie to the east. This provides about 3,000 miles of coastline and a bounty of fish and seafood for the residents of Mexico. The Rio Grande River forms over half of Mexico's 2,000-mile border with the United States.

### DIVERSE TERRAIN

Diverse climate and terrain make up the land of Mexico, which includes tropical rainforests, mountains, valleys, very arid land, and grasslands. Accounting for the intense isolation that existed between the regions, two-thirds of the land in Mexico consists of high, rugged mountains and rolling plateaus. Rivers running from the mountains in the east to the Gulf of Mexico supply ample fish, seafood, and birds for food for the people in the states of Veracruz and Tabasco.

Two volcanic mountain ranges with peaks as high as 17,000 feet run through Mexico. The mountains of the Western Sierra Madre run from the north to the south along the Pacific coast; the Eastern Sierra Madre lies parallel to that range along the Gulf of Mexico. Mountainous terrain and plateaus form the land between these two mountain ranges. In some areas, the mountains yield to coastal plains where crops are planted, but arid land surrounds the mountains in the northern and north-central areas. A wide variety of crops are grown throughout these areas because the great fluctuations in the elevations cause diverse climatic conditions.

The central region primarily consists of dry land with temperatures determined by the altitude. The southern regions receive more rainfall, and, as a result, many types of crops flourish there. Dense forests fill the southwestern coastal area.

Composed of tropical rainforest and grasslands, the Yucatan peninsula is located in southeastern Mexico. Tropical climate dominates the Yucatan Peninsula, as well as all of the coasts of Mexico.

## >> COOKING METHODS

### INDIAN COOKING METHODS

Prior to the Spaniards' arrival in Mexico in the sixteenth century, the Aztecs, Mayans, and other native Indians boiled, stewed, steamed, baked, broiled, or ate their food raw. Like many countries with meager amounts of meat, they commonly stewed and braised both to tenderize the tough meat and to extend it with other ingredients.

### SPANISH INFLUENCE

*Food on comal*
©leonardomarcel

After the Spanish introduced lard and butter in 1521, both sautéing and deep-frying became popular and often-used cooking techniques. Even today, Mexicans fry lots of foods. Most kitchens in Mexico are equipped with a griddle, *comal*, for frying a variety of food items. The preparation of many sauces begins by grinding or puréeing the ingredients together, then sautéing the paste, adding liquid to the paste, and then placing the food item(s) into the sauce.

### COOKING IN A PIT

A precursor to the New England clambake, the Indians dug a pit, made a fire in the pit, let it burn down, and then cooked over the smoldering embers. They sometimes cooked a whole animal slowly in the pit. Other times, they placed pots of food in the pit, covered them with mud and/or leaves, and left them to simmer. This oven/pit functioned to bake or steam foods. Today, most Mexicans steam tamales and other foods in a steamer over simmering water.

## >> REGIONS

### ISOLATION

Two factors account for the extensive differences found among the regional cuisines of Mexico. As mentioned before, the first cause came from the isolation that resulted from the rugged terrain. Mountains, steep valleys, canyons, and desert areas created difficult travel between regions. This led to the formation of about 32 distinct states and territories, and each developed and still retains its own regional cuisine. The second factor rose from the wide range of climates existing in Mexico.

### CLIMATE

The mountainous regions of Mexico experience cool weather, the arid lands are very dry and hot (except those in the mountains), and the tropical areas are hot and humid. Because of these diverse weather conditions, different crops flourish in the various regions. With different food products available in different regions, cooks needed to adapt recipes. For example, although *tamales* are prepared throughout Mexico, they wrap the filling with cornhusks in the cooler climates, while cooks in tropical areas surround the *tamale* filling with banana leaves.

The varied climates of Mexico fall into three distinct zones that are determined by the altitude. Areas with an elevation up to 3,000 feet experience tropical conditions characterized by long, hot summers and mild winters. Temperate climate exists in land with altitudes from 3,000 to 6,000 feet, and these areas are the most conducive to raising crops. The cold zone includes terrain above 6,000 feet.

Because of insufficient rainfall and mountainous terrain, only 12 percent of the land in Mexico is suitable for use as farmland. Basically, the northern part of Mexico is dry, but the southern area receives more rainfall and thus contains much of the farmland. Some of the crops grown in the south include corn, beans, sugar, coffee, vanilla, cacao, potatoes, avocados, chili peppers, tomatoes, coconuts, oranges, bananas, grapes, lemons, mangoes, and pineapples.

## CHARACTERISTICS FOUND IN THE NORTH

The arid land found in northern Mexico provides grasslands for grazing cattle and farmland for growing varieties of wheat adapted to flourish in low moisture. As a result, inhabitants of the north consume a lot of cheese and, unlike the rest of Mexicans, prefer beef instead of pork. Due to the dry climate and availability of beef, *cecina*, dried beef, remains a staple here. In addition, milder, less spicy dishes prevail in the north. With high wheat production, tortillas made from wheat are common here, while residents of the south prefer corn tortillas.

*Cecina*
©Angel Simon

## COASTAL AREAS

Tropical weather reigns in the coastal areas, and a plethora of fruits and vegetables thrive in the hot and humid conditions found there. Many tropical fruits and vegetables, including bananas, plantains, avocados, coconuts, and papayas, flourish throughout the year in these areas.

## MEXICO'S PACIFIC NORTHWEST

This area is divided into six regions. A peninsula lying south of California, the Pacific Northwest consists of dry, desertlike mountains with rolling hills in the interior. The coastal areas contain fertile farmland, producing crops such as grapes and dates, as well as abundant cattle and seafood. With the bounty of fresh seafood, *ceviche*—seafood "cooked" or marinated in lime juice until it turns opaque—hails from this region.

## CENTRAL MEXICO

The largest region, the Plateau of Mexico encompasses the central portion. This varied land contains numerous volcanoes, lakes, plateaus, flatlands, and mountains. The Sierra Madre Mountains and Mexico City lie within this region. In addition to ample seafood, corn, beans, wheat, and barley grow here. All sorts of wild mushrooms thrive in the forests of Central Mexico.

## EAST

The Gulf Coastal Plain lies in the east and consists of diverse land. The Rio Grande River flows through this region. Forests and dry land make up the north, while the south contains rich farmland and tropical rainforests. With rivers and coastline, ample fish and other seafood are available here. In addition to consuming lots of seafood, inhabitants of this region like spicy foods and coconut.

## SOUTHERN UPLANDS

Situated in the south, the resort city of Acapulco lies in the region called the Southern Uplands. Although the many steep ridges and deep gorges in this region make growing crops difficult, people in this region have access to abundant fish and seafood. The state of Oaxaca in the south was a center of Aztec culture, and the cooking here strongly reflects that Aztec heritage.

## CHIAPAS HIGHLANDS

In the southeast of Mexico, east of the Southern Uplands, lies the Chiapas Highlands. Coffee and fruits thrive in this region of flat-topped mountains.

## YUCATAN PENINSULA

Finally, the Yucatan Peninsula lies to the far southeast, dividing the Gulf of Mexico from the Caribbean Sea. This hot, humid area contains lots of plateaus. An isolated region, the Yucatan peninsula was once cut off from the mainland by thick jungles and swamps. The cooking of this region exemplifies the cuisine of the Mayans, with hot and spicy foods predominating. Ample seafood, cacao, coffee, corn, and sugar come from the Yucatan.

## >> CUISINE

From the time of the Mayans and Aztecs to the present, beans and corn formed the foundation of the Mexican cuisine. Both foods appear in numerous guises and are served at almost every meal.

### COMPLEMENTARY PROTEIN

For an explanation of complementary proteins, see the sidebar on page 550 in Chapter 17, South America.

When served separately, legumes (beans) and grains (corn, wheat, rice, etc.) do not contain all of the necessary amino acids to form complete protein; however, combining a legume with a grain creates complete protein. Although meat and dairy products provide complete protein by themselves, both of these foods were scarce in Mexico before the Spanish arrived in the sixteenth century. Typical of people in many countries with limited food resources, the early Mexicans developed mainstays in their diet that formed protein-rich combinations of foods.

Even today, the foods most closely associated with Mexico, such as beans in a corn or wheat tortilla or beans and rice, exemplify the combining of legumes with grain. These food combinations contain all the necessary amino acids to supply complete protein. We call these combinations of foods that create complete protein "complementary proteins."

### BEANS

Beans combined with grain still provide the majority of protein consumed throughout Mexico. Many types of beans are available, and they show up prepared in a countless variety of ways including boiled, mashed, and fried, as well as in stews and soups. In addition to appearing at the breakfast table, beans are served as a separate course after the entrée at *comida*, the main meal of the day.

### CORN

It is said that the average Mexican consumes almost 400 pounds of corn each year!

A sacred plant in the religion of the Aztecs, corn joins beans to form the foundation of most meals. While many soups, appetizers, entrées, and vegetables contain whole corn, *masa* (ground corn) replaces grains like wheat or rye that usually make breads, dumplings, and pasta throughout Europe and the Middle East. To make *masa*, dried corn is processed with lime (the chemical, not the fruit) and water to soften it before grinding.

Mexicans use all parts of the corn plant, even using the husks as the outer wrapper for *tamales*. In the early days, they used the husks to hold the inside ingredients together and protect them from the ashes of the fire during cooking. After cooking in the fire or steaming, they remove and discard the husks, leaving the steamed filling to eat.

### GRAINS

The current trend of serving wraps instead of sandwiches is really a version of the Mexican tortilla wrapped around a filling.

Consumed at every meal, the tortilla is a flat, unleavened disk of bread made from *masa* or wheat flour, and cooked on a *comal*. Before the Spanish arrived and introduced wheat to Mexico, cooks made all tortillas from corn. Today, most wheat tortillas appear in the north because much wheat grows there.

Whether made from corn or wheat, the tortilla encases all varieties of fillings and functions as bread in the Mexican version of a sandwich. The versatile tortilla becomes a wrapper for many dishes (*burrito, tostado, taco, enchilada*), a scoop for dips (cut and served plain or deep-fried as chips), a replacement for noodles in soup (julienne tortilla), or a substitute for croutons on a salad (deep-fried pieces). Served plain or fried, as whole rounds or in pieces, tortillas remain an intrinsic part of the Mexican cuisine.

Another staple grain introduced by the Spaniards in the sixteenth century, rice appears regularly. Often cooked with tomatoes and/or chilies, it accompanies most entrées. Preparation of Mexican rice usually begins by frying the rice like a pilaf. This causes the grains to remain separate in contrast to the sticky rice favored in many Asian countries.

*Tortillas*
© Dorling Kindersley

## MEAT

Pork reigns as the favorite meat throughout most of Mexico, except in the north, where they prefer beef. Because meat is both somewhat scarce and tough, Mexicans tend to cook it a long time and then shred it. Available meat is extended by using it in soups, stews, or as a filling mixed with the ubiquitous beans. A small amount goes a long way in the typical meat taco. To make a taco, a little meat is placed down the middle of a soft corn tortilla, topped with sauce, and then the tortilla is rolled to encase the filling. Myriad fillings include beans, cheese, vegetables, meats, or any combination of these ingredients. Only the American version of the taco is served in a deep-fried corn tortilla shell. In Mexico, burritos are tacos prepared with a wheat tortilla. When deep-fried, the burrito is called a *chimichanga*.

Prepared with the less desirable parts of the animal, sausages serve as another way to extend the meager meat supplies. They play a substantial role in the cuisine of Mexico because a small amount of sausage cooked in a dish adds a lot of flavor. *Chorizo*, a well-known Mexican (and Spanish) spicy pork sausage, appears often.

## FISH AND SEAFOOD

With miles and miles of coastline and many rivers, seafood and fish abound and compose much of the diet in the areas where they are available. Seafood soups similar to the French *bouillabaisse* appear with significant regional variations. Difficult travel caused by the mountains in the interior regions historically prohibited transporting the fish and seafood in its fresh state, but drying or salting seafood made it possible to transport it into the interiors of the country. Dried shrimp is a flavoring used throughout Mexico. As in many countries, including Spain, Italy, and Scandinavia, salted cod is popular and is part of the traditional Christmas Eve dinner.

## CHEESE

First produced after the Spanish introduced dairy cattle, cheese still plays an important role in the Mexican cuisine. Numerous types of *queso* (cheeses) are available, many possessing unique melting properties. Mexican cheeses fall into three categories: fresh, melting, and hard cheeses. Fresh cheeses become soft and hot when heated, but do not melt. Typically these cheeses are used as fillings for meats and vegetables. *Chile relleno*, a mild chili pepper that is stuffed and deep-fried, often features a filling of fresh cheese.

Melting cheeses melt into a smooth consistency and do not separate or become stringy. *Quesadillas*, one example of the many dishes that utilize melting cheeses, consists of a tortilla topped with cheese and strips of roasted, peeled peppers or any other desired ingredients, then folded in half and fried until the cheese melts.

## CHEESES OF MEXICO

### Fresh Cheeses
**Blanco Fresco** Made from cow's milk; mild flavor, firm texture, sometimes called *para freir*

**Fresco** Made from a combination of cow's and goat's milk; mild flavor, soft, crumbly, somewhat grainy texture

**Panela** Salty mild flavor, spongy, soft texture

**Requeson** Mild flavor, spreads easily

### Melting Cheeses
**Asadero** Made from cow's milk; slightly tangy, stretched curd cheese, prevalent in northern Mexico

**Chihuahua** Spongy

**Oaxaca** Made from cow's milk; slightly tangy, stretched curd cheese, braided cheese with soft texture

**Quesillo** Known as string cheese, from Oaxaca

**Queso quesadila** Mild flavor, soft texture

### Hard Cheeses
**Añejo** Made from cow's or goat's milk; salty flavor, crumbly, hard texture, similar to Parmesan cheese; aged; sometimes called *queso Cotija*

---

The third category, hard cheeses, are usually full-flavored cheeses. Most often, they are served in two ways: grated or crumbled and sprinkled over dishes or added to fillings to create a more complex taste. Mexicans also cook and garnish with thick, cultured cream similar to the French *crème frâiche*. To prepare this cream, heavy whipping cream is cultured with yogurt or buttermilk.

## SAUCES

The many sauces used in Mexican cookery differ greatly from those found in Europe. Appearing on most dishes, both spicy and mildly spiced sauces enliven dry fillings, beans, and meat. Mexicans prefer to mix the foods into thick sauces to form a stewlike consistency rather than serve thinner sauces, such as those traditionally poured over the food or used to nap food items in European and other cuisines.

Several techniques/practices make the Mexican sauce different from a typical European sauce. First, they toast or "dry sauté" many of the ingredients in a dry skillet. This changes and intensifies the flavor of the chile or spice involved. After toasting, they purée the ingredients together with a mortar and pestle or food processor. Then, they strain the sauce to remove any larger pieces of pepper, onion, or other ingredients, which leaves a smooth sauce. At this point, they often fry the mixture to amalgamate and concentrate the flavors. To produce a thick, highly concentrated sauce, they add a minimum of liquid to the sauce during preparation. The foods mixed with the thick sauce often are scooped with a tortilla rather than eaten with a fork.

Mexicans grind or crush many ingredients, including whole spices, herbs, seeds, peppers, onions, garlic, and other flavorings, into a paste before incorporating them into the sauce or dish. To facilitate this, most Mexican kitchens are equipped with a *metate*, a type of vessel used for grinding ingredients. Also, most kitchens contain a mortar and pestle. Today, the food processor expedites this grinding or puréeing procedure.

Using indigenous ingredients, many sauces are tomato based and flavored with chilies and cilantro. Salsas provide an excellent example of this flavor combination. First grown by the Mayans, pumpkin seeds appear in many Mexican recipes. A frequent addition to Mexican sauces, ground pumpkin seeds thicken the sauce as well as enhance its flavor. In Mexican cookery, cooks do not thicken sauces with *roux*, flour, or cornstarch. Rather, they thicken with ground seeds, nuts, tortillas, and/or bread, which also adds flavor and texture to the sauce.

## MOLE

A well-known Mexican sauce dating from the Aztecs, *mole* actually contains unsweetened chocolate in addition to chilies, tomatoes, and a variety of spices, herbs, and ground seeds and nuts. Every region makes its own version of *mole*, and any meat, poultry, seafood, or vegetable can be prepared in a *mole* sauce. Depending on the ingredients used, *moles* come in green, red, and black variations. *Mole poblano*, turkey in a *mole* sauce, dates back to pre-Columbian times and remains a favorite holiday dish. Indigenous to Mexico, the turkey appears in *mole* as well as many other preparations.

## SALSA

Salsa, the major condiment of Mexico, plays an important role in the cuisine. Made from an endless assortment of ingredients, salsa usually is prepared with a base of tomatoes or tomatillos. Often referred to as green tomatoes, tomatillos actually are not tomatoes at all. They sometimes replace tomatoes in salsas and sauces, but tomatillos lack the sweetness of tomatoes, so they create a base with a tangier flavor. Although some salsa is quite *picante*, or hot, others contain milder peppers, resulting in a less spicy condiment. A dish of salsa sits on every dining table, where diners use it as a dip for strips of tortillas or deep-fried tortilla chips or add it to any prepared dishes, including eggs, tacos or burritos, entrées, beans, and vegetables.

## CHILI PEPPERS

One of the identifying characteristics of Mexican cooking remains the extensive use of chili peppers. In varying degrees of heat ranging from mild to fiery, more than 100 types of peppers appear in all sorts of dishes. Beans and rice rise to new heights with the addition of chili peppers.

The ribs and seeds of the chili pepper contain the most heat, so removing them greatly reduces their spiciness. Chilies appear in many preparations, including meats, salsas, sauces, and *adobo*, a seasoning paste containing ground chili peppers, herbs, spices, and vinegar. Fresh and dried peppers are used raw, cooked, roasted, and pickled. *Chipotles, jalapeño* peppers that are smoked and then dried, lend a distinctive, smoky flavor to dishes. Known as *escabeche*, pickled peppers and vegetables appear often as condiments.

## HERBS AND SPICES

Other herbs and spices prevalent in Mexican cookery include cilantro, *epazote*, oregano, cumin, cinnamon, anise, cloves, bay leaf, and allspice. Cilantro flavors many dishes found in all parts of the menu. *Epazote* is added to tortilla dishes and beans, particularly black beans. *Achiote*, annatto seeds, give a yellow color to the dish and appear frequently in the Mexican cuisine.

> *Information about the heat of peppers on the Scoville scale is on page 582 in Chapter 18, Caribbean Islands.*

> *Generally, smaller chili peppers contain more heat than larger peppers.*

### SOME OF THE AVAILABLE CHILI PEPPERS

**Fresh Chili Peppers**

*cayenne*—Hot to very hot
*habañero*—Very, very hot
*jalapeño*—Hot
*poblano*—Mild to medium
*Scotch bonnet*—Extremely hot, rated the hottest chili pepper
*serrano*—Hot to very hot
*tabasco*—Very hot

**Dried Chili Peppers**

*ancho*—Dried poblano peppers, mild heat
*chipotle*—Dried, smoked jalapeño peppers, hot to very hot heat
*guajillo*—Dried mirasole peppers, somewhat hot heat
*pasilla*—dried chilaca peppers, medium to hot heat

### HANDLING CHILI PEPPERS

- *Wearing gloves when handling peppers keeps the spicy oils found in the peppers off your hands. Those volatile oils remaining on hands can cause stinging in the eyes or any cuts or sensitive areas when rubbed.*
- *The seeds and veins (or ribs) of the pepper contain the most heat, so removing them from the peppers definitely tones down the spiciness and heat.*

*Chipotle chili*
Dave King © Dorling Kindersley

*Ancho chili*
Richard Embery © Pearson Education

*Pasilla chili*
Philip Dowell © Dorling Kindersley

### PEEL FRESH TOMATOES

*Place whole tomato in pot of boiling water deep enough to cover the tomato for 15 to 20 seconds. Remove tomato from water and place in cold water or allow to cool at room temperature. When cool enough to handle, peel skin with knife.*

*Blanching tomato in boiling water and then placing in cold water to stop the cooking*
Richard Embery/Pearson Education/PH College

*Peeling tomato*
Pearson Education/PH College

## FATS

Imparting a definite flavor to dishes, the most commonly used cooking fat is lard. Other cooking oils and fats are sometimes used, depending on the desired taste of the dish.

## SOUPS

Soups claim an important place in the Mexican diet. Prepared in countless varieties, soups precede the entrée at the main meal of the day. Served both cold and hot, the many types include those with a base of chicken broth, cream soups, and some almost as thick as stews. *Pozole*, a thick stewlike soup containing pork and hominy, remains a favorite throughout the country.

## FRUITS AND VEGETABLES

Local open-air markets selling fresh fruits, vegetables, and often meats, seafood, beans, herbs, spices, and even crafts exist in all but the smallest towns. With limited meat supply here and the profusion of vegetables flourishing throughout the country, zucchini, greens, and *chayote*, sometimes called green pear, are just a few of the available vegetables that are eaten alone or as filling for a tortilla.

As found in the Caribbean and other countries in the tropics, both sweet and savory bananas play a significant role in this cuisine: plantains function as a vegetable and accompany many entrées, banana leaves wrap foods for steaming, and sweet bananas show up fried, boiled, grilled, or eaten raw.

Another favorite throughout Mexico, the indigenous avocado appears often. Incorporated into all sorts of dishes, it is served raw, as well as used in soups, stews, and other dishes. Its best-known preparation remains *guacamole*, a spread made of mashed avocado, onion, tomato, and chilies. Recipes for *guacamole* vary greatly from region to region.

Tomatoes show up constantly as an ingredient in all sorts of sauces, salsas, and dishes prepared throughout Mexico. Used roasted, cooked, and raw, they lend color as well as various flavors and textures to a wide range of dishes.

With lots of arid land, the flourishing cactus plants enter into Mexico's culinary world. Cacti appear in salads, sauces, juices, and either stewed or fried as a vegetable. The popular prickly pear is the fruit of the *nopales* cactus. Tequila is made from the *agave* cactus.

## BEVERAGES

Chocolate originated in this part of the world. Frequently served as a beverage, it is usually paired with cinnamon. Another nonalcoholic drink consumed in huge quantities, coffee functions as a flavoring as well as a beverage. The Mexicans prepare very strong coffee and flavor it with plenty of sugar. With abundant fresh fruits available, fruit juices continue to be popular drinks. Favorite alcoholic beverages remain beer, rum, and tequila.

## DESSERTS

Like their Spanish ancestors who were influenced by the Arabs, Mexicans prefer very sweet desserts. A typical dessert plate served in Mexico even includes candy. Often incorporating fruit in fresh, candied, or paste form, desserts also frequently incorporate nuts and lots of eggs. Some of the available nuts include pine nuts, peanuts, almonds, pecans, and walnuts. Flans and other custardlike confections remain very popular.

## MEALS

The day begins with a breakfast of fruit, tortillas or sweet rolls, and coffee or hot chocolate, but some people also eat meat, eggs, and/or beans with breakfast. Many consume a midmorning snack to hold them until the main meal of the day, which is eaten around two o'clock in the afternoon. Consisting of several courses, *comida* is the largest meal of the day. Soup precedes the entrée that is accompanied by a vegetable or salad. A bowl of beans follows the entrée, and then the dessert, usually consisting of fresh or stewed fruit. Tortillas and salsa are included on the table for *comida*. Much like the traditional English tea, *merienda* features pastries with coffee or hot chocolate served around six in the evening. Eaten at nine or ten o'clock, the light, late evening meal, *cena*, might consist of one or two appetizers and a bowl of soup.

*When Cortez arrived in Mexico City, he learned of the Aztec emperor Montezuma's favorite chocolate drink that contained the indigenous ingredients chocolate, honey, and vanilla. Cortez introduced the drink to Spain, and of course, it became a popular addition to Spain's cuisine and eventually to many cuisines around the world.*

| REGION | AREA | WEATHER | TOPOGRAPHY | FOODS |
|---|---|---|---|---|
| Pacific Northwest | Northwest | Hot | Interior: arid, mountainous Coast: fertile farmland | Cattle, seafood, cheese, wheat, dates, peppers, grapes, prickly pears |
| Plateau of Mexico | Central (includes Mexico City) | Some temperate, some hot | Mountains, lakes, forests, volcanoes, flatlands, plateaus | Seafood, game, goat, barley, wheat, corn, beans, vegetables, squash, pumpkin, chili peppers, mushrooms, fruits, chocolate |
| Gulf Coastal Plain | East (includes Veracruz) | North: arid South: hot, humid | North: coast, forests South: tropical coast, rainforest, rich farmland | Seafood, black beans, sugar, corn, tropical fruits and vegetables |
| Southern Uplands | South (includes Oaxaca) | Hot, humid | Coast, plateaus, forests, grasslands | Seafood, beans, corn, avocado, plantains, squash, tomatoes, chili peppers, pumpkins, bananas |
| Chiapas Highlands | Southeast | Hot, humid | Coast, valleys, flat-topped mountains, farmland | Seafood, game, beans, mushrooms, jalapeños, fruits, coffee, cacao |
| Yucatan | Southeast | Tropical, hot, humid | Coast, grasslands, swamps, plateaus, forest, jungle, rainforest | Seafood, beans, corn, chili peppers, sugar, tropical fruits and vegetables, plantains, bananas, avocado, papaya, mango, vanilla, cacao, coffee |

## >> Review Questions

1. Name at least four foods commonly consumed by the Indians in Mexico before the European explorers arrived.
2. Name at least five foods introduced to Mexico by the Spaniards.
3. Describe the topography and climate found in Mexico. Explain how they influenced the regional cuisines.
4. What is salsa and how is it used in Mexico?
5. Name and describe several Mexican dishes including *mole*, burrito, and taco.
6. Which flavorings are most prevalent in Mexican cookery?
7. Describe the daily meal pattern for inhabitants of Mexico.

## >> Glossary

**achiote** Ground annatto seeds used in cooking that give a yellow color to the dish

**adobo** A seasoning paste containing ground chili peppers, herbs, spices, and vinegar used in many preparations, including meats and salsas

**burrito** A taco prepared with a wheat tortilla

**cecina** Dried beef popular in northern Mexico

**cena** Light evening meal served around nine or ten o'clock

**ceviche** Seafood "cooked" or marinated in lime juice until it becomes opaque

**chayote** A common vegetable in Mexico, sometimes called a green pear

**chili relleno** A chili pepper stuffed with cheese, meat, or another filling, then dipped in batter and deep-fried

**chimichanga** A deep-fried burrito

**chorizo** A well-known Mexican (and Spanish) spicy pork sausage

**comida** The main meal of the day, eaten around two o'clock in the afternoon

**escabeche** Pickled peppers or vegetables

**guacamole** A spread consisting of mashed avocado, onion, tomato, and usually chili peppers, ingredients vary from region to region

**masa** Ground corn used for making tortillas and other foods

**merienda** Similar to the English tea, pastries and coffee or hot chocolate are served around six in the evening

**mole** Savory Mexican sauce containing unsweetened chocolate, chilies, tomatoes, and spices

**picante** Mexican word for "hot and spicy"

**quesadillas** A tortilla topped with cheese and roasted, peeled peppers or other ingredients, folded in half and fried until the cheese melts

**queso** The Mexican word for cheese

**taco** A corn tortilla topped with meat, beans, cheese, vegetables, or any combination of fillings and sauce, then rolled to encase the filling

**tamales** Entrée consisting of corn husks or banana leaves wrapped around filling ingredients then steamed; the husks or leaves are discarded and the filling is eaten

**tortilla** A flat, unleavened disk made from wheat or corn and cooked on a dry griddle; eaten at every meal; Mexican bread

## GUACAMOLE

### AVOCADO DIP

**Note:** Guacamole darkens with exposure to air, so if not serving immediately, cover tightly to avoid oxidation. Many say inserting the avocado pit into the dip helps prevent the guacamole from darkening.

**Number of Servings:** 10
**Serving Size:** 2 oz. (57 g), or 1/4 cup (60 mL)
**Total Yield:** 1 lb., 4 oz. (568 g), or 2 1/2 cups (600 mL)
**Food Balance:** Protein
**Wine Style:** Off-dry, low-oaked whites and soft reds
**Example:** Beringer Chenin Blanc, Penfolds Riesling, Matua Sauvignon Blanc

### TWIST ON THE CLASSIC

For a different presentation, serve the guacamole in a hollow shell of half of an avocado.

Guacamole can function in many areas of the menu. Traditionally served as a dip for warm tortillas or tortilla chips, it is delicious as part of a salad or as a condiment or side dish. The buttery texture of avocado adds a smooth texture to any plate.

| INGREDIENTS | WEIGHT U.S. | WEIGHT METRIC | VOLUME U.S. | VOLUME METRIC |
|---|---|---|---|---|
| avocado, peeled, seeded | 12 1/2 oz. | 355 g | 2 medium | |
| onion, white, minced | 3/4 oz. | 22 g | 2 tablespoons | 30 mL |
| *serrano* chilies, seeds and veins removed if desired, minced | 1/2 oz. | 15 g, or to taste | 1 or 2 each, or to taste | |
| fresh cilantro, minced | 1/2 oz. | 15 g | 2 tablespoons | 30 mL |
| fresh lime juice | | | 2 teaspoons | 10 mL |
| tomato, peeled, seeded, and chopped | 6 oz. | 170 g | 1 medium | |
| salt | | | 1/2 teaspoon | 3 mL |

① Place avocado in bowl, mash with fork against side of bowl until chunky paste.

② Add onion, chilies, cilantro, lime juice, tomato, and salt, mix well.

③ Serve immediately, accompanied by tortilla chips or warm tortillas, as part of a salad, or as a condiment with another dish. If not serving immediately, place avocado pit into dip and cover tightly with plastic wrap to prevent it from turning brown (oxidizing).

Otokimus © Shutterstock

© Olyina

# SALSA CRUDA

## UNCOOKED SPICY TOMATO SAUCE

**Note:** A bowl of salsa sits on the dining table in Mexico as Americans and Europeans have salt and pepper on the table.

### TWIST ON THE CLASSIC

Make a Mexican burger by seasoning the ground beef with cumin and chili powder and topping the cooked hamburger with guacamole and salsa.

**Number of Servings:** 8
**Serving Size:** 2 oz. (57 g), or 1/4 cup (60 mL)
**Total Yield:** 1 lb., 2 oz. (511 g), or 2 cups (480 mL)
**Food Balance:** Sweet/spicy/protein
**Wine Style:** Soft and fruity Gewürztraminer, Sauvignon Blanc, Pinot Blanc, Beaujolais
**Example:** Stone Cellars Shiraz

| INGREDIENTS | WEIGHT | | VOLUME | |
|---|---|---|---|---|
| | *U.S.* | *METRIC* | *U.S.* | *METRIC* |
| tomatoes, peeled and diced | 1 lb. | 454 g | 2 large | |
| *serrano* chilies, seeds and veins removed if desired, minced | 1/4 oz. | 8 g, or to taste | 1 or 2 each, or to taste | |
| fresh cilantro, minced | 1/4 oz. | 8 g | 1 tablespoon | 15 mL |
| white onion, minced | 2 oz. | 57 g | 1/3 cup, or 1/2 small | 80 mL |
| fresh lime juice | | | 2 teaspoons | 10 mL |
| salt | | | 1/2 teaspoon | 3 mL |

1. Mix all ingredients in bowl.
2. Correct seasonings. Serve with tortilla chips or as a condiment with any dish.

© JJAVA

© JJAVA

# SOPA DE ELOTE

## CORN SOUP

**Number of Servings:** 12
**Serving Size:** 8 oz. (227 g)
**Total Yield:** 6 lb., 6 oz. (2.9 kg)
**Food Balance:** Sweet/protein
**Wine Style:** Off-dry, low-oaked whites and soft reds
**Example:** Meridian Santa Barbara Chardonnay or Pinot Noir

**Cooking Method:** Sauté, boil

| | WEIGHT | | VOLUME | |
|---|---|---|---|---|
| **INGREDIENTS** | **U.S.** | **METRIC** | **U.S.** | **METRIC** |
| corn, on cob or frozen kernels | 2 lb., 4 oz. | 1 kg | 9 ears, or 6 cups | 1.4 L |
| chicken stock | | | 2 quarts (8 cups) | 1.9 L |
| fresh *poblano* chilies, charred and peeled | 1 lb., 7 oz. | 653 g | 4 each | |
| OR | | | | |
| canned *poblano* chilies | 9 oz. | 256 g | 2 small cans | |
| tomatoes, fresh or canned, peeled and chopped | 12 oz. | 340 g | 2 medium, or 1 1/3 cup | 320 mL |
| white onion, diced | 6 oz. | 170 g | 1 medium | |
| butter | 1 1/2 oz. | 43 g | 3 tablespoons | 45 mL |
| heavy cream | | 227 g | 1 cup | 240 mL |
| salt | | | to taste | |

**Garnish:**

sour cream

1. If using fresh corn, remove kernels from the cob. Reserve kernels. Cook chicken stock with leftover corn cobs for at least 30 minutes. If using frozen corn, just heat the stock.

2. Remove seeds and veins from chilies. Place chilies, tomatoes, onion, and 2 cups (480 mL) corn in bowl of food processor fitted with knife blade. Pulse until paste.

3. Melt butter in pan over medium to medium-low heat. Add paste and simmer for 10 minutes, stirring often.

4. Remove cobs from stock (if cobs were used). Add sautéed paste and remaining 4 cups (960 mL) corn to stock, simmer until corn is tender, about 25 minutes.

5. Add cream and cook just until warm. Be careful not to curdle the soup. Add salt, if needed. Correct seasonings.

6. Serve immediately, garnished with a dollop of sour cream.

Richard Embery © Pearson Education/PH College

# SOPA DE TORTILLAS
## TORTILLA SOUP

Don Farrall/Getty Images

**Number of Servings:** 10
**Serving Size:** 8 oz. (227 g)
**Total Yield:** 5 lb. (2.3 kg)
**Food Balance:** Sweet-and-sour/spicy
**Wine Style:** Off-dry, low-oaked whites and soft reds
**Example:** Beringer Moscato, Sauvignon Blanc, or Founders' Estate Merlot

**Cooking Method:** Sauté, boil

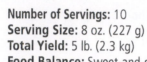

### TWIST ON THE CLASSIC

Add cooked rice to this soup to make it more hearty and filling.

© blueee

| INGREDIENTS | WEIGHT | | VOLUME | |
|---|---|---|---|---|
| | U.S. | METRIC | U.S. | METRIC |
| chicken stock | | | 2 quarts (8 cups) | 1.9 L |
| oil or lard | | 28 g | 2 tablespoons | 30 mL |
| white onion, small dice | 5 oz. | 142 g | 1 medium | |
| garlic, smashed and minced | 1/4 oz. | 8 g | 2 cloves | |
| *jalapeño*, seeds and veins removed, minced | 1/4 oz. | 8 g | 1/2 each | |
| fresh tomato, peeled, seeded, and cut into dice | 12 oz. | 340 g | 2 each | |
| chicken breasts, cooked and cut into medium dice | 7 1/2 oz. | 213 g | 2 cups, or 2 breasts | 480 mL |
| fresh lime juice | | 28 g | 2 tablespoons | 30 mL |
| pepper | | | 1/4 teaspoon | 2 mL |
| dried oregano | | | 1/2 teaspoon | 3 mL |

**Garnish:**

tortilla, cut into strips
oil or lard, for frying
*jalapeño* or *serrano* peppers, minced
Monterey Jack cheese, grated,
    *optional*
avocado, diced, *optional*
fresh lime juice, *optional*

1. Heat chicken stock to simmering.
2. Heat oil in skillet over medium heat, sauté onion about 3 or 4 minutes. Add garlic and *jalapeño*, sauté another couple of minutes, until softened.
3. Add tomato to skillet, sauté another 3 or 4 minutes.
4. Add sautéed vegetables to chicken broth. Add chicken, lime juice, pepper, and oregano. Simmer about 15 minutes. Correct seasonings.

### GARNISH:

1. Fry tortilla strips slowly in hot oil or lard until golden brown.
2. Drain well on absorbent paper.

### ASSEMBLY:

1. Place hot soup in bowl.
2. Top with tortilla strips.
3. Serve accompanied by peppers and bowls of optional garnishes, if desired.

## ENSALADA MIXTA

### MIXED SALAD

**Note:** Chill plates in advance for this salad.

**Number of Servings:** 8
**Cooking Method:** Grill
**Serving Size:** 1 oz. (28 g) poblano
About 1 1/2 oz. (43 g) tomato (1/4 each)
About 1/2 oz. (15 g) avocado (2 slices)
3/4 oz. (22 g) onion
About 3/4 oz. (22 g) hard-boiled egg (1/4 egg)
1 oz. (28 g), or 2 tablespoons (30 mL) dressing
**Food Balance:** Balanced
**Wine Style:** Wine friendly—Pick a winner
**Example:** Château St. Jean Chardonnay or Cabernet Sauvignon

| | *WEIGHT* | | *VOLUME* | |
|---|---|---|---|---|
| ***INGREDIENTS*** | ***U.S.*** | ***METRIC*** | ***U.S.*** | ***METRIC*** |
| **Dressing:** | | | | |
| vinegar, white or cider | | 78 g | 1/3 cup | 80 mL |
| dried oregano | | | 1 teaspoon | 5 mL |
| salt | | | 1/2 teaspoon | 3 mL |
| pepper | | | 1/4 teaspoon | 2 mL |
| oil | | 227 g | 1 cup | 240 mL |
| lettuce, torn into bite-sized pieces | as needed | | | |
| *poblano* chilies, charred, peeled, seeds and veins removed, cut into 1/4-to 1/2-inch (1/2- to 1 1/3-cm) strips | 8 1/4 oz. | 234 g | 3 each | |
| tomato, 1/4-inch (1/2-cm) slices | 13 oz. | 369 g | 2 medium | |
| avocado, slices | 4 3/4 oz. | 135 g | 1 each | |
| onion, thin slices | 6 oz. | 170 g | 1 medium | |
| eggs, hard-boiled and cut into eighths | 3 1/2 oz. | 104 g | 2 each | |

**TWIST ON THE CLASSIC**

Top with blackened salmon or fish of choice to make this into an entrée salad.

**TO PEEL FRESH PEPPERS**

Roast peppers over the open flame of a grill or gas burner or place in a broiler. Turn as needed until charred and blackened all over. Place charred peppers in a bag for a few minutes to soften the skin, then remove them from the bag and peel under cool running water.

*Charring pepper over flame*
Richard Embery © Pearson Education/PH College

*Placing charred pepper in bag to steam*
David Murray and Jules Selmes © Dorling Kindersley

## DRESSING:

1. Mix vinegar, oregano, salt, and pepper in jar with tight-fitting lid, blender, or food processor fitted with knife blade.
2. Slowly add oil to blender or food processor. If using jar, add oil and shake vigorously.
3. Correct seasonings. Refrigerate until needed.

## ASSEMBLY:

1. For each serving, place bed of lettuce on chilled plate.
2. Decoratively arrange all ingredients on top, using about 1 oz. (28 g) *poblanos*, about 1 1/2 oz. (43 g) tomato (1/4 tomato), about 1/2 oz. (15 g) avocado (2 slices), 3/4 oz. (22 g) onion, and about 3/4 oz. (22 g) hard-boiled egg (1/4 egg).
3. Shake dressing well to mix oil and flavorings. Drizzle about 2 tablespoons (28 g or 30 mL) over each salad. Serve.

*Peeling pepper under running water*
Richard Embery © Pearson Education/PH College

# ENSALADA DE NOCHE BUENA

## CHRISTMAS EVE SALAD

**Note:** See page 329 in Chapter 10, Israel, recipe for Orange and Olive Salad, which contains instructions and photographs for removing rind and cutting orange into segments.

**Number of Servings:** 9
**Serving Size:** 6 oz. (170 g)
**Total Yield:** 3 lb., 9 oz. (1.6 kg)

Olaf Speier/Fotolia

| INGREDIENTS | WEIGHT U.S. | METRIC | VOLUME U.S. | METRIC |
|---|---|---|---|---|
| sugar | 3 3/4 oz. | 107 g | 1/2 cup | 120 mL |
| wine vinegar | | 57 g | 1/4 cup | 60 mL |
| beets, fresh or canned, cooked and chopped | 6 oz. | 170 g | 3 medium | |
| oranges, peeled, sectioned, and membrane removed | 8 oz. | 227 g | 3 each | |
| jicama, peeled and sliced | 15 oz. | 426 g | 1 each | |
| tart apple, peeled, cored, and sliced | 8 oz. | 227 g | 1 each | |
| bananas, peeled and sliced | 11 1/2 oz. | 326 g | 3 each | |
| lettuce, *optional* | | | | |
| peanuts, chopped | 3 oz. | 86 g | 1/2 cup | 120 mL |

1. Mix sugar and vinegar together in bowl until sugar dissolves, set aside.
2. Mix beets, oranges, jicama, apple, and bananas in bowl. Add vinegar mixture and mix gently. Refrigerate until needed.
3. To serve, place fruit mixture on bed of lettuce, if desired, sprinkle with peanuts.

> **TWIST ON THE CLASSIC**
>
> For an Italian slant, replace the jicama with fennel and top the salad with toasted hazelnuts instead of peanuts.

# ALBÓNDIGAS

## MEATBALLS

**Note:** There are countless variations of albóndigas in every region of Mexico. Many use half beef and half pork instead of all beef.

**Number of Servings:** 12
**Serving Size:** 6 1/2 oz. (184 g), with 4 meatballs (1 1/2 oz. or 43 g raw meat each)
**Total Yield:** 5 lb., 2 1/2 oz. (2.3 kg), about 55 meatballs
**Food Balance:** Balanced
**Wine Style:** Wine friendly—Choose your favorite wine!
**Example:** Penfolds Chardonnay or Shiraz

**Cooking Method:** Sauté, braise

> **TWIST ON THE CLASSIC**
>
> Serve these meatballs on Cuban or French bread to create a Mexican submarine sandwich. If desired, top meatballs with a melting cheese and heat to melt cheese.

| INGREDIENTS | WEIGHT U.S. | METRIC | VOLUME U.S. | METRIC |
|---|---|---|---|---|
| **Meatballs:** | | | | |
| bay leaves | | | 2 small | |
| whole cloves | | | 6 each | |
| whole allspice | | | 8 each | |

© full image

© dulsita

| INGREDIENTS | WEIGHT | | VOLUME | |
| --- | --- | --- | --- | --- |
| | U.S. | METRIC | U.S. | METRIC |
| whole cumin | 1/4 oz. | 8 g | 1 teaspoon | 5 mL |
| peppercorns | | | 8 each | |
| garlic, minced | 3/4 oz. | 22 g | 6 cloves | |
| salt | 1 oz. | 28 g | 1 tablespoon + 1 teaspoon | 20 mL |
| dried oregano | | | 2 teaspoons | 10 mL |
| fresh mint or cilantro | 2 1/2 oz. | 71 g | 1 cup, packed | 240 mL |
| ground beef | 3 lb. | 1.4 kg | | |
| eggs, beaten | 6 3/4 oz. | 191 g | 4 each | |
| eggs, hard-boiled, peeled, and minced | 7 1/2 oz. | 213 g | 4 each | |
| bread crumbs | 2 1/2 oz. | 71 g | 1/2 cup | 120 mL |
| oil | as needed | | | |

**Sauce:**

| INGREDIENTS | WEIGHT | | VOLUME | |
| --- | --- | --- | --- | --- |
| *pasilla* chilies, cut in half, stems, seeds, and veins removed | 1 oz. | 28 g | 4 each | |
| *guajillo* chilies, cut in half, stems, seeds, and veins removed | 3 1/2 oz. | 104 g | 14 each | |
| tomatillos | 3 lb. | 1.4 kg | | |
| salt | 1/2 oz. | 15 g | 2 teaspoons | 10 mL |
| garlic cloves, peeled | 1 1/2 oz. | 43 g | 12 each | |

**Accompaniments:**
cooked rice
tortillas

## MEATBALLS:

1. Heat *comal* or skillet over medium heat until hot. Add bay leaves, cloves, allspice, cumin, and peppercorns. Toast until they begin to release aromas. Transfer to food processor fitted with knife blade. Process until ground.
2. Add garlic, salt, oregano, and mint or cilantro. Pulse until coarsely chopped. Add meat. Pulse until well mixed.
3. Remove to large bowl. Add raw and hard-boiled egg and bread crumbs. Mix well to thoroughly combine. Divide and shape into 1 1/2-oz. (43-g) or desired size meatballs (about 2 tablespoons or 30 mL each).
4. Heat skillet lightly coated with oil over medium-high heat. Sauté meatballs until browned, about 1 to 2 minutes per side. Transfer to plate, cover, and refrigerate until needed. Reserve skillet for sauce preparation.

## SAUCE:

1. Heat skillet over medium heat. Cook *pasilla* and *guajillo* chilies on inside and outside until they begin to blister and smell. Remove from skillet, place in bowl and cover with hot water for 10 minutes. After soaking, remove from water and place in food processor fitted with knife blade. Pulse to chop.
2. Meanwhile, add tomatillos to hot water and boil until they turn a dull green color, about 5 minutes. Drain, cool until able to handle. Remove skins, place tomatillos in food processor. Add salt and garlic, process until paste.
3. Heat skillet over medium heat. Strain pepper-tomatillo paste; discard pulp remaining in strainer. Add strained paste to skillet. Stirring constantly, cook for 5 minutes.
4. Add meatballs to sauce, cook another 25 minutes. Serve accompanied by rice and/or tortillas.

# ROJO CHILE DE CARNE

## BEEF IN RED CHILE SAUCE

**Number of Servings:** 8
**Serving Size:** 8 oz. (227 g)
**Total Yield:** 4 lb., 6 1/2 oz. (2 kg)
**Wine Style:** Medium-bodied red wine with balanced acidity and well-integrated oak for the beef in chile sauce.
**Example:** Pinot Noir San Andreas Sonoma Coast 2012, Hirsch Vineyard, California, United States

**Cooking Method:** Braise

| | WEIGHT | | VOLUME | |
| --- | --- | --- | --- | --- |
| **INGREDIENTS** | **U.S.** | **METRIC** | **U.S.** | **METRIC** |
| chuck steak, trimmed, cut into 1- to 1 1/2-inch (2 1/2- to 4-cm) cubes or stew meat | 2 lb., 3 1/4 oz. | 1 kg | | |
| flour | as needed for dredging | | | |
| oil | | 57 g or as needed | 1/4 cup or as needed | 60 mL or as needed |
| onion, medium dice | 7 oz. | 199 g | 1 large | |
| garlic, peeled, minced | 3/4 oz. | 22 g | 6 cloves | |
| cumin, ground | 1/4 oz. | 8 g | 2 teaspoons | 10 mL |
| oregano | | | 2 teaspoons | 10 mL |
| pepper | | | 1/2 teaspoon | 3 mL |
| water or light beef stock | | 680 to 908 g | 3 to 4 cups | 720 to 960 mL |
| *Chile Rojo* sauce, *recipe on page 537* | 1 lb., 1 oz. | 482 g | 2 cups | 480 mL |

1. Dredge meat in flour to coat. Heat 1/2 oz. 15 g, 1 tablespoon, or 15 mL oil in large skillet over medium-high heat. Add single layer of meat to pan; sauté meat to brown all sides. Work in batches, removing meat when browned. Add another 1/2 oz. 15 g, 1 tablespoon, or 15 mL oil between batches and/or when needed.

2. Add onion to skillet; stir constantly for about 2 minutes, to soften. Add garlic, cumin, oregano, and pepper. Stir constantly until fragrant, about 1 to 2 minutes.

3. Place meat, onion mixture, and water or stock in large pan. Bring to boil, reduce heat, cover, and simmer for 1 hour.

4. Add *Chile Rojo* sauce and simmer, uncovered until tender, about 1 hour and 30 minutes. Leave pot uncovered to reduce sauce until thick; cover pan when it reaches desired thickness.

5. Correct seasonings. Serve with beans, rice, and tortillas.

© Jayme Burrows

# BIRRIA

## LAMB IN CHILI BROTH

Monkey Business Images © Shutterstock

**Note:** Begin preparation of this dish the day before service to allow time to marinate the lamb shanks.
If desired, prepare this dish with any cut of bone-in lamb, goat, offal, or a combination. The serving size depends on the size/weight of the lamb shanks.

**Number of Servings:** 12      **Cooking Method:** Bake
**Serving Size:** 1 lamb shank with sauce, about 12 1/2 oz. (355 g)
**Total Yield:** 12 lb., 13 oz. (5.8 kg)
**Food Balance:** Spicy/protein
**Wine Style:** Off-dry, low-oaked whites and soft reds
**Example:** Souverain Sauvignon Blanc or Merlot

| | WEIGHT | | VOLUME | |
| --- | --- | --- | --- | --- |
| INGREDIENTS | U.S. | METRIC | U.S. | METRIC |
| *ancho* chilies, stemmed and seeded | 1 oz. | 28 g | 6 each | |
| *guajillos* chilies, stemmed and seeded | 2 oz. | 57 g | 10 each | |
| *pasilla* chilies, stemmed and seeded | 1/2 oz. | 15 g | 2 each | |
| water, hot | | 114 g | 1/2 cup | 120 mL |
| garlic cloves, peeled | 1 oz. | 28 g | 8 each | |
| whole cumin | 1/2 oz. | 15 g | 2 teaspoons | 10 mL |
| bay leaves | | | 2 each | |
| dried oregano | 1/4 oz. | 8 g | 1 tablespoon + 1 teaspoon | 20 mL |
| whole cloves | | | 4 each | |
| peppercorns | | | 16 each | |
| dried thyme | 1/4 oz. | 8 g | 2 teaspoons | 10 mL |
| onion, diced | 4 oz. | 114 g | 1 small | |
| tomatoes, fresh or canned, chopped | 1 lb., 13 oz. | 823 g | two 14 1/2-oz. cans | two 411-g cans |
| salt | 1/4 oz. | 8 g | 1 teaspoon | 5 mL |
| vinegar, cider or white | | 86 g | 1/4 cup + 2 tablespoons | 90 mL |
| oil | | 28 g | 2 tablespoons | 30 mL |
| lamb shanks | 9 lb., 13 oz. | 4.5 kg | 12 each | |
| stock, lamb or beef | | | 1 quart (4 cups) | 960 mL |

**Accompaniments:**
tortillas
steamed rice

① Cut all peppers on one side, so they will lay flat in *comal* or skillet. Heat *comal* or skillet over medium heat. Add peppers and toast lightly. Remove from *comal*, place in nonreactive bowl. Cover with hot water; set aside for at least 20 minutes.

② Toast garlic in comal. Add cumin and toast until fragrant and beginning to brown. Remove from heat.

③ Into food processor fitted with knife blade, place peppers, soaking liquid, garlic, cumin, bay leaves, oregano, cloves, peppercorns, thyme, onion, tomatoes, salt, and vinegar. Process until paste consistency.

④ Heat oil in skillet over medium heat. Add paste. Sauté 1 minute, reduce heat and simmer for 10 to 15 minutes.

⑤ Place washed lamb shanks in nonreactive dish. Coat shanks evenly with paste mixture. Cover pan and refrigerate several hours or overnight.

⑥ Preheat oven to 350 degrees (180°C). Transfer lamb shanks and marinade to ovenproof dish. Pour stock over lamb shanks, cover dish tightly. Bake about 2 hours, until meat is very tender. If needed, add a little water or stock to pan.

⑦ Correct seasonings. Serve lamb shank and sauce, accompanied by tortillas and rice.

## CHILI RELLENOS

### STUFFED CHILI PEPPERS

**Note:** Cheese makes a wonderful alternative to the pork filling, *picadillo*. If available, use queso Oaxaca; otherwise, substitute Muenster cheese. To prepare cheese rellenos, fill peppers with about 2 oz. (57 g) cheese cut into 3 pieces (1/2-inch or 1 1/3-cm strips). Flour and batter rellenos, then fry. Any extra *picadillo* makes a wonderful filling for tortillas.

**Number of Servings:** 10

**Serving Size:** One 6-oz. (170-g) filled pepper
3 oz. (90 mL) sauce

**Total Yield:** 1 lb., 14 oz. (851 g) picadillo
1 lb., 14 oz. (851 g) sauce

**Food Balance:** Protein/sweet/spicy

**Wine Style:** Off-dry, low-oaked whites and soft reds

**Example:** Meridian Vineyards Sauvignon Blanc or Merlot

**Cooking Method:** Boil, sauté, deep fry

**TWIST ON THE CLASSIC**

Replace *picadillo* with any filling. Try a vegetarian, Indian twist by filling with spicy chickpea curry.

| | WEIGHT | | VOLUME | |
|---|---|---|---|---|
| **INGREDIENTS** | **U.S.** | **METRIC** | **U.S.** | **METRIC** |
| *poblano* peppers | 3 lb., 10 oz. | 1.6 kg | 10 each | |
| **Picadillo:** | | | | |
| boneless pork, large cubes | 2 lb. | 908 g | | |
| white onion, slices | 2 oz. | 57 g | 1/2 small | |
| garlic, sliced | 1/4 oz. | 8 g | 2 cloves | |
| oil or lard | | 43 g | 3 tablespoons | 45 mL |
| white onions, small dice | 4 oz. | 114 g | 1 small | |
| garlic, minced | 1/4 oz. | 8 g | 2 cloves | |
| ground cinnamon | | | 3/4 teaspoon | 4 mL |
| ground cloves | | | 3/4 teaspoon | 4 mL |
| salt | 1/4 oz. | 8 g | 1 teaspoon | 5 mL |
| pepper | | | 1 teaspoon | 5 mL |
| tomatoes, fresh or canned, peeled, seeded, and chopped | 1 lb. | 454 g | 2 large, or 1 3/4 cups | 420 mL |
| raisins | 3 1/2 oz. | 104 g | 1/2 cup | 120 mL |
| **Sauce:** | | | | |
| tomatoes, fresh or canned, peeled and chopped | 1 lb. | 454 g | 2 large or 1 3/4 cups | 420 mL |
| white onion, small dice | 2 oz. | 57 g | 1/2 small | |
| garlic, minced | 1/4 oz. | 8 g | 2 cloves | |
| ground cinnamon | | | 1/2 teaspoon | 3 mL |
| ground cloves | | | 1/4 teaspoon | 2 mL |
| pepper | | | 3/4 teaspoon | 4 mL |
| bay leaves | | | 2 each | |
| dried thyme | | | 1/4 teaspoon | 2 mL |
| almonds | 1 oz. | 28 g | 2 tablespoons | 30 mL |
| oil or lard | | 28 g | 2 tablespoons | 30 mL |
| stock, pork or chicken | | 680 g | 3 cups | 720 mL |
| flour | as needed, for dredging | | | |
| **Batter:** | | | | |
| eggs, separated | 5 oz. | 142 g | 3 each | |
| salt | | | 1/4 teaspoon | 2 mL |
| oil, for deep-frying | | | | |

*Removing seeds and veins from peeled pepper*

*Filling pepper with picadillo*

*Coating rellenos (stuffed peppers) with batter*

## PEPPERS:

1. Char peppers on grill or over flame of burner until blackened and blistered, but not soft. Place in bag, seal, and wait about 15 minutes.
2. Remove from bag, peel skin from peppers.* Be careful not to cut peppers.
3. Make slit on one side of pepper just large enough to remove seeds and ribs. Rinse with cold water, set aside until needed.

## *PICADILLO:*

1. Place pork, sliced onion, and sliced garlic in pan. Cover with cold water, bring to boil, lower heat and simmer until tender, about 45 to 50 minutes.
2. Drain meat, reserve liquid (stock). Let stock cool, skim off fat when cold. Shred meat, refrigerate if not using right away.
3. Heat 3 tablespoons (43 g or 45 mL) oil in pan over medium heat. Add cooked pork, cook a few minutes. Add diced onion, minced garlic, cinnamon, cloves, salt, and pepper. Cook another minute or 2.
4. Add tomatoes and raisins. Cook over high heat stirring constantly, about 10 minutes, until almost dry. Correct seasonings. Set aside or refrigerate until needed.

## SAUCE:

1. Purée tomatoes, onion, garlic, cinnamon, cloves, pepper, bay leaves, thyme, and almonds.
2. Heat oil in pan, add purée. Stirring constantly, sauté over high heat for about 5 minutes.
3. Add stock, cook over medium heat for 15 minutes. Correct seasonings.

## CHILI PREPARATION:

1. Stuff each pepper with 3 oz. or 1/3 cup (86 g) *picadillo*. Close, fasten with toothpicks.
2. Place flour on plate, dredge peppers in flour, set aside.

## BATTER:

1. Whip egg whites until stiff peaks form.
2. Add salt and yolks, whisking or mixing one at a time, until blended.

## FRYING AND SERVING:

1. Heat about 1 inch (2 1/2 cm) oil in pan or deep-fryer to 375 degrees (190°C).
2. One at a time, place pepper in batter, turn to coat.
3. Gently place pepper into hot oil, fry until golden brown.
4. Remove from oil, drain well on paper toweling. Remove toothpicks. Repeat until all peppers are fried.
5. Place tomato sauce on each plate and top with Chili Rellenos, or place peppers in pan of sauce, heat over low flame, and then serve.

*See photographs for charring and peeling peppers on page 524 in this chapter.

# TAMALES DE PUERCO CON CHILE ROJA

## PORK TAMALES IN RED SAUCE

**Number of Servings:** 8
**Serving Size:** About 3 tamales
**Scaling:** 2 1/2 oz. (71 g) (1/3 cup or 80 mL) masa per tamale
   1 1/2 oz. (43 g) (2 tablespoons or 30 mL) meat with sauce per tamale
**Total Yield:** 26 tamales
   masa dough: 4 lb., 2 oz. (1.9 kg)
   meat: 1 lb., 11 1/4 oz. (773 g)
   meat + chile sauce: 2 lb., 8 3/4 oz. (1.2 kg)
**Wine Style:** Full-bodied fruit-forward red wine with elegant balance and long finish.
**Example:** Pinot Noir Manchester Ridge Vineyard 2013, Poe, California, United States

**Cooking Method:** Boil, Steam

### TWIST ON THE CLASSIC

- Make a very simple tamale dish by spreading half of the masa dough in a large ovenproof dish. Top with the meat and red chile sauce mixture, then top that with the remaining masa dough. Bake until done, and cut into squares for service. As with tamales, accompany with beans and rice.
- Fill tamales with any imaginable filling from sweet to savory.
- Tamales make a great appetizer—just serve one tamale and garnish with guacamole, sour cream, salsa, and perhaps a 1 1/2-inch (4-cm) cut of corn on the cob.

| INGREDIENTS | WEIGHT | | VOLUME | |
| --- | --- | --- | --- | --- |
| | U.S. | METRIC | U.S. | METRIC |
| cornhusks, dried | | | | |
| water, boiling | | | to cover | |
| pork butt or shoulder | 3 lb., 6 oz. | 1.5 kg | | |
| water | | | 1 quart + 2 cups | 1.4 L |
| salt | 1 1/2 oz. | 43 g | 1 tablespoon + 2 teaspoons | 25 mL |
| **Masa Dough:** | | | | |
| lard or vegetable shortening | 1 lb. | 454 g | | |
| salt | 1/2 oz. | 15 g | 2 teaspoons | 10 mL |
| baking powder | 1 1/2 oz. | 43 g | 1 1/2 teaspoons | 8 mL |
| masa harina, dried* | 15 oz. | 426 g | 4 cups | 960 mL |
| water | | 567 g | 2 1/2 cups | 600 mL |
| pork stock (from above) | | 340 to 454 g | 1 1/2 to 2 cups | 360 to 480 mL |
| red chile sauce, from recipe for Chile Rojo on page 537 | 13 1/2 oz. | 383 g | 1 1/2 cups | 360 mL |

1. Place cornhusks in large bowl. Cover them with boiling water. Place a weight (like a plate) over husks to keep them submerged. Allow to soak at least several hours or overnight. When softened, discard water and drain cornhusks.
2. Cut pork into five or six large pieces. Place in pot with water and salt. Bring to boil, reduce heat and simmer until tender, about 1 1/2 hours.
3. Remove from heat. Leave pork in broth and allow to cool.
4. Remove pork from stock. Using 2 forks, shred meat (remove fat). Refrigerate until needed. (Can be prepared ahead and refrigerated.)
5. Place fat (lard or vegetable shortening), salt, and baking powder in bowl of mixer fitted with whisk attachment. Mix on medium-high speed until light and fluffy, about 2 minutes. Stop mixer and scrape sides, as needed.
6. In separate bowl, mix masa harina and water. Add one-third to fat, beat at medium until well combined. Repeat with remaining 2 one-thirds, beating well after each addition.
7. Add 8 oz. (227 g, 1 cup, or 240 mL) pork stock, mix on medium-low until combined. If refrigerating for long, mix with mixer until fluffy again. Add additional pork stock as needed to make light dough with texture of smooth peanut butter. If necessary, refrigerate until needed. (Can be prepared ahead and refrigerated. If refrigerating for long, mix on mixer until fluffy. Add more pork stock, if needed.)
8. Mix red chile sauce with shredded pork.

*Making tamales*
© Jennifer Boggs/Amy Pa

© shellystuart

© snyfer

**To Form and Finish Tamales:**

1. Use any torn cornhusks, and cut into strips to tie the tamales. This is the traditional method of tying the tamales. Alternately, tie with butcher string.

2. Prepare large steamer for tamales. Line steamer pan with cornhusks to protect tamales from water. If steaming in pan on stove, place water under steamer basket to a level under the basket.

3. Place cornhusk on table with narrow end facing you. Place 2 1/2 oz. (71 g, 1/3 cup, 80 mL) masa dough in center of cornhusk. Spread into square about 1/4-inch (1/2-cm) thick staying at least 2 inches (5 cm) from edges of cornhusk.

4. Place a row of pork filling along right side of masa about an inch (2.5 cm) from the edge of the masa.

5. Bring long sides of cornhusk together so that the edges of masa meet to encase the filling. Fold cornhusk sides over to one side and fold the bottom side up to form a package that is open on one end.

6. Tie with cornhusk strip to secure package. Continue with remaining ingredients to form tamales. (Can be prepared ahead and refrigerated until cooking.)

7. To steam, place tamales with the open side up in prepared steamer basket. Steam over water boiling at a medium level for 1 hour and 15 minutes. If necessary, add more boiling water to pan.

8. Remove from steamer. Let sit a few minutes before unwrapping, so filling continues to set and they will release from the cornhusks easily.

9. Serve accompanied by beans and rice, sour cream, salsa, and (if desired) extra red chile sauce.

- If fresh *masa harina* is available, use 2 pounds (908 g) with no water.
- Reheat leftover cooked tamales by steaming them until hot.

---

## MANCHA MANTELES

### TABLECLOTH STRAINER (CHICKEN AND PORK BRAISED WITH FRUITS)

© tycoon101

**Number of Servings:** 8
**Serving Size:** 1/4 chicken
**Total Yield:** 11 lb., 8 oz. (5.2 kg)
**Food Balance:** Spicy/sweet/protein
**Wine Style:** Off-dry, low-oaked whites and soft reds
**Example:** Beringer Founders' Estate Pinot Grigio or Shiraz

**Cooking Method:** Sauté, braise

| INGREDIENTS | WEIGHT | | VOLUME | |
| --- | --- | --- | --- | --- |
| | U.S. | METRIC | U.S. | METRIC |
| lean pork, 1-inch (2 1/2-cm) cubes | 1 lb., 8 oz. | 681 g | | |
| chicken stock | | | 1 quart + 2 cups (6 cups) | 1.4 L |
| oil or lard | | 71 g | 1/4 cup + 1 tablespoon | 75 mL |
| chicken, cut into serving pieces | about 6 lb. | 2.7 kg | 2 each | |
| almonds | 8 1/2 oz. | 241 g | 1 1/2 cups | 360 mL |
| sesame seeds | 1 1/2 oz. | 43 g | 1/4 cup | 60 mL |
| *ancho* chilies, seeds, veins, and stems removed | 2 oz. | 57 g | 6 each | |
| *pasilla* chilies, seeds, veins, and stems removed | 3/4 oz. | 22 g | 4 each | |
| tomatoes, peeled, seeded, and chopped | 1 lb., 8 oz. | 681 g | 4 each | |
| ground cinnamon | 1/4 oz. | 8 g | 2 teaspoons | 10 mL |
| salt | 1/2 oz. | 15 g | 2 teaspoons | 10 mL |
| plantain, peeled and cut into 1/4-inch (1/2-cm) slices | 9 oz. | 256 g | 2 small | |
| pineapple, fresh or canned cubes | 14 1/2 oz. | 411 g | 2 cups | 480 mL |
| apples, peeled, cored, and cut into large dice | 1 lb. | 454 g | 2 large | |

**Accompaniments:**

tortillas

cooked rice

① Place pork in pan with stock, simmer for 25 minutes. Drain pork, reserve stock.

② Heat oil in large pan, sauté chicken pieces until lightly browned, remove from pan, set aside.

③ In same oil, sauté almonds until lightly browned. Lift from pan with slotted spoon, place in bowl of food processor fitted with knife blade.

④ In same oil, sauté sesame seeds until lightly browned (use lid because they will pop out of pan). Drain, reserving oil, and place seeds in bowl of food processor.

⑤ In same oil, sauté all chilies for about 2 minutes. Drain and place in bowl of food processor.

⑥ Add tomatoes and 2 cups (454 g or 480 mL) of reserved stock to food processor. Process until ingredients form a thick, smooth paste.

⑦ Reheat same pan. Stirring constantly, sauté paste, cinnamon, and salt for about 4 minutes. Add 3 1/2 cups (828 g or 840 mL) stock to paste, stir well.

⑧ Add pork, chicken, plantain, pineapple, and apples to sauce. Cover and simmer for 1 to 1 1/4 hours, until meats are tender. Add more stock if needed.

⑨ Correct seasonings. Serve with tortillas and/or rice.

---

**TWIST ON THE CLASSIC**

Transform this into a fish dish by omitting the pork and chicken. Proceed with the recipe but cook the fruits for about 30 minutes alone. Then add fish and/or shellfish and cook until done.

# MOLE DE GUAJOLOTE

## TURKEY IN MOLE SAUCE

David Murray and Jules Selmes © Dorling Kindersley

**TWIST ON THE CLASSIC**

Give this turkey *mole* a French twist by serving the turkey and *mole* sauce in a *crêpe*.

This dish dates back to the Aztecs. *Mole* sauce complements a variety of dishes besides the traditional turkey, including pork, chicken, duck, enchiladas, and more. The list of ingredients looks intimidating, but the recipe is not that difficult. Basically, ingredients are sautéed, then puréed.

**Note:** The *mole* sauce can be prepared in advance and refrigerated or frozen. Use only the amount of sauce needed to accompany the turkey, save any remaining sauce for other dishes or freeze it for later use.

**Number of Servings:** 22 to 25  
**Cooking Method:** Sauté, braise  
**Serving Size:** 6 to 7 oz. (170 to 199 g)  
**Total Yield:** 4 lb., 10 oz., 8 1/2 cups (2.1 kg) sauce; about 10 lb. (4.5 kg) total  
**Food Balance:** Spicy/protein/sweet  
**Wine Style:** Off-dry, low-oaked whites and soft reds  
**Example:** Rosemount Traminer, Riesling, or Shiraz

| | WEIGHT | | VOLUME | |
|---|---|---|---|---|
| INGREDIENTS | U.S. | METRIC | U.S. | METRIC |
| **Chilies:** | | | | |
| *pasilla* chilies | 1 1/4 oz. | 36 g | 4 each | |
| *mulato* chilies | 2 oz. | 57 g | 5 each | |
| *ancho* chilies | 2 3/4 oz. | 78 g | 6 each | |
| *chipotle* chilies | 1/4 oz. | 8 g | 1 each | |
| oil or lard | | 15 g | 1 tablespoon | 15 mL |
| water, boiling | | | | |
| **Seasoning Paste:** | | | | |
| almonds | 2 1/2 oz. | 71 g | 1/3 cup | 80 mL |
| peanuts, shelled | 2 oz. | 57 g | 1/3 cup | 80 mL |
| hulled pumpkin seeds | 2 oz. | 57 g | 1/3 cup | 80 mL |
| sesame seeds | 2 oz. | 57 g | 1/3 cup | 80 mL |
| raisins | 1 3/4 oz. | 50 g | 1/4 cup | 60 mL |
| peppercorns | | | 6 each | |
| cinnamon stick | | | one 3/4-inch piece | one 2-cm piece |
| whole coriander | | | 1/8 teaspoon | 1 mL |
| aniseed | | | 1/8 teaspoon | 1 mL |
| bay leaf | | | 1 each | |
| whole cloves | | | 4 each | |
| corn tortilla, stale | 1 oz. | 28 g | 1 each | |
| French bread, stale | 1 oz. | 28 g | two 3/4-inch slices | two 2-cm slices |
| garlic cloves, unpeeled | 3/4 oz. | 22 g | 3 to 4 large | |
| white onion, diced | 7 oz. | 199 g | 1 large | |
| **Tomato-Tomatillo Paste:** | | | | |
| tomatillos, fresh or canned | 7 oz. | 199 g | 2 each or 1 cup | 240 mL |
| tomatoes, peeled and chopped | 10 oz. | 284 g | 1 cup | 240 mL |
| **Turkey:** | | | | |
| oil or lard | | 43 g | 3 tablespoons | 45 mL |
| turkey, cut into serving pieces | 10 to 12 lb. | 4.5 to 5.4 kg | 1 each | |
| stock, turkey or chicken | | | 1 quart (4 cups), or more as needed | 960 mL |
| unsweetened chocolate, cut into small pieces | 1 1/2 oz. | 43 g | | |
| **Garnish:** | | | | |
| tortillas, corn or wheat | | | | |
| sesame seeds, toasted | | | | |

## CHILIES:

① Cut chilies open, remove seeds and veins, save 3 tablespoons (45 g) seeds. Tear peppers into pieces.

② Heat 1 tablespoon (15 g or 15 mL) oil in skillet over medium heat. Sauté chilies quickly, stirring constantly so they do not burn.

③ Place chilies in bowl, cover with boiling water, set aside for at least 1 hour.

④ Drain when ready to use, reserving soaking liquid.

© Moreno Novello

## SEASONING PASTE:

① Heat frying pan, add almonds and peanuts, shake pan to keep them moving, toast until lightly browned, pour into bowl of food processor fitted with knife blade.

② Add pumpkin seeds to pan, cover (because they pop and jump from pan), shake pan to keep them moving. Toast until lightly browned; transfer to bowl of food processor.

③ Add sesame seeds to pan, cover (because they pop and jump from pan), shake pan to keep them moving. Toast until lightly browned; transfer to bowl of food processor.

④ Add raisins to pan, shake pan to keep them moving. Toast lightly; transfer to bowl of food processor.

⑤ Add reserved chili seeds, peppercorns, cinnamon, coriander, aniseed, bay leaf, and cloves to pan, shake pan to keep them moving. Toast lightly; pour into bowl of food processor.

⑥ Add soaked chilies and 1/2 cup (114 g or 120 mL) soaking liquid to processor bowl. Pulse until consistency of thick paste, scraping down sides of processor several times, as needed.

⑦ Add tortilla and bread to pan, toast lightly just to dry. Tear into pieces; add to processor bowl.

⑧ Place garlic cloves in pan, toast on all sides until skin darkens, 1 or 2 minutes. Peel garlic, mince, and add to processor bowl.

⑨ Add onion to processor bowl, pulse to process until thick paste, scraping down sides of processor several times. Remove from processor, refrigerate until needed.

## TOMATO-TOMATILLO PASTE:

① If using fresh tomatillos, peel husks, place tomatillos in pan of water. Bring to boil, reduce heat and simmer for 10 minutes. Remove from water, cool slightly. Chop tomatillos coarsely.

② Place tomatillos and tomatoes in bowl of food processor. Pulse until paste. Set aside until ready to use.

## TURKEY:

① Preheat oven to 350 degrees (180°C).

② Heat 2 tablespoons (28 g or 30 mL) of oil in pan over medium heat. Sauté turkey pieces until browned. Do not wash pan, reserve for sautéing seasoning paste.

③ Place turkey in ovenproof pan, cover, and bake for about 1 1/4 hours, until done.

④ Cool slightly, cut into slices or small pieces, as desired.

⑤ Skim fat from pan drippings. On stovetop, deglaze pan by adding enough stock to make 1 quart (960 mL) of stock, scraping pan and whisking over high heat.

## ASSEMBLY:

① Heat pan used to sauté turkey. Add tomato and tomatillo mixture, simmer for 10 minutes, stirring often.

② Add 1 cup (227 g or 240 mL) stock, simmer for 10 minutes, stirring often. Add seasoning paste, remaining stock, and chocolate. Simmer for 40 minutes, stirring occasionally. (*Mole* may be prepared to this point and refrigerated.)

③ Place turkey in pan, turn to cover with *mole* sauce, simmer for about 20 minutes. If necessary, thin sauce with more stock. Sauce should be thick enough to coat spoon. Correct seasonings.

④ Serve accompanied by tortillas. If desired, sprinkle with toasted sesame seeds.

# HUACHINANGO A LA VERACRUZANA
## RED SNAPPER, VERACRUZ STYLE

Pearson Education/PH College

**Note:** This dish makes a great first course. Reduce the amount of *jalapeño* if a less spicy dish is desired. Some recipes for this dish call for dredging the red snapper in flour, frying it, then covering it with the tomato sauce to serve. Some cooks add parboiled potatoes to the tomato sauce.

**Number of Servings:** 8

**Serving Size:** 7 oz. (199 g)

**Total Yield:** 3 lb., 10 oz. (1.6 kg)

**Food Balance:** Balanced

**Wine Style:** Wine friendly—Try your favorite

**Example:** Souverain Sauvignon Blanc or Cabernet Sauvignon

**Cooking Method:** Sauté, bake

| INGREDIENTS | WEIGHT U.S. | WEIGHT METRIC | VOLUME U.S. | VOLUME METRIC |
|---|---|---|---|---|
| red snapper or other ocean fish, fillets or (traditionally) fish with head and tail left on | 1 lb., 13 oz. | 823 g | | |
| fresh lime juice | | 43 g | 3 tablespoons | 45 mL |
| **Tomato Sauce:** | | | | |
| olive oil | | 28 g | 2 tablespoons | 30 mL |
| white onion, small dice | 6 oz. | 170 g | 1 large | |
| garlic, minced | 1/4 oz. | 8 g | 2 cloves | |
| tomatoes, fresh or canned, peeled, seeded, and chopped | 2 lb. | 908 g | 3 3/4 cups | 900 mL |
| bay leaf | | | 1 each | |
| dried oregano | | | 3/4 teaspoon | 4 mL |
| ground cinnamon | | | 1/8 teaspoon | 1 mL |
| ground cloves | | | 1/8 teaspoon | 1 mL |
| sugar | | | 1/2 teaspoon | 3 mL |
| green olives, pitted and cut in half | 1 1/2 oz. | 43 g | 1/4 cup | 60 mL |
| capers | 1 oz. | 28 g | 2 tablespoons | 30 mL |
| *jalapeños* or *escabeche* (pickled *jalapeños*), cut into strips | 1/2 oz. | 15 g, or to taste | 2 each, or to taste | |

**Accompaniment:**

cooked rice or potatoes

① Place fish in ovenproof dish, pour lime juice over fish, cover and refrigerate at least 2 hours.

② Preheat oven to 350 degrees (180°C). Heat oil in skillet over medium heat. Add onion, sauté, stirring often for a couple of minutes. Add garlic, sauté until softened.

③ Add tomatoes, bay leaf, oregano, cinnamon, cloves, sugar, olives, capers, and *jalapeños* or *escabeche*. Cook for 10 minutes over medium-high flame, stirring constantly.

④ Pour sauce over fish, bake for about 30 minutes, until done. Serve immediately, accompanied by rice or potatoes.

# CHILE ROJO

## RED CHILE SAUCE

**Total Yield:** 2 lb. (908 g), 3 1/2 cups (840 mL)  **Cooking Method:** Boil
**Wine Style:** Wonderful smokiness combined with roasted hops flavors are the perfect combination with this chili sauce.
**Example:** Helles Lagerbier, Aecht Schlenkerla, Germany

<table>
<tr><th></th><th colspan="2">WEIGHT</th><th colspan="2">VOLUME</th></tr>
<tr><th>INGREDIENTS</th><th>U.S.</th><th>METRIC</th><th>U.S.</th><th>METRIC</th></tr>
<tr><td>Guajillo or New Mexico chilies, dried; stems, seeds, and veins removed; cut or torn into pieces</td><td>6 oz.</td><td>170 g</td><td></td><td></td></tr>
<tr><td>water, boiling</td><td></td><td></td><td>1 quart + 3/4 cup and as needed</td><td>1.1 L and as needed</td></tr>
<tr><td>garlic, peeled</td><td>1/2 oz.</td><td>15 g</td><td>4 cloves</td><td></td></tr>
<tr><td>cumin</td><td>1/4 oz.</td><td>8 g</td><td>1 teaspoon</td><td>5 mL</td></tr>
<tr><td>pepper</td><td></td><td></td><td>1/2 teaspoon</td><td>3 mL</td></tr>
<tr><td>salt</td><td>1/2 oz.</td><td>15 g</td><td>2 teaspoons</td><td>10 mL</td></tr>
</table>

1. Add chilies to boiling water. Reduce heat and simmer, stirring occasionally, about 10 to 15 minutes until chilies hydrate on all sides.

2. Drop garlic cloves through feed tube of running food processor fitted with knife blade. Pulse and scrape sides as needed.

3. Add chilies, chili water, cumin, pepper, and salt to food processor. Purée until smooth. Add more water if needed to make paste smooth and thin enough to pass through medium strainer. (Do not use a China cap; the holes are too small.)

4. Press chili paste through strainer, pressing to extract as much liquid as possible. Discard pulp. Correct seasonings.

**TWIST ON THE CLASSIC**

Use this sauce to flavor any meat. Add some of this sauce to the cooking liquid when braising short ribs or brisket.

Freeze any remaining Chile Rojo for later use.

# FRIJOLES

## BEANS

**Note:** Begin preparation for this dish the day before to allow time to soak the beans.

**Number of Servings:** 10                    **Cooking Method:** Boil
**Serving Size:** 6 oz. (170 g)
**Total Yield:** 3 lb., 13 oz. (1.7 kg)

|  | WEIGHT | | VOLUME | |
| --- | --- | --- | --- | --- |
| INGREDIENTS | U.S. | METRIC | U.S. | METRIC |
| beans, pinto, black, or any type | 1 lb. | 454 g | 2 1/2 cups | 600 mL |
| white onion, diced | 7 oz. | 199 g | 1 large | |
| oil or lard | | 15 g | 1 tablespoon | 15 mL |
| salt | 1/4 oz. | 8 g, or to taste | 1 teaspoon | 5 mL, or to taste |

**Accompaniments:**

chili pepper, fresh or pickled,
    sliced

salsa

1. Rinse beans well, place in pot, cover with cold water. Refrigerate to soak overnight.
2. Add onion and oil, bring to boil, reduce heat and simmer until done, about 1 1/2 to 2 hours, depending on type of bean.
3. Season with salt to taste. If desired, mash some of the beans to slightly thicken the sauce.
4. Serve beans and some of the bean liquid in a small bowl. If desired, the diner can add chili peppers or salsa to flavor the beans.

© kafka

# FRIJOLES REFRITOS

## REFRIED BEANS

**Note:** Appearing very frequently throughout Mexico, these beans accompany almost any food. Although they are rather bland themselves, refried beans are served with the ever-present bowl of salsa.

**Number of Servings:** 9
**Serving Size:** 4 oz. (114 g)
**Total Yield:** 2 lb., 5 oz. (1.1 kg)

**Cooking Method:** Sauté

Clive Streeter @ Dorling Kindersley

| | WEIGHT | | VOLUME | |
|---|---|---|---|---|
| **INGREDIENTS** | **U.S.** | **METRIC** | **U.S.** | **METRIC** |
| oil or lard | | 71 g | 1/4 cup + 1 tablespoon | 75 mL |
| white onions, small dice | 12 oz. | 454 g | 2 medium to large | |
| beans, any kind, cooked, with some cooking liquid | 2 lb., 6 oz. | 1.1 kg | 6 cups | |

1. Heat oil in heavy pan over medium heat. Add onion and sauté until soft, a few minutes.
2. Reduce heat to medium-low to low. Add 12 oz., or about 2 cups (454 g), beans and cooking liquid to pan, mash well with spoon or spatula.
3. Continue adding beans and liquid, mashing into coarse purée. Sauté until purée starts to dry out.
4. Correct seasonings. Serve, accompanied by salsa.

> **TWIST ON THE CLASSIC**
>
> To create a Mexican eggs Benedict, top Mexican rice with refried beans, then place a poached egg on top. Garnish with sour cream and salsa.

# COLIFLOR EN ADOBO ROJO

## CAULIFLOWER IN RED *ADOBO* SAUCE

**Number of Servings:** 9
**Serving Size:** 4 oz. (114 g)
**Total Yield:** 2 lb., 7 oz. (1.1 kg), with 9 oz. (256 g), or 1 cup (240 mL) sauce
**Food Balance:** Spicy/protein
**Wine Style:** Off-dry, low-oaked whites and soft reds
**Example:** Lindemans Semillion or Shiraz

| | WEIGHT | | VOLUME | |
|---|---|---|---|---|
| **INGREDIENTS** | **U.S.** | **METRIC** | **U.S.** | **METRIC** |
| ***Adobo* Sauce:** | | | | |
| *ancho* chilies, seeded and veins removed | 1 1/2 oz. | 43 g | 5 each | |
| water, boiling | | 227 g | 1 cup | 240 mL |
| garlic cloves, unpeeled | 3/4 oz. | 22 g | 4 large | |
| whole cumin | | | 1/4 teaspoon | 2 mL |
| peppercorns | | | 4 each | |
| whole cloves | | | 2 each | |
| dried oregano | | | 1 teaspoon | 5 mL |
| stock or water | | | 1 cup | 240 mL or as needed |
| oil or lard | | 227 g | 1 tablespoon | 15 mL |
| cauliflower, flowerets | 2 lb., 3 oz. | 994 g | 2 heads | |

Photo courtesy of the California Walnut Board 2013

1. Heat skillet over medium heat. Sauté chilies briefly, flattening with spatula for even cooking, until just beginning to color; do not burn. Remove chilies from pan, tear into pieces, place in bowl, cover with boiling water, set aside for 30 minutes.

2. Place garlic in pan over medium heat. Cook until light brown spots appear on each side, remove from pan. When cool, peel garlic and mince.

3. Place garlic, cumin, peppercorns, cloves, oregano, and 1/2 cup (114 g or 120 mL) of stock or water in bowl of food processor fitted with knife blade. Pulse to break spices.

4. Drain chilies, reserve liquid. Add chilies to processor, process until paste. Add a little soaking water as needed if too thick to process into paste.

5. Heat oil in pan over medium to medium-low heat. Add *adobo* paste and sauté for 5 minutes, stirring constantly.

6. Meanwhile, steam or boil cauliflower in or over pot of boiling water until three-quarters done. Pour off water, return cauliflower to pot.

7. Add *adobo* paste and remaining 1/2 cup (114 g or 120 mL) of stock or water to pot with cauliflower. Heat over medium-low heat and cook until cauliflower is done, about 5 minutes. Add more stock, water, or reserved soaking water, if needed. Serve immediately.

## CALABACITAS CON CREMA
### CREAMED ZUCCHINI

Jacek Chabraszewski © Shutterstock

**Number of Servings:** 9

**Serving Size:** 4 oz. (114 g)

**Total Yield:** 2 lb., 4 oz. (1 kg)

**Cooking Method:** Boil

| | WEIGHT | | VOLUME | |
|---|---|---|---|---|
| INGREDIENTS | U.S. | METRIC | U.S. | METRIC |
| zucchini, diced | 1 lb., 8 oz. | 681 g | 2 medium | |
| tomatoes, peeled and chopped | 12 oz. | 340 g | 2 each, or 1 1/2 cups | 360 mL |
| fresh mint, minced | 1/4 oz. | 8 g | 2 tablespoons | 30 mL |
| fresh cilantro, minced | 3/4 oz. | 22 g | 3 tablespoons | 45 mL |
| *jalapeño*, seeds and veins removed, minced | 1/4 oz. | 8 g | 1/2 each | |
| pepper | | | 1/4 teaspoon | 2 mL |
| ground cinnamon | | | 1/2 teaspoon | 3 mL |
| ground cloves | | | 1/4 teaspoon | 2 mL |
| salt | | | 1/2 teaspoon | 3 mL |
| heavy cream | | 114 g | 1/4 cup | 60 mL |
| stock or water | as needed | | | |

1. Place all ingredients in pan.

2. Stirring occasionally, simmer until zucchini is tender, about 10 to 15 minutes. Add stock or water if too dry. Almost no liquid should remain at end of cooking.

3. Correct seasonings. Serve.

## ARROZ A LA MEXICANA

### MEXICAN RICE

**Note:** To prepare more spicy Mexican rice, add one or two *serrano* peppers to the tomato mixture. Do not overdo it; this rice should not be too *picante*.

**Number of Servings:** 11
**Serving Size:** 4 oz. (114 g)
**Total Yield:** 2 lb., 15 oz. (1.3 kg)

**Cooking Method:** Sauté, boil

Silvia Bogdanski © Shutterstock

| INGREDIENTS | WEIGHT U.S. | WEIGHT METRIC | VOLUME U.S. | VOLUME METRIC |
|---|---|---|---|---|
| tomatoes, fresh or canned, peeled and chopped | 8 oz. | 227 g | 1 large, or 1 cup | 240 mL |
| white onion, small dice | 2 oz. | 57 g | 1/2 small | |
| garlic, minced | | | 1 clove | |
| oil or lard | | 43 g | 3 tablespoons | 45 mL |
| long-grain rice | 10 1/2 oz. | 298 g | 1 1/2 cups | 360 mL |
| chicken stock, hot | | 794 g | 3 1/2 cups | 840 mL |
| peas, *optional* | | | | |

1. Purée tomatoes, onion, and garlic in food processor fitted with knife blade.
2. Heat oil in pan over high heat, add rice, and sauté until lightly browned. Add tomato purée, sauté, stirring constantly until liquid is absorbed.
3. Add stock, bring to boil, lower heat, cover and simmer until most of liquid is absorbed, about 18 to 20 minutes. If desired, add peas to pan for last few minutes of cooking.
4. Remove pan from heat, let rest still covered, about 10 minutes. Serve.

### TWIST ON THE CLASSIC

Turn this into an entrée by adding pieces of cooked chicken to the rice. Another entrée idea is to layer the cooked rice with sautéed ground beef seasoned with cumin and chili powder. Top it with grated cheese and bake it to heat thoroughly.

## PAN DE MUERTO

### "DAY OF THE DEAD" BREAD

**Total Yield:** 3 lb., 13 oz. (1.7 kg) dough
2 each 10-inch (25-cm) round loaves

**Cooking Method:** Bake

© natspel

| INGREDIENTS | WEIGHT U.S. | WEIGHT METRIC | VOLUME U.S. | VOLUME METRIC |
|---|---|---|---|---|
| bread flour | 1 lb., 11 3/4 oz. + as needed | 787 g + as needed | 6 cups + as needed | 1.4 L + as needed |
| yeast, dry | 3/4 oz. | 22 g | 2 tablespoons | 30 mL |
| sugar | 5 1/4 oz. | 149 g | 2/3 cup | 160 mL |
| salt | 1/4 oz. | 8 g | 1 teaspoon | 5 mL |
| orange zest | 1/2 oz. | 15 g | 1 tablespoon | 15 mL |
| anise seed | 1/2 oz. | 15 g | 1 tablespoon | 15 mL |
| butter, cut in pieces | 4 oz. | 114 g | 1/2 cup or 1 stick | 120 mL or 1 stick |
| water | | 284 g | 1 1/4 cups | 300 mL |

### TWIST ON THE CLASSIC

Make a grilled cheese and smoked salmon sandwich with this sweetened bread. Use St. Andre, brie, or mozzarella cheese with smoked salmon and sauté the sandwich in butter.

Also called All Souls' Day, the "Day of the Dead" is celebrated on November 1 and 2. This holiday serves as a time to remember and honor those who have died. Many people create altars in their homes with remembrances from loved ones who have died, and they often place this bread on the altar. Traditionally, they decorate this bread with pieces of dough to resemble bones around the bread and a "ball" of dough is placed on top to represent a skull.

Although this bread reflects the European influence in the use of wheat flour instead of corn, the celebration of All Souls' Day harks from days long before the Spanish came to Mexico. This bread exemplifies the fusing of the indigenous culture with the Spanish influence.

| INGREDIENTS | WEIGHT | | VOLUME | |
| --- | --- | --- | --- | --- |
| | U.S. | METRIC | U.S. | METRIC |
| eggs, room temperature | 8 1/4 oz. | 234 g | 5 each | |

**Garnish:**
sugar, for sprinkling
orange juice glaze, for
   drizzling

1. Pan spray baking sheet. Place 9 oz. (256 g, 2 cups, or 266 mL) flour, yeast, sugar, salt, orange zest, and anise seed in mixing bowl. Stir to combine.
2. Heat butter and water until lukewarm. Add to flour mixture, mix with mixer at low speed or wooden spoon to combine. Beat about 3 minutes at medium speed.
3. Add eggs, one at a time, beating well between each addition.
4. Add 4 1/2 oz. (128 g, 1 cup, or 240 mL) flour, mix at low speed, continue adding flour until it forms soft dough. Either knead with machine or knead by hand for about 10 minutes, until smooth and elastic. Return to bowl, cover and let rise until doubled, about 1 1/4 to 1 1/2 hours.
5. Preheat oven to 350 degrees (180°C). Punch down dough, remove one-quarter of dough for decoration; set aside and cover. Divide remaining dough in half. Form each half into round loaf. Place on prepared pan (leaving room for them to double on the pan).
6. From reserved dough, form 2 golf ball-size rounds. Divide remaining dough in half. Portion each half into 8 pieces. With each of those pieces, roll in center to form pencil-like (elongated) piece with a knob at each end (to look like a bone). Place one "bone" on the side of the loaf on each quarter. Use remaining bone to form a cross with each of them. Place round ball in center at top of loaf (to look like a skull).
7. Cover and let rise until doubled, about 45 minutes. Bake for about 30 minutes, until golden and done.
8. Remove from oven; immediately sprinkle sugar on top. Let cool on rack. If desired, drizzle with an orange juice glaze.

---

## POLVORONES

### SHORTBREAD COOKIES

Clive Streeter © Dorling Kindersley Media Library

**Note:** Traditionally, these cookies are wrapped in tissue paper like a bonbon.

**Total Yield:** 15 oz. (426 g) raw dough;
Forty 2-inch (5-cm) cookies

**Cooking Method:** Bake

| INGREDIENTS | WEIGHT | | VOLUME | |
| --- | --- | --- | --- | --- |
| | U.S. | METRIC | U.S. | METRIC |
| almonds | 3 oz. | 86 g | 1/2 cup | 120 mL |
| all-purpose flour | 8 oz. | 227 g | 1 1/2 cups | 360 mL |
| sugar | 1 1/2 oz. | 43 g | 3 tablespoons | 45 mL |
| baking powder | | | 1 teaspoon | 5 mL |
| salt | | | 1/8 teaspoon | 1 mL |
| unsalted butter or half butter and half shortening, cold, cut into pieces | 5 oz. | 142 g | 10 tablespoons | 148 mL |
| confectioner's sugar, for dusting baked cookies | | | | |

1. Preheat oven to 350 degrees (180°C). Cover baking pans with parchment paper. On separate pans, bake almonds and flour until lightly browned, about 14 to 18 minutes. Remove from oven, cool.
2. Place almonds and sugar in bowl of food processor fitted with knife blade. Pulse until almonds are finely ground.
3. Add flour, baking powder, and salt to processor bowl, pulse to mix well.
4. Place cold butter pieces in processor, pulse to mix until dough comes together. Wrap in plastic wrap, refrigerate several hours or overnight. To chill quickly, place dough in freezer. Check after 20 or 30 minutes for firmness.
5. Position oven rack in top of oven. Preheat oven to 350 degrees (180°C).
6. Remove dough from refrigerator. If using all butter, hit dough with rolling pin to flatten a bit. Place dough on parchment paper or plastic wrap, top with piece of plastic wrap, and roll dough to 1/4-inch (1/2-cm) thickness.
7. Remove plastic wrap, cut out 2-inch (5-cm) cookies. Reroll scraps, continue rolling dough and cutting cookies until all dough is used. Bake on prepared pans in top of oven for 12 to 15 minutes, until lightly browned.
8. Immediately after removing from oven, sift thick layer of confectioner's sugar over cookies. Leave on pans until completely cooled.
9. Carefully transfer to airtight storage container with spatula—these cookies are fragile and break easily.

These fragile cookies resemble "Mexican wedding cookies" with their soft, crumbly texture and coating of confectioner's sugar; however, they are rolled out and cut into rounds rather than baked as balls of dough.

# PASTEL DE TRES LECHES

## THREE MILK CAKE

**Note:** Bake this cake the day before service because it needs to rest in the refrigerator for several hours or overnight.

**Number of Servings:** 9
**Serving Size:** One 3- by 4-inch (8- by 10-cm) piece
**Total Yield:** One 9- by 13-inch (23- by 33-cm) cake
**Food Balance:** Sweet
**Wine Style:** Sweet or off-dry
**Example:** Beringer Moscato, Rosemount Traminer Riesling

**Cooking Method:** Bake

### TWIST ON THE CLASSIC

Place a piece of Pastel de Tres Leches on a bed of warm chocolate sauce. Top the cake with strawberries, raspberries, or a mixture of berries, and finish with a dollop of whipped cream.

| INGREDIENTS | WEIGHT U.S. | METRIC | VOLUME U.S. | METRIC |
|---|---|---|---|---|
| **Soaking Syrup:** | | | | |
| sweetened condensed milk | | | one 14-oz. can | one 420-mL can |
| evaporated milk | | | one 12-oz. can | one 360-mL can |
| heavy cream | | 114 g | 1/2 cup | 120 mL |
| **Cake:** | | | | |
| all-purpose flour, sifted | 8 oz. | 227 g | 2 cups | 480 mL |
| baking powder | 1/4 oz. | 8 g | 2 teaspoons | 10 mL |
| eggs, separated | 10 oz. | 284 g | 6 each | |
| sugar | 13 1/4 oz. | 376 g | 1 3/4 cups | 420 mL |
| whole milk | | 104 g | 1/4 cup + 3 tablespoons | 105 mL |
| vanilla | | | 1 teaspoon | 5 mL |
| **Frosting:** | | | | |
| heavy whipping cream | | 340 g | 1 1/2 cups | 360 mL |
| confectioner's sugar | 1 1/2 oz. | 43 g, or to taste | 3 tablespoons | 45 mL, or to taste |
| vanilla | | | 1 teaspoon | 5 mL |
| **Garnish:** | | | | |
| fresh fruit, *optional* | | | | |

© carloscanlefoto

### SOAKING SYRUP:

1. Whisk condensed milk, evaporated milk, and 1/2 cup (114 g or 120 mL) cream together in bowl.
2. Refrigerate until needed.

### CAKE:

1. Sift flour and baking powder together into bowl. Set aside until needed. Pan-spray 9- by 13-inch (23- by 33-cm) pan. Preheat oven to 350 degrees (180°C).
2. Place egg whites in bowl of mixer fitted with wire beater. Beat at medium-low speed until frothy. Increase to high speed, beat until just starting to stiffen. Slowly add sugar by the tablespoon. Beat until stiff.
3. Add yolks, one at a time, beating well after each addition. Turn off mixer.
4. Sift one-third of flour mixture over eggs. Using rubber spatula, fold in gently and quickly. Add half of milk; fold in gently and quickly. Sift in half of remaining flour; fold in gently and quickly. Fold in remaining milk, and then sift remaining flour over top and fold in. Fold in vanilla.
5. Pour into prepared pan. Bake in preheated oven for 25 to 30 minutes, until a knife inserted into center comes out with only a few crumbs clinging. Allow to cool about 5 minutes. Poke holes over top of cake with toothpick or knife.
6. Slowly spoon soaking syrup over cake. Cool completely. Cover and refrigerate for several hours or overnight.

### FROSTING:

1. Place whipping cream in bowl of mixer fitted with wire beater. Beat at high speed until it starts to hold its shape.
2. Add sugar to taste and vanilla. Continue beating until soft peaks form.
3. Either spread whipped cream over cake before cutting or place a dollop on each piece. Also, garnish with fresh fruit, if desired.

# South America

>> **LEARNING OBJECTIVES**

By the end of this chapter, you will be able to:

- Discuss contributions made by the native Incas that impacted South America and the world
- Discuss the influences of other countries on the cuisines of South America
- Identify differences and similarities in the cuisines of South American countries
- Name food products prevalent in various areas of South America
- Prepare a variety of South American dishes

## >> HISTORY

### EARLY INDIAN TRIBES

By 6000 B.C., various indigenous tribes inhabited the continent of South America. It is believed that these people were originally Asians who traveled through Alaska to North America, and then continued their southern migration from North America through Central America to South America.

The cuisines found in many South American countries reflect heavy influence from the people who inhabited the area long before the Europeans discovered this part of the world. In particular, the Incas exerted a profound effect on the culture that is still widely felt. The heart of the Incan civilization flourished in the area that is now Peru, Ecuador, Bolivia, and Chile. As a result, these countries exhibit very strong remnants of the Incan cuisine.

### SPANISH SETTLERS

*When the Spanish arrived, the Incas ruled Peru. As did the Aztec leader in Mexico, the Incan ruler indulged in huge feasts with many, many dishes prepared for him. In fact, some accounts say those feasts included up to 500 dishes!*

When the Spanish arrived in South America at the beginning of the sixteenth century, they introduced pigs, cows, lamb, chickens, goats, dairy products, wheat, and almonds to this "new" land. In exchange, the European explorers learned of products indigenous to the New World like corn, beans, potatoes, tomatoes, chili peppers, avocados, squash, sweet potatoes, pineapples, chocolate, tobacco, and vanilla. Because several of these products play such a significant role in the cuisines of Europe, it is astounding to realize that the Europeans knew nothing of these foods until the sixteenth century.

When the Spanish came to Venezuela and Colombia around 1500, they found a land with almost impassable terrain inhabited by just a few Indians. Only the quest for gold made them continue on and explore these two countries.

In 1531, the Spanish found Peru. They discovered a land where the little meat available was given to royalty, and the common people had almost none. A diet of beans and grains replaced meat, except for those who lived near the coasts, rivers, and lakes and therefore had access to fish and other seafood.

*Unfortunately, the Spanish brought diseases like smallpox to the Incan population. One hundred years after the Spanish arrived, the number of Incas was reduced by 80 percent.*

The Spanish introduced the Peruvians to butter, cheese, and milk, which they quickly incorporated into their cooking. The introduction of butter allowed the Peruvians, as it did the Mexicans, to fry foods; prior to that time, they had had no source of cooking fat. The cuisine of Peru developed into a melding of Incan and Spanish foods, which is now known as Creole cooking.

### INCAS

The inventive Incas worked extensively with plant breeding to improve their crops, and the European conquerors learned much about agriculture and horticulture from them. Besides adapting existing produce to withstand the climates and conditions in the mountains, they developed many new varieties of vegetables, particularly corn, potatoes, and hot peppers. Realizing the effect of altitude on the plants, they experimented with growing crops at different altitudes to take advantage of the variations that occurred in the vegetables.

The Incas terraced the slopes of the Andes Mountains in Peru, which allowed them to produce bountiful crops on the steep inclines. They then devised an intricate system of canals to irrigate all areas of the mountains. By utilizing the force of water going downhill, they even irrigated the sides of the mountains! Through these innovations, the Incas transformed once barren land into some of the best farmland in the world.

Another of their significant culinary contributions was in the area of food preservation. The Incas figured out methods to air-dry, salt, dehydrate, and freeze-dry foods.

### PORTUGUESE AND AFRICAN IMPACT

Lying east of the Incan settlements, the area that is now Brazil was inhabited by relatively few people. As a result, when the Portuguese arrived in 1533, they had a strong impact on the cuisine there. Because they needed lots of laborers to work on their sugar plantations, the Portuguese imported slaves from western Africa. When the slaves realized that the climate in Brazil was similar to their home in Africa, they planted yams, okra, greens, and other foods from western Africa and then prepared their native recipes. The native Brazilians adopted the use of strong seasonings, *dendê* (palm oil), smoked and dried fish, and the vegetables from these African slaves. Soon, the African foods and recipes became part of the cuisine of Brazil. Although this cuisine shows some of the indigenous influence, the Portuguese and the Africans left the most pronounced effects on the cookery of Brazil. The Portuguese ruled Brazil until 1822 when Brazil received its independence.

Mostly settling in southern Brazil, an influx of immigrants from Germany, Switzerland, Poland, Italy, and more started coming in the late 1800s. Choosing the south because the climate resembled that of their homeland, they planted crops and prepared the dishes from their heritage. The cuisine of each ethnic group melded with the existing Brazilian cookery in the areas where they settled.

Also, Japanese came to work on coffee plantations in the early 1900s. They planted many fruits and vegetables, introduced them to the Brazilians, and they soon became an integral part of the diet in Brazil. In fact, they say São Paulo has the largest Japanese population of any location outside of Japan.

> *Between 1550 and 1888, they believe 3,500,000 African slaves were brought to Brazil. In 1888, they abolished slavery, ending the 350-year history of slavery in Brazil.*

## >> TOPOGRAPHY

From its north to south, South America encompasses 4,750 miles. From east to west at its widest point, the continent stretches for about 3,000 miles. This huge area contains very diverse terrain and climates, including glaciers, mountains, rainforests, and tropical jungle. The equator runs through it, while the icy Atlantic on the south separates this continent from Antarctica.

### BORDERING WATERS

With the exception of land-locked Bolivia and Paraguay, all countries in South America border an ocean or sea. The Pacific Ocean lies to the west, the Caribbean Sea borders on the north, and the Atlantic Ocean is situated on the east. In the south, the Drake Passage separates South America from Antarctica.

### EQUATOR

The equator runs through three countries in South America: Brazil, Ecuador, and Colombia. Moving south from the equator, the temperatures become cooler. Because of their distance from the equator, southern Chile and Argentina experience cold weather and many hours of daylight in the summer, just like Alaska and Scandinavia.

> *The seasons south of the equator are opposite those north of the equator. When it is summer north of the equator, winter reigns south of the equator.*

### ANDES MOUNTAINS

The high mountains of the Andes span 4,500 miles and run parallel to the coast through Venezuela, Colombia, Ecuador, Peru, Bolivia, Paraguay, Chile, and Argentina. With peaks above 20,000 feet, the Andes ranks as the longest chain and second highest group of mountains in the world. Even though some of these mountains lie near the equator, there are cool temperatures at the high altitudes throughout the year. While the Incas terraced the mountains in Peru, allowing them to grow crops, the mountains in Chile were too steep to terrace. As a result, the people of Chile grew significantly fewer vegetables.

### VARIOUS COUNTRIES

Venezuela and Colombia lie in northern South America. Dense jungles line the coasts, and the Andes Mountains run parallel to the coast. The valleys in the Andes provide fertile farmland and a temperate climate for growing crops.

| Ingredients and Foods Commonly Used throughout the Cuisines of South America Include | |
| --- | --- |
| • beef and pork | • squash |
| • game | • chili peppers |
| • guinea pig (Peru) | • cassava |
| • corn | • tropical fruits and vegetables |
| • all sorts of beans | • bananas and plantains |
| • rice | • peanuts |
| • potatoes, yams, and sweet potatoes | • coconuts, coconut milk, and coconut oil |
| • quinoa | • sugar |

*The world's largest rainforest lies in Peru at the Amazon River. Rainforest also covers much of the land in Ecuador.*

Three neighboring countries, Peru, Ecuador, and Chile, lie along the western coast of South America. Each of these countries borders the Pacific Ocean, and mountains from the Andes run parallel to the coast.

Besides mountains, Peru's diverse topography includes desert and rainforest. Between the Pacific and the Andes there lies a narrow strip of desert that is almost devoid of vegetation, except in a spot where more than 50 tiny rivers run in a path from the mountains to the ocean. Irrigation from these many rivers supports the growth of crops.

Forests, arid lands, and grasslands compose Chile's coastal area. Lying in the north of Chile, the Atacama Desert has had no recorded rainfall throughout history.

Brazil is a huge country with varied topography and over 4,650 miles of coastline. Although the north of Brazil contains jungles, savannas, and dry brush country, the south has temperate highlands with fertile farmland. The second longest river in the world, the 4,000-mile Amazon River cuts through Brazil, Bolivia, and Peru, creating dense, tropical forests.

Lying south of Brazil, Uruguay and Argentina have very fertile farmland and a temperate climate. The *pampa* consists of humid grasslands that is ideal for raising livestock. Most of the high-quality meat produced in South America comes from the *pampa* in these two countries.

## >> COOKING METHODS

Because almost no cooking fats existed in South America prior to the arrival of the Spanish in the sixteenth century, foods were boiled, steamed, broiled over an open fire, stewed, or toasted in a dry pan. Frying was not an option. South Americans prepared hearty soups and stews by braising, which, of course, served both to tenderize the tough meat and extend the meager supply of meat with other ingredients.

Traditional ovens did not exist here, but, as in Mexico, they baked and steamed by digging a pit, lining it with stones, burning wood or charcoal in the pit, then baking or steaming the food with the heat radiating from the stones and embers after the fire burned down. A precursor of the New England "clambake," this outdoor barbecue still marks any festive occasion in the mountainous and coastal areas.

*The Incas used the difficult climate of the Andes to extend their stores of food. They left foods outside to naturally freeze during the cold night and thaw during the warmer days until the food dehydrated. This process of freezing and thawing continued for as many days as it took until the moisture was gone, and the foods were dehydrated. With this preservation technique, the Incas dehydrated a number of foods, notably potatoes and corn. Called chuño, the dried potato kept for up to one year. Chuño enabled the Incas to survive through times of drought and famine.*

The barbecue, grilling and cooking over the coals and embers of the fire, came from the *gauchos* (cattlemen or cowboys) who raised cattle in southern Brazil, Patagonia (southern Chile), Argentina, Uruguay, and Paraguay. Traditionally, they butterflied the whole animal, placed it on a metal grate, and cooked it over the fire. If preparing a smaller piece of meat, they skewered it and then cooked it.

In Brazil, this grilling is known as *churrasco*. In Argentina, Chile, Paraguay, and Uruguay, they call it *asada*.

As mentioned before, the Incas preserved foods by air-drying, salting, dehydrating, and freeze-drying. This provided food through the cold winters in the mountains as well as during times of drought and/or poor crops throughout the rest of the land.

## >> REGIONS

### ISOLATION

South America contains very diverse conditions in terms of both terrain and climate. Mountains, dense jungles, tropical rainforests, rivers, arid land, and desert made travel extremely difficult. Isolation played a significant role in the development of cuisines in the different regions.

### PERU AND ECUADOR

Although the climate in the Andes Mountains remains temperate, with seasons, the rest of Peru has no distinct seasons. As a result, crops mature throughout the year. While arid, hot, desertlike conditions prevail in the area west of the mountains by the coast, the land east of the mountains is tropical, hot, and humid.

Peru and Ecuador share similar topography, so the climates and cuisines have much in common. The cuisine in the mountains varied greatly from those in other areas due to two factors: differences in the available foods produced in each area and the isolation created by the difficult terrain. This isolation made the sharing of foods and recipes close to impossible both within the mountains and on either side of them.

*Chile contains more than 2,700 miles of coastline. This long and narrow country would stretch from northern Newfoundland to southern Florida.*

### CHILE

On the southwestern side of South America lies Chile, a narrow country containing even more diverse topography and climate than the rest of South America. The northern third consists of desert with almost no rainfall and nothing growing. The middle section features fertile valleys of rich, sandy soil and a Mediterranean climate with hot, dry summers and cool, wet winters. Ideal for growing grapes, large vineyards yielding some high-quality wines cover the countryside in this part of Chile. Lying near Antarctica, the southern third is cold, mountainous country with thick forests and tremendous rainfall. Glaciers dot some of the mountains.

With more than 2,500 miles of coast, a huge variety of fish and seafood flourishes. Tropical fish thrive in the north, while the cold currents found in some areas support a myriad of nontropical species.

- *Chile provides the United States with 95 percent of its eating grapes in the winter.*
- *In the last 16 years, exports of Chilean fruits and vegetables have increased more than 700 percent.*
- *Chile ranks as the second largest exporter of salmon.*

### BRAZIL

Covering much of eastern South America, Brazil borders every country in South America except Chile and Ecuador. A number of different regions make up this large country. The Amazon River transects the hot, humid, and tropical central portion, which contains dense rainforest. Tropical fruits and vegetables thrive in these hot and humid areas. The southern section consists of mostly grasslands with a few rivers. Directly on the coasts, the land becomes forest. Most of the major cities lie in the coastal areas.

*Ranking as the largest country in Latin America, Brazil is the fifth largest country in the world. About the size of the United States, its vast lands span four time zones.*

### BOLIVIA

About three times the size of Montana, Bolivia is one of the few South American countries not bordering an ocean. Brazil lies to the north and east of Bolivia, Paraguay and Argentina border on the south, Peru and Chili are to the west. Bolivia's land consists of jungles, the Andes Mountains, plateaus, and hills. With varied topography and climate, Bolivians grow many fruits and vegetables, including potatoes, corn, chili peppers, bananas, plantains, and sugarcane.

*In the 1930s and 40s, Bolivia was one of the few countries that allowed war refugees to move there without restrictions. Many fleeing from the Nazis found a home in Bolivia, bringing many European culinary influences to this country.*

### URUGUAY AND ARGENTINA

In the southern portion of South America, Uruguay and most of Argentina contain humid grasslands and a temperate climate ideal for producing a profusion of crops and lots of animals for meat. Called the *pampa*, the richest farmland in South America is

## SOME SOUTH AMERICAN CHEESES

### Argentina

**Regianitto** Made from cow's milk; hard, used for grating and cooking; similar to Parmesan, first made by Italian immigrants

**Sardo** Made from cow's milk; firm texture; similar to Pecorino, often grated

### Brazil

**Catupiry** Soft, mild, low acidity; spreads like cream cheese or Brie; first made in 1911 by Mario Silvestrini, an Italian immigrant

**Minas** Made from cow's milk; becomes more firm as it ages; available in three varieties: *Frescal* (fresh, aged 4 to 10 days), *Meia-Cura* (slightly mature), and *Curado* (mature)

**Queijo Coalho** Salty flavor; firm texture

**Requeijao** Mild and creamy

**Queijo de Brasilia** Made from cow's milk; slightly tangy flavor; similar to Cheddar

### Chile

**Chanco** Made from cow's milk; semi-hard texture; sour to salty flavor

**Pan Quehue** Made from cow's milk; smooth, semisoft texture; mild flavor

**Chilarti** Made from cow's milk; very creamy, soft texture; mild flavor similar to havarti

### Uruguay

**Holland Mill Uruguda** Made from cow's milk; mild flavor; smooth texture; similar to Gouda

---

located here. This area boasts ideal amounts of rainfall and a temperate climate. Uruguay raises both cattle and sheep; Argentina primarily produces beef.

## >> CUISINE

Generally, culinary traits from the early inhabitants as well as from Portugal and Spain appear in the South American cuisines. European cooking methods and ingredients combined with the indigenous foods of South America to create the cuisines of the various countries.

### PROTEIN

Except in the *pampa* of Argentina and Uruguay, meat is not plentiful throughout South America. In the other countries, available meat is often tough for a couple of reasons. First, the animals must forage for sufficient food, so their muscles develop more. Second, their limited diet creates leaner animals. Since lean animals have less fat, their meat is tougher. As a result, cooks shred or chop the meat and slowly braise it in various sauces. This produces stews and hearty soups, which still remain popular throughout South America. Although plentiful seafood and fish exist along the coasts, rivers, and lakes, beans and grains continue to be the most important staples throughout this continent. The combination of legumes and grains forms a complete protein, and is the foundation of the diet in much of South America. Abundant fruits and vegetables grow in the tropical areas. Bananas, plantains, and coconuts serve as mainstays in cuisines found in the tropics.

### CHEESE

In the areas where cattle are raised, cheeses are often produced. As a result, the majority of cheeses in South America are made from cow's milk. Since Italian immigrants made most of the early cheeses, many South American cheeses resemble Italian cheeses. Cheeses are made in countries without lots of cattle, but the cheese production seems more limited.

### PERU

Peru has a rich culinary history based both on the Incan civilization and on its difficult terrain. As a result, two distinct Creole cuisines developed—one in the mountains and

---

### COMPLEMENTARY PROTEIN

*Amino acids make up the structure we call protein. There are nine essential amino acids that the human body cannot produce, so we must obtain these nine from foods we eat. Although meat, dairy, and soy products contain all the necessary amino acids to form complete protein, grains, seeds, and legumes contain only some of the essential amino acids needed to make complete protein. Seeds and grains are low in one group of the essential amino acids and high in another group, but legumes are the opposite. That is, while legumes are high in the group of amino acids that are low in grains, grains are high in the amino acids that are low in legumes. So, when these foods are eaten together, they combine and provide all the essential amino acids necessary to form complete protein. In essence, the amino acids in these foods complement each other.*

the other on the coast. Animal protein included fish, game, llamas, and guinea pigs. In the valleys of the Andes Mountains, the early inhabitants raised many types of potatoes, *quinoa* (a type of grain), amaranth, beans, pumpkins, squash, greens, and other crops that could withstand the cool weather in the mountains.

First cultivated around 200 B.C., potatoes rank supreme in the mountainous portions of Peru. It is said the Incas identified over 4,000 potato varieties. They developed different hybrids for preserving, for a range of cooking situations, and for their multitude of colors including white, purple, yellow, pink, and red. While some varieties cook quickly, they adapted others for slow cooking in soups or stews. In addition, the various potatoes possess differing flavor components.

Peruvians also produce and consume a staggering number of varieties of corn, another favorite food. In fact, the Incas developed more varieties of corn here than are found anywhere in the world. Through their botanical explorations, they produced and raised different types of corn for a wide range of culinary purposes. They developed kernels that remain soft for grinding into meal or flour and others that dry well for long-term storage. In addition, they altered the size of the kernels, creating some kernels the size of marbles and others the size of a fist. The Incas had corn for everyday use, some sweet varieties, some for making into hominy, and others for dehydrating. For consumption, they roasted or boiled the whole kernels or ground them into flour.

As settlers move to Peru, they fused the existing Peruvian cuisine with the foods and recipes from their homeland. The Spanish introduced cattle, pigs, sheep, goats, chicken, dairy products including milk and cheese, fats, wheat, rice, olives, and more. Arab influence brought stuffed vegetables and other foods (like the empanada), sweets, and desserts. Discussed earlier, Africans planted the fruits and vegetables, used spices and recipes from their homeland, and prepared offal. Like many slaves, they received the unwanted parts of the animal from their owners, so they cooked the hearts, kidney, tripe, intestines, or whatever. From the Chinese immigrants, the Peruvians learned to cook stir-fries, served rice with every meal, and flavored with soy sauce and ginger. Peruvians adopted pasta dishes and many fresh vegetables from the Italians. The Japanese taught them great finesse with seafood, which refined the way they prepared *ceviche*. Each group left its mark that created the fusion of Peru's cuisine.

Although Peru is situated near the equator, ocean currents temper the climate. Cooking in the coastal area includes abundant fish and seafood. Fruits and vegetables are available in the coastal areas where irrigation has transformed some of the desert into fertile farmland. A stark contrast from the Andes region, the dishes of the coastal region reflect a richer and more elaborate cuisine than the cookery in the mountains.

The Peruvian chili seasoning *aji* shows up in many dishes, including appetizers, soups, stews, entrées, and vegetables. The ubiquitous *aji* appears as commonly in the cuisine of Peru as chilies appear in Mexican cooking.

Served throughout Latin America, *ceviche* originated in Peru. To prepare *ceviche*, raw fish is marinated in lemon and lime juices flavored with onion, garlic, and other spices. The acid from the citrus juices essentially "cooks" the fish, and the appearance of the fish changes from translucent to opaque. Peruvians typically serve *ceviche* with a garnish of sweet potatoes and small cut pieces of corn on the cob.

Another "raw" seafood dish, *tiradito* is prepared with the same ingredients as *ceviche*. The difference is that they cut the fish for *ceviche* in cubes while *tiradito* contains sliced fish like Japanese sashimi.

People in the tropical northern coastal regions of Peru and coastal Ecuador consume lots of bananas, plantains, and peanuts. Bananas permeate all parts of the menu and are prepared in a variety of ways, including boiled, fried, and even ground into flour for use in breads and pastries. A reflection on the European influence, many dishes from the areas where the Incas once lived incorporate cheese and cream.

## QUINOA

*The Incas first discovered quinoa (pronounced keen-wah) about 5,000 to 6,000 years ago. Because this grain grows well at high altitudes, it thrived throughout the Andes. Called the "mother grain" in the Incan language, quinoa contains the essential amino acids, making it higher in protein than typical grains. In studies, the amino acids found in quinoa compare to that of soy products and dried milk. The Incas consumed quinoa as a cooked whole grain or ground it for use as flour. They also cooked the greens from the plant. Along with potatoes and corn, quinoa served as a staple for the Incas living in the Andes in Peru, Bolivia, and Ecuador.*

*The Incas receive credit for developing popcorn.*

## BRAZIL

Rice continues to be an important staple throughout Brazil. Rather than steaming it and serving it dry as in many Asian cuisines, preparing rice involves first sautéing the rice in the style of pilaf and then mixing in other vegetables and seasonings. Layered with meat, seafood, vegetables, and/or sauce, rice becomes the basis for the Brazilian version of casseroles.

Beans form the foundation of the diet. Black beans are the most popular legume and appear in a myriad of dishes. Considered the national dish of Brazil, *feijoada completa* combines beans with several smoked and cured meats and seasonings.

Crops grown in the hot, humid jungles and the hot, dry grasslands of Brazil include peanuts, bananas, coconuts, yams, and *manioc,* a starchy root vegetable also called *cassava.* The jungles yield a profusion of tropical fruits like mangos, papayas, breadfruit, oranges, bananas, coconuts, and more. Coconut and coconut milk appear in all sorts of dishes, from soups and stews to desserts. Brazilians also use lots of ginger and lemon juice.

The region of Bahia in eastern Brazil exhibits the strongest African influence and is reputed to have the finest cuisine in the country. Seafood abounds, and coconut milk and hot chilies flavor most dishes in Bahia. Fish stews remain standard fare in northeastern Brazil.

Beans accompanied by starchy mashes or rice dominate the diet in the central region. When meat is available in this region, pork, including sausage and bacon, ranks as first choice. Brazilians use many types of chili peppers in all sorts of dishes and condiments. Some of the best cheeses produced in Brazil come from the central region.

The south of Brazil enjoys a temperate climate and actually contains *pampas* like Argentina. Plentiful beef comes from this area, and wine is produced here.

## VENEZUELA AND COLOMBIA

A type of cornbread, *arepa,* is the staff of life in Venezuela and Colombia. Filled with meat, stuffed *arepa* is boiled and used as a dumpling in soup or fried. In the mountainous regions, people consume great quantities of potatoes.

The tropical or semitropical regions feature soups and stews with the starchy root, cassava, replacing the potato that is favored in the higher elevations. Again, in these warmer areas, bananas and plantains serve as staples and often appear in soups and stews, as a side dish, or in dessert. Venezuelans and Colombians grill, fry, or boil bananas and plantains. Wasting no part of the plant, cooks wrap banana leaves around fillings to hold them together while cooking them in coals or steaming. As in Brazil, coconuts and coconut milk appear in many dishes, both sweet and savory.

They raise cattle in Venezuela and Colombia, but the meat is tough by American standards. As a result, stewing and braising remain popular cooking techniques because meat becomes tender when cut it into small pieces and slowly cooked.

## ARGENTINA AND URUGUAY

The cattle from Argentina are a different story. Very high-quality beef is the norm here, and it functions as a staple in the Argentine diet. Served as often as three times a day, beef also often appears in several courses within a meal. Uruguay raises more sheep than beef, so lots of lamb and mutton are consumed in addition to beef. A popular appetizer served as a first course, picnic fare, or a snack, the *empanada* is a small turnover or pie filled with any combination of meats and seasonings. The presence of pumpkin and squash in soups, stews, and desserts shows the influence of the native peoples on the cuisine of these two countries.

*Arepa*
© redav

Most cattle raised in the pampa feed on the grass rather than being fed grain in a feedlot. Many people feel this produces meat that contains less fat. Some describe Argentine beef as having a more gamelike flavor and a more grainy texture than beef from the United States.

## CHILE

With Chile's miles of coastline, seafood makes up for the scarcity of meat there. More seafood is consumed in Chile than in any other Latin American country, but the ubiquitous bean still ranks supreme here. In fact, the national dish of Chile consists of a mixture of beans, corn, and squash called *porotos granados*. Two seasonings are associated with Chile: *color,* an orange-red flavoring that combines garlic, paprika, and melted fat, and *pebre*, a sauce made of onions, garlic, chili peppers, coriander, vinegar, and olive oil.

*Porotos granados*
© instantanea2010

## COFFEE

Coffee, the beverage of choice through most of South America, is served at all meals and between meals, too. Over half of the world's coffee comes from Latin America. Colombia produces very high-quality coffee, but Brazil's coffee is usually blended with another coffee of higher quality.

## SWEETS

Because sugar is plentiful and used generously, sweets play a large role in the cuisines of South America. All fruits and several vegetables, including sweet potatoes and squash, are served candied. Also, South Americans prepare intensely sweet pastes from many fruits, which are used as filling for pastries or eaten plain.

By North American standards, South American desserts are cloyingly sweet. Probably the best-known South American dessert remains flan, a molded custard. Nuts are plentiful and incorporated into many confections. Another popular dessert in Central and South America as well as the Caribbean is sautéed bananas and sugar drizzled with rum or brandy.

## MEALS

The main meal of the day occurs in the afternoon. Consisting of several courses, this large meal is traditionally followed by a *siesta*, a nap. Meals follow the same pattern as those of Mexico: breakfast is composed of fruit, tortillas or sweet rolls, coffee or hot chocolate, and perhaps meat, eggs, and/or beans. Midmorning snacks hold the diner until the main meal in the afternoon. Around six o'clock in the evening, South Americans consume pastries and coffee or hot chocolate. A light evening meal is served at nine or ten o'clock.

| REGION | AREA | WEATHER | TOPOGRAPHY | FOODS |
|---|---|---|---|---|
| Venezuela | West | Cool | Mountains | Cattle, potatoes |
| | North | Hot | Coast, forests | Seafood, bananas, plantains, coconuts, cassava |
| Colombia | Central, west central | Cool | Mountains | Cattle, potatoes, coffee |
| | West | Hot | Coast, rainforest | Seafood, bananas, plantains, coconuts, cassava |
| Ecuador | West (coastal) | Hot | Coast, rainforest | Seafood, plantains, bananas, peanuts, corn, chili peppers, fruits, vegetables |
| | East (Andes) | Cool | Mountains, steep valleys | Llama, beans, quinoa, potatoes, squash, corn, pumpkin |
| Peru | West (coastal) | Arid, hot | Coast, desert, small rivers for irrigation | Seafood, plantains, bananas, peanuts, corn, chili peppers, fruits, vegetables |
| | East (Andes) | Cool | Mountains, steep valleys | Llama, beans, corn, quinoa, amaranth, potatoes, squash, pumpkin |

| REGION | AREA | WEATHER | TOPOGRAPHY | FOODS |
|---|---|---|---|---|
| Brazil | Northern two-thirds | Hot | Tropical rainforest, savannas, dry brush land | Seafood, game, nuts, peanuts, manioc, corn, sweet potatoes, yams, okra, plantains, coconut, oranges, papaya, mangos, breadfruit, bananas, dates, coffee, sugar, cocoa |
| | Lower third | Temperate | Grasslands, fertile farmland | Cattle, many fruits and vegetables |
| Bolivia | Brazil to north and east, Paraguay and Argentina to south, Peru and Chile to west | Tropical to temperate | Andes Mountains, Amazon River, tropical rainforest, plateaus, hills | Many fruits and vegetables including potatoes, corn, quinoa, chili peppers, bananas, plantains, sugarcane |
| Chile | Northern third | Hot, arid | Desert, little or no rainfall | Seafood |
| | Middle third | Hot, dry summers; cool, wet winters | Fertile valleys | Seafood, grapes, wine |
| | Southern third | Cold | Mountains, forest | Seafood |
| Uruguay | *Pampa* | Temperate | Humid grasslands | Sheep, beef, many crops |
| Argentina | *Pampa* | Temperate | Humid grasslands, fertile farmland | Beef, wine, many crops |

## >> Review Questions

1. Discuss the effect of the Andes Mountains on the cuisines of South America.
2. What did the Incas contribute to the cuisines of South America?
3. Name five foods that the Europeans learned about when they discovered South America.
4. Name four food products and flavorings that are prevalent in South America.
5. Discuss which animal proteins are consumed in various areas of South America and why.

## >> Glossary

**aji** Spicy chili seasoning frequently used in the cooking of Peru

**arepa** Type of cornbread

**ceviche** Dish consisting of raw fish marinated in citrus juices with other seasonings; the citrus juice "cooks" the fish, changing its appearance from raw to opaque; originally from Peru, *ceviche* is served throughout Latin America

**color** An orange-red flavoring that combines garlic, paprika, and melted fat; used in Chile

**creole** Style of cooking melding Incan and Spanish culinary components

**dendê** An orange-colored oil made from palm; brought to Brazil by slaves from western Africa, where it is used extensively

**empanada** Small turnover or pie filled with any combination of meats and seasonings

**feijoada completa** Dish combining beans with a variety of smoked and cured meats and seasonings; the national dish of Brazil

**manioc** A starchy root vegetable which is sometimes called *cassava*

**pampa** Humid grasslands that are found in Argentina and Uruguay; ideal lands for raising livestock

**pebre** A sauce made of onions, garlic, chili peppers, coriander, vinegar, and olive oil; used as a seasoning in Chile

**porotos granados** Dish containing a mixture of beans, corn, and squash; the national dish of Chile

**quinoa** A grain that thrives in the mountains; originally raised by the Incas and still consumed today

## EMPANADAS DE HORNO (ARGENTINA)

### MEAT FILLED TURNOVERS

**Serving Size:** 4-inch (10-cm) turnover
**Total Yield:** 18 to 20 turnovers
**Food Balance:** Sweet/spicy/protein
**Wine Style:** Off-dry, low-oaked whites and soft reds
**Example:** Beringer Founders' Estate Pinot Grigio, Black Opal Shiraz

**Cooking Method:** Bake

Courtesy of CanolaInfo.org

| INGREDIENTS | WEIGHT U.S. | WEIGHT METRIC | VOLUME U.S. | VOLUME METRIC |
|---|---|---|---|---|
| **Dough:** | | | | |
| all-purpose flour | 9 oz. | 256 g | 2 cups | 480 mL |
| salt | 1/4 oz. | 8 g | 1 teaspoon | 5 mL |
| butter, cold, cut into 5 pieces | 5 oz. | 142 g | 1/2 cup + 2 tablespoons | 150 mL |
| water, cold | | 78 g | 1/3 cup | 80 mL |
| **Filling:** | | | | |
| raisins | 2 oz. | 57 g | 1/4 cup | 60 mL |
| water, boiling | | 227 g | 1 cup | 240 mL |
| onion, finely chopped | 3 oz. | 86 g | 1 small, or 1/2 cup | 120 mL |
| olive oil | | 15 g | 1 tablespoon | 15 mL |
| water | | 114 g | 1/2 cup | 120 mL |
| sirloin steak, boneless, 1/4-inch (1/2-cm) cubes | 8 oz. | 227 g | | |
| crushed red pepper | | | 1 teaspoon | 5 mL |
| ground cumin | | | 1/4 teaspoon | 2 mL |
| paprika | | | 1/2 teaspoon | 3 mL |
| salt | | | 1/2 teaspoon | 3 mL |
| pepper | | | few grindings | |
| **Assembly:** | | | | |
| all-purpose flour | | | as needed | |
| eggs, hard boiled, each cut into 10 slices | | | 2 each | |
| green olives, pitted, quartered | 2 oz. | 57 g | 20 each | |

> **TWIST ON THE CLASSIC**
>
> Try substituting chicken for the beef, or turn this into a vegetarian appetizer by using tofu or an assortment of vegetables for the filling.

### DOUGH:

1. Place flour and salt in bowl of food processor fitted with knife blade. Pulse a couple of times to mix.
2. Place cold butter on top. Pulse a few times to cut into dough, until mixture forms pea-sized pieces.
3. With machine running, add water through feed tube. Pulse a few times until dough forms a ball.
4. Remove dough from bowl, wrap in plastic wrap. Store in refrigerator while preparing filling.

### FILLING:

1. Soak raisins in 1 cup (227 g or 240 mL) boiling water for 10 minutes. Drain thoroughly. Set aside.
2. Combine onions, olive oil, and 1/2 cup (114 g or 120 mL) water in skillet. Boil over high heat until water is evaporated.
3. Add meat, cook, stirring constantly, until browned. Stir in crushed red pepper, cumin, paprika, salt, pepper, and reserved raisins. Set filling aside.

### ASSEMBLY:

1. Place oven rack in center of oven. Preheat oven to 400 degrees (205°C).
2. Roll out dough on lightly floured surface to about 1/8 inch (30 mm) thick. Cut out 4-inch (10-cm) rounds. Gather scraps and roll only once again or it may become too tough.

③ Place 3/4 ounce, or 1 tablespoon (22 g) filling in center of each round. Top filling with piece of egg and 4 pieces of olive.

④ Using pastry brush, moisten perimeter of dough with water. Fold dough in half, press edges firmly together, and curve to form crescent. Flute joined edges of dough like a pie crust to seal.

⑤ Place pastries on ungreased baking sheet. Bake for 15 to 20 minutes, until golden. Serve.

# ESCABECHE DE PESCADO (THROUGHOUT SOUTH AMERICA)

## FISH ESCABECHE

**Note:** Actually fried, marinated fish, this dish is served as an appetizer or entrée throughout Latin America. Each country prepares its own variation of this popular dish, which features many types of fish, shrimp, or chicken. Traditionally, *escabeche* is served at room temperature.

**Number of Servings:** 6 to 8 appetizers
**Cooking Method:** Deep-fry, boil
**Serving Size:** 3 to 4 oz. (86 to 114 g) fish plus vegetables for appetizer (double for entrée)
**Total Yield:** 2 lb., 10 oz. (1.2 kg)
**Food Balance:** Spicy/acid
**Wine Style:** Off-dry, low-oaked whites and soft reds
**Example:** Campanile or Meridian Vineyards Pinot Grigio, Penfolds Shiraz

| | WEIGHT | | VOLUME | |
|---|---|---|---|---|
| **INGREDIENTS** | **U.S.** | **METRIC** | **U.S.** | **METRIC** |
| boneless fish fillet, cod, haddock, or whitefish | 1 lb., 8 oz. | 681 g | | |
| flour | 2 oz. | 57 g | 1/2 cup | 120 mL |
| kosher salt | 1/4 oz. | 8 g | 1 teaspoon | 5 mL |
| paprika | 1/2 oz. | 15 g | 1 tablespoon + 1 teaspoon | 20 mL |
| ground cayenne | | | 1/8 teaspoon | 1 mL |
| oil, for deep-frying | | | | |
| onion, 3/8-inch (1-cm) slices | 7 oz. | 199 g | 1 large | |
| carrot, peeled and cut on diagonal into 1/2-inch (1 1/3-cm) slices | 3 1/2 oz. | 104 g | 1 each | |
| garlic cloves, peeled | 1 oz. | 28 g | 6 each | |
| *jalapeño* peppers, whole | 3 3/4 oz. | 107 g | 4 each | |
| bay leaves | | | 2 each | |
| red wine vinegar | | 227 g | 1 cup | 240 mL |
| red wine | | 227 g | 1 cup | 240 mL |
| dried thyme | | | 1 teaspoon | 5 mL |
| stock, chicken or fish | | 227 g | 1 cup | 240 mL |

① Cut fish fillet into six or eight pieces, or use whole fish.

② Combine flour, salt, 2 teaspoons (10 mL) of paprika, and cayenne on plate, mix well. Dredge fish in flour mixture.

③ Heat oil for deep-frying in heavy pan 375 degrees (190°C). Fry fish, a few pieces at a time, to maintain proper temperature of oil. Fry fish until golden, about 5 minutes. Remove from pan and drain well on absorbent paper, then place in nonreactive bowl in single layer. Refrigerate until needed.

④ Pour off all but about 1/4 inch (1/2 cm) oil. Heat oil remaining in pan; add onion, carrot, and garlic, sauté until golden.

⑤ Add *jalapeños*, remaining 2 teaspoons (10 mL) paprika, and bay leaves. Sauté for another minute or 2.

⑥ Add vinegar, bring to boil, reduce heat and simmer 5 minutes. Add red wine, bring to boil, reduce heat and simmer 5 minutes.

⑦ Add thyme and stock, bring to boil, reduce heat and simmer 15 minutes. Pour hot liquid over fish, let cool. Serve immediately or cover and refrigerate until ready to serve. Serve fish accompanied by some of the pickled vegetables and marinating liquid.

---

### TWIST ON THE CLASSIC

Turn this into an entrée salad by serving the *escabeche* on top of a bed of greens.

# CREMA FRIA DE PALTA (CHILE)

## COLD CREAM OF AVOCADO SOUP

**Number of Servings:** 8
**Serving Size:** 7 oz. (198 g)
**Total Yield:** 3 lb., 13 3/4 oz. (1.8 kg)

| INGREDIENTS | WEIGHT U.S. | WEIGHT METRIC | VOLUME U.S. | VOLUME METRIC |
|---|---|---|---|---|
| chicken stock | | 908 g | 1 quart | 960 mL |
| lime juice | | 43 g | 3 tablespoons | 45 mL |
| salt | 1/4 oz. | 8 g | 1 teaspoon | 5 mL |
| cayenne pepper | | | 1/4 teaspoon | 2 mL |
| avocado, Florida variety, peeled, diced | 1 lb., 10 1/2 oz. | 752 g | 2 large | |
| half and half | | 227 g | 1 cup | 240 mL |

**Garnish:**

cilantro, minced

① Mix chicken stock, lime juice, salt, cayenne, and avocado in large nonreactive bowl. Chill well.

② In batches, add avocado and the stock mixture to food processor fitted with knife blade. Purée until smooth. Repeat with remaining ingredients. Return to nonreactive bowl.

③ Add half and half. Stir well. Chill until service.

④ Serve, garnished with cilantro.

The Florida variety of avocado is larger than the Hass avocado; they are about double the size. Also, the texture and flavor vary between these varieties; however, Hass avocados will work fine to make this soup.

Cut avocado shortly before needed. Store tightly covered to prevent its turning brown.

This soup can be served as a hot soup. Just be careful not to boil the avocado since it can curdle.

© Yanik Chauvin

© cook_inspire

# SOPA DE FEIJÃO (BRAZIL)

## BRAZILIAN BEAN SOUP

Pearson Education/PH College

## TWIST ON THE CLASSIC

For a vegetarian entrée, add cooked black beans to the puréed soup and serve it over polenta.

**Note:** Use less salt if preparing soup with ham hock.

**Number of Servings:** 10
**Serving Size:** 8 oz. (227 g)
**Total Yield:** 5 lb., 2 oz. (2.3 kg)
**Food Balance:** Balanced
**Wine Style:** Wine friendly—Choose your favorite wine!
**Example:** Beringer Private Reserve Chardonnay or Cabernet Sauvignon

**Cooking Method:** Sauté, boil

| | WEIGHT | | VOLUME | |
|---|---|---|---|---|
| INGREDIENTS | U.S. | METRIC | U.S. | METRIC |
| dried black beans | 1 lb. | 454 g | 2 1/2 cups | 600 mL |
| ham hock, *optional* | | | 1 each | |
| olive oil | | 15 g | 1 tablespoon | 15 mL |
| onion, dice | 10 oz. | 284 g | 2 medium | |
| garlic, minced | 1/2 oz. | 15 g | 4 cloves | |
| *jalapeño* peppers, seeded and deribbed if desired, minced | 1 1/2 oz. | 43 g | 2 each | |
| ground cumin | | | 1 teaspoon | 5 mL |
| ground cloves | | | 1/2 teaspoon | 3 mL |
| salt | 3/4 oz. | 22 g | 1 tablespoon | 15 mL |

**Garnish:**

sour cream
lemon or lime slices

1. Wash beans thoroughly, cover with water, and soak overnight in a pot in refrigerator. If time is limited, place beans in boiling water. Turn off heat and soak for 2 or 3 hours.
2. If using ham hock, boil in water for 15 minutes, then drain and discard water.
3. Heat olive oil over medium heat. Add onions and sauté about 4 minutes. Add garlic and jalapeños, sauté another 2 or 3 minutes, until softened.
4. Add sautéed onions, garlic, peppers, cumin, cloves, and ham hock, if desired, to beans. Bring to boil, reduce heat and simmer until beans are soft, about 1 hour and 15 minutes.
5. Remove ham hock if used, cut meat from bone into bite-sized pieces. Refrigerate until needed.
6. Purée soup in food processor fitted with knife blade until smooth. If too thick, add liquid. Add salt, if needed, and ham pieces, if used. Correct seasonings.
7. Serve hot, topped with sour cream and lemon or lime slice, if desired.

# CHUPE DE CAMARONES (PERU)

## SHRIMP CHOWDER

## TWIST ON THE CLASSIC

Serve this hearty soup as an entrée by allowing the chowder to thicken and placing it over rice.

**Number of Servings:** 15
**Serving Size:** 8 oz. (227 g)
**Total Yield:** 7 lb., 10 oz. (3.5 kg)
**Food Balance:** Protein/spicy
**Wine Style:** Off-dry, low-oaked whites and soft reds
**Example:** Campanile Pinot Grigio, Beringer Founders' Estate Pinot Noir

**Cooking Method:** Boil, sauté

| INGREDIENTS | WEIGHT | | VOLUME | |
| --- | --- | --- | --- | --- |
| | **U.S.** | **METRIC** | **U.S.** | **METRIC** |
| shrimp, unpeeled | 1 lb., 8 oz. | 681 g | | |
| crayfish, unpeeled | 1 lb. | 454 g | | |
| water | | 454 g | 2 cups | 480 mL |
| bay leaves | | | 2 each | |
| olive oil | | 28 g | 2 tablespoons | 30 mL |
| onion, medium dice | 6 oz. | 170 g | 1 large | |
| garlic, minced | 1/2 oz. | 15 g | 4 cloves | |
| celery, medium dice | 4 1/2 oz. | 128 g | 1 cup | 240 mL |
| salt | | | 1/2 teaspoon | 3 mL |
| pepper | | | 1/2 teaspoon | 3 mL |
| ground cumin | | | 1/2 teaspoon | 3 mL |
| dried oregano | | | 1/2 teaspoon | 3 mL |
| crushed red pepper or cayenne (which will be hotter) | | | 1/2 teaspoon | 3 mL |
| tomato purée | 12 oz. | 340 g | one 12-oz. can | one 360-mL can |
| fish stock | | | 1 quart (4 cups) | 960 mL |
| rice | 4 3/4 oz. | 135 g | 1/2 cup | 120 mL |
| potatoes, white, waxy, or all-purpose, peeled and cut into 1/2-inch (1 1/3-cm) dice | 1 lb. | 454 g | 3 large | |
| corn kernels | 5 oz. | 142 g | 1 cup | 240 mL |
| whole milk | | 454 g | 2 cups | 480 mL |
| *queso fresco* or feta cheese | 8 oz. | 227 g | | |

**Garnish:**

fresh parsley, finely chopped

crayfish, *optional*

hot yellow pepper, roasted

1. Peel and devein shrimp, reserving shells. Rinse shrimp, slice on the diagonal into two or three pieces (depending on size of shrimp). Refrigerate until needed. If desired, reserve one crayfish to garnish each serving. Peel and chop remaining crayfish into pieces the size of the shrimp pieces. Reserve crayfish shells.

2. Boil shells with 2 cups (454 g or 480 mL) water and bay leaves for 10 minutes, strain broth and set aside.

3. Heat 1 tablespoon (15 g or 15 mL) of oil in large pot over medium heat. Sauté onions, garlic, and celery for 1 or 2 minutes. Add salt, pepper, cumin, oregano, and crushed pepper or cayenne, stirring until onions are wilted but not browned.

4. Add tomato purée, reserved stock, and fish stock. Bring to boil.

5. Add rice and potatoes. Lower heat and simmer. If using fresh corn, add when potatoes are halfway done. If using frozen corn, add when potatoes are almost tender.

6. When potatoes are cooked, add milk and grated or crumbled cheese. Cook over low heat but do not allow to boil.

7. Heat remaining 1 tablespoon (15 g or 15 mL) of oil in sauté pan over medium heat. Sauté shrimp and crayfish for 1 minute until they just turn opaque, then add to chowder. Correct seasonings.

8. To serve, sprinkle with parsley and garnish with whole crayfish and a piece of roasted pepper, if desired.

# CEBICHE DE HONGOS (PERU)

## MUSHROOM CEVICHE

**Number of Servings:** 8
**Serving Size:** 3 1/2 oz. (104 g)
**Total Yield:** 1 lb., 12 oz. (794 g)

| INGREDIENTS | WEIGHT U.S. | WEIGHT METRIC | VOLUME U.S. | VOLUME METRIC |
|---|---|---|---|---|
| mushrooms, washed and cut into quarters | 1 lb. | 454 g | | |
| olive oil | | 57 g | 1/4 cup | 60 mL |
| red onion, julienne | 6 oz. | 170 g | 1 large | |
| scallions, thin slices | 1 oz. | 28 g | 1/4 cup | 60 mL |
| fresh lemon juice | | 227 g | 1 cup | 240 mL |
| garlic, minced | 1/4 oz. | 8 g | 2 cloves | |
| hot red pepper, seeds and ribs removed if desired, finely chopped | 1/4 oz. | 8 g | 1 each | |
| salt | to taste | | | |
| pepper | to taste | | | |
| celery, small dice | 1 1/2 oz. | 43 g | 1/4 cup | 60 mL |
| dried oregano | | | 1 teaspoon | 5 mL |
| fresh cilantro, minced | 1/4 oz. | 8 g | 1 tablespoon | 15 mL |

**Garnish:**

fresh cilantro, minced
hot pepper, seeds and ribs removed,
    minced, *optional*
sweet potato, cooked and cut into 1-inch
    (2 1/2-cm) slices
corn on the cob, cooked and cut into 1- or
    1 1/2-inch (2 1/2- or 4-cm) pieces

1. Mix mushrooms and olive oil in bowl, set aside.
2. Soak onion and scallions in salted water, set aside.
3. Combine lemon juice, garlic, hot red pepper, salt, and pepper. Add mushrooms and marinate for 30 minutes at room temperature.
4. Add celery, oregano, drained onions, and cilantro to *ceviche* mixture. Toss well and marinate 30 minutes. Correct seasonings.
5. To serve, place *ceviche* on leaf of lettuce, sprinkle with more finely chopped cilantro and hot pepper, if desired. Garnish with pieces of sweet potato and corn on the cob.

### TWIST ON THE CLASSIC

Use this mushroom *ceviche* as an accompaniment to grilled beef. If desired, heat the *ceviche*.

# ENSALADA DE QUINUA CON FRIJOLES NEGROS Y CHOCLO (AREAS IN THE ANDES)

## QUINOA SALAD WITH BLACK BEANS AND CORN

**Note:** Quinoa thrives in the high altitudes of the Andes Mountains.

**Number of Servings:** 23
**Serving Size:** 4 oz. (114 g)
**Total Yield:** 5 lb., 12 oz. (2.6 kg)

**Cooking Method:** Boil

### TWIST ON THE CLASSIC

Heat this dish and serve it as a side dish.

|  | WEIGHT | | VOLUME | |
|---|---|---|---|---|
| INGREDIENTS | U.S. | METRIC | U.S. | METRIC |
| **Dressing:** | | | | |
| sherry vinegar | | 170 g | 3/4 cup | 180 mL |
| Dijon mustard | 1 1/2 oz. | 43 g | 3 tablespoons | 45 mL |
| salt | | | 1 1/2 teaspoons | 8 mL |
| pepper | | | 1 teaspoon | 5 mL |
| olive oil | | 340 g | 1 1/2 cups | 360 mL |
| **Salad:** | | | | |
| quinoa | 1 lb. | 454 g | 2 1/4 cups | 540 mL |
| water | | | 1 quart + 2 cups (6 cups) | 1.4 L |
| carrot, peeled and minced | 1 1/2 oz. | 43 g | 1 small | |
| celery, small dice | 1 1/4 oz. | 36 g | 1 stalk | |
| red onion, small dice | 3 oz. | 86 g | 1/2 small to medium | |
| red bell pepper, seeds and membranes removed, small dice | 3 oz. | 86 g | 1/2 each | |
| green bell pepper, seeds and membranes removed, small dice | 3 oz. | 86 g | 1/2 each | |
| black beans, cooked and drained | 15 oz. | 426 g | one 15-oz. can | one 450-mL can |
| corn, frozen or fresh, cooked | 5 oz. | 142 g | 1 cup | 240 mL |
| salt | | | 1/2 teaspoon | 3 mL |
| pepper | | | 1/2 teaspoon | 3 mL |
| fresh cilantro, minced | 1 1/4 oz. | 36 g | 1/2 cup | 120 mL |

**Garnish:**

tomato *concasse*, grape tomatoes, or cherry tomatoes cut in half

*Cooked quinoa*
Pearson Education/PH College

Courtesy of CanolaInfo.org

### DRESSING:

1. Place vinegar, mustard, salt, and pepper in bowl of food processor fitted with knife blade. Process to mix.
2. Slowly add oil through food tube. Process until dressing emulsifies (thickens). Set aside until needed, or refrigerate for longer storage.

### SALAD:

1. Rinse quinoa well with cold water until rinse water is clear. Place quinoa in pot, cover with 1 1/2 quarts (1.4 L) water. Bring to boil, reduce heat and simmer for 10 minutes, until grains look translucent. Drain. Allow to drain about an hour. If less time is available, place quinoa in pan over low heat. Cover and cook for about 5 minutes to dry.
2. Place quinoa in large bowl. Add carrot, celery, onion, bell peppers, black beans, corn, salt, pepper, and cilantro. Gently mix with rubber spatula to combine vegetables.
3. Add dressing. Mix gently with rubber spatula to combine thoroughly. Correct seasonings.
4. Serve, garnished with tomato. If desired, serve over a bed of lettuce.

# PABELLON CRIOLLO (VENEZUELA, COLUMBIA)

## BEEF IN TOMATO SAUCE WITH BLACK BEANS, RICE, AND PLANTAINS

**Number of Servings:** 12

**Serving Size:** 5 oz. (142 g) meat
4 1/2 oz. (128 g) beans

**Total Yield:** 3 lb., 12 oz. (1.7 kg) meat
3 lb., 6 oz. (1.5 kg) beans

**Food Balance:** Sweet/protein

**Wine Style:** Off-dry, low-oaked whites and soft reds

**Example:** Beringer Founders' Estate Chardonnay, Shiraz, or Merlot

**Cooking Method:** Boil, sauté, broil

### TWIST ON THE CLASSIC

Present this dish by molding it in a PVC pipe or molding ring. Begin with the rice, top that with black beans, and repeat both layers. Unmold from the pipe or ring and arrange the meat on top of the stack. Decorate with plantains.

| | WEIGHT | | VOLUME | |
|---|---|---|---|---|
| **INGREDIENTS** | **U.S.** | **METRIC** | **U.S.** | **METRIC** |
| **Black Beans:** | | | | |
| dried black beans | 1 lb., 4 oz. | 568 g | 3 cups | 720 mL |
| olive oil | | 43 g | 3 tablespoons | 45 mL |
| onions, fine dice | 3 oz. | 86 g | 1 small, or 1/4 cup | 60 mL |
| green bell pepper, fine dice | 7 oz. | 199 g | 1 1/2 cups | 360 mL |
| garlic, minced or pulverized | 1/2 oz. | 15 g | 4 cloves, or 2 teaspoons | 10 mL |
| salt | 1/2 oz. | 15 g | 2 teaspoons | 10 mL |
| fresh cilantro | | | 6 sprigs | |
| **Meat:** | | | | |
| olive oil | | 114 g | 1/2 cup | 120 mL |
| onions, coarsely chopped | 10 oz. | 284 g | 2 cups | 480 mL |
| garlic, minced or pulverized | 1/2 oz. | 15 g | 4 cloves, or 2 teaspoons | 10 mL |
| canned plum tomatoes, drained and chopped | 1 lb., 14 oz. | 851 g | 4 cups | 960 mL |
| ground cumin | 1/4 oz. | 8 g | 2 teaspoons | 10 mL |
| salt | 1/2 oz. | 15 g | 2 teaspoons | 10 mL |
| sirloin of beef, lean top or boneless steak, 1/2 inch (1 1/3 cm) thick | 4 lb. | 1.8 kg | | |
| **Rice:** | | | | |
| olive oil | | 57 g | 1/4 cup | 60 mL |
| whole onion, peeled | 6 oz. | 170 g | 1 large | |
| green bell pepper, cut into quarters, seeds and ribs removed | 8 oz. | 227 g | 1 large | |
| long-grain rice | 1 lb., 10 oz. | 738 g | 4 cups | 960 mL |
| water, boiling | | | 2 quarts (8 cups) | 1.9 L |
| salt | 1 oz. | 28 g | 1 tablespoon + 1 teaspoon | 20 mL |
| **Plantains:** | | | | |
| ripe plantains, peeled | | | 4 large | |
| vegetable oil | | 78 g | 1/3 cup | 80 mL |

## BLACK BEANS:

1. Rinse black beans well. Cover with water and soak overnight or put into a pot of boiling water, turn off heat, and let soak several hours.
2. Bring pot of beans to boil over high heat, reduce heat to low, and simmer, uncovered, for 2 hours until almost tender.
3. In skillet, heat 3 tablespoons (43 g or 45 mL) oil over moderate heat. Add onions, bell pepper, garlic, and salt. Cook for 3 minutes, stirring constantly, then add to beans. Add cilantro and cook for 15 minutes, or until beans are tender. Discard cilantro. Cover and set aside. Refrigerate for longer storage.

## MEAT:

1. In skillet, heat 1/2 cup (114 g or 120 mL) oil over moderate heat. Add onions and garlic, cook about 5 minutes, stirring occasionally until onions are soft and transparent but not brown. Add tomatoes, cumin, and salt. Reduce heat to low and cook, uncovered, for 30 minutes, stirring frequently, until tomato juices evaporate and sauce becomes a thick purée.
2. Meanwhile, grill or broil steak 4 inches (10 cm) above or below heat source for about 5 minutes on each side, until medium rare or desired temperature. Cut meat into strips 1/4 inch (1/2 cm) wide and 1 1/2 inches (4 cm) long.
3. Add strips of beef to tomato mixture, mix well, cover skillet, and put it aside until needed.

## RICE:

1. Preheat oven to 250 degrees (120°C).
2. In heavy pan, heat 1/4 cup (57 g or 60 mL) oil over moderate heat until hot. Add onion and bell pepper, sauté for 5 minutes, stirring frequently. Add rice and stir constantly for 2 or 3 minutes to coat rice with oil.
3. Pour boiling water over rice, add salt, and bring to boil. Stir once or twice, cover pan, reduce heat to low. Simmer undisturbed for 20 minutes, until rice is tender and has absorbed all liquid.
4. Discard onion and pepper. Keep rice warm in oven.

## PLANTAINS:

1. Cut plantains crosswise in half and lengthwise into six or eight slices.
2. Heat 1/3 cup (78 g or 80 mL) oil in skillet over moderate heat. Sauté plantain pieces for 2 or 3 minutes on each side until tender and golden brown.

## ASSEMBLY:

1. Return beans and beef to low heat and cook to heat them thoroughly.
2. Spoon beef into center of heated platter or plate. Surround with alternating mounds of rice and black beans. Decorate with plantain slices and serve.

*Sautéing mushrooms*

Richard Embery © Pearson Education/PH College

# COSTILLITAS DE CORDERO AL HORNO (ARGENTINA)

## BAKED LAMB CHOPS

**Note:** This amount of mushroom accompaniment yields about 3 1/4 oz. (92 g) per serving. If less is desired, use this amount for more chops. Also, this recipe is portioned for two chops per serving. Depending on the size of the chops, the serving size could be three chops.

**Number of Servings:** 8
**Serving Size:** 2 lamb chops with mushroom accompaniment, about 9 to 10 oz. (256 to 284 g)
**Total Yield:** 5 lb., 3 oz. (2.4 kg), including 1 lb., 11 1/4 oz. (773 g) mushroom mixture
**Food Balance:** Balanced
**Wine Style:** Wine friendly—Choose your favorite wine!
**Example:** Penfolds Riesling, Chardonnay, or Shiraz

**Cooking Method:** Sauté, bake

| | WEIGHT | | VOLUME | |
|---|---|---|---|---|
| **INGREDIENTS** | **U.S.** | **METRIC** | **U.S.** | **METRIC** |
| olive oil | | 43 g | 3 tablespoons | 45 mL |
| onion, minced | 4 oz. | 114 g | 1 small, about 3/4 cup | 180 mL |
| garlic, smashed and minced | 1 oz. | 28 g | 8 cloves | |
| mushrooms, finely chopped | 2 lb. | 908 g | | |
| bay leaf | | | 1 each | |
| fresh rosemary leaves, minced | 1/2 oz. | 15 g | 3 tablespoons | 45 mL |
| tomato paste | 1 3/4 oz. | 50 g | 3 tablespoons | 45 mL |
| salt | 1/4 oz. | 8 g | 1 teaspoon | 5 mL |
| pepper | | | 1 teaspoon | 5 mL |
| white wine | | 454 g | 2 cups | 480 mL |
| fresh parsley, minced | 1/2 oz. | 15 g | 1/4 cup | 60 mL |
| bread crumbs | 1/2 oz. | 15 g | 3 tablespoons | 45 mL |
| lamb loin chops, trimmed to thickness of choice | 3 lb., 9 1/4 oz. | 1.6 kg | 16 each | |

**Garnish:**

| | | |
|---|---|---|
| fresh rosemary | | 8 small sprigs |

1. Heat 2 tablespoons (28 g or 30 mL) of olive oil over medium heat. Add onion, sauté for a couple of minutes.
2. Add garlic and sauté, stirring constantly, for another 30 seconds. Add mushrooms and bay leaf, cook about 3 minutes, until mushrooms release liquid.
3. Add rosemary, tomato paste, salt, pepper, and 1 cup (227 g or 240 mL) of white wine. Cook until most of liquid evaporates, about 5 minutes. Remove from heat, stir in parsley and bread crumbs. Remove bay leaf and discard. Cover and refrigerate mushroom mixture until needed. *This can be prepared the day before using.*
4. Place oven rack in center of oven. Preheat oven to 375 degrees (190°C). Heat remaining 1 tablespoon (15 g or 15 mL) oil in skillet over medium-high heat. Quickly sear lamb chops until golden on outside. Turn over and sear other side. Remove from skillet.
5. Reduce heat to medium-low, add remaining 1 cup (227 g or 240 mL) white wine to skillet. Deglaze by scraping any bits from bottom of skillet and reducing wine by about half. Remove from heat.
6. Place mushroom mixture in bottom of ovenproof dish. Top with seared lamb chops, and pour wine from deglazed pan over chops.
7. Cover and bake for 20 to 35 minutes, until proper internal temperature. Cooking time will depend on the thickness of the chops and whether the mushroom mixture is cold (prepared earlier and refrigerated). If desired, uncover chops for last 10 minutes to dry outside of chops.
8. Serve on a bed of mushroom mixture and garnished with a dollop of the mushroom mixture and a sprig of fresh rosemary.

# SECO DE CHANCO (ECUADOR)

## PORK STEW

**Note:** Since the seeds and ribs contain most of the "heat," removing the seeds and ribs from the *serrano* peppers creates a milder dish.

**Number of Servings:** 11

**Serving Size:** 7 oz. (199 g)

**Total Yield:** 5 lb., 1 1/2 oz. (2.3 kg)

**Food Balance:** Balanced

**Wine Style:** Wine friendly—Choose your favorite wine!

**Example:** St. Clement Sauvignon Blanc or Merlot

**Cooking Method:** Braise

Eising © Getty Images

**TWIST ON THE CLASSIC**

Cut the meat into smaller pieces and then wrap the cooked meat and peppers in a tortilla.

| | WEIGHT | | VOLUME | |
|---|---|---|---|---|
| INGREDIENTS | U.S. | METRIC | U.S. | METRIC |
| olive oil | | 57 g | 1/4 cup | 60 mL or as needed |
| boneless pork shoulder, trimmed and cut into 1 1/2- to 2-inch (4- to 5-cm) cubes | 4 lb., 12 1/2 oz. | 2.2 kg | | |
| onion, small dice | 1 lb. | 454 g | 2 large | |
| garlic, smashed and minced | 1/2 oz. | 15 g | 4 cloves | |
| *serrano* chili, seeds and ribs removed if desired, minced | 1/2 oz. | 15 g | 2 each | |
| tomatoes, dice | 1 lb., 2 oz. | 511 g | | |
| salt | 1/2 oz. | 15 g | 2 teaspoons | 10 mL |
| ground cumin | 1/4 oz. | 8 g | 2 teaspoons | 10 mL |
| dried oregano | | | 2 teaspoons | 10 mL |
| fresh cilantro, minced | 1 oz. | 28 g | 1/4 cup + 2 tablespoons | 90 mL |
| beer | | 680 g | two 12-oz. bottles | two 360-mL bottles |
| red bell pepper, seeds and ribs removed, large dice | 14 1/2 oz. | 411 g | 1 large | |

**Accompaniment:**

cooked rice

1. Heat 2 tablespoons (28 g or 30 mL) of oil in large pan over medium heat. Add pork and sauté until brown (seared) on all sides. Remove pork from pan. Set aside until needed; refrigerate for longer storage.
2. If fat remains in pan, discard all except 2 tablespoons (28 g or 30 mL). Add oil, if needed, to cover bottom of pan. Heat until hot.
3. Add onion, cook for several minutes until softened. Add garlic and cook another minute.
4. Add *serrano* chilies, tomatoes, salt, cumin, oregano, and cilantro. Stir well. Bring to boil, reduce heat and cook about 5 minutes.
5. Add pork and beer. Stir to mix. Heat until boiling, reduce heat, cover and simmer for approximately 1 hour and 15 minutes to 1 hour and 30 minutes until meat is tender.
6. Stir in bell pepper. Return to boil, reduce heat and simmer for 15 minutes. Cover pan if sauce is desired thickness. Cook uncovered if sauce is too thin. Correct seasonings. Serve, accompanied by rice.

## ARROZ CON PATO (PERU)
### BRAISED DUCK WITH CILANTRO RICE

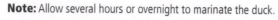

**Note:** Allow several hours or overnight to marinate the duck.

**Note:** This recipe includes a large amount of rice to accompany the duck. As in much of South America, dishes in Peru contain large quantities of grains and/or vegetables with smaller portions of meat or seafood.

**Number of Servings:** 12  
**Serving Size:** 1/4 duck or 2 pieces  
**Food Balance:** Balanced  
**Wine Style:** Wine friendly—Pick a winner  
**Example:** Stags' Leap Chardonnay or Petite Syrah  

**Cooking Method:** Braise

### TWIST ON THE CLASSIC

Since most North Americans are unfamiliar with braised duck, vary this dish by roasting the duck and serving it over the cilantro rice. Another alternative is to serve slices of duck breast fanned on a mound of the cilantro rice.

| INGREDIENTS | WEIGHT U.S. | WEIGHT METRIC | VOLUME U.S. | VOLUME METRIC |
|---|---|---|---|---|
| ducks | 12 to 15 lb. | 5.4 to 6.8 kg | 3 each | |
| fresh lemon juice | | 114 g | 1/2 cup | 120 mL |
| ground cumin | | | 1 1/2 teaspoons | 8 mL |
| salt | 3/4 oz. | 22 g | 1 tablespoon | 15 mL |
| pepper | 1/4 oz. | 8 g | 1 1/2 teaspoons | 8 mL |
| light beer | | | four 12-oz. bottles | four 360-mL bottles |
| dark beer (Guinness or Bock) | | 454 g | 2 cups | 480 mL |
| long-grain rice | 2 lb., 7 oz. | 1.1 kg | 6 cups | 1.4 L |
| fresh cilantro, minced | 4 1/2 oz. | 128 g | 1 1/2 cups | 360 mL |
| green peas, fresh or frozen | 1 lb. | 454 g | 3 cups | 720 mL |

© Christian Vinces

1. Wash ducks thoroughly. Cut each duck into eight serving pieces, trim all visible fat. (This allows serving 2 pieces, or 1/4 duck. If serving the 1/4 duck as one piece, cut duck into quarters.)

2. Mix lemon juice, cumin, 1 1/2 teaspoons (11 g or 8 mL) of salt, and 3/4 teaspoon (4 g or 4 mL) of pepper in stainless-steel or other nonreactive bowl. Add duck pieces, turn to coat, marinate in refrigerator for at least several hours or overnight.

3. In heavy pan, sear duck on all sides until browned. Render as much fat from ducks as possible, drain.

4. Add both beers to duck in pan, bring to boil over high heat. Deglaze pan by scraping drippings from bottom and sides of pan. Reduce heat to low, cover and cook for 45 minutes, or until leg is tender when pierced with knife. Transfer duck to heated plate or low oven, cover to keep warm.

5. Strain cooking liquid, saving 2 quarts + 2 1/2 cups, or 10 1/2 cups (2.5 L). If there is not enough, add water.

6. Bring cooking liquid to boil over high heat, stir in rice and return to boil. Reduce heat to low, cover pan, and simmer undisturbed for 20 minutes, or until the rice has absorbed all liquid. Stir in cilantro, peas, remaining 1 1/2 teaspoons (11 g or 8 mL) salt, and remaining 3/4 teaspoon (4 g or 4 mL) pepper. Correct seasonings.

7. Place duck pieces on rice in pan, cover and return to low heat for a few minutes to thoroughly heat the duck. To serve, mound rice and peas, top with duck pieces.

# VATAPA (BRAZIL)

## FISH STEW

**Number of Servings:** 8
**Serving Size:** 7 oz. (199 g)
**Total Yield:** 3 lb., 10 oz. (1.6 kg)
**Food Balance:** Sweet/spicy/protein
**Wine Style:** Off-dry, low-oaked whites and soft reds
**Example:** Beringer, Château St. Jean, or Penfolds Riesling

**Cooking Method:** Braise

Vinicius Tupinamba © Shutterstock

### TWIST ON THE CLASSIC

To serve like *bouillabaisse*, prepare this dish with a wide variety of seafood and fish.

| | WEIGHT | | VOLUME | |
|---|---|---|---|---|
| **INGREDIENTS** | **U.S.** | **METRIC** | **U.S.** | **METRIC** |
| unsalted peanuts | 3 1/4 oz. | 92 g | 1/2 cup | 120 mL |
| unsweetened coconut | 9 oz. | 256 g | 3 cups | 720 mL |
| milk | | 340 g | 1 1/2 cups | 360 mL |
| water | | 794 g | 3 1/2 cups | 840 mL |
| olive oil | | 57 g | 1/4 cup | 60 mL |
| fish, any white, firm fleshed variety | 2 lb., 8 oz. | 1.1 kg | | |
| shrimp, peeled and deveined | 1 lb. | 454 g | | |
| onion, small dice | 7 oz. | 199 g | 1 large | |
| garlic, smashed and minced | 1/4 oz. | 8 g | 2 cloves | |
| plum tomatoes, canned, chopped | 8 oz. | 227 g | 1 cup | 240 mL |
| ginger, peeled and minced | 1/4 oz. | 8 g | 1 tablespoon | 15 mL |
| hot chili pepper, finely chopped | 1/4 oz. | 8 g | 1 each | |
| fresh cilantro, finely chopped | 1/4 oz. | 8 g | 1 tablespoon | 15 mL |
| salt | 1/2 oz. | 15 g | 2 teaspoons | 10 mL |
| cornmeal | 2 oz. | 57 g | 1/4 cup + 2 tablespoons | 90 mL |

**Accompaniment:**

cooked rice

1. Grind peanuts in coffee grinder or food processor fitted with knife blade by pulsing. Cut fish across grain into pieces about 2 inches (5 cm) wide.

2. Place coconut, milk, and 1 1/2 cups (355 g or 360 mL) of water into saucepan and simmer for 30 minutes. Strain and reserve liquid. Discard coconut.

3. Heat oil in skillet or braising pan over medium heat. Sauté fish and shrimp lightly, do not overcook. Remove fish and seafood to plate, and refrigerate until needed.

4. Sauté onions in same skillet until soft. Add garlic and sauté another minute. Add tomatoes, ginger, chili pepper, cilantro, salt, and remaining 2 cups (439 g or 480 mL) water. Bring to boil, cover skillet and simmer 15 minutes. Strain, pushing on vegetables to remove all juices. Reserve broth, and discard vegetables.

5. Meanwhile simmer coconut milk mixture, peanuts, and cornmeal in skillet for about 10 minutes, until thickened. Stir often to prevent lumping.

6. Return strained broth to skillet. Whisk cornmeal mixture into broth. Heat thoroughly and add seafood. Cook until heated through. Correct seasonings. Serve over rice.

# POROTOS GRANADOS (CHILE)

## BEAN, SQUASH, AND CORN STEW

**Number of Servings:** 12  
**Serving Size:** 10 oz. (284 g)  
**Total Yield:** 8 lb., 1/2 oz. (3.6 kg)

**Cooking Method:** Braise

© gourmet-vision/image BROKER

| INGREDIENTS | WEIGHT | | VOLUME | |
|---|---|---|---|---|
| | U.S. | METRIC | U.S. | METRIC |
| oil | | 28 g | 2 tablespoons | 30 mL |
| onion, small dice | 15 1/2 oz. | 439 g | 2 large | |
| green pepper, seeds and membranes removed, small dice | 6 oz. | 170 g | 2 small | |
| garlic, peeled, minced | 1 oz. | 28 g | 6 cloves | |
| cumin | 1/4 oz. | 8 g | 2 teaspoons | 10 mL |
| paprika | 1/2 oz. | 15 g | 2 tablespoons | 30 mL |
| tomato, peeled, diced, fresh or canned | 1 lb., 1/2 oz. | 469 g | 2 cups | 480 mL |
| salt | 1/2 oz. | 15 g | 2 teaspoons | 10 mL |
| pepper | | | 1 teaspoon | 5 mL |
| pumpkin or winter squash (like butternut), peeled, seeds removed, cut into 1-inch (2 1/2-cm) dice | 2 lb. | 908 g | 2 to 4 cups | 480 to 960 mL |
| chicken stock or water | | | as needed | as needed |
| cranberry beans, lima beans, or beans of choice, cooked | 1 lb., 12 oz. | 794 g | 4 cups | 960 mL |
| corn kernels, fresh or frozen | 1 lb., 4 1/2 oz. | 582 g | 4 cups | 960 mL |

**Garnish:**

basil, chiffonade

hot pepper, minced, *optional*

1. Heat oil over medium heat in large skillet or pan. Add onion, sauté 4 or 5 minutes, until softened.
2. Add green pepper, garlic, cumin, and paprika. Stir and sauté another 2 minutes, until fragrant.
3. Add tomatoes, salt, pepper, pumpkin, and stock to barely cover the contents. Throughout the cooking, add more stock if needed. Cover and simmer for 30 to 40 minutes, until squash is almost tender.
4. Add beans, cook another 20 minutes. Add corn, cook about 10 minutes, until done. Correct seasonings.
5. Serve, garnished with basil and hot pepper, if desired.

## TWIST ON THE CLASSIC

- During the final part of cooking the *Porotos Granados*, top it with dumpling dough.
- Make wells (an indent) on top of the *Porotos Granados*, place a raw egg in each indent to poach the egg. Serve a portion of the *Porotos Granados* with the poached egg on top.

Traditionally, they prepare this recipe with fresh cranberry beans; however, they might be difficult to obtain in many locations. Replace with fresh lima beans or small fava beans or use canned beans. If using canned beans, try black-eyed peas, cannellini beans, or the variety of choice. Typically, they cook the pumpkin or winter squash long enough to begin to break down, so it thickens the stew.

*Porotos Granados* hails from the time before the Europeans came and the indigenous people prepared dishes with the native foods that thrived. In Chile, grilled sausages and a simple salad often accompany this popular vegetarian dish.

# LOCRO (MANY SOUTH AMERICAN COUNTRIES)

## SQUASH STEW

**Note:** This dish varies from country to country. Some omit the cheese and half-and-half; others add a piece of fish; some recipes include other vegetables. Rice usually accompanies *locro*, which functions as an entrée or side dish.

**Number of Servings:** 9
**Serving Size:** 4 oz. (114 g) side dish
**Total Yield:** 2 lb., 5 oz. (1.1 kg)
**Food Balance:** Sweet/protein
**Wine Style:** Off-dry, low-oaked whites and soft reds
**Example:** Souverain Sauvignon Blanc or Merlot

**Cooking Method:** Sauté, braise

| INGREDIENTS | WEIGHT | | VOLUME | |
| --- | --- | --- | --- | --- |
| | U.S. | METRIC | U.S. | METRIC |
| olive oil | | 28 g | 2 tablespoons | 30 mL |
| onion, small dice | 6 oz. | 170 g | 1 large | |
| garlic, minced | | | 1 clove | |
| dried oregano | | | 1/2 teaspoon | 3 mL |
| ground turmeric | | | 1 teaspoon | 5 mL |
| ground cumin | | | 1/2 teaspoon | 3 mL |
| ground cayenne | | | 1/4 teaspoon | 2 mL |
| pepper | | | 1/4 teaspoon | 2 mL |
| butternut squash, peeled, seeded, and cut into 1-inch (2 1/2-cm) cubes | 1 lb., 9 1/2 oz. | 724 g | 1 each, or 4 cups | 960 mL |
| chicken stock | | 114 g | 1/2 cup | 120 mL |
| corn, fresh or frozen | 5 oz. | 142 g | 1 cup | 240 mL |
| half-and-half | | 114 g | 1/2 cup | 120 mL |
| *queso fresco* or feta | 3 oz. | 86 g | 1/2 cup | 120 mL |

**Garnish:**

fresh parsley, minced

**TWIST ON THE CLASSIC**

Substitute beans for the squash to create a South American version of succotash.

1. Heat oil in pan over medium heat, add onion, sauté for 2 or 3 minutes. Add garlic, oregano, turmeric, cumin, cayenne, and pepper, sauté 1 minute.

2. Add squash and stock, simmer for 10 minutes if using fresh corn, 20 minutes if using frozen corn. Add water, as needed, to keep squash from burning.

3. Add corn, cook another 15 minutes for fresh corn, 5 minutes for frozen corn. (The squash should cook a total of 25 minutes.)

4. Add half-and-half and cheese, stir gently, remove from heat. Correct seasonings. Serve immediately, garnished with parsley.

# PAPAS A LA HUANCAINA (PERU)
## POTATOES WITH CHEESE AND CHILI SAUCE

**Number of Servings:** 8
**Serving Size:** 1 potato

**Cooking Method:** Boil

© Ildi

| INGREDIENTS | WEIGHT U.S. | WEIGHT METRIC | VOLUME U.S. | VOLUME METRIC |
|---|---|---|---|---|
| fresh lemon juice | | 57 g | 1/4 cup | 60 mL |
| dried hot pepper, seeds removed, crumbled | 1/8 to 1/4 oz. | 4 to 8 g | 1 1/2 teaspoons | 8 mL |
| salt | | | 1/2 teaspoon | 3 mL |
| black pepper | | | few grindings | |
| onion, thin slices, separated into rings | 6 oz. | 170 g | 1 large | |
| potatoes, white, waxy, or all-purpose, peeled | 2 lb., 3 oz. | 994 g | 8 medium | |
| fresh *queso blanco*, mozzarella, or Muenster cheese, grated | 3 oz. | 86 g | 1 cup | 240 mL |
| heavy cream | | 156 g | 2/3 cup | 160 mL |
| ground turmeric | 1/4 oz. | 8 g | 1 teaspoon | 5 mL |
| fresh red or green hot chili, seeded and minced | 1/4 oz. | 8 g | 1 each | |
| olive oil | | 78 g | 1/3 cup | 80 mL |
| **Garnish:** | | | | |
| fresh red or green hot chili, seeded and cut lengthwise into 1/2-inch (1 1/3-cm) strips | | | 1 each | |
| eggs, hard-cooked and cut lengthwise into halves | | | 4 each | |
| black olives | | | 8 each | |

1. Combine lemon juice, dried hot pepper, 1/2 teaspoon (3 mL) salt, and black pepper in large bowl. Add onion rings, turning to coat evenly. Cover the bowl and set aside to marinate at room temperature.
2. Boil potatoes in pot of water until tender but not falling apart.
3. Combine cheese, cream, turmeric, more black pepper, and chili pepper in food processor fitted with knife blade. Process for 30 seconds, until smooth and creamy.
4. Heat olive oil in heavy skillet over moderate heat. Add cheese mixture, reduce heat to low, and cook, stirring constantly for 5 to 8 minutes, until sauce thickens. Correct seasonings.
5. To assemble, arrange potatoes on heated platter or plate and pour sauce over them. Drain onion rings and place over the potatoes. Garnish with chili strips, eggs, and black olives.

## COUVE A MINEIRA (BRAZIL)

### GREENS

**Note:** This recipe works with almost any green vegetable.

**Number of Servings:** 9

**Cooking Method:** Sauté

**Serving Size:** 4 oz. (114 g)

**Total Yield:** 2 lb., 4 oz. (1 kg)

Eising © Getty Images, Inc.–Jupiterimages

| INGREDIENTS | WEIGHT U.S. | WEIGHT METRIC | VOLUME U.S. | VOLUME METRIC |
|---|---|---|---|---|
| olive oil | | 43 g | 3 tablespoons | 45 mL |
| onion, minced | 1 lb. | 454 g | 3 medium | |
| garlic, minced | 3/4 oz. | 22 g | 6 cloves | |
| fresh kale, stems removed, washed and cut into thin slices | 1 lb., 14 oz. | 851 g | | |
| salt | 1/4 oz. | 8 g | 1 teaspoon | 5 mL |
| pepper | | | 1 teaspoon | 5 mL |
| ground coriander | | | 3/4 teaspoon | 4 mL |
| ground mace | | | 1/8 teaspoon | 1 mL |

1. Heat oil in large pan over medium heat. Add onion, sauté about 3 minutes, until soft.
2. Add garlic, sauté another 1 or 2 minutes.
3. Add kale, salt, pepper, coriander, and mace, cook about 8 to 10 minutes until done. Add a few drops of water if necessary to prevent burning.
4. Correct seasonings. Serve.

### TWIST ON THE CLASSIC

Use any desired greens or a combination of greens in this dish. Also, add pieces of ham or prosciutto for flavoring.

## AREPA (COLOMBIA)

### CORN CAKES

**Number:** 16 *arepa*

**Cooking Method:** Sauté

**Scaling:** 2 oz. (57 g) for 1 each 3- to 4-inch (8- to 10-cm) cake

**Total Yield:** 2 lb., 1 3/4 oz. (958 g)

### TWIST ON THE CLASSIC

Make an arepa about 6 inches (15 cm) in diameter and top it with any filling. Then fold two sides together to hold the filling while eating. Try filling with thick chili, pulled pork, or thick *Porotos Granados*.

| INGREDIENTS | WEIGHT U.S. | WEIGHT METRIC | VOLUME U.S. | VOLUME METRIC |
|---|---|---|---|---|
| *arepa* flour | 12 oz. | 340 g | 2 cups | 480 mL |
| salt | 1/4 oz. | 8 g | 1 teaspoon | 5 mL |
| water, hot | | 454 to 680 g | 2 to 3 cups | 480 to 720 mL |
| oil, butter or pan spray, for frying | | | | |

1. Combine flour and salt in large bowl. Mixing with wooden spoon, add water slowly. Add 2 cups (454 g or 480 mL) water, mix well and add more water, as needed to form a soft dough.
2. Cover with film wrap, let rest for 10 minutes. Knead for about 3 minutes, until soft dough. If dough is too dry, wet hands and continue kneading.
3. Lightly coat bottom of griddle or large skillet with oil, butter, or pan spray. Heat over medium heat until hot.

In Colombia, they pat *arepa* dough to 1/4 inch (1/2 cm). In Venezuela, they make the *arepa* dough 3/4-inch (2-cm) thick.

*Arepa* flour is precooked corn flour that is dehydrated. Often, it is called *masarepa*. Purchase it at a supermarket in many areas or in a Latin market or grocery.

A very popular food, *arepas* are served for breakfast, lunch, snack, or anytime. Often, they serve them with butter or cream cheese at breakfast. *Arepas* also function as a sandwich with cheese or any type of filling. Some split the *arepas* and place the filling in the middle like a sandwich. Others place the filling on top. In Venezuela where they prepare thicker *arepas*, they are often split and filled.

Arepa *with white corn flour*
© rafer 76

Arepa *with yellow corn flour*
© Ildi Papp

④ Form 2 oz. (57 g) dough (about the size of a large golf ball) into ball. Press into a disk about 3- to 4-inches (8- to 10-cm) in diameter and 1/4-inch (0.5-cm) thick. To form, press between slightly wet palms of your hands or between film wrap. If edges of disk crack, the dough is too dry, so wet your hands and smooth the edges to eliminate cracks. Place disk in hot pan.

⑤ Allow to cook about 5 minutes, turn with spatula to cook other side. After another 5 minutes, turn to brown (but not burn) both sides. If it becomes too brown, lower heat. It should have some brown spots on it (somewhat like an English muffin). The *arepa* cooks about 15 minutes.

⑥ Repeat with remaining dough. Cooked *arepas* do not stay well. Instead, cook what is needed, tightly cover and refrigerate remaining dough until needed.

# FLAN

## CARAMEL CUSTARD

**TWIST ON THE CLASSIC**

Prepare the flan in individual molds.
Also, consider adding flavorings and/or fresh fruit to the flan. For example, add
• some amaretto for flavoring
• espresso to create a coffee flan
• pieces of peeled, fresh peach
• raspberries

**Number of Servings:** 6 to 8
**Total Yield:** One 7- to 8-inch (18- to 20-cm) round

**Cooking Method:** Boil, bake

| | WEIGHT | | VOLUME | |
|---|---|---|---|---|
| **INGREDIENTS** | **U.S.** | **METRIC** | **U.S.** | **METRIC** |
| sugar | 2 oz. | 57 g | 1/4 cup | 60 mL |
| water | | 241 g | 1 cup + 1 tablespoon | 255 mL |
| eggs | 6 3/4 oz. | 191 g | 4 each | |
| sweetened condensed milk | | | one 14-oz. can | one 420-mL can |
| vanilla | | | 1 teaspoon | 5 mL |

**Garnish:**
fresh fruit

Martin Brigdale © Dorling Kindersley

© joanna wnuk

1. Preheat oven to 350 degrees (180°C). Prepare pan for *bain-marie*, or hot water bath (a pan large enough to place soufflé dish in—you will add hot water to come halfway up sides of soufflé dish).

2. Place sugar and 1 tablespoon (15 g or 15 mL) of water in small, heavy saucepan, mix just to moisten sugar. Cook over medium-high heat, brush any sugar crystals from side of pan with pastry brush dipped in cold water. Do not stir.

3. Cook until light golden brown in color. Immediately pour into 1-quart (960-mL) soufflé pan, and tilt pan to cover bottom and sides evenly with caramelized sugar.

4. Beat eggs in bowl until frothy. Combine condensed milk, remaining 1 cup (227 g or 240 mL) water, and vanilla in separate bowl. Pour into eggs and mix.

5. Pour mixture into prepared pan. Bake in *bain-marie* for about 1 hour, until knife inserted in center of custard comes out clean. Cool, then refrigerate for several hours or overnight.

6. Unmold onto serving platter. Firm custard will be surrounded by thin caramel from caramelized sugar in pan.

7. To serve, slice like a pie. Spoon some caramel sauce over each piece. Garnish with fresh fruit.

## ALFAJORES (ARGENTINA)

### SANDWICH COOKIES

**Note:** In countless variations, these cookies are prepared throughout South America. When first made, the cookies are crisp. The next day, the cookie softens from the moist filling. Many prefer the softened cookies.

**Serving Size:** 2-inch (5-cm) cookie (3/4 oz. or 22 g dough)  **Cooking Method:** Bake
**Total Yield:** 1 lb., 13 oz. (823 g) raw dough; 19 sandwich cookies

| | WEIGHT | | VOLUME | |
|---|---|---|---|---|
| **INGREDIENTS** | **U.S.** | **METRIC** | **U.S.** | **METRIC** |
| all-purpose flour | 9 3/4 oz. | 276 g | 2 cups | 480 mL |
| cornstarch | 4 1/2 oz. | 128 g | 1 cup | 240 mL |
| baking powder | | | 3/4 teaspoon | 4 mL |
| salt | | | 1/4 teaspoon | 2 mL |
| unsalted butter | 8 oz. | 227 g | 1 cup (2 sticks) | 240 mL |
| sugar | 4 oz. | 114 g | 1/2 cup | 120 mL |
| egg | 1 3/4 oz. | 50 g | 1 each | |
| egg yolk | 3/4 oz. | 22 g | 1 each | |
| vanilla | | | 1 teaspoon | 5 mL |
| brandy | | 15 g | 1 tablespoon | 15 mL |
| *dulce de leche* | at least 12 oz. | 340 g | | |
| coconut, for dipping | as needed | | | |

### TWIST ON THE CLASSIC

For a different taste and visual presentation, dip the *dulce de leche*–filled cookie in chocolate and then coat half of the cookie in coconut.

Very popular throughout South America and all of Latin America, *dulce de leche* is actually caramelized milk. Buy it in cans from the supermarket or Latin stores, or make it from scratch. Making *dulce de leche* requires cooking and stirring the milk for about two hours. Some call it *manjar blanco*.

In-Finity © Shutterstock

1. Sift flour, cornstarch, baking powder, and salt into bowl. Set aside until needed.

2. Cream butter and sugar in bowl until light and fluffy. Add egg, mix well. Add egg yolk, mix until thoroughly incorporated. Add vanilla and brandy, mix until light.

3. Add reserved dry ingredients to butter mixture. Mix just to combine. Divide dough in half. Wrap each half in plastic wrap. Chill at least 30 minutes or as long as overnight.

4. Position oven rack in center of oven. Preheat oven to 350 degrees (180°C). Place sheet of parchment paper on sheet pan or half sheet pan.

5. Place chilled dough on lightly floured work surface. Roll out to 1/4 inch (1/2 cm) thick. Cut into 2-inch (5-cm) rounds. Place rounds on prepared sheet pan. Bake for 10 to 15 minutes, until beginning to brown on edges.

6. Transfer to cooling racks and cool completely.

7. Spread about 2 teaspoons (15 g) *dulce de leche* on bottom side of half of the cookies. Top with remaining cookies so the top sides face out. (The two bottoms of the cookies face each other with the filling in between them.) *Dulce de leche* filling should ooze out of sides a bit so coconut can stick to it.

8. Roll edges of cookies in coconut. Store in tightly covered container.

# Caribbean Islands

## >> LEARNING OBJECTIVES

By the end of this chapter, you will be able to:

- Explain the role of the Arawaks and Caribs in the history of the Caribbean Islands
- Name the European countries that have ruled islands of the Caribbean
- Explain the culinary influences from various nationalities on the cuisines of the Caribbean Islands
- Discuss factors that have limited crops on the islands of the Caribbean
- Name foods that are prevalent on the Caribbean Islands
- Prepare a variety of dishes from the Caribbean Islands

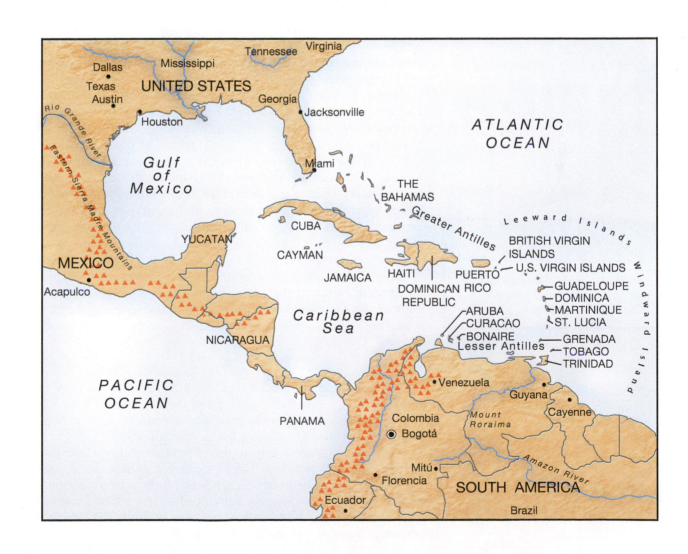

## >> HISTORY

### ARAWAKS AND CARIBS

Originally, two tribes from South America, the peace-loving Arawaks and the more aggressive Caribs, migrated to the islands scattered throughout the Caribbean Sea. Arriving around 600 A.D., the Arawaks survived on the indigenous foods they found on the islands.

Fish, including snapper, grouper, and shrimp; native animals like wild hogs; and abundant tropical fruits and vegetables formed the basis of the Arawaks' diet. Guava, pineapple, cashews, sweet potatoes, pumpkin, papaya, and cassava flourished throughout these tropical islands. Although there are mixed reports about whether the Arawaks found hot peppers growing in the Caribbean Islands or they brought the peppers from South America, we know that they added chili peppers to most of their dishes. Today, hot peppers still flavor many dishes found in the islands of the Caribbean.

The Arawaks and Caribs who inhabited these islands endured intrusions and invasions from the men arriving from various European countries. These Europeans sought two things: the food products that grow in a tropical climate and lands to possess. In the islands of the Caribbean, they discovered both. Besides the herbs, spices, and other native foods here, these islands provided tropical lands to plant the crops they desired. While the island inhabitants learned of new foods from the Europeans, the natives taught the Europeans much about surviving in the islands.

### SPANISH INFLUENCE

Sailing the seas in search of spices, Christopher Columbus discovered islands in the Caribbean around 1490 and claimed the land for Spain. On various islands, Columbus found myriad spices including cinnamon, nutmeg, mace, allspice, cloves, coriander, and peppercorns.

Within 70 years of the Spanish landing, the Arawaks lost all control of their homeland and became slaves to their European rulers. Better fighters, the Caribs held off the Europeans for much longer, but they eventually could not keep them from taking over their lands.

The Spanish introduced pigs, cattle, and goats to these islands. Obtained from the pigs, lard became the favored cooking fat. In addition, the Spanish brought and planted many fruits, vegetables, and herbs, including bananas, plantains, coconuts, ginger, sugarcane, mangoes, citrus fruits, figs, grapes, tamarind, date palms, chickpeas, eggplant, onions, garlic, oregano, and cumin. The Spanish preserved meat by salting and drying, and the Caribbean natives adopted these techniques. These new foods and preservation methods changed the cuisine of the Caribbean Islands.

The Spanish established large sugar plantations that required lots of labor. Soon, the Spanish enslaved the native people to work on the plantations. Unfortunately, many of the Arawaks died from diseases and overwork. To fulfill their need for more slaves, the Spanish settlers imported Africans to the Caribbean Islands to work the land.

*In 1493, Christopher Columbus brought sugarcane to the Caribbean.*

### CUBA

Christopher Columbus landed on Cuba in 1492. A typical story throughout the islands, in less than 20 years, the Spanish ruled there, and the native Arawaks became slaves. Before long, the native population died as a result of diseases brought by the Europeans and from their living conditions under Spanish rule.

Prior to the Spanish arrival, the people inhabiting Cuba had survived by fishing, hunting, and planting crops like black beans, corn, cassava, and sweet potatoes. The Spanish imported their native European foods, which became incorporated into the cookery of Cuba. The Spanish introduced *sofrito*, a mixture of sautéed green bell peppers, onion, garlic, and tomatoes that they used to flavor many dishes. This flavoring mixture still appears in many Cuban dishes.

After the demise of the native population, the Europeans imported slaves from Africa to work on the plantations. These Africans brought plantains, taro, and okra as well as the recipes from their homeland.

When slavery was abolished, many Chinese came to fill the need for cheap labor. Among other things, this resulted in rice being served with many dishes.

Strong Spanish influence still dominates in Cuba, affecting the language, cuisine, and culture. So today, the Cuban cuisine fuses the foods and cookery of the indigenous people, the Spanish, Africans, and Chinese.

Fidel Castro became Cuba's first Communist premier in 1959. From 1962 until 2015, the United States restricted travel to Cuba and prohibited trade.

## TRINIDAD AND TOBAGO

Trinidad lies at the southern end of the islands, near South America. First spotted by Christopher Columbus in 1498, Trinidad was named Isle of Trinidad because of the three mountain peaks standing on the island. Spanish rule began in 1592, and it lasted until the British took control in 1797.

Very lush and green, Tobago contains rainforests. Lots of tropical fruits such as grape-fruit, oranges, mango, and cocoa thrive here. During its history, the Dutch, British, and French all have ruled Tobago. In 1889, Britain placed Tobago under Trinidad's jurisdiction, and the two countries became united. Together, they achieved their independence in 1962.

## OTHER ISLANDS

From the time of the arrival of the first European settlers, Spain, Britain, France, Denmark, and the Netherlands repeatedly exchanged power over many islands. As a result of intense power struggles, European countries actually exchanged control of St. Lucia six different times during a 20-year span.

In their quest for places to produce coffee and sugar, the French took control of Martinique, Haiti, and Guadeloupe. The French influence remains apparent in the cooking, language, and culture of these islands.

The Dutch ruled Bonaire, Curacao, and Aruba. Remnants of the Dutch cuisine are evident in the fondness here for Edam cheese and split pea soup, which are served frequently on these islands. In addition, the Dutch brought many spices to the Caribbean Islands from their other tropical colony, Indonesia.

Through the continual changing of power on the islands, the British won control of many islands, including Jamaica, Grenada, Trinidad, and Tobago. They introduced rum, breadfruit, and mangos to the Caribbean culinary world. Islands with British heritage serve many foods adopted from the British. For example, the Jamaican beef patty is a direct descendant of the Cornish pasties served throughout the British Isles.

## IMPORTING CHEAP LABORERS

With the banning of slavery in the nineteenth century, plantation owners imported cheap laborers from around the world to work on the sugar plantations and other large farms on the islands. Many immigrants came from India, Southeast Asia, and China. Of course, these workers brought their native cuisines with them to their new land, and those cuisines fused with the cookery of the Caribbean. Influences from India remain quite prominent, with the adoption of curries, pilafs, rice, chutneys, and the spices used to flavor Indian dishes. Chinese and Southeast Asians introduced chop suey, stir-fries, sweet-and-sour dishes, and rice.

## U.S. VIRGIN ISLANDS

The U.S. Virgin Islands consists of three islands, St. Croix, St. John, and St. Thomas. Settled by the Arawaks and Caribs as early as 300 B.C., these islands attracted the Spanish, British, French, Danish, and Dutch. After being governed by several European countries, the United States purchased these islands from the Danish in 1917.

*Quite an industrialized country, Trinidad exports lots of oil and produces large amounts of asphalt. Located in southwest Trinidad, Pitch Lake contains a natural basin of asphalt that is the largest in the world. Trinidad is the home of the limbo, calypso, and steel bands.*

*In 1502, Columbus landed in Martinique. The French claimed the island in 1635. With plenty of sugarcane growing, they produced lots of rum on Martinique.*

### RULE OVER SOME OF THE ISLANDS

| **British** | **French** |
|---|---|
| Anguilla | Guadeloupe |
| Barbados | (French) Haiti |
| British Virgin Islands | Martinique |
| Cayman Islands | **Spanish** |
| Grenada | Cuba |
| Jamaica | Dominican |
| (British) Nevis | Republic |
| Tobago | Puerto Rico |
| Trinidad | |
| **Dutch** | |
| Aruba | |
| Bonaire | |
| Curacao | |

### DATES OF INDEPENDENCE FOR ISLANDS

*1804 Haiti*
*1844 Dominican Republic*
*1962 Jamaica*
*1962 Trinidad and Tobago*
*1966 Barbados*
*1973 Bahamas*
*1974 Grenada*

## >> TOPOGRAPHY

Often called the West Indies, the Caribbean Islands are strewn throughout the Caribbean Sea. More than 7,000 islands in the Caribbean form a wide arc stretching from the United States to South America. Of those thousands of islands, only 2 percent are inhabited. About 75 percent of the Caribbean population reside in Cuba, Haiti, and the Dominican Republic.

The Caribbean Islands are divided into two large regions. The Greater Antilles in the north is composed of Cuba, Hispaniola (which contains two countries, Haiti and the Dominican Republic), Jamaica, and Puerto Rico. Lying in the eastern Caribbean, the Lesser Antilles includes numerous islands situated from the Virgin Islands south to Trinidad and west to Aruba.

Located at the southern end of the Caribbean Islands just north of Trinidad and Tobago, Curacao, Aruba, and Bonaire form the Netherlands Antilles. These islands lie close to the coast of Venezuela.

### DIVERSITY IN CLIMATE

The islands in the Caribbean contain diverse terrain and climates. Some of the climatic differences result from ocean breezes known as trade winds. Besides affecting the temperature, trade winds impact the amount of rainfall an area receives, which, of course, affects both the climate and the growing conditions. Some islands are semi arid, with cacti and small scruffy trees and bushes; other islands support lush vegetation; and still others contain rainforests.

### DIVERSITY IN TOPOGRAPHY

Great topographical differences exist among the islands. While some of the islands are perfectly flat, many contain mountainous terrain. Of course, cooler temperatures prevail in the mountainous regions, which affects the crops that can grow there. The famous Blue Mountain coffee variety thrives in the Blue Mountains of Jamaica. Volcanic eruptions created many of the islands, such as Jamaica, and active volcanoes still exist on some of the islands.

Curacao contains arid vistas and desert vegetation such as cacti. Contrarily, the island of Dominica is quite lush, with volcanoes and mountains making up much of the landscape. Cuba, the largest of the Caribbean Islands, lies just south of Florida. Many believe that its landmass once joined to that of the United States.

## >> COOKING METHODS

### ARAWAK INFLUENCE

The Arawaks brought the cooking method of grilling with them from South America. From that heritage, Caribbean cooks frequently grill and spit-roast all sorts of foods.

*The curries found in the Caribbean Islands reflect influence from Indian curries rather than those of Southeast Asia. Caribbean curries contain seasonings like turmeric, black and cayenne pepper, cardamom, cumin, mustard, ginger, cloves, garlic, and/or coriander. Creating a very different flavor palate, curries from Southeast Asia derive their flavorings from various roots and leaves in addition to peppers and herbs.*

*Cuba—Largest Caribbean Island*
*Hispaniola—Second largest Caribbean Island*
*Jamaica—Third largest Caribbean Island*
*While the larger islands have more land available for agriculture, some of the smaller islands do not contain sufficient land to plant enough crops or raise animals. As a result, those islands must rely on importing many food items, which makes the food there very expensive.*

*The Blue Mountains tower as high as 7,400 feet. Mountains dominate the center of Jamaica. Moving away from the mountains, the land changes to rolling hills and then to coastal plains near the sea. Rainforests and springs in the mountains yield more than 120 rivers that flow from the center of Jamaica to the sea. However, while much of the island is lush, the southern coast contains semi arid land.*

**Ingredients and Foods Commonly Used throughout the Cuisines of the Caribbean Islands Include**

- fish and seafood—fresh and salted
- pork and lard
- beans and rice
- bananas and plantains
- coconut
- sweet potatoes, yams, taro, and cassava
- corn
- *callaloo* and greens
- pumpkins
- tropical fruits including mango, papaya, breadfruit, and pineapple
- hot peppers
- herbs and spices including thyme, allspice, peppers, cinnamon, nutmeg, cloves, and oregano

In the well-known Jamaican preparation called jerk, they coat pork, other meats, poultry, or fish with highly spiced seasoning paste, marinate it, and then grill. The birth of jerk came when the West African preference for cooking in earthen pits joined the Arawaks' affinity for flavoring meats by rubbing them with hot pepper seasoning. Although jerk dishes now appear on menus throughout the islands and the United States, most associate jerk seasonings with Jamaica.

## FRYING

Introduced to the islands by the Spanish, frying quickly became a popular and frequently used cooking technique. Abundant vegetable oil and lard provided the necessary medium for both deep-frying and sautéing. Prevalent in Africa, deep-frying was adopted by the Caribbeans for use with all sorts of foods including fish, seafood, meat, vegetables, and fruits. Commonly served, they make deep-fried fritters with almost any ingredients including salted fish, conch, other fish and seafood, as well as all sorts of meats, fruits, and vegetables.

## BRAISING

Like so many other countries with a limited supply of meat, one-pot cookery prevails as a method of extending a small amount of meat into a full meal. The long, slow braising tenderizes tough cuts of meat. This method has the added advantage of using any available meats and vegetables.

## PRESERVATION TECHNIQUES

The native Indians smoked meat to preserve it in the hot climate. Salted fish and meat also extended the protein supply, particularly for the slaves who were allowed only meager amounts of fresh meat.

## >> REGIONS
### ISSUES AFFECTING THE VARIOUS ISLANDS' CUISINES

The cookery differs on each island because of a number of factors. First, the Spanish, English, French, and Dutch controlled various islands of the Caribbean from the 1500s until the twentieth century. Each island exhibits culinary traits adopted from the ruling countries. In many cases, islands had several ruling nations in their history, which resulted in the cuisine reflecting influences from several countries.

Further culinary influences came from the people brought to the islands from Africa, India, China, and Southeast Asia to work as slaves or cheap laborers. These people prepared their native dishes and fused their homeland's cookery with the cuisine of their new land. Finally, the varying topography and climate existing on each of the islands resulted in differences in the type of crops grown and the animals raised.

## CUBA

Cuba's cookery combines elements from various ethnic groups. The European settlers contributed simmered sauces, saffron, garlic, onions, tomatoes, and peppers. Native Indians planted sweet potatoes, corn, squash, and yucca. Africans brought their culinary heritage, which merged with Cuba's existing cuisine. Later influences came from Indian and Chinese immigrants.

Of course, the bounty of fish, other seafood, and tropical fruits and vegetables played an important part in the cuisine. Many describe Cuba's cuisine as a fusion of Spanish and Caribbean cookery.

*The Arawaks created the first grill by arranging strips of green wood to hold the meat while cooking over an open fire. They chose green wood because it contains more moisture and burns much slower than seasoned wood, making it less likely to burn while grilling. Because they cooked the food slowly, it absorbed some of the flavor of the wood. The Arawaks called this barbacoa, which became the word "barbeque."*

*Jerk flavoring encompasses a number of spices. In addition to chili peppers, jerk seasoning may include cinnamon, allspice, nutmeg, thyme, salt, onions, and more. Because of the long, slow grilling or baking (in a pit lined with hot stones) and the generous amounts of hot peppers and salt rubbed on the meat, they say jerked meat lasts longer without spoiling in the hot climate.*

### NATIONAL DISHES OF THE ISLANDS

*Aruba—keshi yena (stuffed cheese shells)*
*Bahamas—cracked conch*
*Cayman Islands—turtle stew*
*Cuba—black beans*
*Jamaica—ackee and saltfish*
*Puerto Rico—arroz con gandules (rice with pigeon peas)*
*Trinidad and Tobago—crab and callaloo*

While Cuban dishes are highly spiced, they are *not* hot from the use of chili peppers. Cubans generously include herbs and spices, but they do not use the hot peppers found in the cookery of many other islands.

Most Cuban meals include rice. They also serve a variety of soups and stews.

## JAMAICA

Arriving in the 900s, the Arawaks called Jamaica, "Xaymaca," meaning land of wood and water. When the Europeans came, they brought tropical fruits, vegetables, and flowers from many places including China, Malaysia, India, and Africa. Breadfruit came from Tahiti, West Africans introduced *ackee* (the fruit of an evergreen tree), and the Europeans brought bananas, citrus fruits, and sugarcane. Because of Jamaica's fertile soil, the imported plants thrived. Today, sugarcane remains a very important crop here. Made from by-products of sugar refining, rum commands a huge role in Jamaica's economy.

The warm waters surrounding Jamaica supported lots of fish and seafood including snapper, turtle, and lobster. The inland swamps and rivers provided oysters, crayfish, and fowl.

Although the Spanish were the first Europeans to occupy Jamaica, they left the island after about 50 years, after enslaving and killing most of the Arawak inhabitants. More than 150 years later, the British arrived and took control. They introduced lots of foods and culinary traditions including curries from India.

## POVERTY

Although the climate throughout the Caribbean is conducive to growing abundant crops, many of the islanders live in poverty. Poor soil, crop devastation by insects, hurricanes, lack of rain, and old agricultural machinery and techniques are some of the problems that plague Caribbean farmers. As a result, the islanders must import at least part of their food supplies, which makes the food expensive.

## SIMILARITIES AND DIFFERENCES IN DISHES

As is true with different regions in other countries, a number of the same dishes are prepared on many islands. Variations on a dish distinguish it on each island. Countless renditions of bean fritters, fish fritters, blood sausage, stuffed crabs, fried cornbread, pepper pot (vegetable soup prepared with any available meat and vegetables), curries, beans and rice, and *callaloo* (a soup made of greens and other ingredients that depend on where it is prepared) appear in homes and on menus throughout the islands.

# >> CUISINE

## AFRICAN INFLUENCE

The African slaves exerted a profound effect on the Caribbean cuisine that still prevails throughout the islands. Because both Africa and the Caribbean Islands experience a tropical climate, similar crops grow in both these areas. As a result, the African immigrants could plant the foods that grew in their homeland, cook their native recipes, and produce their familiar dishes of African origin. They brought plantains, beans, cornmeal dishes, okra, and yams to their new home, and their recipes, cooking techniques, and foods became assimilated into the Caribbean cuisine.

## CREOLE COOKERY

Creole cooking, a fusion of French, Spanish, and African influences, appears throughout the Caribbean, Latin America, and parts of the United States (such as New Orleans). The vegetables and seafood of Africa join Spanish herbs and spices and wonderful

## CHEESES OF THE CARIBBEAN ISLANDS

**Crema Mexicana** Thick rich soft cream, flavor similar to whipping cream

**Duroblando** Strong flavor, firm texture

**Queso Fresco** Made from cow's and goat's milk; mild flavor, soft crumbly texture; does not melt

**Queso Media Luna** Mild taste, semifirm texture; favorite in Puerto Rico; sometimes called *queso de papa*

**Queso para Freír** Mild flavor, firm texture; does not melt

---

French sauces, resulting in a unique cookery. Although many think Creole cookery contains spicy, hot flavorings, it does not. The spicy chilies so prevalent in the African cuisines are absent from Creole dishes.

## FISH AND SEAFOOD

All sorts of fish and seafood abound off these islands. Large, meaty fish such as swordfish, tuna, dolphin, and marlin; smaller fish including grouper, snapper, and mackerel; and a myriad of shellfish such as lobster, conch, shrimp, and crab provide a constant source of protein-rich foods. Many associate conch with the Caribbean because it appears on menus in fritters, chowder, and salads.

*Conch is pronounced "conk."*

Although surrounded by ocean and an abundance of fish and seafood, slaves in the Caribbean had little time to fish. Because salting and drying preserved the fish even in the heat of the tropical islands, this became a mainstay in their diet. Appearing in many traditional dishes, salted fish still plays an important role in the native Caribbean cuisine.

## MEAT

The Arawaks hunted wild hogs before the Spanish introduced the pig. Pork still remains the most popular meat throughout the islands. Chicken, duck, turkey, goat, and beef also are consumed.

*Pigeon peas are preferred in the Bahamas, red beans in Puerto Rico, and black beans in Cuba.*

Goat stew is commonly served on many Caribbean Islands. Considered the national dish of Montserrat, it also is very popular on St. Kitts and Nevis. The version served on these islands combines goat, vegetables, and dumplings in a tomato-based liquid. Jamaicans often prepare goat in a curry sauce.

## LEGUMES AND GRAINS

When the Asian immigrants moved to the Caribbean, they introduced rice, and it was quickly adopted as a mainstay in the cuisine. Today, rice along with all sorts of dried beans forms the foundation of the Caribbean diet. Often called "peas" in the islands, beans appear as salads, side dishes, or combined with rice and served as an entrée. Different versions of beans and rice are prepared on each island.

*Identified with the cookery of Trinidad, pelau is a dish consisting of meat, poultry, fish, and/or pigeon peas with vegetables and rice.*

## FRUITS AND VEGETABLES

The climate and conditions on many of the islands support the growth of a wide range of tropical fruits and vegetables. Generally, coconut trees thrive in the coastal areas, and pineapples grow in the low-lying land. Sugarcane flourishes in the interior regions of numerous islands.

With a year-round growing season, the bounty of vegetables fills the gap left by the limited meat supplies. As a result, many meat dishes contain lots of vegetables and/or rice.

The Arawaks ate corn, and today it is a food that still appears often, both as a vegetable or ground into cornmeal and cooked into porridge or bread. Years ago as well as today, root vegetables also formed a substantial part of the diet of the Caribbean native. Taro, cassava, and yams appear in many preparations.

Plantains and bananas are cooked in a number of ways and often accompany meals. Depending on their ripeness, plantains regularly appear sautéed, boiled, or baked and function as a starch. Even the plantain leaves are used as a wrapper to hold other foods for steaming.

Fruits flourish here and claim a significant place in the cuisine and diet of the islanders. Numerous varieties of fruits grow, including citrus fruits, mango, papaya, pineapple, avocado, coconuts, and more. The grapefruit, guava, and pineapple are indigenous to the islands.

Coconut appears in all sorts of dishes from appetizers to desserts. Islanders use all parts of the coconut, including the milk, meat, and oil.

## FLAVORINGS

A bounty of herbs, spices, and hot peppers flavor dishes in Caribbean cookery. While a profusion of spices thrive in the tropical conditions here, the favorite herb remains thyme. Jamaica produces lots of allspice, which comes from the pimento tree and appears in many dishes on that island. Cinnamon, ginger, peppercorns, and nutmeg grow well throughout the islands. Forty percent of the world's nutmeg and mace comes from Grenada, which is known as the "Spice Island." A plethora of sweet and hot peppers flourish here. Numerous peppers, including the hottest varieties, the Scotch bonnet and *habañero*, flavor many of the dishes prepared throughout the islands. Although many islanders season liberally with chili peppers, several islands, including Cuba and Puerto Rico, do not prepare many spicy dishes.

## DESSERT

Islanders like cloyingly sweet desserts, and they are served often. Since lots of sugarcane grows on many islands, sugar is plentiful and readily available. Evaporated, condensed milk replaces fresh milk in many confections. Numerous desserts contain bananas, coconut, other tropical fruits, and/or rum. British desserts such as puddings, buns, and trifle often appear on the islands that have a history of British rule. Flans remain favorites on islands with Spanish heritage.

## BEVERAGES

With the abundance of fruit growing in the islands, fruit juices are popular and frequently served. Beer and rum reign as the preferred alcoholic beverages. Made from fermented sugar and water, rum was first made in the seventeenth century by the British on the island of Barbados. Many used molasses instead of sugarcane to make rum. The many varieties of rum include dry, dark, light, and heavy. Many islands produce their own brands, and each island's beer and rum has its own characteristics. Rum appears in numerous recipes for food, and many different rum drinks are served throughout the islands.

---

*Mace and nutmeg come from the same plant, the tropical nutmeg tree. Nutmeg is the kernel of the seed, and the outer shell or membrane covering the nutmeg is the mace. Both spices are ground for use in sweet and savory dishes.*

*Reflecting their Spanish heritage, Cubans and Puerto Ricans use lots of garlic and lime for flavoring.*

*Scoville units measure the level of capsaicin in the pepper. Capsaicin contains the heat. Heat levels found in individual peppers fluctuate greatly because the heat level varies from plant to plant.*

| Pepper | Scoville Units |
|---|---|
| bell | 0 |
| pepperoncini | 100–500 |
| poblano | 500–1,000 |
| ancho, pasilla | 1,000–1,500 |
| cascabel | 1,500–2,500 |
| jalapeño, chipotle | 2,500–10,000 |
| serrano | 5,000–20,000 |
| cayenne, piquin, tabasco, aji | 30,000–50,000 |
| Thai | 50,000–100,000 |
| habañero, Scotch bonnet | 80,000–300,000 |

*For information on handling chili peppers, refer to page 515 in Chapter 16, Mexico.*

*The Scotch bonnet and habañero are varieties of the same pepper. Although individual peppers vary widely in appearance, their heat levels are basically the same.*

*white rum—Light-bodied*
*golden rum—Medium-bodied; aged in oak barrels for several years*
*dark rum—Full-bodied; long aging in oak barrels*

| REGION | AREA | WEATHER | TOPOGRAPHY | FOODS |
|---|---|---|---|---|
| **Greater Antilles:** | | | | |
| Cuba | South of Florida | Semitropical; dry, mild winters; wet summers | Mountains, rolling hills, grasslands, farmland, coast | Seafood, pork, rice, cassava, sugar, sweet potatoes, corn, peas, beans, okra, chilies, vegetables, fruits, citrus fruits, rum |
| Jamaica | South of Cuba | Tropical; hot and humid; rainy spring and fall | Rolling hills, mountains, plains, plateaus, coast | Seafood, livestock, poultry, rice, yams, plantains, sugar, vegetables, fruits, bananas, coconuts, ginger, allspice, coffee, cocoa beans, rum |
| **Lesser Antilles:** | | | | |
| Virgin Islands: St. Thomas, St. Croix, and St. John | East of Puerto Rico | Tropical; moderated by trade winds | Hills, fertile land, coast | Seafood, beef, eggs, chickens, vegetables, fruits, nuts |
| Martinique and Guadeloupe | South Caribbean, north of Trinidad and Tobago | Tropical; hot and humid summer and fall; milder winter and spring; trade winds | Hills, mountains, volcanoes, coast | Seafood, livestock, sugar, rice, fruits, vegetables, bananas, pineapple, cocoa, coffee, rum |
| Trinidad and Tobago | South Caribbean, just north of Venezuela | Tropical; hot and humid | Forests, flatlands, farmland, hills, mountains, coast | Seafood, beans, sugar, vegetables, coconuts, sweet potatoes, fruits, cocoa, coffee, rum |

## >> Review Questions

1. Discuss how history has influenced the cuisines of the Caribbean Islands.
2. Explain the exchange of power that occurred between the European nations that occupied the islands in the Caribbean and how that impacted their cuisine.
3. Discuss the effects of climate and weather on the cuisines of the Caribbean Islands.
4. Name five foods that are common ingredients throughout the Caribbean Islands.
5. Name and describe at least three dishes frequently served throughout the islands of the Caribbean.

## >> Glossary

**callaloo** Greens obtained from the taro plant; also the name of a soup made of greens and other ingredients, including salt pork, crab, and/or coconut milk

**pepper pot** Vegetable soup prepared with any available meat and vegetables

**sofrito** Mixture of sautéed green peppers, onion, garlic, and tomatoes

## STAMP AND GO (JAMAICA)

### SALT COD FRITTERS

Nathalie Dulex © Shutterstock

**TWIST ON THE CLASSIC**

For a luncheon or light entrée, prepare small stamp-and-go patties about 1 1/2 inches (4 cm) in diameter. Place three patties in pita bread and top with condiments of choice, such as diced tomato, shredded lettuce, and tartar sauce made with capers, pickle relish, minced green onion, dill, and mayonnaise.

**Note:** Being preparations for this dish a day before serving to allow time to soak the salt cod.

**Number of Servings:** 8  
**Serving Size:** 3 patties  
**Total Yield:** 1 lb., 8 oz. (681 g) raw batter; 24 1-oz. (28-g) patties  
**Food Balance:** Protein/spicy  
**Wine Style:** Off-dry, low-oaked whites and soft reds  
**Example:** Meridian Pinot Grigio/Sauvignon Blanc or Santa Barbara Chardonnay

**Cooking Method:** Deep-fry

| INGREDIENTS | WEIGHT | | VOLUME | |
| --- | --- | --- | --- | --- |
| | U.S. | METRIC | U.S. | METRIC |
| salt cod | 8 oz. | 227 g | | |
| flour | 4 3/4 oz. | 135 g | 1 cup | 240 mL |
| baking powder | | | 1 teaspoon | 5 mL |
| salt | | | 1/2 teaspoon | 3 mL |
| dried thyme | | | 1/4 teaspoon | 2 mL |
| water, cold | | 170 g | 3/4 cup | 180 mL |
| egg | 1 3/4 oz. | 50 g | 1 each | |
| onion, minced | 4 oz. | 114 g | 1 small | |
| garlic, minced | | | 1 clove | |
| hot pepper, seeds and ribs removed, minced | 1/4 oz. | 8 g | 1/2 each | |
| vegetable oil, for frying | | | | |

1. Place salt cod in bowl, cover with cold water, refrigerate at least 12 hours, changing water at least once or twice during that time.

2. Drain fish, place in pan, cover with fresh water, bring to boil, continue boiling about 10 minutes.

3. Drain, shred finely, discarding any skin or bones.

4. Place flour, baking powder, salt, and thyme in bowl. Stir in water and egg.

5. Add onion, garlic, hot pepper, and fish, stir to blend.

6. Heat about 1/2 inch (1 1/3 cm) oil in frying pan until hot, drop in fish mixture by tablespoonful (1 oz., 28 g, or 30 mL), fry until golden brown on both sides, about 2 to 3 minutes.

7. Drain on absorbent paper, serve hot.

Courtesy of Idaho Potato Commission

# COCONUT SHRIMP

**Number of Servings:** 12
**Serving Size:** 4 shrimp, about 3 oz. (86 g)
**Total Yield:** 2 lb., 6 oz. (1.1 kg)
**Wine Style:** Coconut shrimp are very easy to pair with dry Riesling with some weight on it. Because of its minerality and medium palate, it is a perfect combination.
**Example:** Riesling Reserve 2013, Hermann J.Wiemer, Finger Lakes, N.Y.

**Cooking Method:** Fry

## TWIST ON THE CLASSIC

Serve the coconut shrimp fanned around a slice of grilled pineapple accompanied by mango salsa.

| INGREDIENTS | WEIGHT U.S. | WEIGHT METRIC | VOLUME U.S. | VOLUME METRIC |
|---|---|---|---|---|
| shrimp, jumbo (21/25), shells removed with tail shells intact, deveined, washed | 1 lb., 12 oz. | 794 g | | |
| dried salt | | | 1/2 teaspoon | 3 mL |
| pepper | | | 1/2 teaspoon | 3 mL |
| lime juice | | 28 g | 2 tablespoons | 30 mL |
| eggs | 6 3/4 oz. | 191 g | 4 each | |
| water | | 28 g | 2 tablespoons | 30 mL |
| coconut, unsweetened, shredded | 7 oz. | 199 g | 2 cups | 480 mL |
| flour, all purpose | 4 1/2 oz. | 128 g | 1 cup | 240 mL |
| oil for frying | | 170 g | about 3/4 cup | 180 mL |

**Garnish:**

lemon or lime wedge
Chinese duck sauce or sauce of choice

1. Place shrimp in bowl, sprinkle with salt, pepper, and lime juice, toss to mix. Refrigerate to marinate for 5 to 10 minutes while preparing breading station.
2. Mix eggs with water in shallow bowl, place coconut in another shallow bowl or plate, place flour in third shallow bowl or plate.
3. Dip shrimp in flour, shake off excess, dip in egg, and then dip into coconut. Place shrimp on platter until all coated. Cover and refrigerate until needed.
4. Heat 1/4-inch (0.5-cm) (about 2 to 3 oz., 57 to 86 g, 4 to 6 tablespoons, or 60 to 90 mL) oil in skillet until hot.
5. Add shrimp, cook until golden brown, about 1 minute on each side.
6. Remove to pan lined with absorbent paper, keep warm in oven until all fried.
7. Serve, garnished with lemon or lime wedge. Accompany with Chinese duck sauce or sauce of choice.

© Brent Hofacker

## CUBAN SANDWICH (CUBA)

**Note:** Although traditionally served as a full-sized sandwich for lunch, this one is cut into small pieces and served as an hors d'oeuvre. These also work well as a passed hors d'oeuvre. If Cuban bread is unavailable, substitute Italian or French bread.

**Serving Size:** About 2-oz. (57-g) portion  
**Cooking Method:** Sauté  
**Total Yield:** 1 lb., 14 3/4 oz. (872 g), or about fifteen 2-oz. (57-g) pieces  
**Food Balance:** Balanced  
**Wine Style:** Wine friendly—Choose your favorite wine!  
**Example:** St. Clement Chardonnay or Cabernet Sauvignon

| INGREDIENTS | WEIGHT | | VOLUME | |
| --- | --- | --- | --- | --- |
| | U.S. | METRIC | U.S. | METRIC |
| Cuban bread | 11 oz. | 312 g | one 21-inch loaf | one 53-cm loaf |
| prepared mustard | 1 oz. | 28 g | 2 tablespoons | 30 mL |
| dill pickle slices | 3 1/2 oz. | 104 g | about 28 slices | |
| roast pork, sliced, at room temperature, *see recipe that follows* | 6 oz. | 170 g | | |
| baked ham, thin slice, at room temperature | 4 oz. | 114 g | | |
| Swiss cheese, sliced, at room temperature | 5 oz. | 142 g | | |
| butter | 1 oz. | 28 g | 2 tablespoons | 30 mL |

1. Slice bread in half, lengthwise. Spread thinly with mustard.

2. Top one half with a layer of pickles, then place pork slices over pickles. Place ham over pork and then Swiss cheese slices over the ham.

3. Place remaining half of bread over the Swiss cheese. Melt one tablespoon (15 g or 15 mL) of butter on griddle or in large skillet over medium heat.

4. Place sandwich on griddle and top with a weight to press and flatten the sandwich. (Wrap a heavy pan such as cast iron skillet or a braiser with foil and place on top of sandwich to press it.)

5. Sauté slowly to warm the meats and melt the cheese. When first side is toasted, move sandwich to side of pan and melt remaining one tablespoon (15 g or 15 mL) butter in pan. Turn sandwich and sauté other side. *Be careful not to burn bread. Lower heat if needed.*

6. Remove sandwich, cut into sections about 1 1/4 inches (3 cm) wide (about 2 oz., 57g in weight, depending on width of bread). Place toothpick through each piece. Serve immediately.

REDAV © Shutterstock

# PUERCO ASADO (CUBA)

## ROASTED PORK LOIN

**Note:** Allow time to marinate pork loin.

**Note:** Although this recipe is included as an ingredient in a Cuban sandwich, this pork roast makes a delicious entrée on its own. The *mojo* seasoning used as a rub and marinade (the garlic, oregano, salt, pepper, and, traditionally, sour orange, which has been substituted here by a combination of orange juice with lemon and/or lime juice), creates a flavorful piece of meat.

**Serving Size:** 6 oz. (170 g) per loaf of bread
**Total Yield:** 1 lb., 9 1/2 oz. (724 g)
**Food Balance:** Balanced
**Wine Style:** Wine friendly—Pick a winner!
**Example:** Greg Norman Chardonnay or Zinfandel

**Cooking Method:** Bake

| | WEIGHT | | VOLUME | |
|---|---|---|---|---|
| **INGREDIENTS** | **U.S.** | **METRIC** | **U.S.** | **METRIC** |
| garlic, smashed | 1/2 oz. | 15 g | 4 cloves | |
| salt | | | 1/2 teaspoon | 3 mL |
| pepper | | | 1/4 teaspoon | 2 mL |
| dried oregano | | | 1/2 teaspoon | 3 mL |
| lemon or lime juice, or combination | | 57 g | 1/4 cup | 60 mL |
| orange juice | | 57 g | 1/4 cup | 60 mL |
| pork loin, trimmed | 2 lb., 5 3/4 oz. | 1.1 kg | | |

1. Using a mortar and pestle or smashing ingredients on board using the side of the knife, mash garlic, salt, pepper, and oregano together to form a paste. Set aside until needed. Combine lemon and/or lime and orange juices together. Set aside until needed.

2. Cut slits or poke holes in meat. Rub the meat all over with the garlic-spice paste. Place in nonreactive bowl. Pour the juices over the meat. Cover and refrigerate for at least 2 hours and as long as overnight.

3. Place oven rack in center of oven. Preheat oven to 425 degrees (220°C).

4. Remove meat from marinade. Cover and refrigerate marinade for later use. Place meat in baking pan and place in oven. Reduce temperature to 325 degrees (160°C). Bake meat uncovered for 1 hour.

5. Pour marinade over meat and continue baking for another 1 hour and 30 minutes, until it reaches proper internal temperature.

6. Remove from oven. Cover and let rest 10 to 15 minutes before slicing.

Dagmara Ponikiewska © Shutterstock

# JAMAICAN BEEF PATTIES (JAMAICA)

© Brent Hofacker

**Number of Servings:** 16 appetizers, 8 entrées

**Serving Size:** 1 turnover appetizer
2 turnovers entrées

**Scaling:** 1 1/2 oz. (43 g) dough per turnover (4 1/2- to 5-inch, 11- to 13-cm round)
1 1/2 oz. (43 g) filling per turnover (2 tablespoons, 30 mL)

**Total Yield:** 16 turnovers
Dough: 1 lb., 9 oz. (710 g)
Filling: 1 lb., 9 oz. (710 g)

**Cooking Method:** Sauté, bake

**Wine Style:** Medium-bodied red wine with well-integrated oak and a balanced acidity.

**Example:** Pinot Noir La Encantada Vineyard, Sta. Rita Hills 2013, Habit Winery

| | WEIGHT | | VOLUME | |
|---|---|---|---|---|
| **INGREDIENTS** | **U.S.** | **METRIC** | **U.S.** | **METRIC** |
| **Pastry:** | | | | |
| flour, all purpose | 14 oz. | 397 g | 3 cups | 720 mL |
| salt | | | 1/2 teaspoon | 3 mL |
| baking powder | | | 1/2 teaspoon | 3 mL |
| curry powder | 1/4 oz. | 8 g | 2 teaspoons | 10 mL |
| butter, unsalted or margarine, cold or shortening, cut into pieces | 6 oz. | 170 g | 3/4 cup or 1 1/2 sticks | 180 mL |
| water, ice cold | | 114 to 170 g | 1/2 to 3/4 cup | 120 to 180 mL |
| **Filling:** | | | | |
| oil | | 15 g | 1 tablespoon | 15 mL |
| onion, minced | 7 oz. | 199 g | 1 large | |
| garlic, peeled, smashed | 1/2 oz. | 15 g | 2 cloves | |
| hot pepper, serrano or choice, seeds and membranes removed, if desired | 1/2 oz., to taste | 15 g, to taste | 1 or 2 each, to taste | |
| ground beef | 1 lb. | 454 g | | |
| thyme | | | 1 teaspoon | 5 mL |
| allspice | | | 1/4 teaspoon | 2 mL |
| curry powder | 1/4 oz. | 8 g | 2 teaspoons | 10 mL |
| salt | 1/4 oz. | 8 g | 1 teaspoon | 5 mL |
| breadcrumbs | 2 1/2 oz. | 71 g | 1/2 cup | 120 mL |
| water or beef stock | | 284 g | 1 1/4 cups | 300 mL |
| egg | 1 3/4 oz. | 50 g | 1 each | |
| water | | | 1 teaspoon | 5 mL |

## FOR DOUGH:

1. Place flour, salt, baking powder, and curry powder in food processor fitted with knife blade. Pulse to combine.
2. Add cold fat, pulse to combine until the size of peas.
3. Add 4 oz. (114 g, 1/2 cup, or 120 mL) cold water through feed tube; pulse to combine. Add more water as needed, until dough forms a ball.
4. Remove from food processor. Knead a couple of times to mix dough thoroughly. Wrap in plastic wrap and chill. (If time is short, flatten into disk and place in freezer to chill quickly.)

## FOR FILLING:

1. Heat oil in skillet over medium heat. Add onion, sauté a few minutes to soften.
2. Add garlic and pepper; sauté another minute or two to soften.
3. Add ground beef, thyme, allspice, curry powder, and salt. Stir and sauté until meat is done.
4. Add breadcrumbs and water. Stirring occasionally, cook until the liquid is absorbed, and mixture has stew-like consistency. Remove from heat and cool.

## ASSEMBLY:

1. Cover baking sheet with parchment paper. Place baking rack in middle or upper half of oven. Preheat oven to 400 degrees (205°C). Mix egg with water; set aside until needed.
2. Take a portion of the dough; roll on lightly floured surface until 1/8-inch (0.3-cm) thick. Cut into 4 1/2- to 5-inch (11- to 13-cm) rounds (or desired size).
3. Place 1 1/2 oz. (43 g, 2 tablespoons, or 30 mL) of filling in lower half of disk but staying 1/2 inch (1 1/3 cm) from edges. Using a finger dipped in water, wet outer edge of half of the circle. Fold top half over the bottom, press edges to seal. Seal by pressing edge with fork tines to make decorative edge and seal tightly.
4. Place turnover on prepared pan. Repeat with remaining dough and filling. Using a pastry brush, paint each turnover with prepared egg wash.
5. Place pan in oven and bake for 20 to 25 minutes, until golden. Remove from oven; transfer to cooling rack. Serve while still hot.

> In Jamaica, they typically use half of a Scotch bonnet pepper in this recipe. I replaced the fiery, hot Scotch bonnet with a serrano to accommodate the typical American palate. Feel free to use whatever peppers, with or without seeds and membranes, desired.

## CALLALOO (EASTERN CARIBBEAN)

### SOUP WITH GREENS AND CRAB

**Number of Servings:** 14

**Cooking Method:** Sauté, boil

**Serving Size:** 8 oz. (227 g)
**Total Yield:** 7 lb., 4 oz. (3.3 kg)
**Food Balance:** Spicy/sweet
**Wine Style:** Off-dry, low-oaked whites and soft reds
**Example:** Beringer Riesling, Viognier, or Pinot Noir

Pearson Education/PH College

| INGREDIENTS | WEIGHT U.S. | METRIC | VOLUME U.S. | METRIC |
|---|---|---|---|---|
| butter | 1 oz. | 28 g | 2 tablespoons | 30 mL |
| onions, finely chopped | 10 oz. | 284 g | 2 large or 2 cups | 480 mL |
| garlic, minced | 1/2 oz. | 15 g | 4 cloves | |
| *callaloo* greens or spinach, washed, stems removed, and cut into 1/2-inch (1 1/3-cm) strips | 1 lb., 11 oz. | 766 g | | |
| fresh hot pepper, minced, or ground cayenne pepper, *optional* | to taste | | | |
| chicken stock | | | 2 quarts (8 cups) | 1.9 L |
| coconut milk, unsweetened | | 340 g | 1 1/2 cups | 360 mL |
| black pepper | | | 1 teaspoon | 5 mL |
| crabmeat, fresh, canned, or frozen, all shell and cartilage removed | 12 oz. | 340 g | | |

1. Melt butter in large pan over medium heat, add onions, sauté gently for about 3 minutes.
2. Add garlic, sauté another 3 minutes.
3. Add greens and optional hot pepper or cayenne, mix well, cook until soft, about 5 minutes.
4. Add stock, coconut milk, and black pepper, bring to boil, then reduce heat and simmer uncovered until greens are tender, about 10 minutes.
5. Add crabmeat, simmer another 5 minutes. Correct seasonings, serve.

### TWIST ON THE CLASSIC

To make this into an entrée similar to *bouillabaisse*, follow the recipe up to adding the crab. At that point, add an assortment of fish pieces and shellfish like mussels, clams, and shrimp.

# PEPPER POT (WESTERN CARIBBEAN)

**Note:** A cross between soup and stew, this dish hails from the time of the Arawaks. Any available ingredients went in the pot and soon a meal emerged. Every island prepares a different version of this dish.

**Number of Servings:** 9
**Serving Size:** 10 oz. (284 g)
**Total Yield:** 5 lb., 11 oz. (2.6 kg)
**Food Balance:** Spicy/protein
**Wine Style:** Off-dry, low-oaked whites and soft reds
**Example:** Beringer Gewürztraminer, Founders' Estate Merlot

**Cooking Method:** Braise

| | WEIGHT | | VOLUME | |
|---|---|---|---|---|
| **INGREDIENTS** | **U.S.** | **METRIC** | **U.S.** | **METRIC** |
| bacon, diced, or salt pork, cut into thin strips | 3 oz. | 86 g | 3 slices | |
| lean pork, cubes | 8 oz. | 227 g | | |
| onion, thin slices | 13 1/2 oz. | 383 g | 2 large | |
| chicken stock | | | 1 quart + 2 cups (6 cups) | 1.4 L |
| *habañero*, seeds and ribs removed, minced | 1/4 oz. | 8 g | 1 each | |
| or | | | | |
| *jalapeño* chili, seeds and ribs removed, minced | 3/4 oz. | 22 g | 1 each | |
| *callaloo* or spinach, washed, stems removed, and cut roughly | 10 oz. | 284 g | | |
| kale, washed, stems removed, and cut roughly | 1 lb., 5 oz. | 596 g | | |
| okra, sliced | 5 oz. | 142 g | 12 each or 1 1/2 cups | 360 mL |
| yam, peeled, sliced, and cut into quarters | 8 oz. | 227 g | 1 small to medium | |
| dried thyme | 1/4 oz. | 8 g | 2 teaspoons | 10 mL |
| black pepper | | | 1/2 teaspoon | 3 mL |
| salt | to taste | | | |

1. Place bacon or salt pork in large pot, sauté over medium heat to render fat, about 10 minutes.
2. Add pork cubes and onions, sauté about 5 minutes, until pork browns and onions soften.
3. Add stock, bring to boil, reduce heat, cover, simmer 1 1/2 hours.
4. Add remaining ingredients and simmer another 1 hour.
5. Correct seasonings, remove salt pork, if used, serve.

## TWIST ON THE CLASSIC

Transform this into an entrée by adding just enough stock to make it the thickness of stew and serving over wide egg noodles or rice.

## RICE SALAD

**Note:** Allow several hours or overnight to refrigerate this salad before serving.

**Number of Servings:** 8
**Serving Size:** 4 oz. (114 g)
**Total Yield:** 2 lb. (908 g)

**Cooking Method:** Boil (rice)

| INGREDIENTS | WEIGHT U.S. | WEIGHT METRIC | VOLUME U.S. | VOLUME METRIC |
|---|---|---|---|---|
| curry powder | 1/4 oz. | 8 g | 2 teaspoons | 10 mL |
| ground turmeric | | | 1/4 teaspoon | 2 mL |
| salt | | | 1/2 teaspoon | 3 mL |
| pepper | | | 1/4 teaspoon | 2 mL |
| water | | 28 g | 2 tablespoons | 30 mL |
| plain yogurt | 6 oz. | 170 g | 2/3 cup | 160 mL |
| raisins | 1 1/2 oz. | 43 g | 3 tablespoons | 45 mL |
| onion, minced | 1 oz. | 28 g | 1 tablespoon | 15 mL |
| cider vinegar | | 57 g | 1/4 cup | 60 mL |
| green bell pepper, small dice | 3 1/2 oz. | 99 g | 1/2 cup | 120 mL |
| red bell pepper, small dice | 3 1/2 oz. | 99 g | 1/2 cup | 120 mL |
| rice, cooked and cooled | 15 oz. | 426 g | 2 cups | 480 mL |

**Garnish:**

lettuce leaves

1. Mix curry powder, turmeric, salt, pepper, and water in bowl. Add yogurt, raisins, and onion. Mix well.
2. Add vinegar, bell peppers, and rice. Stir gently.
3. Cover and refrigerate several hours or overnight. Correct seasonings, serve on base of lettuce leaves.

nata_vkusidey/Fotolia

# MIXED BEAN SALAD

© Dorling Kindersley

**Note:** Allow time for the flavors to marry.

**Note:** Either cook dried beans or use canned beans.

**Number of Servings:** 15
**Serving Size:** 4 oz. (114 g)
**Total Yield:** 3 lb., 13 oz. (1.7 kg)

**Cooking Method:** Boil (individual ingredients)

| | WEIGHT | | VOLUME | |
|---|---|---|---|---|
| INGREDIENTS | U.S. | METRIC | U.S. | METRIC |
| **Salad:** | | | | |
| black-eyed peas, cooked | 9 1/2 oz. | 270 g | 1 cup | 240 mL |
| kidney beans, cooked | 9 1/2 oz. | 270 g | 1 cup | 240 mL |
| chickpeas, cooked | 7 1/2 oz. | 213 g | 1 cup | 240 mL |
| green beans, cooked *al dente* | 6 oz. | 170 g | 36 each | |
| avocado, firm, ripe, peeled and cut into cubes | 11 oz. | 312 g | 2 each | |
| onion, thin slices | 6 oz. | 170 g | 2 small | |
| red bell pepper, cut into strips | 7 oz. | 199 g | 1 each | |
| fresh chives, minced | 1/4 oz. | 8 g | 6 leaves | |
| **Dressing:** | | | | |
| garlic, smashed and minced | 1/2 oz. | 15 g | 4 cloves | |
| hot red pepper, seeded and minced | 1/4 to 1/2 oz. | 8 to 15 g | 1 small | |
| salt | 1/4 oz. | 8 g | 1 teaspoon | 5 mL |
| black pepper | | | 1/4 teaspoon | 2 mL |
| ground allspice | | | 1 teaspoon | 5 mL |
| cider vinegar | | 86 g | 1/4 cup + 2 tablespoons | 90 mL |
| fresh lemon juice | | 22 g | 1 tablespoon + 1 1/2 teaspoons | 23 mL |
| olive oil | | 156 g | 2/3 cup | 160 mL |
| lettuce leaves, for serving | | | | |

1. Combine all salad ingredients in bowl.
2. Whisk all dressing ingredients together in another bowl, jar, or food processor fitted with knife blade. Whisk or process until dressing thickens.
3. Pour dressing over salad, mix gently.
4. Cover and refrigerate a few hours or overnight, correct seasonings. Serve on lettuce leaves.

## ROPA VIEJA (CUBA AND PUERTO RICO)

### SHREDDED BEEF

**Note:** This dish is served in the islands of the Caribbean with Spanish heritage. *Ropa vieja* literally means "old clothes," and the dish is prepared with leftover or tough cuts of meat. If leftover meat is unavailable, simmer about 4 1/2 lb. (2 kg) meat with bay leaves and diced onion in water until tender, about 2 hours.

**Number of Servings:** 14

**Serving Size:** 6 oz. (170 g)

**Total Yield:** 5 lb., 4 oz. (2.4 kg)

**Food Balance:** Protein/spice

**Wine Style:** Off-dry, low-oaked whites and soft reds

**Example:** Penfolds Riesling or Shiraz

**Cooking Method:** Sauté

| INGREDIENTS | WEIGHT | | VOLUME | |
|---|---|---|---|---|
| | U.S. | METRIC | U.S. | METRIC |
| beef, flank or brisket, cooked | 2 lb., 8 oz. | 1.1 kg | | |
| oil | | 43 g | 3 tablespoons | 45 mL |
| onion, medium dice | 1 lb., 2 oz. | 511 g | 2 large | |
| garlic, minced | 1/2 oz. | 15 g | 4 cloves | |
| green bell pepper, seeded and cut into medium dice | 8 oz. | 227 g | 1 large | |
| *jalapeño* chili, seeds and ribs removed, minced | 1 1/2 oz. | 43 g | 2 each | |
| plum tomatoes, canned, diced | 2 lb., 1 oz. | 936 g | 1 quart (4 cups) | 960 mL |
| dried oregano | | | 1 teaspoon | 5 mL |
| ground allspice | | | 1/2 teaspoon | 3 mL |
| salt | 1/4 oz. | 8 g | 1 teaspoon | 5 mL |
| capers, drained | 1 oz. | 28 g | 2 tablespoons | 30 mL |

**Accompaniment:**

cooked rice

1. Shred beef by cutting into 1/4-inch (1/2-cm) strips with the grain, then cut those strips into 2-inch (5-cm) lengths. Refrigerate until needed.
2. Heat oil in large pan over medium-high heat. Add onion, garlic, bell pepper, and *jalapeño*, sauté about 5 minutes.
3. Add tomatoes, oregano, allspice, salt, capers, and shredded beef, cook about 10 minutes, stirring frequently.
4. Correct seasonings, serve immediately, accompanied by rice.

**TWIST ON THE CLASSIC**

This makes a great filling for a submarine sandwich. If desired, top it with pepper cheese and heat the sandwich until the cheese melts.

# CURRIED LAMB (JAMAICA)

**Note:** Allow at least 3 hours to marinate the meat.

**Note:** Some of the many curry variations include the addition of coconut milk, tomatoes, and/or potatoes. Many islanders make this recipe with goat instead of lamb.

**Number of Servings:** 15
**Serving Size:** 6 oz. (170 g)
**Total Yield:** 5 lb., 13 1/2 oz. (2.7 kg)
**Food Balance:** Spicy/sour
**Wine Style:** Off-dry, low-oaked whites and soft reds
**Example:** Castello di Gabbiano Pinot Grigio or Chianti

**Cooking Method:** Braise

David Murray and Jules Selmes © Dorling Kindersley

© paul_brighton

**TWIST ON THE CLASSIC**

Instead of serving this over rice, serve it in a hollowed round of bread.

| INGREDIENTS | WEIGHT | | VOLUME | |
|---|---|---|---|---|
| | U.S. | METRIC | U.S. | METRIC |
| lamb, trimmed and cut into 1 1/2-inch (4-cm) cubes | 4 lb., 5 oz. | 2 kg | | |
| onion, large dice | 1 lb., 2 oz. | 511 g | 2 large | |
| garlic, smashed and minced | 1/2 oz. | 15 g | 4 cloves | |
| hot chilies, *habañero, serrano,* or pepper of choice, seeds and membranes removed, if desired, and minced | 1/2 oz. | 15 g or to taste | 2 each or to taste | |
| curry powder | 1 1/4 oz. | 36 g | 1/4 cup + 2 tablespoons | 90 mL |
| dried thyme | | | 2 teaspoons | 10 mL |
| bay leaves | | | 4 each | |
| ground allspice | 1/4 oz. | 8 g | 2 teaspoons | 10 mL |
| oil | | 43 g | 3 tablespoons | 45 mL |
| lamb or chicken stock or water | | | 1 quart (4 cups) | 960 mL |
| salt | | | as needed | |
| pepper | | | as needed | |
| fresh lime juice | | 57 g | 1/4 cup | 60 mL |

**Accompaniment:**
cooked rice

**Garnish:**
lime wedges

1. Place lamb, onion, garlic, chilies, curry powder, thyme, bay leaves, and allspice in nonreactive bowl. Mix thoroughly. Cover and refrigerate at least 3 hours or overnight.
2. Cover bottom of large pan with oil and cook over medium to medium-high heat until hot. Add lamb mixture and sauté until meat is browned, about 7 to 10 minutes.
3. Add stock and bring to a boil. Reduce heat, cover and simmer 45 minutes.
4. Remove cover and continue to simmer until meat is tender, about another 45 minutes. If too much liquid evaporates, cover the pan. If curry is too soupy, increase heat to evaporate more liquid. This dish should contain plenty of liquid for the cooked rice to soak up.
5. Correct seasonings, adding salt and pepper as needed. Remove bay leaves. Add lime juice and serve meat and sauce over rice. Garnish with lime wedges.

# JERK PORK (JAMAICA)

## PORK WITH SPICY RUB

**Note:** Adjust the heat of the marinade with the choice of pepper and/or by removing the seeds and ribs of the pepper to make it milder.

**Note:** Allow time to marinate the meat.

**Number of Servings:** 8

**Serving Size:** 5 to 6 oz. (142 to 170 g)

**Total Yield:** 3 lb. (1.4 kg)

**Food Balance:** Spicy/protein

**Wine Style:** Off-dry, low-oaked whites and soft reds

**Example:** Beringer Founders' Estate Sauvignon Blanc or Zinfandel

**Cooking Method:** Grill

**TWIST ON THE CLASSIC**

Use this marinade on chicken, beef, lamb, or fish.

| | WEIGHT | | VOLUME | |
| --- | --- | --- | --- | --- |
| **INGREDIENTS** | **U.S.** | **METRIC** | **U.S.** | **METRIC** |
| **Marinade:** | | | | |
| onion, dice | 6 oz. | 170 g | 1 large | |
| garlic, minced | 1/4 oz. | 8 g | 2 cloves | |
| hot chilies, *jalapeño* or *habañero*, seeds and ribs removed, if desired, minced | 1 3/4 oz. | 50 g | 3 each | |
| fresh ginger, peeled and minced | 1/4 oz. | 8 g | one 1/4-inch piece | one 1/2-cm piece |
| soy sauce | | 15 g | 1 tablespoon | 15 mL |
| ground allspice | | | 1 teaspoon | 5 mL |
| dried thyme | | | 1 teaspoon | 5 mL |
| ground cinnamon | | | 1/2 teaspoon | 3 mL |
| pork fillets or chops | 3 lb., 8 oz. | 1.6 kg | | |

1. Combine all marinade ingredients—onion, garlic, chilies, ginger, soy sauce, allspice, thyme, and cinnamon—in bowl of food processor fitted with knife blade.
2. Process until mixture becomes thick paste, scraping down sides of bowl as needed.
3. Rub mixture over pork, cover and refrigerate several hours or overnight.
4. Preheat grill, place pork on grill without removing marinade. Cook pork until done, having reached proper internal temperature.
5. Serve immediately.

testing © Shutterstock

# CARIBBEAN BAKED CHICKEN

© paul_brighton

**Note:** Allow time to marinate the chicken.

**Number of Servings:** 8
**Serving Size:** 1/4 chicken
**Total Yield:** 7 lb., 2 oz. (3.2 kg)
**Food Balance:** Spicy
**Wine Style:** Off-dry, low-oaked whites and soft reds
**Example:** Château St. Jean Pinot Blanc, Black Opal Shiraz, Meridian Vineyards Syrah

**Cooking Method:** Bake

| | WEIGHT | | VOLUME | |
|---|---|---|---|---|
| **INGREDIENTS** | **U.S.** | **METRIC** | **U.S.** | **METRIC** |
| chicken, cut into quarters, skin removed, if desired | about 6 lb. | 2.7 kg | 2 each | |
| dark rum | | 170 g | 3/4 cup | 180 mL |
| soy sauce | | 170 g | 3/4 cup | 180 mL |
| lime juice | | 78 g | 1/3 cup | 80 mL |
| onions, fine dice | 14 oz. | 397 g | 2 large | |
| garlic, minced | 1 oz. | 28 g | 8 cloves | |
| fresh ginger, peeled and minced | 1 1/2 oz. | 43 g | 1/4 cup | 60 mL |
| hot peppers, seeds and ribs removed, minced | 3 oz. | 86 g or to taste | 4 each or to taste | |
| dried thyme | 1 oz. | 28 g | 1/4 cup | 60 mL |
| dry mustard | | | 1 teaspoon | 5 mL |
| cornstarch | 1/2 oz. | 15 g | 1 tablespoon | 15 mL |
| water, cold | | 28 g | 2 tablespoons | 30 mL |

**Accompaniment:**
cooked rice

1. Wash chicken, place in ovenproof pan.
2. Place rum, soy sauce, lime juice, onions, garlic, ginger, hot peppers, thyme, and mustard in food processor fitted with knife blade. Pulse until paste, about 30 seconds, scraping down sides of bowl as needed. Pour paste over chicken pieces, refrigerate at least 4 hours.
3. Preheat oven to 350 degrees (180°C).
4. Place chicken in oven, bake about 1 hour, until chicken is done. Turn chicken once or twice while cooking and baste with pan juices two or three times.
5. Meanwhile, combine cornstarch with water, mix well, and set aside until needed. Remove roasting pan from oven, and remove chicken from pan.
6. Stirring constantly, add cornstarch mixture to pan on stovetop, cook over medium heat until slightly thickened. Correct seasonings.
7. Add chicken to pan and stir to coat. Serve immediately, accompanied by rice.

# SAUTÉED GROUPER

**Note:** Use this same preparation for snapper or any available fish fillets.

**Number of Servings:** 9
**Serving Size:** 6 oz. (170 g)
**Total Yield:** 3 lb., 10 1/2 oz. (1.7 kg)
**Food Balance:** Balanced
**Wine Style:** Wine friendly—Try your favorite!
**Example:** Rosemount Chardonnay or Shiraz

**Cooking Method:** Sauté

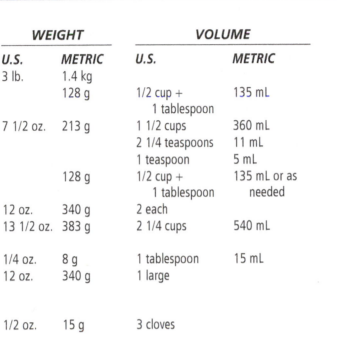

| | WEIGHT | | VOLUME | |
| --- | --- | --- | --- | --- |
| **INGREDIENTS** | **U.S.** | **METRIC** | **U.S.** | **METRIC** |
| grouper fillets | 3 lb. | 1.4 kg | | |
| lime juice | | 128 g | 1/2 cup + 1 tablespoon | 135 mL |
| flour | 7 1/2 oz. | 213 g | 1 1/2 cups | 360 mL |
| salt | | | 2 1/4 teaspoons | 11 mL |
| pepper | | | 1 teaspoon | 5 mL |
| oil | | 128 g | 1/2 cup + 1 tablespoon | 135 mL or as needed |
| onions, medium dice | 12 oz. | 340 g | 2 each | |
| tomatoes, canned or fresh, peeled, seeded, and diced | 13 1/2 oz. | 383 g | 2 1/4 cups | 540 mL |
| dried thyme | 1/4 oz. | 8 g | 1 tablespoon | 15 mL |
| bell pepper, red, green, or mixture, seeds and membranes removed, medium dice | 12 oz. | 340 g | 1 large | |
| garlic, smashed and minced | 1/2 oz. | 15 g | 3 cloves | |

**Accompaniment:**
cooked rice

**Garnish:**
lime wedges

Sautéing grouper
© Alena Yakusheva

© C M Kempin

1. Place grouper fillets in nonreactive bowl or pan. Pour lime juice over them and move fish so lime juice coats each fillet. Cover and refrigerate for at least 1 hour.
2. Mix flour with 1 1/2 teaspoons (8 mL) of salt and 3/4 teaspoon (4 mL) of pepper. Place on plate and dredge fillets to coat.
3. Heat about 2 tablespoons (28 g or 30 mL) of oil in large skillet (use enough oil to coat bottom of pan) over medium-high heat. Sauté fish in batches—depending on the thickness of the fillets, about 4 minutes on the first side and 3 minutes on the other side. When almost done, remove from skillet and keep warm in low oven. Continue sautéing the remaining fish, using additional oil as needed.
4. Coat bottom of skillet with oil and heat over medium heat. Add onions and sauté a few minutes until softened.
5. Add tomatoes, thyme, bell pepper, and garlic. Cook about 10 minutes, until softened. Add remaining 3/4 teaspoon (4 mL) salt and 1/4 teaspoon (2 mL) pepper.
6. Push vegetables aside and add fried fish to skillet. Cook another few minutes until done and thoroughly hot. Correct seasonings.
7. Serve fish with some of the vegetables, accompanied by rice and garnished with lime wedges.

## TWIST ON THE CLASSIC

To add spice, add some minced hot pepper with the bell pepper in this recipe.

# SHRIMP AND MANGO CURRY

**Note:** If ripe mangoes are unavailable, try substituting ripe pineapple for the mango.

**Number of Servings:** 10  **Cooking Method:** Sauté
**Serving Size:** 8 oz. (227 g)
**Total Yield:** 5 lb. (2.3 kg)
**Food Balance:** Sweet/spicy
**Wine Style:** Off-dry, low-oaked whites and soft reds
**Example:** Château St. Jean Riesling or Gewürztraminer, Penfolds Riesling

*Cutting along each side of the pit*
Pearson Education/PH College

| INGREDIENTS | WEIGHT U.S. | WEIGHT METRIC | VOLUME U.S. | VOLUME METRIC |
|---|---|---|---|---|
| butter | 1 oz. | 28 g | 2 tablespoons | 30 mL |
| onions, small dice | 8 oz. | 227 g | 2 small | |
| garlic, minced | 1/2 oz. | 15 g | 4 cloves | |
| fresh ginger, peeled and minced | 1 oz. | 28 g | 2 tablespoons | 30 mL |
| *jalapeño* chili, seeds and ribs removed, minced | 1/2 oz. | 15 g | 1 each | |
| curry powder | 3/4 oz. | 22 g | 3 tablespoons | 45 mL |
| salt | | | 3/4 teaspoon | 4 mL |
| water | | 680 g | 3 cups | 720 mL |
| sweet potatoes, peeled and cut into large dice | 1 lb., 2 oz. | 511 g | 2 large | |
| shrimp, peeled and deveined | 2 lb. | 908 g | | |
| mangoes, peeled and cut into dice | about 1 lb. | 454 g | 2 each | |

**Accompaniment:**

cooked rice

*After making crosscuts, press up on the rind side to create standing cubes*
Pearson Education/PH College

1. Melt butter in saucepan over medium heat, add onions, garlic, ginger, and *jalapeño*. Sauté until soft, about 3 minutes.
2. Add curry powder and salt, stir to mix.
3. Add water and sweet potatoes, continue to cook, uncovered, until almost soft, about 12 to 15 minutes.
4. Add shrimp and mangoes, stir occasionally, cook until shrimp is done, about 5 to 7 minutes. Correct seasonings.
5. Serve immediately over rice.

*Cutting cubes from rind of mango*
Pearson Education/PH College

© paul_brighton

## MOROS Y CRISTIANOS (CUBA)

### BLACK BEANS AND RICE

**Note:** Serve this dish as a side dish to accompany an entrée (particularly a spicy one), or serve it as an entrée.

**Note:** Allow time to soak the beans in advance.

**Number of Servings:** 14
**Serving Size:** 4 oz. (114 g) side dish
**Total Yield:** 3 lb., 8 oz. (1.6 kg)
**Food Balance:** Protein/balanced
**Wine Style:** Wide variety—Pinot Blanc, Sauvignon Blanc, Merlot, Shiraz, or Zinfandel
**Example:** Château Souverain Sauvignon Blanc, Merlot, or Zinfandel

**Cooking Method:** Boil, sauté

| INGREDIENTS | WEIGHT U.S. | WEIGHT METRIC | VOLUME U.S. | VOLUME METRIC |
|---|---|---|---|---|
| dried black beans | 7 1/2 oz. | 213 g | 1 cup | 240 mL |
| vegetable oil | | 15 g | 1 tablespoon | 15 mL |
| onion, medium dice | 6 oz. | 170 g | 1 large | |
| garlic, minced | 1/4 oz. | 8 g | 2 cloves | |
| rice | 10 1/2 oz. | 298 g | 1 1/2 cups | 360 mL |
| water | | 680 g | 3 cups | 720 mL |
| salt | 1/2 oz. | 15 g | 2 teaspoons | 10 mL |
| pepper | | | 1 teaspoon | 5 mL |

1. Wash beans, place in pot, cover with water, soak in refrigerator overnight.
2. Bring beans (covered with water) to boil, reduce heat and simmer until almost tender, about 45 minutes to 1 hour. Add more water, if necessary, to prevent burning.
3. Heat oil in another pot, add onion and garlic, and sauté until soft, about 4 minutes.
4. Add rice, sauté until rice begins to brown.
5. Add water, salt, pepper, beans, and bean liquid. Bring to boil, reduce heat, cover, simmer 20 minutes, and remove from heat. All liquid should be absorbed.
6. Let sit, covered, for 10 minutes. Correct seasonings, serve.

© Dorling Kindersley

# COU-COU (BARBADOS)

## CORNMEAL MUSH WITH OKRA

Ian Cummings © Rough Guides Dorling Kindersley

**Number of Servings:** 13
**Serving Size:** 4 oz. (114 g)
**Total Yield:** 3 lb., 4 oz. (1.5 kg)

**Cooking Method:** Boil

| INGREDIENTS | WEIGHT | | VOLUME | |
|---|---|---|---|---|
| | U.S. | METRIC | U.S. | METRIC |
| cornmeal | 7 1/2 oz. | 213 g | 2 cups | 480 mL |
| water, cold | | | 1 quart + 1 cup (5 cups) | 1.2 L |
| okra, cut into 1/4-inch (1/2-cm) rounds | 12 oz. | 340 g | 3 1/2 cups | 840 mL |
| salt | 1/2 oz. | 15 g | 2 teaspoons | 10 mL |
| hot sauce | | | 1 teaspoon | 5 mL or to taste |
| butter | 1 oz. | 28 g | 2 tablespoons | 30 mL |

1. Combine cornmeal and 2 cups (454 g or 480 mL) of water in bowl, set aside.
2. Bring remaining 3 cups (680 g or 720 mL) water to boil, add okra, and boil until tender, about 4 to 5 minutes.
3. Reduce heat to low, add salt and hot sauce, gradually add cornmeal mixture, stirring constantly with wooden spoon. Cook, stirring constantly, until mixture becomes very thick and begins to leave sides of pan.
4. Correct seasonings. Transfer to bowl, place butter on top to melt, serve immediately.

## TWIST ON THE CLASSIC

Treat *Cou-Cou* like polenta. Place partially cooled *Cou-Cou* in a loaf pan and cool completely. For service, remove from pan, cut into slices, and sauté.

---

# COCONUT BAKE
# (TRINIDAD, TOBAGO, JAMAICA, AND OTHER ISLANDS)

© Tony

**Number of Servings:** 10
**Serving Size:** 1 wedge 1/10th of round
**Dough:** 1 lb., 5 oz. (596 g)

**Cooking Method:** Bake

| INGREDIENTS | WEIGHT | | VOLUME | |
|---|---|---|---|---|
| | U.S. | METRIC | U.S. | METRIC |
| coconut, dried, unsweetened | 2 oz. | 57 g | 3/4 cup | 180 mL |
| flour, all purpose, sifted | 9 oz. | 256 g | 2 1/4 cups | 540 mL |
| baking powder | 1/2 oz. | 15 g | 1 tablespoon | 15 mL |
| sugar | 1 oz. | 28 g | 2 tablespoons | 30 mL |
| salt | | | 3/4 teaspoon | 4 mL |
| butter, unsalted, cold, cut into pieces | 2 oz. | 57 g | 1/4 cup | 60 mL |
| coconut milk, thin, unsweetened | | 170 g | 3/4 cup | 180 mL |

1. Place coconut in food processor fitted with knife blade. Pulse until fine. Add flour, baking powder, sugar, and salt. Pulse to combine.
2. Place butter on top of flour mixture. Pulse until the size of peas.
3. With processor running, add coconut milk through feed tube. Pulse until it forms ball.

## TWIST ON THE CLASSIC

Make this part of an English Tea by serving it with lemon curd. Either serve a wedge of the coconut bake or prepare it as biscuits for an individual portion.

④ Remove from processor and place on lightly floured counter. Knead about 1 minute to combine well. Cover and allow to rest 30 minutes. Meanwhile, place oven rack in middle of oven and preheat oven to 400 degrees (205°C). Place parchment paper on baking sheet.

⑤ Shape dough into 3/4-inch-thick (2-cm-thick) round disk. Prick top with fork to form wedges (like a sliced pie). Bake for 20 to 25 minutes, until golden. Cool on rack.

> Often, coconut bake is eaten for breakfast with butter, cheese, salt fish, or herring.

## CARIBBEAN BANANAS

**Number of Servings:** 10
**Serving Size:** 1 banana

**Cooking Method:** Sauté

| | WEIGHT | | VOLUME | |
|---|---|---|---|---|
| **INGREDIENTS** | **U.S.** | **METRIC** | **U.S.** | **METRIC** |
| butter | 5 oz. | 142 g | 10 tablespoons (1 stick + 2 tablespoons) | 150 mL |
| brown sugar | 10 1/2 oz. | 298 g | 1 1/2 cups | 360 mL |
| fresh lime juice | | 57 g | 1/4 cup | 60 mL |
| dark rum | | 227 g | 1 cup | 240 mL |
| ground allspice | 1/4 oz. | 8 g | 2 teaspoons | 10 mL |
| ground cinnamon | | | 1 teaspoon | 5 mL |
| bananas, peeled and quartered (sliced in half through width and length) or sliced diagonally into slices about 2 1/2 to 3 inches (6 to 8 cm) long | 3 lb., 2 oz. | 1.4 kg | 10 each | |
| ice cream, if desired | | | | |

> **TWIST ON THE CLASSIC**
>
> Serve the bananas in a crêpe and garnish with a dollop of whipped cream or ice cream.
> If desired, try adding other fruits like peaches, cherries, apricots, or apples. If using apples, add them first to allow them extra time to cook.

① Melt butter in skillet over medium heat. Add brown sugar, stirring constantly. Cook until thick and syrup-like, about 2 to 3 minutes.

② Add lime juice, rum, allspice, and cinnamon. Stir constantly and cook until thick, about 2 to 4 minutes. With match, light rum to burn off alcohol, if desired. *Note: If burning off alcohol in rum, be careful with the flame. Hold match to liquid in skillet. Immediately move hand out of the way. Gently shake pan until flame subsides, and then proceed with recipe.*

③ Add banana pieces. Turn gently to coat them thoroughly with syrup, cook until slightly softened, about 1 or 2 minutes.

④ Serve immediately, alone or with ice cream.

*Cooked sugar mixture just before adding bananas*

Courtesy of CanolaInfo.org

# RUM CAKE

Courtesy of CanolaInfo.org

**Note:** This cake improves with aging, so prepare it the day before service. The rum tastes quite strong the day it is made.

**Number of Servings:** 15

**Serving Size:** Two 1-inch (2 1/2-cm) slices

**Total Yield:** One 10-inch (25-cm) Bundt or angel-food pan

**Cooking Method:** Bake

| | WEIGHT | | VOLUME | |
|---|---|---|---|---|
| INGREDIENTS | U.S. | METRIC | U.S. | METRIC |
| **Soaking Liquid:** | | | | |
| butter | 4 oz. | 114 g | 8 tablespoons (1 stick) | 120 mL |
| water | | 28 g | 2 tablespoons | 30 mL |
| sugar | 6 oz. | 170 g | 3/4 cup | 180 mL |
| rum, dark or golden | | 114 g | 1/2 cup | 120 mL |
| **Cake:** | | | | |
| all-purpose flour, sifted | 12 1/4 oz. | 348 g | 3 cups | 720 mL |
| baking powder | 1/4 oz. | 8 g | 2 teaspoons | 10 mL |
| baking soda | | | 1/2 teaspoon | 3 mL |
| salt | | | 1/4 teaspoon | 2 mL |
| butter, softened | 12 oz. | 340 g | 1 1/2 cups (3 sticks) | 360 mL |
| sugar | 12 1/2 oz. | 355 g | 1 1/2 cups | 360 mL |
| vanilla | | | 2 teaspoons | 10 mL |
| lemon peel, minced | 1/4 oz. | 8 g | 1 tablespoon | 15 mL |
| rum, dark or golden | | 170 g | 3/4 cup | 180 mL |
| eggs | 6 3/4 oz. | 191 g | 4 each | |
| milk | | 170 g | 3/4 cup | 180 mL |

**Garnish:**

confectioner's sugar, for
  dusting

effe45 © Shutterstock

## SOAKING LIQUID:

1. Melt butter in saucepan. Add water, sugar, and rum.
2. Bring to boil. Reduce heat and simmer for about 10 to 12 minutes, until slightly thickened. Do not overcook.
3. Remove from heat. Cool. Set aside until needed.

## CAKE:

1. Pan-spray or grease 10-inch (25-cm) tube pan or Bundt pan. Position rack in center of oven. Preheat oven to 350 degrees (180°C).
2. Sift together flour, baking powder, baking soda, and salt. Set aside until needed.
3. Cream softened butter and sugar in mixer until light and fluffy using wire beater, if available.
4. Add vanilla and lemon peel. Mix well. Add rum and mix thoroughly. Add eggs, one at a time, beating well after each addition.
5. Add 1/3 of flour mixture, beat on lowest speed just to incorporate. Add half of milk, mix just to incorporate.
6. Repeat procedure with remaining ingredients: half of remaining flour, remaining milk, then remaining flour. After each addition, mix just to incorporate. *Over-mixing the batter could result in tough cake or uneven texture.*
7. Pour into prepared pan. Bake for 50 to 60 minutes, until knife inserted in cake comes out clean.
8. Place cake, still in pan, on rack. Use skewer or pointed knife to make holes into cake. Spoon soaking liquid over cake. Allow to stand at least 30 minutes, so liquid soaks into cake.
9. While still a bit warm, invert cake on serving plate. Allow to cool completely. Cover and reserve until serving time. Dust with confectioner's sugar and slice into 1-inch (2 1/2-cm) pieces. Serve two slices per serving.

Courtesy King Arthur Flour

### TWIST ON THE CLASSIC

For presentation, prepare individual cakes in miniature ring pans. Surround the cake with cut tropical fruits and garnish with a scoop of coconut ice cream.

# Glossary

*achiote*—Ground annatto seeds used in cooking that give a yellow color to the dish, used frequently in Mexico

*adobo*—A seasoning paste containing ground chili peppers, herbs, spices, and vinegar, used in many preparations, including meats and salsas in Mexico

*aioli*—Mayonnaise flavored with garlic

*aji*—Spicy chili seasoning frequently used in the cooking of Peru

*al dente*—Literally "to the tooth," meaning cooked until done but still crisp; an Italian term

*antipasto*—An assorted appetizer platter usually containing salami, cheese, olives, and grilled vegetables, popular in Italy

*aquavit*—Literally "water of life" in Swedish, a strong liquor made from potatoes or grains, its flavoring comes from caraway, anise, fennel, coriander, star anise, or any combination of these herbs; first made in the 1400s

*arepa*—Type of cornbread commonly eaten in Venezuela and Colombia

*Ashkenazi Jews*—Jewish people with central or Eastern European heritage

*bacala*—Salted codfish prepared in Italy

*Backerei*—German bakeries that sell all sorts of breads and rolls

*bagoong*—Shrimp paste used in the Philippines

*banchan*—Another word sometimes used for *panch'an*; side dishes like vegetables, salads, pickles, and condiments served with Korean meals

*bangers and mash*—Sausages and mashed potatoes served in pubs throughout the British Isles

*barbie*—The Australian term for a barbecue grill

*basmati*—An aromatic type of long-grain rice preferred in India, grown in the foothills of the Himalayas

*beef stroganoff*—A stewlike dish consisting of pieces of beef cooked with mushrooms, onions, and sour cream; originated in Russia

*berbere*—Spicy seasoning mixture used in Ethiopia containing cumin, coriander, ginger, cardamom, nutmeg, cinnamon, allspice, paprika, fenugreek, salt, pepper, and cayenne

*beurre blanc*—Butter sauce often used in France

*bigos*—The national dish of Poland, consists of sauerkraut cooked with a variety of meats and sausages

*biryani*—A baked rice dish that usually contains *basmati* rice flavored with saffron and meat, popular in India

*biscuits*—British word for cookies

*blinis*—Small, buckwheat pancakes traditionally topped with sour cream, smoked salmon, caviar, or other toppings; originated in Russia

*bourekas*—Turnovers of phyllo dough filled with spinach or potato, popular in Israel

*borscht*—Soup made from beets and other ingredients, popular in Eastern Europe

*bourewors*—A popular Afrikaner sausage dish

*braunschweiger*—Liverwurst or liver sausage that originated in the town of Braunschweig in northern Germany

*bredie*—A stew served in South Africa containing lamb or mutton, onions, and other vegetables

*brigades*—Teams of people working in the kitchen who prepare food items according to the type of cooking techniques involved in the preparation

*brodetto*—Italian fish soup resembling the French soup, *bouillabaisse*

*bulgogi*—Marinated strips of beef grilled at the table, a popular Korean dish

*bulgur*—Cracked wheat that is boiled and then dried (dehydrated)

*burrito*—A taco prepared with a wheat tortilla, popular in Mexico

*café au lait*—Strong coffee mixed with warmed milk, served throughout France

*callaloo*—Greens obtained from the taro plant; also the name of a soup served in the Caribbean Islands made with greens and other ingredients, including salt pork, crab, and/or coconut milk

*calvados*—Apple brandy made in Normandy in the northwest of France

*Campari*—Bitter, red liquor served as an aperitif from the region of Lombardy (in Italy)

*cannellini*—White kidney beans frequently consumed in Italy

*caper*—Bud from a shrub that grows in Mediterranean areas; usually preserved by pickling or salting

*carpetbagger steak*—Steak with a pocket cut into side, filled with oysters, and then grilled

*cassoulet*—A one-pot dish containing various meats, white beans, and herbs; originated in Languedoc, France

*caste*—One's social class; four distinct castes, or social levels, exist in Indian society, and relatively little intermingling occurs among these castes

*cawl*—Clear broth containing vegetables, served in Wales (British Isles)

*cecina*—Dried beef popular in northern Mexico

*cena*—Light evening meal served around nine or ten o'clock in Mexico

*ceviche*—Dish consisting of raw fish marinated in citrus juices with other seasonings; the citrus juice "cooks" the fish, changing its appearance from translucent to opaque; originally from Peru, *ceviche* is served throughout Latin America

*challah*—Braided egg bread traditionally served on the Sabbath and all holidays in Israel and in Jewish homes throughout the world

*chao*—Cooking technique known as stir-frying; Chinese term

*chapati flour*—A finely ground whole wheat flour, commonly used in India

*charcuterie*—French word that refers to all sorts of sausages and cured meats

*charlotte russe*—A molded dessert consisting of a core of Bavarian cream folded with whipped cream and surrounded by ladyfinger biscuits; a French confection

*chartreuse*—A molded dish with a decorative outside of colorful vegetables and an inside containing vegetables, game, and/or poultry

*chayote*—A common vegetable in Mexico, sometimes called "green pear"

*chelo*—Steamed rice popular in the Middle East

*chelo kebah*—A dish consisting of rice, marinated lamb, spices, and yogurt; the national dish of Iran

*chili relleno*—A chili pepper stuffed with cheese, meat, or another filling, then dipped in batter and deep-fried, served in Mexico

*chimichanga*—A deep-fried burrito, popular in Mexico

*chips*—Thickly cut french fries served throughout the British Isles

*cholent*—Known as "Sabbath stew," a slowly cooked casserole containing rice or barley, beans, meat, and potatoes; traditionally cooked at a low temperature in an oven in a commercial bakery all Friday night and then eaten on Saturday, as no work may be performed on the Sabbath; served in Israel and Eastern Europe

*chorizo*—A spicy pork sausage flavored with garlic and paprika, popular in Spain and Mexico

*choucroute*—Popular casserole containing sauerkraut, various meats, and sausage,

usually accompanied by boiled potatoes, served in Alsace-Lorraine, France

*churros*—*Choux* pastry dough deep-fried in olive oil and eaten at breakfast; sold by street vendors in Spain

*chutney*—Spicy relish made from one or more fruits or vegetables and used as a condiment to accompany many foods, popular in India

*cockaleekie*—A thick chicken soup containing leeks and barley, from Scotland

*colcannon*—An Irish dish of potatoes mixed with kale or cabbage

*color*—An orange-red flavoring that combines garlic, paprika, and melted fat; used in Chile

*comida*—The main meal of the day in Mexico, eaten around two o'clock in the afternoon

*confit*—A method of slow cooking goose or duck in fat, popular in France

*congee*—Rice (or millet or barley) porridge served in China for breakfast, to babies, and to ill people

*couscous*—A tiny pasta shaped like a grain and made from semolina, popular in the northern part of Africa

*creole*—Style of cooking melding Incan and Spanish culinary components

*crêpes*—Thin, delicate pancakes, served rolled around a savory or sweet filling; originated in Brittany, France

*dal*—Actually means "split legumes," a dish of mildly spiced lentil purée widely consumed in the north of India

*dashi*—Japanese stock made from dried bonito and dried kelp; forms the foundation for much Japanese cookery, including soups and braised dishes

*dendê*—An orange-colored oil derived from the palm; brought to Brazil by slaves from western Africa where it is used extensively

*dhwen-jang*—Korean bean paste

*dim sum*—Snack foods eaten for lunch or any time throughout the day; can include soups, steamed buns, stuffed dumplings, sweet and savory pastries, and much more; originated in the southern region of Canton, China

*dolma*—A filling, usually of meat and/or rice, enclosed in an edible wrapper such as grape leaves or cabbage leaves, popular throughout the Middle East

*Emmentaler*—Type of Swiss cheese from Bavaria

*empanada*—Small turnover or pie filled with any combination of meats and seasonings wrapped in a soft, flaky crust, popular in South America and Spain

*escabeche*—Pickled peppers or vegetables served in Mexico

*falafel*—Fried chickpea patties served in pita bread topped with salad and a *tahini* sauce; known as Israeli hot dogs; served throughout the Middle East

*feijoada completa*—Dish combining beans with a variety of smoked and cured meats and seasonings; the national dish of Brazil

*feta*—A sheep's milk cheese with a salty flavor and crumbly texture, quite popular throughout the Middle East

*fish and chips*—Deep-fried fish and thickly cut french fries, served with malt vinegar; popular throughout the British Isles

*fjords*—Inlets in Scandinavia

*foie gras*—The highly prized goose liver prominent in France, produced by force-feeding geese so they develop large livers

*forellen blau*—Literally meaning "blue trout" in German, this fish is prepared by dropping a live trout in boiling water containing a little vinegar; the vinegar causes the skin of the fish to take on a blue cast, thus the name

*frikadeller*—Ground meat mixture that is made into meatballs, patties, or used as forcemeat; popular in Denmark

*frito misto di Mare*—Assorted deep-fried fish and seafood; Italian term

*gado-gado*—An Indonesian salad consisting of a variety of vegetables accompanied by peanut sauce dressing

*garde manger*—Preparation of cold foods and garnishes

*gazpacho*—Cold tomato vegetable soup; originated in Andalusia, Spain *gefilte fish*—A fish dumpling that is served cold and usually accompanied by horseradish; originated in Eastern Europe, served in Israel

*ghee*—Clarified butter; cooking fat of choice throughout India

*gnocchi*—Potato and flour dumpling served in northern Italy; served with a sauce, like pasta

*golabki*—Polish stuffed cabbage roll cooked in a tomato-based sweet-and-sour sauce

*golubtsi*—Russian stuffed cabbage roll surrounded by a sour cream sauce

*goulash*—Hungarian beef stew containing onions, tomatoes, and potatoes

*grappa*—Clear-colored, sharp-tasting brandy made in Italy

*gravlax*—Salmon cured with salt, sugar, and dill, popular in Scandinavia

*gremolada*—Aromatic ingredients, including lemon zest, parsley, rosemary, sage, and garlic, that are added to braised veal shanks (*ossobuco*) a few minutes before serving; Italian term

*guacamole*—A spread consisting of mashed avocado, onion, tomato, and usually chili peppers; ingredients vary from region to region; popular throughout Mexico

*gyros*—Lamb cooked on a rotisserie, then sliced in thin shavings and served in pita bread or plain; served in Greece

*haggis*—Scottish dish consisting of sheep's heart, liver, and lung mixed with oatmeal, stuffed in a sheep's stomach and boiled

*handai*—Wide wooden bowl used for cooling rice in Japan

*hangi*—Oven dug in the ground by Māori

*haricots*—Thin, tender green beans; French word

*harissa*—Hot pepper paste used in Morocco

*hoisin*—A sweet and spicy sauce made from soybeans; used in cooking, marinades, and dips in China

*holubtsi*—Ukrainian stuffed cabbage rolls filled with meat, kasha, and rice

*hummus*—A spread combining chickpeas with garlic, lemon juice, *tahini,* and other ingredients; served throughout the Middle East

*injera*—A spongy flatbread served in Ethiopia, used to scoop food

*jambon Serrano*—Spanish cured ham with a sweet-salty taste similar to the *prosciutto* of Italy

*kadayif*—A shredded variety of phyllo dough that looks like shredded wheat

*kaeng*—Thai word for liquid, refers to amount of liquid in a dish

*kaffeestunde*—Literally translated "coffee hour" in German, a late afternoon snack consisting of pastry and coffee or other beverage

*karahi*—A wok-type deep pan with a rounded bottom and handles on each side, used for frying in India

*kasha*—Buckwheat groats; a grain

*kashrut*—The rules governing kosher diet and preparation

*katsuo*—Dried bonito shavings (bonito is a fish in the mackerel family), frequently used in Japanese cookery

*kecap*—Sweet soy sauce used in Indonesia

*kibbe*—Ground lamb and grain patty that is served either raw or cooked, popular throughout the Middle East

*kibbutz*—A farm collective in Israel where the people who live and work on the farm own the entire business

*kimch'i*—Spicy, fermented cabbage or vegetable mixture popular in Korea and served at every meal

*kippers*—Smoked herring, frequently served at breakfast or tea in the British Isles

*kirschwasser*—Strong cherry liqueur produced in the Black Forest (in Germany)

*klippfisk*—Popular dish containing salted cod; served in Norway

*knedlíky*—Dumplings served frequently in the Czech Republic

*knish*—A dumpling consisting of dough surrounding one of several fillings; popular in Israel

*kombu*—Dried kelp, a seaweed often used in Japanese cookery

*konditorei*—Bakeries that sell pastries found in Germany; they usually contain tables and chairs where customers can sit and order a slice of pastry or ice cream with coffee or other beverages

*kugel*—Often called noodle pudding, a casserole usually consisting of noodles, cottage cheese, sour cream, raisins, and cinnamon; other vegetables can form a kugel; popular in Israel

*kumara*—Type of sweet potato indigenous to New Zealand

*labaneh*—A cheese made from curdled yogurt, served in the Middle East

*lassi*—A yogurt drink popular in India

*latkes*—Potato pancakes, traditionally served at Chanukah

*lebkuchen*—Spiced honey cookie eaten alone or baked in large pieces and used as the base for gingerbread houses; popular in Germany

*lumpia*—Filipino version of Chinese spring rolls

*mamaliga*—Cornmeal mush served in Romania, resembles the Italian polenta

*manioc*—A starchy root vegetable, sometimes called *cassava*

*marinara*—A tomato-based sauce containing no meat; served often in Italy

*masa*—Ground corn used for making tortillas and other foods in Mexico

*masala*—A mixture of spices frequently used in India

*mazza*—Appetizers served throughout the Middle East

*mealies*—A porridge made from corn, often consumed by poor people in South Africa

*merienda*—Similar to the English tea, a Mexican meal at which pastries and coffee or hot chocolate are served, around six in the evening

*meseta*—High, dry plateaus in Spain

*metzgerie*—Shops carrying cold cuts and sausages in Germany

*mezze*—Appetizers served throughout the Middle East

*millet*—A grain

*minestrone*—Italian vegetable soup

*mirin*—Japanese sweet rice wine used for cooking

*miso*—Fermented bean paste, used as a flavoring for soups or sauces; Japanese

*mititei*—Garlic-infused meatballs from Romania

*mittagessen*—The main meal of the day in Germany, served in the afternoon around twelve or one o'clock

*moa*—Large, flightless bird standing up to 15 feet tall, native to New Zealand, became extinct in early 1770s

*mole*—Savory Mexican sauce containing unsweetened chocolate, chilies, tomatoes, and spices

*molkerien*—Shops selling milk, cheeses, and other dairy products in Germany

*monsoons*—Seasonal winds that affect the weather

*moussaka*—A dish consisting of alternating layers of ground lamb, fried eggplant, and sauce, from Greece

*mutton*—Sheep meat, which has a stronger flavor and tougher texture than younger lamb

*nabémono*—One-pot cookery common in Japan; similar to fondue, diners cook their own food in a pot of stock heating on the dining table

*nám pla*—Fish sauce used extensively in Thailand

*nuoc mam*—Fish sauce used extensively in Vietnam

*olla podrida*—A casserole containing almost anything that can be stewed; literally translated "rotten pot"; originated in central Spain

*ossobuco*—Braised veal shanks popular in Italy

*outback*—The large areas of bush country in the interior sections of Australia

*ouzo*—An anise-flavored alcoholic beverage that turns cloudy when mixed with water; a popular drink in Greece

*paan*—An assortment of aromatic spices and herbs to clear the palate and aid digestion; served at the end of the meal in India

*paella*—A casserole of saffron rice with a variety of meats, chicken, seafood, and vegetables named for the pot in which it is cooked; originated in Valencia (Spain); every region of Spain has its own variation of this national dish

*Pākehā*—Māori word for Europeans

*pampa*—Humid grasslands found in Argentina and Uruguay; ideal lands for raising livestock

*pancetta*—Unsmoked pork used for flavoring in Italy

*panch'an*—Side dishes like vegetables, salads, pickles, and condiments served with Korean meals; sometimes called "*banchan*"

*paprikash*—Hungarian stew–type dish containing plenty of paprika

*parve*—Kosher foods that can accompany either meat or dairy products

*pasta e fagioli*—Tomato-based soup containing pasta and beans; popular in Italy

*pasty*—A turnover usually filled with meat, potatoes, and vegetables served in the British Isles

*patis*—Fish sauce used in the Philippines; salty, thin, and amber in color

*pavlova*—An Australian/New Zealand dessert consisting of a large meringue shell filled with whipped cream and fresh fruits; named for the famous ballerina Anna Pavlova

*pebre*—A sauce made of onions, garlic, chili peppers, coriander, vinegar, and olive oil; used as a seasoning in Chile

*pepper pot*—Vegetable soup prepared with any available meat and vegetables; popular in the Caribbean Islands

*pesto*—Basil-garlic sauce served with pasta and in other dishes, originated in the city of Genoa (in Italy)

*pfefferpotthast*—A stew of beef short ribs containing lots of pepper; served in Germany

*phó'*—Rice noodle soup in a meat broth strongly flavored with cilantro, garlic, and

*nuoc mam;* commonly eaten for breakfast in Vietnam but served at any meal; considered the national dish of Vietnam

*picante*—Mexican word for "hot and spicy"

*piripiri*—Spicy seasoning mixture used in Mozambique

*piroshki*—Baked or fried dumplings filled with meat and cabbage, popular in Russia

*pita bread*—Also called pocket bread, a yeast bread dough formed into a disk then baked in a very hot oven; a pocket forms in the bread during baking; popular throughout the Middle East

*polenta*—Starch made of cornmeal that sometimes replaces pasta in the north of Italy

*polo*—A favorite Iranian dish consisting of steamed rice with combinations of fruits, vegetables, nuts, and meats

*ponzu*—A citrus-based dipping sauce; used in Japan

*porotos granados*—Dish containing a mixture of beans, corn, and squash; the national dish of Chile

*porridge*—Cooked cereal, usually oatmeal; British term

*potato crisps*—British for the American term "potato chips"

*prawns*—Large shrimp

*primo piatto*—Literally "first course" in Italy, this usually consists of soup, pasta, rice, or polenta and is followed by the meat course

*prosciutto*—Salted, air-cured ham from Italy

*quesadillas*—A tortilla topped with cheese and roasted, peeled peppers or other ingredients; if desired, folded in half and fried until the cheese melts; served in Mexico

*queso*—The Mexican word for cheese

*quinoa*—A grain that thrives in the mountains; originally raised by the Inca Indians and still consumed today

*ragu*—Italian tomato-based sauce containing meat

*raita*—Yogurt salad, popular in India

*retsina*—A sharp Greek wine, flavored with resin

*rijsttafel*—Literally meaning "rice table," opulent display of many different dishes accompanied by rice, requiring many servants for preparation and service, developed by the Dutch settlers in Indonesia

*risotto*—Creamy rice dish popular in the north of Italy

*rømmegrøt*—Porridge made with sour cream, popular in Norway

*rôtisseur*—Person in kitchen responsible for foods that require roasting; French word

*sake*—Japanese rice wine, served warm in the winter

*saltimbocca*—Dish consisting of pounded veal with a thin slice of *prosciutto,* seasoned and braised in white wine (Italian)

*sambar*—Spicy lentil dish widely consumed in the south of India

*Sambuca*—Clear, anise-flavored liqueur served as an after-dinner cordial; originated in Italy

*samp*—Cornmeal mush widely consumed in central Africa

*sarmale*—Romanian stuffed cabbage roll

*sashimi*—Raw fish sliced thinly, accompanied by *wasabi;* served in Japan

*satay*—Grilled meat accompanied by a spicy peanut sauce; commonly served in Indonesia

*saucier*—Person in kitchen responsible for preparation of sauces; French word

*sauerbraten*—Beef marinated in an acidic liquid (often vinegar, but it depends on the region), then braised; served throughout Germany

*schnitzel*—Veal cutlets that are pounded thin, sometimes breaded, and then pan-fried, popular in Germany

*Schwartzwälder Kirschtorte*—Black Forest cherry cake, a torte featuring cake layers flavored with *Kirschwasser,* a cherry liquor, and filled with whipped cream and cherry filling; originated in the Black Forest region (in Germany)

*scone*—A slightly sweetened bread product (like an American biscuit) containing dried currants; popular in the British Isles

*selametan*—Ceremonial feast that marks important events in Indonesia

*Sephardic Jews*—Jewish people from Greece, Turkey, Spain, and northern Africa

*shakshouka*—Israeli dish of sautéed tomatoes, onions, garlic, and herbs topped with a poached egg

*shearer's stew*—Lamb stew with dumplings served in Australia

*shepherd's pie*—A dish containing cooked beef topped with mashed potatoes; served throughout the British Isles

*shish kebob*—Smaller cubes of meat and sometimes vegetables placed on a skewer, then grilled over fire; widely consumed in the Middle East

*shwarma*—Grilled slices of meat served in a pita with salad, served in the Middle East

*siomai*—Filipino dumplings

*siopao*—Filipino steamed buns with a variety of fillings

*smörgåsbord*—A buffet laden with all sorts of meats, seafood, vegetables, salads, cheeses, and breads; contains as many as sixty food items; popular in Sweden

*smørrebrød*—Literally "buttered bread," an opened-faced sandwich with a base of thin bread or cracker that is spread with butter, then topped with meat, seafood, or cheese and crowned with an eye-catching garnish; the Danes are known for these sandwiches, which resemble canapés

*soba*—Oriental noodle made from buckwheat

*sofrito*—Mixture of sautéed green peppers, onion, garlic, and tomatoes, commonly used in Spanish cooking

*soju*—Korean distilled grain liquor

*soto*—Indonesian chicken and coconut milk soup

*spaetzle*—A starch that is a cross between a dumpling and a noodle; popular in Germany and areas in France near the German border

*spanakopita*—A dish consisting of phyllo dough layered with a spinach and feta mixture, from Greece

*steak and kidney pie*—A stewlike combination of kidneys and steak topped with a pastry crust, popular in the British Isles

*stollen*—Traditional Christmas bread that originated in Dresden, Germany

*sushi*—Raw or cooked fish, vinegared rice, and, often, vegetable(s) rolled in a wrapper of *nori* seaweed; accompanied by *wasabi;* popular in Japan

*taco*—Meat, beans, cheese, vegetables, or any combination of filling possibilities placed on a soft corn tortilla, topped with sauce, then rolled in the tortilla, which encases the filling; popular in Mexico

*tagine*—A type of stew containing meat and, often, fruit served in Morocco; a pot used for cooking a *tagine* (stew), with a cone-shaped lid containing a hole on the top so steam can escape

*tahini*—Sesame seed paste, sort of like a peanut butter made from sesame seeds; used throughout the Middle East

*tamales*—Mexican entrée consisting of corn husks or banana leaves encasing filling ingredients that are steamed; husks or leaves are discarded and the filling is eaten

*tandoori*—A clay oven used to roast meats, poultry, seafood, or vegetables, as well as to bake flatbreads in very high heat; used in the north of India

*tapas*—Small snacks or appetizers served throughout Iberia

*tarte Tatin*—An upside-down apple pie: apples, butter, and sugar are caramelized, then topped with pie dough and baked; the cooked tart is inverted on a plate after baking; a French confection

*tava*—Concave griddle made of cast iron used in Indian cookery

*teff*—A grain grown at high elevations

*tempura*—Individual food items coated with a very light batter and deep-fried; well-known Japanese dish

*thali*—Actually refers to the platter or tray that holds the small bowls during a meal, but known as the Indian method for eating meals by which each diner receives a platter containing small bowls of the various foods being served

*tilapia*—A rapid-growing freshwater fish that thrives in warm waters

*tofu*—Soybean curd; a cheeselike substance made from soybeans; a complete protein

*töltött kaposzta*—Hungarian stuffed cabbage roll

*tortilla*—A flat, unleavened disk made from wheat or corn and cooked on a dry griddle, eaten at every meal; Mexican bread

*treacle*—A sweet syrup such as maple syrup or molasses; popular in the British Isles

*tsai-fan*—Protein or vegetable served with rice; Chinese term

*tumpeng*—An Indonesian ceremonial rice dish consisting of a cone of rice decorated with a variety of foods, served at all important events

*udon*—Japanese noodle made from wheat

*vareniki*—A sweet dumpling filled with cheese or fruits

*varenyky*—Boiled dumplings with potatoes, sauerkraut, cheese, or fruits, garnished with sour cream, fried onions, or bacon bits; served in the Ukraine

*wasabi*—Very pungent, spicy hot, green horseradish dipping sauce served as a condiment with raw fish in Japan

*Westphalian ham*—A delicate, smoked ham similar to Italian *prosciutto*, prepared in Westphalia, Germany, served sliced very thinly on buttered rye or pumpernickel bread

*wok*—A pan with sloping sides and a rounded bottom used for stir-frying

*wot*—Ethiopian term for stew

*wurst*—Any of the countless varieties of sausages served in Germany

*yin-yang*—Complex philosophy that affects food, art, and other aspects of Chinese life; deals with combining opposites to achieve balance and harmony; *yin* represents the feminine or dark principles, while *yang* stands for the masculine or light; the important issue remains the successful combining of these two forces to achieve the harmony and balance in the food, art, or any medium that leads to balance and harmony in the body and spirit

*Yorkshire pudding*—A savory battercake cooked in meat fat, usually served with roast beef in the British Isles

*zabaglione*—Dessert sauce containing eggs, sugar, and Marsala wine; popular in Italy

*zakuska*—Assorted hors d'oeuvres or bite-size morsels of food, from Russia

*zwiebelkuchen*—Quichelike pie consisting of a pastry shell with a filling of bacon, eggs, cream, and onions; popular in Germany

# Bibliography

Aaron, Jan, and Georgine Sachs Salom. *The Art of Mexican Cooking.* New York: Doubleday, 1965.

Alford, Jeffrey, and Naomi Duguid. *Hot, Sour, Salty, Sweet: A Culinary Journey through Southeast Asia.* New York: Artisan, 2000.

Alford, Jeffrey, and Naomi Duguid. *Mangoes and Curry Leaves: Culinary Travels through the Great Subcontinent.* New York: Artisan, 2005.

Anderson, Jean, and Hedy Würz. *The New German Cookbook: More than 230 Contemporary and Traditional Recipes.* New York: HarperCollins, 1993.

Andoh, Elizabeth. *Washoku: Recipes from the Japanese Home Kitchen.* Berkeley: Ten Speed Press, 2005.

Ansky, Sherry. *The Food of Israel: Authentic Recipes from the Land of Milk and Honey.* Boston: Periplus Editions (HK), 2000.

Argyriou, Ellen, Editor. *The Australian Heritage Cookbook.* Surry Hills, Australia: Gaslight Publishing, 1988.

Atkinson, Catherine, and Trish Davies. *East European Kitchen.* New York: Hermes House, 2001.

Bailey, Adrian, and the Editors of Time-Life Books. *The Cooking of the British Isles.* New York: Time-Life Books, 1969.

Bailey, Adrian, and the Editors of Time-Life Books. *Recipes: The Cooking of the British Isles.* New York: Time-Life Books, 1969.

Bannerman, Colin. *Acquired Tastes: Celebrating Australia's Culinary History.* Canberra, Australia: National Library of Australia, 1998.

Bar-David, Molly Lyons. *The Israeli Cookbook.* New York: Crown, 1964.

Barrenechea, Teresa. *The Cuisines of Spain: Exploring Regional Home Cooking.* Berkeley, CA: Ten Speed Press, 2005.

Bartell, Karen Hulene. *Fine Filipino Food.* New York: Hippocrene Books, 2003.

Bastianich, Lidia Matticchio. *Lidia's Italian Table.* New York: William Morrow, 1998.

Batali, Mario. *Simple Italian Food: Recipes from My Two Villages.* New York: Clarkson Potter, 1998.

Bateman, Michael. *Café Brazil.* Lincolnwood (Chicago), IL: Contemporary Books, 1999.

Bates, Margaret. *The Belfast Cookery Book.* London: Pergamon Press, 1967.

Bayless, Richard Lane. *Rick Bayless's Mexican Kitchen.* New York: Scribner, 1996.

Bayless, Rick with Deann Groen Bayless, and Jeanmarie Brownson. *Rick Bayless's Mexican Kitchen: Capturing the Vibrant Flavors of a World-Class Cuisine.* New York: Scribner, 1996.

Bayless, Rick with Jeanmarie Brownson, and Deann Groen Bayless. *Rick Bayless Mexico One Plate at a Time.* New York: Scribner, 2000.

Beck, Simone. *Food and Friends.* New York: Viking Penguin, 1991.

Bharadwaj, Monisha. *The Indian Spice Kitchen: Essential Ingredients and Over 200 Authentic Recipes.* New York: Dutton, 1997.

Bittman, Mark. *The Best Recipes in the World: More than 1,000 Dishes to Cook at Home.* New York: Broadway Books, 2005.

Black, Maggie, and Deirdre Le Faye. *The Jane Austen Cookbook.* Toronto: McClelland & Stewart, 1995.

Blanc, Raymond. *Simple French Cookery.* London: BBC Books, 2002.

Bonekamp, Gunnevi. *Scandinavian Cooking.* New York: Garland Books, 1973.

Booth, Shirley. *Food of Japan.* London: Interlink Books, 2002.

Brîzová, Joza, et al. *The Czechoslovak Cookbook.* New York: Crown, 1965.

Brown, Dale, and Editors of Time-Life Books. *The Cooking of Scandinavia.* New York: Time-Life Books, 1968.

Bugialli, Giuliano. *Foods of Tuscany.* New York: Stewart, Tabori & Chang, 1992.

Casas, Penelope. *¡Delicioso! The Regional Cooking of Spain.* New York: Alfred A. Knopf, 2000.

Casas, Penelope. *The Foods and Wine of Spain.* New York: Alfred A. Knopf, 1982.

Casas, Penelope. *Tapas, The Little Dishes of Spain.* New York: Alfred A. Knopf, 1989.

Chamberlain, Lesley. *The Food and Cooking of Eastern Europe.* London: Penguin Books, 1989.

Chamberlain, Lesley with Catherine Atkinson, and Trish Davies. *Classic German Cookbook.* London: Southwater, 2007.

Chamberlain, Samuel. *British Bouquet: An Epicurean Tour of Britain.* New York: Gourmet Distributing, 1963.

Chandra, Smita and Sanjeev Chandra. *Cuisines of India: The Art and Tradition of Regional Indian Cooking.* New York: The Ecco Press, 2001.

Chang, Wonona W. and Irving B., and Austin Kutscher. *An Encyclopedia of Chinese Food and Cooking.* New York: Crown, 1979.

Chen, Helen. *Helen Chen's Chinese Home Cooking.* New York: Hearst Books, 1994.

Child, Julia, Louisette Bertholle, and Simone Beck. *Mastering the Art of French Cooking*, Volume I. New York: Alfred A. Knopf, 1961.

Claiborne, Craig, Pierre Franey, and the Editors of Time-Life Books. *Classic French Cooking.* New York: Time-Life Books, 1970.

Clayton, Bernard. *Bernard Clayton's New Complete Book of Breads.* New York: Simon and Schuster, 1973.

Condon, Richard, and Wendy Bennett. *The Mexican Stove.* New York: Doubleday, 1973.

Conran, Caroline. *Under the Sun: Caroline Conran's French Country Cooking.* San Diego: Laurel Glen, 2002.

Conte, Anna Del. *A Casa: Seasonal Italian Home Cooking.* New York: HarperCollins Publishers, 1992.

Copage, Eric V. *Kwanzaa: An African Celebration of Culture and Cooking.* New York: William Morrow, 1991.

Craig, Elizabeth. *The Scottish Cookery Book.* London: Andre Deutsch, 1956.

Croce, Julia della. *The Classic Italian Cookbook*. New York: DK Publishing, 1996.

Cuadra, Morena, and Morena Escardó. *Everything Peruvian Cookbook*. Avon, MA: Adams Media, 2013.

Cullen, Nuala. *Savoring Ireland*. New York: Quadrillion Publishing Ltd., 1998.

*Curry Cuisine: Fragrant dishes from India, Thailand, Vietnam, and Indonesia*. New York: DK Publishing Inc., 2006.

DeMers, John. *Caribbean Cooking*. New York: HP Books, 1997.

DeMers, John. *The Food of Jamaica: Authentic Recipes from the Jewel of the Caribbean*. Boston: Periplus Editions, 1998.

Dewitt, Dave, and Nancy Gerlach. *The Fiery Cuisines: The World's Most Delicious Hot Dishes*. Berkeley: Ten Speed Press, 1991.

Doméneck, Alejandro. *Spanish and Portuguese Cooking*. New York: 'Round the world cooking library, 1973.

Dosti, Rose. *Middle Eastern Cooking*. Tuscon, AZ: HP Books, 1982.

Dosti, Rose. *Mideast and Mediterranean Cuisines*. Tuscon, AZ: Fisher Books, 1993.

Downer, Lesley. *At the Japanese Table: New and Traditional Recipes*. San Francisco: Chronical Books, 1993.

Duff, Gail. *Bread: 150 Traditional Recipes from around the World*. New York: Macmillan Publishing Company, 1993.

Dunlop, Fiona. *The North African Kitchen: Regional Recipes and Stories*. Northampton, MA: Interlink Publishing Group, 2008.

Dunlop, Fuchsia. *Every Grain of Rice: Simple Chinese Home Cooking*. New York: W.W. Norton & Company, Inc., 2012.

Dunlop, Fuchsia. *Revolutionary Chinese Cookbook: Recipes from Hunan Province*. New York: W.W. Norton, 2006.

Duong, Binh, and Marcia Kiesel. *Simple Art of Vietnamese Cooking*. New York: Prentice Hall, 1991.

Dutt, Monica. *The Art of Indian Cooking*. New York: Bantam Books, 1972.

Ellmer, Bruno H. *Classical and Contemporary Italian Cooking for Professionals*. New York: Van Nostrand Reinhold, 1990.

Feibleman, Peter S., and the Editors of Time-Life Books. *The Cooking of Spain and Portugal*. New York: Time-Life Books, 1969.

Feibleman, Peter S., and the Editors of Time-Life Books. *Recipes: The Cooking of Spain and Portugal*. New York: Time-Life Books, 1969.

Fisher, M. F. K., and the Editors of Time-Life Books. *The Cooking of Provincial France*. New York: Time-Life Books, 1968.

Fitzgibbon, Theodora. *A Taste of Ireland*. London: Weidenfeld and Nicolson, 1968.

Franey, Pierre, and Richard Flaste. *Pierre Franey's Cooking in France*. New York: Alfred A. Knopf, 1994.

Freson, Robert. *The Taste of France*. New York: Stewart, Tabori & Chang, 1983.

Ganor, Avi, and Ron Maiberg. *Taste of Israel: A Mediterranean Feast*. New York: Galahad Books, 1993.

Germaine, Elizabeth, and Ann L. Burckhardt. *Cooking the Australian Way*. Minneapolis, MN: Lerner Publications, 1990.

Goodman, Matthew. *Jewish Food: The World at Table*. New York: HarperCollins, 2005.

Gopal, Sharda. *Step by Step Indian Cooking*. New York: Barron's Educational Series, 1987.

Gray, Andrea Lawson, and Adriana Almazán Lahl. *Celebraciones Mexicanas: History, Traditions, and Recipes*. Lanham, MA: AltaMira Press, 2013.

Grossman, Harold J. *Grossman's Guide to Wines, Spirits, and Beers*. New York: Charles Scribner's Sons, 1974.

Guermont, Claude, and Paul Frumkin. *The Norman Table*. New York: Charles Scribner's Sons, 1985.

Gundel, Károly. *Gundel's Hungarian Cookbook*. Budapest: Kossuth Printing House, 1998.

Gupta, Pranati Sen. *The Art of Indian Cuisine*. New York: Hawthorn Books, 1974.

Gur, Janna. *The Book of New Israeli Food: a culinary journey*. New York: Schocken Books, 2007.

Hachten, Harva. *Best of Regional African Cooking*. New York: Hippocrene Books, 1970.

Hafner, Dorinda. *A Taste of Africa*. Berkley, CA: Ten Speed Press, 1993.

Hahn, Emily, and the Editors of Time-Life Books. *The Cooking of China*. New York: Time-Life Books, 1968.

Hahn, Emily, and the Editors of Time-Life Books. *Recipes: The Cooking of China*. New York: Time-Life Books, 1968.

Harbutt, Juliet. *Cheese*. Minocqua, WI: Willow Creek Press, 1999.

Haroutunian, Arto der. *Vegetarian Dishes from Across the Middle East*. New York: The Experiment, LLC, 2008.

Harris, Dunstan A. *Island Cooking: Recipes from the Caribbean*. Freedom, CA: Crossing Press, 1988.

Harris, Jessica. *The Africa Cookbook: Tastes of a Continent*. New York: Simon & Schuster, 1998.

Harris, Jessica B. *Tasting Brazil*. New York: Macmillan, 1992.

Harris, Valentina. *Regional Italian Cooking*. New York: Pantheon Books, 1986.

Hassani, Nadia. *Spoonfuls of Germany: Culinary Delights of the German Regions in 170 Recipes*. New York: Hippocrene Books, 2004.

Hayes, Babetta. *Two Hundred Years of Australian Cooking*. Melbourne, Australia: Thomas Nelson, 1970.

Hazelton, Nika Standen. *Classical Scandinavian Cooking*. New York: Charles Scribner's Sons, 1987.

Hazelton, Nika Standen. *The Cooking of Germany*. New York: Time-Life Books, 1969.

Hazen, Marcella. *Marcella Cucina*. New York: HarperCollins, 1997.

Hazen, Marcella. *More Classic Italian Cooking*. New York: Alfred A. Knopf, 1978.

Heberle, Marianna Olsewska. *Polish Cooking*. New York: HP Books, 2005.

Hillman, Howard. *Great Peasant Dishes of the World*. Boston, MA: Houghton Mifflin, 1983.

Hirigoyen, Gerald, and Cameron Hirigoyen. *The Basque Kitchen: Tempting Food from the Pyrenees*. New York: HarperCollins, 1999.

Hush, Joanne, and Peter Wong. *The Chinese Menu Cookbook*. New York: Holt, Reinhart and Winston, 1976.

ICA Bokförlag Test Kitchen. *Swedish Cakes and Cookies:* New York: Skyhorse Publishing, Inc., 2008.

ICA Test Kitchen. *Swedish Cooking*. Västerrås, Sweden: ICA Bokförlag, 1983.

Ilkin, Nur, and Sheilah Kaufman. *The Turkish Cookbook: Regional Recipes and Stories*. Northampton, Massachusetts: Interlink Books, 2010.

Ingram, Christine. *Breads of the World*. Blaby Road, Wigston, Leicestershire LE18 4SE: Lorenz Books, 2013.

Ingram, Christine, and Jennie Shapter. *The Baker's Guide to Bread.* Blaby Road, Wigston, Leicestershire LE18 4SE: Lorenz Books, 2013.

Jackson, Elizabeth A. *South of the Sahara.* Hollis, NH: Fantail, 1999.

Jacobs, Lauraine. *New Taste New Zealand.* North Shore City, New Zealand: Tandem Press, 1996.

Jaffrey, Madhur. *Far Eastern Cookery.* New York: Harper & Row, 1989.

Jaffrey, Madhur. *Madhur Jaffrey's Indian Cooking.* New York: Barron's Educational Series, 1983.

Jaffrey, Madhur. *A Taste of India.* New York: Atheneum, 1986.

Jenkins, Steven. *Cheese Primer.* New York: Workman, 1996.

Jessel, Camilla. *The Taste of Spain.* New York: St. Martin's Press, 1990.

Johnson, Margaret M. *The Irish Pub Book.* San Francisco: Chronicle Books, 2006.

Kasper, Lynne Rossetto. *The Italian Country Table.* New York: Scribner, 1999.

Katzen, Mollie. *Moosewood Cookbook.* Berkeley, CA: Ten Speed Press, 1977.

Kennedy, Diana. *The Cuisines of Mexico.* New York: Harper & Row, 1972.

Kennedy, Diana. *From My Mexican Kitchen.* New York: Clarkson Potter/Publishers, 2003.

Kennedy, Diana. *My Mexico.* New York: Clarkson Potter, 1998.

Kennedy, Diana. *Recipes from the Regional Cooks of Mexico.* New York: Harper & Row, 1978.

*Kenneseth Israel Sisterhood Cookbook.* Louisville, KY: Kenneseth Israel Sisterhood.

Kijac, Maria Baez. *The South American Table.* Boston: Harvard Common Press, 2003.

Kirchner, Bharti. *The Healthy Cuisine of India: Recipes from the Bengal Region.* Los Angeles: Lowell House, 1992.

Klepper, Nicolae. *Taste of Romania.* New York: Hippocrene, 1999.

Knab, Sophie Hodorowicz. *The Polish Country Kitchen.* New York: Hippocrene Books, 2002.

Koplan, Steven, Brian H. Smith, and Michael A. Weiss. *Exploring Wine.* New York: Van Nostrand Reinhold, 1996.

Kosaki, Takayuki, and Walter Wagner. *The Food of Japan: Authentic Recipes from the Land of the Rising Sun.* Singapore: Periplus Editions (HK), 1995.

Kwak, Jenny, with Liz Fried. *Dok Suni: Recipes from My Mother's Korean Kitchen.* New York: St. Martin's Press, 1998.

Kwong, Kylie. *Simple Chinese Cooking.* New York: Viking Studio, 2007.

Lalbachan, Pamela. *The Complete Caribbean Cookbook.* Boston, MA: Charles E. Tuttle, 1994.

Lane, Rachel. *South American Grill.* Australia: Hardie Grant Books, 2012.

Lang, George. *The Cuisine of Hungary.* New York: Atheneum, 1983.

Laurd, Elisabeth. *The Old World Kitchen.* New York: Bantam Books, 1987.

Law, Ruth. *The Southeast Asia Cookbook.* New York: Donald I. Fine, 1990.

Lee, Cecilia Hae-Jin. *Eating Korean from Barbecue to Kimchi, Recipes from My Home.* Hoboken, NJ: John Wiley & Sons, 2005.

Lenôtre, Gaston. *Lenôtre's Desserts and Pastries.* New York: Barron's, 1975.

Leonard, Jonathan Norton, and the Editors of Time-Life Books. *Latin American Cooking.* New York: Time-Life Books, 1968.

Leonard, Jonathan Norton, and the Editors of Time-Life Books. *Recipes: Latin American Cooking.* New York: Time-Life Books, 1976.

Leung Mai. *The Chinese People's Cookbook.* New York: Harper & Row, 1979.

Levy, Faye. *Faye Levy's International Jewish Cookbook.* New York: Warner Books, 1991.

Levy, Faye. *Feast from the Mideast: 250 Sun-Drenched Dishes from the Lands of the Bible.* New York: HarperCollins, 2003.

Lindgren, Glenn, Raúl Musibay, and Jorge Castillo. *Three Guys from Miami Cook Cuban.* Salt Lake City: Gibbs Smith, 2004.

Lo, Eileen Yin-Fei. *Chinese Kitchen: Recipes, Techniques, Ingredients, History, and Memories from America's Leading Authority on Chinese Cooking.* New York: William Morrow, 1999.

Lo, Eileen Yin-Fei. *Mastering the Art of Chinese Cooking.* San Francisco: Chronicle Books, 2009.

Lo, Kenneth. *Regional Chinese Cookbook.* New York: Larousse, 1981.

MacMillan, Maya Kaimal. *Curried Flavors.* New York: Abbeville Press, 1996.

Magnier-Moreno, Marianne. *Middle Eastern Basics: 70 Recipes.* Buffalo, NY: Firefly Books, 2010.

Malgieri, Nick. *Nick Malgieri's Perfect Pastry.* New York: MacMillan Publishing Company, 1989.

Mark, Theonie. *Greek Islands Cooking.* Boston, MA: Little, Brown, 1974.

Marks, Copeland. *The Indonesian Kitchen.* New York: Atheneum, 1981.

Marquez-Sharpnack, Yvette, Veronica Gonzalez-Smith, and Evangelina Soza. *Muy Bueno: Three Generations of Authentic Mexican Flavor.* New York: Hippocrene Books, 2012.

Martin, Yan Kit. *Chinese Cooking: Step-by-Step Techniques.* New York: Crescent Books, 1984.

McGregor, Mary. *A Wee Taste O'Scotland.* Venice, FL: Westcoast Printing, 1995.

Mendel, Janet. *Cooking from the Heart of Spain: Food of La Mancha.* New York: HarperCollins, 2006.

Mendel, Janet. *My Kitchen in Spain: 225 Authentic Regional Recipes.* New York: HarperCollins, 2002.

Meyer, Arthur L. *Danish Cooking and Baking Traditions:* New York: Hippocrene Books, Inc., 2011.

Michalik, Ewa. *The Food and Cooking of Poland.* London: Anness Publishing Ltd., 2008.

Middione, Carlo. *La Vera Cucina: Traditional Recipes from the Homes and Farms of Italy.* New York: Simon and Schuster, 1996.

Morris, Sallie. *Taste of Indonesia.* London: Anness Publishing Limited, 1996.

Morris, Sally. *British and Irish Cooking.* New York: Garland Books, 1972.

Mostar, Katink. *Das Grosse Katinka Mostar Lockbuch.* München: Sudwest Verlag GmbH & Co, 1978.

Nathan, Joan. *The Foods of Israel Today.* New York: Alfred A. Knopf, 2001.

Nathan, Joan. *Jewish Cooking in America.* New York: Alfred A. Knopf, 1994.

Negrin, Micol. *Rustico: Regional Italian Country Cooking:* New York: Clarkson Potter Publishers, 2002.

Nelson, Kay Shaw. *The Eastern European Cookbook.* New York: Dover Publications, 1973.

Newman, Graeme. *The Down Under Cookbook*. New York: Harrow and Heston, 1987.

Newman, Graeme, and Betsy Newman. *Good Food from Australia*. New York: Hippocrene Books, 1997.

Ngô, Bach, and Gloria Zimmerman. *The Classic Cuisine of Vietnam*. New York: Barron's, 1979.

Nickles, Harry, and the Editors of Time-Life Books. *Middle Eastern Cooking*. New York: Time-Life Books, 1969.

Ojakangas, Beatrice. *Scandinavian Cooking*. Tucson, AZ: HP Books, 1983.

Ortiz, Elisabeth Lambert. *The Complete Book of Mexican Cooking*. New York: J. B. Lippincott, 1965.

Osborne, Christine. *Australian and New Zealand Food and Drink*. New York: Bookwright Press, 1989.

Owen, Sri. *Indonesian Regional Cooking*. New York: St. Martin's Press, 1994.

Owen, Sri. *The Indonesian Kitchen*. Northampton, MA: Interlink Publishing Group, Inc., 2009.

Panjabi, Camellia. *50 Great Curries of India*. Great Britain: Barnes and Noble and Kyle Cathie Limited, 2007.

Papashvily, Helen, George Papashvily, and the Editors of Time-Life Books. *Recipes: Russian Cooking*. New York: Time-Life Books, 1969.

Passmore, Jacki, and Daniel Reid. *The Complete Chinese Cookbook*. New York: Exeter Books, 1982.

Peck, Paula. *The Art of Fine Baking*. New York: Galahad Books, 1961.

*Perfect Spanish*. United Kingdom, Parragon Publishing, 2009.

Peterson, James. *Glorious French Food: A Fresh Approach to the Classics*. Hoboken, NJ: John Wiley & Sons, 2002.

Pizarro, José. *José Pizarro's Spanish Flavors*. Lanham, MD: Kule Cathie Limited, 2012.

Plum, Camilla. *Scandinavian Kitchen:* Great Britain: Kyle Cathie Ltd., 2011.

Quinn, Lucinda Scala. *Jamaican Cooking: 140 Roadside and Homestyle Recipes*. New York: Macmillan, 1997.

Rahamut, Wendy. *Modern Caribbean Cuisine*. Northampton, MA: Interlink Books, 2007.

Ramazanoglu, Gülseren. *Turkish Cookery*. Istanbul, Turkey: Ramazanoglu Publications, 1989.

Rau, Santha Rama, and the Editors of Time-Life Books. *The Cooking of India*. New York: Time-Life Books, 1969.

Reekie, Jennie. *Traditional French Cooking*. New York: St. Martin's Press, 1975.

Richie, Donald. *A Taste of Japan*. New York: Kodansha America, Inc., 1992.

Robertson, Carol. *Portuguese Cooking: The Authentic and Robust Cuisine of Portugal*. Berkeley: North Atlantic Books, 1993.

Robinson, Mark. *izakaya: The Japanese Pub Cookbook*. Tokyo: Kodansha America Inc., 2008.

Rhodes, Gary. *New Classics*. New York: Dorling Kindersley, 2001.

Roden, Claudia. *The Book of Jewish Food*. New York: Alfred A. Knopf, 1996.

Roden, Claudia. *A Book of Middle Eastern Food*. New York: Alfred A. Knopf, 1972.

Roden, Claudia. *The Good Food of Italy Region by Region*. New York: Alfred A. Knopf, 1990.

Roden, Claudia. *The New Book of Middle Eastern Food*. New York: Alfred A. Knopf, 2000.

Rojas-Lombardi, Felipe. *The Art of South American Cooking*. New York: HarperCollins, 1991.

Romagnoli, Margaret, and G. Franco Romagnoli. *The New Italian Cooking*. Boston, MA: Little, Brown, 1980.

Romagnoli, Margaret, and G. Franco Romagnoli. *The Romagnolis' Table*. Boston, MA: Little, Brown, 1975.

Römer, Joachim, and Michael Ditter. *Culinaria European Specialties*. Cologne, Germany: Könemann Verlagsgesellschaft, 1995.

Rose, Evelyn. *The New Complete International Jewish Cookbook*. New York: Carroll & Graf, 1992.

Rosenblatt, Julia Carlson, and Frederic H. Sonnenschmidt. *Dining with Sherlock Holmes*. Indianapolis and New York: Bobbs-Merrill, 1976.

Ruggieri, Luisa de. *Italian Cooking*. New York: 'Round the World Cooking Library, 1972.

Sahni, Julie. *Classic Indian Cooking*. New York: William Morrow, 1980.

Sahni, Julie. *Julie Sahni's Introduction to Indian Cooking*. Berkeley, CA: Ten Speed Press, 1998.

Salloum, Habeeb, and James Peters. *From the Land of Figs and Olives*. New York: Interlink Publishing Group, 1997.

Samuelsson, Marcus. *Aquavit and the New Scandinavian Cuisine*. New York: Houghton Mifflin, 2003.

Samuelsson, Marcus. *The Soul of a New Cuisine*. Hoboken, NJ: John Wiley & Sons, Inc., 2006.

Scharfenberg, Horst. *The Cuisines of Germany*. New York: Poseidon Press, 1980.

Scott, David. *Recipes for an Arabian Night*. New York: Pantheon Books, 1983.

Seranne, Ann, and Eileen Gaden. *The Best of Near Eastern Cookery*. New York: Doubleday, 1964.

Sheffer, Nelli, and Mimi Sheraton. *Food Markets of the World*. New York: Harry N. Abrams, 1997.

Sheraton, Mimi. *The German Cookbook: A Complete Guide to Mastering Authentic German Cooking*. New York: Random House, 1993.

Shimbo, Hiroko. *The Japanese Kitchen: 250 Recipes in a Traditional Spirit*. Boston: Harvard Common Press, 2000.

Sinclair, Pat. *Scandinavian Classic Baking*. Gretna, LA: Pelican Publishing Company, Inc., 2011.

Singh, Balbir. *Mrs. Balbir Singh's Indian Cookery*. London: Mills & Boon Limited, 1971.

Singh, Rohini. *The Wonderful World of Indian Cookery*. Gretna, LA: Pelican, 1994.

Sodsook, Victor. *True Thai, The Modern Art of Thai Cooking*. New York: William Morrow, 1995.

Sokolov, Raymond. *The Jewish-American Kitchen*. Avenel, NJ: Wings Books, 1993.

Solomon, Charmaine. *The Complete Asian Cookbook*. New York: McGraw-Hill, 1976.

Solomon, Jay. *A Taste of the Tropics: Traditional and Innovative Cooking from the Pacific and Caribbean*. Berkeley: Ten Speed Press, 2003.

Steinberg, Rafael, and the Editors of Time-Life Books. *Pacific and Southeast Asian Cooking*. New York: Time-Life Books, 1970.

Steinberg, Rafael, and the Editors of Time-Life Books. *Recipes: Pacific and Southeast Asian Cooking*. New York: Time-Life Books, 1972.

Stellino, Nick. *Nick Stellino's Glorious Italian Cooking*. New York: G.P. Putnam's Sons, 1996.

Sweetser, Wendy. *Asian Flavors: Unlock Culinary Secrets with Spices, Sauces, and Other Exotic Ingredients*. New York: Kodansha International, 2005.

Thiam, Pierre. *Yolele! Recipes from the Heart of Senegal*. New York: Lake Isle Press. Inc., 2008.

Thompson, David. *Thai food*. Berkeley: Ten Speed Press, 2002.

Thompson, Jeanette T. *Bahamian Cuisine "The Spice of Your Life."* Great Exuma, Bahamas: Tract Three Productions, 1996.

Tolvanen, Kirsti. *Finnish Food*. Helsinki: Kustannusosakeyhtiö Otava, 1965.

Trang, Corinne. *Authentic Vietnamese Cooking: Food from a Family Table*. New York: Simon & Schuster, 1999.

Trang, Corinne. *Essentials of Asian Cuisine: Fundamentals and Favorite Recipes*. New York: Simon & Schuster, 2003.

Trang, Corinne, Vivek Singh, Das Sreedharan, Mahmood Akbar, Sri Owen, and David Thompson. *Curry Cuisine: Fragrant Dishes from India, Thailand, Vietnam, and Indonesia*. New York: Dorling Kindersley, 2006.

Trilling, Susana. *Seasons of My Heart: A Culinary Journey through Oaxaca, Mexico*. New York: Ballantine Books, 1999.

Tropp, Barbara. *The Modern Art of Chinese Cooking*. New York: William Morrow, 1982.

Trotter, Christopher. *The Scottish Kitchen:* London: Aurum Press Limited, 2004.

Tsuji, Shizuo. *Japanese Cooking: A Simple Art*. New York: Kodansha International, 1980.

Urakami, Hiroko. *Japanese Family-Style Recipes*. New York: Kodansha America, 1992.

Urrutia, Mary, and Joan Schwartz. *Memories of a Cuban Kitchen: More Than 200 Classic Recipes*. New York: Macmillan, 1992.

Van der Post, Laurens, and the Editors of Time-Life Books. *African Cooking*. New York: Time-Life Books, 1970.

Van Waerebeek-Gonzalez, Ruth. *The Chilean Kitchen: Authentic, Homestyle Foods, Regional Wines, and Culinary Traditions of Chile*. New York: HPBooks, 1999.

Viestad, Andreas. *Kitchen of Light: New Scandinavian Cooking with Andreas Viestad*. New York: Artisan, 2003.

Volokh, Anne. *The Art of Russian Cuisine*. New York: Macmillan, 1983.

Von Bremzen, Anya. *The New Spanish Table*. New York: Workman, 2005.

Von Bremzen, Anya, and John Welchman. *Please to the Table: The Russian Cookbook*. New York: Workman, 1990.

Von Bremzen, Anya, and John Welchman. *Terrific Pacific Cookbook*. New York: Workman, 1995.

von Holzen, Heinz, Lother Arsana, and Wendy Hutton. *The Food of Indonesia: authentic Recipes from the Spice Islands*. Singapore: Periplus Editions Ltd., 1997.

Walden, Hilaire. *Portuguese Cooking*. Edison, NJ: Chartwell Books, 1994.

Wason, Betty. *The Art of German Cooking*. New York: Doubleday, 1967.

Wechsberg, Joseph, and the Editors of Time-Life Books. *The Cooking of Vienna's Empire*. New York: Time-Life Books, 1968.

Wechsberg, Joseph, and the Editors of Time-Life Books. *Recipes: The Cooking of Vienna's Empire*. New York: Time-Life Books, 1974.

Widenfelt, Sam, Editor. *Swedish Food*. Sweden: Esselte, 1956.

Wilde, Mary Poulos. *The Best of Ethnic Home Cooking*. Los Angeles, CA: J. P. Tarcher, 1981.

Willan, Anne. *French Regional Cooking*. New York: William Morrow, 1981.

Wilson, Carol, and Christopher Trotter. *Scottish Traditional Recipes*. London: Anness Publishing Ltd., 2009.

Wilson, Carol, and Christopher Trotter. *A Taste of Scotland*. London: Lorenz Books, 2008.

Wolfe, Linda, and the Editors of Time-Life Books. *The Cooking of the Caribbean Islands*. New York: Time-Life Books, 1970.

Wolfe, Linda, and the Editors of Time-Life Books. *Recipes: The Cooking of the Caribbean Islands*. New York: Time-Life Books, 1970.

Wolfert, Paula. *Cooking of Southwest France*. Hoboken, New Jersey: John Wiley & Sons, Inc., 2005.

Woodward, Sarah. *The Ottoman Kitchen*. New York: Interlink Publishing Group, 2001.

*World Book Encyclopedia*. Chicago: World Book, 1999.

Zane, Eva. *Middle Eastern Cookery*. New York: Charles Scribner's Sons, 1974.

Zaslavsky, Nancy. *A Cook's Tour of Mexico*. New York: St. Martin's Press, 1995.

# Credits

## Chapter 1

**p. 1:** Pearson Education, Inc.; **p. 5:** Elzbieta Sekowska/Shutterstock; **p. 6** (bottom): Joe Gough/Fotolia; **p. 6** (top): Joe Gough/Fotolia; **p. 8:** Pearson Education, Inc.; **p. 10:** Pearson Education, Inc.; **p. 11:** Fotolia; **p. 12:** Joe Gough/Fotolia; **p. 13:** Viktorija/Fotolia; **p. 14:** Pearson Education, Inc.; **p. 15:** Fanfo/Fotolia; **p. 16:** Azurita/Fotolia; **p. 17:** FoodPhotogr Eising/StockFood/AGE Fotostock; **p. 18:** Annamavritta/Fotolia; **p. 19:** Fudio/Fotolia; **p. 20:** Courtesy of the Idaho Potato Commission; **p. 21:** Nicol/Photocuisine/AGE Fotostock; **p. 22:** Courtesy of the Idaho Potato Commission; **p. 23:** Marco Mayer/Fotolia; **p. 24:** Fanfo/Fotolia; **p. 25:** R Embery/Pearson Education, Inc.; **p. 26:** Lilyana Vynogradova/Fotolia; **p. 27** (left): Courtesy of the Idaho Potato Commission; **p. 27** (right): Shutterstock; **p. 28** (bottom): Shutterstock; **p. 28** (top): Courtesy of the Idaho Potato Commission; **p. 29** (bottom left): Jules Selmes/David Murray/Dorling Kindersley, Ltd.; **p. 29** (bottom right): King Arthur Flour; **p. 29** (top): Joe Gough/Fotolia; **p. 30** (bottom): JJAVA/Fotolia; **p. 30** (middle): Constantinos Loumakis/Shutterstock; **p. 30** (top): Pearson Education, Inc.; **p. 31** (top, bottom): Pearson Education, Inc.; **p. 32** (top, middle, bottom): Pearson Education, Inc.

## Chapter 2

**p. 33:** Pearson Education, Inc.; **p. 38:** Gts/Shutterstock; **p. 40:** Pearson Education, Inc.; **p. 41** (top, middle and bottom): Pearson Education, Inc.; **p. 41:** Pearson Education, Inc.; **p. 42** (left, right): Pearson Education, Inc.; **p. 43:** MediablitzImages/Fotolia; **p. 44:** Martiapunts/Fotolia; **p. 45** (bottom): Pearson Education, Inc.; **p. 45** (top): Courtesy of the Idaho Potato Commission; **p. 46:** Mariontxa/Fotolia; **p. 47:** Paul Brighton/Fotolia; **p. 48** (bottom): Mizina/Fotolia; **p. 48** (top): Olyina/Fotolia; **p. 49** (bottom): Shutterstock; **p. 49** (top): Uckyo/Fotolia; **p. 51:** Pearson Education, Inc.; **p. 52:** Mike Richter/Fotolia; **p. 53:** Jb325/Fotolia; **p. 54** (bottom): Pearson Education, Inc.; **p. 54** (middle): Kuvona/Fotolia; **p. 54** (top): Douglas Freer/Fotolia; **p. 55:** Neil Mersh/Dorling Kindersley, Ltd.; **p. 56** (bottom): Pearson Education, Inc.; **p. 56** (top): Pearson Education, Inc.; **p. 57:** Fanfo/Fotolia; **p. 58** (bottom): David Smith/Fotolia; **p. 58** (top): DueDiDenari/Fotolia; **p. 59:** AmpFotoStudio/Shutterstock; **p. 60** (bottom left): Jerry Young//Dorling Kindersley, Ltd.; **p. 60** (bottom right): Pearson Education, Inc.; **p. 60** (top): Pearson Education, Inc.; **p. 61:** Grafvision/Fotolia

## Chapter 3

**p. 62:** Pearson Education, Inc.; **p. 65** (bottom): Maksim Shebeko/Fotolia; **p. 65** (middle): Fanfo/Fotolia; **p. 65** (top): Taratorki/Fotolia; **p. 66:** Sollub/Fotolia; **p. 70:** Pearson Education, Inc.; **p. 72:** Fotogal/Fotolia; **p. 72:** Pearson Education, Inc.; **p. 73:** Fotogal/Fotolia; **p. 73:** Stuart West/DK Images; **p. 74** (top, middle, bottom): Pearson Education, Inc.; **p. 75** (bottom left): Fotolia; **p. 75** (bottom right): Pass/Fotolia; **p. 75** (top): Pearson Education, Inc.; **p. 76 (top, bottom):** Pearson Education, Inc.; **p. 77** (bottom): Jules Selmes/David Murray//Dorling Kindersley, Ltd.; **p. 77** (top): Pearson Education, Inc.; **p. 78** (top, bottom left and right): Jules Selmes/David Murray/Dorling Kindersley, Ltd.; **p. 79:** Natalia Mylova/Fotolia; **p. 80:** Flayols/Age Fotostock; **p. 81:** ComugneroSilvana/Fotolia; **p. 82:** Photographee.eu/Fotolia; **p. 83** (top, bottom): Joe Gough/Fotolia; **p. 84:** Jules Selmes/David Murray/Dorling Kindersley, Ltd.; **p. 85:** Joe Gough/Fotolia; **p. 87:** PhotoEd/Fotolia; **p. 88** (bottom): Chamillew/Fotolia; **p. 88** (top): Gryfot/Fotolia; **p. 89** (top): Vaspakulov/Fotolia; **p. 89:** Alexandre Kuhl de Oliveira/Shutterstock; **p. 90:** Kab Vision/Fotolia; **p. 92:** Pearson Education, Inc.; **p. 93** (bottom): Mathieu Viennet/Getty Images; **p. 93** (top): Alain Wacquier/Fotolia; **p. 94:** Courtesy of the Idaho Potato Commission; **p. 95** (bottom): Courtesy of the Idaho Potato Commission; **p. 95** (top): Pearson Education, Inc.; **p. 96** (left, right): Pearson Education, Inc.; **p. 97** (bottom left): Pearson Education, Inc.; **p. 97** (bottom right): Pearson Education, Inc.; **p. 97** (top): Superfood/Fotolia.

**p. 98** (all): Pearson Education, Inc.; **p. 99** (bottom left): Gerard Brown/Dorling Kindersley, Ltd.; **p. 99** (bottom right): Sugar0607/Fotolia; **p. 99** (top): Pearson Education, Inc.; **p. 99:** recipe for pate brisee © Gaston Lenôtre; **p. 101** (bottom): Martin Brigdale/Dorling Kindersley, Ltd.; **p. 101** (top): Clive Streeter/Dorling Kindersley, Ltd.; **p. 102** (left, right): Pearson Education, Inc.; **p. 103** (left, center, right): Pearson Education, Inc.

## Chapter 4

**p. 104:** Pearson Education, Inc.; **p. 107** (bottom): Silberkorn73/Fotolia; **p. 107** (top): Lsantilli/Fotolia; **p. 109:** Oran Tantapakul/Fotolia; **p. 110:** Pearson Education, Inc.; **p. 111:** Pearson Education, Inc.; **p. 112** (bottom): Lsantilli/Fotolia; **p. 112** (top): Jillian Alexander/Fotolia; **p. 114:** Pearson Education, Inc.; **p. 116:** Pearson Education, Inc.; **p. 116:** Pearson Education, Inc.; **p. 117** (left): Patrick McLeavy, Clive Streeter/Dorling Kindersley, Ltd.; **p. 117** (right): Ramon grosso dolarea/Shutterstock; **p. 118:** David Munns/Dorling Kindersley, Ltd.; **p. 119:** Fotolia; **p. 120:** Pearson Education, Inc.; **p. 121:** Sarsmis/Fotolia; **p. 122** (left): Ekaterina Nikitina/Shutterstock; **p. 122** (right): Courtesy of the Idaho Potato Commission; **p. 123** (top, bottom): Pearson Education, Inc.; **p. 124** (bottom center): Fotolia; **p. 124** (bottom left): Joe Gough/Fotolia; **p. 124** (bottom right): FomaA/Fotolia; **p. 124** (top, middle): Pearson Education, Inc.; **p. 125** (bottom): Schankz/Fotolia; **p. 125** (middle): Pearson Education, Inc.; **p. 125** (top): vladi59/Fotolia; **p. 126** (bottom middle): Piotr Rzeszutek/Shutterstock; **p. 126** (bottom right): Dani Vincek/Fotolia; **p. 126** (top, bottom left): Pearson Education, Inc.; **p. 127** (bottom): Mi.Ti./Fotolia; **p. 127** (top): Morenovel/Fotolia; **p. 129** (bottom right): Pearson Education, Inc.; **p. 129** (top, bottom left): Jules Selmes, David Murray/Dorling Kindersley, Ltd.; **p. 130** (bottom): Msheldrake/Shutterstock; **p. 130** (top): William Shaw/Dorling Kindersley, Ltd.; **p. 131** (bottom): Joe Gough/Fotolia; **p. 131** (top): Pearson Education, Inc.; **p. 132:** Fanfo/Fotolia; **p. 133:** Comugnero Silvana/Fotolia; **p. 134** (bottom): Marco Mayer/Fotolia; **p. 134** (top): Jules Selmes/David Murray/Dorling Kindersley, Ltd.; **p. 135:** Clive Streeter/Dorling Kindersley, Ltd.; **p. 136:** Audaxl/Fotolia; **p. 137:** Comugnero Silvana/Fotolia; **p. 138** (bottom left): PhotoEd/Fotolia; **p. 138** (bottom right): Matteocozzi/Fotolia; **p. 138** (top, middle): Richard Embery/Pearson Education, Inc.; **p. 139** (all): Pearson Education, Inc.; **p. 140** (left): Pearson Education, Inc.; **p. 140** (right): Giotti52/Fotolia; **p. 141** (left, middle): David Murray/Dorling Kindersley, Ltd.; **p. 141** (right): Anneka/Shutterstock; **p. 142:** Neil Mersh/Dorling Kindersley, Ltd.; **p. 143:** EZeePics Studio/Fotolia

## Chapter 5

**p. 144:** Pearson Education, Inc.; **p. 146:** Jörg Lantelme/Fotolia; **p. 148:** Lilyana Vynogradova/Fotolia; **p. 149:** Bernd Jürgens/Fotolia; **p. 150** (bottom): Quade/Fotolia; **p. 150** (middle): Mike Richter/Fotolia; **p. 150** (top): Nataliia Pyzhova/Fotolia; **p. 151:** emf_images/Fotolia; **p. 152:** Pearson Education, Inc.; **p. 154:** Maille; **p. 154:** Pearson Education, Inc.; **p. 155:** Viktorija/Fotolia; **p. 156** (top, bottom): Silencefoto/Fotolia; **p. 157:** Pearson Education, Inc.; **p. 158:** Quade/Fotolia; **p. 159:** Pearson Education, Inc.; **p. 159:** Idaho Potato Commission; **p. 160** (bottom): ExQuisine/Fotolia; **p. 160** (top): M. Schuppich/Fotolia; **p. 161** (left, middle, right): Jules Selmes/David Murray/Dorling Kindersley, Ltd.; **p. 162** (bottom): Pearson Education, Inc.; **p. 162** (top): Jules Selmes/David Murray/Dorling Kindersley, Ltd.; **p. 162:** Quade/Fotolia; **p. 163:** Pearson Education, Inc.; **p. 163:** Viktor1/Shutterstock; **p. 165:** Svry/Shutterstock; **p. 166:** Jerry Young/Dorling Kindersley, Ltd.; **p. 167** (bottom): Kab-vision/Fotolia; **p. 167** (top): Margrit Hirsch/Fotolia; **p. 167:** Jerry Young/Dorling Kindersley, Ltd.; **p. 168:** Creative studio/Fotolia; **p. 169** (left): Pearson Education, Inc.; **p. 169** (right): Tanja/Fotolia; **p.170:** Wiktory/Shutterstock; **p. 171** (bottom right): Bernd Jürgens/Fotolia; **p. 171** (top, bottom left): Pearson Education, Inc.; **p. 172:** Pearson Education, Inc.; **p. 173** (top, bottom left and right): Courtesy of Patricia Heyman; **p. 174** (right, bottom): Jean-Louis Vosgien/Shutterstock; **p. 174:** Courtesy of Patricia Heyman; **p. 175** (bottom): Viperagp/Fotolia; **p. 175** (top): Marina Lohrbach/Fotolia

## Chapter 6

**p. 177:** Pearson Education, Inc.; **p. 180** (bottom): Petersen/Fotolia; **p. 180** (top): Bernd Jürgens/Fotolia; **p. 182** (bottom left, right): Nikitos77/Fotolia; **p. 182** (top): Adisa/Fotolia; **p. 185** (left): Elenathewise/Fotolia; **p. 185** (right): Stevem/Fotolia; **p. 186:** Pearson Education, Inc.; **p. 187** (bottom center): Alexnika/Shutterstock; **p. 187** (top, bottom left): Pearson Education, Inc.; **p. 187**(bottom right): Martin Turzak/Fotolia; **p. 187**(bottom left): Pearson Education, Inc.; **p. 188** (bottom): Brent Hofacker/Fotolia; **p. 188** (top): Dar1930/Fotolia; **p. 189** (bottom): Clive Streeter/Dorling Kindersley, Ltd.; **p. 189**(top): Brent Hofacker/Fotolia; **p. 190:** Cook_inspire/Fotolia; **p. 191:** Courtesy of Canola Oil @ canolainfo.org; **p. 192** (left): Natalikaevsti/Fotolia; **p. 192** (right): Viktor/Fotolia; **p. 192:** Pearson Education, Inc.; **p. 193:** Gayvoronskaya_Yana/Shutterstock; **p. 194:** Aynia/Fotolia; **p. 194:** Dorling Kindersley, Ltd.; **p. 195:** Paul Cowan/Shutterstock; **p. 196** (left, middle and right): Pearson Education, Inc.; **p. 197** (left, middle and right): Pearson Education, Inc.; **p. 198:** Ildi/Fotolia; **p. 198:** Thinkstock/Getty Images; **p. 199:** Arturo Limon/Shutterstock; **p. 200:** Stephanie Frey/Shutterstock; **p. 201:** © Kiselev Andrey Valerevich/Shutterstock; **p. 202:** Clive Streeter/Dorling Kindersley, Ltd.; **p. 203** (bottom): Olaf Speier/Fotolia; **p. 203** (top): Fkruger/Fotolia; **p. 204:** Erik Svensson/Dorling Kindersley, Ltd.; **p. 204:** Vera-g/Fotolia; **p. 205:** Kamenecskly Konstantin/Shutterstock; **p. 206:** Pearson Education, Inc.; **p. 206:** Stocksnapper/Shutterstock; **p. 207:** Pearson Education, Inc.; **p. 208:** Comugnero Silvana/Fotolia; **p. 209:** Brad Pict/Fotolia

## Chapter 7

**p. 210:** Pearson Education, Inc.; **p. 215:** Fanfo/Fotolia; **p. 216:** Dmytro Sukharevskyy /Fotolia; **p. 217** (bottom): Grafvision/Fotolia; **p. 217** (top): Manulito/Fotolia; **p. 218:** Olgavolodina/Fotolia; **p. 219:** Annamavritta/Fotolia; **p. 220:** Pearson Education, Inc.; **p. 222** (top, bottom left): Barbara Dudzinska/Fotolia; **p. 222:** Stormur/Shutterstock; **p. 223** (center): Robert6666/Fotolia; **p. 223** (left): Nestonik/Fotolia; **p. 223** (right): Liaurinko/Fotolia; **p. 224** (bottom): Shutterstock; **p. 224** (top): Pearson Education, Inc.; **p. 225:** Ekaterina Pokrovskaya/Shutterstock; **p. 226:** JJAVA/Fotolia; **p. 227:** Pawel Strykowski/Fotolia; **p. 228** (left): Stuart Monk/Fotolia; **p. 228** (right): PHB.cz/Fotolia; **p. 229** (bottom): Graletta/Fotolia; **p. 229** (top): Nitr/Fotolia; **p. 230:** Brett Mulcahy/Shutterstock; **p. 231:** Pearson Education, Inc.; **p. 232** (bottom): Joe Gough/Fotolia; **p. 232** (top): Blende40/Fotolia; **p. 232:** Pearson Education, Inc.; **p. 233:** Jay/Fotolia; **p. 234** (bottom): Joe Gough/Fotolia; **p. 234:** BGSmith/Shutterstock; **p. 235** (left): Papa1266/Fotolia; **p. 235** (right): Fox17/Fotolia; **p. 236:** Ian O'Leary/Dorling Kindersley, Ltd.; **p. 237:** Clive Streeter/Dorling Kindersley, Ltd.; **p. 238:** Fox17/Fotolia; **p. 239:** Tobik/Shutterstock; **p. 240** (left): Unpict/Fotolia; **p. 240** (right): Mrr/Fotolia; **p. 241:** Maksim Shebeko/Fotolia; **p. 241:** Pearson Education, Inc.; **p. 242:** Pearson Education, Inc.; **p. 243** (top, middle, bottom): Pearson Education, Inc.; **p. 244** (all): Pearson Education, Inc.; **p. 245:** Pelena/Fotolia

## Chapter 8

**p. 247:** Pearson Education, Inc.; **p. 252** (bottom): Laurent Renault/Shutterstock; **p. 252** (top): Joanna Wnuk/Fotolia; **p. 254** (top, bottom): Paul Brighton/Fotolia; **p. 255** (bottom): Teleginatania/Fotolia; **p. 255** (top): Eva Gruendemann/Fotolia; **p. 256:** Pearson Education, Inc.; **p. 258:** Pearson Education, Inc.; **p. 258:** Viktor/Fotolia; **p. 259** (bottom left): Floydine/Fotolia; **p. 259** (bottom right): Fotolia; **p. 259** (top): Mariusz Prusaczyk/Fotolia; **p. 260:** Courtesy of Canola Oil @ canolainfo.org; **p. 261:** Zef/Shutterstock; **p. 262:** Elzbieta Sekowska/Shutterstock; **p. 263:** Mariontxa/Fotolia; **p. 264:** Milarka/Getty Images; **p. 265:** Geff Reis/AGE Fotostock; **p. 266:** Joe Gough/Shutterstock; **p. 267:** Pearson Education, Inc.; **p. 268:** Travellinglight/iStockphoto/Getty Images; **p. 269:** Elzbieta Sekowska/Shutterstock; **p. 271** (all): Pearson Education, Inc.; **p. 272:** Pearson Education, Inc.; **p. 273:** Paul Brighton/Fotolia; **p. 274:** Serghei Velusceac/Fotolia; **p. 275:** Pearson Education, Inc.; **p. 276:** Eva Gruendemann/Shutterstock; **p. 277:** Olinchuk/Shutterstock; **p. 278:** Pawel70/Fotolia; **p. 279:** Hohenhaus/iStockphoto/Getty Images; **p. 280:** Pearson Education, Inc.

## Chapter 9

**p. 281:** Pearson Education, Inc.; **p. 284** (bottom): Joe Gough/Fotolia; **p. 284** (top): VP/Fotolia; **p. 285:** Courtesy of Canola Oil @ canolainfo.org; **p. 286:** Faraways/Fotolia; **p. 287:** Mallivan/Fotolia; **p. 289:** Pearson Education, Inc.;

**p. 291** (left): Jules Selmes/David Murray/Dorling Kindersley, Ltd.; **p. 291** (right): David Murray/Jules Selmes/Dorling Kindersley, Ltd.; **p. 291:** Pearson Education, Inc.; **p. 292** (left): Jules Selmes/David Murray/Dorling Kindersley, Ltd.; **p. 292** (right): Uckyo/Fotolia; **p. 293** (bottom): Pearson Education, Inc.; **p. 293** (top): Keko64/Fotolia; **p. 294:** David Murray/Jules Selmes/Dorling Kindersley, Ltd.; **p. 295:** Elzbieta Sekowska/Fotolia; **p. 296:** Ramzi Hachicho/Fotolia; **p. 297:** Lenushkab/Fotolia; **p. 298:** Kheng Guan Toh/Shutterstock; **p. 299** (bottom): Paul Brighton/Fotolia; **p. 299** (top): Paul Brighton/Fotolia; **p. 300:** Bratwustle/Shutterstock; **p. 301:** Jérôme Rommé/Fotolia; **p. 302:** FoodPhotogr. Eising/ AGE Fotostock; **p. 303:** Evgenyb/Fotolia; **p. 305:** Ian O'Leary/Dorling Kindersley, Ltd.; **p. 306:** Clive Streeter/Dorling Kindersley, Ltd.; **p. 307** (all): Pearson Education, Inc.; **p. 308:** CiprianCB/Shutterstock; **p. 309:** Belaya Katerina/Fotolia; **p. 310** (bottom): Warren Goldswain/Fotolia; **p. 310** (top): Pawel Burgiel/Fotolia; **p. 311** (left, right): Pearson Education, Inc.; **p. 312** (bottom): Maksim Denisenko/Fotolia; **p. 312** (top): David Murray/Dorling Kindersley, Ltd.; **p. 313:** Clive Streeter/Dorling Kindersley, Ltd.

## Chapter 10

**p. 314:** Pearson Education, Inc.; **p. 318** (bottom): Rafael Ben Ari/Fotolia; **p. 318** (middle): Paul Brighton/Fotolia; **p. 318** (top): Signorinac/Fotolia; **p. 319:** Kybele/Fotolia; **p. 320:** Pearson Education, Inc.; **p. 322:** Pearson Education, Inc.; **p. 322:** Rafael Ben Ari/Fotolia; **p. 323** (bottom right): Robert Lerich/Fotolia; **p. 323** (top, bottom left): Pearson Education, Inc.; **p. 325** (left, right): Pearson Education, Inc.; **p. 326:** Elzbieta Sekowska/Fotolia; **p. 327:** Chiyacat/Shutterstock; **p. 328:** Ints Vikmanis/Shutterstock; **p. 329** (center): David Murray/Dorling Kindersley, Ltd.; **p. 329** (left, right): Pearson Education, Inc.; **p. 330:** Ustinova/Fotolia; **p. 331** (left): David Murray/Jules Selmes/Dorling Kindersley, Ltd.; **p. 331** (right): Dave King/Dorling Kindersley, Ltd.; **p. 332** (left): Pearson Education, Inc.; **p. 332** (right): JJAva/Fotolia; **p. 333** (bottom): Brent Hofacker/Fotolia; **p. 333** (top): Clive Streeter/Dorling Kindersley, Ltd.; **p. 334:** Oocoskun/Fotolia; **p. 335:** nito/Fotolia; **p. 336:** Robyn Mackenzie/Shutterstock; **p. 337:** Olaf Speier/Fotolia; **p. 338:** Fanfo/Fotolia; **p. 339:** Lamb Kebabs/Shutterstock; **p. 340** (left): Jeff Smith/Getty Images; **p. 340** (right): Olga Lyubkin/Fotolia; **p. 341** (left): Anayupariam/Fotolia; **p. 341** (right): Ian O'Leary/Dorling Kindersley, Ltd.; **p. 342** (left): Pearson Education, Inc.; **p. 342** (right): Courtesy of the Idaho Potato Commission; **p. 344** (left): Pearson Education, Inc.; **p. 344** (right): Harris Shiffman/Shutterstock; **p. 345:** Clive Streeter/Dorling Kindersley, Ltd.; **p. 346:** Olga Phoenix/Shutterstock; **p. 347** (bottom): King Arthur Flour; **p. 347** (middle): Odelia Cohen/Getty Images; **p. 347** (top): Elzbieta Sekowska/Shutterstock

## Chapter 11

**p. 348:** Pearson Education, Inc.; **p. 349:** Pearson Education, Inc.; **p. 349:** Piai/Fotolia; **p. 352:** Dave King/Dorling Kindersley, Ltd.; **p. 353** (bottom): Superfood/Fotolia; **p. 353** (top): David Murray/Dorling Kindersley, Ltd.; **p. 354** (bottom): Paul Brighton/Fotolia; **p. 354** (top): SS/Fotolia; **p. 355:** Paul Brighton/Fotolia; **p. 356:** Erwinova/Fotolia; **p. 357**(top): Asiancool/Fotolia; **p. 357:** Pearson Education, Inc.; **p. 359:** David Murray/Jules Selmes/Dorling Kindersley, Ltd.; **p. 360** (top, bottom): Dreambigphotos/Fotolia; **p. 361:** Paul Williams/Dorling Kindersley, Ltd.; **p. 362** (bottom): Jjava/Fotolia; **p. 362** (top): Uckyo/Fotolia; **p. 363:** Pearson Education, Inc.; **p. 364:** Jreika/Fotolia; **p. 365** (top, bottom): David Murray/Jules Selmes/Dorling Kindersley, Ltd.; **p. 366** (bottom): Rossa di sera/Shutterstock; **p. 366** (middle): Joshua Resnick/Fotolia; **p. 366** (top left): Jules Selmes/David Murray/Dorling Kindersley, Ltd.; **p. 366** (top right and center): David Murray/Jules Selmes/Dorling Kindersley, Ltd.; **p. 367:** Amallia Eka/Shutterstock; **p. 368:** Pearson Education, Inc.; **p. 369:** visi.stock/Fotolia; **p. 370:** Ian O'Leary/Dorling Kindersley, Ltd.; **p. 371:** Pearson Education, Inc.; **p. 373:** Johnson76/Shutterstock; **p. 374:** Taiftin/Fotolia; **p. 375:** Paul Williams/Dorling Kindersley, Ltd.; **p. 376:** Qingqing/Shutterstock; **p. 378:** © pipop kangsiri/Alamy; **p. 379** (bottom left): Photogrape/Fotolia; **p. 379** (bottom right): Tim Hall/Getty Images; **p. 379** (top): Tanawatpontchour/Fotolia; **p. 380:** Oldamulet/Fotolia; **p. 381:** Paul Williams /Dorling Kindersley, Ltd.

## Chapter 12

**p. 382:** Pearson Education, Inc.; **p. 386** (bottom): Guzel Studio/Fotolia; **p. 386** (top): Xuejun li/Fotolia; **p. 387** (bottom): blue moon images; **p. 387** (top): Vladimir Gerasimov/Fotolia; **p. 388:** Nickola che/Fotolia; **p. 391:**

Pearson Education, Inc.; **p. 393** (bottom): Ian O'Leary/Dorling Kindersley, Ltd.; **p. 393** (top): Pearson Education, Inc.; **p. 394** (bottom left, center): Pearson Education, Inc.; **p. 394** (bottom right): Shellyagami photoar/Shutterstock; **p. 394** (top): David Mager/Pearson Education, Inc.; **p. 395** (bottom): Dave King/Dorling Kindersley, Ltd.; **p. 395** (top center): Richard Embery/Pearson Education, Inc.; **p. 395** (top left): Reika/Fotolia; **p. 395** (top right): Richard Embery/Pearson Education, Inc.; **p. 396** (bottom): Strakovskaya/Shutterstock; **p. 396** (top): Tab62/Fotolia; **p. 397** (bottom): Daj/Getty Images; **p. 397** (top): Lobur Alexey Ivanovich/Shutterstock; **p. 398**: Courtesy of Canola Oil @ canolainfo.org; **p. 399** (top, bottom): Kyogo7002/Fotolia; **p. 400** (bottom): Ben Fink/Dorling Kindersley, Ltd.; **p. 400** (top): © tanawatpontchour/Fotolia; **p. 401**: Pearson Education, Inc.; **p. 402** (bottom): David Murray/Jules SelmesDorling Kindersley, Ltd.; **p. 402** (middle): David Murray/Jules SelmesDorling Kindersley, Ltd.; **p. 402** (top): Jules Selmes/David Murray/Dorling Kindersley, Ltd.; **p. 403**: Clive Streeter/Patrick McLeavy/Dorling Kindersley, Ltd.; **p. 404** (bottom): © portokalis/Fotolia; **p. 404** (top): Paul_brighto/Fotolia; **p. 405**: Paul brighton/Fotolia; **p. 406** (all): Richard Embery/Pearson Education, Inc.; **p. 407**: Wizdata1/Shutterstock; **p. 408**: Wizdata1/Shutterstock; **p. 409** (bottom): JJAVA/Fotolia; **p. 409** (middle): SK/Fotolia; **p. 409** (top): Pearson Education, Inc.; **p. 410**: Arancio/Shutterstock; **p. 412** (bottom): Wizdata1/Shutterstock; **p. 412** (top): Fuchi/Fotolia

## Chapter 13

**p. 414**: Pearson Education, Inc.; **p. 420** (bottom): TuTheLens/Fotolia; **p. 420** (top): Aleksandar Todorovic/Fotolia; **p. 421**: januarandris/Fotolia; **p. 422** (bottom): Jose Gil/Fotolia; **p. 422** (top): bayu harsa/Fotolia; **p. 424**: Pearson Education, Inc.; **p. 426** (left, right, center): Pearson Education, Inc.; **p. 427** (left): Courtesy of Canola Oil @ canolainfo.org; **p. 427** (right): dziewul/Fotolia; **p. 428** (bottom): Pick up AAFNUCB0 from On Cooking, p. 857.; **p. 428** (top): Pearson Education, Inc.; **p. 429** (bottom): Pearson Education, Inc.; **p. 429** (top): wong yu liang/Fotolia; **p. 430**: Lucky Dragon/Fotolia; **p. 431**: sugar0607/Fotolia; **p. 432**: Kasia/Shutterstock; **p. 433** (bottom): MAHATHIR MOHD YASIN/Shutterstock; **p. 433** (top): Fotolia; **p. 434**: Clive Streeter and Patrick McLeavy/Dorling Kindersley; **p. 435**: Annabelle Breakey/Getty Images; **p. 436**: Pearson Education, Inc.; **p. 438** (left): sutichak/Fotolia; **p. 438** (right): kazama14/Fotolia; **p. 439** (all): Pearson Education, Inc.; **p. 440**: Andrea Skjold/Shutterstock; **p. 441**: Pearson Education, Inc.; **p. 442** (bottom): Dave Abram/Rough Guides/DK Images; **p. 442** (top): Dorling Kindersley Limited; **p. 443**: Goytex/Fotolia; **p. 444**: Pearson Education; **p. 445** (left): kicut82/Fotolia; **p. 445** (right): Rifanny/Fotolia; **p. 446** (bottom right): Tony Magdaraog/Shutterstock; **p. 446** (top, bottom left and center): Pearson Education, Inc.; **p. 447**: Alan Newham/Dorling Kindersley Limited; **p. 448** (bottom): Ulyana Khorunzha/Shutterstock; **p. 448** (top): David Murray/Jules Selmes/Dorling Kindersley, Ltd

## Chapter 14

**p. 449**: Pearson Education, Inc.; **p. 452**: aleks/Fotolia; **p. 453** (bottom): paul brighton/Fotolia; **p. 453** (top): Lucky Dragon/Fotolia; **p. 454**: uckyo/Fotolia; **p. 455**: witty/Shutterstock; **p. 458**: Aditya Patankar/Dorling Kindersley Limited; **p. 458**: Pearson Education, Inc.; **p. 460**(top): Tobik/Shutterstock; **p. 461**: Pearson Education, Inc.; **p. 462** (bottom): Barbara Pheby/Shutterstock; **p. 462** (top): Joe Gough/Fotolia; **p. 463**: Szabolcs Szekeres/Fotolia; **p. 464**: Courtesy of Canola Oil @ canolainfo.org; **p. 465**: Courtesy of Canola Oil @ canolainfo.org; **p. 466**: © WITTY /Fotolia; **p. 467**: Pearson Education, Inc.; **p. 468**: Abeer/Fotolia; **p. 469**: manubahuguna/Fotolia; **p. 470**: Shutterstock; **p. 471**: FomaA/Fotolia; **p. 472** (left): paul brighton/Fotolia; **p. 472** (right): Shutterstock; **p. 473**: Clive Streeter Patrick McLeavy/Dorling Kindersley; **p. 474** (left): Joe Gough/Fotolia; **p. 474** (right): Joe Gough/Fotolia; **p. 475**: Fotolia; **p. 476** (bottom): sugar/Fotolia; **p. 476** (top): Pearson Education, Inc.; **p. 477** (bottom): Dave King/Dorling Kindersley Limited; **p. 477** (top): Linda & Colin McKie/Getty Images; **p. 478**: Shutterstock; **p. 479**: Stanjoman/Shutterstock

## Chapter 15

**p. 480**: Pearson Education; **p. 486** (bottom): Jjay beaumont/Fotolia; **p. 486** (top): Ideenkoch/Fotolia; **p. 487**: LianeM/Fotolia; **p. 490** (bottom): Josie Grant/Shutterstock; **p. 490** (top): Tsuboya/Fotolia; **p. 491**: Maille; **p. 492** (bottom): Frits Solvang/Dorling Kindersley, Ltd.; **p. 492** (top): SergioZ/Shutterstock; **p. 493**: Courtesy of Canola Oil @ canolainfo.org; **p. 494**: Pearson Education, Inc.; **p. 495**: Sattriani/Fotolia; **p. 496**: Jabiru/Fotolia; **p. 497**: D. Pimborough/Shutterstock; **p. 498** (bottom): Paul Brighton/Fotolia; **p. 498** (top): Paul Cowan/Shutterstock; **p. 499**: Pearson Education, Inc.; **p. 500**: Jules Selmes/David Murray/Dorling Kindersley, Ldt; **p. 501** (bottom): Stocksolutions/Fotolia; **p. 501** (top): David Murray/Jules Selmes/Dorling Kindersley , Ltd.; **p. 502** (bottom): Rachel Dewis/Getty Images; **p. 502** (top): Pearson Education, Inc.; **p. 503** (bottom): Mackenzie/Shutterstock; **p. 503** (top): Lulu Durand/Shutterstock; **p. 504**: Blue Wren/Fotolia; **p. 505**: David Murray/Dorling Kindersley, Ltd.; **p. 506** (bottom): Fotoca/Fotolia; **p. 506** (top): King Arthur Flour

## Chapter 16

**p. 510**: leonardomarcel/Fotolia; **p. 511**: Angel Simon/Fotolia; **p. 513**: Andy Crawford/Dorling Kindersley, Ltd.; **p. 515** (center): Pearson Education, Inc.; **p. 515** (left): Dave King/Dorling Kindersley, Ltd.; **p. 515** (right): Philip Dowell/Dorling Kindersley, Ltd.; **p. 516** (bottom): Pearson Education, Inc.; **p. 516** (top): Pearson Education, Inc.; **p. 519** (left): Otokimus/Shutterstock; **p. 519** (right): Olyina/Fotolia; **p. 520** (left, right): JJAVA/Fotolia; **p. 521**: R Embery/Pearson Education, Inc.; **p. 522** (bottom): Blueee/Fotolia; **p. 522** (top): Don Farrall/Getty Images; **p. 524** (bottom): R Embery/Pearson Education, Inc.; **p. 524** (top left): R Embery/Pearson Education, Inc.; **p. 524** (top right): Jules Selmes/David Murray/Dorling Kindersley, Ltd.; **p. 525**: Olaf Speier/Fotolia; **p. 526** (bottom): Dulsita/Fotolia; **p. 526** (top): Full image/Fotolia; **p. 527**: Jayme Burrows/Shutterstock; **p. 528**: MBI/Shutterstock; **p. 529**: Pearson Education, Inc.; **p. 530** (left, middle and right): Pearson Education, Inc.; **p. 531**: Jennifer Boggs/Amy Pa/Blend Images/AGE Fotostock; **p. 532** (bottom): Tycoon101/Fotolia; **p. 532** (top left): Shellystuart/Fotolia; **p. 532** (top right): Snyfer/Fotolia; **p. 534**: David Murray/Jules Selmes/Dorling Kindersley, Ltd.; **p. 535**: Morenovel/Fotolia; **p. 536**: Pearson Education, Inc.; **p. 537**: Pearson Education, Inc.; **p. 538**: © kafka/Fotolia; **p. 539** (bottom): zkruger/Getty images; **p. 539** (middle): uckyo/Fotolia; **p. 539** (top): Clive Streeter/Dorling Kindersley, Ltd.; **p. 540**: Jacek Chabraszewski/Shutterstock; **p. 541** (bottom): Natspel/Fotolia; **p. 541** (top): Silvia Bogdanski/Shutterstock; **p. 542**: Clive Streeter/Dorling Kindersley, Ltd.; **p. 544**: Carloscanlefoto/Fotolia

## Chapter 17

**p. 552**: Redav/Fotolia; **p. 553**: Instantanea2010/Fotolia; **p. 555**: Courtesy of Canola Oil @ canolainfo.org; **p. 556**: Pearson Education, Inc.; **p. 557** (left): Yanik Chauvin/Fotolia; **p. 557** (right): Cook_inspire/Fotolia; **p. 558**: Pearson Education, Inc.; **p. 559**: Pearson Education, Inc.; **p. 560**: Pearson Education, Inc.; **p. 561** (bottom): Courtesy of Canola Oil @ canolainfo.org; **p. 561** (top): Pearson Education, Inc.; **p. 562**: Pearson Education, Inc.; **p. 564**: R Embery/Pearson Education, Inc.; **p. 565**: Eising/Getty Images; **p. 566** (bottom): Christian Vinces/Shutterstock; **p. 566** (top): Pearson Education, Inc.; **p. 567**: Vinicius Tupinamba/Shutterstock; **p. 568**: Gourmet-vision/image BROKER/AGE Fotostock; **p. 569**: Pearson Education, Inc.; **p. 570**: lldi/Fotolia; **p. 571**: Eising/Getty Images; **p. 572** (left): Rafer 76/Fotolia; **p. 572** (right): lldi Papp/Shutterstock; **p. 573** (left): Martin Brigdale/Dorling Kindersley, Ltd.; **p. 573** (right): Joanna wnuk/Fotolia; **p. 574**: In-Finity/Shutterstock

## Chapter 18

**p. 575**: Pearson Education; **p. 584** (bottom): Idaho Potato Commission; **p. 584** (top): Nathalie Dulex/Shutterstock; **p. 585**: Brent Hofacker/Fotolia; **p. 586**: Redav/Shutterstock; **p. 587**: Dagmara Ponikiewska/Shutterstock; **p. 588**: Brent Hofacker/Fotolia; **p. 589**: Pearson Education, Inc.; **p. 590**: Pearson Education, Inc.; **p. 591**: nata_vkusidey/Fotolia; **p. 592**: Clive Streeter/Dorling Kindersley, Ltd.; **p. 593**: Pearson Education, Inc.; **p. 594** (bottom): Paul Brighton/Fotolia; **p. 594** (top): Jules Selmes,David Murray/Dorling Kindersley, Ltd.; **p. 595**: Testing/Shutterstock; **p. 596**: Paul Brighton/Fotolia; **p. 597** (bottom): C M Kempin/Gastrofotos/AGE Fotostock; **p. 597** (top): Alena Yakusheva/Fotolia; **p. 598** (bottom right): Paul Brighton/Fotolia; **p. 598** (top, middle, bottom left): Pearson Education, Inc.; **p. 599**: Dave King/Dorling Kindersley, Ltd.; **p. 600** (bottom): Tony/Fotolia; **p. 600** (top): Ian Cummings/Dorling Kindersley, Ltd.; **p. 601** (bottom left): Courtesy of Canola Oil @ canolainfo.org; **p. 601** (bottom right): Pearson Education, Inc.; **p. 601** (top): Pearson Education, Inc.; **p. 602** (bottom): King Arthur Flour; **p. 602** (middle): effe45/Shutterstock; **p. 602** (top): Courtesy of Canola Oil @ canolainfo.org

# Subject Index

# Recipe Index

## AFRICA

## AUSTRALIA AND NEW ZEALAND

## BRITISH ISLES

## CARIBBEAN ISLANDS